T0181812

Lecture Notes in Computer Science   **14083**

Founding Editors

Gerhard Goos
Juris Hartmanis

Editorial Board Members

Elisa Bertino, *Purdue University, West Lafayette, IN, USA*
Wen Gao, *Peking University, Beijing, China*
Bernhard Steffen, *TU Dortmund University, Dortmund, Germany*
Moti Yung, *Columbia University, New York, NY, USA*

The series Lecture Notes in Computer Science (LNCS), including its subseries Lecture Notes in Artificial Intelligence (LNAI) and Lecture Notes in Bioinformatics (LNBI), has established itself as a medium for the publication of new developments in computer science and information technology research, teaching, and education.

LNCS enjoys close cooperation with the computer science R & D community, the series counts many renowned academics among its volume editors and paper authors, and collaborates with prestigious societies. Its mission is to serve this international community by providing an invaluable service, mainly focused on the publication of conference and workshop proceedings and postproceedings. LNCS commenced publication in 1973.

Helena Handschuh · Anna Lysyanskaya
Editors

Advances in Cryptology – CRYPTO 2023

43rd Annual International Cryptology Conference, CRYPTO 2023
Santa Barbara, CA, USA, August 20–24, 2023
Proceedings, Part III

Springer

Editors
Helena Handschuh
Rambus Inc.
San Jose, CA, USA

Anna Lysyanskaya
Brown University
Providence, RI, USA

ISSN 0302-9743 ISSN 1611-3349 (electronic)
Lecture Notes in Computer Science
ISBN 978-3-031-38547-6 ISBN 978-3-031-38548-3 (eBook)
https://doi.org/10.1007/978-3-031-38548-3

© International Association for Cryptologic Research 2023

This work is subject to copyright. All rights are reserved by the Publisher, whether the whole or part of the material is concerned, specifically the rights of translation, reprinting, reuse of illustrations, recitation, broadcasting, reproduction on microfilms or in any other physical way, and transmission or information storage and retrieval, electronic adaptation, computer software, or by similar or dissimilar methodology now known or hereafter developed.
The use of general descriptive names, registered names, trademarks, service marks, etc. in this publication does not imply, even in the absence of a specific statement, that such names are exempt from the relevant protective laws and regulations and therefore free for general use.
The publisher, the authors, and the editors are safe to assume that the advice and information in this book are believed to be true and accurate at the date of publication. Neither the publisher nor the authors or the editors give a warranty, expressed or implied, with respect to the material contained herein or for any errors or omissions that may have been made. The publisher remains neutral with regard to jurisdictional claims in published maps and institutional affiliations.

This Springer imprint is published by the registered company Springer Nature Switzerland AG
The registered company address is: Gewerbestrasse 11, 6330 Cham, Switzerland

Preface

The 43rd International Cryptology Conference (CRYPTO 2023) was held at the University of California, Santa Barbara, California, USA, from August 20th to August 24th, 2023. It is an annual conference organized by the International Association for Cryptologic Research (IACR).

A record 479 papers were submitted for presentation at the conference, and 124 were selected, including two pairs of soft merges, for a total of 122 speaking slots. As a result of this record high, CRYPTO 2023 had three tracks for the first time in its history.

For the first time in its history as well, CRYPTO benefited from the great advice and tremendous help from six area chairs, covering the main areas of focus for the conference. These were Lejla Batina for Efficient and Secure Implementations, Dan Boneh for Public Key Primitives with Advanced Functionalities, Orr Dunkelman for Symmetric Cryptology, Leo Reyzin for Information-Theoretic and Complexity-Theoretic Cryptography, Douglas Stebila for Public-Key Cryptography and Muthuramakrishnan Venkitasubramaniam for Multi-Party Computation. Each of them helped lead discussions and decide which ones of the approximately 80 submissions in their area should be accepted. Their help was invaluable and we could not have succeeded without them.

To evaluate the submissions, we selected a program committee that consisted of 102 top cryptography researchers from all over the world. This was the largest program committee that CRYPTO has ever had, as well. Each paper was assigned to three program committee members who reviewed it either by themselves or with the help of a trusted sub-referee. As a result, we benefited from the expertise of almost 500 sub-referees. Together, they generated a staggering 1500 reviews. We thank our program committee members and the external sub-referees for the hard work of peer review which is the bedrock of scientific progress.

The review process was double-blind and confidential. In accordance with the IACR conflict-of-interest policy, the reviewing software we used (HotCRP) kept track of which reviewers had a conflict of interest with which authors (for example, by virtue of being a close collaborator or an advisor) and ensured that no paper was assigned a conflicted reviewer.

In order to be considered, submissions had to be anonymous and their length was limited to 30 pages excluding the bibliography and supplementary materials. After the first six or so weeks of evaluation, the committee chose to continue considering 330 papers; the remaining 149 papers were rejected, including five desk rejects. The majority of these received three reviews, none of which favored acceptance, although in limited cases the decision was made based on only two reviews that were in agreement. The papers that remained under consideration were invited to submit a response (rebuttal) to clarifications requested from their reviewers. Two papers were withdrawn during this second phase. Each of the 328 remaining papers received at least three reviews. After around five weeks of additional discussions, the committee made the final selection of the 124 papers that appear in these proceedings.

We would like to thank all the authors who submitted their papers to CRYPTO 2023. The vast majority of the submissions, including those that were ultimately not selected, were of very high quality, and we are very honored that CRYPTO was the venue that the authors chose for their work. We are additionally grateful to the authors of the accepted papers for the extra work of incorporating the reviewers' feedback and presenting their papers at the conference.

This year the Best Paper Award was awarded to Keegan Ryan and Nadia Heninger for their paper "Fast Practical Lattice Reduction Through Iterated Compression." The Best Early Career Paper Award went to Elizabeth Crites, Chelsea Komlo and Mary Maller for their paper "Fully Adaptive Schnorr Threshold Signatures." The runner up Best Early Career Paper was by Ward Beullens on "Graph-Theoretic Algorithms for the Alternating Trilinear Form Equivalence Problem." These three papers were subsequently invited to be submitted to the IACR Journal of Cryptology.

In addition to the presentations of contributed papers included in these proceedings, the conference also featured two plenary talks: Hugo Krawczyk delivered the IACR Distinguished Lecture, and Scott Aaronson gave an invited talk titled "Neurocryptography." The traditional rump session, chaired by Allison Bishop, took place on Tuesday, August 22nd, and featured numerous short talks.

Co-located cryptography workshops were held in the preceding weekend; they included the following seven events, "Crypto meets Artificial Intelligence—The Glowing Hot Topics in Cryptography," "MathCrypt—The Workshop on Mathematical Cryptology," "CFAIL—The Conference for Failed Approaches and Insightful Losses in Cryptography," "PPML—The Privacy-Preserving Machine Learning Workshop," "WAC6—The Workshop on Attacks in Cryptography 6," "ACAI—Applied Cryptology and Artificial Intelligence," and "RISE—Research Insights and Stories for Enlightenment." We gladly thank Alessandra Scafuro for serving as the Affiliated Events Chair and putting together such an enticing program.

All of this was possible thanks to Kevin McCurley and Kay McKelly without whom all of our review software would be crashing non-stop, and all of the Crypto presentations would be nothing but static. They are the true pillars of all of our IACR Crypto events and conferences. Last but not least we thank Britta Hale for serving as our General Chair and making sure the conference went smoothly and attendees had a great experience. Thank you to our industry sponsors, including early sponsors a16z, AWS, Casper, Google, JPMorgan, Meta, PQShield, and TII for their generous contributions, as well as to the NSF Award 2330160 for supporting Ph.D. student participants.

August 2023

Helena Handschuh
Anna Lysyanskaya

Organization

General Chair

Britta Hale — Naval Postgraduate School, USA

Program Co-chairs

Helena Handschuh — Rambus Inc., USA
Anna Lysyanskaya — Brown University, USA

Area Chairs

Lejla Batina (*for Efficient and Secure Implementations*) — Radboud University, the Netherlands

Dan Boneh (*for Public Key Primitives with Advanced Functionalities*) — Stanford University, USA

Orr Dunkelman (*for Symmetric Cryptology*) — University of Haifa, Israel

Leo Reyzin (*for Information-Theoretic and Complexity-Theoretic Cryptography*) — Boston University, USA

Douglas Stebila (*for Public-Key Cryptography*) — University of Waterloo, Canada

Muthu Venkitasubramaniam (*for Multi-Party Computation*) — Georgetown University, USA

Program Committee

Shweta Agrawal — IIT Madras, India
Ghada Almashaqbeh — University of Connecticut, USA
Benny Applebaum — Tel-Aviv University, Israel
Marshall Ball — New York University, USA
Fabrice Benhamouda — Algorand Foundation, USA

Nina Bindel	SandboxAQ, USA
Allison Bishop	Proof Trading and City University of New York, USA
Joppe W. Bos	NXP Semiconductors, Belgium
Raphael Bost	Direction Générale de l'Armement, France
Chris Brzuska	Aalto University, Finland
Benedikt Bünz	Stanford and Espresso Systems, USA
David Cash	University of Chicago, USA
Gaëtan Cassiers	TU Graz and Lamarr Security Research, Austria
Yilei Chen	Tsinghua University, China
Chitchanok Chuengsatiansup	The University of Melbourne, Australia
Kai-Min Chung	Academia Sinica, Taiwan
Carlos Cid	Simula UiB, Norway, and Okinawa Institute of Science and Technology, Japan
Sandro Coretti	IOHK, Switzerland
Geoffroy Couteau	CNRS, IRIF, Université Paris-Cité, France
Luca De Feo	IBM Research Europe, Switzerland
Gabrielle De Micheli	University of California, San Diego, USA
Jean Paul Degabriele	Technology Innovation Institute, UAE
Siemen Dhooghe	imec-COSIC, KU Leuven, Belgium
Itai Dinur	Ben-Gurion University, Israel
Christoph Dobraunig	Intel Labs, Intel Corporation, USA
Thomas Eisenbarth	University of Lübeck, Germany
Sebastian Faust	TU Darmstadt, Germany
Ben Fisch	Yale University, USA
Pierre-Alain Fouque	IRISA and University of Rennes, France
Georg Fuchsbauer	TU Wien, Austria
Chaya Ganesh	Indian Institute of Science, India
Rosario Gennaro	City University of New York, USA
Henri Gilbert	ANSSI, France
Niv Gilboa	Ben-Gurion University, Israel
Mike Hamburg	Rambus Inc., the Netherlands
David Heath	University of Illinois Urbana-Champaign, USA
Naofumi Homma	Tohoku University, Japan
Abhishek Jain	Johns Hopkins University, USA
Bhavana Kanukurthi	Indian Institute of Science, India
Shuichi Katsumata	PQShield, UK, and AIST, Japan
Jonathan Katz	University of Maryland and Dfns, USA
Nathan Keller	Bar-Ilan University, Israel
Lisa Kohl	CWI, the Netherlands
Ilan Komargodski	Hebrew University, Israel and NTT Research, USA

Anja Lehmann	Hasso-Plattner-Institute, University of Potsdam, Germany
Tancrède Lepoint	Amazon, USA
Benjamin Lipp	Max Planck Institute for Security and Privacy, Germany
Feng-Hao Liu	Florida Atlantic University, USA
Tianren Liu	Peking University, China
Patrick Longa	Microsoft Research, USA
Julian Loss	CISPA Helmholtz Center for Information Security, Germany
Fermi Ma	Simons Institute and UC Berkeley, USA
Mary Maller	Ethereum Foundation and PQShield, UK
Chloe Martindale	University of Bristol, UK
Alexander May	Ruhr-University Bochum, Germany
Florian Mendel	Infineon Technologies, Germany
Bart Mennink	Radboud University, the Netherlands
Brice Minaud	Inria and ENS, France
Kazuhiko Minematsu	NEC and Yokohama National University, Japan
Pratyush Mishra	Aleo Systems, USA
Tarik Moataz	MongoDB, USA
Jesper Buus Nielsen	Aarhus University, Denmark
Kaisa Nyberg	Aalto University, Finland
Miyako Ohkubo	NICT, Japan
Eran Omri	Ariel University, Israel
David Oswald	University of Birmingham, UK
Omkant Pandey	Stony Brook University, USA
Omer Paneth	Tel-Aviv University, Israel
Alain Passelègue	Inria and ENS Lyon, France
Arpita Patra	IISc Bangalore and Google Research, India
Léo Perrin	Inria, France
Thomas Peters	UCLouvain and FNRS, Belgium
Thomas Peyrin	Nanyang Technological University, Singapore
Stjepan Picek	Radboud University, the Netherlands
David Pointcheval	École Normale Supérieure, France
Antigoni Polychroniadou	J.P. Morgan AI Research, USA
Bart Preneel	University of Leuven, Belgium
Mariana Raykova	Google, USA
Christian Rechberger	TU Graz, Austria
Oscar Reparaz	Block, Inc., USA
Matthieu Rivain	CryptoExperts, France
Mélissa Rossi	ANSSI, France
Guy Rothblum	Apple, USA

Alexander Russell   University of Connecticut, USA
Paul Rösler   FAU Erlangen-Nürnberg, Germany
Kazue Sako   Waseda University, Japan
Alessandra Scafuro   North Carolina State University, USA
Patrick Schaumont   Worcester Polytechnic Institute, USA
Thomas Schneider   TU Darmstadt, Germany
André Schrottenloher   Inria, Univ. Rennes, CNRS, IRISA, France
Dominique Schröder   FAU Erlangen-Nürnberg, Germany
Benjamin Smith   Inria and École Polytechnique, France
Ling Song   Jinan University, China
Mehdi Tibouchi   NTT Social Informatics Laboratories, Japan
Yosuke Todo   NTT Social Informatics Laboratories, Japan
Alin Tomescu   Aptos Labs, USA
Dominique Unruh   University of Tartu, Estonia
Gilles Van Assche   STMicroelectronics, Belgium
Damien Vergnaud   Sorbonne Université, France
Jiayu Xu   Oregon State University, USA
Arkady Yerukhimovich   George Washington University, USA
Yu Yu   Shanghai Jiao Tong University, China

Additional Reviewers

Kasra Abbaszadeh
Behzad Abdolmaleki
Masayuki Abe
Ittai Abraham
Hamza Abusalah
Amit Agarwal
Akshima
Gorjan Alagic
Martin Albrecht
Bar Alon
Miguel Ambrona
Prabhanjan Ananth
Megumi Ando
Yoshinori Aono
Paula Arnold
Gal Arnon
Arasu Arun
Gilad Asharov
Renas Bacho
Matilda Backendal

Christian Badertscher
Shi Bai
David Balbás
Paulo Barreto
James Bartusek
Andrea Basso
Jules Baudrin
Balthazar Bauer
Carsten Baum
Josh Beal
Hugo Beguinet
Amos Beimel
Sana Belguith
Thiago Bergamaschi
Olivier Bernard
Sebastian Berndt
Ward Beullens
Tim Beyne
Rishiraj Bhattacharyya
Ritam Bhaumik

Mengda Bi
Alexander Bienstock
Bruno Blanchet
Olivier Blazy
Maxime Bombar
Xavier Bonnetain
Jonathan Bootle
Samuel Bouaziz-Ermann
Katharina Boudgoust
Alexandre Bouez
Charles Bouillaguet
Christina Boura
Clémence Bouvier
Ross Bowden
Pedro Branco
Anne Broadbent
Olivier Bronchain
Andreas Brüggemann
Anirudh Chandramouli
Eleonora Cagli
Matteo Campanelli
Pedro Capitão
Eliana Carozza
Kévin Carrier
Wouter Castryck
Pyrros Chaidos
Andre Chailloux
Suvradip Chakraborty
Gowri Chandran
Rohit Chatterjee
Albert Cheu
Céline Chevalier
Nai-Hui Chia
Arka Rai Choudhuri
Hien Chu
Hao Chung
Michele Ciampi
Valerio Cini
James Clements
Christine Cloostermans
Benoît Cogliati
Andrea Coladangelo
Jean-Sébastien Coron
Henry Corrigan-Gibbs
Craig Costello

Elizabeth Crites
Eric Crockett
Jan-Pieter D'Anvers
Antoine Dallon
Poulami Das
Gareth Davies
Hannah Davis
Dennis Dayanikli
Leo de Castro
Paola De Perthuis
Rafael del Pino
Cyprien Delpech de Saint Guilhem
Jeroen Delvaux
Patrick Derbez
Zach DeStefano
Lalita Devadas
Julien Devevey
Henri Devillez
Jean-François Dhem
Adam Ding
Yevgeniy Dodis
Xiaoyang Dong
Nico Döttling
Benjamin Dowling
Leo Ducas
Clément Ducros
Céline Duguey
Jesko Dujmovic
Christoph Egger
Maria Eichlseder
Reo Eriguchi
Andreas Erwig
Daniel Escudero
Thomas Espitau
Andre Esser
Simona Etinski
Thibauld Feneuil
Pouria Fallahpour
Maya Farber Brodsky
Pooya Farshim
Joël Felderhoff
Rex Fernando
Matthias Fitzi
Antonio Flórez-Gutiérrez
Cody Freitag

Sapir Freizeit
Benjamin Fuller
Phillip Gajland
Tarek Galal
Nicolas Gama
John Gaspoz
Pierrick Gaudry
Romain Gay
Peter Gaži
Yuval Gelles
Marilyn George
François Gérard
Paul Gerhart
Alexandru Gheorghiu
Ashrujit Ghoshal
Shane Gibbons
Benedikt Gierlichs
Barbara Gigerl
Noemi Glaeser
Aarushi Goel
Eli Goldin
Junqing Gong
Dov Gordon
Lénaïck Gouriou
Marc Gourjon
Jerome Govinden
Juan Grados
Lorenzo Grassi
Sandra Guasch
Aurore Guillevic
Sam Gunn
Aldo Gunsing
Daniel Günther
Chun Guo
Siyao Guo
Yue Guo
Shreyas Gupta
Hosein Hadipour
Mohammad Hajiabadi
Shai Halevi
Lucjan Hanzlik
Aditya Hegde
Rachelle Heim
Lena Heimberger
Paul Hermouet

Julia Hesse
Minki Hhan
Taiga Hiroka
Justin Holmgren
Alex Hoover
Akinori Hosoyamada
Kristina Hostakova
Kai Hu
Yu-Hsuan Huang
Mi-Ying Miryam Huang
Pavel Hubáček
Andreas Hülsing
Akiko Inoue
Takanori Isobe
Akira Ito
Ryoma Ito
Tetsu Iwata
Jennifer Jackson
Joseph Jaeger
Zahra Jafargholi
Jonas Janneck
Stanislaw Jarecki
Zhengzhong Jin
David Joseph
Daniel Jost
Nathan Ju
Seny Kamara
Chetan Kamath
Simon Holmgaard Kamp
Gabriel Kaptchuk
Vukašin Karadžić
Ioanna Karantaidou
Harish Karthikeyan
Mustafa Khairallah
Mojtaba Khalili
Nora Khayata
Hamidreza Khoshakhlagh
Eda Kirimli
Elena Kirshanova
Ágnes Kiss
Fuyuki Kitagawa
Susumu Kiyoshima
Alexander Koch
Dmitry Kogan
Konrad Kohbrok

Sreehari Kollath
Yashvanth Kondi
Venkata Koppula
Marina Krcek
Maximilian Kroschewski
Daniël Kuijsters
Péter Kutas
Qiqi Lai
Yi-Fu Lai
Philip Lazos
Jason LeGrow
Gregor Leander
Ulysse Léchine
Yi Lee
Charlotte Lefevre
Jonas Lehmann
Antonin Leroux
Baiyu Li
Chaoyun Li
Hanjun Li
Wenjie Li
Xin Li
Xingjian Li
Zhe Li
Mingyu Liang
Xiao Liang
Damien Ligier
Wei-Kai Lin
Helger Lipmaa
Guozhen Liu
Jiahui Liu
Linsheng Liu
Meicheng Liu
Qipeng Liu
Zeyu Liu
Chen-Da Liu-Zhang
Alex Lombardi
Johanna Loyer
Ji Luo
Vadim Lyubashevsky
Yiping Ma
Varun Madathil
Bernardo Magri
Luciano Maino
Monosij Maitra

Christian Majenz
Jasleen Malvai
Marian Margraf
Mario Marhuenda Beltrán
Erik Mårtensson
Ange Martinelli
Daniel Masny
Loïc Masure
Takahiro Matsuda
Kotaro Matsuoka
Christian Matt
Krystian Matusiewicz
Noam Mazor
Matthias Meijers
Fredrik Meisingseth
Pierre Meyer
Daniele Micciancio
Elena Micheli
Marine Minier
Helen Möllering
Charles Momin
Atsuki Momose
Hart Montgomery
Tal Moran
Tomoyuki Morimae
Kirill Morozov
Fabrice Mouhartem
Koksal Mus
Saachi Mutreja
Michael Naehrig
Marcel Nageler
Rishub Nagpal
Yusuke Naito
Anand Kumar Narayanan
Shoei Nashimoto
Ky Nguyen
Georgio Nicolas
Raine Nieminen
Valeria Nikolaenko
Oded Nir
Ryo Nishimaki
Olga Nissenbaum
Anca Nitulescu
Julian Nowakowski
Adam O'Neill

Sai Lakshmi Bhavana Obbattu
Maciej Obremski
Arne Tobias Ødegaard
Morten Øygarden
Cavit Özbay
Erdinc Ozturk
Jiaxin Pan
Dimitrios Papachristoudis
Aditi Partap
Anat Paskin-Cherniavsky
Rafael Pass
Sikhar Patranabis
Stanislav Peceny
Chris Peikert
Angelos Pelecanos
Alice Pellet-Mary
Octavio Perez-Kempner
Guilherme Perin
Trevor Perrin
Giuseppe Persiano
Pessl Peter
Spencer Peters
Duong Hieu Phan
Benny Pinkas
Bertram Poettering
Guru Vamsi Policharla
Jason Pollack
Giacomo Pope
Alexander Poremba
Eamonn Postlethwaite
Thomas Prest
Robert Primas
Luowen Qian
Willy Quach
Håvard Raddum
Shahram Rasoolzadeh
Divya Ravi
Michael Reichle
Jean-René Reinhard
Omar Renawi
Joost Renes
Nicolas Resch
Mahshid Riahinia
Silas Richelson
Jan Richter-Brockmann

Doreen Riepel
Peter Rindal
Bhaskar Roberts
Wrenna Robson
Sondre Rønjom
Mike Rosulek
Yann Rotella
Lior Rotem
Ron Rothblum
Adeline Roux-Langlois
Joe Rowell
Lawrence Roy
Keegan Ryan
Mark Ryan
Sherman S. M. Chow
Eric Sageloli
Antonio Sanso
Practik Sarkar
Yu Sasaki
Robert Schaedlich
Jan Schlegel
Martin Schläffer
Markus Schofnegger
Peter Scholl
Jan Schoone
Phillipp Schoppmann
Jacob Schuldt
Mark Schultz
Marek Sefranek
Nicolas Sendrier
Jae Hong Seo
Karn Seth
Srinath Setty
Yannick Seurin
Dana Shamir
Devika Sharma
Yaobin Shen
Yixin Shen
Danping Shi
Sina Shiehian
Omri Shmueli
Ferdinand Sibleyras
Janno Siim
Mark Simkin
Jaspal Singh

Amit Singh Bhati
Sujoy Sinha Roy
Naomi Sirkin
Daniel Slamanig
Christopher Smith
Tomer Solomon
Fang Song
Yifan Song
Pratik Soni
Jesse Spielman
Srivatsan Sridhar
Damien Stehlé
Marc Stevens
Christoph Striecks
Patrick Struck
Adam Suhl
Chao Sun
Siwei Sun
Berk Sunar
Ajith Suresh
Moeto Suzuki
Erkan Tairi
Akira Takahashi
Katsuyuki Takashima
Abdul Rahman Taleb
Quan Quan Tan
Er-Cheng Tang
Qiang Tang
Stefano Tessaro
Justin Thaler
Yan Bo Ti
Tyge Tiessen
Junichi Tomida
Dilara Toprakhisar
Andreas Trügler
Daniel Tschudi
Yiannis Tselekounis
Ida Tucker
Balazs Udvarhelyi
Rei Ueno
Florian Unterstein
Annapurna Valiveti
Gijs Van Laer
Wessel van Woerden
Akhil Vanukuri
Karolin Varner

Javier Verbel
Tanner Verber
Frederik Vercauteren
Corentin Verhamme
Psi Vesely
Fernando Virdia
Quoc-Huy Vu
Benedikt Wagner
Roman Walch
Hendrik Waldner
Han Wang
Libo Wang
William Wang
Yunhao Wang
Zhedong Wang
Hoeteck Wee
Mor Weiss
Weiqiang Wen
Chenkai Weng
Luca Wilke
Mathias Wolf
David Wu
Lichao Wu
Zejun Xiang
Tiancheng Xie
Alex Xiong
Anshu Yadav
Sophia Yakoubov
Hossein Yalame
Shota Yamada
Avishay Yanai
Kang Yang
Qianqian Yang
Tianqi Yang
Yibin Yang
Kan Yasuda
Eylon Yogev
Yang Yu
Arantxa Zapico
Hadas Zeilberger
Bin Zhang
Jiang Zhang
Ruizhe Zhang
Zhenda Zhang
Chenzhi Zhu
Jens Zumbraegel

Contents – Part III

Cryptanalysis

Fast Practical Lattice Reduction Through Iterated Compression 3
Keegan Ryan and Nadia Heninger

Does the Dual-Sieve Attack on Learning with Errors Even Work? 37
Léo Ducas and Ludo N. Pulles

Exploring Decryption Failures of BIKE: New Class of Weak Keys and Key
Recovery Attacks 70
Tianrui Wang, Anyu Wang, and Xiaoyun Wang

Graph-Theoretic Algorithms for the Alternating Trilinear Form
Equivalence Problem 101
Ward Beullens

Analysis of the Security of the PSSI Problem and Cryptanalysis
of the Durandal Signature Scheme 127
Nicolas Aragon, Victor Dyseryn, and Philippe Gaborit

Finding Short Integer Solutions When the Modulus Is Small 150
Léo Ducas, Thomas Espitau, and Eamonn W. Postlethwaite

Practical-Time Related-Key Attack on GOST with Secret S-Boxes 177
Orr Dunkelman, Nathan Keller, and Ariel Weizmann

On Perfect Linear Approximations and Differentials over Two-Round SPNs ... 209
*Christof Beierle, Patrick Felke, Gregor Leander, Patrick Neumann,
and Lukas Stennes*

Differential Meet-In-The-Middle Cryptanalysis 240
*Christina Boura, Nicolas David, Patrick Derbez, Gregor Leander,
and María Naya-Plasencia*

Moving a Step of ChaCha in Syncopated Rhythm 273
Shichang Wang, Meicheng Liu, Shiqi Hou, and Dongdai Lin

Cryptanalysis of Symmetric Primitives over Rings and a Key Recovery
Attack on Rubato 305
   Lorenzo Grassi, Irati Manterola Ayala, Martha Norberg Hovd,
   Morten Øygarden, Håvard Raddum, and Qingju Wang

Side Channels

Prouff and Rivain's Formal Security Proof of Masking, Revisited: Tight
Bounds in the Noisy Leakage Model 343
   Loïc Masure and François-Xavier Standaert

Combined Fault and Leakage Resilience: Composability, Constructions
and Compiler 377
   Sebastian Berndt, Thomas Eisenbarth, Sebastian Faust, Marc Gourjon,
   Maximilian Orlt, and Okan Seker

Learning with Physical Rounding for Linear and Quadratic Leakage
Functions 410
   Clément Hoffmann, Pierrick Méaux, Charles Momin, Yann Rotella,
   François-Xavier Standaert, and Balazs Udvarhelyi

Unifying Freedom and Separation for Tight Probing-Secure Composition 440
   Sonia Belaïd, Gaëtan Cassiers, Matthieu Rivain,
   and Abdul Rahman Taleb

Symmetric Constructions

Twin Column Parity Mixers and Gaston: A New Mixing Layer
and Permutation 475
   Solane El Hirch, Joan Daemen, Raghvendra Rohit,
   and Rusydi H. Makarim

New Design Techniques for Efficient Arithmetization-Oriented Hash
Functions: Anemoi Permutations and Jive Compression Mode 507
   Clémence Bouvier, Pierre Briaud, Pyrros Chaidos, Léo Perrin,
   Robin Salen, Vesselin Velichkov, and Danny Willems

Coefficient Grouping for Complex Affine Layers 540
   Fukang Liu, Lorenzo Grassi, Clémence Bouvier, Willi Meier,
   and Takanori Isobe

Horst Meets *Fluid*-SPN: Griffin for Zero-Knowledge Applications 573
   Lorenzo Grassi, Yonglin Hao, Christian Rechberger,
   Markus Schofnegger, Roman Walch, and Qingju Wang

On the Security of Keyed Hashing Based on Public Permutations   607
   Jonathan Fuchs, Yann Rotella, and Joan Daemen

Revisiting the Indifferentiability of the Sum of Permutations   628
   Aldo Gunsing, Ritam Bhaumik, Ashwin Jha, Bart Mennink,
   and Yaobin Shen

When Messages Are Keys: Is HMAC a Dual-PRF?   661
   Matilda Backendal, Mihir Bellare, Felix Günther, and Matteo Scarlata

Layout Graphs, Random Walks and the *t*-Wise Independence of SPN
Block Ciphers   694
   Tianren Liu, Angelos Pelecanos, Stefano Tessaro,
   and Vinod Vaikuntanathan

Isogenies

CSI-Otter: Isogeny-Based (Partially) Blind Signatures from the Class
Group Action with a Twist   729
   Shuichi Katsumata, Yi-Fu Lai, Jason T. LeGrow, and Ling Qin

Weak Instances of Class Group Action Based Cryptography
via Self-pairings   762
   Wouter Castryck, Marc Houben, Simon-Philipp Merz, Marzio Mula,
   Sam van Buuren, and Frederik Vercauteren

Author Index   793

Cryptanalysis

Fast Practical Lattice Reduction Through Iterated Compression

Keegan Ryan[(✉)] [iD] and Nadia Heninger [iD]

University of California, San Diego, La Jolla, USA
kryan@ucsd.edu, nadiah@cs.ucsd.edu

Abstract. We introduce a new lattice basis reduction algorithm with approximation guarantees analogous to the LLL algorithm and practical performance that far exceeds the current state of the art. We achieve these results by iteratively applying precision management techniques within a recursive algorithm structure and show the stability of this approach. We analyze the asymptotic behavior of our algorithm, and show that the heuristic running time is $O(n^\omega(C + n)^{1+\varepsilon})$ for lattices of dimension n, $\omega \in (2, 3]$ bounding the cost of size reduction, matrix multiplication, and QR factorization, and C bounding the log of the condition number of the input basis B. This yields a running time of $O\left(n^\omega(p + n)^{1+\varepsilon}\right)$ for precision $p = O(\log \|B\|_{max})$ in common applications. Our algorithm is fully practical, and we have published our implementation. We experimentally validate our heuristic, give extensive benchmarks against numerous classes of cryptographic lattices, and show that our algorithm significantly outperforms existing implementations.

1 Introduction

Lattice basis reduction is a fundamental technique in cryptanalysis. The celebrated LLL algorithm [36] achieves a $2^{O(n)}$ approximation factor for lattice reduction in time $O(n^{5+\varepsilon}(p + \log n)^{2+\varepsilon})$ for a lattice of dimension n with entries of size $p = O(\log \|B\|_{max})$. This is polynomial time, but the large exponents ensure that this algorithm quickly becomes infeasible in practice for even moderately sized lattices.

The current gold standard lattice basis reduction algorithm used in practice is the L^2 algorithm [45] implemented in fpLLL [54], which improves the dependence on p by carefully managing precision for a runtime of $O(n^{4+\varepsilon}(p + \log n)(p + n))$. Current implementations take advantage of hardware floating-point support and are fast up to a few hundred dimensions, but the running time again becomes an obstacle beyond this point.

A separate line of work reduces the running time dependence on n by developing reduction algorithms with a recursive structure [33,41]. These algorithms have impressive performance, but have practical drawbacks in that they only output a single short vector and lack practical implementations.

Kirchner, Espitau, and Fouque [31] combined both approaches by giving an algorithm with a recursive structure that decreases the working precision as the

© International Association for Cryptologic Research 2023
H. Handschuh and A. Lysyanskaya (Eds.): CRYPTO 2023, LNCS 14083, pp. 3–36, 2023.
https://doi.org/10.1007/978-3-031-38548-3_1

lattice basis is reduced. They report impressive performance numbers on lattice bases of high dimension and precision, and claim a running time of $\tilde{O}(n^\omega C)$ for $C > \log(\|B\|\|B^{-1}\|)$ and ω equaling the matrix multiplication exponent. These results are based on a very strong heuristic assumption about linear regressions of log-Gram-Schmidt norms related to the Geometric Series Assumption (GSA). They use this assumption to argue that the required precision decreases exponentially throughout execution of their algorithm.

Heuristic precision issues. Unfortunately, the heuristic of [31] fails for large classes of cryptanalytically relevant lattices that include some of the most canonical applications of the LLL algorithm in cryptography: NTRU [15], Coppersmith lattices for solving low-degree polynomials modulo integers [13,27], and factoring with partial information [28]. These deviations from the GSA result in either unfavorable running times or computational errors due to insufficient precision. In practice, their implementation simply fails to reduce many of these lattices.

Our contribution. In this work, we give a new recursive variant of the LLL algorithm with a novel iterative strategy for managing precision. Our algorithm is extremely fast in practice and parallelizes naturally. We benchmark its performance against a diverse collection of families of lattices of theoretical and practical interest to showcase how the wildly differing structures of these lattices exhibit differing behaviors during lattice reduction. We find that our algorithm significantly outperforms fpLLL in every test case, and the algorithm of [31] on almost all families of lattices. Our test cases included a three-gigabyte lattice basis of dimension 8192, which we were able to reduce in 6.4 core-years.

Existing analysis tools are incompatible with our algorithm, so we develop new theoretical results to explain the behavior of and increase confidence in the stability and correctness of our approach. Our asymptotic running time matches the claimed running time of [31] while requiring significantly weaker heuristic assumptions, and our approximation guarantees for the reduced basis match those of the LLL algorithm.

We have made our implementation[1] available to the community with the aim for it to become a practical drop-in replacement for fpLLL.

1.1   Overview of Techniques

Iterated Compression. We develop several new tools to support the implementation and analysis of our algorithm. Our algorithm uses a new metric for lattice reduction distinct from prior work, which we call the *drop* of a lattice basis. Our new definition is used analogously to the Lovász condition of traditional LLL reduction. We say a basis B of rank n is α-lattice-reduced if it is size-reduced and $\mathrm{drop}(B) \le \alpha n$.

In addition, we apply a type of lattice basis "compression", which transforms a lattice basis into one with similar geometric properties but with smaller

---

[1] Our implementation is available at https://github.com/keeganryan/flatter.

entries and superior numerical stability. This compression is largely akin to [50], although our analysis is new.

Our algorithm is summarized by the pseudocode in Algorithm 1.

Algorithm 1: Reduce (sketch)

Input : Lattice basis B of rank n and reduction quality α
Output: Unimodular matrix U such that BU is α-lattice-reduced
1 **while** $drop(B) > \alpha n$ **do**
2   **for** *Proj. sublattice indices* $[i:j]$ *in* $\{[\frac{n}{4}:\frac{3n}{4}], [0:\frac{n}{2}], [\frac{n}{2}:n]\}$ **do**
3       $U_k \leftarrow$ Reduce$(B_{[i:j]}, \alpha')$ for improved reduction quality $\alpha' < \alpha$.
4       $B \leftarrow$ Compress(BU_k) to decrease entry size
5 **return** $U \leftarrow$ accumulation of all previous unimodular transformations

---

While the general description of the algorithm is simple and reminiscent of prior algorithms, the details and its analysis are not. The design of the compression function is critical to achieving numerical stability in practice, and, like [50], it is more sophisticated than simply taking the most significant bits. Unlike [50], our algorithm iterates the compression process, so extra care is needed to ensure accumulating rounding errors remain manageable. We develop first-order and asymptotic results using perturbation theory to bound the entry size of compressed bases and the accuracy of iterated compression.

Using heuristic assumptions, we prove the following running time for our algorithm, given here in a simplified form.

Theorem 1 (Simplified). *Let B be an integer lattice basis of dimension n and let $C > \log(\|B\|\|B^{-1}\|)$. If the running time of size reduction, matrix multiplication, and QR factorization has a $O(n^\omega)$ dependence on the dimension for some $\omega \in (2,3]$, and our heuristic assumptions are true, then the running time of our algorithm is*

$$O\left(n^\omega(C+n)^{1+\varepsilon}\right).$$

For B that are also upper triangular and size-reduced, as is common in cryptanalytic attacks, this is $O\left(n^\omega(\log\|B\|_{max} + n)^{1+\varepsilon}\right)$.

A deep dive into profiles. We analyze the behavior of our algorithm without relying upon the Geometric Series Assumption (GSA), which is clearly false for major classes of lattices of cryptanalytic importance, including Coppersmith, NTRU, LWE, and hidden number problem lattices. We do this by studying the evolution of the *profile*, or the log-norms of the Gram-Schmidt vectors, during lattice reduction. Unlike [31], which assumed via heuristic that the profile closely followed a linear trend of known slope, our analysis considers all possible profile shapes and their evolutions. We use the basis drop, as computed from the profile, to relate the change in lattice potential to the change in required precision.

In addition to its utility in analyzing the behavior of our algorithm, our redefinition of reduction quality in terms of the basis drop leads to bases with the same properties as LLL-reduced bases, and we achieve results analogous to [43, Theorem 9]. In practice, our algorithm returns approximations of equivalent quality to LLL.

Theorem 2. *Let B be a α-lattice-reduced rank-n basis satisfying our new definition of reduction quality. Let $\vec{b}_i^*$ denote the ith Gram-Schmidt vector and $\lambda_i(B)$ denote the ith successive minimum of the lattice spanned by B. Then B satisfies*

1. $\|\vec{b}_1\| \leq 2^{\alpha n}(\det B)^{1/n}$.
2. $\|\vec{b}_n^*\| \geq 2^{-\alpha n}(\det B)^{1/n}$.
3. For all $i \in \{1, \ldots, n\}, \|\vec{b}_i\| \leq 2^{\alpha n + O(n)}\lambda_i(B)$.
4. $\|\vec{b}_1\| \times \cdots \times \|\vec{b}_n\| \leq 2^{\alpha n^2 + O(n^2)} \det B$.

A focus on applications. Finally, we benchmark our algorithm against a wide variety of lattice families. We comprehensively analyze the behavior of our implementation on lattices of research interest, particularly lattice constructions from numerous cryptanalytic applications. Our selected test cases exhibit profiles that evolve in wildly different ways, and our implementation significantly outperforms existing tools on these lattices.

The main goal of this work is to produce a fully practical, implementable algorithm that outperforms existing lattice reduction implementations, and is intended to be used in practice. To that end, our theoretical results characterize the behavior of the algorithm and give confidence in the numerical stability of our approach with the help of weaker heuristic assumptions than prior work. We experimentally justify our heuristics.

2   Background

2.1   Notation

In this work, we represent bases in column notation, with the columns of B being basis vectors of the lattice. We index the vectors from 1 to n and denote the ith vector by $\vec{b}_i$. We use $\|\cdot\|$ to refer to the Euclidean norm for vectors and spectral norm for matrices, unless otherwise specified. We use log to denote the base-2 logarithm. We use $\kappa(B) = \|B\|\|B^{-1}\|$ to represent the condition number of matrix B. We use $B_{[i:j]}$ for $0 \leq i < j \leq n$ to denote the projected sublattice of rank $j - i$ formed by taking the lattice generated by the first j vectors projected orthogonally to the first i vectors. For brevity, we may use the term "sublattice" when we refer to a projected sublattice, as our algorithm does not consider sublattices in the non-projected sense.

2.2   History of Lattice Reduction Algorithms

The running time to reduce a lattice basis B is typically given in terms of the dimension n of the lattice and the size of the largest basis vector $\beta = \log \max_i \|\vec{b}_i\| = O(\log \|B\|_{max} + \log n)$. The goal of lattice reduction is to find a reduced basis where the n output vectors approximate the optimally smallest basis by an exponential factor $2^{O(n)}$. The original LLL algorithm [36] terminates in $O(n^{5+\varepsilon}\beta^{2+\varepsilon})$ bit operations where $\varepsilon > 0$ allows fast integer arithmetic. Two main lines of work have made progress towards reducing the running time of lattice reduction.

One line of work reduces the dependence on the dimension by using a recursive algorithm structure. Koy and Schnorr [33] proposed minimizing the cost by iteratively reducing overlapping sublattices, and the resulting algorithm required $O(n^{3+\varepsilon}\beta^{2+\varepsilon})$ bit operations. However, the output of the algorithm only bounded the length of the first vector by a factor of $2^{O(n\log n)}$ and made no guarantees on the other vectors. While their reported performance is impressive, to our knowledge the algorithm has not been implemented since. The recursive reduction idea was improved upon by Neumaier and Stehlé [41], achieving a proven runtime of $O(n^{4+\varepsilon}\beta^{1+\varepsilon})$ and bounding the first vector by a factor of $2^{O(n)}$. This algorithm uses exact precision, so the algorithm may need to compute with integers of bit-size $O(n\beta)$. For this reason, the algorithm is not considered practical, and to our knowledge, it has never been implemented.

A second line of work reduces the running time by carefully managing precision [9,39]. The L^2 algorithm of Nguyen and Stehlé [45] takes time $O(n^{4+\varepsilon}\beta(n+\beta))$ and returns a basis of essentially the same quality as LLL. Essentially, the L^2 algorithm progressively reduces the first k basis vectors and observes that $O(k)$ bits suffice to represent the reduced partial basis. This algorithm is implemented in fpLLL, is fast, and is the tool most commonly used in practice. The $\tilde{L}^1$ algorithm [46] uses numerical stability results to reduce the runtime to $O(n^{5+\varepsilon}\beta + n^{\omega+1+\varepsilon}\beta^{1+\varepsilon})$ and achieves essentially the same reduction quality as LLL. Here, ω is an exponent for matrix multiplication. However, this algorithm is also considered impractical and to our knowledge has not been implemented. An alternative approach of Bi et al. [4] and Saruchi et al. [50] improves lattice reduction running time in practice by reducing the bit sizes of entries to form an approximate basis with smaller vector precision $\beta' < \beta$, then applying lattice reduction algorithms to reduce the smaller basis.

It has long been a goal to unify these two lines of research, but there are many challenges to doing so. Kirchner, Espitau, and Fouque [31] recently published an algorithm that has a recursive structure and also decreases the working precision as the lattice basis becomes more reduced. Their algorithm is fast in practice for certain classes of bases, and they claim a running time of $\tilde{O}(n^{\omega}C)$ for $C > \log(\|B\|\|B^{-1}\|)$ by using strong heuristics to bound the necessary precision at each step. Unfortunately, their heuristic assumptions do not hold for important classes of lattice bases like NTRU and Coppersmith lattices, and their implementation does not work on these lattices in practice.

An orthogonal line of work, which includes sieving and enumeration (see [43]), and BKZ [10,51], achieves better approximation factors than LLL, although not in polynomial time. These algorithms are typically used to set parameter sizes for post-quantum cryptography. The exponential approximation factors achieved in this work do not impact the security of modern lattice-based cryptography. However, LLL is used as a preprocessing step for these SVP algorithms, and our parallelized reduction algorithm can be used as a drop-in improvement.

2.3   Lattice Reduction Basics

Many algorithms based on LLL operate on the Gram-Schmidt orthogonalization (GSO) of a lattice basis B, or the closely related QR-factorization which represents $B = QR$ as the product of an orthogonal matrix Q and upper triangular R. For a Gram-Schmidt vector $\vec{b}_i^*$, note that we have $\|\vec{b}_i^*\| = |R_{i,i}|$. Recursive lattice reduction algorithms frequently consider projected sublattices; that is, the lattice generated by vectors $\vec{b}_{i+1}, \ldots, \vec{b}_j$ projected onto the vector space orthogonal to $\vec{b}_1, \ldots, \vec{b}_i$. Using the upper triangular Gram-Schmidt coefficient matrix or R-factor, such a projected sublattice basis is easily computed from a block matrix of dimension $n_2 = j - i$ along the diagonal.

The basic steps of the LLL algorithm are a swap operation on neighboring vectors $\vec{b}_i$ and $\vec{b}_{i+1}$ followed by a size-reduction step to ensure the new vector at index $i + 1$ is small relative to indices 1 through i. This size reduction step ensures the GSO coefficients are not too large. The process repeats until the reduction criteria are satisfied and the algorithm terminates.

Variants of the LLL algorithm have a similar structure. Recursive algorithms determine a projected sublattice basis B_{sub} of dimension n_2 from R, and use a lattice reduction algorithm to find unimodular $U \in \mathbb{Z}^{n_2 \times n_2}$ such that $B_{sub}U$ is reduced. This U is applied to n_2 columns of the lattice of dimension n, and the Gram-Schmidt norms $\|\vec{b}_k^*\|, \ldots, \|\vec{b}_{k+n_2}^*\|$ are changed in the exact same way as the Gram-Schmidt norms of B_{sub}. In essence, recursive algorithms are more efficient because they avoid having to update the full basis, and instead batch together many swapping and size-reduction operations in dimension n_2 into a single efficient update U to apply to dimension n. We say an algorithm is LLL-like if it generates update matrices U through a combination of neighbor swaps and size reductions.

There are multiple definitions of size reduction in the literature. We will not restrict ourselves to a particular one, and instead allow any definition that satisfies the following property:

Definition 1 (Size reduction).   *Let B be a basis of rank n and let $B = QDM$ be the Gram-Schmidt orthogonalization where Q is orthogonal, $D = diag(\|\vec{b}_1^*\|, \ldots, \|\vec{b}_n^*\|)$, and M is unitriangular. B is size-reduced if $\|M\| = 2^{O(n)}$ and $\|M^{-1}\| = 2^{O(n)}$.*

This property is satisfied by the η size reduction of L^2 (see [50, Lemma 12]) and the Seysen block size reduction of [31] (see Theorem 2), and it allows us to bound matrix condition numbers and norms easily.

2.4 Heuristic Assumptions

Heuristic assumptions are frequently used to understand the empirical behavior of lattice algorithms.

The geometric series assumption (GSA) states that reduced lattice bases heuristically have $\|\vec{b}_i^*\|/\|\vec{b}_{i+1}^*\|$ constant. While this holds for some applications, it is false in general. Our results do not depend on the GSA.

The heuristic assumption of [31] states that the slope of a linear regression of the $\log\|\vec{b}_i^*\|$ values decreases exponentially quickly throughout lattice reduction, and in its limit it approximates a known, small value. This assumption is used recursively to bound the maximum and minimum Gram-Schmidt norm, which is in turn used to conclude that an exponentially decreasing working precision suffices for their algorithm. Their assumption is validated against Knapsack and NTRU-like lattices.

This assumption is violated when the final profile does not closely follow the GSA. For example, consider overstretched NTRU. We note that NTRU-like [54] bases are not generated in the same way as genuine NTRU bases, and their empirical behavior during lattice reduction is different. Kirchner and Fouque [32] use a lemma by Pataki and Tural [47] to prove by contradiction that genuine NTRU bases do not follow the GSA, and the Gram-Schmidt norms are shorter than the GSA predicts. As a result, the required working precision does not decrease exponentially.

It is also claimed in [31] that QR factorization (Cholesky decomposition to be precise) and size reduction can heuristically be performed with the same asymptotic running time as matrix multiplication. We do not evaluate this claim in our work, but we observe that if it is true, it lowers the asymptotic running time of our algorithm as well.

3 Lattice Profiles and Their Application

Define the profile of a lattice basis as a vector $\vec{\ell}$ with $\ell_i = \log\|\vec{b}_i^*\|$. The origin of this name is unclear; we note the term has been used in various forms by Kirchner, Espitau, and Fouque [29,30], and Ducas and van Woerden [20,21]. The profile of a lattice basis encodes a wealth of information about its properties and its behavior under lattice reduction, and it can vary significantly across different problems. Works by Kirchner and Fouque [32], Albrecht and Ducas [1], and Ducas and van Woerden [21] have used the behavior of the lattice profile to analyze specific problems, for example to identify dense sublattices and uniquely short vectors for NTRU and LWE lattices that allow solving these problems more efficiently. In our case, we will use the profile to characterize the behavior of lattice reduction algorithms on general lattices. This section recounts some properties of lattice profiles found in prior work, and also develops our new concept of lattice reduction.

3.1   Example Profiles

The cryptanalytic applications of lattice reduction vary significantly, and so too do the input and output profiles of the bases involved in solving these problems, computed before and after performing lattice reduction. Example input and output pairs are given in Fig. 1.

We can observe that there are several common input shapes for these profiles. Input bases for q-ary lattices, LWE lattices, and NTRU lattices [38] all resemble a step function, where the first half of the profile is large ($\log q$), and the second half is small (0). We loosely classify these input bases as being "balanced." On the other hand, input profiles for Goldstein-Mayer lattices [25], Gentry-Halevi lattices [24], and knapsack-lattices [34] consist of a single large entry, and the remaining ones are small. Input bases with such profiles were named "knapsack-like" by [31]. Finally, we note several cases where the input profile is neither balanced or knapsack-like, such as the Coppersmith lattices for RSA [37], Elliptic Curve Hidden Number Problem (ECHNP) [56], Modular Inversion Hidden Number Problem (MIHNP) [8], Ajtai bases [44], or Goldreich-Goldwasser-Halevi encryption lattices [42]. We call such profiles irregular. These categories are not formal or strict; rather they aid in understanding the spectrum of profiles that appear in lattice cryptanalysis.

The output profiles for these cryptanalytic problems are similarly diverse. One class of output profiles seems to follow the GSA. We use the term "GSA-like" to describe the output profiles of lattice problems which follow such a pattern. The output profiles for random q-ary lattices, Goldstein-Mayer lattices, and Ajtai lattices are all GSA-like. A second class of output profiles consists of a single small element followed by a GSA-like decay. Output profiles of this shape imply that lattice reduction has found a single short vector $\vec{b}_0$ with small norm, and all other vectors are significantly longer. This context appears when solving the unique SVP problem, so we call such output profiles "uSVP-like." Finally, we observe that several output bases are neither GSA-like nor uSVP-like. Instead, we observe the presence of two or more levels where the profile is basically flat within a level before increasing to the start of the next level. We call these output profiles "structured" because their shape implies the presence of unexpectedly dense sublattices within a lattice, demonstrating additional structure when compared to random lattices. Output profiles for NTRU lattices, NTRU-like lattices [54], and Coppersmith lattices are all structured.

One important observation is that different lattice problems may have identical input profiles, but completely different output profiles. Random q-ary, LWE, and NTRU lattices all have balanced input profiles, but their outputs are GSA-like, uSVP-like, and structured respectively. Representing a lattice basis by its profile therefore discards information about the lattice and makes it impossible to exactly predict the properties and behavior of the lattice profile during lattice reduction. Although the lattice profile does not encode every property about a lattice basis, our analysis demonstrates that the lattice profile is a powerful tool for analyzing general lattice problems.

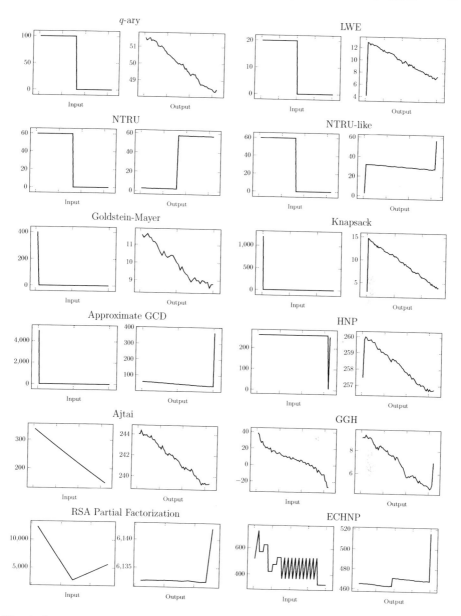

Fig. 1. Sample Lattice Input and Output Profiles. We generated sample lattices for a number of cryptanalytic problems, then LLL-reduced them. There is a wide variety of input types and output types. Note that the scales on the y-axes vary enormously across different problem instances.

3.2   Functions of the Lattice Profile

The profile of a lattice basis encodes significant information about how the profile might evolve during reduction by an LLL-like algorithm. While in some applications it is justified to use the geometric series assumption to predict the results of lattice reduction, it is clear from Fig. 1 that this assumption is false for many lattices of interest. For our algorithm to perform well on generic lattices, we must consider all possible ways the profile can change during lattice reduction.

One useful quantity is the *spread* of a basis, which we define in terms of its profile $\vec{\ell}$ as $\text{spread}(B) = \max_i \ell_i - \min_i \ell_i$. Kirchner et al. [31] use the spread to set the working precision of their algorithm, and they use their heuristic assumption to argue that the spread decreases exponentially quickly.

Neumaier and Stehlé give a key result about the spread [41, Lemma 2]. During every profile-altering step in an LLL-like algorithm that updates $\vec{\ell} \to \vec{\ell}'$, we have $\max_i \ell'_i \leq \max_i \ell_i$. Similarly, $\min_i \ell'_i \geq \min_i \ell_i$. That is, $\text{spread}(B)$ never increases. Unfortunately, the spread is not guaranteed to decrease: consider the basis $\begin{bmatrix} 2^p & 0 \\ 0 & 1 \end{bmatrix}$. The spread is p, and the spread of reduced basis $\begin{bmatrix} 0 & 2^p \\ 1 & 0 \end{bmatrix}$ is also p.

In this work, we consider the lattice potential $\Pi(B)$ of a basis in the logarithmic domain

$$\text{Potential: } \Pi(B) = \sum_{i=1}^{n} (n - i + 1)\ell_i.$$

With every swap in an LLL-like algorithm, the potential decreases. Additionally, if we have a sublattice B_{sub} and reduce to B'_{sub}, the change in potential of the sublattice equals the change in potential of the updated full lattice: $\Pi(B_{sub}) - \Pi(B'_{sub}) = \Pi(B) - \Pi(B')$.

Although not directly used in this work, many useful properties of the profile are found in the work of Ducas and van Woerden [20].

3.3   Profile Compression and Profile Drop

The profile of a lattice basis also encodes information about how individual vectors of that basis may be scaled without interfering with the behavior of an LLL-like algorithm. This scaling was first described by Saruchi et al. [50] and plays a central role in our ability to bound the precision required of our lattice reduction algorithm. We recount their technique here, and this motivates the definition of a new function of the lattice profile we call the *drop*.

At a high level, the number of bits of precision required to reduce an arbitrary basis B depends on the log-condition number of B. If B is size-reduced, the log-condition number depends on the spread. If B is also compressed by the scaling method, the spread depends on the drop. We show that the drop decreases during reduction, bounding the precision necessary at each step.

The key observation from the work of Saruchi et al. [50] is that some lattice bases can naturally be split into contiguous blocks where no LLL swaps are ever performed between neighboring blocks. When the profile is known, as in the case of upper-triangular bases, these blocks can be detected and exploited to reduce the number of bits of precision needed to represent the lattice.

Consider a profile $\vec{\ell}$ of dimension n where there exists index k satisfying

$$\max_{1 \leq i \leq k} \ell_i < \min_{k+1 \leq i \leq n} \ell_i.$$

This naturally splits the lattice into one projected sublattice of dimension k and one of dimension $n - k$. Because the profile-altering swaps of an LLL-like algorithm will never increase the maximum profile value of the first sublattice and will never decrease the minimum of the second, there will never be a point at which an LLL swap occurs at indices $(k, k + 1)$.

We can make changes to the basis without interfering with this property. For any $d < \min_{k+1 \leq i \leq n} \ell_i - \max_{1 \leq i \leq k} \ell_i$, we may scale vectors $\vec{b}_{k+1}, \ldots, \vec{b}_n$ by 2^{-d}, and the resulting basis still has the property that no LLL swaps occur at $(k, k+1)$. Since the vectors reduced within a block are scaled uniformly, this operation does not interfere with the order of LLL swaps within a projected sublattice. We call any scaling that preserves this block structure and the relative differences within a block a *valid* scaling. This operation is depicted in Fig. 2, and Saruchi et al. give an example method for computing valid scalings [50, Algorithm 2].

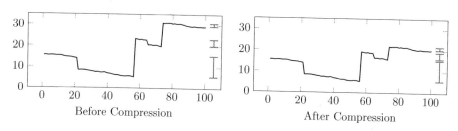

Fig. 2. Example scaling operation. The profile on the left is scaled with integer scaling factors to create the profile on the right. These profiles can be divided into three blocks: 1 to 55, 56 to 72, and 73 to 100. These three blocks can be scaled independently, so the second and third blocks are scaled down so that the gaps between blocks are small. The blue bars on the right depict the different components of the drop. Although the spread decreases with compression, the drop is unchanged.

Similar to how the Lovász condition ensures the decrease between ℓ_i and ℓ_{i+1} is bounded, the drop is used to ensure that the decrease within each disjoint region of the lattice profile is bounded. The drop is the infimum of the spread of a valid scaling of the profile, or equivalently it is the sum of the spreads of each independent block in the profile. A formal definition is given below.

Definition 2 (Profile drop). *Let $\vec{\ell}$ be the profile of a lattice of dimension n, and define the set*

$$D = \cup_{1 \leq i \leq n-1, \ell_{i+1} < \ell_i} [\ell_{i+1}, \ell_i].$$

Then the drop of the profile is the volume of this set.

A few properties are apparent. First, the drop is invariant under valid scaling. Second, by rescaling the regions so the gap between each region is $O(1)$, there is a way to create a scaled lattice with profile $\vec{\ell}' = \vec{\ell} - \vec{d}$ such that spread($\vec{\ell}'$) = drop($\vec{\ell}$) + $O(n)$. Finally, just as Neumeier and Stehlé show the spread never increases during LLL swaps, the same is true of the drop.

3.4   Lattice Reduction Condition

We use the newly defined drop of a lattice profile to specify our reduction condition. The Lovász condition of LLL reduction is unsuitable for our application because it bounds the decrease between all neighboring profile elements by the same amount. For our recursive algorithm, reducing a projected sublattice results in two large decreases between the profile elements directly neighboring the sublattice. Although possible, it is prohibitively expensive to iterate the algorithm until all decreases between neighbors are small. By weakening the definition of a reduced lattice, we obtain an algorithm that is asymptotically and practically more powerful.

Definition 3 (α lattice reduction). *A basis B is α-lattice-reduced for $\alpha > 0$ if it is size-reduced and if* drop(B) $\leq \alpha n$.

Theorem 2 shows that bases reduced in our sense are just as useful as bases reduced in the traditional sense, and we find the same to be true in practice.

Proof of Theorem 2. The proof of this theorem proceeds in much the same way as in [43, Theorem 9]. One key observation that makes our proof different is that drop(B) $\leq \alpha n \Rightarrow \max_{i<j}(\ell_i - \ell_j) \leq \alpha n$. The other is that $\log \|\vec{b}_i\| \leq \max_{j \leq i} \ell_j + O(n)$ by size reducedness. Additional details are in the full version [49]. □

4   Improved Lattice Reduction Algorithm

A crucial component of our algorithm is how we manage the growth of numerical error as we repeatedly scale, rotate, and round lattice bases. This is analogous to tracking floating point error in a computation, except we apply the concept to entire lattices. While many works [39, 46, 50] rely on the rigorous numerical bounds of Chang et al. [9] to analyze the effects of small perturbations, we unfortunately cannot rely on their results here. They require an analog of the Lovász condition which is prohibitively strict for our algorithm, and there seems to be no easy way to adapt their results to support our weaker condition on reduced bases. As a consequence, our results are asymptotic and to first order; we leave the important goal of developing rigorous bounds to future work.

Our approach to relating two lattice bases comes from normwise perturbation analysis [53], which uses an exponentially small parameter $\gamma = 2^{-u}$ to quantify the maximum deviation between two values. Frequently analysis is done up to first order in γ, and terms involving γ^2 are assumed to be negligibly small.

Definition 4 (Similar Lattice Bases). *Let B and $\hat{B}$ be two bases of the same rank and dimension, and let γ be a small parameter. We say B and $\hat{B}$ are similar if there exists orthogonal Q such that for all nonzero $\vec{x}$, up to first order in γ,*

$$\frac{\|B\vec{x} - Q\hat{B}\vec{x}\|}{\|B\vec{x}\|} \leq \gamma.$$

For simplicity, we write $B \approx_\gamma \hat{B}$.

For integer values of $\vec{x}$, note that $B\vec{x}$ and $Q\hat{B}\vec{x}$ are lattice vectors; the definition therefore states that every vector in lattice $\mathcal{L}(B)$ is normwise close to a particular (rotated) vector in the lattice $\mathcal{L}(\hat{B})$. This is different from [9], which considers matrix perturbations and basis vector perturbations, but our definition implies that if U is invertible, $B \approx_\gamma \hat{B} \Leftrightarrow BU \approx_\gamma \hat{B}U$. The above definition leads to several other useful results.

Lemma 1. *Let $B_1, B_2, B_3 \in \mathbb{R}^{n \times n}$, and let $\gamma, \gamma' \geq 0$. Then*

1. *$B_1 \approx_\gamma B_2 \Leftrightarrow B_2 \approx_\gamma B_1$*
2. *$B_1 \approx_\gamma B_2$ and $B_2 \approx_{\gamma'} B_3 \Rightarrow B_1 \approx_{\gamma+\gamma'} B_3$.*
3. *If $B_1 \approx_\gamma B_2$, then to first order*

$$\|B_2\| \leq (1+\gamma)\|B_1\| \quad and \quad \|B_2^{-1}\| \leq (1+\kappa(B_1)\gamma)\|B_1^{-1}\|$$

4. *Let $\vec{\ell}_1$ and $\vec{\ell}_2$ be the profiles of B_1 and B_2, and let $B_1 \approx_\gamma B_2$. Then*

$$|\ell_{1,i} - \ell_{2,i}| < \sqrt{2n^3}\kappa(B_1)\gamma \text{ for all } i \in \{1, \dots, n\}.$$

The proofs are not particularly enlightening, and they involve routine applications of perturbation theory. These proofs are included in the full version of this paper [49].

There are a few important things to note with this lemma. First, lattice basis similarity is symmetric, and error grows slowly when considering transitive similarity. This fact allows us to bound the accumulated error after calculating a chain of multiple similar lattice bases. Second, for $\gamma \ll 1/\kappa(B)$, we see that lattice similarity implies that the condition number and profiles of similar bases are provably close. This shows how the condition number $\kappa(B)$ plays an important role in similarity, and it justifies our focus on constraining the condition number during lattice reduction.

4.1 Basis Compression

The central object in our algorithm is a *compressed* lattice basis which plays an analogous role to the size reduction and Gram-Schmidt orthogonalization in the original LLL algorithm. In particular, we use lattice compression to convert an arbitrary basis B into a new basis $\hat{B}$ that captures the same geometric properties with respect to lattice reduction, except $\hat{B}$ is upper-triangular with small integer entries and has a small condition number, making it easier to work with.

Definition 5 (γ-Compressed Lattice Basis). *Let $B \in \mathbb{R}^{n \times n}$ be a basis of rank n. We say $\hat{B} \in \mathbb{Z}^{n \times n}$ is a γ-compressed basis of B if it satisfies the following:*

- *$\hat{B} \approx_\gamma BUD$ for some unimodular U and diagonal D.*
- *$\hat{B} \in \mathbb{Z}^{n \times n}$ is upper-triangular with nonzero diagonal.*
- *$\hat{B}$ is size-reduced: $\log \kappa(\hat{B}) = drop(\hat{B}) + O(n)$.*
- *Entries are small: $\log \|\hat{B}\|_{max} = O(drop(B) - \log \gamma + n)$*
- *If U_2 is a unimodular matrix obtained by performing LLL swaps or size-reduction operations on $\hat{B}$, then DU_2D^{-1} is unimodular.*

The last property is related to the scaling technique of Saruchi et al. [50, Theorem 2], and it is due to U_2 having a block upper triangular structure that respects the independent blocks described in Sect. 3.3. It is possible to efficiently compute a γ-compressed basis given an estimate of $\kappa(B)$. We outline the basic compression operation in Algorithm 2, and give additional details in the full version [49].

Algorithm 2: CompressLattice (Simplified)

Input : $B \in \mathbb{Z}^{n \times n}$, $\gamma \leq 1/2$, $C > \log \kappa(B)$
Output: $\hat{B}$ compressed, $U \in \mathbb{Z}^{n \times n}$, $D = diag(2^{d_1}, \ldots, 2^{d_n})$ with $d_i \in \mathbb{Z}$
   satisfying $\hat{B} \approx_{2^{-O(drop(B)+n)}\gamma} BUD$. The profile of $\hat{B}$ is close to the
   (D-scaled) profile of B with absolute error γ.

1 QR-Factorize B to get an upper-triangular, floating point, γ-similar basis.
2 Compute profile $\vec{\ell}$ from the diagonal of the R-factor.
3 Compute integer scaling vector $\vec{d}$ using the profile and the technique of [50].
4 Scale and round the entries to integer values.
5 Size reduce to get basis $\hat{B}$ and unimodular U.
6 **return** $\hat{B}, U, diag(2^{d_1}, \ldots, 2^{d_n})$

Lemma 2. *Let $\omega \in (2,3]$ and ε be global parameters bounding the complexity of algorithms as follows. We assume there exists algorithm QR that on input B, $C > \log \kappa(B)$, returns a γ-similar basis R with $\kappa(R) = 2^{O(C)}$ in time $O(n^\omega(C - \log \gamma + \log n)^{1+\varepsilon})$. We also assume that there exists algorithm SizeReduce that size reduces an integer, upper-triangular basis B (with $C > \log \kappa(B)$) in time $O(n^\omega(C + \log \|B\|_{max} + n)^{1+\varepsilon})$. Finally, we assume there exists a matrix multiplication algorithm which computes product A_1A_2 of two $n \times n$ matrices in time $O(n^\omega(\log \|A_1\|_{max} + \log \|A_2\|_{max})^{1+\varepsilon})$.*

Algorithm CompressLattice returns a compressed basis $\hat{B}$, diagonal $D = diag(2^{d_1}, \ldots, 2^{d_n})$, and unimodular U satisfying $\hat{B} \approx_{2^{-O(drop(B)+n)}\gamma} BUD$. In addition, if $\vec{\ell}_B$ is the profile of B and $\vec{\ell}_{\hat{B}}$ is the profile of $\hat{B}$, then we have $\left|\vec{\ell}_{\hat{B},i} - (\vec{\ell}_{B,i} + d_i)\right| \leq \gamma$. This algorithm takes time $O(n^\omega(C - \log \gamma + n)^{1+\varepsilon})$.

Example QR factorization and size reduction algorithms satisfying the condition with $\omega = 3$ are provided in the full version [49], and heuristic algorithms for $\omega < 3$ are suggested in [31].

The proof of this lemma involves tracking how the condition number changes after each operation, showing how each operation results in a similar lattice. The resulting lattice has small condition number and is upper-triangular as a result of the size-reduction and QR operations. The scaling operation ensures that $\mathrm{spread}(\hat{\ell}_i) = \mathrm{drop}(B) + O(n)$, which in turn bounds the resulting precision.

4.2   Reducing Sublattices

An important feature of recursive lattice reduction algorithms is the ability to compute projected sublattices B_{sub}, reduce them to obtain unimodular U_{sub}, then use U_{sub} to apply the same transformation to the original lattice basis [33, 41]. For completeness, we include a description of this operation using our notation of compression and γ-similarity.

Algorithm 3: ReduceSublattice

Input   : Compressed basis $B^{(k)} \in \mathbb{Z}^{n \times n}$, sublattice index $1 \leq i < j \leq n$, reduction quality $\alpha(\cdot)$, approximation quality $\gamma \leq 2^{-1}$, reduction function LatRed

Output: Compressed basis $B^{(k+1)}$, unimodular U, and diagonal D such that $B^{(k+1)} \approx_{\gamma'} B^{(k)} U D$ for $\gamma' = 2^{-O(\mathrm{drop}(B^{(k+1)})+n)} \gamma$ and $\mathrm{drop}(B^{(k+1)}_{[i:j]}) \leq (\alpha(j-i)+\gamma)(j-i)$.

1 $B'_{sub}, U'_{sub}, D_{sub} \leftarrow$ CompressLattice$(B^{(k)}_{[i:j]}, \gamma)$
2 $U''_{sub} \leftarrow$ LatRed$(B'_{sub}, \alpha, \gamma)$
3 $U' \leftarrow \mathrm{diag}(I_{i-1}, U'_{sub} D_{sub} U''_{sub} D^{-1}_{sub}, I_{n-j})$
4 $B^{(k+1)}, U'', D \leftarrow$ CompressLattice$(B^{(k)} U', \gamma)$
5 $U \leftarrow U' U''$
6 **return** $B^{(k+1)}, U, D$

Lemma 3 (Correctness of Algorithm 3 (ReduceSublattice)). *Consider compressed basis $B^{(k)}$, sublattice index $[i : j]$, approximation quality γ, lattice reduction function LatRed, and lattice reduction quality α. Algorithm 3 returns compressed basis $B^{(k+1)}$, unimodular U, and diagonal D such that for $\gamma' = 2^{-O(\mathrm{drop}(B^{(k+1)})+n)} \gamma$, we have $B^{(k+1)} \approx_{\gamma'} B^{(k)} U D$. In addition, the profile of $B^{(k+1)}$ matches the (D-scaled) profile of $B^{(k)}$ outside of index $[i : j]$ to absolute error γ and has bounded drop on index $[i : j]$: $\mathrm{drop}(B^{(k+1)}_{[i:j]}) \leq (\alpha(j-i)+\gamma)(j-i)$. The running time of this algorithm, excluding the call to LatRed, is*

$$O\left(n^\omega (\mathrm{drop}(B^{(k)}) - \log\gamma + n)^{1+\varepsilon}\right).$$

The Global Profile. In both the practical implementation and theoretical analysis of our algorithm, it is helpful to make use of a concept we call the "global profile." As explored in Lemma 3, sublattice reduction returns a new basis whose (scaled) profile is almost unchanged outside of the sublattice index, and the drop is almost bounded within the sublattice index, where the absolute error scales with γ. We note that the cost of this algorithm scales with $-\log \gamma$, so it is exceedingly cheap to trade off running time for accuracy.

The closeness of these profiles means that we can relate the explicitly computed profile of the current (local) sublattice to the (global) profile of the original input had we applied the same unimodular transformations to the input basis. If we are currently reducing the sublattice B_{sub} of input B at global index $[i:j]$ with profiles $\vec{\ell}_{sub}$ and $\vec{\ell}$ respectively, then there exist unimodular U, $D = diag(2^{d_1}, \ldots, 2^{d_n})$, and similarity γ such that

$$|\bar{\ell}_{i+k} - (\ell_{sub,k} - d_{i+k})| \leq \gamma \text{ for } k \in \{1, \ldots, j - i\}.$$

For the purpose of our practical implementation and asymptotic analysis, we assume γ is parameterized so that the absolute error in the profile is negligibly small. This makes the notation much cleaner and more intuitive. We revisit this assumption later when we use our heuristic assumptions to select γ, but we note that the accumulated error is swallowed by the γ' term in Algorithm 3, is offset by the strictly decreasing α in Lemma 4, and does not affect the reducedness of bases, since similarity to a basis with drop $O(\alpha n)$ implies a drop of $O((\alpha+\gamma)n) = O(\alpha n)$. We leave rigorous analyses to future work.

This definition is practically useful, since $\vec{d}$ can be efficiently computed by tracking how the bases have been scaled during compression. Therefore at any point in the computation, the global profile is known to high accuracy. We use $\bar{\Pi}$ to refer to the potential computed from the global profile $\vec{\ell}$, and we observe that this is a useful tool for understanding the remaining work to be done during lattice reduction. For more information, we refer to the full version [49].

4.3   Lattice Reduction of Partially Reduced Bases

So far, we have demonstrated how to take a specified sublattice and reduce it, all while efficiently maintaining a "compressed" representation whose size depends on the current profile drop. Depending on the profile of the compressed basis, the choice of sublattice can have a large impact on the running time. It is important to select these sublattices carefully, and in this section we develop a particular strategy that is efficient for input bases whose profiles are slightly constrained. Section 4.5 uses this subroutine to reduce arbitrary input bases.

Our constraints enable us to construct a simple recursive algorithm that maintains these properties, and we use this invariance to argue that our algorithm makes progress no matter the particular evolution of the profile. This definition and recursive subroutine is the core of our algorithm, and we show how it is used to reduce generic lattice bases in Sect. 4.5. We call such constrained bases *LR-reduced*, since we require that the *Left* ($B_{[0:\frac{n}{2}]}$) and *Right* ($B_{[\frac{n}{2}:n]}$) projected sublattices each have bounded drop.

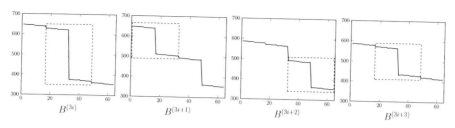

Fig. 3. Changes in Profile during LR Reduction. We logged the profile (without compression scalings) at different stages while running Algorithm 4 on a q-ary lattice basis. The dashed box indicates the profile of the sublattice reduce in each step, corresponding to the Middle, Left, and Right sublattices. Observe that $B^{(3i)}$ and $B^{(3i+3)}$ are LR-reduced, and all sublattices are LR-reduced.

Definition 6 (LR-reduced basis). *We consider a basis B of rank $n = 2^k$ and a reduction parameter $\alpha(\cdot)$. B is LR-reduced if $k = 0$ or:*

- *$B_{[0:\frac{n}{2}]}$ and $B_{[\frac{n}{2}:n]}$ have bounded drop $\leq \alpha(n/2)n/2$, and*
- *$B_{[0:\frac{n}{2}]}$ and $B_{[\frac{n}{2}:n]}$ are LR-reduced with parameter α.*

Algorithm 4: ReduceLR

Input : Compressed LR-reduced basis $B^{(3i)}$ of rank $n \geq 2$ a power of 2, reduction quality α, similarity quality γ

Output: Unimodular U such that $B^{(3i)}UD \approx_{2^{-O(\alpha n)}\gamma} B^{(3r)}$ for diagonal D and number of rounds $r - i$. $B^{(3r)}$ is LR-reduced and $\alpha(n)$-lattice-reduced.

1 **if** $n = 2$ **then**
2 $\quad$ **return** $U \leftarrow$ output of Schönhage's reduction algorithm [52]
3 $B^{(3i+1)}, U_M, D_M \leftarrow$ ReduceSublattice$(B^{(3i)}, \frac{n}{4}, \frac{3n}{4}, \alpha, \gamma, \text{ReduceLR})$
4 $B^{(3i+2)}, U_L, D_L \leftarrow$ ReduceSublattice$(B^{(3i+1)}, 0, \frac{n}{2}, \alpha, \gamma, \text{ReduceLR})$
5 $B^{(3i+3)}, U_R, D_R \leftarrow$ ReduceSublattice$(B^{(3i+2)}, \frac{n}{2}, n, \alpha, \gamma, \text{ReduceLR})$
6 **if** $drop(B^{(3i+3)}) > \alpha(n)n$ **then**
7 $\quad$ $U_2 \leftarrow$ ReduceLR$(B^{(3i+3)}, \alpha, \gamma)$
8 **else**
9 $\quad$ $U_2 \leftarrow I_n$
10 $U \leftarrow U_M D_M U_L (D_L U_R (D_R U_2 D_R^{-1}) D_L^{-1}) D_M^{-1}$
11 **return** U

We describe a method to fully reduce LR-reduced bases in Algorithm 4, and we depict the behavior in Fig. 3. The main appeal of this construction is how the inputs to each recursive call are LR-reduced, so we can temporarily avoid some of the complexity of analyzing the behavior of our algorithm on completely arbitrary lattice bases. We conclude this section by exploring how to set some of the input arguments for this algorithm, and investigate the behavior in Sect. 4.4.

Setting Reduction Parameter α. We have so far used $\alpha(\cdot)$ to represent the approximation factors used to bound the quality of reduced sublattices of different sizes. The particular choice of α has significant impact on the behavior of the algorithm. If $\alpha(n/2) \approx \alpha(n)$, then the process depicted in Fig. 3 takes too many rounds to converge, since we require the overall slope in this example to match the slope in both the left and right halves of the profile. Ideally, we want the sublattices to be reduced to higher quality, so we want $\alpha(n/2) < \alpha(n)$. Fewer rounds are needed to reduce a basis of rank n, but if $\alpha(n/2)$ is too small, the high-quality sublattice reductions become prohibitively expensive. In addition, we require $\alpha(2) \geq \alpha^* = \log(4/3)$, a bound determined by Hermite's constant for rank-2 lattices.

A similar phenomenon was observed by Kirchner, Espitau, and Fouque [31], and they suggest asymptotic ranges for determining the reduction quality of sublattices. Since our main goal is to have a practical algorithm that concretely achieves comparable reduction quality to LLL, we develop an entirely new, concrete method for setting this parameter. In particular, if our end goal is reducing a lattice of rank N to quality α, we reduce sublattices of rank n to quality

$$\alpha(n) = \alpha^* + \left(\frac{n}{N}\right)^{\log g} (\alpha - \alpha^*)$$

for some fixed parameter $1 < g < 2^{\omega-2}$. This choice of α geometrically interpolates between α^* and α, and it guarantees $\alpha(2) \geq \alpha^*$ and $\alpha(N) = \alpha$.

Bounding the Number of Rounds. The description of Algorithm 4 references the number of rounds r, which counts how many iterations the cycle of three sublattice reduction steps are applied to input basis $B^{(0)}$. Understanding r is crucial to bounding the running time and numerical error of the algorithm, but although r is small in practice, it is challenging to bound this value for all possible lattice bases without making heuristic assumptions.

Koy and Schnorr [33, Theorem 3] bound the number of iterations of their recursive algorithm with a block variant of the potential function, but they find it is "impractical" to bound the spread of Gram-Schmidt norms between blocks, so their approach fails to bound the profile drop and is incompatible with our algorithm. Neumaier and Stehle [41, Lemma 5] use dynamical systems to bound the number of iterations, but the resulting bases are similarly ill-behaved. Kirchner et al. [31, Section 4.2] suggest using six iterations in practice.

We make the following heuristic assumptions involving r. These assumptions hold for the diverse suite of lattice families we tested our algorithm on, and we were unable to create any pathological counterexamples.

Heuristic 1. The potential reduced in the current round is bounded by the potential reduced in all remaining rounds. In particular,

$$\bar{\Pi}(B^{(3i)}) - \bar{\Pi}(B^{(3(i+1))}) = \Omega\left(\bar{\Pi}(B^{(3i)}) - \bar{\Pi}(B^{(3r)})\right).$$

Heuristic 2. The change in potential in the current round is bounded in all except the last two rounds. That is, for all $i < r - 2$,

$$\bar{\Pi}(B^{(3i)}) - \bar{\Pi}(B^{(3(i+1))}) = \Omega\left(n^3(\alpha(n) - \alpha(n/2))\right).$$

Recalling Fig. 3, the first heuristic assumption captures the idea that the bulk of the remaining reduction work happens in the next three sublattice reductions. Intuitively, since the left and right sublattices are already reduced, all of the remaining potential must be between these two halves; reducing the middle sublattice decreases much of this potential. The second heuristic is designed to handle cases where the change in potential is small, like when there is a solitary long vector in the left sublattice of an otherwise reduced basis. Although we cannot completely avoid these cases, this heuristic states that if no sublattice reduction in a round removes much potential, the profile is very nearly reduced.

As can be found in the full version [49], it is possible to show by induction that our heuristic assumptions imply that the number of rounds r is

$$O\left(\log\left(\frac{\bar{\Pi}(B^{(3i)}) - \bar{\Pi}(B^{(3r)})}{n^3(\alpha - \alpha^*)}\right)\right) = O\left(\log(\mathrm{drop}(B^{(3i)})/n) + \log\left(\frac{1}{\alpha - \alpha^*}\right)\right).$$

Setting the Similarity Parameter γ. Algorithm 3 returns a γ'-similar basis where $\gamma' = 2^{-O(\mathrm{drop}(B^{(k+1)})+n)}\gamma$; since Algorithm 4 calls this subroutine a total of $3r$ times within the r rounds of reduction, this creates a similarity relationship with parameter $\sum_{i=0}^{r-1} 2^{-O(\mathrm{drop}(B^{(i+1)})+n)}\gamma \le 3r2^{-O(\mathrm{drop}(B^{(3r)})+n)}\gamma = 3r2^{-O(\alpha n)}\gamma$, and this achieves that the profiles of $B^{(0)}$ and $B^{(3r)}$ are the same up to scaling and absolute error $3r\gamma$.

This suggests setting the working value of γ at each round i to $-\log(\gamma) = \Theta(\log r)$. The heuristic contribution of $\log r = O(\log(\log \mathrm{drop}(B^{(3i)}) + \log n))$ is small, so we infer that the heuristic assumptions about the number of rounds does not matter much when it comes to evaluating the numerical stability. In fact, any choice of γ satisfying

$$\gamma = 2^{-O(\mathrm{drop}(B^{(3i)})+n)}.$$

does not affect the $O(\mathrm{drop}(B^{(k)}) - \log \gamma + n)$ term in the running time.

4.4 Analyzing the Behavior of Left-Right Reduction

Relating the Potential to the Profile Drop. The lattice potential is a useful tool for bounding the remaining work, but the cost of performing basis compression and matrix multiplication depends on the profile drop. We wish to relate these two quantities, but this is challenging. If a lattice does not follow the GSA, large changes in potential do not necessarily imply large changes in the drop, and large changes in the drop do not imply large changes in potential.

While [31, Section 4.2] bounds the cost complexity per unit reduction in potential, it does so using the heuristic assumption which predicts exponentially decreasing spread. This fails to consider the common cases where sublattice reduction finds vectors shorter than predicted by the GSA. We require a new approach to relate the change in lattice potential to the cost of future updates.

The following lemma shows that the three sublattice reductions in Algorithm 4 either decrease the drop (and therefore future update cost) by a large amount or decrease the potential by a large amount. We prove this by using the LR-reduction property to bound the maximum and minimum values of the profile in sublattices of rank $n/4$ after each of the three sublattice reductions.

Lemma 4. *Let $B^{(3i)}$ be the compressed LR-reduced basis of rank n at round i used as input to Algorithm 4, and let $B^{(3i+3)}$ be the basis after the three sublattice reductions. The drop of the input basis for the next round is bounded by the current round's change in global potential $\bar{\Pi}$:*

$$n^2 \left(drop(B^{(3i+3)}) - 5\alpha(n)n/2 \right) = O \left(\bar{\Pi}(B^{(3i)}) - \bar{\Pi}(B^{(3i+3)}) \right).$$

We will use this lemma to amortize the cost of expensive update steps with the overall change in lattice potential.

Bounding the Running Time. There are many factors that go into bounding the running time of Algorithm 4. Our goal in analyzing this algorithm is to find a cost function T that can bound the running time at all levels. One piece of the running time on input B is the cost of the nonrecursive steps, which by Lemma 3 and our choice of γ is $O(n^\omega(drop(B) + n)^{1+\varepsilon})$. We write this as $O(n^\omega p^{1+\varepsilon})$ for $p = \Theta(drop(B) + n)$. Note that $\log(\|B\|_{max}) = O(p)$ and $\log(\|U\|_{max}) = O(p)$, so it is natural to think of p as the working precision. Note also that in the base case, the cost of Schönhage reduction [52] takes time $O(p^{1+\varepsilon}) = O(n^\omega p^{1+\varepsilon})$.

The cost function T also contains the recursive cost of Algorithm 4, which calls itself three times on sublattices of rank $n/2$, and once on a lattice of rank n. A cost function T is therefore a valid bound on the running time if

$$T(B^{(3i)}) \geq T(B_M) + T(B_L) + T(B_R) + C_u n^\omega p^{1+\varepsilon} + T(B^{(3i+3)}) \geq 0 \quad (1)$$

for some constant $C_u > 0$ bounding the cost of the base case and nonrecursive steps. We have found that the cost function naturally depends on three values.

1. **Potential Change.** Like in the original LLL algorithm, the potential of a lattice basis conveys important information about how much work remains. Including this term allows us to distinguish between lattice bases that require the same amount of precision but different amounts of remaining potential. We set this term to

$$T_{\bar{\Pi}}(B^{(3i)}) = n^{\omega-2} \left(\bar{\Pi}(B^{(3i)}) - \bar{\Pi}(B^{(3r)}) \right) p^\varepsilon.$$

2. **Precision.** Lattice basis potential does not capture the entire picture. A lattice basis may have asymptotically small potential, but require arbitrarily large precision. Since the nonrecursive steps depend on the precision, this term must be present. We set this term to

$$T_{prec}(B^{(3i)}) = n^\omega p^{1+\varepsilon}.$$

3. **Approximation.** We require at least one term to depend on the approximation factor of lattice reduction. Otherwise, this would imply that it is possible to achieve lattice bases with arbitrarily good approximation. We set this term to

$$T_A(B^{(3i)}) = \left(\frac{\bar{\Pi}(B^{(3i)}) - \bar{\Pi}(B^{(3r)})}{n^3(\boldsymbol{\alpha}(n) - \boldsymbol{\alpha}(n/2))} + c_1 \right) n^\omega (n + \boldsymbol{\alpha}(n)n) p^\varepsilon$$

for $i < r$ for some $c_1 > 0$ and $T_A(B^{(3r)}) = 0$.

We define function $T(B^{(3i)}) = C_{\bar{\Pi}} T_{\bar{\Pi}}(B^{(3i)}) + C_{prec} T_{prec}(B^{(3i)}) + C_A T_A(B^{(3i)})$ for some constants $C_{\bar{\Pi}}, C_{prec}, C_A$. While the first two terms make intuitive sense, the third is more difficult to explain. As the basis becomes more reduced, the approximation factor of sublattice reduction remains a fixed cost that always contributes to the drop. To bound the contribution of this fixed cost in each node of the recursion tree, we use the heuristic assumptions to bound the recursive behavior and show that this choice of $T_A(\cdot)$ satisfies the requirements. Our conclusion does not rule out the possibility of simpler constructions; we only aim to give a reasonable construction that works.

Lemma 5. *Let $\omega \in (2,3]$ be a parameter bounding the complexity of matrix multiplication, size reduction, and QR factorization as described in Lemma 2. If the heuristic assumptions 1 and 2 are correct, then there exists appropriate choice of constants $C_{\bar{\Pi}}, C_{prec}, C_A > 0$ such that $T(\cdot)$ satisfies Eq. 1.*

As a corollary, this means that for input B and reduction goal α, it is possible to instantiate $\boldsymbol{\alpha}$ and γ such that the running time of Algorithm 4 on these inputs is $O(T(B)) =$

$$O\left(\left(\frac{\alpha}{\alpha - \alpha^*} \right) n^\omega p^{1+\varepsilon} + \alpha n^{\omega+1} p^\varepsilon \right)$$

where $p = O(drop(B) + n)$.

4.5 Reducing Generic Lattice Bases

Algorithm 4 provides a method for α-reducing bases with rank $n = 2^k$ that are LR-reduced and compressed, but most lattice bases do not satisfy this condition. Fortunately, it is comparatively easy to reduce generic bases using this method.

We begin by *padding* the lattice with a number of large, orthogonal vectors in higher-dimensional space until the rank of the padded lattice is a power of 2. These extraneous vectors are chosen so that they are never modified by lattice reduction. In particular, for an input basis B of rank n with $\kappa(B) < 2^C$, we generate the padded basis of dimension $N = 2^{\lceil \log(n) \rceil}$

$$
B_{pad} = \begin{bmatrix} B & 0 \\ 0 & \lceil 2n \|B\|_{max} \rceil I_{N-n} \end{bmatrix}.
$$

We have $\text{drop}(B) = \text{drop}(B_{pad})$ and $\kappa(B_{pad}) = 2^{C+O(\log n)}$. The latter statement is because the singular values of B_{pad} are the singular values of B and $\lceil 2n \|B\|_{max} \rceil$. The largest singular value of B_{pad} is only up to $O(n)$ times larger than the largest of B, and the smallest singular value is unchanged.

We next compress B_{pad} to obtain a compressed basis for input to Algorithm 3. This basis is not LR-reduced, however. We recursively reduce the left sublattice to quality α, and then do the same with the right. Now that the basis is LR-reduced and compressed, we use Algorithm 4 to reduce it the rest of the way. Although this algorithm is also recursive, its recursive structure is simply a binary tree, and it is fully analyzable.

Lattice reduction of B_{pad} returns U_{pad} such that, for some scaling D_{pad}, $\text{drop}(B_{pad}U_{pad}) = \text{drop}(B_{pad}U_{pad}D_{pad}) \leq \alpha N/2$. In addition, the padding scheme yields the special structure

$$
U_{pad} = \begin{bmatrix} U' & 0 \\ 0 & I_{N-n} \end{bmatrix},
$$

so $\text{drop}(BU') \leq \alpha n$. We finally size-reduce BU' to obtain U which α-lattice-reduces B. These operations are described in detail in the full version [49]. We arrive at the following result.

Theorem 1 (Full). *Let $B \in \mathbb{Z}^{n \times n}$ be a lattice basis and $C > \log(\kappa(B))$ a bound on its condition number. Let α^* be a constant determined by the Hermite constant in small dimension, and let $\alpha > 2\alpha^*$ be the desired reduction quality. Finally, let $\omega \in (2,3]$ and $\varepsilon > 0$ be parameters bounding the runtime of size reduction, matrix multiplication, and QR factorization as described in Lemma 2. If the heuristic assumptions 1 and 2 are correct, then our algorithm returns unimodular U such that BU is $O(\alpha)$-lattice-reduced. The running time of our reduction algorithm is*

$$
O\left(\left(\frac{\alpha}{\alpha - \alpha^*} \right) n^\omega (C + n)^{1+\varepsilon} \right).
$$

5   Implementation Details

We implemented our algorithm in C++. Our implementation is currently about 14,000 lines of code. We have two versions of our algorithm: the "provable" version, where the padding scheme, recursion decisions, and reduction parameters match those described in our proofs, and the "heuristic" version, which we use to evaluate the practical performance in our running time experiments.

Heuristic and optimization improvements. Our heuristic implementation does not implement the padding scheme from Sect. 4.5. Rather than limit ReduceLR to operate on bases of rank 2^k, we simply round when subdividing the lattice. In addition, we also use an approach similar to [31] to reduce sublattices to quality $\alpha \gg \alpha(n/2)$ in early rounds, avoiding expensive reductions of sublattices that have little effect on global potential. Until the drop is sufficiently small, we reduce sublattices to quality $\Theta(\text{drop}(B)/n)$, which improves running time considerably.

We also do not always recurse down to rank 2. Instead, if the dimension is ≤ 32 and required precision is at most 128 bits, we use fpLLL to reduce that basis using LLL or BKZ, depending on the desired reduction quality. This allows us to achieve α better than $\log(4/3)$ in practice.

Typically, we perform compression so the resulting size is $2 \cdot \text{drop}(B) + 3n + 30$ bits and find that our algorithm is stable for all of our test cases. For some of the ultra-large test cases, we aggressively set the precision to $\text{drop}(B) + 30$ bits. This is more memory efficient, but it is not stable for some of the lattice bases with structured output, so we do not do this by default.

Many optimizations are found in the compression function, as this is a significant cost in our algorithm. We note that $B^{(k)}U'$ in Algorithm 3 is block-upper-triangular, with $B_{2,2}$ corresponding to $B^{(k)}_{[i:j]}$ in the following example:

$$B^{(k)}U' = \begin{bmatrix} B_{1,1} & B_{1,2} & B_{1,3} \\ 0 & B_{2,2} & B_{2,3} \\ 0 & 0 & B_{3,3} \end{bmatrix}.$$

The only non-upper-triangular block on the diagonal is $B_{2,2}$, so $\begin{bmatrix} B_{2,2} & B_{2,3} \end{bmatrix}$ can be QR-factorized on its own. If $B^{(k)}$ was η-size-reduced before sublattice reduction, then $B_{1,1}$ and $B_{3,3}$ remain size-reduced. $B_{1,2}$ changed with multiplication by U', but only $B_{1,1}$ is needed to size-reduce $B_{1,2}$. This is independent of the QR-factorization in the second row, so we are able to exploit the data dependencies to do multiple operations in parallel, including reducing multiple sublattices simultaneously. If we use do a variant of Seysen size reduction, we avoid a potentially unstable inversion of $B_{1,1}$ by exploiting its triangularity [26, Chapter 8] to size-reduce $B_{1,2}$.

We additionally adopt a version of [31, Algorithm 8] to make a basis LR-reduced, rather than exactly implement the method described in Sect. 4.5. This is because in practice, knapsack-like lattices often behave like random, GSA-like lattices at the beginning of computation. The first sublattice reduction of rank 2 often decreases the drop by half, and it is cheaper to recompress the entire rank-n basis now since only two rows are not η-size-reduced. However, it is easy to construct knapsack-like counterexamples that do not behave like random lattices (a diagonal knapsack-like basis is one example), so while this is a worthwhile case to optimize for, and there is no downside to performing early reduction in this way, it is not possible to prove that our algorithm runs faster on knapsack-like input bases.

6   Experimental Evaluation

We conducted a series of experiments to demonstrate the performance of our algorithm. All of our experiments were carried out on a single core of a 2.20 GHz Intel Xeon E5-2699v4 processor of a machine with 512 GB of RAM unless noted otherwise. This machine was built in 2016. For fpLLL, we used version 5.4.2 available on GitHub, compiled and run on this same machine. For the Kirchner, Espitau, and Fouque (KEF) algorithm, the authors kindly shared their source code with us, which we also compiled and ran on this same machine.

The specific details of a problem determine what approximation factor is required to solve the problem, and we configure all three implementations to heuristically obtain equivalently short vectors. Typically, this corresponds to a root Hermite factor of 1.02 or 1.03, as is achieved by the default L^2 implementation of fpLLL. Better approximation factors are achieved using fpLLL's BKZ implementation, and worse approximation factors are achieved by doing L^2 with a smaller value of δ. Each measurement is collected over a single instance of the respective problem, since the running time does not vary significantly across multiple trials. Additional experiments are found in the full version [49].

6.1   Knapsack Lattices

Knapsack lattices are one of the canonical applications of lattice reduction in cryptography and cryptanalysis, and one of the most common classes of lattices encountered in lattice reduction problems. One of the first applications of lattice reduction in cryptography was to solve the low-density subset sum problem to attack knapsack public-key cryptography. We use the lattice basis construction of [34], which is knapsack-like in input and uSVP-like in output, since the solution to the subset sum problem corresponds to a uniquely short vector.

We constructed the lattice bases for the knapsack instances in [31] and reduced them using our implementation, fpLLL, and the implementation of [31]. Because their implementation crashes partway through the reduction process, we present their reported values. All examples were run single-threaded and reduced to quality $\alpha = 0.0852$, equivalent to root Hermite factor 1.03 (Table 1).

Table 1. Performance on knapsack lattices.

Dimension	Bit size	fpLLL (s)	[31, reported] (s)	Ours (s)
128	100000	3831	400	69
256	10000	2764	200	83
384	10000	10855	780	246

We conjecture that the presence of this uniquely short vector, which means that the heuristic assumption of [31] does not hold at all recursion levels, leads to their algorithm requiring more bits of precision than ours, and therefore a longer runtime.

6.2   Gentry-Halevi Fully Homomorphic Encryption

Gentry proposed a Fully Homomorphic Encryption (FHE) scheme based on ideal lattices in 2009 [23] with concrete parameters suggested by Gentry and Halevi in [24]. The scheme relied on two hardness assumptions. First, the difficulty of breaking the underlying somewhat homomorphic encryption scheme was based on ideal lattice problems, and the hardness of the transformation that made it bootstrappable was based on the sparse subset sum problem (SSSP). Gentry and Halevi have created several public keys for this scheme as a cryptanalytic key recovery challenge.[2]

Due to a polynomial-time quantum algorithm [5] and subexponential-time classical algorithms [6, 7] solving the principal ideal problem, FHE based on ideals is no longer considered secure. The SSSP challenges were solved in practice by [35], breaking the bootstrapping argument of Gentry and Halevi's scheme. We are unaware of a practical break of the underlying ideal lattice problems for the proposed small, medium, and large parameters in the main challenges.

Gentry and Halevi propose different security levels s that naturally lead to lattices in Hermite Normal Form of dimension $n = 2^{s+1}$ and bit size $380(2^{s+1})$. The goal of lattice reduction is finding a basis with $\|\vec{b}_n^*\|$ sufficiently large. Gentry-Halevi lattices are knapsack-like in input and GSA-like in output.

Chen and Nguyen reduced the toy parameters (dimension 512) in 30 core-days in 2011 using generic lattice reduction algorithms [10]. They estimated that the small parameters (dimension 2048) would take 45 core-years and the medium parameters (dimension 8192) would take 68582 core-years. Plantard, Susilo, and Zhang exploited extra algebraic structure to solve the toy challenge in 24 core-days in 2015 and estimated 15.7 years to solve the small parameters [48].

Our implementation solves the toy parameters in 15 core-minutes and the small parameters in under 31 core-hours running single-threaded on the 2.2GHz processors. We additionally broke the small parameters in 4 h 10 min wall time running in multithreaded mode on an AMD EPYC 72F3 8-core processor running at up to 4.1GHz. Gentry and Halevi's small main challenge has solution 201 216 186 242 353 55 335 420 104 13 299 262 510 414 239.

We solved the medium parameters in about 6.4 core-years running in multi-threaded mode on a 2.6GHz Intel Xeon E7-4860v2 processor of a machine with one terabyte of RAM, taking 151 days of wall time. The calculation required over 400 gigabytes of RAM and minor manual intervention to calibrate the working precision and stopping point. To solve the challenge, we reduced an 8192-dimensional knapsack-like lattice with 375-kilobyte entries, and we achieved a root Hermite factor of 1.033 with $\|\vec{b}_n^*\| > 16$. The medium main challenge has solution 137 215 285 520 251 145 157 205 510 389 110 38 203 248 116.

The KEF implementation [31] ran on lattices up to dimension 128, and fpLLL ran up to dimension 256. As shown in Fig. 4, our implementation is both faster than the alternatives and terminates for larger parameter sizes.

---

[2] https://shaih.github.io/pubs/FHE-challenge-2010.html.

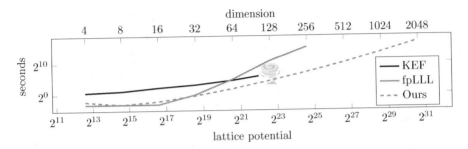

Fig. 4. Gentry-Halevi Ideal FHE. We compare the single-threaded performance of our lattice reduction algorithm on Gentry-Halevi ideal lattices. The 512-dimensional parameters correspond to the "toy" parameter settings in the original scheme, and 2048 dimensions were the "small" parameters.

6.3 Univariate Coppersmith

Coppersmith's method can be used to find small roots of low-degree polynomials modulo integers of possibly unknown factorization. This method is particularly interesting in cryptanalysis because it is fully provable using only the approximation guarantees of LLL, and is one of the canonical applications for LLL in cryptanalysis. However, the dimension and parameters increase quickly as the size of the problem approaches the asymptotic limits.

We implemented Howgrave-Graham's version [27] of Coppersmith's original method [13,14] to solve the problem of decrypting low public exponent RSA with stereotyped messages. We set $e = 3$ for a 2048-bit modulus N, and varied the number of unknown bits of the message from 400 (solvable with a dimension 5 lattice) and 678 (solvable with a 382-dimensional lattice with 430,000 bit entries). The asymptotic limit for the method with these parameters (without additional brute forcing) would be expected to be $\approx \lfloor (\log N)/3 \rfloor = 682$ bits.

These lattices violate the GSA, and the heuristic assumption in [31] does not hold for them. These lattices have irregular input and structured output. We note that this application only requires finding a single short vector, so the provable guarantees of some of the recursive algorithms would suffice to solve it.

We compare our algorithm to fpLLL, the KEF algorithm [31], and these implementations with the rounding approach of Bi et al. [4] which achieves an asymptotic improvement over LLL for this lattice construction.

The experimental results are shown in Fig. 5. We can see that the LLL with rounding technique achieves an asymptotic improvement over plain LLL, and our algorithm improves further. The implementation of [31] crashed on all instances after dimension 20, even when using the rounding technique.

We attempted to determine why their implementation crashed to rule out simple programming errors. The most common cause of failure occurred while performing size reduction; an assertion failed, indicating that the function failed to converge on a stable solution within 1000 iterations. We hypothesize that the lack of stability is due to incorrectly setting the working precision of their

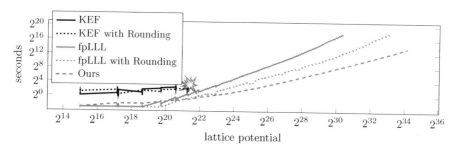

Fig. 5. RSA with Stereotyped Messages. We generated Coppersmith/Howgrave-Graham lattices for 2048-bit RSA plaintext recovery from stereotyped messages, and compare our running time to the KEF algorithm, fpLLL, and both with the rounding approach of Bi et al. [4]. The KEF algorithm crashed on instances above dimension 20.

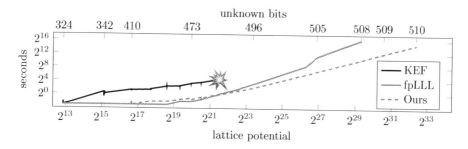

Fig. 6. RSA Partial Factorization. We generated Howgrave-Graham lattices for 2048-bit RSA factorization with high bits known. The dimension and potential grow quickly as the number of unknown bits approaches the asymptotic limit of 512. The KEF code crashed after 487 unknown bits, solvable with a 19-dimensional lattice. The largest parameters we were able to solve required a 265-dimensional lattice with 270,000-bit entries.

algorithm. Occasionally, their implementation exhausted the 512GB RAM on our test machines, and the process was killed by the operating system. These failures appear to stem from weaknesses in the algorithm rather than the programming of the implementation.

6.4   RSA Factorization with High Bits Known

In [13], Coppersmith gave a polynomial-time algorithm for factoring an RSA modulus from half of the most or least significant bits of one of the factors, assuming only the approximation guarantee of LLL.

Later, Howgrave-Graham gave an alternative formulation of factoring with partial information as an instance of the problem of computing approximate common divisors [28], with an alternative lattice construction that has become the preferred method of solving this problem in practice. This method has seen several real-world applications, including cryptanalysis of broken random number generation in Taiwanese smartcards [3], cryptanalyzing broken Infineon prime generation [40], and cryptanalyzing MEGA encryption [2].

In theory, using this method it is possible to factor an RSA modulus in polynomial time with knowledge of half of the most or least significant bits of one of the factors. In practice, this method can be remarkably efficient when relatively few bits need to be recovered, but the parameters required to solve the problem increase quickly as the number of bits to solve for approaches half the bits of a factor. To be concrete, for a 2048-bit RSA modulus, a 3-dimensional lattice with 2048-bit entries suffices to solve for 341 unknown bits of one of the 1024-bit factors, but if one wishes to solve for 511 unknown bits, the minimum parameters that result in a solvable problem instance dictate that one needs to reduce a 545-dimensional lattice with 557,000-bit entries, assuming that the reduction achieves an approximation factor of $1.02^{\dim L}$.

Figure 6 shows experimental results comparing algorithm performance on Howgrave-Graham lattices of minimal parameters to solve each problem size. The largest problem instance we were able to solve recovered 510 bits of a 1024-bit factor; this required reducing a 265-dimensional lattice with 270,000-bit entries in under 8 h of computation time. The largest instance fpLLL was able to solve recovered 508 unknown bits by reducing a lattice of dimension 135 with 133,000-bit entries. For this problem size, fpLLL took around 20 h of computational time; our implementation reduced the same lattice in 20 min. The implementation of [31] crashed on all instances larger than the 19-dimensional lattice that solves the problem for 487 unknown bits.

In practice, one can brute force some of these unknown bits to avoid prohibitively expensive lattice reduction times, and apply the "chaining" approach of Bi et al. [4] to the successive lattice reductions. Improving the runtime of the lattice reduction step is an important step in reducing the total runtime of this process. The lattice for this problem has irregular input and structured output, violates the GSA, and falsifies the heuristic of [31].

6.5 q-Ary Lattice Reduction

Lattice-reduction algorithms are frequently run on q-ary lattices of the form

$$B = \begin{bmatrix} qI & A \\ 0 & I \end{bmatrix}.$$

It is easy to generate lattices of this form uniformly at random by sampling A from $\mathbb{Z}_q^{m \times n}$. Input bases like this are balanced, but their outputs types can vary depending on the problem. Although the profiles for LWE and NTRU lattices behave in the same way as for a random q-ary lattice, there is a "phase transition" where the extra structure in these lattices becomes apparent [1,21]. For LWE and NTRU, this divergence from randomness occurs when the secret vector is found, and lattice reduction can terminate early. It is therefore interesting to consider the performance of our algorithm on random q-ary lattice bases, and the output of these bases is GSA-like.

We ran our lattice reduction implementation on the same parameter sizes as reported in [31] and to approximation quality equivalent to root Hermite factor 1.02. We reduced the same lattices using fpLLL and the implementation from [31]. All experiments were single-threaded (Fig. 7).

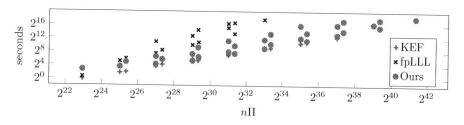

Fig. 7. *q*-ary. The algorithm of [31] has been optimized for the case of *q*-ary lattices, and performs quite well on them. Our implementation shows similar asymptotic behavior. [31] did not terminate for instance sizes above 1024 dimensions.

Our implementation is significantly faster than fpLLL, but slower than [31]. The implementation of [31] did not terminate for instance sizes above dimension 1024 with precision 512, dimension 512 with precision 4096. The largest basis successfully reduced by fpLLL had dimension 256 with 2048-bit entries. The implementation of [31] has been aggressively optimized for this lattice profile, and such optimizations could likely be used to speed up our own implementation even further. We also note that our implementation was capable of running on even larger instances. The largest *q*-ary basis we successfully reduced had dimension 1536 with 3072-bit entries.

6.6 Approximate GCD

Numerous FHE and multilinear map schemes [11,16–19,55] have been proposed which rely on the hardness of the approximate greatest common divisor (AGCD) [28] problem. There are many different lattice constructions for solving AGCD (see [55, Appendix B] and [12,22,31]), and the solvability depends on both the number of samples and the approximation factor. While Kirchner et al. mention that they vary the approximation factor and dimension out of memory concerns, they do not document the final parameters for each test case. We derive and run experiments for our own construction and parameters.

We build and reduce the dual of the lattice construction (3.1) presented in van Dijk et al. [55] to solve AGCD, which we note is related to the multiplicity-one Coppersmith construction [12]. We focus on the dual because the resulting unimodular update matrices are smaller in practice, and computing the update matrices for the primal is prohibitively expensive. It is efficient to compute the dual of the reduced dual and recover the secret short vector in the primal.

Like [31], we observe a tradeoff between approximation quality α, dimension, and attack time. As predicted by Theorem 1, we experimentally observe that

Table 2. Performance on AGCD lattices. We perform a lattice attack on FHE and multilinear map schemes by solving instances of the AGCD problem. The reported size is the maximum size of entries in the basis in millions of bits.

Scheme	Sec. Lvl	Size (Mb)	Our dim	Our α	KEF (s)	Our time (s)
CMNT [18]	42	0.16	152	0.220	300	59
	52	0.86	556	0.210	3300	1406
	62	4.2	2156	0.179		52016
CNT [19]	42	0.06	204	0.199	200	54
	52	0.27	876	0.135	1700	1673
	62	1.02	3422	0.065		531005
CLT [17]	42	0.27	144	0.314	780	85
	52	1.1	600	0.213	10560	1946
	62	4.2	2486	0.167		68940
CCK [11]	52	0.9	621	0.209	4400	1665
	62	4.6	2478	0.172	82920	116400
CLT [16]	52	0.99	601	0.210	4000	1779
	62	4.26	2514	0.167	79320	67599

both high dimension and small α can lead to long running times. We find a curve that fits the behavior on small instances to predict parameter settings that lead to fast reduction times for large instances. Our choice of parameters may not be optimal, but our strategy is effective for solving AGCD in practice.

We generated lattice bases for the same schemes described in [31] and attempted to reduce them using both their implementation and our implementation in multithreaded mode to match the original evaluation. Their implementation crashed partway through reduction on all instances, so we present their running times as originally reported. We present the results in Table 2.

We see that our implementation is faster in almost all cases. However, since we do not have the full details of their construction, we are unsure if the improved performance is due to the nature of our algorithm, the details of our implementation, or the parametrization of our attack. Regardless of the reason, we also note that our implementation successfully broke larger instances of the AGCD problem than previously reported for three of the schemes, corresponding to a 62-bit security level.

Acknowledgments. We are grateful to Thomas Espitau for helpful discussions and sharing source code, we thank Jonathan M. Smith for graciously providing computing time on different, modern processors for our experiments, and we thank Daniel J. Bernstein for numerous discussions and grantwriting. We also thank Léo Ducas for informative discussions and Shai Halevi for finding and reuploading an offline copy of the Gentry and Halevi FHE challenges. Finally, we thank the anonymous reviewers for their extensive comments on an earlier version of this work. This work was supported by NSF grant no. 1913210.

References

1. Albrecht, M., Ducas, L.: Lattice attacks on NTRU and LWE: a history of refinements. Cryptology ePrint Archive, Report 2021/799 (2021). https://eprint.iacr.org/2021/799
2. Backendal, M., Haller, M., Paterson, K.G.: MEGA: malleable encryption goes awry. In: 2023 IEEE Symposium on Security and Privacy (SP), pp. 450–467, May 2023. https://doi.org/10.1109/SP46215.2023.00026
3. Bernstein, D.J., et al.: Factoring RSA keys from certified smart cards: coppersmith in the wild. In: Sako, K., Sarkar, P. (eds.) ASIACRYPT 2013. LNCS, vol. 8270, pp. 341–360. Springer, Heidelberg (2013). https://doi.org/10.1007/978-3-642-42045-0_18
4. Bi, J., Coron, J.-S., Faugère, J.-C., Nguyen, P.Q., Renault, G., Zeitoun, R.: Rounding and chaining LLL: finding faster small roots of univariate polynomial congruences. In: Krawczyk, H. (ed.) PKC 2014. LNCS, vol. 8383, pp. 185–202. Springer, Heidelberg (2014). https://doi.org/10.1007/978-3-642-54631-0_11
5. Biasse, J.F., Song, F.: Efficient quantum algorithms for computing class groups and solving the principal ideal problem in arbitrary degree number fields. In: Krauthgamer, R. (ed.) 27th SODA, pp. 893–902. ACM-SIAM, January 2016. https://doi.org/10.1137/1.9781611974331.ch64
6. Biasse, J.F.: Subexponential time relations in the class group of large degree number fields. Adv. Math. Commun. **8**(4), 407–425 (2014). https://doi.org/10.3934/amc.2014.8.407
7. Biasse, J.F., Fieker, C.: Subexponential class group and unit group computation in large degree number fields. LMS J. Comput. Math. **17**(A), 385–403 (2014). https://doi.org/10.1112/S1461157014000345
8. Boneh, D., Halevi, S., Howgrave-Graham, N.: The modular inversion hidden number problem. In: Boyd, C. (ed.) ASIACRYPT 2001. LNCS, vol. 2248, pp. 36–51. Springer, Heidelberg (2001). https://doi.org/10.1007/3-540-45682-1_3
9. Chang, X.W., Stehlé, D., Villard, G.: Perturbation analysis of the QR factor R in the context of LLL lattice basis reduction. Math. Comput. **81**(279), 1487–1511 (2012). https://hal-ens-lyon.archives-ouvertes.fr/ensl-00529425
10. Chen, Y., Nguyen, P.Q.: BKZ 2.0: better lattice security estimates. In: Lee, D.H., Wang, X. (eds.) ASIACRYPT 2011. LNCS, vol. 7073, pp. 1–20. Springer, Heidelberg (2011). https://doi.org/10.1007/978-3-642-25385-0_1
11. Cheon, J.H., et al.: Batch fully homomorphic encryption over the integers. In: Johansson, T., Nguyen, P.Q. (eds.) EUROCRYPT 2013. LNCS, vol. 7881, pp. 315–335. Springer, Heidelberg (2013). https://doi.org/10.1007/978-3-642-38348-9_20
12. Cohn, H., Heninger, N.: Approximate common divisors via lattices. ANTS X p. 271 (2012). https://doi.org/10.2140/obs.2013.1.271
13. Coppersmith, D.: Small solutions to polynomial equations, and low exponent RSA vulnerabilities. J. Cryptol. **10**(4), 233–260 (1997). https://doi.org/10.1007/s001459900030
14. Coppersmith, D.: Finding small solutions to small degree polynomials. In: Silverman, J.H. (ed.) CaLC 2001. LNCS, vol. 2146, pp. 20–31. Springer, Heidelberg (2001). https://doi.org/10.1007/3-540-44670-2_3
15. Coppersmith, D., Shamir, A.: Lattice attacks on NTRU. In: Fumy, W. (ed.) EUROCRYPT 1997. LNCS, vol. 1233, pp. 52–61. Springer, Heidelberg (1997). https://doi.org/10.1007/3-540-69053-0_5

16. Coron, J.-S., Lepoint, T., Tibouchi, M.: Practical multilinear maps over the integers. In: Canetti, R., Garay, J.A. (eds.) CRYPTO 2013. LNCS, vol. 8042, pp. 476–493. Springer, Heidelberg (2013). https://doi.org/10.1007/978-3-642-40041-4_26

17. Coron, J.-S., Lepoint, T., Tibouchi, M.: Scale-invariant fully homomorphic encryption over the integers. In: Krawczyk, H. (ed.) PKC 2014. LNCS, vol. 8383, pp. 311–328. Springer, Heidelberg (2014). https://doi.org/10.1007/978-3-642-54631-0_18

18. Coron, J.-S., Mandal, A., Naccache, D., Tibouchi, M.: Fully homomorphic encryption over the integers with shorter public keys. In: Rogaway, P. (ed.) CRYPTO 2011. LNCS, vol. 6841, pp. 487–504. Springer, Heidelberg (2011). https://doi.org/10.1007/978-3-642-22792-9_28

19. Coron, J.-S., Naccache, D., Tibouchi, M.: Public key compression and modulus switching for fully homomorphic encryption over the integers. In: Pointcheval, D., Johansson, T. (eds.) EUROCRYPT 2012. LNCS, vol. 7237, pp. 446–464. Springer, Heidelberg (2012). https://doi.org/10.1007/978-3-642-29011-4_27

20. Ducas, L., van Woerden, W.: A note on a claim of Eldar & Hallgren: LLL already solves it. Cryptology ePrint Archive, Report 2021/1391 (2021). https://eprint.iacr.org/2021/1391

21. Ducas, L., van Woerden, W.: NTRU fatigue: how stretched is overstretched? In: Tibouchi, M., Wang, H. (eds.) ASIACRYPT 2021. LNCS, vol. 13093, pp. 3–32. Springer, Cham (2021). https://doi.org/10.1007/978-3-030-92068-5_1

22. Galbraith, S.D., Gebregiyorgis, S.W., Murphy, S.: Algorithms for the approximate common divisor problem. LMS J. Comput. Math. **19**(A), 58–72 (2016). https://doi.org/10.1112/S1461157016000218

23. Gentry, C.: Fully homomorphic encryption using ideal lattices. In: Mitzenmacher, M. (ed.) 41st ACM STOC, pp. 169–178. ACM Press (2009). https://doi.org/10.1145/1536414.1536440

24. Gentry, C., Halevi, S.: Implementing Gentry's fully-homomorphic encryption scheme. In: Paterson, K.G. (ed.) EUROCRYPT 2011. LNCS, vol. 6632, pp. 129–148. Springer, Heidelberg (2011). https://doi.org/10.1007/978-3-642-20465-4_9

25. Goldstein, D., Mayer, A.: On the equidistribution of Hecke points **15**(2), 165–189 (2003). https://doi.org/10.1515/form.2003.009

26. Higham, N.J.: Accuracy and Stability of Numerical Algorithms, 2nd edn. Society for Industrial and Applied Mathematics, Philadelphia, PA, USA (2002)

27. Howgrave-Graham, N.: Finding small roots of univariate modular equations revisited. In: Darnell, M. (ed.) Cryptography and Coding 1997. LNCS, vol. 1355, pp. 131–142. Springer, Heidelberg (1997). https://doi.org/10.1007/BFb0024458

28. Howgrave-Graham, N.: Approximate integer common divisors. In: Silverman, J.H. (ed.) CaLC 2001. LNCS, vol. 2146, pp. 51–66. Springer, Heidelberg (2001). https://doi.org/10.1007/3-540-44670-2_6

29. Kirchner, P., Espitau, T., Fouque, P.A.: Algebraic and Euclidean lattices: optimal lattice reduction and beyond. Cryptology ePrint Archive, Report 2019/1436 (2019). https://eprint.iacr.org/2019/1436

30. Kirchner, P., Espitau, T., Fouque, P.-A.: Fast reduction of algebraic lattices over cyclotomic fields. In: Micciancio, D., Ristenpart, T. (eds.) CRYPTO 2020. LNCS, vol. 12171, pp. 155–185. Springer, Cham (2020). https://doi.org/10.1007/978-3-030-56880-1_6

31. Kirchner, P., Espitau, T., Fouque, P.-A.: Towards faster polynomial-time lattice reduction. In: Malkin, T., Peikert, C. (eds.) CRYPTO 2021. LNCS, vol. 12826, pp. 760–790. Springer, Cham (2021). https://doi.org/10.1007/978-3-030-84245-1_26

32. Kirchner, P., Fouque, P.-A.: Revisiting lattice attacks on overstretched NTRU parameters. In: Coron, J.-S., Nielsen, J.B. (eds.) EUROCRYPT 2017. LNCS, vol. 10210, pp. 3–26. Springer, Cham (2017). https://doi.org/10.1007/978-3-319-56620-7_1

33. Koy, H., Schnorr, C.P.: Segment LLL-reduction of lattice bases. In: Silverman, J.H. (ed.) CaLC 2001. LNCS, vol. 2146, pp. 67–80. Springer, Heidelberg (2001). https://doi.org/10.1007/3-540-44670-2_7

34. Lagarias, J.C., Odlyzko, A.M.: Solving low-density subset sum problems. In: 24th FOCS, pp. 1–10. IEEE Computer Society Press (1983). https://doi.org/10.1109/SFCS.1983.70

35. Lee, M.S.: On the sparse subset sum problem from gentry-Halevi's implementation of fully homomorphic encryption. Cryptology ePrint Archive, Report 2011/567 (2011). https://eprint.iacr.org/2011/567

36. Lenstra, A.K., Lenstra, H.W., Lovász, L.: Factoring polynomials with rational coefficients. Math. Ann. **261**(4), 515–534 (1982). https://doi.org/10.1007/BF01457454

37. May, A.: Using LLL-reduction for solving RSA and factorization problems. In: Nguyen, P., Vallée, B. (eds.) ISC, pp. 315–348. Springer, Heidelberg (2010). https://doi.org/10.1007/978-3-642-02295-10

38. Micciancio, D., Regev, O.: Lattice-based cryptography. In: Bernstein, D.J., Buchmann, J., Dahmen, E. (eds.) Post-Quantum Cryptography, pp. 147–191. Springer, Heidelberg (2009). https://doi.org/10.1007/978-3-540-88702-7_5

39. Morel, I., Stehlé, D., Villard, G.: H-LLL: using householder inside LLL. In: Proceedings of the 2009 International Symposium on Symbolic and Algebraic Computation, ISSAC 2009, pp. 271–278. Association for Computing Machinery, New York (2009). https://doi.org/10.1145/1576702.1576740

40. Nemec, M., Sýs, M., Svenda, P., Klinec, D., Matyas, V.: The return of coppersmith's attack: practical factorization of widely used RSA moduli. In: Thuraisingham, B.M., Evans, D., Malkin, T., Xu, D. (eds.) ACM CCS 2017, pp. 1631–1648. ACM Press (2017). https://doi.org/10.1145/3133956.3133969

41. Neumaier, A., Stehlé, D.: Faster LLL-type reduction of lattice bases. In: Proceedings of the ACM on International Symposium on Symbolic and Algebraic Computation, ISSAC 2016, pp. 373–380. Association for Computing Machinery, New York (2016). https://doi.org/10.1145/2930889.2930917

42. Nguyen, P.Q.: The two faces of lattices in cryptology. In: Vaudenay, S., Youssef, A.M. (eds.) SAC 2001. LNCS, vol. 2259, p. 313. Springer, Heidelberg (2001). https://doi.org/10.1007/3-540-45537-X_24

43. Nguyen, P.Q.: Hermite's constant and lattice algorithms. In: Nguyen, P., Vallée, B. (eds.) The LLL Algorithm. Information Security and Cryptography, ISC, pp. 19–69. Springer, Heidelberg (2010). https://doi.org/10.1007/978-3-642-02295-1

44. Nguyen, P.Q., Stehlé, D.: LLL on the average. In: Hess, F., Pauli, S., Pohst, M. (eds.) ANTS 2006. LNCS, vol. 4076, pp. 238–256. Springer, Heidelberg (2006). https://doi.org/10.1007/11792086_18

45. Nguyen, P.Q., Stehlé, D.: An LLL algorithm with quadratic complexity. SIAM J. Comput. **39**(3), 874–903 (2009). https://doi.org/10.1137/070705702

46. Novocin, A., Stehlé, D., Villard, G.: An LLL-reduction algorithm with quasi-linear time complexity: extended abstract. In: Proceedings of the Forty-Third Annual ACM Symposium on Theory of Computing, STOC 2011, pp. 403–412. Association for Computing Machinery, New York (2011). https://doi.org/10.1145/1993636.1993691

47. Pataki, G., Tural, M.: On sublattice determinants in reduced bases (2008). https://doi.org/10.48550/ARXIV.0804.4014

48. Plantard, T., Susilo, W., Zhang, Z.: LLL for ideal lattices: re-evaluation of the security of Gentry–Halevi's FHE scheme. Des. Codes Crypt. **76**(2), 325–344 (2014). https://doi.org/10.1007/s10623-014-9957-1
49. Ryan, K., Heninger, N.: Fast practical lattice reduction through iterated compression. Cryptology ePrint Archive, Report 2023/237 (2023). https://eprint.iacr.org/2023/237
50. Saruchi, Morel, I., Stehlé, D., Villard, G.: LLL reducing with the most significant bits. In: Proceedings of the 39th International Symposium on Symbolic and Algebraic Computation, ISSAC 2014, pp. 367–374. Association for Computing Machinery, New York (2014). https://doi.org/10.1145/2608628.2608645
51. Schnorr, C.P., Euchner, M.: Lattice basis reduction: improved practical algorithms and solving subset sum problems. Math. Programm. **66**(1), 181–199 (1994). https://doi.org/10.1007/BF01581144
52. Schönhage, A.: Fast reduction and composition of binary quadratic forms. In: Proceedings of the 1991 International Symposium on Symbolic and Algebraic Computation, ISSAC 1991. Association for Computing Machinery, New York (1991). https://doi.org/10.1145/120694.120711
53. Stewart, G.W., Sun, J.G.: Matrix perturbation theory (1990)
54. The FPLLL development team: FPLLL, a lattice reduction library, Version: 5.4.2 (2022). https://github.com/fplll/fplll
55. van Dijk, M., Gentry, C., Halevi, S., Vaikuntanathan, V.: Fully homomorphic encryption over the integers. In: Gilbert, H. (ed.) EUROCRYPT 2010. LNCS, vol. 6110, pp. 24–43. Springer, Heidelberg (2010). https://doi.org/10.1007/978-3-642-13190-5_2
56. Xu, J., Hu, L., Sarkar, S.: Cryptanalysis of elliptic curve hidden number problem from PKC 2017. Des. Codes Crypt. **88**(2), 341–361 (2019). https://doi.org/10.1007/s10623-019-00685-y

Does the Dual-Sieve Attack on Learning with Errors Even Work?

Léo Ducas[1,2]([✉]) [iD] and Ludo N. Pulles[1] [iD]

[1] CWI, Cryptology Group, Amsterdam, The Netherlands
ducas@cwi.nl
[2] Mathematical Institute, Leiden University, Leiden, The Netherlands

Abstract. Guo and Johansson (ASIACRYPT 2021), and MATZOV (tech. report 2022) have independently claimed improved attacks against various NIST lattice candidates by adding a Fast Fourier Transform (FFT) trick on top of the so-called Dual-Sieve attack. Recently, there was more follow up work in this line adding new practical improvements.

However, from a theoretical perspective, all of these works are painfully specific to Learning with Errors, while the principle of the Dual-Sieve attack is more general (Laarhoven & Walter, CT-RSA 2021). More critically, all of these works are based on heuristics that have received very little theoretical and experimental attention.

This work attempts to rectify the above deficiencies of the literature. We first propose a generalization of the FFT trick by Guo and Johansson to arbitrary Bounded Distance Decoding instances. This generalization offers a new improvement to the attack.

We then theoretically explore the underlying heuristics and show that these are in contradiction with formal, unconditional theorems in some regimes, and with well-tested heuristics in other regimes. The specific instantiations of the recent literature fall into this second regime.

We confirm these contradictions with experiments, documenting several phenomena that are not predicted by the analysis, including a "waterfall-floor" phenomenon, reminiscent of Low-Density Parity-Check decoding failures.

We conclude that the success probability of the recent Dual-Sieve-FFT attacks are presumably significantly overestimated. We further discuss the adequate way forward towards fixing the attack and its analysis.

Keywords: Lattices · Cryptanalysis · Heuristics · Learning with Errors · Dual Attack · Fast Fourier Transform

1 Introduction

The idea of using short dual vectors for distinguishing between points close to or far from a lattice was put forward, in a complexity theoretic context, by Aharonov and Regev [2], and can even be traced back in a pure geometric context to earlier work by Håstad [19]. The problem at hand here is coined the decisional Bounded Distance Decoding problem (BDD). This idea is not even limited to

© International Association for Cryptologic Research 2023
H. Handschuh and A. Lysyanskaya (Eds.): CRYPTO 2023, LNCS 14083, pp. 37–69, 2023.
https://doi.org/10.1007/978-3-031-38548-3_2

lattices, and was already implicit in the very construction of Low-Density Parity-Check codes dating back to [17].

This idea made its way into cryptanalysis of cryptosystems based on the Learning with Errors (LWE) problem in a survey of Micciancio and Regev [27]. Indeed, Learning with Errors is a special case of BDD, for a specific family of random lattices. An attack on LWE (or BDD) using this idea is a so-called *dual attack*, in contrast with the other type of attacks that operate solely in the *primal* lattice. The best dual and primal attacks are then typically used by the lattice cryptanalyst to instantiate LWE cryptosystems.

Since then, two fundamental developments have happened. The first, initially suggested by Alkim, Ducas, Pöppelmann, and Schwabe [6], consisted of exploiting the fact that lattice sieving [10, 28, 30]—a class of algorithms for finding short lattice vectors—naturally provides not only the shortest vector, but exponentially many short vectors. The hope is that the information of these exponentially many short dual vectors can be leveraged to improve a distinguisher, for example by summing a score function over them [23].

We refer to this style of attack as a *Dual-Sieve* attack. The concrete cryptanalytic impact of this idea can be further improved by guessing multiple coordinates of the secret rather than just one [3, 16], and then finding the right solution among these candidates rather than just a few.

The second development is also reminiscent from a cryptanalytic technique of code-based cryptography by Levieil and Fouque [24]. The idea is to batch the score evaluation of a large number of algebraically related candidates via a Fast Fourier Transform. For carefully crafted parameters, the cost of getting all those scores is barely larger than the cost of naïvely computing a single score. This led Guo and Johansson [18] to claim an improved attack on various NIST post-quantum standardization candidates, followed quickly by an independent technical report of MATZOV [25]. We refer to this style of attack as a *Dual-Sieve-FFT* attack. The latter has already been followed up upon, with a quantum variant [5] and a coding-theoretic enhanced variant [11].

1.1 Contributions

Abstraction and Generalization of the FFT trick (Sect. 3). We note that the original principle of the dual attack [2, 19] is general: it applies to the bounded distance decoding problem (BDD) in arbitrary lattices. However, the recent instances of the Dual-Sieve attack [3, 6, 16] and the Dual-Sieve-FFT attacks [5, 11, 18, 25] are described in a very specialized way to Learning with Errors. The only exception is the work of [23], which we find geometrically enlightening, although their work is limited to the Dual-Sieve attack.

Our first contribution (Sect. 3) is therefore to also generalize the FFT trick of [18] to the general setting. Beyond the theoretical satisfaction of abstracting the technique to its mathematical core, this generalization also offers further improvement over the work of [18]: for the same algorithmic price, we can further improve the shortness of the dual vectors and therefore their distinguishing power.

Contradictions from the Heuristic Analysis (Sect. 4). A second observation regarding this literature is that the analysis of the Dual-Sieve attack (with or without FFT) relies on one specific independence heuristic, which has received essentially no attention so far. Namely, it is assumed that all the individual scores, given by each dual vector, are mutually independent.

We approach the analysis of this heuristic by looking at the conclusions it leads to. The geometric point of view offered by the work of Laarhoven and Walter [23] is pivotal in that respect: judging the reasonability of a heuristic conclusion is very much enabled by the language of geometry. In particular, their work concludes with a heuristic algorithm that distinguishes a noisy lattice point from random, even when the noise slightly exceeds the Gaussian Heuristic, *i.e.* the expected minimal distance of a random lattice. This should raise suspicion, as even random points are not expected to be much further away from the lattice than this minimal distance. This suspicion of invalidity becomes an undeniable contradiction by considering a recent result of Debris, Ducas, Resch, and Tillich [12], stating that the above task is statistically impossible, even to an unbounded attacker.

The contradiction above is, however, limited to a rather theoretical regime of the Dual-Sieve attack, which is not that of the recent concrete cryptanalytic claims [5,11,16,18,25]. In their context, the BDD error is below the Gaussian Heuristic but the actual BDD sample needs to be discovered among a large number T of uniform samples. We will show that this also leads to a contradiction. Namely, for large T, we argue that many of those random targets will lie closer to the lattice than the BDD target itself. The claim that the BDD target can be successfully identified among so many random targets contradicts the very principle of the attack, namely that the expected score of a target increases with its closeness to the lattice. It turns out that the parameters used in [18,25] specifically fall into that contradictory regime that uses a large number T of targets.

Experiments (Sect. 5). To understand what is going on, we zoom in on the distribution of scores for random targets and BDD targets. We ran extensive experiments, and discovered that both distributions deviate from the predictions made under the independence heuristic. First, the *body* of the distribution of scores for random targets is properly predicted, but not its *tail*: after a predicted rapid decrease (visually, a *waterfall*), this distribution hits a *floor*. This is perfectly in line with our second contradictory regime: some random targets will be close to the lattice, and should therefore have a high score.

However, that is not all. The distribution of scores for BDD target is also mispredicted, and this is no longer just a matter of the tail. Contrary to prediction, this distribution is not gaussian-like. It is in fact not even symmetric around its average, and its variance appears exponentially larger than predicted. In particular, the probability of the score of a BDD target being low is higher than predicted.

All of the code that is used for the experiments, as well as the results of the experiments are publicly available at:

https://github.com/ludopulles/DoesDualSieveWork.

These experiments are implemented in python using the G6K and FPyLLL libraries [4,34], and there is a binding to some C code to accelerate the FFT.

1.2   Conclusion

Our theoretical contradictions and our experiments both demonstrate that the underlying heuristic of the Dual-Sieve attack is invalid. Both phenomena uncovered by the experiments point to the success probability of the Dual-Sieve attack (with or without FFT) being presumably over-estimated by the current heuristic, at least in certain regimes of interest.

In particular, the concrete cryptanalytic claims of numerous works [5,6,11, 16,18,25] should be considered at least unsubstantiated, as these are currently based on a flawed heuristic. Still, some of those claims might not be that far from reality, but those of [5,11,18,25], being so deep in the contradictory regime, are presumably significantly far away from reality.

Afterthoughts (Sect. 6). We conclude our work with various discussions. First, we mention the prior occurrence of a similar *waterfall-floor* phenomenon in the coding literature [7,33,35] and relate to it. We then reflect on the source of the issue in the independence heuristic, and highlight the effect of these dependencies with a toy example. We finally discuss a suitable way forward in fixing the Dual-Sieve attack and its analysis.

2   Preliminaries

In this paper, we will make clear which heuristics are used by referring to these as *Heuristics*. Any statement that is derived using one or more heuristics will be called a *Heuristic Claim*, which will be motivated by a *Heuristic Justification* explaining why it is believed to be true.

Geometric objects. The n-dimensional (closed) ball of radius 1 is denoted by $\mathcal{B}^n$; the $(n-1)$-dimensional sphere (residing in the n-dimensional ambient space) is denoted by $\mathcal{S}^{n-1}$. In particular the unit circle is denoted by $\mathcal{S}^1$ and is naturally a subgroup of $\mathbb{C}^*$.

2.1   Probabilities and Distributions

Probabilities are denoted by $\mathbb{P}$, expectations by $\mathbb{E}$. The variance of a random variable X is $\mathbb{V}[X] = \mathbb{E}\left[X^2\right] - (\mathbb{E}\left[X\right])^2$, and its standard deviation is $\sigma_X = \sqrt{\mathbb{V}[X]}$. The *cumulative density function* (CDF) at $x \in \mathbb{R}$ of a distribution $\mathcal{D}$ is $\mathbb{P}_{X \leftarrow \mathcal{D}}[X \leq x]$, and the *survival function* (SF) of $\mathcal{D}$ is $\mathbb{P}_{X \leftarrow \mathcal{D}}[X \geq x] = 1 - \mathbb{P}_{X \leftarrow \mathcal{D}}[X < x]$, where X is drawn from $\mathcal{D}$.

The uniform distribution on a set X is denoted by $U(X)$. The continuous gaussian $\mathcal{N}(c, \sigma^2)$ of average $c \in \mathbb{R}$ and standard deviation $\sigma \in \mathbb{R}_{>0}$ has a probability density at $x \in \mathbb{R}$ proportional to $\rho_{c,\sigma}(x) = \exp\left(-\frac{(x-c)^2}{2\sigma^2}\right)$.

The (gaussian) *error function* is erf and the *complementary error function* is $\mathrm{erfc}(x) = 1 - \mathrm{erf}(x)$, for a random variable $X \leftarrow \mathcal{N}(c, \sigma^2)$ we have for all $x \in \mathbb{R}$

$$\mathbb{P}[X < x] = \frac{1}{2}\left(1 + \mathrm{erf}\left(\frac{x - c}{\sigma\sqrt{2}}\right)\right). \tag{1}$$

Lemma 1 ([1, 7.1.23]). *It holds that*

$$\mathrm{erfc}(x) = e^{-x^2} \cdot \left(\frac{1}{\sqrt{\pi} \cdot x} + O\left(\frac{1}{x^3}\right)\right) \qquad \text{as } x \to \infty.$$

2.2 Lattices

A *lattice* Λ is a discrete subgroup of $\mathbb{R}^n$, its *rank* is the dimension of its $\mathbb{R}$-linear span, and the *volume* of a full rank lattice is $\det \Lambda = \mathrm{Vol}(\mathbb{R}^n/\Lambda)$. For $1 \le k \le n$, a *basis* $\mathbf{B} \in \mathbb{R}^{n \times k}$ consisting of $\mathbb{R}$-linearly independent column vectors $\mathbf{b}_1, \ldots, \mathbf{b}_k$ defines the rank-k lattice

$$\mathcal{L}(\mathbf{B}) = \{\mathbf{v} \in \mathbb{R}^n | \exists \mathbf{c} \in \mathbb{Z}^k : \mathbf{v} = c_1 \mathbf{b}_1 + \cdots + c_k \mathbf{b}_k\},$$

of volume $\sqrt{\det \mathbf{B}^\mathsf{T} \mathbf{B}}$. For $1 \le \ell \le r \le n$, we use $\mathbf{B}_{[\ell,r]}$ for the basis consisting of vectors $\pi_\ell(\mathbf{b}_\ell), \ldots, \pi_\ell(\mathbf{b}_r)$, where π_ℓ is the projection map that projects away from $\mathbf{b}_1, \ldots, \mathbf{b}_{\ell-1}$. The length of a shortest nonzero vector of a lattice $\Lambda \subset \mathbb{R}^n$ is denoted by $\lambda_1(\Lambda)$.

Duality. There are two ways to define the dual of a lattice, the first one being geometric and specific to lattices, while the second is inherited from groups. In the context of the FFT trick, it is useful to consider both definitions, and relate them.

Definition 1. *The* dual lattice $\Lambda^\vee$ *of a full rank lattice* $\Lambda \subset \mathbb{R}^n$ *is the set of all* $\mathbf{w} \in \mathbb{R}^n$ *such that* $\langle \mathbf{w}, \Lambda \rangle \subseteq \mathbb{Z}$.

Definition 2. *For a full rank lattice* $\Lambda \subset \mathbb{R}^n$, *let*

$$\widehat{\Lambda} = \{\chi \colon \mathbb{R}^n/\Lambda \to \mathcal{S}^1 | \chi \text{ continuous group hom.}\}$$

denote the group of characters on the torus $\mathbb{R}^n/\Lambda$.

The following lemma shows that we may interchange these two notions of duality, i.e. any dual vector defines a character and vice versa.

Lemma 2. *The map from* $\Lambda^\vee$ *to* $\widehat{\Lambda}$ *that sends a dual vector* $\mathbf{w}$ *to the character*

$$\chi_\mathbf{w} \colon \mathbf{t} \mapsto \exp(2\pi i \cdot \langle \mathbf{t}, \mathbf{w} \rangle), \tag{2}$$

is a group isomorphism.

For a finite abelian group G, the dual group $\widehat{G}$ is the group of the homo-morphisms $\chi\colon G \to \mathcal{S}^1$. For a sublattice $\Lambda' \subset \Lambda$, the dual of Λ/Λ' has a natural connection to the dual lattices of Λ' and Λ by the following lemma.

Lemma 3. *For two full rank lattices $\Lambda_1 \subset \Lambda_2 \subset \mathbb{R}^n$, there is a canonical group isomorphism of abelian groups,*

$$\widehat{\Lambda_1/\Lambda_2} \to \widehat{\Lambda_2/\Lambda_1},$$

given by restricting a character $\chi\colon \mathbb{R}^n/\Lambda_1 \to \mathcal{S}^1$ (modulo $\widehat{\Lambda_2}$) to Λ_2/Λ_1.

Dual basis and dual blocks. Given a basis $\mathbf{B}$ of the primal lattice Λ, one can construct an associated dual basis $\mathbf{B}^\vee = \mathbf{B} \cdot (\mathbf{B}^\mathsf{T} \cdot \mathbf{B})^{-1}$ of the dual lattice $\Lambda^\vee$. Consider the *reversed dual basis* $^\vee\mathbf{B} = [\mathbf{b}_n^\vee, \ldots, \mathbf{b}_1^\vee]$ in which the order-ing of the basis vectors is reversed. A basis for the dual of $\mathcal{L}(\mathbf{B}_{[\ell,r]})$ is given by $\tau(\mathbf{b}_r^\vee), \ldots, \tau(\mathbf{b}_\ell^\vee)$ where τ is the map projecting away from $\mathbf{b}_{r+1}^\vee, \ldots, \mathbf{b}_n^\vee$, denoted by $(^\vee\mathbf{B})_{[n+1-r, n+1-\ell]}$. Informally, this shows that projecting in the primal lattice corresponds to sectioning in the dual lattice. More details on dual bases can be found in the course of Micciancio [26].

Fourier Transforms. For any set S let $\mathbb{C}^S$ be the group of sequences $(x_s)_{s \in S}$ having complex coefficients x_s, where the group operation is given by pointwise addition. The *Discrete Fourier Transform* (DFT) of a sequence $(x_g)_{g \in G} \subset \mathbb{C}$ is the $\mathbb{C}$-linear map

$$\mathrm{DFT}_G\colon \qquad \mathbb{C}^G \to \mathbb{C}^{\widehat{G}},$$
$$(x_g)_{g \in G} \mapsto \left(\sum_{g \in G} x_g \cdot \overline{\chi(g)} \right)_{\chi \in \widehat{G}}. \tag{3}$$

The m-dimensional *Fast Fourier Transform* (FFT) is an algorithm that, upon input a group G, given as $n_1, \ldots, n_m \in \mathbb{Z}_{\geq 2}$ such that $G \cong \bigoplus_{j=1}^m (\mathbb{Z}/n_j\mathbb{Z})$, and $(x_g)_{g \in G}$, outputs $\mathrm{DFT}_G\big((x_g)_{g \in G}\big)$ in time $O(|G| \log |G|)$. There are various FFTs known for any finite group G (even when an n_i is a large prime) [15,32]. When the group G is not cyclic, the algorithm is often referred to as a multi-dimensional FFT. When $G \cong (\mathbb{Z}/2\mathbb{Z})^k$, the algorithm is a *Walsh–Hadamard Transform* (WHT), which is more efficient in practice. For a finite group G, the inverse of DFT_G is given by

$$\mathrm{DFT}_G^{-1}\left((y_\chi)_{\chi \in \widehat{G}}\right) = \frac{1}{|G|} \cdot \left(\sum_{\chi \in \widehat{G}} y_\chi \chi(g) \right)_{g \in G}.$$

Identifying an element $g \in G$ with the evaluation map $\mathrm{ev}_g \colon \chi \mapsto \chi(g)$ gives the canonical isomorphism $G \cong \widehat{\widehat{G}}$, so an inverse DFT is basically a DFT, up to some reordering.

Gaussian Heuristic. The *Gaussian Heuristic* states that the number of lattice points in a measurable set $S \subset \mathbb{R}^n$ is approximately $\mathrm{Vol}(S) / \det \Lambda$. This leads to the following heuristic on the length of a shortest vector.

Heuristic 1 (Gaussian Heuristic). *Given a random lattice $\Lambda \subset \mathbb{R}^n$ of volume 1, then $\lambda_1(\Lambda)$ is approximately*

$$\mathrm{GH}(n) := \mathrm{Vol}(\mathcal{B}^n)^{-1/n} = \frac{\Gamma(1 + \frac{n}{2})^{1/n}}{\sqrt{\pi}} \approx \sqrt{\frac{n}{2\pi e}} \cdot (\pi n)^{1/n},$$

where we use Stirling's formula in the approximation step.

Note that Minkowski's theorem states $\lambda_1(\Lambda) \leq 2 \cdot \mathrm{GH}(n)$.

Heuristic 2. *Given a random lattice $\Lambda \subset \mathbb{R}^n$ of volume 1, for $r > 1$ we have*

$$|\{\mathbf{v} \in \Lambda \mid \|\mathbf{v}\| \leq r \cdot \mathrm{GH}(n)\}| \approx r^n.$$

In particular, the ith shortest lattice point $\mathbf{v}$ has length $\|\mathbf{v}\| \approx \mathrm{GH}(n) \sqrt[n]{i}$.

Bounded Distance Decoding. The following computational problems are considered hard for specific parameters, on which the security of LWE cryptosystems is based.

Problem 1 (BDD, Lattice Form). For $r > 0$, *Bounded Distance Decoding* (BDD_r) is the task of, given a lattice Λ and a target $\mathbf{t} \in \mathbb{R}^n$ with the promise that there exists a nearby lattice point $\mathbf{v} \in \Lambda$ at distance at most $r\lambda_1(\Lambda)$ away from $\mathbf{t}$, finding the point $\mathbf{v} \in \Lambda$.

By considering $\mathbf{t}$ modulo the lattice and demanding $\mathbf{t} - \mathbf{v}$ as a result, we get the syndrome form.

Problem 2 (BDD, Syndrome Form). For $r > 0$, (syndrome) *Bounded Distance Decoding* (BDD_r) is the task of, given a lattice Λ and target $\mathbf{t} \in \mathbb{R}^n/\Lambda$ in the torus with the promise that there exists $\mathbf{e} \in \mathbf{t}$ such that $\|\mathbf{e}\| < r\lambda_1(\Lambda)$, finding this error $\mathbf{e}$.

Concretely, to solve a BDD instance, one is given some basis $\mathbf{B}$ of the lattice together with the target $\mathbf{t}$ being expressed in terms of the basis $\mathbf{B}$ with coefficients in the interval $[0, 1)$.

When BDD is instantiated with $r < \frac{1}{2}$, it is guaranteed that there is only one lattice point close enough to $\mathbf{t}$. For random lattices, there is still one lattice point close enough with high probability when you move up to $r < 1$ by the following heuristic.

Heuristic Claim 1. *Let Λ be a random lattice of volume 1, $r \in (0, 1)$. The probability that a target $\mathbf{t} \leftarrow U(R\mathcal{B}^n)$ is at a distance of at most R from some nonzero lattice point $\mathbf{v} \in \Lambda$ is at most $O(n\sqrt{n})r^n$, where $R = r\,\mathrm{GH}(n)$.*

This Heuristic can be justified with the Gaussian Heuristic and an upper bound on spherical domes, cf. [28, Lem. 4.1].

Heuristic Justification. Note that only lattice points $\mathbf{v} \in \Lambda \setminus \{\mathbf{0}\}$ are relevant with $\|\mathbf{v}\| \leq 2R = 2r\,\mathrm{GH}(n)$ by the triangle inequality. For such a $\mathbf{v} \in \Lambda \setminus \{\mathbf{0}\}$, we are interested in $\mathrm{Vol}(R\mathcal{B}^n \cap (\mathbf{v} + R\mathcal{B}^n))$, which is twice the volume of the spherical dome $\{\mathbf{t} \in R\mathcal{B}^n \mid \langle \mathbf{t}, \mathbf{v} \rangle \geq \frac{1}{2}\|\mathbf{v}\|^2\}$. This spherical dome is contained in a cylinder with base $R\sqrt{1-\alpha^2} \cdot \mathcal{B}^{n-1}$ and height $R(1 - \alpha)$, which has volume at most $R^n(1-\alpha^2)^{n/2}\mathrm{Vol}(\mathcal{B}^{n-1})$, where $\alpha = \|\mathbf{v}\|/2R$. One can show that $\mathrm{Vol}(\mathcal{B}^{n-1}) \leq \frac{\sqrt{en}}{2}\mathrm{Vol}(\mathcal{B}^n)$ holds, which implies $\mathrm{Vol}(R\mathcal{B}^n \cap (\mathbf{v} + R\mathcal{B}^n)) \leq O(\sqrt{n})r^n(1-\alpha^2)^{n/2}$.

The Gaussian Heuristic predicts approximately ℓ^n lattice points in a ball of radius $\ell\,\mathrm{GH}(n)$. By using this estimate for $\ell \in (1, 2r)$, the volume of all the spherical domes is roughly

$$\int_1^{2r} n\ell^{n-1} \cdot O(\sqrt{n})r^n \left(1 - \frac{\ell^2}{4r^2}\right)^{n/2} d\ell \leq O(n\sqrt{n})r^n \int_1^{2r} \left(\ell^2 - \frac{\ell^4}{4r^2}\right)^{n/2} d\ell. \quad (4)$$

The integrand reaches the maximum r^n at $\ell = \sqrt{2}r$ so Eq. (4) is at most $O(n\sqrt{n})r^{2n}(2r-1)$. For the desired probability, we consider the ratio of volumes, which is at most $O(n\sqrt{n})r^{2n}/\mathrm{Vol}(R\mathcal{B}^n) = O(n\sqrt{n})r^n$.

2.3   Dual Distinguishing

The idea of using short dual vectors for distinguishing between BDD samples and random samples can be traced back at least to [2] in the lattice literature, and can be viewed as a lattice analog to an old decoding technique [17,22,31]. Given a BDD sample $\mathbf{t} = \mathbf{v} + \mathbf{e}$ with $\mathbf{v} \in \Lambda$, for any dual vector $\mathbf{w} \in \Lambda^\vee$ one has,

$$\langle \mathbf{t}, \mathbf{w} \rangle = \langle \mathbf{v}, \mathbf{w} \rangle + \langle \mathbf{e}, \mathbf{w} \rangle \equiv \langle \mathbf{e}, \mathbf{w} \rangle \pmod 1. \quad (5)$$

In particular, if the error $\mathbf{e}$ and the dual vector $\mathbf{w}$ are of small enough ℓ_2 norm, $\langle \mathbf{t}, \mathbf{w} \rangle$ should be close to an integer. Moreover, $\langle \mathbf{t}, \mathbf{w} \rangle \pmod 1$ is thus well-defined for any $\mathbf{t} \in \mathbb{R}^n/\Lambda$. A natural score to consider, as some indication that the target $\mathbf{t}$ is close to the lattice Λ, is therefore given by,

$$f_{\mathbf{w}}(\mathbf{t}) := \frac{\chi_{\mathbf{w}}(\mathbf{t}) + \chi_{-\mathbf{w}}(\mathbf{t})}{2} = \cos(2\pi \cdot \langle \mathbf{t}, \mathbf{w} \rangle), \quad (6)$$

reusing $\chi_{\mathbf{w}}$ from Lemma 2.

If $\mathbf{t}$ is indeed close to the lattice, $f_{\mathbf{w}}(\mathbf{t})$ should be close to 1, but the converse does not need to be true. To boost one's confidence in the fidelity of this score, one may naturally consider the total score over many dual vectors $\mathcal{W} \subset \Lambda^\vee$ given by,

$$f_{\mathcal{W}}(\mathbf{t}) := \sum_{\mathbf{w} \in \mathcal{W}} f_{\mathbf{w}}(\mathbf{t}). \quad (7)$$

This function is referred to as the simple decoder f_{simple} by Laarhoven and Walter [23], and resembles the Aharonov-Regev [2] decoder closely which is given by $f_{\mathbf{w}}^{AR}(\mathbf{t}) := \rho_{1/\sigma}(\mathbf{w}) f_{\mathbf{w}}(\mathbf{t})$.

In carefully crafted circumstances, in particular regarding the construction of the set of short dual vectors $\mathcal{W}$, this approach can give a provable worst-case distinguisher [2] or certificate [19].

More recent works [18,23,25] have reused this idea more heuristically, in a context where $\mathcal{W}$ simply is the set of all the dual vectors smaller than a certain radius (typically given by running a sieve algorithm [10]), and for a random error $\mathbf{e}$.

The Analysis of [23]. First, Laarhoven and Walter analyze in [23, Lem. 6] the distribution of the score $f_{\mathbf{w}}(\mathbf{t})$ of BDD targets $\mathbf{t}$ with a distance of exactly r to the primal lattice. In the derivation, they approximate this distribution by targets sampled from a continuous gaussian with $\sigma = r/\sqrt{n}$.

Lemma 4 (cf. [23, Lemma 6]). *Let $\Lambda \subset \mathbb{R}^n$ be a full rank lattice and $\mathbf{w} \in \Lambda^{\vee}$ be a dual vector.*

(a) If $\mathbf{t} \leftarrow U(\mathbb{R}^n/\Lambda)$, then $\mathbb{E}[f_{\mathbf{w}}(\mathbf{t})] = 0$, and $\mathbb{V}[f_{\mathbf{w}}(\mathbf{t})] = 1/2$,
(b) If $\mathbf{t} \leftarrow \mathcal{N}(0,\sigma^2)^n \pmod{\Lambda}$ with $\sigma \in \mathbb{R}_{>0}$, then

$$\mathbb{E}[f_{\mathbf{w}}(\mathbf{t})] = e^{-2\pi^2\sigma^2\|\mathbf{w}\|^2}, \quad \text{and} \quad \mathbb{V}[f_{\mathbf{w}}(\mathbf{t})] = \frac{1}{2} - \Theta\left(e^{-4\pi^2\sigma^2\|\mathbf{w}\|^2}\right). \quad (8)$$

Proof. For the variance, we will use $f_{\mathbf{w}}(\mathbf{t})^2 = \frac{1}{2} + \frac{1}{2}\cos(4\pi\langle\mathbf{w},\mathbf{t}\rangle) = \frac{1}{2} + \frac{1}{2}f_{2\mathbf{w}}(\mathbf{t})$.

(a) Integrating over a fundamental region $\mathbf{B}\cdot[0,1]^n$ shows $\mathbb{E}[f_{\mathbf{w}}(\mathbf{t})] = 0$ since $\int_0^1 \cos(\alpha + 2\pi kx) = 0$ for all $k \in \mathbb{Z}$ and $\alpha \in \mathbb{R}$. Then by the above, it readily follows,

$$\mathbb{V}[f_{\mathbf{w}}(\mathbf{t})] = \frac{1}{2} + \frac{1}{2}\mathbb{E}[f_{2\mathbf{w}}(\mathbf{t})] = \frac{1}{2}.$$

(b) Because a gaussian is a radial distribution,

$$\mathbb{E}[f_{\mathbf{w}}(\mathbf{t})] = \mathbb{E}_{x \leftarrow \mathcal{N}(0,\sigma^2)}[\cos(2\pi x\|\mathbf{w}\|)] = \exp\left(-2\pi^2\sigma^2\|\mathbf{w}\|^2\right),$$

and $\mathbb{V}[f_{\mathbf{w}}(\mathbf{t})] = \frac{1}{2} + \frac{1}{2}\mathbb{E}[f_{2\mathbf{w}}(\mathbf{t})] - \mathbb{E}[f_{\mathbf{w}}(\mathbf{t})]^2 = \frac{1}{2} + \frac{1}{2}\varepsilon^4 - \varepsilon^2$, where $\varepsilon = \exp(-2\pi^2\sigma^2\|\mathbf{w}\|^2) \in (0,1)$.

However, to conclude on the behavior of the total score, one must resort to the following heuristic.

Heuristic 3 (Independence Heuristic). *For any fixed set $\mathcal{W} \subset \Lambda^{\vee}$ and any distribution for $\mathbf{t}$ considered in Lemma 4, the random variables $(\langle\mathbf{w},\mathbf{t}\rangle \bmod 1)_{\mathbf{w} \in \mathcal{W}}$ are mutually independent.*

We will refer to this heuristic as the Independence Heuristic.

By combining the above heuristic with a central limit approximation—which is fair, given the exponential size of $\mathcal{W}$ in the context of interest—one can model the total score $f_{\mathcal{W}}(\mathbf{t})$ of each type of sample as a gaussian of center $|\mathcal{W}| \cdot E$ and variance $|\mathcal{W}| \cdot V$, where E and V are the expectation and variance given by the above Lemma 4.

One may then deduce the distinguishing advantage of the score function using the following lemma.

Lemma 5. *Let $X \leftarrow \mathcal{N}(E_X, V_X)$ and $Y \leftarrow \mathcal{N}(E_Y, V_Y)$ be independent gaussian random variables. Then*

$$\mathbb{P}[X > Y] = \frac{1}{2}\left[1 + \operatorname{erf}\left(\frac{E_X - E_Y}{\sqrt{2(V_X + V_Y)}}\right)\right] \tag{9}$$

Proof. Consider the variable $Z = X - Y$, which is also gaussian, specifically $Z \sim \mathcal{N}(E_Z, V_Z)$ where $E_Z = E_X - E_Y$ and $V_Z = V_X + V_Y$. Conclude noting that the event $X > Y$ is equivalent to $Z > 0$.

This lemma leads Laarhoven and Walter to roughly the following claim.

Heuristic Claim 2 (cf. [23, Lem. 9]). *Let $\Lambda \subset \mathbb{R}^n$ be a random lattice of volume 1, $r > 0$ and $\mathcal{W} \subset \Lambda^{\vee}$ a set consisting of the α^n shortest vectors of $\Lambda^{\vee}$, where $\alpha = \min\{\beta \mid e^2 \ln(\beta) = \beta^2 r^2\}$. Then, we have*

$$\mathbb{P}\left[f_{\mathcal{W}}(\mathbf{t}_{\mathrm{BDD}}) > f_{\mathcal{W}}(\mathbf{t}_{\mathrm{unif}})\right] \geq \frac{1}{2} + \frac{1}{2}\operatorname{erf}\left(\frac{1}{\sqrt{2}}\right) \approx 0.84,$$

where $\mathbf{t}_{\mathrm{unif}} \leftarrow U(\mathbb{R}^n/\Lambda)$ and $\mathbf{t}_{\mathrm{BDD}} \leftarrow U(r\mathrm{GH}(n)\,\mathcal{S}^{n-1})$ are sampled independently.

Heuristic Justification. First, we approximate the uniform distribution of BDD samples $\mathbf{t}_{\mathrm{BDD}} \leftarrow U(r\mathrm{GH}(n)\,\mathcal{S}^{n-1})$ by a gaussian distribution with $\sigma = r\mathrm{GH}(n)/\sqrt{n}$. According to the Gaussian Heuristic, the lengths of the vectors in $\mathcal{W}$ are concentrated around $\alpha \cdot \mathrm{GH}(n)$. By the Independence Heuristic and Lemma 4, the score function for the BDD sample follows a gaussian distribution $\mathcal{N}(E_X, V_X)$, where

$$E_X = \alpha^n \exp\left(-\frac{2\pi^2\alpha^2 r^2 \cdot \mathrm{GH}(n)^4}{n}\right) = \alpha^n \exp\left(-\frac{\alpha^2 r^2 \cdot n}{2e^2}\right) = \alpha^{n/2},$$

by construction of α. The variance is $V_X \approx \frac{1}{2} \cdot \alpha^n$.

On the other hand, uniform samples give a score distribution Y following a gaussian distribution $\mathcal{N}(E_Y, V_Y)$ where $E_Y = 0$ and $V_Y = \alpha^n/2$ by case (a) of Lemma 4.

Hence by Lemma 5, the probability of having $X > Y$ equals

$$\frac{1}{2} + \frac{1}{2}\operatorname{erf}\left(\frac{\alpha^{n/2}}{\sqrt{2 \cdot \alpha^n}}\right) \approx 0.84.$$

The analysis of [18] *and* [25]. The analysis proposed by Guo–Johansson [18] is somewhat less explicit. Instead of analyzing the score directly, they consider the statistical distance between the distribution of $\langle \mathbf{t}, \mathbf{w} \rangle$ mod 1 for $\mathbf{t}$ uniform and gaussian.

Using the same Independence Heuristic, they then conclude on the statistical distance between the tuples $(\langle \mathbf{t}, \mathbf{w} \rangle \bmod 1)_{\mathbf{w} \in \mathcal{W}}$ for $\mathbf{t}$ uniform and gaussian. While there exist optimal distinguishers (introduced in [23] using a lemma dating back to Neyman-Pearson [29]), it differs from the score function $f_{\mathcal{W}}$, but they seem to assume that the scoring function is not that far from optimal. An argument for such a statement is given by Laarhoven and Walter [23, Corollary 2], but it is not mentioned by Guo and Johansson [18].

The analysis of MATZOV [25] is on the contrary quite explicit on computing the distribution of scores, while taking into account the severe technical complications introduced by their *modulus switching*. Namely, they increase the number of dual vectors with a factor D_{round} in [25, Section 5] to account for the effect of rounding the Fourier coefficients after performing a modulus switch. Another factor D_{arg} is also introduced, but we view it as dubious (see Appendix A.4 of the full version [14]).

In any case, we can essentially recover the key claims of [18,25] directly from the above analysis as well, using the following lemma. Note that we express the result more generally in terms of BDD in an arbitrary lattice rather than a specific LWE instance.

Lemma 6. *Let* $X \leftarrow \mathcal{N}(E_X, V_X)$ *and* $Y_i \leftarrow \mathcal{N}(E_Y, V_Y)$ *be independent gaussian random variables for* $i \in \{1, \dots, T\}$. *Then*

$$\mathbb{P}\left[X > \max_{i \in \{1,\dots,T\}} (Y_i)\right] \geq 1 - \frac{T}{2} \operatorname{erfc}\left(\frac{E_X - E_Y}{\sqrt{2 \cdot (V_X + V_Y)}}\right) \tag{10}$$

Proof. Follows directly from a union bound on the complementary events with Lemma 5.

This leads to the following heuristic claim, underlying the work of [18,25]. Note that we state this key claim here for a *projected sublattice* with renormalization of the volume, where the dual vectors are in the dual of this projected sublattice. Indeed, the general setting of the Dual-Sieve attack [6,16,18,25] first applies BKZ on the dual of a lattice of dimension d, obtaining a reversed dual basis $^{\vee}\mathbf{B}$. Then the set $\mathcal{W}$ is obtained by running a sieve in dimension β_{sieve} on the first dual block, that is the β_{sieve}-dimension dual sublattice $\Lambda^{\vee} \subset \Lambda_{\mathrm{LWE}}^{\vee}$ generated by the partial reversed dual basis $(^{\vee}\mathbf{B})_{[1,\beta_{\mathrm{sieve}}]}$. This is the dual of the projected sublattice generated by $\mathbf{B}_{[d+1-\beta_{\mathrm{sieve}}, d]}$ of the full primal lattice Λ_{LWE}.

Heuristic Claim 3 (Key claim of [18,25], reconstructed). *Let* $\Lambda \subset \mathbb{R}^n$ *be a random lattice of volume 1,* $\mathcal{W} \subset \Lambda^{\vee}$ *the set consisting of the* $(4/3)^{n/2}$ *shortest vectors of* $\Lambda^{\vee}$. *For some* $\sigma > 0$ *and* $T \in \mathbb{Z}_{\geq 1}$, *consider* $\mathbf{t}_{\mathrm{BDD}} \leftarrow \mathcal{N}(0, \sigma^2)^n$

and i.i.d. $\mathbf{t}_{\mathrm{unif}}^{(i)} \leftarrow U(\mathbb{R}^n/\Lambda)$ where $i \in \{1,\ldots,T\}$. Set $\ell = \sqrt{4/3} \cdot \mathrm{GH}(n)$ and $\varepsilon = \exp(-2\pi^2\sigma^2\ell^2)$. If $\ln T \leq |\mathcal{W}|\,\varepsilon^2$, we have

$$\mathbb{P}\left[\forall i \in \{1,\ldots,T\}: f_\mathcal{W}(\mathbf{t}_{\mathrm{BDD}}) > f_\mathcal{W}(\mathbf{t}_{\mathrm{unif}}^{(i)})\right] \geq 1 - O\left(\frac{1}{\sqrt{\ln T}}\right).$$

Heuristic Justification. Similar to the Heuristic Justification of Heuristic Claim 2, the score distribution for $\mathbf{t}_{\mathrm{BDD}}$ is approximately $X \sim \mathcal{N}\left(\varepsilon \cdot |\mathcal{W}|, \frac{1}{2}|\mathcal{W}|\right)$, as lengths of vectors in $\mathcal{W}$ are concentrated around $\ell = \sqrt{4/3} \cdot \mathrm{GH}(n)$ by the Gaussian Heuristic. The uniform samples $\mathbf{t}_{\mathrm{unif}}^{(i)}$ each give a score distribution that is approximately $Y_i \sim \mathcal{N}(0, \frac{1}{2}|\mathcal{W}|)$.

Thus by Lemma 6, the probability that $f_\mathcal{W}(\mathbf{t}_{\mathrm{BDD}})$ is bigger than every score of the uniform errors equals

$$1 - \frac{T}{2}\,\mathrm{erfc}\left(\frac{|\mathcal{W}| \cdot \varepsilon}{\sqrt{|\mathcal{W}|}}\right) \geq 1 - \frac{T}{2}\,\mathrm{erfc}\left(\sqrt{\ln T}\right).$$

Hence, with Lemma 1 we conclude,

$$\mathbb{P}\left[X > \max_{i \in \{1,\ldots,T\}}(Y_i)\right] \geq 1 - \frac{1}{2\sqrt{\pi \ln T}}\left(1 + O\left(\frac{1}{\ln T}\right)\right) \geq 1 - O\left(\frac{1}{\sqrt{\ln T}}\right).$$

3   Dual-Sieve-FFT Distinguishing, Generalized

As established by the literature [2,19,23], scoring target points to obtain information about their distance to a primal lattice Λ using short dual vectors is very general, and not limited to LWE lattices.

In this section, we will show that this is also the case of the extra FFT trick as proposed in recent work of Guo and Johansson [18].

3.1   Abstracting the Dual-Sieve-FFT Attack of Guo–Johansson

The general idea is as follows. Given a lattice Λ, one first crafts a sparsification Λ' of Λ, i.e. a sublattice $\Lambda' \subset \Lambda$ of finite index. This gives rise to a finite abelian group of cosets $G := \Lambda/\Lambda'$. Now, to solve BDD for a target $\mathbf{t} \in \mathbb{R}^n/\Lambda$ on the lattice Λ, one solves BDD for the target $\mathbf{t}$ on all the cosets $\Lambda' + g$, or equivalently, solve BDD for all the targets $\mathbf{t} - g$ with $g + \Lambda' \in G$ on the sublattice Λ'. For the correct choice of coset $g + \Lambda'$, the distance to $\mathbf{t}$ is the same as in the initial BDD problem, but the sublattice is sparser, making this BDD problem easier than the original one. However, we now have $|G|$ instances to consider.

With the help of the DFT, the score function f_W can be computed for all targets $\mathbf{t} - g$ in a batch. That is, applying the DFT_G in Eq. (3) on a sequence $(\chi_{\mathbf{w}'}(g - \mathbf{t}))_{g \in G}$ for some $\mathbf{w}' \in (\Lambda')^\vee$ gives another sequence that at index $\chi_{\mathbf{w}} \in \widehat{G}$ has a value of,

$$\sum_{g \in G} \chi_{\mathbf{w}'}(g - \mathbf{t}) \overline{\chi_{\mathbf{w}}(g)} = \chi_{\mathbf{w}'}(-\mathbf{t}) \cdot \sum_{g \in G} \frac{\chi_{\mathbf{w}'}(g)}{\chi_{\mathbf{w}}(g)}, \tag{11}$$

where $\mathbf{w} + \Lambda^\vee \in (\Lambda')^\vee / \Lambda^\vee$ as $\widehat{G}$ is isomorphic to $(\Lambda')^\vee / \Lambda^\vee$ by Lemmata 2 and 3. Note that $\chi_{\mathbf{w}'}(g)$ is well defined for $g \in \Lambda/\Lambda'$ as $\chi_{\mathbf{w}'}$ is Λ'-periodic. By the orthogonality of characters, note that

$$\sum_{g \in G} \frac{\chi_{\mathbf{w}'}(g)}{\chi_{\mathbf{w}}(g)} = \begin{cases} |G|, & \text{if } \mathbf{w}' \in \mathbf{w} + \Lambda^\vee, \\ 0, & \text{otherwise.} \end{cases}$$

Hence, Eq. (11) is zero everywhere except at index $\chi_{\mathbf{w}'}$, where it is equal to $|G| \cdot \chi_{\mathbf{w}'}(-\mathbf{t})$.

By $\mathbb{C}$-linearity of the DFT, one can obtain an expression for the DFT of $f_W(g - \mathbf{t})$ for any finite set of dual vectors $W \subset (\Lambda')^\vee$. More specifically, if for all $\mathbf{w} \in W$ we have $-\mathbf{w} \in W$, i.e. it is *symmetric*, we have

$$\mathrm{DFT}_G \left((f_W(\mathbf{t} - g))_{g \in G} \right) = |G| \cdot \left(\sum_{\mathbf{w}' \in W \cap (\mathbf{w} + \Lambda^\vee)} f_{\mathbf{w}'}(\mathbf{t}) \right)_{\mathbf{w} + \Lambda^\vee \in \widehat{G}}.$$

Neglecting this scalar $|G|$, we therefore construct a batch of score functions, by performing an inverse FFT on the sequence $\sum_{\mathbf{w}' \in \mathbf{w} + \Lambda^\vee} f_{\mathbf{w}'}(-\mathbf{t})$ for all (dual) cosets $\mathbf{w} + \Lambda^\vee \in (\Lambda')^\vee / \Lambda^\vee$. Then, the entry with $g + \Lambda' \in G$ that has the highest score is most likely the coset $g + \Lambda'$ containing the lattice point in Λ that is closest to $\mathbf{t}$.

3.2 Implementation of the General Dual-Sieve-FFT Attack

In this section, we will give a concrete implementation of an algorithm that performs the general Dual-Sieve-FFT attack on a lattice Λ.

Concretely, the lattice Λ is specified by a basis $\mathbf{B} = [\mathbf{b}_1, \ldots, \mathbf{b}_n]$, and one can take a simple sparsification such as $\Lambda' = \mathcal{L}([d_1 \mathbf{b}_1, \ldots, d_n \mathbf{b}_n])$ for suitable $d_1, \ldots, d_n \in \mathbb{N}$.

In fact, any sparsification is, after a basis change, of this shape. When the sublattice $\Lambda' = \mathbf{B}' \cdot \mathbb{Z}^n \subset \mathbf{B} \cdot \mathbb{Z}^n = \Lambda$ is described by a matrix $\mathbf{B}'$, we can express the basis $\mathbf{B}'$ in terms of $\mathbf{B}$, i.e. find the matrix $\mathbf{A} \in \mathbb{Z}^{n \times n}$ such that $\mathbf{B}' = \mathbf{B} \cdot \mathbf{A}$.

Then, put $\mathbf{A}$ in the Smith Normal Form, i.e. find matrices $\mathbf{S}, \mathbf{T} \in \mathrm{GL}_n(\mathbb{Z})$ and a diagonal matrix $\mathbf{D}$ such that $\mathbf{A} = \mathbf{SDT}$ and thus, we have $\mathbf{B}'\mathbf{T}^{-1} = (\mathbf{BS}) \cdot \mathbf{D}$. As $\mathbf{A}$ was full rank, $\mathbf{D}$ is full rank (i.e. invertible over $\mathbb{Q}$), so here Λ' is described by the basis $[d_1\mathbf{b}'_1, \ldots, d_n\mathbf{b}'_n]$, where $\mathrm{diag}(d_1, \ldots, d_n) = \mathbf{D}$ and $\mathbf{BS} = [\mathbf{b}'_1, \ldots, \mathbf{b}'_n]$ is a basis for Λ.

Hence, without loss of generality, we have a sparsification $\Lambda' \subset \Lambda$, where $\mathbf{B}$ is a basis for Λ and $\mathbf{B}' = [d_1\mathbf{b}_1, \ldots, d_n\mathbf{b}_n]$ is a basis for Λ'. Then Algorithm 1 will find the coset of Λ' containing the closest lattice vector to some target $\mathbf{t}$.

Algorithm 1. DualFFT$(\mathbf{B}, \mathbf{B}', \mathcal{W}, \mathbf{t})$

Require:
1: A basis $\mathbf{B}$ of a full rank lattice $\Lambda \subset \mathbb{R}^n$,
2: A basis $\mathbf{B}' = \mathbf{B} \cdot \mathrm{diag}(d_1, \ldots, d_n)$ of $\Lambda' \subset \Lambda$,
3: A set of short dual vectors $\mathcal{W} \subset (\Lambda')^\vee$,
4: A target $\mathbf{t} \in \mathbb{R}^n / \Lambda'$

Ensure:
5: A lattice coset $g \in \Lambda/\Lambda'$ closest to $\mathbf{t}$

6: _____
7: Initialize a table T with zeros of dimension $d_1 \times d_2 \times \cdots \times d_n$
8: **for** $\mathbf{w} \in \mathcal{W}$ **do**
9:     Write $\mathbf{w} \equiv \frac{j_1}{d_1}\mathbf{b}_1^\vee + \cdots + \frac{j_n}{d_n}\mathbf{b}_n^\vee \pmod{\Lambda^\vee}$, where $0 \le j_i < d_i$
10:    $\mathsf{T}[j_1, j_2, \ldots, j_n] \leftarrow \mathsf{T}[j_1, j_2, \ldots, j_n] + \cos(2\pi \langle \mathbf{w}, \mathbf{t} \rangle)$
11: **end for**
12: $\mathsf{S} = \mathrm{DFT}^{-1}_{\mathbb{Z}/d_1\mathbb{Z} \times \cdots \times \mathbb{Z}/d_n\mathbb{Z}}(\mathsf{T})$
13: $(j_1, j_2, \cdots, j_n) \leftarrow \underset{\substack{k_1, k_2, \cdots, k_n \\ 0 \le k_i < d_i}}{\mathrm{argmax}} \{\mathsf{S}[k_1, k_2, \cdots, k_n]\}$
14: **return** $j_1\mathbf{b}_1 + \cdots + j_n\mathbf{b}_n$

Structure of the Quotient Group. From a geometric perspective, concerning the length of the vectors in $\mathcal{W}$, the structure of the group $G = \Lambda/\Lambda'$ does not appear to matter at all, only its size does. On the other hand, while asymptotically all group structures allow to compute DFT_G in time $O(|G| \log |G|)$, the structure of the group matters quite a lot in practice and the case $G = (\mathbb{Z}/2\mathbb{Z})^k$, *i.e.* the Walsh–Hadamard Transform, should definitely be the best choice. That is, one should construct the sublattice Λ' as generated by $\mathbf{B}' = [2\mathbf{b}_1, \ldots, 2\mathbf{b}_k, \mathbf{b}_{k+1}, \ldots, \mathbf{b}_n]$, which has index 2^k in Λ.

Randomized Sparsification. Note that the analysis of the length of the vectors in $\mathcal{W}$ requires applying Gaussian Heuristic to the densification of the dual, induced by the sparsification of the primal.

This might require care. Indeed, if the basis is well reduced before we apply the dual densification $\mathrm{diag}\left(\frac{1}{d_1}, \ldots, \frac{1}{d_n}\right)$, this might create a dual lattice which is not random-looking; in particular it might contain a few vectors shorter than predicted by Gaussian Heuristic, with an unclear impact on the rest of $\mathcal{W}$.

We do not expect this to be an issue if the basis $\mathbf{B}$ is adequately randomized before constructing the sparsification.

3.3   Advantages of the Generalization

Not only is it theoretically more satisfying to apply the FFT trick to the general decoding problem rather than to the specific LWE problem, it also makes recursion more straightforward.

Shorter Dual Vectors. The algorithm of Guo and Johansson [18] seems to perfectly fit this formalization, where the basis $\mathbf{B}$ is the standard basis associated with the q-ary representation of the lattice, and $\mathbf{B}' = \mathbf{B} \cdot \mathrm{diag}(\gamma, \ldots, \gamma, 1, \ldots 1)$ (with k many γ's). The set of short dual vectors is obtained by first running BKZ-reduction with block size β_{BKZ} on the dual of $\mathbf{B}'$, and then sieving in the sublattice generated by the first β_{sieve} vectors of this reduced dual basis. The impact of the sparsification $\mathbf{B}' = \mathbf{B} \cdot \mathrm{diag}(\gamma, \ldots, \gamma, 1, \ldots 1)$ on the length of the vectors in $\mathcal{W}$ is to shorten them by a factor $\gamma^{k/n}$. That is, the sparsification has been *diluted* over n many dimension.

Instead, consider first applying dual-BKZ-reduction with block size β_{BKZ} on $\mathbf{B}$, and then taking $\mathbf{B}' = \mathbf{B} \cdot \mathrm{diag}(1, \ldots 1, \gamma, \ldots, \gamma)$. In this way, the densification of the reversed dual basis is given by $^{\vee}(\mathbf{B}') = {^{\vee}\mathbf{B}} \cdot \mathrm{diag}\left(\frac{1}{\gamma}, \ldots, \frac{1}{\gamma}, 1, \ldots 1\right)$ remains concentrated on the k first dual vectors![1] Therefore, its effect is now to shorten the length of the vectors in $\mathcal{W}$ by a factor $\gamma^{k/\beta_{\mathrm{sieve}}}$ (assuming $k < \beta_{\mathrm{sieve}}$).

We leave the concrete exploitation of this improvement to future work, given that the next section of this work will invalidate the current success probability analysis of the dual attack as a whole. Before the improved concrete cryptanalysis claims are made, the attack should first be convincingly fixed!

Open Question 1. *Produce estimates of the gain of the above improvement of the Dual-Sieve-FFT attack on relevant concrete lattice-based schemes, once the general analysis of Dual-Sieve attacks has been fixed (cf. Open Question 2).*

4   Contradictions from the Heuristic Analysis

In the following, we will show two regimes where the analyses of [18, 23, 25] give rise to absurd conclusions.

The first one is concerned with distinguishing a target from a single uniform sample, when its expected distance to the lattice exceeds the Gaussian Heuristic, a task that was recently proven statistically impossible in a random lattice [12].

The second one is concerned with the case of finding a planted solution among many candidates. For certain parameters, the analysis of [18, 25] predicts a successful guess of the desired target, despite the existence of many other candidates that are even closer to the lattice than the planted solution. We would like to stress that this contradiction is independent of whether or not one uses the FFT trick, but merely arises from the large number of candidates that is used.

---

[1] The warning on randomized sparsification from Sect. 3.2 still applies here; the basis randomization should be applied to the block $\mathbf{B}_{[n-\beta_{\mathrm{sieve}}+1,n]}$.

Recall that in this section, as in [23], we implicitly renormalize the lattice Λ to have volume 1.

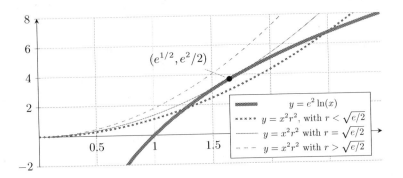

Fig. 1. The equation $e^2 \ln(x) = x^2 r^2$ for various r.

4.1   Distinguishing the Indistinguishable

Set Up. Recall that the main result of Laarhoven and Walter [23, Lem. 9], reformulated as Heuristic Claim 2, provides an algorithm to distinguish a BDD instance at distance $r \cdot \mathrm{GH}(n)$ from a uniform target modulo the lattice. After a precomputation depending solely on the lattice Λ, this algorithm has exponential complexity α^n where $e^2 \ln(\alpha) = \alpha^2 r^2$, and the heuristic analysis claims that it is successful with probability ≈ 0.84, that is, with constant advantage.

Lemma 7. *The equation $e^2 \ln(x) = x^2 r^2$ admits a real solution in x if and only if $r^2 \le e/2$.*

Proof. The statement and its proof is illustrated by Fig. 1. First, note that $x \mapsto e^2 \ln(x)$ is concave, while $x \mapsto x^2 r^2$ is convex for any $r \in \mathbb{R}$. We discuss three cases.

Case 1: $r^2 = e/2$. The parabola $y = r^2 x^2$ intersects tangentially the curve $y = e^2 \ln x$ at $(x, y) = (\sqrt{e}, \frac{1}{2}e^2)$, with slope $\left.\frac{dy}{dx}\right|_{x=\sqrt{e}} = e^{3/2}$. By convexity, we have $e^2 \ln(x) < x^2 r^2$ for any $x \ne \sqrt{e}$.

Case 2: $r^2 > e/2$. Note that $r^2 x^2$ is strictly increasing in r^2 for any x. Reusing Case 1, we see that $e^2 \ln(x) < x^2 r^2$ for all x: there are no solution in that case.

Case 3: $r^2 < e/2$. We have $e^2 \ln(x) > x^2 r^2$ at $x = \sqrt{e}$. We also have $e^2 \ln(x) < x^2 r^2$ when $x = 1$. The Intermediate Value Theorem then tells there is a solution with $x \in (1, \sqrt{e})$.

Note that $\sqrt{e/2} \approx 1.1658 > 1$. The fact that the algorithm is supposed to work beyond $r > 1$ raises suspicion: the average number of points at distance at most $r \cdot \mathrm{GH}(n)$ for a uniform target is exactly r^n by the Gaussian Heuristic.

More formally, it is a theorem[2] that for any measurable set $V \subset \mathbb{R}^n$, it holds that

$$\mathop{\mathbb{E}}_{\mathbf{t} \leftarrow U(\mathbb{R}^n/\Lambda)} \left[|(V + \mathbf{t}) \cap \Lambda| \right] = \frac{\mathrm{Vol}(V)}{\det \Lambda}.$$

Still, one could imagine a scenario where with small probability a target has few close vectors, but most likely it will not, making distinguishing statistically possible.

The Contradiction. It has been shown recently by Debris et al. [12] that the above scenario does not occur with random lattices. More specifically, for a formally defined notion of random lattices, it is proven that for errors from a uniform distribution on the ball of radius $r\mathrm{GH}(n)$ $(r > 1)$, the statistical distance between the error modulo the lattice and $U(\mathbb{R}^n/\Lambda)$ is exponentially small as a function of the dimension [12, Prop. 4.3].

That is, for all $r > 1$, no algorithm, whatever its complexity, can even succeed with probability greater than $\frac{1}{2} + O(1) \cdot r^{-n/2}$. Yet, [23, Lem. 9] (reformulated as Heuristic Claim 2) claims a constant advantage.   ⚡

Discussion. One could counter-argue that the claim [23, Lem. 9] is given for uniform distributions over a sphere, a case not contradicted by Debris et al. [12]. However, the actual analysis in [23] is done for a Gaussian distribution, a case which *is* also covered by Debris et al. [12, Theorem 4.6].

The Suspect Heuristic. We note that this counter-argument applies only to the (heuristic) [23, Lem. 9], that is given a single sample, and not to [23, Lem. 8]. Indeed, in the context of the (heuristic) [23, Lem. 8] where exponentially many samples, either all uniform or all BDD, are given, the exponentially small statistical distance can be compensated for with a large number of samples, as discussed between both Lemmata.

We note in particular that [23, Lem. 8] does not require the Independence Heuristic, as it uses only one dual vector. In fact, after close inspection of the reasoning behind [23, Lem. 8], we could not identify any step that should be too hard to make formally provable, up to minor conditions and small losses in the concrete efficiency of the distinguisher. Indeed, with enough effort, it appears that all the other heuristics and approximations could be dealt with formally.

This sets the Independence Heuristic as the prime suspect leading to the erroneous [23, Lem. 9].

4.2   Candidates Closer Than the Solution (Asymptotic)

Set Up. Recall that the key claim of [18] and [25], reconstructed as Heuristic Claim 3 considers the case where the set of dual vectors comes from a lattice

---

[2] The difference with the Gaussian Heuristic being the presence of a uniform random shift $\mathbf{t} \leftarrow U(\mathbb{R}^n/\Lambda)$.

sieve [10, 28, 30], that is, it consists of $N = (4/3)^{n/2}$ vectors of length $\ell = \sqrt{4/3} \cdot$ GH(n). Given one BDD instance with the error sampled from a gaussian with parameter σ and T uniform samples, the claim is made that the BDD sample can be detected with probability close to 1, whenever $\ln T \leq N\varepsilon^2$ where $\varepsilon = \exp(-2\pi^2\sigma^2\ell^2)$.

Let us consider the constraint the other way around, that is, how large can one take σ for a given number of targets T? The condition translates to $\frac{1}{\varepsilon} \leq \sqrt{N/\ln T}$, and this constrains σ to satisfy

$$\sigma \leq \sqrt{\frac{\ln(1/\varepsilon)}{2\pi^2\ell^2}} = \sqrt{\frac{\ln N - \ln\ln T}{4\pi^2\ell^2}} = \frac{1}{2\pi\sqrt{\frac{4}{3} \cdot \text{GH}(n)}} \cdot \sqrt{\frac{n}{2}\ln\frac{4}{3} - \ln\ln T}.$$

With GH$(n) \approx \sqrt{\frac{n}{2\pi e}}$, one then arrives at $\sigma \leq \sqrt{C - \frac{C'\ln\ln T}{n}}$ for some constants $C = \frac{3e\ln(4/3)}{16\pi} \approx 0.047$ and $C' = \frac{3e}{8\pi} \approx 0.32$. This means that Heuristic Claim 3 supposedly still finds a BDD sample at expected distance $\sqrt{C \cdot n} \approx 0.89\,\text{GH}(n)$, even among a number of random candidates as large as doubly-exponential $T = \exp(\exp(n^{.99}))$.

The Contradiction (Asymptotic). We will show that the above claim leads to a contradiction, already for a single-exponential $T = 2.05^n$ number of random candidates.

Lemma 8. *Let Λ be a lattice of volume 1, and $r > 0$ such that $r < \frac{\lambda_1(\Lambda)}{2\,\text{GH}(n)}$. Then, for a target $\mathbf{t}$ uniform in $\mathbb{R}^n/\Lambda$, it holds with probability r^n that $\mathbf{t}$ is at distance at most $r\,\text{GH}(n)$ from the lattice.*

Proof. Note that the volume of the ball of radius $r \cdot \text{GH}(n)$ is exactly r^n by definition of GH(n). Furthermore, because $r \cdot \text{GH}(n) < \lambda_1(\Lambda)/2$, all translations of this ball by points in Λ are disjoint. Said otherwise, this ball does not intersect itself modulo the lattice. More formally, its projection onto the torus $\mathbb{R}^n/\Lambda$ is injective. Hence, the ball modulo the lattice also has volume r^n in $\mathbb{R}^n/\Lambda$. The probability of $\mathbf{t}$ falling into that ball is therefore $r^n/\text{Vol}(\mathbb{R}^n/\Lambda) = r^n/\det\Lambda = r^n$.

Let us use this lemma in the case of a random lattice of volume 1, or more specifically, one where we expect $\lambda_1(\Lambda) \approx \text{GH}(n)$. Using Lemma 8 with $r = 0.49$, the probability that a uniform target lies in the ball of radius $r\,\text{GH}(n)$ equals r^n. When taking $T = 2.05^n$ uniform samples, on expectation we have $T \cdot r^n > 1.004^n \gg 1$ of the uniform samples to fall in this ball and therefore with high probability there will be one such target at most $r\,\text{GH}(n)$ away from a lattice point. More concretely, the probability that none of these targets lies in this ball is $(1 - r^n)^T \to e^{-1.004^n}$ (as $n \to \infty$), so with overwhelming probability there is a uniform target in the ball of radius $r\,\text{GH}(n)$.

On the other hand, recall that the actual BDD target had an expected length of $\sigma\sqrt{n} \approx 0.89\,\text{GH}(n) > r\,\text{GH}(n)$. We note that $0.89 > r$, so we expect one uniformly sampled candidate lying closer to the lattice than the solution we are looking for. However, the score function f_W is precisely meant to associate larger score to closer targets, so we expect that this uniform sample will get a higher score than the BDD sample and thus, the algorithm gives with overwhelming probability a wrong result.   ⚡

Discussion. One might counter-argue that f_W only probabilistically classifies vectors by their distance to the lattice and might somehow still give the particularly close uniform sample a lower score than the BDD sample. However, if we consider super-exponential number of uniform samples, for example $T = n^{2n}$, with the same argument, for some constant probability, there exists a random target $\mathbf{t}$ lying at distance $\frac{1}{n^2}\mathrm{GH}(n) = O(n^{-3/2})$ from the lattice. In this case we have $\langle \mathbf{t}, \mathbf{w} \rangle \leq O(1/n)$ for any $\mathbf{w} \in W$ output by a sieve, and approximating the cosine we know the score of $\mathbf{t}$ will be $f_W(\mathbf{t}) \geq N(1 - O(1/n^2))$, which is essentially maximal.

The Suspect Heuristic. The discussion above points to the same suspect as Sect. 4.1, namely, the Independence Heuristic. Indeed, under independence the probability of one uniform target reaching a constant fraction of the maximal score N should decrease as fast as $\exp(-\Theta(N))$, but we have shown that this probability is in fact at least $\exp(-\Theta(n \log n))$. Independence can not hold for such large choices of $N = \omega(n \log n)$, and this should be visible in the tail of the score distribution of uniform targets.

4.3   Candidates Closer Than the Solution (Concrete)

Set Up. In the contradiction above, we have chosen T as large as 2.05^n to be able to invoke Lemma 8 to have a uniform sample at distance $r\,\mathrm{GH}(n) < \frac{1}{2}\lambda_1(\Lambda)$, quantifying the probability that a random target in $\mathbb{R}^n/\Lambda$ falls close to the lattice. This leads to an *over-contradiction*: we exhibited the existence of a random target at distance $0.49\,\mathrm{GH}(n)$ from the lattice, much closer than the planted solution, at distance $0.89\,\mathrm{GH}(n)$. However, even when there is a uniform sample at distance e.g. $0.88\,\mathrm{GH}(n)$ from the lattice, this sample can get a higher score than the BDD sample resulting in an incorrect guess of which one the BDD sample was.

To extend Lemma 8 up to radii $r < 1$, we will resort to a heuristic instead. In this regime, translations of the ball by points in Λ may start to intersect. In practice, however, the volume of this intersection remains rather small and should not affect the volume so much.

Heuristic Claim 4. *Let Λ be a random lattice of volume 1, and $r \in (0,1)$. For a target $\mathbf{t}$ sampled uniformly in the torus $\mathbb{R}^n/\Lambda$, we have a probability of $r^n \cdot (1 - n^{O(1)}r^n)$ that $\mathbf{t}$ is at distance at most $r\,\mathrm{GH}(n)$ from the lattice.*

Heuristic Justification. Contrary to the proof of Lemma 8, we now have to subtract from r^n the probability that a target $\mathbf{t}$ has at least two lattice points at distance less than $r\,\mathrm{GH}(n)$ away, which by Heuristic Claim 1 happens with probability $O(n\sqrt{n})r^{2n}$.

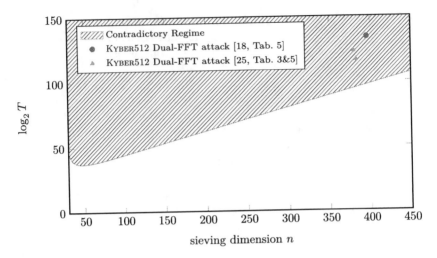

Fig. 2. Concrete Contradictory Regime: Maximum number of targets T before one is expected to be closer to a random lattice of dimension d than the planted solution. Obtained with script `volumetric_contr.py`.

The Contradiction. The idea now is that we end up at a contradiction whenever we instantiate the claim from above with the smallest possible r such that it is likely there is such a point among the T uniform samples.

For a given number of random samples T, we will pick σ for the BDD sample as before, i.e. such that $\ln T = N\varepsilon^2$ where $\varepsilon = \exp(-2\pi^2\sigma^2\ell^2)$. By the above Heuristic Claim 4, among those T targets, with constant probability there exists a target at distance at most $r \cdot \mathrm{GH}(n)$ from the lattice, where $r = 1/\sqrt[n]{T}$. When for a given T, the length $r\,\mathrm{GH}(n)$ is smaller than the expected length of the BDD sample, i.e. $\sqrt{n} \cdot \sigma$, this contradicts Heuristic Claim 3 and we say it is in the contradictory regime. This concrete contradictory regime is depicted in Fig. 2. ⚡

Contradictory Regime, in the Context of Concrete Attacks Against LWE. Above, we have determined the contradictory regime when obtaining the set $\mathcal{W}$ by a sieve over the full lattice, and assuming its volume was 1. It is not hard to see that scaling the lattice up or down is not going to affect the conclusion: the gaussian heuristic of the primal, σ and r will scale with the lattice, while the length ℓ of the dual vectors will scale inversely; this leaves ϵ and T unaffected.

In the context of the cryptanalytic literature [16,18,25], the set $\mathcal{W}$ does not come from the full dual lattice $\Lambda_{\mathrm{LWE}}^{\vee} \subset \mathbb{R}^n$. Instead, the full dual basis is first BKZ-reduced with blocksize β_{BKZ}, and then a sieve is run on the lattice $\Lambda^{\vee} \subset \Lambda_{\mathrm{LWE}}^{\vee}$ generated by the β_{sieve} first basis vectors of that BKZ-reduced basis. Effectively, this means that the dual distinguishing is not performed with respect to the whole LWE lattice Λ_{LWE}, but with respect to the projected sublattice Λ of it. Indeed, let $W \subset \mathbb{R}^n$ be the β_{sieve}-dimensional real vector space spanned by $\mathcal{W}$, and let π_W denote the orthogonal projection onto W. Then, for any $\mathbf{w} \in \mathcal{W}$, and any target $\mathbf{t} \in \mathbb{R}^n / \Lambda_{\mathrm{LWE}}$, it holds that

$$\langle \mathbf{w}, \mathbf{t} \rangle = \langle \mathbf{w}, \pi_W(\mathbf{t}) \rangle. \tag{12}$$

Therefore, $f_{\mathcal{W}}(\mathbf{t}) = f_{\mathcal{W}}(\pi_W(\mathbf{t}))$ for any target $\mathbf{t} \in \mathbb{R}^n / \Lambda_{\mathrm{LWE}}$. Note that $\pi_W(\mathbf{t})$ now lies in the β_{sieve}-dimensional torus $W / \pi_W(\Lambda_{\mathrm{LWE}})$. Hence we are effectively running the dual-distinguishing here over a projected sublattice of dimension β_{sieve}.

In this scenario, the contradictory regime is solely determined by β_{sieve} and T, and not by other quantities such as the LWE parameters, β_{BKZ}. Indeed the LWE parameters and β_{BKZ} are going to influence the volume of the lattice on which we run the final sieve to obtain $\mathcal{W}$, but if the parameters are tuned optimally, we still have $\ln T \approx N\varepsilon^2$ where $\varepsilon = \exp(-2\pi^2\sigma^2\ell^2)$.

This might not perfectly be representative of the exact analysis of MAT-ZOV [25] in that we do not make a special analysis of the modulus switching effect on the score distribution. Instead, this treats modulus switching as adding an implicit error, increasing σ. This remains a strong signal on the credibility of the heuristic analysis in that regime.

Another point raising discussion is the fact that our contradiction is established in the case where the uniform targets $\mathbf{t}$ are independent. This is not formally the case when those targets comes from a partial enumeration, though such a heuristic has been used in the past, for example underlying the analysis of the hybrid attack [21]. More critically, we see no mention of such dependence and how they would affect the algorithm in the existing analysis [16,18,25]. While we do not claim that it is impossible, we view the notion that such dependences could fix the algorithm as quite doubtful, and requiring specific substantiation with analysis and experiments.

In other words, while our contradiction does not formally disprove the recent claims on the Dual-Sieve attack [16,18,25], it does invalidate the reasoning leading to these claims. And in the absence of an obvious reason why this or that detail would solve the issues raised here, it seems reasonable to presume that these claims are indeed incorrect.

The Parameters of Guo–Johansson and MATZOV. We now turn to the instantiations from [18] and [25], focusing on the KYBER512 [8] parameter set, in the "asymptotic model" for dimensions for free.[3]

In [18, Table 5], we find a sieving dimension $\beta_{\mathrm{sieve}} = 396$ (where all the dual vectors come from), a guessing dimension $t_1 = 20$, and an FFT dimension $t = 78$. The guessing part considers all 7 possible values $\{-3, \ldots, 3\}$ of each coordinate, while the FFT is done with $\gamma = 2$, giving rise to $T = 7^{20} \cdot 2^{78} \approx 2^{134.1}$ targets.

In [25, Table 3], we find a sieving dimension $\beta_{\mathrm{sieve}} = 380$ (where all the dual vectors come from), a guessing dimension $k_{\mathrm{enum}} = 19$, and an FFT dimension

---

[3] This is the optimistic estimate in [13]. The other "G6K model" used in [18,25] is debated in Appendix A.2 of the full version [14].

$k_{\text{fft}} = 34$. The guessing part enumerates over $\{-3, \ldots, 3\}^{\text{enum}}$ in order of decreasing probability from the used binomial distribution, while the FFT is done with $p = 5$, giving rise to, according to [25], $T = 2^{19 \cdot H(\chi_s)} \cdot 5^{34} \approx 2^{123.3}$ many targets. Using an improved cost metric, they also give [25, Table 5] another set of parameter where $\beta_2 = 383$ and $T = 2^{17 \cdot H(\chi_s)} \cdot 5^{33} \approx 2^{116.3}$.[4]

For both instantiations [18,25] the dual attack is used rather deep in its contradictory regime, as depicted in Fig. 2.   ⚡

Remark. At this point, we clarify that it would be a mistake to consider the analysis still valid whenever it is not in the contradictory regime. The existence of the contradictory regime shows a fundamental flaw in the Independence Heuristic, that may very well have an impact beyond the contradictory regime. If it does not, this should be thoroughly substantiated with analysis and experiments.

5 Experiments

In this section, we provide further substantiation of the concrete contradiction (Sect. 4.2) with experimental evidence. We hope that the experiments will provide insight on what exactly goes wrong, and will show how the analysis can be fixed. We focus our analysis on the case where $\mathcal{W}$ is the output of a full sieve, namely it contains all the $(4/3)^{n/2}$ vectors of length less than $\sqrt{4/3} \cdot \text{GH}(n)$.

We look at three distributions: the score of uniform targets, the score of BDD targets with a gaussian error, and finally, the score of BDD targets with a gaussian error and modulus switching. There are two plausible diagnoses for how the contradictory regime appears: either the BDD scores are smaller than predicted, or the uniform scores are higher than predicted.

Because the contradictory regime only kicks in for rather large values of T (say 2^{40} even in small dimension) these unpredicted high scores might be very rare and we are interested in the tail of that distribution. Naïvely, it would take a long time to run such large scale experiments, but the same FFT trick from [18] (cf. Sect. 3) makes it feasible to run experiments on this scale!

5.1 Implementation Details

We used the G6K software [4] for running the experiments, using Python on a high-level but with a binding to some C code for computing the WHT. For the uniform targets we wrote the script `unif_scores.py`, which computes scores for many points sampled uniformly from $(\mathbb{Z}/q\mathbb{Z})^n$, where $\mathcal{W}$ is the output of a full sieve on the dual of $\mathbf{B} \cdot \text{diag}(2, \ldots, 2, 1, \ldots, 1)$ with the number of 2s equal to the FFT dimension. This setup allowed us to get roughly 2^{25} samples per second per CPU core. The scores were stored in buckets of width 1 while the exceptionally

---

[4] We are not quite sure how this quantity was derived, and it seems incorrect. See Appendix A.5 of the full version [14].

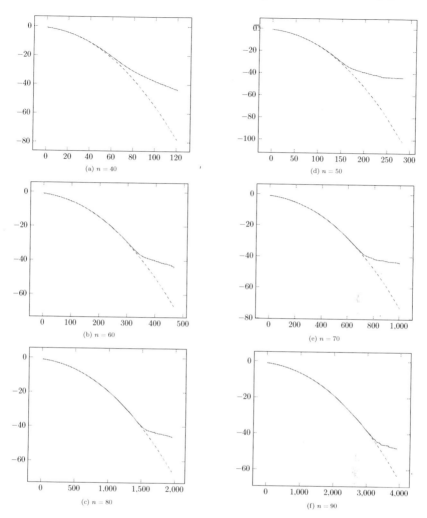

Legend: distribution of the scores on the x-axis and the logarithm (base 2) of the survival function (SF) on the y-axis. Dashed blue line: prediction from the heuristic analysis. Red line: experimental distribution. 2^{45} samples per curve.

Fig. 3. The distribution of scores according to the prediction and determined experimentally. The experimental data is obtained with `unif_scores.py` and listed in `data/unif_scores_nX.csv` of the auxiliary files. (Color figure online)

high scores were kept in a list. Here, we sieve using the dual mode built into G6K which only works with the dual basis implicitly.[5]

In addition, the BDD scores are obtained with the script `bdd_scores.py`, which computed the score function for a BDD sample that samples from a

---

[5] cf. https://github.com/fplll/fplll/wiki/FPLLL-Days-5-Summary.

gaussian of parameter $\sigma = \text{ghf}\,\text{GH}(n)/\sqrt{nq}$ where $\text{ghf} \in (0,1)$ and $\sqrt{q}$ is the normalization factor for the LWE lattice.

Lastly, the modulus switching scores are obtained with the script `mod_switch.py`, which performs the dual attack of [25, Alg. 2]. In particular, it samples one random q-ary lattice, and then computes the score for targets that are sampled as in KYBER [8].

In G6K, we set the saturation ratio of the sieve to 90% and then extracted the $\lceil 0.90 \cdot (4/3)^{n/2} \rceil$ shortest dual vectors from the database.

Remark 1. The G6K software [4] implicitly considers symmetry, and only outputs one out each pair of $\mathbf{w}, -\mathbf{w}$. Yet, both define the same individual score $f_\mathbf{w} = f_{-\mathbf{w}}$. Hence, only one of them should be used and the second is purely redundant.

Therefore, when using a saturation ratio of 90%, G6K provides only $0.45 \cdot (4/3)^{n/2}$ pairs of vectors of length below $\sqrt{4/3} \cdot \text{GH}(n)$. The remaining dual vectors, we extracted, are therefore slightly larger than $\sqrt{4/3} \cdot \text{GH}(n)$, and the whole database is rather concentrated around this length. This does *not* affect our conclusions, as the prediction under the heuristic analysis plotted in Fig. 3 does not depend on the length of dual vectors, and Fig. 5 has a prediction that takes the exact experimental length of each dual vector into account.

We further note that this halving of the number of short vectors was missed in the prior works of [18,25], leading to some irrelevant complication in the analysis of [25], as discussed in Appendix A.4 of the full version [14].

5.2   Distribution of Scores of Uniform Targets

We measured the score distribution for uniform targets over lattices of various dimension, and plotted our result in Fig. 3. On each of these curves, we see a clear deviation from prediction for rare events: large scores are more likely to occur than predicted. After following a *waterfall* shape, i.e. a quadratic decay in logarithmic scale, the score probability seems to reach a *floor*, where it decays much slower than a normal distribution predicts. This is perfectly in accordance with the contradiction discussed in Sects. 4.2 and 4.3: we start encountering vectors that are quite close to the lattice, which should have a rather high score.

In this light, it seems insightful to compare the number of samples needed to reach the floor in practice, to the number of samples where the contradictory regime starts according to Sect. 4.3. For this, we first need to define precisely when the distribution enters the floor region: we consider the floor to start when the experimental SF of a score exceeds the predicted SF by an arbitrary factor of 2. Graphically, this corresponds in Fig. 3 to a vertical gap of 1 unit between both curves. This comparison is depicted in Fig. 4.

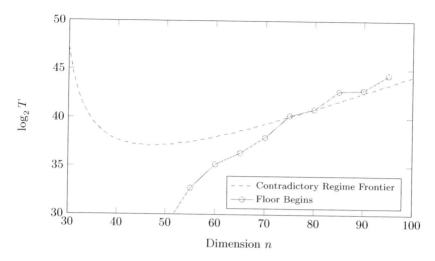

Fig. 4. Comparison of the Floor of the score of uniform samples with the Frontier of the contradictory regime of Sect. 4.3.

Conclusion. We notice in Fig. 4 that in small dimensions, the floor begins quite earlier than the contradictory regime, vindicating the notion that the analysis might fail even in an earlier regime than our predicted contradiction. In larger dimension both curves appear to converge, but at this point, one *should not* extrapolate this behavior to higher dimensions without providing any theoretical justification. Furthermore, as we will see in the next Sect. 5.3, this floor behaviour is not the only thing the analyses of [23,25] mispredict.

5.3 Distribution of Scores of BDD Targets

We measured the score distribution for BDD targets sampled from a gaussian of parameter $\sigma = 0.7 \cdot \mathrm{GH}(n) / \sqrt{n}$, over lattices of various dimensions n, and plotted our result in Fig. 3. The predicted score distribution is based on the Independence Heuristic, but also takes into account the exact lengths of each dual vector in Eq. (8), instead of approximating all the lengths to be equal to $\sqrt{4/3} \cdot \mathrm{GH}(n)$, to make the prediction more accurate.

The first thing one notices is that the distribution is significantly more spread out than predicted. The variance is significantly higher. In fact, the ratio between the actual and predicted variance appears to grow exponentially with the dimension, as visible on Table 1.

One might also want to consider the average. However, since the average is linear, its prediction does not require the Independence Heuristic. And indeed, the prediction is close to the measured average.

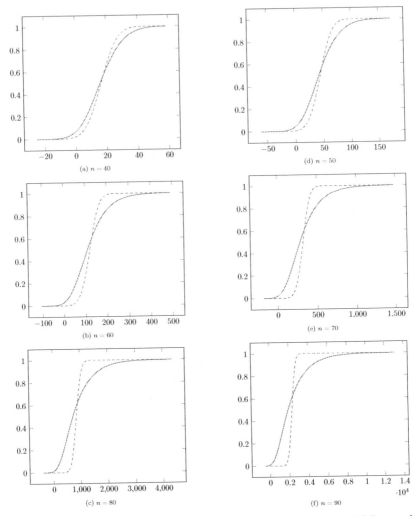

Legend: Cumulative distribution function of the score for gaussian BDD samples, with parameter $\sigma = 0.7 \cdot GH(n)/\sqrt{n}$. Probability ($y$-axis) is given on a linear scale. Dashed blue line: prediction from the Heuristic Analysis. Red line: experimental. 2^{15} samples per curve.

Fig. 5. The distribution of scores according to the prediction and the distribution determined experimentally. The experimental data is obtained with `bdd_scores.py` and listed in `data/bdd_scores_nX.csv` of the auxiliary files. (Color figure online)

A more interesting statistic is the median. According to the standard analysis [23,25] reconstructed in Sect. 2.3, the median is predicted to be equal to the average. In practice, however, the median is noticeably lower. This partially implies that the distribution is quite asymmetric around its average, contrary to the analysis' prediction.

Table 1. Variance of the BDD score distribution

Dimension n	40	50	60	70	80	90
predicted std. dev.	8.31	17.19	35.41	72.80	149.52	307.01
measured std. dev.	11.86	30.24	80.19	221.03	614.16	1732.72
ratio meas./pred.	1.43	1.76	2.26	3.04	4.11	5.64
predicted average	16.71	44.68	120.26	320.53	859.99	2310.28
measured average	16.75	45.32	120.60	322.51	863.15	2325.99
ratio meas./pred.	1.00	1.01	1.00	1.01	1.00	1.01
measured average	16.75	45.32	120.60	322.51	863.15	2325.99
measured median	16.13	42.27	108.74	282.54	735.47	1914.36
ratio med./avg.	0.96	0.93	0.90	0.88	0.85	0.82

Conclusion. All in all, it is fair to say that the standard analysis [23, 25], reconstructed in Sect. 2.3 of the dual attack is completely off when it comes to predicting the score of BDD targets. The distribution is definitely *not* gaussian, nor even symmetric around its average, and its variance is hugely underestimated.

5.4 Distribution of Scores, with Modulus Switching

Lastly, we ran experiments on the score distribution when using modulus switching in [25, Alg. 2]. We compare these experiments to the given bounds: a lower bound for the average [25, Lem. 5.4 and 5.5] and an upper bound on the variance [25, Lem. 5.7]. We also test asymmetry by comparing the average and the median.

As in the case of BDD target without modulus switching (Table 1), we note that the standard deviation is significantly underestimated: the given upper bound is significantly violated. Additionally, the upper bound is constant as a function of p, but we see that the standard deviation increases with p for the values listed in Table 2.

Regarding asymmetry, we see the experimental median is a bit lower than the average for $p \geq 4$, displaying the similar asymmetry than without modulus switching. The case $p = 3$ stands out with an extreme asymmetry: here the median is more than ten times smaller than the average. While the case $p = 3$ might not be of interest in practice, it appears as a good test case for a robust fix of the prediction. One may further wonder whether this phenomenon for $p = 3$ might extend to larger p when changing other parameters.

Table 2. Predicted vs. measured average, standard deviation and median for scores using modulus switching. Used parameters: $k_{\text{enum}} = 0$, $k_{\text{fft}} = 20$, $k_{\text{lat}} = 45$, $q = 3329$, $\eta = 3$ and 100 samples. A sieve ran in dimension 110 giving 13,393,776 dual vectors.

p	3	4	5	6	7
std. dev. upper bound	4317	4317	4317	4317	4317
measured		$2.53 \cdot 10^5$	$7.42 \cdot 10^5$	$1.19 \cdot 10^6$	$1.42 \cdot 10^6$	$1.47 \cdot 10^6$
ratio meas./u.b.	58.60	171.9	275.7	328.9	340.5
average lower bound	$8.08 \cdot 10^4$	$4.26 \cdot 10^5$	$1.61 \cdot 10^6$	$3.15 \cdot 10^6$	$4.66 \cdot 10^6$
measured average	$9.46 \cdot 10^4$	$6.81 \cdot 10^5$	$1.89 \cdot 10^6$	$3.36 \cdot 10^6$	$4.79 \cdot 10^6$
ratio meas./l.b.	1.17	1.60	1.17	1.07	1.03
measured average	$9.46 \cdot 10^4$	$6.81 \cdot 10^5$	$1.89 \cdot 10^6$	$3.36 \cdot 10^6$	$4.79 \cdot 10^6$
measured median	$6.84 \cdot 10^3$	$4.32 \cdot 10^5$	$1.57 \cdot 10^6$	$3.06 \cdot 10^6$	$4.54 \cdot 10^6$
ratio med./avg.	0.0723	0.63	0.83	0.91	0.95

Conclusion. The prediction for the distribution of scores of BDD targets with modulus switching seems to naturally inherit the issues of the same prediction without modulus switching (i.e. unpredicted asymmetry, underestimated variance), but seems to also raise new ones: an unpredicted growth of variance as p increases, and a very extreme case of asymmetry for certain choices of p.

6   Afterthoughts

As shown in the experiments, the heuristic analysis underlying the dual attack does not match practice. In order to get a precise cost on the dual attack, the analysis has to be fixed, in a way that correctly predicts both distribution of scores, for uniform and for BDD targets.

In this section, we propose a possible explanation of what is happening, while mentioning a similar phenomenon in coding theory. Ultimately, there are some fixes that need to be made to the dual attack and we mention some pitfalls to look out for when fixing the attack.

6.1   A Similar Result from Coding Theory

The *waterfall-floor* phenomenon visible in Fig. 4 is something coding theory has encountered before in a rather similar context, namely the error failure probability when decoding Low-Density Parity-Check (LDPC) codes [7,33,35]. We recall that the principle of LDPC decoding is to exploit the low-weight from the parity check matrix, or, said otherwise, the shortness of some vectors of the dual code. The analogy is striking.

6.2 The Origin of Correlation

Formally, the quantities $\langle \mathbf{w}, \mathbf{e} \rangle$ mod 1 for $\mathbf{w} \in \mathcal{W}$ can only be independent if the set $\mathcal{W}$ is linearly independent. Yet, it appears in Fig. 6(a) that the "length" of the linear relation matters when it comes to the impact of such dependencies on the total score $f_\mathcal{W}$. Indeed, we see that a long relation $\mathbf{w}_3 = 5\mathbf{w}_1 + 7\mathbf{w}_2$ is not that far off from the linearly independent case. On the contrary, a short relation $\mathbf{w}_3 = \mathbf{w}_1 + \mathbf{w}_2$ changes that distribution severely.

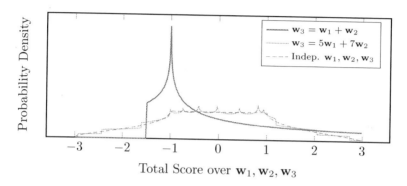

Fig. 6. Distribution of the total score $f_\mathcal{W}(\mathbf{t})$ where $|\mathcal{W}| = 3$, for a uniform $\mathbf{t}$ mod Λ when the $\mathbf{w}$'s are linearly independent versus related. Measured over 2^{25} samples.

Since $\mathcal{W}$ is taken as the output of a sieve [10,28,30], i.e. the set of the $(4/3)^{n/2}$ shortest vectors, we get many short relations. Namely, we expect a constant fraction of vectors to belong to a triple of the form $\mathbf{w}_3 = \pm\mathbf{w}_1 \pm \mathbf{w}_2$. For $k \geq 4$, each vector will belong to an exponential amount of such k-tuple $\mathbf{w}_k = \pm\mathbf{w}_1 \pm \mathbf{w}_2 \pm \cdots \pm \mathbf{w}_{k-1}$, the precise quantity of such tuples should be analyzable following the theory underlying tuple-sieves [9,20].

We clarify that this discussion and experiments are only meant to illustrate where the correlations come from. Fixing the analysis via this angle would require understanding the much harder question of how these correlations compound, and we are doubtful if this would be a tractable route.

6.3 Is the Dual Attack Fixable?

The theoretical analysis of Sect. 4 and the experiments of Sect. 5 unequivocally invalidate the standard analysis of the Dual-Sieve attack (with or without FFT) as found in [5,11,18,23,25]. In the context of the Dual-Sieve-FFT attack, as instantiated in [5,11,18,25], our work point out a presumably large number of false positive, i.e. incorrect answers having a higher score than that of the desired target.

However, if this number of false positives in the current parametrization is reasonable, all might not be lost. Indeed, one may consider the Dual-Sieve-FFT technique as a first filtering stage in an attack with multiple stages; the leftover problem is still the problem of finding one BDD target among many candidates, but in an easier lattice (smaller in dimension, and/or sparser). If the leftover problem becomes sufficiently easier to accommodate all these targets, the Dual-Sieve-FTT attack might be salvaged.

Nevertheless, to substantiate such a fix, one must first produce a new convincing model for the score distribution of both BDD and random targets. This should be backed both by theoretical arguments, and by experimental validation.

We insist that pulling the parameters of the attack outside of the contradictory regime is not a convincing way of substantiating a fix. We need a sound analysis that precisely predicts the score behavior, and it should specifically be tested on the regime where the prior analysis made mispredictions. That is, we should have theoretically justified predictions that match with the experimental behavior measured in Figs. 3 and 5 and beyond.

In particular, we warn against a flawed argument for a fix, that would consist of constructing the set $\mathcal{W} = \mathcal{W}_1 \cup \mathcal{W}_2$ from two BKZ reductions and sieves instead of just one. One might argue that the dual distinguishing is now happening in a lattice of dimension 2β instead of β, which would push points of Fig. 2 outside of the contradictory regime. But considering the experiments of Sect. 5.2 in Fig. 3 we should see that this does not really fix the issue. Each half $f_{\mathcal{W}_i}$ of the score distribution $f_{\mathcal{W}}$ is going to hit its floor, and the sum of those two distribution will also have a floor at essentially the same height. Indeed, it would suffice to hit the floor of one of the functions, to hit the floor of the aggregate.

A more credible approach however is indeed to run two (or a few) BKZ reduction and sieves, obtaining two sets of short dual vectors $\mathcal{W}_1, \mathcal{W}_2$ then considering the aggregate score as the *minimum* of both scores $f' = \min(f_{\mathcal{W}_1}, f_{\mathcal{W}_2})$ rather than its sum. To hit the floor of this new aggregate, a uniform sample would need to hit *both* floors simultaneously. If $f_{\mathcal{W}_1}, f_{\mathcal{W}_2}$ are sufficiently independent (an assumption that would need substantiation), that should be much more unlikely than hitting either floor.

Note however that taking such a minimum aggregate of scores might also amplify the issues with low scores for BDD targets observed in Sect. 5.3. A robust model for all the distributions at hand is therefore still required. Also note that taking the smallest of both scores is conceptually not that far off from the prior fix idea of first filtering with $f_{\mathcal{W}_1}$ and then filtering the survivors again with a new stage of the attack.

Open Question 2. *Convincingly fix the analysis of the Dual-Sieve-FFT attack with robust predictions for both score distributions, matching experiments from Fig. 3 and 5 and beyond. Then, consider if one of the suggested fixes above allows to recover a complexity close to that of the original claims [5, 11, 18, 23, 25].*

We further invite future work to fix other minor oddities, listed in Appendix A of the full version [14].

Acknowledgments. We would like to thank Martin Albrecht, Qian Guo, Thomas Johansson, Eamonn Postlethwaite, Yixin Shen, Michael Walter, Wessel van Woerden for helpful discussion and feedback. Some of them might not endorse our conclusions. Authors Léo Ducas and Ludo Pulles are supported by ERC Starting Grant 947821 (ARTICULATE).

References

1. Abramowitz, M., Stegun, I.A.: Handbook of mathematical functions with formulas, graphs, and mathematical tables. Nat. Bureau Stan. Appl. Math. Ser. **55** (1964). https://archive.org/details/AandS-mono600
2. Aharonov, D., Regev, O.: Lattice problems in NP cap coNP. In: 45th Annual Symposium on Foundations of Computer Science, pp. 362–371. IEEE Computer Society Press, Rome, Italy, 17–19 October 2004. https://doi.org/10.1109/FOCS.2004.35
3. Albrecht, M.R.: On dual lattice attacks against small-secret LWE and parameter choices in HElib and SEAL. In: Coron, J.-S., Nielsen, J.B. (eds.) EUROCRYPT 2017. LNCS, vol. 10211, pp. 103–129. Springer, Cham (2017). https://doi.org/10.1007/978-3-319-56614-6_4
4. Albrecht, M.R., Ducas, L., Herold, G., Kirshanova, E., Postlethwaite, E.W., Stevens, M.: The general sieve kernel and new records in lattice reduction. In: Ishai, Y., Rijmen, V. (eds.) EUROCRYPT 2019. LNCS, vol. 11477, pp. 717–746. Springer, Cham (2019). https://doi.org/10.1007/978-3-030-17656-3_25
5. Albrecht, M.R., Shen, Y.: Quantum augmented dual attack. arXiv preprint arXiv:2205.13983 (2022)
6. Alkim, E., Ducas, L., Pöppelmann, T., Schwabe, P.: Post-quantum key exchange - a New Hope. In: USENIX security symposium, vol. 2016 (2016)
7. Arpin, S., Billingsley, T.R., Hast, D.R., Lau, J.B., Perlner, R., Robinson, A.: A study of error floor behavior in QC-MDPC codes. In: Cheon, J.H., Johansson, T. (eds.) Post-Quantum Cryptography: 13th International Workshop, PQCrypto 2022, Virtual Event, 28–30 September 2022, Proceedings. LNCS, pp. 89–103. Springer, Cham (2022). https://doi.org/10.1007/978-3-031-17234-2_5
8. Avanzi, R., et al.: CRYSTALS-Kyber algorithm specifications and supporting documentation. NIST PQC Round **2**(4), 1–43 (2019)
9. Bai, S., Laarhoven, T., Stehlé, D.: Tuple lattice sieving. LMS J. Comput. Math. **19**(A), 146–162 (2016). https://doi.org/10.1112/S1461157016000292
10. Becker, A., Ducas, L., Gama, N., Laarhoven, T.: New directions in nearest neighbor searching with applications to lattice sieving. In: Krauthgamer, R. (ed.) 27th Annual ACM-SIAM Symposium on Discrete Algorithms, pp. 10–24. ACM-SIAM, Arlington, VA, USA, 10–12 January 2016. https://doi.org/10.1137/1.9781611974331.ch2
11. Carrier, K., Shen, Y., Tillich, J.P.: Faster dual lattice attacks by using coding theory. Cryptology ePrint Archive, Paper 2022/1750 (2022). https://eprint.iacr.org/2022/1750
12. Debris-Alazard, T., Ducas, L., Resch, N., Tillich, J.P.: Smoothing codes and lattices: systematic study and new bounds. Cryptology ePrint Archive, Paper 2022/615 (2022). https://eprint.iacr.org/2022/615
13. Ducas, L.: Shortest vector from lattice sieving: a few dimensions for free. In: Nielsen, J.B., Rijmen, V. (eds.) EUROCRYPT 2018. LNCS, vol. 10820, pp. 125–145. Springer, Cham (2018). https://doi.org/10.1007/978-3-319-78381-9_5

14. Ducas, L., Pulles, L.: Does the dual-sieve attack on learning with errors even work? Cryptology ePrint Archive, Paper 2023/302 (2023). https://eprint.iacr.org/2023/302

15. Duhamel, P., Vetterli, M.: Fast Fourier transforms: a tutorial review and a state of the art. Sig. Process. **19**(4), 259–299 (1990). https://infoscience.epfl.ch/record/59946

16. Espitau, T., Joux, A., Kharchenko, N.: On a Dual/Hybrid approach to small secret LWE. In: Bhargavan, K., Oswald, E., Prabhakaran, M. (eds.) INDOCRYPT 2020. LNCS, vol. 12578, pp. 440–462. Springer, Cham (2020). https://doi.org/10.1007/978-3-030-65277-7_20

17. Gallager, R.: Low-density parity-check codes. IRE Trans. Inf. Theory **8**(1), 21–28 (1962). https://doi.org/10.1109/TIT.1962.1057683

18. Guo, Q., Johansson, T.: Faster dual lattice attacks for solving LWE with applications to CRYSTALS. In: Tibouchi, M., Wang, H. (eds.) ASIACRYPT 2021. LNCS, vol. 13093, pp. 33–62. Springer, Cham (2021). https://doi.org/10.1007/978-3-030-92068-5_2

19. Håstad, J.: Dual vectors and lower bounds for the nearest lattice point problem. Combinatorica **8**(1), 75–81 (1988). https://doi.org/10.1007/BF02122554

20. Herold, G., Kirshanova, E.: Improved algorithms for the approximate k-list problem in Euclidean Norm. In: Fehr, S. (ed.) PKC 2017. LNCS, vol. 10174, pp. 16–40. Springer, Heidelberg (2017). https://doi.org/10.1007/978-3-662-54365-8_2

21. Howgrave-Graham, N.: A hybrid lattice-reduction and meet-in-the-middle attack against NTRU. In: Menezes, A. (ed.) CRYPTO 2007. LNCS, vol. 4622, pp. 150–169. Springer, Heidelberg (2007). https://doi.org/10.1007/978-3-540-74143-5_9

22. Jabri, A.A.: A statistical decoding algorithm for general linear block codes. In: Honary, B. (ed.) Cryptography and Coding 2001. LNCS, vol. 2260, pp. 1–8. Springer, Heidelberg (2001). https://doi.org/10.1007/3-540-45325-3_1

23. Laarhoven, T., Walter, M.: Dual lattice attacks for closest vector problems (with preprocessing). In: Paterson, K.G. (ed.) CT-RSA 2021. LNCS, vol. 12704, pp. 478–502. Springer, Cham (2021). https://doi.org/10.1007/978-3-030-75539-3_20

24. Levieil, É., Fouque, P.-A.: An improved LPN algorithm. In: De Prisco, R., Yung, M. (eds.) SCN 2006. LNCS, vol. 4116, pp. 348–359. Springer, Heidelberg (2006). https://doi.org/10.1007/11832072_24

25. MATZOV: Report on the security of LWE: Improved dual lattice attack, April 2022. https://doi.org/10.5281/zenodo.6493704

26. Micciancio, D.: Lattice algorithms and applications, lecture 3: the dual lattice (2014). https://cseweb.ucsd.edu/classes/sp14/cse206A-a/lec3.pdf

27. Micciancio, D., Regev, O.: Lattice-based cryptography. In: Bernstein, D.J., Buchmann, J., Dahmen, E. (eds.) Post-Quantum Cryptography, pp. 147–191. Springer, Heidelberg (2009). https://doi.org/10.1007/978-3-540-88702-7_5

28. Micciancio, D., Voulgaris, P.: Faster exponential time algorithms for the shortest vector problem. In: Charika, M. (ed.) 21st Annual ACM-SIAM Symposium on Discrete Algorithms, pp. 1468–1480. ACM-SIAM (2010). https://doi.org/10.1137/1.9781611973075.119

29. Neyman, J., Pearson, E.S.: On the problem of the most efficient tests of statistical hypotheses. Philos. Trans. Roy. Soc. London Ser. A Containing Papers Math. Phys. Charact. **231**(694–706), 289–337 (1933). https://doi.org/10.1098/rsta.1933.0009

30. Nguyen, P.Q., Vidick, T.: Sieve algorithms for the shortest vector problem are practical. J. Math. Cryptol. **2**(2), 181–207 (2008). https://doi.org/10.1515/JMC.2008.009

31. Overbeck, R.: Statistical decoding revisited. In: Batten, L.M., Safavi-Naini, R. (eds.) ACISP 2006. LNCS, vol. 4058, pp. 283–294. Springer, Heidelberg (2006). https://doi.org/10.1007/11780656_24
32. Rader, C.M.: Discrete Fourier transforms when the number of data samples is prime. Proc. IEEE **56**(6), 1107–1108 (1968)
33. Richter, G.: Finding small stopping sets in the Tanner graphs of LDPC codes. In: 4th International Symposium on Turbo Codes & Related Topics; 6th International ITG-Conference on Source and Channel Coding, pp. 1–5. VDE, Munich, Germany, 3–7 April 2006
34. The FPLLL development team: FPyLLL, a Python wrapper for the FPLLL lattice reduction library, Version: 0.5.9 (2023). https://github.com/fplll/fpylll
35. Vasić, B., Chilappagari, S.K., Nguyen, D.V.: Failures and error floors of iterative decoders. In: Declerq, D., Fossorier, M., Biglieri, E. (eds.) Channel Coding: Theory, Algorithms, and Applications: Academic Press Library in Mobile and Wireless Communications, pp. 299–341. Academic Press, December 2014. https://doi.org/10.1016/B978-0-12-396499-1.00006-6

Exploring Decryption Failures of BIKE: New Class of Weak Keys and Key Recovery Attacks

Tianrui Wang[1], Anyu Wang[2,3,4(✉)], and Xiaoyun Wang[2,3,4,5,6]

[1] Institute for Network Sciences and Cyberspace, Tsinghua University, Beijing, China
wangtr22@mails.tsinghua.edu.cn
[2] Institute for Advanced Study, BNRist, Tsinghua University, Beijing, China
{anyuwang,xiaoyunwang}@tsinghua.edu.cn
[3] Zhongguancun Laboratory, Beijing, China
[4] National Financial Cryptography Research Center, Beijing, China
[5] Shandong Institute of Blockchain, Jinan, China
[6] Key Laboratory of Cryptologic Technology and Information Security (Ministry of Education), School of Cyber Science and Technology, Shandong University, Qingdao, China

Abstract. Code-based cryptography has received a lot of attention recently because it is considered secure under quantum computing. Among them, the QC-MDPC based scheme is one of the most promising due to its excellent performance. QC-MDPC based schemes are usually subject to a small rate of decryption failure, which can leak information about the secret key. This raises two crucial problems: how to accurately estimate the decryption failure rate and how to use the failure information to recover the secret key. However, the two problems are challenging due to the difficulty of geometrically characterizing the bit-flipping decoder employed in QC-MDPC, such as using decoding radius.

In this work, we introduce the gathering property and show it is strongly connected with the decryption failure rate of QC-MDPC. Based on this property, we present two results for QC-MDPC based schemes. The first is a new construction of weak keys obtained by extending the keys that have gathering property via ring isomorphism. For the set of weak keys, we present a rigorous analysis of the probability, as well as experimental simulation of the decryption failure rates. Considering BIKE's parameter set targeting 128-bit security, our result eventually indicates that the average decryption failure rate is lower bounded by $\mathrm{DFR}_{\mathrm{avg}} \geq 2^{-116.61}$. The second entails two key recovery attacks against CCA secure QC-MDPC schemes using decryption failures in a multi-target setting. The two attacks consider whether or not it is allowed to reuse ciphertexts respectively. In both cases, we show the decryption failures can be used to identify whether a target's secret key satisfies the gathering property. Then using the gathering property as an extra information, we present a modified information set decoding algorithm that efficiently retrieves the target's secret key. For BIKE's parameter set targeting 128-bit security, we show a key recovery

© International Association for Cryptologic Research 2023
H. Handschuh and A. Lysyanskaya (Eds.): CRYPTO 2023, LNCS 14083, pp. 70–100, 2023.
https://doi.org/10.1007/978-3-031-38548-3_3

attack with complexity $2^{116.61}$ can be mounted if ciphertexts reusing is not permitted, and the complexity can be reduced to $2^{98.77}$ when ciphertexts reusing is permitted.

Keywords: Post-quantum cryptography · Code-based cryptography · Decryption failure · BIKE · QC-MDPC · Information set decoding

1 Introduction

Shor's algorithm [46] can solve the problems of integer factorization and discrete logarithm in quantum polynomial time. Then once large-scale quantum computer that implements Shor's algorithm becomes a reality, traditional public-key systems based on factorization and discrete logarithm will run the risk of being broken. As a result, developing public-key systems that can withstand quantum attacks has become a pressing concern. In 2016, NIST (*National Institute of Standards and Technology*) was motivated to start a process of standardizing post-quantum public-key cryptographic algorithms [1]. In this process, code-based cryptography plays an important role.

Code-based cryptography can be traced back to the invention of McEliece public-key encryption scheme [39] and its variation Niederreiter scheme [42]. These schemes are built on Goppa codes, and their security can be reduced to the hardness of decoding binary linear codes [6]. Other types of codes can also be used to construct public key encryption schemes, and those based on QC-MDPC (*quasi-cyclic moderate density parity check*) codes are in an competitive class in terms of efficiency and bandwidth [40]. BIKE [3] is a representative QC-MDPC based scheme that has advanced to the fourth round of the NIST standardization process [2].

QC-MDPC based schemes are typically subject to decryption failures, which means that even when the protocol is correctly executed, it is still possible for the decryption to fail to recover the intended message. It is well known that decryption failures can leak information about the secret key, and different types of decryption failure attacks have been proposed for various lattice-based and code-based schemes. One type of such attacks was introduced by Jaulmes and Joux in [35] and extended in [27,34], which is against CPA (*chosen plaintext attack*) secure schemes and recovers the secret key by choosing certain ciphertexts that fail based on characteristics of the secret key. Another type of decryption failure attack can be carried out against CCA (*chosen ciphertext attack*) secure schemes, which is typically mounted in three stages: a precomputation stage in which special ciphertexts are generated randomly, a decryption stage in which the ciphertexts are submitted for decryption and some decryption failures are observed, and a key recovery stage in which the secret key is retrieved based on a statistical analysis of the decryption failures [14]. In [29], Guo et al. presented such an attack against the CCA secure QC-MDPC based scheme in [40] by using the "distance spectrum" to retrieve the secret key. Later, decryption failure attacks against other code-based schemes were also proposed for, e.g., HQC [28], QC-LDPC [24] and LRPC [4].

In [13,15], D'Anvers et al. investigated the decryption failure attacks for LWE-based schemes and proposed a technique called "directed failure boosting", which significantly speeds up the ciphertext search when several decoding failures have already been obtained. In addition to focusing solely on how to recover the secret key, Bindel and Schanck [7] demonstrated that successful decryption can also be utilized to speed up the search for ciphertexts. D'Anvers et al. [16] used the correlation of individual mistake bits to demonstrate that the decryption failure rate for specific algorithms could be underestimated.

To protect a scheme against decryption failure attacks, a natural solution is to reduce the probability of decoding failure so that it is unlikely to occur for an allowed number of decryptions. In QC-MDPC based schemes, the bit-flipping decoding algorithm [26] is employed to handle the errors involved in the decryption procedure. Since the bit-flipping algorithm is originally developed to decode LDPC (*Low Density Parity Check*) codes, numerous efforts have been made to enhance it to handle slightly denser errors in MDPC codes [9–11,31, 37,40]. Another major problem is how to accurately estimate the failure rate of QC-MDPC based schemes. In [47], an asymptotic upper bound on the decoding failure rate is derived for MDPC codes. Sendrier and Vasseur [44] propose a framework to estimate the failure rate by adopting a Markov chain model. On the other hand, weak keys that result in higher decryption failure rate in QC-MDPC based schemes were also studied [45,48].

In BIKE, the Black-Gray-Flip (BGF) decoder [19] is adopted, and the decryption failure rate is believed to be low enough to make the scheme δ-correct, that is, the decryption failure rate δ is less than $2^{-\lambda}$ for λ-bit security. Under this condition, the CCA security of BIKE can be guaranteed via the Fujisaki-Okamoto transformation [25,32].

1.1   Our Results

In this work, we reinvestigate the decryption failure rate for QC-MDPC based schemes by introducing the *gathering property*. $(y_0, y_1) \in \mathcal{R}^2$ is said to satisfy the (m, ϵ)-gathering property if there are $(w_H(y_0) - \epsilon)$ 1's of y_0 gathering in some m consecutive positions (see Fig. 1), where $\mathcal{R} = \mathbb{F}_2[x]/(x^r - 1)$. The gathering property exhibits a strong connection with the decryption failure rate of QC-MDPC. Experimental result demonstrates that when both the secret keys and the errors satisfy the gathering property, the decryption failure rate is significantly higher than the average. Based on the gathering property, we are able to give the following two results on the decryption failure rate for QC-MDPC based schemes.

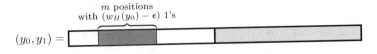

Fig. 1. An illustration of the gathering property.

A New Construction of Weak Keys. Our first contribution is a new construction of weak keys for QC-MDPC based schemes. Let $K_{m,\epsilon}(w)$ be the set of secret keys satisfying the (m, ϵ)-gathering property. Through experiments, it can be proved that the decryption failure rate for the keys drawn from $K_{m,\epsilon}(w)$ is higher than the average. Furthermore, $K_{m,\epsilon}(w)$ can be extended to a larger set of weak keys $K_{m,\epsilon}^{\text{union}}(w)$ by using the ring isomorphisms of $\mathcal{R}$.

We provide a rigorous approach to calculate the probability that a random key is in $K_{m,\epsilon}^{\text{union}}(w)$, as well as experimental simulations of the decryption failure rates for keys drawing from $K_{m,\epsilon}^{\text{union}}(w)$. These directly lead to a lower bound on the average decryption failure rate for BIKE's parameter set targeting 128-bit security, i.e.,

$$\text{DFR}_{\text{avg}} \geq 2^{-116.61} . \tag{1}$$

Taking the simulation error into account, we can still conclude that $\text{DFR}_{\text{avg}} \geq 2^{-117.77}$ at 95% confidence level by using the normal approximation framework.

Key Recovery Attack. Our second contribution entails two key recovery attacks using decryption failures against CCA secure QC-MDPC schemes. The attacks are carried out in the multi-target setting, i.e., numerous targets are queried with the goal of recovering the secret key for at least one of these targets.

First, we consider an attack model that assumes multi-target protection where ciphertexts reusing is not allowed. For each target, the attacker randomly generates a set of ciphertexts, and then queries the target's decryption oracle to decrypt these ciphertexts. Once a decryption failure occurs for a target T, the attacker has an advantage of identifying whether T's secret key belongs the set of weak keys $K_{m,\epsilon}^{\text{union}}(w)$, i.e., there exists an isomorphism of $\mathcal{R}$ such that the secret key satisfies the (m, ϵ)-gathering property after the action of isomorphism. Then we propose a *modified information set decoding* algorithm, which can efficiently recover T's secret key from the public key by using the gathering property as extra information. On the other hand, the current version of BIKE does not offer multi-target protection, prompting us to explore an attack model where ciphertexts reusing is permissible. In this model, the attacker first constructs a set of ciphertexts such that the errors satisfying the (m, ϵ)-gathering property. Then the attacker queries each target's decryption oracle to decrypt the same set of ciphertexts. For a target T that has a decryption failure, the attacker has an advantage of identifying whether T's secret key satisfies the (m, ϵ)-gathering property and can thus be efficiently recovered by the modified information set decoding algorithm.

Again we focus on BIKE's parameter set targeting 128-bit security. For the attack model that ciphertexts reusing is not allowed, we show that a key recovery attack can be performed with complexity

$$C_{\text{total}} = 2^{116.61}. \tag{2}$$

Furthermore, when considering the attack model allowing for ciphertexts reusing, we show that the complexity of the key recovery attack can be reduced to $2^{98.77}$. Table 1 lists more detailed attack complexity of our attacks.

The source code for our experiments on decryption failure rates is available at https://github.com/1234wangtr/BIKE_weakey.

Table 1. The time complexity of the key recovery attacks against BIKE's parameter set targeting 128-bit security. The complexity of identifying failures is primarily determined by the complexity of accessing decryption oracles for all targets. The complexity of the key recovery step is determined by the total time complexity associated with all calls made to the ISD algorithm. The preprocessing complexity is associated with constructing the set of ciphertexts that satisfy the (m, ϵ)-gathering property.

	Attack model *without* ciphertexts reusing	Attack model *with* ciphertexts reusing
Total Complexity	$2^{116.61}$	$2^{98.77}$
Number of Targets	$2^{87.28}$	$2^{76.69}$
Queries per Target	$2^{29.33}$	$2^{22.08}$
Complexity of Identifying Failures	$2^{116.61}$	$2^{98.77}$
Complexity of the Key Recovery Step	$2^{111.96}$	$2^{94.81}$
Complexity of Preprocessing	—	$2^{97.66}$

1.2 Related Works

Guo Et Al's Attack on MDPC. In [29], Guo et al. find a strong correlation between the decryption failure rate and the secret key's distance spectrum, which is defined to be the set of distances between any two 1's in the secret key. From decryption failures, one can collect enough information about the secret key's distance spectrum, and then recover the secret key from the distance spectrum by the algorithm given in [29].

Weak Keys in QC-MDPC Schemes. In [18,45], the authors figure out that there exist weak secret keys in QC-MDPC for which the decryption failure rates are higher than the average. Vassuer [49] gives a classification of known weak keys in QC-MDPC, and presents simulation results for BIKE with parameter set targeting 128-bit security. In fact, lower bounds on the average decryption failure rate can be deduced via the formula $\text{DFR}_{\text{avg}} \geq \frac{|W|}{|K|} \cdot \text{DFR}_{\text{W}}$ where K is the set of keys and W is a set of weak keys, DFR_{W} represents the decryption failure rate for the keys drawn uniformly from W. However, the lower bounds provided in [49] are all below 2^{-128}, which has no effect on BIKE's CCA security [2].

1.3   Summary of Our Work

As noted in [2,3], BIKE's security under decryption failures raises two critical questions: whether there exist weak keys that can affect the current estimate of the average decryption failure rate, and whether it is possible to launch a successful attack by utilizing the decryption failures. Our work confirms positive answers to both questions.

Weak Keys and Average DFR. We present a set of weak keys that impacts BIKE's current estimate of the average decryption failure rate for the first time. For BIKE's parameter set targeting 128-bit security, our results indicate that the average decryption failure rate is higher than 2^{-128}. This is concerning because the CCA security of BIKE relies on the δ-correctness assumption, which our findings suggest is not fully established.

Decryption Failure Attacks. Applying previous decryption failure attacks, such as [29], to BIKE faces a major challenge due to the low average decryption failure rate. Our new attack framework provides a solution by utilizing the gathering property. The gathering property exhibits a significant impact on the decryption failure rate, making our attack framework effective. Moreover, our framework permits a rigorous derivation or experimental confirmation of the relevant probability and decryption failure rates. This enables us to calculate the explicit attack complexity, and can give some insight into the concrete security of BIKE under decryption failure attacks.

1.4   Organizations

Section 2 introduces some preliminary concepts. In Sect. 3, we define the gathering property and provide experimental results on the decryption failure rate, assuming both the secret key and error satisfy this property. Section 4 presents a new construction of weak keys and derives lower bounds on the average decryption failure rate based on these weak keys. Section 5 and Sect. 6 describe key recovery attacks leveraging the gathering property, while Sect. 7 offers concluding remarks.

2   Preliminary

The following notations will be used in this paper.

- For a vector $\mathbf{y} = (y_0, \cdots, y_{n-1}) \in \mathbb{F}_2^n$, denote $w_H(\mathbf{y})$ to be the Hamming weight of $\mathbf{y}$, denote $\mathrm{Supp}(\mathbf{y})$ to be the support of $\mathbf{y}$, and denote $\mathbf{y}^{[a,b)} := (y_a, y_{a+1}, \cdots, y_{b-1})$, where the subscripts are taken mod n.
- Let $\mathcal{R} := \mathbb{F}_2[x]/(x^r - 1)$. An element in the ring $\mathcal{R}$ is represented in a polynomial form, i.e., $y = y_0 + y_1 x + \cdots + y_{r-1} x^{r-1}$, and the bold-case letter

$\mathbf{y} = (y_0, \cdots, y_{r-1})$ will be used to denote the coefficient vector of y. A circulant matrix corresponding the coefficients of y can be defined as

$$\mathbf{rot(y)} = \begin{pmatrix} y_0 & y_{r-1} & \cdots & y_1 \\ y_1 & y_0 & \cdots & y_2 \\ \vdots & \vdots & \ddots & \vdots \\ y_{r-1} & y_{r-2} & \cdots & y_0 \end{pmatrix}. \tag{3}$$

Then for any $y, z \in \mathcal{R}$, the coefficient vector of yz equals to $\mathbf{rot(y)} \cdot \mathbf{z}$.

– Suppose i is co-prime to r, then the map

$$\phi_i : y(x) \rightarrow y(x^i) \tag{4}$$

defines an isomorphism of $\mathcal{R}$ to $\mathcal{R}$. Particularly, this isomorphism preserves the Hamming weight.

– Denote
  • $K(w) := \{(h_0, h_1) \in \mathcal{R}^2 | w_H(h_0) = w_H(h_1) = w/2\}$,
  • $E(t) := \{(e_0, e_1) \in \mathcal{R}^2 | w_H(e_0) + w_H(e_1) = t\}$,
  • $E(t_0, t_1) := \{(e_0, e_1) \in \mathcal{R}^2 | w_H(e_0) = t_0, w_H(e_1) = t_1\}$.

Let $K_{m,\epsilon}(w)$ and $E_{m,\epsilon}(t_0, t_1)$ to be subsets of $K(w)$ and $E(t_0, t_1)$ respectively, such that their elements satisfy the (m, ϵ)-gathering property in Definition 1. Denote

$$p_{m,\epsilon} := \frac{|K_{m,\epsilon}(w)|}{|K(w)|} \text{ and } q_{m,\epsilon} := \frac{|E_{m,\epsilon}(t/2, t/2)|}{|E(t)|}. \tag{5}$$

2.1   Estimate of the Probability from the Frequency

How to estimate the probability from the frequency is a basic problem in statistics. In this paper, we mainly focus on the simulation of the decryption failures, which can be treated as a Bernoulli trial. Suppose we repeat the decryption for N times and find F failures while the actual decryption failure rate is p. Then the ratio F/N is an estimate of p. In the framework of normal approximation, the standard deviation of this estimate is

$$\sigma = \frac{\sqrt{F(N-F)}}{N\sqrt{N}} \approx \frac{\sqrt{F}}{N} \text{ for } F \ll N. \tag{6}$$

Then it has

$$\Pr[F/N - 2\sigma < p < F/N + 2\sigma] \approx 95\%, \tag{7}$$

and the confidence level will increase to 99.7% if 3σ is adopted in (7).

2.2   BIKE

In this work, we use BIKE to demonstrate our results. The gathering property and the key recovery attack can be directly applied to the QC-MDPC based schemes such as [41]. BIKE is built by first constructing a PKE (*public-key encryption*) using the Niederreiter framework, and then obtaining a KEM (*key encapsulation encapsulation*) following the method proposed in [20]. Let $n = 2r, w = 2v = O(\sqrt{n}), t = O(\sqrt{n})$ be a set of parameters, and let H, L, K be hash functions with proper outputs. Then BIKE KEM can be described as follows.

- KeyGen ():
    - Randomly generate $h_0, h_1 \in \mathcal{R}$ such that $w_H(h_0) = w_H(h_1) = w/2$.
    - Compute $h = h_1 h_0^{-1} \in \mathcal{R}$.
    - Output (h_0, h_1, σ) as the secret key, and h as the public key.
- Encaps (h):
    - Randomly choose $m \in \{0,1\}^{256}$.
    - Compute $(e_0, e_1) = \mathtt{H}(m) \in \mathcal{R}^2$ such that $w_H(e_0) + w_H(e_1) = t$.
    - Output the ciphertext $c = (e_0 + e_1 h, m \oplus \mathtt{L}(e_0, e_1))$, and the shared secret $\mathcal{K} = \mathtt{K}(m, c)$.
- Decaps ((h_0, h_1, σ), c):
    - Compute $e' = \mathtt{decoder}(c_0 h_0, h_0, h_1) \in \mathcal{R}^2$.
    - Compute $m' = c_1 \oplus L(e')$.
    - If $e' = \mathtt{H}(m')$ then output $\mathtt{K}(m', c)$, else output $\mathtt{K}(\sigma, c)$.

The $\mathtt{decoder}$ in BIKE is the Black-Gray-Flip (BGF) algorithm proposed in [19]. BIKE provides three classes of parameters targeting 128-bit, 192-bit and 256-bit security respectively, which are listed in Table 2.

Table 2. BIKE parameter sets.

Security Level	r	w	t	Decryption Failure Rate
128-bit	12323	142	134	2^{-128}
192-bit	24659	206	199	2^{-192}
256-bit	40973	274	264	2^{-256}

2.3   The Bit-Flipping Algorithm

The bit-flipping algorithm is initially introduced in [26] for the decoding of LDPC codes. Taking inputs as an LDPC matrix $\mathbf{H} \in \mathbb{F}_2^{m \times n}$ and a syndrome vector $\mathbf{s} \in \mathbb{F}_2^m$, it iteratively finds the error vector $\mathbf{e} \in \mathbb{F}_2^n$ s.t. $\mathbf{He} = \mathbf{s}$ as follows. The algorithm starts with a zero vector $\mathbf{e} = \mathbf{0}$. In each iteration, it computes the number of *unsatisfied parity checks*

$$\mathtt{UPC}(\mathbf{e}, i) := |\mathrm{Supp}(\mathbf{He} + \mathbf{s}) \cap \mathrm{Supp}(\mathbf{h_i})| \tag{8}$$

for each position $i \in [0, n-1]$, where $\mathbf{h_i}$ is the i-th column of $\mathbf{H}$, and flips the i-th position of $\mathbf{e}$ if $\mathtt{UPC}(\mathbf{e}, i)$ exceeds a pre-set threshold τ. The algorithm terminates when the maximum number of iterations NIter is achieved. We refer to Algorithm 1 for the details.

Algorithm 1: The Bit Flipping Algorithm

Input: $\mathbf{H} \in \mathbb{F}_2^{m \times n}, \mathbf{s} \in \mathbb{F}_2^m$

Output: $\mathbf{e} \in \mathbb{F}_2^n$ s.t. $\mathbf{He} = \mathbf{s}$

1: $\mathbf{e} = \mathbf{0}$
2: **while** $i <$ NIter **do**
3:    **for** j from 0 to $n - 1$ **do**
4:       **if** UPC$(\mathbf{e}, j) \geq \tau$ **then**
5:          Flip the j-th position of $\mathbf{e}$
6:       **end if**
7:    **end for**
8:    $i = i + 1$
9: **end while**
10: **return** $\mathbf{e}$

When dealing with QC-MDPC codes, the bit-flipping algorithm takes $s, h_0, h_1 \in \mathcal{R}$ as inputs and finds the error vector $e_0, e_1 \in \mathcal{R}$ by solving

$$\begin{bmatrix} \text{rot}(\mathbf{h}_0) & \text{rot}(\mathbf{h}_1) \end{bmatrix} \begin{bmatrix} e_0 \\ e_1 \end{bmatrix} = \mathbf{s} \qquad (9)$$

via Algorithm 1. Several optimizations have been proposed for MDPC codes, such as improved selection of the threshold and flipping the bits in parallel. The BGF algorithm in BIKE adopts a BG iteration, in which the positions with UPCs that exceed a high threshold (black) are flipped and checked first, and the positions with UPCs that are close but below a high threshold (gray) are flipped afterwards. Then some standard bit-flipping iterations are performed. The complete BGF algorithm can be found in the full version of this work.

3   The Gathering Property for QC-MDPC

In this section we focus on the decryption failure rate of QC-MDPC based schemes when both the secret key (h_0, h_1) and the error (e_0, e_1) satisfy the *gathering property* defined as below.

Definition 1 (gathering property). *Let $m < r$ be a positive integer and let $\epsilon \geq 0$ be a small integer, then $(y_0, y_1) \in \mathcal{R}^2$ is said to have the (m, ϵ)-gathering property if there exists an integer a such that*

$$w_H(\mathbf{y}_0^{[a,a+m)}) = w_H(\mathbf{y}_0) - \epsilon. \qquad (10)$$

The gathering property means that all but ϵ 1's of y_0 gather in some m consecutive positions (in the cyclic sense). We note that there is no requirement on the right side element y_1. In this paper, we are particularly interested in the case $\epsilon = 0, 1$.

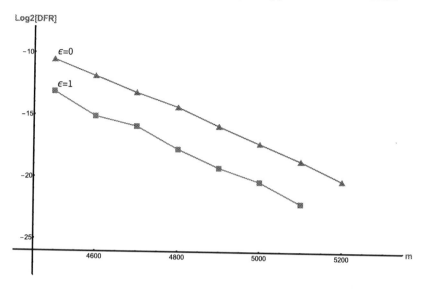

Fig. 2. The decryption failure rates for (h_0, h_1) and (e_0, e_1) satisfy the (m, ϵ)-gathering property.

3.1 The Frequency of Decryption Failures

The gathering property has a significant impact on the decryption failure rates of QC-MDPC based schemes. We experimentally simulate the decryption failure rates for BIKE with BGF algorithm and parameter set targeting 128-bit security. In the experiment, we sample (h_0, h_1) from $\mathrm{K}_{m,\epsilon}(w)$ and sample (e_0, e_1) from $\mathrm{E}_{m,\epsilon}(t/2, t/2)$ uniformly at random, where the specific sampling method is discussed in Sect. 3.1. By taking $(s = h_0 e_0 + h_1 e_1, h_0, h_1)$ as input, the BGF algorithm outputs a vector $\mathbf{e}$. Then we count a decryption failure if and only if $\mathbf{e} \neq (e_0, e_1)$. For $4500 \leq m \leq 5100$ and $\epsilon = 0, 1$, the frequency of decryption failures in our experiment is listed in Table 3, and their trend is depicted in Fig. 2. From the figure, we can see that the decryption failure rates are significantly higher than the average when both the secret key (h_0, h_1) and the error (e_0, e_1) satisfy the gathering property.

How to Sample Keys and Errors. Directly sampling $(h_0, h_1), (e_0, e_1)$ from $\mathrm{K}_{m,\epsilon}(w)$ and $\mathrm{E}_{m,\epsilon}(t/2, t/2)$ uniformly is difficult. We observe that the decryption failures are preserved by cyclic shifting. That is, $(h_0, h_1), (e_0, e_1)$ gives a decryption failure if and only if $(x^i h_0, x^i h_1), (x^j e_0, x^j e_1)$ gives a decryption failure for any $i, j \in \mathbb{Z}$. As a result, we can take the following strategy, which samples the keys and errors such that 1's of h_0 and e_0 roughly gather in $[0, m)$. Note that we are interested in $m \leq r/2, \epsilon \in \{0, 1\}$ in experiments.

Firstly, we focus on the case $\epsilon = 0$. To sample (h_0, h_1), we first set the 0-th position of h_0 to 1 and then randomly choose $(w/2 - \epsilon - 1)$ positions from $[1, m)$ and set them to 1. Denoting j to be the last position of h_0 with a value of 1,

Table 3. The frequency of decryption failures for (h_0, h_1) and (e_0, e_1) satisfying the (m, ϵ)-gathering property. N represents the number of decryptions performed, and F represents the number of decryption failures observed.

(m, ϵ)	$(4500, 0)$	$(4600, 0)$	$(4700, 0)$	$(4800, 0)$	$(4900, 0)$	$(5000, 0)$	$(5100, 0)$	$(5200, 0)$
N	240393	595827	1496235	3330070	952115	2507712	6605312	19727185
F	160	160	160	160	16	16	16	16

(m, ϵ)	$(4500, 1)$	$(4600, 1)$	$(4700, 1)$	$(4800, 1)$	$(4900, 1)$	$(5000, 1)$	$(5100, 1)$
N	139443	491647	911967	2957650	9176502	19197539	28910000
F	15.5^*	14	15	13.5^*	15	14.5^*	6.5^*

* The '.5' comes from the rejection sampling in Algorithm 2, where a decryption failure in the overlapping area counts as 0.5.

then we randomly choose ϵ positions from $[j+1, r)$ and set them to 1.[1] h_1 is just generated randomly such that $w_H(h_1) = w/2$. Such procedure is summarized in Algorithm 2. (e_0, e_1) is sampled in the same way as (h_0, h_1), while the input of the algorithm is set to be $(t, m, \epsilon = 0)$.

It can be proved that the decryption failure rate for keys and errors sampled as above equals to that for $K_{m,\epsilon}(w)$ and $E_{m,\epsilon}(t/2, t/2)$. Let $K_{m,\epsilon}^{(0)}(w)$ and $E_{m,\epsilon}^{(0)}(t)$ denote the set of (h_0, h_1) and (e_0, e_1) generated as above respectively. Denote $K_{m,\epsilon}^{(b)}(w) = \{(x^b h_0, x^b h_1) : (h_0, h_1) \in K_{m,\epsilon}^{(0)}(w)\}$ and $E_{m,\epsilon}^{(b)}(t) = \{(x^b e_0, x^b e_1) : (e_0, e_1) \in E_{m,\epsilon}^{(0)}(t)\}$. Then it is clear that

$$\mathrm{DFR}_{\substack{(h_0, h_1) \overset{\$}{\leftarrow} K_{m,\epsilon}^{(0)}(w) \\ (e_0, e_1) \overset{\$}{\leftarrow} E_{m,\epsilon}^{(0)}(t)}} = \mathrm{DFR}_{\substack{(h_0, h_1) \overset{\$}{\leftarrow} K_{m,\epsilon}^{(b)}(w) \\ (e_0, e_1) \overset{\$}{\leftarrow} E_{m,\epsilon}^{(b')}(t)}} \tag{11}$$

for any $b, b' \in \mathbb{Z}$ because of the cyclic property. Additionally, for $\epsilon = 0$, $K_{m,\epsilon}(w)$ is exactly the disjoint union of $K_{m,\epsilon}^{(b)}(w), 0 \le b < r$, and $E_{m,\epsilon}(t/2, t/2)$ is the disjoint union of $E_{m,\epsilon}^{(b)}(t), 0 \le b < r$. As a result, for $\epsilon = 0$ we can deduce that

$$\mathrm{DFR}_{\substack{(h_0, h_1) \overset{\$}{\leftarrow} K_{m,\epsilon}(w) \\ (e_0, e_1) \overset{\$}{\leftarrow} E_{m,\epsilon}(t/2, t/2)}} = \mathrm{DFR}_{\substack{(h_0, h_1) \overset{\$}{\leftarrow} K_{m,\epsilon}^{(0)}(w) \\ (e_0, e_1) \overset{\$}{\leftarrow} E_{m,\epsilon}^{(0)}(t)}} . \tag{12}$$

For $\epsilon = 1$, Eq. (11) still holds. However, the sets $K_{m,\epsilon}^{(b)}(w), 0 \le b < r$, intersect with each other, which makes Eq. (12) no longer holds. We solve this issue by rejection sampling. Specifically, we observe that there is no (h_0, h_1) simultaneously drops into more than 2 of $K_{m,\epsilon}^{(b)}(w)$, i.e., each element in the overlapping area $K_{m,\epsilon}^{(0)}(w) \cap (\cup_{1 \le b < r} K_{m,\epsilon}^{(b)}(w))$ appears exactly twice in the complete union $\cup_{0 \le b < r} K_{m,\epsilon}^{(b)}(w)$. A similar conclusion also holds for the sets $E_{m,\epsilon}^{(b)}(t)$. Therefore,

---

[1] For $\epsilon = 0$ there is nothing to do in this step.

by accepting the (h_0, h_1) and (e_0, e_1) that drop in the overlapping area with probability $1/2$ (see Algorithm 2),[2] we can obtain a result similar to Eq. (12). A complete proof can be found in the full version of this work.

Algorithm 2: Sampling the keys and errors

Input: w, m and $\epsilon = 0$ or 1
Output: $(h_0, h_1) \in \mathcal{R}^2$
1: Randomly generate $h_1 \in \mathcal{R}$ such that $w_H(h_1) = w/2$
2: $h_0 \leftarrow 0 \in \mathcal{R}$
3: Set the 0-th position of h_0 to 1
4: Randomly choose $w/2 - \epsilon - 1$ positions $\subseteq [1, m)$ and set them to 1
5: $j \leftarrow$ the last position of h_0 whose value is 1
6: Randomly choose ϵ positions $\subseteq [j + 1, r)$ and set them to 1.
7: **if** $\epsilon = 1$ **then**
8:     **if** (h_0, h_1) is in the overlapping area **then**
9:         Accept (h_0, h_1) with probability $1/2$
10:    **end if**
11: **end if**
12: **return** (h_0, h_1)

Lemma 1. *Denote* $\mathrm{F}(w, m, \epsilon)$ *to be the random function corresponding to Algorithm 2. Then for* $m \leq \frac{r}{2}$ *and* $\epsilon \in \{0, 1\}$, *it has*

$$\mathrm{DFR}_{\substack{(h_0,h_1) \xleftarrow{\$} \mathrm{K}_{m,\epsilon}(w) \\ (e_0,e_1) \xleftarrow{\$} \mathrm{E}_{m,\epsilon}(t/2, t/2)}} = \mathrm{DFR}_{\substack{(h_0,h_1) \leftarrow \mathrm{F}(w,m,\epsilon) \\ (e_0,e_1) \leftarrow \mathrm{F}(t,m,\epsilon)}} . \tag{13}$$

For $m > \frac{r}{2}$ or $\epsilon \geq 2$, the rejection sampling approach may be extended by first determining how many sets $\mathrm{K}_{m,\epsilon}^{(b)}(w)$ an element (h_0, h_1) drops in, and then accepting it with proper probability. However, determining the exact number of sets is complicated and time consuming, and better solutions to this problem have yet to be devised.

3.2 An Explanation of the Gathering Property

Our basic observation is that the gathering property considerably raises the numbers of unsatisfied parity checks for partial positions. Then the number of bits that are incorrectly flipped can be increased for these positions, which makes the decoding more likely to fail.

Specifically, we consider an example that both $(h_0, h_1), (e_0, e_1) \in \mathcal{R}^2$ satisfy the (m, ϵ)-gathering property such that $\epsilon = 0$ and all the 1's of h_0 and e_0 gather in their first m positions. As depicted in Fig. 3, there is a diagonal area of the

---

[2] An equivalent way is to not perform reject sampling but to count each decryption failure in the overlapping area as 0.5.

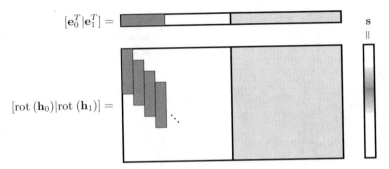

Fig. 3. An explanation of the gathering property. The shadow parts represent that the 1's gather in these positions.

matrix $\mathbf{H} = [\mathbf{rot}(\mathbf{h_0})|\mathbf{rot}(\mathbf{h_1})]$ in which the 1's gather. As a result, the syndrome $s = h_0 e_0 + h_1 e_1$ will be denser around the m-th position. Now we consider the first iteration of the bit-flipping algorithm, in which the number of unsatisfied parity checks $\mathtt{UPC}(\mathbf{0}, i) = |\mathrm{Supp}(\mathbf{s}) \cap \mathrm{Supp}(\mathbf{h_i})|$ is computed at first. Due to the property of $\mathbf{s}$, the numbers of unsatisfied parity checks $\mathtt{UPC}(\mathbf{0}, i), 0 \leq i \leq m - 1$, are more likely to be greater than other positions. This eventually increases the risk of a correct bit being mistakenly flipped in the first m positions. In fact, this phenomenon does happen when decryption failure occurs. For BIKE's parameter set targeting 128-bit security, we set $m = 4500$ and test the average unsatisfied parity check number of the first m positions and that of all positions, and find that the local unsatisfied parity check number is much higher than the global one in each iteration of the BGF algorithm, see Table 4.

Table 4. A comparison of the local UPC and the global UPC.

Iteration	Average UPC of the first m positions	Average UPC of all positions
0	31.3864	26.4111
1	57.2082	42.7164
2	83.5507	56.5557
3	114.588	73.0108
4	148.179	93.1936

3.3 Number of Keys and Errors Satisfying the Gathering Property

The purpose of this subsection is to prove the following statement.

Lemma 2. *Suppose $m < r/2$ and $\epsilon \in \{0,1\}$, then it has*

$$1 - \xi \leq \frac{|\mathrm{K}_{m,\epsilon}(w)|}{\tau(w/2, m, \epsilon)} \leq 1 \ and \ 1 - \xi \leq \frac{|\mathrm{E}_{m,\epsilon}(t/2, t/2)|}{\tau(t/2, m, \epsilon)} \leq 1 \ , \tag{14}$$

where

$$\tau(x, m, \epsilon) := r \sum_{d=x-\epsilon}^{m} \binom{d-2}{x-2-\epsilon}\binom{r-d}{\epsilon}\binom{r}{x}. \tag{15}$$

For $\epsilon = 0$, it has $\xi = 0$. For $\epsilon = 1, m \leq 5200$ and BIKE's parameter set with 128-bit security, it has $\xi < 0.05$.

Proof. For $\epsilon = 0$, $\mathrm{K}_{m,\epsilon}(w)$ is the disjoint union of $\mathrm{K}_{m,\epsilon}^{(b)}(w), 0 \leq b < r$, then it has $|\mathrm{K}_{m,\epsilon}(w)| = \sum_{0 \leq b < r} |\mathrm{K}_{m,\epsilon}^{(b)}(w)| = r|\mathrm{K}_{m,\epsilon}^{(0)}(w)|$. To count the number of (h_0, h_1) in $\mathrm{K}_{m,\epsilon}^{(0)}(w)$, we enumerate the position $d \in (0, m)$ such that the d-th position of h_0 is 1 and there are exactly $(w/2 - \epsilon - 2)$ 1's in the $(0, d)$ positions of h_0. Clearly for a fixed d there are $\binom{d-2}{w/2-2-\epsilon}\binom{r-d}{\epsilon}\binom{r}{w/2}$ distinct (h_0, h_1) in $\mathrm{K}_{m,\epsilon}^{(0)}(w)$, and then the lemma follows directly.

For $\epsilon = 1$, $\cup_{0 \leq b < r} \mathrm{K}_{m,\epsilon}^{(b)}(w)$ is not a disjoint union. Then counting the overlapping area gives an estimate of $\mathrm{K}_{m,\epsilon}(w)$, where the complete proof can be found in the full version of this work. □

In this paper, we only consider BIKE's parameter set with 128-bit security, and focus on the parameters $\epsilon = 1, m \leq 5200$ or $\epsilon = 0$. For $\epsilon = 1, m = 5200$, it can be calculated from Lemma 2 that $\xi < 0.05$, which means that the error is no more than $|\log_2(1 - \xi)| < 0.08$ bits. The error is further reduced when m decreases. Using Lemma 2, we calculate the probability $p_{m,\epsilon} = |\mathrm{K}_{m,\epsilon}(w)|/|\mathrm{K}(w)|$ and $q_{m,\epsilon} = |\mathrm{E}_{m,\epsilon}(t/2, t/2)|/|\mathrm{E}(t)|$ for the (m, ϵ) involved in our experiments of Sect. 3.1, which are listed in Table 5.

Table 5. The probability $p_{m,\epsilon}$ and $q_{m,\epsilon}$ for the (m, ϵ) involved in our experiment and BIKE's parameter set targeting 128-bit security. The numbers are presented in their logarithmic form.

(m, ϵ)	$(4500, 0)$	$(4600, 0)$	$(4700, 0)$	$(4800, 0)$	$(4900, 0)$	$(5000, 0)$	$(5100, 0)$	$(5200, 0)$
$p_{m,\epsilon}$	-96.09	-93.86	-91.67	-89.53	-87.43	-85.37	-83.36	-81.39
$q_{m,\epsilon}$	-94.17	-92.06	-90.0	-87.98	-86.0	-84.06	-82.16	-80.3

(m, ϵ)	$(4500, 1)$	$(4600, 1)$	$(4700, 1)$	$(4800, 1)$	$(4900, 1)$	$(5000, 1)$	$(5100, 1)$
$p_{m,\epsilon}$	-89.13	-86.95	-84.81	-82.72	-80.67	-78.66	-76.69
$q_{m,\epsilon}$	-87.29	-85.23	-83.22	-81.25	-79.32	-77.43	-75.58

4   A New Class of Weak Keys

In this section, we focus on the construction of weak keys that have decryption failure rate higher than the average. Our basic observation is that the set of keys satisfying the (m, ϵ)-gathering property (i.e., $K_{m,\epsilon}(w)$) may have higher decryption failure rate. Specifically, denote

$$\mathrm{DFR}^{K}_{m,\epsilon} := \mathrm{DFR}_{(h_0,h_1) \xleftarrow{\$} K_{m,\epsilon}(w), (e_0,e_1) \xleftarrow{\$} E(t)} \tag{16}$$

as the decryption failure rate for the key drawn from $K_{m,\epsilon}(w)$ and the error drawn from $E(t)$. Then we can deduce a lower bound by

$$\mathrm{DFR}^{K}_{m,\epsilon} \geq \mathrm{DFR}_{\substack{(h_0,h_1) \xleftarrow{\$} K_{m,\epsilon}(w) \\ (e_0,e_1) \xleftarrow{\$} E_{m,\epsilon}(\frac{t}{2},\frac{t}{2})}} \cdot \Pr_{(e_0,e_1) \xleftarrow{\$} E(t)} [(e_0,e_1) \in E_{m,\epsilon}(\frac{t}{2},\frac{t}{2})] . \tag{17}$$

For example, using the experimental results in Sect. 3.1, we have $\mathrm{DFR}^{K}_{m,\epsilon} \geq 2^{-22.08} \cdot 2^{-75.58} = 2^{-97.66}$ for $m = 5100$ and $\epsilon = 1$, which is much higher than the average decryption failure rate 2^{-128} given in BIKE. However, the probability of a random key (h_0, h_1) falling in $K_{m,\epsilon}(w)$ is too small to impact the average decryption failure rate. Next, we focus on the case $\epsilon = 1$, and show the following two facts.

(i) The set of weak keys $K_{m,\epsilon}(w)$ can be extended by using the isomorphisms of the ring $\mathcal{R}$.
(ii) Based on the extended weak keys, a lower bound greater than 2^{-128} on the average decryption failure rate can be derived for BIKE's parameter set targeting 128-bit security.

4.1   Extending Weak Keys Using Isomorphism

Let ϕ_i be an isomorphism of $\mathcal{R}$, and denote $K^{\phi_i}_{m,\epsilon}(w)$ to be the set of keys obtained by applying ϕ_i to $K_{m,\epsilon}(w)$, i.e.,

$$K^{\phi_i}_{m,\epsilon}(w) := \{(\phi_i(h_0), \phi_i(h_1)) : (h_0, h_1) \in K_{m,\epsilon}(w)\}. \tag{18}$$

Note that ϕ_i preserves decryption failures, i.e., $(h_0, h_1), (e_0, e_1)$ gives a decryption failure if and only if $(\phi_i(h_0), \phi_i(h_1)), (\phi_i(e_0), \phi_i(e_1))$ gives a decryption failure. Thus we have the following lemma.

Lemma 3. *For any isomorphism* $\phi_i : \mathcal{R} \to \mathcal{R}$, *it has*

$$\mathrm{DFR}_{\substack{(h_0,h_1) \xleftarrow{\$} K^{\phi_i}_{m,\epsilon}(w) \\ (e_0,e_1) \xleftarrow{\$} E(t)}} = \mathrm{DFR}_{\substack{(h_0,h_1) \xleftarrow{\$} K_{m,\epsilon}(w) \\ (e_0,e_1) \xleftarrow{\$} E(t)}} = \mathrm{DFR}^{K}_{m,\epsilon} . \tag{19}$$

Next we focus on the decryption failure rate for the keys drawn uniformly from the union

$$K^{\mathrm{union}}_{m,\epsilon}(w) := \bigcup_{1 \leq i < r/2} K^{\phi_i}_{m,\epsilon}(w). \tag{20}$$

Note that only half of the isomorphisms are considered due to $K^{\phi_i}_{m,\epsilon}(w) = K^{\phi_{-i}}_{m,\epsilon}(w)$. To begin with, we show for proper choices of (m, ϵ), the above union is 'roughly' disjoint. That is, denote $K_{m,\epsilon}^{\text{overlap}}(w) = \cup_{i,j}(K_{m,\epsilon}^{\phi_i}(w) \cap K_{m,\epsilon}^{\phi_j}(w))$ as the overlapping area of the union in (20), then it has

$$\frac{|K_{m,\epsilon}^{\text{overlap}}(w)|}{|K_{m,\epsilon}^{\text{union}}(w)|} \leq \frac{|K_{m,\epsilon}^{\phi_i}(w) \cap K_{m,\epsilon}^{\text{overlap}}(w)|}{|K_{m,\epsilon}^{\phi_i}(w)|} \leq \delta , \tag{21}$$

where δ is a small number. The detailed proof can be found in the full version of this work. For example, when $m = 4000, \epsilon = 1$, δ is as small as 2^{-35}. Based on this observation, we can prove the following result.

Theorem 1. *Suppose the error (e_0, e_1) is drawn from $E(t)$ uniformly at random, then for the set of keys $K_{m,\epsilon}^{\text{union}}(w) = \cup_{1 \leq i < r/2} K_{m,\epsilon}^{\phi_i}(w)$ it has*

$$\text{DFR}_{(h_0,h_1) \xleftarrow{\$} K_{m,\epsilon}^{\text{union}}(w)} \geq \text{DFR}_{(h_0,h_1) \xleftarrow{\$} K_{m,\epsilon}(w)} - \delta , \tag{22}$$

and $|K_{m,\epsilon}^{\text{union}}(w)| \geq (1 - \delta)(r - 1)/2 \cdot |K_{m,\epsilon}(w)|$.

Proof. Since $|K_{m,\epsilon}^{\text{union}}(w)| \geq \sum_i (|K_{m,\epsilon}^{\phi_i}(w)| - |K_{m,\epsilon}^{\phi_i}(w) \cap K_{m,\epsilon}^{\text{overlap}}(w)|)$, then it follows directly from (21) that $|K_{m,\epsilon}^{\text{union}}(w)| \geq (1 - \delta)(r - 1)/2 \cdot |K_{m,\epsilon}(w)|$. It remains to show (22). Denote $\bar{h} = (h_0, h_1)$, $\tilde{K}_{m,\epsilon}^{\phi_i}(w) = K_{m,\epsilon}^{\phi_i}(w) \cap K_{m,\epsilon}^{\text{overlap}}(w)$ and $\bar{K}_{m,\epsilon}^{\phi_i}(w) = K_{m,\epsilon}^{\phi_i}(w) - \tilde{K}_{m,\epsilon}^{\phi_i}(w)$, then

$$\text{DFR}_{\bar{h} \xleftarrow{\$} K_{m,\epsilon}^{\text{union}}(w)} \geq \sum_{1 \leq i \leq \frac{r}{2}} \text{DFR}_{\bar{h} \xleftarrow{\$} \bar{K}_{m,\epsilon}^{\phi_i}(w)} \cdot \Pr_{\bar{h} \xleftarrow{\$} K_{m,\epsilon}^{\text{union}}(w)} [\bar{h} \in \bar{K}_{m,\epsilon}^{\phi_i}(w)] . \tag{23}$$

Note that

$$\text{DFR}_{\bar{h} \xleftarrow{\$} K_{m,\epsilon}^{\phi_i}(w)} = \text{DFR}_{\bar{h} \xleftarrow{\$} \bar{K}_{m,\epsilon}^{\phi_i}(w)} \cdot \Pr_{\bar{h} \xleftarrow{\$} K_{m,\epsilon}^{\phi_i}(w)} [\bar{h} \in \bar{K}_{m,\epsilon}^{\phi_i}(w)]$$

$$+ \text{DFR}_{\bar{h} \xleftarrow{\$} \tilde{K}_{m,\epsilon}^{\phi_i}(w)} \cdot \Pr_{\bar{h} \xleftarrow{\$} K_{m,\epsilon}^{\phi_i}(w)} [\bar{h} \in \tilde{K}_{m,\epsilon}^{\phi_i}(w)]$$

$$\leq \text{DFR}_{\bar{h} \xleftarrow{\$} \bar{K}_{m,\epsilon}^{\phi_i}(w)} \cdot \Pr_{\bar{h} \xleftarrow{\$} K_{m,\epsilon}^{\phi_i}(w)} [\bar{h} \in \bar{K}_{m,\epsilon}^{\phi_i}(w)] + \delta ,$$

then it follows from (23) that

$$\text{DFR}_{\bar{h} \xleftarrow{\$} K_{m,\epsilon}^{\text{union}}(w)} \geq \sum_{1 \leq i \leq \frac{r}{2}} (\text{DFR}_{\bar{h} \xleftarrow{\$} K_{m,\epsilon}^{\phi_i}(w)} - \delta) \cdot \Pr_{\bar{h} \xleftarrow{\$} K_{m,\epsilon}^{\text{union}}(w)} [\bar{h} \in K_{m,\epsilon}^{\phi_i}(w)]$$

$$= (\text{DFR}_{\bar{h} \xleftarrow{\$} K_{m,\epsilon}(w)} - \delta) \cdot \sum_{1 \leq i \leq \frac{r}{2}} \Pr_{\bar{h} \xleftarrow{\$} K_{m,\epsilon}^{\text{union}}(w)} [\bar{h} \in K_{m,\epsilon}^{\phi_i}(w)]$$

$$\geq \text{DFR}_{\bar{h} \xleftarrow{\$} K_{m,\epsilon}(w)} - \delta,$$

which completes the proof.   □

4.2   Lower Bound on the Average DFR

In this subsection we give lower bounds on the average decryption failure rate by using Theorem 1 and the formula

$$\mathrm{DFR}_{\mathrm{avg}} \geq 2 \cdot \mathrm{DFR}_{(h_0,h_1) \xleftarrow{\$} \mathrm{K}^{\mathrm{union}}_{m,\epsilon}(w)} \cdot \frac{|\mathrm{K}^{\mathrm{union}}_{m,\epsilon}(w)|}{|\mathrm{K}(w)|}, \tag{24}$$

where the '$2\times$' comes from the gathering property defined for the right side of (h_0, h_1), i.e., the 1's of h_1 are gathering while h_0 is chosen freely. We note that there is a very little chance that both sides of (h_0, h_1) have the property that their 1's gathering. However, the probability is too small to have any effect on (24), and a rigorous treatment can be performed in a way similar to that of Theorem 1.

Next, we consider BIKE's parameter set targeting 128-bit security, and focus on $2900 \leq m \leq 4000, \epsilon = 1$. By Theorem 1, $\mathrm{DFR}_{(h_0,h_1) \xleftarrow{\$} \mathrm{K}^{\mathrm{union}}_{m,\epsilon}(w)}$ can be estimated by simulating the decryption failure rate $\mathrm{DFR}_{(h_0,h_1) \xleftarrow{\$} \mathrm{K}_{m,\epsilon}(w)}$. In our experiments, we sample (h_0, h_1) and (e_0, e_1) from $\mathrm{K}_{m,\epsilon}(w)$ and $\mathrm{E}(t)$ uniformly at random. For each (m, ϵ), the number of decryption performed and the number of decryption failures are listed in Table 6. Note that for these set of parameters, it has $\delta \approx 2^{-35}$, which is negligible with respect to $\mathrm{DFR}_{(h_0,h_1) \xleftarrow{\$} \mathrm{K}_{m,\epsilon}(w)}$. On the other hand, lower bound on $|\mathrm{K}^{\mathrm{union}}_{m,\epsilon}(w)|/|\mathrm{K}(w)|$ can be derived by using Theorem 1 and Lemma 2.

Table 6. Estimates of the decryption failure rates for the set of weak keys $\mathrm{K}^{\mathrm{union}}_{m,\epsilon}(w)$. N represents the number of decryptions, and F represents the number of decryption failures. p is 2 times the probability that a random key (h_0, h_1) is in $\mathrm{K}^{\mathrm{union}}_{m,\epsilon}(w)$.

(m, ϵ)	$(2900, 1)$	$(3100, 1)$	$(3200, 1)$	$(3400, 1)$	$(3500, 1)$	$(3600, 1)$	$(4000, 1)$
N	2996871	5459695	32903584	165860000	214960000	315470000	8745860000
F	16	16	31.5*	25.5*	13.5*	11	13
DFR	-17.52	-18.38	-19.99	-22.63	-23.92	-24.77	-29.33
p	-119.45	-112.76	-109.58	-103.51	-100.62	-97.80	-87.28

* The '.5' comes from the rejection sampling in Algorithm 2, where a decryption failure in the overlapping area counts as 0.5.

Combining the above results, we can give estimated lower bounds on the average decryption failure rate by using (24). Figure 4 depicts the corresponding results. From the figure, $(m = 4000, \epsilon = 1)$ yields an estimated lower bound for the average decryption failure rate such that

$$\mathrm{DFR}_{\mathrm{avg}} \geq 2^{-29.33} \cdot 2^{-87.28} = 2^{-116.61}. \tag{25}$$

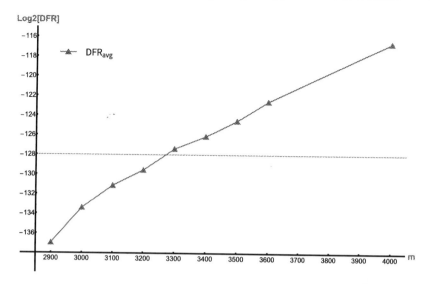

Fig. 4. Lower bounds on the average decryption failure rate for BIKE's parameter set targeting 128-bit security.

Taking the simulation error into consideration, we note that 13 decryption failures are observed from 8745860000 decryptions. Then using the framework in Sect. 2.1, we have

$$\mathrm{DFR}_{(h_0,h_1) \overset{\$}{\leftarrow} \mathrm{K}_{m,\epsilon}(w)} \geq F/N - 2 \cdot \sqrt{F}/N \approx 2^{-30.49} \tag{26}$$

at 95% confidence level. As a result, we can deduce that the average decryption failure rate for BIKE's parameter set targeting 128-bit security is lower bounded by $\mathrm{DFR}_{\mathrm{avg}} \geq 2^{-30.49} \cdot 2^{-87.28} = 2^{-117.77}$ at 95% confidence level. For larger $m > 4000$, we should expect better lower bounds according to Fig. 4. However, in this case $\mathrm{DFR}_{(h_0,h_1) \overset{\$}{\leftarrow} \mathrm{K}_{m,\epsilon}^{\mathrm{union}}(w)}$ is very small and difficult to simulate experimentally.

5 A Key Recovery Attack Using Decryption Failures

In this section, we demonstrate how the class of weak keys introduced in Sect. 4 can be utilized to launch a key recovery attack against QC-MDPC schemes with CCA security. The attack is in a multi-target mode, which means that numerous targets are queried, each with its own query limit, with the goal of recovering the key for at least one of these targets. Additionally, we assume that a ciphertext is only valid for a single target, i.e., the scheme provides multi-target protection.

5.1 Attack Model

The attack can be modeled as follows.

Step 0 (*Setup*). To begin with, we choose the proper parameters m, ϵ. Let $\mathrm{K}_{m,\epsilon}^{\mathtt{weak}}(w)$ to be the set of weak keys defined in Sect. 4, i.e., the set of all $(h_0, h_1) \in \mathrm{K}_{m,\epsilon}(w)$ such that (h_0, h_1) or (h_1, h_0) satisfying the (m, ϵ)-gathering property. Denote

$$p_{m,\epsilon}^{\mathtt{weak}} := \frac{|\mathrm{K}_{m,\epsilon}^{\mathtt{weak}}(w)|}{|\mathrm{K}(w)|} \qquad (27)$$

to be the probability that a random secret key is in $\mathrm{K}_{m,\epsilon}^{\mathtt{weak}}(w)$, and denote $\mathrm{DFR}_{m,\epsilon}^{\mathtt{weak}}$ to be the decryption failure rate for key drawn from $\mathrm{K}_{m,\epsilon}^{\mathtt{weak}}(w)$ and error drawn from $E(t)$.

Step 1 (*Construct Ciphertexts for a Target*). For a target T, initialize the set of ciphertexts to be $C_T = \{\}$. Randomly generate $1/\mathrm{DFR}_{m,\epsilon}^{\mathtt{weak}}$ seeds $m \in \{0,1\}^{256}$, then compute $(e_0, e_1) = \mathrm{H}(m)$ according to the error generation step of BIKE, and add the corresponding ciphertext to C_T. Clearly $|C_T| = 1/\mathrm{DFR}_{m,\epsilon}^{\mathtt{weak}}$.

Step 2 (*Query and Collect Decryption Failures*). Query the target T's decryption oracle to decrypt all ciphertexts in C_T. If a decryption failure occurs, then go to the key recovery step. Else, choose another target and then repeat the ciphertexts construction and query steps.

Step 3 (*Recover the Secret Key*). For a target T that has a decryption failure, there is a probability $p_{\mathtt{true}}$ that T's secret key (h_0, h_1) is in $\mathrm{K}_{m,\epsilon}^{\mathtt{weak}}(w)$. In the case that $(h_0, h_1) \in \mathrm{K}_{m,\epsilon}^{\mathtt{weak}}(w)$, there exists an isomorphism $\phi_i, 1 \le i < r/2$, such that $(\phi_i^{-1}(h_0), \phi_i^{-1}(h_1))$ or $(\phi_i^{-1}(h_1), \phi_i^{-1}(h_0))$ satisfying the (m, ϵ)-gathering property. With the gathering property as extra information, the secret key can be efficiently recovered using a modified information set decoding (ISD) algorithm presented in the next subsection. Then the attacker enumerates the isomorphisms $\phi_i, 1 \le i < r/2$ and tries to recover $(\phi_i^{-1}(h_0), \phi_i^{-1}(h_1))$ or $(\phi_i^{-1}(h_1), \phi_i^{-1}(h_0))$ from

$$\phi_i^{-1}(h) = \phi_i^{-1}(h_1) \cdot (\phi_i^{-1}(h_0))^{-1} \qquad (28)$$

utilizing the modified ISD algorithm. If T's secret key (h_0, h_1) is in $\mathrm{K}_{m,\epsilon}^{\mathtt{weak}}(w)$, then for some ϕ_i the modified ISD algorithm can efficiently recovers T's secret key and the attack terminates. If T's secret key (h_0, h_1) is not in $\mathrm{K}_{m,\epsilon}^{\mathtt{weak}}(w)$, it is unlikely the modified ISD algorithm can efficiently recover the secret key for any $1 \le i < r/2$. Then the attacker chooses another target and repeats the ciphertexts construction, query and key recovery steps.

Analysis of the Probability $p_{\mathtt{true}}$. Let 'FAIL' denote the event that a decryption failure occurs for the secret key $\bar{h} := (h_0, h_1)$, and denote $\mathrm{X} := \mathrm{K}(w) \times \mathrm{E}(t)$. Then it can be deduced that

$$p_{\mathtt{true}} = \Pr_{(\bar{h}, \bar{e}) \xleftarrow{\$} \mathrm{X}} [\bar{h} \in \mathrm{K}_{m,\epsilon}^{\mathtt{weak}}(w) \mid \mathrm{FAIL}]$$

$$= \Pr_{(\bar{h}, \bar{e}) \xleftarrow{\$} \mathrm{X}} [\mathrm{FAIL} \mid \bar{h} \in \mathrm{K}_{m,\epsilon}^{\mathtt{weak}}(w)] \cdot \Pr_{(\bar{h}, \bar{e}) \xleftarrow{\$} \mathrm{X}} [\bar{h} \in \mathrm{K}_{m,\epsilon}^{\mathtt{weak}}(w)] / \Pr_{(\bar{h}, \bar{e}) \xleftarrow{\$} \mathrm{X}} [\mathrm{FAIL}]$$

$$= \mathrm{DFR}_{m,\epsilon}^{\mathtt{weak}} \cdot p_{m,\epsilon}^{\mathtt{weak}} / \mathrm{DFR}_{\mathrm{avg}}$$

by Bayes' theorem, where $\mathrm{DFR}_{\mathrm{avg}} = \Pr_{(\bar{h}, \bar{e}) \xleftarrow{\$} \mathrm{X}} [\mathrm{FAIL}]$ is the average decryption failure rate.

5.2 Information Set Decoding Using Extra Information

Efficiently retrieving the secret key given extra information is a well-known topic in public key cryptography [8,12,17,30,50]. Several effects have been developed to address this issue in code-based cryptography. Horlemann et al. [33] present a general framework for recovering the key by employing hint information such as certain erroneous or error-free locations, or the Hamming weight of error blocks. Esser et al. [22] demonstrate that when a fraction of the secret key bits are erased or faulty, the key recovery for BIKE can be greatly accelerated. Kirshanova and May [36] show that a small portion of the secret key at any known positions can be used to successfully recover the entire secret key for McEliece. The purpose of this subsection is to develop an effective approach for using the gathering property to improve the key recovery in QC-MDPC.

Our goal is to recover a target's secret key (h_0, h_1) from the public key $h = h_1 h_0^{-1}$ using the fact that (h_0, h_1) satisfies the (m, ϵ)-gathering property. Denote $\mathbf{H} = (\mathbf{I}_r, \mathtt{rot}(h))$, $\mathbf{e} = (\mathbf{h}_1^T, \mathbf{h}_0^T)^T$ and $\mathbf{s} = \mathbf{0}$. Then the problem can be stated as follows.

Problem 1. Given $\mathbf{H} \in \mathbb{F}_2^{r \times 2r}, \mathbf{s} \in \mathbb{F}_2^r$ and positive integers w, m and $\epsilon \geq 0$, find $\mathbf{e} = (\mathbf{h}_1^T, \mathbf{h}_0^T)^T$ such that $\mathbf{He} = \mathbf{s}$, $w_H(\mathbf{h}_0) = w_H(\mathbf{h}_1) = w/2$ and there exists an integer a such that $w_H(\mathbf{h}_0^{[a, a+m)}) = w/2 - \epsilon$.

Without the extra information of the gathering property, the above problem is typically solved using the information set decoding (ISD) algorithm.

Classical ISD Algorithm. The ISD algorithm iteratively finds a vector $\mathbf{e}$ such that $\mathbf{He} = \mathbf{s}$ and $w_H(\mathbf{e}) = w$. Suppose l, p are two integers, each iteration of the ISD algorithm is as follows.

- *Random Permutation*: Choose a random permutation matrix $\mathbf{P}$, and compute $\mathbf{HP}^{-1}$.
- *Gauss Elimination*: Apply Gauss elimination to the matrix $\mathbf{HP}^{-1}$ and obtain a matrix of the form

$$\mathbf{H}' := \mathbf{THP}^{-1} = \begin{bmatrix} \mathbf{I}_{r-l} & \mathbf{H_1} \\ \mathbf{O} & \mathbf{H_2} \end{bmatrix}, \tag{29}$$

where $\mathbf{T}$ is the corresponding Gauss elimination matrix, $\mathbf{O}$ is an $l \times (r - l)$ zero matrix. Denote $\mathbf{Pe} = (\mathbf{e}_1^T, \mathbf{e}_2^T)^T$ and $\mathbf{Ts} = (\mathbf{s}_1^T, \mathbf{s}_2^T)^T$ such that $\mathbf{e}_1, \mathbf{s}_1 \in \mathbb{F}_2^{r-l}, \mathbf{e_2} \in \mathbb{F}_2^{r+l}$ and $\mathbf{s_2} \in \mathbb{F}_2^l$. Then the problem can be written as

$$\mathbf{H}_2 \mathbf{e}_2 = \mathbf{s}_2, \mathbf{e}_1 = \mathbf{H}_1 \mathbf{e}_2 + \mathbf{s}_1. \tag{30}$$

- *Column Match*: In this step, an algorithm $\mathtt{COLUMNMATCH}(\mathbf{H_2}, \mathbf{s_2}, p)$ is called to generate a set $\mathrm{L} = \{\mathbf{e_2} : \mathbf{H_2 e_2} = \mathbf{s_2}, w_H(\mathbf{e_2}) = p\}$. The $\mathtt{COLUMNMATCH}$ algorithm differs depending on the ISD algorithms, e.g., Stern-Dumer [21], MMT [38], BJMM [5], etc.

– *Recover* $\mathbf{e}$: For all $\mathbf{e_2} \in L$, compute $\mathbf{e_1} = \mathbf{H_1 e_2} + \mathbf{s_1}$. If $w_H(\mathbf{e_1}) = w - p$, then the algorithm returns $\mathbf{e} = \mathbf{P}^{-1} \cdot (\mathbf{e_1}^T, \mathbf{e_2}^T)^T$. Else goes to the *Random Permutation* step and try another permutation matrix.

For a random $\mathbf{P}$, the probability that the Hamming weight of $\mathbf{Pe} = (\mathbf{e_1}^T, \mathbf{e_2}^T)^T$ splits to $w - p$ and p is

$$P_{ISD} = \frac{\binom{r-l}{w-p}\binom{n-r+l}{p}}{\binom{n}{w}} . \tag{31}$$

Thus the ISD algorithm outputs the vector $\mathbf{e}$ after P_{ISD}^{-1} iterations in average. For each iteration, the time and space costs are mainly the costs of COLUMNMATCH, which we denote by T_{MATCH} and S_{MATCH} respectively. For example, in the Stern-Dumer ISD algorithm [21], it has $T_{MATCH} = S_{MATCH} = \max\{\binom{(r+l)/2}{p/2}, \binom{(r+l)/2}{p/2}^2/2^l\}$. The total time complexity of the ISD algorithm can be represented as $T_{MATCH} \cdot P_{ISD}^{-1}$ and the space complexity is S_{MATCH}.

Remark 1. It is required that the Hamming weight of $\mathbf{e}$ can be split into $w/2$ and $w/2$ in Problem 1, whereas the ISD algorithm just returns a vector of Hamming weight w. In the context of key recovery, w is usually small enough such that the vector $\mathbf{e}$ is unique (up to cyclic shifting in the quasi-cyclic case), making the two conditions equivalent.

Using the Extra Information. Our basic idea is to use the extra information to increase the probability P_{ISD}. We note that the permutation $\mathbf{P}$ actually gives a random partition of all the positions $[0, 2r) = Q_l \cup Q_r$ such that $|Q_l| = r - l$ and $|Q_r| = r + l$, and the ISD algorithm outputs the vector $\mathbf{e}$ if $w_H(\mathbf{e}^{Q_l}) = w - p$ and $w_H(\mathbf{e}^{Q_r}) = p$.

Suppose $p \geq \epsilon$ and $l \leq r - m$. By using the extra information, we construct the partition as follows. First, randomly choose $b \in [0, r - 1)$, then put the m positions $\mathbf{h_0}^{[b, b+m)}$ into Q_l, and put the other $r - m$ positions of $\mathbf{h_0}$ into Q_r. After that, randomly choose $r - l - m$ positions of $\mathbf{h_1}$ and put them into Q_l, and put the other $l + m$ positions of $\mathbf{h_1}$ into Q_r. The next steps are then carried out in the same manner as the classical ISD algorithm.

Note that with probability at least $1/r$, it has $w_H(\mathbf{h_0}^{[b,b+m)}) = w/2 - \epsilon$. In this case, the ISD algorithm outputs the correct vector $\mathbf{e}$ whenever the $r - l - m$ positions of $\mathbf{h_1}$ have exactly $(w/2 - p + \epsilon)$ 1's and the other $l + m$ positions of $\mathbf{h_1}$ have $(p - \epsilon)$ 1's. As a result, the success probability when using the extra information is

$$P_{extra} = \frac{1}{r} \frac{\binom{l+m}{p-\epsilon}\binom{r-l-m}{w/2-p+\epsilon}}{\binom{r}{w/2}} , \tag{32}$$

And the total complexity is as follows.

Proposition 4 (ISD with extra information). *The above algorithm gives a solution to Problem 1 in average time complexity $T_{MATCH} P_{extra}^{-1}$ and space complexity S_{MATCH}. When using the COLUMNMATCH in the Stern-Dumer ISD algorithm, it has $T_{MATCH} = S_{MATCH} = \max\{\binom{(k+l)/2}{p/2}, \binom{(k+l)/2}{p/2}^2/2^l\}$.*

For the quasi-cyclic case, each cyclic shift of (h_0, h_1) is also a solution to $h = h_1 h_0^{-1}$ [23,43]. As a result, the step that randomly chooses $b \in [0, r-1)$ can be skipped, and we just put the first m positions $\mathbf{h}_0^{[0,m)}$ into Q_l, and put the other $r - m$ positions of $\mathbf{h}_0$ into Q_r. This enables us to obtain an $r\times$ speedup for the quasi-cyclic case.

Corollary 5. *Given $h \in \mathcal{R}$, then (h_0, h_1) satisfying $h = h_1 h_0^{-1}$ and the (m, ϵ)-gathering property can be recovered in time complexity $T_{MATCH} P_{extra}^{-1}/r$ and space complexity S_{MATCH}.*

5.3   Complexity Analysis

We present an analysis of the complexity of the key recovery attack in Sect. 5.1. The total complexity can be divided into two parts: the complexity of identifying decryption failures (Step 1 and Step 2) and the complexity of the key recovery step (Step 3).

The complexity of identifying decryption failures. On average, $1/p_{m,\epsilon}^{\text{weak}}$ targets are required to obtain a secret key falling in $K_{m,\epsilon}^{\text{weak}}(w)$, which should result in a successful key recovery in Step 3. Thus both Step 1 and Step 2 are called $1/p_{m,\epsilon}^{\text{weak}}$ times. On the other hand, for a single target, the complexity of the ciphertexts construction and the decryption query is $|C_T| = 1/\text{DFR}_{m,\epsilon}^{\text{weak}}$. Thus the complexity of identifying decryption failures is

$$1/p_{m,\epsilon}^{\text{weak}} \cdot 1/\text{DFR}_{m,\epsilon}^{\text{weak}} \ . \tag{33}$$

The complexity of the key recovery step. For the key recovery step, the attacker calls the ISD algorithm $2 \cdot r/2$ times for each secret key, and the probability that a secret key (in this step) falls in $K_{m,\epsilon}^{\text{weak}}(w)$ is p_{true}. Thus the complexity of the key recovery step is

$$1/p_{\text{true}} \cdot r \cdot T_{ISD} \ , \tag{34}$$

where $p_{\text{true}} = p_{m,\epsilon}^{\text{weak}} \cdot \text{DFR}_{m,\epsilon}^{\text{weak}}/\text{DFR}_{avg}$ and T_{ISD} is the time complexity of a single call of the ISD algorithm as in Corollary 5.

Besides, note that Step 1 and Step 2 can be performed in polynomial space complexity, thus the total space complexity of the key recovery attack is S_{ISD}, which is the space complexity of a single call of the ISD algorithm. Therefore, the total complexity of the key recovery attack is as follows.

Theorem 2. *The key recovery attack in Sect. 5.1 can be mounted in time complexity*

$$C_{total} = (\text{DFR}_{m,\epsilon}^{weak} \cdot p_{m,\epsilon}^{weak})^{-1} + p_{true}^{-1} \cdot r \cdot T_{ISD}, \tag{35}$$

and space complexity S_{ISD}, where $p_{true} = p_{m,\epsilon}^{weak} \cdot \text{DFR}_{m,\epsilon}^{weak} \cdot \text{DFR}_{avg}^{-1}$. The number of targets required is $1/p_{m,\epsilon}^{weak}$, and the number of queries required for a single target is $1/\text{DFR}_{m,\epsilon}^{weak}$.

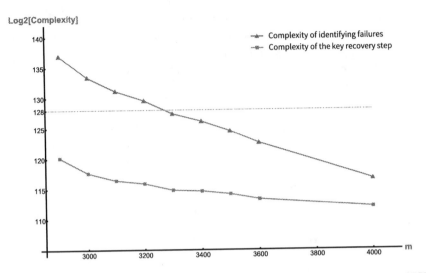

Fig. 5. The complexity of identifying a decryption failure and the complexity of ISD. The complexity of the key recovery attack can be viewed as their maximum.

Concrete Attack Complexity for BIKE. Next, we consider BIKE's parameter set targeting 128-bit security, and give the concrete complexity of the key recovery attack. We should note that the precise value of the average decryption failure rate DFR_{avg} is yet unknown for BIKE. Nonetheless, an upper bound on DFR_{avg} suffices for estimating the total complexity using Theorem 2. In the following analysis we assume that $DFR_{avg} < 2^{-80}$ for BIKE's parameter set targeting 128-bit security. We believe this upper bound is almost certain because the estimated value of DFR_{avg} is about 2^{-128} in [3]. Despite the fact that our conclusion in Sect. 4 indicates that $DFR_{avg} \geq 2^{-116.61}$, there is no evidence that DFR_{avg} can be as large as 2^{-80}.

In this attack, we initialize (m, ϵ) such that $(2900 \leq m \leq 4000, \epsilon = 1)$. The $DFR_{m,\epsilon}^{weak}$ and $p_{m,\epsilon}^{weak}$ have been simulated experimentally in Sect. 4.2, and their values are listed in Table 6. In Fig. 5, we illustrate the complexity of identifying a decryption failure and the complexity of the key recovery step. The complexity of the key recovery attack can be viewed as their maximum. It can be deduced from the figure that the total complexity is less than 2^{128} for $3300 \leq m \leq 4000$. For example, when $m = 4000$, it has $DFR_{m,\epsilon}^{weak} = 2^{-29.33}$, $p_{m,\epsilon}^{weak} = 2^{-87.28}$, $T_{ISD} = 2^{75.35}$ and the total complexity is

$$C_{total} = 2^{116.61}. \qquad (36)$$

In this case, the number of targets required is $1/p_{m,\epsilon}^{weak} = 2^{87.28}$, and the number of queries required for a single target is $1/DFR_{m,\epsilon}^{weak} = 2^{29.33}$ (see Table 1 for the details).

Moreover, it can be observed from Fig. 5 that both the complexity of identifying failures and the complexity of the key recovery step decrease as m increases.[3] So better total complexity can be expected when (m, ϵ)-gathering property is considered for m slightly larger than 4000. However, large m leads to low decryption failure rate which is difficult to be simulated via experiment.

6 A Key Recovery Attack with Ciphertexts Reusing

We note that BIKE does not offer protection against multiple targets in its current version. As described in Sect. 2.2, each target shares the same generation of error $(e_0, e_1) = \mathtt{H}(m)$ without binding to the public key. Thus it is possible to mount an attack by reusing the ciphertexts. Specifically, the results in Sect. 3.1 demonstrate that the decryption failure rate is greatly increased when both the secret key (h_0, h_1) and the error (e_0, e_1) satisfy the (m, ϵ)-gathering property. Thus the attacker first constructs a set of ciphertexts C of which the corresponding errors satisfy the (m, ϵ)-gathering property. Then by querying a target T's decryption oracle to decrypt the ciphertexts C, the attacker has an advantage of identifying whether T's secret key (h_0, h_1) satisfies the (m, ϵ)-gathering property by identifying whether a decryption failure occurs. Then use the (m, ϵ)-gathering property as an extra information, the attacker is able to recover T's secret key by using the ISD algorithm in Sect. 5.2.

6.1 Attack Model (with Ciphertexts Reusing)

The attack can be modeled as follows.

Step 0 (*Setup*). To begin with, we choose the proper parameters m, ϵ. Let $\mathrm{DFR}_{m,\epsilon}$ denote the decryption failure rate when both the secret key and error satisfying the (m, ϵ)-gathering property. Denote

$$p_{m,\epsilon} := \frac{|\mathrm{K}_{m,\epsilon}(w)|}{|\mathrm{K}(w)|} \text{ and } q_{m,\epsilon} := \frac{|\mathrm{E}_{m,\epsilon}(t/2, t/2)|}{|\mathrm{E}(t)|} \tag{37}$$

to be the probability that a random secret key (or a random error) satisfies the (m, ϵ)-gathering property.

Step 1 (*Ciphertexts Construction*). Initialize the set of ciphertexts to be C = {}. Randomly generate $1/(\mathrm{DFR}_{m,\epsilon} \cdot q_{m,\epsilon})$ seeds $m \in \{0,1\}^{256}$, then compute the errors $(e_0, e_1) = \mathtt{H}(m)$ according to the error generation step of BIKE. If an error (e_0, e_1) satisfies $w_H(e_0) = w_H(e_1) = t/2$ and the (m, ϵ)-gathering property, then add the corresponding ciphertext to C. On average, there will be $1/\mathrm{DFR}_{m,\epsilon}$ ciphertexts in C.

---

[3] To be more specific, the complexity of the key recovery step is the product of p_{true}^{-1} and $r \cdot T_{\mathrm{ISD}}$. For m around 4000, p_{true} increases faster than T_{ISD}, leading to a drop in the complexity of the key recovery step. But as m becomes very large, the complexity of the key recovery step will eventually approaches to 2^{128}.

Step 2 (*Query and Collect Decryption Failures*). For a target T, query T's decryption oracle to decrypt the ciphertexts in C. If a decryption failure occurs, then go to the key recovery step. Else, choose another target T', and repeat the query step.

Step 3 (*Recover the Secret Key*). For a target T that has a decryption failure, there is a probability p_{true} that T's secret key (h_0, h_1) satisfies the (m, ϵ)-gathering property. In this case, (h_0, h_1) can be efficiently recovered by using the modified ISD algorithm in Sect. 5.2. On the other hand, if (h_0, h_1) does not satisfy the (m, ϵ)-gathering property, it is unlikely the modified ISD algorithm can efficiently recover (h_0, h_1). Thus the attacker simply try to recover (h_0, h_1) by using the modified ISD algorithm. If (h_0, h_1) is recovered successfully, the attack terminates. Otherwise, the attacker chooses another target and repeats the query and key recovery steps.

Analysis of the Probability p_{true}. Let 'FAIL' denote the event that a decryption failure occurs for the secret key $\bar{h} := (h_0, h_1)$, and denote X := $\mathrm{K}(w) \times \mathrm{E}_{m,\epsilon}(t/2, t/2)$. Then it can be deduced that

$$p_{\text{true}} = \Pr_{(\bar{h}, \bar{e}) \xleftarrow{\$} X}[\bar{h} \in \mathrm{K}_{m,\epsilon}(w) \mid \text{FAIL}]$$
$$= \Pr_{(\bar{h}, \bar{e}) \xleftarrow{\$} X}[\text{FAIL} \mid \bar{h} \in \mathrm{K}_{m,\epsilon}(w)] \cdot \Pr_{(\bar{h}, \bar{e}) \xleftarrow{\$} X}[\bar{h} \in \mathrm{K}_{m,\epsilon}(w)] / \Pr_{(\bar{h}, \bar{e}) \xleftarrow{\$} X}[\text{FAIL}]$$
$$= \mathrm{DFR}_{m,\epsilon} \cdot p_{m,\epsilon} / \mathrm{DFR}_{\text{avg}}^{e \sim (m,\epsilon)}$$

by Bayes' theorem, where $\mathrm{DFR}_{\text{avg}}^{e \sim (m,\epsilon)} = \Pr_{(\bar{h}, \bar{e}) \xleftarrow{\$} X}[\text{FAIL}]$ is the average decryption failure rate for error drawn from $\mathrm{E}_{m,\epsilon}(t/2, t/2)$ and random key.

6.2   Complexity Analysis

The total complexity consists of three parts: the complexity of preprocessing (Step 1), the complexity of identifying decryption failures (Step 2) and the complexity of the key recovery step (Step 3).

The complexity of preprocessing. The complexity of preprocessing is determined by the total number of errors computed in Step 1, which is equal to

$$1/(\mathrm{DFR}_{m,\epsilon} \cdot q_{m,\epsilon}) \ . \tag{38}$$

The complexity of identifying decryption failures. On average, $1/p_{m,\epsilon}$ targets are required to obtain a secret key satisfying the (m, ϵ)-gathering property, which should result in a successful key recovery in Step 3. Thus Step 2 is called $1/p_{m,\epsilon}$ times. On the other hand, the number of decryption queries for a single target is $|\mathrm{C}| = 1/\mathrm{DFR}_{m,\epsilon}$. Thus the complexity of identifying decryption failures is

$$1/p_{m,\epsilon} \cdot 1/\mathrm{DFR}_{m,\epsilon} \ . \tag{39}$$

The complexity of the key recovery step. For the key recovery step, the probability that a secret key satisfying the (m, ϵ)-gathering property is p_{true}. Thus the complexity of the key recovery step is

$$1/p_{\text{true}} \cdot T_{\text{ISD}} , \tag{40}$$

where $p_{\text{true}} = \text{DFR}_{m,\epsilon} \cdot p_{m,\epsilon}/\text{DFR}_{\text{avg}}^{e\sim(m,\epsilon)}$ and T_{ISD} is the time complexity of a single call of the ISD algorithm as in Corollary 5.

Besides, note that the space complexity of Step 1 is $(\text{DFR}_{m,\epsilon})^{-1}$, thus the total space complexity of the key recovery attack is $(\text{DFR}_{m,\epsilon})^{-1} + S_{\text{ISD}}$, where S_{ISD} is the space complexity of a single call of the ISD algorithm. Therefore, the total complexity of the key recovery attack is as follows.

Theorem 3. *The key recovery attack in Sect. 6.1 can be mounted in time complexity*

$$C_{total} = (\text{DFR}_{m,\epsilon} \cdot q_{m,\epsilon})^{-1} + (\text{DFR}_{m,\epsilon} \cdot p_{m,\epsilon})^{-1} + p_{true}^{-1} \cdot T_{ISD}, \tag{41}$$

and space complexity $S_{MATCH} + \text{DFR}_{m,\epsilon}^{-1}$ where $p_{true} = \text{DFR}_{m,\epsilon} \cdot p_{m,\epsilon}/\text{DFR}_{avg}^{e\sim(m,\epsilon)}$. The number of targets required is $1/p_{m,\epsilon}$, the number of queries required for a single target is $1/(\text{DFR}_{m,\epsilon})$.

Concrete Attack Complexity for BIKE. Next, we consider BIKE's parameter set targeting 128-bit security. In this attack, we initialize $m = 5100, \epsilon = 1$. Then from Table 3 and Table 5 it has $p_{m,\epsilon} = 2^{-76.69}, q_{m,\epsilon} = 2^{-75.58}$, $\text{DFR}_{m,\epsilon} = 2^{-22.08}$, $T_{\text{ISD}} = 2^{75.86}$. To determine the concrete complexity of the key recovery attack, an upper bound on $\text{DFR}_{\text{avg}}^{e\sim(m,\epsilon)}$ must be established. Our experiments suggest that $\text{DFR}_{\text{avg}}^{e\sim(m,\epsilon)}$ is very close to the average decryption failure rate DFR_{avg} for small parameters. Additionally, through extrapolation method it can be deduced that $\text{DFR}_{\text{avg}}^{e\sim(m,\epsilon)} < 2^{-80}$ for BIKE's parameter set targeting 128-bit security. We refer to the full version of this work for further details. Therefore, it can be deduced from Theorem 3 that the total complexity is

$$C_{\text{total}} = 2^{98.77}, \tag{42}$$

where the number of targets required is $1/p_{m,\epsilon} = 2^{76.69}$, and the number of queries required for a single target is $1/(\text{DFR}_{m,\epsilon}) = 2^{22.08}$ (see Table 1 for the details).

7   Conclusion

We propose the gathering property for QC-MDPC and demonstrate its strong correlation with the decryption failure rate. By considering the secret keys satisfying the gathering property, we construct a new set of weak keys by using isomorphisms of the ring $\mathcal{R}$. For BIKE's parameter set targeting 128-bit security, we derive a lower bound on the average decryption failure rate $\text{DFR}_{\text{avg}} \geq 2^{-116.61}$.

We present two multi-target key recovery attacks against QC-MDPC based schemes with CCA security, as well as an analysis of their complexity for BIKE's parameter set targeting 128-bit security. The first attack prohibits ciphertexts reusing and has a complexity of $2^{116.61}$, while the second attack allows ciphertexts reusing and can attain a complexity of $2^{98.77}$.

There are many issues should be addressed in future work. For example, we exclusively consider $\epsilon = 0, 1$ due to the need for rigorous calculations of probability. A natural concern is whether $\epsilon \geq 2$ leads to stronger results on weak keys and better key recovery attacks. Besides, for the sake of simplicity, in our attack the filtered ciphertexts will satisfy $w_H(\mathbf{e_0}) = w_H(\mathbf{e_1}) = t/2$. It is expected that the gathering property performs better for unbalanced error weights, resulting in attacks with improved complexity.

Acknowledgments. We thank the anonymous reviewers from CRYPTO 2023 for the valuable comments. This work is supported by the National Key R&D Program of China (2020YFA0309705, 2018YFA0704701), Shandong Key Research and Development Program (2020ZLYS09), the Major Scientific and Technological Innovation Project of Shandong, China (2019JZZY010133), the Major Program of Guangdong Basic and Applied Research (2019B030302008), and Tsinghua University Dushi Program.

References

1. National institute of standards and technology: post-quantum cryptography project (2016). http://csrc.nist.gov/projects/post-quantum-cryptography
2. Alagic, G., et al.: Status report on the third round of the NIST post-quantum cryptography standardization process. US Department of Commerce, NIST (2022)
3. Aragon, N., et al.: BIKE. Technical report, National Institute of Standards and Technology (2022). http://csrc.nist.gov/Projects/post-quantum-cryptography/round-4-submissions
4. Aragon, N., Gaborit, P.: A key recovery attack against LRPC using decryption failures. In: International Workshop on Coding and Cryptography, WCC, vol. 2019 (2019)
5. Becker, A., Joux, A., May, A., Meurer, A.: Decoding random binary linear codes in $2^{n/20}$: how $1 + 1 = 0$ improves information set decoding. In: Pointcheval, D., Johansson, T. (eds.) EUROCRYPT 2012. LNCS, vol. 7237, pp. 520–536. Springer, Heidelberg (2012). https://doi.org/10.1007/978-3-642-29011-4_31
6. Berlekamp, E.R., McEliece, R.J., van Tilborg, H.C.A.: On the inherent intractability of certain coding problems (corresp.). IEEE Trans. Inf. Theor. **24**(3), 384–386 (1978). https://doi.org/10.1109/TIT.1978.1055873
7. Bindel, N., Schanck, J.M.: Decryption failure is more likely after success. In: Ding, J., Tillich, J.-P. (eds.) PQCrypto 2020. LNCS, vol. 12100, pp. 206–225. Springer, Cham (2020). https://doi.org/10.1007/978-3-030-44223-1_12
8. Blömer, J., May, A.: New partial key exposure attacks on RSA. In: Boneh, D. (ed.) CRYPTO 2003. LNCS, vol. 2729, pp. 27–43. Springer, Heidelberg (2003). https://doi.org/10.1007/978-3-540-45146-4_2
9. Chaulet, J.: Étude de cryptosystèmes à clé publique basés sur les codes MDPC quasi-cycliques. Ph.D. thesis, Paris 6 (2017)

10. Chaulet, J., Sendrier, N.: Worst case QC-MDPC decoder for McEliece cryptosystem. In: IEEE International Symposium on Information Theory, ISIT 2016, Barcelona, Spain, 10–15 July 2016, pp. 1366–1370. IEEE (2016). https://doi.org/10.1109/ISIT.2016.7541522

11. Chou, T.: QcBits: constant-time small-key code-based cryptography. In: Gierlichs, B., Poschmann, A.Y. (eds.) CHES 2016. LNCS, vol. 9813, pp. 280–300. Springer, Heidelberg (2016). https://doi.org/10.1007/978-3-662-53140-2_14

12. Coppersmith, D.: Small solutions to polynomial equations, and low exponent RSA vulnerabilities. J. Cryptol. **10**(4), 233–260 (1997). https://doi.org/10.1007/s001459900030

13. D'Anvers, J., Batsleer, S.: Multitarget decryption failure attacks and their application to saber and kyber. In: Hanaoka, G., Shikata, J., Watanabe, Y. (eds.) Proceedings of the 25th IACR International Conference on Practice and Theory of Public-Key Cryptography, PKC 2022, Virtual Event, Part I. LNCS, 8–11 March 2022, vol. 13177, pp. 3–33. Springer, Heidelberg (2022). https://doi.org/10.1007/978-3-030-97121-2_1

14. D'Anvers, J.P., Guo, Q., Johansson, T., Nilsson, A., Vercauteren, F., Verbauwhede, I.: Decryption failure attacks on IND-CCA secure lattice-based schemes. In: Lin, D., Sako, K. (eds.) 22nd International Conference on Theory and Practice of Public Key Cryptography, PKC 2019, Part II. LNCS, Beijing, China, 14–17 April 2019, vol. 11443, pp. 565–598. Springer, Heidelberg (2019). https://doi.org/10.1007/978-3-030-17259-6_19

15. D'Anvers, J.P., Rossi, M., Virdia, F.: (One) failure is not an option: bootstrapping the search for failures in lattice-based encryption schemes. In: Canteaut, A., Ishai, Y. (eds.) Advances in Cryptology, EUROCRYPT 2020, Part III. LNCS, Zagreb, Croatia, 10–14 May 2020, vol. 12107, pp. 3–33. Springer, Heidelberg (2020). https://doi.org/10.1007/978-3-030-45727-3_1

16. D'Anvers, J.P., Vercauteren, F., Verbauwhede, I.: The impact of error dependencies on ring/mod-LWE/LWR based schemes. In: Ding, J., Steinwandt, R. (eds.) 10th International Conference on Post-Quantum Cryptography, PQCrypto 2019, Chongqing, China, 8–10 May 2019, pp. 103–115. Springer, Heidelberg (2019). https://doi.org/10.1007/978-3-030-25510-7_6

17. den Boer, B., Bosselaers, A.: An attack on the last two rounds of MD4. In: Feigenbaum, J. (ed.) Advances in Cryptology, CRYPTO 1991. LNCS, Santa Barbara, CA, USA, 11–15 August 1992, vol. 576, pp. 194–203. Springer, Heidelberg (1992). https://doi.org/10.1007/3-540-46766-1_14

18. Drucker, N., Gueron, S., Kostic, D.: On constant-time QC-MDPC decoding with negligible failure rate. Cryptology ePrint Archive (2019)

19. Drucker, N., Gueron, S., Kostic, D.: QC-MDPC decoders with several shades of gray. In: Ding, J., Tillich, J.P. (eds.) 11th International Conference on Post-Quantum Cryptography, PQCrypto 2020, Paris, France, 15–17 April 2020, pp. 35–50. Springer, Heidelberg (2020). https://doi.org/10.1007/978-3-030-44223-1_3

20. Drucker, N., Gueron, S., Kostic, D., Persichetti, E.: On the applicability of the Fujisaki-Okamoto transformation to the BIKE KEM. Int. J. Comput. Math. Comput. Syst. Theor. **6**(4), 364–374 (2021). https://doi.org/10.1080/23799927.2021.1930176

21. Dumer, I.: On minimum distance decoding of linear codes. In: Proceedings of the 5th Joint Soviet-Swedish International Workshop on Information Theory, pp. 50–52 (1991)

22. Esser, A., May, A., Verbel, J.A., Wen, W.: Partial key exposure attacks on bike, rainbow and NTRU. In: Dodis, Y., Shrimpton, T. (eds.) Proceedings of the 42nd Annual International Cryptology Conference Advances in Cryptology, CRYPTO 2022, Part III. LNCS, Santa Barbara, CA, USA, 15–18 August 2022, vol. 13509, pp. 346–375. Springer, Heidelberg (2022). https://doi.org/10.1007/978-3-031-15982-4_12

23. Esser, A., May, A., Zweydinger, F.: McEliece needs a break - solving McEliece-1284 and quasi-cyclic-2918 with modern ISD. In: Dunkelman, O., Dziembowski, S. (eds.) Advances in Cryptology, EUROCRYPT 2022, Part III. LNCS, Trondheim, Norway, 30 May–3 June 2022, vol. 13277, pp. 433–457. Springer, Heidelberg (2022). https://doi.org/10.1007/978-3-031-07082-2_16

24. Fabsic, T., Hromada, V., Stankovski, P., Zajac, P., Guo, Q., Johansson, T.: A reaction attack on the QC-LDPC McEliece cryptosystem. In: Lange, T., Takagi, T. (eds.) 8th International Workshop on Post-Quantum Cryptography, PQCrypto 2017, Utrecht, The Netherlands, 26–28 June 2017, pp. 51–68. Springer, Heidelberg (2017). https://doi.org/10.1007/978-3-319-59879-6_4

25. Fujisaki, E., Okamoto, T.: How to enhance the security of public-key encryption at minimum cost. In: Imai, H., Zheng, Y. (eds.) 2nd International Workshop on Theory and Practice in Public Key Cryptography, PKC'99. LNCS, Kamakura, Japan, 1–3 March 1999, vol. 1560, pp. 53–68. Springer, Heidelberg (1999). https://doi.org/10.1007/3-540-49162-7_5

26. Gallager, R.: Low-density parity-check codes. IRE Trans. Inf. Theor. **8**(1), 21–28 (1962)

27. Gama, N., Nguyen, P.Q.: New chosen-ciphertext attacks on NTRU. In: Okamoto, T., Wang, X. (eds.) 10th International Conference on Theory and Practice of Public Key Cryptography, PKC 2007. LNCS, Beijing, China, 16–20 April 2007, vol. 4450, pp. 89–106. Springer, Heidelberg (2007). https://doi.org/10.1007/978-3-540-71677-8_7

28. Guo, Q., Johansson, T.: A new decryption failure attack against HQC. In: Moriai, S., Wang, H. (eds.) Advances in Cryptology, ASIACRYPT 2020, Part I. LNCS, Daejeon, South Korea, 7–11 December 2020, vol. 12491, pp. 353–382. Springer, Heidelberg (2020). https://doi.org/10.1007/978-3-030-64837-4_12

29. Guo, Q., Johansson, T., Stankovski, P.: A key recovery attack on MDPC with CCA security using decoding errors. In: Cheon, J.H., Takagi, T. (eds.) Advances in Cryptology, ASIACRYPT 2016, Part I. LNCS, Hanoi, Vietnam, 4–8 December 2016, vol. 10031, pp. 789–815. Springer, Heidelberg (2016). https://doi.org/10.1007/978-3-662-53887-6_29

30. Henecka, W., May, A., Meurer, A.: Correcting errors in RSA private keys. In: Rabin, T. (ed.) Advances in Cryptology, CRYPTO 2010. LNCS, Santa Barbara, CA, USA, 15–19 August 2010, vol. 6223, pp. 351–369. Springer, Heidelberg (2010). https://doi.org/10.1007/978-3-642-14623-7_19

31. Heyse, S., von Maurich, I., Güneysu, T.: Smaller keys for code-based cryptography: QC-MDPC McEliece implementations on embedded devices. In: Bertoni, G., Coron, J.S. (eds.) Cryptographic Hardware and Embedded Systems, CHES 2013. LNCS, Santa Barbara, CA, USA, 20–23 August 2013, vol. 8086, pp. 273–292. Springer, Heidelberg (20123). https://doi.org/10.1007/978-3-642-40349-1_16

32. Hofheinz, D., Hövelmanns, K., Kiltz, E.: A modular analysis of the Fujisaki-Okamoto transformation. In: Kalai, Y., Reyzin, L. (eds.) 15th Theory of Cryptography Conference, TCC 2017, Part I. LNCS, Baltimore, MD, USA, 12–15 November 2017, vol. 10677, pp. 341–371. Springer, Heidelberg (2017). https://doi.org/10.1007/978-3-319-70500-2_12

33. Horlemann, A.L., Puchinger, S., Renner, J., Schamberger, T., Wachter-Zeh, A.: Information-set decoding with hints. In: Wachter-Zeh, A., Bartz, H., Liva, G. (eds.) Code-Based Cryptography, CBCrypto 2021. LNCS, vol. 13150, pp. 60–83. Springer, Cham (2022). https://doi.org/10.1007/978-3-030-98365-9_4

34. Howgrave-Graham, N., et al.: The impact of decryption failures on the security of NTRU encryption. In: Boneh, D. (ed.) Advances in Cryptology, CRYPTO 2003. LNCS, Santa Barbara, CA, USA, 17–21 August 2003, vol. 2729, pp. 226–246. Springer, Heidelberg (2003). https://doi.org/10.1007/978-3-540-45146-4_14

35. Jaulmes, É., Joux, A.: A chosen-ciphertext attack against NTRU. In: Bellare, M. (ed.) Advances in Cryptology, CRYPTO 2000. LNCS, vol. 1880, pp. 20–35, Santa Barbara, CA, USA, 20–24 August 2000. Springer, Heidelberg (2020). https://doi.org/10.1007/3-540-44598-6_2

36. Kirshanova, E., May, A.: Decoding McEliece with a hint - secret Goppa key parts reveal everything. In: Galdi, C., Jarecki, S. (eds.) Proceedings of the 13th International Conference on Security and Cryptography for Networks, SCN 2022, Amalfi, Italy, 12–14 September 2022. LNCS, vol. 13409, pp. 3–20. Springer, Heidelberg (2022). https://doi.org/10.1007/978-3-031-14791-3_1

37. von Maurich, I., Güneysu, T.: Towards side-channel resistant implementations of QC-MDPC McEliece encryption on constrained devices. In: Mosca, M. (ed.) 6th International Workshop on Post-Quantum Cryptography, PQCrypto 2014, Waterloo, Ontario, Canada, 1–3 October 2014, pp. 266–282. Springer, Heidelberg (2014). https://doi.org/10.1007/978-3-319-11659-4_16

38. May, A., Meurer, A., Thomae, E.: Decoding random linear codes in $\tilde{\mathcal{O}}(2^{0.054n})$. In: Lee, D.H., Wang, X. (eds.) Advances in Cryptology, ASIACRYPT 2011. LNCS, Seoul, South Korea, 4–8 December 2011, vol. 7073, pp. 107–124. Springer, Heidelberg (2011). https://doi.org/10.1007/978-3-642-25385-0_6

39. McEliece, R.J.: A public-key cryptosystem based on algebraic Coding Theory, pp. 114–116. The Deep Space Network Progress Report, DSN PR 42-44 (1978)

40. Misoczki, R., Tillich, J., Sendrier, N., Barreto, P.S.L.M.: MDPC-McEliece: new McEliece variants from moderate density parity-check codes. In: Proceedings of the 2013 IEEE International Symposium on Information Theory, Istanbul, Turkey, 7–12 July 2013, pp. 2069–2073. IEEE (2013). https://doi.org/10.1109/ISIT.2013.6620590

41. Misoczki, R., Tillich, J.P., Sendrier, N., Barreto, P.S.: MDPC-McEliece: New McEliece variants from moderate density parity-check codes. In: 2013 IEEE International Symposium on Information Theory, pp. 2069–2073. IEEE (2013)

42. Niederreiter, H.: Knapsack-type cryptosystems and algebraic coding theory. Prob. Contr. Inform. Theor. **15**(2), 157–166 (1986)

43. Sendrier, N.: Decoding one out of many. In: Yang, B.Y. (ed.) 4th International Workshop on Post-Quantum Cryptography, PQCrypto 2011, Tapei, Taiwan, 29 November–2 December 2011, pp. 51–67. Springer, Heidelberg (2011). https://doi.org/10.1007/978-3-642-25405-5_4

44. Sendrier, N., Vasseur, V.: On the decoding failure rate of QC-MDPC bit-flipping decoders. In: Ding, J., Steinwandt, R. (eds.) 10th International Conference on Post-Quantum Cryptography, PQCrypto 2019, Chongqing, China, 8–10 May 2019, pp. 404–416. Springer, Heidelberg (2019). https://doi.org/10.1007/978-3-030-25510-7_22

45. Sendrier, N., Vasseur, V.: On the existence of weak keys for QC-MDPC decoding. Cryptology ePrint Archive (2020)

46. Shor, P.W.: Algorithms for quantum computation: discrete logarithms and factoring. In: 35th Annual Symposium on Foundations of Computer Science, Santa Fe, NM, USA, 20–22 November 1994, pp. 124–134. IEEE Computer Society Press (1994). https://doi.org/10.1109/SFCS.1994.365700

47. Tillich, J.: The decoding failure probability of MDPC codes. In: 2018 IEEE International Symposium on Information Theory, ISIT 2018, Vail, CO, USA, 17–22 June 2018, pp. 941–945. IEEE (2018). https://doi.org/10.1109/ISIT.2018.8437843

48. Vasseur, V.: Post-quantum cryptography: a study of the decoding of QC-MDPC codes. Ph.D. thesis, Université de Paris (2021)

49. Vasseur, V.: QC-MDPC codes DFR and the IND-CCA security of bike. HAL (2022)

50. Zhou, Y., van de Pol, J., Yu, Y., Standaert, F.X.: A third is all you need: extended partial key exposure attack on CRT-RSA with additive exponent blinding. In: Proceedings of the 28th International Conference on the Theory and Application of Cryptology and Information Security, Advances in Cryptology (ASIACRYPT 2022, Part IV), Taipei, Taiwan, 5–9 December 2022, pp. 508–536. Springer, Heidelberg (2023). https://doi.org/10.1007/978-3-031-22972-5_18

Graph-Theoretic Algorithms
for the Alternating Trilinear Form
Equivalence Problem

Ward Beullens[✉] [iD]

IBM Research, Zurich, Switzerland
wbe@zurich.ibm.com

Abstract. At Eurocrypt'22 Tang, Duong, Joux, Plantard, Qiao, and Susilo proposed a digital signature algorithm based on the hardness of the isomorphism problem of alternating trilinear forms. They propose three concrete parameters in dimensions 9, 10, and 11 respectively. We give new heuristic algorithms that solve this problem more efficiently. With our new algorithms, the first parameter set can be broken in less than a day on a laptop. For the second parameter set, we show there is a 2^{-17} fraction of the public keys that can also be broken in less than a day. We do not break the third parameter set in practice, but we claim it falls short of the target security level of 128 bits.

1 Introduction

We are interested in the Alternating Trilinear Form Equivalence (ATFE) problem, which is defined as follows:

Definition 1 (ATFE). *Given a pair of equivalent alternating trilinear forms $\phi_1, \phi_2 \in ATF(\mathbb{F}_q^n)$, the ATFE problem asks to find an equivalence $S \in GL(\mathbb{F}_q^n)$ such that $\phi_2(x, y, z) = \phi_1(Sx, Sy, Sz)$.*

This problem was shown to be complete for the Tensor Isomorphism complexity class (TI) [15,26], and believed to be hard on average, even for quantum algorithms. Therefore, the authors of [25] argued that ATFE is a good basis for post-quantum cryptography, and they proposed a digital signature algorithm based on the hardness of the ATFE problem. They propose three concrete instances of the ATFE problem, using alternating trilinear forms in dimensions 9, 10, and 11 over fields of order $524287, 131071$, and 65521 respectively. Their signature scheme fits in a family of signature schemes based on the GMW zero-knowledge proof protocol for Graph isomorphisms [14], which has been generalized to many isomorphism problems, resulting in isogeny-based [5,11,13], multivariate [22], and code-based [6] signature algorithms. Some of these signature schemes have been broken in practice because the isomorphism problems turned out to be easier to solve than expected [3,7].

Ward Beullens holds Junior Post-Doctoral fellowship 1S95620N from the Research Foundation Flanders (FWO).

© International Association for Cryptologic Research 2023
H. Handschuh and A. Lysyanskaya (Eds.): CRYPTO 2023, LNCS 14083, pp. 101–126, 2023.
https://doi.org/10.1007/978-3-031-38548-3_4

After the work of [25], the ATFE problem has been used to construct ring signatures independently by D'Alconzo and Gangemi [12] and Chen *et al.* [10], both using the framework of Beullens, Katsumata, and Pintore [4]. Leroux and Roméas [20] construct an updateable encryption scheme based on the hardness ATFE. To have confidence in the security of these cryptographic systems, and to be able to pick secure parameter sets, it is important to investigate the concrete hardness of the ATFE problem.

Contributions. In this paper we give new heuristic algorithms for solving the ATFE problem. Since our main motivation is to break the cryptosystem proposed by [25] we focus on dimensions 9, 10 and 11. Our results are summarized in Table 1. Our new algorithms are more efficient than existing algorithms and can solve the ATFE problems proposed by [25] in dimension 9 in at most 4 h. We also show that a $1/q$ fraction of the proposed ATFE problems in dimension 10 can be solved in practice in approximately 1.5 h. We do not break the proposed parameter set in dimension 11, but we estimate that it can be broken in 2^{60} core-hours on modern CPUs, which means that the signature scheme is less secure than the target security level of 128 bits. Our algorithm of Sect. 7 exploits a connection between alternating trilinear forms in dimension 9 and Abelian surfaces.

Implementations of some (parts of) of our algorithms, including a complete implementation of our $O(q)$ algorithm for solving the ATFE problem in dimension 9, and the algorithms to reproduce Table 2 are publicly available through the following link:

https://github.com/WardBeullens/BreakingATFE .

Table 1. Algorithms for solving the ATFE problem in dimensions 9, 10 and 11.

Dimension n	Algorithm	Complexity (# field ops.)	Note
9	Tang *et al.* [25]	$O(q^7)$	At rank $R = 6$
	Section 5.3	$O(q^2)$	At rank $R = 4$
	Section 7	$O(q)$	Practical for $q = 524287$.
10	Tang *et al.* [25]	$O(q^7)$	At rank $R = 6$
	Section 5.3	$O(q^6)$	At rank $R = 6$
	Section 6	$O(1)$	Works only for $1/q$-fraction of instances. Practical for $q = 131071$
11	Tang *et al.* [25]	$O(q^9)$	At rank $R = 6$
	Section 5.3	$O(q^4)$	At rank $R = 6$

2 Preliminaries

Let $\mathbb{F}_q$ be a prime field of odd characteristic. We denote by $\mathcal{S}(q,n)$ be the space of skew-symmetric n-by-n matrices over $\mathbb{F}_q$.

Projective space and projective frames. Let V be an n-dimensional vector space over a field $\mathbb{F}_q$. This defines a projective space $\mathbb{P}(V) := V \setminus \{0\} \mod \sim$, where $\mathbf{u} \sim \mathbf{v}$ if there exists $\alpha \in \mathbb{F}_q$ such that $\mathbf{u} = \alpha \mathbf{v}$. We denote the equivalence class of $\mathbf{u} \in V$ as $\bar{\mathbf{u}}$. It is well known that if $\mathbf{b}_1, \ldots, \mathbf{b}_n$ is a basis for V, we can uniquely represent vectors $\mathbf{v}$ in V with n coordinates $\alpha_1, \ldots, \alpha_n \in \mathbb{F}_q$, such that $\mathbf{v} = \sum_{i=1}^{n} \alpha_i \mathbf{b}_i$. Analogously, we call a sequence of $n+1$ projective points $\bar{\mathbf{b}}_1, \ldots, \bar{\mathbf{b}}_{n+1} \in \mathbb{P}(V)$ a projective frame (or projective basis) if no n of them are contained in a hyperplane of $\mathbb{P}(V)$. One can always pick representatives for the projective points in a frame such that $\sum_{i=1}^{n} \mathbf{b}_i = \mathbf{b}_{n+1}$, and this choice of representatives is unique up to multiplication by a scalar in $\mathbb{F}_q$. So, given a projective frame, we can represent any projective point $\bar{\mathbf{v}} \in \mathbb{P}(V)$ in terms of homogeneous coordinates α_i such that $\sum_i \alpha_i \mathbf{b}_i = \mathbf{v}$, and this representation is unique up to multiplication by a scalar in $\mathbb{F}_q$.

Alternating trilinear forms. A trilinear form on V is a function $\phi : V \times V \times V \to \mathbb{F}_q$ that is linear in each of its three arguments, e.g., $\phi(\alpha \mathbf{u} + \mathbf{u}', \mathbf{v}, \mathbf{w}) = \alpha \phi(\mathbf{u}, \mathbf{v}, \mathbf{w}) + \phi(\mathbf{u}', \mathbf{v}, \mathbf{w})$ for all $\mathbf{u}, \mathbf{u}', \mathbf{v}, \mathbf{w} \in V$ and all $\alpha \in \mathbb{F}_q$. We say a trilinear form ϕ is *alternating* if $\phi(\mathbf{u}, \mathbf{v}, \mathbf{w}) = 0$ when at least two of the three inputs are equal. Let $\mathbf{b}_1, \ldots, \mathbf{b}_n$ be a basis for V, and let $\mathbf{b}_1^*, \ldots, \mathbf{b}_n^*$ be the corresponding dual basis. The alternating trilinear forms make up an $\mathbb{F}_q$-vectorspace, and a basis is given by trilinear forms $\mathbf{b}_i^* \wedge \mathbf{b}_j^* \wedge \mathbf{b}_k^*$, where $1 \le i < j < k \le n$, which are defined as

$$(\mathbf{b}_i^* \wedge \mathbf{b}_j^* \wedge \mathbf{b}_k^*)(\mathbf{u}, \mathbf{v}, \mathbf{w}) := \begin{vmatrix} \mathbf{b}_i^*(\mathbf{u}) & \mathbf{b}_j^*(\mathbf{u}) & \mathbf{b}_k^*(\mathbf{u}) \\ \mathbf{b}_i^*(\mathbf{v}) & \mathbf{b}_j^*(\mathbf{v}) & \mathbf{b}_k^*(\mathbf{v}) \\ \mathbf{b}_i^*(\mathbf{w}) & \mathbf{b}_j^*(\mathbf{w}) & \mathbf{b}_k^*(\mathbf{w}) \end{vmatrix},$$

which implies that the space of alternating trilinear forms has dimension $\binom{n}{3}$. We denote the space of alternating trilinear forms on V by $\mathrm{ATF}(V)$.

Radicals. If ϕ is an alternating trilinear form and $\mathbf{u} \in V$, then we denote by $\phi_{\mathbf{u}}$ the alternating bilinear form $\phi_{\mathbf{u}}(\mathbf{v}, \mathbf{w}) := \phi(\mathbf{u}, \mathbf{v}, \mathbf{w})$. Similarly, for $\mathbf{u}, \mathbf{v} \in V$ we define the linear form $\phi_{\mathbf{u}, \mathbf{v}}(\mathbf{w}) := \phi(\mathbf{u}, \mathbf{v}, \mathbf{w})$. We define the *radical* $\mathrm{Rad}(\phi)$ of a trilinear form ϕ as the space $\{\mathbf{x} \mid \phi_{\mathbf{x}} = 0\}$. We say ϕ is *non-degenerate* if $\mathrm{Rad}(\phi)$ is trivial. For a vector $\mathbf{u} \in V$ we define $\mathrm{Rad}_\phi(\mathbf{u}) := \{\mathbf{x} \mid \phi_{\mathbf{u}, \mathbf{x}} = 0\}$, and we say the *rank* of $\mathbf{u}$ (with respect to ϕ) is the rank of $\phi_{\mathbf{u}}$, which equals the codimension of $\mathrm{Rad}_\phi(\mathbf{u})$. Note that $\mathrm{Rad}_\phi(\mathbf{u})$ always contains $\langle \mathbf{u} \rangle$ (because ϕ is alternating), so the rank of $\mathbf{u}$ is always strictly smaller than n. Moreover, $\mathrm{rank}(\mathbf{u})$ is always even.

Solving the MinRank problem. Our algorithms for solving the equivalence problem of alternating trilinear forms will use a subroutine to solve the MinRank problem. Given k matrices $\mathbf{M}_1, \ldots, \mathbf{M}_k \in \mathbb{F}_q^{n \times n}$ and a target rank r, the MinRank problem asks to find a linear combination $\sum_i \alpha_i \mathbf{M}_i$ with rank at most r. This problem has been studied relatively well because it is relevant for the security of many cryptosystems. We will use the MinRank-solving algorithm of [1]. Let $\mathbf{M} = \sum_i \alpha_i \mathbf{M}_i$ be the rank-r linear combination that we are looking for, and let $\mathbf{M} = \mathbf{HC}$ with $\mathbf{H} \in \mathbb{F}_q^{n \times r}$ and $\mathbf{C} \in \mathbb{F}_q^{r \times n}$ be a rank-decomposition of $\mathbf{M}$. If $\mathbf{M}^{(j)} = \sum \alpha_i \mathbf{M}_i^{(j)}$ is the j-th row of $\mathbf{M}$, then the matrix

$$\begin{pmatrix} \mathbf{M}^{(j)} \\ C \end{pmatrix}$$

obtained by adding $\mathbf{M}^{(j)}$ on top of $\mathbf{C}$ has rank r, so all $\binom{n}{r+1}$ of its $(r+1)$-by-$(r+1)$ minors vanish. The idea behind the algorithm of [1] is that after doing a cofactor expansion along the top row we get a bilinear equation in the coefficients α_i and the r-by-r minors of C of which there are $\binom{n}{r}$. We then try to solve a system of equations, whose variables are the α_i and the minors of C, by linearization. We expect this system of equations to have a unique solution if the number of equations $n\binom{n}{r+1}$ is at least the number of monomials $k\binom{n}{r}$, which happens if $n(n-r) \geq (r+1)k$ and if the MinRank problem has a unique solution. The bottleneck of the algorithm is doing linear algebra on a square matrix of size $k\binom{n}{r}$, which would take $O(k^3\binom{n}{r}^3)$ field operations with Gaussian elimination. However, we can take advantage of the sparsity of the matrix and solve the system with the Wiedemann solver in $O(k^3 r \binom{n}{r}^2)$ field operations instead [1].

3   The Graph of Alternating Trilinear Forms

Let $\phi \in \text{ATF}(V)$ be an alternating trilinear form, then we can define a graph G_ϕ, as the undirected graph with vertex set $\mathbb{P}(V)$, and where $(\bar{\mathbf{u}}, \bar{\mathbf{v}}) \in \mathbb{P}(V)^2$ is an edge in G_ϕ if and only if $\phi_{\mathbf{u},\mathbf{v}} = 0$. This graph is an invariant of alternating trilinear forms, introduced by Hora and Pudlák to classify all the trilinear forms over $\mathbb{F}_2$ in dimensions 8 and 9 [18,19].[1] Hora and Pudlák observed that

$$\deg(\bar{\mathbf{v}}) = \frac{q^{n-\text{rank}(\mathbf{v})} - q}{q - 1},$$

because $\bar{\mathbf{u}}$ is a neighbour of $\bar{\mathbf{v}}$ precisely if $\bar{\mathbf{u}} \neq \bar{\mathbf{v}}$ and $\mathbf{u} \in \text{Rad}_\phi(\mathbf{v})$.

In the remainder of this section, we compute the average number of points of each rank, and the number of edges between them.

Theorem 2. *Let $n \in \mathbb{N}$ and let $n - d$, $n - d_1$, and $n - d_2$ be non-negative even numbers less than n. Then, as q goes to infinity, the average number of projective*

---

[1] For dimension 8 over $\mathbb{F}_2$, the graph invariant distinguishes all the alternating trilinear forms up to isomorphism, in dimension 9 more invariants are needed.

points $\bar{\mathbf{u}} \in \mathbb{P}(\mathbb{F}_q^n)$ with $\text{rank}(\bar{\mathbf{u}}) = n - d$ of a uniformly randomly trilinear form $\phi \in ATF(\mathbb{F}_q^n)$ tends to

$$q^{(-d^2+3d)/2+n-2},$$

and the average number of ordered edges $(\bar{\mathbf{u}}_1, \bar{\mathbf{u}}_2)$ in the graph G_ϕ with $\bar{\mathbf{u}}_1$ of rank $n - d_1$ and $\bar{\mathbf{u}}_2$ of rank $n - d_2$ tends to

$$q^{\frac{-d_1^2 - d_2^2 + 5(d_1 + d_2)}{2} + n - 6}.$$

Examples. We apply the theorem to dimensions $9, 10$, and 11, because those are the parameters proposed by [25].

- In dimension $n = 9$, the graph of a random form ϕ has on average close to q^2 points of rank 4, q^7 points of rank 6, the average number of $(4, 4)$-edges and $(4, 6)$-edges tends to q^3 and q^6 respectively. This means that rank-4 points have on average q rank-4 neighbours and q^4 rank-6 neighbours, and each rank 6 point has on average $1/q$ neighbours of rank 4.
- In dimension $n = 10$, the average number of rank-4 points tends to $1/q$. We exploit this in Sect. 6 by giving a very efficient key-recovery attack that works for a $1/q$ fraction of all keys. The average number of rank-6 points is q^6.
- In dimension $n = 11$, the average number of rank-6 and rank-8 points tends to q^4 and q^9 respectively, each rank-6 point has on average close to q rank-6 neighbours and q^4 rank-8 neighbours. Rank-8 points have on average $1/q$ rank-6 neighbours.

Note that the first part of the statement agrees with the experimental observations in [25] (Table 3), where the authors observed that for randomly chosen ϕ, there are close to $q^{n-1}, q^{n-3}, q^{n-6}$, and q^{n-10} vectors of rank $n - 3, n - 4, n - 5$, and $n - 6$ respectively. Finding a proof for these rank statistics was left as an open problem. Before we prove the theorem, we first give an approximation for the probability that a random-skew symmetric matrix has a certain rank.

Lemma 3. Let n, d be integers, such that $0 \leq n - d \leq n$ and $n - d$ is even, then

$$\Pr_{M \leftarrow \mathcal{S}(q,n)} [M \text{ has rank } n - d] \sim q^{(-d^2+d)/2} \text{ as } q \to \infty$$

Proof. This approximation can be obtained by starting from a theorem by Carlitz [9] that says that the number of skew-symmetric n-by-n matrices over $\mathbb{F}_q$ with rank $2r$ is

$$q^{r(r-1)} \frac{\prod_{i=0}^{2r-1}(q^{m-i} - 1)}{\prod_{i=1}^{r}(q^{2i} - 1)}.$$

Dividing this quantity by $q^{n(n-1)/2}$ (the total number of skew-symmetric matrices) we get an exact expression for the probability of interest. Then, we replace the $(q^{m-i}-1)$ and $(q^{2i}-1)$ factors by q^{m-i} and q^{2i} respectively and simplify the result to get a nicer-looking approximation that is valid for q going to infinity. $\square$

Now we give the proof of Theorem 2.

Proof. For the first part of the theorem, it suffices to compute the probability that an arbitrary $\mathbf{v} \in \mathbb{P}(\mathbb{F}_q^n)$ has rank $r = n - d$, so let $\mathbf{v} \neq 0$ be an arbitrary non-zero vector in $\mathbb{F}_q^n$.

Extend $\mathbf{v}$ to a basis $\mathbf{v} = \mathbf{v}_1, \mathbf{v}_2, \dots, \mathbf{v}_n$ of $\mathbb{F}_q^n$. Then, with respect to this basis, the bilinear form $\phi_\mathbf{v}$ has a matrix representation $\phi_\mathbf{v}(\sum_i y_i \mathbf{v}_i, \sum_i z_i \mathbf{v}_i) = \mathbf{y}^t M \mathbf{z}$, with

$$M = \begin{pmatrix} 0 & 0_{1 \times (n-1)} \\ 0_{(n-1) \times 1} & M' \end{pmatrix},$$

where M' is a uniformly random $(n-1)$-by-$(n-1)$ skew-symmetric matrix. Therefore, it follows from Lemma 3 that if $n - d$ is even, the probability that $\phi_\mathbf{v}$ has rank $n - d$ tends to

$$q^{(-(d-1)^2 + (d-1))/2} = q^{(-d^2 + 3d - 2)/2}.$$

The number of projective points in $\mathbb{P}(\mathbb{F}_q^n)$ tends to q^{n-1}, so by the linearity of expectation, the average number of points of rank $n - d$ tends to

$$q^{(-d^2 + 3d)/2 + n - 2}.$$

To prove the second part of the theorem, we similarly compute the probability that an arbitrary pair of distinct projective points $\mathbf{v}_1, \mathbf{v}_2 \in \mathbb{P}(\mathbb{F}_q^n)$ is an edge in G_ϕ, with $\mathbf{v}_1$ of rank $n - d_1$ and $\mathbf{v}_2$ of rank $n - d_2$.

Extend $\mathbf{v}_1, \mathbf{v}_2$ to a basis $\mathbf{v}_1, \dots, \mathbf{v}_n$ of $\mathbb{F}_q^n$. With respect to this basis, the bilinear forms $T_{\mathbf{v}_1}$ and $T_{\mathbf{v}_2}$ have matrix representations

$$M_{\mathbf{v}_1} = \begin{pmatrix} 0 & 0 & 0 \\ 0 & 0 & \mathbf{a}^t \\ 0 & -\mathbf{a} & M'_1 \end{pmatrix} \text{ and } M_{\mathbf{v}_2} = \begin{pmatrix} 0 & 0 & -\mathbf{a}^t \\ 0 & 0 & 0 \\ \mathbf{a} & 0 & M'_2 \end{pmatrix},$$

where $\mathbf{a} \in \mathbb{F}_q^{n-2}$ and $M'_{\mathbf{v}_1}, M'_{\mathbf{v}_2} \in \mathbb{F}_q^{(n-2) \times (n-2)}$ are uniformly random. Now $([\mathbf{v}_1], [\mathbf{v}_2])$ is an edge in the graph G_T if and only if $\mathbf{a} = 0$, which happens with probability q^{-n+2}. And if this is the case, then $[\mathbf{v}_1]$ and $[\mathbf{v}_2]$ have ranks r_1 and r_2 if $M'_{\mathbf{v}_1}$ and $M'_{\mathbf{v}_2}$ have ranks r_1 and r_2 respectively. Lemma 3 says that this happens with probabilities that tend to

$$q^{\frac{(d_1-2)^2 + (d_1-2)}{2}} \text{ and } q^{\frac{(d_2-2)^2 + (d_2-2)}{2}}$$

respectively. Since the number of ordered pairs of projective points tends to q^{2n-n}, it follows from the linearity of expectation that the average number of

$(n - d_1, n - d_2)$-edges in G_ϕ tends to

$$q^{2n-2}q^{-n-2}q^{\frac{(d_1-2)^2+(d_1-2)}{2}}q^{\frac{(d_2-2)^2+(d_2-2)}{2}} = q^{n-6+\frac{-d_1^2-d_2^2+5(d_1+d_2)}{2}}.$$

$\square$

4 Solving **ATFE** with Auxiliary Information via Gröbner Bases

This section describes the Gröbner basis-based approach to solving the ATFE problem with auxiliary information, which we will use as a subroutine for our algorithms to solve ATFE without auxiliary information. We also give some improvements that make the subroutine run faster in practice.

The algorithm of [7]. Bouillaguet, Faugère, Fouque, and Perret suggest solving the ATFE problem, using a Gröbner basis approach [7]. This works as follows: let S be an n-by-n matrix whose entries $\{s_{ij}\}$ we consider to be formal variables and use a system-solving algorithm to find the solutions of the system

$$\phi_2(x, y, z) = \phi_1(Sx, Sy, Sz).$$

This is a system of $\binom{n}{3}$ cubic equations in the n^2 variables $\{s_{ij}\}$, and the solutions precisely correspond to the isomorphisms from ϕ_1 to ϕ_2. We can also consider a second matrix T (which represents the inverse of S) with entries $\{t_{ij}\}$, and then solve the system

$$\begin{cases} ST = TS = \mathbf{1}_n \\ \phi_2(x, y, z) = \phi_1(Sx, Sy, Sz) \\ \phi_2(x, y, Tz) = \phi_1(Sx, Sy, z) \\ \phi_2(x, Ty, Tz) = \phi_1(Sx, y, z) \\ \phi_2(Tx, Ty, Tz) = \phi_1(x, y, z) \end{cases}.$$

This is a system of $2n^2 + 4\binom{n}{3}$ equations in $2n^2$ variables. It turns out that solving the second system is more efficient because we now have many quadratic equations, which are generally easier to solve than cubic equations. Nevertheless, it seems that solving the systems of equations is still exponentially hard. An instance of the problem with $n = 7, q = 16$ was solved by [7] in five hours with 3 GB of RAM, but the same approach failed for $n = 8$ after running out of memory (74 GB was available). However, Bouillaguet *et al.* observed that the problem becomes much easier when some auxiliary information in the form of $\mathbf{u}, \mathbf{v} \in \mathbb{F}_q^n$ such that $S\mathbf{v} = \mathbf{u}$ is available. In this case, after adding the n linear equations $S\mathbf{v} = \mathbf{u}$ to the system, the system can be solved at degree 2 with time complexity $O(n^6)$. This makes it possible to solve an instance with $n = 16, q = 2$ in only 90 s [7].

Improvements and experiments. We observe that we can use slightly less auxiliary information and still have an efficient algorithm: we can use a pair of projective points $\bar{\mathbf{u}}, \bar{\mathbf{v}} \in \mathbb{P}(\mathbb{F}_q^n)$ such that $S\bar{\mathbf{u}} = \bar{\mathbf{v}}$, rather than affine points $\mathbf{u}, \mathbf{v}$ such that $S\mathbf{u} = \mathbf{v}$ exactly. This means that the system of equations has just one fewer linear equation, which does not seem to affect the running time of the Gröbner basis algorithm too much. This is advantageous because finding projective points $\bar{\mathbf{u}}$ and $\bar{\mathbf{v}}$ such that $S\bar{\mathbf{u}} = \bar{\mathbf{v}}$, is easier than finding affine points $\mathbf{u}, \mathbf{v}$ such that $S\mathbf{u} = \mathbf{v}$.

The algorithm of [25] and our algorithms of Sect. 5.3 solve instances of the ATFE problem with auxiliary information $\bar{\mathbf{v}} = S\bar{\mathbf{u}}$, where $\bar{\mathbf{u}}$ and $\bar{\mathbf{v}}$ are points of low rank for ϕ_1 and ϕ_2 respectively. We can exploit this to speed up the system-solving approach because we know that $S\operatorname{Rad}_{\phi_2}(\mathbf{v}) = \operatorname{Rad}_{\phi_1}(\mathbf{u})$ and $\operatorname{Rad}_{\phi_2}(\mathbf{v}) = T\operatorname{Rad}_{\phi_1}(\mathbf{u})$. This gives $2R(n - R - 1)$ additional linear equations on the variables $\{s_{ij}\}$ and $\{t_{ij}\}$, which can be used to eliminate some variables to make the system solving approach more efficient in practice.

We do some experiments on a laptop (intel i9-10885H CPU and 64 GB of RAM), using the Gröbner basis implementation of the Giac library which is accessible through Sage [21,27]. We solve some instances of the ATFE problem with auxiliary information that we will need in Sect. 5.3. Unlike Bouillaguet *et al.* , who did experiments for trilinear forms that were not necessarily alternating and with auxiliary points that did not have low rank, we notice that the Gröbner basis algorithm does not always terminate at degree 2. Nevertheless, the algorithm is efficient enough to run in practice in a reasonable amount of time. The results are given in Table 2. We notice that the Gröbner-basis solving algorithm always finds three solutions, because if (S, T) is a solution, then $(\alpha S, \alpha^2 T)$ and $(\alpha^2 S, \alpha T)$ are also solutions, where $\alpha \in \overline{\mathbb{F}}_q$ is a third root of unity.

Table 2. Solving several ATFE problems with auxiliary information with SAGE.

(n, q)	Rank of $\bar{\mathbf{u}}$ and $\bar{\mathbf{v}}$	Number of variables	Time (seconds)	Memory (MB)
$(9, 524287)$	6	122	270	4312
	4	114	5	305
$(10, 131071)$	6	146	1000	8971
	4	142	4800	18486
$(11, 65521)$	6	174	200	1097

5   Algorithms for the Alternating Trilinear Form Equivalence Problem

This section describes some heuristic algorithms for the ATFE problem. We first revisit the algorithms of [7,25], before introducing new algorithms.

5.1   The Algorithms of [7, 25]

$O(q^n n^6)$ **algorithm.** It follows from the algorithm in the previous section that to solve the ATFE problem it suffices to find a good pair of vectors $\mathbf{u}, \mathbf{v}$ such that $S\mathbf{v} = \mathbf{u}$. Just taking a pair $(\mathbf{e}_1, \mathbf{u})$ where $\mathbf{u} \in \mathbb{F}_q^n$ is uniformly random has a success probability of $|\mathrm{Aut}(\phi)|q^{-n}$. Randomly chosen alternating trilinear forms in dimension $n \geq 10$ seem to have no non-trivial automorphisms, so for random trilinear forms, the algorithm of [7] runs in time $O(q^n n^6)$.

$O(q^{2n/3}\mathrm{poly}(n))$ **algorithm.** The authors of [25] improve on this approach, using the fact that if $\mathbf{u}$ has rank r for ϕ_2, then $S\mathbf{u}$ must also have rank r for ϕ_1. Their algorithm is parametrized by a rank R. Let N_R be the number of vectors in $\mathbb{F}_q^n$ with rank R for ϕ_1. Then in the first phase the algorithm computes two lists L_1, L_2 of $O(N_R^{1/2})$ vectors of rank R for ϕ_1 and ϕ_2 respectively. This is done by brute force: repeatedly pick $\mathbf{u} \in \mathbb{F}_q^n$ at random, compute the rank of $\phi_{1\mathbf{u}}$ and keep the vector if the rank is equal to R. This takes on average q^n/N_R attempts per vector, so it makes for a total cost of $O(q^n N_R^{-1/2}\mathrm{poly}(n))$. Then, with high probability, there is a vector $\mathbf{u} \in L_1$ and $\mathbf{v} \in L_2$ such that $S\mathbf{u} = \mathbf{v}$. We do not know which pair is the good one, so in the second phase, we run the system-solving algorithm of Sect. 4 for every pair $(\mathbf{u}, \mathbf{v}) \in L_1 \times L_2$, for a total cost of $O(N_R n^6)$. The complexity of the algorithm is optimal if the rank R is chosen such that $N_R \approx q^{3n/2}$. If such an R exists, we get an algorithm that runs in time $O(q^{2n/3}\mathrm{poly}(n))$.

5.2   A General MinRank-Based Algorithm

Using MinRank solving algorithms. We generalize the algorithm of [25] to allow for more efficient algorithms to build the lists L_1 and L_2. From the trilinearity of ϕ, we have that $\phi_{\mathbf{v}} = \sum_i v_i \phi_{\mathbf{e}_i}$, where v_i is the i-th coordinate of $\mathbf{v}$ with respect to the standard basis $\mathbf{e}_i, \ldots, \mathbf{e}_n$. Therefore, as observed by [25], finding the coefficients of a low-rank vector $\mathbf{v}$ for ϕ is equivalent to finding a low-rank linear combination of the alternating bilinear forms $\phi_{\mathbf{e}_1}, \ldots \phi_{\mathbf{e}_n}$, which is an instance of the MinRank problem which we discussed in Sect. 2. The algorithm uses a target rank R, and samples $O(\sqrt{N_R})$ (projective) solutions to the MinRank instances corresponding to ϕ_1 and ϕ_2. Then we try all the $O(N_R)$ pairs of points $(\bar{\mathbf{u}}, \bar{\mathbf{v}}) \in L_1 \times L_2$. This makes for a complexity of

$$O(\sqrt{N_R}\,\mathsf{MR}_{n,r} + N_R n^6),$$

where N_R is now the number of *projective* points of rank R, and where $\mathsf{MR}_{n,R}$ denotes the complexity of sampling a solution to the MinRank instance derived from an alternating trilinear form ϕ in dimension n, and with target rank R. Unfortunately, it seems cumbersome to get good estimates of $\mathsf{MR}_{n,R}$. This is because the matrices in our MinRank problem are structured: they represent the bilinear forms $\phi_{\mathbf{e}_i}$, so the matrices are antisymmetric, have zeroes on the i-th row and column, and $(\phi_{\mathbf{e}_i})_{j,k} = -(\phi_{\mathbf{e}_j})_{i,k} = (\phi_{\mathbf{e}_k})_{i,j}$. This seems to adversely affect the performance of the MinRank solving algorithm of Bardet et al. [1], because there are non-trivial linear dependencies between the equations in the support minors modeling. It would be interesting to rigorously investigate how this structure affects the performance of existing MinRank-solving algorithms, and perhaps design more efficient MinRank-solving algorithms that can take advantage of this structure, especially for large n. We do not estimate the running time of this algorithm and we move on to the more efficient approach of the next subsection where rather than solving MinRank instances to populate the lists L_1 and L_2 directly, we use an approach that is more efficient for small n which exploits walking in the G_ϕ graph. This approach only uses the MinRank subroutine on instances from Table 2, which are easy enough so that we can implement the MinRank solver and observe the running time of the solver directly, so we do not need a thorough theoretical understanding of the efficiency of the MinRank solver for the purpose of estimating the cost of breaking the parameter sets proposed by [25].

5.3   Graph-Walking Algorithms for Small n

In this section, we exploit the fact that once a low-rank point $\bar{\mathbf{v}} \in \phi$ is found, we can look for its low-rank neighbours in the graph G_ϕ to find additional low-rank vectors more efficiently.

Odd dimensions. In odd dimensions, according to Theorem 2, there are approximately q^{n-2} points of rank $n-3$, which makes a $1/q$ fraction of all points. So, to sample a point of rank $n-3$ by brute force takes $O(q\,\mathrm{poly}(n))$ work. However, once a single point $\bar{\mathbf{v}}$ of rank $n-3$ is found, we can sample additional rank-$(n-3)$ vectors with only $O(\mathrm{poly}(n))$ effort, by just sampling one of the neighbours of $\bar{\mathbf{v}}$.

Lemma 4. *Let n be odd, and let $\bar{\mathbf{v}}$ be a projective point with rank at most $n-3$ for an alternating trilinear form ϕ. Then the neighbours of $\bar{\mathbf{v}}$ in the graph G_ϕ also have rank at most $n-3$.*

Proof. Suppose $\bar{\mathbf{v}}$ is a neighbour of $\bar{\mathbf{u}}$, then we have that $\langle \bar{\mathbf{u}}, \bar{\mathbf{v}} \rangle \in \mathrm{Rad}(\bar{\mathbf{v}})$, so the rank of $\bar{\mathbf{v}}$ is $n - \dim(\mathrm{Rad}(\bar{\mathbf{v}})) < n-2$, but the rank has to be even, so $\bar{\mathbf{v}}$ must have rank at most $n-3$. $\qquad\square$

Is it useful to generate many points of rank $n-3$? We could use the algorithm from the previous subsection at rank $R = n-3$, but that would get a complexity q^{n-2}, which does not improve on the brute-force algorithm of [25]. However, rank-$(n-3)$ points are quite likely to have rank-$(n-5)$ neighbours! Theorem 2 says that the number of $(n-3, n-5)$-edges in G_ϕ is approximately q^{n-3}. Recall that there are q^{n-2} rank $(n-3)$ points, so we expect that a $1/q$-fraction of rank $n-3$ points have a rank-$(n-5)$ neighbour.

This suggests the following approach for sampling rank $n-5$ points: starting from a point of rank $n-3$, do a random walk in G_ϕ, and at each point $\bar{\mathbf{v}}$ check if $\bar{\mathbf{v}}$

has a neighbour of rank $n-5$. We expect this to succeed after $O(q)$ steps. Checking if $\bar{\mathbf{v}}$ has a rank $n-5$ neighbour is efficient, because the neighbours of $\bar{\mathbf{v}}$ form a space of dimension 3, so we only have to solve a MinRank instance with 3 matrices of size n-by-n and target rank $n-5$. We can do this with the support-minors algorithm of [1] with a complexity of $O(k^3 r \binom{n}{r}^2) = O(n\binom{n}{n-5}^2) = O(n^{11})$. The complexity $O(n^{11})$ might seem impractical, but the bottleneck of the algorithm is doing linear algebra on a sparse matrix with $3\binom{n}{5}$ columns, which for $n=9$ and $n=11$ is only 378 and 1386 columns respectively, which is still very practical.

If we run the algorithm from the previous section at rank $R = n-5$ with the graph-walking approach we get a complexity of

$$O(q^{(n-5)/2}n^{11} + q^{n-7}n^6).$$

Which for small n is better than the algorithm of [25]. For large enough q, the running time of the algorithm is dominated by the second phase, which runs Gröbner basis algorithms for each of the approximately $N_{n-5} = q^{n-7}$ pairs $(\bar{\mathbf{u}}, \bar{\mathbf{v}}) \in L_1 \times L_2$. Two of the three parameter sets proposed by [25] have odd n, these are $(n, q) = (9, 524287)$ and $(n, q) = (11, 65521)$. For these parameters the bottleneck of the algorithm is running $524287^2 \approx 2^{38}$ and $65521^4 \approx 2^{64}$ executions of the Gröbner basis algorithm respectively. Given that a Sage implementation of the Gröbner basis algorithm takes approximately 5 s and 200 s for these parameter sets (see Table 2), we can conclude that these parameters fall short of their target security level of 128 bits of security. Nevertheless, a practical break still seems out of reach.

Even dimension. We now adapt the attack to the case of an even dimension. Note that in this case, all points have rank at most $n-2$, since the rank has to be even, and less than n. Moreover, according to Theorem 2, the number of $(n-2, n-4)$ edges and the number of rank-$(n-2)$ points are both q^{n-1}, so we expect most rank-$(n-2)$ points to have one rank-$(n-4)$ neighbour. Finding a rank-$(n-4)$ neighbour of a rank-$(n-2)$ point $\bar{\mathbf{u}}$ comes down to solving a MinRank problem with only 2 n-by-n matrices M_1, M_2, corresponding to $\phi_{\mathbf{u}}, \phi_{\mathbf{v}}$, where $\mathbf{u}, \mathbf{v}$ is a basis for $\mathrm{Rad}_\phi(\mathbf{u})$. This problem can be solved by computing and factoring the gcd of a few determinants of $(n-3)$-by-$(n-3)$ minors of $M_1 + \lambda M_2$. This approach allows us to sample points of rank $n-4$ with $O(n^3)$ field operations, resulting in an algorithm for the ATFE problem with complexity

$$O(\sqrt{N_{n-4}}\, n^3 + N_{n-4}\, n^6) = O(q^{(n-4)/2}n^3 + q^{n-4}\, n^6).$$

For $n = 10$, this becomes a $O(q^6)$ algorithm, only slightly better than the algorithm of [25] which has a complexity of $O(q^7)$. We believe it is better to use rank $R = n-6$ for larger n, but we leave an analysis of the complexity for future work since we are mostly interested in dimensions $n = 9, 10$ and 11.

5.4   A (Sketch of An) Algorithm Using Graph-Neighbourhood Invariants

We would like to have more invariants to distinguish points in alternating trilinear forms, by which we mean functions

$$F : \mathrm{ATF}(\mathbb{F}_q^n) \times \mathbb{P}(\mathbb{F}_q^n) \to X : (\phi, \bar{\mathbf{v}}) \mapsto F(\phi, \bar{\mathbf{v}}),$$

such that $F(\phi, \bar{\mathbf{v}}) = F(\phi \circ S, S^{-1}\bar{\mathbf{v}})$ for all $S \in GL(\mathbb{F}_q^n)$. We already heavily used one of these invariants, namely $\mathrm{rank}_\phi(\bar{\mathbf{v}})$, but if we had a more powerful invariant we could speed up the second phase of our ATFE algorithm. Instead of running the Gröbner basis algorithm for all pairs $(\bar{\mathbf{u}}, \bar{\mathbf{v}}) \in L_1 \times L_2$, we only need to consider pairs $(\bar{\mathbf{u}}, \bar{\mathbf{v}})$ such that $F(\phi_1, \bar{\mathbf{u}}) = F(\phi_2, \bar{\mathbf{v}})$. If the invariant is sufficiently powerful such that there are no false positives, then we would only have to do a single Gröbner basis computation. This would reduce the complexity of the attack to

$$O(\sqrt{N_R} \,(\mathsf{MR}_{n,R} + T_F) + n^6),$$

where T_F is the time it takes to compute the invariant F. We have a few candidates for invariants, based on the graphs of alternating trilinear forms. We know that if $\phi_2 = \phi_1 \circ S$, then the graphs G_{ϕ_1} and G_{ϕ_2} are isomorphic, and we have an explicit isomorphism given by $\Psi_S : G_{\phi_2} \to G_{\phi_1} : \bar{\mathbf{v}} \mapsto S\bar{\mathbf{v}}$. Similarly, the restrictions of G_{ϕ_1} and G_{ϕ_1} to points of rank R are also isomorphic with the same isomorphism. Therefore, following the approach of Bouillaguet et al. [8] for the closely related "Isomorphism of Polynomials" problem, we can define a family of invariants $F_{k,r}(\phi, \bar{\mathbf{v}})$ that outputs a canonical representation of the radius-k-neighbourhood of $\bar{\mathbf{u}}$ in the restriction of G_ϕ to points of rank r.

In dimension 9, it turns out that with high probability the graph is vertex-transitive, which means the graph invariants do not have any distinguishing power. However, for larger n, preliminary experiments suggest that the graphs invariants can distinguish points quite well, even for small radii (e.g. 1 or 2), so we conjecture that this approach gives rise to an algorithm that runs in time $O(q^{n/2+c} \,\mathrm{poly}(n))$ for some constant c.

6   A Class of Weak Keys for $n = 10$

Theorem 2 says that a random alternating trilinear form in dimension $n = 10$ has on average q^{-1} points of rank 4, which suggests that a random trilinear form has a unique rank-4 point with probability close to $1/q$. We can confirm this experimentally for small q. Moreover, if the rank-4 point exists, we can find it efficiently by solving a MinRank problem with 10 matrices of dimensions 10-by-10 and a target rank of 4. This gives an efficient 2-step attack on a $1/q$ fraction of all public keys: Firstly, try to find the unique rank-4 points $\bar{\mathbf{u}}, \bar{\mathbf{v}}$ in ϕ_1 and ϕ_2 respectively. Secondly, if the points exist, run the Gröbner basis algorithm from Sect. 4 to find the equivalence S such that $\phi_2 = \phi_1 \circ S$, using the auxiliary information that $\bar{\mathbf{u}} = S\bar{\mathbf{v}}$.

We observe that this works quite well in practice for the $(n, q) = (10, 131071)$ parameter set proposed in [25]. Our Sage script can find the rank-4 point in ϕ_1 and ϕ_2 in roughly 16 min each, by solving the associated MinRank problem. After finding the two rank-4 points (which can be done in parallel using two cores) we can solve for the equivalence $S \in GL(\mathbb{F}_q^{10})$ such that $\phi_2 = \phi_1 \circ S$ with the Gröbner basis approach from Sect. 4. This takes approximately 1 h and 20 min (see Table 2). The total attack takes approximately one hour and 36 min on the author's laptop.[2]

7   The Curious Case of $n = 9$

In this section, we observe that for randomly chosen alternating trilinear forms in dimension 9, the restriction of G_ϕ to points of rank 4 has a lot of structure, which we can exploit to formulate a heuristic algorithm for the ATFE problem in dimension 9. Our algorithm runs in time $O(q)$ and works well in practice. We can solve the ATFE problem for the $n = 9$ parameter set proposed by [25] in at most 4 h on the author's laptop. We also observe that if the number of points of rank 4 is divisible by 2^r, then the attack runs in time $O(q/\sqrt{2^r})$. This gives a family of weak keys for which the attack is slighty faster. Empirically, the number of points seems to be divisible by 2^r with a probability that is slightly larger than 2^{-r}.

7.1   Graph-Neighbourhood Invariants

According to Theorem 2, a random alternating trilinear form $\phi \in \text{ATF}(\mathbb{F}_q^9)$ has on average close to q^2 points of rank 4, and the graph G_ϕ, restricted to the rank-4 points has on average $q^3/2$ edges, meaning that the average point in the graph has degree q. We start our investigation by computing and plotting the rank-4 graphs for some 9-dimensional alternating trilinear forms: Figure 1 displays the rank-4 graphs of a selection of five typical alternating trilinear forms modulo $q = 5$. We see that the graphs are surprisingly nice:

Observation 1. *Let $\phi \in \text{ATF}(\mathbb{F}_q^9)$ be a uniformly random form, let $G_{4,\phi}$ be the restriction of G_ϕ to points of rank 4, and let $N_4 = |G_{4,\phi}|$ be the number of points of rank 4. Then with high probability $G_{4,\phi}$ has dihedral symmetry Dih_{N_4}. In particular, $G_{4,\phi}$ is vertex-transitive and has at least $2N_4$ automorphisms.*

Figure 2 shows some counterexamples, where the graphs are not regular or do not have the dihedral symmetry, but even these counterexamples are 'nice' in the

---

[2] To do the experiments, we deliberately generate weak keys with a point of rank 4, by first generating a random alternating trilinear form ϕ' for which $\text{Rad}'_\phi(e_1) = \langle e_1, \ldots, e_6 \rangle$, so that e_1 has rank 4 and then composing ϕ with a random invertible map $T \in GL(\mathbb{F}_q^{10})$ to send the rank-4 point to some random position. Every form with a point of rank-4 is isomorphic to a form ϕ' where $\text{Rad}_{\phi'}(e_1) = \langle e_1, \ldots, e_6 \rangle$, so this method of generating instances does not introduce additional structure that could affect the hardness of finding the rank-4 point or the Gröbner basis step.

sense that they have a lot of automorphisms and that they are almost regular: there are at most two distinct degrees. For $q = 5$ the irregular graphs are still fairly common, making up about 20% of the randomly sampled forms, but for larger q the irregular graphs seem to become increasingly rare. We computed the rank-4 graph for 25 randomly chosen forms with $q = 31$, and they were all regular with dihedral symmetry Dih_{N_4}. This is unfortunate because it means the graph-based invariants from Sect. 5.4 are completely useless in dimension $n = 9$. Since the graph is vertex-transitive, the neighbourhoods of any two vertices look the same, so we can not use the graphs to distinguish good pairs $(\mathbf{u}, \mathbf{v})$ from bad pairs.

7.2   A Mysterious Function H

Since the graph-based invariants fail, we try to construct some other invariants. We start only from a form ϕ and a point $\bar{\mathbf{v}} \in \mathbb{P}(\mathbb{F}_q^9)$ of rank 4. What objects can we build from this information? We have $K = \mathrm{Rad}_\phi(\mathbf{v})$, which is a 5-dimensional space, so it is natural to look at $\phi|_K$, the restriction of ϕ to K. The isomorphism class of this 5-dimensional form is an invariant. Unfortunately, this invariant is not very powerful, because $\phi|_K$ is degenerate ($\phi(\mathbf{v}, \mathbf{x}, \mathbf{y}) = 0$ for all $\mathbf{x}, \mathbf{y} \in K$), and it turns out that up to isomorphism there are only two degenerate forms in dimension 5, namely 0 and $\mathbf{e}_1^* \wedge \mathbf{e}_2^* \wedge \mathbf{e}_3^*$, so we get at most one bit of information from the invariant. Even worse, $\phi|_K = 0$ is extremely unlikely, so we get essentially no information from the isomorphism class of $\phi|_K$. However, $\mathrm{Rad}(\mathbf{e}_1^* \wedge \mathbf{e}_2^* \wedge \mathbf{e}_3^*) = \langle \mathbf{e}_4, \mathbf{e}_5 \rangle$ is two-dimensional, so we have identified a new space $R = \mathrm{Rad}(\phi|_K) \subset K$.

We can use this space R to speed up the system-solving algorithm from Sect. 4. We know that if $\phi_2 = \phi_1 \circ S$ and if $(\bar{\mathbf{u}}, \bar{\mathbf{v}})$ is a good pair of points (i.e., $\bar{\mathbf{u}} = S\bar{\mathbf{v}}$), then we must have that $SR_{\phi_2, \mathbf{v}} = R_{\phi_1, \mathbf{u}}$ and $R_{\phi_2, \mathbf{v}} = TR_{\phi_1, \mathbf{u}}$, which gives us some additional linear constraints on the entries of S and T, meaning that we can eliminate some more variables before applying the generic system-solving algorithm.

Encouraged by this small victory, we keep looking for more canonical spaces that we can construct from a 9-dimensional form ϕ and a rank-4 point $\bar{\mathbf{u}}$. We have $q + 1$ points in R, namely $\bar{\mathbf{u}}$ and q new points. Let $\bar{\mathbf{v}} \in R$ be one of the new points. We can look at its radical $\mathrm{Rad}_\phi(\bar{\mathbf{v}})$, which has dimension at least 3, because it has to be odd, and it includes R. This space is not canonical, because it relies on the choice of $\bar{\mathbf{u}}$ in $R \setminus \{\bar{\mathbf{u}}\}$, but the sum of all these spaces is canonical. This suggests we define a new space

$$W = \sum_{\substack{\bar{\mathbf{v}} \in R \\ \bar{\mathbf{v}} \neq \bar{\mathbf{u}}}} \mathrm{Rad}_\phi(\bar{\mathbf{v}}) \, .$$

According to our experiments, this space is four-dimensional with high probability, and not included in K. This space W is canonical, so it also gives us

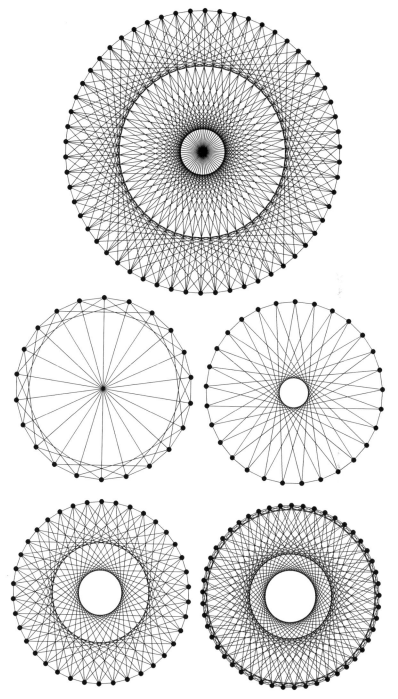

Fig. 1. Five typical rank-4 subgraphs of G_ϕ for randomly chosen alternating trilinear forms $\phi \in \mathrm{ATF}(\mathbb{F}_5^9)$. The graphs are regular and have Dihedral symmetry.

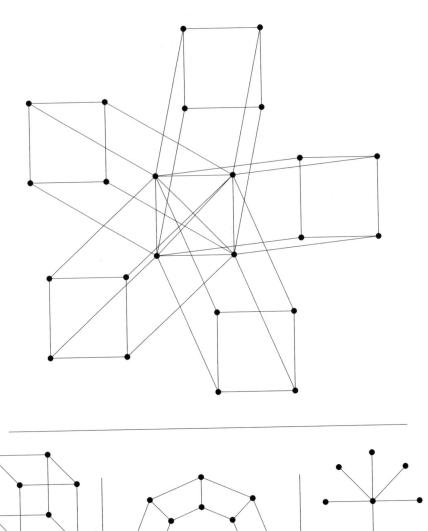

Fig. 2. A selection of four 'atypical' rank-4 graphs for alternating trilinear forms on $\mathbb{F}_5^9$. The top graph has graph automorphism group $Dih_4 \times S_5$, and the bottom graphs have automorphism groups (from left to right) $\mathbb{Z}_2 \times (\mathbb{Z}_2 \times S_4)^2$, $\mathbb{Z}_2 \times Dih_8$, and $\mathbb{Z}_2 \times S_5^2$.

some extra linear constraints on S and T that help speed up the system-solving algorithm. However, we observe something remarkable:

Observation 2. *For random $\phi \in ATF(\mathbb{F}_q^9)$ and $\bar{\mathbf{u}} \in \mathbb{P}(\mathbb{F}_q^9)$ of rank 4, with high probability, we have that the space W contains exactly two points of rank 4, $\bar{\mathbf{u}}$ and some other point that we call $H_\phi(\bar{\mathbf{u}})$. If $\bar{\mathbf{u}}$ is the only rank-4 point in W, we define $H_\phi(\bar{\mathbf{u}}) := \bar{\mathbf{u}}$. With high probability this defines a function H_ϕ, mapping the set of rank-4 points of ϕ to itself.*

For small q, it happens sometimes that the function H_ϕ is not well-defined, because some W contains more than 2 rank-4 points. However, we observe that as q grows, the function H_ϕ seems well defined at every point with increasingly high probability.

The meaning of H. To investigate this a priori mysterious function H, we calculate and plot the directed graph of H_ϕ whose nodes are the rank-4 points of ϕ, and where there is an edge from $\bar{\mathbf{v}}$ to $\bar{\mathbf{u}}$ if $H_\phi(\bar{\mathbf{v}}) = \bar{\mathbf{u}}$. (Self edges are not drawn.) Some results can be seen in Fig. 3. Even though the definition of H might seem arbitrary, we can see that the graphs have remarkable structure! We observe that if the number of rank-four points is $2^d k$, with k odd, then the graph of H_ϕ is typically a collection of 2-volcano graphs with height d. That is, the nodes of each connected component can be partitioned in $d+1$ levels $V_0, \ldots, V_d$, where V_0 is a regular graph of degree $0, 1$ or 2, where $H(V_{i+1}) = V_i$ for $0 \leq i < d$, where each node in V_0 has exactly one incoming edge from V_1, and where each node in V_i has exactly two incoming edges from V_{i+1} for $1 \leq i < d$. The subgraph V_0 is called the *crater*, and V_d is called the *floor*. These ℓ-volcano graphs also appear in the study of isogenies between elliptic curves over finite fields [24]. The graphs on the left side of Fig. 3 are drawn in a way to emphasize the 2-volcano structure. The same graphs are drawn on the right-hand side where the points are arranged in the circle according to the dihedral symmetry of G_ϕ. More precisely, we pick an elementary rotation r in $D_{N_4} \subset \mathrm{Aut}(G_\phi)$, and an arbitrary base point $\bar{\mathbf{u}}_0$. Then, since r acts transitively, we can label the rank-4 points as $\bar{\mathbf{u}}_i = r^i(\bar{\mathbf{u}}_0)$ for i going from 0 to $N_4 - 1$. We plot the point $\bar{\mathbf{u}}_i$ on the i-th location along a circle. From this plot, it is clear that $H_\phi(\bar{\mathbf{u}}_i) = \bar{\mathbf{u}}_{-2i+a \mod N_4}$ for some value of a. Note that this explains the 2-volcano structure. The value of a is not meaningful since it depends on the elementary rotation r and the base point $\bar{\mathbf{u}}_0$ that we chose to label the points.

This picture suggests that there is a group structure on the set of point of rank-4, and that our function H is $\bar{\mathbf{v}} \mapsto [-2]\bar{\mathbf{v}} + \bar{\mathbf{u}}$ for some rank-4 point $\bar{\mathbf{u}}$, and it turns out that this is indeed the case. It seems well known to algebraic geometers that to each alternating nine-dimensional trilinear form $\phi \in \mathrm{ATF}(\mathbb{F}_q^9)$, one can associate a torsor over an abelian surface A_ϕ in $\mathbb{P}(\mathbb{F}_q^9)$ [2,16,17,23]. Moreover, the set of rank-4 nodes for ϕ that we are using in our attack are exactly the $\mathbb{F}_q$-rational points on the abelian surface A_ϕ. After promoting an arbitrary point of A_ϕ to be the identity, we get a group structure on A_ϕ, and Proposition 6.1 of the work of Benedetti, Manivel, and Tanturri [2] give a concrete description of this group law which is analogous to the well-known chord-tangent group law for elliptic curves:

Given two generic rank-4 points $\bar{\mathbf{u}}$ and $\bar{\mathbf{v}}$, there exists a unique third rank-4 point $\bar{\mathbf{w}} \in \mathbb{P}(\mathbb{F}_q^9)$ such that

$$\phi_{\bar{\mathbf{u}},\bar{\mathbf{v}}} \sim \phi_{\bar{\mathbf{u}},\bar{\mathbf{w}}} \sim \phi_{\bar{\mathbf{v}},\bar{\mathbf{w}}} \, ,$$

which we can think of as "the third point on A_ϕ and on the line through $\bar{\mathbf{u}}$ and $\bar{\mathbf{v}}$". After fixing an identity elements, we get a group law in the same way as in the elliptic curve case. Our H-function fits into this analogy as $H(\bar{\mathbf{u}})$ being "the second point on A_ϕ and the line tangent to A_ϕ at $\bar{\mathbf{u}}$", which is indeed the function $\bar{\mathbf{u}} \mapsto [-2]\bar{\mathbf{u}} + \bar{\mathbf{v}}$, where $\bar{\mathbf{v}}$ is some fixed point that depends on the choice of the identity element. (In the elliptic curve setting where the elliptic curve is in Weierstass form and the identity is chosen to be the point at infinity the second point on the line tangent at P is $[-2]P$, but if we choose a different identity the second point on the tangent is in general $[-2]P + Q$ for some Q that is not necessarily O.)

It turns out that for the three examples in Fig. 3 the rational 2-torsion of A_ϕ is cyclic (trivial in the third example), which explains the 2-volcano structure of the graphs. We have also found examples (see Fig. 4) where H is 4-to-1 and 8-to-1, which correspond to the case where the rational 2-torsion of A_ϕ is $(\mathbb{Z}/2\mathbb{Z})^2$ or $(\mathbb{Z}/2\mathbb{Z})^3$ respectively. So far, we have not seen any examples where the 2-torsion is $(\mathbb{Z}/2\mathbb{Z})^4$.

7.3 Turning H into an Invariant

Since the function H does not depend on a choice of a coordinate system, we have that H is covariant, i.e.

$$H_{\phi \circ S}(S^{-1}\bar{\mathbf{v}}) = S^{-1}H_\phi(\bar{\mathbf{v}})$$

for any $S \in GL(\mathbb{F}_q^n)$. We can turn this into an invariant by iterating the function and using projective frames. Starting from $\bar{\mathbf{v}}$, we build a canonical projective frame by iterating the function H_ϕ on $\bar{\mathbf{v}}$. This gives a sequence $\bar{\mathbf{v}}, H_\phi(\bar{\mathbf{v}}), H_\phi^2(\bar{\mathbf{v}}), \ldots$ from which we can drop an element if it is not independent of its predecessors. We continue this procedure until we have full projective frame $\bar{\mathbf{v}}_1, \ldots, \bar{\mathbf{v}}_{10}$. It could happen that we never get a full projective frame, e.g. if the sequence is periodic with a period less than 10, but this does not seem to happen often for large enough q.

Now, to create an invariant, we sample one additional element $\bar{\mathbf{v}}_{11}$ from the sequence $\{H_\phi^i(\bar{\mathbf{v}})\}$ and we write it in homogeneous coordinates with respect to our canonical frame. If we were to compute the invariant for $\phi \circ S, S^{-1}\bar{\mathbf{u}}$, then we get the sequence $H_{\phi \circ S}(S^{-1}\bar{\mathbf{u}})$, which is equal to $S^{-1}H_\phi(\bar{\mathbf{u}})$. This means that the canonical projective frame is just $S^{-1}\bar{\mathbf{v}}, \ldots, S^{-1}\bar{\mathbf{v}}_{10}$ and the additional point is $S^{-1}\bar{\mathbf{v}}_{11}$. The homogeneous coordinates of $S^{-1}\bar{\mathbf{v}}_{11}$ with respect to the frame $S^{-1}\bar{\mathbf{v}}, \ldots, S^{-1}\bar{\mathbf{v}}_{10}$ are the same as those of $\bar{\mathbf{v}}_{11}$ with respect to $\bar{\mathbf{v}}_1, \ldots, \bar{\mathbf{v}}_{10}$, so

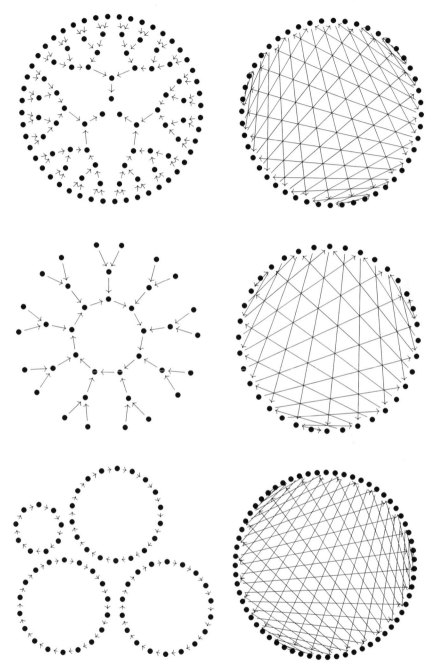

Fig. 3. Directed graphs corresponding to the H-function for three alternating trilinear forms. Each graph is drawn twice: once on the left in a way to make the 2-volcano structure of the graph clear, and once on the right where we arrange the rank-4 points in a circle according to the symmetry of G_ϕ. The three forms have 48, 36, and 63 points of rank 4 respectively.

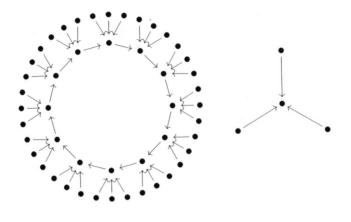

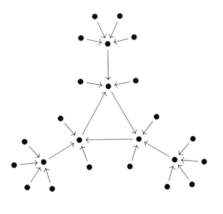

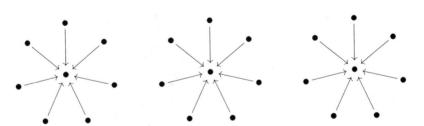

Fig. 4. Directed graphs corresponding to the H-function for three alternating trilinear forms (separated by horizontal lines) ϕ whose corresponding abelian surfaces A_ϕ have a 2-torsion that is non-cyclic. The first two surfaces have 2-torsion $(\mathbb{Z}/2\mathbb{Z})^2$, and the last one $(\mathbb{Z}/2\mathbb{Z})^3$, which you can tell because the H-functions are 4-to-1 and 8-to-1 respectively.

they are indeed an invariant. We observe that with high probability, this invariant is perfect.

Observation 3. *Let $\phi \in ATF(\mathbb{F}_q^9)$ be a uniformly random form. Let $F(\phi, \bar{\mathbf{v}})$ be the invariant that outputs the homogeneous coordinates of $\bar{\mathbf{v}}_{11}$ with respect to the canonical frame $\bar{\mathbf{v}}_1, \ldots, \bar{\mathbf{v}}_{10}$ as described above. We observe that this invariant is well-defined with high probability if q is large enough. Moreover, with high probability, the invariant is perfect, in the sense that $F(\phi, \bar{\mathbf{v}}) = F(\phi, \bar{\mathbf{v}}')$ if and only if there is an automorphism of ϕ that sends $\bar{\mathbf{v}}$ to $\bar{\mathbf{v}}'$.*

7.4   Using F to Solve the ATFE Problem

Now that we have a perfect invariant that is efficiently computable, we can instantiate the algorithm of Sect. 5.4. The idea is to compute lists L_1 containing pairs $(\bar{\mathbf{v}}, F(\phi_1, \bar{\mathbf{v}}))$, and L_2 containing $(\bar{\mathbf{u}}, F(\phi_2, \bar{\mathbf{u}}))$ where the $\bar{\mathbf{v}}$ and $\bar{\mathbf{u}}$ are rank-4 points for ϕ_1 and ϕ_2 respectively. We keep extending the lists until we have a collision $F(\phi_1, \bar{\mathbf{v}}) = F(\phi_2, \bar{\mathbf{u}})$, which happens after computing an expected number of $O(\sqrt{N_4})$ invariants. Since the invariant is perfect with high probability, we can assume that if a collision occurs, then there exists an isomorphism $S \in GL(\mathbb{F}_q^9)$ such that $\phi_2 = \phi_1 \circ S$ and $S\bar{\mathbf{u}} = \bar{\mathbf{v}}$, so given $\bar{\mathbf{v}}$ and $\bar{\mathbf{u}}$ we can efficiently find S with the system-solving approach of Sect. 4.

We can apply three optimizations: first, instead of computing the invariants for randomly chosen rank-4 points $\bar{\mathbf{u}}$ and $\bar{\mathbf{v}}$, we first take $s = \lceil 2\log_2 q \rceil$ steps in the H_ϕ-graph. That is, we sample an rank-4 element $\bar{\mathbf{u}}$, but we compute the invariant for $H_\phi^s(\bar{\mathbf{u}})$. This ensures that we compute the invariant for points on the crater of one of the 2-volcanoes. If the number of rank-4 points is $N_4 = 2^d k$, then there are only k points on the craters, so we will find the first collision after computing in expectation only $O(\sqrt{k})$ invariants, a speedup of a factor $O(\sqrt{2^d})$.

Secondly, recall that to compute a single invariant we need to compute a chain $\bar{\mathbf{v}}, H_\phi^1(\bar{\mathbf{v}}), H_\phi^2(\bar{\mathbf{v}}), \ldots$ of length at least $s + 11$. We can speed up the construction of the list L_1 by roughly a factor $s + 11$, by first computing a chain of length $L \gg s + 11$ (e.g. $L = 20(s + 11)$), and then extracting roughly $L - s - 11$ invariants from this long chain. We should only use this optimization for the list L_1. The probability that $F(\phi_2, H_\phi^s(\bar{\mathbf{v}}))$ collides with an invariant in L_1 is strongly correlated with the probability that $F(\phi_2, H_\phi^{s+1}(\bar{\mathbf{v}}))$ results in a collision, so if we were to use the optimization also for L_2 we can no longer expect to find a collision after computing $O(\sqrt{k})$ invariants. Since extending the list L_1 is a factor $s + 11$ cheaper than extending the list L_2, we get an optimal running time if we choose $|L_1| \approx (s + 11)|L_2|$.

Finally, we can avoid the system-solving approach of [7]. If $S\bar{\mathbf{v}} = \bar{\mathbf{u}}$, then also $SH_{\phi_2}^i(\bar{\mathbf{v}}) = H_{\phi_1}^i(\bar{\mathbf{u}})$ for all i. Therefore we can just recompute the canonical projective frame for $\bar{\mathbf{v}}$ and $\bar{\mathbf{u}}$, and output the unique linear map that sends the frame of $\bar{\mathbf{u}}$ to the frame of $\bar{\mathbf{v}}$. This is simpler and more efficient than the system-solving approach of [7], but it does not make a significant difference to the overall cost of running the algorithm, since this last step was cheap compared to the cost of finding the collision $(\bar{\mathbf{u}}, \bar{\mathbf{v}})$.

The optimized algorithm goes as follows:

Input: Two isomorphic alternating trilinear forms $\phi_1, \phi_2 \in \text{ATF}(\mathbb{F}_q^n)$.
Output: $S \in GL(\mathbb{F}_q^n)$ such that $\phi_2 = \phi_1 \circ S$.

0. Initialize empty lists L_1, L_2. Set $s = \lceil 2 \log_2(q) \rceil$ and $L = 20(s + 11)$.
1. Find a point $\bar{\mathbf{w}}_1$ of rank 6 for ϕ_1 e.g., by brute force or by solving a MinRank problem. Similarly, find $\bar{\mathbf{w}}_2$ of rank 6 for ϕ_2.
2. (Grow list L_1)

2a. Sample $\bar{\mathbf{u}}_0$ of rank 4 by walking in the G_{ϕ_1} graph: Set $\bar{\mathbf{w}}_1 \xleftarrow{\$}$ $\text{Rad}_{\phi_1}(\bar{\mathbf{w}}_1)$, and check if there exists $\bar{\mathbf{u}} \in \text{Rad}_{\phi_1}(\bar{\mathbf{w}}_1)$ of rank 4 by solving a MinRank problem with 3 matrices and target rank 4. Repeat until a $\bar{\mathbf{u}}_0$ of rank 4 is found.
2b. Compute a chain $\bar{\mathbf{u}}_0, \bar{\mathbf{u}}_1 = H_{\phi_1}(\bar{\mathbf{u}}), \bar{\mathbf{u}}_2 = H_{\phi_1}^2(\bar{\mathbf{u}}), \ldots, \bar{\mathbf{u}}_L = H_{\phi_1}^L(\bar{\mathbf{u}})$ of length $L + 1$.
2c. For i from s to $L - 11$, compute $F(\phi_1, \bar{\mathbf{u}}_i)$, by extracting a projective frame from the sequence starting at $\bar{\mathbf{u}}_i$, and writing the next point in the sequence in homogeneous coordinates with respect to this frame. Add all the pairs $(\bar{\mathbf{u}}_i, F(\phi_1, \bar{\mathbf{u}}_i))$ to the list L_1.

3. (Grow list L_2)

3a. Sample $\bar{\mathbf{v}}$ of rank 4 by walking in the G_{ϕ_2} graph: Set $\bar{\mathbf{w}}_2 \xleftarrow{\$}$ $\text{Rad}_{\phi_1}(\bar{\mathbf{w}}_2)$, and check if there exists $\bar{\mathbf{v}} \in \text{Rad}_{\phi_2}(\bar{\mathbf{w}}_2)$ of rank 4 by solving a MinRank problem with 3 matrices and target rank 4. Repeat until a $\bar{\mathbf{v}}$ of rank 4 is found.
3b. Compute $F(\phi_2, H_{\phi_2}^s(\bar{\mathbf{v}}))$ and add $(H_{\phi_2}^s(\bar{\mathbf{v}}), F(\phi_2, H_{\phi_2}^s(\bar{\mathbf{v}})))$ to the list L_2.
3c. Repeat step **3** until $|L_1| < (s + 11)|L_2|$.

4. If there is a pair $(\bar{\mathbf{u}}, F(\phi_1, \bar{\mathbf{u}})) \in L_1$ and $(\bar{\mathbf{v}}, F(\phi_2, \bar{\mathbf{v}})) \in L_2$ such that $F(\phi_1, \bar{\mathbf{u}}) \sim F(\phi_2, \bar{\mathbf{v}})$ continue to step **5** otherwise go to step **2**.
5. Recompute the canonical projective frames $\bar{\mathbf{u}}_1, \ldots, \bar{\mathbf{u}}_{10}$ and $\bar{\mathbf{v}}_1, \bar{\mathbf{v}}_{10}$ by iterating H_{ϕ_1} and H_{ϕ_2}. Finally, output the unique $S \in GL(\mathbb{F}_q^9)$ such that $S\bar{\mathbf{v}}_i = \bar{\mathbf{u}}_i$ for all i from 1 to 10.

Experiments. We implement the algorithm in C++ and use it to solve random instances of the ATFE problem with the parameter set $n = 9, q = 524287$ proposed by [25], aiming for 128 bits of security level. For these instances, we can generate between 100 and 140 invariants per second for the list L_1, and between 3 and 4.5 invariants per second for L_2. If the number of rank-4 points is $N_4 = 2^d k$, then we are looking for collisions in a space of size approximately $k/|\mathrm{Aut}(\phi_1)|$ invariants[3]. So, we expect to find the first collision when

$$|L_1| \approx \sqrt{\frac{(s+11)k}{|\mathrm{Aut}(\phi)|}}, \text{ and } |L_2| \approx \sqrt{\frac{k}{(s+11)|\mathrm{Aut}(\phi)|}}.$$

The worst case solving time is when $|\mathrm{Aut}(\phi_1)|$ is small (2 is the smallest that we observed) and $N_4 \approx q^2$ odd. In that case, we would have an expected running time of 8 h. We solved five ATFE problems and the solving time varied between 40 minutes and 4 hours. The large variability in solving time is to be expected. Some small amount of variability is due to the stochastic nature of the collision finding, sometimes we are lucky and find a collision early on, and sometimes we have to do more work, but most of the variability is due to the distribution of $k/|\mathrm{Aut}(\phi_1)|$. If ϕ_1 and ϕ_2 have more automorphisms (we observe that $|\mathrm{Aut}(\phi_1)|$ is usually between 2 and 6) or if the number of rank-4 points N_4 is divisible by a large power of 2, then the search space can be considerably smaller.

Breaking alternating trilinear form digital signatures. A public key of the [25] signature scheme consists of C isomorphic alternating trilinear forms $\phi_1, \cdots, \phi_C$, where for the $n = 9$ parameter set we have $C = 32$. The corresponding secret key consists of $C-1$ isomorphisms connecting all the forms. To recover the secret key, an attacker needs to solve 31 ATFE problems. Naively solving each problem with our algorithm would take roughly between 31 times 40 min and 31 times 4 h, i.e. between one and five days on a laptop. We can do better: To find the isomorphisms between a set of C forms $\phi_1, \ldots, \phi_C$, we first compute a list L_1 of rank-4 points and their invariants for ϕ_1 that is a factor $\sqrt{C-1}$ larger than optimal for a single execution of the ATFE-solving algorithm. Then, when we look for the isomorphism between ϕ_1 and ϕ_i for $i > 1$ the second list can be smaller by a factor $\sqrt{C-1}$. The total cost of finding the $C-1$ isomorphisms is then only a factor $\sqrt{C-1}$ more expensive than solving an individual ATFE problem. With this strategy, we expect to be able to do a full key recovery using between 4 and 22 h, depending on the number of invariants on the craters.

To forge a single signature, we do not need to recover the entire secret key. We can start the signing procedure like an honest signer, then the attacker receives a set of challenges $b_1, \ldots, b_r \in [C]$ by hashing the message and the commitment $M|\psi_1|\ldots|\psi_r$. To finish the signature, the attacker only needs to solve the ATFE problem for the pairs of forms (ϕ_C, ϕ_{b_i}). In the $n = 9$ parameter set we have $r = 26$, so in the worst case the attacker needs to solve 26 ATFE problems, but this only happens if all the 26 challenges $b_1, \ldots, b_{26}$ are distinct and different from C. In general, the number of ATFE problems that an attacker needs to solve is $|\{b_1, \ldots, b_r, C\}| - 1$. For the $r = 26, c = 32$ parameter set the attacker

---

[3] This is only approximate, because some of the points on the crater could be fixed points of some of the automorphisms.

can hash a few commitments (on average a few thousand) until it gets a set of challenges with $|\{b_1, \ldots, b_r, C\}| - 1 \leq 12$. So to forge a signature it suffices to solve only 12 simultaneous ATFE problems, which we expect to be able to do using between 2.5 and 14 h.

Open Problems

Our work shows that the ATFE parameters proposed by [25] are insecure, especially the $n = 9$ parameters. But there is still a lot of work to be done to understand the hardness of the ATFE problem. Can the $n = 9$ attack be generalized to higher dimensions? Instantiating the algorithm sketched in Sect. 5.4 and evaluating its complexity is also left for future work. Lastly, can the torsor on A_ϕ be used for constructive purposes?

Acknowledgements. We thank Simon-Phillip Merz, Luca De Feo, Péter Kutas, and Wouter Castryck for the helpful discussions, and in the case of Wouter also for pointing me in the direction of the work of Benedetti, Manivel, and Tanturri [2], which demystified the function H.

References

1. Bardet, M., et al.: Improvements of algebraic attacks for solving the rank decoding and MinRank problems. In: Moriai, S., Wang, H. (eds.) ASIACRYPT 2020. LNCS, vol. 12491, pp. 507–536. Springer, Cham (2020). https://doi.org/10.1007/978-3-030-64837-4_17
2. Benedetti, V., Manivel, L., Tanturri, F.: The geometry of the Coble cubic and orbital degeneracy loci. Mathe. Ann. **379**(1–2), 415–440 (2021)
3. Beullens, W.: Not enough LESS: an improved algorithm for solving code equivalence problems over $\mathbb{F}_q$. In: Dunkelman, O., Jacobson, Jr., M.J., O'Flynn, C. (eds.) SAC 2020. LNCS, vol. 12804, pp. 387–403. Springer, Cham (2021). https://doi.org/10.1007/978-3-030-81652-0_15
4. Beullens, W., Katsumata, S., Pintore, F.: Calamari and Falafl: logarithmic (linkable) ring signatures from isogenies and lattices. In: Moriai, S., Wang, H. (eds.) ASIACRYPT 2020. LNCS, vol. 12492, pp. 464–492. Springer, Cham (2020). https://doi.org/10.1007/978-3-030-64834-3_16
5. Beullens, W., Kleinjung, T., Vercauteren, F.: CSI-FiSh: efficient isogeny based signatures through class group computations. In: Galbraith, S.D., Moriai, S. (eds.) ASIACRYPT 2019. LNCS, vol. 11921, pp. 227–247. Springer, Cham (2019). https://doi.org/10.1007/978-3-030-34578-5_9
6. Biasse, J.-F., Micheli, G., Persichetti, E., Santini, P.: LESS is more: code-based signatures without syndromes. In: Nitaj, A., Youssef, A. (eds.) AFRICACRYPT 2020. LNCS, vol. 12174, pp. 45–65. Springer, Cham (2020). https://doi.org/10.1007/978-3-030-51938-4_3
7. Bouillaguet, C., Faugère, J.-C., Fouque, P.-A., Perret, L.: Practical cryptanalysis of the identification scheme based on the isomorphism of polynomial with one secret problem. In: Catalano, D., Fazio, N., Gennaro, R., Nicolosi, A. (eds.) PKC 2011. LNCS, vol. 6571, pp. 473–493. Springer, Heidelberg (2011). https://doi.org/10.1007/978-3-642-19379-8_29

8. Bouillaguet, C., Fouque, P.-A., Véber, A.: Graph-theoretic algorithms for the "Isomorphism of Polynomials" problem. In: Johansson, T., Nguyen, P.Q. (eds.) EUROCRYPT 2013. LNCS, vol. 7881, pp. 211–227. Springer, Heidelberg (2013). https://doi.org/10.1007/978-3-642-38348-9_13

9. Carlitz, L.: Representations by quadratic forms in a finite field (1954)

10. Chen, Z., Duong, D.H., Nguyen, N.T., Qiao, Y., Susilo, W., Tang, G.: QROM security and ring signatures. Cryptology ePrint Archive, On digital signatures based on isomorphism problems (2022)

11. Couveignes, J.-M.: Hard homogeneous spaces. Cryptology ePrint Archive, Report 2006/291 (2006). https://eprint.iacr.org/2006/291

12. D'Alconzo, G., Gangemi, A.: TRIFORS: Linkable trilinear forms ring signature. Cryptology ePrint Archive (2022)

13. De Feo, L., Galbraith, S.D.: SeaSign: compact isogeny signatures from class group actions. In: Ishai, Y., Rijmen, V. (eds.) EUROCRYPT 2019. LNCS, vol. 11478, pp. 759–789. Springer, Cham (2019). https://doi.org/10.1007/978-3-030-17659-4_26

14. Goldreich, O., Micali, S., Wigderson, A.: Proofs that yield nothing but their validity or all languages in NP have zero-knowledge proof systems. J. ACM **38**(3), 691–729 (1991)

15. Grochow, J.A., Qiao, Y.: On the complexity of isomorphism problems for tensors, groups, and polynomials I: tensor isomorphism-completeness. In: 12th Innovations in Theoretical Computer Science Conference (ITCS 2021). Schloss Dagstuhl-Leibniz-Zentrum für Informatik (2021)

16. Gruson, L., Sam, S.V.: Alternating trilinear forms on a nine-dimensional space and degenerations of (3,3)-polarized Abelian surfaces. Proc. London Math. Soc. **110**(3), 755–785 (2015)

17. Gruson, L., Sam, S.V., Weyman, J.: Moduli of Abelian varieties, Vinberg θ-groups, and free resolutions. In: Peeva, I. (ed.) Commutative Algebra: Expository Papers Dedicated to David Eisenbud on the Occasion of His 65th Birthday, pp. 419–469. Springer, New York (2013). https://doi.org/10.1007/978-1-4614-5292-8_13

18. Hora, J., Pudlák, P.: Classification of 8-dimensional trilinear alternating forms over GF(2). Comm. Algebra **43**(8), 3459–3471 (2015)

19. Hora, J., Pudlák, P.: Classification of 9-dimensional trilinear alternating forms over GF(2). Finite Fields Appl. **70**, 101788 (2021)

20. Leroux, A., Roméas, M.: Updatable encryption from group actions. Cryptology ePrint Archive (2022)

21. Parisse, B., De Graeve, R.: Giac/Xcas, version 1.9.0 (2022). https://www-fourier.univ-grenoble-alpes.fr/parisse/giac.html

22. Patarin, J.: Hidden fields equations (HFE) and isomorphisms of polynomials (IP): two new families of asymmetric algorithms. In: Maurer, U. (ed.) EUROCRYPT 1996. LNCS, vol. 1070, pp. 33–48. Springer, Heidelberg (1996). https://doi.org/10.1007/3-540-68339-9_4

23. Rains, E., Sam, S.: Invariant theory of $\bigwedge^3(9)$ and genus-2 curves. Algebra Number Theory **12**(4), 935–957 (2018)

24. Sutherland, A.: Isogeny volcanoes. Open Book Ser. **1**(1), 507–530 (2013)

25. Tang, G., Duong, D.H., Joux, A., Plantard, T., Qiao, Y., Susilo, W.: Practical post-quantum signature schemes from isomorphism problems of trilinear forms. In: Dunkelman, O., Dziembowski, S. (eds.) EUROCRYPT 2022, Part III. LNCS, vol. 13277, pp. 582–612. Springer, Heidelberg (2022). https://doi.org/10.1007/978-3-031-07082-2_21

26. Tang, G., Qiao, Y., Grochow, J.A.: Average-case algorithms for testing isomorphism of polynomials, algebras, and multilinear forms. J. Groups Complex. Cryptol. **14** (2022)
27. The Sage Developers: SageMath, the Sage Mathematics Software System (Version 9.7) (2022). https://www.sagemath.org

Analysis of the Security of the PSSI Problem and Cryptanalysis of the Durandal Signature Scheme

Nicolas Aragon[1(✉)], Victor Dyseryn[2], and Philippe Gaborit[2]

[1] Naquidis Center, Talence, France
nicolas.aragon@protonmail.com
[2] XLIM, Université de Limoges, Limoges, France

Abstract. We present a new attack against the PSSI problem, one of the three problems at the root of security of Durandal, an efficient rank metric code-based signature scheme with a public key size of 15 kB and a signature size of 4 kB, presented at EUROCRYPT'19. Our attack recovers the private key using a leakage of information coming from several signatures produced with the same key. Our approach is to combine pairs of signatures and perform Cramer-like formulas in order to build subspaces containing a secret element. We break all existing parameters of Durandal: the two published sets of parameters claiming a security of 128 bits are broken in respectively 2^{66} and 2^{73} elementary bit operations, and the number of signatures required to finalize the attack is 1,792 and 4,096 respectively. We implemented our attack and ran experiments that demonstrated its success with smaller parameters.

Keywords: Rank-based cryptography · code-based cryptography · post-quantum cryptography · digital signatures · cryptanalysis

1 Introduction

Background on Post-Quantum Cryptography. Recent advances in quantum computing demonstrate an increase in the number of qubits available in a single quantum processor. While this does not represent an immediate threat for classical cryptography, it calls for a rapid transition to *quantum-resistant cryptography* (also called *post-quantum cryptography*, or PQC).

The main focus of this article is digital signatures, one of the most important cryptographic algorithms. The NIST PQC team announced in July 2022 that three digital signatures candidates were selected for standardization: two are based on euclidean lattices [8,11] and the third one is a hash-based signature [7]. NIST also announced a new standardization project, starting in 2023, calling for efficient signatures not based on structured lattices. Code-based signatures represent an efficient alternative to lattices.

Presentation of the Durandal Signature Scheme. Durandal [5] is a code-based signature scheme published in 2019 and could be a promising candidate for

© International Association for Cryptologic Research 2023
H. Handschuh and A. Lysyanskaya (Eds.): CRYPTO 2023, LNCS 14083, pp. 127–149, 2023.
https://doi.org/10.1007/978-3-031-38548-3_5

this new standardization project, with a public key size of 15 kB and a signature size of 4 kB. It uses the rank metric instead of the usual Hamming metric. Durandal is based on an adaptation of the Lyubashevsky proof of knowledge [13] in a rank metric context. Then, the Fiat-Shamir heuristic [10] is used to turn the proof of knowledge into a signature scheme.

The security proof of Durandal relies on the difficulty of three problems: (i) the Ideal Rank Syndrome Decoding (IRSD) [2], a variant of the generic decoding problem in rank metric (RSD) where the objects have ideal structure; (ii) the Rank Support Learning (RSL) [12], another variant of RSD where the attacker is given several syndromes with the same support; and (iii) the Product Spaces Subspaces Indistinguishability (PSSI) problem, which was published in the same paper than Durandal. While the first two problems are slight variants of generic ones and appear in other code-based algorithms [1,4], the third one is an ad-hoc problem which is very specific to this signature scheme, hence was somewhat less studied. PSSI has no known reduction to a well-established difficult problem. All these factors may explain why we could find an attack on the PSSI problem and present it in this work.

Presentation of PSSI. The PSSI problem, which will be defined formally later in this paper, consists in deciding whether pairs (F, Z) of subspaces of the finite field $\mathbb{F}_{q^m}$ (seen as an $\mathbb{F}_q$-vector space) were generated randomly or with a special pattern, namely that the subspace Z contains a subspace U of the product space EF, where E is a private space, fixed across the pairs. Pairs generated in this fashion are contained in a Durandal signature, that is why we will call such pairs (F, Z) "*signatures*".

In the Durandal paper [5], a security analysis of PSSI was given. First, it was noticed that an easy attack is avoided by *filtering* the subspace U inside the subspace EF, meaning that it does not contain any non-zero product element of the form ef where $e \in E$ and $f \in F$. Second, a distinguisher is presented which consists in multiplying Z by a subspace of F of dimension 2, and spotting a loss of dimension. The parameters were chosen so as to make the probability of such a loss of dimension negligible. However, all these considerations were securing only one signature and no security analysis was presented when the attacker disposed of several samples of PSSI problem, i.e. several signatures. The attack on PSSI presented in this work exploits leakage of information due to several signatures sharing the same space E, which is part of the private key.

Our Contributions. The purpose of this article is to present a new attack against the PSSI problem. Our approach is to combine signatures two by two and to perform Cramer-like formulas – but with vector spaces on the numerator – in order to build subspaces containing a secret element. The process is repeated until the entire space E is found. Then, a chain of intersections allows to recover this secret element. This method is efficient against a wide range of parameters. In the Durandal paper [5], two sets of parameters were presented, claiming 128 bits of security. Our attack breaks both parameter sets in 2^{66} and

2^{73} elementary bit operations respectively. The average number of signatures necessary to finalize the attack remains reasonable; less than a few thousands.

In light of this new attack, new parameters must be found that are likely to increase the public key and signature sizes of Durandal. It is questionable whether this scheme will remain competitive as compared to other possible rank-based digital signature candidates for the upcoming NIST standardization project, which are already smaller than Durandal and rely on more generic difficult problems, see for example [9].

Organization of the Paper. The paper is organized as follows. Section 2 contains definitions and preliminary lemmas. Background on the attacked scheme is given in Sects. 3 and 4 which present Durandal and PSSI problem. For understanding the gist and the main steps of the attack, the reader should read Sect. 5 and 6.1. The rest of Sect. 6 provides full details on the correctness and complexity of the attack. Finally, experimental results supporting our attack are shown in Sect. 7.

2 Preliminaries

2.1 Notation and General Definitions

Let $\mathbb{F}_q$ denote the finite field of q elements where q is the power of a prime and let $\mathbb{F}_{q^m}$ denote the field of q^m elements i.e., the extension field of degree m of $\mathbb{F}_q$. $\mathbb{F}_{q^m}$ is also an $\mathbb{F}_q$-vector space of dimension m; we denote by capital letters the $\mathbb{F}_q$-subspaces of $\mathbb{F}_{q^m}$ and by lower-case letters the elements of $\mathbb{F}_{q^m}$.

Let $X \subset \mathbb{F}_{q^m}$. We denote by $\langle X \rangle$ the $\mathbb{F}_q$-subspace generated by the elements of X:

$$\langle X \rangle = \mathrm{Vect}_{\mathbb{F}_q}(X).$$

If $X = \{x_1, \ldots, x_n\}$, we simply use the notation $\langle x_1, \ldots, x_n \rangle$.

Vectors are denoted by bold lower-case letters and matrices by bold capital letters (e.g., $\boldsymbol{x} = (x_1, \ldots, x_n) \in \mathbb{F}_{q^m}^n$ and $\boldsymbol{M} = (m_{ij})_{\substack{1 \leqslant i \leqslant k \\ 1 \leqslant j \leqslant n}} \in \mathbb{F}_{q^m}^{k \times n}$).

If S is a finite set, we denote by $x \xleftarrow{\$} S$ when x is chosen uniformly at random from S.

We now give the definition of the rank metric and the associated definition of support in this metric.

Definition 1 (Rank metric over $\mathbb{F}_{q^m}^n$). *Let $\boldsymbol{x} = (x_1, \ldots, x_n) \in \mathbb{F}_{q^m}^n$ and $(\beta_1, \ldots, \beta_m) \in \mathbb{F}_{q^m}^m$ be a basis of $\mathbb{F}_{q^m}$ viewed as an m-dimensional vector space over $\mathbb{F}_q$. Each coordinate x_j is associated to a vector of $\mathbb{F}_q^m$ in this basis: $x_j = \sum_{i=1}^{m} m_{ij}\beta_i$. The $m \times n$ matrix associated to $\boldsymbol{x}$ is given by $\boldsymbol{M}(\boldsymbol{x}) = (m_{ij})_{\substack{1 \leqslant i \leqslant m \\ 1 \leqslant j \leqslant n}}$. The rank weight $\|\boldsymbol{x}\|$ of $\boldsymbol{x}$ is defined as the rank of its associated matrix:*

$$\|\boldsymbol{x}\| := \mathrm{rank}\, \boldsymbol{M}(\boldsymbol{x}).$$

The rank weight is independent from the choice of the basis $(\beta_1, \ldots, \beta_m)$.

The associated distance $d(\boldsymbol{x}, \boldsymbol{y})$ between elements $\boldsymbol{x}$ and $\boldsymbol{y}$ in $\mathbb{F}_{q^m}^n$ is defined by $d(\boldsymbol{x}, \boldsymbol{y}) = \|\boldsymbol{x} - \boldsymbol{y}\|$.

Definition 2 (Rank support of a word). *Let $\boldsymbol{x} = (x_1, \ldots, x_n) \in \mathbb{F}_{q^m}^n$. The support of $\boldsymbol{x}$, denoted $\mathrm{Supp}(\boldsymbol{x})$, is the $\mathbb{F}_q$-subspace of $\mathbb{F}_{q^m}$ generated by the coordinates of $\boldsymbol{x}$:*

$$\mathrm{Supp}(\boldsymbol{x}) := \langle x_1, \ldots, x_n \rangle.$$

This definition is coherent with the definition of the rank weight since we have $\dim \mathrm{Supp}(\boldsymbol{x}) = \|\boldsymbol{x}\|$.

The number of supports of dimension r, i.e. the number of $\mathbb{F}_q$-subspaces of dimension r of $\mathbb{F}_{q^m}$, is given by the Gaussian coefficient

$$\begin{bmatrix} m \\ r \end{bmatrix}_q = \prod_{i=0}^{r-1} \frac{q^m - q^i}{q^r - q^i}.$$

The Grassmannian $\mathbf{Gr}(\mathbb{F}_{q^m}, r)$ represents the set of all subspaces of $\mathbb{F}_{q^m}$ of dimension r.

Definition 3 (Ideal matrix). *Let $P \in \mathbb{F}_q[X]$ be a polynomial of degree n. Let $G \in \mathbb{F}_{q^m}[X]$ be a polynomial of degree $n-1$ at most. An ideal matrix generated by G is a square matrix $\boldsymbol{M}$ of size $n \times n$ such that for all $1 \le i \le n$, its i-th row can be identified to the polynomial $X^{i-1}G \mod P$, i.e.*

$$\sum_{j=1}^{n} m_{i,j} X^{j-1} \equiv X^{i-1}G \mod P.$$

Remark 1. By extension, a $n \times 2n$ matrix consisting of two ideal square blocks of size n is also called an ideal matrix.

2.2   Dimension of an Intersection of Subspaces

In this subsection, we prove some lemmas on the probability distribution of the dimension of an intersection of two or more random subspaces of $\mathbb{F}_{q^m}$. These lemmas will be useful for a fine analysis of our attack.

Lemma 1. *Let $x \in \mathbb{F}_{q^m} \setminus \{0\}$. Let $B \xleftarrow{\$} \mathbf{Gr}(\mathbb{F}_{q^m}, b)$ a random subspace of dimension b. Then*

$$\mathrm{Prob}(x \in B) = \frac{q^b - 1}{q^m - 1}.$$

Proof. The set of subspaces of $\mathbb{F}_{q^m}$ of dimension b containing x is in bijection with the set of subspaces of the projective hyperplane $\mathbb{F}_{q^m}/\langle x \rangle$ of dimension $b-1$. $\mathbb{F}_{q^m}/\langle x \rangle$ is an $\mathbb{F}_q$-vector space of dimension $m-1$, hence the number of subspaces of $\mathbb{F}_{q^m}$ of dimension b containing x is $\begin{bmatrix} m-1 \\ b-1 \end{bmatrix}_q$.

Then we divide this number by the total number $\begin{bmatrix} m \\ b \end{bmatrix}_q$ of subspaces of $\mathbb{F}_{q^m}$ of dimension b, to get the desired probability:

$$\text{Prob}(x \in B) = \frac{\begin{bmatrix} m-1 \\ b-1 \end{bmatrix}_q}{\begin{bmatrix} m \\ b \end{bmatrix}_q}$$

$$= \prod_{i=0}^{b-2} \frac{q^{m-1} - q^i}{q^{b-1} - q^i} \prod_{i=0}^{b-1} \frac{q^b - q^i}{q^m - q^i}$$

$$= \frac{q^b - 1}{q^m - 1}.$$

$\square$

Lemma 2. *Let $A \in \mathbf{Gr}(\mathbb{F}_{q^m}, a)$ and $B \xleftarrow{\$} \mathbf{Gr}(\mathbb{F}_{q^m}, b)$ be subspaces of $\mathbb{F}_{q^m}$. Then*

$$\text{Prob}(\dim(A \cap B) > 0) \leq q^{a+b-m}.$$

Proof. Notice that

$$\dim(A \cap B) > 0 \Leftrightarrow \exists x \in A \backslash \{0\}, x \in B$$

hence:

$$\text{Prob}(\dim(A \cap B) > 0) = \text{Prob}\left(\bigvee_{x \in A \backslash \{0\}} x \in B \right)$$

$$\leq \sum_{x \in A \backslash \{0\}} \text{Prob}(x \in B)$$

$$= \sum_{x \in A \backslash \{0\}} \frac{q^b - 1}{q^m - 1} \qquad \text{(Lemma 1)}$$

$$\leq \sum_{x \in A \backslash \{0\}} q^{b-m}$$

$$= (q^a - 1)q^{b-m}$$

$$\leq q^{a+b-m}.$$

$\square$

Remark 2. When $a + b > m$, $\dim(A \cap B)$ is always greater than 0 according to Grassmann's formula on dimensions. Note that the above lemma still holds in that case, since the right-hand side of the equality is larger than 1.

We can generalize this lemma to an arbitrary family of independent random subspaces.

Lemma 3. *For $1 \leq i \leq n$, let $A_i \xleftarrow{\$} \mathbf{Gr}(\mathbb{F}_{q^m}, a_i)$ be random independent (in the sense of probability) subspaces of $\mathbb{F}_{q^m}$. Then*

$$\mathrm{Prob}(\dim(\cap_i A_i) > 0) \leq q^{\sum_i a_i - (n-1)m}.$$

Proof. As before, $\dim(\cap_i A_i) > 0$ if and only if there exists $x \neq 0$ such that $x \in \cap_i A_i$, hence:

$$
\begin{aligned}
\mathrm{Prob}(\dim(\cap_i A_i) > 0) &= \mathrm{Prob}\left(\bigvee_{x \in \mathbb{F}_{q^m} \setminus \{0\}} x \in \cap_i A_i \right) \\
&= \mathrm{Prob}\left(\bigvee_{x \in \mathbb{F}_{q^m} \setminus \{0\}} \left(\bigwedge_{i=1}^{n} x \in A_i \right) \right) \\
&\leq \sum_{x \in \mathbb{F}_{q^m} \setminus \{0\}} \mathrm{Prob}\left(\bigwedge_{i=1}^{n} x \in A_i \right) \\
&= \sum_{x \in \mathbb{F}_{q^m} \setminus \{0\}} \prod_{i=1}^{n} \mathrm{Prob}(x \in A_i) \qquad \text{(by independency of spaces A_i)} \\
&= \sum_{x \in \mathbb{F}_{q^m} \setminus \{0\}} \prod_{i=1}^{n} \frac{q^{a_i} - 1}{q^m - 1} \\
&\leq \sum_{x \in \mathbb{F}_{q^m} \setminus \{0\}} \prod_{i=1}^{n} q^{a_i - m} \\
&= \sum_{x \in \mathbb{F}_{q^m} \setminus \{0\}} q^{\sum_i a_i - nm} \\
&= (q^m - 1) q^{\sum_i a_i - nm} \\
&\leq q^{\sum_i a_i - (n-1)m}.
\end{aligned}
$$

$\square$

Remark 3. Similarly to the previous remark, when $\sum_i a_i > (n-1)m$, $\dim(\cap_i A_i) > 0$ and the lemma is still valid.

We now present a slight variation of the above lemma when the random subspaces A_i all share a common element x. Let us introduce the following notation:

Definition 4. *Let $U \in \mathbf{Gr}(\mathbb{F}_{q^m}, u)$ a subspace of dimension u. For $a \geq u$, we define*

$$\mathbf{Gr}(\mathbb{F}_{q^m}, U, a) := \{ A \in \mathbf{Gr}(\mathbb{F}_{q^m}, a) \mid U \subset A \},$$

the set of all subspaces of $\mathbb{F}_{q^m}$ of dimension a containing U.

$\mathbf{Gr}(\mathbb{F}_{q^m}, U, a)$ is in bijection with $\mathbf{Gr}(\mathbb{F}_{q^m}/U, a - u)$, hence is of cardinality $\begin{bmatrix} m - u \\ a - u \end{bmatrix}_q$.

Lemma 4. *Let* $x \in \mathbb{F}_{q^m} \backslash \{0\}$. *For* $1 \leq i \leq n$, *let* $A_i \xleftarrow{\$} \mathbf{Gr}(\mathbb{F}_{q^m}, \langle x \rangle, a_i)$ *be random independent subspaces of* $\mathbb{F}_{q^m}$ *all containing* x. *Then,* $\dim(\cap_i A_i) \geq 1$ *and*

$$\mathrm{Prob}(\dim(\cap_i A_i) > 1) \leq q^{\sum_i a_i - (n-1)m - 1}.$$

Proof. Since the subspaces A_i all contain x, we have immediately $\dim(\cap_i A_i) \geq 1$. Next, we note that

$$\dim \left(\bigcap_i A_i \right) > 1 \Leftrightarrow \dim \left(\bigcap_i A_i / \langle x \rangle \right) > 0.$$

Therefore, we can apply Lemma 3 with the space $\mathbb{F}_{q^m}/\langle x \rangle$ (of dimension $m - 1$) and subspaces $A'_i \xleftarrow{\$} \mathbf{Gr}(\mathbb{F}_{q^m}/\langle x \rangle, a_i - 1)$, to get

$$\mathrm{Prob}(\dim(\cap_i A_i) > 1) \leq q^{\sum_i (a_i - 1) - (n-1)(m-1)}$$
$$= q^{\sum_i a_i - (n-1)m - 1}.$$

$\square$

2.3 Product Spaces

Definition 5 (Product space). *Let* E *and* F *be two* $\mathbb{F}_q$-*subspaces of* $\mathbb{F}_{q^m}$ *(seen as an* $\mathbb{F}_q$-*vector space of dimension* m*). The product space* EF *is defined as the* $\mathbb{F}_q$-*subspace generated by all the products of an element of* E *with an element of* F:

$$EF := \langle \{ ef \mid e \in E, f \in F \} \rangle.$$

Remark 4. When E and F are of $\mathbb{F}_q$-dimension r and d respectively, the dimension of the product space EF is upper bounded by rd. Indeed, for a basis $(e_1, ..., e_r)$ of E and a basis $(f_1, ..., f_d)$ of F, it is clear that the tensor product of these basis $(e_i f_j)_{1 \leq i \leq r, 1 \leq j \leq d}$ is a generating family of EF.

When r and d are small with respect to m, this family is also linearly independent with great probability, meaning that the dimension of EF is exactly rd in the typical case (see [6], Sect. 3 for more detailed results on this probability).

The following proposition states that it is easy to compute E from F and EF (when $\dim(EF) \ll m$). It is analogue to the division $\frac{ef}{f} = e$, but in a vector space setting. It will be necessary for a fine understanding of the PSSI problem, and is also used extensively for the decoding of LRPC codes, a family of rank-metric codes not used in Durandal but found in other rank-metric cryptographic algorithms.

Proposition 1 ([6], Proposition 3.5). *Suppose m is prime. Let $E \xleftarrow{\$}$* $\mathbf{Gr}(\mathbb{F}_{q^m}, r)$ *and* $F \xleftarrow{\$} \mathbf{Gr}(\mathbb{F}_{q^m}, d)$. *Let* (f_i) *be a basis of* F. *Then*

$$E = \bigcap_i f_i^{-1} EF$$

with probability at least

$$1 - rq^{r\frac{d(d+1)}{2} - m}.$$

Remark 5. The above result requires m to be prime, which is always the case for parameters of rank-based cryptographic primitives, including Durandal.

Remark 6. This proposition shows that it is possible to recover E with probability close to 1 when $rd \ll m$. In the other extreme case where $rd \geq m$ (i.e. $EF = \mathbb{F}_{q^m}$), we get $f_i^{-1} EF = \mathbb{F}_{q^m}$ so the chain of intersections will always be $\mathbb{F}_{q^m}$ and no information on E can be retrieved.

Definition 6 (Filtered subspace). *Let E and F be two $\mathbb{F}_q$-subspaces of $\mathbb{F}_{q^m}$. A strict subspace $U \subsetneq EF$ of the product space EF is said to be filtered when it contains no non-zero product elements of the form ef with $e \in E$ and $f \in F$:*

$$\{ef, e \in E, f \in F\} \cap U = \{0\}.$$

3   Durandal Signature Scheme

3.1   Description of the Scheme

We recap briefly in Fig. 1 the Durandal signature scheme, although no deep understanding of the scheme is required for the rest of the article, since our attack targets more specifically the PSSI problem defined in the next section. The reader is referred to [5] for more details on Durandal. The scheme is parametrized with variables m, n, k, l, l', r, d, and λ. In Durandal, only half-rate codes are considered, therefore $n = 2k$.

Key Generation. The secret key consists of two matrices $\boldsymbol{S} \in E^{lk \times n}$ and $\boldsymbol{S}' \in E^{l'k \times n}$ whose coordinates belong to the same secret support $E \subset \mathbb{F}_{q^m}$ of dimension r. $\boldsymbol{S}$ and $\boldsymbol{S}'$ are composed of ideal blocks of size $k \times k$.

The public key consists of a random $(n - k) \times n$ ideal matrix $\boldsymbol{H}$, together with the matrices $\boldsymbol{T} = \boldsymbol{H}\boldsymbol{S}^\top$ and $\boldsymbol{T}' = \boldsymbol{H}\boldsymbol{S}'^\top$.

Signature of a Message μ. Similar to the Lyubashevsky approach, the signer first computes to a vector $\boldsymbol{z} = \boldsymbol{y} + \boldsymbol{c}\boldsymbol{S}'$, where $\boldsymbol{y}$ is a vector whose coordinates are sampled in a space $W + EF$ depending on the secret key and $\boldsymbol{c}$ is a challenge depending on the message μ.

However, in order to avoid an attack, the vector $\boldsymbol{z}$ must be corrected with a corrective term $\boldsymbol{p}\boldsymbol{S}$ such that $\mathrm{Supp}(\boldsymbol{z}) \subset W + U$, where U is a filtered subspace of the product space EF of dimension $rd - \lambda$. $\boldsymbol{p}$ is a vector with coordinates in F and is computed through linear algebra during the signing process.

The signature is the tuple $(\boldsymbol{z}, F, \boldsymbol{c}, \boldsymbol{p})$. The signature consists therefore of the challenge $\boldsymbol{c}$, computed through a hash function, together with the answer to this challenge.

Verification of a Signature ($\mu, \boldsymbol{z}, F, \boldsymbol{c}, \boldsymbol{p}$). To verify the signature, we have to check the rank weight of $\boldsymbol{z}$ and that $\mathcal{H}(\boldsymbol{x}, F, \mu) = \boldsymbol{c}$. The vector $\boldsymbol{x}$ is recomputed using $\boldsymbol{z}, \boldsymbol{c}, \boldsymbol{p}$ and the public key.

Key generation: $E \xleftarrow{\$} \mathbf{Gr}(\mathbb{F}_{q^m}, r)$

Secret key: $\boldsymbol{S} \in E^{lk \times n}$, $\boldsymbol{S}' \in E^{l'k \times n}$

Public key: $\boldsymbol{H} \xleftarrow{\$}$ ideal matrix $\in \mathbb{F}_{q^m}^{(n-k) \times n}$, $\boldsymbol{T} = \boldsymbol{H} \boldsymbol{S}^T$, $\boldsymbol{T}' = \boldsymbol{H} \boldsymbol{S}'^T$

Sign($\mu, \boldsymbol{S}, \boldsymbol{S}'$):

1. $W \xleftarrow{\$} \mathbf{Gr}(\mathbb{F}_{q^m}, w)$,
   $F \xleftarrow{\$} \mathbf{Gr}(\mathbb{F}_{q^m}, d)$
2. $\boldsymbol{y} \xleftarrow{\$} (W + EF)^n$, $\boldsymbol{x} = \boldsymbol{H} \boldsymbol{y}^T$
3. $\boldsymbol{c} = \mathcal{H}(\boldsymbol{x}, F, \mu)$, $\boldsymbol{c} \in F^{l'k}$
4. $U \xleftarrow{\$}$ filtered subspace of EF of dimension $rd - \lambda$
5. $\boldsymbol{z} = \boldsymbol{y} + \boldsymbol{c}\boldsymbol{S}' + \boldsymbol{p}\boldsymbol{S}$, $\boldsymbol{z} \in (W + U)^n$
6. Output $(\boldsymbol{z}, F, \boldsymbol{c}, \boldsymbol{p})$

Verify($\mu, \boldsymbol{z}, F, \boldsymbol{c}, \boldsymbol{p}, \boldsymbol{H}, \boldsymbol{T}, \boldsymbol{T}'$):

1. Accept if and only if :
   $\|\boldsymbol{z}\| \leqslant w + rd - \lambda$ and
   $\mathcal{H}(\boldsymbol{H}\boldsymbol{z}^T - \boldsymbol{T}'\boldsymbol{c}^T + \boldsymbol{T}\boldsymbol{p}^T, F, \mu) = \boldsymbol{c}$

Fig. 1. The Durandal Signature scheme

3.2   Parameters

The parameters of Durandal, as presented in [5], are shown in Table 1.

Table 1. Parameters for Durandal. The sizes of public key (pk) and signature (σ) are in bytes.

	m	n	k	l	l'	d	r	w	λ	q	pk size	σ size	Security
Durandal-I	241	202	101	4	1	6	6	57	12	2	15,245	4,064	128
Durandal-II	263	226	113	4	1	7	7	56	14	2	18,606	5,019	128

4   PSSI Problem

The security of the Durandal signature scheme relies on the hardness of several problems: I-RSL, ARSD and PSSI. (see Theorem 20 in [5]).

While the first two problems are slight variants of the well-known *syndrome decoding problem in the rank metric* (RSD) and are widely used among rank-based cryptographic primitives, the PSSI is an ad-hoc problem that was also introduced in Durandal paper [5]. This latter problem will be the main focus for the rest of the article.

The PSSI problem appears naturally when we try to prove the indistinguishability of the signatures. Remember that we wrote in the previous section that the first two components of a Durandal signature are a subspace $F \in \mathbf{Gr}(\mathbb{F}_{q^m}, d)$ and a vector z whose coordinates belong to the subspace $Z = W + U$, where U is a filtered subspace of EF. When a signer signs N times with the same key, it produces several subspaces $(F_i, Z_i)_{1 \leq i \leq N}$, the space E being fixed since it is linked to the private key. It is natural to require that pairs of such subspaces (F_i, Z_i) are indistinguishable from random subspaces of the same dimension. This is captured in the following definition:

Problem 1 (Product Spaces Subspaces Indistinguishability). Let E be a fixed $\mathbb{F}_q$-subspace of $\mathbb{F}_{q^m}$ of dimension r. Let F_i, U_i and W_i be subspaces defined as follows:

- $F_i \xleftarrow{\$} \mathbf{Gr}(\mathbb{F}_{q^m}, d)$;
- $U_i \xleftarrow{\$} \mathbf{Gr}(EF_i, rd - \lambda)$ such that $\{ef, e \in E, f \in F_i\} \cap U_i = \{0\}$;
- $W_i \xleftarrow{\$} \mathbf{Gr}(\mathbb{F}_{q^m}, w)$.

The $\mathrm{PSSI}_{r,d,\lambda,w,m,N}$ problem consists in distinguishing N samples of the form (Z_i, F_i) where $Z_i = W_i + U_i$ from N samples of the form (Z_i', F_i) where Z_i' is a random subspace of $\mathbb{F}_{q^m}$ of dimension $w + rd - \lambda$.[1]

Remark 7. An easy distinguisher could be to guess randomly unless $\dim(Z_i) < w + rd - \lambda$, in which case Z_i is of the first form $W_i + U_i$ described above. However, this can occur only if spaces U_i and W_i have a non-zero intersection, which happens with a probability dominated by $q^{w+rd-\lambda-m}$ (cf. Lemma 2). As a result, with practical parameters of Durandal, as presented in Table 1, this easy distinguisher gets a negligible advantage of less than 2^{-128}. Therefore, in the rest of this document, we consider the intersection $W_i \cap U_i$ to be trivial.

We define more precisely the two distributions between which a PSSI attacker must discriminate.

---

[1] In the original paper of Durandal, the first component of the samples are vectors z_i of length n and support Z_i but this has been proven equivalent to the version defined in this paper (see beginning of Sect. 4.1 in [5]).

Definition 7 (PSSI distribution $\mathcal{D}_{\mathsf{PSSI}}$). *Let E be a $\mathbb{F}_q$-subspace of $\mathbb{F}_{q^m}$ of dimension r. Let $\mathcal{D}_{\mathsf{PSSI}}(E)$ the distribution that outputs samples (F_i, Z_i) defined as follows:*

- $F_i \xleftarrow{\$} \mathbf{Gr}(\mathbb{F}_{q^m}, d)$;
- $U_i \xleftarrow{\$} \mathbf{Gr}(EF_i, rd - \lambda)$ *such that* $\{ef, e \in E, f \in F\} \cap U_i = \{0\}$;
- $W_i \xleftarrow{\$} \mathbf{Gr}(\mathbb{F}_{q^m}, w)$;
- $Z_i = W_i + U_i$.

Definition 8 (Random distribution $\mathcal{D}_{\mathsf{Random}}$). *Let $\mathcal{D}_{\mathsf{Random}}$ the distribution that outputs samples (F_i, Z_i) where F_i and Z_i are independent random variables picked uniformly in, respectively, $\mathbf{Gr}(\mathbb{F}_{q^m}, d)$ and $\mathbf{Gr}(\mathbb{F}_{q^m}, w + rd - \lambda)$.*

The problem PSSI now simply consists in distinguishing N independent samples from the PSSI distribution or from the random distribution.

We can now define the search version of this problem which will be attacked in the next sections. It is obviously harder than PSSI.

Problem 2 (Search-PSSI). Given N independent samples (F_i, Z_i) from $\mathcal{D}_{\mathsf{PSSI}}(E)$ with $\dim(E) = r$, the Search-PSSI$_{r,d,\lambda,w,m,N}$ problem consists in finding the vector space E.

Why Filtering U?

There exists a simple attack on Search-PSSI in the case where U is equal to the entire space EF and is not a strict subspace of it. In such a problematic setting, we can use Proposition 1 to recover E from the knowledge of EF and F.

The filtration condition is a stronger constraint than having U being a strict subspace of EF. The objective is to avoid an attacker gaining information from intersections I of the form $f^{-1}Z \cap f'^{-1}Z$ with $(f, f') \in F^2$. If Z contains some product elements ef then the probability that $\dim I \neq 0$ is much higher than if Z were truly random. With the filtration of the space U, such techniques would not be useful.

Recovering the Private Key from Search-PSSI

In Durandal, from the public key $(\boldsymbol{H}, \boldsymbol{T}, \boldsymbol{T}')$ and the space E it is easy to recover the private key $(\boldsymbol{S}, \boldsymbol{S}')$. Indeed, the equations $\boldsymbol{t}_i = \boldsymbol{H}\boldsymbol{s}_i^T$ with coefficients in $\mathbb{F}_{q^m}$ can be rewritten as linear systems in $\mathbb{F}_q$. The number of equations $m(n-k)$ is way larger than the number of unknowns rn, so with overwhelming probability the syndromes $\boldsymbol{s}_i$ of the private key will be the unique solution.

Existing Attacks on PSSI

A security analysis of PSSI was presented in Durandal paper (see Sect. 4.1 in [5]). The analysis relied on a distinguisher, whose idea is to consider product spaces of the form $Z_i G_i$ where G_i is a subspace of F_i of dimension 2. The probability that $\dim Z_i G_i = 2(w + rd - \lambda)$ depends on whether Z_i is random or not. The claimed work factor of this distinguisher was

$$2^{m-2(rd-\lambda)}$$

and the authors of Durandal chose their parameters such that this work factor is above the security level. Up to the present work, the above distinguisher was the state-of-the-art attack on PSSI and it seemed that a large value for m was enough to prevent an attacker from breaking PSSI. As we will see next, that is not the case, and on the contrary, the larger m is, the more attackable the parameters are.

5   An Observation When m Is High

Before unveiling a practical attack against PSSI, we first make an interesting observation which reveals the secret space E to an attacker who has no constraint on m. **Therefore, in this section, we place ourselves in the simplified situation where $2d(w + rd - \lambda) \ll m$.** Even though it is unrealistic as compared to practical parameters of the Durandal signature scheme, it gives a first glimpse of the ideas that will be used for a practical attack against PSSI in the next section.

The idea is the following: suppose an attacker has two instances from the PSSI distribution (F_1, Z_1) and (F_2, Z_2). They can compute a "cross-product" of these instances

$$A := F_1 Z_2 + F_2 Z_1$$

Even though for $i \in \{1, 2\}$, Z_i contains a subspace U_i that is filtered and does not contain any product element $e f_i$ with $e \in E$ and $f_i \in F_i$, nothing guarantees that A is not filtered, meaning it can contain product elements of the form eg with $e \in E$ and $g \in F_1 F_2$. Indeed, we observed empirically with great probability that the entire product space $E(F_1 F_2)$ is contained in A:

$$E(F_1 F_2) \subset A.$$

The dimension of A is upper bounded by $2d(w + rd - \lambda)$ (which is by hypothesis greatly less than m) and since an attacker can compute very easily a basis of the vector space $F_1 F_2$, one can use Proposition 1 to recover E by computing

$$\bigcap_{g \in F_1 F_2} g^{-1} A.$$

An informal explanation for why A contains some product elements lies in the fact that, even though Z_i contains no product elements, it contains "2-sums" of product elements of the form $ef_i + e'f_i'$ for $(e, e') \in E^2$ and $(f_i, f_i') \in F_i^2$.

More problematically, we will see in the next section that one can find 2-sums in both Z_1 and Z_2 for the *same pair* (e, e'), meaning that there exists $(e, e') \in E^2, (f_1, f_1') \in F_1^2$ and $(f_2, f_2') \in F_2^2$ such that

$$ef_1 + e'f_1' = z_1 \in Z_1,$$
$$ef_2 + e'f_2' = z_2 \in Z_2.$$

Notice that, in that case, the cross product $f_1'z_2 - f_2'z_1$, which is an element of A, is also a product element because:

$$f_1'z_2 - f_2'z_1 = ef_2f_1' + e'f_2'f_1' - ef_1f_2' - e'f_1'f_2'$$
$$= e(f_2f_1' - f_1f_2').$$

This explains why A contains product elements. As said earlier, we observed furthermore that A contains all of them.

As said at the beginning of the section, computing A is only useful when m is high enough. With practical parameters of PSSI, m is much less than $2d(w + rd - \lambda)$, and the computation of $F_1Z_2 + F_2Z_1$ would lead to $A = \mathbb{F}_{q^m}$. It does not give any information on E (see Remark 6).

The next section overcomes this limitation on parameters; we refine the observation to give a practical attack against PSSI.

6   An Attack Against PSSI

Since the vector space $F_1Z_2 + F_2Z_1$ is too large for a practical attack, we turn our initial observation into a combinatorial attack where the attacker picks individual elements $f_1 \in F_1$ and $f_2 \in F_2$ and computes spaces $f_1Z_2 + f_2Z_1$. If the attacker is lucky enough, they can obtain a product element eg with $e \in E$ and $g \in F_1F_2$. Since the vector spaces F_1 and F_2 are of small dimension d, the combinatorial factor in the attack is manageable.

6.1   General Overview of the Attack

Our combinatorial attack against PSSI consists in repeatedly applying Algorithm 1. The algorithm returns an element of $\mathbb{F}_{q^m}$, which is most of the time 0. We will show later on that, with a non negligible probability, it returns a non-zero element of $\mathbb{F}_{q^m}$ and in that case, this element belongs to the secret space E with overwhelming probability.

Algorithm 1. Attack against PSSI

Input: Four PSSI samples $(F_1, Z_1), (F_2, Z_2), (F_3, Z_3), (F_4, Z_4)$
Output: An element $x \in \mathbb{F}_{q^m}$

1: Choose $(f_1, f_1') \xleftarrow{\$} F_1^2$
2: Choose $(f_2, f_2') \xleftarrow{\$} F_2^2$
3: Choose $(f_3, f_3') \xleftarrow{\$} F_3^2$
4: Choose $(f_4, f_4') \xleftarrow{\$} F_4^2$
5: **for** $(i, j) \in [\![1, 4]\!]^2$ with $i < j$ **do**
6:    **if** $\begin{vmatrix} f_i & f_i' \\ f_j & f_j' \end{vmatrix} = 0$ **then** go back to step 1
7:    **else**
8:        Compute
$$A_{i,j} := \frac{f_j' Z_i + f_i' Z_j}{\begin{vmatrix} f_i & f_i' \\ f_j & f_j' \end{vmatrix}}$$
9:    **end if**
10: **end for**
11: Compute
$$B := \bigcap_{\substack{(i,j) \in [\![1,4]\!]^2 \\ i < j}} A_{i,j}$$
12: **if** $\dim(B) = 1$ **then**
13:    **return** a non-zero element of B
14: **else**
15:    **return** 0
16: **end if.**

The attacker starts by drawing random pairs in the subspaces F_i. If they are lucky, there exists a pair $(e, e') \in E^2$, such that a system $(\mathcal{S})$ of four conditions is verified:

$$(\mathcal{S}) : \begin{cases} e f_1 + e' f_1' = z_1 \in Z_1 \\ e f_2 + e' f_2' = z_2 \in Z_2 \\ e f_3 + e' f_3' = z_3 \in Z_3 \\ e f_4 + e' f_4' = z_4 \in Z_4 \end{cases}$$

Because the matrix $\begin{pmatrix} f_i & f_i' \\ f_j & f_j' \end{pmatrix}$ is chosen invertible (if not, the attacker retries with new random pairs), the element e can be recovered using Cramer's formula

$$e = \frac{\begin{vmatrix} z_i & f_i' \\ z_j & f_j' \end{vmatrix}}{\begin{vmatrix} f_i & f_i' \\ f_j & f_j' \end{vmatrix}}.$$

However, only the space Z_i is known to the attacker, not the exact element z_i. The attack thus consists in computing **a Cramer-like formula with vector spaces**, in order to get vector spaces containing e:

$$e \in A_{i,j} = \frac{\begin{vmatrix} Z_i & f_i' \\ Z_j & f_j' \end{vmatrix}}{\begin{vmatrix} f_i & f_i' \\ f_j & f_j' \end{vmatrix}}.$$

Finally, the attacker intersects all the spaces $A_{i,j}$. Two cases can then happen:

- If the attacker was lucky in the random sampling of (f_i, f_i'), there exists $(e, e') \in E^2$ such that conditions $(\mathcal{S})$ are verified, and then the intersection will be almost surely $\langle e \rangle$.
- In the other case, the intersection will be almost surely of dimension 0 and the attacker can retry with other samples.

The following subsections will be dedicated to proving our main result on the probability of success of the attack. It relies on one equality on parameters, which is verified for Durandal, as well as on an assumption which is discussed in the next subsection and is supported by simulations.

Theorem 1. *Under the equality* $\lambda = 2r$ *and under Assumption 1, the attack presented in Algorithm 1 outputs:*

- *0 with a probability* $\geq 1 - \alpha$;
- *an element* $x \in E \setminus \{0\}$ *with a probability* $\geq \beta$;
- *an element* $x \in \mathbb{F}_{q^m} \setminus E$ *with a probability* $\leq \alpha - \beta$.

with

$$\begin{cases} \alpha = q^{-6r} + q^{12(w+rd-\lambda)-5m} - q^{12(w+rd-\lambda)-5m-6r} \\ \beta = q^{-6r} - q^{12(w+rd-\lambda)-5m-6r-1} \end{cases}$$

Note that $\alpha - \beta$ is always greater than 0 and that for existing parameters of Durandal, both α and β weigh approximately q^{-6r}, therefore the probability that the third case happens is negligible in front of the chances of being in one of the two first cases.

Before delving into the details of the proof, we need technical results about the existence of 2-sums in a product space.

6.2 Technical Results About 2-Sums

For this subsection, let E be a subspace of $\mathbb{F}_{q^m}$ of dimension r and let $(F_1, Z_1), (F_2, Z_2), (F_3, Z_3), (F_4, Z_4)$ be four PSSI samples.

Definition 9. *For a pair (e, e') of linearly independent elements in E, we define $X_{e,e',F,Z}$ the boolean random variable*

$$X_{e,e',F,Z} : F^2 \longrightarrow \{0,1\}$$
$$(f, f') \longmapsto \mathbf{1}_Z(ef + e'f')$$

where $\mathbf{1}_Z$ refers to the indicator function of the set Z.

The element $ef + e'f'$ belongs to the product space EF and it is natural to think that its statistical distribution is close to uniformly random inside the space EF, therefore the probability that it falls in the space Z is expected to be $q^{-\lambda}$, since Z is of codimension λ in EF. We formalize it in the following assumption, alongside with an additional hypothesis on the independence of the random variables defined above.

Assumption 1. *The family of random variables (X_{e,e',F_i,Z_i}), parametrized by all the pairs (e, e') of linearly independent elements in E and the four PSSI samples, form a family of independent Bernoulli variables of parameter $q^{-\lambda}$.*

This assumption was validated by numerous simulations. Using the above assumption, we can prove the following lemma which explicitly gives the probability of fulfilling conditions from $(\mathcal{S})$. We present in Sect. 7 an experimental validation of Lemma 5.

Lemma 5. *Let $(f_i, f_i') \xleftarrow{\$} F_i$ for $i \in [\![1, 4]\!]$. Under the condition $\lambda = 2r$ and under Assumption 1, the probability ε that there exists a pair $(e, e') \in E^2$, such that the system $(\mathcal{S})$ of four conditions is verified:*

$$(\mathcal{S}) : \begin{cases} ef_1 + e'f_1' = z_1 \in Z_1 \\ ef_2 + e'f_2' = z_2 \in Z_2 \\ ef_3 + e'f_3' = z_3 \in Z_3 \\ ef_4 + e'f_4' = z_4 \in Z_4 \end{cases}$$

admits an asymptotic development

$$\varepsilon = q^{-6r} + o_{r\to\infty}(q^{-10r}).$$

Proof. The system $(\mathcal{S})$ is verified for a pair (e, e') when the four boolean variables X_{e,e',F_i,Z_i} (defined above) are all true for $i \in [\![1, 4]\!]$. Therefore,

$$\varepsilon = \text{Prob}(\bigvee_{(e,e') \in E^2} (\bigwedge_{i=1}^{4} X_{e,e',F_i,Z_i}))$$

$$= 1 - \text{Prob}(\bigwedge_{(e,e') \in E^2} (\bigvee_{i=1}^{4} \overline{X}_{e,e',F_i,Z_i}))$$

$$= 1 - \prod_{(e,e') \in E^2} \text{Prob}(\bigvee_{i=1}^{4} \overline{X}_{e,e',F_i,Z_i})$$

$$= 1 - \prod_{(e,e') \in E^2} (1 - \text{Prob}(\bigwedge_{i=1}^{4} X_{e,e',F_i,Z_i}))$$

$$= 1 - \prod_{(e,e') \in E^2} (1 - q^{-4\lambda})$$

$$= 1 - (1 - q^{-4\lambda})^{q^{2r}}$$

$$= 1 - (1 - q^{-8r})^{q^{2r}}$$

$$= 1 - (1 - q^{-6r} + o_{r \to \infty}(q^{-10r}))$$

$$= q^{-6r} + o_{r \to \infty}(q^{-10r}).$$

$\square$

In the rest of the paper we will omit the residue in $o_{r \to \infty}(q^{-10r})$.

6.3   Proof of the Probability of Success of the Attack

We can now finalize the proof of success of the attack.

Proof (of Theorem 1). The three cases of Theorem 1 form a partition of the possible outputs of Algorithm 1, hence we only need to prove the first two inequalities on the probabilities of the theorem and the third inequality will follow immediately.

For $i \in [\![1, 4]\!]$, let $(f_i, f_i') \in F_i^2$ be the pairs sampled at random during the first four steps of the attack.

We will consider two separate cases depending on whether conditions from $(\mathcal{S})$ are fulfilled. Each case will yield one of the equalities to be proven.

First Case. Suppose that there exists $(e, e') \in E^2$ such that the conditions from $(\mathcal{S})$ are verified. According to Lemma 5, this happens with probability q^{-6r}.

In that case, we can assume the vector spaces $A_{i,j}$ are independent (as random variables) subspaces of $\mathbb{F}_{q^m}$, all containing e, of dimension $a_{i,j} \leq 2(w + rd - \lambda)$, hence $\sum_{i,j} a_{i,j} \leq 12(w + rd - \lambda)$. By using Lemma 4, $\langle e \rangle \subset B$

and the probability that B is exactly $\langle e \rangle$ is greater than $1 - q^{12(w+rd-\lambda)-5m-1}$. As a result, Algorithm 1 outputs an element of E with a probability greater or equal to

$$q^{-6r}(1 - q^{12(w+rd-\lambda)-5m-1}) = \beta.$$

Second Case. If there does not exist a pair $(e, e') \in E$ such that the conditions from $(\mathcal{S})$ are verified (it happens with probability $1 - q^{-6r}$), then the vector spaces $A_{i,j}$ can be seen as random independent subspaces of $\mathbb{F}_{q^m}$ of dimension $a_{i,j} \leq 2(w + rd - \lambda)$, so this time we use Lemma 3.

It proves that Algorithm 1 returns 0 with a probability of at least

$$(1 - q^{-6r})(1 - q^{12(w+rd-\lambda)-5m}) = 1 - \alpha.$$

$\square$

6.4   Complexity of the Attack

Algorithm 1 returns only one element of E with a small probability of success. In order to fully solve the Search-PSSI problem, the attacker has to recover the whole space E, i.e. at least r elements of the secret space. In this subsection we study the complexity of the full attack, which recovers E totally.

Let us first study the complexity of one call to Algorithm 1. The most costly operation is Step 11, which consists in five intersections of subspaces of $\mathbb{F}_{q^m}$, each of dimension less than $2(w + rd - \lambda)$. An intersection of two subspaces is usually computed through the Zassenhaus algorithm, and is essentially a Gaussian elimination of a binary matrix of size $4(w + rd - \lambda) \times 2m$, which costs $2m \times (4(w + rd - \lambda))^2 = 32m(w + rd - \lambda)^2$ operations in $\mathbb{F}_q$. Repeating the operation five times yields a total complexity of

$$160m(w + rd - \lambda)^2$$

operations in $\mathbb{F}_q$.

It remains to evaluate the number of calls to Algorithm 1. To simplify, because the probability that Algorithm 1 returns an element outside the space E is negligible, we will consider that the algorithm either

– returns a random element of E with probability q^{-6r}, or
– returns $\emptyset$ with probability $1 - q^{-6r}$.

On average, the number of times Algorithm 1 must be run is q^{6r} multiplied by the expectancy of the number of elements needed to recover E, which is given by the following lemma.

Lemma 6. *Let E be a subspace of $\mathbb{F}_{q^m}$ of dimension r. Let $\mathcal{O}$ be an oracle which, on each call i, returns an independent $x_i \overset{\$}{\leftarrow} E$. The average number n of calls to the oracle such that $\langle x_1, ..., x_n \rangle = E$ is upper bounded as follows:*

$$n \leq r + \frac{1}{q-1}.$$

Proof. Let X be the integer-value random variable defined as the number of calls to the oracle until it generates E, i.e. $\langle x_1, ..., x_{X-1} \rangle \subsetneq E$ and $\langle x_1, ..., x_X \rangle = E$.

It is clear that $X \geq r$ with probability 1. For $i > r$, $X \geq i$ if and only if $\langle x_1, ..., x_i \rangle \subsetneq E$, which is equivalent to having a uniformly random $r \times i$ matrix with entries in $\mathbb{F}_q$ not of full rank. This happens with a probability upper bounded by q^{r-i} (see for example [1, Lemma 1]).

To finish the proof, we calculate the expectancy n of X:

$$n = \mathbb{E}(X)$$

$$= r + \sum_{i=r+1}^{\infty} \mathrm{Prob}(X \geq i)$$

$$\leq r + \sum_{i=r+1}^{\infty} q^{r-i}$$

$$\leq r + \frac{1}{q-1}.$$

$\square$

Therefore, we can formulate the following result.

Proposition 2 (Complexity of the attack). *Under the same conditions of validity than Theorem 1, the average complexity of the attack is given by*

$$160m(w + rd - \lambda)^2(r + \frac{1}{q-1})q^{6r}$$

operations in $\mathbb{F}_q$.

Applying the above formula to parameters of Durandal, it gives the following table (Table 2):

Table 2. Theoretical base-2 logarithm of the average number of bit operations necessary to run our attack against Search-PSSI.

	Theoretical complexity	Security
Durandal-I	66	128
Durandal-II	73	128

6.5   Number of Signatures

In the previous subsection, we saw that Algorithm 1 must be run on average $(r + \frac{1}{q-1})q^{6r}$ to finalize the attack. Since 4 PSSI samples are used in Algorithm 1, it could seem that an average number of $4(r + \frac{1}{q-1})q^{6r}$ of signatures would be necessary to recover the private key. This would be a very large number of signatures with the considered parameters.

Fortunately, the same signatures can be reused by running Algorithm 1 several times with the same 4 PSSI samples. Indeed, this algorithm starts by choosing at random 8 elements in vector spaces of $\mathbb{F}_q$-dimension d, which makes q^{8d} possibilities.

We can assume that if the algorithm is run with the same set of 4 signatures a number of times greatly less than q^{8d}, the event that one run outputs an element of E remains probabilistically independent from the other runs with the same samples.

Empirically, we set to q^{5d} the number of reuses of the same signatures in Algorithm 1, which makes an average number of signatures necessary to finalize the attack of:

$$4\left(r + \frac{1}{q-1}\right)\frac{q^{6r}}{q^{5d}}.$$

Applying the above formula to parameters of Durandal, it gives the following table (Table 3):

Table 3. Excepted number of signatures to perform our attack on Search-PSSI.

	Expected signatures
Durandal-I	1,792
Durandal-II	4,096

7   Experimental Results

We implemented the attack in C language, using the RBC library [3] which provides useful functions when working with finite field subspaces. Our implementation is publicly available in the following Github repository:

https://github.com/victordyseryn/pssi-security-implementation

All of our experiments were performed on a laptop equipped with an Intel Core i5-7440HQ CPU and 16 GB RAM.

Since we didn't have a sufficient computing power at our disposal to run the 2^{66} attack on the actual parameters of Durandal in reasonable time, we tried to run experiments with lower parameter sets, which are represented in the following table (Table 4):

Table 4. Reduced parameter sets for experiments on PSSI attack

Experiment number	q	m	d	r	λ	w
A2	2	83	2	2	3	19
A3	2	127	3	3	6	28
A4	2	163	4	4	8	38
A5	2	199	5	5	10	47

Table 5. Experimental results on PSSI attack

Experiment	q	m	d	r	λ	w	Number of tests	Number of signatures (avg)	Experimental complexity	Theoretical complexity
A2	2	83	2	2	3	19	1,000	10	$2^{32.4}$	$2^{35.9}$
A3	2	127	3	3	6	28	100	301	$2^{44.9}$	2^{44}
A4	2	163	4	4	8	38	1	502	$2^{51.2}$	$2^{51.7}$

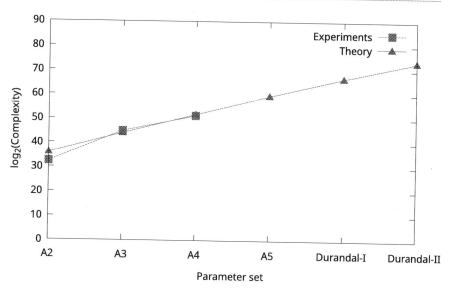

Fig. 2. Comparison between experimental and theoretical complexities for different values of r.

For each experiment, we ran the attack a number of times depending on the complexity of the attack, and we recorded the average number of cycles to recover the entire secret space E, as well as the average number of PSSI samples needed. We were able to complete the attack up to the parameter set A4. Experiment A5 was out of reach in a reasonable time. We computed the experimental complexity of our experiments as the average number of cycles required to recover the secret key, and then multiplying this cycle count by 64 to obtain an approximation of the number of bit operations performed by our 64-bit processor. Our experimental results are presented in Table 5.

Figure 2 shows the comparison between the experimental and theoretical complexities, as well as the expected complexities for parameter sets A5, Durandal-I and Durandal-II.

Finally, we also validated the result from Lemma 5 by running the following experiment: we randomly generated PSSI samples, and checked whether a pair $(e, e') \in E^2$ such that the system described in the definition of Lemma 5 exists or not by enumerating every possible pair (e, e'). Results are presented in Table 6.

Table 6. Experimental results validating Lemma 5

q	m	d	r	λ	w	Number of tests	Experimental probability	Theoretical probability
2	83	3	3	6	19	2^{24}	$2^{-18.6}$	2^{-18}
2	127	3	3	6	28	2^{24}	$2^{-18.9}$	2^{-18}

8   Conclusion and Perspectives

We presented an attack against Durandal signature scheme that combines pairs of signatures into Cramer-like formulas to build secret subspaces. It would be an interesting research problem to investigate whether the approach can be extended to combining triples of signatures (or even arbitrary tuples of signatures).

Such a refinement of the attack is not trivial; a naive generalization would lead to build subspaces of the form $\langle f_1, f_2 \rangle Z_3 + \langle f_1, f_3 \rangle Z_2 + \langle f_2, f_3 \rangle Z_1$ whose typical dimension is so large that it would almost surely cover the ambient space $\mathbb{F}_{q^m}$. However, by replacing Z_i by strict subspaces of them, the dimension of the calculated subspace would decrease, although it is unclear yet whether this subspace would still contain secret elements with a non-negligible probability.

References

1. Aguilar-Melchor, C., Aragon, N., Dyseryn, V., Gaborit, P., Zémor, G.: LRPC codes with multiple syndromes: near ideal-size KEMs without ideals. In: Cheon, J.H., Johansson, T. (eds.) Post-Quantum Cryptography, PQCrypto 2022. LNCS, vol 13512. Springer, Cham (2022). https://doi.org/10.1007/978-3-031-17234-2_3
2. Aguilar-Melchor, C., Blazy, O., Deneuville, J.-C., Gaborit, P., Zémor, G.: Efficient encryption from random quasi-cyclic codes. IEEE Trans. Inf. Theor. **64**(5), 3927–3943 (2018)
3. Aragon, N., et al.: The rank-based cryptography library. In: Wachter-Zeh, A., Bartz, H., Liva, G. (eds.) Code-Based Cryptography, CBCrypto 2021. LNCS, vol. 13150. Springer, Cham (2022). https://doi.org/10.1007/978-3-030-98365-9_2

4. Aragon, N., et al.: ROLLO (merger of Rank-Ouroboros, LAKE and LOCKER). Second round submission to the NIST post-quantum cryptography call, March 2019

5. Aragon, N., Blazy, O., Gaborit, P., Hauteville, A., Zémor, G.: Durandal: a rank metric based signature scheme. In: Ishai, Y., Rijmen, V. (eds.) EUROCRYPT 2019. LNCS, vol. 11478, pp. 728–758. Springer, Cham (2019). https://doi.org/10.1007/978-3-030-17659-4_25

6. Aragon, N., Gaborit, P., Hauteville, A., Ruatta, O., Zémor, G.: Low rank parity check codes: new decoding algorithms and applications to cryptography. IEEE Trans. Inf. Theor. **65**(12), 7697–7717 (2019)

7. Aumasson, J.-P., et al.: SPHINCS+. Submission to the 3rd round of the NIST post-quantum project (v3.1), June 2022

8. Ducas, L., et al.: CRYSTALS-Dilithium. Algorithm Specifications and Supporting Documentation (Version 3.1), February 2021

9. Feneuil, T.: Building MPCitH-based Signatures from MQ, MinRank. Rank SD and PKP. Cryptology ePrint Archive (2022)

10. Fiat, A., Shamir, A.: How to prove yourself: practical solutions to identification and signature problems. In: Odlyzko, A.M. (ed.) CRYPTO 1986. LNCS, vol. 263, pp. 186–194. Springer, Heidelberg (1987). https://doi.org/10.1007/3-540-47721-7_12

11. Fouque, P.-A., et al.: Falcon: fast-Fourier lattice-based compact signatures over NTRU. Algorithm Specifications and Supporting Documentation (Version 1.2), October 2020

12. Gaborit, P., Hauteville, A., Phan, D.H., Tillich, J.-P.: Identity-based encryption from codes with rank metric. In: Katz, J., Shacham, H. (eds.) CRYPTO 2017. LNCS, vol. 10403, pp. 194–224. Springer, Cham (2017). https://doi.org/10.1007/978-3-319-63697-9_7

13. Lyubashevsky, V.: Lattice signatures without trapdoors. In: Pointcheval, D., Johansson, T. (eds.) EUROCRYPT 2012. LNCS, vol. 7237, pp. 738–755. Springer, Heidelberg (2012). https://doi.org/10.1007/978-3-642-29011-4_43

Finding Short Integer Solutions When the Modulus Is Small

Léo Ducas[1,2], Thomas Espitau[3], and Eamonn W. Postlethwaite[1(✉)]

[1] CWI, Cryptology Group, Amsterdam, The Netherlands
ewp@cwi.nl
[2] Mathematical Institute, Leiden University, Leiden, The Netherlands
[3] PQShield, Paris, France

Abstract. We present cryptanalysis of the inhomogenous short integer solution (ISIS) problem for anomalously small moduli q by exploiting the geometry of BKZ reduced bases of q-ary lattices.

We apply this cryptanalysis to examples from the literature where taking such small moduli has been suggested. A recent work [Espitau–Tibouchi–Wallet–Yu, CRYPTO 2022] suggests small q versions of the lattice signature scheme Falcon and its variant Mitaka. For one small q parametrisation of Falcon we reduce the estimated security against signature forgery by approximately 26 bits. For one small q parametrisation of Mitaka we successfully forge a signature in 15 s.

1 Introduction

The Short Integer Solution (SIS) problem is a computational problem that requires one to find a non-zero short vector in a lattice from a specific class of random lattices, known as random q-ary lattices. It was first introduced by Ajtai [1,20] along with reductions to worst-case lattice problems. The SIS problem has emerged as fundamental to lattice-based cryptography in both theory and practice. The above worst-case hardness reductions require the modulus q of the SIS instance to be significantly larger than ν, its Euclidean length bound on solutions. Given that concrete cryptographic design can be thought as a rarefied game of chicken, one sees this requirement on q ignored with parameters pushed towards maximal efficiency, and only constrained by documented cryptanalytic attacks.

The SIS problem has an inhomogeneous variant (ISIS), which often holds greater relevance in cryptanalytic contexts. In particular, forging a signature in lattice-based signature schemes commonly constitutes solving a particular ISIS instance.

One notable difference between the SIS and ISIS problems is that SIS becomes trivial once $q \leqslant \nu$. This can be demonstrated by the solution vector $q \cdot \mathbf{e}_1$ which is non-zero, in all random q-ary lattices and has length not greater than ν.

© International Association for Cryptologic Research 2023
H. Handschuh and A. Lysyanskaya (Eds.): CRYPTO 2023, LNCS 14083, pp. 150–176, 2023.
https://doi.org/10.1007/978-3-031-38548-3_6

However, $q \cdot \mathbf{e}_1$ is not a solution vector for ISIS provided its target $\mathbf{u}$ is not the zero vector. If $\mathbf{u} = \mathbf{0}$ then SIS and ISIS coincide. Nevertheless, ISIS also eventually becomes trivial as q decreases. For example, consider the ISIS instance $\mathbf{A}\mathbf{x} = \mathbf{u} \bmod q$, where $\mathbf{A} \in \mathbb{Z}_q^{n \times m}$ with $m \geqslant n$ and $\mathbf{u} \in \mathbb{Z}_q^n \setminus \{\mathbf{0}\}$ are chosen uniformly. Assuming that $\mathbf{A} = (\mathbf{A}_1 \,|\, \mathbf{A}_2)$ is such that $\mathbf{A}_1 \in \mathbb{Z}_q^{n \times n}$ is invertible over $\mathbb{Z}_q$, then $\mathbf{x}^t = (\mathbf{u}^t \mathbf{A}_1^{-t} \,|\, \mathbf{0})$ is non-zero and satisfies $\mathbf{A}\mathbf{x} = \mathbf{u} \bmod q$. The first n entries of $\mathbf{x}$ are uniform in $\mathbb{Z}_q^n \setminus \{\mathbf{0}\}$. By reducing the coefficients of $\mathbf{x}$ modulo q around 0 this solution has an expected square length of $nq^2/12$.[1] If this is sufficiently below ν^2 then it is likely that $\mathbf{x}$ is an ISIS solution. As such, the following approximate observations can be made:

1. for $\nu < q$, SIS and ISIS are similar problems and are both subject to lattice reduction attacks,
2. for $\nu \geqslant q$, SIS becomes trivial, but not necessarily ISIS, and
3. for $\nu \geqslant q\sqrt{n/12}$, ISIS also becomes trivial.

This naturally leads to the question of the security of ISIS in the regime where $\nu \in (q, q\sqrt{n/12})$. We do not expect ISIS to be hard as soon as $\nu < q\sqrt{n/12}$. Indeed, if ν is slightly below $q\sqrt{n/12}$ then one can attempt an Information Set Decoding (ISD) style of attack by randomising the columns of $\mathbf{A}_1$ and hoping that after a few trials the solution $\mathbf{x}^t = (\mathbf{u}^t \mathbf{A}_1^{-t} \,|\, \mathbf{0})$ reduced modulo q around $\mathbf{0}$ has a length slightly below its expectation.

While we find this gap in our cryptanalytic knowledge to be motivating in its own right, recent works have proposed ISIS parameters where $\nu > q$. In particular small q parameter sets for the lattice signatures Falcon [22] and its variant Mitaka [15] were proposed in [16], as well as for early parameters of a blind signature scheme [11].[2]

Contributions. For the regime $\nu \in (q, q\sqrt{n/12})$ we give an attack that is essentially a hybrid of the standard lattice reduction attack when $\nu < q$ with the ISD style attack when $\nu \approx q\sqrt{n/12}$. We improve this hybrid by exploiting the many short vectors given by a lattice sieve, providing in essence many ISD attempts with a single lattice reduction effort.

The core of the attack lies in noticing that after lattice reduction on a SIS lattice basis, we get a profile often referred to as having a Z-shape. This reduced basis has a number of q vectors as its first columns, $q \cdot \mathbf{e}_1, \ldots, q \cdot \mathbf{e}_{\ell-1}$. By performing lattice sieving in the first projected sublattice after the q vectors and lifting the discovered short vectors to the non-projected lattice, we reduce the first $\ell - 1$ entries of these short vectors modulo q around 0. The square length of a vector lifted in this manner is then the square length of the projected vector that lifted to it, plus the square length of its first $\ell - 1$ entries. These first $\ell - 1$ entries lie in $\lceil -(q-1)/2 \rceil, \ldots, \lfloor q/2 \rfloor$.

On the technical level, our attack requires us to model the Z-shape of a SIS lattice basis after lattice reduction and to count the number of integer points in

---

[1] For simplicity we consider the expected square length of the region $[-q/2, q/2]^n$.
[2] Given early communication with the authors the parameters of [11] were revised.

the intersection of certain hyperballs and hypercubes. We achieve the first by using models that exist in the literature [2, 14] and the latter via the efficient convolution of truncated theta series of $\mathbb{Z}$. Our model also assumes that the lifted entries of projected vectors are independently and uniformly distributed in $\lceil -(q-1)/2 \rceil, \ldots, \lfloor q/2 \rfloor$. Both our modelling of the Z-shape after reduction and our assumption on the uniformity of lifted entries are verified experimentally.

As another technical contribution we introduce an intermediate problem between SIS and ISIS that we call SIS*. The SIS* problem is identical to SIS except it disallows solutions that are $\mathbf{0} \bmod q$. In particular, if $\nu < q$ then SIS and SIS* coincide, and if $\nu \geq q$ then it allows us to argue about the homogeneous version of our attack. We give a generic reduction from ISIS to SIS* that increases the rank of the instance by one from m to $m+1$ and has a probability loss factor approximately mq. We then give a reduction using the SIS* attack we outline above that performs better: it still increments the rank but has a probability loss factor of $q/2$.

As a final contribution, we present the performance of our attack against several small q parameter sets suggested in [16]. For one parameter set suggested for Falcon we reduce the forgery security in the CoreSVP model [4] from 118 to 92 bits. For another parameter set suggested for Mitaka we reduced the BKZ blocksize required for forgery to $\beta \approx 40$ and implement the attack. We also explicitly state that we believe the attacks presented in this work are far from optimised. As such, we suggest that appealing to the practical security of ISIS instances with $\nu \geq q$ is approached with great care and, if possible, not at all. Our code is available at https://github.com/verdiverdiverdi/ISIS-small-q.

Application Beyond SIS. An alternative interpretation of our attack can be made directly on SIS in systematic form; $\mathbf{A} = (\mathbf{I}_n \parallel \mathbf{A}_2) \in \mathbb{Z}_q^{n \times m}$ and one searches for a short $\mathbf{x} \in \mathbb{Z}^m \setminus \{\mathbf{0}\}$ such that $\mathbf{A}\mathbf{x} = 0 \bmod q$. The attacker may ignore carefully chosen rows or columns of $\mathbf{A}$. Ignoring columns is standard, and is equivalent to fixing entries of $\mathbf{x}$ to 0. Let $\mathbf{A}'$ denote $\mathbf{A}$ with some rows removed. Assuming solutions to the original SIS instance exist, we may find a short non-zero $\mathbf{x} \in \{0\}^n \times \mathbb{Z}^{m-n}$ such that $\mathbf{A}'\mathbf{x} = \mathbf{0} \bmod q$. Such an $\mathbf{x}$ does not guarantee $\mathbf{A}\mathbf{x} = \mathbf{0} \bmod q$. Due to the systematic form of $\mathbf{A}$ one can choose x_i for $1 \leq i \leq n$ to ensure $\mathbf{A}\mathbf{x} = \mathbf{0} \bmod q$, but these x_i may not be small. Our attack consists of using the many outputs of a sieve to brute force this approach, hoping that one solution has small enough x_i.

However, we find our geometric description preferable, because it also hints that this attack is not fundamentally limited to SIS type problems. For example, this attack would also be applicable to Hawk [9, 13] if the parameter σ_{pk} (η in the specification version) was small. One would need to replace reduction modulo q by Babai lifting [7], and it might no longer be possible to calculate the success probability of the attack via theta series, but the principle remains valid. That is, if the adversary is given vectors that are shorter than what they can find using generic lattice reduction, then these vectors may be abused to improve attacks. The design of Hawk anticipated this, and set σ_{pk} precisely so that the vectors given to the attacker are not too short. To account for the variance in the length of sampled vectors, keys that would be too short are also rejected.

Related Work. The general principle of considering the Z-shape basis structure is not new and is discussed in the cryptanalysis of Dilithium [19]. Due to Dilithium's use of the ℓ_∞ version of ISIS the Z-shape structure did not lead to the best attacks. We take inspiration to consider the Z-shape in q-ary bases from [2,14,17].

Organisation of the Paper. Section 2 introduces the necessary preliminaries. Section 3 outlines our attack and our model for it against SIS*, and Sect. 3.5 describes how we mount it on ISIS. Section 4 outlines an optimisation to the basic attack. Section 5 provides experimental verification of two of the heuristics in our attack, namely our modelling of the Z-shape of a SIS lattice basis after reduction and the distribution of lifted entries. Section 6 discusses how our attack affects the security of recent cryptosystems in the $\nu \geqslant q$ regime.

2   Preliminaries

2.1   Lattices and Computational Problems

Definition 1 (Lattice). Let $\mathbf{B} \in \mathbb{R}^{d \times m}$ have linearly independent columns. A lattice $\mathbf{\Lambda}$ is the integer span of the columns of $\mathbf{B}$, $\{\mathbf{B} \cdot \mathbf{x} \colon \mathbf{x} \in \mathbb{Z}^m\}$. We say $\mathbf{B}$ is a basis for $\mathbf{\Lambda}$, $\mathbf{\Lambda}$ has dimension d and rank m, and $\mathbf{\Lambda}$ is full rank if $d = m$.

Definition 2 (Lattice Volume). The volume of lattice $\mathbf{\Lambda}$ with basis $\mathbf{B}$ is $\text{vol}(\mathbf{\Lambda}) = \sqrt{\det(\mathbf{B}^t \mathbf{B})}$.

If $\mathbf{\Lambda}$ is full rank then $\text{vol}(\mathbf{\Lambda}) = \det(\mathbf{B})$. Note that the lattices generated by $\mathbf{B}, \mathbf{C} \in \mathbb{R}^{d \times m}$ are equal if and only if there exists $\mathbf{U} \in \text{Gl}_m(\mathbb{Z})$ such that $\mathbf{B} = \mathbf{CU}$, and therefore volume is well defined.

Definition 3 (First minimum). For lattice $\mathbf{\Lambda}$ we define

$$\lambda_1(\mathbf{\Lambda}) = \min_{\mathbf{x} \in \mathbf{\Lambda} \setminus \{\mathbf{0}\}} \|\mathbf{x}\|.$$

We can estimate the first minimum via the Gaussian heuristic which calculates the radius of ball whose volume equals that of the lattice.

Definition 4 (Gaussian heuristic). Let $v_m = \pi^{m/2}/\Gamma(1 + m/2)$ be the volume of the m dimensional unit ball. For rank m lattice $\mathbf{\Lambda}$ we estimate $\lambda_1(\mathbf{\Lambda})$ as $\text{gh}(\mathbf{\Lambda}) = v_m^{-1/m} \cdot \text{vol}(\mathbf{\Lambda})^{1/m} \approx \sqrt{m/2\pi e} \cdot \text{vol}(\mathbf{\Lambda})^{1/m}$.

Throughout we will consider projected sublattices, for which we need the following projections.

Definition 5 (Projections). Given a lattice basis $\mathbf{B} \in \mathbb{R}^{d \times m}$ and an index $1 \leqslant i \leqslant m+1$, define $\pi_{\mathbf{B},i} \colon \mathbb{R}^d \to \mathbb{R}^d$ as the orthogonal projection *against* $\mathrm{span}_{\mathbb{R}}(\mathbf{b}_1, \ldots, \mathbf{b}_{i-1})$ (i.e. *onto* $\mathrm{span}_{\mathbb{R}}(\mathbf{b}_1, \ldots, \mathbf{b}_{i-1})^{\perp}$).

For any $\mathbf{B}$ we have $\pi_{\mathbf{B},1} = \mathrm{Id}_{\mathbb{R}^d}$ and, if $m = d$, $\pi_{\mathbf{B},m+1}(\mathbb{R}^d) = \{\mathbf{0}\}$. If $\mathbf{x} \in \mathrm{span}_{\mathbb{R}}(\mathbf{b}_1, \ldots, \mathbf{b}_{i-1})$ and $\mathbf{y} \in \mathbb{R}^d$ then $\langle \mathbf{x}, \pi_{\mathbf{B},i}(\mathbf{y}) \rangle = 0$. If the basis is clear from context we write π_i. To compute these projections one can use the Gram–Schmidt basis related to a lattice basis $\mathbf{B}$.

Definition 6 (Gram–Schmidt). Given a basis $\mathbf{B} \in \mathbb{R}^{d \times m}$ the Gram–Schmidt basis $\mathbf{B}^* \in \mathbb{R}^{d \times m}$ has pairwise orthogonal columns and is related to $\mathbf{B}$ via an upper triangular matrix $\mathbf{M}$ with a unit diagonal as $\mathbf{B} = \mathbf{B}^* \cdot \mathbf{M}$.

For $1 \leqslant i \leqslant m$ we have $\mathrm{span}_{\mathbb{R}}(\mathbf{b}_1, \ldots, \mathbf{b}_i) = \mathrm{span}_{\mathbb{R}}(\mathbf{b}_1^*, \ldots, \mathbf{b}_i^*)$ and for $\mathbf{x} \in \mathbb{R}^d$ one can calculate $\pi_{\mathbf{B},i}(\mathbf{x})$ via

$$\mathbf{x}_1 = \mathbf{x}, \quad \mathbf{x}_{j+1} = \mathbf{x}_j - \frac{\langle \mathbf{b}_j^*, \mathbf{x}_j \rangle}{\langle \mathbf{b}_j^*, \mathbf{b}_j^* \rangle} \mathbf{b}_j^*,$$

for $1 \leqslant j \leqslant i-1$ so that $\pi_{\mathbf{B},i}(\mathbf{x}) = \mathbf{x}_i$. Note that $\pi_i(\mathbf{b}_i) = \mathbf{b}_i^*$ and $\mathrm{vol}(\mathbf{\Lambda}) = \prod_i \|\mathbf{b}_i^*\|$. We use the following shorthand for projected lattices and lattice bases.

Definition 7 (Projected lattices and bases). Given basis $\mathbf{B} \in \mathbb{R}^{d \times m}$ and $1 \leqslant \ell < r \leqslant m+1$ let $\mathbf{B}_{[\ell:r]} = (\pi_\ell(\mathbf{b}_\ell) | \cdots | \pi_\ell(\mathbf{b}_{r-1}))$ and $\mathbf{\Lambda}_{[\ell:r]} = \{\mathbf{B}_{[\ell:r]} \cdot \mathbf{x} \colon \mathbf{x} \in \mathbb{Z}^{r-\ell}\}$. If $r = m+1$ we write $\mathbf{B}_{[\ell]}$ and $\mathbf{\Lambda}_{[\ell]}$.

For example

$$\mathbf{B}_{[1]} = \mathbf{B},$$
$$\mathbf{B}_{[1:r]} = (\mathbf{b}_1 | \cdots | \mathbf{b}_{r-1}),$$
$$\mathbf{B}_{[\ell:r]} = (\mathbf{b}_\ell^* | \pi_\ell(\mathbf{b}_{\ell+1}) | \cdots | \pi_\ell(\mathbf{b}_{r-1})).$$

One quantity of a basis we use throughout it its profile.

Definition 8 (Basis profile). Given a basis $\mathbf{B} \in \mathbb{R}^{d \times m}$ its profile is the tuple $(\log \|\mathbf{b}_i^*\|)_{i=1}^m \in \mathbb{R}^m$.

Often we consider lattices of a particular form.

Definition 9 (q-ary lattice). For some $q \in \mathbb{Z}_{>0}$ a rank m lattice $\mathbf{\Lambda}$ is a q-ary lattice if $q\mathbb{Z}^m \subseteq \mathbf{\Lambda} \subseteq \mathbb{Z}^m$.

Solving the following (I)SIS problems can be achieved by performing certain lattice reduction tasks over related q-ary lattices.

Definition 10 ((I)SIS). Let $n \in \mathbb{N}$, m, q, ν be functions with domain $\mathbb{N}$ and $\mathbf{A} \leftarrow U(\mathbb{Z}_q^{n \times m})$. We suppress the dependence of m, q and ν on n.

The $\mathsf{SIS}_{n,m,q,\nu}$ problem is to find a vector $\mathbf{x} \in \mathbb{Z}^m \setminus \{\mathbf{0}\}$ such that $\|\mathbf{x}\| \leqslant \nu$ and $\mathbf{A}\mathbf{x} = \mathbf{0} \bmod q$.

Given also $\mathbf{u} \leftarrow U(\mathbb{Z}_q^n)$ the $\mathsf{ISIS}_{n,m,q,\nu}$ problem is to find a vector $\mathbf{x} \in \mathbb{Z}^m \setminus \{\mathbf{0}\}$ such that $\|\mathbf{x}\| \leqslant \nu$ and $\mathbf{A}\mathbf{x} = \mathbf{u} \bmod q$.

If $\varphi_{\mathbf{A}} : \mathbb{Z}^m \to \mathbb{Z}_q^n$, $\mathbf{x} \mapsto \mathbf{A}\mathbf{x} \bmod q$ then $\ker(\varphi_{\mathbf{A}})$ forms a lattice called the kernel lattice of $\mathbf{A}$. Note that $\mathbf{A}$ is not in general a basis for this lattice.

Definition 11 (Kernel lattice and basis). Let $\Lambda_q^\perp(\mathbf{A}) = \{\mathbf{x} \in \mathbb{Z}^m : \mathbf{A}\mathbf{x} = \mathbf{0} \bmod q\}$ be the kernel lattice of $\mathbf{A}$. If one can permute the columns of $\mathbf{A}$ (which relates to a known entrywise permutation of the lattice $\Lambda_q^\perp(\mathbf{A})$) to $(\mathbf{A}_1 \mid \mathbf{A}_2)$ such that $\mathbf{A}_1 \in \mathrm{Gl}_n(\mathbb{Z}_q)$ then one can form the basis

$$\mathbf{B}_{\mathbf{A}} = \begin{pmatrix} q\mathbf{I}_n & -\mathbf{A}_1^{-1}\mathbf{A}_2 \\ \mathbf{0} & \mathbf{I}_{m-n} \end{pmatrix},$$

of $\Lambda_q^\perp(\mathbf{A})$.

Throughout, we will assume that such a permutation of the columns of $\mathbf{A}$ exists and note that for prime q, if $m = 2n$ then one exists with overwhelming probability in n. Note that $\Lambda_q^\perp(\mathbf{A})$ has (full) rank m and volume q^n. Solving a $\mathsf{SIS}_{n,m,q,\nu}$ instance given by $\mathbf{A}$ is equivalent to finding $\mathbf{x} \in \Lambda_q^\perp(\mathbf{A})$ with $\|\mathbf{x}\| \leqslant \nu$. Solving an $\mathsf{ISIS}_{n,m,q,\nu}$ instance given by $\mathbf{A}$ and $\mathbf{u}$ is equivalent to finding $\mathbf{b} \in \mathbb{Z}^m$ such that $\mathbf{A}\mathbf{b} = \mathbf{u} \bmod q$ and $\mathbf{x} \in \Lambda_q^\perp(\mathbf{A})$ with $\|\mathbf{b} - \mathbf{x}\| \leqslant \nu$ since $\mathbf{A}(\mathbf{b} - \mathbf{x}) = \mathbf{u} - \mathbf{0} \bmod q$.

For clarity of exposition we introduce the SIS^* problem, which we give a reduction from ISIS to in Sect. 3.5. Trivial SIS solutions of the form $q \cdot \mathbf{e}_i$ are disallowed for SIS^*.

Definition 12 (SIS^*). Let $n \in \mathbb{N}$, m, q, ν be functions with domain $\mathbb{N}$ and $\mathbf{A} \leftarrow \mathsf{U}(\mathbb{Z}_q^{n \times m})$. The $\mathsf{SIS}^*_{n,m,q,\nu}$ problem is to find a vector $\mathbf{x} \in \mathbb{Z}^m \setminus q\mathbb{Z}^m$ such that $\|\mathbf{x}\| \leqslant \nu$ and $\mathbf{A}\mathbf{x} = \mathbf{0} \bmod q$.

If $\nu < q$ then SIS and SIS^* are equivalent problems. We make use of a particular instance of theta functions on a lattice.

Definition 13 (Theta function of a lattice). Given a lattice Λ we write

$$\Theta_{\Lambda}(\tau) = \sum_{\mathbf{x} \in \Lambda} e^{\pi i \tau \|x\|^2},$$

for any $\tau \in \mathbb{C}$ with $\mathrm{Im}\,\tau > 0$.

Letting $X = e^{\pi i \tau}$ and suppressing the dependence on τ we see that the coefficient of X^{j^2} in Θ_{Λ} denotes the number of lattice vectors in Λ with length j. We have

$$\Theta_{\mathbb{Z}} = 1 + 2 \sum_{j \in \mathbb{Z}_{>0}} X^{j^2},$$

and note that $(\Theta_{\mathbb{Z}})^m = \Theta_{\mathbb{Z}^m}$ for $m \in \mathbb{N}$.

2.2 Reduction Algorithms

Lattice reduction algorithms take as input a basis $\mathbf{B}_{\mathrm{pre}} \in \mathbb{R}^{d \times m}$ of lattice Λ, some control parameters, and upon termination output a pair $(\mathbf{B}, \mathbf{U}) \in \mathbb{R}^{d \times m} \times \mathrm{Gl}_m(\mathbb{Z})$ such that $\mathbf{B} = \mathbf{B}_{\mathrm{pre}} \mathbf{U}$ and $\mathbf{B}$ is a "better" basis of Λ. For our cryptanalytic purpose we are interested in the properties of the profile after lattice reduction. We consider the celebrated LLL [18] and BKZ [24] reduction algorithms and heuristics that describe their behaviour on "random" lattices, see [2] for a survey. The relevant information here is that LLL is an efficient form of prereduction, and that BKZ is parametrised by a parameter β, where BKZ-β finds short vectors in rank β lattices. As such, given that lattice sieves (see Sect. 2.3) are the most efficient method known to achieve this, the cost of BKZ grows exponentially in β.

An important quantity is the root Hermite factor which can be used to determine $\|\mathbf{b}_1\|$ of a basis after BKZ-β reduction.

Definition 14 (Root Hermite factor [10]). *For $\beta \geqslant 50$ let*

$$\delta_\beta = \left(\frac{\beta}{2\pi e} (\pi \beta)^{1/\beta} \right)^{1/2(\beta-1)}.$$

For smaller values of β the root Hermite factor δ_β is determined experimentally. After BKZ-β reduction on basis $\mathbf{B} \in \mathbb{R}^{d \times m}$ of lattice Λ we estimate $\|\mathbf{b}_1\| \approx \delta_\beta^{m-1} \cdot \mathrm{vol}(\Lambda)^{1/m}$. The other heuristic we use is the Geometric Series Assumption (GSA) [25]. This asserts that after lattice reduction the Gram–Schmidt norms decrease as a geometric series.

Definition 15 (Geometric Series Assumption). *After lattice reduction on basis $\mathbf{B} \in \mathbb{R}^{d \times m}$ there exists $\gamma \in (0, 1)$ such that for $1 \leqslant i \leqslant m$ we have $\|\mathbf{b}_i^*\| = \gamma^{i-1} \|\mathbf{b}_1\|$.*

Given a basis $\mathbf{B}^{d \times m}$ of lattice Λ, and assuming both $\|\mathbf{b}_1\| = \delta_\beta^{m-1} \cdot \mathrm{vol}(\Lambda)^{1/m}$ and the GSA after BKZ-β reduction, since $\mathrm{vol}(\Lambda) = \prod_i \|\mathbf{b}_i^*\| = \|\mathbf{b}_1\|^{m-1} \cdot (\gamma \cdots \gamma^{m-1})$ we have $\gamma(\beta) = 1/\delta_\beta^2$.

For our final assumption we specialise to q-ary lattices, specifically those of the form $\Lambda_q^{\perp}(\mathbf{A})$ for $\mathbf{A} \in \mathbb{Z}_q^{n \times m}$ with basis $\mathbf{B_A}$, recall Definition 11. We note that for $1 \leqslant i \leqslant n$ we have $\pi_i(\mathbf{b}_i) = \mathbf{b}_i^* = q \cdot \mathbf{e}_i$. Under the root Hermite factor and GSA heuristics we assume that after BKZ-β reduction $\|\mathbf{b}_i^*\| = \delta_\beta^{m-1} \cdot \mathrm{vol}(\Lambda) \cdot \gamma(\beta)^{i-1} = \delta_\beta^{m-2i+1} \cdot \mathrm{vol}(\Lambda)^{1/m}$ [4, Sect. 6.3]. However in Sect. 3, we assume that for $1 \leqslant i \leqslant n$, if $q < \delta_\beta^{m-2i+1} \cdot \mathrm{vol}(\Lambda)^{1/m}$ then the q vector remains and the decrease in the profile begins only bounded away from the first indices of the basis. This "Z-shape" phenomenon was first observed in [17] and is discussed more in [2] and [19, App. C]; we give more detail on our use of it in Sect. 3.

2.3 Lattice Sieves

In this work a lattice sieve is an algorithm that takes as input a basis $\mathbf{B} \in \mathbb{R}^{d \times m}$ of lattice Λ and outputs in time exponential in m a constant fraction, which we can control, of vectors in $\{\mathbf{x} \in \Lambda \setminus \{\mathbf{0}\}: \|\mathbf{x}\| \leqslant \sqrt{4/3} \cdot \mathrm{gh}(\Lambda)\}$. We call the set of vectors output by a sieve its *database*. One expects $(4/3)^{m/2}$ vectors in a sieve database and for their lengths to concentrate around $\sqrt{4/3} \cdot \mathrm{gh}(\Lambda)$.

In our attack we sieve in projected sublattices $\Lambda_{[\ell]}$ of Λ determined by some $\mathbf{B}_{[\ell]}$ and then "lift" these vectors from $\Lambda_{[\ell]}$ to Λ following [12]. Let $1 \leqslant \ell - 1 < m$ and m' be such that $\ell - 1 + m' = m$. If a sieve is performed on $\mathbf{B}_{[\ell]}$ then we have a database of short vectors $L \subset \Lambda_{[\ell]}$. Let $\mathbf{w} \in \Lambda$ be such that $\mathbf{w} = \mathbf{B}\mathbf{v}$ for some $\mathbf{v} \in \mathbb{Z}^m$. We may split $\mathbf{B} = (\mathbf{B}' \mid \mathbf{B}'')$ with $\mathbf{B}' \in \mathbb{R}^{d \times (\ell - 1)}$ and $\mathbf{B}'' \in \mathbb{R}^{d \times m'}$ and $\mathbf{v}$ similarly. Then $\pi_\ell(\mathbf{w}) = \pi_\ell(\mathbf{B}'\mathbf{v}') + \pi_\ell(\mathbf{B}''\mathbf{v}'') = \mathbf{0} + \mathbf{B}_{[\ell]}\mathbf{v}''$. We see therefore that for $\mathbf{w}_{[\ell]} \in L$ with $\mathbf{w}_{[\ell]} = \mathbf{B}_{[\ell]}\mathbf{v}_{[\ell]}$, each lift of $\mathbf{w}_{[\ell]}$ to Λ is of the form $\mathbf{B}'\mathbf{v}' + \mathbf{B}''\mathbf{v}_{[\ell]}$ for $\mathbf{v}' \in \mathbb{Z}^{\ell - 1}$.

The shortest $\mathbf{w} \in \Lambda$ such that $\pi_\ell(\mathbf{w}) = \mathbf{w}_{[\ell]}$ is given by a particular choice of $\mathbf{v}'$. In our case, due to the geometry of our reduced bases, for every $\mathbf{w}_{[\ell]}$ we are able to find this choice of $\mathbf{v}'$. In particular, we consider bases $\mathbf{B}_{\mathbf{A}}$ of $\Lambda_q^\perp(\mathbf{A})$ for $\mathbf{A} \in \mathbb{Z}_q^{n \times m}$. Let $\mathbf{B} = \mathbf{B}_{\mathbf{A}}\mathbf{U}$ be the basis after BKZ-β reduction and ℓ be maximal such that $\mathbf{B}' = (q \cdot \mathbf{e}_1 \mid \cdots \mid q \cdot \mathbf{e}_{\ell - 1})$. In this case we have

$$\mathbf{B}'' = \begin{pmatrix} \mathbf{C} \\ \mathbf{D} \end{pmatrix}, \qquad \mathbf{B}_{[\ell]} = \begin{pmatrix} \mathbf{0} \\ \mathbf{D} \end{pmatrix},$$

with $\mathbf{C} \in \mathbb{Z}^{(\ell - 1) \times m'}$ and $\mathbf{D} \in \mathbb{Z}^{m' \times m'}$. If $\mathbf{w}_{[\ell]} = \mathbf{B}_{[\ell]}\mathbf{v}_{[\ell]}$ then its shortest lift is some

$$\mathbf{w} = \mathbf{B}'\mathbf{v}' + \mathbf{B}''\mathbf{v}_{[\ell]} = \begin{pmatrix} qv_1' \\ \vdots \\ qv_{\ell-1}' \\ 0 \\ \vdots \\ 0 \end{pmatrix} + \begin{pmatrix} \mathbf{C}\mathbf{v}_{[\ell]} \\ \mathbf{B}_{[\ell]}\mathbf{v}_{[\ell]} \end{pmatrix}. \tag{1}$$

To find the shortest lift we reduce $\mathbf{C}\mathbf{v}_{[\ell]}$ modulo q centred around 0.

2.4   Elements of High Dimensional Geometry

Definition 16. We define the following geometric figures for $n \geqslant 1$,

i $B_n(r) = \{\mathbf{x} \in \mathbb{R}^n : \|\mathbf{x}\| \leqslant r\}$, the n dimensional ball of radius r, i.e. the dilatation of the ℓ_2 norm unit ball by a factor of r,

ii $\mathsf{Cube}_n(q) = \begin{cases} \{-(q-1)/2, \ldots, (q-1)/2\}^n, & q \text{ odd}, \\ \{-(q-2)/2, \ldots, q/2\}^n, & q \text{ even}. \end{cases}$

Our $\mathsf{Cube}_n(q)$ represents the region of shortest reductions of $\mathbf{x} \in \mathbb{Z}^n$ modulo q, with an arbitrary choice made in the case of even q.

3   Attack on Small Modulus SIS

Our attack is based on two main ingredients: on the one hand a precise prediction of the geometry of BKZ reduced bases of q-ary lattices, and on the other calculating the number of integer points in the intersection of hyperballs and hypercubes in high dimensions.

3.1   On the Z-Shape of BKZ Reduced Bases for q-ary Lattices

The Three Zones of the Z-Shape. As in the SIS problem we consider a uniform matrix $\mathbf{A} \in \mathbb{Z}_q^{n \times m}$ and its associated kernel lattice $\Lambda_q^\perp(\mathbf{A})$. We refer to its basis $\mathbf{B_A}$ as $\mathbf{B}$ and apply some amount of lattice reduction to it. Initially, the profile $(\ell_i)_{i=1}^m$ of the basis has $\ell_i = \log q$ for $i \in [n]$ and $\ell_i = 0$ for $i > n$, resulting in a "Z-shape", see Fig. 1. The profile indices are divided into three distinct zones: Zone I, comprising of the q vectors with $\ell_i = \log q$, Zone II, the "slope", currently empty, and Zone III, the "flat tail", with $\ell_i = 0$.

LLL Reduction. As lattice reduction is applied, starting with LLL, the profile may change, with the vector corresponding to the last vector in Zone I potentially having a projection shorter than q and the vector corresponding to the first index in Zone III potentially having a projection longer than 1. These indices are now part of Zone II, where $\ell_i \in (0, \log q)$. Additionally, we assume that the GSA applies to Zone II. The LLL algorithm is partially self-dual, reducing both the basis and the corresponding dual basis, resulting in all ℓ_i falling into these three distinct and ordered zones, as discussed in greater detail in [2, Sect. 4.3].

BKZ Profile. We then use the stronger lattice reduction algorithm BKZ. Unlike LLL, BKZ does not possess this partially self-dual property. However, if BKZ-β fails to find a vector of length shorter than q within the first β columns of the basis $\mathbf{B}$, it can be asserted that $\ell_1 = \log q$. It has been observed that BKZ-β reduction preserves the Z-shape and its three zones, up to a small "kink" just

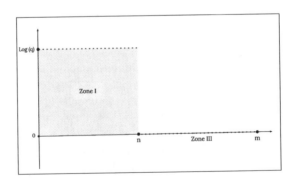

Fig. 1. Initial profile of basis $\mathbf{B}$.

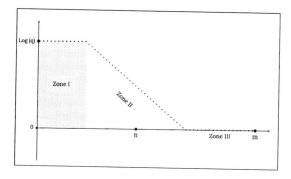

Fig. 2. Profile after some BKZ reduction.

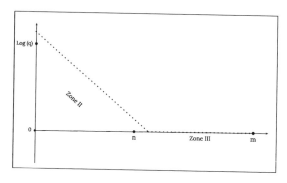

Fig. 3. Profile after rerandomisation and then some BKZ reduction.

before Zone III [2], with the slope of Zone II decreasing according to the GSA, see Fig. 2. This observation was first documented in [17]. Additionally, randomising **B** can remove the q vectors from the first n columns of the basis. Applying BKZ to such randomised bases is depicted in Fig. 3. We note that the use of the q vectors is fundamental to our attack, so we do not randomise bases in this manner. The application of BKZ-β to bases of the form $\mathbf{B_A}$, with and without randomisation, is discussed in more detail in [19, App. C]. In what follows we present a model for BKZ-β reduction on bases of the form $\mathbf{B_A}$ that captures the aforementioned Z-shape phenomenon, similar to the model presented in [14, Heuristic. 2.8].

A Predictive Model for BKZ Profiles. Our model for predicting the basis profile after BKZ reduction is based on the volume invariance of a lattice under a change of basis, as in [19, App. C]. To determine the output profile, we make two assumptions:

i. the GSA holds in Zone II, with the slope determined solely by the BKZ blocksize β, specifically $\gamma(\beta) = 1/\delta_\beta^2$,
ii. despite not being a self-dual algorithm, upon completion BKZ reduction preserves Zones I, II, and III, and their order.

Using these assumptions, we construct a preliminary "extended" profile that has more indices than the rank of the lattice. Specifically, let n_q, n_{GSA}, and n_1 represent the number of vectors in Zone I, Zone II and Zone III, respectively. The input basis has $n_q = n$ and $n_1 = m - n$ and we use the GSA to determine n_{GSA}. Under the GSA after BKZ-β reduction and in a log scale, Zone II begins at index $n + 1$ with value $\log q - 2 \log \delta_\beta$ and decreases by $-2 \log \delta_\beta$ per subsequent index. This continues until the profile takes a value in the range $(2 \log \delta(\beta), 0]$, which allows us to calculate n_{GSA} as $\lfloor \log q / (2 \log \delta_\beta) \rfloor$. On a profile plot, Zone II therefore consists of the points $(n_q + i, \log q - 2i \log \delta_\beta)$ for $i \in \{1, \ldots, n_{\mathsf{GSA}}\}$. The global shape of the profile is quite accurate, but the resulting (logarithm of the) volume, that is to say, the sum of all the values in the three zones

$$\sum_{i=1}^{n_q} \log q + \sum_{i=1}^{n_{\mathsf{GSA}}} (\log q - 2i \log \delta_\beta) + \sum_{i=n_q+n_{\mathsf{GSA}}+1}^{m} 0$$
$$= (n + n_{\mathsf{GSA}}) \log q - n_{\mathsf{GSA}}(n_{\mathsf{GSA}} + 1) \log \delta_\beta,$$

is not equal to that of the lattice; $n \log(q)$. What remains is to find the correct starting index of Zone II, i.e. some index smaller than n. To do so we shift a window of indices of length m, the rank of the lattice, in increments of one, right from $\{1, \ldots, m\}$ to $\{1 + j, \ldots, m + j\}$ for some $j \in \mathbb{N}$. The shift j is chosen such that the volume implied by the profile is as close to the volume of the lattice as the discretisation of indices allows. Finally, we renormalise the profile in Zone II so that the volume of the profile we have constructed equals the volume of the lattice. A schematic of the entire process is given in Fig. 4. We note that one can directly compute n_q and n_{GSA} by solving an easy system of equations, but that this requires considering four different cases depending on the existence of Zones I and III.

3.2 Exploiting the Z-Shape

Let $\mathbf{B}$ be the output of BKZ-β reduction on some basis $\mathbf{B_A}$ and let $r = \min\{n_q + \beta + 1, m + 1\}$. Our ability to predict the behaviour of the profile of $\mathbf{B}$ leads to the following observation. When the modulus q is relatively small compared to the length bound ν in $\mathsf{SIS}^*_{n,m,q,\nu}$ instances, the discovery of short vectors in $\Lambda_{[n_q+1:r]}$ via sieving on $\mathbf{B}_{[n_q+1:r]}$ opens up avenues for new attack strategies through the lifting techniques of [12].

Lifting Vectors in q-ary Lattices. Recall the notation of (1) and let $\ell = n_q + 1$. We make the slight alteration of considering $\mathbf{B}_{[\ell:r]}$ defining the projected sublattice $\Lambda_{[\ell:r]}$ rather than $\mathbf{B}_{[\ell]}$ defining $\Lambda_{[\ell]}$, and so $\mathbf{B}' \in \mathbb{Z}^{m \times (\ell-1)}$ and $\mathbf{B}'' \in \mathbb{Z}^{m \times (r-\ell)}$. Let $\mathbf{w}_{[\ell:r]} = \mathbf{B}_{[\ell:r]} \mathbf{v}_{[\ell:r]} \in \Lambda_{[\ell:r]}$ have square norm η^2. Each lift $\mathbf{w}$ of $\mathbf{w}_{[\ell:r]}$ is of the form $\mathbf{B}'\mathbf{v}' + \mathbf{B}''\mathbf{v}_{[\ell:r]}$ where $\mathbf{B}' = (q \cdot \mathbf{e}_1 \mid \cdots \mid q \cdot \mathbf{e}_{\ell-1})$.

Following (1) let $\mathbf{w}$ be the shortest lift of $\mathbf{w}_{[\ell:r]}$. The maximum square length of $\mathbf{w}$ is therefore $\eta^2 + n_q q^2 / 4$ and the average case length, when the first $\ell - 1$ entries of $\mathbf{w}$ are uniformly distributed mod q around 0, is approximately $\eta^2 + n_q q^2 / 12$. We note this approach relies on q vectors remaining at the beginning of the basis over which to lift (Fig. 5).

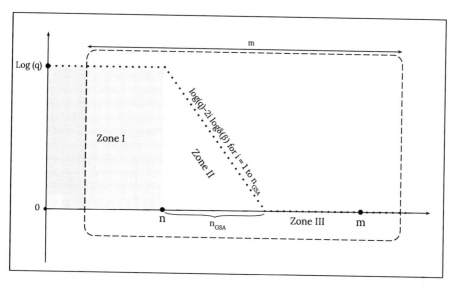

Fig. 4. Illustration of the moving window technique to estimate the profile of a BKZ reduced basis $\mathbf{B}$. The initial profile is constructed by setting the starting index of Zone II as $n + 1$ and letting the subsequent slope be given by the GSA. Zone III continues beyond m. Then a sliding window of length m (the dashed box) moves from its leftmost position to the right until the closest approximation to the lattice volume is found.

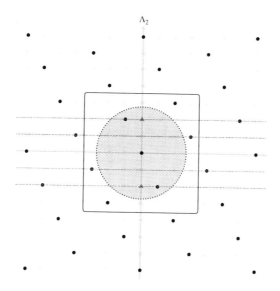

Fig. 5. Illustration of the attack in dimension 2, where we look at the projection $\Lambda_{[2]}$ of the lattice $\Lambda = \Lambda_q^\perp(\mathbf{A})$ for $\mathbf{A} \in \mathbb{Z}_q^{1 \times 2}$ against the q vector $(q\ 0)^t$. Lifts for the projections within an ℓ_2 ball are depicted by horizontal dotted lines. The only two points of $\Lambda_{[2]}$ which can be lifted to a vector of Λ in the ℓ_2 ball are highlighted by triangles.

On Success Probability. The above procedure returns a $\mathsf{SIS}^*_{n,m,q,\nu}$ solution if $\|\mathbf{w}\|^2 \leqslant \nu^2$, i.e. when the lifted entries have square norm less than $\nu^2 - \eta^2$. We make the assumption, which we experimentally verify in Sect. 5, that the first n_q entries of $\mathbf{w}$ are uniformly distributed in $\mathsf{Cube}_{n_q}(q)$, so this success condition is equivalent to a uniform element of $\mathsf{Cube}_{n_q}(q)$ lying in $\mathsf{B}_{n_q}\left(\sqrt{\nu^2 - \eta^2}\right)$. This probability is precisely

$$p(\nu, \eta, q, n_q) = \frac{\left|\mathsf{Cube}_{n_q}(q) \cap \mathsf{B}_{n_q}\left(\sqrt{\nu^2 - \eta^2}\right)\right|}{\left|\mathsf{Cube}_{n_q}(q)\right|}, \tag{2}$$

3.3   On Balls and Cubes

The denominator of (2) is q^{n_q}, but we require an efficient method to compute the numerator. For this, we appeal to the theta series of $\mathbb{Z}$.

Convolution of Truncated Theta. We now present a method to calculate the number of lattice points of $\mathbb{Z}^{n_q}$ contained in the intersection of a centered cube and ball. Our method revolves around considering convolutions of the function $\Theta_{\mathbb{Z}}$.

We define $\Theta_{\mathbb{Z},N} = 1 + \sum_{1 \leqslant j \leqslant N} 2X^{j^2}$, and for any polynomial $p(X) = \sum_{i \in \mathbb{N}} \alpha_i X^i \in \mathbb{Z}[X]$, we define $p_N(X) = \sum_{0 \leqslant i \leqslant N^2} \alpha_i X^i$. Note this truncates a polynomial at its degree N^2 term, similar to $\Theta_{\mathbb{Z},N}$. By definition of the product of polynomials, $\Theta_{\mathbb{Z},N} \cdot \Theta_{\mathbb{Z},N}$ is a polynomial whose j^{th} coefficient is the number of integer points of squared norm j and whose coordinates are all smaller than or equal to N in absolute value. Hence, truncating the polynomial at its degree M^2 term and evaluating it at 1 gives exactly the number of points in $\mathbb{Z}^2$ inside the ℓ_2 ball of radius M and with coefficients smaller than or equal to N in absolute value. That is to say, if N is even, the number of points in $\mathsf{Cube}_2(2N + 1) \cap \mathsf{B}_2(M)$.[3]

This simple observation leads to a recursive approach that generalises it to arbitrary dimensions. We seek to compute $\Theta^{(n)}$, defined by $\Theta^{(1)} = \Theta_{\mathbb{Z},N}$ and $\Theta^{(i)} = \left(\Theta^{(i-1)} \cdot \Theta^{(1)}\right)_M$ for some n, N, M. In words, this process counts the integer points introduced by increasing the dimension of the cube and removes the points outside of the ball.

One may think of this truncated convolution as a product in the ring $\mathbb{Z}[X]/(X^M)$. It is therefore tempting to accelerate the calculation of $\Theta^{(n)}$ using fast exponentiation (square-and-multiply). It turns out that the naïve iterative approach is also competitive for the parameters at hand if one exploits the fact that $\Theta^{(1)}$ is a rather sparse polynomial with only $\sqrt{N}$ non zero coefficients out of $M > N$. Indeed, the former approach has a complexity of $O(M^2 \log n)$ arithmetic operations and the latter $O(n \cdot M \cdot \sqrt{N})$. With some implementation effort,

---

[3] Even N relates to odd $q = 2N + 1$. Allowing for even q, where $\mathsf{Cube}_n(q)$ is non-symmetric, requires slightly more care. We are concerned with odd q in this work.

the former approach could be accelerated using the Fast Fourier Transform for convolution, leading to $O(M \log M \log n)$ complexity, though this was not necessary for our parameters. Furthermore, to explore the attack parameters, we will generally want to compute $\Theta^{(n)}$ for increasing values of n; the iterative approach with caching perfectly fits this use case.

Alternative Approach. We also mention an alternative approach we considered for computing this numerator, at least approximately. One might forget the discrete aspect of the problem, and simply compute the volume of the intersection between a hyperball and a hypercube. An efficient method exists [5,23] and we implemented it,[4] but found it difficult to use: it requires floating-point computation with high precision and the careful truncation of infinite series. This approach might still be preferable when the modulus q is large.

3.4 Putting It All Together

We now give the full attack in Algorithm 1. We then outline how we estimate the success probability of our attack, which is experimentally verified in Sect. 5, and give its cost.

To estimate the success probability of Algorithm 1, we propose with two conservative assumptions:

i. the maximum length of vectors in the projected sieve database $\mathcal{P}$ is $\sqrt{4/3}\,q$, rather than the slightly smaller $\sqrt{4/3}\,\|\mathbf{b}_\ell^*\|$ that we would approximately expect via the Gaussian heuristic,
ii. all $(4/3)^{(r-\ell)/2}$ vectors in $\mathcal{P}$ are of this maximum length.

Recalling (2) and setting $n_q = \ell - 1$ and $\eta = \sqrt{4/3}\,q$, given that (q, ν) are parameters of our SIS* instance, we compute $p = p(\nu, \eta, q, n_q)$ via the methods of Sect. 3.3. We now make the assumption that the first $\ell-1$ entries of each shortest lift $\mathbf{w}$ of $\mathbf{w}_{[\ell:r]} \in \mathcal{P}$ are independent and identically distributed, implying in particular that each lift has length shorter than ν with probability p. Hence, the expected number of successes of the lifting event over the $4/3^{(r-l)/2}$ candidates of $\mathcal{P}$ corresponds to the expectation of a binomial random variable with $(4/3)^{(r-\ell)/2}$ trials and success probability p. It is therefore $(4/3)^{(r-\ell)/2}p$.

---

[4] https://github.com/verdiverdiverdi/ball-box.

Algorithm 1: Z-attack outline

Input: A matrix $\mathbf{A} \in \mathbb{Z}_q^{n \times m}$, a threshold value $\nu > 0$, a BKZ
   blocksize β.
Output: A solution $\mathbf{x} \in \mathbb{Z}^m \setminus q\mathbb{Z}^m$ such that $\mathbf{A}\mathbf{x} = 0 \bmod q$ and
   $\|\mathbf{x}\| \leqslant \nu$, or $\perp$ if the attack is unsuccessful.

1 Write $\mathbf{A}$ as $(\mathbf{A}_1 \mid \mathbf{A}_2) \in \mathbb{Z}_q^{n \times n} \times \mathbb{Z}_q^{n \times (n-m)}$
2 Assert $\mathbf{A}_1 \in \mathrm{Gl}_n(\mathbb{Z}_q)$
3 $\mathbf{B_A} \leftarrow \begin{pmatrix} q\mathbf{I}_n & -\mathbf{A}_1^{-1}\mathbf{A}_2 \\ \mathbf{0} & \mathbf{I}_{m-n} \end{pmatrix}$
4 Run BKZ-β algorithm on $\mathbf{B_A}$, receive $\mathbf{B}$
5 Let ℓ be maximal such that $\mathbf{B}$ begins $(q \cdot \mathbf{e}_1 \mid \cdots \mid q \cdot \mathbf{e}_{\ell-1})$
6 **if** $\ell = 1$ **then return** $\mathbf{b}_1$ when $\mathbf{b}_1 \leqslant \nu$ **else** $\perp$
7 Let $r \leftarrow \min\{\ell + \beta, m + 1\}$
8 Let $\mathbf{B} = (\mathbf{B}' \mid \mathbf{B}'' \mid *) \in \mathbb{Z}^{m \times (\ell-1)} \times \mathbb{Z}^{m \times (r-\ell)} \times \mathbb{Z}^{m \times (m-r+1)}$
9 $\mathcal{P} \leftarrow$ **Sieve** $(\mathbf{\Lambda}_{[\ell:r]})$ using $\mathbf{B}_{[\ell:r]}$
10 **for** $\mathbf{w}_{[\ell:r]} \in \mathcal{P}$ **do**
11 $\quad$ Let $\mathbf{v}_{[\ell:r]} \in \mathbb{Z}^{r-\ell}$ such that $\mathbf{w}_{[\ell:r]} = \mathbf{B}_{[\ell:r]}\mathbf{v}_{[\ell:r]}$
12 $\quad$ Find shortest $\mathbf{w} = \mathbf{B}'\mathbf{v}' + \mathbf{B}''\mathbf{v}_{[\ell:r]}$, i.e. reduce the first $\ell - 1$
   $\quad$ entries of $\mathbf{B}''\mathbf{v}_{[\ell:r]}$ around $0 \bmod q$
13 $\quad$ **if** $\|\mathbf{w}\| \leqslant \nu$ **then return** $\mathbf{w}$
14 **end for**
15 **return** $\perp$

If this expected value is less than one, we rerandomise Zone II of $\mathbf{B}$ (in particular, leaving the q vectors and Zone III unaltered) and repeat once again lattice reduction to retrieve the Z-shape profile and restart the attack. Note that p is non-decreasing if the number of q vectors remaining at the beginning of the basis decreases. We assume that performing the sieving and lifting operation again is independent of previous attempts.

The cost of the attack under consideration is evaluated by adopting the CoreSVP methodology [4]. Specifically, we assume that the total cost of the BKZ reduction and sieve in the projected sublattice can be approximated by a single SVP oracle call. By leveraging lattice sieves, we estimate this cost to be of the order $2^{c\beta + o(\beta)}$, where $c = 0.292$ [8] for a classical lattice sieve. We acknowledge that this estimate is a simplification and underestimate, but we employ it to facilitate comparisons to the security levels of signature schemes proposed in [16]. We note the conventional technique of unbalancing the reduction and sieving dimensions could, in a more precise cost model, optimise our attack.

3.5 Extension to ISIS

For convenience, the attack under consideration has thus far been discussed in the homogeneous setting. Cryptanalysing signature schemes typically requires one to solve ISIS. From a complexity-theoretic perspective, we demonstrate that the inhomogeneous variant is not inherently more difficult. However, our proposed reduction loses a factor of approximately mq in the success probability of the attack. We contend that this loss is largely a consequence of the reduction and posit that we can achieve the significantly smaller factor $q/2$.

A Reduction from ISIS to SIS*. While the following reduction from ISIS to SIS in instances where $\nu < q$ seems folklore, it has not been extensively documented beyond a comment by Peikert.[5] Below we give a similar reduction that does not require $\nu < q$.

Lemma 1. *For prime q, if there exists adversary $\mathcal{A}$ solving $\mathsf{SIS}^*_{n,m+1,q,\nu}$ in time T with success probability p, then there exists adversary $\mathcal{B}$ solving $\mathsf{ISIS}_{n,m,q,\nu}$ in time $T + \mathrm{poly}(n, m, \log q)$ with probability at least*

$$\frac{p}{(m+1)(q-1)} - \frac{1}{q^n}.$$

Proof. Set $m' = m+1$. For an $\mathsf{ISIS}_{n,m,q,\nu}$ instance $(\mathbf{A}, \mathbf{u})$, $\mathcal{B}$ proceeds by sampling $f \leftarrow \mathsf{U}(\mathbb{Z}_q^\times)$ and a uniform permutation matrix $\mathbf{P} \in \mathbb{Z}^{m' \times m'}$. Subsequently, $\mathcal{B}$ creates $\mathbf{A}' = [\mathbf{A}|f\mathbf{u}] \cdot \mathbf{P}$ and transmits it to $\mathcal{A}$. Note that the invertibility of f and $\mathbf{P}$ implies that the distribution of $\mathbf{A}'$ remains uniform based on the uniformity of $(\mathbf{A}, \mathbf{u})$. Furthermore, the distribution of $\mathbf{A}'$ is independent of $\mathbf{P}$ and f and follows the correct input distribution for $\mathcal{A}$.

Upon receiving $\mathbf{A}'$, $\mathcal{A}$ produces $\mathbf{x}'$. With probability p, it holds that $\mathbf{A}'\mathbf{x}' = \mathbf{0} \bmod q$, $\|\mathbf{x}'\| \leqslant \nu$, and $\mathbf{x}' \notin q\mathbb{Z}^{m'}$. Specifically, at least one coordinate of $\mathbf{x}'$ must be non-zero modulo q. As such, with probability at least $1/m'$, $\mathbf{P}\mathbf{x}'$ is of the form $(\mathbf{x}, y)$, where $\mathbf{x} \in \mathbb{Z}^m$ and $y \in \mathbb{Z} \setminus q\mathbb{Z}$. It further holds with probability $1/(q-1)$ that $f = -y^{-1}$. Notably, $\mathbf{x}$ has $\|\mathbf{x}\| \leqslant \|\mathbf{P}\mathbf{x}'\| = \|\mathbf{x}'\| \leqslant \nu$, and if $\mathbf{x} \neq \mathbf{0}$, it constitutes a solution to the $\mathsf{ISIS}_{n,m,q,\nu}$ instance. To conclude, remark that $\mathbf{x} = \mathbf{0}$ only when $\mathbf{u} = \mathbf{0}$, which occurs with probability $1/q^n$. $\square$

A Heuristic Improvement. We note that the above reduction transforms generic adversaries. Our Z-shape attack implements a particular SIS* solver, with a specific property on the distribution of its output: in our model some number, greater than one, of the first entries of the output solution $\mathbf{x}'$ are uniform mod q around 0. Hence, let us assume that the SIS* adversary $\mathcal{A}$ above has the same property and design a better reduction. In the notation of Lemma 1 we fix $f = 1$ and $\mathbf{P}$ to a be permutation matrix that sets $\mathbf{u}$ as the first column of $\mathbf{A}'$ and ensures the first n columns are in $\mathrm{Gl}_n(\mathbb{Z}_q)$, in particular let $\mathbf{A}' = (\mathbf{u} \,|\, \bar{\mathbf{A}})$. Let the SIS* solution be $\mathbf{x}' = (x_1' \,|\, \mathbf{x}'')$. If $x_1' \in \{1, -1\}$ then we have solved our ISIS instance as $\mathbf{A}'\mathbf{x}' = \pm\mathbf{u} + \bar{\mathbf{A}}\mathbf{x}'' = \mathbf{0} \bmod q$ and one may use the relevant submatrix of $\mathbf{P}$ and potentially negation to recover $\mathbf{x}$ such that $\mathbf{A}\mathbf{x} = \mathbf{u} \bmod q$. Note $\|\mathbf{x}\| = \|\mathbf{x}''\| \leqslant \|\mathbf{x}'\| \leqslant \nu$.

---

[5] https://crypto.stackexchange.com/questions/87097/.

In the above our SIS* solver must function in one rank higher than the original ISIS instance and the probability that a given $x_1' \in \{1, -1\}$ is $2/q$, i.e. the success probability is $2/q$ rather than approximately $1/mq$ as in Lemma 1.

4   Optimisations

In this section, we introduce an optimisation to enhance the generic attack of Algorithm 1. It employs a technique from the lattice sieving literature referred to as "on-the-fly lifting". This approach considers more lifts over the q vectors, albeit at slightly longer lengths.

4.1   On the Fly Lifting

During the execution of a lattice sieve, pairs of vectors are added together to search for new and shorter vectors. There are two main methods for this process: a double loop over the entire current database of vectors [21] or the use of locality-sensitive techniques to consider only pairs of vectors with a high probability of summing to a new, shorter vector [8]. Regardless of the method used, the process is iterative, and the lengths of vectors in the sieve database decrease over many such searches for pairs. This means that many more vectors are considered than ultimately inhabit the terminal sieving database. The on-the-fly lifting technique is introduced to consider lifting some subset of these vectors, as well as those in the terminal database, in the hope that some well-chosen excess computation can improve the sieve's performance [3].

We model on-the-fly lifting by considering the terminal sieve database and performing one more iteration. Each vector encountered in that iteration, regardless of its length, is lifted. The number and length of these extra vectors will vary depending on the style of sieve used. It is important to note that this surplus iteration is not necessary in practice, as vectors of the appropriate length can simply be lifted during the sieving procedure. However, it is conceptually cleaner.

Nguyen–Vidick Style Sieves. In Nguyen–Vidick style sieves [21] each iteration of the sieve is a double loop over the database where all distinct pairs of vectors are added and the shortest sums kept.[6] Given our assumption that a terminal sieving database on a rank β lattice $\mathbf{\Lambda}$ has size $(4/3)^{\beta/2}$ and maximum length $\sqrt{4/3}\,\mathrm{gh}(\mathbf{\Lambda})$, performing a final sieving iteration visits $(4/3)^{\beta}$ vectors of length less than $\sqrt{2} \cdot \sqrt{4/3}\,\mathrm{gh}(\mathbf{\Lambda})$. Specialising to Algorithm 1 this means performing the lifting during the sieve operation, and altering our conservative assumptions on the success probability to stating that each vector we attempt to lift has length $\sqrt{2} \cdot \sqrt{4/3}\,q$ and that there are $(4/3)^{r-\ell}$ of them. We note that while, when not considering on the fly techniques, we took complexity exponent $c = 0.292$ because there was no reason to not consider the fastest lattice sieve,

---

[6] For simplicity, one may think of including $\mathbf{0}$ in the database to allow the iteration to keep short vectors already present in the database.

Nguyen–Vidick sieves have asymptotic time complexity given by the exponent $c = 0.415$ [21].

The Becker–Ducas–Gama–Laarhoven Sieve. Sieves that use locality sensitive techniques achieve lower time complexities by considering fewer pairs of vectors in an iteration [8]. This means that in our model that considers repeating the final iteration of sieving on the terminal sieve database, such sieves give fewer opportunities for on the fly lifting. On the positive side, the ability of such sieves to forego trying so many pairs of vectors comes from mechanisms to select only pairs that are more likely to have a short sum. In particular, the distribution of the lengths of sums of pairs that *are* selected is concentrated on shorter values than for Nguyen–Vidick style sieves. The following lemma examines the time optimal parameters of [8]. Here a vector $\mathbf{u}$ is compared only with vectors $\mathbf{w}$ that take angular distance not more than $\pi/3$ with some vector $\mathbf{r}$, which itself takes angular distance not more than $\pi/3$ with $\mathbf{u}$.

Lemma 2. *Following the notation of [8, Sect. 2] let $\alpha = 1/2$ and $\mathbf{u} \in S^{n-1}$ be the centre of spherical cap $\mathcal{C}_{\mathbf{u},\alpha}$. Let $\mathbf{r} \in \mathcal{C}_{\mathbf{u},\alpha}$ be the centre of another spherical cap $\mathcal{C}_{\mathbf{r},\alpha}$. The probability that uniform $\mathbf{w} \in \mathcal{C}_{\mathbf{r},\alpha}$ is such that $\|\mathbf{u} - \mathbf{w}\| \leqslant \sqrt{3/2}$ is at least one half.*

Proof. Rotate such that $\mathbf{r} = \mathbf{e}_1$ and decompose $\mathbf{u} = \mathbf{u}' + u_1\mathbf{r}$, $\mathbf{w} = \mathbf{w}' + w_1\mathbf{r}$ such that $\langle \mathbf{u}', \mathbf{r} \rangle = \langle \mathbf{w}', \mathbf{r} \rangle = 0$. We have $\|\mathbf{u} - \mathbf{w}\|^2 = \|\mathbf{u}' - \mathbf{w}'\|^2 + (u_1 - w_1)^2$ with $u_1 \in [1/2, 1]$ and $\|\mathbf{u}'\|^2 = 1 - u_1^2$, and similarly for $(w_1, \mathbf{w}')$. Then $\|\mathbf{u} - \mathbf{w}\|^2 = \|\mathbf{u}'\|^2 + \|\mathbf{w}'\|^2 - 2\langle \mathbf{u}', \mathbf{w}' \rangle + (u_1 - w_1)^2 \leqslant 3/2 - 2\langle \mathbf{u}', \mathbf{w}' \rangle$. We project $\mathbf{u}, \mathbf{w}$ in the cap $\mathcal{C}_{\mathbf{r},\alpha}$ onto the ball of one less dimension $B_{n-1}\left(\sqrt{3/4}\right) \subset \{0\} \times \mathbb{R}^{n-1}$. By the rotational symmetry of $\mathcal{C}_{\mathbf{r},\alpha}$ around the axis $\mathbf{r}$, for any $\mathbf{u}$ and uniform $\mathbf{w} \in \mathcal{C}_{\mathbf{r},\alpha}$, the angle between $\mathbf{u}'$ and $\mathbf{w}'$ is uniform in $[0, 2\pi)$, and therefore the inner product above is non negative with probability one half. In this case, $\|\mathbf{u} - \mathbf{w}\| \leqslant \sqrt{3/2}$. □

By scaling onto the sphere of radius $\sqrt{4/3}\,\mathrm{gh}(\Lambda)$ we have $\sqrt{3/2} \cdot \sqrt{4/3}\,\mathrm{gh}(\Lambda) = \sqrt{2}\,\mathrm{gh}(\Lambda)$. We therefore change our assumptions on the success probability of Algorithm 1, when using the sieve of [8], to each vector we attempt to lift having length $\sqrt{2}\,q$ and there being $(3/2)^{(r-\ell)/2}$ of them. This number of vectors comes from the $\alpha = \beta = 1/2$ case of [8, Sect. 7] and is less than the $(4/3)^{r-\ell}$ of the Nguyen–Vidick sieves. Here we have complexity exponent $c = 0.292$.

A Possible Improvement. We note that when considering on the fly lifting it is not necessarily the case that the lengths of vectors are concentrated around their maximum, as opposed to the terminal database of a sieve. For example, in a Nguyen–Vidick style sieve, if the lengths of the vectors considered during on the fly lifting have lengths concentrated below $\sqrt{2} \cdot \sqrt{4/3}\,\mathrm{gh}(\Lambda)$ then our model is pessimistic; taking a shorter length as an upper bound for our projected vectors would better match reality and lower the cost of the attack.

5   Experimental Verification

In this section we experimentally verify two heuristics used in our attack. The first is on the behaviour of the lengths of lifted entries of vectors from a projected sieve database, which are expected to follow the uniform distribution over $\mathsf{Cube}_{n_q}(q)$. As an extension, we also verify that the total lengths of lifted vectors match our expectations. The second heuristic of our model relates to the simulation of the Z-shape after BKZ reduction. We note that we are considering the lengths of lifted vectors without considering on-the-fly lifting, as introduced in Sect. 4.

Experimental Toolkit. The `fpylll` library [26] is used for BKZ reduction algorithm and the general sieve kernel [3,27] is used for sieving in projected sublattices. We use the progressive BKZ algorithm [6], in which a subset of block sizes $(\beta'_i)_i \subset \{3, \dots, \beta - 1\}$ are used in some number of BKZ-β' tours as a prereduction process prior to BKZ-β.

5.1   The Lengths of Lifts

In these experiments we use progressive BKZ-β with a decreasing number of iterations as $\beta' < \beta$ increases. Specifically, we denote the process of running t iterations of BKZ-β' for $\beta' \in \{l, \dots, u\}$ by the pair $(t, [l, u])$, resulting in the following sequence: $(8, [3, 5]), (4, [6, 10]), (2, [11, 20]), (1, [40, \infty))$.

Uniformity in $\mathsf{Cubd}_n(q)$. Following the selection of parameters n, m, q, and a reduction parameter β for BKZ reduction such that we expect q vectors to remain at the beginning of the basis, we perform BKZ-β reduction on a uniform $\mathbf{B_A}$, resulting in $\mathbf{B}$. The number of remaining q vectors in $\mathbf{B}$ is denoted by n_q. Next, by setting $\ell - 1 = n_q$ and $r = \max\{\ell + \beta, m + 1\}$, we sieve in $\Lambda_{[\ell:r]}$ using $\mathbf{B}_{[\ell:r]}$, following Algorithm 1. We ensure that $r \leqslant m + 1$ so that we sieve in a rank β projected sublattice. The number of vectors having length less than or equal to $4/3\,q$ is denoted as N, and we ensure that this quantity is greater than $(4/3)^{\beta/2}$. Subsequently, the sieve database is lifted to $\mathbf{B}$ over the q vectors, and the length of each lifted vector, limited to its first n_q entries, is recorded as $\{L_i\}_{i=1}^N$. As in Sect. 3.3, we can calculate the fraction of $\mathsf{Cube}_{n_q}(q)$ having length less than a given radius R, i.e.

$$p'(R, q, n_q) = \frac{|\mathsf{Cube}_{n_q}(q) \cap \mathsf{B}_{n_q}(R)|}{|\mathsf{Cube}_{n_q}(q)|},$$

similarly to (2). Further, $\{L_i\}_{i=1}^N$ is sorted as $L_1 \leqslant \cdots \leqslant L_n$, and for any i, if there exists $j < i$ such that $L_j = L_i$, then we remove L_j. Ultimately, for the remaining L_i the coordinates $(L_i, p'(L_i, q, n_q))$ and $(L_i, i/N)$ are plotted. These represent the proportion of lifts with length that is less than or equal to L_i according to our model ("Modelled proportion" in Fig. 6), and observed in our experiments ("Experimental proportion" in Fig. 6).

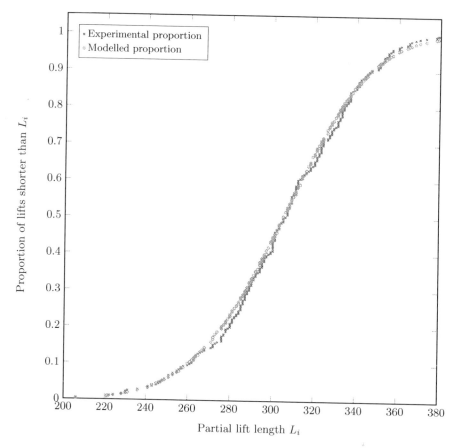

Fig. 6. For $(n, m, q, \beta) = (120, 240, 257, 40)$ we check the distribution of the length of only the lifted entries of lifted vectors, following the description of the first experiment in Sect. 5.1.

Distribution of Total Lengths. Given the above approach we can also consider, given a particular distribution of lengths of projected vectors in the database of $\text{Sieve}(\Lambda_{[\ell:r]})$, the distribution of lengths of the full lifted vectors expected by our model. Note that we must consider the distribution of the lengths of the projected vectors since, under our model, the distributions of the lifts of projected vectors of different lengths are themselves different. In this case we let $\{L_{proj,i}\}_{i=1}^{N}$ represent the lengths of the vectors in the projected sieve database, and for each index i let $\{L_{total,i}\}_{i=1}^{N}$ represent the length of the respective entire lifted vector. We sort $\{L_{total,i}\}_{i=1}^{N}$ as $L_{total,1} \leqslant \cdots \leqslant L_{total,N}$ and for all i if there exists $j < i$ such that $L_{total,j} = L_{total,i}$ we remove $L_{total,j}$. For given $\{L_{proj,i}\}_{i=1}^{N}$ and length $L_{total,k}$, the expected number of lifted vectors

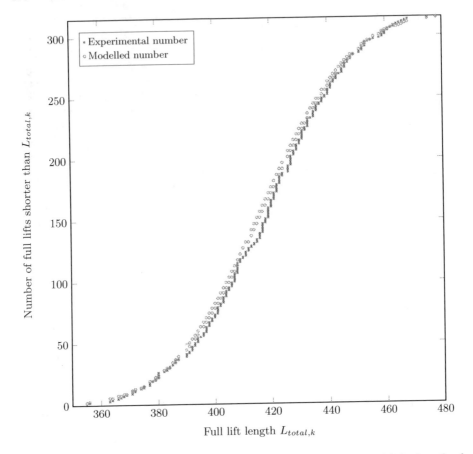

Fig. 7. For $(n, m, q, \beta) = (120, 240, 257, 40)$ we check the distribution of the length of the entire lifted vectors, following the description of the second experiment in Sect. 5.1.

of length less than or equal to $L_{total,k}$ is given by

$$E_k = \sum_{i=1}^{N} p'\left(\sqrt{L_{total,k}^2 - L_{proj,i}^2}, q, n_q\right).$$

We plot coordinates $(L_{total,k}, E_k)$ and $(L_{total,k}, k)$ as "Modelled number" and "Experimental number" respectively in Fig. 7, the latter of which represents the number of lifts from our experiments which have length less than or equal to $L_{total,k}$.

Table 1. For $(n, m, q, \beta) = (120, 240, 257, \beta)$ we run the altered progressive BKZ-β reduction described in Sect. 5.2. After $\beta' \in \{5, 10, 20, 30, 40\}$ we compute the average number of q vectors and the standard deviation of this number over 60 experimental trials and denote these quantities as $\mathbb{E}[X]$ and $\sqrt{\mathbb{V}[X]}$. In the final column we give the number of q vectors expected by the model of Sect. 3.1.

β	$\mathbb{E}[X]$	$\sqrt{\mathbb{V}[X]}$	Sect. 3.1
5	41.4	2.2	45
10	31.6	1.7	33
20	19.4	1.4	22
30	13.9	1.4	15
40	9.8	1.5	12

5.2 The Z-Shape Basis

To achieve the Z-shape of Sect. 3.1 is unfortunately not a matter of simply applying lattice reduction to a basis $\mathbf{B_A}$. As described in [2, Fig. 6] there is a phenomenon whereby, rather than Zone III consisting of Gram–Schmidt vectors of length 1, a kink appears with vectors of Gram–Schmidt norm strictly less than 1. These shorter than expected Gram–Schmidt vectors introduce, in the log scale, negative terms to the sum $\sum_i \log\|\mathbf{b}_i^*\| = n \log q$. This in turn, due to the invariance of the sum, means some $\log\|\mathbf{b}_i^*\|$ must be greater, potentially leading to more q vectors than expected. Having a larger Zone I means that on average more length is added during the lifting process, lowering the efficacy of our attack. To avoid this we take the number of indices we expect to be in Zone III according to our model of Sect. 3.1 and perform no lattice reduction on them. These indices are then unchanged, and since lattice reduction preserves the real span of the vectors of Zone I and Zone II, their Gram–Schmidt norms remain 1. We also perform slightly heavier progressive BKZ in these experiments, denoted by the single pair $(8, [3, \infty))$. With the above, slightly artificial, alterations we are able to experimentally achieve the number of q vectors expected by our model, see Table 1. In Fig. 8 we also plot the average profile of the same experiments against the Z-shape profile expected by our model in Sect. 3.1.

Our modified BKZ reduction process is seemingly capable of producing bases with the expected number of q vectors, as predicted by our model. However, the aforementioned kinks are still to some degree present for $\beta \in \{20, 30, 40\}$. The accurate modelling of Z-shape bases remains an open question. Nevertheless, we maintain that it would be unsatisfactory to rely on the presence of such kinks in a basis profile for the practical security of a cryptographic scheme.

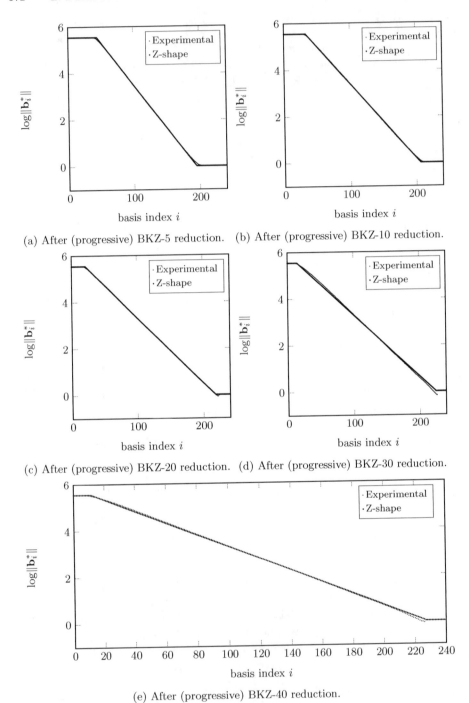

(a) After (progressive) BKZ-5 reduction.   (b) After (progressive) BKZ-10 reduction.

(c) After (progressive) BKZ-20 reduction.   (d) After (progressive) BKZ-30 reduction.

(e) After (progressive) BKZ-40 reduction.

Fig. 8. For $(n, m, q, \beta) = (120, 240, 257, 40)$ we run the altered progressive BKZ-β reduction described in Sect. 5.2 and plot the profile expected by our Z-shape model against the average of 60 experimental profiles.

6   Application and Practical Cryptanalysis

6.1   Small q Hash and Sign Signatures

In [16] a simple technique to reduce the bandwidth of hash and sign based signatures such as Falcon [22] and Mitaka [15] was proposed: reduce the size of the modulus q. Even though this technique is simple and effective, care must be taken with regards to the choice of q, as the best attacks are dependent on q. By framing Falcon and Mitaka as particular ISIS instances, we propose a revision of the cryptanalysis of [16] with the attack and optimisations introduced in Sect. 3 and Sect. 4.

On Hash and Sign Signatures as ISIS. We review the underlying principles of hash and sign signatures such as Falcon and Mitaka. The scheme involves two keys: the signing key, which acts as a trapdoor, and enables one to solve the approximate closest vector problem via discrete Gaussian sampling over the lattice, and the verification key $\mathbf{H}$, which can only verify whether a point belongs to the lattice.

We provide a high-level, but incomplete, description of the signing process for both Falcon and Mitaka. In both schemes, the public key $\mathbf{H}$ can be expressed as an integer matrix with specific structure. While we do not delve into the details of the matrix construction, the security argument crucially relies on the decisional NTRU assumption, which loosely states that $\mathbf{H}$ can be viewed as a random matrix.[7]

Let $m = 2n$. The signing algorithm hashes a message to $\mathbf{c} \in \mathbb{Z}_q^n$ and employs the signing key to sample $\mathbf{s}_1, \mathbf{s}_2 \in \mathbb{Z}^n$ such that $\mathbf{s}_1 + \mathbf{H}\mathbf{s}_2 = \mathbf{c} \bmod q$, as described in [22, Sect. 3.9.1]. If we concatenate $\mathbf{s}_1$ and $\mathbf{s}_2$ to form $\mathbf{s}$, the signature is valid if $\|\mathbf{s}\| \leqslant \nu$ for some length bound ν. This can be viewed as an $\mathsf{ISIS}_{n,m,q,\nu}$ instance with added structure, where $\mathbf{A} = (\mathbf{I}_n \,|\, \mathbf{H})$. If we can differentiate this ISIS instance from a uniform $\mathbf{A}$, we can break the decisional NTRU assumption discussed earlier. Note that if we express $\mathbf{A} = (\mathbf{A}_1 \,|\, \mathbf{A}_2)$, where $\mathbf{A}_1 \in \mathbb{Z}_q^{n \times n}$ and $\mathbf{A}_1 \in \mathrm{Gl}_n(\mathbb{Z}_q)$, we can transform this ISIS instance into one that is semantically similar to those implied by Falcon and Mitaka via $\mathbf{A}_1^{-1}\mathbf{A} = (\mathbf{I}_n \,|\, \mathbf{A}_1^{-1}\mathbf{A}_2)$. With this view of Falcon and Mitaka as ISIS instances, we can apply our attack.

Attack Costs. In Table 2 when considering on the fly lifting we only consider the faster sieve of [8], and recall that this optimisation was *not* subject to experimental validation in Sect. 5. For the second entry of each pair of estimated costs we incorporate the probability loss factor into our script by assuming each lift is short enough with probability reduced by a factor $q/2$.

An Overestimated Loss. In the next paragraph we report on experiments that mount the above attack. In these experiments we did not multiply by the

---

[7] Strictly speaking, the NTRU assumption only states that the number ring element from which the matrix $\mathbf{H}$ can be reconstructed is indistinguishable from uniform.

Table 2. Classical complexities of variants of our attack against signature forgery on small q parameter sets for Falcon and Mitaka. Our n relates to d in [16], we fix $m = 2n$, and F and M denote Falcon and Mitaka respectively. We report two pairs of complexities, one without on the fly lifting and one with, denoted "no otf" and "otf" respectively. In each pair we report in order the cost of the SIS* attack and the cost of the ISIS attack, accounting for the reduction loss factor of $q/2$ on success probability. The former is given between parenthesis. The final column is the suggested bit security of the parameter set in the CoreSVP model according to [16, Table 2]. The lowest ISIS attack cost is in boldface in each row.

$(n, q, \nu,$ scheme)	no otf		otf		[16, Table 2]
	(SIS*)	ISIS	(SIS*)	ISIS	
$(512, 257, 801,$ F)	(95)	98	(90)	**92**	118
$(512, 257, 1470,$ M)	(8)	14	(8)	**12**	94
$(512, 521, 1141,$ F)	(113)	115	(110)	**111**	121
$(512, 521, 2094,$ M)	(55)	58	(51)	**54**	97
$(512, 1031, 1606,$ F)	(117)	**119**	(120)	121	122
$(512, 1031, 2945,$ M)	(81)	84	(78)	**80**	99

randomising scalar f in Lemma 1 for the reasons discussed below the lemma. The success probability of the attack appears to be higher than even the heuristic $2/q$ we suggest. This can be explained by the fact that vectors output by SIS* solvers are short, hence their coordinates are biased toward smaller values such as 1 and -1.

We therefore reiterate our warning that the concrete results given in this paper are only meant as a cautionary tale, and certainly not as definitive cost estimates usable for claiming concrete security. Most likely our attack and its analysis can be further improved. This optimisation effort is left to whoever dares venture into the low modulus ISIS regime.

Practical Attack on Mitaka with Small q. As seen in Table 2 the cost of the attack on the small q variant of Mitaka with $n = 512$ and $q = 257$ appears very low, so low that not mounting the attack in practice would be indefensible. Without on the fly lifting our script proposes as the optimal attack a blocksize of 25 repeated $2^{6.5}$ times. Due to various overheads, one might prefer to choose a blocksize of 45 and repeat only once.

In practice, it is generally preferable to run BKZ with a smaller blocksize and run a final sieve on a projected sublattice of a larger rank to better balance the cost of the two procedures. We chose (by trial and error) a BKZ blocksize of 12 and a sieving rank of 60 and did not perform any on the fly lifting techniques, rather we lifted every vector in our terminal sieve database. We also restricted the sloped portion of the Z-shape on which we ran lattice reduction to dimension 160 to avoid having to resort to high precision floating point arithmetic in LLL.

We implemented this attack on ISIS with parameters derived from the small q parameters for Mitaka of [16]: $m = 1024$, $n = 512$, $q = 257$ and $\nu = 1470$. This implementation is provided in the sage script `attack.sage`, and relies on the libraries fpylll and g6k [3,26,27]. It ran successfully on all 20 random instances we launched, each taking less than 15 s on a single core (Intel(R) Core(TM) i7-4790 CPU, 3.60 GHz).

Acknowledgements. The authors thank Damien Stehlé and Yang Yu for useful discussions, and the reviewers for their comments. The research of L. Ducas and E.W. Postlethwaite was supported by the ERC-StG-ARTICULATE project (no. 947821).

References

1. Ajtai, M.: Generating hard instances of lattice problems (extended abstract). In: 28th ACM STOC, pp. 99–108. ACM Press, May 1996. https://doi.org/10.1145/237814.237838

2. Albrecht, M.R., Ducas, L.: Lattice Attacks on NTRU and LWE: A History of Refinements. London Mathematical Society Lecture Note Series, pp. 15–40. Cambridge University Press (2021). https://doi.org/10.1017/9781108854207.004

3. Albrecht, M.R., Ducas, L., Herold, G., Kirshanova, E., Postlethwaite, E.W., Stevens, M.: The general sieve kernel and new records in lattice reduction. In: Ishai, Y., Rijmen, V. (eds.) EUROCRYPT 2019. LNCS, vol. 11477, pp. 717–746. Springer, Cham (2019). https://doi.org/10.1007/978-3-030-17656-3_25

4. Alkim, E., Ducas, L., Pöppelmann, T., Schwabe, P.: Post-quantum key exchange - a new hope. In: Holz, T., Savage, S. (eds.) USENIX Security 2016, pp. 327–343. USENIX Association, August 2016

5. Aono, Y., Nguyen, P.Q.: Random sampling revisited: lattice enumeration with discrete pruning. In: Coron, J.-S., Nielsen, J.B. (eds.) EUROCRYPT 2017, Part II. LNCS, vol. 10211, pp. 65–102. Springer, Cham (2017). https://doi.org/10.1007/978-3-319-56614-6_3

6. Aono, Y., Wang, Y., Hayashi, T., Takagi, T.: Improved progressive BKZ algorithms and their precise cost estimation by sharp simulator. In: Fischlin, M., Coron, J.-S. (eds.) EUROCRYPT 2016, Part I. LNCS, vol. 9665, pp. 789–819. Springer, Heidelberg (2016). https://doi.org/10.1007/978-3-662-49890-3_30

7. Babai, L.: On Lovász' lattice reduction and the nearest lattice point problem. Combinatorica **6**(1), 1–13 (1986). https://doi.org/10.1007/BF02579403

8. Becker, A., Ducas, L., Gama, N., Laarhoven, T.: New directions in nearest neighbor searching with applications to lattice sieving. In: Krauthgamer, R. (ed.) 27th SODA, pp. 10–24. ACM-SIAM, January 2016. https://doi.org/10.1137/1.9781611974331.ch2

9. Bos, J.W., et al.: HAWK. Technical report, National Institute of Standards and Technology (2023, to appear). https://csrc.nist.gov/projects/pqc-dig-sig

10. Chen, Y.: Réduction de réseau et sécurité concrète du chiffrement complètement homomorphe. Ph.D. thesis, Paris, July 2013. http://www.theses.fr/2013PA077242, thèse de doctorat dirigée par Nguyen, Phong-Quang Informatique Paris 7 2013

11. Devevey, J., Fawzi, O., Passelègue, A., Stehlé, D.: On Rejection Sampling in Lyubashevsky's Signature Scheme. In: Agrawal, S., Lin, D. (eds.) Advances in Cryptology, ASIACRYPT 2022. LNCS, vol. 13794, pp. 34–64. Springer, Cham (2022). https://doi.org/10.1007/978-3-031-22972-5_2

12. Ducas, L.: Shortest vector from lattice sieving: a few dimensions for free. In: Nielsen, J.B., Rijmen, V. (eds.) EUROCRYPT 2018, Part I. LNCS, vol. 10820, pp. 125–145. Springer, Cham (2018). https://doi.org/10.1007/978-3-319-78381-9_5

13. Ducas, L., Postlethwaite, E.W., Pulles, L.N., Woerden, W.: Hawk: module LIP makes lattice signatures fast, compact and simple. In: Agrawal, S., Lin, D. (eds.) Advances in Cryptology, ASIACRYPT 2022, Part IV. LNCS, vol. 13794, pp. 65–94. Springer, Cham (2022). https://doi.org/10.1007/978-3-031-22972-5_3

14. Ducas, L., van Woerden, W.: NTRU fatigue: how stretched is overstretched? In: Tibouchi, M., Wang, H. (eds.) ASIACRYPT 2021. LNCS, vol. 13093, pp. 3–32. Springer, Cham (2021). https://doi.org/10.1007/978-3-030-92068-5_1

15. Espitau, T., et al.: MITAKA: a simpler, parallelizable, maskable variant of falcon. In: Dunkelman, O., Dziembowski, S. (eds.) EUROCRYPT 2022, Part III. LNCS, vol. 13277, pp. 222–253. Springer, Heidelberg, May/June 2022. https://doi.org/10.1007/978-3-031-07082-2_9

16. Espitau, T., Tibouchi, M., Wallet, A., Yu, Y.: Shorter hash-and-sign lattice-based signatures. In: Dodis, Y., Shrimpton, T. (eds.) CRYPTO 2022, Part II. LNCS, August 2022, vol. 13508, pp. 245–275. Springer, Heidelberg (2022). https://doi.org/10.1007/978-3-031-15979-4_9

17. Howgrave-Graham, N.: A hybrid lattice-reduction and meet-in-the-middle attack against NTRU. In: Menezes, A. (ed.) CRYPTO 2007. LNCS, August 2007, vol. 4622, pp. 150–169. Springer, Heidelberg (2007). https://doi.org/10.1007/978-3-540-74143-5_9

18. Lenstra, A.K., Lenstra, H.W., Lovász, L.: Factoring polynomials with rational coefficients. Mathematische Annalen **261**(4), 515–534 (1982). https://doi.org/10.1007/BF01457454

19. Lyubashevsky, V., et al.: CRYSTALS-DILITHIUM. Technical report, National Institute of Standards and Technology (2022). https://csrc.nist.gov/Projects/post-quantum-cryptography/selected-algorithms-2022

20. Micciancio, D., Regev, O.: Worst-case to average-case reductions based on gaussian measures. SIAM J. Comput. **37**(1), 267–302 (2007). https://doi.org/10.1137/S0097539705447360

21. Nguyen, P.Q., Vidick, T.: Sieve algorithms for the shortest vector problem are practical. J. Math. Cryptol. **2**(2), 181–207 (2008). https://doi.org/10.1515/JMC.2008.009

22. Prest, T., et al.: FALCON. Technical report, National Institute of Standards and Technology (2022). https://csrc.nist.gov/Projects/post-quantum-cryptography/selected-algorithms-2022

23. Rousseau, C.C., Ruehr, O.G.: Problems and solutions. SIAM Rev. **39**(4), 761–789 (1997). https://doi.org/10.1137/SIREAD000039000004000761000001

24. Schnorr, C.P., Euchner, M.: Lattice basis reduction: improved practical algorithms and solving subset sum problems. Math. Program. **66**(1), 181–199 (1994). https://doi.org/10.1007/BF01581144

25. Schnorr, C.P.: Lattice reduction by random sampling and birthday methods. In: Alt, H., Habib, M. (eds.) STACS 2003. LNCS, vol. 2607, pp. 145–156. Springer, Heidelberg (2003). https://doi.org/10.1007/3-540-36494-3_14

26. development team, T.F.: fpylll, a Python wrapper for the fplll lattice reduction library, Version: 0.5.9 (2023). https://github.com/fplll/fpylll

27. The G6K development team: The general sieve kernel, Version: 0.1.2 (2023). https://github.com/fplll/g6k

Practical-Time Related-Key Attack on GOST with Secret S-Boxes

Orr Dunkelman[1][✉], Nathan Keller[2], and Ariel Weizmann[2]

[1] Computer Science Department, University of Haifa, Haifa, Israel
orrd@cs.haifa.ac.il
[2] Department of Mathematics, Bar-Ilan University, Ramat Gan, Israel
Nathan.Keller@biu.ac.il

Abstract. The block cipher GOST 28147-89 was the Russian Federation encryption standard for over 20 years, and is still one of its two standard block ciphers. GOST is a 32-round Feistel construction, whose security benefits from the fact that the S-boxes used in the design are kept secret. In the last 10 years, several attacks on the full 32-round GOST were presented. However, they all assume that the S-boxes are known. When the S-boxes are secret, all published attacks either target a small number of rounds, or apply for small sets of weak keys.

In this paper we present the first practical-time attack on GOST with secret S-boxes. The attack works in the related-key model and is faster than all previous attacks in this model which assume that the S-boxes are known. The complexity of the attack is less than 2^{27} encryptions. It was fully verified, and runs in a few seconds on a PC. The attack is based on a novel type of related-key differentials of GOST, inspired by local collisions.

Our new technique may be applicable to certain GOST-based hash functions as well. To demonstrate this, we show how to find a collision on a Davies-Meyer construction based on GOST with an arbitrary initial value, in less than 2^{10} hash function evaluations.

Keywords: Related-key differential cryptanalysis · GOST · Local collision

1 Introduction

The block cipher GOST 28147-89 (usually shortened to GOST) was developed in the USSR in the 1970's, as an alternative for DES. From 1989 to 2015, it was

O. Dunkelman—Supported in part by the Center for Cyber, Law, and Policy in conjunction with the Israel National Cyber Bureau in the Prime Minister's Office and by the Israeli Science Foundation through grants No. 880/18 and 3380/19.
N. Keller and A. Weizmann—Supported by the European Research Council under the ERC starting grant agreement n. 757731 (LightCrypt) and by the BIU Center for Research in Applied Cryptography and Cyber Security in conjunction with the Israel National Cyber Bureau in the Prime Minister's Office.
A. Weizmann—Supported by the President Scholarship for Ph.D. students at the Bar-Ilan University.

ⓒ International Association for Cryptologic Research 2023
H. Handschuh and A. Lysyanskaya (Eds.): CRYPTO 2023, LNCS 14083, pp. 177–208, 2023.
https://doi.org/10.1007/978-3-031-38548-3_7

the official encryption standard of the USSR, and then of the Russian Federation (RF), and was obligatory to use in the RF in all data processing systems providing public services [16]. Since 2015, an instantiation of GOST with specified S-boxes named Magma is one of the two ciphers in the RF encryption standard GOST R 34.12-2015 [15]. Consequently, GOST is still very widely used in the Russian Federation.

GOST is a 32-round Feistel construction whose round function uses eight 4-to-4 bit S-boxes. The structure of the S-boxes was kept secret, and reportedly, different sets of S-boxes were used in different industry branches. The set used in the banking industry had leaked and was published in [31], and most previous attacks on GOST used that set of S-boxes. In the new standard GOST R 34.12-2015, the S-boxes were specified (to another set of values). Another central feature of the design of GOST is the key schedule. The 256-bit key is represented as an array of eight 32-bit words $(K_1, K_2, \ldots, K_8)$, and the subkeys used in the 32 rounds are taken directly from the array in a structured form. This property was exploited in several attacks on GOST.

Previous Works. In the last 30 years, GOST has been the target of numerous cryptanalytic attempts. Most of these attempts assumed that the S-boxes are known (thus, not targeting the original strong version of the cipher). Under this assumption, in the standard single-key model, several attacks can break the full 32-round GOST faster than exhaustive key search [11,12,20], but all of them have an impractical time complexity of at least 2^{179} encryptions (see also [10] and the multiple references therein). In the related-key model (in which the adversary may request encryptions under pairs of unknown keys with a known relation and her goal is to recover the keys), several practical-time attacks on the full 32-round GOST were obtained. After two works that could attack only reduced-round variants [21,32], Ko et al. [24] were the first to obtain a related-key attack on the full 32-round variant. Their attack, which uses the related-key differential technique [21], requires 2^{36} chosen plaintexts and time of 2^{36} encryptions. Biryukov and Nikolic [7] presented an attack on the full 32 rounds which uses complementation properties and requires 2^{38} chosen plaintexts and 2^{38} encryptions. Rudskoy [29] and Pudovkina and Khoruzhenko [27] presented related-key boomerang attacks [22] with semi-practical complexities. The best among these attacks, by Ko et al. [24], has a complexity of 2^{36}.

Only several papers targeted the original variant of GOST, with secret S-boxes. Saarinen [30] presented an attack with a complexity of 2^{32} that applies for the 2^{32} keys of the form $(K, K, \ldots, K, K)$. Bar-On et al. [2] presented an attack on 24 rounds that applies for all keys and has a complexity of 2^{63}, as well as an attack on the full 32-round version that applies for the 2^{128} keys of the form $(K_1, K_2, K_3, K_4, K_4, K_3, K_2, K_1)$ and has a complexity of 2^{40}. All these attacks are based on variants of the slide technique [8]. Ko et al. [24] presented a related-key differential with probability 1 on an arbitrary number of rounds which can be used for distinguishing GOST from a random permutation. Zhao et al. [35] presented an attack on the full 32-round variant using algebraic fault analysis. They showed that insertion of 270 faults and time of a few hours are sufficient to recover the secret S-boxes. Neither of these attacks endanger the security of the full GOST with secret S-boxes – the attacks either target partial encryption, or apply only for a small set of weak keys, or provide only a distinguishing ability, or require using the side-channel attack model.

Our Contributions. In this paper we present the first practical-time attack on the full GOST with secret S-boxes. Our attack, which works in the related-key model, recovers the secret S-boxes and the secret key, requiring only 2^{27} chosen plaintexts and time of 2^{27} encryptions in the worst case (among 100 experiments), and about 2^{24} chosen plaintexts and time of 2^{24} encryptions on average. Thus, our attack is significantly faster than all previously known related-key attacks on GOST, although those attacks assume that the S-boxes are known. Needless to say, our attack is significantly stronger than all previous attacks on GOST with secret S-boxes, as none of those attacks can break the full GOST for all keys. The attack was fully verified experimentally and runs in a few seconds on a PC. A comparison of the complexity of our attack with the complexities of previously known attacks on GOST is presented in Table 1.[1]

Like the attack of Ko et al. [24], our attack uses the related-key differential technique [21]. However, the differential characteristic we use differs significantly from the characteristic used in [24]. Our characteristic has the form of *local collisions* between two encryption processes over three rounds of GOST, in which in the first round, a state difference is created by a subkey difference, in the second round the state difference is 'kept from spreading', and in the third round the state difference is canceled by another properly selected subkey difference. Such local collisions, first proposed by Chabaud and Joux [9], were very effective in collision attacks against hash functions from the SHA family (e.g., [5,33,34]). We use them for the GOST block cipher at the first time.

Being a collision-based related-key attack, our attack is naturally effective against certain types of GOST-based hash functions. We demonstrate this effectiveness by showing that for a Davies-Meyer hash function based on GOST, one can find a collision in less than 2^{10} hash function evaluations, for an arbitrary initial value. Previously, the techniques from Mendel et al.'s attack [26] on the GOST hash function [17] could be used to find a collision in a Davies-Meyer hash function based on GOST almost instantly, but only if the 64-bit initial value is of the form (x, x) for a 32-bit value x. Otherwise, no ways to find a collision in less than 2^{32} hash function evaluations were known.

We present two additional applications of our techniques: the first S-box recovery attack on the cipher GOST2 [13], and a simplification of the S-box recovery attack of Bar-On et al. [2] on GOST with a palindromic key schedule.

---

[1] While the focus of this paper is on GOST with secret S-boxes, we note that in the known S-box setting, a related-key attack with complexity of 2^{16} chosen plaintexts and less than 2^{20} encryptions can be obtained by using the probability-one 25-round related-key differential characteristic with input difference $(e_{31}, 0, e_{31}, 0, e_{31}, 0, e_{31}, 0)$ and key difference $(e_{31}, 0)$ used in [24] and extending it to almost the entire cipher in a truncated manner, like was done in [2]. As the description of the attack includes many fine details and is of less interest, we omit it here.

Table 1. Comparison of Our Results with Previous Attacks on GOST

No. of Rounds	Fraction of Keys	Secret S-boxes?	Data[a]	Time[b]	Technique and Source[c]
21	all	no	2^{56} CP	2^{56}	RK Diff. [32]
24	all	no	?[d]	?[d]	RK Diff. [21]
25	all	no	5 CP	2^{32}	RK Diff. [28]
32	all	no	2^{36} CP	2^{36}	RK Diff. [24]
32	all	no	2^{38} CP	2^{38}	Complementation [7]
32	all	no	2^{10} ACPC	2^{71}	RK Boom. [29]
32	all	no	?[d] ACPC	?[d]	RK Boom. [27]
24	all	yes	2^{63} CP	2^{63}	Slide [2]
32	2^{-224}	yes	2^{32} CP	2^{32}	Slide [30]
32	2^{-128}	yes	2^{40} CP	2^{40}	Slide [2]
32	all	yes	2^{27} CP	2^{27}	RK Diff. (Sect. 4)

[a] Time is measured in GOST encryptions
[b] "CP"—Chosen plaintext, "ACPC"—Adaptive Chosen Plaintext and Ciphertext
[c] "RK"—Related-Key, "Diff."—Differential, "Boom."—Boomerang
[d] The notation '?' means that the attack complexity was not specified

Organization of the Paper. In Sect. 2 we describe the structure of GOST and briefly recall the related-key differential technique used in the paper. In Sect. 3 we present the new type of differentials of GOST we employ. The related-key attack on the full 32-round GOST is presented in Sect. 4. Potential applications of the techniques to hash functions based on GOST, including the GOST hash function [17], are discussed in Sect. 5. We conclude the paper with a summary and discussion in Sect. 6.

2   Preliminaries

2.1   The Structure of GOST

GOST 28147-89 is a 64-bit block size, 256-bit key size block cipher, composed of 32 Feistel rounds. For each $1 \le i \le 32$, the i'th round is defined as follows (see Fig. 1):

$$F_{K_i}(X_L, X_R) = (X_R, X_L \oplus \lll_{11} (S(X_R \boxplus K_i))),$$

where:

- $\oplus$ denotes bit-wise XOR and $\boxplus$ denotes modular addition modulo 2^{32}.
- For each 32-bit word A, $\lll_{11} (A)$ denotes cyclic left-rotation of A by 11 bits.
- K_i is the round key. The key schedule is very simple: Divide the 256-bit key into eight 32-bit subkeys $K_1, \ldots, K_8$. These subkeys are used in this order

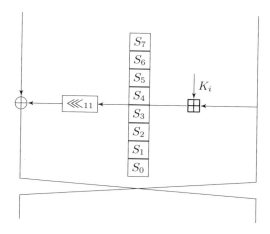

Fig. 1. One GOST Round.

three times in rounds 1–24, and in the reverse order $K_8, \ldots, K_1$ in the last 8 rounds 25–32.

- S is an S-box layer of eight 4-to-4 bit S-boxes[2] $S_0 \ldots, S_7 : \{0, 1\}^4 \to \{0, 1\}^4$, where S_0 is performed on the four least significant bits, and S_7 is performed on the four most significant bits. These S-boxes are kept secret. In addition, they are not necessarily permutations.

2.2 Related-Key Differential Attacks

Differential Attacks. Differential cryptanalysis was introduced by Biham and Shamir [6]. It analyzes the development of differences through the encryption process of pairs of plaintexts.

Let E be an n-bit block cipher consisting of r rounds. A differential with probability p of E is a statistical property of the form $\Pr[E(P) \oplus E(P') = \Omega_O \mid P \oplus P' = \Omega_I] = p$, denoted by $\Omega_I \xrightarrow{p} \Omega_O$. If $p \gg 2^{-n}$, the differential can be used to distinguish E from a random permutation, given $O(p^{-1})$ pairs of plaintexts with difference Ω_I.

Differentials can be used for key-recovery attacks as well, in a procedure called iR-attack. In this procedure, the adversary finds a differential $\Omega_I \xrightarrow{p} \Omega_O$ for the first $r - i$ rounds of E and uses it to recover key material in the last i rounds. First, the adversary asks for the encryption of $O(p^{-1})$ pairs (P, P') of plaintexts that satisfy $P \oplus P' = \Omega_I$. Then, she guesses some of the subkey bits used in the last i rounds, partially decrypts the ciphertext pairs through the last i rounds and checks whether the difference at the input to the $(r - i + 1)$'th round is equal to Ω_O at least several times. As the data is expected to contain

---

[2] The somewhat nonstandard notations used here follow the notations presented in the up-to-date official document describing GOST [15].

several plaintext pairs that satisfy the differential, it is expected that the check succeeds for the correct key guess and fails for wrong key guesses with a high probability.

Related-Key Differential Cryptanalysis. Related-key (in short, RK) attacks were introduced by Biham [3] and by Knudsen [23], independently. The attack model in these attacks is that the adversary may obtain the encryption of plaintexts under several related unknown keys, where the relation between the keys is known to (or can be chosen by) the adversary. The goal of the adversary is to recover the keys.

In [21], Kelsey et al. introduced the related-key differential cryptanalysis. In a related-key differential attack, the adversary can ask for the encryption of plaintext pairs with a chosen difference Ω_I (i.e., $P, P' = P \oplus \Omega_I$), under unknown keys with a chosen difference Ω_K (i.e., $K, K' = K \oplus \Omega_K$). A related-key differential with a probability of p of a block cipher E under two keys $K, K' = K \oplus \Omega_K$ is a statistical property of the form $\Pr[E_K(P) \oplus E_{K'}(P') = \Omega_O \mid P \oplus P' = \Omega_I] = p$, denoted by $\Omega_I \xrightarrow[\Omega_K]{p} \Omega_O$. Related-key differentials can be used for key-recovery in a similar way to ordinary differentials.

3   The New Related-Key Differential of GOST

In this section we present the new related-key differential of GOST which we use in our attacks. The differential is based on a 3-round 'local collision', inspired by local collisions in hash functions, first proposed by Chabaud and Joux [9].

For the sake of concreteness, we first present the differential for the special case of GOST with the S-boxes used in the banking industry, which was considered in most previous works on GOST. Afterwards, we show how to use the differential when the S-boxes are unknown.

3.1   The Basic 3-Round Iterative Related-Key Differential

Consider the encryption through the first three rounds of GOST of a plaintext P under two related keys K, K' such that $K_1' = K_1 \oplus e_{31}, K_2' = K_2 \oplus e_{10}, K_3' = K_3 \oplus e_{31}$ (see Fig. 2).

At the first round, since the state difference is zero and the subkey difference is in the most significant bit, the modular addition behaves like XOR with respect to differences, and thus, the XOR difference after the key addition is e_{31}. As the S-box S_7 in the set used in the banking industry satisfies the differential $8 \xrightarrow{1/4} 8$, with a probability of $\frac{1}{4}$ the difference after the S-box layer is e_{31}, which is mapped to e_{10} by the left rotation. At the second round, the input difference e_{10} is canceled by the sub-key difference with a probability of $\frac{1}{2}$. At the third round, the difference after the key addition is e_{31} (like in the first round), and thus, with a probability of $\frac{1}{4}$ the difference after the rotation is e_{10}, which is canceled in the XOR operation at the end of the round, resulting in a zero state

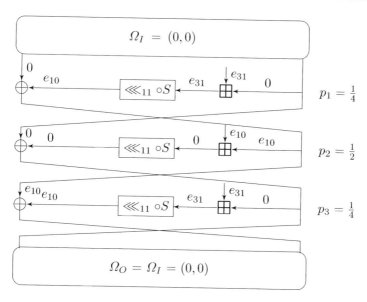

Fig. 2. Our 3-Round iterative RK differential characteristic on GOST (using the banking industry S-boxes).

difference at the input of the fourth round. Hence, we get the following 3-round iterative differential characteristic:

$$(0,0) \xrightarrow[\Omega_{K_1}=e_{31}]{\frac{1}{4}} (0,e_{10}) \xrightarrow[\Omega_{K_2}=e_{10}]{\frac{1}{2}} (e_{10},0) \xrightarrow[\Omega_{K_3}=e_{31}]{\frac{1}{4}} (0,0),$$

as depicted in Fig. 2. Since this related-key differential characteristic is of the form $0 \rightarrow 0$, it can be viewed as a *local collision*.

3.2 The Full 32-Round Differential

Consider the encryption of a plaintext P under two keys K, K' with key difference

$$\Omega_K = (e_{31}, e_{10}, e_{31}, 0, 0, 0, 0, 0).$$

By the 3-round iterative differential characteristic described above we have the following 8-round iterative differential:

$$(0,0) \xrightarrow[\Omega_K]{2^{-5}} (0,0).$$

Since the eight sub-keys used in rounds 9–16 and 17–24 are the same as in rounds 1–8, we obtain the 24-round iterative differential:

$$(0,0) \xrightarrow[\Omega_K]{2^{-15}} (0,0).$$

In rounds 25–32, the subkeys are used in reverse order, and hence, there is no key difference until round 29 (inclusive). Thus, we get the following 29-round differential:

$$(0,0) \xrightarrow[\Omega_K]{2^{-15}} (0,0).$$

At the last three rounds, the subkey differences are e_{31}, e_{10}, e_{31}, respectively. Hence, we may apply again the basic three-round differential characteristic, to obtain a 32-round related-key differential with probability of 2^{-20}. In order to reduce the data complexity of attacks exploiting the differential, we prefer to use in these rounds a truncated differential characteristic (i.e., a differential characteristic that predicts the difference only in part of the state) which holds with a probability close to 1.

For this sake, we examine the development of the difference in the last three rounds. The input difference to round 30 is zero and the subkey difference is e_{31}. Thus, after the key addition the difference is e_{31}, and after the S-box layer the difference is of the form $?0000000_x$ (where ? is an unknown 4-bit value), which is mapped by the left rotation to $00000XY0_x$ (where $X \in \{0, \ldots, 7\}, Y \in \{0, 8\}$).

At round 31, with a probability of over 99% the truncated difference after the key addition (in which the subkey difference is e_{10}) is of the form $000???Q0_x$ (where $Q \in \{0, 8\}$), since we require the addition carry to go through at most 9 bits. After the S-box layer the difference is $000????0_x$, which is mapped to $Z???W000_x$ (where $W \in \{0, 8\}, Z \in \{0, \ldots, 7\}$) by the left rotation. This difference is copied to the right half of the ciphertext.

At round 32, the difference after the key addition (in which the subkey difference is e_{31}) is $????T000_x$. After the S-box layer, the difference is $?????000_x$ which is mapped by the left rotation to $??U00V??_x$ (where $V \in \{0, \ldots, 7\}, U \in \{0, 8\}$). This is the difference in the left half of the ciphertext.

Hence, we have a related key truncated differential on the entire cipher

$$(0,0) \xrightarrow[\Omega_K]{2^{-15}} (??U00V??_x, Z???W000_x),$$

where $U, W \in \{0, 8\}, V, Z \in \{0, \ldots, 7\}$, and ? is an unknown value, as depicted in Fig. 3. To conclude, this related-key truncated differential predicts a zero difference in 28 bits with a probability of about 2^{-15}.

3.3   The Related-Key Differential for GOST with Secret S-boxes

Recall that our 3-round iterative differential characteristic,

$$(0,0) \xrightarrow[\Omega_{K_1}=e_{31}]{\frac{1}{4}} (0, e_{10}) \xrightarrow[\Omega_{K_2}=e_{10}]{\frac{1}{2}} (e_{10}, 0) \xrightarrow[\Omega_{K_3}=e_{31}]{\frac{1}{4}} (0,0),$$

relies on the differential transition $8 \xrightarrow{\frac{1}{4}} 8$ in the S-box S_7. When S_7 is a secret S-box, this differential might be impossible, and we have no direct way to check its probability.

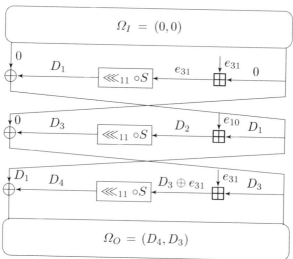

$D_1 = 00000XY0_x, D_2 = 000???Q0_x, D_3 = Z???W000_x, D_4 = ??U00V??_x$, where
$X, Z, V \in \{0, \ldots, 7\}, Q, Y, W, U \in \{0, 8\}.$

Fig. 3. The last three Rounds of our RK truncated differential characteristic on the full GOST (considering the banking industry S-boxes).

To overcome this, we consider four additional related keys, obtained by changing the difference in K_2. Namely, while we leave the key difference in K_1, K_3 fixed at e_{31}, we consider four differences in K_2:

$$\Omega^0_{K_2} = e_7, \Omega^1_{K_2} = e_8, \Omega^2_{K_2} = e_9, \Omega^3_{K_2} = e_{10}.$$

If in S_7, a differential of the form $8 \xrightarrow{p} (2^i + 2^{i+1} + \ldots + 2^{i+b-1})$ is satisfied (where $i \in \{0, 1, 2, 3\}$ and $b \in \{1, \ldots, 4-i\}$; note that the sum contains between one and four terms), then the following 3-round differential characteristic holds,[3] with overall probability of $p^2 2^{-b}$:

$$(0,0) \xrightarrow[\Omega_{K_1}=e_{31}]{p} (0, e_{7+i,7+i+1,\ldots,7+i+b-1}) \xrightarrow[\Omega^i_{K_2}=e_{7+i}]{2^{-b}} (e_{7+i,7+i+1,\ldots,7+i+b-1}, 0)$$

$$\xrightarrow[\Omega_{K_3}=e_{31}]{p} (0,0).$$

Furthermore, as we are interested only in the probability of having a zero output difference after three rounds for a given subkey difference (formally called 'probability of a differential') and not in the probability of the exact transition sequence

---

[3] If a differential of the form $8 \xrightarrow{p} 0$ is satisfied, then an even stronger 1-round iterative differential characteristic of GOST can be constructed, as is described in Sect. 3.4. We note that the existence of such a transition implies that the S-boxes are not bijective, but the official document describing GOST [16] permits using such S-boxes.

from the zero input difference to the zero output difference (formally called 'probability of a differential characteristic'), we can enjoy several differential characteristics at the same time. Indeed, when we consider the encryption of two identical plaintexts under the subkey difference $\Omega(K_1, K_2, K_3) = (e_{31}, e_{7+i}, e_{31})$, the probability of having a zero difference after three rounds is at least $\sum_{b=1}^{4} p_b^2 2^{-j}$, where p_b is the probability of the transition $8 \rightarrow (2^i + 2^{i+1} + \ldots + 2^{i+b-1})$ in S_7.

Note that out of the 15 possible non-zero output differences of S_7, 10 are of the prescribed form (for some b, i). Hence, for a random S-box, with an overwhelming probability at least one of these differentials is possible.

Among the differential characteristics we consider, the lowest probability is obtained in the case $p = 2^{-3}, b = 4$, in which the probability of the entire truncated differential is about $\left(p^2 \cdot 2^{-b}\right)^3 = 2^{-30}$. (Note that in a 4-bit S-box, the lowest possible non-zero probability of a differential is 2^{-3}). The highest probability is obtained in the case $p = 1, b = 1$, in which the probability of the entire truncated differential is at least $\left(p^2 \cdot 2^{-b}\right)^3 = 2^{-3}$.

In practice (as we have verified by running experiments on many randomly chosen S-boxes), in most cases for at least one of the four key differences, the overall probability of the truncated differential is at least 2^{-24}. Thus, by repeating the attack procedure for at most 5 key differences, we will be able to use the differential in the secret S-box setting (also obtaining some information on the S-box on the way).

3.4   Other Variants of the Differential

Besides the variants described above, many other variants of the differential can be considered. For example, instead of inserting the local collision at the first three rounds, one may insert it at any three other consecutive rounds. The active S-box S_7 can be replaced with any other S-box, and the input difference 8 can be replaced with any other input difference. The key difference in the third round can differ from the difference in the first round, as long as it is contained in the same S-box. Some of these changes affect the probability of the differential (e.g., when the subkey difference at the first and the third rounds is e_i for $i \neq 31$, we have to 'pay' probability of $(1/2)^2$ to bypass the key addition operations at the first and the third rounds).

The following additional variant could be useful in the case of non-invertible S-boxes (which are allowed by the design of GOST). If a differential of the form $(2^i + 2^{i+1} + \ldots + 2^{i+b-1}) \xrightarrow[S_j]{p} 0$ (where $i \in \{0, 1, 2, 3\}$ and $b \in \{1, \ldots, 4-i\}$) is satisfied, then we get an 1-round iterative differential characteristic $(0,0) \xrightarrow[\Omega_{K_1} = e_{4j+i}]{p \cdot 2^{-b} \geq 2^{-7}} (0,0)$. Using this characteristic, one can easily construct a related-key differential for the full cipher of the form $(0,0) \xrightarrow[\Omega_K = (e_{4j+i}, 0,0,0,0,0,0,0)]{p^3 \cdot 2^{-3b} \geq 2^{-21}} (D,0)$, where D has a few active bits. Alternatively, one may reach a ciphertext difference with more active bits by inserting the key difference e_{4j+i} in the subkey K_2. Using this variant of the differential, the adaptation of the attack described in Sect. 4

to the setting of non-invertible S-boxes is very simple. Hence, from now on we focus on the case of invertible S-boxes.

We use several of these variants in our attack (see Sects. 4.3 and 4.4). Other variants may be useful for future attacks on GOST and on other related cryptosystems. As a concrete application, we note that a variant of the differential applies to GOST2 – a variant of GOST with a modified key schedule that was proposed in [13] and studied in [1,14]. While the primary goal of the modified key schedule proposed in GOST2 was to thwart attacks based on the key schedule, a slight change of our differential holds for the modified key schedule as well. Specifically, using the same key difference, the only significant change is that the last occurrence of the 'local collision' is in rounds 29–31 instead of 30–32. This slightly increases the complexity of our attack (as one has to assume some probabilistic differential transition at round 29 in order to control the avalanche in round 32), but the attack works and requires less than 2^{30} encryptions.

4   The New Related-Key Attack on GOST with Secret S-boxes

In this section we present our new attack on GOST with secret S-boxes. The attack uses several variants of the related-key differential presented in Sect. 3 to gradually recover the bits of the subkey K_1 (used at the last round) and the secret S-boxes. Once all the S-boxes and the full subkey K_1 are recovered (up to a few candidates), the other subkeys can be recovered in a similar way with a lower complexity, by attacking a reduced-round variant of GOST and using the knowledge of the S-boxes. For the sake of simplicity, we present the attack in the case where all S-boxes of GOST are permutations (see Sect. 3.4 regarding non-invertible S-boxes), and use adaptively chosen plaintext queries in order to reduce the number of related-keys used in the attack. We describe the modifications needed for using only chosen plaintexts (which were fully verified experimentally) in Sect. 4.6.

This section is organized as follows. In Sect. 4.1 we describe the strategy we use to recover the S-boxes. In Sects. 4.2, 4.3, 4.4, and 4.5 we present the attack (divided into four main steps for the sake of convenience), and in Sect. 4.6 we report on the experimental verification of the attack. The code we use in the attack is enclosed to the paper and will be made publicly available.

4.1   The Strategy Used for S-box Recovery

In order to recover the secret S-boxes, we examine the last round of encryption (i.e., round 32). As we shall see in Sect. 4.2, the related-key differential allows us to find pairs (v_i, v_i') of inputs/outputs of the round function of round 32, for which we know the inputs and the XOR difference between the outputs. We claim that given a secret S-box $S : \{0,1\}^n \to \{0,1\}^n$, the number of such random pairs (v_i, v_i') needed to recover S, up to an XOR of all outputs of S with the same constant (which we cannot distinguish since at the output of S, we know only XOR differences), is $O(n2^n)$. Indeed, we can use the following simple algorithm to recover S.

First,[4] we assume w.l.o.g. that $S(0) = 0$ (since we recover S only up to an XOR with a constant). Secondly, we sort the pairs (v_i, v_i') according to v_i, and look for pairs of the form $(v_i, v_i') = (0, x)$. The assumption $S(0) = 0$ implies $S(x) = S(v_i) \oplus S(v_i')$. Then, we look for pairs of the form $(v_j, v_j') = (x, y)$, which yield $S(y) = S(v_j) \oplus S(v_j')$, where $S(v_j) = S(x)$ was already found at the previous stage. We continue in this fashion until all values $S(\cdot)$ are recovered.

When does this process recover the full S-box? Let G be a graph whose vertex set is $\{0, 1\}^n$, where v_i and v_i' are connected by an edge if the pair (v_i, v_i') exists in our data set. The process recovers S if and only if the graph is connected. It is well-known that a graph on 2^n vertices that has $m = 2^{n-1}(n + c)$ edges which are chosen uniformly at random, is connected with probability that tends to $e^{-e^{-c}}$ as $n \to \infty$ (see, e.g., [19, Theorem 4.1]). Hence, the process is expected to recover the full S-box with a high probability, once significantly more than $n2^{n-1}$ pairs (which is equal to 32 for $n = 4$) are given.

In our case, the value of n is relatively small and the pairs are not random (as they stem from plaintext pairs that satisfy a related-key differential). Hence, the number of required pairs may be somewhat larger than in the general asymptotic result. Our experiments (presented in Sect. 4.6) show that on average, with 256 pairs, the S-box is recovered with a fairly high probability.

The S-box recovery algorithm is described in Algorithm 1, where at the j'th iteration, we find the value of $S(v)$ for each vertex v whose distance from the vertex 0 in the graph G is j. In addition, the algorithm outputs 'Failure' if it encounters two equal pairs of inputs which lead to different output differences. Thus, the algorithm can be used also for filtering out wrong subkey guesses which lead to such a contradiction.

This simple S-box recovery algorithm is not tailor-made for our attack, and can be used in other differential-based S-box recovery attacks as well. For example, it can be used in the S-box recovery step of the attack of Bar-On et al. on GOST with palindromic key schedule [2, Sect. 5], instead of the more complex and more data-consuming algorithm of Dunkelman and Huang [18] which recovers the S-box from its difference distribution table. Indeed, once the differential part of the attack provides us with right pairs for which the actual input values are known and only the knowledge of the outputs is differential (as is commonly the case, e.g., in attacks on Feistel networks), there is no need to pass through the difference distribution table and our algorithm is sufficient. In the specific case of the attack of [2], this does not affect the overall complexity since the S-box recovery part is not the heaviest part of the attack. However, this might have effect in other cases.

---

[4] We alert the reader that this algorithm is different (and much simpler) than the algorithm presented in [18]. The reason for the difference is that in our case we know the inputs to the S-box and the output differences, while the algorithm of [18] assumes only knowledge of the input and output differences.

Algorithm 1. S-box Recovery.

Input: A table T of m triples (v_i, v'_i, d_i) where for each i, (v_i, v'_i) is a pair of input values to an S-box $S : \{0, 1\}^4 \to \{0, 1\}^4$ and $d_i = S(v_i) \oplus S(v'_i)$ is the corresponding output difference.

Sort T according to the first value.
Set $S(0) = 0$.
for all $v \in \{1, \ldots, 15\}$ **do**
    Set $S(v) = -1$.
end for
for all i such that $v_i = 0$ **do**
    Set $S(v'_i) = d_i$.
end for
for all $j \in \{1, \ldots, 15\}$ **do**
    for all $i \in \{0, \ldots, m - 1\}$ **do**
        if $S(v_i) \geq 0 \wedge S(v'_i) = -1$ **then**
            Set $S(v'_i) = S(v_i) \oplus d_i$.
        end if
        if $S(v_i) = -1 \wedge S(v'_i) \geq 0$ **then**
            Set $S(v_i) = S(v'_i) \oplus d_i$.
        end if
        if $S(v_i) \geq 0 \wedge S(v'_i) \geq 0 \wedge S(v_i) \oplus S(v'_i) \neq d_i$ **then**
            Abort the algorithm and output 'Failure'.
        end if
    end for
end for
Output

4.2   First Stage of the Attack – Recovering Two S-boxes

In this subsection we present the first stage of the attack. At this stage, we use the related-key differential presented in Sect. 3, along with a partial guess of the subkey K_1 used at round 32, to obtain 256 pairs of inputs to each of the S-boxes S_4, S_5, for which we know the output differences. This will allow us to significantly reduce the number of possible candidates for the guessed subkey bits, and for each remaining guess, to recover these two S-boxes (up to an output XOR with a constant) using Algorithm 1.

The success probability of the attack and its complexity significantly depend on the differential properties of the S-boxes on which we make no assumptions. For the sake of convenience, in this subsection and in the following subsections we give a rough estimate of the success probability and of the complexity at the end of each step, and present the exact figures obtained experimentally in Sect. 4.6. When the differential we consider is clear from the context, we call a pair that satisfies it a right pair.

Step 1: Finding the First Right Pair. As described in Sect. 3.3, if we consider GOST encryptions of the same plaintext P under five related keys: $K, \{K \oplus \Omega^i_{K1}\}_{i \in \{0,1,2,3\}}$, where $\Omega^i_{K1} = (e_{31}, e_{7+i}, e_{31}, 0, 0, 0, 0, 0)$, then for most choices of the secret S-box, the following RK truncated differential holds for one of the key differences:

$$(0,0) \xrightarrow[\Omega^i_{K1}]{\bar{p} \geq 2^{-24}} (??U00V??_x, Z???W000_x),$$

where $U, W \in \{0, 8\}, V, Z \in \{0, \ldots, 7\}$, and ? is an unknown value. To exploit the differential, we generate plaintexts P_j one by one, and ask for their encryption using the five related keys until one of the following occurs:

1. We find a plaintext P and $i \in \{0, 1, 2, 3\}$ such that $E_K(P) \oplus E_{K \oplus \Omega^i_{K1}}(P) = (??U00V??_x \parallel Z???W000)_x$. In this case we continue to the next step, in which many more right pairs will be found.
2. After the generation of 2^{27} ciphertexts, no pair that satisfies the RK truncated differential was found. We refer to such a case as a failure and abort the attack.

Assuming that $\bar{p} = 2^{-24}$, after trying 2^{24} plaintexts P_j we obtain 2^{26} pairs that satisfy the zero input difference and the key difference of one of the related-key differentials we try in parallel. Hence, with a probability of $1 - (1 - 2^{-24})^{2^{26}} \approx 1 - e^{-4} \approx 0.98$, we obtain at least one right pair. (Note that as the input difference of the differential is zero, the right pair is composed of the same plaintext, encrypted under two different keys.)

Step 2: Finding Many More Right Pairs at a Reduced Cost. Once we find a single right pair, we can find many right pairs at a significantly lower cost, using the concept of *neutral bits* that was introduced by Biham and Chen [4] and used in the collision attacks on the hash functions SHA-0 and SHA-1 [4,5]. We observe that there are many plaintext bits that have almost no effect on the first three rounds of the differential. Specifically, a change in bits 12–22 (which are included in the right half of the plaintext) and/or in bits 32–38, 52–63 (which are included in the left half of the plaintext) affect the differential at most with a very small probability. (This effect occurs only in case of a very long carry chains). Therefore, given a single right pair, we can generate 2^{30} more pairs that satisfy the first 3 rounds of the differential with a probability close to 1, by changing the value of some of the 30 neutral bits listed above. Each of these 2^{30} additional pairs satisfies the differential with probability of at least 2^{-16} (instead of 2^{-24}).

Therefore, after checking 2^{25} of the 2^{30} additional pairs, we are expected to find at least $2^{25} \cdot 2^{-16} = 2^9$ additional right pairs. Note that as the probability that a random plaintext pair satisfies the truncated ciphertext difference is 2^{-28}, with a high probability *all* pairs which remain at this stage are indeed right pairs.

Step 3: Partially Guessing the Subkey K_1 and Recovering the S-boxes S_4, S_5. At this point, we have 256 plaintext-ciphertext pairs $(P_j, C_j), (P_j, C'_j)$ such that

$E_K(P_j) = C_j, E_{K'}(P_i) = C'_i, K \oplus K' = \Omega^i_{K1} = (e_{31}, e_{7+i}, e_{31}, 0, 0, 0, 0, 0)$ for some $i \in \{0, 1, 2, 3\}$, and $C_j \oplus C'_j = (??U00V??_x \parallel Z???W000)_x$, where $U, W \in \{0, 8\}, V, Z \in \{0, \ldots, 7\}$, and ? is an unknown value.

We guess the 24 least significant bits of K_1 and partially decrypt the ciphertext pairs through the last round to obtain the input values to the S-boxes S_4, S_5. Assuming that the pair is a right pair, the corresponding output difference must be equal to bits 59–63, 32–34 of $C_j \oplus C'_j$ (which correspond to a left rotation by 11 bits of bits 16–23 in the output of the 32'th round function), since the difference in the corresponding bits in the differential is zero (as $D_1 = 00000XY0_x$). This allows using Algorithm 1 to recover the S-boxes S_4, S_5 (up to XOR of the output with a constant), under the assumption that the subkey guess is correct.[5]

This step can be performed efficiently, such that its complexity will be less than 2^{27} encryptions, as we explain at the end of the next step.

Step 4: Eliminating Wrong Subkey Guesses. As mentioned in Sect. 4.1, Algorithm 1 not only recovers the S-boxes, but also allows us to filter out wrong subkey guesses, as those guesses lead to a contradiction between the values of S.

In order to further reduce the number of possible subkey guesses, we use three additional subkey filtering steps. These steps are based on checking whether there is an addition carry that affects the input difference to one of the S-boxes S_4, S_5, S_6, and each of them can be applied to some of the right pairs.

1. Assume that the ciphertexts (C_i, C'_i) in some right pair satisfy $C_i \oplus C'_i = (??U00V??_x \parallel Z??0W000_x)$, where $U, W \in \{0, 8\}, V, Z \in \{0, \ldots, 7\}$, and ? is an unknown value. (This means that in addition to being a right pair, we require that the difference in bits 16–19 is zero.) If bits 59–62 of the difference $C_i \oplus C'_i$ are not all equal to zero, then the inputs to the S-box S_4 that correspond to C_i and C'_i cannot be equal (as bits 59–62 correspond to a left shift by 11 bits of the output of S_4). Since we assume that C_i and C'_i are equal in bits 16–19, this may happen only if in exactly one of the addition operations $C_i \boxplus K_1, C'_i \boxplus K_1$ there is a carry into bit 16. In other words, we have either

$$(K_1 \pmod{2^{16}}) \boxplus (C_i \pmod{2^{16}}) \geq 2^{16}$$

and

$$(K_1 \pmod{2^{16}})) \boxplus (C'_i \pmod{2^{16}}) < 2^{16},$$

or vice versa. This yields an inequality of the form $a_i < K_1 \pmod{2^{16}} < b_i$.

2. By the same reasoning, if $C_i \oplus C'_i = (??U00V??_x \parallel Z?0?W000_x)$ (meaning that in addition to being a right pair, we require that the difference in bits 20–23 is zero), and bits 63 and 32–34 of the difference $C_i \oplus C'_i$ are not all equal to zero, then we have either

$$(K_1 \pmod{2^{20}}) \boxplus (C_i \pmod{2^{20}}) \geq 2^{20}$$

---

[5] We note that while we can use the same strategy to obtain 256 pairs of known input values with known output differences for S_6 as well, it turns out that due to addition carries, many of these pairs are equal and so we do not obtain enough information for recovering this S-box. Instead, we recover it at a later stage.

and

$$(K_1 \pmod{2^{20}})) \boxplus (C_i' \pmod{2^{20}}) < 2^{20},$$

or vice versa.

3. By the same reasoning, if $C_i \oplus C_i' = (??U00V??_x \parallel Z0??W000)_x$ (meaning that in addition to being a right pair, we require that the difference in bits 24–27 is zero), and bits 35–38 of the difference $C_i \oplus C_i'$ are not all equal to zero, then we have either

$$(K_1 \pmod{2^{24}}) \boxplus (C_i \pmod{2^{24}}) \geq 2^{24}$$

and

$$(K_1 \pmod{2^{24}})) \boxplus (C_i' \pmod{2^{24}}) < 2^{24},$$

or vice versa.

For sake of efficiency, we perform the key filtering of Step 4 before the S-box recovery process of Step 3, and divide the key guessing into several steps. That is, first we guess the 16 least significant bits of K_1 and perform the first key filtering step. Then, for the remaining values of bits 0–15 of K_1, we guess bits 16–19 of K_1 and perform the second key filtering step. Then, for the remaining values of bits 0–19 of K_1, we guess bits 20–23 of K_1 and perform the third key filtering step. For the remaining subkey values, we perform the S-box recovery procedure of Step 3 along with the additional key filtering it provides.

According to our experiments (using 100 different keys and S-boxes), about $2^{14.2}$ possible values of bits 0–23 of K_1 pass this filtering. Among these values, about $2^{7.8}$ possible values pass the additional filtering of Algorithm 1, and for each of them, we recover the S-boxes S_4 and S_5, up to XOR of the output with a constant. (Among the 100 experiments, the highest number of surviving keys was $2274 \approx 2^{11.2}$). The time complexity of this step is significantly smaller than 2^{27} encryptions.

4.3   The Second Stage of the Attack – Recovering Two Additional S-boxes

In this subsection we present the second stage of the attack. At this stage, we use a variant of the related-key differential presented in Sect. 3 to further reduce the number of possible values of the subkey K_1 and to recover the S-boxes S_1, S_2 (up to an output XOR with a constant).

The Differential we Use at this Stage. In the choice of the differential, we can exploit the fact that the S-box S_4 was already recovered at the first stage.[6] As follows from the analysis presented in Sect. 3.3, for any input difference of S_4 of the form $2^i + 2^{i+1} + \ldots + 2^{i+\ell-1}$ (where $i \in \{0, 1, 2, 3\}$ and $\ell \in \{1, \ldots, 4-i\}$) and

---

[6] Although theoretically S_4 depends on the 24 least significant bits of K_1, our experiments show that in most of the cases the same S-box is suggested by all the remaining keys. We thus use the S-box S_4 of the first remaining key.

any output difference of the form $2^j + 2^{j+1} + \ldots + 2^{j+b-1}$ (where $j \in \{0,1,2,3\}$ and $b \in \{1, \ldots, 4-j\}$), the following 3-round iterative differential characteristic holds:

$$(0,0) \xrightarrow[\Omega^i_{K_1}=e_{16+i}]{2^{-\ell} \cdot \mathrm{DDT}_{S_4}[(i..i+\ell-1)][(j..j+b-1)]} \left(0, e_{27+j,27+j+1,\ldots,27+j+b-1}\right)$$

$$\xrightarrow[\Omega^j_{K_2}=e_{27+j}]{2^{-b}} \left(e_{27+j,27+j+1,\ldots,27+j+b-1}, 0\right) \xrightarrow[\Omega^i_{K_3}=e_{16+i}]{2^{-\ell} \cdot \mathrm{DDT}_{S_4}[(i..i+\ell-1)][(j..j+b-1)]} (0,0),$$

where $\mathrm{DDT}_{S_4}[(i..i+\ell-1)][(j..j+b-1)]$ denotes the probability of the transition

$$(2^i + 2^{i+1} + \ldots + 2^{i+\ell-1}) \xrightarrow[S_4]{} (2^j + 2^{j+1} + \ldots + 2^{j+b-1}).$$

Here, the characteristic of the first and the third round holds since in the modular addition operation, the difference 2^i is transformed to $2^i + 2^{i+1} + \ldots + 2^{i+\ell-1}$ with probability $2^{-\ell}$. (Note that such addition carries are not considered in Sect. 3.3, as there the difference is in bit e_{31} for which modular addition does not have carry).

The probability of the 3-round iterative differential

$$(0,0) \xrightarrow[]{\Omega_{K2}=(e_{16+i},e_{27+j},e_{16+i})} (0,0) \tag{1}$$

is much higher than the probability of each separate differential characteristic, since it enjoys the contributions of all differential characteristics that correspond to these values of i,j and all possible values of ℓ, b.

In order to choose the key difference of the differential, we compute a lower bound on the probability of the differential (1) for all i,j:

$$p_{i,j} = \sum_{b=1}^{4-j} 2^{-b} \left(\sum_{\ell=1}^{4-i} 2^{-\ell} \mathrm{DDT}_{S_4}[(i..i+\ell-1)][(j..j+b-1)] \right)^2.$$

Then, we choose i,j such that $p_{i,j}$ is maximal and ask for the encryption of the same plaintext under keys with difference $\Omega_{K2} = (e_{16+i}, e_{27+j}, e_{16+i})$.

We performed an experiment with 100 randomly chosen S-boxes. The largest value $p_{i,j}$ was about 2^{-6} on average, and for 99 out of the 100 S-boxes it was larger than $2^{-7.3}$. We therefore assume that $p_{i,j} \geq 2^{-7.3}$. Using the key difference

$$\Omega_{K2} = (e_{16+i}, e_{27+j}, e_{16+i}, 0, 0, 0, 0, 0),$$

we get the 29-round related-key differential

$$(0,0) \xrightarrow[\Omega_K]{p^3_{i,j} \geq 2^{-22}} (0,0).$$

As in the differential presented in Sect. 3, we do not use probabilistic differential transitions in the last three rounds, in which the subkey differences are

$e_{16+i}, e_{27+j}, e_{16+i}$ (respectively), and instead, we use a truncated differential based on following the possible differences.

At round 30, the input difference is zero and the subkey difference is e_{16+i}. Thus, after the key addition the difference is $00??0000_x$ with a high probability. This truncated difference is preserved by the S-box layer, and then is mapped by the left rotation to $?Y00000X_x$ (where $X \in \{0, \ldots, 7\}, Y \in \{0, 8\}$).

At round 31, the truncated difference after the key addition (in which the subkey difference is e_{27+j}) is $?Q00000?_x$ (where $Q \in \{0, 8\}$). After the S-box layer, the difference is $??00000?_x$, which is mapped to $0000Z??W_x$ (where $W \in \{0, 8\}, Z \in \{0, \ldots, 7\}$) by the left rotation. This difference is copied to the right half of the ciphertext.

At round 32, the difference after the key addition (in which the subkey difference is e_{16+i}) is $00?????T_x$ (where $T \in \{0, 8\}$). After the S-box layer, the difference is $00??????_x$ which is mapped by the left rotation to $?????U0V_x$ (where $V \in \{0, \ldots, 7\}, U \in \{0, 8\}$). This is the difference in the left half of the ciphertext.

Hence, we have a related key truncated differential on the entire cipher:

$$(0,0) \xrightarrow[\Omega_{K2}]{p_{i,j}^3 \geq 2^{-22}} (?????U0V_x, 0000Z??W_x),$$

where $V, Z \in \{0, \ldots, 7\}, U, Y \in \{0, 8\}$, and ? is an unknown 4-bit value. We use this characteristic to recover two additional S-boxes, S_1, S_2, and to eliminate more wrong keys.

The following steps are similar to the corresponding steps of Stage 1. As there are many small differences, we provide a detailed description.

Step 1: Finding the First Right Pair. We generate plaintexts one by one, and ask for their encryption using the two related keys, $K, K' = K \oplus \Omega_{K2}$, until one of the following occurs:

1. We find a plaintext P such that the difference $E_K(P) \oplus E_{K \oplus \Omega_{K2}}(P)$ is of the form $(?????U0V_x \parallel 0000Z??W_x)$. In this case we continue to the next step, in which many more right pairs are found.
2. After the generation of 2^{25} ciphertexts, no pair that satisfies the RK truncated differential was found. We refer to such a case as a failure and abort the attack.

Assuming that $p_{i,j}^3 = 2^{-22}$, after trying 2^{24} plaintexts P_j we obtain 2^{24} pairs that satisfy the zero input difference and the key difference of the related-key differentials. Hence, with a probability of $1 - (1 - 2^{-22})^{2^{24}} \approx 1 - e^{-4} \approx 0.98$, we obtain at least one right pair.

Step 2: Finding Many More Right Pairs at a Reduced Cost. Again, once we find a single right pair, we can find many right pairs at a lower cost, using neutral bits. We observe that a change in bits 4–12 and/or in bits 44–58, 63 of the plaintext affects the differential with a very small probability. (This effect occurs only in case of a very long carry chain). Therefore, given a single right pair, we can generate 2^{25} more pairs that satisfy the first 3 rounds of the differential with a probability close to 1, by changing the value of some of the 25 neutral bits listed above. Each of these 2^{25} additional pairs satisfies the differential with probability of about $p_{i,j}^2 \geq 2^{-14.6}$ (instead of $p_{i,j}^3$).

Therefore, after checking $2^{22.6}$ additional pairs, we are expected to find $2^{22.6} \cdot 2^{-14.6} = 2^8$ additional right pairs. Note that as the probability that a random plaintext pair satisfies the truncated ciphertext difference is 2^{-28}, with a high probability *all* pairs which remain at this stage are indeed right pairs.

Step 3: Recovering the S-boxes S_1, S_2. At this point, we have 256 plaintext-ciphertext pairs $(P_j, C_j), (P_j, C'_j)$ such that $E_K(P_j) = C_j, E_{K'}(P_i) = C'_i, K \oplus K' = \Omega_{K2} = (e_{16+i}, e_{27+j}, e_{16+i}, 0, 0, 0, 0, 0)$ for the chosen $i, j \in \{0, 1, 2, 3\}$, and $C_j \oplus C'_j = (?????U0V_x \parallel 0000Z??W_x)$, where $U, W \in \{0, 8\}, V, Z \in \{0, \ldots, 7\}$, and ? is an unknown value.

For each remaining value of the 12 least significant bits of K_1, we partially decrypt the ciphertext pairs through the last round to obtain the input values to the S-boxes S_1, S_2. Assuming that the pair is a right pair, the corresponding output difference must be equal to bits 47–54 of $C_j \oplus C'_j$ (which are a left rotation by 11 bits of bits 4–11, and are of the left half of the ciphertext), since the difference in the corresponding bits in the differential is zero. This allows using Algorithm 1 to recover S-boxes S_1, S_2 (up to XOR of the output with a constant), under the assumption that the subkey guess is correct.

Step 4: Eliminating Wrong Subkey Guesses. As mentioned in Sect. 4.1, Algorithm 1 not only recovers the S-boxes, but also allows us to filter out wrong subkey guesses, as those guesses lead to a contradiction between the values of S.

In order to further reduce the number of possible subkey guesses, we use an additional subkey filtering step, which we apply for each of the 256 pairs.

Assume that the ciphertexts (C_i, C'_i) in some right pair satisfy $C_i \oplus C'_i = (?????U0V_x \parallel 00000??W_x)$, where $U, W \in \{0, 8\}, V \in \{0, \ldots, 7\}$, and ? is an unknown value. (This means that in addition to being a right pair, we require that the difference in bits 12–14 is zero.) If bits 55–58 of the difference $C_i \oplus C'_i$ are not all equal to zero, then the inputs to the S-box S_4 that correspond to C_i and C'_i cannot be equal (as bits 55–58 correspond to a left shift by 11 bits of the output of S_4). Since we assume that C_i and C'_i are equal in bits 12–15, this may happen only if in exactly one of the addition operations $C_i \boxplus K_1, C'_i \boxplus K_1$ there is a carry into bit 12. In other words, we have either

$$(K_1 \pmod{2^{12}}) \boxplus (C_i \pmod{2^{12}}) \geq 2^{12}$$

and

$$(K_1 \pmod{2^{12}})) \boxplus (C'_i \pmod{2^{12}}) < 2^{12},$$

or vice versa. This yields an inequality of the form $a_i < K_1 \pmod{2^{12}} < b_i$.

For the sake of efficiency, we first perform the key filtering of Step 4, and then we perform the S-box recovery process of Step 3, along with the additional key filtering it provides. According to our experiments (using 100 randomly selected keys and S-boxes), about 1.2 keys remain out of 2^{24} possible values of the 24 least significant bits of K_1. For each of them we recover the S-boxes S_1, S_2, up to XOR of the output with a constant.

4.4   The Third Stage of the Attack – Recovering One Additional S-box

In this subsection we present the third stage of the attack. At this stage, we use another variant of the related-key differential presented in Sect. 3 to further reduce the number of possible values of the subkey K_1 and to recover the S-box S_7 (up to an output XOR with a constant). As this stage is very similar to the second stage, we present it briefly.

The Differential We Use at this Stage. In the choice of the differential, we exploit the fact that the S-box S_2 was already recovered at the second stage.[7]

We choose the key difference $\Omega_{K3} = (e_{8+i}, e_{19+j}, e_{8+i}, 0, 0, 0, 0, 0)$, where (i, j) is chosen such that

$$p_{i,j} = \sum_{b=1}^{4-j} 2^{-b} \left(\sum_{\ell=1}^{4-i} 2^{-\ell} \text{DDT}_{S_2}[(i..i + \ell - 1)][(j..j + b - 1)] \right)^2$$

is maximal. For this key difference, we obtain the 32-round related-key truncated differential

$$(0, 0) \xrightarrow[\Omega_{K3}]{p_{i,j}^3 \geq 2^{-22}} (0V?????U_x, ?W0000Z?_x),$$

where $V, Z \in \{0, \ldots, 7\}, U, Y \in \{0, 8\}$, and ? is an unknown 4-bit value.

Steps 1,2: Finding 256 Right Pairs. To find one right pair, we generate plaintexts one by one, and ask for their encryption using the two related keys, $K, K' = K \oplus \Omega_{K3}$, until either we find a right pair with respect to the differential, or we try 2^{26} pairs and don't find a right one (in which case we abort the attack and declare 'Failure'). By the same analysis as in the second stage, with probability of 98% we obtain a right pair after trying at most 2^{24} plaintexts.

To find many additional right pairs at a reduced cost, we again use neutral bits. We observe that a change in bits 0–4, 28–31 and/or in bits 36–50, 63 of the plaintext affects the differential at most with a very small probability. Therefore, given a single right pair, we can generate 2^{25} more pairs that satisfy the first 3 rounds of the differential with a probability close to 1, by changing the value of some of these 25 neutral bits. Each of these 2^{25} additional pairs satisfies the

---

[7] Although S_2 depends on the 12 least significant bits of K_1, since only about 1.2 keys remain out of 2^{24} possible values of the 24 least significant bits of K_1, we assume that the S-box S_2 suggested by all remaining keys is the same. This assumption was verified experimentally. We thus use the S-box S_2 suggested by the first remaining key.

differential with probability of about $p_{i,j}^2 \geq 2^{-14.6}$. Therefore, after checking $2^{22.6}$ additional pairs, we are expected to find $2^{22.6} \cdot 2^{-14.6} = 2^8$ additional right pairs. As above, with a high probability *all* pairs which remain at this stage are indeed right pairs.

Steps 3,4: Guessing the Rest of the Bits of K_1, and Recovering S-box S_7. At this point, we have 256 plaintext-ciphertext pairs $(P_j, C_j), (P_j, C_j')$ such that $E_K(P_j) = C_j, E_{K'}(P_i) = C_j', K \oplus K' = \Omega_{K3} = (e_{8+i}, e_{19+j}, e_{8+i}, 0, 0, 0, 0, 0)$ for the chosen $i, j \in \{0, 1, 2, 3\}$, and $C_j \oplus C_j' = (0V?????U_x \| ?W0000Z?_x)$, where $U, W \in \{0, 8\}, V, Z \in \{0, \ldots, 7\}$, and ? is an unknown value.

We guess the 8 most significant bits of K_1, and for each remaining value of the 24 least significant bits of K_1 we get a candidate for the entire subkey K_1. For each candidate, we partially decrypt the ciphertext pairs through the last round to obtain the input values to the S-box S_7. Assuming that the pair is a right pair, the corresponding output difference must be equal to bits 39–42 of $C_j \oplus C_j'$ (which are a left rotation by 11 bits of bits 28–31, and are of the left half of the ciphertext), since the difference in the corresponding bits in the differential is zero. This allows using Algorithm 1 to recover S-box S_7 (up to XOR of the output with a constant), under the assumption that the subkey guess is correct. Algorithm 1 also allows us to filter out wrong subkey guesses, as those guesses lead to a contradiction between the values of S_7.

According to our experiments (using 100 different keys and S-boxes), $2^{4.1}$ suggestions for the full subkey K_1 remain, and for each of them, we obtain a unique suggestion for the S-boxes S_1, S_2, S_4, S_5, and S_7, up to XOR of the output with a constant.

4.5 The Fourth Stage of the Attack – Recovering the Rest of the S-Boxes and Eliminating More Wrong Candidates of K_1

In this subsection we present the fourth stage of the attack. At this stage, we reuse ciphertext pairs obtained at the previous stages to fully recover the S-boxes and the subkey K_1.

Step 1: Recovering the Rest of the S-boxes (S_0, S_3, S_6), up to XOR of the Output with a Constant. While neither of the three differentials used in the attack does not provide enough data for recovering S-boxes S_0, S_3, S_6, we can recover them by combining ciphertext pairs obtained from two differentials.

1. At the first and second stages together, we obtain 512 plaintext-ciphertext pairs $(P_j, C_j), (P_j, C_j')$ such that bits 12–15 (which form the input to S_3) of $C_j \oplus C_j'$ are of the form $W \in \{0, 8\}$ (at the first stage) or $Z \in \{0, \ldots, 7\}$ (at the second stage). For each remaining candidate of K_1, we partially decrypt these ciphertext pairs through the last round to obtain the input values to the S-box S_3. Assuming that the pair is a right pair, the corresponding output difference must be equal to bits 55–58 of $C_j \oplus C_j'$ (which are a left rotation by 11 bits of bits 12–15, and are of the left half of the ciphertext), since the

difference in the corresponding bits in both differentials is zero. This allows using Algorithm 1 to recover the S-box S_3 (up to XOR of the output with a constant), under the assumption that the subkey guess is correct, and also to filter out wrong subkey guesses, as those guesses lead to a contradiction between the values of S_3.

2. Similarly, at the first and the third stages together, we obtain 512 pairs $(P_j, C_j), (P_j, C_j')$ such that the bits 24–27 (which form the input to S_6) of $C_j \oplus C_j'$ can obtain any value (at the first stage) or are of the form $W \in \{0, 8\}$ (at the third stage). This allows using Algorithm 1 to recover the S-box S_6 (up to XOR of the output with a constant), under the assumption that the subkey guess is correct, and also to filter out wrong subkey guesses, as those guesses lead to a contradiction between the values of S_6.

3. Similarly, at the second and the third stages together, we obtain 512 pairs $(P_j, C_j), (P_j, C_j')$ such that the bits 0–3 (which form the input to S_0) of $C_j \oplus C_j'$ are of the form $W \in \{0, 8\}$ (at the second stage) or can obtain any value (at the third stage). This allows using Algorithm 1 to recover the S-box S_0 (up to XOR of the output with a constant), under the assumption that the subkey guess is correct, and also to filter out wrong subkey guesses.

According to our experiments, in most of the cases, at this stage a unique value of bits 0–27 of K_1 remains. (Specifically, among 100 experiments, only in a single experiment two values remained).

Step 2: Fully Recovering the S-boxes, and Recovering the Rest of K_1 up to a Few Remaining Candidates. Due to the differential nature of the attack, analysis of the last round recovers the S-boxes only up to XOR of the output with a constant, and also cannot recover bits 28–31 of K_1 (as these bits affect no addition carries to other S-boxes). In order to recover the missing key/S-box material, we analyze round 31. Note that at this stage, for each guess of bits 28–31 of K_1, we are able to decrypt the ciphertexts through the last round, to obtain inputs to the round function of round 31, which are correct up to XOR with the same 32-bit constant A. We recover A and filter out wrong guesses of bits 28–31 of K_1, in the following steps.

1. In the plaintext-ciphertext pairs $(P_j, C_j), (P_j, C_j')$ obtained at the first stage, the difference at the input to the round function of round 31 is of the form $00000XY0_x$, where $X \in \{0, \ldots, 7\}, Y \in \{0, 8\}$. Hence, by guessing the 12 least significant bits of A and of K_2, we can obtain the input values to the S-boxes S_1, S_2 in round 31. Assuming that the pair is a right pair, the corresponding output difference must be equal to bits 15–22 of $C_j \oplus C_j'$ (which are a left rotation by 11 bits of bits 4–11), since the difference in the corresponding bits in the differential is zero. As the S-boxes S_1, S_2 are known (up to XOR of the output with a constant, which does not affect output differences), this provides a very strong filtering condition on the guessed values.

For the sake of efficiency, we apply this filtering in a two-stage process. First we guess bits 0–7 of A and K_2 and check the filtering condition in S_1, and then we guess bits 8–11 of A and K_2 and check the filtering condition in S_2.

2. In a similar manner, in the plaintext-ciphertext pairs $(P_j, C_j), (P_j, C'_j)$ obtained at the third stage, there is a non-zero difference at the inputs of the S-boxes S_4, S_5. This allows guessing bits 12–23 of A and K_2 and obtain an additional strong filtering condition on the guessed values by checking output differences of S_4, S_5 (whose inputs are known for each guess of the bits of A, K_2).

3. Finally, in the plaintext-ciphertext pairs $(P_j, C_j), (P_j, C'_j)$ obtained at the second stage, there is a non-zero difference at the inputs of the S-boxes S_6, S_7. This allows guessing bits 24–31 of A and K_2 and obtaining an additional strong filtering condition on the guessed values by checking output differences of S_6, S_7 (whose inputs are known for each guess of the bits of A, K_2).

Step 3: Discarding the Remaining Wrong Candidates. We remain with a few values of the most significant bits of A and of K_2 which cannot be recovered by examining merely rounds 31,32, due to the differential nature of the attack. In order to recover them, we analyze round 30. Note that at this stage, we can decrypt the ciphertexts through rounds 32,31 to obtain inputs to the round function of round 30, up to a few possible values which stem from the remaining possible values for A and K_2. Since these values are different from each other on the most significant bits, we need to perform the filtering using differences between inputs to S-box S_7 in round 30.

In a similar manner to *Step 2*, we divide the elimination of the subkey K_3 used at round 30 into three steps, using the three differentials. First, in the third differential we use, at round 30, the S-box S_2 has a non-zero input difference. Hence, we can guess bits 0–11 of K_3, compute the inputs to this S-box, and check whether its output difference is equal to bits 51–54 of the difference at the input to round 30 (which correspond to a left rotation by 11 bits of bits 8–11). By the same reasoning as above, this equality must hold for any right pair with respect to the third differential. As the S-box S_2 is known, this provides us with a strong filtering condition on bits 0–11 of K_3. Then, in the second differential, at round 30, the S-box S_4 has non-zero input difference, which provides a filtering condition on bits 12–19 and the remaining values of bits 0–11. Finally, in the first differential, at round 30, the S-box S_7 has non-zero input difference, which provides a filtering condition on bits 20–31 and the remaining values of bits 0–19.

This completes the recovery of bits 0–27 of the subkey K_1, and the S-boxes 0–6. In addition, for each possible value of bits 28–31 of the subkey K_1, we recover S_7 and the subkey K_2, up to a swap between their most significant bits (which we cannot recognize). Our experiments show that in about 74% of the cases (i.e., in 65 out of the 88 successful experiments), 8 possible vales of bits 28–31 of K_1 remain, and in the rest of the cases, all of the 16 possible values of these four bits remain. As all the S-boxes are known at this stage, the few remaining subkey candidates can be easily discarded by attacking a reduced-round version of GOST.

Table 2. The success rate and the data, time, and memory complexities of the attack (average over 100 experiments), using 7 related keys and 256 right pairs for each characteristic.

	1st stage	2nd stage	3rd stage	4th stage	Overall
Success rate	97/100	94/97	92/94	88/92	88%
Data complexity	$2^{22.2}$	$2^{22.4}$	$2^{23.2}$	0	$2^{24.2}$
Time complexity	$2^{22.2}$	$2^{22.4}$	$2^{23.2}$	negligible	$2^{24.2}$
Memory complexity	$2^{9.5}$	2^9	2^9	0	$3 \cdot 2^9 = 2^{10.6}$

This stage does not require additional data, and is significantly faster than the previous steps.

4.6   Experimental Verification of the Attack

In this section we describe the experimental verification of the full attack, using 100 different randomly chosen keys and randomly chosen S-boxes. (All S-boxes were chosen to be permutations, following the discussion in Sect. 3.4).

General Information. The code for the experiments is written in C++, uses a Microsoft Visual C++ (MSVC) compiler, and the operating system we use is Windows. The 100 experiments together took 1121 s on a single PC, where the longest experiment took 91 s and the median experiment took 7 s. The code is available in https://github.com/ArielWeizman/GOST.git.

Results. Table 2 describes the success rate and the average complexity of the experiments, for each of the four stages of the attack. The maximal time complexity of the full attack was 2^{27} encryptions, while the minimum was $2^{18.7}$ encryptions. The bulk of the memory is used to store the 2^9 ciphertexts (i.e., 2^8 pairs) at each stage and the remaining keys. Our experiments show that on average, after the first stage there are about $2^{7.8}$ remaining keys. (The highest number of remaining keys after the first stage was about $2^{11.2}$). Therefore, the memory required for the first stage is about $2^9 + 2^{7.8} \approx 2^{9.5}$ 64-bit blocks on average (with a maximum of about $2^9 + 2^{11.2} \approx 2^{11.4}$ 64-bit blocks). After the second and the third stages only a few key candidates remain, and therefore, a few memory cells are sufficient for storing them.

The Number of Related Keys Required in the Attack. To minimize the number of related keys, we used in the experiments adaptive chosen plaintexts, as the key differences at the second and the third stages are chosen according to the previous stages. Our attack uses 7 related keys: four key differences for the first characteristic, and one for each of the two additional characteristics.

Table 3. A comparison between chosen plaintext (CP) and adaptively chosen plaintext (ACP) modes, in terms of the number of related keys used and the average complexity.

CP/ACP	ACP	ACP	CP
Number of RK	4.2	7	13
Data and time complexity	$2^{26.3}$	$2^{24.2}$	$2^{25.1}$

Table 4. The effect of the number of right pairs on the success rate and on the average data and time complexity of the full attack.

Number of right pairs	128	192	256	384	512
Success rate	84%	88%	88%	91%	83%
Data and time complexity	$2^{23.9}$	$2^{24.2}$	$2^{24.2}$	$2^{24.5}$	2^{25}

One can minimize the number of related keys used in the first stage, by trying the four options one by one (instead of trying them in parallel). This method uses about 4.2 related keys on average. On the other hand, the data and the time complexity of the first stage are somewhat increased: the average is $2^{26.3}$ encryptions and the maximum is $2^{29.7}$ encryptions.

We performed also experiments of the attack in the chosen plaintext model, by using 13 related keys (i.e., trying the four options of the key difference in round 2 for each characteristic). The success rate of the full attack was 89%, and the time and the data complexity of the full attack was about $2^{25.1}$ encryptions on average, with a maximum of $2^{27.3}$ encryptions. The memory complexity was the same as in the adaptive chosen plaintext model. These results are summarized in Table 3.

The Number of Right Pairs. We also examined the effect of the number of right pairs we use for each characteristic on the success rate and on the data and time complexity. Table 4 reports the results for some values of the number of right pairs. While it may seem that an increase in the amount of right pairs should increase the success rate, this is not always the case, since once the data complexity is increased, more wrong pairs pass the filtering and undermine the attack. In particular, increasing the number of right pairs from 256 to 512 decreases the success rate of the attack. Switching the algorithm to accept the majority of the suggestions (e.g., by discarding inconsistent pairs) would result in a higher success rate, at the expense of significantly slowing down the attack.

5   Possible Application to GOST-Based Hash Functions

In this section we discuss possible applications of our techniques to GOST-based hash functions. First, we present an extremely efficient collision attack on a hash function based on GOST in the Davies-Meyer mode, and then we present observations that may be useful in future attacks on the actual GOST hash function [17].[8]

5.1   Collision Attack on a Davies-Meyer Construction Using GOST

Davies-Meyer Construction Instantiated by GOST and its Security. The Davies-Meyer construction is a way to transform a block cipher into a compression function. Let $E : \{0,1\}^n \cdot \{0,1\}^k \to \{0,1\}^n$ be a block cipher, one can transform it into a compression function $f : \{0,1\}^n \cdot \{0,1\}^k \to \{0,1\}^n$, which accepts an n-bit chaining value and a k-bit message block to produce a new n-bit chaining value using the transformation: $f(cv, m) = E_m(cv) \oplus cv$, where cv is the chaining value and m is the message block. Such a hash function can be used in the Merkle-Damgård mode of iteration to produce a hash function using a standard padding scheme to make the message M a multiple of k-bit blocks, and selecting an IV which is set as H_0, the first chaining value. Then, take the padded message $M' = (M_1|| \ldots ||M_t)$ composed of t blocks, and set $H_0 = IV$, and iteratively apply $H_i = E_{M_i}(H_{i-1}) \oplus H_{i-1}$ for $i = 1, \ldots, t$ until H_t, the digest is computed.

It is clear from the construction that regardless of the block cipher used, a collision in the constructions can be found in time $2^{n/2}$. Thus, the proposed construction is not secure, as the 64-bit block length of GOST allows finding a collision generically with time complexity of about 2^{32}.

Collision Attack Using Mendel et al.'s Technique. A possible way to find a collision faster by exploiting the structure of GOST is to use the technique presented by Mendel et al. [25,26] in their attacks on the GOST hash function. This technique assumes that for some i, the chaining value H_{i-1} is of the form (x, x), for some 32-bit value x, and aims at finding two messages M_i, M_i' such that

$$H_i = E_{M_i}(H_{i-1}) \oplus H_{i-1} = E_{M_i'}(H_{i-1}) \oplus H_{i-1} = H_i'.$$

By the structure of GOST, the 256-bit word M_i, which can be chosen by the adversary, is divided into eight 32-bit words, which are used as the subkeys of the first eight rounds of GOST. Using this property, the adversary can easily find two different values M_i, M_i' for which the intermediate value after eight rounds of GOST is (x, x). (For this, one can choose the first six subkeys arbitrarily and find the unique value (on average) of the last two subkeys that leads to (x, x) by examining 1-round GOST.) For both values, the adversary obtains a fixed point of 8-round GOST. As rounds 9–16 and 17–24 of GOST are identical to

---

[8] We remind the reader that the GOST hash function uses 4 parallel applications of the GOST block cipher, has a 256-bit chaining value and a 256-bit message block. See more details in Sect. 5.2.

rounds 1–8, the intermediate value after 24 rounds is equal to (x, x) as well. Finally, at the last 8 rounds of GOST, the subkeys are used in a reversed order. As GOST is a Feistel construction, this means that when the intermediate value after 24 rounds is (x, x), the last 8 rounds 'undo' the previous 8 rounds, and the resulting ciphertext is a swapped version of the intermediate value after 16 rounds, which in our case is (x, x). Hence, $E_{M_i}(H_{i-1}) = E_{M'_i}(H_{i-1}) = (x, x)$, which yields a collision in H_i.

This attack strongly uses the assumption that $H_{i-1} = (x, x)$. In the attack of Mendel et al. on the actual GOST hash function, they check 2^{32} chaining values H_j until they obtain a chaining value of the form (x, x) and only then they apply the attack. It is unclear whether this attack strategy can be applied to find a collision with complexity of less than 2^{32} when the initial value does not have the specific form (x, x).

Efficient Collision Attack Using Our Technique. We show that with our technique, we can find a collision in time of less than 2^{10} hash function evaluations, for any value of H_{i-1}.

We examine the encryption process $E_{M_i}(H_{i-1})$, where the block cipher E is GOST and the key M_i is the i'th message block that can be chosen by the adversary. We find two values $M_i = (M_{i,1}, \ldots, M_{i,8})$ and $M'_i = (M'_{i,1}, \ldots, M'_{i,8})$ such that in the encryption processes $E_{M_i}(H_{i-1})$ and $E_{M'_i}(H_{i-1})$:

1. The basic 3-round differential of GOST presented in Sect. 3 is satisfied in rounds 1–3,
2. We have $M_{i,j} = M'_{i,j}$ for $j = 4, 5, 6, 7, 8$, and
3. The intermediate value after 8 rounds in the encryption process $E_{M_i}(H_{i-1})$ is H_{i-1}.

Once such two values M_i, M'_i are found, we track the intermediate differences between the encryption processes $E_{M_i}(H_{i-1})$ and $E_{M'_i}(H_{i-1})$. We denote the value of the intermediate states at the end of round ℓ in the encryption processes $E_{M_i}(H_{i-1})$ and $E_{M'_i}(H_{i-1})$ by X_ℓ, X'_ℓ (respectively), and the difference between them by $\Delta X_\ell = X_\ell \oplus X'_\ell$.

First, we claim that M_i, M'_i that satisfy the three above conditions can be found in time which is significantly faster than 2^9 hash function evaluations. Indeed, as was explained in Sect. 3, by looking at the S-box S_7 of GOST we can choose the difference between the words $M_{i,1}, M_{i,2}, M_{i,3}$ and the corresponding words of M'_i such that the differential will hold with probability of at least 2^{-8}. (This holds for most of the possible choices of the S-box S_7.) Then, we can try 2^{10} pairs (M_i, M'_i) with the prescribed difference and check whether the intermediate difference ΔX_3 is zero. With a high probability, a pair that satisfies the differential will be found, thus achieving (1). In order to achieve (3), we can fix the value of $M_{i,4}, M_{i,5}, M_{i,6}$ and find the unique value of the words $M_{i,7}, M_{i,8}$ (on average) such that $X_8 = H_{i-1}$, by assuming that (3) holds and separately examining rounds 7 and 8 of GOST, for which we know the input and the output values. Words $M'_{i,j}$ for $4 \leq j \leq 8$ are taken to be equal to the corresponding words of M_i, in order to satisfy (2).

Due to (1), (2) and (3), we have $X_8' = H_{i-1}$ as well. This means that H_{i-1} is a fixed point of the first 8 rounds of GOST, for both keys M_i and M_i'. Since rounds 9–16 and 17–24 of GOST are identical to rounds 1–8, it follows that $X_{24} = X_{24}' = H_{i-1}$. The zero difference between the encryption processes is preserved until the input of round 30 (as there is no subkey difference and no state difference), and at the last three rounds, the subkeys generated by the keys M_i, M_i' (which are $M_{i,3}, M_{i,2}, M_{i,1}$ and $M_{i,3}', M_{i,2}', M_{i,1}'$, respectively) satisfy the subkey difference of the 3-round related-key differential. Hence, the ciphertext difference is equal to 0 (which means that we get a collision) with probability of at least 2^{-8}.

Finally, we observe that once we obtain one pair (M_i, M_i') that satisfies the differential in rounds 1–3, we can easily generate 2^9 additional pairs that satisfy the differential by leaving $M_{i,1}, M_{i,2}, M_{i,3}$ unchanged, slightly altering $M_{i,4}, M_{i,5}, M_{i,6}$, recomputing $M_{i,7}, M_{i,8}$, and setting M_i' such that (1), (2) are satisfied. With a high probability, one of these pairs satisfies the differential in rounds 30–32, and thus, provides a collision. Thus, we obtain a collision in the hash function, in time complexity of less than 2^{10} hash function evaluations.

5.2   Observations on the GOST Hash Function

The GOST Hash Function. The GOST hash function, defined in the standards GOST R 34.11-94 [17] and GOST 34.311-95, was the Russian Federation hash function standard for almost 20 years, until it was replaced by the hash function Streebog in 2012. It is a 256-bit hash function based on a parallel application of four instances of the GOST block cipher to related inputs, followed by a mixing transformation. The exact description of the hash function is rather complex. We briefly describe the details required for our observations, and refer the reader to [17] for the complete specification.

Similarly to the construction described above, the message M is padded to M' whose length is a multiple of 256 bits, then M' is divided to 256-bit blocks $M' = (M_1 || \ldots || M_t)$, and then a serial application of $f : \{0, 1\}^{256} \times \{0, 1\}^{256} \to \{0, 1\}^{256}$ is used to compute $H_i = f(M_i, H_{i-1})$ for $i = 1, \ldots, t$. We omit the way in which the digest is generated from H_t, as we concentrate on the compression function f.

The structure of f is the following. First, the 256-bit word M_i is used to generate four 256-bit words $K_{i,1}, \ldots, K_{i,4}$, using XORs of iterated applications of a linear transformation A that mixes 64-bit chunks of M_i and a permutation P that changes the order of 8-bit chunks of the resulting words. Then, H_{i-1} is partitioned into 64-bit blocks as $H_{i-1} = (H_{i-1,1} || \ldots || H_{i-1,4})$ and the GOST block cipher is applied four times in parallel, to obtain the 256-bit value $S_i = (GOST_{K_{i,1}}(H_{i-1,1}) || \ldots || GOST_{K_{i,4}}(H_{i-1,4}))$. Finally, an LFSR-based mixing function χ which depends on S_i but also on M_i and H_{i-1} is used to produce $H_i = \chi(H_{i-1}, M_i, S_i)$.

The Attack of Mendel et al. At Crypto'2008, Mendel et al. [26] presented an attack on the GOST hash function, which allows finding a collision with time complexity of 2^{105} hash function evaluations and finding a preimage with time complexity of 2^{192} hash function evaluations. While the attack is far from being practical, it breaks the collision and preimage resistance of the GOST hash function.

The basic observation behind the attack is that when $H_{i-1,1}$ is of the form (x, x), one can easily generate many 256-bit keys $K_{i,1}$ such that $H_{i-1,1}$ is a fixed point of $GOST_{K_{i,1}}(\cdot)$. Specifically, one can generate up to about 2^{192} such keys, with a cost of a few operations for generating each key (as one can arbitrarily choose the first six 32-bit words of $K_{i,1}$ and find the unique value of the last two words which yields a fixed point by analyzing rounds 7, 8 separately).

As $K_{i-1,1}$ is obtained from M_i by a simple linear transformation, the adversary can compute 2^{192} values of M_i which lead to the same 64 initial bits of S_i, with a cost of a few operations for generating each such value M_i. If the value H_i would depend only on S_i and H_{i-1} like in the Davies-Meyer construction, one could obtain a collision in H_i after observing 2^{96} such values M_i, by the birthday paradox. (In fact, if this was the case, one could use the attack of Dinur et al. on GOST [12] to obtain 2^{64} values of M_i which lead to the same 128 initial bits of S_i in time 2^{64}, by combining multi-collisions in two instances of GOST, and then obtain a collision in H_i in time 2^{64} using the birthday paradox). Mendel et al. show that by adding a 64-bit linear restriction, one can leverage the collision in 64 bits of S_i into a collision in 64 bits of H_i despite the existence of the mixing function χ. (This additional restriction is the reason why the strategy of combining multi-collisions in two instances of GOST cannot be applied, due to lack of degrees of freedom). The overall complexity of the collision attack of Mendel et al. is higher than 2^{96} (specifically, it is 2^{105}) due to the need to overcome the finalization that was not described above. The preimage attack of Mendel et al. is based on the same technique.

The Possibility of Applying Our Technique to the GOST Hash Function. As described in Sect. 5.1, our technique can be used to find efficiently pairs $K_{i,1}, K'_{i,1}$ such that $GOST_{K_{i,1}}(H_{i-1,1}) = GOST_{K'_{i,1}}(H_{i-1,1})$. Each such pair can be found at the cost of less than 2^{10} GOST evaluations, even if $H_{i-1,1}$ does not have the form (x, x). A natural strategy for applying this technique to attack the GOST hash function is to find pairs of values (M_i, M'_i) such that collisions in two instantiations of GOST occur simultaneously, thus yielding a collision in 128 bits of H_i.

The first obstacle on the way of this strategy is that the words $K_{i,j}$ are related through the transformations A, P, and thus, it is not clear a-priori that one can obtain differences that comply with our related-key differential in both $K_{i,1}$ and $K_{i,2}$ simultaneously. However, it turns out that the exact structure of A, P does allow to achieve this, at least to some extent. Specifically, let us call a difference of the form e_{31}, e_7, e_{31} in three subsequent subkey words or a cyclic rotation of it a local collision, and observe that if the subkey difference can be decomposed as the sum of two such local collisions (probably, in different words), then the probability of the related-key differential is only squared, which still allows finding collisions efficiently in many cases. Examination of A, P shows that there are many ways to choose a difference in M_i such that in two of the words $K_{i,j}$ the difference will form a local collision. For example, if the nonzero bits in the difference in M_i are the most significant bits of xi_4, xi_5, xi_8 (using the notation of [17]), then the differences in the words $K_{i,1}$ and $K_{i,2}$ form local collisions and the difference in the word $K_{i,3}$ is the sum of two local collisions. This may allow finding many pairs of values (M_i, M_i') which lead to a collision in the 128 initial bits of S_i.

The second obstacle in the way of this strategy is the mixing transformation χ. Examination of the structure of χ (or more specifically, of the transformation $\Psi^{-12}(\Delta(M_i))$ which affects it; note that the effect of H_{i-1} can be neglected, as we assume that there is no difference in H_{i-1}) shows that for the input difference described above, the partial collision in S_i does not lead to a collision in any of the four 64-bit parts of H_i, due to the mixing. A possible way to overcome this obstacle is to modify the difference $\Delta(M_i)$ in such a way that the effect of $\Psi^{-12}(\Delta(M_i))$ will be smaller. For example, if the nonzero bits in $\Delta(M_i)$ are the most significant bits of xi_9, xi_{11}, xi_{18}, then a collision in $S_{i,4}$ leads to a collision in $H_{i,4}$. For this value of $\Delta(M_i)$, the difference in $K_{i,4}$ forms the sum of two local collisions, and thus, one may find collisions in $S_{i,4}$ (and thus, also in $H_{i,4}$) with a reduced cost. However, we could not find a way to obtain collisions in two words of H_i simultaneously, due to the effect of χ.

Finally, the third obstacle is that while the attack of Mendel et al. uses huge multi-collisions due to GOST's mode of iteration (that contains an additive checksum of all chaining values H_i), our attack provides us only with pairs of values of M_i which yield collisions in part of the state H_i. This makes leveraging a partial collision into a full collision significantly more expensive.

To summarize, it seems that the mixing function χ thwarts the natural strategy of using our technique to attack the GOST hash function. However, more sophisticated applications might be possible, especially as the structure of A, P allows obtaining local collisions or their combinations in several words $K_{i,j}$ simultaneously.

6   Summary and Conclusions

In this paper we presented a related-key attack on GOST with secret S-boxes, which is the first known attack on the full GOST with secret S-boxes that works for all keys. We fully verified our attack, and it runs in about 11 s on a PC, with a success rate of 88%. The main technique we used in the attack is a new related-key differential of GOST, which is based on 3-round local collisions, in the spirit of the collision attacks on the SHA-0 and SHA-1 hash functions. We showed that our techniques apply to other variants of GOST as well, such as a Davies-Meyer hash function based on GOST. The main open question for further research is, whether our techniques can be applied to attack the GOST hash function.

References

1. Ashur, T., Bar-On, A., Dunkelman, O.: Cryptanalysis of GOST2. IACR Trans. Symmetric Cryptol. **2017**(1), 203–214 (2017)
2. Bar-On, A., Biham, E., Dunkelman, O., Keller, N.: Efficient slide attacks. J. Cryptol. **31**(3), 641–670 (2018)
3. Biham, E.: New types of cryptanalytic attacks using related keys. J. Cryptol. **7**(4), 229–246 (1994)
4. Biham, E., Chen, R.: Near-collisions of SHA-0. In: Franklin, M. (ed.) CRYPTO 2004. LNCS, vol. 3152, pp. 290–305. Springer, Heidelberg (2004). https://doi.org/10.1007/978-3-540-28628-8_18
5. Biham, E., Chen, R., Joux, A.: Cryptanalysis of SHA-0 and reduced SHA-1. J. Cryptol. **28**(1), 110–160 (2015)
6. Biham, E., Shamir, A.: Differential cryptanalysis of DES-like cryptosystems. J. Cryptol. **4**(1), 3–72 (1991)
7. Biryukov, A., Nikolić, I.: Complementing Feistel ciphers. In: Moriai, S. (ed.) FSE 2013. LNCS, vol. 8424, pp. 3–18. Springer, Heidelberg (2014). https://doi.org/10.1007/978-3-662-43933-3_1
8. Biryukov, A., Wagner, D.: Slide attacks. In: Knudsen, L. (ed.) FSE 1999. LNCS, vol. 1636, pp. 245–259. Springer, Heidelberg (1999). https://doi.org/10.1007/3-540-48519-8_18
9. Chabaud, F., Joux, A.: Differential collisions in SHA-0. In: Krawczyk, H. (ed.) CRYPTO 1998. LNCS, vol. 1462, pp. 56–71. Springer, Heidelberg (1998). https://doi.org/10.1007/BFb0055720
10. Courtois, N.: An improved differential attack on full GOST - extended version. IACR Cryptology ePrint Archive, 2012/138 (2012)
11. Courtois, N.T.: An improved differential attack on full GOST. In: Ryan, P.Y.A., Naccache, D., Quisquater, J.-J. (eds.) The New Codebreakers. LNCS, vol. 9100, pp. 282–303. Springer, Heidelberg (2016). https://doi.org/10.1007/978-3-662-49301-4_18
12. Dinur, I., Dunkelman, O., Shamir, A.: Improved attacks on full GOST. In: Canteaut, A. (ed.) FSE 2012. LNCS, vol. 7549, pp. 9–28. Springer, Heidelberg (2012). https://doi.org/10.1007/978-3-642-34047-5_2
13. Dmukh, A., Dygin, D., Marshalko, G.: A lightweight-friendly modification of GOST block cipher. IACR Cryptology ePrint Archive, 2015/65 (2015)
14. Dmukh, A., Trifonov, D., Chookhno, A.: Modification of the key schedule of the 2-GOST block cipher and its implementation on FPGA. J. Comput. Virol. Hacking Tech. **18**(1), 49–59 (2022)
15. Dolmatov, V., Baryshkov, D.: RFC 8891, GOST R 34.12-2015: Block cipher "Magma" (2020). https://www.ietf.org/rfc/rfc8891.pdf
16. Dolmatov, V.: RFC 5830, GOST 28147-89: encryption, decryption, and message authentication code (MAC) algorithms (2010). https://www.rfc-editor.org/rfc/rfc5830.html
17. Dolmatov, V.: RFC 5831, GOST R 34.11-94: hash function algorithm (2010). https://datatracker.ietf.org/doc/html/rfc5831
18. Dunkelman, O., Huang, S.: Reconstructing an S-box from its difference distribution table. IACR Trans. Symmetric Cryptol. **2019**(2), 193–217 (2019)
19. Frieze, A., Karoński,M.: Introduction to Random Graphs. Cambridge University Press (2015)

20. Isobe, T.: A single-key attack on the full GOST block cipher. J. Cryptol. **26**(1), 172–189 (2013)
21. Kelsey, J., Schneier, B., Wagner, D.: Key-schedule cryptanalysis of IDEA, G-DES, GOST, SAFER, and Triple-DES. In: Koblitz, N. (ed.) CRYPTO 1996. LNCS, vol. 1109, pp. 237–251. Springer, Heidelberg (1996). https://doi.org/10.1007/3-540-68697-5_19
22. Kim, J., Hong, S., Preneel, B., Biham, E., Dunkelman, O., Keller, N.: Related-key boomerang and rectangle attacks: theory and experimental analysis. IEEE Trans. Inf. Theor. **58**(7), 4948–4966 (2012)
23. Knudsen, L.R.: Cryptanalysis of LOKI 91. In: Seberry, J., Zheng, Y. (eds.) AUSCRYPT 1992. LNCS, vol. 718, pp. 196–208. Springer, Heidelberg (1993). https://doi.org/10.1007/3-540-57220-1_62
24. Ko, Y., Hong, S., Lee, W., Lee, S., Kang, J.-S.: Related key differential attacks on 27 rounds of XTEA and full-round GOST. In: Roy, B., Meier, W. (eds.) FSE 2004. LNCS, vol. 3017, pp. 299–316. Springer, Heidelberg (2004). https://doi.org/10.1007/978-3-540-25937-4_19
25. Mendel, F., Pramstaller, N., Rechberger, C.: A (Second) preimage attack on the GOST hash function. In: Nyberg, K. (ed.) FSE 2008. LNCS, vol. 5086, pp. 224–234. Springer, Heidelberg (2008). https://doi.org/10.1007/978-3-540-71039-4_14
26. Mendel, F., Pramstaller, N., Rechberger, C., Kontak, M., Szmidt, J.: Cryptanalysis of the GOST hash function. In: Wagner, D. (ed.) CRYPTO 2008. LNCS, vol. 5157, pp. 162–178. Springer, Heidelberg (2008). https://doi.org/10.1007/978-3-540-85174-5_10
27. Pudovkina, M.A., Khoruzenko, G.I.: An attack on the GOST 28147-89 block cipher with 12 related keys. Math. Aspect. Crypt. (Russ.) **4**(2), 127–152 (2013)
28. Pudovkina, M.: A related-key attack on block ciphers with weak recurrent key schedules. In: Garcia-Alfaro, J., Lafourcade, P. (eds.) FPS 2011. LNCS, vol. 6888, pp. 90–101. Springer, Heidelberg (2012). https://doi.org/10.1007/978-3-642-27901-0_8
29. Rudskoy, V.: On zero practical significance of "Key recovery attack on full GOST block cipher with zero time and memory". IACR Cryptology eprint archive, 2010:111 (2010)
30. Saarinen, M.J.: A chosen key attack against the secret S-boxes of GOST. IACR Cryptology ePrint Archive, 2019/540 (1998)
31. Schneier, B.: Applied Cryptography, 2nd edn. Wiley (1996)
32. Seki, H., Kaneko, T.: Differential cryptanalysis of reduced rounds of GOST. In: Stinson, D.R., Tavares, S. (eds.) SAC 2000. LNCS, vol. 2012, pp. 315–323. Springer, Heidelberg (2001). https://doi.org/10.1007/3-540-44983-3_23
33. Stevens, M., Bursztein, E., Karpman, P., Albertini, A., Markov, Y.: The first collision for full SHA-1. In: Katz, J., Shacham, H. (eds.) CRYPTO 2017. LNCS, vol. 10401, pp. 570–596. Springer, Cham (2017). https://doi.org/10.1007/978-3-319-63688-7_19
34. Wang, X., Yin, Y.L., Yu, H.: Finding collisions in the full SHA-1. In: Shoup, V. (ed.) CRYPTO 2005. LNCS, vol. 3621, pp. 17–36. Springer, Heidelberg (2005). https://doi.org/10.1007/11535218_2
35. Zhao, X., et al.: Algebraic fault analysis on GOST for key recovery and reverse engineering. In: Proceedings of FDTC 2014, pp. 29–39. IEEE Computer Society (2014)

On Perfect Linear Approximations and Differentials over Two-Round SPNs

Christof Beierle[1]($\boxtimes$), Patrick Felke[2]($\boxtimes$), Gregor Leander[1]($\boxtimes$),
Patrick Neumann[1]($\boxtimes$), and Lukas Stennes[1]($\boxtimes$)

[1] Ruhr University Bochum, Bochum, Germany
{christof.beierle,gregor.leander,patrick.neumann,lukas.stennes}@rub.de
[2] University of Applied Sciences Emden/Leer, Emden, Germany
patrick.felke@hs-emden-leer.de

Abstract. Recent constructions of (tweakable) block ciphers with an embedded cryptographic backdoor relied on the existence of probability-one differentials or perfect (non-)linear approximations over a reduced-round version of the primitive. In this work, we study how the existence of probability-one differentials or perfect linear approximations over two rounds of a substitution-permutation network can be avoided by design. More precisely, we develop criteria on the s-box and the linear layer that guarantee the absence of probability-one differentials for all keys. We further present an algorithm that allows to efficiently exclude the existence of keys for which there exists a perfect linear approximation.

Keywords: differential cryptanalysis · linear cryptanalysis · decomposition · boomerang connectivity table · weak keys

1 Introduction

The vast majority of data is protected by symmetric cryptography due to its performance advantage, typically in a hybrid setting with public-key components surrounding the actual encryption. Almost all designs in symmetric cryptography can be subsumed as performance driven. Indeed, beyond security, the main criteria and innovation incentive for symmetric cryptography is efficiency. Consequently, as a community we have made impressive improvements when it comes to designing performant ciphers. We managed to design primitives that allow the encryption of data significantly faster than AES on modern CPUs, even on platforms where AES is directly supported in hardware. For other criteria, e.g., chip-size, latency, code size, side-channel protection, or multiplicative depth, the improvement is even bigger.

With respect to understanding the security of symmetric cryptographic primitives, not much progress has been made in recent years. Even if we look at the resilience against dedicated attack vectors, we still rely on unproven assumptions. One fundamental example is that we often assume independence of the inputs to all parts of a cipher. This is obviously not true as the output of one part serves as the direct input for the next part. Another classical example is

© International Association for Cryptologic Research 2023
H. Handschuh and A. Lysyanskaya (Eds.): CRYPTO 2023, LNCS 14083, pp. 209–239, 2023.
https://doi.org/10.1007/978-3-031-38548-3_8

that we study weaknesses, e.g., differential and linear properties or (non-linear) invariants, by studying all parts of a cipher separately, while we actually only want to exclude that the weaknesses in question apply to the cipher as a whole.

Resistance Against Linear and Differential Attacks. To be more specific, to argue about the resistance of a given cipher with respect to the most important attack vectors, differential [9] and linear cryptanalysis [22], we basically have to give arguments that, for almost all keys, no exploitable differential resp., linear approximation exists, i.e., to bound the probability resp., bias for an overwhelming fraction of all keys. However, in almost all cases we only manage to bound the average probability for a differential or linear characteristic assuming independent round keys.

The case of linear approximations with absolute correlation one and differentials with probability one that work *for all keys* of a key-alternating cipher are trivial to avoid. Indeed, they imply one round linear approximations and differentials with the same property. That is a round function with non-maximal linearity or differential uniformity is enough to rule out those cases.

While for one round of almost any modern design the problem is trivial, already two rounds (as depicted in Fig. 1) have not been thoroughly considered in the past. Given a keyed (or tweaked) two-round construction, not even the question whether there exists a key for which the construction allows a probability-one differential resp., affine approximation has been answered in general.

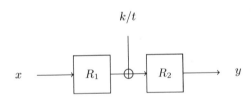

Fig. 1. Two rounds of a key-alternating block cipher.

For one key, while no good arguments for the non-existence of such maximally biased linear and differential properties where given, such properties indeed occurred in designs, either unintentionally or on purpose. For the former cases, the cipher SKINNY [4] is a good example as it actually has perfect two-round linear approximations as has been shown by carefully tracing the bits through the circuit of the s-box recently in [19]. For the latter, the cipher Boomslang [2] is a recent example. Here, a non-linear two-round iterative characteristic has been planted as a backdoor. A closer look at this construction actually reveals that this is based on a two-round linear approximation that has absolute correlation one for the backdoor tweak. As we will see below, further examples exist.

However, intriguingly, such examples only appear for linear approximations, while no (non-trivial) example of a keyed two-round construction is known that exhibits a key for which there is a probability-one differential. One example is the Malicious framework [24] that builds upon a probability-one differential through a partial non-linear layer. Since the probability-one differential appears already over a single round, it belongs to the class of trivial examples.

Our Contribution. In this work we manage to derive conditions under which no key exists such that a differential with probability one occurs in two-round substitution-permutation networks (SPNs). This is captured in Theorem 2 and turns out to be surprisingly technical. However, it is possible to derive several special cases, for mild and natural conditions on the s-box and the linear-layer, that we state in Corollary 7, Corollary 8, and Corollary 9. Besides our results on the non-existence, we further construct several non-trivial examples of two-round SPNs with probability-one differentials, e.g., Example 1.

Interestingly, the boomerang connectivity table (BCT), introduced in [11] appears in our conditions. With this, the most straightforward way of ensuring that no probability-one differential exists for two rounds is to use any linear layer with a non-trivial branch number and any s-box with a non-trivial boomerang uniformity. Our conditions are applicable to virtually any modern SPN design and we give various examples in Table 1.

For the case of a linear approximation, we are able to give efficient algorithms that allow an efficient computation of all keys and the corresponding input and output masks of a linear approximation with absolute correlation one. Using this, we show that Boomslang actually exhibits several other weak tweaks that lead to probability-one linear approximations. Another interesting example is CRAFT [5], where our approach allows an automated way of reproducing results given previously in [18,21].

Table 1 summarizes our results of both the differential and linear parts.

From a technical viewpoint, we deploy recent results on decomposing an s-box layer [20] and in particular conditions for the uniqueness of such a decomposition.

Related Work. There is a large variety of work related to one or another aspect of arguing resistance against differential and linear attacks, starting with the seminal wide-trail strategy [12,13] focusing on linear and differential characteristics. The decorrelation theory [25] is a mean to ensure security against linear and differential attacks (or in general statistical attacks using only a few numbers of plaintext/ciphertext pairs at a time) on average. It does not cover the existence of weak keys or tweaks.

The key-dependent behavior was treated for a large class of two-round SPNs for the case of characteristics in [14] where it was observed that the right pairs can often be seen as the intersection of linear spaces translated by the round key. More recently, the key-dependent behavior of differentials has been approximated using the notion of quasidifferential trails in [8].

Regarding the algorithmic detection of highly-biased linear approximations or highly-probable differentials, we like to mention [17] that deploys links to coding theory or, very recently, [15] from EUROCRYPT 2023 that allow to detect such approximations and differentials in a black-box manner. Thus, from

Table 1. Overview of our results. ✓ indicates that we can exclude the existence of non-trivial perfect linear approximations resp., differentials whereas ✗ means that there are non-trivial perfect linear approximations. ⊥ indicates that our computations aborted and - indicates that the cipher is not AES-like and therefore was not tested for four rounds. r is the number of rounds.

Cipher	Linear			Differential for $r = 2$			
	$r = 2$	$r = 3$	$r = 4$	Corollay 7	Corollay 8	Corollay 9	Theorem 2 & Corollay 10
Boomslang	✗	✓	✗	✓			✓
CRAFT	✗	✓	✓				✓
MANTIS	✗	✓	✗	✓			✓
Midori64	✗	✓	✗	✓			✓
SKINNY-64	✗	✓	✓				✓
SKINNY-128	✗	⊥	⊥				✓
AES	✓	✓	⊥	✓	✓		✓
GIFT-64	✓	✓	✓			✓	✓
GIFT-128	✓	✓	✓			✓	✓
LED	✓	✓	✓	✓			✓
PRESENT	✓	✓	✓			✓	✓
PRINCE	✓	✓	✓		✓		✓
Streebog	✓	✓	⊥	✓	✓		✓
Ascon	✓	✓	-	✓	✓		✓
iSCREAM	✓	⊥	-	✓			✓
Keccak-100	✓	✓	-		✓		✓
Kuznechik	✓	⊥	-	✓	✓		✓
PRIDE	✓	✓	-				✓
RECTANGLE	✓	✓	-			✓	✓

our perspective, the limitation here is that those results do not allow to tackle keyed primitives without iterating over all (round) keys.

For Feistel ciphers, one concrete example that allows to make statements about weak keys is the KN cipher [23]. This construction allows to bound the differential uniformity for any key for two (Feistel) rounds.

Outline. In Sect. 2, we start by fixing notations and recalling the basic properties needed. We then first describe the results for the case of linear approximations in Sect. 3, focusing more on algorithmic solutions. The differential case, with the general statement given in Theorem 2, that leads to various more accessible conditions given in Corollaries 7 to 9, is explained in Sect. 4. As is shown in Table 1, for many SPNs those arguments are sufficient to exclude the existence of probability-one differentials. We conclude the paper in Sect. 5 with some open questions and possible improvements of our work.

2   Preliminaries

We recall some basic properties needed throughout the paper and we fix our notation. We work with bits, which we understand as elements in the field with two elements $\mathbb{F}_2$, and with bit strings, which we understand as vectors in $\mathbb{F}_2^n$, the n-dimensional vector space over $\mathbb{F}_2$. The addition of vectors in $\mathbb{F}_2^n$ is simply denoted by $+$ and corresponds to an xor of bit strings. The canonical inner product of vectors $x, y \in \mathbb{F}_2^n$ is denoted by

$$\langle x, y \rangle = \sum_{i=1}^{n} x_i y_i$$

and used in particular for defining an *affine approximation* for a function $E \colon \mathbb{F}_2^n \to \mathbb{F}_2^n$ by the equation

$$\langle \alpha, x \rangle + \langle \beta, E(x) \rangle = c \tag{1}$$

for $\alpha \in \mathbb{F}_2^n$, $\beta \in \mathbb{F}_2^n$ and $c \in \mathbb{F}_2$. If $c = 0$ we call the approximation *linear*. The *correlation* of a linear approximation is given by

$$\mathrm{cor}_E(\alpha, \beta) := \frac{1}{2^n} \sum_{x \in \mathbb{F}_2^n} (-1)^{\langle \alpha, x \rangle + \langle \beta, E(x) \rangle}.$$

If Eq. (1) holds with absolute correlation equal to one, i.e., there exists a constant c such that it is fulfilled for all x, we say it is a *perfect linear approximation* which we also denote simply by the tuple (α, β, c) or just (α, β) in case we do not care about the constant. We call a perfect linear approximation *non-trivial* if $(\alpha, \beta) \neq (0, 0)$. The *linearity* of E is defined as $\max_{\alpha \neq 0, \beta}(2^n \cdot |\mathrm{cor}_E(\alpha, \beta)|)$ and we call it *maximal* if it is equal to the size of the domain of E, i.e., 2^n.

For E as above and $\alpha \in \mathbb{F}_2^n$, we say that

$$\Delta_\alpha E(x) := E(x) + E(x + \alpha)$$

is the *(first-order) derivative* of E at point x along α. A *probability-one differential* over E is a tuple (α, β), with $\alpha \in \mathbb{F}_2^n, \beta \in \mathbb{F}_2^n$, for which $\Delta_\alpha E(x)$ is equal to β for all x. We call a probability-one differential *non-trivial* if $(\alpha, \beta) \neq (0, 0)$. The *differential uniformity* of E is defined as $\max_{\alpha \neq 0, \beta} |\{x \in \mathbb{F}_2^n \mid \Delta_\alpha E(x) = \beta\}|$ and we call it *maximal* if it is equal to the size of the domain of E.

A perfect linear approximation of a derivative with input mask zero, that is an equation of the form

$$\langle \beta, E(x) + E(x + \alpha) \rangle = c$$

holding for all x, defines a *linear structure* (β, α, c) of E, and we call it non-trivial if $\alpha \neq 0$. The following notation is in particular used when we discuss SPNs. For a convenient handling of the *addition of constants*, and in particular keys, we call

$$T \colon \mathbb{F}_2^n \to \mathbb{F}_2^n \text{ with } T_\alpha(x) = x + \alpha$$

the *translation by* α.

For $n = dm$ and an s-box $S \colon \mathbb{F}_2^m \to \mathbb{F}_2^m$, we denote by $\bar{S}$ the *parallel application of the s-box S*, i.e.,

$$\bar{S}(x_1, \ldots, x_d) = (S(x_1), \ldots, S(x_d)).$$

As we will later deal with more general decompositions, we need the notion of a direct sum of vector spaces. Given vector spaces $U_1, ..., U_d \subseteq \mathbb{F}_2^n$ such that $U_i \cap U_j = \{0\}$ for all $i \neq j$, we define $\bigoplus_i U_i := \sum_i U_i$ and call $\bigoplus_i U_i$ the *direct sum* of the U_i. Recall that for every $x \in \bigoplus_i U_i$ there exist unique $x_i \in U_i$ such that $x = \sum_i x_i$.

We shall call the map (well-)defined by $x \mapsto x_i$ the *projection onto U_i (and along $\bigoplus_{j \neq i} U_j$)* and denote it by π_i^U, where $U = (U_1, ..., U_d)$. For convenience, we may also write $\pi_{l \neq i}^U$ instead of $\sum_{l \neq i} \pi_i^U$, effectively considering the direct sum of $\bigoplus_{l \neq i} U_l$ and U_i.

For a simple s-box layer, the U_i have the form $0^{(i-1)m} \times \mathbb{F}_2^m \times 0^{(d-i)m}$, meaning that they are aligned with the parallel application of d m-bit s-boxes. If we have such a canonical direct sum, and the spaces U_i are clear from the context, we may simply write π_i instead of π_i^U.

Finally, for a vector space $U \subseteq \mathbb{F}_2^n$ we denote by $U^\perp$ the *orthogonal space of* U, i.e.,

$$U^\perp = \{x \mid \langle x, u \rangle = 0 \; \forall u \in U\}.$$

3   Perfect Linear Approximations

Our main result is captured in Theorem 1 and leads to an algorithm that can exclude the existence of weak keys, i.e., keys for which there is a perfect linear approximation. We applied this algorithm to several ciphers and report the results in Table 1. For most of the ciphers, we exclude the existence of non-trivial perfect linear approximations for up to four rounds. For others, we rediscover perfect linear approximations which were previously known in the literature in an automatised fashion.

3.1   Unkeyed Permutations

We start with the rather simple case of an unkeyed permutation $E: \mathbb{F}_2^n \to \mathbb{F}_2^n$. Given oracle access to E, we want to decide whether there exists a non-trivial perfect linear approximation (α, β) for E, i.e., to decide whether there exist $\alpha, \beta \in \mathbb{F}_2^n \setminus \{0\}$ and a constant $c \in \mathbb{F}_2$ such that, for all $x \in \mathbb{F}_2^n$, we have $\langle \alpha, x \rangle = \langle \beta, E(x) \rangle + c$. If such a linear approximation exists, we also want to determine the masks α and β. Of course, multiple choices of (α, β) might be possible and if this is the case we might want to determine all solutions.

To find a perfect linear approximation, we can build a system of linear equations with variables α, β, c by querying E on some random choices for x. If this system has only the trivial solution, we conclude that there is no non-trivial perfect linear approximation for E. On the other hand, a solution (α, β, c) does not necessarily imply a perfect linear approximation, unless E is queried for (almost) all $x \in \mathbb{F}_2^n$. But such false positives would imply a linear approximation with a high absolute correlation and hence would also be of cryptographic interest. Therefore, we do not analyze the possibility of false positives in detail.

Notice that this scenario is mostly interesting in the context of permutation-based cryptography. Hence, we exemplary applied this approach to the Ascon permutation [16] and, unsurprisingly, found that there is no non-trivial perfect linear approximation.

3.2   Two Rounds

We now analyse keyed permutations $E_k \colon \mathbb{F}_2^n \to \mathbb{F}_2^n$. We are interested for which (if any) keys k the permutation E_k has a non-trivial perfect linear approximation. We call such keys weak and, for given masks (α, β) we define the set of weak keys $W_E(\alpha, \beta)$ as

$$W_E(\alpha, \beta) = \{k \mid \mathrm{cor}_{E_k}(\alpha, \beta) = 1\} \cup \{k \mid \mathrm{cor}_{E_k}(\alpha, \beta) = -1\}.$$

Notice that this scenario does not only apply to block ciphers but also to cryptographic permutations again. In that case, instead of weak keys we would be interested in weak constants.

If E is (close enough to) a family of permutations drawn independently and uniformly from the set of all permutations, then applying the approach from Sect. 3.1 to each of those permutations is essentially the best we can do. Here, we consider permutations restricted to the form depicted in Fig. 1, i.e., $E_k(x) = R_2(R_1(x) + k)$ where $R_1, R_2 \colon \mathbb{F}_2^n \to \mathbb{F}_2^n$. The following lemma shows that if there is a perfect linear approximation (α, β) for E_k, then all trails in the corresponding linear hull are such that the correlation over the first permutation R_1 is the same as over the second permutation R_2 up to a sign.

Lemma 1. *Let $R_1, R_2 \colon \mathbb{F}_2^n \to \mathbb{F}_2^n$ be bijective and let $k \in \mathbb{F}_2^n$ be fixed. Then (α, β, c) is a perfect linear approximation for $E_k = R_2(R_1(x) + k)$ if and only if, for all $\gamma \in \mathbb{F}_2^n$, we have $\mathrm{cor}_{R_1}(\alpha, \gamma) = (-1)^{\langle \gamma, k \rangle + c} \mathrm{cor}_{R_2}(\gamma, \beta)$.*

Proof. Let us start with a perfect linear approximation (α, β, c), i.e.,

$$\langle \alpha, x \rangle = \langle \beta, E_k(x) \rangle + c = \langle \beta, R_2(R_1(x) + k) \rangle + c.$$

The statement follows by considering the definition of the correlation of R_1 and replacing the $\langle \alpha, x \rangle$ term with the right-hand side from above. That is, for all $\gamma \in \mathbb{F}_2^n$ we have

$$\mathrm{cor}_{R_1}(\alpha, \gamma) = 2^{-n} \sum_{x \in \mathbb{F}_2^n} (-1)^{\langle \alpha, x \rangle + \langle \gamma, R_1(x) \rangle}$$

$$= 2^{-n} \sum_{x \in \mathbb{F}_2^n} (-1)^{\langle \beta, R_2(R_1(x) + k) \rangle + c + \langle \gamma, R_1(x) \rangle}$$

$$= 2^{-n} \sum_{x \in \mathbb{F}_2^n} (-1)^{\langle \gamma, x + k \rangle + \langle \beta, R_2(x) \rangle + c}$$

$$= (-1)^{\langle \gamma, k \rangle + c} \mathrm{cor}_{R_2}(\gamma, \beta).$$

Conversely, if for all $\gamma \in \mathbb{F}_2^n$ it holds that

$$\text{cor}_{R_1}(\alpha, \gamma) = (-1)^{\langle \gamma, k \rangle + c} \text{cor}_{R_2}(\gamma, \beta)$$

then the claim follows by Parseval's relation (see, e.g., [10, Corollary 5]) since

$$\text{cor}_{E_k}(\alpha, \beta) = \sum_{\gamma \in \mathbb{F}_2^n} \text{cor}_{R_1}(\alpha, \gamma)(-1)^{\langle \gamma, k \rangle} \text{cor}_{R_2}(\gamma, \beta)$$

$$= (-1)^c \cdot \sum_{\gamma \in \mathbb{F}_2^n} \text{cor}_{R_1}(\alpha, \gamma)^2 = (-1)^c.$$

$\square$

From Lemma 1 it is clear that if there is a weak key for (α, β) with constant c, then the set of all weak keys $W_E(\alpha, \beta)$ is given by the solution to the linear system of equations given by $\langle \gamma, k \rangle = c + b_\gamma$ for all $\gamma \in \mathbb{F}_2^n$ such that $\text{cor}_{R_1}(\alpha, \gamma) \neq 0$, where

$$b_\gamma := \begin{cases} 0 & \text{cor}_{R_1}(\alpha, \gamma) = \text{cor}_{R_2}(\gamma, \beta) \\ 1 & \text{cor}_{R_1}(\alpha, \gamma) \neq \text{cor}_{R_2}(\gamma, \beta) \end{cases}.$$

Hence, the weak keys form an affine subspace. Moreover, $W_E(\alpha, \beta)$ is closely related to the linear structures of $\langle \alpha, R_1^{-1} \rangle$ and $\langle \beta, R_2 \rangle$. We record this in the following lemma.

Lemma 2. *Let* $R_1, R_2 \colon \mathbb{F}_2^n \to \mathbb{F}_2^n$ *be bijective and let* $E_k(x) = R_2(R_1(x) + k)$. *For a pair of input and output masks* (α, β) *such that* $W_E(\alpha, \beta)$ *is non-empty, let* $k \in W_E(\alpha, \beta)$. *Then, for every* $u \in \mathbb{F}_2^n$, *the following three statements are equivalent.*

(1) $(k + u) \in W_E(\alpha, \beta)$.
(2) u *is a linear structure of* $\langle \beta, R_2 \rangle$.
(3) u *is a linear structure of* $\langle \alpha, R_1^{-1} \rangle$.

The proof is straightforward and given in the full version of this paper [3].

3.3 SPNs

SPNs are arguably the most important design pattern in symmetric cryptography and hence are of special interest. Considering the special case of SPNs allows us to make exhaustive statements for up to four rounds. To illustrate this, recall our approach from Sect. 3.1. With this, we can, e.g., show that for the AES with some *fixed key* there is no non-trivial perfect linear approximation. In contrast to this, our approach from this section allows us to show that, e.g., for two and three rounds of AES, and for two to four rounds PRESENT there is *no weak key* at all.

We first explain our approach for two round SPNs and then show how the resulting algorithm transfers to three and in the case of AES-like ciphers also to four round SPNs. The results were already given in the introduction in Table 1. We discuss those in more detail in the corresponding paragraphs below.

Two Rounds. As an example, consider the most basic form of a two round SPN;[1] an SPN consisting of two parallel s-boxes, a key addition, a linear layer and another two parallel s-boxes as depicted below.

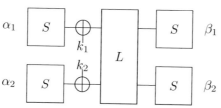

We are interested in perfect linear approximations $(\alpha = (\alpha_1, \alpha_2), \beta = (\beta_1, \beta_2), c)$ for a weak key $k = (k_1, k_2)$. In other words, for all $x = (x_1, x_2) \in \mathbb{F}_2^n$ where n is twice the bit width of the s-box S, it holds that

$$\langle \alpha, x \rangle = \langle \beta, \bar{S}(L(\bar{S}(x) + k)) \rangle + c.$$

Now, our claim (which we prove in Theorem 1 more generally) is that the above equation implies that for all x

$$\langle \beta, \bar{S}(L((x_1, x_2))) \rangle = \langle \beta, \bar{S}(L((x_1, 0))) + \bar{S}(L((0, x_2))) + \bar{S}(L((0, 0))) \rangle$$

which in turn implies an easy way to find all candidates for β by simply evaluating the equation above for some random x to build a system of linear equations. If there are no solutions $\beta \neq 0$ then there is no non-trivial perfect linear approximation. To understand why the claim holds, first notice that instead of inputs we can consider intermediate states directly after the key addition. Then, the upper part of the cipher still decomposes into two parallel s-boxes with key addition. Now the key insight is that the perfect linear approximation implies that the lower part, i.e., $\langle \beta, \bar{S} \circ L \rangle$ must also decompose into two parallel functions. We generalise this example to an arbitrary number of s-boxes in the theorem below.

Theorem 1. *Let $\bar{S} \colon \mathbb{F}_2^n \to \mathbb{F}_2^n$ be the parallel application of d s-boxes S and $L \colon \mathbb{F}_2^n \to \mathbb{F}_2^n$ linear. $E_k(x) = \bar{S}(L(\bar{S}(x) + k))$ has a perfect linear approximation (α, β, c) if and only if the following two assertions are both fulfilled*

1. For all $x \in \mathbb{F}_2^n$ and for all $i \in \{1, 2, \ldots, d\}$, we have

$$\langle \alpha_i, S^{-1}(x_i + k_i) \rangle = \langle \beta, \bar{S} \circ L(\pi_i(x)) \rangle + \sum_{\substack{j=1 \\ j \neq i}}^{d} \langle \alpha_j, S^{-1}(k_j) \rangle + c. \quad (2)$$

2. For all $x \in \mathbb{F}_2^n$, we have

$$\langle \beta, \bar{S} \circ L(x) \rangle = \begin{cases} \langle \beta, \sum_{i=1}^{d} (\bar{S} \circ L(\pi_i(x))) + \bar{S}(0) \rangle & d \text{ even} \\ \langle \beta, \sum_{i=1}^{d} \bar{S} \circ L(\pi_i(x)) \rangle & d \text{ odd} \end{cases}. \quad (3)$$

---

[1] For simplicity, we omit whitening keys and the linear layer in the final round. Adding those have no effect on the (non-)existence of perfect linear approximations.

Proof. We start by assuming the perfect linear approximation (α, β, c) for E_k. That is, for all $x \in \mathbb{F}_2^n$, we have

$$\langle \alpha, x \rangle = \langle \beta, \bar{S} \circ L(\bar{S}(x) + k) \rangle + c,$$

and move one s-box layer and the key addition to the left-hand side:

$$\langle \alpha, \bar{S}^{-1}(x + k) \rangle = \langle \beta, \bar{S} \circ L(x) \rangle + c.$$

We make use of the fact that the s-box layer $\bar{S}$ consists of d parallel applications of the s-box S:

$$\sum_{i=1}^{d} \langle \alpha_i, S^{-1}(x_i + k_i) \rangle = \langle \beta, \bar{S} \circ L(x) \rangle + c. \tag{4}$$

Next, we consider the above equation for x with $x = \pi_i(x)$ and get, for all i,

$$\langle \alpha_i, S^{-1}(x_i + k_i) \rangle = \langle \beta, \bar{S} \circ L(\pi_i(x)) \rangle + c + \sum_{\substack{j=1 \\ j \neq i}}^{d} \langle \alpha_j, S^{-1}(k_j) \rangle. \tag{5}$$

Now we combine Eqs. (4) and (5) by replacing each term on the left-hand side of Eq. (4) with right-hand side term from Eq. (5). This yields

$$\langle \beta, \bar{S} \circ L(x) \rangle + c = \sum_{i=1}^{d} \left(\langle \beta, \bar{S} \circ L(\pi_i(x)) \rangle + c + \sum_{\substack{j=1 \\ j \neq i}}^{d} \langle \alpha_j, S^{-1}(k_j) \rangle \right)$$

$$= \langle \beta, \sum_{i=1}^{d} \bar{S} \circ L(\pi_i(x)) \rangle + d \cdot c + (d - 1) \cdot \sum_{j=1}^{d} \langle \alpha_j, S^{-1}(k_j) \rangle$$

$$= \langle \beta, \sum_{i=1}^{d} \bar{S} \circ L(\pi_i(x)) \rangle + (2d - 1) \cdot c + (d - 1) \cdot \langle \beta, \bar{S}(0) \rangle$$

$$= \begin{cases} \langle \beta, \sum_{i=1}^{d}(\bar{S} \circ L(\pi_i(x))) + \bar{S}(0) \rangle + c & d \text{ even} \\ \langle \beta, \sum_{i=1}^{d} \bar{S} \circ L(\pi_i(x)) \rangle + c & d \text{ odd} \end{cases},$$

where in the last but one step we used Eq. (4). This concludes the first part. Conversely, consider the sum of Eq. (2) over every value of i which yields

$$\langle \alpha, \bar{S}^{-1}(x + k) \rangle = \langle \beta, \sum_{i=1}^{d} \bar{S} \circ L(\pi_i(x)) \rangle + (d - 1) \cdot \langle \alpha, \bar{S}^{-1}(k) \rangle + d \cdot c$$

$$= \begin{cases} \langle \beta, \sum_{i=1}^{d} \bar{S} \circ L(\pi_i(x)) \rangle + \langle \alpha, \bar{S}^{-1}(k) \rangle & d \text{ even} \\ \langle \beta, \sum_{i=1}^{d} \bar{S} \circ L(\pi_i(x)) \rangle + c & d \text{ odd} \end{cases}.$$

Further, Eq. (2) for any i and $x = 0$ gives $\langle \alpha, \bar{S}^{-1}(k) \rangle = \langle \beta, \bar{S}(0) \rangle + c$ and hence we combine the above equation with Eq. (3) to get

$$\langle \alpha, \bar{S}^{-1}(x + k) \rangle = \langle \beta, \bar{S} \circ L(x) \rangle + c,$$

which concludes the proof. $\qquad\qquad\qquad\qquad\qquad\qquad\qquad\qquad\qquad\qquad$ □

Notice that Theorem 1 does *not* directly lead to simple criteria for the s-box and linear layer. Instead it gives rise to efficient algorithms to find or exclude the existence of non-trivial perfect linear approximations. That is, from Theorem 1 it follows that for a perfect linear approximation (α, β) it is necessary that

$$\langle \beta, \bar{S} \circ L(x) + \sum_{i=1}^{d} \bar{S} \circ L(\pi_i(x)) \rangle = \begin{cases} \langle \beta, \bar{S}(0) \rangle & d \text{ even} \\ 0 & d \text{ odd} \end{cases}$$

holds for all $x \in \mathbb{F}_2^n$. Similar to the unkeyed case (Sect. 3.1), we can use this to build a system of linear equations. We record this in Algorithm 1. If there is no non-zero solution β, then we conclude that there is no non-trivial perfect linear approximation. Otherwise, we get candidate output masks which we examine further. Notice that we can apply the same algorithm to the inverse of the two-round SPN to get candidates for the input masks.

Algorithm 1. Search for perfect linear approximations for a two-round SPN

Input
E two round SPN $E \colon \mathbb{F}_2^n \to \mathbb{F}_2^n$ including the description of the s-box layer $\bar{S}$ with d parallel s-boxes and the linear layer L
Output
    B list of candidates for output mask β of a perfect linear approximation
$M \leftarrow (n + 5) \times n$ matrix
for $i = 1$ to $n + 5$ **do**
    $x \leftarrow$ sample uniform random vector from $\mathbb{F}_2^n$
    $z \leftarrow \bar{S}(L(x))$
    for $j = 1$ to d **do**
        $z \leftarrow z + \bar{S}(L(\pi_j(x)))$
    end for
    if d even **then**
        $z \leftarrow z + \bar{S}(L(0))$
    end if
    replace i-th row of M with z
end for
return the (right) kernel of M

We applied[2] Algorithm 1 to a variety of ciphers and report the results in Table 1 together with our results on three and four rounds. We divide the results for two rounds into two groups. First, there are ciphers for which our algorithm

---

[2] See https://doi.org/10.5281/zenodo.7934977.

shows that the only output mask candidate for a perfect linear approximation is $\beta = 0$, i.e., there is no non-trivial perfect linear approximation. As expected, this is the case for most of the examined ciphers.

There are also ciphers for which our automatized analysis indeed finds non-zero candidates for β. This is the case for Boomslang, CRAFT, Midori64, MAN-TIS[3] and SKINNY. For all of these ciphers, non-trivial perfect linear approximation over two rounds were known before. However, an automatized weak key search based on Eq. (2) reveals that some weak keys (or tweaks) were overlooked by the prior works. On closer inspection and with Lemma 2 in mind these additional findings are to no surprise as they correspond to linear structures of the s-boxes and their inverses. Hence, we omit a detailed description of those but briefly recap the prior works. Boomslang [2] was explicitly designed to contain a non-trivial perfect linear approximation. For CRAFT, the perfect linear approximations immediately follow from the representation as a Feistel cipher which was observed in [21]. For Midori64/MANTIS and SKINNY, the approximations were previously reported in [7] and [19] respectively.

Three and Four Rounds. There are two approaches to extend Algorithm 1 to three rounds. We can consider non-linear instead of linear equations or we can make use of superboxes. Combining both enables us to cover four rounds. The resulting variation of Theorem 1 and Algorithm 1 is rather straightforward and the key differences are given below.

First, we examine the approach based on superboxes which of course requires that the cipher has a superbox structure. Here we focus on AES-like designs. That is, the linear layer L can be represented as $L = SC \circ MC$ where MC is a mix column and SC a shuffle cells operation. With standard transformations, we write the three-round SPN as $E_k(x) = \bar{S}(L_2(\bar{Z}_{k^{(1)}}(x) + k^{(2)})))$ where $L_2 = SC \circ MC \circ SC$ and $\bar{Z}_{k^{(1)}} = \bar{S}(MC(\bar{S}(x) + k^{(1)}))$ is a keyed superbox layer. Recall Theorem 1 and notice it still applies if we replace the first s-box layer $\bar{S}$ with a keyed superbox layer $\bar{Z}_{k^{(1)}}$ and redefine π superbox-wise instead of s-box-wise.

The second approach is based on the idea of considering non-linear equations. On the one hand, this is more generic since it does not require a superbox structure but on the other hand it is computationally more demanding. Again consider a three round SPN $E_k = \bar{S}(L(\bar{S}(L(\bar{S}(x) + k^{(1)})) + k^{(2)}))$. Along the lines of Theorem 1, we first get

$$\langle \alpha, \bar{S}^{-1}(x + k^{(1)}) \rangle = \langle \beta, \bar{S}(L(\bar{S} \circ L(x)) + k^{(2)\prime}) \rangle + c$$

where $k^{(2)\prime} = L(k^{(2)})$ and then, for $H = L \circ \bar{S} \circ L$, we get that $\langle \beta, \bar{S}(H(x) + k^{(2)\prime}) \rangle$ is equal to

$$\begin{cases} \langle \beta, \sum_{i=1}^{d} (\bar{S}(H(\pi_i(x)) + k^{(2)\prime})) + \bar{S}(H(0) + k^{(2)\prime}) \rangle & d \text{ even} \\ \langle \beta, \sum_{i=1}^{d} \bar{S}(H(\pi_i(x)) + k^{(2)\prime}) \rangle & d \text{ odd} \end{cases}.$$

The resulting system contains non-linear equations in $k^{(2)\prime}$. But $\bar{S}$ is just the parallel application of s-boxes S, so the non-linearity corresponds to a single

---

[3] Notice that for our analysis Midori64 and MANTIS are equivalent because their s-boxes and linear layers are identical.

s-box and hence can be solved by standard techniques such as linearization, Gröbner bases or SAT solvers.

To cover four rounds, we combine both ideas from before, i.e., we consider superboxes and non-linear equations. Consider a four round SPN with super-boxes Z as

$$E_k(x) = \bar{S}(MC(\bar{S}(SC(MC(SC(\bar{S}(MC(\bar{S}(x) + k^{(1)})) + k^{(2)})))))) + k^{(3)\prime})$$
$$= \bar{S}(MC(\bar{S}(SC(MC(SC(\bar{Z}_{k^{(1)}}(x) + k^{(2)})))))) + k^{(3)\prime}).$$

Then, we get $\langle \alpha, \bar{Z}_{k^{(1)}}^{-1}(x + k^{(2)}) \rangle = \langle \beta, \bar{S}(MC(\bar{S}(SC(MC(SC(x)))))) + k^{(3)\prime}) \rangle + c$ and once again continue analogous to Theorem 1. But keep in mind that we swapped s-boxes for superboxes and hence redefine d to the number of superboxes and π accordingly.

We applied our algorithm for three and four rounds to the same ciphers as before (see Table 1). Some resulting systems were too complex to solve. Those are marked with $\bot$. Ciphers that are not AES-like were not tested for four rounds and hence the corresponding entries are marekd with -. Other than that, we can exlude the existence of weak keys for most ciphers either directly with the adapted versions of Algorithm 1 or with an additional weak key search based on Eq. (2). Exceptions are four rounds of Boomslang, Midori64 and MANTIS. For those, the perfect approximation over two rounds are iterative and hence perfect for four rounds again.

4   Probability-One Differentials

In contrast to the linear case, until now, there are, to the best of our knowledge, no known non-trivial probability-one differentials over two rounds aside from trivial edge cases such as the s-boxes having maximal differential uniformity or the linear layer only working locally on one s-box. While it is easy to see that maximal differential uniformity is a condition for the s-boxes if the differential should hold for all keys (see Corollary 2), the same is not the case if it should only hold a subset of (weak) keys, as the following example will illustrate.

Example 1. Let us consider the 5-bit s-box defined by the following lookup table.

x	0x00 0x01 0x02 0x03 0x04 0x05 0x06 0x07 0x08 0x09 0x0a 0x0b 0x0c 0x0d 0x0e 0x0f
S(x)	0x1c 0x1b 0x1e 0x09 0x17 0x15 0x1d 0x04 0x19 0x00 0x08 0xa 0x0d 0x13 0x0f 0x11
x	0x10 0x11 0x12 0x13 0x14 0x15 0x16 0x17 0x18 0x19 0x1a 0x1b 0x1c 0x1d 0x1e 0x1f
S(x)	0x0c 0x12 0x0e 0x10 0x1f 0x16 0x05 0x07 0x1a 0x18 0xb 0x02 0x14 0x03 0x06 0x01

Note that S has differential uniformity 20 and linearity 24. But, together with a specially crafted linear layer $L : \mathbb{F}_2^{15} \to \mathbb{F}_2^{15}$, $(\texttt{0x1d}^{\times 3}, \texttt{0x1d}^{\times 3})$ is a probability-one differential over two rounds. In a nutshell, this example was constructed by choosing S such that translating the input of S (resp. S^{-1}) by some constants is the same as an affine transformation A of S (resp. S^{-1}), i.e.,

$$S(x + \alpha) = A \circ S(x) \text{ and } S^{-1}(x + \alpha') = A \circ S^{-1}(x), \tag{6}$$

and choosing L such that this affine mapping A commutes with L. More details on this can be found in the full version of this paper [3].[4]

Hence, the question arises under which conditions such a non-trivial differential with probability one can exist and whether we are able to find easy arguments to show non-existence. As we will see, conditions on the differential branch number of the linear layer, together with conditions on the s-boxes, e.g. non-trivial boomerang uniformity and/or all linear structures being trivial, are enough to show that no such differential can exist, see Corollaries 7 to 9.

To actually show our main result, Theorem 2, and the corresponding corollaries, we rely on recent advances on decomposing round functions into a linear and non-linear layer [20]. We will therefore provide the proof of Theorem 2 in a more abstract fashion, and later give a simpler interpretation of this result in Sect. 4.3.

First of all, let us take a look at some general implications of probability-one differentials by abstracting differentials as functionals. For this, we first need the definition of the graph of a function.

Definition 1 (Graph of a Function). *For two sets U, V and $F: U \to V$, we call*

$$\mathcal{G}_F := \{(x, F(x)) \mid x \in U\} \subseteq U \times V$$

the graph *of F.*

It is easy to see that a function and its graph determine each other uniquely.

Then, differential cryptanalysis can be generalized to analyzing the evolution of graphs throughout the cipher E, i.e. for $(x, y) \in \mathcal{G}_F$ we consider the probability that $(E(x), E(y)) \in \mathcal{G}_G$ for two functions F and G. This has been coined *functional cryptanalysis* [6].

Definition 2 (Functional [6]). *For two finite sets U, V and $F: U \to U$ and $G: V \to V$, as well as $E: U \to V$, we call $F \xrightarrow{E}_{p} G$ a functional of E of probability p if*

$$p = \frac{|\{(x, y) \in \mathcal{G}_F \mid (E(x), E(y)) \in \mathcal{G}_G\}|}{|U|}.$$

If $p = 1$, we will just write $F \xrightarrow{E} G$.

In particular any differential (α, β) over E with probability p is a functional $T_\alpha \xrightarrow{E}_{p} T_\beta$. Note that we only consider the unkeyed case here, but the definition could easily be extended by simply taking the average probability over the key.

Lemma 3. *Let U, V be finite sets and $E: U \to V$ be bijective. Then, for any $F: U \to U$ and $G: V \to V$, the functional $F \xrightarrow{E} G$ holds (with probability one) if and only if $G = E \circ F \circ E^{-1}$.*

---

[4] An implementation of this example is also provided together with the source code.

Proof. By definition, $F \xrightarrow{E} G$ if and only if, for any $x \in U$, the tuple $(E(x), E \circ F(x))$ is an element of the graph of G, i.e.

$$\forall x \in U \; \exists! \; y \in V : (E(x), E \circ F(x)) = (y, G(y)) \iff G(y) = E \circ F \circ E^{-1}(y).$$

Since E is bijective, the last equation completely defines G and therefore $G = E \circ F \circ E^{-1}$. $\qquad \square$

In addition, any probability-one functional over multiple rounds can be seen as a trail of probability-one functionals, as the next corollary will show. But first, let us formally define a (probability-one) trail of functionals.

Definition 3 (Functional Trail (of Probability One)). *Let $W_1, ..., W_{r+1}$ be finite sets and $H_1 : W_1 \to W_1, ..., H_{r+1} : W_{r+1} \to W_{r+1}$, as well as $R_1 : W_1 \to W_2, R_2 : W_2 \to W_3, ..., R_r : W_r \to W_{r+1}$. We call $H_1 \xrightarrow{R_1} H_2 \xrightarrow{R_2} ... \xrightarrow{R_r} H_{r+1}$ a functional trail (of probability one) over $R_r \circ ... \circ R_1$ if, for every $i = 1, ..., r$, $H_i \xrightarrow{R_i} H_{i+1}$ is a functional over R_i (of probability one).*

While functional trails can also be defined for probabilities of the functionals that are lower than one, one has to be careful about assuming independence of the transitions $H_i \xrightarrow{R_i} H_{i+1}$, as even the addition of independent keys would, in general, not suffice to achieve this independence. If, one the other hand, every transition happens deterministically, the whole trail has to hold deterministically.

Corollary 1. *Let U, V, W be finite sets and let $E : U \to W$ be bijective. Furthermore, let $F : U \to U$ and $H : W \to W$ such that $F \xrightarrow{E} H$. For any $R_1 : U \to V$ and $R_2 : V \to W$ with $E = R_2 \circ R_1$ we find a unique $G : V \to V$ such that $F \xrightarrow{R_1} G \xrightarrow{R_2} H$. Moreover, $G = R_1 \circ F \circ R_1^{-1} = R_2^{-1} \circ H \circ R_2$.*

Proof. We know from the previous lemma that $F \xrightarrow{E = R_2 \circ R_1} H$ is a functional with probability one if and only if

$$R_2 \circ R_1 \circ F \circ R_1^{-1} \circ R_2^{-1} = H \iff R_1 \circ F \circ R_1^{-1} = R_2^{-1} \circ H \circ R_2.$$

In addition, the lemma also tells us that $F \xrightarrow{R_1} G$ if and only if $G = R_1 \circ F \circ R_1^{-1}$, and $G \xrightarrow{R_2} H$ if and only if $H = R_2 \circ G \circ R_2^{-1}$. $\qquad \square$

This can be iterated in case of E being the composition of more than two functions.

Remark 1. While the intuition for R_1 and R_2 should be that they represent consecutive rounds (or parts of rounds, e.g. for superboxes) of a cipher, they do not necessarily have to be, but could be any consecutive parts of a cipher such that $F \xrightarrow{R_2 \circ R_1} G$.

With this, it is easy to see that if a non-trivial probability-one differential should hold for all keys, there need to exist non-trivial probability-one differentials over R_1 and R_2 individually.

Lemma 4. *Let* $F, G, R \colon \mathbb{F}_2^n \to \mathbb{F}_2^n$, R *bijective, and let us define* $R_k \colon \mathbb{F}_2^n \to \mathbb{F}_2^n$ *as the map* $x \mapsto R(x) + k$ *for* $k \in \mathbb{F}_2^n$. *If* $F \xrightarrow{R_k} G$ *is a probability-one functional for all* $k \in \mathbb{F}_2^n$, *then* G *actually corresponds to the difference* $G = T_{G(0)}$.

Proof. Since $F \xrightarrow{R_k} G$ for all $k \in \mathbb{F}_2^n$, we know from Lemma 3 that this is equivalent to

$$F = R_k^{-1} \circ G \circ R_k$$

for all keys $k \in \mathbb{F}_2^n$. As the left-hand side is independent of k, and holds especially for zero, this gives us that, for all $x \in \mathbb{F}_2^n$,

$$R^{-1} \circ G \circ R(x) = R_k^{-1} \circ G \circ R_k(x) = R^{-1}\left(G\left(R(x) + k\right) + k\right)$$
$$\iff G(x) = G(x + k) + k.$$

Hence, for $x = 0$ we get that $G(k) = k + G(0)$ holds for all $k \in \mathbb{F}_2^n$. □

Corollary 2. *Any probability-one differential over two rounds that holds for all keys is actually a trail of probability-one differentials over the individual rounds.*

In other words we rediscover that, for reasonable s-boxes, there cannot exist a non-trivial differential with probability one over two rounds that holds for all keys.

Note that the left- and right-hand side of the equation $R_1 \circ F \circ R_1^{-1} = R_2^{-1} \circ H \circ R_2$ from Corollary 1 only depend on R_1 and R_2 respectively. If R_1 is a simple s-box layer, and $F = T_\alpha$ for some α, this shows that $R_2^{-1} \circ H \circ R_2$ has in some sense to be aligned with those s-boxes. To make this more precise, we will utilize the results from [20].

4.1   Recent Results Regarding Round Function Decompositions

The basic idea of decomposing a round function into a linear and s-box layer is that we can write an s-box layer as the sum of independent functions defined by the s-boxes, i.e.

$$\begin{pmatrix} S_1(x_1) \\ S_2(x_2) \\ \vdots \\ S_d(x_d) \end{pmatrix} = \begin{pmatrix} S_1(x_1) \\ 0 \\ \vdots \\ 0 \end{pmatrix} + \begin{pmatrix} 0 \\ S_2(x_2) \\ \vdots \\ 0 \end{pmatrix} + \ldots + \begin{pmatrix} 0 \\ 0 \\ \vdots \\ S_d(x_d) \end{pmatrix}.$$

Any linear layer will only change the subspaces induced by the s-boxes.

Definition 4 (Decomposition [20]). *Let* $F : \mathbb{F}_2^n \to \mathbb{F}_2^n$ *bijective. Furthermore, let* $U_1, \ldots, U_d$ *and* $V_1, \ldots, V_d$ *be non-trivial[5] subspaces of* $\mathbb{F}_2^n$ *with* $\bigoplus_i U_i = \mathbb{F}_2^n = \bigoplus_i V_i$, *as well as* $F_i \colon U_i \to V_i$ *with*

$$F(x) = F\left(\sum_i \pi_i^U(x)\right) = \sum_i F_i \circ \pi_i^U(x).$$

We call $\{(U_i, V_i, F_i) \mid 1 \le i \le d\}$ *a decomposition of* F.

---

[5] More precisely, we allow the subspaces to be equal to $\mathbb{F}_2^n$ but not to be $\{0\}$.

As is shown in [20, Lemma 1], knowing the U_i is enough to recover the complete decomposition.

Lemma 5 (Induction of decomposition [20]). *Let $F : \mathbb{F}_2^n \to \mathbb{F}_2^n$ bijective. Let further $U_1, ..., U_d$ be non-trivial subspaces of $\mathbb{F}_2^n$ with $\bigoplus_i U_i = \mathbb{F}_2^n$ and let us define $V_i := F(U_i) + F(0)$. If the V_i are subspaces with $\bigoplus_i V_i = \mathbb{F}_2^n$ and if*

$$F = \sum_i F \circ \pi_i^U + (d+1) \cdot F(0)$$

then $D = \{(U_i, V_i, F_i) \mid 1 \le i \le d\}$ with $F_i := F_{|U_i} + \pi_{l \ne i}^V \circ F(0)$ is a decomposition of F. In this case, we say that $\{U_i \mid 1 \le i \le d\}$ induces the decomposition D.

Additionally, let us recall some basic properties that are useful when working with decompositions.

Corollary 3 ([20]). *Let $F : \mathbb{F}_2^n \to \mathbb{F}_2^n$ bijective and let $\{(U_i, V_i, F_i) \mid 1 \le i \le d\}$ be a decomposition of F. Then, for all i and all $x \in \mathbb{F}_2^n$, we have*

1. *$\pi_i^V \circ F = F_i \circ \pi_i^U$, and*
2. *$\Delta_{\pi_i^U(x)} F = \pi_i^V(\Delta_x F)$, and*
3. *$\Delta_{\pi_i^U(x)} F \in V_i$.*

We can also say something about the decomposition of composite functions.

Corollary 4. *Let $F, G : \mathbb{F}_2^n \to \mathbb{F}_2^n$ be bijective. Further, let $\{(U_i, V_i, F_i) \mid 1 \le i \le d\}$ be a decomposition of F, as well as $\{(V_i, W_i, G_i) \mid 1 \le i \le d\}$ be a decomposition of G. Then $\{(U_i, W_i, G_i \circ F_i) \mid 1 \le i \le d\}$ is a decomposition of $G \circ F$.*

Proof. Since $\{(V_i, W_i, G_i) \mid 1 \le i \le d\}$ is a decomposition of G, we have

$$G \circ F = \sum_i G_i \circ \pi_i^V \circ F = \sum_i G_i \circ F_i \circ \pi_i^U,$$

where the last equality follows from Corollary 3, which completes the proof. $\square$

Finally, let us recall the implications of having two different decompositions. For this, let us recall Lemma 5 and 6, as well as Corollary 9 from [20] in condensed form.[6]

Lemma 6 ([20]). *Let $F : \mathbb{F}_2^n \to \mathbb{F}_2^n$ bijective and let $\{(U_i, V_i, F_i) \mid 1 \le i \le d\}$ and $\{(W_i, X_i, G_i) \mid 1 \le i \le e\}$ be two decompositions of F. Then, we have that F_i is affine on $\mathrm{Im}(\pi_i^U \circ \pi_j^W \circ \pi_{l \ne i}^U)$ for every i, j. Furthermore, if it holds that $\mathrm{Im}(\pi_i^U \circ \pi_j^W \circ \pi_k^U) \ne \{0\}$ for some i, j and $k \ne i$ then*

1. *F_i has maximal differential uniformity, and*
2. *F_k has maximal linearity.*

Knowing this, we can finally move on to analysing the implications that $R_2^{-1} \circ H \circ R_2$ has two different decompositions, as implied by the probability-one differential.

---

[6] For convenience of the reader, we slightly reformulate them by making use of the fact that $\mathrm{Im}(\pi_i^U \circ \pi_j^W) \cap \mathrm{Im}(\pi_i^U \circ \pi_{k \ne j}^W) = \mathrm{Im}(\pi_i^U \circ \pi_j^W \circ \pi_{l \ne i}^U)$ (see [20, Corollary 8]).

4.2   Implications of Two Different Decompositions

Corollary 5. *Let $F, G, R \colon \mathbb{F}_2^n \to \mathbb{F}_2^n$ be all bijective and let $\{(U_i, V_i, H_i) | 1 \le i \le d\}$ be a decomposition of R, as well as $F \xrightarrow{R} G$. Then $\{(U_i, U_i, F_i) | 1 \le i \le d\}$ is a decomposition of F if and only if $\{(V_i, V_i, G_i) | 1 \le i \le d\}$ is a decomposition of G, where F_i and G_i define each other by the equation $G_i = H_i \circ F_i \circ H_i^{-1}$.*

Proof. This is a direct consequence of Corollary 4 and Lemma 3.   □

Remark 2. $\{(U_i, U_i, T_{\pi_i^U(\alpha)}) \mid 1 \le i \le d\}$ is always a decomposition of T_α (for any $\alpha \in \mathbb{F}_2^n$). Hence, for any differential (α, β) over $R_2 \circ R_1$ that holds with probability one, we can always decompose $R_1 \circ T_\alpha \circ R_1^{-1} = R_2^{-1} \circ T_\beta \circ R_2$ according to any decomposition of R_1, but also according to any decomposition of R_2.

Remark 3. Even if $\{(U_i, V_i, F_i) \mid 1 \le i \le d\}$ is a maximal decomposition[7] of R this does not mean that $\{(V_i, V_i, G_i) \mid 1 \le i \le d\}$ is a maximal decomposition of $R \circ T_\alpha \circ R^{-1}$. Trivial examples are the cases in which not all s-boxes are active, i.e. $\pi_i^U(\alpha) = 0$ for some i, as then $G_i := F_i \circ T_{\pi_i^U(\alpha)} \circ F_i^{-1}$ is the identity and can be further decomposed.[8]

With this we can break down the question of the existence of a non-trivial probability-one differential over $R_2 \circ R_1$ into two parts.

Lemma 7. *Let $R_1, R_2 \colon \mathbb{F}_2^n \to \mathbb{F}_2^n$ both be bijective. Then (α, β) is a probability-one differential over $R_2 \circ R_1$ if and only if for any decomposition $\{(U_i, V_i, H_i) \mid 1 \le i \le d\}$ of R_1 it holds that*

1. *$\{V_i \mid 1 \le i \le d\}$ induces a decomposition of $R_2^{-1} \circ T_\beta \circ R_2$, and*
2. *for any j it holds that $\left(R_1 \circ T_\alpha \circ R_1^{-1}\right)_{|V_i} = \left(R_2^{-1} \circ T_\beta \circ R_2\right)_{|V_i}$.*

Proof. Let us assume that (α, β) is a probability-one differential over $R_2 \circ R_1$, i.e. $T_\alpha \xrightarrow{R_2 \circ R_1} T_\beta$. By Corollary 1, this is equivalent to $R_1 \circ T_\alpha \circ R_1^{-1} = R_2^{-1} \circ T_\beta \circ R_2$. Hence, equality has especially to hold for any restriction. Additionally, we know that, for any decomposition $\{(U_i, V_i, H_i) \mid 1 \le i \le d\}$ of R_1, $\{V_i \mid 1 \le i \le d\}$ has to induce a decomposition of $R_1 \circ T_\alpha \circ R_1^{-1}$ and therefore of $R_2^{-1} \circ T_\beta \circ R_2$.

Now, let $\{(U_i, V_i, H_i) \mid 1 \le i \le d\}$ be a decomposition of R_1 such that $\{V_i \mid 1 \le i \le d\}$ induces a decomposition of $R_2^{-1} \circ T_\beta \circ R_2$ and for any j it holds that $\left(R_1 \circ T_\alpha \circ R_1^{-1}\right)_{|V_i} = \left(R_2^{-1} \circ T_\beta \circ R_2\right)_{|V_i}$. Since we know that $\{V_i \mid 1 \le i \le d\}$ also induces a decomposition of $R_1 \circ T_\alpha \circ R_1^{-1}$, we get that

$$R_1 \circ T_\alpha \circ R_1^{-1} = \sum_i R_1 \circ T_\alpha \circ R_1^{-1} \circ \pi_i^V + (d+1) \cdot R_1 \circ T_\alpha \circ R_1^{-1}(0)$$

$$= \sum_i R_2^{-1} \circ T_\beta \circ R_2 \circ \pi_i^V + (d+1) \cdot R_2^{-1} \circ T_\beta \circ R_2(0)$$

$$= R_2^{-1} \circ T_\beta \circ R_2,$$

---

[7] Intuitively, a maximal decomposition means that no s-box can be seen as the composition of two s-boxes. For a precise definition of a maximal decomposition, we refer the interested reader to [20].

[8] As long as $\dim(U_i) \ne 1$ of course, which would already mean that F_i would be affine.

where $R_1 \circ T_\alpha \circ R_1^{-1}(0) = R_2^{-1} \circ T_\beta \circ R_2(0)$ follows from the fact that $0 \in V_i$ for any choice of i. $\qquad\qquad\qquad\qquad\qquad\qquad\qquad\qquad\qquad\qquad\qquad\qquad\qquad\quad\Box$

Note that, if α and β are both zero, those conditions are trivially true, but otherwise they may be not. We will later give a more palatable version of Condition 2, but for now, we will focus on Condition 1.

Recall that Lemma 6 tells us that, under some condition, $R_2^{-1} \circ T_\beta \circ R_2$ has maximal differential uniformity, meaning that (at least) one (first-order) derivative would be constant. This shows a direct link to the boomerang connectivity table (BCT).

Definition 5 ([11]). *Let $U, V \subseteq \mathbb{F}_2^n$ be vector spaces and $R\colon U \to V$ be bijective, then the* boomerang connectivity table (BCT) *is defined as*

$$BCT_F[\alpha, \beta] := \big|\{x \in U | R^{-1}(R(x) + \beta) + R^{-1}(R(x + \alpha) + \beta) = \alpha\}\big|$$

for $\alpha \in U$, $\beta \in V$. Furthermore, the boomerang uniformity is defined as

$$\max_{\alpha \in U \setminus \{0\}, \beta \in V \setminus \{0\}} BCT_R[\alpha, \beta]$$

and we say that it is maximal if it is equal to $|U|$.

The following lemma makes the connection between the BCT and $R_2^{-1} \circ T_\beta \circ R_2$ having maximal differential uniformity more clear, and also provides a similar connection between $R_2^{-1} \circ T_\beta \circ R_2$ having maximal linearity and the existence of linear structures.

Lemma 8. *Let $U, V \subseteq \mathbb{F}_2^n$ be vector spaces and $R\colon U \to V$ be bijective. Then*

1. *for any $\beta \in V \setminus \{0\}$, $R^{-1} \circ T_\beta \circ R$ having maximal differential uniformity is equivalent to R having maximal boomerang uniformity (for output difference β). More precisely, $R^{-1} \circ T_\beta \circ R$ having maximal differential uniformity implies the existence of $\delta \in U \setminus \{0\}$ such that $BCT_R[\delta, \beta] = |U|$, which trivially implies $\Delta_\delta R^{-1} \circ T_\beta \circ R = \delta$, and*
2. *for any $\alpha \in U \setminus \{0\}$, $R \circ T_\alpha \circ R^{-1}$ having maximal linearity is equivalent to R having (at least) one linear structure (with difference α). More precisely, $R \circ T_\alpha \circ R^{-1}$ having maximal linearity implies the existence of $\gamma \in \mathbb{F}_2^n \setminus V^{\perp}$ such that $\langle \gamma, R(x) + R(x + \alpha) \rangle = c$ for any $x \in U$ and some $c \in \mathbb{F}_2$, which trivially implies $\langle \gamma, R \circ T_\alpha \circ R^{-1}(x) \rangle = \langle \gamma, x \rangle + c$ for any $x \in U$.*

Proof. First, let us assume that $R^{-1} \circ T_\beta \circ R$ has maximal differential uniformity, i. e. there exist $\delta, \hat{\delta} \in U \setminus \{0\}$ such that

$$R^{-1} \circ T_\beta \circ R(x) + R^{-1} \circ T_\beta \circ R(x + \delta) = \hat{\delta}.$$

If $\delta = \hat{\delta}$ would hold, then it would already follow that $BCT_R[\delta, \beta] = |U|$. Hence, let us assume that $\delta \neq \hat{\delta}$. As $R^{-1} \circ T_\beta \circ R$ is an involution, it also holds that

$$R^{-1} \circ T_\beta \circ R(x) + R^{-1} \circ T_\beta \circ R(x + \hat{\delta}) = \delta$$

holds for all $x \in U$. Adding those two equations, and substituting x by $x + \delta$, this gives

$$R^{-1} \circ T_\beta \circ R(x) + R^{-1} \circ T_\beta \circ R(x + \delta + \hat{\delta}) = \delta + \hat{\delta}.$$

Now, let us assume that $R \circ T_\alpha \circ R^{-1}$ has maximal linearity, i.e. there exist $\gamma, \hat{\gamma} \in \mathbb{F}_2^n \setminus V^\perp$ such that, for $c = \langle \gamma, R \circ T_\alpha \circ R^{-1}(0) \rangle$, it holds that

$$\langle \gamma, R \circ T_\alpha \circ R^{-1}(x) \rangle = \langle \hat{\gamma}, x \rangle + c \; \forall x \in V.$$

Similar to above, we either have that $\hat{\gamma} = \gamma$, meaning that, by substituting x by $R(x)$

$$\langle \gamma, R(x) + R(x + \alpha) \rangle = c \; \forall x \in U,$$

or we use once more that $R \circ T_\alpha \circ R^{-1}$ is an involution and therefore

$$\langle \hat{\gamma}, R \circ T_\alpha \circ R^{-1}(x) \rangle = \langle \gamma, x \rangle + c \; \forall x \in V.$$

Hence, adding the equations leads to

$$\langle \gamma + \hat{\gamma}, R \circ T_\alpha \circ R^{-1}(x) \rangle = \langle \gamma + \hat{\gamma}, x \rangle \; \forall x \in V,$$

which completes the proof. $\square$

With this, we can state our main result for the differential setting, of which we will provide a more digestible version in Corollary 6.

Theorem 2. *Let $R_1, R_2 \colon \mathbb{F}_2^n \to \mathbb{F}_2^n$ all be bijective. Furthermore, let $\{U_1, U_2\}$ induce a decomposition of R_1^{-1} and let $\{(W_i, X_i, G_i) \mid 1 \leq i \leq e\}$ be a decomposition of R_2. Then (α, β) being a probability-one differential over $R_2 \circ R_1$ has the following implications (for any i).*

1. *If it holds that $\mathrm{Im}(\pi_i^W \circ \pi_1^U \circ \pi_{k \neq i}^W) = \{0\}$, and also $1 \leq \dim(W_i \cap U_1) \leq 2$, as well as $\pi_i^X(\beta) \neq 0$, then it has to hold that*
   (a) *$BCT_{G_i}[\delta, \pi_i^X(\beta)]$ is maximal for some $\delta \in (W_i \cap U_1) \setminus \{0\}$, and*
   (b) *$(\gamma, \pi_j^X(\beta), \langle \gamma, G_j^{-1} \circ T_{\pi_j^X(\beta)} \circ G_j(0) \rangle)$ is a non-trivial linear structure of G_i^{-1} for some $\gamma \in (W_{k \neq i} \oplus (W_i \cap U_2))^\perp \setminus \{0\}$.*
   If $\dim(W_i \cap U_1) = 1$, then δ and γ are unique.
2. *If it holds that $\mathrm{Im}(\pi_i^W \circ \pi_1^U \circ \pi_k^W) \neq \{0\}$ for some $k \neq i$ then it holds that*
   (a) *$\pi_i^X(\beta) = 0$ or $BCT_{G_i}[\delta, \pi_i^X(\beta)]$ is maximal for some $\delta \in W_i$, and*
   (b) *$\pi_k^X(\beta) = 0$ or $(\gamma, \pi_k^X(\beta), c)$ is a non-trivial linear structure of G_k^{-1} for some some $\gamma \in \mathbb{F}_2^n \setminus W_k^\perp$ and $c = \langle \gamma, G_k^{-1}(0) + G_k^{-1}(\pi_k^X(\beta)) \rangle$.*
3. *If it holds that $\mathrm{Im}(\pi_i^W \circ \pi_1^U \circ \pi_{k \neq i}^W) = W_i$ then the map $G_i^{-1} \circ T_{\pi_i^X(\beta)} \circ G_i$ is affine.*

Note that those implications are trivial if $\beta = 0$, but they can be quite strong for non-trivial probability-one differentials. Before we can prove this, we need the following lemma.

Lemma 9. *Let $U_1, U_2, W_1, W_2 \subseteq \mathbb{F}_2^n$ be subspaces with $U_1 \oplus U_2 = \mathbb{F}_2^n = W_1 \oplus W_2$. Then it holds that $\pi_1^W \circ \pi_1^U \circ \pi_2^W = 0$ if any only if $(W_1 \cap U_1) \oplus (W_1 \cap U_2) = W_1$.*

Proof. First, let us assume that $(W_1 \cap U_1) \oplus (W_1 \cap U_2) = W_1$. This means that we are able to find a basis $b_1, ..., b_n$ of $\mathbb{F}_2^n$ such that $\{b_1, ..., b_n\}$ contains a basis of U_1, W_1 and W_2. Since $\pi_1^W \circ \pi_1^U \circ \pi_2^W$ is a composition of linear functions and therefore linear, we will show that every basis vector b_l is mapped to 0. Let us start with looking at $\pi_2^W(b_l)$. We either have $b_l \in W_2$, and therefore $\pi_2^W(b_l) = b_l$, or $\pi_2^W(b_l)$ is already zero. Hence, let us assume that $b_l \in W_2$. Moving to π_1^U, we once more have that either $b_l \in U_1$, thus $\pi_1^U(b_l) = b_l$, or $\pi_1^U(b_l) = 0$. Again, let us assume that $b_l \in U_1$. But then we know that $\pi_1^W(b_l) = 0$, as $b_l \in W_2$ by assumption.

Now, let us assume that $\pi_1^W \circ \pi_1^U \circ \pi_2^W = 0$. According to [20, Corollary 8] this is equivalent to $\mathrm{Im}(\pi_1^W \circ \pi_1^U) \cap \mathrm{Im}(\pi_1^W \circ \pi_2^U) = \{0\}$. Hence, by [20, Corollary 7], $\pi_1^W \circ \pi_1^U = \pi_1^U \circ \pi_1^W$ and $\pi_1^W \circ \pi_2^U = \pi_2^U \circ \pi_1^W$. Similar to how it was done in the proof of [20, Lemma 3], this means that $\mathrm{Im}(\pi_1^W \circ \pi_1^U) = W_1 \cap U_1$ and $\mathrm{Im}(\pi_1^W \circ \pi_2^U) = W_1 \cap U_2$. Hence, $(W_1 \cap U_1) \oplus (W_1 \cap U_2) = W_1$. □

Proof of Theorem 2. Let us start with showing Item 2, i.e. let us assume that $\mathrm{Im}(\pi_i^W \circ \pi_1^U \circ \pi_k^W) \neq \{0\}$ for some $k \neq i$. From Lemma 6 we know that $G_i^{-1} \circ T_{\pi_i^W(\beta)} \circ G_i$ has maximal differential uniformity and $G_k^{-1} \circ T_{\pi_k^W(\beta)} \circ G_k$ has maximal linearity. Hence, the claim follows from Lemma 8.

Next, let us show Item 3, i.e. let us assume that $\mathrm{Im}(\pi_i^W \circ \pi_1^U \circ \pi_{k \neq i}^W) = W_i$. Then it directly follows from Lemma 6 that $G_i^{-1} \circ T_{\pi_i^W(\beta)} \circ G_i$ is affine on $\mathrm{Im}(\pi_i^W \circ \pi_1^U \circ \pi_{k \neq i}^W) = W_i$.

Finally, let us show Item 1, i.e. let us assume that $\mathrm{Im}(\pi_i^W \circ \pi_1^U \circ \pi_{k \neq i}^W) = \{0\}$ holds. By the previous lemma, we know that this is equivalent to $(W_i \cap U_1) \oplus (W_i \cap U_2) = W_i$. Note that, by Corollary 3, for any $w \in W_i$ we have that $\Delta_w R_2^{-1} \circ T_\beta \circ R_2(0) \in W_i$, and for any $v \in W_{k \neq i}$ we have $\Delta_v R_2^{-1} \circ T_\beta \circ R_2(0) \in W_{k \neq i}$. Also, by Corollary 1, for any $u \in U_1$ we have that

$$\Delta_u R_2^{-1} \circ T_\beta \circ R_2(0) = \Delta_u R_1 \circ T_\alpha \circ R_1^{-1}(0) \in U_1.$$

Hence, for any $x \in W_i \cap U_1$ we get that $\Delta_x R_2^{-1} \circ T_\beta \circ R_2(0) \in W_i \cap U_1$. Similar, for any $y \in W_i \cap U_2$ we get $\Delta_y R_2^{-1} \circ T_\beta \circ R_2(0) \in W_i \cap U_2$. Additionally, we know from [20, Lemma 4] that $\{W_{k \neq i}, W_i \cap U_1, W_i \cap U_2\}$ induces a decomposition of $R_2^{-1} \circ T_\beta \circ R_2$, i.e. if we denote the corresponding projections onto $W_i \cap U_1$ and $W_i \cap U_2$ by τ_1 and τ_2 respectively we get

$$\Delta_z R_2^{-1} \circ T_\beta \circ R_2(0) = \Delta_{\pi_{k \neq i}^W(z)} R_2^{-1} \circ T_\beta \circ R_2(0) + \sum_{j=1,2} \Delta_{\tau_j(z)} R_2^{-1} \circ T_\beta \circ R_2(0).$$

Those observations now implies that, for any $z \in \mathbb{F}_2^n$ and any j,

$$\tau_j \left(\Delta_z R_2^{-1} \circ T_\beta \circ R_2(0) \right) = \Delta_{\tau_j(z)} R_2^{-1} \circ T_\beta \circ R_2(0).$$

Moreover, by Corollary 3, for any $w \in W_i$, we have that $\Delta_w R_2^{-1} \circ T_\beta \circ R_2(0) = \Delta_w G_i^{-1} \circ T_{\pi_i^X(\beta)} \circ G_i(0)$, which means that, for any $w \in W_i$ and any j, we can rewrite the equation above to

$$\tau_j \left(\Delta_w G_i^{-1} \circ T_{\pi_i^X(\beta)} \circ G_i(0) \right) = \Delta_{\tau_j(w)} G_i^{-1} \circ T_{\pi_i^X(\beta)} \circ G_i(0).$$

Now, let us assume that $\dim(W_i \cap U_1) \leq 2$. We know that the map $M \colon W_i \cap U_1 \to W_i \cap U_1$ defined by $x \mapsto \Delta_x G_i^{-1} \circ T_{\pi_i^X(\beta)} \circ G_i(0)$ is a bijection, and $M(0) = 0$. Together, this implies that this function must have algebraic degree one, and therefore has to be linear. But this means that, for any $w \in W_i$, we get that

$$\Delta_w G_i^{-1} \circ T_{\pi_i^X(\beta)} \circ G_i(0) = \sum_{j=1,2} \Delta_{\tau_j(w)} G_i^{-1} \circ T_{\pi_i^X(\beta)} \circ G_i(0)$$

$$= \Delta_{\tau_2(w)} G_i^{-1} \circ T_{\pi_i^X(\beta)} \circ G_i(0) + M \circ \tau_1(w).$$

Hence, it is easy to see that for any $\delta \in (W_i \cap U_1) \setminus \{0\}$ the differential $(\delta, M(\delta))$ over $G_i^{-1} \circ T_{\pi_i^X(\beta)} \circ G_i$ holds with probability one, since $\tau_2(\delta) = 0$. Therefore, similar to the proof of Lemma 6, we either get $\delta = M(\delta)$, i.e. $\mathrm{BCT}_{G_i}[\delta, \pi_i^X(\beta)]$ is maximal, or we use that $G_i^{-1} \circ T_{\pi_i^X(\beta)} \circ G_i$ is an involution and get that $\mathrm{BCT}_{G_i}[\delta', \pi_i^X(\beta)]$ is maximal with $\delta' = M(\delta) + \delta \in (W_i \cap U_1) \setminus \{0\}$. Additionally, we know that, for any $w \in W_i$ and any $\hat{\gamma} \in (W_{k \neq i} \oplus (W_i \cap U_2))^{\perp} \setminus \{0\}$,

$$\langle \hat{\gamma}, \Delta_w G_i^{-1} \circ T_{\pi_i^X(\beta)} \circ G_i(0) \rangle = \langle \hat{\gamma}, \Delta_{\tau_2(w)} G_i^{-1} \circ T_{\pi_i^X(\beta)} \circ G_i(0) \rangle + \langle \hat{\gamma}, M \circ \tau_1(w) \rangle$$

$$= \langle \hat{\gamma}, M \circ \tau_1(w) \rangle = \langle (M \circ \tau_1)^T (\hat{\gamma}), w \rangle,$$

as $\Delta_{\tau_2(w)} G_i^{-1} \circ T_{\pi_i^X(\beta)} \circ G_i(0) \in W_i \cap U_2$. Again, similar to the proof of Lemma 6, we either get $\hat{\gamma} = (M \circ \tau_1)^T (\hat{\gamma})$, or we consider $\gamma' = (M \circ \tau_1)^T (\hat{\gamma}) + \hat{\gamma} \in (W_{k \neq i} \oplus (W_i \cap U_2))^{\perp} \setminus \{0\}$. Hence, we know that, for some $\gamma \in (W_{k \neq i} \oplus (W_i \cap U_2))^{\perp} \setminus \{0\}$ and any $w \in W_i$,

$$\langle \gamma, G_i^{-1} \circ T_{\pi_i^X(\beta)} \circ G_i(w) \rangle = \langle \gamma, w \rangle + \langle \gamma, G_i^{-1} \circ T_{\pi_i^X(\beta)} \circ G_i(0) \rangle,$$

and substituting w by $G_i^{-1}(w)$ completes the proof.   □

Note that, by Lemma 8, $G_i^{-1} \circ T_{\pi_i^X(\beta)} \circ G_i$ being affine implies that G_i has maximal boomerang uniformity and G_i^{-1} has (at least) one linear structure. But it even implies more.

Lemma 10. *Let $U, V \subseteq \mathbb{F}_2^n$ be vector spaces and $R \colon U \to V$ be bijective. Furthermore, let $\beta \in V \setminus \{0\}$ such that $R^{-1} \circ T_\beta \circ R$ is affine and let $\alpha := R^{-1} \circ T_\beta \circ R(0)$, i.e. $L \colon U \to U$ with $L := R^{-1} \circ T_\beta \circ R + \alpha$ is linear. Then it holds that*

1. *(α, β) is a differential with probability $2^{-\dim(\mathrm{Im}(L+I))} \geq 2^{-\dim(U)/2}$ over R, where I denotes the identity, and*
2. *$\mathrm{BCT}_R[\delta, \beta] \in \{0, |U|\}$ for all $\delta \in U$, and*
3. *$(\gamma, \beta, \langle \gamma, \alpha \rangle)$ is either a linear structure of R^{-1} or $\mathrm{cor}_{R^{-1} + R^{-1} \circ T_\beta}(0, \gamma) = 0$.*

Proof. Let us start with the first statement. By the definition of L, we have, for all $x \in U$,

$$R^{-1} \circ T_\beta \circ R(x) + x + \alpha = (L + I) \cdot x,$$

which in turn means that

$$R^{-1}(x + \beta) + R^{-1}(x) + \alpha = (L + I) \cdot R^{-1}(x)$$

holds for all $x \in V$. In other words, $R^{-1}(x) + R^{-1}(x + \beta) = \alpha$ holds if and only if $R^{-1}(x) \in \ker(L + I)$. In addition, it is well known that $\dim(U) = \dim(\ker(I + L)) + \dim(\mathrm{Im}(I + L))$. Hence, (β, α) is a differential with probability $2^{\dim(\ker(L+I)) - \dim(U)} = 2^{-\dim(\mathrm{Im}(L+I))}$ over R^{-1}, meaning that (α, β) is a differential with the same probability over R. In addition, it holds that $(I + L)^2 = I + L^2 = 0$ as L has to be an involution, i. e. $\mathrm{Im}(I + L) \subseteq \ker(I + L)$. Hence, $\dim(U) \geq 2 \cdot \dim(\mathrm{Im}(I + L))$, or equivalent $\dim(\mathrm{Im}(I + L)) \leq \frac{\dim(U)}{2}$.

Now, let us prove the second statement. Since $R^{-1} \circ T_\beta \circ R$ is affine, any derivative is constant and the equation $R^{-1} \circ T_\beta \circ R(x) + R^{-1} \circ T_\beta \circ R(x + \delta) = \delta$ is either fulfilled by every or no $x \in U$.

The last statement directly follows from

$$2^{\dim(V)} \cdot \mathrm{cor}_{R^{-1} + R^{-1} \circ T_\beta}(0, \gamma) = \sum_{x \in V} (-1)^{\langle \gamma, R^{-1}(x) + R^{-1} \circ T_\beta(x) \rangle}$$

$$= \sum_{x \in V} (-1)^{\langle \gamma, R^{-1}(x) + L \circ R^{-1}(x) + \alpha \rangle}$$

$$= (-1)^{\langle \gamma, \alpha \rangle} \sum_{x \in V} (-1)^{\langle (I+L)^T \cdot \gamma, R^{-1}(x) \rangle}$$

$$= (-1)^{\langle \gamma, \alpha \rangle} \sum_{y \in U} (-1)^{\langle (I+L)^T \cdot \gamma, y \rangle}$$

$$= \begin{cases} (-1)^{\langle \gamma, \alpha \rangle} \cdot 2^{\dim(U)} & \text{if } \gamma \in \ker\left((I + L)^T\right) \\ 0 & \text{if } \gamma \notin \ker\left((I + L)^T\right) \end{cases}$$

and the fact that $\dim(U) = \dim(V)$ as R is bijective.   □

Next, we will provide more intuition on the result presented above and also give some easy to check conditions that allow to prove the non-existence of probability-one differentials over multiple rounds no matter the key. To make the arguments more easily applicable to standard descriptions of symmetric primitives, we will represent R_1 and R_2 each as an SPN round function in the remainder of this section.

4.3 A Less Technical Interpretation

Remember that a decomposition just means that we can write the functions R_1 (resp. R_2) as the composition of linear layer L_1' (resp. L_2), the parallel application of s-boxes N_1 (resp. N_2) and another linear layer L_1 (resp. L_2'), i. e. $R_1 = L_1 \circ$

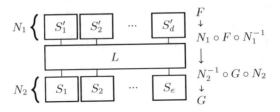

Fig. 2. Probability-one functional trail over a two-round SPN

$N_1 \circ L'_1$ and $R_2 = L'_2 \circ N_2 \circ L_2$. Since the existence of a probability-one differential over $R_2 \circ R_1$ is invariant under linear transformations, we can, without loss of generality, assume that L'_1 and L'_2 are the identity. Also, we can see $L_2 \circ L_1$ as one linear layer L, meaning that we look at $N_2 \circ L \circ N_1$ instead of $R_2 \circ R_1$. Figure 2 shows this well known view of such a two round SPN. Here, we write $N_1 = S'_1 \times S'_2 \times ... \times S'_d$ and $N_2 = S_1 \times S_2 \times ... \times S_e$ where $S'_i : \mathbb{F}_2^{m'_i} \to \mathbb{F}_2^{m'_i}$ and $S_i : \mathbb{F}_2^{m_i} \to \mathbb{F}_2^{m_i}$, i.e. if we define $U_i := 0^{\sum_{l<i} m'_l} \times \mathbb{F}_2^{m'_i} \times 0^{\sum_{l>i} m'_l}$ then $\{(U_i, U_i, 0^{\sum_{l<i} m'_l} \times S'_i \times 0^{\sum_{l>i} m'_l}) \mid 1 \leq i \leq d\}$ is a decomposition of N_1, and if we define $W_i := 0^{\sum_{l<i} m_l} \times \mathbb{F}_2^{m_i} \times 0^{\sum_{l>i} m_l}$ then $\{(W_i, W_i, 0^{\sum_{l<i} m_l} \times S_i \times 0^{\sum_{l>i} m_l}) \mid 1 \leq i \leq e\}$ is a decomposition of N_2.

Let us assume that there exist $F, G : \mathbb{F}_2^n \to \mathbb{F}_2^n$ with $F \xrightarrow{N_2 \circ L \circ N_1} G$. We know from Corollary 1 that there exists an unique trail

$$F \xrightarrow{N_1} N_1 \circ F \circ N_1^{-1} \xrightarrow{L} N_2^{-1} \circ G \circ N_2 \xrightarrow{N_2} G,$$

and we know that the probability-one functional over L is equivalent to

$$N_2^{-1} \circ G \circ N_2 = L \circ N_1 \circ F \circ N_1^{-1} \circ L^{-1}. \tag{7}$$

If we assume that $\{W_i \mid 1 \leq i \leq e\}$ induces a decomposition of G (as it is the case for any translation by an output difference), then we know from Corollary 4 that $\{W_i \mid 1 \leq i \leq e\}$ also induces a decomposition of $N_2^{-1} \circ G \circ N_2$. Similar, assuming that $\{U_i \mid 1 \leq i \leq d\}$ induces a decomposition of F (as it is the case for any translation by an input difference), we know that $\{U_i \mid 1 \leq i \leq d\}$ induces a decomposition of $N_1 \circ F \circ N_1^{-1}$. Note that, by construction, the input and output spaces are identical for each of the two decompositions.

With that, we would like to give an alternative version of Theorem 2 that is plainly based on the linear layer L and the s-boxes of N_2. For this, let us recall how bijective affine transformations impact a decomposition.

Lemma 11 (Lemma 2 of [20]). *Let $F, G : \mathbb{F}_2^n \to \mathbb{F}_2^n$ be bijective and affine equivalent, i.e. $F = A \circ G(B + b) + a$ for invertible matrices $A, B \in \mathbb{F}_2^{n \times n}$ and constants $a, b \in \mathbb{F}_2^n$. Then $\{U_i | 1 \leq i \leq d\}$ induces a decomposition of F if and only if $\{B \cdot U_i | 1 \leq i \leq d\}$ induces a decomposition of G.*

Hence, $\{U_i \mid 1 \le i \le d\}$ inducing a decomposition of $N_1 \circ F \circ N_1^{-1}$ means that $\{L(U_i) \mid 1 \le i \le d\}$ induces a decomposition of $N_2^{-1} \circ G \circ N_2$, and that the corresponding projections onto $L(U_i)$ are $L \circ \pi_i^U \circ L^{-1}$. With that, we can reduce the properties imposed on compositions of the projections to ones imposed on the linear layer L. For this, let us write L and L^{-1} (or more precisely their matrix representation with respect to the standard basis) as block matrices, where the blocks are aligned with the s-boxes in N_1 and N_2, i.e.

$$L = \begin{pmatrix} L_{1,1} & \cdots & L_{1,d} \\ \vdots & & \vdots \\ L_{e,1} & \cdots & L_{e,d} \end{pmatrix} \text{ and } L^{-1} = \begin{pmatrix} (L^{-1})_{1,1} & \cdots & (L^{-1})_{1,e} \\ \vdots & & \vdots \\ (L^{-1})_{d,1} & \cdots & (L^{-1})_{d,e} \end{pmatrix}.$$

With that, the blocks of L and L^{-1} composed with the projections π_i^W and π_j^U are

$$\left(\pi_i^W \circ L \circ \pi_j^U\right)_{a,b} = \begin{cases} L_{i,j} & \text{if } (a,b) = (i,j) \\ 0 & \text{else} \end{cases}$$

and

$$\left(\pi_j^U \circ L^{-1} \circ \pi_l^W\right)_{a,b} = \begin{cases} (L^{-1})_{j,l} & \text{if } (a,b) = (i,j) \\ 0 & \text{else} \end{cases}.$$

Hence,

$$\left(\pi_i^W \circ L \circ \pi_j^U \circ L^{-1} \circ \pi_{l \ne i}^W\right)_{a,b}$$

$$= \left(\sum_{l \ne i} \left(\pi_i^W \circ L \circ \pi_j^U\right) \circ \left(\pi_j^U \circ L^{-1} \circ \pi_l^W\right)\right)_{a,b}$$

$$= \begin{cases} L_{i,j} \cdot (L^{-1})_{j,b} & \text{if } a = i \text{ and } b \ne i \\ 0 & \text{else} \end{cases}.$$

For convenience, let us denote row j of L^{-1} without block $(L^{-1})_{j,i}$ by $(L^{-1})_{j,l \ne i}$. Then our observations above mean that

1. $\text{Im}(\pi_i^W \circ L \circ \pi_j^U \circ L^{-1} \circ \pi_{l \ne i}^W) = 0 \iff \forall l \ne i: L_{i,j} \cdot (L^{-1})_{j,l} = 0$,
2. $\text{Im}(\pi_i^W \circ L \circ \pi_j^U \circ L^{-1} \circ \pi_k^W) \ne 0 \iff L_{i,j} \cdot (L^{-1})_{j,k} \ne 0$,
3. $\text{Im}(\pi_i^W \circ L \circ \pi_j^U \circ L^{-1} \circ \pi_{l \ne i}^W) = W_i \iff L_{i,j} \cdot (L^{-1})_{j,l \ne i}$ has full rank.

With that, we can reformulate Theorem 2 into the following corollary.

Corollary 6. *Let $N_1, N_2, L \colon \mathbb{F}_2^n \to \mathbb{F}_2^n$ be as above. Then the existence of a probability-one differential $((\alpha_1, ..., \alpha_d), (\beta_1, ..., \beta_e))$ over $N_2 \circ L \circ N_1$ has the following implications (for any pair i, j).*

1. *If it holds that $L_{i,j} \cdot (L^{-1})_{j,k \ne i} = 0$, and also $1 \le \text{rank}(L_{i,j}) \le 2$, as well as $\beta_i \ne 0$, then it has to hold that*

(a) $BCT_{S_i}[\delta, \beta_i]$ is maximal for some $\delta \in \mathrm{Im}(L_{i,j}) \setminus \{0\}$, and
(b) $(\gamma, \beta_i, \langle \gamma, S_i^{-1} \circ T_{\beta_i} \circ S_i(0) \rangle)$ is a linear structure of S_i^{-1} for some $\gamma \in$
   $\ker\left(\left(L_{i,k \neq j}\right)^T\right) \setminus \{0\}$.
   If $\mathrm{rank}(L_{i,j}) = 1$, then δ and γ are unique.
2. If it holds that $L_{i,j} \cdot \left(L^{-1}\right)_{j,k} \neq 0$ for some $k \neq i$ then it holds that
   (a) $\beta_i = 0$ or $BCT_{S_i}[\delta, \beta_i]$ is maximal for some $\delta \in \mathbb{F}_2^{m_i}$, and
   (b) $\beta_k = 0$ or (γ, β_k, c) is a linear structure of S_i^{-1} for some $\gamma \in \mathbb{F}_2^{m_k}$ and
      $c = \langle \gamma, S_i^{-1}(0) + S_i^{-1}(\beta_k) \rangle$.
3. If it holds that $L_{i,j} \cdot \left(L^{-1}\right)_{j,k \neq i}$ has full rank, then the map $x \in \mathbb{F}_2^{m_i} \mapsto$
   $S_i^{-1}(S_i(x) + \beta_i)$ is affine.

Remark 4. Note that we do not make any assumptions about the s-boxes in N_1 other than the spaces U_i that they define. Hence, we can see any key/constant addition that happens right before (or right after) the linear layer as part of the s-boxes of N_1, as a simple translation does not affect those spaces.

Now, let us assume that all s-boxes are of equal size m, i.e. $m = m_i = m'_j$ for any i, j, as it is usually the case. Then we can argue based on the differential branch number of L.

Definition 6 (Differential Branch Number [13]). *Let $w \colon (\mathbb{F}_2^m)^d \to \mathbb{N}$ map a vector $(x_1, \ldots, x_d)$ to the number of non-zero coordinates x_i. For a linear map $L \colon (\mathbb{F}_2^m)^d \to (\mathbb{F}_2^m)^d$ the differential branch number of L (over $\mathbb{F}_2^m$) is defined as*

$$\mathcal{B}_d(L) := \min_{x \neq 0} \left(w(x) + w(L(x))\right).$$

Let us also recall [1, Lemma 1].

Lemma 12 ([1]). *Let L be a $dm \times dm$ matrix, decomposed into $m \times m$ submatrices $L_{i,j}$ as above. Then L has differential branch number b (over $\mathbb{F}_2^m$) if and only if all $i \times (d-b+i+1)$ block submatrices of L have full rank for $1 \leq i < b-1$. Moreover, L has linear branch number b if and only if all $(d-b+i-1) \times i$ block submatrices of L have full rank for $1 \leq i < b-1$.*

If the differential branch number of L is at least 3, then Corollary 6 implies the following two corollaries.

Corollary 7. *Let us assume that L has differential branch number of at least 3 and every row of L has a block of full rank. If every s-box $S \colon \mathbb{F}_2^m \to \mathbb{F}_2^m$ of the second non-linear layer has*

1. *differential uniformity smaller than $2^{-m/2}$, or*
2. *no column in the BCT such that each entry is either zero or 2^m, or*
3. *no linear structure (γ, β, c) such that $\mathrm{cor}_{S^{-1}+S^{-1} \circ T_\beta}(0, \gamma') \in \{-1, 0, 1\}$*

then there cannot exist any non-trivial probability-one differential over two rounds.

Proof. Let us fix i. As L, and therefore L^{-1}, has differential branch number of at least 3, we know from the previous lemma that for any j the submatrix $\left(L^{-1}\right)_{j,l\neq i}$ has full rank. Hence, $L_{i,j} \cdot \left(L^{-1}\right)_{j,l\neq i}$ has full rank if and only if $L_{i,j}$ has full rank. By assumption, we know that for every i there exists a j such that $L_{i,j}$ has full rank, which means that we can apply Item 3 of Corollary 6, which, together with Lemma 10, completes the proof. $\square$

Table 1 gives examples where this corollary can be used to directly show that there cannot exist a non-trivial probability-one differential, not matter the key.

Corollary 8. *If L has differential branch number of at least 3 and if the s-boxes of the second non-linear layer either all do not have*

1. *maximal boomerang uniformity, or*
2. *linear structures*

then there cannot exist any non-trivial probability-one differential over two rounds.

Proof. Let i and $l \neq i$ be arbitrary. Since L has differential branch number of at least 3, we know from the lemma above that, for any k, the matrices $L_{i,j\neq k}$ and $\left(L^{-1}\right)_{j\neq k,l}$ both have full rank, which means that

$$L_{i,j\neq k} \cdot \left(L^{-1}\right)_{j\neq k,l} = \sum_{j\neq k} L_{i,j} \cdot \left(L^{-1}\right)_{j,l}$$

must have full rank. But this implies that there exists a j such that $L_{i,j} \cdot \left(L^{-1}\right)_{j,l} \neq 0$, which means that we can apply Item 2 of Corollary 6. If now all s-boxes do not have maximal differential uniformity, we get that the output difference must be zero, i.e. there does not exist a probability-one differential over two rounds. Similar, if all s-boxes do not have linear structures, there also cannot exist a probability-one differential over two rounds. $\square$

Examples of ciphers covered by this corollary are once more given in Table 1. We also get the following corollary.

Corollary 9. *If L is a bit-permutation that maps every output bit of one s-box to a different s-box and if each s-box of the second non-linear layer does not have maximal differential uniformity, then there cannot exist any non-trivial probability-one differential over two rounds.*

Proof. L being a bit-permutation means that its rows and columns are permutations of the standard basis. Together with the fact that L maps every output bit of one s-box to a different s-box this means that $\text{rank}(L_{i,j})$ is either zero or one. Every rank one block now must itself contain a vector of the standard basis (but of $\mathbb{F}_2^m$ instead of $\mathbb{F}_2^{dm}$), which means that the only non-zero elements in the images of the $L_{i,j}$ are standard basis vectors. Note that, as each row of L must have full rank, we actually get the complete standard basis. Hence, if we apply

Item 1 of Corollary 6, we get that there exists a β such that for any s-box S and any i, $\mathrm{BCT}_S[e_i, \beta]$ is maximal, i. e.

$$S^{-1} \circ T_\beta \circ S(x) + S^{-1} \circ T_\beta \circ S(x + e_i) = e_i \ \forall x \in \mathbb{F}_2^m, i.$$

It is now easy to see that, by adding such equations, we get that

$$S^{-1} \circ T_\beta \circ S(x) + S^{-1} \circ T_\beta \circ S(x + y) = y \ \forall x, y \in \mathbb{F}_2^m.$$

By fixing $x = 0$, this gives us

$$S^{-1} \circ T_\beta \circ S(y) + y = S^{-1} \circ T_\beta \circ S(0) \ \forall y \in \mathbb{F}_2^m$$
$$\iff S^{-1}(y + \beta) + S^{-1}(y) = S^{-1} \circ T_\beta \circ S(0) \ \forall y \in \mathbb{F}_2^m.$$

In other words, if $\beta \neq 0$, $(\beta, S^{-1} \circ T_\beta \circ S(0))$ would be a probability-one differential over S^{-1}, meaning that S^{-1}, and therefore S would have maximal differential uniformity, which would be a contradiction to our assumption □

Examples where this corollary is applicable are PRESENT and GIFT, see Table 1.

While Corollaries 7 to 9 already cover a large variety of ciphers, there still exist some, like CRAFT, PRIDE and SKINNY, that are not already covered. For CRAFT and SKINNY, there exist some cells of the output that each only depend on a single cell of the input. As Theorem 2 is based on having two different decompositions, but as one cell of the output depending on only one input-cell means that parts of the two decompositions are identical, it is only reasonable that this theorem cannot directly be used to restrict the output differences for this cell. Still, Theorem 2 can be used to restrict the input and output differences that could potentially lead to a non-trivial probability-one differential to the ones depicted in Table 2 (more details, in addition to an algorithmic interpretation of Theorem 2,[9] are given in the full version of this paper [3]). In order to show that none of those candidates yield a probability-one differential, we can get additional conditions based on the second item of Lemma 7.

Corollary 10. *Let* $N_1, N_2, L \colon \mathbb{F}_2^n \to \mathbb{F}_2^n$ *be as above. If* $((\alpha_1, ..., \alpha_d), (\beta_1, ..., \beta_e))$ *is a probability-one differential over* $N_2 \circ L \circ N_1$ *then it has to hold that*

$$L_{i,j} \cdot S_j' \left((S_j')^{-1}(x) + \alpha_j \right) + \sum_{k \neq j} L_{i,k} \cdot S_k' \left((S_k')^{-1}(0) + \alpha_k \right) = S_i^{-1} \left(S \left(L_{i,j} \cdot x \right) + \beta_i \right)$$

for any i, j *and any* $x \in \mathbb{F}_2^m$.

Proof. From Lemma 7 we know that, for any j, $\left(N_1 \circ T_{(\alpha_1, ..., \alpha_d)} \circ N_1^{-1} \right)_{U_j} = \left(L^{-1} \circ N_2^{-1} \circ T \circ N_2 \circ L \right)_{U_j}$. If we multiply from the left by L this means that, for any i,

$$L_{i,j} \cdot S_j' \left((S_j')^{-1}(x) + \alpha_j \right) + \sum_{k \neq j} L_{i,k} \cdot S_k' \left((S_k')^{-1}(0) + \alpha_k \right) = S_i^{-1} \left(S \left(L_{i,j} \cdot x \right) + \beta_i \right).$$

□

---

[9] This algorithmic version of Theorem 2 is also part of the provided source code.

Table 2. In-/output difference candidates (by Theorem 2).

Cipher	Input Differences	Output Differences	Prob. One Differentials
CRAFT	$0^4 \times 0^4 \times \mathbb{F}_2^4 \times \mathbb{F}_2^4$	$0^4 \times 0^4 \times \mathbb{F}_2^4 \times \mathbb{F}_2^4$	None
PRIDE	$\{\texttt{0x0}, \texttt{0x1}, \texttt{0x8}\}^{16}$	$\{\texttt{0x0}, \texttt{0x1}, \texttt{0x8}\}^{16}$	None
SKINNY-64	$\mathbb{F}_2^4 \times 0^4 \times 0^4 \times 0^4$	$0^4 \times \mathbb{F}_2^4 \times 0^4 \times 0^4$	None
SKINNY-128	$\mathbb{F}_2^8 \times 0^8 \times 0^8 \times 0^8$	$0^8 \times \mathbb{F}_2^8 \times 0^8 \times 0^8$	None

Remark 5. Recall that we moved a potential key/constant addition in the s-boxes S_j'. Hence, instead of directly checking the equation above, one can instead check

$$L_{i,j} \cdot \left(S_j' \left(\left(S_j' \right)^{-1} (x + \kappa) + \alpha_j \right) + S_j' \left(\left(S_j' \right)^{-1} (\kappa) + \alpha_j \right) \right)$$
$$= S_i^{-1} \left(S \left(L_{i,j} \cdot x \right) + \beta_i \right) + S_i^{-1} \left(S \left(0 \right) + \beta_i \right)$$

for any key/constant κ.

For CRAFT and SKINNY, the implications of this corollary are quite obvious, as all blocks $L_{i,j} \in \{0, I\}$, and therefore $\alpha_j \neq 0 \Rightarrow \beta_i \neq 0 \; \forall i$ s.t. $L_{i,j} = I$. As no non-zero difference from Table 2 fulfills this condition, this shows that there cannot exist a non-trivial probability-one differential for CRAFT and SKINNY. Similarly, Corollary 10 can be used to show that the differences from Table 2 for PRIDE are also not possible. For details on this, we refer the interested reader to the full version of this paper [3].

5 Conclusion

We presented algorithms (in the linear case) and conditions (in the differential case) to exclude the existence of weak keys for optimal distinguishers for a few rounds of SPN ciphers. There are several obvious questions that arise, most prominently to generalize to either more rounds or smaller probability or both. We expect that in particular studying non-optimal distinguishers immediately gets very complicated in general. However, we think that generalizing the probability-one differential case from two to more rounds is worth trying. For four rounds, continuing the track we laid out here, one would have to consider superboxes instead of s-boxes and one of the technical question becomes how to ensure that a superbox, i.e., two rounds of an SPN, does not have maximal boomerang uniformity.

From a technical perspective, the striking difference of the differential case, where we can give rather compact criteria, and the linear case, where we have to rely on algorithms to check the properties, can also be seen as a vectorial vs. Boolean variant of the uniqueness property. More precisely while for the vectorial case we can rely on Lemma 6, there does not seem to be a corresponding version for the Boolean case. More general, understanding under which condition a Boolean function allows two essentially different compositions is an interesting future research topic on its own. In terms of questions for Boolean functions and s-boxes, we feel that the s-box property considered in Eq. (6) could be of independent interest in the design of s-boxes and many natural questions in the area of Boolean functions could be discussed in the future.

Acknowledgments. This work was funded by the by the projects *Analysis and Protection of Lightweight Cryptographic Algorithms* (432878529), *Symmetric Cipher Design with Inherent Physical Security* (406956718) and by the Deutsche Forschungs-gemeinschaft (DFG, German Research Foundation) under Germany's Excellence Strategy - EXC 2092 CASA - 390781972.

References

1. Albrecht, M.R., Driessen, B., Kavun, E.B., Leander, G., Paar, C., Yalçın, T.: Block ciphers – focus on the linear layer (feat. PRIDE). In: Garay, J.A., Gennaro, R. (eds.) CRYPTO 2014, Part I. LNCS, vol. 8616, pp. 57–76. Springer, Heidelberg (2014). https://doi.org/10.1007/978-3-662-44371-2_4
2. Beierle, C., Beyne, T., Felke, P., Leander, G.: Constructing and deconstructing intentional weaknesses in symmetric ciphers. In: Dodis, Y., Shrimpton, T. (eds.) Proceedings of the 42nd Annual International Cryptology Conference on Advances in Cryptology, CRYPTO 2022, Part III. LNCS, Santa Barbara, CA, USA, 15–18 August 2022, vol. 13509, pp. 748–778. Springer, Heidelberg (2022). https://doi.org/10.1007/978-3-031-15982-4_25
3. Beierle, C., Felke, P., Leander, G., Neumann, P., Stennes, L.: On perfect linear approximations and differentials over two-round SPNs. Cryptology ePrint Archive, Paper 2023/725 (2023). https://eprint.iacr.org/2023/725
4. Beierle, C., et al.: The SKINNY family of block ciphers and its low-latency variant MANTIS. In: Robshaw, M., Katz, J. (eds.) CRYPTO 2016, Part II. LNCS, vol. 9815, pp. 123–153. Springer, Heidelberg (2016). https://doi.org/10.1007/978-3-662-53008-5_5
5. Beierle, C., Leander, G., Moradi, A., Rasoolzadeh, S.: CRAFT: lightweight tweakable block cipher with efficient protection against DFA attacks. IACR Trans. Symmetric Cryptol. **2019**(1), 5–45 (2019). https://doi.org/10.13154/tosc.v2019.i1.5-45
6. Bellini, E., Makarim, R.H.: Functional cryptanalysis: application to reduced-round Xoodoo. IACR Cryptol. ePrint Arch., p. 134 (2022). https://eprint.iacr.org/2022/134
7. Beyne, T.: Block cipher invariants as eigenvectors of correlation matrices. J. Cryptol. **33**(3), 1156–1183 (2020). https://doi.org/10.1007/s00145-020-09344-1
8. Beyne, T., Rijmen, V.: Differential cryptanalysis in the fixed-key model. In: Dodis, Y., Shrimpton, T. (eds.) Proceedings of the42nd Annual International Cryptology Conference Advances in Cryptology, CRYPTO 2022, Part III. LNCS, Santa Barbara, CA, USA, 15–18 August 2022, vol. 13509, pp. 687–716. Springer, Heidelberg (2022). https://doi.org/10.1007/978-3-031-15982-4_23
9. Biham, E., Shamir, A.: Differential cryptanalysis of DES-like cryptosystems. In: Menezes, A.J., Vanstone, S.A. (eds.) CRYPTO 1990. LNCS, vol. 537, pp. 2–21. Springer, Heidelberg (1991). https://doi.org/10.1007/3-540-38424-3_1

10. Carlet, C. (ed.): Boolean Functions for Cryptography and Coding Theory. Cambridge University Press (2020). https://doi.org/10.1017/9781108606806

11. Cid, C., Huang, T., Peyrin, T., Sasaki, Yu., Song, L.: Boomerang connectivity table: a new cryptanalysis tool. In: Nielsen, J.B., Rijmen, V. (eds.) EUROCRYPT 2018. LNCS, vol. 10821, pp. 683–714. Springer, Cham (2018). https://doi.org/10.1007/978-3-319-78375-8_22

12. Daemen, J.: Cipher and hash function design, strategies based on linear and differential cryptanalysis, Ph.D. Thesis. K.U. Leuven (1995). http://jda.noekeon.org/

13. Daemen, J., Rijmen, V.: The wide trail design strategy. In: Honary, B. (ed.) Cryptography and Coding 2001. LNCS, vol. 2260, pp. 222–238. Springer, Heidelberg (2001). https://doi.org/10.1007/3-540-45325-3_20

14. Daemen, J., Rijmen, V.: Plateau characteristics. IET Inf. Secur. 1(1), 11–17 (2007). https://doi.org/10.1049/iet-ifs:20060099, https://doi.org/10.1049/iet-ifs:20060099

15. Dinur, I., Dunkelman, O., Keller, N., Ronen, E., Shamir, A.: Efficient detection of high probability statistical properties of cryptosystems via surrogate differentiation. In: Advances in Cryptology, EUROCRYPT 2023. LNCS, Lyon, France, 23–27 April 2023, vol. 14007. Springer, Heidelberg (2023). https://doi.org/10.1007/978-3-031-30634-1_4

16. Dobraunig, C., Eichlseder, M., Mendel, F., Schläffer, M.: ASCON v1.2: lightweight authenticated encryption and hashing. J. Cryptol. 34(3), 33 (2021). https://doi.org/10.1007/s00145-021-09398-9

17. Fourquet, R., Loidreau, P., Tavernier, C.: Finding good linear approximations of block ciphers and its application to cryptanalysis of reduced round DES. In: Workshop on Coding and Cryptography, WCC 2009 (2009). https://perso.univ-rennes1.fr/pierre.loidreau/articles/wcc_2009/wcc_2009.pdf

18. Guo, H., et al.: Differential attacks on CRAFT exploiting the involutory s-boxes and tweak additions. IACR Trans. Symmetric Cryptol. 2020(3), 119–151 (2020). https://doi.org/10.13154/tosc.v2020.i3.119-151

19. Kuijsters, D., Verbakel, D., Daemen, J.: Weak subtweakeys in SKINNY. IACR Cryptol. ePrint Arch., p. 1042 (2022). https://eprint.iacr.org/2022/1042

20. Lambin, B., Leander, G., Neumann, P.: Pitfalls and shortcomings for decompositions and alignment. In: Hazay, C., Stam, M. (eds.) Advances in Cryptology, EUROCRYPT 2023. LNCS, vol. 14007. Springer, Cham (2023). https://doi.org/10.1007/978-3-031-30634-1_11

21. Leander, G., Rasoolzadeh, S.: Weak tweak-keys for the CRAFT block cipher. IACR Trans. Symmetric Cryptol. 2022(1), 38–63 (2022). https://doi.org/10.46586/tosc.v2022.i1.38-63

22. Matsui, M.: Linear cryptanalysis method for DES cipher. In: Helleseth, T. (ed.) EUROCRYPT 1993. LNCS, vol. 765, pp. 386–397. Springer, Heidelberg (1994). https://doi.org/10.1007/3-540-48285-7_33

23. Nyberg, K., Knudsen, L.R.: Provable security against a differential attack. J. Cryptol. 8(1), 27–37 (1995). https://doi.org/10.1007/BF00204800

24. Peyrin, T., Wang, H.: The MALICIOUS framework: embedding backdoors into tweakable block ciphers. In: Micciancio, D., Ristenpart, T. (eds.) CRYPTO 2020, Part III. LNCS, vol. 12172, pp. 249–278. Springer, Cham (2020). https://doi.org/10.1007/978-3-030-56877-1_9

25. Vaudenay, S.: Provable security for block ciphers by decorrelation. In: Morvan, M., Meinel, C., Krob, D. (eds.) STACS 1998. LNCS, vol. 1373, pp. 249–275. Springer, Heidelberg (1998). https://doi.org/10.1007/BFb0028566

Differential Meet-In-The-Middle Cryptanalysis

Christina Boura[1][✉], Nicolas David[2], Patrick Derbez[3], Gregor Leander[4], and María Naya-Plasencia[2]

[1] Université Paris-Saclay, UVSQ, CNRS, Laboratoire de mathématiques de Versailles, 78000 Versailles, France
christina.boura@uvsq.fr
[2] Inria, Paris, France
{nicolas.david,maria.naya-plasencia}@inria.fr
[3] Univ Rennes, Inria, CNRS, IRISA, Rennes, France
patrick.derbez@irisa.fr
[4] Ruhr University Bochum, Bochum, Germany
gregor.leander@rub.de

Abstract. In this paper we introduce the differential meet-in-the-middle framework, a new cryptanalysis technique for symmetric primitives. Our new cryptanalysis method combines techniques from both meet-in-the-middle and differential cryptanalysis. As such, the introduced technique can be seen as a way of extending meet-in-the-middle attacks and their variants but also as a new way to perform the key recovery part in differential attacks. We apply our approach to SKINNY-128-384 in the single-key model and to AES-256 in the related-key model. Our attack on SKINNY-128-384 permits to break 25 out of the 56 rounds of this variant and improves by two rounds the previous best known attacks. For AES-256 we attack 12 rounds by considering two related keys, thus outperforming the previous best related-key attack on AES-256 with only two related keys by 2 rounds.

Keywords: differential cryptanalysis · meet-in-the-middle cryptanalysis · SKINNY, AES

1 Introduction

Since the 1970's and the standarization of the DES block cipher hundreds of different symmetric primitives have been designed to address special needs and industrial requirements or to provide an answer to particular research problems. A fundamental procedure that permits to decide which among those primitives can be trusted and safely deployed is cryptanalysis. The first modern symmetric cryptanalysis techniques were developed in the late 1970's, 1980's and in the beginning of the 1990's. Among these first and most important attacks are, of course meet-in-the-middle [21], differential [8] and linear cryptanalysis [39], but also boomerang [46] and rectangle attacks [6], impossible differential [5,35], higher-order differential [36] or differential-linear attacks [37]. More attacks appeared

© International Association for Cryptologic Research 2023
H. Handschuh and A. Lysyanskaya (Eds.): CRYPTO 2023, LNCS 14083, pp. 240–272, 2023.
https://doi.org/10.1007/978-3-031-38548-3_9

in succession to new designs, as for example the square attack [17], particularly well-adapted to AES-like constructions or the subspace invariant attacks [38] that worked well against some particular lightweight ciphers. In parallel, some techniques, as the division property [44], permitted to define a new algorithmic framework to generalize older attacks. As the field is well advanced, nowadays, it is more and more rare to come up with entirely new cryptanalysis techniques, while improvements of the known ones are more common.

Among the existing cryptanalysis techniques, differential attacks [8] are among the oldest and the best studied cryptanalysis methods. Their idea is to exploit an input difference that propagates through the cipher to an output difference with a high probability. Through the years, these attacks have been refined and many improvements to different parts of the attack procedure have been introduced: the use of structures to build up the plaintext or ciphertext pairs [9], the use of truncated differentials [36], conditional differentials [34], the technique of probabilistic neutral bits [16] or refinements in the key recovery process, to mention only a few. A first research question in link with our work is the following:

Question 1. Do there exist alternative methods for doing the key recovery step of a differential attack more efficiently?

Another popular – and actually even older – technique that has been useful in many cryptanalysis applications, and the subject of a large number of improvements and further studies is meet-in-the-middle (MITM) cryptanalysis [21]. The idea of basic MITM attacks is to split the cipher into two parts, where each part can be computed with partial knowledge of the key. An attacker can then validate partial key guesses by checking for a match in the middle. Again, many extensions and refinements of the basic attack exist today: the technique of partial matching, where only a part of the middle state is known, guessing some bits of the internal state [24], the all-subkeys approach [31], the splice-and-cut technique [1,2,28] and the sieve-in-the-middle (SITM) approach [14] that permits to extend the length of a MITM attack by searching for a match through an extra S-box layer in the middle. Finally, the method of bicliques is a cryptanalysis technique [12] that aims at extending MITM attacks by some rounds. A second research problem of interest to us and that motivated our initial work is:

Question 2. Can we find a new way to extend a MITM attack to more rounds?

In this paper we provide a positive answer to both questions simultaneously by proposing a new cryptanalysis technique that we call the *differential meet-in-the-middle attack*. The idea of this new technique is to use a differential to cover several middle rounds of the cipher while running a meet-in-the-middle attack on its external rounds. In a nutshell, this combination has many potential advantages. In particular, with our new technique, a middle part of the cipher is covered by a differential and thus we have to apply MITM techniques on much less rounds than with all previous MITM-type attacks. Note that Demirci-Selçuk MITM attacks [19] applied with the differential enumeration technique [23] also combine to some extent truncated differentials and the MITM approach, but in this case the guess is done in parallel on the inner part (with a truncation-based distinguisher) and the external part, trying to match some particular properties of the differential set. Interestingly, our new method can also be interpreted as a differential attack where the key recovery step is done in a different way. Indeed, starting from a given plaintext-ciphertext pair, we guess in parallel the input keys that allow us to compute a matching plaintext ensuring the given input difference of the differential, and the output keys that allow us to compute the ciphertext that ensures the output difference of the differential, and compute the associated plaintext for all these ciphertexts by making calls to the oracle. Next, we try to match the list of plaintexts computed with the guesses of the input key bits and the list of plaintexts computed with the list of output keys by finding a collision. We repeat this for enough plaintexts so that we can expect one of them to satisfy the differential. All collisions found will imply a potential candidate for the associated guess of keys. The matching can usually be done efficiently with list merging algorithms like the ones in [41].

In order to demonstrate the efficiency of our new cryptanalysis technique, we provide two applications. First, we apply the attack in the single-key setting to the block cipher SKINNY and we show how to break 25 out of the 56 rounds of SKINNY-128-384, the 128-bit block variant employing a 384-bit key. Our attack improves by two the number of rounds of the previous best attack against this variant in the single-key model. A summary of the best attacks against SKINNY-128-384 is given in Table 1.[1] Then, we provide an application to AES-256 by breaking 12 rounds of the cipher in the related-key model. Our attack uses only 2 related keys, whereas the best previous attacks with this number of related keys could reach at most 10 rounds. A summary of the best attacks against AES-256 is given in Table 2.

Table 1. Best attacks against SKINNY-128-384 in the single-key (SK) model together with the results presented in this paper. ID stands for impossible differentials, MITM for meet-in-the-middle attacks and DS-MITM for Demirci-Selçuk-type MITM.

# Rounds	Data	Time	Memory	Type	Ref.
21	2^{123}	$2^{353.6}$	2^{341}	ID	[47]
21	$2^{122.89}$	$2^{347.35}$	2^{336}	ID	[30]
22	2^{96}	$2^{382.46}$	$2^{330.99}$	DS-MITM	[43]
22	$2^{92.22}$	$2^{373.48}$	$2^{147.22}$	ID	[45]
23	2^{104}	2^{376}	2^{8}	MITM	[22]
23	2^{117}	$2^{361.9}$	$2^{118.5}$	Diff-MITM	Sect. 3.2
24	2^{117}	$2^{361.9}$	2^{183}	Diff-MITM	Sect. 3.4
24	$2^{122.3}$	$2^{372.5}$	$2^{123.8}$	Diff-MITM	Sect. 3.5
25	$2^{122.3}$	$2^{372.5}$	$2^{188.3}$	Diff-MITM	Sect. 3.5

---

[1] Note that [30] provides a 26-round integral attack against SKINNY-128-384 but it relies on differences in the tweak.

Table 2. Best attacks against `AES-256` together with the results presented in this paper. † The parameter s should be such that $0 \leq s \leq 7.5$.

# Rounds	Data	Time	Memory	# Related-key	Type	Ref.
9	2^{120}	2^{203}	2^{203}	0	MITM	[20]
10	2^{114}	2^{173}	2^{64}	64	Rectangle	[7,33]
14	$2^{99.5}$	$2^{99.5}$	2^{56}	4	Boomerang	[11]
14	2^{91+s}	2^{92+s}	2^{89-s}	2^{19-s}	Boomerang	[29] †
14	$2q$	$q2^{66}$	-	$2q$	q-multicollisions	[27]
14	2^{125}	2^{125}	2^{65}	2^{32}	basic RK differential	[27]
12	2^{89}	2^{206}	$2^{71.6}$	2	Diff-MITM	Sect. 4

The rest of the paper is organized as follows. Section 2 describes the general framework of our new cryptanalysis technique, compares it to both differential and MITM attacks and provides several improvements. Our attacks against `SKINNY-128-384` are described in Sect. 3 and our application on `AES-256` is given in Sect. 4. Finally, several open problems are discussed in Sect. 5.

2   The New Attack: Differential MITM

We propose in this work a new cryptanalysis technique against symmetric primitives. This new attack aims at combining meet-in-the-middle (MITM) attacks together with differential cryptanalysis, and we will call this new technique *differential MITM*. The original motivation of our work was to investigate whether there exists a method for reaching more rounds than the sieve-in-the-middle attack [14,15], an extension of classical MITM attacks. However, our technique can also be interpreted as a new key-recovery method to apply in differential cryptanalysis, that can be sometimes combined with MITM improvements for reaching more rounds. We will present in this section a high-level description of the new technique. More precisely, we will provide a general framework that describes how to mount a differential MITM attack in a generic and simple way, and we will show how to combine this generic method with two techniques: the parallel treatment of data partitions in order to add one round mostly for free (idea that inherits from MITM attacks, like bicliques, and that cannot be applied to classical differential attacks), as well as a technique to reduce the data complexity.

2.1   General Framework

Consider a n-bit cipher E decomposed into three sub-ciphers: $E_{out} \circ E_m \circ E_{in}$, as depicted in Fig. 1. Let the number of rounds of E_{in}, E_m and E_{out} be r_{in}, r_m and r_{out} respectively. Finally, let Δ_x be the input difference to the middle part E_m, Δ_y the output difference of E_m and suppose that the differential $\Delta_x \to \Delta_y$, covering the r_m middle rounds, has probability 2^{-p}.

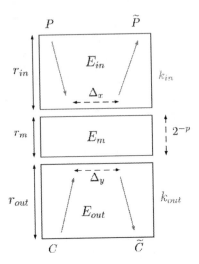

Fig. 1. A high-level description of the Differential MITM technique.

We start our analysis with a first randomly chosen plaintext P and its associated ciphertext C, and we aim at generating a second plaintext-ciphertext pair $(\widetilde{P}, \widetilde{C})$ such that together they satisfy the differential on the middle rounds. Our new idea is to generate $(\widetilde{P}, \widetilde{C})$ with a meet-in-the-middle approach. For this, candidate plaintexts $\widetilde{P}$ are computed from both the plaintext P and the difference Δ_x for each possible value of the associated key k_{in}, while candidate ciphertexts $\widetilde{C}$ are computed from C and Δ_y for each possible value of the involved key, k_{out}. The match is then performed on the relation $E(\widetilde{P}) = \widetilde{C}$ (or $\widetilde{P} = E^{-1}(\widetilde{C})$). Note that the roles of the upper and lower part can be interchanged without loss of generality in order to optimize the data and memory complexity, if we consider that the access to both the encryption and the decryption oracles is granted.

Upper Part. Given P, the aim is to guess the minimal amount of key information, that we will denote by k_{in}, such that we can compute the associated $\widetilde{P}$ that ensures $E_{in}(P) \oplus E_{in}(\widetilde{P}) = \Delta_x$ if the guess of k_{in} corresponds to the secret key. For each guess i for k_{in}, we obtain a different candidate for $\widetilde{P}$, that we denote by $\widetilde{P}^i$, leading to a total of $2^{|k_{in}|}$ such values. From them, we can compute the $2^{|k_{in}|}$ associated ciphertexts $\widehat{C}^i = E(\widetilde{P}^i)$ with calls to the encryption oracle and store them in a hash table H.

Lower Part. Similarly, given C, we can guess some key material k_{out}, of bitlength $|k_{out}|$, and compute a new ciphertext $\widetilde{C}$ that satisfies the equation $E_{out}^{-1}(C) \oplus E_{out}^{-1}(\widetilde{C}) = \Delta_y$ if the key guess is correct. We obtain $2^{|k_{out}|}$ values for $\widetilde{C}^j$, each associated to a guess j for k_{out}.

Number of Pairs and Match. For the correct key guess, the transition $\Delta_x \to \Delta_y$ will happen with a probability 2^{-p}. Therefore, we will repeat the upper and lower procedures 2^p times with 2^p different messages P_ℓ so that we can expect one pair $(P_\ell, \widetilde{P}_\ell^i)$ to satisfy the differential together with the associated pair $(C_\ell, \widetilde{C}_\ell^j)$. When this is the case, we will find a collision for a certain ℓ between a $\widehat{C}_\ell^i$ computed in the upper part and stored in H and a $\widetilde{C}_\ell^j$ computed from the lower part. Each collision (i, j) has an associated key guess $k_{in} = i, k_{out} = j$, that we will consider as a potential candidate. The number of expected collisions for each fixed P_ℓ is $2^{|k_{in}|+|k_{out}|-|k_{in}\cap k_{out}|-n}$.

Algorithm 1. Differential MITM attack

---

    while right key not found **do**   ▷ 2^p trials expected
        Randomly pick P
        $C \leftarrow E(P)$ ▷ Oracle call
        $H \leftarrow \emptyset$ ▷ hash table initialization
        for each guess i for k_{in} **do**   ▷ Forward computation
            Compute $\widetilde{P}^i$ from i and P
            $\widehat{C}^i \leftarrow E(\widetilde{P}^i)$ ▷ Oracle call
            $H[\widehat{C}^i] \leftarrow H[\widehat{C}^i] \cup \{i\}$
        end for
        for each guess j for k_{out} **do**   ▷ Backward computation
            Compute $\widetilde{C}^j$ from j and C
            for each $i \in H[\widetilde{C}^j]$ **do**
                Complete (i, j) to retrieve the master key
                Try candidates against extra data
            end for
        end for
    end while

Complexity. The time complexity of this attack can be estimated as

$$\mathcal{T} = 2^p \times \left(2^{|k_{in}|} + 2^{|k_{out}|}\right) + 2^{|k_{in}|+|k_{out}|-|k_{in}\cap k_{out}|-n+p},$$

where the first term corresponds to the computations done in E_{in} and E_{out}, and the last one to the number of expected key candidates. With this, we recover $k_{in} \cup k_{out}$, so if we expect fewer key candidates than the whole set $k_{in} \cup k_{out}$, (i.e. $|k_{in}| + |k_{out}| - |k_{in} \cap k_{out}| - n + p < |k_{in} \cup k_{out}|$, which holds as long as $p < n$), we can guess the remaining bits of the master key and test the guess with additional pairs. Thus we recover the whole key with a complexity smaller than the cost of an exhaustive key search, and an additional cost of

$$2^{k-(|k_{in}\cup k_{out}|)} \times \max\{1, 2^{|k_{in}|+|k_{out}|-|k_{in}\cap k_{out}|-n+p}\}$$

to be added to the time complexity $\mathcal{T}$. In the expected case where $|k_{in}| + |k_{out}| - |k_{in} \cap k_{out}| - n + p \geq 0$, the total time complexity is thus

$$\mathcal{T} = 2^p \times \left(2^{|k_{in}|} + 2^{|k_{out}|}\right) + 2^{|k_{in}\cup k_{out}|-n+p} + 2^{k-n+p}.$$

The (naive) data complexity of this first version of the attack can be estimated as

$$\mathcal{D} = \min(2^n, 2^{p+\min(|k_{in}|,|k_{out}|)}).$$

Finally, the naive memory complexity is given by $\mathcal{M} = 2^{\min(|k_{in}|,|k_{out}|)}$, though it can be improved to $2^{\min(|k_{in}|-|k_{in}\cap k_{out}|,k_{out}-|k_{in}\cap k_{out}|)}$ by first guessing the common key material before running the attack.

2.2   Improvement: Parallel Partitions for Layers with Partial Subkeys

We will show now that in the case where the round key addition does not affect the whole state but only a part of it (as is for instance the case in Feistel constructions [25], or in the SKINNY [4] and GIFT [3] ciphers), we can extend the attack by one round. As we will show, if the m bits of the state affected by the key addition are such that $m < p$ (where p is the $-\log_2$ of the probability of the differential distinguisher), the time complexity of adding this round will not be affected. However, the exact data complexity of the attack has to be checked case-by-case, as it might depend on the configuration of the differences in the external states. A technique on how to reduce the data complexity will be further discussed in Sect. 2.3. The memory complexity might be a priori increased.

The main idea here is to consider, in addition to guessing in parallel the key bits intervening in the lower and upper parts, a partial parallel guess of the final states. More precisely, 2^m penultimate and final states (or the initial state, without loss of generality) will be guessed in parallel, without needing to guess the key that allows the transition from the penultimate one to the final. When performing the final match, we will take into account this key transition. Actually, it can be seen as considering 2^m plaintexts P_i and ciphertexts C_j in parallel, without knowing which ones would match together, as this transition is determined by the last round-key.

Since we expect to try on average 2^p plaintexts in order to find one that will satisfy the differential of probability 2^{-p}, we can divide the final state of size 2^n into two parts. The part without the key addition will take 2^{p-m} different values, and the attack will be repeated for each one of those.

On the other hand, the part affected by the key addition will take 2^m possible values for X, the state before the key addition, and for each we can compute the state S_{r-1} in Fig. 2 from the output of the differential MITM attack. From this state, we will guess the k_{out} bits, in order to compute the associated state potentially generating the output difference of the middle differential, obtaining $2^{|k_{out}|+m}$ candidates to match. In parallel, the state Y after the key addition will also take all the 2^m possibilities, and with them we decrypt in order to obtain the plaintext, and do the upper key guessing procedure to deduce the good pairs, obtaining $2^{|k_{in}|+m}$ candidates. The number of possible solutions might seem higher by a factor of 2^{2m}, but note that we have to match X and Y, as well as their associated pairs X' and Y', and they must satisfy $X \oplus X' = Y \oplus Y'$. This adds m bit-conditions, or more if this final subkey was already determined by k_{in} and k_{out}, which is usually the case. This implies m additional conditions, and $2^{2m}2^{-m}2^{-m} = 1$, so the cost, given by the number of solutions, stays exactly the same as the attack with one round less. We will see how this technique can be applied in practice in Sect. 3.

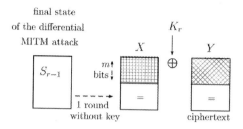

Fig. 2. Partial guess of the final state to add one round for free. S_{r-1} is the final state of the simple differential MITM attack.

2.3 Improvement: Reducing Data with Imposed Conditions

We explain here a way to obtain time-data-memory trade-offs for the original attack. If when choosing the plaintext P, we force x of its bits, that might have been active otherwise, to a certain value, and if we expect the same from the associated plaintext $\widetilde{P}$, the overall probability of the attack will decrease to 2^{-p-x}, as we will have to repeat the procedure until a $\widetilde{P}$ that satisfies this constraint is found. More precisely, if $\widetilde{P}$ does not fit this condition, the corresponding tuple will not be stored in the hash table since we do not have access to its ciphertext. However by doing so, the data complexity will be reduced by a factor of 2^x as well as the memory complexity. When combining this technique with the previous one, we can derive the following two inequalities for x:

$$p + x \le n - x \quad \text{and} \quad 2^{p+x}(2^{|k_{in}|} + 2^{|k_{out}|}) < 2^k.$$

This type of trade-off applies in particular when all the code book of size 2^n is needed before fixing the x bits, and the data complexity becomes 2^{n-x}.

Data Reduction Without Time Increase. As the total number of candidates for the key of the input part (respectively output) will be $2^{|k_{in}|-x}$ (respectively $2^{|k_{out}|-x}$), if we are able to find these candidates with their associated $\widetilde{P}$ (respectively $\widetilde{C}$) in a complexity given by the number of solutions, the time complexity would become:

$$2^{p+x}(2^{|k_{in}|-x} + 2^{|k_{out}|-x}) = 2^p(2^{|k_{in}|} + 2^{|k_{out}|}),$$

which allows us to reduce the data complexity to 2^{n-x} while not increasing the time complexity. The optimal data complexity in this case will be $2^{\frac{n+p}{2}}$, obtained with x equal to $\frac{n-p}{2}$.

This can actually be done in many cases using rebound-like techniques [40]. This is the case for all our attacks summarized in Table 1. An example can be seen in Sect. 3.

2.4   Discussion and Comparison

As argued before, our new cryptanalysis technique is closely related to two families of techniques: MITM attacks and differential attacks. In this section we will discuss similarities and differences between these families and will try to identify cases where our new technique might be efficient or cases where it permits to reach better results compared to the best known attacks.

Relation to MITM Attacks. In relation to MITM attacks and its variants, like the sieve-in-the-middle technique, our attack, already if using a differential with probability one, could have, a priori, the potential of reaching more rounds. The starting point of our research was whether it was possible to add even more rounds in the middle of a MITM-like attack and this is how we came up with the new attack. The data complexity of the new attack could be higher than a classical MITM one as now we compute a new $\widetilde{P}$ from each guess of the key, and this plaintext can take many different values, besides the 2^p different plaintexts P_ℓ taken as starting points in order to find one that satisfies the differential. On the other hand, despite the fact that the sets of bits k_{in} or k_{out} involved in the parallel computations of the differential MITM attack are not determined in the same way as the key bits involved in MITM attacks, we expect those quantities to be relatively close under similar settings, as this principally depends on the propagation properties of the round function. More precisely, it seems that more aligned [13] the round function is, closer the sets will be.

Therefore, we expect that ciphers where classical MITM attacks work well, can also be interesting targets for differential MITM attacks. This is actually how we found the application shown in Sect. 3 on SKINNY. Indeed, the best known attack against SKINNY-384-128 previous to ours was a MITM one [22].

Relation to Differential Attacks. Curiously enough, our new attack can also be seen as a new way of performing the key-recovery part associated to a differential distinguisher.

Classical Differential Attacks. A differential attack starts with a differential distinguisher on r_m rounds of relatively high probability 2^{-p}. One then typically extends the distinguisher by r_{in} rounds to reach the plaintext state and by r_{out} rounds to reach the ciphertext state, with probability 1 as depicted in Fig. 3. Structures are then used to build plaintext (or ciphertext) pairs. A structure of size 2^s allows to build 2^{2s-1} pairs (though building all these pairs is rarely needed), but for each structure we need to consider typically an additional probability so that the pairs from the structure satisfy the input difference of the distinguisher. If we are not considering truncated but fixed differentials, as it will be our case, the probability of reaching a fixed difference Δ_x is approximately 2^{-s}. In order to expect that at least one pair will satisfy the distinguisher, we will need to consider 2^{p-s+1} structures, each of size 2^s, and for each structure, 2^{s-1} pairs will reach the input difference Δ_x, leading to a total of $2^{p-s+1+s-1} = 2^p$ pairs reaching Δ_x. Typically, for determining a priori potential good pairs, one performs some sieving that will allow not to try all the pairs from all the structures. This sieving is done by looking at the activity pattern of the ciphertexts and can be estimated as $2^{-c} = 2^{-n+a}$, where a is the bit-size of the active part in the ciphertext. The key recovery part depends on the particular properties of the round function. Its complexity can be often accurately lower bounded by the number of the partial key candidates in the key-recovery rounds, thanks to early abort and divide-and-conquer techniques.

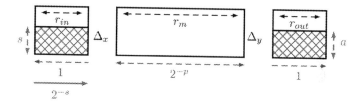

Fig. 3. Framework of a classical differential attack.

The data complexity of such an attack is 2^{p+1} and the time complexity can be estimated as

$$2^{p+1} + 2^{p-s+1}2^{2s-1}2^{-c}C_k \approx 2^{p+s-n+a}, \tag{1}$$

where C_k is the average cost of determining the key bits for each candidate pair. This quantity can be lower bounded by the number of partial key candidates in the key-recovery rounds and this number can be much greater than 1 if the key is bigger than the state.

We can see that if s and a are big enough, i.e. $a + s \gg n$, which can happen when several rounds are appended, the complexity of a differential MITM attack for an equivalent number of rounds might be more interesting. Indeed, the influence of the input and output extensions to the complexity are added and not multiplied. In particular, our attack can become much more efficient when the key size of the cipher is bigger than the state size, otherwise 2^p might already be close to the limit.

3 Differential Meet-the-Middle Attacks Against SKINNY-128-384

We provide in this section our applications to SKINNY-128-384. We start by recalling the specifications of the SKINNY family of ciphers.

3.1   Specifications of SKINNY

The SKINNY family of tweakable block ciphers was designed by Beierle et al. [4]. It is a family of lightweight ciphers following a classical SPN structure but implementing a very compact S-box, a linear layer based on a sparse non-MDS binary matrix and a lightweight key schedule. The block size n can be 64 or 128 bits and for both versions the state is seen as a 4×4 matrix of 4-bit or 8-bit cells. Row 0 is considered the uppermost one and column 0 is taken to be the leftmost one. The numbering of the words inside the state matrix is as follows.

0	1	2	3
4	5	6	7
8	9	10	11
12	13	14	15

SKINNY follows the tweakey framework [32] and XORs a tweakey to the two upmost rows of the state. There exist three main variants for the tweakey size: $t = n$, $t = 2n$ and $t = 3n$ and the corresponding variant is denoted by SKINNY-n-t. Furthermore, the tweakey to block size ratio is denoted by $z = t/n$. The tweakey state is viewed also as a set of z 4×4 arrays of cells. For $z = 3$, which is the variant of interest to us, the three tweakey arrays are denoted by **TK1**, **TK2** and **TK3**.

The round function of SKINNY is depicted on Fig. 4, and the number of times this function is iterated depends on both n and t, as shown in Table 3.

Table 3. Number of rounds for each of the main variants SKINNY-n-t.

Block size n	$t = n$	$t = 2n$	$t = 3n$
64	32	36	40
128	40	48	56

One round of SKINNY is composed of five operations applied in the following order: SubCells (SC), AddConstants (AC), AddRoundTweakey (ART), ShiftRows (SR) and MixColumns (MC). We now briefly describe the operations that are of interest to us.

SubCells (SC) This operation applies an S-box to all cells of the state. The table representation of the 8-bit S-box S used in the 128-bit variants is

```
S = [ 65 4c 6a 42 4b 63 43 6b 55 75 5a 7a 53 73 5b 7b
      35 8c 3a 81 89 33 80 3b 95 25 98 2a 90 23 99 2b
      e5 cc e8 c1 c9 e0 c0 e9 d5 f5 d8 f8 d0 f0 d9 f9
      a5 1c a8 12 1b a0 13 a9 05 b5 0a b8 03 b0 0b b9
      32 88 3c 85 8d 34 84 3d 91 22 9c 2c 94 24 9d 2d
      62 4a 6c 45 4d 64 44 6d 52 72 5c 7c 54 74 5d 7d
      a1 1a ac 15 1d a4 14 ad 02 b1 0c bc 04 b4 0d bd
      e1 c8 ec c5 cd e4 c4 ed d1 f1 dc fc d4 f4 dd fd
      36 8e 38 82 8b 30 83 39 96 26 9a 28 93 20 9b 29      ·
      66 4e 68 41 49 60 40 69 56 76 58 78 50 70 59 79
      a6 1e aa 11 19 a3 10 ab 06 b6 08 ba 00 b3 09 bb
      e6 ce ea c2 cb e3 c3 eb d6 f6 da fa d3 f3 db fb
      31 8a 3e 86 8f 37 87 3f 92 21 9e 2e 97 27 9f 2f
      61 48 6e 46 4f 67 47 6f 51 71 5e 7e 57 77 5f 7f
      a2 18 ae 16 1f a7 17 af 01 b2 0e be 07 b7 0f bf
      e2 ca ee c6 cf e7 c7 ef d2 f2 de fe d7 f7 df ff ] .
```

AddRoundTweakey (ART). We describe this step only for the variants with $z = 3$. Here, the first and second rows of the 3 tweakey arrays **TK1**, **TK2** and **TK3** are extracted and XORed to the internal state, respecting the bit positions inside the arrays. More formally, if $IS_{i,j}$ is the cell at the intersection of row i and j of the state, we have that for $(i, j) \in \{0, 1\} \times \{0, 1, 2, 3\}$:

$$IS_{i,j} = TK1_{i,j} \oplus TK2_{i,j} \oplus TK3_{i,j}.$$

ShiftRows (SR). This operation rotates the cells inside a row to the right by a certain offset that depends on the row. More precisely, cells in row i, where $0 \leq i < 4$, are rotated by i positions to the right.

MixColumns (MC). This operation updates the state by multiplying each column by a binary matrix **M**. This matrix, as well as its inverse are as follows.

$$\mathbf{M} = \begin{pmatrix} 1 & 0 & 1 & 1 \\ 1 & 0 & 0 & 0 \\ 0 & 1 & 1 & 0 \\ 1 & 0 & 1 & 0 \end{pmatrix}, \quad \mathbf{M}^{-1} = \begin{pmatrix} 0 & 1 & 0 & 0 \\ 0 & 1 & 1 & 1 \\ 0 & 1 & 0 & 1 \\ 1 & 0 & 0 & 1 \end{pmatrix}.$$

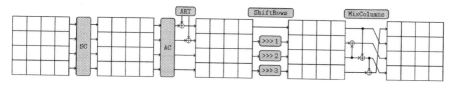

Fig. 4. Round function of SKINNY [4].

Next we describe the tweakey schedule of SKINNY-128-384, the variant we analyse in this work.

Tweakey Schedule of SKINNY-128-384. At each round, all tweakey arrays are updated as follows (see also Fig. 5). First, the same permutation P_T is applied on the cell positions of the 3 tweakey arrays: for all $0 \leq i \leq 15$, we have that $\mathbf{TK1}_i \leftarrow \mathbf{TK1}_{P_T[i]}$ with

$$P_T = [9, 15, 8, 13, 10, 14, 12, 11, 0, 1, 2, 3, 4, 5, 6, 7],$$

and the same exact permutation is applied to the cells of $\mathbf{TK2}$ and $\mathbf{TK3}$. Finally, the cells of the first two rows of $\mathbf{TK2}$ and $\mathbf{TK3}$ are individually updated by the LFSR:

$$(x_7||x_6||x_5||x_4||x_3||x_2||x_1||x_0) \rightarrow (x_0 \oplus x_6||x_7||x_6||x_5||x_4||x_3||x_2||x_1),$$

where x_0 is the LSB in a byte.

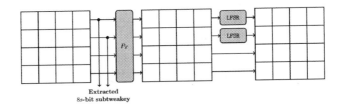

Extracted
$8s$-bit subtweakey

Fig. 5. Tweakey schedule of SKINNY. All tweakey arrays $\mathbf{TK1}$, $\mathbf{TK2}$ and $\mathbf{TK3}$ follow the same transformation with the only exception that no LFSR is applied to $\mathbf{TK1}$. [4]

Property. In most attacks, including ours, it is more efficient to guess round-key bits than key bits. Since the key-schedule of SKINNY is fully linear, guessing enough (e.g. 384 in the $\mathbf{TK3}$ model) independent round-key bits allows to uniquely determine the master key and thus all remaining round-key bits. SKINNY has a unique property that makes the evaluation of the dimension of any set of round-key bytes easy: in the $\mathbf{TKx}$ model, a round-key byte $K_r[i]$ always depends on exactly x master key bytes, one from each $\mathbf{TK}$ key and they all have the same index. Furthermore, given x round-key bytes from the 30 first rounds and depending on the same x master key bytes, they are always independent and allow to uniquely determine their x corresponding master key bytes.

We present now 3 attacks against round-reduced variants of SKINNY-128-384 by using our new differential meet-in-the-middle technique. We first describe a simple attack against 23 rounds as well as several improvements and trade-offs. We then explain how this attack can be extended to an attack on 24 rounds without increasing the attack's overall complexity. Finally, we describe a new attack against 25 rounds.

3.2 An Attack Against 23-Round SKINNY-128-384

As explained in Sect. 2, differential meet-in-the-middle attacks rely on two classical cryptanalysis techniques: differential attacks and meet-in-the-middle attacks. The main idea is to use a meet-in-the-middle attack to generate a pair following a given differential in the middle rounds. Thanks to this procedure, we are able to extend a differential distinguisher by more rounds than with a classical early-abort procedure, as discussed in Sect. 2.4.

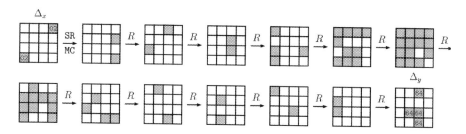

Fig. 6. Truncated differential trail for the attack on 23 rounds.

Differential. The truncated differential used in our attack against 23 rounds of SKINNY-128-384 is depicted in Fig. 6. It has 56 active S-boxes, without counting those of the first and the last round. We verified that this truncated differential can be successfully instantiated by using the constrained programming Choco-solver [42], and more precisely the model developed by Delaune *et al.* to search for the best differential characteristics for the SKINNY family of block ciphers [18].

The best instantiation of this truncated differential has a probability of 2^{-119} and there are in total 2048 instantiations with this same probability. These instantiations can be divided into four groups $(\Delta_x^{(i)}, \Delta_y^{(i)})$, for $i = 1, 2, 3, 4$, each one having 512 trails inside, starting with the same difference $\Delta_x^{(i)}$ and terminating after 13 rounds with the same difference $\Delta_y^{(i)}$. We found as well many more differential trails with the same input/output differences but smaller probabilities: 2560 with probability 2^{-120}, 7168 with probability 2^{-121}, 18432 with probability 2^{-122} and 44800 with probability 2^{-123}. Thus the probability of the differential depicted on Fig. 6 is higher than $2^{-105.9}$.

The Attack. We describe now our core attack against 23-round SKINNY-128-384.

1. Ask for the encryption of the whole codebook.
2. Randomly pick one plaintext/ciphertext pair (P, C).
3. For each possible value i of k_{in} compute the tuple $(P, \widetilde{P}, i)$ so that the difference on the state after the 6th S-box layer is $[0\ 0\ 0\ 2\ 0\ 0\ 0\ 0\ 0\ 0\ 0\ 2\ 0\ 0\ 0]$ (see Fig. 6). Doing so requires to know the values of all the active S-boxes involved in the probability 1 transition $\Delta_x \rightarrow \Delta_P$, where Δ_P is the plaintext difference, and k_{in} is the set of subkey bytes needed to compute them from the plaintext.

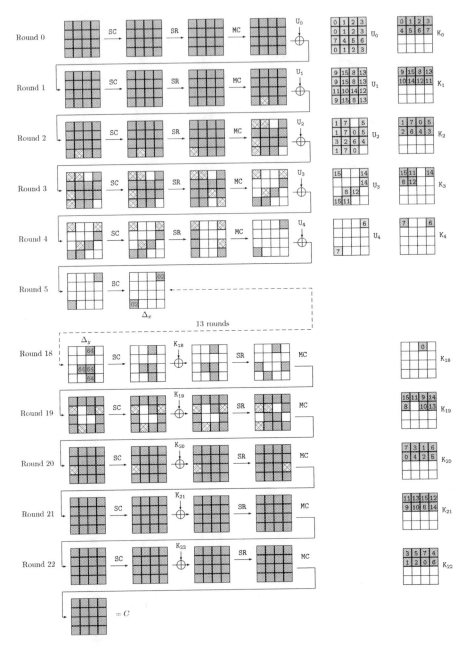

Fig. 7. Core attack against 23 rounds of SKINNY-128/384. Knowledge of blue key bytes allows to compute values of green ones and thus to propagate differences. No difference in both white and red bytes, but the red ones are required to compute green bytes. Indexes in subkey bytes are the indexes of the corresponding master key bytes. The equivalent subkeys U$_i$ are computed as MC(SR(K$_i$)), from the original subkeys K$_i$. (Color figure online)

4. Store all these tuples in a hash table. This step requires to guess 31 subkey bytes as depicted in Fig. 7.
5. Similarly, for each possible value j of k_{out} compute the tuple $(C, \widetilde{C}, j)$ so that the difference on the state before the 19th S-box layer is 0x64 on all active bytes. The set k_{out} involves 32 bytes and thus there are 2^{256} such tuples.
6. For each of them check for possible matches on the hash table. The match is performed on both the new ciphertext (i.e. $(\widetilde{P}, \widetilde{C})$ must be a valid plaintext/ciphertext pair) as well as on the linear relations between the subkey bytes of the upper and lower guess.
7. Each match leads to a (full) key candidate that can be tried against very few additional plaintexts (3 in our case).
8. Repeat from Step 2 until the right key is retrieved.

Table 4. Subkey bytes involved in the 23-round core attack.

Byte	k_{in}	k_{out}	# equations
0	$K_0[0], K_2[2]$	$K_{18}[2], K_{20}[4], K_{22}[6]$	2
1	$K_0[1], K_2[0]$	$K_{20}[2], K_{22}[4]$	1
2	$K_0[2], K_2[4]$	$K_{20}[6], K_{22}[5]$	1
3	$K_0[3], K_2[7]$	$K_{20}[1], K_{22}[0]$	1
4	$K_0[4], K_2[6]$	$K_{20}[5], K_{22}[3]$	1
5	$K_0[5], K_2[3]$	$K_{20}[7], K_{22}[1]$	1
6	$K_0[6], K_2[5], K_4[3]$	$K_{20}[3], K_{22}[7]$	2
7	$K_0[7], K_2[1], K_4[0]$	$K_{20}[0], K_{22}[2]$	2
8	$K_1[2], K_3[4]$	$K_{19}[4], K_{21}[6]$	1
9	$K_1[0]$	$K_{19}[2], K_{21}[4]$	0
10	$K_1[4]$	$K_{19}[6], K_{21}[5]$	0
11	$K_1[7], K_3[1]$	$K_{19}[1], K_{21}[0]$	1
12	$K_1[6], K_3[5]$	$K_{21}[3]$	0
13	$K_1[3]$	$K_{19}[7], K_{21}[1]$	0
14	$K_1[5], K_3[3]$	$K_{19}[3], K_{21}[7]$	1
15	$K_1[1], K_3[0]$	$K_{19}[0], K_{21}[2]$	1

The data complexity of this attack is 2^{128} since in Step 1 we ask for the encryption of the full codebook. The memory complexity is determined by Step 3 in which 2^{248} words of $128 + 248 = 376$ bits each are stored. Note that we do not need to store C_1 since it is common to all tuples. Thus the memory complexity is $2^{249.5}$ 128-bit words. The time complexity is 2^{248} for computing the hash table, 2^{256} for performing Step 4, and, as shown in Table 4, $k_{in} \cup k_{out}$ is the full key so that the complexity of Step 6 is $2^{384-128} = 2^{256}$. Finally, the attack has to be repeated $2^{105.9}$ times (the probability of the distinguisher) in order to construct one right differential pair. Hence, the overall complexity of our attack is $2^{105.9} \times 2^{256} = 2^{361.9}$.

Decreasing Memory Complexity. It is possible to decrease the memory complexity of the attack by avoiding the match on the linear relations between both k_{in} and k_{out}. Indeed, since the key-schedule of SKINNY is fully linear, we can first guess the intersection of k_{in} and k_{out}, and only then run the attack. The dimension of the intersection is $248 + 256 - 384 = 120$ and thus the memory complexity can be decreased to $2^{249.5-120} = 2^{129.5}$.

Data-Time-Memory Trade-Off. To decrease the data complexity of our attack, as described in Sect. 2.3, it is possible to only ask for the encryption of a portion of the whole codebook, let say 2^{128-x} plaintext/ciphertext pairs. In this case, the probability that we have access to the corresponding ciphertext of $\widetilde{P}$ is 2^{-x} and the attack has to be ran 2^x times to compensate. Overall, the complexity of our 23-round attack is then $\mathcal{D} = 2^{128-x}$ plaintext/ciphertext pairs, $\mathcal{M} = 2^{129.5-x}$ 128-bit words and $\mathcal{T} = 2^{361.9+x}$ encryptions. To expect at least one pair following the differential under the extra constraint on the plaintexts, x cannot be higher than $(128 - 105.9)/2 = 11.05$.

As explained in Sect. 2.3, in practice, given any pair of ciphertexts, we can enumerate the possible values for both k_{in} and k_{out} with a complexity roughly equivalent to the number of solutions. Such a procedure is described in Sect. 3.3. Thus, the trade-off does not increase the time complexity and the overall complexity of our attack is $D = 2^{117}$, $T = 2^{361.9}$ and $M = 2^{118.5}$.

3.3   Enumeration Procedure of k_{out} for the 23-Round Attack

In this section we describe a procedure to retrieve the possible values of k_{out} in the case where the pair of ciphertexts is given. Its complexity is 2^{128} simple operations, showing that the data/time/memory trade-off described in Sect. 2.3 can be applied without increasing the time complexity. Since the key is not applied on the full state, the procedure is more complex than a classical rebound but still relies on the fact that, on average, knowing the differences at both the input and output of an Sbox leads to one pair of actual values.

The steps of our enumeration procedure are depicted on Fig. 8. The main idea is to propagate differences from the ciphertexts to Round 18, get the actual values since differences in this internal state are fully known, and propagate them back to the ciphertexts to obtain the key material we want. Except from Step 1 in which we guess 8 values, all following steps perform one guess each. Steps 7 and 8 have both a probability of success of 2^{-8} and thus we expect only $2^{13 \times 8} = 2^{104}$ partial solutions at the end of Step 8.

3.4   Extension to 24 Rounds

Our differential meet-in-the-middle attack against 23-round SKINNY can be extended to an attack against 24 rounds without increasing its overall complexity by using the generic improvement presented in Sect. 2.2. This can be achieved since on one hand the key-schedule is linear (and enough subkey bytes are involved in our attack so that the master key is fully retrieved) and on the

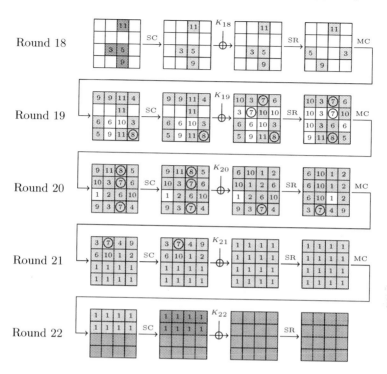

Fig. 8. Enumeration procedure of k_{out} for the 23-round attack. Differences in blue cells and actual values in red cells are known. No difference in white cells. (Color figure online)

other hand the subkey is only applied on half of the state in each round. The scenario of this new attack is quite similar to the original one:

1. Ask for the encryption of the whole codebook.
2. Pick 2^{64} plaintext/ciphertext pairs (P_ℓ, C_ℓ) such that $\text{MC}^{-1}(C_\ell)$ is constant on the last two rows as depicted in Fig. 9. Here we exploit the fact that the round key is only applied on the first two rows of the internal state.
3. As for this original attack, compute all possible tuples $(P_\ell, \widetilde{P}^i_\ell, i)$ for each value i of k_{in} and each P_ℓ from the structure defined at the previous step such that the state difference after the 6th S-box layer is 0x02 on both active bytes.
4. Store them in a hash table. Note that the tuples are computed for all the 2^{64} plaintexts selected at Step 2 so the memory complexity is $2^{248+64} = 2^{312}$ 504-bit words.
5. For each value j of k_{out} and each state $S_{23,\ell}$ coherent with Step 2 (i.e. 2^{64} states, one for each possible value of the subkey K_{23}), compute all possible tuples $(S_{23,\ell}, \widetilde{S}^j_{23,\ell}, j)$ so that the difference on the state before the 19th S-box layer is 0x64 on the four active bytes.
6. Check for possible matches on the hash table. The match is now performed on three quantities:

- the difference between the last states: $C \oplus \widetilde{C} = \mathtt{MC} \circ \mathtt{SR}(\mathtt{SC}(S_{23}) \oplus \mathtt{SC}(\widetilde{S}_{23}))$. This is a 64-bit filter because the difference is zero on the two last rows since $\mathtt{MC}^{-1}(C)$ is constant on these rows.
- the filter on the keys (from key schedule equations): a 120-bit filter as for the original attack against 23 rounds (15 equations on 8 bits each, see Table 4).
- the filter on the keys (from equations describing the last round). Indeed, since $k_{in} \cup k_{out}$ generates the master key, K_{23} can be rewritten as $f(k_{in}) \oplus g(k_{out})$ where f and g are both linear and, because of the linearity of all the operations, the equation $C = \mathtt{MC}(\mathtt{SR}(\mathtt{SC}(S_{23}) \oplus K_{23}))$ can thus be rewritten as $C \oplus \mathtt{MC}(\mathtt{SR}(f(k_{in}))) = \mathtt{MC}(\mathtt{SR}(\mathtt{SC}(S_{23}) \oplus g(k_{out})))$. This represents a 64-bit filter.

7. Repeat from Step 2 until the right key is retrieved.

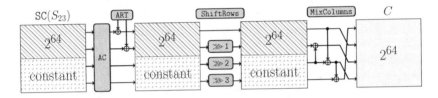

Fig. 9. Last round of the attack against 24 rounds.

The attack has to be repeated enough times so that the structure contains at least one pair following the differential. Since during Step 2 we generate 2^{64} pairs and since the probability of the differential is $2^{-105.9}$, the procedure has to be repeated $2^{41.9}$ times. Thus the data complexity is 2^{128} (i.e. the whole codebook is needed), the memory complexity is around 2^{314} 128-bit words and the time complexity $2^{256+64+41.9} = 2^{361.9}$ encryptions.

Note that previous improvements regarding both the memory and data complexities still apply and thus our attack has complexity: $\mathcal{D} = 2^{128-11} = 2^{117}$ plaintext/ciphertext pairs, $\mathcal{M} = 2^{194-11} = 2^{183}$ 128-bit words and $\mathcal{T} = 2^{361.9}$ encryptions.

3.5   An Attack Against 25 Rounds of SKINNY-128-384

To mount a differential meet-in-the-middle attack against 25 rounds of SKINNY, we used the differential depicted in Fig. 10. The best instantiation of this truncated differential has a probability of 2^{-131}. By fixing the difference of the active bytes to 0x32 at the input and to 0x64 at the output, we found several instantiations with a high enough probability: 2048 with probability 2^{-131}, 10240 with 2^{-132}, 28672 with 2^{-133} and finally 73728 trails with probability 2^{-134}. Thus, the probability of the depicted differential is higher than $2^{-116.5}$. This differential is then extended by 4 rounds to the plaintext and 5 rounds to the ciphertext to reach 24 rounds as depicted in Fig. 11.

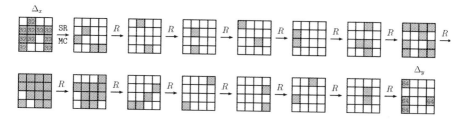

Fig. 10. Truncated differential trail for the attack on 25 rounds.

The key bytes involved in the attack are given in Table 5, leading to a complexity of $\mathcal{D} = 2^{128}$ data, $\mathcal{T} = 2^{256} \times 2^{116.5} = 2^{372.5}$ encryptions and $\mathcal{M} = 2^{249.5}$ 128-bit words. Furthermore, the dimension of the intersection between both k_{in} and k_{out} is once again $248 + 256 - 384 = 120$, which allows to reduce the memory complexity to $2^{129.5}$ 128-bit words.

Table 5. Subkey bytes involved in the 24-round core attack.

Byte	k_{in}	k_{out}	# equations
0	$K_0[0], K_2[2]$	$K_{20}[4], K_{22}[6]$	1
1	$K_0[1], K_2[0]$	$K_{20}[2], K_{22}[4]$	1
2	$K_0[2], K_2[4]$	$K_{20}[6], K_{22}[5]$	1
3	$K_0[3], K_2[7]$	$K_{20}[1], K_{22}[0]$	1
4	$K_0[4], K_2[6]$	$K_{20}[5], K_{22}[3]$	1
5	$K_0[5], K_2[3]$	$K_{22}[1], K_{24}[0]$	1
6	$K_0[6], K_2[5]$	$K_{20}[3], K_{22}[7]$	1
7	$K_0[7], K_2[1]$	$K_{20}[0], K_{22}[2]$	1
8	$K_1[2], K_3[4]$	$K_{21}[6], K_{23}[5]$	1
9	$K_1[0], K_3[2]$	$K_{21}[4], K_{23}[6]$	1
10	$K_1[4], K_3[6]$	$K_{21}[5], K_{23}[3]$	1
11	$K_1[7], K_3[1]$	$K_{21}[0], K_{23}[2]$	1
12	$K_1[6]$	$K_{21}[3], K_{23}[7]$	0
13	$K_1[3], K_3[7]$	$K_{21}[1], K_{23}[0]$	1
14	$K_1[5], K_3[3]$	$K_{21}[7], K_{23}[1]$	1
15	$K_1[1], K_3[0]$	$K_{19}[0], K_{21}[2], K_{23}[4]$	2

As for the 23-round attack described above, this attack can be extended by one round without increasing its overall complexity. As a consequence, and after applying the data/time/memory trade-off presented in Sect. 2.3, the complexity of our attack against 25 rounds is $\mathcal{D} = 2^{128-x}$ plaintext/ciphertext pairs, $\mathcal{M} = 2^{194-x}$ 128-bit words and $\mathcal{T} = 2^{372.5+x}$ encryptions. In this case, x cannot be higher than $(128 - 116.5)/2 = 5.75$. Furthermore, we can again apply this trade-off without increasing the time complexity and thus the final complexity is $D = 2^{122.3}$, $T = 2^{372.5}$ and $M = 2^{188.3}$.

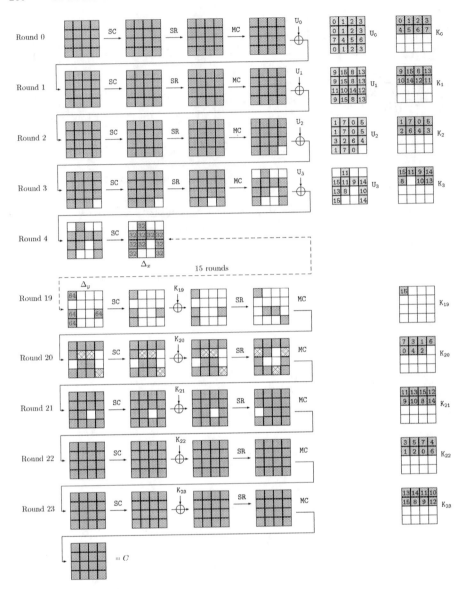

Fig. 11. Core attack against 24 rounds of SKINNY-128-384. Knowledge of blue key bytes allows to compute values of green ones and thus to propagate differences. No difference in both white and red bytes, but the red ones are required to compute green bytes. Indexes in subkey bytes are the indexes of the corresponding master key bytes. (Color figure online)

3.6   Comparison of the Attacks on SKINNY-128-384 with Differential Attacks

One may wonder whether the improved attacks on SKINNY-128-384 and in particular the one reaching 25 rounds, are exclusively due to the quality and the length of the differential distinguisher used. In this section we show that this is not the case, and that the best classical differential attacks that we could build using the same differential reached strictly less rounds than our attack. We show that even when considering optimal lower bounds for the complexities of classical differential attacks, it is not possible to reach more than 24 rounds for SKINNY-128-384 this way. This shows that differential MITM attacks can reach more rounds than differential ones in certain scenarios.

A lower bound on the complexity of differential attacks can be determined in part by the number of partial key candidates. When the key schedule is linear, as in SKINNY, the partial candidates for the key can be obtained optimally and in parallel for the input and the output, and can then be merged with respect to the common information between both partial keys, given by the key schedule.

In particular, for 24 rounds of SKINNY-128-384 starting from the differential of Fig. 10, and considering all the possible combinations for the number of input, r_{in}, and output, r_{out} rounds, the complexity, given by Eq. (1), cannot be smaller than:

$$2^{116+128}(2^{120} + 2^{128} + 2^{120+128-120}) = 2^{373},$$

where the parameters (with respect to Eq. (1)) are $p = 116$, $s = 128$, $c = 0$, and $C_k = (2^{120} + 2^{128} + 2^{120+128-120})$. As the number of pairs needed to find one pair that verifies the input difference and also the differential path is $2^{116+128}$, we need a structure of size 2^{122}. If we solve both parts sequentially, the complexity will exceed exhaustive search, as the most of the external keys are independent of those in the other part. Instead, considering both parts in parallel, we have $64 + 64 + 64 + 56$ keybits involved in the input for a condition on 128 bits of recovering the input difference (so 2^{120} key candidates), and $64 + 64 + 64 + 56 + 8$ keybits involved in the output part, with 128-bit conditions (so 2^{128} key candidates). The memory need is 2^{128} for the parallel computation. The linear relations between both partial keys are $64 + 56$, given by the even and odd subkeys respectively. So the previous result provides a lower bound on the complexity that such an attack would obtain. If we try to add one extra round and attack 25 rounds, a minimal additional factor of 2^{64} has to be added to one of the parallel computations, as the number of partial solutions will increase by this amount. This would be too expensive and we can therefore conclude that we cannot build classical differential attacks on 25 rounds of SKINNY-128-384 based on this distinguisher.

This extra round can be added in our case due to the different nature of the attack, and its relation to MITM cryptanalysis. Therefore, it is fair to conclude that in this case, differential meet-in-the-middle attacks are more powerful than classical differential attacks, reaching one extra round while having a similar complexity.

4   New Attack Against 12-Round AES-256 in the related-key setting

To show how powerful our new cryptanalysis technique is, we propose an application against AES-256 in the related-key model. It is well known that this version of AES was fully broken by Biryukov and Khovratovich in [11]. However, this attack is a boomerang one and thus requires 4 related keys as well as both encryption and decryption oracles. In our case, we propose an attack in the chosen plaintext setting and requiring only 2 related keys. It is depicted in Fig. 14 and uses a differential characteristic similar to the one from [10].

In this section we first give a short description of AES-256, then we explain the key generation process that has to be performed by the adversary and finally we explain the whole attack.

4.1   Description of AES-256

The Advanced Encryption Standard [26] is a Substitution-Permutation Network (SPN) that can be instantiated using three different key sizes: 128, 192, and 256 bits. The 128-bit plaintext initializes the internal state viewed as a 4×4 matrix of bytes, i.e. values in the finite field $\mathbb{F}_{256}$, which is defined using the irreducible polynomial $x^8 + x^4 + x^3 + x + 1$ over $\mathbb{F}_2$. Depending on the version of the AES, N_r rounds are applied to that state and $N_r = 14$ for the 256-bit version. Each of the N_r rounds (see Fig. 12) applies four operations to the state matrix (except in the last round where the MixColumns operation is omitted):

- AddRoundKey (AK) adds a 128-bit subkey to the state.
- SubBytes (SB) applies the same 8-bit to 8-bit invertible S-Box **S** 16 times in parallel on each byte of the state.
- ShiftRows (SR) shifts the i-th row left by i positions.
- MixColumns (MC) replaces each of the four columns C of the state by $M \times C$ where M is a constant 4×4 maximum distance separable matrix over $\mathbb{F}_{256}$.

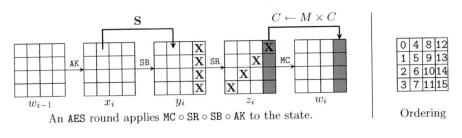

An AES round applies MC ∘ SR ∘ SB ∘ AK to the state.   Ordering

Fig. 12.   Description of one AES round and the ordering of bytes in an internal state

After the N_r-th round has been applied, a final subkey is added to the internal state to produce the ciphertext. The key expansion algorithm to produce the

$N_r + 1$ subkeys is described in Fig. 13. We refer to the original publication [26] for further details.

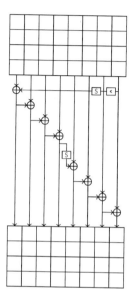

Fig. 13. Key schedule of AES-256

4.2   Generation of the Related Keys

Because the key schedule of AES involves S-boxes, it is impossible to control the difference of each key byte, otherwise the possible values of some key bytes would be restricted, limiting the choice of the master key for the adversary and thus leading to weak-key attacks.

In our attack, the adversary is free to pick any master key K and we assume that he can then perform the following procedure to generate a related key K'. First, we choose the difference a to any non-zero value and another value b such that the differential transition b → a through the S-box happens with probability 2^{-6}. In the case of our attack, as depicted in Fig. 14, the adversary applies the difference b on the first byte of k_8 and the difference MC$((a, 0, 0, 0))$ to the first column of k_9. He finally reconstructs K' from (k'_8, k'_9).

4.3   The Attack

The distinguisher we use for the attack starts from columns 0 and 3 of state w_0 and columns 1 and 2 of z_1 and stops at state x_{11}. Both transitions $\Delta x_1[0] \to \Delta z_1[0]$ and $\Delta x_2[0] \to \Delta z_2[0]$ depend on uncontrollable differences from the key and thus there is a probability of 2^{-2} that the characteristic does not hold.

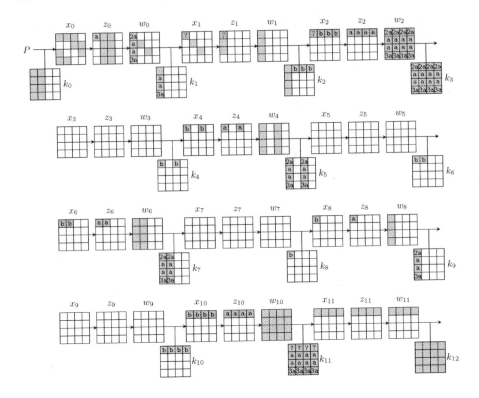

Fig. 14. Differential characteristic used in our 12-round attack. No difference in white cells. Transitions in blue belong to the distinguisher.

However, if it does, the average probability of the distinguisher is $2^{-(7\times2+6\times12)} = 2^{-86}$.

Step 1. The difference on P belongs to a vector space of dimension 11 since the differences on bytes 10, 11, 12 and 15 have to be 0 and $\Delta P[1] = \Delta P[5]$ (because they are both equal to $\Delta k_2[1]$). Thus, we start by asking for the encryption of a structure of 2^{88} messages under the key K and a similar one under the key K'.

Step 2. We then pick a message P and the goal is to generate all the possible $\widetilde{P}$ and to associate to each of them the corresponding key values. First, we guess 9 bytes of k_0 and 2 bytes of k_1 to compute $z_0[0]$ and both $z_1[1]$ and $z_1[2]$. We then guess the difference in the first column of k_2 and propagate backwards the differences and values to obtain $\widetilde{P}$. Furthermore, guessing the difference of k_2 gives us the values of the last column of k_3 since both the difference at the input and output of the S-box would be known for each byte of this column. As a result, we generate $2^{(9+2+4)\times8} = 2^{120}$ tuples for

$$(\widetilde{P}, k_0[0,2,3,4,7,8,9,13,14], k_1[5,10], k_3[12,13,14,15]).$$

Step 3. Starting from the same message P as above and taking its corresponding ciphertext C, the goal is now to generate all the possible $\widetilde{C}$. The procedure is quite straightforward. First, we guess the difference of $k_{11}[0]$ as well as the difference on the first column of k_{12}. This gives us the difference on both k_{11} and k_{12}. Then we guess the first line of k_{12} except the last byte (which is obtained by computing $k_{12}[8] \oplus k_{10}[12]$) and we can compute $\widetilde{C}$. As a result, we generate $2^{(5+3)\times 8} = 2^{64}$ tuples for

$$(\widetilde{C}, k_{10}[12], k_{11}[12, 13, 14, 15], k_{12}[0, 4, 8, 12]).$$

Step 4. We now look at matches between both lists of tuples so that $(\widetilde{P}, \widetilde{C})$ is a valid plaintext-ciphertext pair. We expect around $2^{120+64-128} = 2^{56}$ matches, each leading to a possible value for $\widetilde{P}, \widetilde{C}$, $k_0[0, 2, 3, 4, 7, 8, 9, 13, 14]$, $k_1[5, 10]$, $k_3[12, 13, 14, 15]$, $k_{10}[12]$, $k_{11}[12, 13, 14, 15]$, $k_{12}[0, 4, 8$ and $12]$.

Using a simple Gaussian elimination, we found that it is enough to guess 9 extra key bytes to fully reconstruct the master key, which then has to be checked against few additional data.

Complexity. The time complexity of Steps 2 to 4 is $\max(2^{120}, 2^{64}, 2^{72}) = 2^{120}$ and the memory complexity is around 2^{64} tuples of $128 + 64 = 192$ bits since only the list built at Step 3 has to be stored. The attack has to be repeated 2^{86} times (the probability of the distinguisher), leading to an overall complexity of 2^{206}. The data complexity is 2^{89} chosen plaintexts, 2^{88} messages for each of both keys.

Note that the probability that the trail holds is 2^{-2} because of the transitions $\Delta x_1[0] \rightarrow \Delta z_1[0]$ and $\Delta x_2[0] \rightarrow \Delta z_2[0]$. Thus, it might be needed to repeat the attack several times to retrieve the key, either by asking another key K' computed with another value of (a, b) or by modifying the position of the zero difference on the first column of z_1 (3 possible choices).

5   Conclusion and Open Problems

We introduced in this work a new cryptanalysis technique, that we called the differential MITM attack. We managed to successfully apply this new technique to SKINNY-128-384 and AES-256 in two different settings. Our attack against SKINNY allowed us to provide the best single-key attack against the analyzed variant by reaching two more rounds than the previously best known attack. Our application on AES-256 permitted to break 2 rounds more than the previously best attack that used two related keys or less.

The introduction of this new technique releases naturally numerous questions and opens many new research directions. First, we would like to further understand the link between the new attack and classical MITM attacks and how these two attacks can be compared. For example, we would like to identify for what kind of primitives the quantity of the involved key material in the differential MITM attack would be typically smaller compared to a classical MITM attack applied to the same cipher in a similar setting. We did some preliminary experiments on different ciphers by mounting both types of attacks in a comparable way and in some cases the amount of key bits to be guessed was smaller for the new attack while in some other cases this same amount was smaller for a classical MITM attack. It would therefore be interesting to be able to predict in an easy way, how this quantity compares for the two attacks. It would also be interesting to understand the details that allow our technique to be more performant than classical differential attacks and the other way round.

As MITM attacks combine particularly well with the technique of bicliques, another natural question is whether differential MITM attacks combine well with bicliques as well. Furthermore, is it possible to find any concrete application where the combination of a differential MITM with bicliques could improve previous MITM or other attacks? Finally, can the technique of bicliques be combined with the method of partitions we proposed in the case of partial subkey additions, and how do they compare?

A last open question is whether instead of combining MITM techniques with differential attacks, one could successfully combine MITM with some other well-known family of cryptanalysis, such as for example linear or differential-linear attacks.

Acknowledgements. This project has received funding from the European Research Council (ERC) under the European Union's Horizon 2020 research and innovation programme (grant agreement no. 714294 - acronym QUASYModo). It was also partially supported by the French Agence Nationale de la Recherche through the SWAP project under Contract ANR-21-CE39-0012, through the DeCrypt project under Contract ANR-18-CE39-0007, and by the Deutsche Forschungsgemeinschaft (DFG, German Research Foudation) under Germany's Excellence Strategy - EXC 2092 CASA - 390781972. Finally, the authors would like to thank the Dagstuhl Seminar 22141 on Symmetric Cryptography that gave the opportunity to the authors to advance this collaboration.

A   Automatic Detection of Involved Keys

We provide here a simple algorithm to search, given a differential, for efficient applications of the new attack. Indeed, in many cases, it is technically very easy to exactly determine which information about the key is required in the forward or backward computation. As often, when it comes to the question of dependency only, the easiest and less error-prone method is to experimentally determine which bits have an actual influence. Assume we are given (the implementation of) a function $F : \mathbb{F}_2^n \to \mathbb{F}_2^m$ and want to determine if the ith input bit of x has an influence on the output of $F(x)$, that is if there exist an input x such that

$$F(x) \neq F(x \oplus e_i),$$

where e_i is the vector that has a one exactly at position i.

For this, we could simply take a random input x and compute $F(x) \oplus F(x \oplus e_i)$. If the result is non-zero, we know that the output depends on the ith input bit.

After repeating this process a few times and if we always get zero as a result, we conclude that the ith bit does not have an influence on the output. The later decision might of course be wrong (while the former never is). However, for our applications this is (i) very unlikely to happen due to the construction of the round functions and (ii) irrelevant for the attacks as a key bit that influences the output only in one out of many outputs usually does not have to be guessed.

Focusing on our target, given the implementation of the cipher, i.e. in particular the (round-reduced) encryption and decryption procedures along with the key schedule, we can easily process as represented in Algorithm 2.

Algorithm 2. CHECK DEPENDENCIES

Input: An Implementation of the round reduced encryption and decryption E_r, a difference Δ
Output: The set of key bits $\mathcal{K}$ required to propagate Δ through E_r^{-1}
1: $\mathcal{K} \leftarrow \emptyset$
2: **for** each i from 0 to $n-1$ **do**
3:     **for** each t from 1 to tries **do**
4:         $x \leftarrow$ random message
5:         $k \leftarrow$ random key
6:         $y_1 \leftarrow E_r(k, x)$ $\triangleright$ Query Encryption
7:         $z_1 \leftarrow E_r^{-1}(k, y_1 \oplus \Delta)$ $\triangleright$ Query Decryption
8:         $y_2 \leftarrow E_r(k \oplus e_i, x)$ $\triangleright$ Query Encryption with bit flipped
9:         $z_2 \leftarrow E_r^{-1}(k \oplus e_i, y_2 \oplus \Delta)$ $\triangleright$ Query Decryption with bit flipped
10:        **if** $z_1 \neq z_2$ **then**
11:            Include key bit i to $\mathcal{K}$
12:        **end if**
13:     **end for**
14: **end for**
15: Return $\mathcal{K}$

The nice feature of the algorithm is that it works for any cipher structure and without the need to know or implement any internal details. However, on this generality we might miss many possible improvements. As an example, consider the key schedule of SKINNY. Here, every round-tweak-key bit is the sum of three bits of (updated) master tweak-key bits. The algorithm above would (correctly) detect the dependence of the output on those three bits, but obviously guessing the sum of the bits is enough. We can easily adopt the above algorithm to take into account linear (tweak) key-schedules. The main idea is not to flip master key-bits directly, but rather round-key bits.

Let us denote the linear key schedule by $L : \mathbb{F}_2^\kappa \rightarrow \mathbb{F}_2^{n\hat{r}}$. The ith bit of the expanded key can thus be written as $\langle L_i, k \rangle$ where L_i denotes the ith row of the matrix corresponding to L. Furthermore we denote by $\widehat{E}_r$ the encryption excluding the key schedule, i.e.

$$E_r(k, x) = \widehat{E}_r(L(k), x).$$

Instead of master key-bits, we now aim at computing the round-key bits that the encryption depends on and collecting the corresponding linear combinations of the master-key.

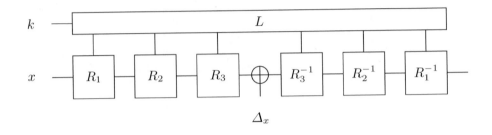

Algorithm 3. CHECK LINEAR-DEPENDENCIES

Input: An Implementation of the round reduced encryption and decryption $\widehat{E}_r$, the key-schedule L and a difference Δ

Output: A linear subspace of key bits $\mathcal{K}$ required to propagate Δ through $\widehat{E}_r^{-1}$

1: $\mathcal{K} \leftarrow \{\}$
2: **for** each i from 0 to $n \ldots r - 1$ **do**
3:      **for** each t from 1 to tries **do**
4:          $x \leftarrow$ random message
5:          $k \leftarrow$ random key
6:          $y_1 \leftarrow \widehat{E}_r(L(k), x)$ ▷ Query Encryption
7:          $z_1 \leftarrow \widehat{E}_r^{-1}(L(k), y_1 \oplus \Delta)$ ▷ Query Decryption
8:          $y_2 \leftarrow \widehat{E}_r(L(k) \oplus e_i, x)$ ▷ Query Encryption with bit flipped
9:          $z_2 \leftarrow \widehat{E}_r^{-1}(L(k) \oplus e_i, y_2 \oplus \Delta)$ ▷ Query Decryption with bit flipped
10:        **if** $z_1 \neq z_2$ **then**
11:            Include L_i to $\mathcal{K}$
12:        **end if**
13:      **end for**
14: **end for**
15: Return span($\mathcal{K}$)   ▷ Vector space spanned by the corresponding L_i

---

The vector-space contains the information that is sufficient to guess in order to compute the upper part of the attack. The dimension of $\mathcal{K}$ corresponds to the amount of information that has to be guessed, its Gauss-Jordan-basis contains information on which master key bits can be guessed equivalently. This algorithm again is easy to adapt given an implementation of a cipher. In practice, given a differential $\Delta_x \rightarrow \Delta_y$, we can apply this algorithm on both (E_{in}, Δ_x) and (E_{out}^{-1}, Δ_y) to respectively get the sets k_{in} and k_{out} required in our new framework.

For SKINNY, Algorithm 3 allows to complete both the differential trails given in Sect. 3 into attacks against 23 and 24 rounds, that we will finally extend by one additional round at the end to get the currently best known results on SKINNY-128-384.

References

1. Aoki, K., Sasaki, Y.: Preimage attacks on one-block MD4, 63-step MD5 and more. In: Avanzi, R.M., Keliher, L., Sica, F. (eds.) SAC 2008. LNCS, vol. 5381, pp. 103–119. Springer, Heidelberg (2008). https://doi.org/10.1007/978-3-642-04159-4_7
2. Aoki, K., Sasaki, Yu.: Meet-in-the-middle preimage attacks against reduced SHA-0 and SHA-1. In: Halevi, S. (ed.) CRYPTO 2009. LNCS, vol. 5677, pp. 70–89. Springer, Heidelberg (2009). https://doi.org/10.1007/978-3-642-03356-8_5
3. Banik, S., Pandey, S.K., Peyrin, T., Sasaki, Yu., Sim, S.M., Todo, Y.: GIFT: a small present. In: Fischer, W., Homma, N. (eds.) CHES 2017. LNCS, vol. 10529, pp. 321–345. Springer, Cham (2017). https://doi.org/10.1007/978-3-319-66787-4_16
4. Beierle, C., et al.: The SKINNY family of block ciphers and its low-latency variant MANTIS. In: Robshaw, M., Katz, J. (eds.) CRYPTO 2016, Part II. LNCS, vol. 9815, pp. 123–153. Springer, Heidelberg (2016). https://doi.org/10.1007/978-3-662-53008-5_5
5. Biham, E., Biryukov, A., Shamir, A.: Miss in the middle attacks on IDEA and Khufu. In: Knudsen, L. (ed.) FSE 1999. LNCS, vol. 1636, pp. 124–138. Springer, Heidelberg (1999). https://doi.org/10.1007/3-540-48519-8_10
6. Biham, E., Dunkelman, O., Keller, N.: The rectangle attack — rectangling the serpent. In: Pfitzmann, B. (ed.) EUROCRYPT 2001. LNCS, vol. 2045, pp. 340–357. Springer, Heidelberg (2001). https://doi.org/10.1007/3-540-44987-6_21
7. Biham, E., Dunkelman, O., Keller, N.: Related-Key boomerang and rectangle attacks. In: Cramer, R. (ed.) EUROCRYPT 2005. LNCS, vol. 3494, pp. 507–525. Springer, Heidelberg (2005). https://doi.org/10.1007/11426639_30
8. Biham, E., Shamir, A.: Differential cryptanalysis of DES-like cryptosystems. In: Menezes, A.J., Vanstone, S.A. (eds.) CRYPTO 1990. LNCS, vol. 537, pp. 2–21. Springer, Heidelberg (1991). https://doi.org/10.1007/3-540-38424-3_1
9. Biham, E., Shamir, A.: Differential cryptanalysis of the full 16-round DES. In: Brickell, E.F. (ed.) CRYPTO 1992. LNCS, vol. 740, pp. 487–496. Springer, Heidelberg (1993). https://doi.org/10.1007/3-540-48071-4_34
10. Biryukov, A., Dunkelman, O., Keller, N., Khovratovich, D., Shamir, A.: Key recovery attacks of practical complexity on AES-256 variants with up to 10 rounds. In: Gilbert, H. (ed.) EUROCRYPT 2010. LNCS, vol. 6110, pp. 299–319. Springer, Heidelberg (2010). https://doi.org/10.1007/978-3-642-13190-5_15
11. Biryukov, A., Khovratovich, D.: Related-key cryptanalysis of the full AES-192 and AES-256. In: Matsui, M. (ed.) ASIACRYPT 2009. LNCS, vol. 5912, pp. 1–18. Springer, Heidelberg (2009). https://doi.org/10.1007/978-3-642-10366-7_1
12. Bogdanov, A., Khovratovich, D., Rechberger, C.: Biclique cryptanalysis of the full AES. In: Lee, D.H., Wang, X. (eds.) ASIACRYPT 2011. LNCS, vol. 7073, pp. 344–371. Springer, Heidelberg (2011). https://doi.org/10.1007/978-3-642-25385-0_19
13. Bordes, Nicolas, Daemen, Joan, Kuijsters, Daniël, Van Assche, Gilles: Thinking outside the superbox. In: Malkin, Tal, Peikert, Chris (eds.) CRYPTO 2021, Part III. LNCS, vol. 12827, pp. 337–367. Springer, Cham (2021). https://doi.org/10.1007/978-3-030-84252-9_12

14. Canteaut, A., Naya-Plasencia, M., Vayssière, B.: Sieve-in-the-middle: improved MITM attacks. In: Canetti, R., Garay, J.A. (eds.) CRYPTO 2013, Part I. LNCS, vol. 8042, pp. 222–240. Springer, Heidelberg (2013). https://doi.org/10.1007/978-3-642-40041-4_13

15. Canteaut, A., Naya-Plasencia, M., Vayssière, B.: Sieve-in-the-middle: improved MITM attacks (full version). IACR Cryptology ePrint Archive, p. 324 (2013). http://eprint.iacr.org/2013/324

16. Choudhuri, A.R., Maitra, S.: Differential cryptanalysis of Salsa and ChaCha - an evaluation with a hybrid model. Cryptology ePrint Archive, Paper 2016/377 (2016). https://eprint.iacr.org/2016/377

17. Daemen, J., Knudsen, L., Rijmen, V.: The block cipher square. In: Biham, E. (ed.) FSE 1997. LNCS, vol. 1267, pp. 149–165. Springer, Heidelberg (1997). https://doi.org/10.1007/BFb0052343

18. Delaune, S., Derbez, P., Huynh, P., Minier, M., Mollimard, V., Prud'homme, C.: Efficient methods to search for best differential characteristics on SKINNY. In: Sako, K., Tippenhauer, N.O. (eds.) ACNS 2021, Part II. LNCS, vol. 12727, pp. 184–207. Springer, Heidelberg (2021). https://doi.org/10.1007/978-3-030-78375-4_8

19. Demirci, H., Selçuk, A.A.: A meet-in-the-middle attack on 8-round AES. In: Nyberg, K. (ed.) FSE 2008. LNCS, vol. 5086, pp. 116–126. Springer, Heidelberg (2008). https://doi.org/10.1007/978-3-540-71039-4_7

20. Derbez, P., Fouque, P.-A., Jean, J.: Improved key recovery attacks on reduced-round AES, in the single-key setting. In: Johansson, T., Nguyen, P.Q. (eds.) EUROCRYPT 2013. LNCS, vol. 7881, pp. 371–387. Springer, Heidelberg (2013). https://doi.org/10.1007/978-3-642-38348-9_23

21. Diffie, W., Hellman, M.: Special feature exhaustive cryptanalysis of the NBS Data Encryption Standard. Computer **10**(6), 74–84 (1977)

22. Dong, X., Hua, J., Sun, S., Li, Z., Wang, X., Hu, L.: Meet-in-the-middle attacks revisited: key-recovery, collision, and preimage attacks. In: Malkin, T., Peikert, C. (eds.) CRYPTO 2021, Part III. LNCS, vol. 12827, pp. 278–308. Springer, Heidelberg (2021). https://doi.org/10.1007/978-3-030-84252-9_10

23. Dunkelman, O., Keller, N., Shamir, A.: Improved single-key attacks on 8-round AES-192 and AES-256. In: Abe, M. (ed.) ASIACRYPT 2010. LNCS, vol. 6477, pp. 158–176. Springer, Heidelberg (2010). https://doi.org/10.1007/978-3-642-17373-8_10

24. Dunkelman, O., Sekar, G., Preneel, B.: Improved meet-in-the-middle attacks on reduced-round DES. In: Srinathan, K., Rangan, C.P., Yung, M. (eds.) INDOCRYPT 2007. LNCS, vol. 4859, pp. 86–100. Springer, Heidelberg (2007). https://doi.org/10.1007/978-3-540-77026-8_8

25. Feistel, H.: Cryptography and computer privacy. Sci. Am. **228**(5), 15–23 (1973)

26. FIPS 197: Announcing the Advanced Encryption Standard (AES). National Institute for Standards and Technology, Gaithersburg, MD, USA, November 2001

27. Gérault, D., Lafourcade, P., Minier, M., Solnon, C.: Revisiting AES related-key differential attacks with constraint programming. Inf. Process. Lett. **139**, 24–29 (2018)

28. Guo, J., Ling, S., Rechberger, C., Wang, H.: Advanced meet-in-the-middle preimage attacks: first results on Full Tiger, and improved results on MD4 and SHA-2. In: Abe, M. (ed.) ASIACRYPT 2010. LNCS, vol. 6477, pp. 56–75. Springer, Heidelberg (2010). https://doi.org/10.1007/978-3-642-17373-8_4

29. Guo, J., Song, L., Wang, H.: Key structures: improved related-key boomerang attack against the full AES-256. In: Nguyen, K., Yang, G., Guo, F., Susilo, W. (eds.) ACISP 2022. LNCS, vol. 13494, pp. 3–23. Springer, Heidelberg (2022). https://doi.org/10.1007/978-3-031-22301-3_1

30. Hadipour, H., Sadeghi, S., Eichlseder, M.: Finding the impossible: automated search for full impossible-differential, zero-correlation, and integral attacks. In: Hazay, C., Stam, M. (eds.) EUROCRYPT 2023, Part IV. LNCS, vol. 14007, pp. 128–157. Springer, Heidelberg (2023). https://doi.org/10.1007/978-3-031-30634-1_5

31. Isobe, T., Shibutani, K.: All subkeys recovery attack on block ciphers: extending meet-in-the-middle approach. In: Knudsen, L.R., Wu, H. (eds.) SAC 2012. LNCS, vol. 7707, pp. 202–221. Springer, Heidelberg (2012). https://doi.org/10.1007/978-3-642-35999-6_14

32. Jean, J., Nikolić, I., Peyrin, T.: Tweaks and keys for block ciphers: the TWEAKEY framework. In: Sarkar, P., Iwata, T. (eds.) ASIACRYPT 2014. LNCS, vol. 8874, pp. 274–288. Springer, Heidelberg (2014). https://doi.org/10.1007/978-3-662-45608-8_15

33. Kim, J., Hong, S., Preneel, B.: Related-key rectangle attacks on reduced AES-192 and AES-256. In: Biryukov, A. (ed.) FSE 2007. LNCS, vol. 4593, pp. 225–241. Springer, Heidelberg (2007). https://doi.org/10.1007/978-3-540-74619-5_15

34. Knellwolf, S., Meier, W., Naya-Plasencia, M.: Conditional differential cryptanalysis of NLFSR-based cryptosystems. In: Abe, M. (ed.) ASIACRYPT 2010. LNCS, vol. 6477, pp. 130–145. Springer, Heidelberg (2010). https://doi.org/10.1007/978-3-642-17373-8_8

35. Knudsen, L.: DEAL-a 128-bit block cipher. Complexity **258**(2), 216 (1998)

36. Knudsen, L.R.: Truncated and higher order differentials. In: Preneel, B. (ed.) FSE 1994. LNCS, vol. 1008, pp. 196–211. Springer, Heidelberg (1995). https://doi.org/10.1007/3-540-60590-8_16

37. Langford, S.K., Hellman, M.E.: Differential-linear cryptanalysis. In: Desmedt, Y.G. (ed.) CRYPTO 1994. LNCS, vol. 839, pp. 17–25. Springer, Heidelberg (1994). https://doi.org/10.1007/3-540-48658-5_3

38. Leander, G., Abdelraheem, M.A., AlKhzaimi, H., Zenner, E.: A cryptanalysis of PRINTCIPHER: the invariant subspace attack. In: Rogaway, P. (ed.) CRYPTO 2011. LNCS, vol. 6841, pp. 206–221. Springer, Heidelberg (2011). https://doi.org/10.1007/978-3-642-22792-9_12

39. Matsui, M.: Linear cryptanalysis method for DES cipher. In: Helleseth, T. (ed.) EUROCRYPT 1993. LNCS, vol. 765, pp. 386–397. Springer, Heidelberg (1994). https://doi.org/10.1007/3-540-48285-7_33

40. Mendel, F., Rechberger, C., Schläffer, M., Thomsen, S.S.: The rebound attack: cryptanalysis of reduced whirlpool and Grøstl. In: Dunkelman, O. (ed.) FSE 2009. LNCS, vol. 5665, pp. 260–276. Springer, Heidelberg (2009). https://doi.org/10.1007/978-3-642-03317-9_16

41. Naya-Plasencia, M.: How to improve rebound attacks. In: Rogaway, P. (ed.) CRYPTO 2011. LNCS, vol. 6841, pp. 188–205. Springer (2011)

42. Prud'homme, C., Fages, J.G., Lorca, X.: Choco Solver Documentation. TASC, INRIA Rennes, LINA CNRS UMR 6241, COSLING S.A.S. (2016). http://www.choco-solver.org

43. Shi, D., Sun, S., Derbez, P., Todo, Y., Sun, B., Hu, L.: Programming the Demirci-Selçuk meet-in-the-middle attack with constraints. In: Peyrin, T., Galbraith, S.D. (eds.) ASIACRYPT 2018, Part II. LNCS, vol. 11273, pp. 3–34. Springer, Heidelberg (2018). https://doi.org/10.1007/978-3-030-03329-3_1

44. Todo, Y.: Structural evaluation by generalized integral property. In: Oswald, E., Fischlin, M. (eds.) EUROCRYPT 2015, Part I. LNCS, vol. 9056, pp. 287–314. Springer, Heidelberg (2015). https://doi.org/10.1007/978-3-662-46800-5_12
45. Tolba, M., Abdelkhalek, A., Youssef, A.M.: Impossible differential cryptanalysis of reduced-round SKINNY. In: Joye, M., Nitaj, A. (eds.) AFRICACRYPT 2017. LNCS, vol. 10239, pp. 117–134. Springer, Cham (2017). https://doi.org/10.1007/978-3-319-57339-7_7
46. Wagner, D.: The boomerang attack. In: Knudsen, L. (ed.) FSE 1999. LNCS, vol. 1636, pp. 156–170. Springer, Heidelberg (1999). https://doi.org/10.1007/3-540-48519-8_12
47. Yang, D., Qi, W., Chen, H.: Impossible differential attacks on the SKINNY family of block ciphers. IET Inf. Secur. 11(6), 377–385 (2017)

Moving a Step of ChaCha in Syncopated Rhythm

Shichang Wang[1,2], Meicheng Liu[1,2($\boxtimes$)], Shiqi Hou[1,2], and Dongdai Lin[1,2]

[1] State Key Laboratory of Information Security, Institute of Information Engineering, Chinese Academy of Sciences, Beijing, People's Republic of China
`{wangshichang,liumeicheng,houshiqi,ddlin}@iie.ac.cn`
[2] School of Cyber Security, University of Chinese Academy of Sciences, Beijing, People's Republic of China

Abstract. The stream cipher ChaCha is one of the most widely used ciphers in the real world, such as in TLS, SSH and so on. In this paper, we study the security of ChaCha via differential cryptanalysis based on probabilistic neutrality bits (PNBs). We introduce the *syncopation* technique for the PNB-based approximation in the backward direction, which significantly amplifies its correlation by utilizing the property of ARX structure. In virtue of this technique, we present a new and efficient method for finding a good set of PNBs. A refined framework of key-recovery attack is then formalized for round-reduced ChaCha. The new techniques allow us to break 7.5 rounds of ChaCha without the last XOR and rotation, as well as to bring faster attacks on 6 rounds and 7 rounds of ChaCha.

Keywords: Stream Ciphers · ChaCha · Differential Cryptanalysis · PNB · Syncopation

1 Introduction

Symmetric key cryptosystems play an indispensable role in cryptography. Owing to the significant performance advantage of symmetric cryptographic primitives, there are massive deployment of symmetric primitives, including stream ciphers, block ciphers, hash functions, and cryptographic permutations, in virtually all real-world applications and scenarios related to cryptography. Among them, ARX-based design is one important and attractive branch with simplicity and efficiency in both software and hardware implementations, especially in consideration of the persistent focus on lightweight cryptography. ARX is short for modular Addition, Rotation and bit-wise XOR. ARX-based designs not only have very high efficiency, but also provide good security properties. The algebraic

Supported by the National Natural Science Foundation of China (Grant No. 62122085, 12231015 and 61936008) and the Youth Innovation Promotion Association of Chinese Academy of Sciences.

© International Association for Cryptologic Research 2023
H. Handschuh and A. Lysyanskaya (Eds.): CRYPTO 2023, LNCS 14083, pp. 273–304, 2023.
https://doi.org/10.1007/978-3-031-38548-3_10

degree of ARX ciphers is usually high after a very few rounds since the function of carry bit within one modular addition already reaches almost maximal degree. With regard to differential [7] and linear [23] attacks, the probabilities of differentials and absolute correlations of linear approximations decrease very quickly when the numbers of rounds increase.

One of the most important set of ARX ciphers is the family consisting of Salsa20, ChaCha and their variants. In 2005, Bernstein proposed the stream cipher Salsa20 [5] as a candidate for the eSTREAM competition [17], and its 12-round variant was accepted into the final software portfolio. Later, as a variant of Salsa20, ChaCha [4] was proposed by Bernstein in 2008 to provide better diffusion and cryptanalytic resistance without slowing down encryption. The stream cipher ChaCha has a total of 20 rounds. In addition, the ChaCha family also includes reduced-round ciphers—the 8-round version ChaCha8 and the 12-round version ChaCha12. In the following, we mainly concentrate on the version of ChaCha with a 256-bit key due to its wide deployment.

ChaCha, along with the message authentication code Poly1305 [3], is adopted as one of the cipher suites of Transport Layer Security (TLS) [20], which has been supported by Google on both Chrome and Android. Also, the RFC 7634 [25] proposes the use of ChaCha along with Poly1305 for IKEv2 and IPsec. In addition, it has been implemented in many other protocols such as SSH, Noise, QUIC, WireGard, S/MIME 4.0 and so on. Apart from the usage of encryption, ChaCha has also been used as a pseudo-random number generator in the operating system with Linux kernel. Up to now, there are plenty of protocols and software which have implemented the stream cipher ChaCha, and please refer to [18] for details. In a nutshell, ChaCha is one of the most widely-used ciphers in practice.

Related Works. Because of the wide range of usage and deployment of ChaCha, it is crucial to systematically and deeply analyze its security. And indeed, cryptanalysts have advanced lots of important and profound works on the security evaluation of round reduced ChaCha.

At FSE 2008, Aumasson et al. [1] proposed a significant improvement on the differential cryptanalysis of both Salsa20 and ChaCha with introducing a new concept called *probabilistic neutral bits* (shortcut PNBs). In most cases, the attacks are launched by a meet-in-the-middle approach, in which for forward direction one applies some input difference to the initial state to observe the output difference after certain rounds, and for backward direction once a set of key bits with less influence on the output difference is identified using the PNB method, attackers can obtain the output difference at the middle from the final state. Since most of the attacks on Salsa and ChaCha to date have been carried out under based on PNBs, this idea will be reviewed detailedly in Sect. 3.1.

Several further enhancements have been proposed following this line of research. In 2012, Shi et al. [26] achieved some incremental advancements for both Salsa20 and ChaCha by introducing the concept of *column chaining distinguisher* (CCD). Maitra [22] provided the idea of chosen IV cryptanalysis to obtain certain improvements in the key-recovery attacks of both ciphers. In 2017,

Choudhuri and Maitra [8] improved the attacks with the idea of extending single-bit differentials to multi-bit differentials using linear approximations derived theoretically, which is essentially a differential-linear cryptanalysis [19]. Dey and Sarkar [15] improved the attacks by giving an algorithm for constructing a good PNB set, and then in [16] they provided a theoretical justification of the distinguishers of both ciphers. At CRYPTO 2020, Beierle, Leander and Todo [2] provided the first 3.5-round single-bit distinguisher, and improved the attacks for ChaCha7 with time complexity of $2^{230.86}$. Later, Coutinho and Souza Neto [10] presented a few more distinguishers for 3.5 rounds of ChaCha, and provided a further improvement on the differential-linear attacks including the distinguishers and key-recovery attacks for 7 rounds of ChaCha. However, in a recent work [12], Dey et al. showed that the correlation of differential at 3.5-th round in [10] is much smaller than their claim which results to inaccurate complexities of the attacks. The authors of [10] immediately corrected this mistake and reevaluated the complexities in [9]. In [12], Dey et al. also provided a theoretical explanation of the issue that not all keys have available IV's to satisfy the given differential, called *strong keys* at [2], mainly for two special cases, and provided experimental results for the other six cases without theoretical explanations. Subsequently, at EUROCRYPT 2022, Dey et al. [14] further improved the attack on ChaCha7 with time complexity of $2^{221.95}$ by introducing a concept of *exploitable keys* and constructing a list to store combinations of exploitable keys with a favorable IV for each key. At ASIACRYPT 2022, Coutinho et al. [11] presented a differential-linear distinguisher against 7 rounds of ChaCha by improving its linear part, with both time and data complexities of 2^{214}. Very recently, Dey et al. [13] presented a full key recovery attack on ChaCha6 with a complexity of $2^{99.48}$.

Since the first published analysis of ChaCha in 2008 by Aumasson et al. [1], its valid attacks in the literatures have stayed within 7 rounds [2,8,14,15,26]. In [24], Miyashita et al. presented an attack on 7.25 rounds of ChaCha with time complexity of $2^{255.62}$ and success probability of 0.5. However, as declared in [24], this attack is less efficient than a brute force attack.

Contributions. So far, the best results of key-recovery attacks against ChaCha are obtained by the PNB-based differential cryptanalysis, which is composed of two parts: forward truncated differential and backward PNB-based approximation. For the two parts, we have proposed several new techniques and improvements, which are summarized as follows.

Backward PNB-based Approximation: In the PNB-based approximation, the essential problem is how to find numerous PNBs with a large correlation of backward approximation. Unfortunately, more PNBs and larger correlation are usually contradictory. To simplify the problem, we first show that the backward approximation $\Delta f = \Delta g$ connected with the forward differential corresponding to two initializations can be seen as applying twice an approximation $f = g$ in a single initialization, and thus its correlation is the square of the correlation of the latter (see also Proposition 1). This fact is simple and was not illuminated in the previous analysis but it is surprising that it significantly simplifies calculations of the backward correlation. By this observation, we can treat the PNB-based approximation similar to the linear part in differential-linear cryptanalysis. However, the PNB-based approximation is much more complicated. We then introduce the technique called *syncopation* that takes advantage of ARX structures to analyze the propagation characteristic of PNBs and amplify the approximation correlation. To further simplify the analysis, the approximated part f is divided into two parts f_0 and f_1, that is, $f = f_1 \circ f_0$. The PNB-based approximating function g is a restriction of f with PNBs to be a fixed value, and this relationship also applies to g_0 and f_0. The *syncopation* technique is used in the g_0 (to say f_0) part for reducing its dependence on PNBs so that the correlation between g_0 and f_0 is high. We analyze the properties of syncopation in the basic operations of ARX designs, especially including modular subtraction and modular addition. We also present a tool for determining syncopations, which leads to a new and efficient method for finding a good set of PNBs with a large correlation by restrictions on non-PNBs. In virtue of the new observations and techniques, a refined framework of the PNB-based differential attack is formalized as described in Sect. 4.

Forward Differential: By analysis of the equations that control differential propagation, we achieve two main improvements in the differential part. Firstly, we show several useful observations on these differential equations, and propose a concise and effective way to satisfy the given differential. This treatment leads to a save of time by 2^{-2} in the key recovery at the cost of 2^4 times of data, compared with the work of Beierle, Leander and Todo [2]. Compared with Dey et al.'s technique [14], it does not require restrictions on exploitable keys (which shrink the space of all possible PNBs) and saves up to 2^{22} times of data. Secondly, a more comprehensive theoretical explanation is presented for the proportion of *strong keys* (about 30%) reported in [2], which covers all the remaining six (out of eight) cases lacked in the previous theoretical analysis [12]. The details are shown in Sect. 5.

Comparison of Results. As applications of our techniques, we present several attacks on the round-reduced versions of ChaCha with a 256-bit key. To be more specific, for ChaCha6, we show a partial key-recovery attack with time complexity of $2^{75.7}$ and data complexity of $2^{73.7}$, where nine more key bits (total 45 key bits) can be recovered with less time complexity than the previous best known partial key recovery [2]. With regard to ChaCha7, several attacks are obtained with different complexities. Specifically, we can launch a key-recovery attack on ChaCha7 with a time complexity of $2^{210.3}$ using a data complexity of $2^{103.3}$. With a data complexity of $2^{68.9}$, our attack on ChaCha7 takes a time complexity of $2^{216.9}$. The data and time complexity of this attack are both less than the previous best known attack with a time complexity of $2^{221.95}$ [14]. Towards a closer analysis of ChaCha8, we present two attacks against ChaCha7.5$^{\oplus}$, which is defined as a round-reduced version without the last bit-wise XOR and rotation compared with ChaCha7.5. Our attack on ChaCha7.5$^{\oplus}$ is launched with the time complexity of $2^{244.9}$ and data complexity of $2^{104.9}$. We also obtain another attack on ChaCha7.5$^{\oplus}$, which requires time complexity of $2^{242.9}$ with an increasing data complexity of $2^{125.8}$.

As far as we know, these attacks are the best known (partial) key-recovery attacks on ChaCha6, ChaCha7 and ChaCha7.5$^{\oplus}$. In particular, our attacks on ChaCha7 and ChaCha7.5$^{\oplus}$ are both several thousands times faster than the previous best known key-recovery attack or a brute force attack. Moreover, this is the first time that a key recovery attack is achieved beyond 7 rounds of ChaCha. As mentioned earlier, since the first 7-round attack was presented by Aumasson et al. [1] in 2008, nearly fifteen years have passed while no public cryptanalytic results superior to a brute force have been proposed on more than 7 rounds of ChaCha. In consequence, we take a small but difficult step towards the security analysis of ChaCha.

Our key-recovery attacks on round-reduced ChaCha are summarized in Table 1, with a comparison of the best known attacks that are better than a brute force attack. Last but not least, it is important to emphasize that our attacks do not pose any threat on ChaCha with full 20 rounds in the actual deployment.

Table 1. Key-recovery attacks on ChaCha

Round-reduced ChaCha	Time	Data	Reference
ChaCha6	2^{139}	2^{30}	[1]
	2^{136}	2^{28}	[26]
	$2^{127.5}$	$2^{37.5}$	[8]
	$2^{99.48}$	-	[13]
	$2^{77.4}$†	2^{58}	[2]
	$2^{75.7}$†	$2^{73.7}$	Sect. 6.3
ChaCha7	2^{248}	2^{27}	[1]
	$2^{246.5}$	2^{27}	[26]
	$2^{237.7}$	2^{96}	[8]
	$2^{230.86}$	$2^{48.83}$	[2]
	$2^{221.95}$	$2^{90.20}$‡	[14]
	$2^{216.9}$	$2^{68.9}$	Sect. 6.1
	$2^{210.3}$	$2^{103.3}$	Sect. 6.1
ChaCha7.5$^{\oplus}$	$2^{244.9}$	$2^{104.9}$	Sect. 6.2
	$2^{242.9}$	$2^{125.8}$	Sect. 6.2

† In the analysis of ChaCha6, the partial key-recovery attacks are launched where 36 key bits are restored in [2], and nine more bits (i.e. 45 bits) are recovered in our attack.

‡ By our evaluation, it can be cut down to $2^{75.89}$.

The full version of this paper and all codes of verification experiments can be found at https://eprint.iacr.org/2023/1087 and https://github.com/desert-oasis/chacha_syncopation.git respectively.

Organization of the Paper. In Sect. 2, we briefly recall the specification of ChaCha, and list the notations used throughout this paper. In Sect. 3, we review the framework of differential attacks based on PNB method, and recent advances on cryptanalysis of ChaCha. Then in Sect. 4, we introduce the *syncopation* technique for the PNB-based approximation in the backward direction and refine the PNB-based differential attack taking this technique into account. Next in Sect. 5, the analysis of differential part in the forward direction is provided. In Sect. 6, we present the attacks on ChaCha7, ChaCha7.5$^{\oplus}$ and ChaCha6 with our proposed techniques. Finally, Sect. 7 concludes this paper.

2 Preliminaries

In this section, we first take a look at the stream cipher ChaCha, and then summarize the notations used throughout this paper.

In 2008, the stream cipher ChaCha [4] was introduced by Bernstein, as a variant of Salsa20 aiming at bringing better diffusion for similar performance. To start with, we give a brief description of ChaCha. The cipher operates on 32-bit words, takes as input a 256-bit secret key $k = (k_0, k_1, \cdots, k_7)$, a 96-bit nonce $v = (v_0, v_1, v_2)$ and a 32-bit block counter t_0, and produces a sequence of 512-bit keystream blocks. In the subsequent content, we will refer to the nonce and block counter words together as IV words. The operations consist of bit-wise XOR ($\oplus$), left rotation ($\lll$) and addition modulo 2^{32} ($\boxplus$). The state of ChaCha consists of sixteen 32-bit words, which can be represented as a 4×4 matrix

$$\mathbf{X} = \begin{pmatrix} x_0 & x_1 & x_2 & x_3 \\ x_4 & x_5 & x_6 & x_7 \\ x_8 & x_9 & x_{10} & x_{11} \\ x_{12} & x_{13} & x_{14} & x_{15} \end{pmatrix} = \begin{pmatrix} c_0 & c_1 & c_2 & c_3 \\ k_0 & k_1 & k_2 & k_3 \\ k_4 & k_5 & k_6 & k_7 \\ t_0 & v_0 & v_1 & v_2 \end{pmatrix}. \tag{1}$$

As for the initial state, it is built by placing the four predefined constants (c_0, c_1, c_2, c_3), secret key $k = (k_0, k_1, \cdots, k_7)$, block counter t_0 and nonce (v_0, v_1, v_2) as in the above matrix, where the four constants for the version with a 256-bit key are $c_0 = 0 \times 61707865$, $c_1 = 0 \times 3320646e$, $c_2 = 0 \times 79622d32$, $c_3 = 0 \times 6b206574$.

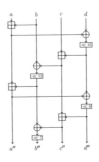

Fig. 1. The function *quarterround* of ChaCha.

The round function *Round* consists of 4 parallel applications of the function *quarterround*. The function *quarterround* uses 4 modular additions and 4 XOR's and 4 rotations to update four 32-bit state words. Specifically, the function *quarterround* transforms a 4-word vector (a, b, c, d) into (a'', b'', c'', d'') via an intermediate vector (a', b', c', d'):

$$a' = a \boxplus b; \quad d' = (d \oplus a') \lll 16;$$
$$c' = c \boxplus d'; \quad b' = (b \oplus c') \lll 12;$$
$$a'' = a' \boxplus b'; \quad d'' = (d' \oplus a'') \lll 8;$$
$$c'' = c' \boxplus d''; \quad b'' = (b' \oplus c'') \lll 7.$$

As depicted in Fig. 1, this transformation is invertible and updates each word twice, so the round function of ChaCha is also invertible. Let $X^{(r)}$ denote the state after r rounds, i.e. $X^{(r)} = Round^r(X^{(0)})$. The inverse of round function is denoted as $Round^{-1}$, then $X^{(0)} = Round^{-r}(X^{(r)})$. In the odd rounds, called column rounds, the function *quarterround* is applied to the four columns (x_0, x_4, x_8, x_{12}), (x_1, x_5, x_9, x_{13}), $(x_2, x_6, x_{10}, x_{14})$ and $(x_3, x_7, x_{11}, x_{15})$. In the even rounds, called diagonal rounds, the *quarterround* function is applied to the four diagonals $(x_0, x_5, x_{10}, x_{15})$, $(x_1, x_6, x_{11}, x_{12})$, (x_2, x_7, x_8, x_{13}) and (x_3, x_4, x_9, x_{14}). The keystream block Z of ChaChaR is obtained as the word-wise modular addition of the initial state and the state after R rounds, which means $Z = X^{(0)} \boxplus X^{(R)}$ and $X^{(R)} = Round^R(X^{(0)})$.

Next, we list the notations mainly used throughout this paper in Table 2.

Table 2. Notations.

Notation	Description
x	An n-bit word, i.e., an n-bit vector $x = (x[n-1], x[n-2], \cdots, x[0]) \in \mathbb{F}_2^n$
$X^{(r)}$	State matrix after applications of r round functions
x_i or $X[i]$	The i-th word of state matrix X
$x_i[j_2 : j_1]$	The consecutive $(j_2 - j_1 + 1)$-bit vector of the i-th word of state matrix X, starting from $x_i[j_1]$ ending to $x_i[j_2]$, $j_2 \geq j_1$
$x \boxplus y$	Addition of x and y modulo 2^n
$x \boxminus y$	Subtraction of x and y modulo 2^n
$x \oplus y$	Bit-wise XOR of x and y
$x \lll l$	Rotation of x by l bits to the left
Δx	XOR difference of x and x', i.e. $\Delta x = x \oplus x'$

3 Reviewing Differential Cryptanalysis of ChaCha

In this section, we first review the differential attack proposed by Aumasson et al. [1], which is based on the technique called *probabilistic neutral bits* (shortcut PNBs). Then, we summarize the recent advances on cryptanalysis of ChaCha.

3.1 Differential Attack Based on PNB Method

In general, the differential attacks based on PNB method in [1] use a meet-in-the-middle idea. Usually, one selects a truncated differential with some (single-bit) input/output differences after certain rounds for forward direction. Then one identifies the set of PNBs with less influence over the output difference from backward direction. As for the significant key bits, we just guess and recover them in the key recovery phase of the attacks. The framework of differential attack based on PNB method is illustrated in Fig. 2, where we use the shortcuts ID and OD for input and output difference.

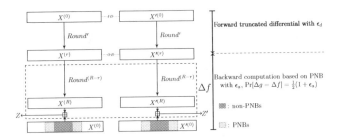

Fig. 2. Framework of PNB-based differential attack.

Assume that we use a truncated differential with a single-bit input difference at $X^{(0)}[i][j]$ of IV and a single-bit output difference at $X^{(r)}[p][q]$ of middle state after r rounds, denoted by $(\Delta X^{(r)}[p][q], \Delta X^{(0)}[i][j])$, which is actually a differential-linear (DL) approximation, and its correlation ε_d is defined by

$$\Pr_{v,t}\left\{\Delta X^{(r)}[p][q] = 0 \mid \Delta X^{(0)} = e_{ij}\right\} = \frac{1}{2}\left(1 + \varepsilon_d\right), \tag{2}$$

where e_{ij} is a state whose j-th bit of i-th word is one and other bits are zero. Note that regarding key as a random variable, the median of correlation over all keys is used in the following analysis.

The corresponding output Z is observed for a nonce v, counter t and the given secret key k. Having k, v and t, one can invert the operations to access internal state from backward direction. Given the above forward differential, let

$$\Delta f(k, v, t, Z, Z') \triangleq (Round^{-(R-r)}(Z \boxminus X^{(0)}) \oplus Round^{-(R-r)}(Z' \boxminus X'^{(0)}))[p][q], \tag{3}$$

then $\Delta X^{(r)}[p][q] = \Delta f(k, v, t, Z, Z')$. To obtain a more efficient attack than exhaustive search over all possibilities of secret key, we need to find an approximation Δg of Δf which effectively depends on $m = 256 - n$ key bits. More formally, let k^1 correspond to the subkey of m bits of secret key $k = (k^1, k^0)$ and Δf be correlated to Δg with correlation ε_a,

$$\Pr_{v,t}\left\{\Delta f\left(k, v, t, Z, Z'\right) = \Delta g\left(k^1, v, t, Z, Z'\right)\right\} = \frac{1}{2}\left(1 + \varepsilon_a\right) \tag{4}$$

Denote the correlation of Δg by ε, i.e. $\Pr_{v,t}\left\{\Delta g(k^1, v, t, Z, Z') = 0\right\} = \frac{1}{2}(1+\varepsilon)$.
Under a reasonable independence assumption, the equality $\varepsilon = \varepsilon_d \cdot \varepsilon_a$ holds.

Probabilistic Neutral Bits. Generally speaking, PNBs are these non-significant key bits with less influence (of size n), and on the opposite side non-PNBs are these significant key bits with great influence (of size m). To identify the set of PNBs (or non-PNBs), Aumasson et al. [1] gave a formal definition of a suitable measure for the amount of influence which every key bit has on output of Δf.

Definition 1 (Neutrality measure [1]). *The neutrality measure of k_i with respect to the function $\Delta f(k, W)$ is defined as γ_i, where $W = (v, t, Z, Z')$ and $\Pr\left\{\Delta f(k, W) = \Delta f(k \oplus e_i, W)\right\} = \frac{1}{2}(1+\gamma_i)$, i.e. the probability (over all k and W) that complementing the key bit k_i does not change the output of $\Delta f(k, W)$, where e_i is the unit vector of which i-th bit is one and other bits are all zero.*

In practice, a threshold γ is set, and $PNB = \{i \mid |\gamma_i| > \gamma\}$ and $Non\text{-}PNB = \{i \mid |\gamma_i| \le \gamma\}$. Assuming that k^1 denotes the significant key bits, i.e. non-PNBs, we simply define $\Delta g(k^1, W)$ as $\Delta f(k, W)$ with setting all PNBs into a fixed value (e.g. all zeros). Then the correlation ε_a is measured experimentally by using enough random IVs under many randomly chosen keys.

The Neyman-Pearson decision theory gives the results for estimating the number of samples N required to get the bounds on probabilities of false alarm p_{fa} and non-detection p_{nd}. It can be shown that $N \approx \left(\dfrac{\sqrt{\alpha \log 4} + 3\sqrt{1 - (\varepsilon_a \varepsilon_d)^2}}{\varepsilon_a \varepsilon_d}\right)^2$
samples suffices to achieve that $p_{nd} = 1.3 \times 10^{-3}$ and $p_{fa} = 2^{-\alpha}$. With using the median correlation ε^* in the above equation, we have a success probability of at least $\frac{1}{2}(1 - p_{nd}) \approx \frac{1}{2}$ for the attack.

Subsequently, a two-step key-recovery procedure can be launched, where the non-PNBs are first recovered according to the given single-bit differential and then PNBs are found by exhaustive search. The time complexity of this key-recovery attack is calculated as $T = 2^m N + (2^m p_{fa} + (1 - p_{nd}))2^n \approx 2^m N + 2^{256-\alpha} + 2^n$, where $m + n = 256$. For details about this procedure, please refer to [1]. As applications of the PNB-based differential cryptanalysis, Aumasson et al. [1] presented the analysis of Salsa, ChaCha and Rumba, especially including the first attacks on 6 and 7 rounds of ChaCha.

3.2   Recent Advances in Cryptanalysis of ChaCha

In the following, we recall recent advances in cryptanalysis of ChaCha in [2,14].

At CRYPTO 2020, Beierle et al. [2] presented the first 3.5-round differential-linear (DL) approximation for ChaCha, leading to further improvements on attacks on ChaCha6 and ChaCha7. More precisely, the DL distinguisher is divided into two parts, the differential characteristic in E_1 and the middle DL approximation in E_m. For the new distinguisher of ChaCha in [2], the first part E_1 consists of one round and the second part E_m covers 2.5 rounds.

The four *quarterround* functions are independent in the first round and we pay our attention on only one of them in the following analysis. The differential characteristics of E_1 can be presented over one *quarterround* function as $\Delta_{in} = ([], [], [], [6]) \rightarrow \Delta_m = ([2], [5, 9, 17, 29], [10, 22, 30], [10, 30])$, where Δ_m has the minimal Hamming weight of 10. Then with Δ_m as input difference of middle part E_m, they found the following DL approximation with probability $\Pr[(\Delta X_j^{(1)}, \Delta X_{j+4}^{(1)}, \Delta X_{j+8}^{(1)}, \Delta X_{j+12}^{(1)}) = \Delta_m \rightarrow \Delta X_{(j+1) \bmod 4}^{(3.5)}[0]] = \frac{1}{2}(1+\varepsilon_d)$, for $j \in \{0, 1, 2, 3\}$, where the correlation is evaluated experimentally as $\varepsilon_d = 2^{-8.3}$. The experimental distinguisher of E_m is combined with the differential characteristic of E_1, and the resulting distinguisher covers 3.5 rounds with single-bit input difference and output linear mask, which is summarized in Table 3 for the case $j = 1$. To find a right pair in the first round, one can repeatedly choose random IVs with some fixed iterations. As evaluated in [2], the probability that pairs with the input difference Δ_{in} satisfy the given differential in the first round is $p = 2^{-5}$ on average for about 70% of the keys. Therefore, on average we need repeat the procedure of attacks for $p^{-1} = 2^5$ times with varying IVs in the input difference column (ID column) on which the input difference is imposed.

To avoid the cost of iterations for getting a right pair, Dey et al. [14] proposed another alternative way to find the right pairs with the help of a pre-computed list. Actually, one should pre-compute all the needed right pairs offline and keep them in a list. To achieve this goal, they introduced the concept of *exploitable key*, which was restated as the following in the case of ChaCha.

Definition 2 (Exploitable key [14]). *Let $k_{ID} \in \mathbb{F}_2^{64}$ and a subspace $\mathbb{S}_{K_{nmem}} = \{(a_{63}, a_{62}, \cdots, a_0) \mid a_i = 0 \text{ for } i \notin K_{nmem}\} \subseteq \mathbb{F}_2^{64}$, if there exists at least one IV $v \in \mathbb{F}_2^{32}$ such that for any key $k'_{ID} \in k_{ID} \oplus \mathbb{S}_{K_{nmem}}$, $((k'_{ID}, v), (k'_{ID}, v'))$ forms a right pair, k_{ID} is an exploitable key with respect to the subspace $\mathbb{S}_{K_{nmem}}$, and the corresponding v is a favorable IV for k_{ID}.*

They constructed a subset K_{nmem} with dimension 18, and evaluated that there are approximately 62% exploitable keys among all the keys. Then one should construct a pre-computed list to store about $0.62 \times 2^{64-18} = 2^{45.31}$ possible exploitable keys along with their favorable IVs. They used the same forward differential of [2] for the attack on ChaCha7. With their systematic three-step strategy, they found a set of 79 PNBs with the backward correlation $\varepsilon_a = 0.00057$. When $\alpha = 38.8$, this gives $N = 2^{44.89}$, and the time complexity is $2^{221.95}$. Since there are $2^{45.31}$ exploitable keys in the ID column, they estimated the overall data complexity as $2^{45.31} \times N = 2^{90.2}$.[1]

4   The PNB-Based Attack with Syncopation

In this paper, we describe a refined framework of differential attack based on the PNB method for ARX ciphers. In this section, we focus on the PNB-based

---

[1] Noting that there are at most 2^{32} IVs in the ID column, the number N_{ID} of different IV pairs stored in the pre-computed list is less than 2^{31}, and therefore the overall data complexity can be cut down to $2^{31} \times N = 2^{75.89}$.

approximation in the backward direction. The analysis of differential part in the forward direction will be discussed in the next section.

Table 3. The 3.5-round DL approximation in [2].

ID	OD	$|\varepsilon_d|$
$\Delta X_{13}^{(0)}[6]$ satisfying $\Delta_{in} \to \Delta_m$	$\Delta X_2^{(3.5)}[0]$	$2^{-8.3}$

In the following, we will discuss the calculation of approximation correlation and searching for PNBs using properties of the ARX structure in the PNB-based approximation, along with the attack framework.

First, we show a simple but useful observation about the correlation of backward approximation, which significantly cuts down the workload of estimation of backward correlation. More precisely, we observe that the backward approximation of the differential described in (4) is actually the sum of the same approximation with two different inputs in initialization, and thus its correlation is the square of the correlation of the latter, which is shown in Proposition 1. This fact is simple and was not illuminated in the previous analysis, but it is surprising that it is powerful in the calculation of backward correlation.

After that, a technique called *syncopation* is introduced for the PNB-based approximation of ARX ciphers, to amplify the correlation of the approximation. For simplifying the analysis, the approximated part of an ARX cipher, denoted by f, is divided into two parts f_0 and f_1, that is, $f = f_1 \circ f_0$. The PNB-based approximating function g is a function of f with assigning PNBs to be a fixed value, and the same relationship holds between g_0 and f_0. The *syncopation* technique is applied to the part g_0 (to say f_0) for reducing its dependence on PNBs so that the correlation between g_0 and f_0 is high. The syncopations split the input of f_0 into different segments such that each segment of output of f_0 only depends on the same segment of the input under some restrictions. A syncopation consists of a few non-PNBs following by PNBs, and a split segment consists of several non-PNBs. In the other words, the output of f_0 excluding the syncopations does not depend on PNBs, and therefore the approximation correlation between g_0 and f_0 is high. In this section, we analyze the properties of syncopation in modular subtraction and modular addition, and present a tool for determining syncopations, which leads to a new and efficient method for finding a good set of PNBs with a large correlation.

The attack framework is depicted as in Fig. 3.

In the backward computations with PNBs, we observe that computing the backward correlation of output difference at middle states can be simplified into the computation of the correlation of the middle state in one initialization. This treatment is always used in the linear part when one constructs a differential-linear approximation. More precisely, let

$$f(k, v, t, Z) \triangleq Round^{-(R-r)}(Z \boxminus X^{(0)})[p][q], \tag{5}$$

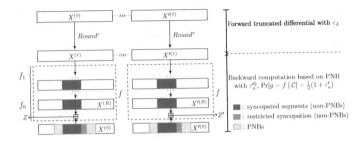

Fig. 3. Refined framework of PNB-based differential attack.

and then by (3) we have $\Delta f(k, v, t, Z, Z') = f(k, v, t, Z) \oplus f(k, v', t', Z')$. Let g an approximation of f which effectively depends on $m = 256 - n$ key bits, more formally, let k^1 correspond to the m-bit subkey of secret key $k = (k^1, k^0)$, in general, g is constructed by assigning a fixed value $\hat{k}^0$ to k^0, i.e.,

$$g(k^1, v, t, Z) \triangleq f(k, v, t, Z) \mid_{k^0 = \hat{k}^0}. \tag{6}$$

Then we can use g to construct an approximation for the function Δf, i.e. $g(k^1, v, t, Z) \oplus g(k^1, v', t', Z')$, which is always the same to the one constructed directly by Δg. Under the assumption of independence, the square relationship is established between the correlation of this treatment and the traditional one, which is summarized in the following.

Proposition 1. *Let f and g be the functions as defined in* (5) *and* (6), *where Round is the round function, $X^{(0)}$ the state as defined in* (1) *and k^1 corresponds to the m-bit subkey of secret key k. Let ϵ_a be the correlation of f and g,*

$$\Pr_{v,t}\{f(k, v, t, Z) = g(k^1, v, t, Z)\} = \frac{1}{2}(1 + \epsilon_a), \tag{7}$$

and ε_a the correlation of backward approximation in the differential using g,

$$\Pr_{v,t}\{f(k, v, t, Z) \oplus f(k, v', t', Z') = g(k^1, v, t, Z) \oplus g(k^1, v', t', Z')\} = \frac{1}{2}(1 + \varepsilon_a).$$

If Z and Z' are statistically independent, then it holds that $\varepsilon_a = \epsilon_a^2$.

Proof. If Z and Z' are statistically independent, then $Z \boxminus X^{(0)}$ and $Z' \boxminus X'^{(0)}$ are statistically independent. Therefore, by the definitions of f and g, $f(k, v, t, Z) \oplus g(k^1, v, t, Z)$ and $f(k, v', t', Z') \oplus g(k^1, v', t', Z')$ are statistically independent, and both equal to zero with probability of $\frac{1}{2}(1 + \epsilon_a)$. By Piling-up Lemma, $f(k, v, t, Z) \oplus g(k^1, v, t, Z)) \oplus (f(k, v', t', Z') \oplus g(k^1, v', t', Z') = 0$ holds with probability of $\frac{1}{2}(1 + \epsilon_a^2)$. Thus, we have $\varepsilon_a = \epsilon_a^2$. $\square$

By Proposition 1, we can detect the correlation ϵ_a instead of ε_a in practice. It takes about the square root of the amount of computations to detect the correlation ϵ_a in experiments compared with detecting ε_a by using the conventional method. In the following, we usually refer to ϵ_a as the correlation of backward single approximation $f = g$ in one initialization, and correspondingly, to ε_a as the correlation of backward double approximation $\Delta f = \Delta g$ in the differential.

4.1 Syncopation Technique

In the PNB-based approximation, the essential problem is how to find numerous PNBs with a large correlation. Unfortunately, more PNBs and larger correlation are contradictory in most cases. In the literatures, as far as we know, the methods for handling this problem are limited to the naive threshold rule [1] and greedy-like method recently shown in [14, 15], though the seminal attack was proposed fifteen years ago. Both methods treat the cipher as a black box, and yet the ARX structure of the cipher has been unexploited. In the existing similar work, this structure has been utilized by the partitioning technique [2, 6, 21] in linear cryptanalysis and differential-linear cryptanalysis. The idea of partitioning technique is to divide the input or output space into different subsets each of which corresponds to a good differential or linear characteristic. The PNB-based approximation is much more complicated than the cases of differential and linear characteristic, and the technique is not applicable to the PNB-based attack. Even in linear and differential-linear cryptanalysis, some ARX designs might be too complicated to use the partitioning technique, as stated by Beierle et al. in [2], *"unfortunately, 7-round ChaCha is too complicated to apply our (partitioning) technique for the linear part"*. However, we find that some similar properties of the ARX structure utilized by the partitioning technique can be used in the PNB-based approximation though with a different way.

Inspired by the partitioning technique, we introduce the *syncopation* technique for the PNB-based attack, which exploits the properties of ARX structure. As mentioned above, in linear or differential-linear attacks, to increase the correlation of linear approximation, one can use the partitioning technique to choose corresponding linear masks for different subsets of ciphertexts. In the PNB-based attack, a much more complicated function is used to approximate the targeted function. For simplifying the analysis, we divide the approximating function g into two parts g_0 and g_1, that is, $g = g_1 \circ g_0$. The *syncopation* technique is applied to the first part g_0 for reducing its dependence on PNBs so that the correlation of the approximation g_0 is high with the corresponding part f_0.

Before the description of *syncopation* technique, some notations and definitions are provided in the following. The consecutive bits in each word operated by the cipher is called a segment. Let the secret key k consist of two parts, the PNBs k^0 and non-PNBs k^1, as defined prevously. Let u be a positive integer. We denote by $k^\mathcal{R}$ the least u significant bits of a non-PNB segment that are adjacent to PNBs in a word, and define $k^\# = (k^\mathcal{R}, k^0)$. We call $k^\#$ *syncopation bits*, $k^\mathcal{R}$ *restricted bits*, and k^0 *syncopation bits*. The *syncopated bits*, denoted by k^o, are defined as the bits obtained by removing $k^\#$ from k.

A bit of an internal state S also belongs to one of the three types: syncopated bit, restricted bit and syncopation bit. A syncopation bit is considered as unknown. The syncopated bit is known when the restricted bits satisfy some conditions independent on syncopation bits. The set of all restricted and syncopation bits in S is denoted by $S^\#$, and each segment of $S^\#$ whose bits are consecutive in the state S is called a *syncopation*. The *syncopated state* obtained by removing $S^\#$ from S is denoted by S^o, and each segment of S^o whose bits are consecutive in the state S is called a *syncopated segment*. A simple example for syncopation technique is given in Fig. 4, where these terms and notations are illustrated in Fig. 4(b).

We restrict conditions on non-PNBs $k^{\mathcal{R}}$ so that the syncopated output of a PNB approximating function does not depend on PNBs, and therefore the approximation correlation will be amplified.

Before analyzing the propagation of syncopation property, like differential and linear characteristic, we provide the basic properties of modular addition and subtraction which are the nonlinear operations in ARX designs.

Property of Modular Addition. Let us consider two n-bit words s and k and a modular addition operation $x = s \boxplus k$, where k is secret and unknown, s is public for attackers. Assume that the consecutive key bits $k[t + w - 1 : t]$ are nonPNBs and known in backward computation, we are interested in under what conditions $x[t+w-1 : t]$ are independent on front PNBs and determinedly calculated from k and s. To this end, Lemma 1 is derived.

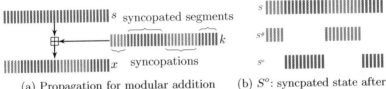

(a) Propagation for modular addition

(b) S^o: syncpated state after removing $S^{\#}$ from state S

Fig. 4. A simple example for syncopation technique of modular addition, where the blue lines represent for syncopated bits, red lines for restricted bits and gray lines for syncopation bits, from left to right for a word.

Lemma 1. *Let* $x = s \boxplus k$ *and* $x, k, s \in \mathbb{F}_2^n$. *If* $k[t-1 : t-u] \oplus s[t-1 : t-u] \neq \vec{1}$ *for* $1 \leq u \leq t$, *then we have*

$$x[t + w - 1 : t] = s[t + w - 1 : t] + k[t + w - 1 : t] + Carry[t] - Carry[t + w] \cdot 2^w,$$

$$Carry[t + w] = \begin{cases} 0 \ if \ \ s[t + w - 1 : t] + k[t + w - 1 : t] + k[t - \iota] < 2^w, \\ 1 \ if \ \ s[t + w - 1 : t] + k[t + w - 1 : t] + k[t - \iota] \geq 2^w, \end{cases}$$

$$Carry[t] = s[t-\iota] \ if \ k[t-1 : t-\iota+1] \oplus s[t-1 : t-\iota+1] = \vec{1} \ and \ k[t-\iota] \oplus s[t-\iota] = 0$$

where the width of segment $w \geq 0$, $1 \leq \iota \leq u$ *and* $Carry[i]$ *denotes the i-th bit of carry vector, i.e.* $s \boxplus k = s \oplus k \oplus Carry$.

In Fig. 4, according to Lemma 1, the syncopated segment $x[26 : 16]$ of internal state is independent on the syncopation $k[14 : 6]$ of secret key when the condition on restricted bits $k[15] = s[15]$ holds. The proof of Lemma 1 is provided in the full version. Note that the parameter u is actually the number of restricted bits in conditions, and ι is an auxiliary parameter that identifies the minimum index such that the premise of lemma holds. In the above lemma, when $w = 0$, only $Carry[t]$ is computed. Actually, Lemma 1 generalizes the property of modular addition utilized by the partitioning technique in [21] which can be seen as the special case of $w = 1$ and $u = 2$ in Lemma 1, see also the full version.

Property of Modular Subtraction. Let us consider two n-bit words x and k and a modular addition operation, $F_k : \mathbb{F}_2^n \to \mathbb{F}_2^n, x \mapsto s = x \boxplus k$, where s is known and k is secret and unknown, for instance, F_k serving as the last operation in branches b and c of ChaCha. Similarly, the property of modular subtraction is derived as Lemma 2.

Lemma 2. *Let* $s = x \boxplus k$ *and* $x, k, s \in \mathbb{F}_2^n$. *If* $k[t-1 : t-u] \oplus s[t-1 : t-u] \neq \vec{0}$ *for* $1 \leq u \leq t$, *then we have*

$$x[t+w-1 : t] = Carry[t+w] \cdot 2^w + s[t+w-1 : t] - k[t+w-1 : t] - Carry[t],$$

$$Carry[t+w] = \begin{cases} 0 & if \quad s[t+w-1:t] > k[t+w-1:t], \\ Carry[t] & if \quad s[t+w-1:t] = k[t+w-1:t], \\ 1 & if \quad s[t+w-1:t] < k[t+w-1:t], \end{cases}$$

$Carry[t] = s[t-\iota] \oplus 1$ *if* $k[t-1 : t-\iota+1] \oplus s[t-1 : t-\iota+1] = \vec{0}$ *and* $k[t-\iota] \oplus s[t-\iota] = 1$

where the width of segment $w \geq 0$, $1 \leq \iota \leq u$, *and* $Carry[t]$ *denotes the t-th bit of carry vector, i.e.* $x \boxplus k = x \oplus k \oplus Carry$.

The proof of Lemma 2 is provided in the full version. Lemma 2 generalizes the property of modular subtraction utilized by partitioning technique in linear or differential-linear attacks. More exactly, Lemma 2 in [2] falls into the case of $w = 1$ and $u = 2$ in Lemma 2, and please refer to the full version for details.

Here in after, we assume that there is a set of syncopated segments of internal state with carries $\mathcal{X} = \{(x[t+w-1 : t], Carry[t+w])\}$ in f_0. A syncopated segment is usually obtained by imposing conditions on restricted bits. Let $\mathcal{C}$ be the set of corresponding conditions of $\mathcal{X}$, that is, $\mathcal{C} = \{C(k[t-1 : t-u], s[t-1 : t-u])\}$, where $C(k[t-1 : t-u], s[t-1 : t-u])$ denotes $k[t-1 : t-u] \oplus s[t-1 : t-u] \neq \vec{0}$ and $k[t-1 : t-u] \oplus s[t-1 : t-u] \neq \vec{1}$ for modular subtraction and modular addition respectively.

Propagation for Modular Addition and Subtraction. According to Lemmas 1 and 2, the syncopated segment $x[t+w-1 : t]$ is known if $k[t+w-1 : t-u]$ and $s[t+w-1 : t-u]$ are given and conditions on restricted bits hold. For modular addition and subtraction, the syncopation property is unchange but brings restricted bits, if k and s have the same syncopation property or one of them is known. As depicted in Fig. 4(a), the sum of top augend which is known and right addend has the same syncopation property with the right addend. Here the one restricted bit is introduced by modular addition.

Propagation for Rotation and XOR. For the rotation operation, the propagation of syncopation is almost equivalent in terms of rotation, that is the pattern of syncopation after rotation is almost equivalent to rotation of the one before rotation. The propagation of syncopation on the XOR operation has the following property: the set of the syncopations is the union of input syncopations and the set of the syncopated segments is the intersection of input segments.

By analysis of syncopation propagation on the basic operations, we can get a general property for ARX structures.

Proposition 2. *Let $f(k, s)$ be a function consisting of ARX operations, and $k = (k^o, k^{\mathcal{R}}, k^0)$ with $k^o, k^{\mathcal{R}}$ and k^0 being the syncopated bits, restricted and syncopation bits respectively. Let g be a restriction of f with k^0 to be a fixed value. If $k^{\mathcal{R}}$ satisfies the syncopation property propagating from k to f, that is, the restricted equations introduced by modular operations are satisfied, then any syncopated segment in the output of f is independent with k^0 and thus equals the corresponding segment in the output of g.*

Instead of finding a linear mask in partitioning technique, the goal of syncopation technique is to find a PNB set consisting of as many as possible PNBs (to say syncopation bits), as well as maximize the overall length of syncopated segments of internal state in the ARX function for a fixed size of PNB set.

The first question is how to determine the syncopated segments in the PNB-based attack. Subsequently, an algorithm is given to determine all the profitable syncopated segments which are obtained by imposing conditions on corresponding restricted segments.

A Tool for Determining Syncopated Segments and Restricted Segments. First we find all the possible positions of secret key where the syncopation technique can be applied on. Then all the profitable syncopated segments and corresponding conditions are determined by the syncopated segments and restricted segments of secret key according to the specific structure of target cipher. Algorithm 1 summarizes the procedure, and note that $u = 1$ or $u = 2$ are usually used in our attacks.

Example of Algorithm 1. Here an example is given to explain Algorithm 1. As shown in Fig. 4, the bits $\{k[31 : 27], k[14 : 6]\}$ are PNBs and the bits $\{k[26 : 15], k[5 : 0]\}$ are nonPNBs for the secret key word k. Then after running the steps 2 – 10 of Algorithm 1 with $u = 1$, we get the profitable syncopated segment $k^o = \{k[26 : 16]\}$ and restricted segment $k^{\mathcal{R}} = \{k[15]\}$ of the word k. Next, a simple structure in Fig. 4(a) is used to illustrate the step 12 of Algorithm 1, i.e. $x = s \boxplus k$ where s is public and know. According to the propagation for modular addition (Lemma 1), the profitable syncopated segment of internal state is $x[26 : 16]$ and its condition is $k[15] = s[15]$.

Algorithm 1. Determining syncopated segments given a set of PNBs

---

Input: A set of PNBs.
Output: The syncopated segments with u-bit restricted segments.
1: **for** $0 \leq i \leq 7$ **do**
2:     **for** $0 \leq j < 31 - u$ **do**
3:         **if** $k_i[j]$ is a PNB and $k_i[j + u : j + 1]$ are all non-PNBs **then**
4:             $k^{\mathcal{R}} \leftarrow k^{\mathcal{R}} \cup \{k_i[j + u : j + 1]\}$, $j_0 \leftarrow j + u + 1$
5:             **while** $j + u + 1 \leq 31$ and $k_i[j + u + 1]$ is a non-PNB **do**
6:                 $j \leftarrow j + 1$
7:             **end while**
8:             $k^o \leftarrow k^o \cup \{k_i[j + u : j_0]\}$, $j \leftarrow j + u$
9:         **end if**
10:     **end for**
11: **end for**
12: According to k^o and $k^{\mathcal{R}}$, find the profitable syncopated segments $\mathcal{X}$ and conditions $\mathcal{C}$ on restricted segments with analyzing the specific structure of cipher. ▷ Refer to Sects. 6.1, 6.2 and 6.3 for details.
13: Return $\mathcal{X}$ and $\mathcal{C}$.

4.2 Refined PNB-Based Attack with Syncopation

First, we present a new and efficient method to find a good set of PNBs with greedy algorithm. Then, a refined procedure of key-recovery attack is summarized, along with the analysis of complexities.

New Efficient Method to Construct PNB Set. In our method, we experimentally estimate the backward correlation of $f = g$ as described in Proposition 1, i.e., the correlation ϵ_a in (7) instead of ε_a in (4). This trick saves lots of computations as explained before and makes our method very efficient. With the tool of determining syncopated segments, we take the syncopation technique into account, which results in a new criteria of identifying PNBs. The resulting key bits by new criteria are called the conditional PNBs (CPNBs for short). Specifically, we first generalize the definition of neutrality measure to conditional neutrality measure, and propose a greedy algorithm to find a good set of CPNBs.

Definition 3 (Conditional neutrality measure). *The conditional neutrality measure of the key bit k_i with respect to the function $f(k, v, t, Z)$ and condition $C_i(k, v, t, Z)$ is defined as γ_i', and $\Pr\{f(k, v, t, Z) = f(k \oplus e_i, v, t, \ Z) \mid C_i(k, v, t, Z)\} = \frac{1}{2}(1 + \gamma_i')$ i.e. the probability (over all k and (v, t)) that complementing the key bit k_i does not change the output of $f(k, v, t, Z) \mid_{C_i(k,v,t,Z)}$. Here e_i is the unit vector where the i-th bit is one and other bits are all zeros.*

In practice, the condition $C_i(k, v, t, Z)$ of key bit k_i is obtained by Algorithm 1 with treating only k_i as a PNB and other key bits as non-PNBs. In the traditional way, one could construct a set of CPNBs by setting a threshold γ for conditional neutrality measure, i.e. $CPNB = \{i \mid |\gamma_i'| \geq \gamma\}$. However, there may raise the incompatibility between CPNBs that suppose that the key bits k_i and k_j are separately derived as CPNBs, if the condition $C_i(k, v, t, Z)$ of k_i being a CPNB depends on k_j, then then k_i should not be CPNB. Therefore, we always treat all the CPNBs as a whole when constructing a set of CPNBs in the following.

In general, the procedure of finding a good set of CPNBs is divided into two steps as the following. First, in the preprocessing step, those key bits are excluded whose conditional neutrality measure is less than a threshold γ_{cNeutr}, which will not become good CPNBs. As a result, we get a preliminary short-listing of CPNBs, denoted by $CPNB^{shortlist}$ of which elements are the key bits with conditional neutrality measure greater than γ_{cNeutr}. Note that the value of γ_{cNeutr} is set to quite lower than the ones used in the conventional method, e.g. $\gamma_{cNeutr} = 2^{-5.0}$. In the second step, a greedy algorithm is launched to find a good set of CPNBs from $CPNB^{shortlist}$, which is described in detail below.

Algorithm 2. A greedy algorithm for searching a conditional PNB set

---

Input: The size n of CPNB set and $CPNB^{shortlist}$.
Output: The CPNB set, its correlation, syncopated segments and conditions.
1: Initialize a set $CPNB_0 = \emptyset$.
2: **for** $i \in \{0, 1, \cdots, n-1\}$ **do**
3:     **for** $j \in CPNB^{shortlist}$ and $j \notin CPNB_i$ **do**
4:         $CPNB_{temp} \leftarrow CPNB_i \cup \{j\}$.   ▷ The bit positions of k^0 in the key k.
5:         Update $\mathcal{X}_{i,j}$ and $\mathcal{C}_{i,j}$ by performing Algorithm 1 with $CPNB_{temp}$ as input.
6:         Under the conditions $\mathcal{C}_{i,j}$ of $\mathcal{X}_{i,j}$, estimate backward correlation $\epsilon_a'^{(i,j)}$ in (7), assigning k^0 by setting key bits of $CPNB_i$ to zero and flipping key bit j.
7:     **end for**
8:     Choose index j_i with maximal correlation, and $CPNB_{i+1} \leftarrow CPNB_i \cup \{j_i\}$.
9: **end for**
10: Determine $\mathcal{X}_n$ and $\mathcal{C}_n$ of $CPNB_n$ by Algorithm 1.
11: Under the conditions $\mathcal{C}_n$ of $\mathcal{X}_n$, estimate backward correlation ϵ_a' in (7), assigning k^0 by setting key bits of $CPNB_n$ to zero.
12: Return $CPNB_n$, ϵ_a', $\mathcal{X}_n$ and $\mathcal{C}_n$.

Greedy Algorithm With New Criteria. Once the size of CPNB set is specified, we construct the set of CPNB by selecting PNB one by one as shown in Algorithm 2. In the i-th iteration, the index of key bit with maximal conditional correlation in backward direction, i.e. minimizing the time complexity, is selected and added into CPNB set. To be accurate, we declare a temporary CPNB set $CPNB_{temp}$ to include a new key bit j, and update the set of syncopated segments $\mathcal{X}_{i,j}$ and its condition set $\mathcal{C}_{i,j}$ by performing Algorithm 1. Then under the conditions $\mathcal{C}_{i,j}$, the correlation $\epsilon_a'^{(i,j)}$ in (7) is estimated with assigning k^0 by flipping the new bit and setting other bits in $CPNB_{temp}$ to zeros. This iteration is repeated until enough CPNBs are identified. The detailed procedure is presented in Algorithm 2, where ϵ_a' is the conditional backward correlation in a single initialization, that is, $\Pr[f = g \mid \mathcal{C}] = \frac{1}{2}(1 + \epsilon_a')$.

When the number of conditions C for syncopated segments $\mathcal{X}$ is very large, it takes a lot of time overhead to satisfy them, and we will not be able to explore further the impact of conditions on backward correlation. However, according to the propagation of modular addition and subtraction (Lemmas 1 and 2), we know that the values of syncopated segments $\mathcal{X}$ are independent on PNBs and determinedly computed under the conditions C of $\mathcal{X}$. In practice, we theoretically estimate the backward correlation at the steps 6 and 11 of Algorithm 2 on the premise that the values of $\mathcal{X} = \{(x[t + w - 1 : t], Carry[t + w])\}$ are known, that is estimating the correlation between g_1 and f_1 with fixing the values of $\mathcal{X}$ in g_0 to the ones in f_0. Moreover, our experiments show that the theoretically estimated value is very close to the actual value, and we can always use the theoretical value instead of the actual value. It is worth noting that the use of theoretical evaluation of conditional backward correlation makes our method for finding CPNBs very efficient in practice.

Algorithm 3. Recovery of the full secret key

Input: N pairs $\{(M, M')\}$ of accessible data with IV satisfying ID, the set of n CPNBs denoted by k^0 and corresponding conditions C.
Output: The full secret key.
1: Classify N pairs into subsets according to the values of $S^{\mathcal{R}}$.   ▷ Pre-process data where no key bits are involved.
2: **for all** $\hat{k}^1 \in \{0, 1\}^m$ **do** ▷ Identify secret key $k = (k^1, k^0)$, $|k^1| = m$ and $|k^0| = n$.
3:     Set $\hat{k} = (\hat{k}^1, 0^n)$, according to the values of $k^{\mathcal{R}}$, choose subsets of $\{(M, M')\}$ whose values of $S^{\mathcal{R}}$ satisfying conditions C, about $N^* = qN$ pairs.
4:     Compute the correlation at OD with filtered N^* pairs.
5:     **if** the optimal decision rule legitimates $\hat{k}^1$ as a (possibly) correct one **then**
6:         Perform an additional exhaustive search over remaining n-bit subkey k^0. Once that the right key is found, output it.
7:     **end if**
8: **end for**

New Key-Recovery Attack with Syncopation Technique. In a chosen-IV attack, an attacker can get the keystream blocks by xoring given plaintexts and ciphertexts. Therefore, the accessible in-and-out data consists of public values, e.g. constants, IV and keystream block Z, which are collectively denoted by M for simplicity. Assume that there is a set of n CPNBs generated by our new method along with the set of syncopated segments $\mathcal{X}$ and set of corresponding conditions C. Once an attacker obtains a pair of accessible in-and-out data (M, M'), according to its values of $S^{\mathcal{R}}$, we classify it into the corresponding subset. In the online phase, since the non-PNB key bits are guessed, the values of key bits in $k^{\mathcal{R}}$ are known due to the requirement $k^{\mathcal{R}} \subseteq NonPNB$. The pairs are then filtered under the conditions C. Suppose that N pairs are given, about $N^* = qN$ pairs will be remaining for subsequent statistic testing according to Lemmas 1 and 2, where $q = (\prod(1 - \frac{1}{2^u})^{\theta_u})^2$ and θ_u be the number of syncopated segments with an u-bit restricted segment. The detailed procedure of key-recovery attack is summarized as Algorithm 3.

Analysis of Complexities. The total time complexity of Algorithm 3 is $T = T_0 + T_1$, where the complexity T_0 of step 1 is N, and T_1 of step 2 to 8 can be estimated as done in [1]. Therefore,

$$T = N + 2^m N^* + 2^{\kappa - \alpha} + 2^n,$$

where $N = \frac{1}{q} N^*$, $N^* \approx (\frac{\sqrt{\alpha \log 4} + 3\sqrt{1 - (\varepsilon_a \varepsilon_d)^2}}{\varepsilon_a \varepsilon_d})^2$, $q = (\prod(1 - \frac{1}{2^u})^{\theta_u})^2$, θ_u is the number of syncopated segments with an u-bit restricted segment, ε_d is the forward correlation, $\varepsilon_a = \epsilon_a'^2$ is the conditional backward correlation utilizing syncopation technique, and κ is the size of secret key, $\kappa = 256$ for ChaCha. The data complexity is of N. The memory complexity is mainly consumed in step 1 of at most N, and if we only keep these subsets used later, it takes memory of $2^{|k^{\mathcal{R}}|} N^*$, please refer Sect. 6.1 for details.

5   Theoretical Analysis of Differential Equations

In this section, we describe our improvements on forward differential, which are obtained by an in-depth analysis of the equations controlling differential propagation in ARX structure. More precisely, a concise and effective way is found to satisfy the given differential, resulting in a reduced complexity in key-recovery attacks. Besides, a more comprehensive theoretical explanation of *strong keys* is presented, which covers all the remaining six (out of eight) cases lacked in previous analysis.

According to the experiments of [2], for about 70% of the keys, called *weak keys*, there exists at least one IV satisfying the differential characteristic $\Delta_{in} \rightarrow \Delta_m$ in the first round, which is the differential characteristic of *quarterround* function described in Sect. 3.2. On the flip side, their experiments imply the existence of *strong keys* for which we can not find such IV. Recently, Dey et al. [12] provided a theoretical explanation about the differential characteristic mainly for two (out of eight) special cases, especially pointing out the case in which 12.5% of all keys becomes strong keys. But, for the other six cases, there is no theoretical explanation now. In the direction of finding a right pair, Dey et al. [14] proposed to achieve the right pairs by constructing a list consisting of at least one favorable IV for these *exploitable keys*. However, this treatment view the differential propagation as a black box, which results in a lot of data and storage overhead. In the following, it is shown that we fill in the missing parts of the previous work and overcome the shortcomings of existing method to some extent based on the deeper analysis of differential equations of ARX structure.

For the given differential characteristic $\Delta_{in} \rightarrow \Delta_m$ in the first round, which is described in Sect. 3.2, there are totally five differential equations to satisfy:

$$
\begin{cases}
c[22] = Carry_{(c,d')}[22], & (8) \\
a'[2] = Carry_{(a',b')}[2], & (9) \\
c'[10] = Carry_{(c',d'')}[10], & (10) \\
c'[30] = Carry_{(c',d'')}[30], & (11) \\
d''[22] = Carry_{(c',d'')}[22], & (12)
\end{cases}
$$

where $Carry_{(x,y)}[i]$ denotes the i-th bit of carry vector $Carry_{(x,y)}$ of modular addition between x and y, i.e. $x \boxplus y = x \oplus y \oplus Carry_{(x,y)}$. As shown in Fig. 1, Eq. (8) and (9) guarantee that the difference is not propagated to next bits in the second and third addition modular of *quarterround* function respectively, Eqs. (10), (11) and (12) guarantee that the difference is not propagated to next bits in the fourth addition of *quarterround* function.

In the initialization of ChaCha, a fixed constant is loaded into branch a, an unknown secret key is loaded into branches b and c. Therefore, we can not control branches a, b and c. Only branch d can be varied to satisfy the differential equations given the secret key. First, it is observed that at least one bit of d is almost linearly involved in Eqs. (10), (11) and (12). Therefore, we can always flip the linear bits to satisfy corresponding equations. We summarized this observation in the following.

Observation of Last Three Differential Equations.

- Eq. (10): $d[26] = Carry_{(c',d'')}[10] \oplus Carry_{(c,d')}[10] \oplus c[10] \oplus a'[26]$.
- Eq. (11): $d[14] = Carry_{(c',d'')}[30] \oplus Carry_{(c,d')}[30] \oplus c[30] \oplus a'[14]$.
- Eq. (12): $d[30] \oplus d[18] = Carry_{(c',d'')}[22] \oplus Carry_{(a',b')}[14] \oplus Carry_{(c,d')}[2] \oplus a'[30] \oplus a'[14] \oplus b[2] \oplus c[2] \oplus a'[18]$.

Thus, based on the above observation, the last three equations are satisfied by flipping $d[26]$, $d[14]$ and $d[30]$, which is verified by experiments given later.

As for the first two differential equations, no obvious linear bits of b are involved in equations. Therefore, we could not simply flip some bits of d to satisfy the two equations. It is noted that the two equations can not always be satisfied, and specially, Dey et al. [12] discussed two special cases where Eq. (9) is always established and must not be established, i.e. $a'[2:0] \in \{000, 100\}$. For details about their results, please refer to Theorems 5 and 6 in [12]. Next, we give a more in-depth analysis of Eqs. (8) and (9) by considering them together, which results in a theoretical interpretation for other six complex cases. The analysis stems from an observation of interaction between the first two equations which control differential propagation of two consecutive modular addition.

Observation of the First Two Differential Equations. Considering an internal variable $c'[21:20]$, we further analyze the interaction between constraints of Eqs. (8) and (9). Since the relation $b' = (b \oplus c') \lll 12$, we can obtain the range of $c'[21:20]$ from the constraints of $b'[1:0]$

derived by the assumption that Eq. (9) holds. Precisely, assume that Eq. (9) holds, we have that $c'[21 : 20] \in C_{a'[2:0]}^{'b[21:20]} \triangleq \{b'[1 : 0] \oplus b[21 : 20] \mid a'[2] = \lfloor (a'[1 : 0] + b'[1 : 0])/2^2 \rfloor\}$. Due to the fact that $Carry_{(c,d')}[22] =$

$$\begin{cases} 0, & if \quad c'[21:20] > c[21:20], \\ 1, & if \quad c'[21:20] < c[21:20], \\ Carry_{(c,d')}[20], & if \quad c'[21:20] = c[21:20], \end{cases}$$ Eq. (8) also restricts the range

of $c'[21 : 20]$, i.e. if $c[22] = 1$ then $c'[21 : 20] \leq c[21 : 20]$; otherwise $c[22] = 0$ then $c'[21 : 20] \geq c[21 : 20]$. Therefore, the two constraints of Eqs. (8) and (9) may contradict.

Taking the two equations into account together, it is first identified that the cases Eqs. (8) and (9) can not hold at the same time. For this, a function $sign(\cdot, \cdot) : \{\alpha \mid \alpha \in \mathbb{Z}\} \times \mathbb{Z} \to \{1, -1, 0\}$ is defined as

$$sign(S, \beta) = \begin{cases} 1 \, if \quad \forall \alpha \in S, \alpha > \beta, \\ -1 \, if \quad \forall \alpha \in S, \alpha < \beta, \\ 0 \, otherwise, \end{cases}$$

where $sign(\cdot) \neq 0$ implies a contradiction between Eq.s (8) and (9) . Otherwise, a heuristically optimal setting of d is given such that as few bits of b and c as possible are involved in. Formally, we write in a form of lemma below.

Lemma 3. *Given two words* $a'[2 : 0] \in \{0, 1\}^3$ *and* $b[21 : 20] \in \{0, 1\}^2$, *let* $C_{a'[2:0]}^{'b[21:20]} \triangleq \{b'[1 : 0] \oplus b[21 : 20] \mid a'[2] = \lfloor (a'[1 : 0] + b'[1 : 0])/2^2 \rfloor\}$.

- *For* $a'[2 : 0] = 000$ *and* $\forall b[21 : 20] \in \{0, 1\}^2$, $a'[2 : 0] \in \{111, 001\}$ *and* $b[21 : 20] \in \{01, 10\}$, *no matter what value of* $c[22 : 20]$, *Eqs. (8) and (9) can hold simultaneously, specially with the following setting.*
  If $c[21 : 20] = min(C_{a'[2:0]}^{'b[21:20]})$ *and* $c[22] = 1$, *or* $c[21 : 20] = max(C_{a'[2:0]}^{'b[21:20]})$ *and* $c[22] = 0$,

$$\begin{cases} d[5 : 4] = a'[5 : 4] \oplus (3 \times c[22]) \\ d[3 - i] = a'[3 - i] \oplus c[19 - i] \oplus 1, \quad i \in \{0, 1, \cdots, t - 1\} \\ d[3 - t] = a'[3 - t] \oplus c[19 - t] \end{cases} \quad (13)$$

  where $t \in \{0, 1, \cdots, 19\}$ *is the minimum integer such that* $c[19 - t] = c[22]$. *Otherwise,*

$$\begin{cases} d[5 : 4] = a'[5 : 4] \oplus (2 \times c[22] + 1 - c[19]) \\ d[3] = a'[3] \oplus c[19] \end{cases} \quad (14)$$

- *For* $a'[2 : 0] = 100$, *Eq (9) must not be satisfied.*
- *For* $a'[2 : 0] \in \{101, 110, 010, 011\}$ *and* $\forall b[21 : 20] \in \{0, 1\}^2$, $a'[2 : 0] \in \{111, 001\}$ *and* $b[21 : 20] \in \{00, 11\}$,
  - *When* $c[21 : 20] \notin C_{a'[2:0]}^{'b[21:20]}$, *if* $c[22] = \frac{1}{2}(1 + sign(C_{a'[2:0]}^{'b[21:20]}, c[21 : 20]))$ *then Eqs. (8) and (9) can not hold simultaneously; otherwise, then Eqs. (8) and (9) can hold simultaneously, specially with the following setting,*

$$\begin{cases} d[5 : 4] = a'[5 : 4] \oplus \left(min(C_{a'[2:0]}^{'b[21:20]}) - c[21 : 20] + c[22] \times 4 - c[19] \right) \\ d[3] = a'[3] \oplus c[19] \end{cases}$$
$$(15)$$

- *When $c[21:20] \in C'^{b[21:20]}_{a'[2:0]}$, Eqs. (8) and (9) can hold simultaneously, specially with the following setting. If $c[21:20] = min(C'^{b[21:20]}_{a'[2:0]})$ and $c[22] = 1$, or $c[21:20] = max(C'^{b[21:20]}_{a'[2:0]})$ and $c[22] = 0$, the setting is same to Eqs. (13); otherwise, the setting is same to Eqs. (14).*

The proof of Lemma 3 is given in the full version. In an attack, it is necessary to know how many unknown bits need to guess and how many public bits are consumed to satisfy the first two equations. For this purpose, the following corollary is directly derived from the above lemma.

Corollary 1. *For $a'[2:0] \in \mathbb{F}_2^3$ and $a'[2:0] \neq 100$, with the setting of Lemma 3,*

- *In Eqs. (13), there are at most 22 bits of d i.e. $d[5:0]$ and $d[31:16]$, and at most 32 bits of b and 23 bits of c i.e. $c[22:0]$ are needed to guess. If $t \leq 3$, with probability $\frac{15}{16}$, at most 6 bits of d i.e. $d[5:0]$ are restricted, and at most 8 bits of b i.e. $a'[5:0]$ and $b[21:20]$ and 7 bits of c i.e. $c[22:16]$ are needed to guess. Note that this setting is used only when $c[21:20] = min(C'^{b[21:20]}_{a'[2:0]})$ and $c[22] = 1$, or $c[21:20] = max(C'^{b[21:20]}_{a'[2:0]})$ and $c[22] = 0$, which are 25% of all cases.*
- *In Eqs. (14) and (15), there are 3 bits of d i.e. $d[5:3]$, and at most 8 bits of b i.e. $a'[5:0]$ and $b[21:20]$ and 4 bits of c i.e. $c[22:19]$ needed to guess.*

5.1 Reducing Complexities

Based on our observations of the five differential equations, we propose to use a concise and efficient way to generate a right pair in the first round. Given a weak key, from Corollary 1, we know that with probability greater than $\frac{15}{16}$ one can use at most six IV bits $\{0:5\}$ to satisfy the first two equations, and flip three IV bits $\{14, 26, 30\}$ to satisfy the last three equations based on the aforementioned observation. Inspired by the analysis of five differential equations, a proposition is presented as follows.

Proposition 3. *Let $k_{ID} \in \mathbb{F}_2^{64}$, if k_{ID} is a weak key that there exists at least one $v \in \mathbb{F}_2^{32}$ satisfying the given differential, then with probability greater than $\frac{15}{16} = 93.75\%$, one can find v in a subspace $\mathbb{S}_{V_{nfree}} \subseteq \mathbb{F}_2^{32}$ with 2^9 IVs such that $((k_{ID}, v), (k_{ID}, v'))$ forms a right pair, where the subspace $\mathbb{S}_{V_{nfree}} = \{(a_{31}, a_{30}, \cdots , a_0) \mid a_i = 0 \text{ for } i \notin V_{nfree}\}$ and the index subset $V_{nfree} = \{0:5, 14, 26, 30\}$.*

The experiment has been conducted to verify the above proposition, and its codes have been public. As a result, for 66.4% keys among all the keys we find one v in the subspace in Proposition 3 that satisfies the given differential, which confirms Proposition 3, i.e. $\geq 70\% \times \frac{15}{16} = 65.6\%$.

5.2   Theoretical Interpretation of Strong Key

According to Lemma 3, we derive a lower bound for the percentage of strong keys $k_{ID} \in \mathbb{F}_2^{64}$ that there is no IV $v \in \mathbb{F}_2^{32}$ satisfying the given differential for each case of $a'[2:0]$.

Theorem 1. *Among all the keys, there are at least 29.6875% strong keys $k_{ID} \in \mathbb{F}_2^{64}$ that there is no IV $v \in \mathbb{F}_2^{32}$ satisfying the given differential, for different $a'[2:0]$ we have*

$$
\tau = \begin{cases}
0 & \text{if } a'[2:0] = 000, \quad 1 \quad\;\; \text{if } a'[2:0] = 100, \\
0.0625 \text{ if } a'[2:0] = 001, \quad 0.375 \text{ if } a'[2:0] = 101, \\
0.25 \;\;\text{ if } a'[2:0] = 010, \quad 0.25 \;\; \text{if } a'[2:0] = 110, \\
0.375 \text{ if } a'[2:0] = 011, \quad 0.0625 \text{ if } a'[2:0] = 111.
\end{cases}
$$

where τ denotes the percentage of strong keys derived by Lemma 3.

We give the proofs of Theorem 1 in the full version, along with two examples of strong keys. With analyzing six more complex cases, our theoretical derivation of strong keys is basically consistent with the experimental result 30%.

6   Applications: ChaCha7/7.5$^{\oplus}$/6

In this section, we present several key-recovery attacks on ChaCha7, 7.5$^{\oplus}$ and ChaCha6 utilizing the new proposed techniques in Sects. 4 and 5. In the attacks, we use the forward differential characteristic in Table 3.

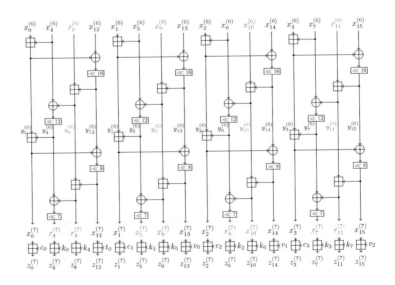

Fig. 5. Last round of ChaCha7.

6.1   Attacks Against ChaCha7

The inverse structure of ChaCha7 is first analyzed for Algorithm 1 to determine all the syncopated segments, and the procedure of last round of ChaCha7 is illustrated in Fig. 5. For the inversion of last *quarterround* function, since the following relationships,

$$
\begin{cases}
x_7^{(7)} = z_7^{(7)} \boxminus k_3 \\
x_{11}^{(7)} = z_{11}^{(7)} \boxminus k_7 \\
y_{11}^{(6)} = (z_{11}^{(7)} \boxminus x_{15}^{(7)}) \boxminus k_7 \\
x_{11}^{(6)} = (z_{11}^{(7)} \boxminus x_{15}^{(7)} \boxminus y_{15}^{(6)}) \boxminus k_7
\end{cases}
,
\qquad
\begin{cases}
x_3^{(7)} = z_3^{(7)} \boxminus c_3 \\
x_{15}^{(7)} = z_{15}^{(7)} \boxminus v_2 \\
y_{15}^{(6)} = (x_{15}^{(7)} \ggg 8) \oplus x_3^{(7)}
\end{cases}
$$

the syncopation technique can be applied on words $x_7^{(7)}$, $x_{11}^{(7)}$, $y_{11}^{(6)}$, and $x_{11}^{(6)}$ with using the property of modular subtraction, i.e. Lemma 2, where words underlined by x are known since that they can be derived from constants, IV and keystream blocks. The analysis is similar for other three *quarterround* functions, and all the words on which the syncopation technique can be applied are marked by color red in Fig. 5. Given a PNB set, Algorithm 1 is performed and the syncopated segments is determined for all the words labeled by red in Fig. 5 according to syncopated segments and restricted segments of secret key. The attacks with better parameters are obtained for ChaCha7 by setting $u = 1$, i.e. only using the syncopated segments with a one-bit restricted segment.

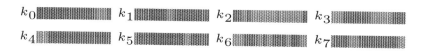

Fig. 6. The classification of all key bits for 74 CPNBs, where gray line represents CPNBs, and blue and red lines represent non-PNBs, from left to right for $k_i[31:0]$.

The Set of CPNBs. In the first step, a preliminary shortlisting of 151 possible CPNBs is obtained by setting a threshold 2^{-5} for conditional neutrality measure, which are given in the full version. Then Algorithm 2 is executed with input of the preliminary shortlisting, and the size of CPNB set is exhaustively searched. As a result, two sets with 74 CPNBs and 89 CPNBs are selected by minimizing time complexity under the requirement that data complexity does not exceed the amount of available IV. The set of 74 CPNBs is $\{2, 3, 4, 5, 47, 48, 49, 66, 67, 68, 69, 70, 71, 72, 73, 74, 75, 77, 78, 79, 80, 81, 82, 83, 84,$ $85, 86, 87, 90, 91, 102, 103, 104, 105, 106, 107, 108, 109, 110, 123, 124, 125, 126, 127,$ $155, 156, 157, 158, 159, 168, 169, 191, 192, 193, 194, 199, 200, 207, 208, 211, 212, 219,$ $220, 221, 222, 223, 224, 225, 226, 244, 245, 246, 247, 255\}$. In Fig. 6, the 74 gray lines represent 74 CPNBs according to their indexes of secret key i.e. the

Table 4. Syncopated segments of 74 CPNBs, where"-" denotes $w = 0$.

syncopated segment ← condition	(i, j_1, j_2)
T0: $x_4^{(7)}[j_2 : j_1] \leftarrow k_0[i] \neq z_4^{(7)}[i]$	$(6, 7, 31)$
T0: $x_5^{(7)}[j_2 : j_1] \leftarrow k_1[i] \neq z_5^{(7)}[i]$	$(18, 19, 31)$
T0: $x_6^{(7)}[j_2 : j_1] \leftarrow k_2[i] \neq z_6^{(7)}[i]$	$\{(12, -, -), (24, 25, 25), (28, 29, 31)\}$
T0: $x_7^{(7)}[j_2 : j_1] \leftarrow k_3[i] \neq z_7^{(7)}[i]$	$(15, 16, 26)$
T0: $x_9^{(7)}[j_2 : j_1] \leftarrow k_5[i] \neq z_9^{(7)}[i]$ T1: $y_9^{(6)}[j_2 : j_1] \leftarrow k_5[i] \neq (z_9^{(7)} \boxminus x_{13}^{(7)})[i]$ T2: $x_9^{(6)}[j_2 : j_1] \leftarrow k_5[i] \neq (z_9^{(7)} \boxminus x_{13}^{(7)} \boxminus y_{13}^{(6)})[i]$	$(10, 11, 30)$
T0: $x_{10}^{(7)}[j_2 : j_1] \leftarrow k_6[i] \neq z_{10}^{(7)}[i]$ T1: $y_{10}^{(6)}[j_2 : j_1] \leftarrow k_6[i] \neq (z_{10}^{(7)} \boxminus x_{14}^{(7)})[i]$ T2: $x_{10}^{(6)}[j_2 : j_1] \leftarrow k_6[i] \neq (z_{10}^{(7)} \boxminus x_{14}^{(7)} \boxminus y_{14}^{(6)})[i]$	$\{(3, 4, 6), (9, 10, 14), (17, 18, 18), (21, 22, 26)\}$
T0: $x_{11}^{(7)}[j_2 : j_1] \leftarrow k_7[i] \neq z_{11}^{(7)}[i]$ T1: $y_{11}^{(6)}[j_2 : j_1] \leftarrow k_7[i] \neq (z_{11}^{(7)} \boxminus x_{15}^{(7)})[i]$ T2: $x_{11}^{(6)}[j_2 : j_1] \leftarrow k_7[i] \neq (z_{11}^{(7)} \boxminus x_{15}^{(7)} \boxminus y_{15}^{(6)})[i]$	$\{(3, 4, 19), (24, 25, 30)\}$

syncopation bits, and the remaining blue and red lines represent non-CPNBs where the syncopated segments k^o and restricted segments $k^{\mathcal{R}}$ of secret key are denoted by areas of blue and red lines respectively. The syncopated segments for the 74 CPNBs are summarized in Table 4 along with 27 conditions, where we ignore the carry bits after syncopated segments. The set of 89 CPNBs is $\{2, 3, 4, 5, 6, 14, 15, 26, 47, 48, 49, 51, 66, 67, 68, 69, 70, 71, 72, 73, 74, 75, 77, 78, 79,$ $80, 81, 82, 83, 84, 85, 86, 87, 90, 91, 95, 102, 103, 104, 105, 106, 107, 108, 109, 110, 111,$ $115, 123, 124, 125, 126, 127, 135, 136, 147, 155, 156, 157, 158, 159, 168, 169, 170, 191,$ $192, 193, 194, 195, 199, 200, 207, 208, 211, 212, 219, 220, 221, 222, 223, 224, 225, 226,$ $227, 232, 244, 245, 246, 247, 255\}$. The syncopated segments of the 89 CPNBs are given in Table 5 along with their 40 conditions.

From Table 4, we remove 13 inessential conditions whose coordinates in table are $\{(T0, 8), (T0, 11), (T1, 8), (T1, 9), (T1, 10), (T1, 11), (T1, 12), (T2, 6), (T2, 8),$ $(T2, 9), (T2, 10), (T2, 11), (T2, 12)\}$, where (Ti, j) locates a condition with type Ti and top-to-bottom order j in right column of table, $0 \leq i \leq 2$ and $0 \leq j \leq 12$. For example, coordinate $(T0, 8)$ locates the syncopated segment and its condition $x_{10}^{(7)}[14 : 10] \leftarrow k_6[9] \neq z_{10}^{(7)}[9]$. In the experiment of 2^{10} random keys and $2^{16.3}$ IVs for each key, the conditional correlation is theoretically estimated as $\epsilon'_a = 0.2365$. We have conducted a verification experiment for this theoretical calculation, in which 2^6 random keys are used with $2^{32.6}$ IVs for each key. The result of experiment shows that the conditional correlation is $\epsilon'_a = 0.2369$, which is very close to the theoretical one and justifies theoretical calculation of conditional correlation. The codes of experiments have been public. Therefore, the conditional backward correlation is $\varepsilon_a = 2^{-4.2}$, when $n = 74$ and $\alpha = 48$, the time and data complexities are $T = 2^{213.9}$ and $N = 2^{59.9}$ respectively.

Table 5. Syncopated segments of 89 CPNBs, where "-" denotes $w = 0$.

syncopated segment ← condition	(i, j_1, j_2)
T0: $x_4^{(7)}[j_2 : j_1] \leftarrow k_0[i] \neq z_4^{(7)}[i]$	$\{(7, 8, 13), (16, 17, 25), (27, 28, 31)\}$
T0: $x_5^{(7)}[j_2 : j_1] \leftarrow k_1[i] \neq z_5^{(7)}[i]$	$\{(18, -, -), (20, 21, 31)\}$
T0: $x_6^{(7)}[j_2 : j_1] \leftarrow k_2[i] \neq z_6^{(7)}[i]$	$\{(12, -, -), (24, 25, 25), (28, 29, 30)\}$
T0: $x_7^{(7)}[j_2 : j_1] \leftarrow k_3[i] \neq z_7^{(7)}[i]$	$\{(16, 17, 18), (20, 21, 26)\}$
T0: $x_8^{(7)}[j_2 : j_1] \leftarrow k_4[9] \neq z_8^{(7)}[9]$ T1: $y_8^{(6)}[j_2 : j_1] \leftarrow k_4[9] \neq (z_8^{(7)} \boxminus x_{12}^{(7)})[9]$ T2: $x_8^{(6)}[j_2 : j_1] \leftarrow k_4[9] \neq (z_8^{(7)} \boxminus x_{12}^{(7)} \boxminus y_{12}^{(6)})[9]$	$\{(9, 10, 18), (20, 21, 26)\}$
T0: $x_9^{(7)}[j_2 : j_1] \leftarrow k_5[i] \neq z_9^{(7)}[i]$ T1: $y_9^{(6)}[j_2 : j_1] \leftarrow k_5[i] \neq (z_9^{(7)} \boxminus x_{13}^{(7)})[i]$ T2: $x_9^{(6)}[j_2 : j_1] \leftarrow k_5[i] \neq (z_9^{(7)} \boxminus x_{13}^{(7)} \boxminus y_{13}^{(6)})[i]$	$(11, 12, 30)$
T0: $x_{10}^{(7)}[j_2 : j_1] \leftarrow k_6[i] \neq z_{10}^{(7)}[i]$ T1: $y_{10}^{(6)}[j_2 : j_1] \leftarrow k_6[i] \neq (z_{10}^{(7)} \boxminus x_{14}^{(7)})[i]$ T2: $x_{10}^{(6)}[j_2 : j_1] \leftarrow k_6[i] \neq (z_{10}^{(7)} \boxminus x_{14}^{(7)} \boxminus y_{14}^{(6)})[i]$	$\{(4, 5, 6), (10, 11, 14), (17, 18, 18), (21, 22, 26)\}$
T0: $x_{11}^{(7)}[j_2 : j_1] \leftarrow k_7[i] \neq z_{11}^{(7)}[i]$ T1: $y_{11}^{(6)}[j_2 : j_1] \leftarrow k_7[i] \neq (z_{11}^{(7)} \boxminus x_{15}^{(7)})[i]$ T2: $x_{11}^{(6)}[j_2 : j_1] \leftarrow k_7[i] \neq (z_{11}^{(7)} \boxminus x_{15}^{(7)} \boxminus y_{15}^{(6)})[i]$	$\{(4, 5, 7), (9, 10, 19), (24, 25, 30)\}$

Analysis of Complexities. According to Corollary 1, we should know the fifteen key bits $\{32 : 37, 52, 53, 176 : 182\}$ to determine the first two differential equations, and they are not involved in the set of 74 CPNBs. Therefore, we can freely satisfy the first two differential equations by setting at most six IV bits $\{0 : 5\}$ as done in Lemma 3. The overall attack process is as follows: in step 1 of Algorithm 3 one prepares 2^6 structures of data with N pairs in each structure by traversing six IV bits $\{0 : 5\}$, and in step 3 of Algorithm 3 first selects one structure according to guessed key, and then as specified in Algorithm 3 choose subsets satisfying 28 conditions and performs the statistic testing. To satisfy the last three differential equations, this process needs to be performed 2^3 times. The N pairs should be generated by varying other three branches at which no input difference is imposed, i.e. $N \leq 2^{96}$, without affecting the propagation of differential in the first round. As a result, the total time complexity is $2^{213.9+3} = 2^{216.9}$, and data complexity is $2^{59.9+9} = 2^{68.9}$. As for the memory complexity is of $2^{6+|k^{\mathcal{R}}|} N^* = 2^{48.9}$, where we ignore the subsets that must not satisfy 28 conditions and only store the subsets used later in each structure.

Similarly, we remove 13 inessential conditions from the 40 conditions of 89 CPNBs, and their coordinates in Table 5 are $\{(T0, 14), (T0, 17), (T1, 14), (T1, 15), (T1, 16), (T1, 18), (T1, 19), (T2, 11), (T2, 12), (T2, 15), (T2, 16), (T2, 18), (T2, 19)\}$, where (Ti, j) locates a condition with type Ti and top-to-bottom order j in right column of table, $0 \leq i \leq 2$ and $0 \leq j \leq 19$. By the experiment with 2^{10} random keys and $2^{20.3}$ IVs for each key, the conditional correlation ϵ_a' is theoretically estimated as $2^{-4.14}$, and the codes of experiment have been public. Therefore, the conditional backward correlation is $\varepsilon_a = 2^{-8.28}$, when $n = 89$ and $\alpha = 54$, we obtain another attack with less time complexity of $2^{207.3+3} = 2^{210.3}$ and data complexity of $2^{94.3+9} = 2^{103.3}$.

6.2 Attacks Against ChaCha7.5$^{\oplus}$

To get closer to ChaCha8, ChaCha7.5$^{\oplus}$ is defined as a round-reduced version without last bit-wise XOR and left rotation in the last round function compared with ChaCha7.5.

Since the analysis of ChaCha7.5$^{\oplus}$ is similar to the one of ChaCha7, we only focus on different points and present specific attack parameters against ChaCha7.5$^{\oplus}$ in the following. The last round of ChaCha7.5$^{\oplus}$ is illustrated in Fig. 7 where the notation $1^{\oplus}$ means no last XOR and left rotation in one round. For the inversion of last *quarterround* function in the 7-th round, the relationship is that $x_3^{(7)} = (x_3^{(7.5^{\oplus})} \boxminus z_4^{(7.5^{\oplus})}) \boxplus k_0$ and $x_3^{(7.5^{\oplus})} = z_3^{(7.5^{\oplus})} \boxminus c_3$, and then the syncopation technique can be applied on $x_3^{(7)}$ with using the property of modular addition, i.e. Lemma 1. In Fig. 7, we mark all the words on which the syncopation technique can be applied with using the property of modular addition (Lemma 1) and subtraction (Lemma 2) which are marked by color green and red respectively. Similarly, we set $u = 1$ and use the syncopated segments with a one-bit restricted segment in Algorithm 1.

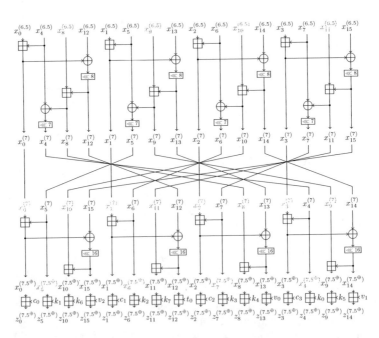

Fig. 7. Last $1^{\oplus}$ round of ChaCha7.5$^{\oplus}$.

The Set of CPNBs. A preliminary shortlisting of 119 possible CPNBs is obtained by setting 2^{-5} as a threshold for conditional neutrality measure, which is given in the full version. Then Algorithm 2 is executed with the preliminary shortlisting, and a set of 54 CPNBs is selected to launch the key-recovery attack. The 54 CPNBs are $\{74, 75, 83, 90, 91, 92, 95, 108, 109, 110, 111, 115, 123, 124, 125,$ $126, 127, 155, 156, 157, 158, 159, 168, 169, 170, 191, 192, 193, 194, 195, 199, 200, 204,$ $207, 208, 211, 212, 213, 216, 219, 220, 221, 222, 223, 224, 225, 226, 227, 232, 244, 245,$ $246, 247, 255\}$, and its syncopated segments and 30 conditions are given in the full version.

Analysis of Complexities. Two inessential conditions are removed from the 30 conditions of 54 CPNBs. By the experiment with 2^{10} random keys and $2^{20.3}$ IVs for each key, the conditional correlation ϵ'_a is theoretically estimated as $2^{-4.3}$. Therefore, the conditional backward correlation is $\varepsilon_a = 2^{-8.6}$, when $n = 54$ and $\alpha = 19$, an attack is obtained with time complexity of $2^{241.9+3} = 2^{244.9}$ and data complexity of $2^{95.9+9} = 2^{104.9}$.

Another attack on ChaCha7.5$^{\oplus}$. Another alternative way is to find the right pairs with help of a pre-computed list, as proposed in [14]. The attacker pre-computes all the needed right pairs offline and keep them in a list. In order to find a favorable IV in the pre-computed list for every exploitable key, we should ensure that all the CPNBs of ID column, denoted by $CPNB_{ID}$, satisfy $CPNB_{ID} \subseteq K_{nmem}$, i.e. $K_{mem} \subseteq NonCPNB_{ID}$. Next, we list the main results of the way of pre-computing a list to find right pairss in the first round. A set of 49 CPNBs is selected, that is $CPNB = \{74, 75, 83, 90, 91, 95, 108, 109, 110, 111, 115, 123, 124,$ $125, 126, 127, 155, 156, 157, 158, 159, 168, 169, 170, 191, 192, 193, 194, 199, 204, 207,$ $208, 211, 212, 216, 219, 220, 221, 222, 223, 224, 225, 226, 232, 244, 245, 246, 247, 255\}$. There are four CPNBs in the ID column, i.e. $CPNB_{ID} = \{168, 169, 170, 191\}$. A greedy algorithm is used to construct K_{nmem} such that K_{nmem} includes as many key bits as possible, especially for bits in $CPNB_{ID}$, while the probability of exploitable keys is high. A subset of size 20 is obtained, i.e. $K_{nmem} = \{168, 191, 169, 171, 183, 172, 173, 184, 174, 175, 185, 163, 176, 40, 41, 164, 59, 177,$ $186, 160\}$. Among of them three bits are from $CPNB_{ID}$, and one key bit should be excluded from the CPNB set for a high probability of exploitable keys, i.e. $K_{exclude} = \{170\}$. As a result, there are about $p_{exp} = 55.4\%$ exploitable keys among all keys with respect to the subspace $\mathbb{S}_{K_{nmem}}$. Since the dimension of $\mathbb{S}_{K_{mem}}$ is $64 - 20 = 44$, we should construct a pre-computed list of approximately $p_{exp} \times 2^{44} \approx 2^{43.1}$ possible exploitable keys and their favorable IVs. The final set of 48 CPNBs is $CPNB_{final} = CPNB \setminus K_{exclude}$ and its syncopated segments and 30 conditions are given in the full version.

Analysis of Complexities. The conditional backward correlation of final set of 48 CPNB's is theoretically estimated as $\varepsilon_a = 2^{-6.1}$. Therefore, with $\varepsilon_d = 2^{-8.3}$, $\alpha = 17$, the corresponding data and time complexities of attack are $2^{94.8+31} = 2^{125.8}$ and $2^{242.9}$ respectively.

6.3 Attack Against ChaCha6

Here, we give a new analysis of ChaCha6 under the refined framework. The analysis of ChaCha6 is similar to the one of ChaCha7, and next we only show the main parameters of the attack, and for details please refer to the full version. A partial key-recovery attack is presented in [2], where 36 key bits can be restored. For a better comparison, only the significant key bits are recovered in our attack whose procedure only consists of steps from 1 to 5 in Algorithm 3. As estimated in [2], the attack should be repeated for 2^5 times to find right pairs in the first round. There are two main parameters which affect the complexities of attack, the number m of significant key bits, and the backward correlation ε_a. Given the above main parameters, we determine $N^* = (\frac{\sqrt{(m+5)\log 4}+3\sqrt{1-(\varepsilon_a\varepsilon_d)^2}}{\varepsilon_a\varepsilon_d})^2$, the data complexity $N = 2^5 \times \frac{1}{q} \times 2N^*$, and time complexity $T = 2^5 \times \frac{1}{q} \times 2N^* + 2^5 \times 2N^* \times 2^{m2}$, where $q = ((\frac{1}{2})^{\theta_1}(\frac{3}{4})^{\theta_2})^2$, θ_1 and θ_2 are the numbers of syncopated segments with one-bit and two-bit restricted segments respectively. By performing Algorithm 2 with a greedy criteria of minimizing time complexity, we obtain an attack parameter of ChaCha6, which has 211 CPNBs with 27 syncopated segments ($\theta_1 = 18$, $\theta_2 = 9$). Our experiment has checked the conditional backward correlation of 211 CPNBs, that is $|\varepsilon_a| = 0.81$. Therefore, our attack on ChaCha6 takes time and data complexities of $2^{75.7}$ and $2^{73.7}$ respectively, which is faster and recovers nine more key bits, i.e. 45 key bits, than previous one [2]. The specific significant key bits and corresponding CPNB's syncopated segments and conditions are given in the full version.

7 Conclusion

In this paper, we present PNB-based differential cryptanalysis of ChaCha with *syncopation*. Specifically, we propose the *syncopation* technique, and refine the key-recovery attack based on PNB method with this new technique. The attacks on ChaCha6 and ChaCha7 are improved using the new technique in the PNB-based cryptanalysis. Furthermore, ChaCha7.5$^\oplus$ is defined for getting closer to ChaCha8, and several attacks are presented on ChaCha7.5$^\oplus$. As far as we know, this is the first attack on ChaCha7.5$^\oplus$ which is much more efficient than brute force. In a nutshell, we move a small but important step forward towards the analysis of ChaCha8. It is interesting and worth to consider how to apply the new techniques on the other ARX ciphers, such as Salsa and Chaskey.

Acknowledgements. We are very grateful to the anonymous reviewers for their detailed comments and helpful suggestions of our manuscript. We would also like to thank Chengan Hou for his careful proofreading of this manuscript.

---

[2] The complexity was doubled in the analysis of [2], we multiply it by a factor of two here for a fair comparison.

References

1. Aumasson, J.-P., Fischer, S., Khazaei, S., Meier, W., Rechberger, C.: New features of Latin dances: analysis of salsa, chacha, and rumba. In: Nyberg, K. (ed.) FSE 2008. LNCS, vol. 5086, pp. 470–488. Springer, Heidelberg (2008). https://doi.org/10.1007/978-3-540-71039-4_30

2. Beierle, C., Leander, G., Todo, Y.: Improved differential-linear attacks with applications to ARX ciphers. In: Micciancio, D., Ristenpart, T. (eds.) CRYPTO 2020. LNCS, vol. 12172, pp. 329–358. Springer, Cham (2020). https://doi.org/10.1007/978-3-030-56877-1_12

3. Bernstein, D.J.: The poly1305-AES message-authentication code. In: Gilbert, H., Handschuh, H. (eds.) FSE 2005. LNCS, vol. 3557, pp. 32–49. Springer, Heidelberg (2005). https://doi.org/10.1007/11502760_3

4. Bernstein, D.J.: Chacha, a variant of salsa20 (2008). https://cr.yp.to/chacha/chacha-20080128.pdf

5. Bernstein, D.J.: The Salsa20 family of stream ciphers. In: Robshaw, M., Billet, O. (eds.) New Stream Cipher Designs. LNCS, vol. 4986, pp. 84–97. Springer, Heidelberg (2008). https://doi.org/10.1007/978-3-540-68351-3_8

6. Biham, E., Carmeli, Y.: An improvement of linear cryptanalysis with addition operations with applications to FEAL-8X. In: Joux, A., Youssef, A. (eds.) SAC 2014. LNCS, vol. 8781, pp. 59–76. Springer, Cham (2014). https://doi.org/10.1007/978-3-319-13051-4_4

7. Biham, E., Shamir, A.: Differential cryptanalysis of DES-like cryptosystems. In: Menezes, A.J., Vanstone, S.A. (eds.) CRYPTO 1990. LNCS, vol. 537, pp. 2–21. Springer, Heidelberg (1991). https://doi.org/10.1007/3-540-38424-3_1

8. Choudhuri, A.R., Maitra, S.: Significantly improved multi-bit differentials for reduced round salsa and chacha. IACR Trans. Symmetric Cryptol. **2016**(2), 261–287 (2016). https://doi.org/10.13154/tosc.v2016.i2.261-287

9. Coutinho, M., Neto, T.C.S.: Improved linear approximations to ARX ciphers and attacks against chacha. Cryptology ePrint Archive, Paper 2021/224 (2021). https://eprint.iacr.org/2021/224

10. Coutinho, M., Souza Neto, T.C.: Improved linear approximations to ARX ciphers and attacks against chacha. In: Canteaut, A., Standaert, F.-X. (eds.) EUROCRYPT 2021. LNCS, vol. 12696, pp. 711–740. Springer, Cham (2021). https://doi.org/10.1007/978-3-030-77870-5_25

11. Coutinho, M., Passos, I., Vásquez, J.C.G., de Mendonça, F.L.L., de Sousa, R.T., Borges, F.: Latin dances reloaded: improved cryptanalysis against salsa and chacha, and the proposal of Forró. In: Agrawal, S., Lin, D. (eds.) Advances in Cryptology - ASIACRYPT 2022. ASIACRYPT 2022. Lecture Notes in Computer Science, vol. 13791, pp. 256–286. Springer, Cham (2022). https://doi.org/10.1007/978-3-031-22963-3_9

12. Dey, S., Dey, C., Sarkar, S., Meier, W.: Revisiting cryptanalysis on chacha from crypto 2020 and Eurocrypt 2021. IEEE Trans. Inf. Theory **68**(9), 6114–6133 (2022). https://doi.org/10.1109/TIT.2022.3171865

13. Dey, S., Garai, H.K., Maitra, S.: Cryptanalysis of reduced round chacha- new attack and deeper analysis. Cryptology ePrint Archive, Paper 2023/134 (2023). https://eprint.iacr.org/2023/134

14. Dey, S., Garai, H.K., Sarkar, S., Sharma, N.K.: Revamped differential-linear cryptanalysis on reduced round chacha. In: Dunkelman, O., Dziembowski, S. (eds.) Advances in Cryptology – EUROCRYPT 2022. EUROCRYPT 2022. Lecture Notes in Computer Science, vol. 13277, pp. 86–114. Springer, Cham (2022). https://doi.org/10.1007/978-3-031-07082-2_4

15. Dey, S., Sarkar, S.: Improved analysis for reduced round salsa and chacha. Discret. Appl. Math. **227**, 58–69 (2017). https://doi.org/10.1016/j.dam.2017.04.034

16. Dey, S., Sarkar, S.: Proving the biases of Salsa and ChaCha in differential attack. Des. Codes Crypt. **88**(9), 1827–1856 (2020). https://doi.org/10.1007/s10623-020-00736-9

17. eSTREAM: The ecrypt stream cipher project. https://www.ecrypt.eu.org/stream/

18. IANIX: Chacha usage & deployment. https://ianix.com/pub/chacha-deployment.html

19. Langford, S.K., Hellman, M.E.: Differential-linear cryptanalysis. In: Desmedt, Y.G. (ed.) CRYPTO 1994. LNCS, vol. 839, pp. 17–25. Springer, Heidelberg (1994). https://doi.org/10.1007/3-540-48658-5_3

20. Langley, A., Chang, W., Mavrogiannopoulos, N., Strömbergson, J., Josefsson, S.: Chacha20-poly1305 cipher suites for transport layer security (TLS). RFC **7905**(1–8), 10 (2016). https://doi.org/10.17487/RFC7905

21. Leurent, G.: Improved differential-linear cryptanalysis of 7-round Chaskey with partitioning. In: Fischlin, M., Coron, J.-S. (eds.) EUROCRYPT 2016. LNCS, vol. 9665, pp. 344–371. Springer, Heidelberg (2016). https://doi.org/10.1007/978-3-662-49890-3_14

22. Maitra, S.: Chosen IV cryptanalysis on reduced round chacha and salsa. Discret. Appl. Math. **208**, 88–97 (2016). https://doi.org/10.1016/j.dam.2016.02.020

23. Matsui, M.: Linear cryptanalysis method for DES cipher. In: Helleseth, T. (ed.) EUROCRYPT 1993. LNCS, vol. 765, pp. 386–397. Springer, Heidelberg (1994). https://doi.org/10.1007/3-540-48285-7_33

24. Miyashita, S., Ito, R., Miyaji, A.: PNB-focused differential cryptanalysis of chacha stream cipher. In: Nguyen, K., Yang, G., Guo, F., Susilo, W. (eds.) Information Security and Privacy, pp. 46–66. Springer International Publishing, Cham (2022)

25. Nir, Y.: Chacha20, poly1305, and their use in the internet key exchange protocol (IKE) and IPsec. RFC **7634**(1–13), 10 (2015). https://doi.org/10.17487/RFC7634

26. Shi, Z., Zhang, B., Feng, D., Wu, W.: Improved key recovery attacks on reduced-round Salsa20 and ChaCha. In: Kwon, T., Lee, M.-K., Kwon, D. (eds.) ICISC 2012. LNCS, vol. 7839, pp. 337–351. Springer, Heidelberg (2013). https://doi.org/10.1007/978-3-642-37682-5_24

Cryptanalysis of Symmetric Primitives over Rings and a Key Recovery Attack on **Rubato**

Lorenzo Grassi[1(✉)], Irati Manterola Ayala[2(✉)], Martha Norberg Hovd[2(✉)],
Morten Øygarden[2(✉)], Håvard Raddum[2(✉)], and Qingju Wang[3(✉)]

[1] Ruhr University Bochum, Bochum, Germany
`lorenzo.grassi@ruhr-uni-bochum.de`
[2] Simula UiB, Bergen, Norway
{`irati,martha,morten.oygarden,haavardr`}`@simula.no`
[3] Telecom Paris, Institut Polytechnique de Paris, Palaiseau, France
`qingju.wang@telecom-paris.fr`

Abstract. Symmetric primitives are a cornerstone of cryptography, and have traditionally been defined over fields, where cryptanalysis is now well understood. However, a few symmetric primitives defined over *rings* $\mathbb{Z}_q$ for a composite number q have recently been proposed, a setting where security is much less studied. In this paper we focus on studying established algebraic attacks typically defined over fields and the extent of their applicability to symmetric primitives defined over the ring of integers modulo a composite q. Based on our analysis, we present an attack on full Rubato, a family of symmetric ciphers proposed by Ha et al. at Eurocrypt 2022 designed to be used in a transciphering framework for approximate fully homomorphic encryption. We show that at least 25% of the possible choices for q satisfy certain conditions that lead to a successful key recovery attack with complexity significantly lower than the claimed security level for five of the six ciphers in the Rubato family.

Keywords: Algebraic cryptanalysis · composite modulus · Rubato, Key recovery attack, Arithmetization oriented primitives

1 Introduction

Symmetric cryptography is the most fundamental form of encryption and its history goes back thousands of years. In modern times, the first cipher to be standardized was the symmetric encryption algorithm DES in 1977 [59], and since then many other symmetric ciphers have been proposed and standardized. The continued development of other areas of cryptography has often required symmetric ciphers with particular properties, which prompts the proposals of new schemes. This cycle of demand and proposal continues to this day.

As symmetric cryptography evolves, so does its cryptanalysis. Security claims and notions have been formalized, and it has long been standard to assess the

---

Author list in alphabetical order.

© International Association for Cryptologic Research 2023
H. Handschuh and A. Lysyanskaya (Eds.): CRYPTO 2023, LNCS 14083, pp. 305–339, 2023.
https://doi.org/10.1007/978-3-031-38548-3_11

security of new primitives by examining their susceptibility to known attacks, e.g., linear [57] and differential [16,17] attacks as well as refined and generalized versions of them [14,15,18,52,68]. Another class of attacks is algebraic attacks, such as interpolation [48], higher-order differential [52,54], or computing Gröbner bases for a set of polynomials representing the encryption function.

However, the procedure and success of many attacks depend on the ring or field over which the symmetric primitive is defined, especially algebraic attacks. This dependency is the main topic of our paper, as we assess how attacks on primitives defined over *fields* may carry over to primitives defined over *rings*.

1.1   From Traditional Symmetric Primitives to Symmetric Primitives over Integer Rings Modulo Composites

Traditional Symmetric Primitives. Since computers work with bits, the traditional symmetric ciphers (from DES and onwards) have been built on bit-strings, which must be embedded with mathematical operations in order to perform any cryptographic algorithm. The natural algebraic structure for these ciphers has therefore been the binary field $\mathbb{F}_2$, or one of its extensions $\mathbb{F}_{2^n}$. These fields are very convenient for computers, as addition is simply the XOR operation, and multiplication is simply the AND for $\mathbb{F}_2$, or a particular matrix/vector multiplication over $\mathbb{F}_2$ for multiplying elements of $\mathbb{F}_{2^n}$.

The non-linear operations in these types of ciphers may be performed using S-boxes: permutations on short bit-strings that can easily be implemented via a look-up table. S-boxes should be designed such that describing them with polynomials over the base field produces polynomials of the highest possible degree which the S-box size will permit, as security may be compromised if this is not the case. There are alternative ways of performing non-linear operations, for example the method of ARX ciphers, which uses addition modulo 2^n as an operation in the cipher (see [10–12] for examples). However, S-boxes are by far the most common way to perform non-linear operations.

The linear operations in symmetric ciphers should combine the outputs from different non-linear operations as a means to thwart attacks. Iterating the non-linear and linear operations over several rounds quickly makes the polynomials describing encryption depend on all unknown key variables and have the maximum possible degree for the given number of unknowns and the base field. The fields $\mathbb{F}_2$ and the more general $\mathbb{F}_{2^n}$ are well understood for algebraic cryptanalysis, and it has become increasingly easy to argue convincingly that ciphers defined over either these fields are secure against algebraic attacks.

Arithmetization-Oriented Symmetric Primitives. The traditional ciphers work very well for simple encryption/decryption of binary data. However, with the evolution of more sophisticated cryptographic constructions like multi-party computation (MPC), fully homomorphic encryption (FHE), and zero-knowledge (ZK) protocols there has been an increasing demand for *arithmetization-oriented* symmetric primitives to be used together with MPC, ZK, or FHE. While traditional primitives have been designed to be efficient in software and hardware, the

MPC-/ZK-/FHE-friendly primitives are subject to a different efficiency metric. Instead of minimizing the number of bitwise operations, these designs aim to minimize the cost related to the number of non-linear operations. Roughly:

- MPC-friendly schemes aim to minimize the number of non-linear operations necessary to evaluate them;
- ZK-friendly schemes aim to minimize the number of non-linear operations necessary to verify them;
- FHE-friendly schemes aim to minimize the multiplicative depth of their representation when encryption and decryption are expressed as circuits.

Several specialized MPC-/ZK-/FHE-friendly symmetric primitives have recently been proposed, for example MiMC [4], *Vision/Rescue* [5], Chaghri [6], Rasta [29], Ciminion [30], Reinforced Concrete [41], HadesMiMC/Poseidon [42,44]. All these primitives are characterized by the following:

- they are usually defined over a prime field $\mathbb{F}_p$ for a large prime p (usually $\log_2(p) \geq 64$), whereas traditional schemes are defined over binary fields;
- they can be described by a simple algebraic expression over their natural field, whereas classical schemes require a more complex algebraic expression.

The first point is motivated by the fact that MPC/ZK/FHE protocols often also rely on primitives from public-key cryptography, which are usually defined over prime fields. It is therefore more convenient to deal with a symmetric primitive that works directly over a prime field, rather than one instantiated over a binary field, which would require conversion to/from the prime field.

The second point is related both to the cost metric of MPC/ZK/FHE protocols, and to the fact that any sub-component (such as the non-linear S-boxes) that defines the symmetric primitive must be computed on the fly. Indeed, due to the huge size of the field these primitives are typically defined over, functions such as the S-box cannot be pre-computed and stored as a look-up table. Some simple non-linear algebraic function is therefore used instead of a look-up table, which leads to a simpler algebraic description, making the scheme potentially vulnerable to algebraic attacks [3,13,31,43,49].

Symmetric Primitives over Quotient Rings with Composite Modulus. The areas of MPC, ZK, FHE, and their associated symmetric primitives are constantly evolving. While traditionally defined over fields such as $\mathbb{F}_p$ and $\mathbb{F}_{p^n}$, there has recently been a surge of new MPC-protocols defined over a ring $\mathbb{Z}_{2^n}$ [25, 27,53,58,67]. One method for creating such a ring-based protocol is to construct a MAC over a ring, then apply it in an adapted framework [25].

As with MPC, the vast majority of ZK protocols are also based over fields, but there has recently been a handful of suggestion over rings here as well, e.g., proof systems based on VOLEs over rings [8,9], and the SNARK Rinocchio [35].

The story is slightly different for FHE, as these schemes have most often been defined over polynomial rings, but also here the associated primitives have typically been defined over fields. There are, however, two recently proposed symmetric schemes defined over rings: Elisabeth [24] and Rubato [47]. Furthermore, these schemes are not used to construct an FHE scheme, but rather combined with already existing FHE schemes as part of a larger framework.

Elisabeth is a family of stream ciphers proposed by Cosseron et al. at Asiacrypt 2022, designed and optimized to be used in combination with the TFHE scheme in a Hybrid Homomorphic Encrypton (HHE) framework. Whereas previous ciphers designed for HHE are defined over fields, Elisabeth is defined over the ring $\mathbb{Z}_{16}$. This definition impacts the design of the scheme from a security perspective, which we discuss briefly in Sect. 4 in the bigger picture of how to design a non-linear function over a ring. However, defining the cipher over the ring $\mathbb{Z}_{16}$ also has positive impacts on efficiency, as it allows Elisabeth to exploit the various subroutines of TFHE to the fullest, and runs significantly faster than comparable FHE-friendly ciphers for TFHE.

Rubato is a family of ciphers proposed by Ha et al. at Eurocrypt 2022 designed to be used in a transciphering framework for approximate FHE. The cipher is based on the novel idea of introducing noise to a symmetric cipher of a low algebraic degree, which the authors use to argue that very few rounds is sufficient for achieving security. The design of Rubato is very similar to HERA [23], another FHE-friendly cipher. A critical difference is that HERA is defined over a field $\mathbb{F}_p$ for p a prime, while this condition is relaxed to a ring $\mathbb{Z}_q$ for any 25- or 26-bit integer q in the design of Rubato. We refer to Sect. 5 for a detailed description of the cipher and the framework wherein it is designed to be used.

1.2   Our Contributions

Even though symmetric primitives over rings have been proposed, the cryptanalysis used to argue for their security is developed for primitives over fields. Since symmetric primitives over rings are rather new in the literature, knowledge of cryptanalysis specific to the ring setting is limited. It is therefore timely that the cryptanalysis of symmetric primitives is developed to also assess their security when they are defined over rings, not just fields. In this paper, we aim to start filling this gap.

Security of Symmetric Primitives over the Ring $\mathbb{Z}_q$. First of all, we aim to better understand the differences in the security of a symmetric primitive defined over a ring $\mathbb{Z}_q$ with respect to one defined over a field $\mathbb{F}_p$. We focus first on adapting the brute force attack in Sect. 2, whilst the algebraic attacks based on linearizaton, Gröbner bases, interpolation, and higher-order differential are discussed in Sect. 3.

The reason we focus on algebraic attacks is twofold. First, the main focus of this paper is arithmetization-friendly symmetric schemes. These schemes admit a simple algebraic expression, which in general implies that algebraic attacks are much more powerful than statistical attacks. Second, many statistical attacks (e.g., differential [16]) only exploit the property that $(\mathbb{F}_q, +)$ or $(\mathbb{Z}_q, +)$ are groups, and they work whether the analyzed primitive admits a polynomial representation or not. Hence, it is very likely that such attacks work in a similar way over both rings and fields. We leave the problem of analyzing this aspect in more detail for future work.

Most of the mentioned algebraic attacks can be adapted to work when the cryptographic function admits a polynomial representation over $\mathbb{Z}_q$, though they are not as straightforward as in the finite field case. We report the following:

- Brute force attack: perhaps surprisingly, we note that an adaptation of the brute force attack can be significantly cheaper than the straightforward $\mathcal{O}(q^n)$ for a primitive over $\mathbb{Z}_q$ with n secret elements. For instance, if $q = p^y$, the cost is $\mathcal{O}(y \cdot p^n)$, as opposed to $\mathcal{O}(p^{y \cdot n})$.
- Linearization: this attack works similarly to that of the finite field case, though there are subtle difference. In particular, if other linear algebra methods than (an adaptation of) Gaussian elimination is to be used, the solving procedure for a linear equation system over $\mathbb{Z}_q$ must be repeated for every prime factor of q.
- Gröbner bases: if the polynomial system is overdetermined and admits a unique solution, it can be solved through Gröbner basis techniques, albeit at a higher cost than what we expect when solving it over finite fields. Whether solutions to more general polynomial systems over $\mathbb{Z}_q$ can be found by Gröbner basis methods is an open problem;
- Interpolation: there exist dedicated methods for interpolating polynomials over $\mathbb{Z}_q$. Moreover, for some compositions of q, the maximal degree of polynomials can be significantly smaller than q, which could make interpolation attacks competitive.
- Higher-order differential: beyond restricting to prime factors of q, we have not been able to find good generalizations of zero sums. We therefore do not expect higher-order differential attacks to pose much of a threat to ciphers designed over $\mathbb{Z}_q$.

Based on this analysis we discuss how to design the non-linear components of a symmetric scheme over $\mathbb{Z}_q$ for preventing these attacks in Sect. 4.

Key Recovery Attack on Full Rubato. We present Rubato in Sect. 5, and give an attack on full Rubato in Sect. 6. We exploit the fact that Rubato can, in fact, be described by polynomials of low degree in $\mathbb{Z}_q$. As already mentioned, the designers of Rubato introduced adding random noise drawn from a Gaussian distribution to the Rubato key stream to make algebraic attacks much harder. We show how to overcome the addition of random noise by making use of a brute force attack on the key modulo small factors of q. If some factors are small enough the brute force attack has complexity much lower than the claimed security level and allows the attacker to identify positions in the key stream where no noise has been added, leaving the cipher open to a full key recovery with a linearization attack. We provide experimental data verifying that the brute-force method we introduce works as intended and can be used to remove the noise.

We further discuss the assumptions underlying the attack in Sect. 7 and show that for all but one Rubato variant, at least 25% of the possible choices for q leads to a cipher that can be broken with time complexity less than the claimed security level. For example, if q contains the factor 12, the secret key in Rubato-80M can be successfully recovered with time complexity $2^{57.06}$ using less than 250.000 known key stream elements and less than 25 GB of memory.

Restoring the Security of Rubato. Lastly, in Sect. 8 we discuss some countermeasures that allow to reestablish the security of Rubato, and which could be crucial for the design of new symmetric primitives over rings $\mathbb{Z}_q$. These include increasing the width of the noise distribution, increasing the number of rounds, and using non-polynomial S-boxes.

A Note on Sections Dependency. Sections 2 through 4 are in large parts general discussion on cryptanalysis and security, whilst Sects. 5 through 8.1 deal specifically with Rubato. However, the attack on Rubato does not rely on all the material discussed in the former sections. A reader mainly interested in Rubato may therefore turn to Sect. 5 after having read Sect. 3.1, and similarly a reader mainly interested in more general findings on cryptanalysis may find themselves content with skimming Sects. 5 through 8.1.

2   General Security of Symmetric Primitives: Fields Versus Integers Modulo q

In this section, we recall fundamental properties of polynomial functions over $\mathbb{Z}_q$, and discuss their immediate security impact. We show that polynomials over $\mathbb{Z}_q$ are generally more restricted in their degrees than polynomials over finite fields. On top of that, we shall see that a symmetric primitive that can be written out as a polynomial in $\mathbb{Z}_q$ will offer less resistance against a brute force attack when compared to a primitive defined over a finite field of similar size.

2.1   Notation and Preliminaries

Notation. We fix the following notation for the rest of the paper. Let q denote a composite integer with prime factorization $q = p_1^{y_1} \cdots p_a^{y_a}$, where p_i is prime and $y_i \geq 1$ for $i = 1, \ldots, a$. Lowercase letters refers to single integers, and boldface lowercase letters refers to vectors or sequences of integers. Uppercase letters indicate functions, including matrices. A table of frequently used notation is found in [39, Appendix A].

Polynomial Functions. It is well known that not every function over $\mathbb{Z}_q$ admits a polynomial representation when q is composite. The existence of null polynomials, i.e., non-trivial elements in $\mathbb{Z}_q[x]$ that evaluate to 0 for all $x \in \mathbb{Z}_q$, then follows from a quick counting argument. Univariate polynomial functions and null polynomials have been well-studied in the literature, see e.g., [50,62] for general $\mathbb{Z}_q$, and [36] for the important case of $\mathbb{Z}_{p^y}$. Let $\rho = \rho(q)$ be the smallest integer such that $\rho! \equiv 0 \mod q$. Then there are $\prod_{i=0}^{\rho} q/\gcd(i!, q)$ distinct polynomial functions $\mathbb{Z}_q \to \mathbb{Z}_q$, each of which has a canonical representation as a polynomial in $\mathbb{Z}_q[x]$ of degree at most ρ [62, Corollary 9 and Theorem 10]. Note that ρ can be significantly smaller than q. Indeed, we have $\rho(q) = \max\{\rho(p_i^{y_i}) | 1 \le i \le a\}$, and $y(p-1)+1 \le \rho(p^y) \le py$ [37, Lemma 8]. Finally, a classification of null polynomials is also known [62, Theorem 6], [36, Theorem 1]. While we are not aware of similar studies of *multivariate* polynomial functions over $\mathbb{Z}_q$, a coordinate-wise application of the aforementioned result implies an upper bound of degree $n\rho$ for polynomials in n variables.

Univariate permutation polynomials have also been studied in the literature. An exact characterization is known for $q = 2^y$ [60]. For more general values of q, a formula counting the number of permutation polynomials is given in [65].

A necessary condition for a function F defined over $\mathbb{Z}_q$ to admit a polynomial representation is preservation of congruence. We state the multivariate version in the following, with the proof given in [39, Appendix B].

Lemma 1. *Let u be a divisor of q, and F a polynomial function $\mathbb{Z}_q^n \to \mathbb{Z}_q$.*

i) *For any $\mathbf{x} \in \mathbb{Z}_q^n$:* $F(\mathbf{x}) \mod u \equiv F(\mathbf{x} \mod u) \mod u.$
ii) *$\forall \mathbf{n}_1, \mathbf{n}_2, \mathbf{n}_3 \in \mathbb{N}^n$:* $F(\mathbf{n}_1 \cdot u + \mathbf{n}_2) \mod u \equiv F(\mathbf{n}_3 \cdot u + \mathbf{n}_2) \mod u.$

The Chinese Remainder Theorem. Many problems in $\mathbb{Z}_q$ can be simplified by working over the (powers of) prime factors of q. The classical tool for this is the Chinese Remainder Theorem (CRT), which we recall in the following.

Theorem 1. *Let $q = \prod_{i=1}^{a} p_i^{y_i}$ where $\gcd(p_i, p_j) = 1$ for all $i \ne j$. Let $b_1, \ldots, b_a \in \mathbb{Z}$ such that $0 \le b_i < p_i^{y_i}$ for $1 \le i \le a$. Then there exists a unique integer x that satisfies the two following conditions:*

- *$0 \le x < q$, and*
- *for all $1 \le i \le a$: $x \equiv b_i \mod p_i^{y_i}$.*

Suppose that we want to recover an element $x \in \mathbb{Z}_q$, for $q = p_1^{y_1} \cdot p_2^{y_2}$, from its values modulo $p_i^{y_i}$. By Bézout's identity, there exist $\mu_1, \mu_2 \in \mathbb{Z}$ such that $\mu_1 \cdot p_1^{y_1} + \mu_2 \cdot p_2^{y_2} = 1$, which can be computed via the extended Euclidean algorithm. Then, the solution x to $x \equiv b_1 \mod p_1^{y_1}$ and $x \equiv b_2 \mod p_2^{y_2}$ is given by $x = b_1 \cdot \mu_2 \cdot p_2^{y_2} + b_2 \cdot \mu_1 \cdot p_1^{y_1}$. This strategy can easily be generalized to values of q with more distinct prime factors.

2.2 Solving Polynomial Systems Modulo q

Let $F_1, \ldots, F_n : \mathbb{Z}_q^n \to \mathbb{Z}_q$ be n polynomial functions and consider the following system of equations

$$F_1(x_1, \ldots, x_n) = b_1$$
$$\vdots \quad\quad\quad\quad\quad (1)$$
$$F_n(x_1, \ldots, x_n) = b_n.$$

The discussion in the previous subsection prompts the following strategy for solving such a system of equations.

1. For $i \in \{1, \ldots, a\}$, rewrite Eq. (1) modulo $p_i^{y_i}$.
2. Solve each of the systems modulo $p_i^{y_i}$.
3. Reconstruct a solution in $\mathbb{Z}_q^n$ using CRT.

In the case of $y_i = 1$, solving the system modulo p_i can be done using any algorithm for solving polynomial systems over finite fields. Greater care is needed if $y_i \geq 2$. In the following, we describe a way to further break down the problem.

It is well-known that any $x \in \mathbb{Z}_{p^y}$ can be written as $x = \sum_{i=0}^{y-1} x^{(i)} \cdot p^i$, where $x^{(0)}, \ldots, x^{(y-1)} \in \mathbb{Z}_p$. Based on this, one strategy for solving the equation system modulo p^y is the following:

i) rewrite the equations in Eq. (1) modulo p and solve the system (by exhaustive search if necessary), finding $x_1^{(0)}, \ldots, x_n^{(0)}$;

ii) rewrite the equations modulo p^2. It is simple to note that the only variables appearing in the system are those with superscript (0) and (1), i.e. $x_1^{(0)}, \ldots, x_n^{(0)}$ and $x_1^{(1)}, \ldots, x_n^{(1)}$. Since $x_1^{(0)}, \ldots, x_n^{(0)}$ are known from the previous step, one only needs to solve for $x_1^{(1)}, \ldots, x_n^{(1)}$;

iii) more generally, given $x_1^{(0)}, \ldots, x_n^{(0)}, x_1^{(1)}, \ldots, x_n^{(1)}, \ldots, x_1^{(i-1)}, \ldots, x_n^{(i-1)}$, rewrite the equations modulo p^i, and solve the system in order to find $x_1^{(i)}, \ldots, x_n^{(i)}$.

By working iteratively, one finds a solution $(x_1, \ldots, x_n) \in \mathbb{Z}_{p^y}^n$ to the system of equations modulo p^y. There is the possibility that the reduced systems contain parasitic solutions, i.e., solutions modulo p^i for some $i < y$, that do not lift to a solution modulo p^y. In this case, one can always go back to a smaller modulus and look for a different solution.

While this approach puts a restriction on what values $x_1^{(i)}, \ldots, x_n^{(i)}$ can take, there is still the problem that the system solving routine must be done in the ring $\mathbb{Z}_{p^i}$, where the usual field-based algorithms cannot be readily applied. For now we have mentioned exhaustive search as one possible solving method; more sophisticated methods will be discussed in Sect. 3.

2.3   Impact on Security

It is well known that the cost of a brute force attack on a symmetric primitive defined over a field $\mathbb{F}_{p^y}$ with a secret key consisting of n field elements should be $\mathcal{O}(p^{n \cdot y})$ if the primitive is well-designed. The following result shows that the cost of breaking any symmetric primitive defined over $\mathbb{Z}_{p^y}$ with a secret key of n elements is significantly lower, $\mathcal{O}(y \cdot p^n)$, if the primitive can be described by a system of polynomial equations

Theorem 2. *Let $q = p_1^{y_1} \cdots p_a^{y_a}$ and consider a symmetric primitive over $\mathbb{Z}_q$ relying on the secrecy of n elements. If the primitive can be described by a system of polynomials that admits a constant number of solutions modulo p_i^j, for $1 \leq$*

$i \leq a$ and $1 \leq j \leq y_i$, then the number of evaluations of the primitive needed to perform a brute force attack is

$$\mathcal{O}\left(\sum_{i=1}^{a} y_i \cdot p_i^n\right)$$

Proof. The proof follows the procedure proposed in Sect. 2.2. We focus on finding a solution modulo p^y; the final complexity statement is obtained by summing over all cases on this form.

By Lemma 1, it is not necessary to write the polynomials representing the primitive out in full. Rather, the solving procedure used in $i) - iii)$ in Sect. 2.2, at step i_0 for $0 \leq i_0 \leq y - 1$, is done by evaluating the primitive for all possible values $(x_1^{(i_0)}, \ldots, x_n^{(i_0)}) \in \mathbb{Z}_p^n$. For $i_0 \geq 1$, this search has to be repeated for each solution that was found modulo p^{i_0-1}. Since we assume a constant number of solutions at every step, the cost of finding all solutions modulo p^y is $\mathcal{O}(yp^n)$. Finally, we note that the last step of combining the solutions with CRT will never be a dominant step, as the run time of the extended Euclidean algorithm is logarithmic in the p_i's. $\square$

We emphasize that it is not necessary for an attacker to know the polynomial representation of the primitive in order to apply the attack. Moreover, we do not expect the restriction on solutions for the various moduli to pose much of a practical limitation. For instance, in the case of a block cipher (resp. stream cipher), any would-be parasitic solution is likely to disappear by including a few extra plaintext-ciphertext pairs (resp. key stream elements).

3   Algebraic Methods over $\mathbb{Z}_q$ for Composite q

We now study the applicability of algebraic attacks on symmetric primitives defined over $\mathbb{Z}_q$. As we are unaware of a generalization of algebraic attacks for primitives that do not admit a polynomial representation, we only concern ourselves with the cases where such a representation exists. As we shall see, there are several differences between applying algebraic attacks to a primitive over a ring and over a field, both with regards to efficiency and success. In fact, some of these algebraic attacks may not work at all *even if* the targeted symmetric primitive admits a polynomial representation over the ring.

We start by discussing linearization and Gröbner basis techniques. Both of these are polynomial system solving methods, and can thus be used in the framework described in Sect. 2.2. We then go on to investigate attacks based on interpolation and higher-order differentials.

3.1   Linearization Attacks

Linearization is a well-known class of techniques used to solve multivariate polynomial systems of equations over finite fields (see, e.g., [51]). The core idea is to turn a system of non-linear equations into a linear system by treating each monomial as a separate variable. In general, the method generates polynomials of some degree, up to the point where the number of equations exceeds the number of monomials so a solution can be found by linear algebra.

In symmetric cryptography, it is usually assumed that an attacker has access to sufficiently many equations to directly linearize the system. Recall that the number of possible monomials in a degree d polynomial in $\mathbb{F}[x_1, \ldots, x_n]$, where $|\mathbb{F}| > d$, is $b_{n,d} := \binom{n+d}{n}$. If the symmetric primitive admits a polynomial representation of degree d in n variables, the linearization attack requires $\mathcal{O}(b_{n,d}^\omega)$ multiplications in $\mathbb{F}$, where $2 < \omega \leq 3$ is the linear algebra constant. The memory cost of the linearization attack is $\mathcal{O}(b_{n,d}^2)$, and the data complexity is $\mathcal{O}(b_{n,d})$.

Linear Algebra Modulo q. When the polynomial system is defined over $\mathbb{Z}_q$ for a composite $q = p_1^{y_1} \ldots p_a^{y_a}$ the usual linear algebra techniques cannot be readily applied. The straightforward Gaussian elimination method can, however, be adapted by restricting to multiplications by units in $\mathbb{Z}_q$ (as opposed to nonzero elements for the field case). When performing the ensuing reduction, one furthermore requires the involved rows to have a unit in their pivot position to guarantee a successful row echelon form. Note that this puts a stronger condition on which rows can contribute in a row-reduction process, but it is unlikely to pose much of a problem in the setting of a linearization attack where extra rows may be sampled. More advanced linear algebra techniques, like Strassen's algorithm [64], can also be applied under stronger assumptions on the underlying matrix.

The idea is to recover solutions over $\mathbb{Z}_{p^v}$ for the various prime factors p of q, and combine them using CRT. For $y = 1$, the solution is found by following the normal algorithm over fields. For $y > 1$, we suggest following the first half of a technique by Dixon, which uses p-adic expansion to recover exact rational solutions from systems of integer coefficients [28]. We recall the method below:

For an invertible matrix A over $\mathbb{Z}_{p^v}$ consider the problem of finding $\mathbf{x}$ so that

$$A\mathbf{x} \equiv \mathbf{b} \mod p^y. \tag{2}$$

Start by finding $C \equiv A^{-1} \mod p$, which is done by solving $CA \equiv I \mod p$, using any algorithm that works over the field $\mathbb{F}_p$. For $0 \leq i \leq y - 1$ and $\mathbf{b}_0 = \mathbf{b}$, we then compute $\mathbf{x}_i \equiv C\mathbf{b}_i \mod p$ and $\mathbf{b}_{i+1} = (\mathbf{b}_i - A\mathbf{x}_i)/p$.

Note that, by construction, we have $\mathbf{b}_i - A\mathbf{x}_i \equiv \mathbf{0} \mod p$, so the coordinates in $\mathbf{b}_{i+1}$ are well-defined elements in $\mathbb{Z}_{p^v}$. The solution to Eq. (2) is now given by $\mathbf{x} = \sum_{i=0}^{y-1} \mathbf{x}_i p^i$. This is verified by computing

$$A\mathbf{x} = \sum_{i=0}^{y-1} p^i A\mathbf{x}_i = \sum_{i=0}^{y-1} p^i(\mathbf{b}_i - p\mathbf{b}_{i+1}) = \mathbf{b}_0 - p^y\mathbf{b}_y \equiv \mathbf{b} \mod p^y.$$

3.2   Gröbner Basis Attack

Some of the most powerful techniques for finding a solution to a polynomial equation system involve computing a Gröbner basis of the associated polynomial ideal. While the majority of work in this direction considers polynomial rings over fields, the theory of Gröbner basis computation has also been generalized to work over more general rings. An overview of this generalization can be found in [2, Sect. 4]. A reader familiar with the theory of polynomial rings over fields should note that there are several differences between the two cases. In fact, the definitions of fundamental concepts such as S-polynomials, polynomial reductions and even that of a Gröbner basis itself, must be adapted when working over rings, due to the existence of zero divisors and lack of multiplicative inverses. Still, with the proper adaptations in place, it can be shown that there exists a Gröbner basis for any ideal in a polynomial ring over $\mathbb{Z}_q$.

One of the most efficient algorithms for computing Gröbner bases, the F_4 algorithm [33], has also been extended to polynomial rings over $\mathbb{Z}_q$ in the computer algebra system Magma [19]. It is not clear whether the typical procedure for complexity estimation of the F_4 algorithm (c.f. [7]) can be generalized to polynomial rings over the integers modulo q. We have run several experiments with the F_4 algorithm on randomly generated polynomial systems over both $\mathbb{Z}_{p^y}$ and $\mathbb{F}_{p^y}$, and report the results in [39, Appendix C]. In all experiments we observe that both time and memory costs are significantly larger for the polynomial systems over $\mathbb{Z}_{p^y}$, than it is for their finite field counterpart. Further investigations of the complexity of Gröbner basis computation over $\mathbb{Z}_q$, beyond this qualitative comparison, are out of scope for this work.

Solutions from Gröbner Bases. If the polynomial system is sufficiently overdetermined and has a unique solution, we expect to be able to read the solution directly from the Gröbner basis when the coefficients are in a field. We also observed this in all the $\mathbb{Z}_{p^y}$-experiments in [39, Appendix C]. The process of recovering a solution from a Gröbner basis of more general polynomials systems, however, is more involved (see, e.g., [21]).

When working over a field, the typical strategy is to change the monomial order of the Gröbner basis with the FGLM-algorithm [34] into an order where a univariate polynomial can be found. A solution to one of the variables is then found by factoring this univariate polynomial, and the remainder of the (multivariate) solution is found by back-substitution and repeated solving of univariate polynomial equations. There are several reasons why the same strategy cannot be applied to polynomials over $\mathbb{Z}_q$. Firstly, we are not aware of any work that has adapted the FGLM-algorithm to Gröbner bases over rings. Secondly, factorization in $\mathbb{Z}_q$ is not as well-behaved as in the finite field case, and there are polynomials where no better factorization method than brute-force is known [66]. Finally, it is not even clear whether the theoretical foundations of this strategy (c.f. [21, Sect. 2]) can be extended to rings.

3.3 Interpolation Attack

The goal of the interpolation attack [48] is to construct a polynomial that describes a cryptographic function. Given the interpolation polynomial, the attacker can use it to set up distinguishers, forgeries, or key recovery attacks.

If the cryptographic function is described by a univariate polynomial of degree d over a finite field, then this polynomial can be constructed from the Lagrange interpolation formula using d distinct input-output pairs. This formula relies on the existence of inverses of non-zero elements, and thus cannot be readily applied to polynomials over $\mathbb{Z}_q$. That said, the problem of interpolating polynomials modulo q has been studied in several papers, and some of these techniques can be applied in an attack.

Interpolation of Univariate Polynomials Modulo q. Recall from Sect. 2.1 that univariate polynomial functions have a canonical representation of degree $d \leq \rho = \rho(q)$. This representation can be recovered from the evaluations of the values $0, 1, \ldots, d - 1$, by following the procedure described in the proof of [37, Corollary 7]. Another interpolation method, based on Newton interpolation, is described in [36] for $\mathbb{Z}_{p^v}$. While this is a different approach, it still requires the evaluation of all inputs $0, 1, \ldots, d - 1$. We remark that only knowing the polynomial function modulo factors $p_i^{y_i}$ of q does not pose much of a drawback for an attacker. Indeed, Lemma 1 ensures that an attacker can evaluate any $x \in \mathbb{Z}_q$ modulo these factors, and find the correct output using the CRT.

As noted in Sect. 2.1, the upper degree bound $\rho(q)$ can be significantly smaller than q. Therefore, in order to ensure that interpolation attacks will not pose a problem, any cryptographic function with a polynomial representation over $\mathbb{Z}_q$ should be careful in its choice of q.

3.4 Higher-Order Differential Attack

Given a vectorial Boolean function F over $\mathbb{F}_2^n$ of degree d, the higher-order differential attack [52,54] traditionally exploits the fact that $\bigoplus_{\mathbf{x} \in \mathcal{V}} F(\mathbf{x}) = 0$ for any affine subspace $\mathcal{V} \subseteq \mathbb{F}_2^n$ of dimension strictly larger than d. A generalization of the attack to any prime field $\mathbb{F}_p$ has recently been proposed in [13]. For this version, it is shown that if $F : \mathbb{F}_p^n \to \mathbb{F}_p$ is of degree $\deg(F) < h(p - 1)$, then

$$\sum_{\mathbf{x} \in \mathcal{W}} F(\mathbf{x}) = 0 \tag{3}$$

where $\mathcal{W} \subseteq \mathbb{F}_p^n$ is an affine subspace of dimension at least h [13, Corollary 1]. The result can be generalized further to polynomials over $\mathbb{F}_{p^n}$ using the existence of a vector space isomorphism $\mathbb{F}_{p^n} \cong \mathbb{F}_p^n$.

Differentials of Polynomials over $\mathbb{Z}_q$. For polynomials over $\mathbb{Z}_q$, a zero-sum similar to that of Eq. (3) can be set up by restricting to a prime factor modulus in the following manner.

Proposition 1. *Let p be a prime divisor of q, and $F \in \mathbb{Z}_q[x_1, \ldots, x_n]$ be a polynomial of degree $< h(p - 1)$, and let $\mathcal{V} \subseteq \mathbb{F}_p^n \cong \mathbb{Z}_p^n \subseteq \mathbb{Z}_q^n$ be an affine subspace of dimension at least h. Then:*

$$\sum_{\mathbf{x} \in \mathcal{V}} F(\mathbf{x}) \equiv 0 \mod p.$$

Proof. Due to Lemma 1 and the result in [13], we have that

$$\sum_{\mathbf{x}\in\mathcal{V}} F(\mathbf{x}) \mod p \equiv \sum_{\mathbf{x}\in\mathcal{V}} F(\mathbf{x} \mod p) \mod p \equiv \sum_{\mathbf{x}\in\mathcal{V}\subseteq\mathbb{F}_p^n} F(\mathbf{x}) = 0.$$

□

Unlike the finite field case, this result cannot be generalized to prime powers, since there is no vector space isomorphism between $\mathbb{Z}_p^n$ and $\mathbb{Z}_{p^n}$. Indeed, we have performed small-scale experiments on low degree polynomials F over $\mathbb{Z}_{2^n}$ which generally does not sum to zero, even when the sum is taken over all of $\mathbb{Z}_{2^n}$.

The zero-sum in Eq. (3) crucially relies on the fact that $\sum_{x\in\mathbb{F}_p} x^i = 0$ for each $i < p - 1$. One may ask whether it is possible to obtain a similar result, and thus a better generalization than Proposition 1, when working over $\mathbb{Z}_q$ directly. In [39, Appendix D] we answer this question in the negative when q is the product of distinct primes, by giving an exact characterization of $\sum_{x\in\mathbb{Z}_q} x^i$, for any i.

4 Designing a Non-linear (S-box) Function over $\mathbb{Z}_q$

We discussed possible algebraic attacks on symmetric primitives over rings $\mathbb{Z}_q$ in the previous section. Based on this, we now discuss three possible strategies for designing the S-boxes and/or non-linear functions with the goal of making algebraic attacks as hard as possible. A similar discussion for the linear layer is presented in [39, Appendix E].

4.1 Polynomial Non-linear Function over $\mathbb{Z}_q$

As in the field case, one possible design strategy is to simply define the non-linear invertible S-box function via an invertible polynomial function. Note that it is well-known how to design invertible polynomial functions over a ring $\mathbb{Z}_q$, see e.g. [60,61,69] for some concrete examples.

The advantage of this design is the possibility to define the S-box function in a very efficient way, especially when the polynomial function is sparse. The obvious downside is that it is possible to describe the complete encryption function as a polynomial system, making the brute force attack described in Theorem 2 possible. The algebraic attacks described in the previous section should also be considered in this case.

4.2 Learning from Elisabeth: Look-Up Tables

Another possible way of designing the non-linear function is via a look-up table, which is exactly what is proposed for the Elisabeth stream cipher [24]. Its non-linear layer is defined using 8 different S-box functions $S_1, S_2, \ldots, S_8$ that are defined over $\mathbb{Z}_{16}$ via look-up tables (not invertible in Elisabeth's case), such that they do not admit any polynomial representation over $\mathbb{Z}_{16}$.

The advantage of using look-up tables is the possibility to set up a non-linear function that does not admit any polynomial representation over the ring $\mathbb{Z}_q$, which immediately makes the cipher immune to any algebraic attack working over $\mathbb{Z}_q$. The disadvantage of this strategy is that the ciphers are less applicable, for example in the HHE setting, which combines a symmetric cipher with an FHE scheme. Although FHE schemes are defined to evaluate any polynomial homomorphically, there is no guarantee that a symmetric cipher which does *not* admit a polynomial representation is possible to evaluate, much less that it will be efficient. TFHE, the FHE scheme Elisabeth is designed to be combined with, is able to evaluate a look-up table very efficiently for the parameter choices set by Elisabeth, but it is currently the only FHE scheme able to do so, and hence the only FHE scheme Elisabeth may practically be combined with.

4.3 "Cut and Sew" Approach

Either of the two strategies just proposed have their own pros and cons. Defining an S-box as a simple polynomial allows one to evaluate large S-boxes efficiently, while a non-polynomial S-box is immune to direct algebraic attacks. The best scenario would be to have a design approach that incorporates the advantages of both methods, and the "cut and sew" approach we propose, inspired by ideas from [41], aims to do this.

In the following, we consider two concrete examples, one where $q = p_1 \cdot p_2$ with $p_1 \neq p_2$ and one where $q = p^2$. By combining and generalizing them, it is possible to design a non-linear function for any composite q. Given $x \in \mathbb{Z}_q$, the "cut and sew" approach works as follows:

1. decompose $x \in \mathbb{Z}_q$ to its components with respect to the factors of q;
2. apply a non-linear function on each component of x;
3. recompose the new components together.

Let us consider the two cases in more detail.

Case: $q = p_1 \cdot p_2$. Let us decompose each $x \in \mathbb{Z}_q$ as

$$x = x_2 \cdot p_2 + x_1$$

where $x_1 \in \{0, 1, \ldots, p_2 - 1\}$ and $x_2 \in \{0, 1, \ldots, p_1 - 1\}$. An S-box S over $\mathbb{Z}_q$ can be then defined as

$$S(x) = S_2(x_2) \cdot p_2 + S_1(x_1),$$

where $S_1 : \mathbb{F}_{p_2} \to \mathbb{F}_{p_2}$ and $S_2 : \mathbb{F}_{p_1} \to \mathbb{F}_{p_1}$. It is easy to see that if both S_1 and S_2 are invertible, then S is invertible as well.

Both S_1 and S_2 can be instantiated with either a look-up table or a polynomial function, keeping in mind that both S_1 and S_2 are defined over fields. In particular, by instantiating S_1 and S_2 with polynomials over $\mathbb{F}_{p_2}$ and $\mathbb{F}_{p_1}$, it is possible to efficiently evaluate these functions even if p_1 and p_2 are large.

In order to prevent the algebraic attacks previously discussed, it makes sense to choose S_1 and S_2 such that S does not admit any polynomial representation over $\mathbb{Z}_q$. By Lemma 1, S admits a polynomial representation only if

$$\forall i \in \{1, 2\} : \qquad S(x \cdot p_i + y) \mod p_i \equiv S(z \cdot p_i + y) \mod p_i \qquad (4)$$

for all relevant tuples (x, y, z). It is easy to verify that this equality always holds for $i = 2$. Indeed, $S(x \cdot p_2 + y) \equiv S(z \cdot p_2 + y) \equiv S_1(y) \mod p_2$ by the definition of S.

For the case $i = 1$, one has to prove that such an equality is not satisfied for at least one relevant tuple (x, y, z), depending on the details of S_1 and S_2. For instance, if S_1 and S_2 are chosen as random permutations, then Eq. (4) is not satisfied with probability $1 - 1/p_1$ for any given tuple (x, y, z). Since $1 - 1/p_1 \geq 1/2$, a few tests should be sufficient for verifying that an S-box S does not admit a polynomial representation. We show how to construct an S-box S that does not admit a polynomial representation given an orthomorphism over $\mathbb{F}_{p_2}$ and only in the case $p_1 > p_2$ in [39, Appendix F]. We give this construction for completeness, and leave the problem to generalize such strategy, or to propose new ones, open for future research.

While the method described above ensures that S cannot be described as a polynomial over $\mathbb{Z}_q$, we note that S still reduces to S_1 modulo p_2. Thus, some care is needed in the construction to ensure that this cannot be exploited in an attack. A possible way to prevent this exploitation is by using two different S-boxes S, S' over $\mathbb{Z}_q$ defined as follows

$$x = x_2 \cdot p_2 + x_1 \mapsto S(x) = S_2(x_2) \cdot p_2 + S_1(x_1)$$
$$x = x_1' \cdot p_1 + x_2' \mapsto S'(x) = S_1'(x_1') \cdot p_1 + S_2'(x_2')$$

where $x_2, x_2' \in \mathbb{F}_{p_1}$, $x_1, x_1' \in \mathbb{F}_{p_2}$, $S_2, S_2' : \mathbb{F}_{p_1} \to \mathbb{F}_{p_1}$, and $S_1, S_1' : \mathbb{F}_{p_2} \to \mathbb{F}_{p_2}$. Hence, S admits a polynomial representation modulo p_2, while S' admits it modulo p_1. As a result, a symmetric primitive depending on both S and S' will not admit a polynomial representation modulo any of p_1 or p_2. Note that many MPC-/ZK-/FHE-friendly symmetric primitives (e.g., [5,20,40,41,45,46]) are all defined via multiple S-boxes.

Case: $q = p^2$. Let $x = x_2 \cdot p + x_1$ as before for $x_1, x_2 \in \{0, 1, \ldots, p-1\}$. Here, we suggest to define

$$S(x) = S_2(x_1) \cdot p + S_1(x_2),$$

where $S_1, S_2 : \mathbb{F}_p \to \mathbb{F}_p$, and where we note that x_1 and x_2 are "swapped", in the sense that the output element that is multiplied by p depends only on x_1, while the input element multiplied by p depends only on x_2.[1] As before, such an S-box is invertible if and only if both S_1, S_2 are invertible. Moreover:

---

[1] Note that the subspace $\{x \cdot p + x \in \mathbb{Z}_{p^2} \mid \forall x \in \mathbb{F}_p\}$ is invariant if $S_1 = S_2$. However, it is possible to break such invariant subspace via a proper choices of round constants (see e.g. [55,56] for details).

Lemma 2. *Let p be a prime integer. The function S over $\mathbb{Z}_{p^2}$ defined as $S(x = x_2 \cdot p + x_1) = S_2(x_1) \cdot p + S_1(x_2)$, where $x_1, x_2 \in \{0, 1, \ldots, p-1\}$ and S_1 is invertible, never admits a polynomial representation over $\mathbb{Z}_{p^2}$.*

Proof. If S has a polynomial representation, then it must satisfy Lemma 1, that is, $S(y \cdot p + x) \mod p = S(z \cdot p + x) \mod p$, which implies $S_1(y) = S_1(z)$ for each $x, y, z \in \{0, 1, \ldots, p-1\}$. Obviously, this condition is never satisfied if S_1 is bijective and $y \neq z$. □

The statistical properties of an S-box constructed using the cut-and-sew approach may very well be sub-optimal. This should not cause a big problem when the S-box is large since probabilities of differential or linear trails should still be easy to make small enough to rule out differential or linear attacks. However, it is something a designer should keep in mind and check if using this approach for any particular construction.

5   Rubato

An HHE framework involves the homomorphic evaluation of some cryptographic function, e.g., encryption of a symmetric cipher, and it is therefore desirable that this function has a low multiplicative depth so the evaluation can be done efficiently. However, a low depth is not advisable from a security perspective, as it makes the cipher susceptible to the attacks described in Sect. 3. Furthermore, the strategies described in Sect. 4 do not combine well with FHE, except in specialized circumstances.

Rubato [47] is an attempt to strike a balance between low multiplicative depth and security, as it is a family of symmetric cipher which admits a polynomial representation of low degree, but with the addition of Gaussian noise to the key stream to prevent algebraic attacks. We describe the ciphers in this section, as well as the transciphering framework it is intended for. The notation of the original paper is mostly adapted to ours.

5.1   Description of Rubato

For an integer $q \geq 2$, let $\mathbb{Z}_q := \mathbb{Z} \cap (-q/2, q/2]$ and $\mathbb{Z}_q^\times$ be the multiplicative group of $\mathbb{Z}_q$. We view the state X of Rubato as a $v \times v$ matrix over $\mathbb{Z}_q$, where $x_{i,j}$ denotes the entry in the i-th row and in the j-th column. Let the block size n be the square of some $v \in \mathbb{Z}_{>0}$.

For λ-bit security Rubato takes a symmetric key $\mathbf{k} \in \mathbb{Z}_q^n$, a nonce $\mathbf{nc} \in \{0, 1\}^\lambda$ and a counter $i \in \mathbb{Z}_{\geq 0}$ as input, and returns a block of key stream

$$\mathbf{z} = \mathsf{Rubato}[\mathbf{k}, \mathbf{nc}, i](\mathbf{is}) \in \mathbb{Z}_q^\ell$$

for some $\ell < n$, where $\mathbf{is} = (1, 2, \ldots, n) \in \mathbb{Z}_q^n$ denotes an initial (fixed) state. Encryption of a message vector $\boldsymbol{\mu} \in \mathbb{R}^\ell$ by Rubato is defined by

$$\mathbf{c} = \lfloor \Delta \cdot \boldsymbol{\mu} \rceil + \mathbf{z} \mod q,$$

where $\Delta \in \mathbb{R}$ is a scaling factor dependent on the norm of the message.

Components. We introduce the following components of Rubato:

Add-Round Key and the Key-Schedule: the Add-Round Key function (ARK) over $\mathbb{Z}_q^n$ is defined as

$$\text{ARK}[\mathbf{k}, i](\mathbf{x}) = \mathbf{x} + \mathbf{k} \bullet \mathbf{rc_i},$$

where $\bullet$ denotes component-wise multiplication modulo q and $\mathbf{rc_i} \in (\mathbb{Z}_q^\times)^n$ are round constants defined via an XOF that takes the nonce $\mathbf{nc}$ and the counter i as input.

Mix Columns and Mix Rows: The linear transformation in Rubato is composed of two consecutive operations: MixColumns and MixRows. Let $X \in \mathbb{Z}_q^{v \times v}$ be the state of Rubato. The linear layer is simply defined as

$$X \xrightarrow{\text{MixColumns}} M_v \times X \xrightarrow{\text{MixRows}} (M_v \times X) \times M_v^T$$

where M_v^T denotes the transpose of a particular matrix $M_v \in \mathbb{Z}_q^{v \times v}$. For the particular cases $v \in \{4, 6, 8\}$, M_v is defined as

$$M_v = \begin{bmatrix} \mathbf{y_v} \\ \mathbf{y_v} \lll 1 \\ \vdots \\ \mathbf{y_v} \lll v - 1 \end{bmatrix},$$

where $\mathbf{y_4} = [2, 3, 1, 1]$, $\mathbf{y_6} = [4, 2, 4, 3, 1, 1]$ and $\mathbf{y_8} = [5, 3, 4, 3, 6, 2, 1, 1]$, and $\mathbf{y_v} \lll j$ denotes the cyclic rotation of $\mathbf{y_v}$ by j positions.

Feistel: A quadratic type-III Feistel [70] is applied on the state. Given the input $\mathbf{x} = (x_1, \ldots, x_n) \in \mathbb{Z}_q^n$, the output is

$$\text{Feistel}(\mathbf{x}) = (x_1, x_2 + x_1^2, x_3 + x_2^2, \ldots, x_n + x_{n-1}^2).$$

Rubato. Using the components described above, we illustrate the round function of Rubato in Fig. 1 and define the function as follows:

$$\text{RF}[\mathbf{k}, i] = \text{ARK}[\mathbf{k}, i] \circ \text{Feistel} \circ \text{MixRows} \circ \text{MixColumns}.$$

The final round differs slightly from the rest in that a second linear transformation is applied, together with the truncation function $\text{Tr}_{n,\ell}$, which simply cuts away the last $n - \ell$ entries of the state (i.e., $\text{Tr}_{n,\ell}(x_1, \ldots, x_n) = (x_1, \ldots, x_\ell)$):

$$\begin{aligned} \text{Fin}[\mathbf{k}, i + r] &= \text{Tr}_{n,\ell} \circ \text{ARK}[\mathbf{k}, i + r] \circ \text{MixRows} \circ \text{MixColumns} \circ \\ &\quad \text{Feistel} \circ \text{MixRows} \circ \text{MixColumns}, \end{aligned}$$

This final round is followed by the last function AGN, which adds Gaussian noise. Let $\mathbf{x} = (x_1, \ldots, x_\ell) \in \mathbb{Z}_q^\ell$ and $e_1, \ldots, e_\ell \leftarrow D_{\alpha q}$ be sampled independently

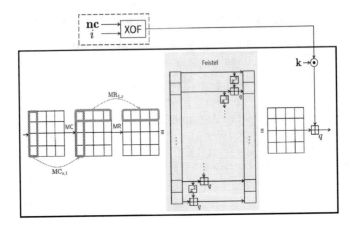

Fig. 1. The round function of Rubato.

Table 1. Proposed parameters of Rubato. λ is the security level, n is the block size, ℓ is the length of the keystream, $\lceil \log_2 q \rceil$ is the bit length of q with $\mathbb{Z}_q$ being the ring Rubato instances operate on, $(\alpha q)^2/2\pi$ is the variance of the Gaussian distribution the noise is sampled from, r is the total number of rounds.

Parameter	λ	n	ℓ	$\lceil \log_2 q \rceil$	αq	r
Par-80S	80	16	12	26	11.1	2
Par-80M	80	36	32	25	2.7	2
Par-80L	80	64	60	25	1.6	2
Par-128S	128	16	12	26	10.5	5
Par-128M	128	36	32	25	4.1	3
Par-128L	128	64	60	25	4.1	2

according to an one-dimensional discrete Gaussian distribution $D_{\alpha q}$ with zero mean and variance $(\alpha q)^2/2\pi$. Then,

$$\text{AGN}(\mathbf{x}) = (x_1 + e_1, \ldots, x_\ell + e_\ell).$$

All in all, the r-round stream cipher Rubato is defined as follows:[2]

$$\text{Rubato}[\mathbf{k}, \mathbf{nc}, i] = \text{AGN} \circ \text{Fin}[\mathbf{k}, i+r] \circ \text{RF}[\mathbf{k}, i+r-1] \circ \cdots \circ \text{RF}[\mathbf{k}, i+1] \circ \text{ARK}[\mathbf{k}, i].$$

The parameters of Rubato proposed by the authors are given in Table 1.

5.2   About the Value of q: Rubato in the RtF Framework

The choice of the parameter q greatly impacts the security of Rubato, and so to better understand the different aspects of this choice, we recall the RtF (Real-to-Finite field) transciphering framework, which is the greater context the Rubato

---

[2] For completeness, we present an equivalent version of Rubato in [39, Appendix G].

ciphers are intended for. We stress, in particular, that there is no requirement for q to be prime from an applicability perspective of this framework.

The RtF framework is a type of HHE framework for the approximate homomorphic encryption scheme CKKS. The framework lets a client encrypt their data using a symmetric cipher, a (comparatively) cheap operation, and the encrypted result is sent to a server which performs the heavy, homomorphic encryption and further cloud computation. The framework was originally proposed by Cho et al. with the symmetric cipher HERA [23], which is a more traditional stream cipher than Rubato. HERA consists of several rounds of linear and non-linear operations, it does not add Gaussian noise to the key stream, and it is explicitly defined over a prime field for security. However, HERA is used in the RtF framework in the same way as Rubato is in the description below.

On the client side of the RtF framework, the client will feed a key $\mathbf{k}$ into Rubato, use the resulting key stream to encrypt a message, and finally send this encrypted message to the server. The client will also encode and encrypt the key $\mathbf{k}$ using the homomorphic encryption scheme FV and send the resulting ciphertext to the server. Upon receiving this encryption of $\mathbf{k}$, the server runs Rubato *homomorphically* to produce an FV-encryption of the key stream, whilst the encryption of the message is transformed into an FV ciphertext. The FV-encryption of the key stream is then subtracted from the FV-encryption of the symmetrically encrypted message, producing an FV-encryption of just the message. Finally, an operation termed 'half bootstrapping' is performed to transform the FV ciphertext into a CKKS ciphertext. After this step is completed, the RtF framework has served its purpose, and the server may evaluate the ciphertext further using only the CKKS scheme.

Since the RtF framework uses Rubato in combination with the FV and CKKS schemes, there are some overlaps in the parameters of the three schemes. Of most importance to us is that the modulus q of Rubato has to match the plaintext modulus of FV, as the key $\mathbf{k}$ is encrypted using FV, and the plaintext modulus of FV must therefore accommodate for this. There is no restriction on this plaintext modulus other than requiring it to be an integer larger than 1 [32]. In practice, however, it is usually taken to be a prime congruent to 1 modulo $2N$, where N is the dimension of the ring FV is defined over, but this choice is made *purely* for efficiency reasons, as the choice of plaintext modulus has no impact on the security of the FV scheme [1,32]. This is in great contrast to Rubato, where the choice of q may severely compromise the security.

5.3   Non-invertible And/Or Non-MDS Matrices for Rubato

Before presenting the attack on Rubato, we point out that the matrices that define the linear layer of Rubato are not always invertible and/or not always MDS for several values of q. We recall that a matrix $M \in \mathbb{Z}_q^{n \times n}$ is *invertible* if and only if its determinant $\det(M)$ is co-prime with q, i.e., $\gcd(\det(M), q) = 1$.

Definition 1 (MDS [26]). *The branch number of* $M \in \mathbb{Z}_q^{n \times n}$ *is defined as* $\mathcal{B}(M) = \min_{x \in \mathbb{Z}_q^n \setminus \{0\}} \{\mathrm{hw}(x) + \mathrm{hw}(M(x))\}$, *where* $\mathrm{hw}(\cdot)$ *is the bundle weight* *in wide trail terminology. A matrix $M \in \mathbb{Z}_q^{n \times n}$ is called a Maximum Distance Separable (MDS) matrix if and only if $\mathcal{B}(M) = n + 1$.*

In the case of Rubato, we check all the possible integer values for q that are 25 or 26 bits. The number of q's such that M_v for $v \in \{4, 6, 8\}$ is invertible or MDS and the corresponding frequencies are provided in Table 2. In the 'Invertible' part, where M_v is invertible over $\mathbb{Z}_q$, the column 'Total' gives the total number of such q's, the column 'Prime' gives the number of such prime q's, and the column 'Composite' gives the number of such composite q's. The corresponding frequencies among all the possible $3 \cdot 2^{24}$ q values are given below the numbers. The 'MDS' columns are similar. We discuss these results in detail in [39, Appendix H].

Table 2. The number of invertible matrices and MDS matrices of Rubato matrices M_v ($v = 4, 6, 8$) over all possible q-values of 25 or 26 bits.

Matrix	Property					
	Invertible			MDS		
	Total	Prime	Composite	Total	Prime	Composite
$v = 4$	$2^{25.04}$	$2^{21.46}$	$2^{24.91}$	$2^{23.23}$	$2^{21.46}$	$2^{22.73}$
	68.57%	5.72%	62.85%	19.56%	5.72%	13.85%
$v = 6$	$2^{23.68}$	$2^{21.46}$	$2^{23.33}$	$2^{22.62}$	$2^{21.46}$	$2^{21.77}$
	26.67%	5.72%	20.95%	12.83%	5.72%	7.11%
$v = 8$	$2^{25.0}$	$2^{21.46}$	$2^{24.87}$	$2^{22.11}$	$2^{21.46}$	$2^{20.64}$
	66.72%	5.72%	61.00%	8.96%	5.72%	3.24%

Impact on the Security. At the current state of the art, we are not aware of any attack on Rubato (or RASTA-like schemes) that exploits the possible non-invertibility of the linear layers that instantiate Rubato. For example, both MASTA and the RASTA-like variant designs proposed in [38] are defined using non-invertible components. Still, no attacks have been proposed on them. This is related to the fact that the encryption function changes at every evaluation for these ciphers. Hence, even if an internal collision is found, different round functions are applied on the same state, with the results of different outputs.

However, using the same non-MDS matrix twice in one round of Rubato might lead to weaker diffusion than expected by the designers, especially due to the small number of rounds. We leave the open problem of exploiting non-invertible and/or non-MDS matrices for future work.

6   Key Recovery Attack on Rubato

We present a key recovery attack on Rubato, which breaks the claimed security level of five of the six proposed variants of Rubato when the modulus q belongs to a certain class. The steps of the attacks are as follows:

1. First, we recover the correct key and noise modulo m, when m is a factor of q lying in a particular interval.
2. Then, we recover the positions in the key stream where the noise added by $AGN(\cdot)$ is exactly 0.
3. Finally, we recover the secret key by setting up a system of polynomial equations using the knowledge of positions with no noise, and solving the system by re-linearization.

For ease of exposition, we specify some further notation:

- We denote the Rubato algorithm without the final $AGN(\cdot)$ operation as $Ru = Ru[\mathbf{k}, nc, i]$.
- The stream of $\mathbb{Z}_q$-elements produced by running Ru is denoted as $\mathbf{w} = (w_1, w_2, \ldots)$.
- For either Rubato or Ru, we let $Rubato_m$ or Ru_m denote that we are executing all the steps of the cipher in the ring $\mathbb{Z}_m$ rather than $\mathbb{Z}_q$, producing a stream of elements in $\mathbb{Z}_m$.

After presenting the attack, we will present the necessary assumptions q must meet in order to have an attack with complexity less than 2^λ given the parameter sets of the different Rubato variants, and the fraction of the valid choices for q that results in weak instances of Rubato.

6.1 Recovering Key and Noise Modulo a Small Factor of q

First, we describe how to recover the correct key values and noise values modulo m, where m is a factor of q lying in a particular interval. The upper and lower bounds on the interval depend on the Rubato variant and will be determined in Sect. 7.1.

Assume the attacker is given s elements of known key stream $z_1, \ldots, z_s$ generated by an unknown secret key $(k_1, \ldots, k_n) \in \mathbb{Z}_q^n$, where

$$s := \left\lceil \binom{n + 2^r}{2^r} \cdot \alpha q \right\rceil.$$

We then have the equations

$$z_i = w_i + e_i \mod q, \text{ for } 1 \leq i \leq s,$$

where the noise values e_i are drawn from $D_{\alpha q}$.

Let m be a non-trivial factor of q, and let $\tilde{\mathbf{k}} = (\tilde{k}_1, \ldots, \tilde{k}_n) \in \mathbb{Z}_m^n$ denote a guess for the values of the secret key modulo m. Note that if m satisfies $m^n < 2^\lambda$ it is possible to do an exhaustive search over all possible $(\tilde{k}_1, \ldots, \tilde{k}_n)$ and compute the $Rubato_m$ key stream with complexity lower than the claimed security level. Furthermore, from Lemma 1 we have the equality

$$Rubato_m[\mathbf{k} \mod m, nc, i] = Rubato[\mathbf{k}, nc, i] \mod m.$$

For each guess $(\tilde{k}_1, \ldots, \tilde{k}_n)$, let $\tilde{w}_1, \ldots, \tilde{w}_s$ be the stream generated by $\mathsf{Ru}_m[\tilde{\mathbf{k}}]$.

In order to check the correctness of a guess, we note the following. If the guess is wrong we expect the values $\tilde{w}_i$ to be distributed uniformly at random over $\mathbb{Z}_m$, and in particular, we expect the candidate noise values computed as

$$\tilde{e}_i = (z_i \mod m) - \tilde{w}_i \text{ for } i = 1, \ldots, s$$

to be distributed uniformly at random over $\mathbb{Z}_m$. This assumption stems from the common expectation that a good cipher behaves like a random permutation. If the guess $(\tilde{k}_1, \ldots, \tilde{k}_n)$ is equal to $(k_1 \mod m, \ldots, k_n \mod m)$ where $(k_1, \ldots, k_n)$ is the correct secret key, we have

$$\tilde{e}_i = (e_i \mod m) \text{ for } i = 1, \ldots, s,$$

where the e_i-values are the actual noise values drawn from $D_{\alpha q}$ when producing the key stream $\mathbf{z}$.

If m is large enough relative to the αq parameter, we can distinguish between a correct and incorrect guess. In other words, the non-uniformity of the Gaussian distribution shines through even if the numbers drawn from $D_{\alpha q}$ are only given modulo m. In Sect. 7.1 we establish the exact bounds on m for five of the six Rubato variants that result in brute force attacks on $\mathbf{k}$ where we can distinguish the correct guess from the wrong ones with complexity smaller than 2^λ. As we shall see, this bound cannot be established in the case of Rubato-128L. After performing this part of the attack, we learn the correct values of $e_i \mod m$ for $i = 1, \ldots, s$, and of $k_j \mod m$ for $j = 1, \ldots, n$.

6.2 Recovering the Key Modulo a Larger Factor of q and Positions in the Key Stream with No Noise

After recovering $e_i \mod m$ for $1 \le i \le s$ and $k_j \mod m$ for $1 \le j \le n$ for some factor m of q, we proceed to identify every position in the key stream where the noise added by $\mathsf{AGN}(\cdot)$ is 0. In the following, let f be a non-trivial factor of q/m.

Case: $f \le m$. If $f \le m$ we can repeat the attack from Sect. 6.1, this time running Rubato$_{fm}$. Similar to the attack described in Sect. 2, the attacker can use the knowledge of the correct key values modulo m to speed up the exhaustive search. For each $k_i \mod fm$, the attacker does not guess on all values $0, \ldots, fm - 1$, but only on the values $(k_i \mod m) + j \cdot m$ for $0 \le j < f$.

Note that there is no lower bound on the size of f. If the attacker is able to distinguish the $D_{\alpha q}$ distribution modulo m from the uniform distribution, the attacker is certainly able to distinguish $D_{\alpha q}$ from uniform modulo $2m$, or any higher multiple of m. The attacker learns the correct key values modulo fm, and the correct e_i-values modulo fm after doing the exhaustive search modulo fm, with a complexity that is no higher than the initial step.

Case: $f = f_1 \cdots f_b$ where all $f_i \leq m$. In this case, it is possible to repeat the exhaustive search for each factor f_i of q/m where $2 \leq f_i \leq m$. The complexity of this is at most $b \cdot m^n$. However, our aim in this step is not to maximize the modulus fm for which one can recover the correct key modulo fm. Rather, we are interested in just having a large enough f such that all noise values e_i for $i = 1, \ldots, s$ will satisfy the bound $|e_i| < fm$ with high probability. In Sect. 7.1 we determine a threshold t depending on αq such that when $fm \geq t$ and e_i is drawn from $D_{\alpha q}$, then $|e_i| < fm$ for all $i = 1, \ldots, s$ with probability higher than 99%. So when we find $e_i \equiv 0 \mod fm$, we have that $e_i \equiv 0 \mod q$ with high probability as well, and not $e_i = \pm fm$. In other words, when the attacker finds $e_i \equiv 0 \mod fm$ where e_i is drawn from $D_{\alpha q}$, the attacker knows that, with high probability, there has been no noise added by $\mathrm{AGN}(\cdot)$ for this particular index i. No added noise will be a rather common occurrence, as the noise value 0 will be sampled from $D_{\alpha q}$ at a rate of $1/\alpha q$.

We define $\mathcal{I}$ to be the set of indices where no noise has been added by $\mathrm{AGN}(\cdot)$:

$$\mathcal{I} = \{i \mid e_i \equiv 0 \mod q\}.$$

So when $fm|q$, $fm > t$ and all prime factors of f are smaller than or equal to m, the attacker can recover the correct $\mathcal{I}$ with probability higher than 99%.

6.3 Key-Recovery of the Full Rubato Key

Assuming the attacker knows $\mathcal{I}$, the set of indices in the Rubato key stream where no noise has been added, it is fairly straightforward to set up a system of polynomial equations in the unknown key variables that can be solved by linearization. As Rubato is designed to have very low multiplicative complexity, and hence have very few iterations of the round function, we will see that the size of the polynomial equations in $k_1, \ldots, k_n$ and the complexity for solving them is small compared to the security parameter.

Treating the unknown $k_1, \ldots, k_n$ as variables, the attacker starts by evaluating all operations for producing the Ru stream in sequence. This yields the expressions $F_i(k_1, \ldots, k_n) = w_i$ for $1 \leq i \leq s$.

When $i \in \mathcal{I}$, the attacker knows that $w_i = z_i$, so they can extract exactly these equations to set up the system

$$
\begin{aligned}
F_{i_1}(k_1, \ldots, k_n) &= z_{i_1} \\
F_{i_2}(k_1, \ldots, k_n) &= z_{i_2} \\
&\vdots \qquad\qquad \vdots \\
F_{i_b}(k_1, \ldots, k_n) &= z_{i_b},
\end{aligned}
\tag{5}
$$

for all $i_j \in \mathcal{I}$. Recall that we assume the attacker knows s elements of key stream where $s = \left\lceil \binom{n+2^r}{2^r} \cdot \alpha q \right\rceil$. Since the noise value 0 is sampled at a rate of $1/\alpha q$ we expect the size of $\mathcal{I}$ to be $|\mathcal{I}| \geq \binom{n+2^r}{2^r}$.

Each polynomial in Eq. (5) has degree 2^r. For instance, since every Rubato variant with 80-bit security has $r = 2$, the degree of the polynomials in Eq. (5)

Table 3. The time complexities for solving a linearizied system of equations modulo one factor of q. To recover the secret Rubato key solving the linearized systems must be repeated at most 26 times, depending on q.

Rubato variant	Degree	# of monomials	Solving complexity
Rubato-80S	4	4845	$2^{34.28}$
Rubato-80M	4	91390	$2^{46.14}$
Rubato-80L	4	814385	$2^{54.98}$
Rubato-128S	32	$2^{41.04}$	$2^{114.90}$
Rubato-128M	8	$2^{27.40}$	$2^{76.72}$
Rubato-128L	4	814385	$2^{54.98}$

is 4. The number of monomials appearing in F_i is given by $\binom{n+2^r}{2^r}$. Since we expect to have more equations than monomials in Eq. (5) we can solve the system by Gaussian elimination. Here we also keep in mind that we are working with a composite q, so we need to use the method explained in Sect. 3.1, and in particular, we must solve the linearized system once for every prime factor of q.

The complexity of solving Eq. (5) for one prime factor is $\mathcal{O}\left(\binom{n+2^r}{2^r}^{\omega}\right)$, where $\omega \leq 3$ is the linear algebra constant. A conservative (and realistic) choice for ω is $\omega = 2.8$. Table 3 gives the degrees, number of monomials, and complexities for solving one linearized system modulo $p|q$ for the six different variants.

As we can see from Table 3, all complexities for breaking noise-less Rubato by linearization are significantly smaller than the security bounds 2^{80} and 2^{128}, even when this step has to be repeated a small number of times. Assuming q satisfies the assumptions necessary for doing steps 1 and 2 of the attack, the attacker can do a full key recovery attack on Rubato with complexity lower than 2^{λ}. Pseudo-code for the complete key recovery attack on Rubato is given in [39, Appendix I], where we also use the notation introduced in the next section.

7   Assumptions and Cost of the Attack on **Rubato**

7.1   Assumptions on q

The following assumptions on the integer q that defines the ring $\mathbb{Z}_q$ used in Rubato must hold in order for the attack in Sect. 6 to be successful.

Assumption 1. *There exists an integer m such that $m|q$ and $m_{min} \leq m \leq m_{max}$, where m_{min} and m_{max} will be determined below.*

For Rubato with claimed λ-bit security, m cannot be too large, as we need $m^n < 2^{\lambda}$ in order to have a valid attack. Moreover, m cannot be too small as this makes the noise modulo m impossible to distinguish from random, hence the bounds $m_{\min}$ and $m_{\max}$.

Assumption 2. *There exists an integer f such that all prime factors of f are at most m, $fm|q$, and $fm > t$, where the threshold t will be determined below.*

This condition is necessary to be able to recover the positions where we know the noise value is exactly 0.

There exist values of q such that both these assumptions hold. These q-values give weak instances of Rubato, and must be avoided in an actual use case. Before looking into the weak choices for q, we compute the bounds m_{min}, m_{max}, and the threshold t mentioned above for a general Rubato variant with claimed λ-bit security.

Determining t. In order to determine the threshold t, recall that the aim is to find the smallest value $t \in \mathbb{Z}$ for each Rubato variant such that

$$e \quad \mathrm{mod}\ (fm) \equiv 0 \qquad \Rightarrow \qquad e \quad \mathrm{mod}\ q \equiv 0$$

with overwhelming probability when $fm > t$ and $fm | q$. This reduces to finding the smallest integer t such that, with high probability, the error values satisfy $|e_i| \le t$ for all $1 \le i < s$. In the analysis below we specify "high probability" to mean above 99%.

Let $G(x) = \frac{1}{\alpha q} \cdot e^{-x^2/2\sigma^2}$ be the Gaussian function describing the discrete Gaussian distribution $D_{\alpha q}$ the noise in Rubato is drawn from, where $\sigma = \alpha q/\sqrt{2\pi}$. Then $G(x)$ gives the probability that we sample $x \leftarrow D_{\alpha q}$. Thus, the probability that we sample $e_i \leftarrow D_{\alpha q}$ such that $|e_i| \le t$ can be computed as

$$\Pr(|e_i| \le t) = \sum_{x=-t}^{t} G(x).$$

We want to make sure that after sampling s noise values, the probability that all of them lie in the interval $[-t, t]$ is at least 0.99. This condition translates into finding the smallest $t \in \mathbb{Z}$ such that $0.99 \le \left(\sum_{x=-t}^{t} G(x) \right)^s$. We then get the desired bounds by finding the smallest t that satisfies this inequality for the different Rubato variants. These values are listed in Table 4.

Determining m_{min} and m_{max}. As already stated, we must have $m^n < 2^\lambda$ in order to have a valid attack. This inequality provides the upper bound m_{max}:

$$m_{max} := \lfloor 2^{\lambda/n} \rfloor.$$

The lower bound m_{min} is the smallest value where it is possible to distinguish the correct key guess $\tilde{\mathbf{k}}$ modulo m_{min} from all the wrong ones. To find this lower bound, we first compute the probability that $e \mod m = x$ for $0 \le x < m$ when e is sampled from $D_{\alpha q}$:

$$\Pr_m(x) = \sum_{i=-\infty}^{\infty} G(im + x).$$

Secondly, for a given modulus m we split the set $\{0, \ldots, m-1\}$ into two disjoint subsets $\mathcal{I}_1$ and $\mathcal{I}_2$ as

$$\mathcal{I}_1 := \{x \mid \Pr_m(x) \geq 1/m\} \qquad \text{and} \qquad \mathcal{I}_2 := \{x \mid \Pr_m(x) < 1/m\}. \qquad (6)$$

For a given stream $\tilde{\mathbf{e}} = \tilde{e}_1, \ldots, \tilde{e}_s$ of candidate noise values (that may or may not be sampled from $D_{\alpha q}$) and $0 \leq i < m$, let $u_i(\tilde{\mathbf{e}})$ be the frequency of observing the value i in the stream $\tilde{\mathbf{e}}$ modulo m, that is,

$$u_i(\tilde{\mathbf{e}}) = \frac{|\{\tilde{e}_j \in \tilde{\mathbf{e}} \mid \tilde{e}_j \mod m = i\}|}{s}.$$

Note that when $\tilde{\mathbf{e}}$ is sampled from $D_{\alpha q}$, we expect $u_i(\tilde{\mathbf{e}}) \approx \Pr_m(i)$ for $0 \leq i < m$.

Score Value for $\tilde{\mathbf{k}}$. For a given key guess $\tilde{\mathbf{k}} = (\tilde{k}_1, \ldots, \tilde{k}_n)$ modulo m, we now define a score value for $\tilde{\mathbf{k}}$. First, execute $\mathsf{Ru}_m[\tilde{\mathbf{k}}]$ producing the stream $\tilde{w}_1, \ldots, \tilde{w}_s$. From the known key stream $z_1, \ldots, z_s$, compute the candidate noise value modulo m as $\tilde{e}_i = (z_i - \tilde{w}_i) \mod m$, for $1 \leq i \leq s$. We define the score for the key guess $\tilde{\mathbf{k}}$ as

$$\mathrm{Sc}(\tilde{\mathbf{k}}) = \sum_{i \in I_1} (u_i(\tilde{\mathbf{e}}) - 1/m) + \sum_{i \in I_2} (1/m - u_i(\tilde{\mathbf{e}})) \,.$$

The score function gives a measure of how much the candidate noise value produced by $\tilde{\mathbf{k}}$ deviates from the uniform distribution in the same way as values drawn from $D_{\alpha q}$ modulo m will deviate from uniform. When $\tilde{\mathbf{k}}$ is the correct guess modulo m, we expect $\mathrm{Sc}(\tilde{\mathbf{k}}) = \sum_{i=0}^{m} |\Pr_m(i) - 1/m|$. This value will be significantly greater than 0, provided m is large enough relative to αq. When $\tilde{\mathbf{k}}$ is a wrong key guess, we expect the noise values in $\tilde{\mathbf{e}}$ to be distributed uniformly at random, and hence a score value of $\mathrm{Sc}(\tilde{\mathbf{k}}) = 0$.

If the assumption that all wrong key guesses give uniformly distributed noise values modulo m holds, it is possible to compute the probability that the correct key guess gives the unique highest score value of all guesses for the key modulo m. However, we have observed that wrong key guesses in 2-round Rubato do *not* produce noise values that are distributed uniformly at random (see Fig. 2e and Fig. 2f). Therefore we have found $m_{\min}$ heuristically, listed in Table 4, by checking the smallest m that produces a score value for the correct key guess that clearly stands out among many (at least 14640) wrong key guesses.

Set of Susceptible Values. We list the bounds $m_{\min}$ and $m_{\max}$ and the threshold t that allow attacks with complexity lower than 2^λ for each parameter set defined for Rubato in Table 4. We performed an exhaustive search on 26-bit numbers (for Rubato-80S and Rubato-128S) and 25-bit numbers (for the other variants) to find the percentage of q's satisfying Assumptions 1 and 2. The last column of Table 4 shows the percentage of vulnerable choices of q. For Rubato-128L we have $m_{\min} > m_{\max}$, so we do not have an attack on this Rubato variant.

(a) **Rubato-80S**: distinguishing correct key guess modulo 11 using 14641 key samples.

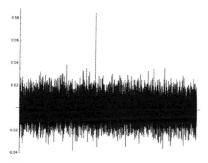

(b) **Rubato-128S**: distinguishing correct key guess modulo 11 using 14641 key samples.

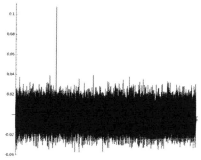

(c) **Rubato-80M**: distinguishing correct key guess modulo 3 using 59049 key samples.

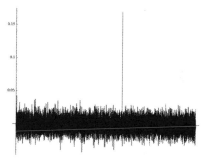

(d) **Rubato-128M**: distinguishing correct key guess modulo 5 using 15625 key samples.

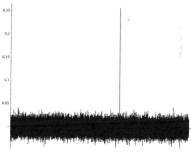

(f) **Uniformly random noise**: score values for 65536 noise vectors modulo 2, produced by the random() function in C. The maximum score value from Fig. 2e is also inserted in the data set.

(e) **Rubato-80L**: distinguishing correct key guess modulo 2 using 65536 key samples.

Fig. 2. Plots of score values computed for key guesses modulo m. The correct guess can be distinguished from all the wrong guesses. Comparing Fig. 2e and 2f shows that wrong key guesses in 2-round Rubato do not produce candidate noise that is uniformly random.

Table 4. Lower and upper bounds for the modulus m, threshold t and percentage of choices of q vulnerable to the attack for the various Rubato variants.

Rubato variant	m_{min}	m_{max}	t	Fraction of vulnerable q's
Rubato-80S	11	31	24	42.05%
Rubato-80M	3	4	7	25%
Rubato-80L	2	2	4	25%
Rubato-128S	11	255	35	58.47%
Rubato-128M	5	11	12	37.25%
Rubato-128L	–	–	–	0%

7.2 Practical Verification of the Attack

We have verified the attack described in Sect. 6 experimentally[3]. We also report on the experiments determining the smallest m for which we can distinguish a correct key guess modulo m from the wrong ones.

In all experiments, we selected a 25- or 26-bit q with some small factors, a key **k** at random, and produced 10000 elements of Rubato key stream. In an actual full key recovery attack, we need s to be higher for the relinearization part, but $s = 10000$ is sufficient for distinguishing the $D_{\alpha q}$ distribution from a (supposedly) uniform distribution modulo m.

Next, we fixed a value of m and made between $11^4 = 14641$ and $2^{16} = 65536$ guesses on the key modulo m, including the correct guess, and stored their score values in a file. Finally, we made plots of the score values in each file as a bar chart and verified that the maximum score value seen indeed corresponds to the correct key modulo m. The plots of the score values observed for the values m_{min} in Table 4 for the different Rubato variants are given in Figs. 2a–2e.

In Fig. 2f we have also included a plot of score values computed from noise values modulo 2, sampled by the random() function in C, together with the maximum score value from Fig. 2e. If the noise values produced by wrong key guesses in Rubato-80L were truly distributed uniformly at random, the plots of Figs. 2e and 2f should look the same. The fact that there is a significantly higher variance in Fig. 2e shows that 2-round Rubato does not behave like a random permutation. This makes it somewhat harder to distinguish wrong key guesses from the correct one, but the attack still works for all values of m given in Table 4.

7.3 Attack Complexities

Finally, we investigate the lowest possible attack complexities of the Rubato attack in concrete numbers. For Rubato-80 and Rubato-128M, the lowest attack

---

[3] The code can be found at https://github.com/Simula-UiB/RubatoAttack.

Table 5. Lowest time complexities of key recovery attack, where q has particular factors.

Rubato variant	Assumption on q	Time	Data	Memory
Rubato-80S	$44\|q$	$2^{55.35}$	$2^{15.71}$	$2^{24.48}$
Rubato-80M	$12\|q$	$2^{57.06}$	$2^{17.91}$	$2^{32.96}$
Rubato-80L	$4\|q$	2^{65}	$2^{20.31}$	$2^{39.27}$
Rubato-128S	$q = 11 \cdot 2^{22}$	$2^{55.35}$	$2^{44.43}$	$2^{44.43}$
Rubato-128M	$20\|q$	$2^{83.59}$	$2^{29.44}$	$2^{39.27}$

complexities occur when $m = m_{min}$ and $f = 2^g$ for $g = \lceil \log_2(t/m) \rceil$. The time complexities are given as the number of times we guess on $\mathbf{k}$ and produce a sufficient amount of key stream to distinguish a correct key guess from the wrong ones. The total key recovery attack complexity C_{kr} is then given as

$$C_{kr} = m^n + g \cdot 2^n + C_{relin},$$

where C_{relin} is the complexity of doing the relinearization step. The complexities for relinearization in Table 3 are given in terms of number of multiplications and additions in $\mathbb{Z}_q$, and not as computing key stream for a particular key guess. When recomputing the complexities in Table 3 to make them comparable to the work done for each guess of $\tilde{\mathbf{k}}$, it becomes clear that apart from Rubato-128S, C_{relin} is negligibly small compared to doing steps 1 and 2 of the attack.

For Rubato-128S, the relinearization step is the dominant part of the attack. For $m = 11$ and the particular value $q = 11 \cdot 2^{22}$ (a 26-bit number) it is much faster to recover the complete key by guessing modulo 11 in step 1, followed by 22 successive key guesses modulo 2 in step 2, and skip solving the linearized system in step 3 altogether. So for this particular value of q the complexity of recovering the complete key in Rubato-128S is given as $C_{kr} = 11^{16} + 22 \cdot 2^{16}$.

Table 5 shows particular conditions on q that give attacks with the smallest possible time complexities. For completeness, we also list the memory and data complexities, where both of these are given as the number of $\mathbb{Z}_q$-elements the attacker needs to store.

8 Final Remarks

8.1 Restoring the Security of **Rubato**

There are several ways Rubato can be made secure against the attack presented in Sect. 6. Here we discuss some of them.

Restricting q to Prime Numbers. The easiest way to prevent our attack is to simply restrict q to be prime. Since our attack is based on the assumption that q contains small factors, this restriction immediately gives Rubato instances that are immune to any small-factor attack. As already mentioned in Sect. 5.2, it is most common to choose the plaintext modulus of FV, the other part q plays in the RtF framework, to be prime. However, we stress that this choice is made for efficiency [22] *not* security in the FV scheme [1,32]. As our attack has demonstrated, restricting q to be prime is a choice made for security in Rubato, not convenience.

Increasing the Width of the Noise Distribution. Another way to protect the scheme against the small-factor attack is to increase the width of the noise distributions. If the value of αq is sufficiently high so that one cannot distinguish the correct key modulo m for $m \le 2^{\lambda/n}$, then one cannot perform the initial exhaustive key search modulo m with a complexity that is lower than the claimed security level. This approach allows keeping Rubato defined for general values of q. The drawback of increasing the αq parameter is that there will be more noise added to the key stream, and hence less accuracy in the decrypted plaintext values. This loss of precision will also compound when doing further operations in the CKKS scheme.

Increasing the Number of Rounds. A third alternative is to increase the number of rounds used in Rubato such that the solving complexity of the relinearization step is high enough to make the scheme secure against our attack. Recall that the total complexity C_{kr} of the key recovery attack depends on the complexity C_{relin} of doing the relinearization step, which in turn depends on the number of monomials appearing in the polynomials defining the stream produced by Ru. More rounds will produce more monomials and therefore a higher solving complexity, as one can see in Table 3. The main disadvantage of this approach is the loss of efficiency, as applying more rounds would result in a higher multiplicative depth. This would be detrimental to Rubato's use case in a transciphering framework, where a low multiplicative depth of the decryption function is necessary for efficiency reasons.

Using Non-polynomial S-Boxes. Lastly, avoiding the use of polynomial S-boxes is yet another way to provide security against our attack, since it requires that the S-boxes in the scheme admit a polynomial representation. As mentioned in Sect. 4.2, this is the case for the stream cipher Elisabeth, whose S-box functions are defined using look-up tables. A full discussion on how to design such S-box functions can be found in Sect. 4. However, using a look-up table rather than a polynomial function in Rubato would result in a severe efficiency loss. The Elisabeth ciphers are defined specifically to be combined with the TFHE scheme, which can very efficiently evaluate a look-up table homomorphically *for free* during a bootstrapping operation [63]. The strategy of using a look-up table as the S-box is therefore very well suited for the TFHE scheme, but not for stream ciphers designed to be combined with any other FHE scheme, such as Rubato.

8.2   Conclusion

Symmetric primitives over rings is a rapidly growing area of cryptography, in part spurred on by the development in MPC, ZK, and FHE. Constructing primitives over rings instead of fields might prove advantageous in certain cases, exemplified by the efficiency of Elisabeth compared to other FHE-friendly ciphers. However, as our key recovery attack on Rubato shows, it is important to take care when choosing the ring the primitive is defined over, since the ring greatly affects how susceptible the primitive is to attacks. We stress that we do not mean to suggest that rings should be avoided as a base structure for symmetric primitives, since several of the proposed schemes have useful properties. Rather, we emphasize that a more thorough cryptanalysis over rings is needed to ensure that proposed primitives are secure, and hope to see more work in this direction.

Acknowledgments. Lorenzo Grassi is supported by the German Research Foundation (DFG) within the framework of the Excellence Strategy of the Federal Government and the States - EXC 2092 CaSa - 39078197.

References

1. Lattigo v4, August 2022. EPFL-LDS, Tune Insight SA. https://github.com/tuneinsight/lattigo
2. Adams, W.W., Loustaunau, P.: An Introduction to Gröbner Bases, vol. 3. American Mathematical Society (1994)
3. Albrecht, M.R., et al.: Algebraic cryptanalysis of STARK-friendly designs: application to MARVELLous and MiMC. In: Galbraith, S.D., Moriai, S. (eds.) ASIACRYPT 2019. LNCS, vol. 11923, pp. 371–397. Springer, Cham (2019). https://doi.org/10.1007/978-3-030-34618-8_13
4. Albrecht, M., Grassi, L., Rechberger, C., Roy, A., Tiessen, T.: MiMC: efficient encryption and cryptographic hashing with minimal multiplicative complexity. In: Cheon, J.H., Takagi, T. (eds.) ASIACRYPT 2016. LNCS, vol. 10031, pp. 191–219. Springer, Heidelberg (2016). https://doi.org/10.1007/978-3-662-53887-6_7
5. Aly, A., Ashur, T., Ben-Sasson, E., Dhooghe, S., Szepieniec, A.: Design of symmetric-key primitives for advanced cryptographic protocols. IACR Trans. Symmetric Cryptol. **2020**(3), 1–45 (2020)
6. Ashur, T., Mahzoun, M., Toprakhisar, D.: Chaghri - a FHE-friendly block cipher. In: Proceedings of the 2022 ACM SIGSAC Conference on Computer and Communications Security, CCS 2022, pp. 139–150. ACM (2022)
7. Bardet, M., Faugère, J.-C., Salvy, B.: On the complexity of Gröbner basis computation of semi-regular overdetermined algebraic equations. In: Proceedings of the International Conference on Polynomial System Solving, pp. 71–74 (2004)
8. Baum, C., Braun, L., Munch-Hansen, A., Razet, B., Scholl, P.: Appenzeller to Brie: efficient zero-knowledge proofs for mixed-mode arithmetic and $\mathbb{Z}_{2^k}$. In: Proceedings of the 2021 ACM SIGSAC Conference on Computer and Communications Security, pp. 192–211 (2021)
9. Baum, C., Braun, L., Munch-Hansen, A., Scholl, P.: MozZ$_{2^k}$arella: efficient vector-OLE and zero-knowledge proofs over $\mathbb{Z}_{2^k}$. In: Dodis, Y., Shrimpton, T. (eds.) Advances in Cryptology - CRYPTO 2022. LNCS, vol. 13510, pp. 329–358. Springer, Cham (2022). https://doi.org/10.1007/978-3-031-15985-5_12

10. Beaulieu, R., Shors, D., Smith, J., Treatman-Clark, S., Weeks, B., Wingers, L.: The SIMON and SPECK lightweight block ciphers. In: Proceedings of the 52nd Annual Design Automation Conference, pp. 175:1–175:6. ACM (2015)
11. Beierle, C., et al.: Lightweight AEAD and hashing using the SPARKLE permutation family. Submission to the NIST lightweight cryptographic standardization process (Finalist)
12. Bernstein, D.J.: The Salsa20 family of stream ciphers. In: Robshaw, M., Billet, O. (eds.) New Stream Cipher Designs. LNCS, vol. 4986, pp. 84–97. Springer, Heidelberg (2008). https://doi.org/10.1007/978-3-540-68351-3_8
13. Beyne, T., et al.: Out of oddity – new cryptanalytic techniques against symmetric primitives optimized for integrity proof systems. In: Micciancio, D., Ristenpart, T. (eds.) CRYPTO 2020. LNCS, vol. 12172, pp. 299–328. Springer, Cham (2020). https://doi.org/10.1007/978-3-030-56877-1_11
14. Biham, E., Biryukov, A., Shamir, A.: Cryptanalysis of skipjack reduced to 31 rounds using impossible differentials. In: Stern, J. (ed.) EUROCRYPT 1999. LNCS, vol. 1592, pp. 12–23. Springer, Heidelberg (1999). https://doi.org/10.1007/3-540-48910-X_2
15. Biham, E., Dunkelman, O., Keller, N.: The rectangle attack — rectangling the serpent. In: Pfitzmann, B. (ed.) EUROCRYPT 2001. LNCS, vol. 2045, pp. 340–357. Springer, Heidelberg (2001). https://doi.org/10.1007/3-540-44987-6_21
16. Biham, E., Shamir, A.: Differential cryptanalysis of DES-like cryptosystems. J. Cryptol. 4(1), 3–72 (1991)
17. Biham, E., Shamir, A.: Differential Cryptanalysis of the Data Encryption Standard. Springer, New York (1993). https://doi.org/10.1007/978-1-4613-9314-6
18. Bogdanov, A., Khovratovich, D., Rechberger, C.: Biclique cryptanalysis of the full AES. In: Lee, D.H., Wang, X. (eds.) ASIACRYPT 2011. LNCS, vol. 7073, pp. 344–371. Springer, Heidelberg (2011). https://doi.org/10.1007/978-3-642-25385-0_19
19. Bosma, W., Cannon, J.J., Fieker, C., Steel, A. (eds.): Gröbner bases over Euclidean rings. In: Magma Handbook, vol. 2.27. Computational Algebra Group, School of Mathematics and Statistics, University of Sydney. https://magma.maths.usyd.edu.au/magma/handbook/text/1259#14396
20. Bouvier, C., et al.: New design techniques for efficient arithmetization-oriented hash functions: anemoi permutations and Jive compression mode. Cryptology ePrint Archive, Paper 2022/840 (2022). https://eprint.iacr.org/2022/840
21. Caminata, A., Gorla, E.: Solving multivariate polynomial systems and an invariant from commutative algebra. In: Bajard, J.C., Topuzoğlu, A. (eds.) WAIFI 2020. LNCS, vol. 12542, pp. 3–36. Springer, Cham (2021). https://doi.org/10.1007/978-3-030-68869-1_1
22. Chen, H., Laine, K., Player, R.: Simple encrypted arithmetic library - SEAL v2.1. Cryptology ePrint Archive, Paper 2017/224 (2017). https://eprint.iacr.org/2017/224
23. Cho, J., et al.: Transciphering framework for approximate homomorphic encryption. In: Tibouchi, M., Wang, H. (eds.) ASIACRYPT 2021. LNCS, vol. 13092, pp. 640–669. Springer, Cham (2021). https://doi.org/10.1007/978-3-030-92078-4_22
24. Cosseron, O., Hoffmann, C., Méaux, P., Standaert, F.: Towards case-optimized hybrid homomorphic encryption - featuring the Elisabeth stream cipher. In: Agrawal, S., Lin, D. (eds.) Advances in Cryptology - ASIACRYPT 2022. LNCS, vol. 13793, pp. 32–67. Springer, Cham (2022). https://doi.org/10.1007/978-3-031-22969-5_2

25. Cramer, R., Damgård, I., Escudero, D., Scholl, P., Xing, C.: SPD$\mathbb{Z}_{2^k}$: efficient MPC mod 2^k for dishonest majority. In: Shacham, H., Boldyreva, A. (eds.) CRYPTO 2018. LNCS, vol. 10992, pp. 769–798. Springer, Cham (2018). https://doi.org/10.1007/978-3-319-96881-0_26

26. Daemen, J., Rijmen, V.: The wide trail design strategy. In: Honary, B. (ed.) Cryptography and Coding 2001. LNCS, vol. 2260, pp. 222–238. Springer, Heidelberg (2001). https://doi.org/10.1007/3-540-45325-3_20

27. Dalskov, A.P., Escudero, D., Keller, M.: Fantastic four: honest-majority four-party secure computation with malicious security. In: USENIX Security Symposium, pp. 2183–2200 (2021)

28. Dixon, J.D.: Exact solution of linear equations using P-Adic expansions. Numer. Math. **40**(1), 137–141 (1982)

29. Dobraunig, C., et al.: Rasta: a cipher with low ANDdepth and few ANDs per bit. In: Shacham, H., Boldyreva, A. (eds.) CRYPTO 2018. LNCS, vol. 10991, pp. 662–692. Springer, Cham (2018). https://doi.org/10.1007/978-3-319-96884-1_22

30. Dobraunig, C., Grassi, L., Guinet, A., Kuijsters, D.: CIMINION: symmetric encryption based on Toffoli-gates over large finite fields. In: Canteaut, A., Standaert, F.-X. (eds.) EUROCRYPT 2021. LNCS, vol. 12697, pp. 3–34. Springer, Cham (2021). https://doi.org/10.1007/978-3-030-77886-6_1

31. Eichlseder, M., et al.: An algebraic attack on ciphers with low-degree round functions: application to full MiMC. In: Moriai, S., Wang, H. (eds.) ASIACRYPT 2020. LNCS, vol. 12491, pp. 477–506. Springer, Cham (2020). https://doi.org/10.1007/978-3-030-64837-4_16

32. Fan, J., Vercauteren, F.: Somewhat practical fully homomorphic encryption. Cryptology ePrint Archive, Paper 2012/144 (2012). https://eprint.iacr.org/2012/144

33. Faugère, J.-C.: A new efficient algorithm for computing Gröbner bases (F₄). J. Pure Appl. Algebra **139**(1–3), 61–88 (1999)

34. Faugère, J.-C., Gianni, P., Lazard, D., Mora, T.: Efficient computation of zero-dimensional Gröbner bases by change of ordering. J. Symb. Comput. **16**(4), 329–344 (1993)

35. Ganesh, C., Nitulescu, A., Soria-Vazquez, E.: Rinocchio: SNARKs for ring arithmetic. Cryptology ePrint Archive, Paper 2021/322 (2021). https://eprint.iacr.org/2021/322

36. Geelen, R., Iliashenko, I., Kang, J., Vercauteren, F.: On polynomial functions modulo p^e and faster bootstrapping for homomorphic encryption. In: Hazay, C., Stam, M. (eds.) Advances in Cryptology - EUROCRYPT 2023. LNCS, vol. 14006, pp. 257–286. Springer, Cham (2023). https://doi.org/10.1007/978-3-031-30620-4_9

37. Gopalan, P.: Query-efficient algorithms for polynomial interpolation over composites. SIAM J. Comput. **38**(3), 1033–1057 (2008)

38. Grassi, L.: Bounded surjective quadratic functions over $\mathbb{F}_p^n$ for MPC-/ZK-/HE-friendly symmetric primitives. Cryptology ePrint Archive, Paper 2022/1313 (2022). https://eprint.iacr.org/2022/1313

39. Grassi, L., Ayala, I.M., Hovd, M.N., Øygarden, M., Raddum, H., Wang, Q.: Cryptanalysis of symmetric primitives over rings and a key recovery attack on Rubato. Cryptology ePrint Archive, Paper 2023/822 (2023). https://eprint.iacr.org/2023/822

40. Grassi, L., Hao, Y., Rechberger, C., Schofnegger, M., Walch, R., Wang, Q.: Horst meets fluid-SPN: Griffin for zero-knowledge applications. Cryptology ePrint Archive, Paper 2022/403 (2022). https://eprint.iacr.org/2022/403

41. Grassi, L., Khovratovich, D., Lüftenegger, R., Rechberger, C., Schofnegger, M., Walch, R.: Reinforced concrete: a fast hash function for verifiable computation. In: Proceedings of the 2022 ACM SIGSAC Conference on Computer and Communications Security, CCS 202, pp. 1323–1335. ACM (2022)

42. Grassi, L., Khovratovich, D., Rechberger, C., Roy, A., Schofnegger, M.: Poseidon: a new hash function for zero-knowledge proof systems. In: 30th USENIX Security Symposium, USENIX Security 2021, pp. 519–535. USENIX Association (2021)

43. Grassi, L., Khovratovich, D., Rønjom, S., Schofnegger, M.: The Legendre symbol and the Modulo-2 operator in symmetric schemes over $\mathbb{F}_p^n$ preimage attack on full Grendel. IACR Trans. Symmetric Cryptol. **2022**(1), 5–37 (2022)

44. Grassi, L., Lüftenegger, R., Rechberger, C., Rotaru, D., Schofnegger, M.: On a generalization of substitution-permutation networks: the HADES design strategy. In: Canteaut, A., Ishai, Y. (eds.) EUROCRYPT 2020. LNCS, vol. 12106, pp. 674–704. Springer, Cham (2020). https://doi.org/10.1007/978-3-030-45724-2_23

45. Grassi, L., Onofri, S., Pedicini, M., Sozzi, L.: Invertible quadratic non-linear layers for MPC-/FHE-/ZK-friendly schemes over $\mathbb{F}_p^n$ application to Poseidon. IACR Trans. Symmetric Cryptol. **2022**(3), 20–72 (2022)

46. Grassi, L., Øygarden, M., Schofnegger, M., Walch, R.: From Farfalle to Megafono via Ciminion: the PRF hydra for MPC applications. In: Hazay, C., Stam, M. (eds.) Advances in Cryptology - EUROCRYPT 2023. LNCS, vol. 14007, pp. 255–286. Springer, Cham (2023). https://doi.org/10.1007/978-3-031-30634-1_9

47. Ha, J., Kim, S., Lee, B., Lee, J., Son, M.: Rubato: noisy ciphers for approximate homomorphic encryption. In: Dunkelman, O., Dziembowski, S. (eds.) Advances in Cryptology - EUROCRYPT 2022. LNCS, vol. 13275, pp. 581–610. Springer, Cham (2022). https://doi.org/10.1007/978-3-031-06944-4_20

48. Jakobsen, T., Knudsen, L.R.: The interpolation attack on block ciphers. In: Biham, E. (ed.) FSE 1997. LNCS, vol. 1267, pp. 28–40. Springer, Heidelberg (1997). https://doi.org/10.1007/BFb0052332

49. Keller, N., Rosemarin, A.: Mind the middle layer: the HADES design strategy revisited. In: Canteaut, A., Standaert, F.-X. (eds.) EUROCRYPT 2021. LNCS, vol. 12697, pp. 35–63. Springer, Cham (2021). https://doi.org/10.1007/978-3-030-77886-6_2

50. Kempner, A.J.: Polynomials and their residue systems. Trans. Am. Math. Soc. **22**(2), 240–266 (1921)

51. Kipnis, A., Shamir, A.: Cryptanalysis of the HFE public key cryptosystem by relinearization. In: Wiener, M. (ed.) CRYPTO 1999. LNCS, vol. 1666, pp. 19–30. Springer, Heidelberg (1999). https://doi.org/10.1007/3-540-48405-1_2

52. Knudsen, L.R.: Truncated and higher order differentials. In: Preneel, B. (ed.) FSE 1994. LNCS, vol. 1008, pp. 196–211. Springer, Heidelberg (1995). https://doi.org/10.1007/3-540-60590-8_16

53. Koti, N., Pancholi, M., Patra, A., Suresh, A.: SWIFT: super-fast and robust privacy-preserving machine learning. In: USENIX Security Symposium, pp. 2651–2668 (2021)

54. Lai, X.: Higher Order Derivatives and Differential Cryptanalysis. Springer, New York (1994). https://doi.org/10.1007/978-1-4615-2694-0_23

55. Leander, G., Abdelraheem, M.A., AlKhzaimi, H., Zenner, E.: A cryptanalysis of PRINTCIPHER: the invariant subspace attack. In: Rogaway, P. (ed.) CRYPTO 2011. LNCS, vol. 6841, pp. 206–221. Springer, Heidelberg (2011). https://doi.org/10.1007/978-3-642-22792-9_12

56. Leander, G., Minaud, B., Rønjom, S.: A generic approach to invariant subspace attacks: cryptanalysis of Robin, iSCREAM and Zorro. In: Oswald, E., Fischlin, M. (eds.) EUROCRYPT 2015. LNCS, vol. 9056, pp. 254–283. Springer, Heidelberg (2015). https://doi.org/10.1007/978-3-662-46800-5_11
57. Matsui, M.: Linear cryptanalysis method for DES cipher. In: Helleseth, T. (ed.) EUROCRYPT 1993. LNCS, vol. 765, pp. 386–397. Springer, Heidelberg (1994). https://doi.org/10.1007/3-540-48285-7_33
58. Mohassel, P., Rindal, P.: ABY3: a mixed protocol framework for machine learning. In: Proceedings of the 2018 ACM SIGSAC Conference on Computer and Communications Security, pp. 35–52 (2018)
59. National Institute of Standards and Technology. FIPS-46: Data Encryption Standard (DES) (1999). https://csrc.nist.gov/csrc/media/publications/fips/46/3/archive/1999-10-25/documents/fips46-3.pdf
60. Rivest, R.L.: Permutation polynomials modulo 2^w. Finite Fields Appl. **2001**(7), 287–292 (2001)
61. Singh, R.P., Maity, S.: Permutation polynomials modulo p^n. Cryptology ePrint Archive, Paper 2009/393 (2009). https://eprint.iacr.org/2009/393
62. Singmaster, D.: On polynomial functions (mod m). J. Num. Theory **6**(5), 345–352 (1974)
63. Smart, N.: Bootstrapping for dummies. Zama Research Blog (2022). https://www.zama.ai/post/what-is-bootstrapping-homomorphic-encryption
64. Strassen, V.: Gaussian elimination is not optimal. Numer. Math. **13**(4), 354–356 (1969)
65. Vasiliev, N.N., Kanzheleva, O.: Polynomial interpolation over the residue rings $\mathbb{Z}_n$. J. Math. Sci. **209**(6), 845–850 (2015)
66. von zur Gathen, J., Hartlieb, S.: Factoring modular polynomials. J. Symbol. Comput. **26**, 583–606 (1998)
67. Wagh, S., Tople, S., Benhamouda, F., Kushilevitz, E., Mittal, P., Rabin, T.: Falcon: honest-majority maliciously secure framework for private deep learning. Proc. Privacy Enhancing Technol. **2021**(1), 188–208 (2021)
68. Wagner, D.: The boomerang attack. In: Knudsen, L. (ed.) FSE 1999. LNCS, vol. 1636, pp. 156–170. Springer, Heidelberg (1999). https://doi.org/10.1007/3-540-48519-8_12
69. Yu, Y., Wang, M.: Permutation polynomials and their differential properties over residue class rings. Cryptology ePrint Archive, Paper 2013/251 (2013). https://eprint.iacr.org/2013/251
70. Zheng, Y., Matsumoto, T., Imai, H.: On the construction of block ciphers provably secure and not relying on any unproved hypotheses. In: Brassard, G. (ed.) CRYPTO 1989. LNCS, vol. 435, pp. 461–480. Springer, New York (1990). https://doi.org/10.1007/0-387-34805-0_42

Side Channels

Prouff and Rivain's Formal Security Proof of Masking, Revisited
Tight Bounds in the Noisy Leakage Model

Loïc Masure[✉] and François-Xavier Standaert

ICTEAM Institute, Université catholique de Louvain, Louvain-la-Neuve, Belgium
loic.masure@uclouvain.be

Abstract. Masking is a counter-measure that can be incorporated to software and hardware implementations of block ciphers to provably secure them against side-channel attacks. The security of masking can be proven in different types of threat models. In this paper, we are interested in directly proving the security in the most realistic threat model, the so-called *noisy leakage* adversary, that captures well how real-world side-channel adversaries operate. Direct proofs in this leakage model have been established by Prouff & Rivain at EUROCRYPT 2013, Dziembowski *et al.* at EUROCRYPT 2015, and Prest *et al.* at CRYPTO 2019. These proofs are complementary to each other, in the sense that the weaknesses of one proof are fixed in at least one of the others, and conversely. These weaknesses concerned in particular the strong requirements on the noise level and the security parameter to get meaningful security bounds, and some requirements on the type of adversary covered by the proof—*i.e.*, chosen or random plaintexts. This suggested that the drawbacks of each security bound could actually be proof artifacts. In this paper, we solve both issues, by revisiting Prouff & Rivain's approach.

1 Introduction

1.1 Context

Side-Channel Analysis (SCA) represents an important threat for cryptographic implementations on embedded devices such as smart-cards, Micro-Controller Units (MCUs), *etc.* [35,36]. In such attacks, the adversary has a physical access to the target device. More precisely, the adversary is assumed to measure some physical metrics of the device called *leakages*—*e.g.* the power consumption of the device or the Electro-Magnetic (EM) emanations around the target—during one or several encryptions. It is then possible to use this side information—beside leveraging plaintexts and ciphertexts—to guess the values of *sensitive* variables, *i.e.* the values of intermediate calculations depending on some chunks of secret. This way, an SCA adversary may independently recover the secret in a divide-and-conquer approach, making the typical complexity of such attacks often negligible compared to a regular cryptanalysis. That is why the SCA threat should carefully be taken into account in the design of cryptographic implementations.

© International Association for Cryptologic Research 2023
H. Handschuh and A. Lysyanskaya (Eds.): CRYPTO 2023, LNCS 14083, pp. 343–376, 2023.
https://doi.org/10.1007/978-3-031-38548-3_12

Thankfully, this does not prevent the deployment and the use of embedded cryptography, as this threat can be mitigated by incorporating counter-measures in the implementation. At a very high level, most of the counter-measures such as *masking* or *shuffling* turn a deterministic cryptographic primitive into a non-deterministic implementation by injecting some randomness during the execution of the primitive, either at a physical level or at an algorithmic level. In this paper, we focus on the main counter-measure considered so far in SCA, namely masking [16, 27], a.k.a. "Multi-Party Computation (MPC) on silicon" [32]. In a nutshell, any sensitive variable is submitted to a $(d + 1)$-linear secret-sharing, where d is the security parameter that the designer may control in order to achieve the desired security level. The implementation is then modified in a way such that all the subsequent calculations involving a sensitive variable are now replaced by some *gadgets* operating on the shares separately, as in multi-party computation. As a result, any SCA adversary must have access to the *noisy* observation of every share of secret to be able to recover any piece of information about a sensitive variable. If any noisy observation induces some uncertainty on the actual value of the corresponding share, it results in an *amplified* uncertainty on the actual value of the target sensitive variable—an intuition that dates back to the seminal works of Chari *et al.* at CRYPTO 99 [16]. As a consequence, the complexity of any SCA attack increases exponentially fast with the security parameter d, at the price of quadratic (or super-linear) runtime and memory overheads in the implementation only [32].

1.2 Provable Security of Masking

The latter intuition has been formalized over the past few years by masking security proofs. Generally speaking, a masking security proof takes as inputs an abstract representation of the implementation, the number of shares $d + 1$ (where d act as he security parameter) and a measure of the noisiness of the leakage, usually characterized from the device embedding the implementation. The masking security proof then returns an upper bound on a metric depicting the security level of the implementation.

There exists different strategies to establish a masking security proof. In this paper, we focus on masking security bounds directly stated in the most realistic threat model. This approach has been first considered by Chari *et al.* [16], before being formalized by Prouff and Rivain [43]. Concretely, a *noisy* observation of an intermediate calculation is a Probability Mass Function (p.m.f.) over all the hypothetical values that the operands may take: the closer the p.m.f. to the uniform distribution, the noisier the leakage.

The idea of security proofs in the noisy leakage model is to assume that any noisy leakage accessed by the adversary is δ-close to the uniform distribution, for some real-valued parameter δ stated in a metric that can be measured by the practitioner.[1] Then, the goal is to prove that the p.m.f. of the secret key, given an

---

[1] *e.g.*, the Statistical Distance (SD), the Euclidean Norm (EN), or the Mutual Information (MI). Notice that in our context, "noisier" means a *lower* δ.

access to the full leakage, is in turn ϵ-close to the p.m.f. that an adversary without access to side-channel would get, for some real-valued parameter ϵ depending on δ, the security parameter d, and some other specifications of the implementation.

This direct approach has gained the reputation of being "not convenient" [8, 10] to work with, up to the point that most masking security proofs are now established in much simpler yet unrealistic threat models [6,8,9,15,32], relying on a non-tight reduction from the noisy leakage model to such simpler threat models [23]. As a result, only three previous works tackled masking security proofs through this direct way so far. These works, from Prouff and Rivain at EUROCRYPT 2013 [43], Dziembowski et al. at EUROCRYPT 2015 [25], and Prest et al. at CRYPTO 2019 [42], considered implementations of block ciphers protected with an Ishai-Sahai-Wagner (I.S.W.) masking scheme [32,45], assuming leak-free refreshings. The latter assumption is a drawback, as it is unrealistic—otherwise studying leaky computations would not be relevant—and some real-world refreshings could critically decrease the security level [19]. Interestingly, these three proofs are quite complementary to each other, in the sense that the weaknesses of one proof are fixed in at least one of the others, and conversely. We give hereafter a brief overview of these pros and cons—also synthesized in Table 1:

1. **Strong noise requirements** [43]. Prouff and Rivain's bound required the baseline noise parameter δ to scale *polynomially* with the field size, which is prohibitive for concrete block ciphers, *e.g.*, the Advanced Encryption Standard (AES) whose field size is 256. On the opposite, Dziembowski et al.'s bound have a nearly tight noise requirement that does not depend on the field size.

2. **Lack of incentive for noisier leakage** [25]. In Dziembowski et al.'s security bound assuming that the noise requirement is verified, the bound no longer depends on the actual baseline noise level δ. This suggests that to reach the desired security level ϵ, the designer would have no incentive in choosing a noisier device on which implementing the block cipher, which sounds unrealistic. In the extreme case where the device is so noisy enough that $\delta \leq \epsilon$, masking would not be necessary, whereas Dziembowski et al.'s bound would still require a prohibitive number of shares to be meaningful. On the opposite, the bounds of Prouff and Rivain and Prest et al. still carry some incentive towards noisier baseline leakage.

3. **Too conservative and hard to estimate metric** [42]. Contrary to the other proofs, the baseline noise in Prest et al.'s security bound is assumed to be measured in a *worst-case* metric, the so-called Relative Error (RE). This contrasts with all the other works considering *average-case* metrics, such as the MI [43] or the SD [25], and does not fit either with SCA security metrics such as Guessing Entropy (GE) or Success Rate (SR) [48] that are averaged metrics as well. Using worst-case metrics has two main drawbacks. First, a baseline noise characterization made with a worst-case metric necessarily results in more conservative requirements than with average-case metrics. Second, worst-case metrics are by definition harder to estimate

on concrete devices by evaluators, and hereupon the RE may not be efficiently tractable—especially for high-dimensional leakage—nor even be formally defined in some cases. As an example, Prest *et al.* even needed to use tedious tail-cut arguments on the exemplary leakage distributions of their case study [42, Remark 2].

4. **Random message attacks** [43]. Last but not least, Prouff and Rivain's security bounds are given for random message attacks, whereas Dziembowski *et al.* and Prest *et al.* state security bounds for chosen plaintext attacks. Even if most of state-of-the-art SCA adversaries consider random plaintext attacks, this contrasts with the common practice in cryptography, where the adversary is assumed to (adaptively) choose the message or the ciphertext.

Table 1. Comparison between all proofs in the Noisy Leakage model: Prouff & Rivain [43], Dziembowski *et al.* [25], Prest *et al.* [42].

Feature	[43]	[25]	[42]	Our work
Strong noise requirement	Yes	No	No	No
Leak-free refreshing	Yes	Yes	Yes (Sec. 6)	Yes
Incentive to small δ	✓	✗	✓	✓
Average-case metric	✓	✓	✗	✓
Adaptive attacks	✗	✓	✓	✓

1.3   Recent Improvements on Security Bounds for Encodings only

In light of the previous drawbacks listed so far, Duc *et al.* conjectured at EURO-CRYPT 2015 that the weaknesses (1–3) were actually proof artifacts [24]. More precisely, it would be possible to prove a masking security bound in terms of MI with tight noise requirement, and tight amplification rates, while covering the leakage of the full block cipher. In a recent line of works, Ito *et al.* [33], Masure *et al.* [40], and Béguinot *et al.* [11] have been able to prove a reduced version of Duc *et al.*'s conjectured security bound, for the leakage of one encoding *only*. While these works represent a first milestone, they were limited in that they did not cover the leakage coming from the *computations*, and Duc *et al.*'s conjecture remained to be proven for the leakage of a full block cipher.

1.4   Our Contribution

In this paper, we prove new masking security bounds stated in the noisy leakage model, in the same setting as the one of the previous works discussed so far— namely Rivain-Prouff's masking scheme, with leak-free refreshings [43]. To this end, we revisit Prouff and Rivain's approach, by showing that some drawbacks of their results can be circumvented.

- **A tight bound with respect to the noise parameter** δ. We leverage the recent results of Ito *et al.* [33], Masure *et al.* [40] and Béguinot *et al.* [11], to bound the amount of informative leakage of computations coming from a full block cipher, masked with an I.S.W.-like masking scheme. As a result, our noise requirement is tight [31], while carrying a much higher incentive to noisier leakage than in the previous works.
- **A security bound with low dependency on the field size.** With the previous contribution alone, our final security bound would still carry a constant factor scaling *quadratically* with the size of the field over which the block cipher operates, regardless of the number of shares. While this is much better than Prouff & Rivain's bound and competitive with Dziembowski *et al.*'s bound, this still sounds unnatural, as it does not perfectly fit Duc *et al.*'s conjecture [24], and might be fatal for block ciphers operating over large fields. To tackle this problem, we show how a careful scrutiny of the implementation, under mild assumptions on the Sbox, can allow us to make this constant factor *quasi-linear* with the field size. We even show how this constant factor overhead can further be made almost independent of the field size, by combining the Rivain-Prouff masking scheme with *blinding*, a well-known counter-measure in asymmetric cryptography.
- **Security Bound with Average Metric.** In our masking security proof, any metric, be it the baseline noise δ or the final security bound ϵ, is expressed in MI. This contrasts with Prouff & Rivain's work where the parameters δ and ϵ are not expressed in the same metric. Since MI is an averaged metric, it is quite easy to estimate by evaluators when characterizing the behavior of the target device in worst-case evaluations [4].
- **Attacks with Chosen Messages.** Eventually, we argue how our security bounds stated for random plaintext attacks can be extended to the case of chosen plaintext attacks, using a similar argument as the one stated by Dziembowski *et al.* in their follow-up work at Tcc 2016 [26].

Overall, our work is the first to state a masking proof with meaningful security bounds, *i.e.*, for which the desired security level can be reached with a reasonable amount of masking shares, and requiring a reasonable amount of noise from the device. Therefore, our masking security bound can be practically used by an SCA evaluator to upper bound current state-of-the-art SCA adversaries. This suggests that masking proofs directly stated in the noisy leakage model can be seen as complementary to the more generic proofs in other threat models. The only shortcoming of our proof, in line of the previous works, concerns the use of leak-free refreshings. We hope future works may allow to relax this assumption, and thereby provide a comparable setting with masking security proofs in the indirect approach taking advantage of reductions between models.

2 Preliminaries

In this paper, we denote sets by calligraphic letters, *e.g.*, $\mathcal{X}$. In particular, the letter $\mathcal{Y}$ denotes a finite field $(\mathcal{Y}, \oplus, \times)$ of characteristic two. Upper-case letters are used to denote random variables, while lower-case letters denote observations of random variables. In this paper, we adopt the following convention: A, B stand for independent random variables uniformly distributed over $\mathcal{Y}$, while G, H denote random variables that are not necessarily uniform over $\mathcal{Y}$, nor assumed to be independent. The letter L will be used to denote a random function $\mathcal{Y} \to \mathcal{L}$, were the set $\mathcal{L}$ is assumed without loss of generality to be discrete. When the context does not carry any ambiguity, we will often denote the random variable L(Y) by omitting the reference to Y. Finally, bold letters denote vectors of random variables.

Mutual Information. Let $Y \in \mathcal{Y}$ be a discrete random variable. The *entropy* of Y, denoted by H(Y), defined by: $H(Y) = -\sum_{s \in \mathcal{Y}} \Pr(Y = s) \log_2 \Pr(Y = s)$. Moreover, we define MI between two discrete random variables Y and L as:

$$MI(Y; L) = H(Y) - \mathbb{E}_l \left[H(Y \mid L = l) \right] \ .$$

2.1   Model of Noisy Leaking Computation

We describe hereafter the frame in which Prouff and Rivain's result is established, that is mostly adapted from their seminal work [43].[2]

Block Cipher. A block cipher over a finite field $\mathcal{Y}$ is defined by a pair of inputs **K**, **P** seen as vectors of $\mathcal{Y}$, and by a sequence of T *elementary calculations* $(C_i)_{1 \le i \le T}$ defined either over $\mathcal{Y}$ or $\mathcal{Y} \times \mathcal{Y}$. More precisely, since $\mathcal{Y}$ is assumed to be a finite field, we consider the elementary calculations to be either an addition $\oplus$ or a field multiplication $\times$, whether the operands are constant or random variables.[3]

Leakage and SCA Adversary. When processed on some input Y (resp. a pair of inputs A, B), an elementary calculation C_i reveals $L_i(Y)$ (resp. L(A, B)) to the adversary, for some *noisy leakage* function L_i, that depends both on Y (resp. A, B), and on some internal randomness assumed to be drawn independently each time L_i leaks. Whenever the context does not carry any ambiguity, we may simply denote the leakage $L_i(Y)$ by L_i. In this paper, we consider an adversary having access to the full leakage induced by each elementary calculation and trying to recover a chunk of secret key.

Definition 1 (SCA key recovery adversary). *An SCA adversary for a block cipher defined over $\mathcal{Y}$ is an algorithm that, upon a sequence of N_a plaintexts* $\mathbf{P} = (P_1, \ldots, P_{N_a})$, *takes as an input a sequence* $\{(L_i)_{1 \le i \le T}\}_{1 \le j \le N_a}$ *of leakages*

---

[2] The interested reader may also refer to Rivain's habilitation thesis for a thorough discussion about the leakage model [44].

[3] As argued by Prouff & Rivain, any mapping over a finite field can be decomposed as a sequence of additions and multiplications, using Lagrange interpolation.

induced by each elementary calculation of a block cipher, and that returns a guess $\widehat{K}$ of one chunk $K \in \mathcal{Y}$ of the secret key **K**. *We say that the adversary is* random-plaintext *if* **P** *is chosen randomly and uniformly over* $\mathcal{Y}^{N_a}$, *whereas we say that the adversary is* chosen-plaintext *if the adversary can arbitrarily choose the sequence* **P**—*possibly adaptively.*

Notice that $\widehat{K}$ depends on the plaintexts used by the adversary (and on the internal randomness of the leakage functions). Accordingly, the accuracy of the key guessing is expected to increase with the number N_a of queries. We formalize this in the definition hereafter.

Definition 2 (Success Rate). *The* success rate *of an SCA key recovery adversary is the quantity*

$$\mathsf{SR}(N_a) = \Pr\left(\widehat{K} = K\right) \ . \tag{1}$$

Similarly, for any probability threshold $\frac{1}{|\mathcal{Y}|} \leq \beta \leq 1$, we define the efficiency *$N_a^\star(\beta)$ of an SCA key recovery adversary as the minimal amount of queries necessary to get a success rate higher than β.*

MI-Noisy Leakage. The success of an SCA key recovery adversary depends on how informative the leakage is about the underlying secret data processed. To measure this, we assume that the evaluator may determine how *noisy* any leakage function is. To this end, we formally define hereafter the concept of MI-noisy leakage.

Definition 3 (Noisy leakage for unary gates). *Let* $\mathsf{C} : \mathcal{Y} \to \mathcal{Y}$ *be an elementary calculation associated with the leakage function L. L is said to be δ-MI-noisy, for some $\delta \geq 0$, if for any input random variable A of C, uniformly distributed over $\mathcal{Y}$,*

$$\mathsf{MI}(A; L(A)) \leq \delta \ .$$

Definition 4 (Noisy leakage for binary gates). *Let* $\mathsf{C} : \mathcal{Y}^2 \to \mathcal{Y}$ *be an elementary calculation associated with the leakage function L. L is said to be δ-MI-noisy, for some $\delta \geq 0$, if for any input random variables A, B of C, uniformly distributed over $\mathcal{Y}$,*

$$\mathsf{MI}(A, B; L(A, B)) \leq \delta \ .$$

We chose the MI as a metric of reference in our proof, because it is at the core of Prouff & Rivain's security bound that we revisit in this paper, and also because we can therefore rely on the recent improvement of Ito *et al.* [33], Masure *et al.* [40] and Béguinot *et al.* [11]. Moreover, the MI is known to be tightly linked to the complexity of Differential Power Analysis (DPA) attacks [17,22,37–39], and "generally carries more intuition (see, *e.g.*, [5] in the context of linear cryptanalysis)" [24]. We discuss this choice of metric in Sect. 5.

2.2   Rivain-Prouff's Masking Scheme

We recall hereafter the definition of masking, mostly taken from Prouff and Rivain's paper [43, Def. 2].

Definition 5. *Let d be a positive integer. The d-encoding of $Y \in \mathcal{Y}$ is a $(d+1)$-tuple $(Y_i)_{0 \leq i \leq d}$ satisfying $\bigoplus_{i=0}^{d} Y_i = Y$ and such that for any strict subset $\mathcal{I}$ of $[\![0, d]\!]$, $(Y_i)_{\mathcal{I}}$ is uniformly distributed over $\mathcal{Y}^{|\mathcal{I}|}$.*

Algorithm 1. Linear gadget in Prouff & Rivain's proof.

Require: A: $(d+1)$-sharing of A, C: elementary calculation linear with its input.
Ensure: B : $(d+1)$-sharing of C(A).
1: **for** $i = 0, \ldots, d$ **do**
2:      $B_i \leftarrow C(A_i)$ ▷ Type 1 or 2
3: **end for**
4: **B** $\leftarrow$ Refresh(**B**)   ▷ Assumed to be leak-free
5: **A** $\leftarrow$ Refresh(**A**)   ▷ Only if A used subsequently.

The parameter d in Definition 5 refers here to the security parameter of the counter-measure. In their paper, Prouff and Rivain explain how to turn any block cipher into a d-order secure implementation—*i.e.* such that any intermediate computation depending on a secret has a $(d+1)$-encoding [43]. First, the plaintext and the secret key are split into $d+1$ shares. Then, each elementary calculation of the block cipher is transformed as follows. If the elementary calculation is linear with respect to its inputs, then it is replaced by the sequence of elementary calculations listed in Algorithm 1. If the elementary calculation is an Sbox, then it can first be decomposed as a sequence of linear calculations and field multiplications. Then the linear calculations can be processed as in Algorithm 1, and the field multiplications can be replaced by the procedure listed in Algorithm 2. It is a variant of the actual I.S.W. scheme revisited by Rivain and Prouff at CHES 2010, up to a permutation between independent operations, so it does not change the amount of informative leakage. Overall, Rivain-Prouff's masked implementation can be decomposed as subsequences of any of the following types:

1. $(z_i \leftarrow g(x_i))_{0 \leq i \leq d}$, with g being a linear function (of the block-cipher);
2. $(z_i \leftarrow g(x_i))_{0 \leq i \leq d}$, with g being an affine function (within an Sbox evaluation);
3. $(v_{i,j} \leftarrow a_i \times b_j)_{0 \leq i,j \leq d}$ (cross-products computation step in multiplication);
4. $(t_{i,j} \leftarrow t_{i,j-1} \oplus v_{i,j})_{0 \leq i,j \leq d}$ (compression step multiplication).

For concreteness, we list two examples of schemes of the AES Sbox (at least its non-linear part) with this method in Algorithms 3 and 4. Algorithm 3 is the one initially proposed by Rivain and Prouff at CHES 2010. Recently, Cardoso

Algorithm 2. Multiplication gadget in Prouff & Rivain's proof.

Require: $\mathbf{A}, \mathbf{B}$: $(d+1)$-sharing of A, B.
Ensure: $\mathbf{C}$: $(d+1)$-sharing of A × B.
1: **for** $i = 0, \ldots, d$ **do**
2:     **for** $j = 0, \ldots, d$ **do**
3:         $V_{i,j} \leftarrow A_i \times B_j$ ▷ Cross products (type 3)
4:     **end for**
5: **end for**
6: $\mathbf{V} \leftarrow \mathsf{Refresh}(\mathbf{V})$ ▷ Assumed to be leak-free
7: **for** $i = 0, \ldots, d$ **do**
8:     $C_i = 0$
9:     **for** $j = 0, \ldots, d$ **do**
10:         $C_i \leftarrow C_i \oplus V_{i,j}$ ▷ Compression (type 4)
11:     **end for**
12: **end for**
13: $\mathbf{C} \leftarrow \mathsf{Refresh}(\mathbf{C})$ ▷ Assumed to be leak-free
14: $\mathbf{A}, \mathbf{B} \leftarrow \mathsf{Refresh}(\mathbf{A}), \mathsf{Refresh}(\mathbf{B})$ ▷ Only if A, B used subsequently.

et al. proposed at CARDIS 2022 an alternative exponentiation scheme depicted in Algorithm 4 which, combined with other implementation tricks, improved upon Rivain-Prouff's exponentiation [46]. Both exponentiations contain the same number of I.S.W. multiplications.[4]

Algorithm 3. R&P's Exp254 [45].

Require: $\mathbf{X}$: $(d+1)$-sharing of X
Ensure: $\mathbf{C}$: $(d+1)$-sharing of X^{254}
1: $\mathbf{Z} \leftarrow \mathsf{SecLin}(s \mapsto s^2, \mathbf{X})$ ▷ $\mathrm{Z} = \mathrm{X}^2$
2: $\mathbf{X} \leftarrow \mathsf{Refresh}(\mathbf{X})$
3: $\mathbf{Y} \leftarrow \mathsf{SecMult}(\mathbf{Z}, \mathbf{X})$ ▷ $\mathrm{Y} = \mathrm{X}^3$
4: $\mathbf{V} \leftarrow \mathsf{SecLin}(s \mapsto s^4, \mathbf{Y})$ ▷ $\mathrm{V} = \mathrm{X}^{12}$
5: $\mathbf{V} \leftarrow \mathsf{Refresh}(\mathbf{V})$
6: $\mathbf{Y} \leftarrow \mathsf{SecMult}(\mathbf{Y}, \mathbf{V})$ ▷ $\mathrm{Y} = \mathrm{X}^{15}$
7: $\mathbf{Y} \leftarrow \mathsf{SecLin}(s \mapsto s^{16}, \mathbf{Y})$ ▷ $\mathrm{Y} = \mathrm{X}^{240}$
8: $\mathbf{Y} \leftarrow \mathsf{SecMult}(\mathbf{Y}, \mathbf{W})$ ▷ $\mathrm{Y} = \mathrm{X}^{252}$
9: $\mathbf{C} \leftarrow \mathsf{SecMult}(\mathbf{Y}, \mathbf{Z})$ ▷ $\mathrm{C} = \mathrm{X}^{254}$

Algorithm 4. Cardoso's Exp254 [46].

Require: $\mathbf{X}$: $(d+1)$-sharing of X
Ensure: $\mathbf{C}$: $(d+1)$-sharing of X^{254}
1: $\mathbf{Z} \leftarrow \mathsf{SecLin}(s \mapsto s^2, \mathbf{X})$ ▷ $\mathrm{Z} = \mathrm{X}^2$
2: $\mathbf{Z} \leftarrow \mathsf{Refresh}(\mathbf{Z})$
3: $\mathbf{Y} \leftarrow \mathsf{SecMult}(\mathbf{Z}, \mathbf{X})$ ▷ $\mathrm{Y} = \mathrm{X}^3$
4: $\mathbf{Z} \leftarrow \mathsf{SecLin}(s \mapsto s^2, \mathbf{Y})$ ▷ $\mathrm{Y} = \mathrm{X}^6$
5: $\mathbf{Y} \leftarrow \mathsf{SecMult}(\mathbf{Z}, \mathbf{X})$ ▷ $\mathrm{Y} = \mathrm{X}^7$
6: $\mathbf{Z} \leftarrow \mathsf{SecLin}(s \mapsto s^2, \mathbf{Y})$ ▷ $\mathrm{Z} = \mathrm{X}^{14}$
7: $\mathbf{Y} \leftarrow \mathsf{SecMult}(\mathbf{Z}, \mathbf{X})$ ▷ $\mathrm{Y} = \mathrm{X}^{15}$
8: $\mathbf{Y} \leftarrow \mathsf{SecLin}(s \mapsto s^{16}, \mathbf{Y})$ ▷ $\mathrm{Y} = \mathrm{X}^{240}$
9: $\mathbf{C} \leftarrow \mathsf{SecMult}(\mathbf{Y}, \mathbf{Z})$ ▷ $\mathrm{C} = \mathrm{X}^{254}$

3 Revisiting Prouff and Rivain's Bound

We are now ready to revisit Prouff and Rivain's formal security proof in this section. To this end we briefly recall the outline of their proof—that we follow as well—based on three steps. First, they leverage the assumption that refresh gadgets are leak-free in order to reduce the MI of a sequence of elementary computations to the sum of the MIs between the secret and each subsequence of leakage. Second, some of these elementary computations—*e.g.*, the non-linear operations

---

[4] There are other generic methods to securely compute an Sbox with masking [30], which are out of the scope of this paper.

of the Sbox—may process non-uniform secrets. That is why the authors make an intermediate reduction to the case where every elementary computation processes uniform secrets—and mutually independent as well, in the case of binary gates. Finally, the authors apply some noise amplification lemma from the literature. Our revisited proof applies the same outline. We now dig into the details of these steps.

3.1   Step 1: Decomposition into Subsequences

We first recall that the MI of a sequence of mutually independent leakages can be bounded by the sum of MIs of each leakage.

Theorem 1 (Subsequence decomposition [43]**).** *Let Y be a random variable over a finite set $\mathcal{Y}$, not necessarily uniform. Let $\mathbf{L} = (L_1, \ldots, L_t)$ be t random variables such that the random variables $(L_i \mid Y = y)_i$ are mutually independent for every $y \in \mathcal{Y}$. Then, we have*

$$\mathsf{MI}(Y; \mathbf{L}) \leq \sum_{i=1}^{t} \mathsf{MI}(Y; L_i) \ . \tag{2}$$

Although we do not claim any improvement in this first step, we reproduce the proof in Sect. B for completeness.

3.2   Step 2(a): Reduction to Uniform Secrets for Unary Gates

We now revisit the second step of Prouff and Rivain's work, namely the reduction from non-uniform secrets to uniform secrets. To this end, we will split our results into two cases. The first case processed in this subsection deals with non-uniform inputs of unary calculations, such as Line 4 in Algorithm 3. The second case deals with non-uniform and non-independent inputs of binary calculations, such as Line 6 in Algorithm 3, and will be deferred in Subsect. 3.3.

The results presented in this section aim at bounding the MI between $\mathsf{C}(Y)$, where $\mathsf{C} : \mathcal{Y} \to \mathcal{Y}$ and its corresponding leakage. We first state the following theorem that relies on a technical lemma from Shulman and Feder [47].

Theorem 2 (Generic Bound for Non-Uniform Secrets [47]**, p. 1360).** *Let $L : \mathcal{Y} \to \mathcal{L}$ be a random function denoting a leakage, and let Y be uniformly distributed over $\mathcal{Y}$. Then, there exists a constant α such that for all random variables G arbitrarily distributed over $\mathcal{Y}$, the following inequality holds true:*

$$\mathsf{MI}(G; L(G)) \leq \alpha \cdot |\mathcal{Y}| \cdot \mathsf{MI}(Y; \mathbf{L}(Y)) \ . \tag{3}$$

Moreover, the smallest value α such that Eq. 3 holds true belongs to the interval $\alpha \in \left[\frac{\log_2(e)}{e}, 1 - e^{-1} \right] \approx [0.53, 0.63]$.

Theorem 2 introduces an overhead scaling with $|\mathcal{Y}|$, which could decrease the final security level by one or several orders of magnitude (*e.g.*, for the AES, $|\mathcal{Y}| = 2^8$). Note that Eq. 3 is nearly tight in the general case, in the sense that the range of α is narrow. Shulman and Feder exhibit an example of worst case leakage function, such that Eq. 3 becomes an equality, for $\alpha \approx 0.53$ [47].

The Power Map Trick. However, such worst-case C functions are not likely to be used in cryptographic primitives, since, *e.g.*, the input and output of Sbox are expected to be uniformly distributed, for cryptographic reasons. That is why we refine hereafter the generic statement of Theorem 2, and we present some examples where this refinement could remove the dependency on the field size. To this end, we revisit Theorem 2 by relying on an intermediate result of Shulman and Feder's proof.

Lemma 1 ([47], **Lemma 6**). *Given a leakage function L and two random variables Y, Y' distributed (non-necessarily uniformly) over the finite set $\mathcal{Y}$, and such that the support of $\Pr(Y')$ contains the support of $\Pr(Y)$. Then, the following inequality holds:*

$$\frac{\mathsf{MI}(Y; L(Y))}{\mathsf{MI}(Y'; L(Y'))} \geq \min_{y \in \mathcal{Y}} \frac{\Pr(Y = y)}{\Pr(Y' = y)} \ .$$

As a result, we straightforwardly get the following corollary.

Corollary 1. *In the same setting as in Lemma 1, if now the support of $\Pr(Y)$ contains the support of $\Pr(Y')$, the following inequality holds true:*

$$\frac{\mathsf{MI}(Y'; L(Y'))}{\mathsf{MI}(Y; L(Y))} \leq \max_{y \in \mathcal{Y}} \frac{\Pr(Y' = y)}{\Pr(Y = y)} \ . \tag{4}$$

Proof. Straightforward, using Lemma 1 and the identity $\max_{x \in \mathcal{X}} x = \frac{1}{\min_{x \in \mathcal{X}} \frac{1}{x}}$, for some finite ordered set $\mathcal{X}$. □

We will leverage Corollary 1 in the case where the Sbox is a monomial, *i.e.* is of the shape $y \mapsto y^k$. Admittedly, this makes our proof slightly more specific than Prouff and Rivain's one, as the latter one can handle any Sbox expressed as a polynomial. Nevertheless, this assumption remains mild, as it covers many Sboxes used in practical ciphers, including the AES, and will allow us to remove a constant factor equal to the field size.

We have seen in Algorithms 3 and 4 that the monomial $y \mapsto y^k$ can be computed in the Rivain-Prouff masking scheme by computing intermediate power maps $y \mapsto y^{k'}$ for some $k' \leq k$, through some square-and-multiply schemes [45]. The bound on the leakage induced by such an intermediate computation is handled by the following corollary.

Corollary 2. *Let Y be a uniform random variable over a finite field $\mathcal{Y}$ of size $M \geq 2$. For any $k \in [\![1, M-1]\!]$, define the function $\mathsf{C} : y \in \mathcal{Y} \mapsto y^k$. Let $L : \mathcal{Y} \to \mathcal{L}$ be a δ-MI-noisy leakage. Then:*

$$\mathsf{MI}\Big(Y; L(Y^k)\Big) \leq \frac{M}{M-1} \cdot \gcd\{k, M-1\} \cdot \delta \ . \tag{5}$$

Proof. Using the Data Processing Inequality (DPI) (stated in Lemma 2 in Appendix A), we are reduced to upper bound $\mathsf{MI}\Big(Y^k; L(Y^k)\Big)$. To this end, we shall compute the p.m.f. of Y^k. The result will then follow from Lemma 1 and

Lemma 2. First, notice that by definition of a field, $y^k = 0$ if and only if (i.f.f.) $y = 0$, so $\Pr\left(Y^k = 0\right) = \frac{1}{M}$. Second, notice that since $(\mathcal{Y}, \oplus, \times)$ is a finite field, the group $(\mathcal{Y}^*, \times)$ is cyclic, hence isomorphic with $\mathbb{Z}_{M-1}$. As a result, for any $s \neq 0$ for which there exists $y \in \mathcal{Y}$ verifying $y^k = s$, we have

$$\Pr\left(Y^k = s\right) = \frac{\gcd(k, M - 1)}{M - 1} ,$$

and $\Pr\left(Y^k = s\right) = 0$ otherwise. To summarize, for all $s \in \mathcal{Y}$, we have

$$\frac{\Pr\left(Y^k = s\right)}{\Pr(Y = s)} \leq \frac{M}{M - 1} \cdot \gcd(k, M - 1) . \tag{6}$$

$\square$

Comparing the universal bound of Eq. 3 to the specific bound in Eq. 5, we can see that we replaced a factor $0.63 \cdot M$ by a factor $\gcd(k, M - 1)$ (ignoring the factor $\frac{M}{M-1}$ for large values of M). As an example Table 2 reports the different constant factors induced by Eq. 5 for the exponentiation scheme of Algorithms 3 and 4, and how they compare to the generic bound of Equation 3. Our power-map-specific bound is between one and two orders of magnitude lower than the generic bound in Equation 3.

Table 2. Factor overheads from Eq. 5, and ratio between the generic bound of Eq. 3 and the refined bound of Eq. 5.

Scheme	k	$\gcd(k, 255)$	$\frac{(1-e^{-1}) \cdot 256}{\gcd(k, 255)}$
Rivain-Prouff [45]	2, 3, 12, 15, 240, 252	1, 3, 3, 15, 15, 3	**161.3**, 53.8, 53.8, **10.8**, 10.8, 53.8
Cardoso et al. [46]	2, 3, 6, 7, 14, 15, 240, 252	1, 3, 3, 1, 1, 15, 15	**161.3**, 53.8, 53.8, 161.3, 161.3, **10.8**, 10.8, 53.8

Admittedly, the numbers reported in Table 2 depend on the exponentiation scheme, and thereby depend on the underlying power-map we aim at computing—which may differ for other block ciphers with power-map-based Sbox beyond the AES. We may therefore wonder how $\gcd(k, M - 1)$ generally scales when M grows. It is not hard to find some integer k such that $\gcd(k, M-1)$ scales linearly with M,[5] so our improved bound could marginally improve the one from Eq. 3 in some worst-case exponentiation schemes. Still, the following theorem suggests that this is not likely to happen.

---

[5] As an example, for the AES field $M - 1 = 255$, which is divided by 3 so there exists some k, e.g., $k = 85$, such that $\gcd(k, M - 1) = \frac{M-1}{3}$.

Theorem 3 ([13], **Thm. 3.2**). *Let $M > 2$ be an integer. Then, for all $\epsilon > 0$, we have $\underset{k}{\mathbb{E}}\left[\gcd(k, M)\right] = \mathcal{O}(M^\epsilon)$, where the expectation is taken with respect to k uniformly distributed in $[\![1, M]\!]$.*

The practical interpretation of Theorem 3 is that if a given exponentiation scheme gives high constant factors, then it should not be hard to modify it, in order to make the constant factor in the right hand-side of Eq. 5 arbitrarily low. As a consequence, we may treat the right hand-side of Eq. 5 as asymptotically independent of M with high probability. That is why in the remaining of this paper, we will abuse notation by denoting any gcd factor as scaling as $\mathcal{O}(M^\epsilon)$—which is confirmed on our implementations of interest by Table 2.

3.3   Step 2(b): Reduction to Uniform Secrets for Binary Gates

We have shown in Subsect. 3.2 how to significantly decrease the loss in the reduction from non-uniform secrets to uniform secrets for leakage coming from unary gates dealing with power maps. In order to have a complete toolbox for reductions to uniform secrets, we also need to deal with leakages coming from gadgets with two input operands, *e.g.*, I.S.W. multiplications. Hereupon, Theorem 2 straightforwardly applies, although spanning a loss of $0.63 |\mathcal{Y}|^2$ in the reduction.

That is why we may naturally think of extending the power map trick introduced before. But contrary to Theorem 2, Corollary 2 does not extend as straightforwardly for binary gates. Indeed, calculations with more than one operand add another difficulty: not only the operands may not be uniformly distributed, but they might also be non-independent. This results in the following corollary.

Corollary 3. *Let Y be a random variable uniformly distributed over the finite field $\mathcal{Y}$. For $p, q \in [\![2, M - 2]\!]$, let $\mathbf{Z} = (Y^p, Y^q)$. Let $L : \mathcal{Y}^2 \to \mathcal{L}$ be a δ-MI-noisy leakage. Then,*

$$\mathsf{MI}(Y; L(\mathbf{Z})) \leq \frac{M}{M - 1} \cdot \min\left\{\gcd(p, M - 1), \gcd(q, M - 1)\right\} \cdot M \cdot \delta . \quad (7)$$

Proof. We apply Lemma 1 for the random vector $\mathbf{Z}' = (Y, Y')$, where Y' is an independent copy of Y. For any $x, y \in \mathcal{Y}$, the total probability formula implies that

$$\frac{\Pr(Y^p = x, Y^q = y)}{\Pr(Y = x, Y' = y)} \leq \frac{\sum_{y'} \Pr(Y^p = x, Y^q = y')}{\Pr(Y = x, Y' = y)} = \frac{\Pr(Y^p = x)}{\Pr(Y = x)\Pr(Y' = y)} .$$

Using Eq. 6, we get that

$$\frac{\Pr(Y^p = x, Y^q = y)}{\Pr(Y = x)\Pr(Y' = y)} \leq \frac{M}{M - 1} \cdot \gcd(p, M - 1) \cdot M . \quad (8)$$

By symmetry, we can obtain the same bound by permuting the roles of p and q, which gives Eq. 7.

Remark 1. Note that the inequality in Eq. 8 is tight, *e.g.*, if p divides q, or inversely. Likewise, we argued that Eq. 3 is generally tight—unless considering further assumptions on the prior distribution. Nevertheless, both facts do not necessarily imply that Eq. 7 is tight. Whether the latter inequality could be refined for binary gates with non-independent operands remains an open-question that we will briefly discuss in Subsect. 3.4.

3.4   Step 3: The Amplification Theorems

We now revisit the third step of Prouff & Rivain's approach. To this end, like in Subsect. 3.2 and Subsect. 3.3, we make a discrepancy between the unary gates and the binary gates.

For Unary Gates. The following amplification theorem is at the core of our direct proof in the noisy leakage model, and holds the name of Mrs. Gerber's Lemma (MGL). It has initially been stated by Wyner and Zyv [50] for binary random variables, and has been recently extended by Jog and Anantharam to random variables in Abelian groups whose size is a power of two [34]. This result has recently been pointed out to the SCA community by Béguinot *et al.* at COSADE 2023 [11].

Theorem 4 (Mrs. Gerber's Lemma (MGL) *[11], Cor. 1).* *Let* $|\mathcal{Y}| = 2^n$ *for some bit-size n and d be a positive integer. Let $Y_0, \ldots, Y_d$ be a $(d+1)$-encoding of the uniform random variable Y over $\mathcal{Y}$, and $\mathbf{L} = (L_0, \ldots, L_d)$ be such that, conditionally to Y_i, the variable L_i is independent of the others. Assume that for all $i \in [\![0, d]\!]$, $\mathsf{MI}(Y_i; L_i) \leq \delta_i$ for some parameter $0 \leq \delta_i \leq 1$. Then*

$$\mathsf{MI}(Y; \mathbf{L}) \leq \mathsf{f}_{\mathsf{MI}}(\delta_0, \ldots, \delta_d) \quad , \tag{9}$$

where $\mathsf{f}_{\mathsf{MI}}(\cdot)$ is Mrs. Gerber's function.

We refer to the works of Béguinot *et al.* for more details about Mrs. Gerber's function [11]. In our context, we only need the properties summarized hereafter.

Proposition 1 (The MGL function [11] Thm. 1, Prop. 3). *The Mrs. Gerber's function $\mathsf{f}_{\mathsf{MI}}(\cdot)$ is concave with respect to any of its variables, when the remaining ones are kept fixed. Let $\eta = (2\log 2)^{-1} \approx 0.72$. Then for all $\delta_0, \ldots, \delta_d \in [0, 1]$, we have*

$$\mathsf{f}_{\mathsf{MI}}(\delta_0, \ldots, \delta_d) \leq \eta \prod_{i=0}^{d} \frac{\delta_i}{\eta} \quad . \tag{10}$$

For Binary Gates. We now extend Béguinot *et al.*'s Theorem 4 to the case of binary gates, as stated hereafter by the following theorem that we prove in Appendix B.1, following a similar outline as Prest *et al.* [42, Thm. 6].

Theorem 5. *Let A, B be two independent and uniform random variables, over a finite field $\mathcal{Y}$. Let $(A_i)_{0 \leq i \leq d}, (B_j)_{0 \leq j \leq d}$ be d-encodings of A and B respectively. Let $L_{i,j} : A_i, B_j \mapsto L_{i,j}(A_i, B_j)$ be a family of randomized and mutually independent leakage functions such that for every i, j, $\mathsf{MI}(A_i, B_j; L_{i,j}(A_i, B_j)) \leq \delta_{i,j}$, for some $\delta_{i,j} \in [0, 1]$. Denote the concatenation of the leakages $\{L_{i,j}\}_{0 \leq i,j \leq d}$ by $\mathbf{L}$. Then,*

$$\mathsf{MI}(A, B; \mathbf{L}) \leq \mathsf{f_{MI}}\left(\sum_{j=0}^{d} \delta_{0,j}, \ldots, \sum_{j=0}^{d} \delta_{d,j}\right) + \mathsf{f_{MI}}\left(\sum_{i=0}^{d} \delta_{i,0}, \ldots, \sum_{i=0}^{d} \delta_{i,d}\right) . \quad (11)$$

3.5   Security Bound for Each Type of Subsequence

In this section, we leverage the noise amplification result to bound the amount of leakage in each subsequence.

Type 1 subsequences occur for linear elementary calculations over uniform secrets, and are already covered by Theorem 4, which is a straightforward application of the MGL.

Corollary 4 (Type 1 subsequences). *Let Y be a uniform random variable over a finite field $\mathcal{Y}$ and $(Y_i)_{0 \leq i \leq d}$ be a d-encoding of Y. Let $\delta \geq 0$ and $L_0, \ldots, L_d$ be δ-MI-noisy leakage functions over $\mathcal{Y}$. Denote $(L_0(Y_0), \ldots, L_d(Y_d))$ by $\mathbf{L}$. Then we have:*

$$\mathsf{MI}(Y; \mathbf{L}) \leq \eta \cdot \left(\frac{\delta}{\eta}\right)^{d+1} . \quad (12)$$

Likewise, type 2 subsequences cover linear elementary calculations over non-uniform secrets, *e.g.*, occurring inside Sboxes. Such subsequences are covered by the following corollary.

Corollary 5 (Type 2 subsequences). *Let Y be a uniform random variable over a finite field $\mathcal{Y}$. Let k, d be positive integers and $(G_i)_{0 \leq i \leq d}$ be a $(d+1)$-sharing of Y^k. Let $0 \leq \delta \leq 1$ and let $L_0(G_0), \ldots, L_d(G_d)$ be δ-MI-noisy leakages. Denote the concatenation of the leakages $\{L_i\}_{0 \leq i \leq d}$ by $\mathbf{L}$. Then, we have:*

$$\mathsf{MI}(Y; \mathbf{L}) \leq \frac{|\mathcal{Y}|}{|\mathcal{Y}| - 1} \cdot \gcd(k, |\mathcal{Y}| - 1) \cdot \eta \cdot \left(\frac{\delta}{\eta}\right)^{d+1} . \quad (13)$$

Proof. Straightforward, by combining Theorem 4 with Corollary 2.   □

We now focus on the more involved type of subsequences, namely type 3, which is a binary gate. It occurs in the cross-products of the I.S.W. multiplication.

Corollary 6 (Type 3 subsequences). *Let Y be a uniform random variable over a finite field $\mathcal{Y}$, let d, p, q be positive integers. Let $(G_i)_i$, $(H_j)_j$ be $d+1$-additive sharings of Y^p, Y^q respectively. Let $0 \leq \delta$, and $\{G_i, H_j \mapsto L_{i,j}(G_i, H_j)\}_{i,j}$ be δ-MI-noisy leakage functions. Let us denote the concatenation of the leakages*

$\{L_{i,j}\}_{0 \leq i,j \leq d}$ *by* $\mathbf{L}$, *and denote* $\varphi(p, q, M) = \min(\gcd(p, M - 1), \gcd(q, M - 1))$. *Then we have:*

$$\mathsf{MI}(Y; \mathbf{L}) \leq 2 \cdot |\mathcal{Y}| \cdot \frac{|\mathcal{Y}|}{|\mathcal{Y}| - 1} \cdot \varphi(p, q, |\mathcal{Y}|) \cdot \eta \cdot \left(\frac{(d + 1) \cdot \delta}{\eta} \right)^{d+1} . \qquad (14)$$

Proof. Combining Theorem 5 with Corollary 3.   □

It now remains to give some upper bounds for type 4 subsequences. These subsequences can be observed in the compression phase of I.S.W. multiplications (after cross-products and refreshings). This is the aim of the following result that we prove in Appendix B.1.

Theorem 6. *Let* $Y_0, \ldots, Y_d$ *be* $d + 1$ *independent uniformly random variables over a finite set* $\mathcal{Y}$. *Let* $L_1, \ldots, L_d$ *be a family of* δ_i-*MI leakage functions, defined over* $\mathcal{Y} \times \mathcal{Y}$, *for some* $0 \leq \delta_i \leq 1$. *We have:*

$$\mathsf{MI}(Y_d; L_1(Y_0, Y_1), \ldots, L_d(Y_{d-1}, Y_d)) \leq \delta_d . \qquad (15)$$

Corollary 7 (Type 4 subsequences). *Let* Y *be a secret, such that for* $p, q \in \mathbb{N}$ *the product of the multiplication* $Y^p \times Y^q$ *is processed by an I.S.W. gadget. For* $0 \leq i, j \leq d$ *and for* $T_{i,j}, V_{i,j} \in \mathcal{Y}$, *let* $\mathbf{L} = \{L_{i,j}(T_{i,j-1}, V_{i,j})\}_{0 \leq i,j \leq d}$ *denote the corresponding type 4 leakages such that for all* i, j, *the leakage* $L_{i,j}(T_{i,j-1}, V_{i,j})$ *is* $\delta_{i,j}$-*MI-noisy, for* $\delta_{i,j} \leq \delta \leq 1$. *Then the following inequality holds true:*

$$\mathsf{MI}(Y; \mathbf{L}_{i,j}(T_{i,j-1}, V_{i,j})_{0 \leq i,j \leq d}) \leq \frac{|\mathcal{Y}|}{|\mathcal{Y}| - 1} \cdot \gcd(p + q, M - 1) \cdot \eta \cdot \left(\frac{\delta}{\eta} \right)^{d+1} . \qquad (16)$$

Proof. Using Corollary 2, we reduce to the case where $Y^p \times Y^q$ is uniformly distributed over $\mathcal{Y}$, inducing a $\gcd(p + q, M - 1)$ factor overhead. Then, by gathering the leakages $\mathbf{L}_{i,j}$ sharing the same index i by batches, we may notice that each batch of index only depends on one share of Y. We may therefore invoke Theorem 4 as follows:

$$\mathsf{MI}(Y; \mathbf{L}) \leq \mathsf{f}(\delta'_0, \ldots, \delta'_d) , \qquad (17)$$

where $\delta'_i = \mathsf{MI}\left(Y_i; \{L_{i,j}(T_{i,j-1}, V_{i,j})\}_{0 \leq j \leq d}\right)$. Finally, we can upper bound each δ'_i by $\delta_{i,d}$ using Theorem 6.   □

3.6   From Subsequences to a Complete Computation

We can now combine the three previous steps to state the main result, in a similar way as Prouff and Rivain [43, Thm. 4] and as Prest *et al.* [42, Sec. 6.3].

Theorem 7. *Consider a* $\mathcal{Y}$-*block cipher with monomial Sboxes, where a sequence of elementary calculations depends on a random variable Y uniformly distributed. Assume that these elementary calculations are protected by a d-encoding masking scheme as described in Subsect. 2.2, resulting in T elementary* *calculations giving access to the leakage* $\mathbf{L} = (L_i)_{1 \le i \le T}$, *where each leakage function* L_i *is assumed to be* δ-*MI-noisy. Then, the following inequality is verified:*

$$\mathsf{MI}(Y; \mathbf{L}) \le t_3 \cdot \eta \cdot \left(\frac{(d+1)\delta}{\eta}\right)^{d+1} + t_{1,2,4} \cdot \eta \cdot \left(\frac{\delta}{\eta}\right)^{d+1} ,$$

such that

$$t_3 = \sum_{(p,q) \in \mathcal{M}} \varphi(p, q, |\mathcal{Y}|), \ \ t_{1,2,4} = \sum_{(p,q) \in \mathcal{M}} \phi(p, q, |\mathcal{Y}|) + \sum_{k \in \mathcal{S}} \psi(k, |\mathcal{Y}|) , \quad (18)$$

where $\mathcal{M}$ *is the sequence of pairs* (p, q) *of exponents in the operands of the I.S.W. multiplication gadgets,* $\mathcal{S}$ *is the sequence of exponents* (k) *of operands over which a linear transformation is applied, and*

- $\varphi(p, q, M) = 2 \cdot M \cdot \frac{M}{M-1} \cdot \min(\gcd(p, M-1), \gcd(q, M-1))$,
- $\phi(p, q, M) = \frac{M}{M-1} \cdot \gcd(p + q, M-1)$,
- $\psi(k, M) = \gcd(k, M-1)$.

Proof. We apply Theorem 1 to decompose the MI into a sum of MIs for each subsequence. Since by assumption Y is uniformly distributed over $\mathcal{Y}$, Corollaries 4, 5, 6, 7 directly apply to bound each term in the sum. □

Note that in (18), $t_3 = \mathcal{O}\left(|\mathcal{Y}|^{1+\epsilon} \cdot |\mathcal{M}|\right)$, and $t_{1,2,4} = \mathcal{O}(|\mathcal{Y}|^{\epsilon} \cdot (|\mathcal{M}| + |\mathcal{S}|))$.

Corollary 8. *For any random-plaintext SCA key recovery adversary targeting a* $\mathcal{Y}$-*block cipher protected by the masking scheme described in Subsect. 2.2, the efficiency verifies the following bound:*

$$N_a^{\star}(\mathsf{SR}) \ge \frac{f(\mathsf{SR}, |\mathcal{Y}|)}{t_3 + t_{1,2,4}} \cdot \frac{1}{\eta} \cdot \left(\frac{\eta}{(d+1)\delta}\right)^{d+1} ,$$

where $f(\mathsf{SR}, M) = \log_2(M) - (1 - \mathsf{SR}) \log_2(M - 1) - \mathsf{H}_2(\mathsf{SR})$, *where* H_2 *is the binary entropy function, and where the constants* t_3 *and* $t_{1,2,4}$ *are the ones defined in Theorem 7.*

Proof. Chérisey *et al.*'s security bound allows to link the SCA key recovery efficiency to the MI between $Y = K \oplus P$ and the corresponding leakage:

$$N_a^{\star}(\beta) \ge \frac{f(\mathsf{SR}, |\mathcal{Y}|)}{\mathsf{MI}(Y; \mathbf{L})} .$$

Plugging Theorem 7 into the latter inequality gives the result. □

In other words, any random plaintext attack on the masked implementation will require at least $\Omega\left(|\mathcal{Y}|^{-(1+\epsilon)} \cdot \log|\mathcal{Y}| \cdot \left(\frac{\eta}{(d+1)\delta}\right)^{d+1}\right)$ queries to the target device.

4   A Tweaked ISW Gadget with Tight Security Bounds

In Remark 1 we have discussed the fact that the bound in Eq. 7 might not be tight, despite the different inequalities used to reach this result are individually tight. Therefore, whether Eq. 7 could be further tightened remains an open question. To tackle this challenge, one should directly state an amplification result similar to Theorem 5 without going through the intermediate reduction to uniform and independent operands. Unfortunately, to the best of our knowledge, all the amplification lemmata used so far in direct proofs in the noisy leakage model [43, Thm. 1], [26, Thm. 2], [42, Lemma 6] always assume the shares to be mutually independent and *uniformly* distributed, in order to prove the noise amplification.[6] To the best of our knowledge, there is no amplification result for non-uniform secret yet. So the question our challenge opens may be seen as the challenge of finding such amplification results for non-uniform secrets.

4.1   The Blinding Counter-Measure to the Rescue

Rather than trying to tackle the challenge raised in Sect. 4, we propose hereafter to circumvent it: if we cannot improve the bounds, we may still tweak the implementation. We instantiate this idea by proposing in Algorithm 5 a tweaked variant of the I.S.W. multiplication, relying on a similar idea as the so-called *blinding* counter-measure for asymmetric cryptography [38, p. 225].

Algorithm 5. "Blinded" I.S.W.

Require: $\mathbf{G}, \mathbf{H}$: $(d+1)$-sharing of $g(\mathrm{Y}), h(\mathrm{Y})$.
Ensure: $\mathbf{I}$: $(d+1)$-sharing of $g(\mathrm{Y}) \times h(\mathrm{Y})$.
  1: $\mathbf{R} \leftarrow \$(1^{d+1})$
  2: $\mathbf{G}' \leftarrow \mathbf{G} \oplus \mathbf{R}$
  3: $\mathbf{G}', \mathbf{R} \leftarrow \mathsf{Refresh}(\mathbf{G}'), \mathsf{Refresh}(\mathbf{R})$
  4: $\mathbf{M} \leftarrow \mathsf{ISW}_1(\mathbf{G}', \mathbf{H})$ ▷ $\mathbf{G}' \perp\!\!\!\perp \mathbf{H}$
  5: $\mathbf{H} \leftarrow \mathsf{Refresh}(\mathbf{H})$
  6: $\mathbf{H}' \leftarrow \mathsf{ISW}_2(\mathbf{H}, \mathbf{R})$ ▷ $\mathbf{H} \perp\!\!\!\perp \mathbf{R}$
  7: $\mathbf{M}, \mathbf{H}' \leftarrow \mathsf{Refresh}(\mathbf{M}), \mathsf{Refresh}(\mathbf{H}')$
  8: $\mathbf{I} \leftarrow \mathbf{M} \oplus \mathbf{H}'$ ▷ $\mathbf{M}, \mathbf{H}'$ linked
  9: $\mathbf{I} \leftarrow \mathsf{Refresh}(\mathbf{I})$
 10: $\mathbf{G}, \mathbf{H} \leftarrow \mathsf{Refresh}(\mathbf{G}), \mathsf{Refresh}(\mathbf{H})$

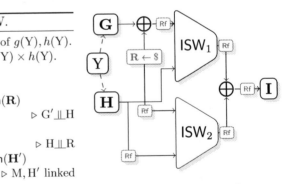

Fig. 1. "Blinded" I.S.W. "Rf" denote the Refresh gadgets.

---

[6] Proofs via reduction to the random probing model do not require the underlying secret to be uniformly distributed, as the reduction is applied to the leakage for each share anyway [23, Lemma 2]. Hence, it ensures that the d-encoding is uniformly distributed over $\mathcal{Y}^{d+1}$, which corresponds to a uniform secret.

The idea, depicted in Fig. 1, is to enforce the input operands of the I.S.W. multiplication gadget to be independent. This is done by *blinding* one operand of the ISW_1 gadget in Fig. 1, by adding it with the $(d+1)$-sharing of a random nonce. Using a second I.S.W. gadget, we can keep the overall output correct by leveraging the identity: $\mathsf{G} \times \mathsf{H} = (\mathsf{G} \oplus \mathsf{R}) \times \mathsf{H} \oplus (\mathsf{R} \times \mathsf{H})$. At first glance, one may think that this trick somewhat shifts the problem without fixing it, since the input operands of both I.S.W. are independent, but now the input operands of the final Xor in line 8 of Algorithm 5 are no longer independent. Surprisingly, the prior joint distribution of the outputs $(\mathsf{M}, \mathsf{H}')$ of the two I.S.W. multiplications has a much lower bias with respect to the joint uniform distribution, compared to the bias of the joint distribution of (G, H). This is formalized in the following theorem, proven in Appendix B.2.

Theorem 8. *Let $Y \in \mathcal{Y}$ be uniformly distributed, and let $\mathbf{L}$ corresponding to the leakage of Algorithm 5. Then, assuming leak-free refreshings, and that $g(Y) = Y^p$ and $h(Y) = Y^q$, for p, q positive integers, the following inequality is satisfied:*

$$\mathsf{MI}(Y; \mathbf{L}) \leq \varphi(p, q, |\mathcal{Y}|) \cdot \eta \cdot \left(\frac{(d+1)\delta}{\eta} \right)^{d+1} + \phi(p, q, |\mathcal{Y}|) \cdot \eta \cdot \left(\frac{\delta}{\eta} \right)^{d+1} ,$$

where

- $\varphi(p, q, M) = 4 \cdot \frac{M}{M-1} \cdot \gcd(q, M-1)$,
- $\phi(p, q, M) = 4 + \frac{M}{M-1} \cdot \gcd(p, M-1) + \max\left(2, \frac{M}{M-1} \cdot \gcd(p+q, M-1) \right)$.

Note that in Theorem 8, both φ and ϕ are almost independent of the field size, whereas t_3 in Theorem 7 scales at least linearly with the field size. From Theorem 8 follows the corollary stated hereafter.

Corollary 9. *In the same setting as in Corollary 8, if the I.S.W. multiplication gadgets are replaced by the scheme in Algorithm 5, then*

$$N_a^\star(\mathsf{SR}) \geq \Omega\left(|\mathcal{Y}|^{-\epsilon} \cdot \log |\mathcal{Y}| \cdot \left(\frac{\eta}{(d+1)\delta} \right)^{d+1} \right) .$$

Proof. The proof follows the one of Corollary 8, by updating the functions φ and ϕ in Eq. 18 with the new values in Theorem 8. $\qquad\square$

5   Discussion

We have established our main results in Sect. 3 and Sect. 4. We propose hereafter to discuss some features of our results, and to compare them to previous works. To this aim, we first compare in Subsect. 5.1 our bounds to previous works. We then discuss in Subsect. 5.2 how we can extend our results to security bounds in terms of chosen plaintext attacks. We conclude this section by discussing the advantages and drawbacks of the blinded I.S.W. gadget presented in Sect. 4.

5.1 Comparison with Related Works

We compare in this section our security bounds with related works. To this end, we first discuss the noise requirements in the different security bounds in the literature. We synthesize in Table 3 the different noise requirements of masking security bounds. We can see that our security bound gets a similar noise requirement as the proofs of Dziembowski *et al.* [25] and Prest *et al.* [42], although stated in different metrics. Notice that the dependency of our noise requirement in d is tight, since it depicts the potential ability of an adversary to increase its success of recovering each share through *horizontal attacks*, as argued by Battistello *et al.* [7] and Grosso and Standaert [31]. Nevertheless, it is still possible to relax this dependency by using other multiplication gadgets [1–3,8,28,29].

Moreover, we also extend Prest *et al.*'s case study on the exemplary leakage distribution in which each intermediate calculation is assumed to leak its Hamming weight with an additive Gaussian noise of standard deviation σ [42, Table 1]. We complete Table 3 with our new result, by using the fact that for such a leakage model, $\mathsf{MI} = \Theta\left(\frac{\log(M)}{\sigma^2}\right)$. It can be noticed that on this particular leakage distribution, our requirement on the minimal noise level is now the weakest of all security proofs based on the I.S.W. masking scheme.

Table 3. Noise requirements, and illustration on a case study on a Hamming weight leakage model with additive Gaussian noise.

Work (year)	Noise requirement	Equivalent Gaussian noise
[43] (2013)	$\mathsf{EN} \leq \mathcal{O}\left(\frac{1}{dM^3}\right)$	$\sigma \geq \Omega\left(dM^{5/2}\sqrt{\log(M)}\right)$
[23] (2014)	$\mathsf{SD} \leq \mathcal{O}\left(\frac{1}{dM^2}\right)$	$\sigma \geq \Omega\left(dM^2\sqrt{\log(M)}\right)$
[25] (2015)	$\mathsf{SD} \leq \mathcal{O}\left(\frac{1}{d}\right)$	$\sigma \geq \Omega\left(d\sqrt{\log(M)}\right)$
[42] (2019)	$\mathsf{RE} \leq \mathcal{O}\left(\frac{1}{d}\right)$	$\sigma \geq \Omega(d\log(M))^{\mathrm{a}}$
This work	$\mathsf{MI} \leq \mathcal{O}\left(\frac{1}{d}\right)$	$\sigma \geq \Omega\left(\sqrt{d\log(M)}\right)$

[a] As explained by Prest *et al.* [42, Remark 2], the RE is not even formally defined for leakage models with Gaussian noise, unless requiring to a tail-cut argument that adds another constant factor hidden in the $\Omega(\cdot)$ notation.

At first glance, Table 3 suggests that Prest *et al.*'s RE-based security bound remains quite competitive with the other works based on the noise requirements. However, we emphasize that the RE is a *worst-case* metric, whereas all the other metrics in Table 3 are *averaged* metrics. Estimating worst-case metrics may not always be efficiently tractable by practitioners, especially for high-dimensional leakage. In addition, worst-case metrics are by definition much more conservative than averaged metrics, which contrasts with the concrete SCA security metrics like the GE or the SR [48] that are also averaged metrics. To illustrate this, let us consider another example of leakage distribution, namely the now famous *random probing* model considered by Duc *et al.* in their groundbreaking work [23]. In this leakage model, the adversary can recover the exact value of any intermediate calculation, each with probability $0 \leq \kappa \leq 1$, where the parameter κ denotes the baseline noise level here. It can be verified that the MI of this leakage model is $\log |\mathcal{Y}| \cdot \kappa$, whereas its RE is always fixed to $|\mathcal{Y}| - 1$ regardless of the value of κ, so that the MI can be set arbitrarily close to zero—by setting κ accordingly— while the RE remains constant. In other words, the random probing model can *never* be proven secure with masking by using a security bound involving the RE, whereas our masking security bound remains meaningful for the random probing leakage model, as long as $\kappa \leq \mathcal{O}\left(\frac{1}{\log |\mathcal{Y}| \cdot d}\right)$.[7]

As a result, the only security bound comparable with ours in terms of noise requirements remains Dziembowski *et al.*'s bound [25]. Their bound is obtained using Chernoff-like concentration inequalities [12]. Although this approach has been fruitful in Duc *et al.*'s elegant reduction to the probing model [23] due to its genericity, it has a major drawback since the convergence rate of the security bound no longer depends on the actual baseline noise level δ. This is highlighted in their final bound [25, Eq. (42)]: it can be verified that the bound is even always increasing for values of d between 0 and 8, and becomes non-trivial—*i.e.*, lower than one—only for $d \geq 142$ if $|\mathcal{Y}| = 256$. On the opposite, our security bounds do not suffer from this caveat, since they depend on the actual baseline noise level δ, which makes our bounds non-trivial for arbitrarily small value of d, provided that δ is small enough as we will depict later in Fig. 2.

5.2   Beyond Random Plaintext Attacks

One may argue that the latter comparison with the works of Dziembowski *et al.* is not completely fair, since their bound is stated for SCA adversary with chosen plaintext. Hereupon, the authors stated later at TCC 2016 that by leveraging a reduction from non-uniform secrets to uniform secrets [26, Lemma 2],

> "The cryptographic interpretation of [reductions from non-uniform to uniform secrets] is that it suffices to consider only random-plaintext attacks, instead of chosen-plaintext attacks" [26, p. 297].

We notice that our Theorem 2 actually represents such a reduction. Accordingly, our main results Theorem 7 and Theorem 8 can be extended to cover adversaries with chosen plaintexts, by multiplying the constant factors by $(1 - e^{-1}) \cdot |\mathcal{Y}|$, as pointed out in the following Corollary 10.

Corollary 10. *Let Y be a random variable arbitrarily distributed over $\mathcal{Y}$, and protected by a masking scheme with $d + 1$ shares as described in Subsect. 2.2 resulting in T elementary calculations. Assume that the scheme protects $|\mathcal{S}|$ linear operations, and $|\mathcal{M}|$ I.S.W. multiplications that are part of a monomial Sbox, and protected according to Algorithm 5. Let $\mathbf{L} = (L_i)_{1 \leq i \leq T}$ be the random vector*

---

[7] This condition could even be relaxed to $\kappa \leq \mathcal{O}(\frac{1}{d})$ in the particular case of leakage in the random probing model, if one would directly state a security bound for this leakage model, *e.g.*, by extending Eq. (9) of Duc *et al.* [24].

denoting the leakage of the full masking scheme, and let $\delta \geq 0$ be such that every L_i is δ-MI-noisy. Then, the inequality in Theorem 7 is verified for:

$$t_3 = (1 - e^{-1}) \cdot |\mathcal{Y}| \cdot \sum_{(p,q) \in \mathcal{M}} \varphi(p, q, |\mathcal{Y}|) ,$$

$$t_{1,2,4} = (1 - e^{-1}) \cdot |\mathcal{Y}| \cdot \left(\sum_{(p,q) \in \mathcal{M}} \phi(p, q, |\mathcal{Y}|) + \sum_{k \in \mathcal{S}} \psi(k, |\mathcal{Y}|) \right) ,$$

where φ and ϕ are the functions defined in Theorem 8, and ψ is the function defined in Theorem 7.

5.3   Beyond Monomial Sboxes

Likewise, we can extend our previous results to random or chosen plaintext attacks on block ciphers whose Sbox is not a monomial, as stated by Corollary 11.

Corollary 11. *Let Y be a random variable arbitrarily distributed over $\mathcal{Y}$, and protected by a masking scheme with $d + 1$ shares as described in Subsect. 2.2, resulting in T elementary calculations. Assume that the scheme protects $|\mathcal{S}|$ linear operations, and $|\mathcal{M}|$ I.S.W. multiplications. Let $\mathbf{L} = (L_i)_{1 \leq i \leq T}$ be the random vector denoting the leakage of the full masking scheme, and let $\delta \geq 0$ be such that every L_i is δ-MI-noisy. Then, the inequality of Theorem 7 is verified for:*

$$t_3 = 2 \cdot (1 - e^{-1}) \cdot |\mathcal{Y}|^2 \cdot |\mathcal{M}|, \quad t_{1,2,4} = (1 - e^{-1}) \cdot |\mathcal{Y}| \cdot (|\mathcal{S}| + |\mathcal{M}|).$$

Proof. We apply Theorem 1, then we group the type 1, 2, and 4 subsequences together and we apply the reduction to uniform secrets using Theorem 2. Likewise, we apply Theorem 2 for type 3 subsequences over the domain $\mathcal{Y} \times \mathcal{Y}$. We can then directly apply Theorem 4 and Theorem 5 respectively.   □

Notice that the only difference in the assumptions of Corollary 10 and Corollary 11 is that we no longer need any particular assumption on the Sbox in the latter case. Whether we could leverage further assumptions on the Sbox for arbitrarily distributed secrets is left as an open question for further works.

Table 4 synthesizes the different constant factors t_3, whether the SCA adversary is assumed to operate with random or chosen plaintexts, or whether the blinded I.S.W. multiplication gadget is used or not. Likewise, we may notice that the constant factor of Corollary 11 scaling quadratically with the field size seems at first glance worse than the one of Dziembowski *et al.* [25, Thm. 1], whereas their security bound only scales linearly with the field size $|\mathcal{Y}|$. Nevertheless, our work considers the paradigm where the leakage comes from the *computations* [41], where Dziembowski *et al.*'s result considers the simulation paradigm where the leakage comes from the *wires*. Duc *et al.* argue that security bounds stated with the simulation paradigm with leakage from the wires can be converted into security bounds in the "leakage from computations" paradigm by

Table 4. Constant factor overhead, depending on the attack scenario, and on the multiplication gadget used.

Sbox \ Plaintext	Random	Chosen
Any Sbox	$\mathcal{O}(|\mathcal{Y}|^2)$	$\mathcal{O}(|\mathcal{Y}|^2)$
Monomial Sbox	$\mathcal{O}(|\mathcal{Y}|^{1+\epsilon})$	$\mathcal{O}(|\mathcal{Y}|^2)$
Monomial Sbox + Blinding	$\mathcal{O}(|\mathcal{Y}|^{\epsilon})$	$\mathcal{O}(|\mathcal{Y}|^{1+\epsilon})$

considering wires defined over $\mathcal{Y} \times \mathcal{Y}$ rather than $\mathcal{Y}$ [23, Sec. 5.5]. This would convert the $|\mathcal{Y}|$ constant factor in Dziembowski *et al.*'s result into $|\mathcal{Y}|^2$.[8]

5.4   On the Tweaked ISW Gadget

We finally discuss some aspects of our blinded I.S.W. multiplication gadget. For concreteness, we present hereafter in Table 5 a comparison of the constant factors in Theorem 7 and Theorem 8, for the AES Sbox exponentiation only. We can observe that while using the blinded I.S.W. gadget doubles the $t_{1,2,4}$ constant factor, it decreases the t_3 constant factor by a factor of $|\mathcal{Y}|/2$, which is of at least two orders of magnitude for the AES field. Interestingly, the t_3 constant factor in Cardoso *et al.*'s scheme is even close to 16, which is the tightest possible, given that their exponentiation scheme contains four multiplications. This is because each multiplication in Cardoso *et al.*'s scheme involves either Y or Y^{14}, but both 1 and 14 are coprime with $|\mathcal{Y}| - 1 = 255$.

Table 5. Constant factors for the whole AES Sbox exponentiation.

Scheme	Corollary 10		Theorem 7		Theorem 8	
	t_3	$t_{1,2,4}$	t_3	$t_{1,2,4}$	t_3	$t_{1,2,4}$
Rivain-Prouff [45]	$331,413$	$1,132$	**4096**	41.1	**32.1**	80.3
Cardoso *et al.* [46]	$331,413$	$1,294$	**2048**	40.1	**16.1**	78.2

We end this subsection by discussing whether blinding would have a significant practical interest for current masked implementations of AES. Admittedly, the significant gain in the constant factor comes though with an increased cost in terms of field multiplications and fresh randomness (by a factor two). Figure 2 compares the security bounds for the whole AES Sbox Rivain-Prouff scheme (stated in bits) with respect to the number of field multiplications. We can see on Fig. 2a, that for the AES field and $\delta = 10^{-2}$, the dotted curve is below the

---

[8] We also recall that their bound is stated in terms of SD, whereas ours is stated in terms of MI.

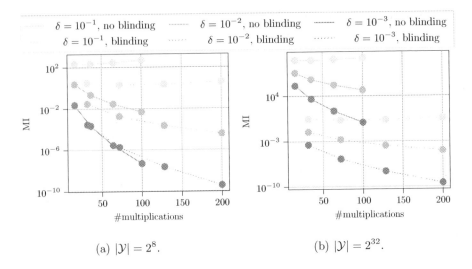

Fig. 2. Security bounds without and with blinding, with respect to the number of field multiplications, for $d \in [1,5]$. The number of multiplications is calculated over the Rivain-Prouff scheme for the AES Sbox.

plain curve, by one order of magnitude. This means that the blinded I.S.W. multiplication implies tighter security bounds for a comparable implementation cost. However, this gain vanishes for noisier implementations, e.g., for $\delta = 10^{-3}$. The advantage of our blinded I.S.W. becomes more significant when working on larger fields, as depicted on Fig. 2b where the field is of size 2^{32}. Whether the advantage of our blinded I.S.W. in terms of *provable* security also translates in terms of actual practical security gains remains an open questions and is let for further investigations in the future.

5.5   Perspectives

The main limitation of our work remains the leak-free assumption for the mask refreshings, like in the previous works [25,42,43]. It remains an open problem whether this assumption could be relaxed. Likewise, our masking security proof only covers the I.S.W. masking scheme, as in the previous works, whereas the generic approach through the probing model can cover any type of masking scheme. Nevertheless, we do not see any prior reason why our security proof could not be used to extend over different masking gadgets, beyond the I.S.W. multiplication gadget, and in particular for table-based masking schemes [18,20], that are known to be efficiently secure in the probing model, but much less in the noisy leakage [14,49]. Overall, this leaves the door open for good opportunities of improvement in the next few years.

Acknowledgment. François-Xavier Standaert is a Senior Associate Researcher of the Belgian Fund for Scientific Research (FNRS-F.R.S.). This work has been funded in part by the ERC project number 724725 (acronym SWORD).

A   Utilitary Lemma

Proposition 2. (MGL properties). *Let* $f(\cdot)$ *be the MGL function defined in Eq. 9, and let* $\delta_0, \ldots, \delta_d$ *be* $d + 1$ *mutually independent random variables. Then the following inequality holds:*

$$\underset{\delta_0, \ldots, \delta_d}{\mathbb{E}} \left[f(\delta_0, \ldots, \delta_d) \right] \leq f\left(\mathbb{E}\left[\delta_0 \right], \ldots, \mathbb{E}\left[\delta_d \right] \right) \quad . \tag{19}$$

Lemma 2. *Let* $Y \in \mathcal{Y}$ *be a discrete random variable, and let* $g : Y \mapsto g(Y)$ *be a mapping* $\mathcal{Y} \to \mathcal{Y}$. *Let* $\mathbf{L} : \mathcal{Y} \to \mathcal{L}$ *be a random variable. Then:*

$$\mathsf{MI}(Y; \mathbf{L}(g(Y))) = \mathsf{MI}(g(Y); \mathbf{L}(g(Y))) \quad .$$

Proof (Proof of Lemma 2). First, notice that we have the two following Markov chains:

$$Y \to g(Y) \to \mathbf{L}(g(Y)) \quad ,$$
$$g(Y) \leftarrow Y \to \mathbf{L}(g(Y)) \quad .$$

By the DPI [21, Sec. 2.8] on the first two chains, we have $\mathsf{MI}(Y; \mathbf{L}(g(Y))) \underset{>}{\lessgtr} \mathsf{MI}(g(Y); \mathbf{L}(g(Y)))$, hence:

$$\mathsf{MI}(Y; \mathbf{L}(g(Y))) = \mathsf{MI}(g(Y); \mathbf{L}(g(Y))) \quad .$$

Lemma 3. *Let* Y, R *be two independent random variables, uniformly distributed over a field* $\mathcal{Y}$ *of size* M. *For all* $a, b \in \mathcal{Y}$, *we have*

$$\Pr\left(Y^{p+q} \oplus RY^q = a, RY^q = b \right) \leq \frac{1}{M^2} \cdot \max\left\{ 2, \frac{M}{M-1} \cdot \gcd(p+q, M-1) \right\} \quad . \tag{20}$$

Proof. Denote by p the left hand-side of Eq. 20. Notice that we may restate p as follows:

$$\mathsf{p} = \Pr\left(Y^{p+q} = a \oplus b \mid RY^q = b \right) \Pr(RY^q = b)$$

Let us distinguish the following cases, in which we will show that p is always upper bounded by the right hand-side of Eq. 20.
Case $a = b = 0$. Here, $\Pr\left(Y^{p+q} = 0 \mid RY^q = 0 \right) = \Pr\left(Y^{p+q} = 0 \right) = \frac{1}{M}$, and

$$\begin{aligned}
\Pr(RY^q = 0) &= \Pr(R = 0 \cup Y^q = 0) \\
&= \Pr(R = 0) + \Pr(Y^q = 0) - \Pr(R = 0 \cap Y^q = 0) \\
&= \Pr(R = 0) + \Pr(Y^q = 0) - \Pr(R = 0) \cdot \Pr(Y^q = 0) \quad ,
\end{aligned}$$

where the first equality comes from the property of the field multiplication, the second equality is an application of the inclusion/exclusion formula, and the last equality comes from the independence between R and Y. Therefore, it comes that

$$\Pr(RY^q = 0) = \frac{2}{M} - \frac{1}{M^2} \leq \frac{2}{M} \quad . \tag{21}$$

Hence, $\mathsf{p} \leq \frac{2}{M^2}$.

Case $a \neq 0, b = 0$. Using Bayes' theorem, we may restate p as follows:

$$\begin{aligned}
\mathsf{p} &= \Pr\left(RY^q = 0 \mid Y^{p+q} = a\right) \cdot \Pr\left(Y^{p+q} = a\right) \\
&= \Pr\left(R = 0 \cup Y = 0 \mid Y^{p+q} = a\right) \cdot \Pr\left(Y^{p+q} = a\right) \\
&= \Pr(R = 0) \cdot \Pr\left(Y^{p+q} = a\right) \\
&= \frac{1}{M} \cdot \Pr\left(Y^{p+q} = a\right) \ ,
\end{aligned}$$

where the third equality comes from R and Y being independent, and necessarily $Y \neq 0$. Using Eq. 6 and Eq. 21, it comes that

$$\mathsf{p} \leq \frac{\gcd(p+q, M-1)}{M(M-1)} \leq 2\frac{\gcd(p+q, M-1)}{M^2} \ .$$

Case $b \neq 0$. Here, RY^q is uniformly distributed over the non-zero values of $\mathcal{Y}$, so $\Pr(RY^q = b) \leq \frac{1}{M-1}$, and is independent of Y. As a consequence, we have

$$\Pr\left(Y^{p+q} = a \oplus b \mid RY^q = b\right) = \Pr\left(Y^{p+q} = a \oplus b\right) \ ,$$

so $\mathsf{p} = \Pr\left(Y^{p+q} = a \oplus b\right) \cdot \Pr(RY^q = b)$. It remains to bound the first factor of p using Eq. 6, and we get $\mathsf{p} \leq \frac{\gcd(p+q, M-1)}{(M-1)^2}$. Finally, using the inequality $\frac{1}{M-1} \leq \frac{2}{M}$, for $M \geq 2$, we obtain $\mathsf{p} \leq 2\frac{\gcd(p+q, M-1)}{M^2}$. □

B   Proofs of Main Results

(Proof of Theorem 1). By definition, we have

$$\mathsf{H}(\mathbf{L} \mid Y) = \mathbb{E}_y \left[\mathsf{H}(L_1, \dots, L_t \mid Y = y)\right] \ . \tag{22}$$

By assumption, all the leakages, conditioned to $Y = y$ are mutually independent so

$$\mathsf{H}(\mathbf{L} \mid Y = y) = \sum_{i=1}^{t} \mathsf{H}(L_i \mid Y = y) \ .$$

Hence, combining with Eq. 22, $\mathsf{H}(\mathbf{L} \mid Y) = \sum_{i=1}^{t} \mathsf{H}(L_i \mid Y)$. Thereby,

$$\mathsf{MI}(\mathbf{L}; Y) \leq \sum_{i=1}^{t} \mathsf{MI}(L_i; Y)$$

□

(Proof of Theorem 2). Now, we can see $\mathbf{L}$ as an—undesired—communication channel. By definition of the capacity C of the channel $\mathbf{L}$, and using Lemma 2, we get that

$$\mathsf{MI}(Y; \mathbf{L}(g(Y))) = \mathsf{MI}(g(Y); \mathbf{L}(g(Y))) \leq \max_{\Pr(Z)} \mathsf{MI}(Z; \mathbf{L}(Z)) = C \ .$$

Using [47, Thm. 1, Eq. (17)], we get that

$$\frac{C}{\mathsf{MI}(Y;\mathbf{L}(Y))} \leq |\mathcal{Y}| \cdot \min\left\{2^{-C}, 1 - e^{-1}\right\} \leq |\mathcal{Y}| \cdot \left(1 - e^{-1}\right)$$

$\square$

B.1 Proof of Theorem 5 and Theorem 6

(Proof of Theorem 5). Using the chain rule of MI [21, Thm. 2.5.2], we have:

$$\mathsf{MI}((A,B);\mathbf{L}) = \mathsf{MI}(A;\mathbf{L}) + \mathsf{MI}(B;\mathbf{L} \mid A) \ . \tag{23}$$

Let us bound the first term of Eq. 23. The bound on the second term will straight-forwardly follow.

Bounding $\mathsf{MI}(A;\mathbf{L})$.
Observe that since A and B are independent, it follows that A and **B** are also independent. As a result,

$$\mathsf{MI}(A;\mathbf{L}) \leq \mathsf{MI}(A;\mathbf{L} \mid \mathbf{B}) = \mathop{\mathbb{E}}_{\mathbf{b}}\left[\mathsf{MI}(A;\mathbf{L} \mid \mathbf{B} = \mathbf{b})\right] \ . \tag{24}$$

Let $\mathbf{b} = (b_0, \ldots, b_d)$ be fixed for now, and let us bound $\mathsf{MI}(A;\mathbf{L} \mid \mathbf{B} = \mathbf{b})$. To this end, notice that we may now gather the leakages $\mathbf{L}_{i,j}$ by batches sharing the same index i as follows:

$$\mathsf{MI}(A;\mathbf{L} \mid \mathbf{B} = \mathbf{b}) = \mathsf{MI}\left(A; \{\mathbf{L}_{0,j}(A_0, b_j)\}_{0 \leq j \leq d}, \ldots, \{\mathbf{L}_{d,j}(A_d, b_j)\}_{0 \leq j \leq d}\right) \ . \tag{25}$$

By assumption, each batch of leakages $\{\mathbf{L}_{i,j}(A_i, b_j)\}_{0 \leq j \leq d}$ only depends on the share A_i. Hence, we may use Theorem 4 to bound the right hand-side of Eq. 25 as follows. Let us define $\mathsf{MI}\left(A_i; \{\mathbf{L}_{i,j}\}_{0 \leq j \leq d}\right) = \delta_i'$—notice that δ_i' depends on b_i. Then we have

$$\mathsf{MI}\left(A; \{\mathbf{L}_{0,j}\}_{0 \leq j \leq d}, \ldots, \{\mathbf{L}_{d,j}\}_{0 \leq j \leq d}\right) \underset{(9)}{\leq} \mathsf{f}_{2^n}(\delta_0', \ldots, \delta_d') \ . \tag{26}$$

Substituting Eq. 26 in Eq. 25, and then plugging into Eq. 24 gives

$$\mathsf{MI}(A;\mathbf{L}) \leq \mathop{\mathbb{E}}_{\mathbf{b}}\left[\mathsf{f}_{2^n}(\delta_0', \ldots, \delta_d')\right] \leq \mathsf{f}_{2^n}\left(\mathop{\mathbb{E}}_{b_0}[\delta_0'], \ldots, \mathop{\mathbb{E}}_{b_d}[\delta_d']\right) \ , \tag{27}$$

where the second inequality comes from Proposition 2. We are then reduced to upper bound $\mathbb{E}[\delta_i']$ for all $0 \leq i \leq d$. To this end, notice that for i fixed, the batch of leakages $\{\mathbf{L}_{i,j}(A_i, b_j) \mid A_i\}_{0 \leq j \leq d}$ are mutually independent. Hence, we can now leverage Theorem 1 to upper bound δ', as follows:

$$\mathsf{MI}\left(A_i; \{\mathbf{L}_{i,j}(A_i, b_j)\}_{0 \leq j \leq d}\right) \underset{(2)}{\leq} \sum_{j=0}^{d} \mathsf{MI}(A_i; \mathbf{L}_{i,j}(A_i, b_j)) \ . \tag{28}$$

Using the chain rule of MI [21, Thm. 2.5.2] the other way around, we get that

$$\mathsf{MI}(A_i; \mathbf{L}_{i,j}(A_i, b_j)) \leq \mathsf{MI}(A_i, B_j; \mathbf{L}_{i,j}(A_i, B_j)) = \delta_{i,j} \ . \tag{29}$$

Hence, combining Eq. 28 with Equation 29, and taking the expectation, we get that

$$\mathbb{E}\left[\delta_i'\right] \leq \sum_{j=0}^{d} \delta_{i,j} \ . \tag{30}$$

Finally, plugging Eq. 30 into Eq. 27 gives the first term in the right hand-side of Eq. 11.

Bounding $\mathsf{MI}(B; \mathbf{L} \mid A)$. Using the chain rule of the MI again, we may bound $\mathsf{MI}(B; \mathbf{L} \mid A)$ by conditioning on the d last shares of $\mathbf{A}$ (except the share of index 0):

$$\mathsf{MI}(B; \mathbf{L} \mid A) \leq \mathsf{MI}\left(B; \mathbf{L} \mid A, \{A_i\}_{1 \leq i \leq d}\right)$$

Using the same argument as Dziembowski *et al.* [26, Lemma 3], we may notice that since A is assumed to be uniform:

$$\left(A, \{A_i\}_{1 \leq i \leq d}\right) \stackrel{d}{=} \left(A \oplus \left(\bigoplus_{i=1}^{d} A_i\right), \{A_i\}_{1 \leq i \leq d}\right) \stackrel{d}{=} \{A_i\}_{0 \leq i \leq d} \ ,$$

it implies that $\mathsf{MI}\left(B; \mathbf{L} \mid A, \{A_i\}_{1 \leq i \leq d}\right) = \mathsf{MI}(B; \mathbf{L} \mid \mathbf{A})$. By symmetry of the roles, the latter term can be bound in the same way as the right hand-side of Eq. 24, by permuting the roles of the indices i and j. □

(Proof of Theorem 6). Let $\mathbf{L} = (L_1(Y_0, Y_1), \ldots, L_d(Y_{d-1}, Y_d))$ for short. Expanding $\mathsf{MI}(Y_d; \mathbf{L})$, we have

$$\mathsf{MI}(Y_d; \mathbf{L}) = \mathsf{MI}(Y_d; L_d(Y_{d-1}, Y_d) \mid L_{d-1}(Y_{d-2}, Y_{d-1}), \ldots, L_1(Y_0, Y_1))$$
$$+ \mathsf{MI}(Y_d; L_{d-1}(Y_{d-2}, Y_{d-1}), \ldots, L_1(Y_0, Y_1))$$

Notice first that the second term in the right hand-side equals 0, since by assumption Y_d is independent of the $\{Y_i\}_{0 \leq i \leq d-1}$. Likewise, the first term of the right hand-side can be upper bounded by $\overline{\mathsf{MI}}(Y_d; L_d(Y_{d-1}, Y_d) \mid Y_{d-1})$, which can in turn be upper bounded by δ_d. □

B.2   Proofs for the Blinded ISW Gadget

(Proof of Theorem 8). We now show how to bound the MI between Y and the whole leakage. Notice that we may not directly use Theorem 1 to upper bound $\mathsf{MI}(Y; \mathbf{L})$ by the sum of the MIs over all the elementary subsequences of the gadget in Fig. 1, since they are not all independent due to the presence of R. This problem can be easily circumvented by using the DPI:

$$\mathsf{MI}(Y; \mathbf{L}) \leq \mathsf{MI}(Y, R; \mathbf{L}) \ . \tag{31}$$

Since the encodings of each sharing is refreshed by the leak-free refresh oracle, all the subsequences in the blinded I.S.W. are now mutually independent, so we may now use Theorem 1:

$$\begin{aligned} \mathsf{MI}(Y, R; \mathbf{L}) = {}& \mathsf{MI}(Y, R; \mathbf{L}_{\oplus_1}) + \mathsf{MI}(Y, R; \mathbf{L}_{\oplus_2}) \\ & + \mathsf{MI}\big(Y, R; \mathbf{L}_{\mathsf{ISW}_{1,in}}\big) + \mathsf{MI}\big(Y, R; \mathbf{L}_{\mathsf{ISW}_{1,out}}\big) \\ & + \mathsf{MI}\big(Y, R; \mathbf{L}_{\mathsf{ISW}_{2,in}}\big) + \mathsf{MI}\big(Y, R; \mathbf{L}_{\mathsf{ISW}_{2,out}}\big) \end{aligned} \tag{32}$$

We shall upper bound each term in the right hand-side of Eq. 32.

Bounding $\mathsf{MI}(Y, R; \mathbf{L}_{\oplus_1})$. Recall that $\mathbf{L}_{\oplus_1}$ is the random variable denoting the leakage of the input operands of the first Xor in Fig. 1, namely Y^p and R. Using Lemma 2, we get that $\mathsf{MI}(Y, R; \mathbf{L}_{\oplus_1}(Y^p, R)) = \mathsf{MI}(Y^p, R; \mathbf{L}_{\oplus_1}(Y^p, R))$. Observe that G and R are independent, so we may refine Corollary 3 . To this end, let A be uniformly distributed over $\mathcal{Y}$, and independent of R. Observe that for any $g, r \in \mathcal{Y}^2$,

$$\frac{\Pr(Y^p = g, R = r)}{\Pr(A = g, R = r)} = \frac{\Pr(Y^p = g) \Pr(R = r)}{\Pr(A = g) \Pr(R = r)} \leq \frac{|\mathcal{Y}|}{|\mathcal{Y}| - 1} \cdot \gcd(p, |\mathcal{Y}| - 1) \ . \tag{33}$$

Therefore, injecting Eq. 33 into Eq. 4 gives

$$\mathsf{MI}(Y^p, R; \mathbf{L}_{\oplus_1}(Y^p, R)) \leq \frac{|\mathcal{Y}|}{|\mathcal{Y}| - 1} \cdot \gcd(p, |\mathcal{Y}| - 1) \cdot \mathsf{MI}(A, R; \mathbf{L}_{\oplus_1}(A, R)) \ .$$

We are then reduced to bound $\mathsf{MI}(A, R; \mathbf{L}_{\oplus_1})$. Applying Corollary 4 on the pair of variables (A, R), we get that:

$$\mathsf{MI}(A, R; \mathbf{L}_{\oplus_1}) \leq \mathsf{f}(\delta, \dots, \delta) \ .$$

Putting everything together, we get that

$$\mathsf{MI}(Y^p, R; \mathbf{L}_{\oplus_1}) \leq \frac{|\mathcal{Y}|}{|\mathcal{Y}| - 1} \cdot \gcd(p, |\mathcal{Y}| - 1) \cdot \mathsf{f}(\delta, \dots, \delta) \ . \tag{34}$$

Bounding $\mathsf{MI}(Y, R; \mathbf{L}_{\oplus_2})$. Using Lemma 2, we get that

$$\mathsf{MI}\big(Y, R; \mathbf{L}_{\oplus_2}(H', M)\big) = \mathsf{MI}\big(H', M; \mathbf{L}_{\oplus_2}(H', M)\big) \ .$$

Using Lemma 3, we deduce that

$$\mathsf{MI}\big(H', M; \mathbf{L}_{\oplus_2}(H', M)\big) \leq \max\left\{2, \frac{M}{M-1} \cdot \gcd(p+q, M-1)\right\} \cdot \mathsf{MI}(A, B; \mathbf{L}_{\oplus_2}(A, B)) \ ,$$

where A, B are independent and uniformly distributed over $\mathcal{Y}$. We may then apply Corollary 4 to get

$$\mathsf{MI}(A, B; \mathbf{L}_{\oplus_2}(A, B)) \leq \mathsf{f}(\delta, \dots, \delta) \ .$$

Putting everything together, we get that

$$\mathsf{MI}(Y, R; \mathbf{L}_{\oplus_2}) \leq \max\left\{2, \frac{M}{M-1} \cdot \gcd(p+q, M-1)\right\} \cdot \mathsf{f}(\delta, \dots, \delta) \ . \tag{35}$$

Bounding $\mathsf{MI}(Y, R; \mathbf{L}_{\mathsf{ISW}_{1,in}})$. Using Lemma 2, we get that

$$\mathsf{MI}\big(Y, R; \mathbf{L}_{\mathsf{ISW}_{1,in}}(G', H)\big) = \mathsf{MI}\big(G', H; \mathbf{L}_{\mathsf{ISW}_{1,in}}(G', H)\big) \ .$$

Observe that the input operands of ISW_1 are independent, and that G' is uniformly distributed over $\mathcal{Y}$. Moreover, for all $h \in \mathcal{Y}$ we have $\Pr(H = h) \leq \frac{\gcd(q, |\mathcal{Y}| - 1)}{|\mathcal{Y}| - 1}$, which implies that

$$\mathsf{MI}\big(G', H; \mathbf{L}_{\mathsf{ISW}_{1,in}}(G', H)\big) \leq \frac{|\mathcal{Y}|}{|\mathcal{Y}| - 1} \cdot \gcd(q, |\mathcal{Y}| - 1)\, \mathsf{MI}\big(G', B; \mathbf{L}_{\mathsf{ISW}_{1,in}}(G', B)\big) \ ,$$

where $B \in \mathcal{Y}$ is uniform and independent of G'. We may then apply Corollary 5 to get

$$\mathsf{MI}\big(G', B; \mathbf{L}_{\mathsf{ISW}_{1,in}}(G', B)\big) \leq 2\,\mathsf{f}((d+1)\delta, \ldots, (d+1)\delta) \ .$$

Putting everything together, we have that

$$\mathsf{MI}\big(Y, R; \mathbf{L}_{\mathsf{ISW}_{1,in}}\big) \leq \frac{2\,|\mathcal{Y}|}{|\mathcal{Y}| - 1} \cdot \gcd(q, |\mathcal{Y}| - 1) \cdot \mathsf{f}((d+1)\delta, \ldots, (d+1)\delta) \ . \quad (36)$$

Bounding $\mathsf{MI}(Y, R; \mathbf{L}_{\mathsf{ISW}_{2,in}})$. In this case, we get exactly the same bound as in Eq. 36, by changing G' with R. The same arguments then apply.

Bounding $\mathsf{MI}(Y, R; \mathbf{L}_{\mathsf{ISW}_{1,out}})$. Using Lemma 2, we get that

$$\mathsf{MI}\big(Y, R; \mathbf{L}_{\mathsf{ISW}_{1,out}}(M)\big) = \mathsf{MI}\big(M; \mathbf{L}_{\mathsf{ISW}_{1,out}}(M)\big) \ .$$

Then, notice that $M = (G \oplus R)H$, and that we argued that $G \oplus R = G'$ is uniformly distributed, and independent of H. Therefore, M is uniformly distributed over the non-zero values of $\mathcal{Y}$, provided that $M \neq 0$. If not, then we have $\Pr(M = 0) = \frac{1}{M}$. Overall, for all $y \in \mathcal{Y}$,

$$\frac{\Pr(M = y)}{\Pr(Y = y)} \leq 2 \ .$$

By virtue of Eq. 6, we have that

$$\mathsf{MI}\big(M; \mathbf{L}_{\mathsf{ISW}_{1,out}}(M)\big) \leq 2\,\mathsf{MI}\big(Y; \mathbf{L}_{\mathsf{ISW}_{1,out}}(Y)\big) \ .$$

We can now apply the remaining of the proof of Corollary 7 (starting after the reduction from non-uniform to uniform secrets) to deduce that

$$\mathsf{MI}\big(Y; \mathbf{L}_{\mathsf{ISW}_{1,out}}(Y)\big) \leq \mathsf{f}(\delta, \ldots, \delta) \ .$$

Putting everything together, we have that

$$\mathsf{MI}\big(Y, R; \mathbf{L}_{\mathsf{ISW}_{1,out}}(M)\big) \leq 2\,\mathsf{f}(\delta, \ldots, \delta) \ . \quad (37)$$

Bounding $\mathsf{MI}(Y, R; \mathbf{L}_{\mathsf{ISW}_{2,out}})$. Observing that $G \oplus R$ may be replaced by R in the previous case of $\mathbf{L}_{\mathsf{ISW}_{1,out}}$ without any loss of generality, we get the same bound as in Eq. 37. □

References

1. Ajtai, M.: Secure computation with information leaking to an adversary. In: Fortnow, L., Vadhan, S.P. (eds.) 43rd Annual ACM Symposium on Theory of Computing, pp. 715–724. ACM Press, San Jose, CA, USA, 6–8 June 2011. https://doi.org/10.1145/1993636.1993731

2. Ananth, P., Ishai, Y., Sahai, A.: Private circuits: a modular approach. In: Shacham, H., Boldyreva, A. (eds.) CRYPTO 2018. LNCS, vol. 10993, pp. 427–455. Springer, Cham (2018). https://doi.org/10.1007/978-3-319-96878-0_15

3. Andrychowicz, M., Dziembowski, S., Faust, S.: Circuit compilers with $O(1/\log(n))$ leakage rate. In: Fischlin, M., Coron, J.-S. (eds.) EUROCRYPT 2016. LNCS, vol. 9666, pp. 586–615. Springer, Heidelberg (2016). https://doi.org/10.1007/978-3-662-49896-5_21

4. Azouaoui, M., et al.: A systematic appraisal of side channel evaluation strategies. Cryptology ePrint Archive, Report 2020/1347 (2020). https://eprint.iacr.org/2020/1347

5. Baignères, T., Junod, P., Vaudenay, S.: How far can we go beyond linear cryptanalysis? In: Lee, P.J. (ed.) ASIACRYPT 2004. LNCS, vol. 3329, pp. 432–450. Springer, Heidelberg (2004). https://doi.org/10.1007/978-3-540-30539-2_31

6. Barthe, G., et al.: Strong non-interference and type-directed higher-order masking. In: Weippl, E.R., Katzenbeisser, S., Kruegel, C., Myers, A.C., Halevi, S. (eds.) ACM CCS 2016: 23rd Conference on Computer and Communications Security, pp. 116–129. ACM Press, Vienna, Austria, 24–28 October 2016. https://doi.org/10.1145/2976749.2978427

7. Battistello, A., Coron, J.-S., Prouff, E., Zeitoun, R.: Horizontal side-channel attacks and countermeasures on the ISW masking scheme. In: Gierlichs, B., Poschmann, A.Y. (eds.) CHES 2016. LNCS, vol. 9813, pp. 23–39. Springer, Heidelberg (2016). https://doi.org/10.1007/978-3-662-53140-2_2

8. Belaïd, S., Coron, J.-S., Prouff, E., Rivain, M., Taleb, A.R.: Random probing security: verification, composition, expansion and new constructions. In: Micciancio, D., Ristenpart, T. (eds.) CRYPTO 2020. LNCS, vol. 12170, pp. 339–368. Springer, Cham (2020). https://doi.org/10.1007/978-3-030-56784-2_12

9. Belaïd, S., Rivain, M., Taleb, A.R.: On the power of expansion: more efficient constructions in the random probing model. In: Canteaut, A., Standaert, F.-X. (eds.) EUROCRYPT 2021. LNCS, vol. 12697, pp. 313–343. Springer, Cham (2021). https://doi.org/10.1007/978-3-030-77886-6_11

10. Belaïd, S., Rivain, M., Taleb, A.R., Vergnaud, D.: Dynamic random probing expansion with quasi linear asymptotic complexity. In: Tibouchi, M., Wang, H. (eds.) ASIACRYPT 2021. LNCS, vol. 13091, pp. 157–188. Springer, Cham (2021). https://doi.org/10.1007/978-3-030-92075-3_6

11. Béguinot, J., et al.: Removing the field size loss from Duc et al'.s conjectured bound for masked encodings. Cryptology ePrint Archive, Paper 2022/1738 (2022). https://eprint.iacr.org/2022/1738

12. Boucheron, S., Lugosi, G., Massart, P.: Concentration Inequalities: A Nonasymptotic Theory of Independence. Oxford University Press (2013)

13. Broughan, K.A.: The GCD-sum function. J. Integer Seq. 4(2.2) (2001)

14. Bruneau, N., Guilley, S., Najm, Z., Teglia, Y.: Multivariate high-order attacks of shuffled tables recomputation. J. Cryptol. **31**(2), 351–393 (2017). https://doi.org/10.1007/s00145-017-9259-7

15. Cassiers, G., Faust, S., Orlt, M., Standaert, F.-X.: Towards tight random probing security. In: Malkin, T., Peikert, C. (eds.) CRYPTO 2021. LNCS, vol. 12827, pp. 185–214. Springer, Cham (2021). https://doi.org/10.1007/978-3-030-84252-9_7

16. Chari, S., Jutla, C.S., Rao, J.R., Rohatgi, P.: Towards sound approaches to counteract power-analysis attacks. In: Wiener, M. (ed.) CRYPTO 1999. LNCS, vol. 1666, pp. 398–412. Springer, Heidelberg (1999). https://doi.org/10.1007/3-540-48405-1_26

17. Cheng, W., Liu, Y., Guilley, S., Rioul, O.: Attacking masked cryptographic implementations: information-theoretic bounds. In: IEEE International Symposium on Information Theory, ISIT 2022, Espoo, Finland, 26 June–1 July 2022, pp. 654–659. IEEE (2022). https://doi.org/10.1109/ISIT50566.2022.9834556

18. Coron, J.-S.: Higher order masking of look-up tables. In: Nguyen, P.Q., Oswald, E. (eds.) EUROCRYPT 2014. LNCS, vol. 8441, pp. 441–458. Springer, Heidelberg (2014). https://doi.org/10.1007/978-3-642-55220-5_25

19. Coron, J.-S., Prouff, E., Rivain, M., Roche, T.: Higher-order side channel security and mask refreshing. In: Moriai, S. (ed.) FSE 2013. LNCS, vol. 8424, pp. 410–424. Springer, Heidelberg (2014). https://doi.org/10.1007/978-3-662-43933-3_21

20. Coron, J.S., Rondepierre, F., Zeitoun, R.: High order masking of look-up tables with common shares. IACR Trans. Cryptographic Hardware Embed. Syst. 2018(1), 40–72 (2018). https://doi.org/10.13154/tches.v2018.i1.40-72. https://tches.iacr.org/index.php/TCHES/article/view/832

21. Cover, T.M., Thomas, J.A.: Elements of Information Theory, 2 edn. Wiley (2006)

22. de Chérisey, E., Guilley, S., Rioul, O., Piantanida, P.: Best information is most successful. IACR Trans. Cryptographic Hardware Embed. Syst. 2019(2), 49–79 (2019). https://doi.org/10.13154/tches.v2019.i2.49-79. https://tches.iacr.org/index.php/TCHES/article/view/7385

23. Duc, A., Dziembowski, S., Faust, S.: Unifying leakage models: from probing attacks to noisy leakage. In: Nguyen, P.Q., Oswald, E. (eds.) EUROCRYPT 2014. LNCS, vol. 8441, pp. 423–440. Springer, Heidelberg (2014). https://doi.org/10.1007/978-3-642-55220-5_24

24. Duc, A., Faust, S., Standaert, F.-X.: Making masking security proofs concrete. In: Oswald, E., Fischlin, M. (eds.) EUROCRYPT 2015. LNCS, vol. 9056, pp. 401–429. Springer, Heidelberg (2015). https://doi.org/10.1007/978-3-662-46800-5_16

25. Dziembowski, S., Faust, S., Skorski, M.: Noisy leakage revisited. In: Oswald, E., Fischlin, M. (eds.) EUROCRYPT 2015. LNCS, vol. 9057, pp. 159–188. Springer, Heidelberg (2015). https://doi.org/10.1007/978-3-662-46803-6_6

26. Dziembowski, S., Faust, S., Skórski, M.: Optimal amplification of noisy leakages. In: Kushilevitz, E., Malkin, T. (eds.) TCC 2016. LNCS, vol. 9563, pp. 291–318. Springer, Heidelberg (2016). https://doi.org/10.1007/978-3-662-49099-0_11

27. Goubin, L., Patarin, J.: DES and differential power analysis the "Duplication" method. In: Koç, Ç.K., Paar, C. (eds.) CHES 1999. LNCS, vol. 1717, pp. 158–172. Springer, Heidelberg (1999). https://doi.org/10.1007/3-540-48059-5_15

28. Goudarzi, D., Joux, A., Rivain, M.: How to securely compute with noisy leakage in quasilinear complexity. In: Peyrin, T., Galbraith, S. (eds.) ASIACRYPT 2018. LNCS, vol. 11273, pp. 547–574. Springer, Cham (2018). https://doi.org/10.1007/978-3-030-03329-3_19

29. Goudarzi, D., Prest, T., Rivain, M., Vergnaud, D.: Probing security through input-output separation and revisited quasilinear masking. IACR Trans. Cryptographic Hardware Embed. Syst. 2021(3), 599–640 (2021). https://doi.org/10.46586/tches.v2021.i3.599-640. https://tches.iacr.org/index.php/TCHES/article/view/8987

30. Goudarzi, D., Rivain, M.: How fast can higher-order masking be in software? In: Coron, J.-S., Nielsen, J.B. (eds.) EUROCRYPT 2017. LNCS, vol. 10210, pp. 567–597. Springer, Cham (2017). https://doi.org/10.1007/978-3-319-56620-7_20

31. Grosso, V., Standaert, F.-X.: Masking proofs are tight and how to exploit it in security evaluations. In: Nielsen, J.B., Rijmen, V. (eds.) EUROCRYPT 2018. LNCS, vol. 10821, pp. 385–412. Springer, Cham (2018). https://doi.org/10.1007/978-3-319-78375-8_13

32. Ishai, Y., Sahai, A., Wagner, D.: Private circuits: securing hardware against probing attacks. In: Boneh, D. (ed.) CRYPTO 2003. LNCS, vol. 2729, pp. 463–481. Springer, Heidelberg (2003). https://doi.org/10.1007/978-3-540-45146-4_27

33. Ito, A., Ueno, R., Homma, N.: On the success rate of side-channel attacks on masked implementations: information-theoretical bounds and their practical usage. In: Yin, H., Stavrou, A., Cremers, C., Shi, E. (eds.) ACM CCS 2022: 29th Conference on Computer and Communications Security, pp. 1521–1535. ACM Press, Los Angeles, CA, USA, 7–11 November 2022. https://doi.org/10.1145/3548606.3560579

34. Jog, V.S., Anantharam, V.: The entropy power inequality and Mrs. Gerber's lemma for groups of order 2^n. IEEE Trans. Inf. Theory **60**(7), 3773–3786 (2014). https://doi.org/10.1109/TIT.2014.2317692

35. Kocher, P.C.: Timing attacks on implementations of Diffie-Hellman, RSA, DSS, and other systems. In: Koblitz, N. (ed.) CRYPTO 1996. LNCS, vol. 1109, pp. 104–113. Springer, Heidelberg (1996). https://doi.org/10.1007/3-540-68697-5_9

36. Kocher, P., Jaffe, J., Jun, B.: Differential power analysis. In: Wiener, M. (ed.) CRYPTO 1999. LNCS, vol. 1666, pp. 388–397. Springer, Heidelberg (1999). https://doi.org/10.1007/3-540-48405-1_25

37. Mangard, S.: Hardware countermeasures against DPA – a statistical analysis of their effectiveness. In: Okamoto, T. (ed.) CT-RSA 2004. LNCS, vol. 2964, pp. 222–235. Springer, Heidelberg (2004). https://doi.org/10.1007/978-3-540-24660-2_18

38. Mangard, S., Oswald, E., Popp, T.: Power Analysis Attacks - Revealing the Secrets of Smart Cards. Springer, New York (2007). https://doi.org/10.1007/978-0-387-38162-6

39. Mangard, S., Oswald, E., Standaert, F.: One for all - all for one: unifying standard differential power analysis attacks. IET Inf. Secur. **5**(2), 100–110 (2011)

40. Masure, L., Rioul, O., Standaert, F.X.: A nearly tight proof of Duc et al'.s conjectured security bound for masked implementations. Cryptology ePrint Archive, Paper 2022/600 (2022). https://eprint.iacr.org/2022/600

41. Micali, S., Reyzin, L.: Physically observable cryptography. In: Naor, M. (ed.) TCC 2004. LNCS, vol. 2951, pp. 278–296. Springer, Heidelberg (2004). https://doi.org/10.1007/978-3-540-24638-1_16

42. Prest, T., Goudarzi, D., Martinelli, A., Passelègue, A.: Unifying leakage models on a Rényi day. In: Boldyreva, A., Micciancio, D. (eds.) CRYPTO 2019. LNCS, vol. 11692, pp. 683–712. Springer, Cham (2019). https://doi.org/10.1007/978-3-030-26948-7_24

43. Prouff, E., Rivain, M.: Masking against side-channel attacks: a formal security proof. In: Johansson, T., Nguyen, P.Q. (eds.) EUROCRYPT 2013. LNCS, vol. 7881, pp. 142–159. Springer, Heidelberg (2013). https://doi.org/10.1007/978-3-642-38348-9_9

44. Rivain, M.: On the provable security of cryptographic implementations: Habilitation thesis. Personal website (2022). https://www.matthieurivain.com/hdr.html

45. Rivain, M., Prouff, E.: Provably secure higher-order masking of AES. In: Mangard, S., Standaert, F.-X. (eds.) CHES 2010. LNCS, vol. 6225, pp. 413–427. Springer, Heidelberg (2010). https://doi.org/10.1007/978-3-642-15031-9_28

46. Cardoso dos Santos, L., Gérard, F., Großschädl, J., Spignoli, L.: Rivain-Prouff on steroids: faster and stronger masking of the AES. In: Buhan, I., Schneider, T. (eds.) Smart Card Research and Advanced Applications, pp. 123–145. Springer, Cham (2023). https://doi.org/10.1007/978-3-031-25319-5_7

47. Shulman, N., Feder, M.: The uniform distribution as a universal prior. IEEE Trans. Inf. Theory **50**(6), 1356–1362 (2004)

48. Standaert, F.-X., Malkin, T.G., Yung, M.: A unified framework for the analysis of side-channel key recovery attacks. In: Joux, A. (ed.) EUROCRYPT 2009. LNCS, vol. 5479, pp. 443–461. Springer, Heidelberg (2009). https://doi.org/10.1007/978-3-642-01001-9_26

49. Tunstall, M., Whitnall, C., Oswald, E.: Masking tables—an underestimated security risk. In: Moriai, S. (ed.) FSE 2013. LNCS, vol. 8424, pp. 425–444. Springer, Heidelberg (2014). https://doi.org/10.1007/978-3-662-43933-3_22

50. Wyner, A.D., Ziv, J.: A theorem on the entropy of certain binary sequences and applications-I. IEEE Trans. Inf. Theory **19**(6), 769–772 (1973). https://doi.org/10.1109/TIT.1973.1055107

Combined Fault and Leakage Resilience: Composability, Constructions and Compiler

Sebastian Berndt[1], Thomas Eisenbarth[2], Sebastian Faust[3](✉),
Marc Gourjon[4,5], Maximilian Orlt[3], and Okan Seker[5]

[1] Institute for Theoretical Computer Science, University of Lübeck, Lübeck, Germany
s.berndt@uni-luebeck.de
[2] Institute for IT Security, University of Lübeck, Lübeck, Germany
thomas.eisenbarth@uni-luebeck.de
[3] TU Darmstadt, Darmstadt, Germany
{sebastian.faust,maximilian.orlt}@tu-darmstadt.de
[4] Hamburg University of Technology, Hamburg, Germany
marc.gourjon@tuhh.de
[5] NXP Semiconductors, Hamburg, Germany

Abstract. Real-world cryptographic implementations nowadays are not only attacked via classical cryptanalysis but also via implementation attacks, including passive attacks (observing side-channel information about the inner computation) and active attacks (inserting faults into the computation). While countermeasures exist for each type of attack, countermeasures against combined attacks have only been considered recently. Masking is a standard technique for protecting against passive side-channel attacks, but protecting against active attacks with additive masking is challenging. Previous approaches include running multiple copies of a masked computation, requiring a large amount of randomness or being vulnerable to horizontal attacks. An alternative approach is polynomial masking, which is inherently fault-resistant.

This work presents a compiler based on polynomial masking that achieves linear computational complexity for affine functions and cubic complexity for non-linear functions. The resulting compiler is secure against attackers using region probes and adaptive faults. In addition, the notion of fault-invariance is introduced to improve security against combined attacks without the need to consider all possible fault combinations. Our approach has the best-known asymptotic efficiency among all known approaches.

1 Introduction

In classical cryptography, the security of cryptographic primitives is often analyzed in the black-box model. In this model, the adversary attacks the cryptographic algorithm via access to inputs and outputs but has no knowledge and no control over the inner workings of the algorithms. In particular, sensitive

© International Association for Cryptologic Research 2023
H. Handschuh and A. Lysyanskaya (Eds.): CRYPTO 2023, LNCS 14083, pp. 377–409, 2023.
https://doi.org/10.1007/978-3-031-38548-3_13

information such as the secret key is hidden from and out of the control of the adversary. Unfortunately, when running cryptographic algorithms on real-world devices countless attacks demonstrate that the black-box model is far too optimistic. Examples include *passive attacks*, where the adversary exploits physical phenomena such as the power consumption or running time of a device to extract sensitive information; or *active attacks*, where the adversary modifies temporary values via a laser or via heating up the device to introduce faulty computation.

Masking Schemes. Masking schemes are a classical countermeasure to protect against passive side-channel attacks. Masking conceals sensitive information by secret sharing each value v from some finite field $\mathbb{F}$ into shares $v_0, \ldots, v_{n-1}$ such that $d + 1$ shares are required to reconstruct the secret, while $\leq d$ shares reveal nothing about the sensitive value v. The most common sharing scheme is *additive* masking. Here, we choose $v_0, \ldots, v_{n-2}$ randomly from $\mathbb{F}$ and define v_{n-1} such that $v = v_0 \oplus v_2 \ldots \oplus v_{n-1}$, where $\oplus$ is the addition of the underlying field $\mathbb{F}$. The main challenge in designing masking schemes is to securely compute on the shared values. To this end, we design masked subcircuits, called *gadgets*, that securely compute on sharings and devise methods for securely composing such gadgets without violating overall security.

The security of a masking scheme is typically analyzed in the so-called probing model originally introduced by Ishai, Sahai and Wagner [ISW03]. In this model, the adversary can learn up to d values that are produced during the computation. The security proof is typically done by analyzing the d-probing security of the gadgets and then extending it towards security of an entire masked circuit via *composition*. To argue secure composition in the probing model, an important property is *(strong) non-interference (SNI)*. Intuitively, this property guarantees that all information gained by the attacker by probing d internal values of a gadget can also be obtained by probing at most d shares of the masked input. Furthermore, probes on the output sharing can be simulated from scratch in the case of the stronger notion.

Beyond Passive Security. As mentioned above, passive side-channel attacks are not the only threat to cryptographic implementations. In practice, an adversary may also be able to induce faults into the computation thereby breaking the cryptographic implementation. Even worse, a physical adversary may launch combined attacks, where the adversary both passively observes side-channel leakage and introduces faults to break the cryptographic implementation. While a masking scheme can be used to protect against the passive adversary, it is easy to see that it fails to offer security against faults. For instance, if an adversary succeeds in adding an offset $c \in \mathcal{F}$ to only one of the shares, the result of the computation is faulty, which may have catastrophic consequences for security [BS97]. Hence, we need to extend probing security to also include fault attacks, where in addition to placing d probes, the adversary is allowed to induce ϵ faults. In this work, we consider arbitrary *adaptive* faults that might even depend on the information obtained via previous probes.

With adaptive faults, we cover attacks where the adversary uses information from previous leakage to insert faults. While such attackers seem unrealistically strong, they are possible in the context of side-channel attacks: Firstly, the adversary has access to the device and could stop or slow down regions of the devices similar as in cold boot attacks. Secondly, the adversary could use the leaked information not immediately but in the next cycle of a circuit that uses multiple cycles, such as AES and Present. Finally, we note that adaptive adversaries are a stronger adversarial model. Thus, from a theoretical point of view it is interesting to explore what security can be achieved in this model.

In order to protect against combined attacks, two main approaches have been considered in the literature – duplicated masking and polynomial masking. The most common one is duplicated masking to replicate the masked computation [DN20b, FRSG22].

Duplicated Approach. In this setting, the masked circuit $\hat{C}$ is executed $\epsilon + 1$ times in parallel. After each gate, the masked outputs of the computation are checked for equality to detect faults. This requires that the $\epsilon + 1$ copies use the same randomness internally. Otherwise, the output sharings would not be equal. Moreover, re-using the randomness has an additional advantage. As generating randomness is costly, by re-using randomness in all $\epsilon + 1$ copies, the overall randomness used can be reduced by a factor of $O(\epsilon)$.

The duplication approach described above has two important shortcomings. First, affine operations that traditionally can be masked at very low cost (typically at an $O(n)$ complexity overhead for $n = \epsilon + d$) get significantly more expensive as each such masked affine operation is now computed $\epsilon + 1$ times. This is especially problematic, as many modern primitives, e.g., [BDPA13, GLR+20, ARS+15, AGR+16, AAB+20, HKL+22, GKR+21] aim to reduce the number of non-linear operations by increasing the number of affine operations significantly. Even worse, in terms of security, the duplication approach is very vulnerable to so-called horizontal attacks [BCPZ16].

Horizontal Attacks. Horizontal attacks are attacks in which an adversary exploits the fact that multiple computations share the same randomness or secret key material. In the context of side-channel attacks, horizontal attacks can be particularly devastating as the attacker can amplify the leaked information and thus recover sensitive information more easily [CFG+10, ORSW12, VGS14, BS21]. To protect against horizontal attacks, it is essential to ensure that different instances of computation use independent and fresh randomness or secret key material.

Clearly, the duplication method is particularly vulnerable to horizontal attacks, as all copies share the same randomness to ensure fault detection. This drawback was already observed and explicitly stated in [FRSG22]. To illustrate this issue more clearly, the full version contains calculations describing the influence of the duplication on attacks in the random probing model. The random probing model is the standard method to analyze security of the masking countermeasure against horizontal attacks. In this model, the adversary can choose an *unbounded number of wires* and receives the value on each chosen wire with probability p. Alternatively, such attacks can be modeled in the region probing model, also introduced in [ISW03]. Here, the threshold model is extended so that the threshold of probes applies to each gadget (or regions) in the circuit.

In other words, the total number of probes increases with the number of gadgets. It has been shown by Duc et.al. [DDF14] that security in this model also implies security in the random probing model. Recently, this property has been used to construct secure compilers e.g. [ADF16,GPRV21]. In this work, we also allow up to t probes in each gadget to model horizontal attacks. One possible way to improve security against horizontal attacks is to use fresh randomness in each copy, but (a) it is not straightforward to detect faults in such randomized computation, and (b) the randomness complexity increases to $O(|C|n^3)$.

An alternative approach to executing the masked computation multiple times is to use an different sharing scheme. Recall that additive secret sharing is highly vulnerable to fault attacks as already a single fault is undetectable. Hence, using an additive sharing intuitively requires a large number of independent copies of the same computation to avoid these faults. To tackle this problem, an obvious idea is to resort to error detection codes, where one of the most promising candidates are Reed Solomon codes (often also called Shamir's secret sharing), which in addition to error detection also offer linearity. The latter is particularly useful for carrying out computation with sharings. In the literature, masking schemes based on Shamir's secret sharing are often called *polynomial masking*.

Polynomial Masking. Here, we need $|\mathbb{F}| \geq n + 1$ and choose pairwise different support points $\alpha_0, \ldots, \alpha_{d-1} \neq 0$. To share a value v, we construct a polynomial $f \in \mathbb{F}[x]$ of degree d such that $f(0) = v$. The i-th share v_i is now defined as $f(\alpha_i)$. Polynomial masking [CPR12,GM11,RP12] is a well-known countermeasure against side channel attacks, which offers advantages over additive secret sharing based schemes due to its higher algebraic complexity. Moreover, they allow for a simple protection against faults: We can add *redundant* points $\alpha_d, \alpha_{d+1}, \ldots \alpha_{n-1}$ and corresponding shares $v_{d+1}, v_{d+2}, \ldots, v_{n-1}$, but will still use a polynomial of degree d. Due to the error-correcting properties of these polynomial codes, *valid* codewords, i.e., those sharings describing a polynomial of degree d, will differ in at least $n - d$ positions. If an attacker modifies less than $n - d$ shares, the underlying polynomial (which can be interpolated from the shares v_i) will have degree at least $d + 1$ due to the fundamental theorem of algebra. Hence, modification of only $n - d$ shares results in an *invalid sharing*.

The idea of using polynomial sharing was already used in the context of multiparty computations in the now classical work of Ben-Or, Goldwasser, and Wigderson [BGW88]. Using a more complicated scheme, called *verifiable secret sharing*, they show how to achieve perfect security if the number of corrupted parties is strictly less than $n/3$. Inspired by this, Seker, Fernandez-Rubio, Eisenbarth, and Steinwandt [SFRES18] adapted the BGW scheme to protect against combined attackers. Their main idea is to simplify the BGW multiplication to avoid using verifiable secret sharing in such a way that faulted inputs will lead to a faulted output with high probability. This allowed them to show that $n = 2d + \epsilon + 1$ shares are sufficient to protect against d probes and ϵ *additive faults*, i.e., faults where the attacker can add an arbitrary value to a wire (independently from the actual value on that wire). Both the randomness requirement and the computational complexity of their multiplication gadgets are asymptotical identical to those using the duplication approach, i.e., $O(n^2)$ and $O(n^3)$ respectively. But, due to their linear number of shares, they can compute affine operations in *linear* time. In this work, we show that $n = d + \epsilon + 1$ are both sufficient and necessary to protect against combined attacks. In particular, in contrast to earlier works [SFRES18, DN20b, FRSG22, RFSG22], we show security in a stronger adversarial model where the adversary can induce *adaptive* faults into the computation and security holds in the *region probing* model.

Our approach has the same asymptotical complexities for multiplication as both the duplicated approach and the approach of [SFRES18] and a linear complexity for affine operations. Furthermore, in contrast to the duplicated approach, our solution is provably resistant against horizontal attacks.

1.1   Contribution

Our contributions are threefold. First, we present combined security notions suitable for *polynomial masking*. Second, we propose the notion of *fault-invariance*, that allows us to transform gadgets secure against probing attacks into ones that are secure against combined attacks. Third, we propose two new compilers which use the optimal (*linear*) number of $n = e + d + 1$ shares and show security against horizontal attacks in the region probing model.

Combined Security Notions for Polynomial Sharing. In previous works [SFRES18, DN20b, FRSG22, RFSG22], an (d, ϵ)-attacker was able to choose d wires for probes and ϵ wires for faults (and corresponding fault operations from a class of possible faults). Then, the circuit was faulted according to these faults and the values of the d chosen wires were given to the attacker aiming to extract some sensitive information from these values. We strengthen the attackers significantly with regard to both probes and faults by allowing *region probes* and *adaptive faults*. Informally, region probes allow to perform d probes per *gadget*, in contrast to d probes in total. Furthermore, our attacker can choose the fault applied to a wire based on the already observed probes adaptively. A formal description about the attacker model is presented in Sect. 3.

A careful analysis of the differences between additive masking and polynomial masking reveals that the previously used security definitions do not transfer easily. In additive masking, we want to give an upper bound on the number of faulty outputs, while in polynomial masking we want to give a lower bound on the *degree* of the polynomial described by the sharing. We present new definitions adapted to this difference that allow to argue the composability of two secure gadgets. Here, composability means if gadgets satisfy certain security properties, these properties also hold for more complex computation that is composed of such gadgets.

Simplification of Combined Security Analyzes. The previous approach to prove the security against combined attackers was to verify probing security of these gadget for *all* possible fault combinations [RFSG22]. This often leads to very complicated proofs with many case distinctions and many optimizations developed cannot be reused. We introduce the notion of *fault-invariance* of a gadget that allows us to *lift* probing-secure gadgets to also be secure against combined attacks *without* the need to consider all possible fault combinations. A fault-invariant gadget that is (S)NI stays (S)NI even in the presence of faults and thus allows us to reuse existing probing-secure gadgets.

A New Countermeasure for Combined Attacks. Finally, we present two new compilers secure against combined attackers using adaptive faults in the region probing model. These are the first such compilers as the existing countermeasures using additive masking are very vulnerable to such attacks. Compared to [SFRES18], we significantly reduce the number of needed shares from $2e+d+1$ down to $n = e + d + 1$ (which we also show as *optimal*). Along the way, we also show how to fix their approach by presenting an SNI-secure refresh. Compared to [DN19], we significantly reduce the number of needed random values down to $O(n^2)$ and the computational complexity down to $O(n^3)$. Finally, we also show that our compilers are secure against *horizontal attacks*, a feature explicitly not shared by [DN20b,FRSG22]. All of the approaches using duplicated sharing [DN20b,FRSG22] need a *quadratic* number of shares, hence their complexity will always be suboptimal for affine circuits or circuits with a very large number of affine gates, a feature of many modern blockciphers, e.g., [AGR+16,AAB+20,HKL+22,GKR+21].

For a comparison of our work to other works protecting against combined attacks, we refer to Table 1 Analyzing the cryptographic primitives Keccak [BDPA13], LowMC [ARS+15] or HadesMiMc [GLR+20] yields complexity estimations shown in Table 2. These estimations show that our approach outperforms the duplication approach due to the large number of linear operations.

Table 1: A comparison of the complexity of the addition, multiplication and refresh gadgets with regard to $n = e + d$.

	# Shares	Multiplication		Addition	Refresh		Horizontal Att
		Rand	Compl	Compl	Rand	Compl	Security
[DN20b, FRSG22]	$O(n^2)$	$O(n^2)$	$O(n^3)$	$O(n^2)$	$O(n^2)$	$O(n^3)$	✗
[SFRES18]	$O(n)$	$O(n^2)$	$O(n^3)$	$O(n)$	insecure		✗
[DN19][a]	$O(n)$	$O(n^3)$	$O(n^5)$	$O(n)$	$O(n^3)$	$O(n^5)$	✗
This Work	$O(n)$	$O(n^2)$	$O(n^3)$	$O(n)$	$O(n^2)$	$O(n^3)$	$O(n^{-2})$

[a]This result is only present in the version 20190603:070457 of the eprint paper.

1.2 Related Work

The study of private circuits was initiated by the work of Ishai, Sahai, and Wagner who presented a generic compiler to protect against probing attacks [ISW03]. In a follow-up work, Ishai, Prabhakaran, Sahai, and Wagner also considered fault attacks and presented a corresponding compiler [IPSW06]. Note that a combination of two protection mechanisms against probing attacks and fault attacks might actually *lower* the security of the protection mechanisms [REB+08,LFZD14]. Similar to the work of Ishai, Prabhakaran, Sahai,

Table 2: A rough estimation of the number of operations of our approach compared to the duplication approach of [DN20b, FRSG22] for $n = 8$ for Keccack [BDPA13], LowMC ($R = 55, m = 20$) [ARS+15], and HadesMiMc ($R_F = 10$) [GLR+20]. The numbers given here depend on estimations given in the corresponding works.

	#Add	#Mult	#Ops [DN20b, FRSG22]	#Ops This Work
Keccak	422 400	38 400	46 694 400	23 040 000
LowMC	28 894 643	3 300	1 850 946 752	232 846 744
HadesMiMc	1 820	150	193 280	91 360

and Wagner, the use of error-detection codes together with threshold implementations was studied by Schneider, Moradi, and Güneysu [SMG16] and by De Cnudde and Nikova [CN16]. Recently, the use of explicit multi-party computation protocols as protection mechanisms was studied by Reparaz, De Meyer, Bilgin, Arribas, Nikova, Nikov, and Smart [RDB+18] and by Dhooghe and Nikova [DN20a]. Closest to this paper is the work of Seker, Fernandez-Rubio, Eisenbarth, and Steinwandt that introduced the model of statistical security against fault attacks [SFRES18][1]. They also showed that the classical multi-party protocol of Ben-Or, Goldwasser, and Wigderson [BGW88] can be adapted to this scenario and reduced the number of shares need from $n \geq 3d + 1$ down to $2d + e + 1$.

Previous security notion. The most common security notions against probing-only attacks are *non-interference (NI)* and its stronger counterpart *SNI*. The stronger security notion provides very useful composition results. Namely, it guarantees that the composition of d-SNI gadgets is d-SNI again. Now, using d-SNI gadgets prevents a probing-only attacker (where $e = 0$) from obtaining any information, but faults might still be used to obtain information. Security notions against probing-only attackers have been studied intensively and it was shown that the non-interference notions indeed prevent realistic attacks (see also Duc, Dziembowski, and Faust [DDF14]). An alternative approach, called *probe-isolating non-interference (PINI)* was introduced by Cassiers and Standaert [CS20] and also allows composability.

For fault attacks, the situation is not as easy, as different strategies might lead to different properties that are non-comparable. The simplest behavior, *fault detection*, aims to detect possible faults. Now, one can regularly check for the existence of these faults and abort the computation to prevent information leakage. In a more complex setting, *fault correction*, the computation would try to correct possible faults. While fault correction is a very useful property, it usually comes at prohibitive cost. We thus only focus on the detection of faults. Adding fault checks after every gate would detect the presence of faults

---

[1] In the full version we show that the construction has a bug.

as early as possible, but would increase the cost of the computation severely. Our first goal is thus to minimize the number of fault checks. The existence of multiple successive gates where no fault detection is used opens up the danger of *ineffective faults*, i.e., faults that only change some parts of the computation, but do not change the output. More informally, these faults cancel out at some point in the computation. As shown, e.g., by Clavier [Cla07] or Dobraunig, Eichlseder, Korak, Mangard, Mendel, and Primas [DEK+18] these (statistical) ineffective faults can be used by attackers in a devastating way. To protect against such faults, we design *fault-robust* gadgets: If these gadgets are given faulted inputs, their outputs will also contain faults.

As described earlier, Dhooghe and Nikova [DN20b] introduced the notion of (S)NINA, a combination of (strong) non-interference and non-accumulation, to protect against combined attackers using d probes and ϵ faults. They showed that a duplicate additive sharing is sufficient to obtain security by presenting a multiplication gadget and a refresh gadget that provided security against combined attacks. Richter-Brockmann, Feldtkeller, Sasdrich, and Güneysu [RFSG22] extended the (S)NINA notion to provide accurate definitions for the hardware context and constructed a tool, VERICA, to analyze gadgets with regard to (S)NINA. Finally, Feldtkeller, Richter-Brockmann, Sasdrich, and Güneysu [FRSG22] adapted the related notion of probe-isolating non-interference (PINI) presented by Cassiers and Standaert [CS20] to fault attacks and combined attacks. Similar to the work of Dhooghe and Nikova, they also used duplicate additive sharing and designed corresponding multiplication and refresh gadgets for these sharings that are secure against combined attacks. In contrast to our work, they only allowed static non-adaptive faults and a total number of d probes (i.e., their attacker only worked in the classical threshold probing model and not in the region probing model). Furthermore, as each copy of the computation uses the same randomness, their approach is very vulnerable to horizontal attacks, as shown in the full version. We summarize the efficiency with regard to $n = e + d$ of the constructions of the previous works in Table 1.

2   Background

In this section, we fix the notation used throughout this paper and give the needed background on polynomials and circuits.

Notation. We denote the set of the numbers between 0 and $n - 1$ by $[n]$, i.e., $[n] = \{0, \ldots, n - 1\}$. We write $r \leftarrow_{\$} S$ to denote that r is a random, uniformly distributed element from the finite set S. To simplify notation, if we are given a vector $(v_0, \ldots, v_{n-1})$, we write $(v_i)_{i \in I}$ to denote a vector only consisting of the elements v_i with $i \in I$ for $I \subseteq [n]$ and thus also $(v_i)_{i \in [n]}$ instead of $(v_0, \ldots, v_{n-1})$. If D and D' are probability distribution over domain X, we write $D \equiv D'$, if $D(x) = D'(x)$ for all $x \in X$, i.e., if the distributions agree at each point. Random variables $X_0, X_1, \ldots X_{n-1}$ over a set $\mathbb{F}$ are independent if it holds for any $a_0, a_1, \ldots a_{n-1} \in \mathbb{F}$ that $\Pr[X_0 = a_0, X_1 = a_1, \ldots X_{n-1} = a_{n-1}] = \prod_{i \in [n]} \Pr[X_i = a_i]$. We write that $X_0, X_1, \ldots X_{n-1}$ are

k-wise independent if for any subset $I \subset [n]$ with $|I| \leq k$, the random variables $(X_i)_{i \in I}$ are independent. For a matrix A, its rank is denoted by $\text{rank}(A)$ and its kernel by $\ker(A)$. The dimension of a linear subspace H is denoted by $\dim(H)$. The weight of a vector $(a_i)_{i \in [n]}$ is the number of non-zero elements $\text{weight}((a_i)_{i \in [n]}) = |\{a_i : a_i \neq 0\}|$. Further, we use polynomials in $\mathbb{F}[x]$ that are functions $f : \mathbb{F} \to \mathbb{F}$ with $f(x) = \sum_{i=0}^{k} f_i x^i$ for a natural number k and for all $f_i \in \mathbb{F}$. The degree $\deg(f)$ of f is the highest index of the non-zero f_i's. In detail, $\deg(f) = \max_i \{i : \text{with } f_i \neq 0\}$.

We say that a probability distribution D is *perfectly simulatable* from a set S, if there exists a simulator Sim such that the output of $\mathsf{Sim}(S)$ has the same distribution as D. In detail, it holds for any possible x in the domain of D that $\Pr[\mathsf{Sim}(S) = x] = \Pr[D = x]$. In the following we denote this with $\mathsf{Sim}(S) \equiv D$.

Polynomial Sharing. Throughout this work, we will fix a finite field $(\mathbb{F}, \oplus, \odot)$ with addition $\oplus$ and multiplication $\odot$ such that $|\mathbb{F}| \geq n+1$, where n will be clear from the application. For the sake of simplicity, we will often also write $\cdot$ instead of $\odot$ and $+$ instead of $\oplus$. Throughout this paper, we fix n pairwise different support points $\alpha_0, \dots, \alpha_{n-1} \in \mathbb{F}$ with $\alpha_i \neq 0$. We will often represent a polynomial $f \in \mathbb{F}[x]$ via the shares $(F_i)_{i \in [n]}$ with $F_i = f(\alpha_i)$ and say that $(F_i)_{i \in [n]}$ is a degree d sharing. To see that $(F_i)_{i \in [n]}$ is indeed a valid representation of f, consider the *Vandermonde matrix* $V_{n,d} := V_{n,d}[\alpha_0, \dots, \alpha_{n-1}]$, where the i-th row has the form $(1, \alpha_i, \alpha_i^2, \dots, \alpha_i^d)$. It is now easy to see that $V_{n,d} \cdot (f_0, \dots, f_d)^T = (f(\alpha_0), f(\alpha_2), \dots, f(\alpha_{n-1}))^T = (F_0, \dots, F_{n-1})^T$, i.e., the Vandermonde matrix can be used to evaluate the polynomial on the public support points α_i. Furthermore, it is well known that $\det(V_{n,d}) = \prod_{0 \leq i < j \leq n-1} (\alpha_i - \alpha_j)$. As the α_i are pairwise different and belong to a field $\mathbb{F}$ (which is free of nonzero zero divisors), this determinant is non-zero. Hence, $V_{n,d}$ is regular and the inverse matrix $V_{n,d}^{-1}$ thus exists. As $V_{n,d} \cdot (f_0, \dots, f_d)^T = (F_0, \dots, F_{n-1})^T$, we have $(f_0, \dots, f_d)^T = V_{n,d}^{-1} \cdot (F_0, \dots, F_{n-1})^T$. Hence, the inverse Vandermonde matrix can interpolate the coefficients f_i from the shares F_i via a linear operator.

To share a sensitive value $s \in \mathbb{F}$ into n shares, we will construct a polynomial f with $f(x) = \sum_{i=0}^{n-1} f_i x^i$ of degree $n-1$ where the coefficients $f_1, f_2, \dots, f_{n-1}$ are chosen randomly and f_0 is equal to the sensitive value s. Then, the value $F_i = f(\alpha_i)$ is the ith share. We denote this randomized procedure that outputs $(F_i)_{i \in [n]}$ from s by $(s_i)_{i \in [n]} \leftarrow \mathsf{Enc}(s)$ with $s_i = f(\alpha_i)$. To recover the sensitive value $f_0 = s$, we only need the first row of $V_{n,d}^{-1}$. We denote the i-th element of the first row of $V_{n,d}^{-1}$ by $\lambda_i^{(0)}$. To reconstruct the shared value, we use the well-known *interpolation lemma*.

Lemma 1 (Interpolation Lemma). *Let $f \in \mathbb{F}[x]$ be a polynomial of degree $d \leq n$, let $\alpha_0, \dots, \alpha_{n-1}$ be pairwise different support points in $\mathbb{F} \setminus \{0\}$, and let $\lambda_i^{(0)}$ be the entries of the first row of the inverse Vandermonde matrix $V_{n,d}[\alpha_0, \dots, \alpha_{n-1}]$. Then $(\lambda_1^{(0)}, \dots, \lambda_n^{(0)}) \cdot (f(\alpha_0), \dots, f(\alpha_{n-1})) = f(0)$.*

To simplify notation, we also write $v \leftarrow \mathsf{Dec}((v_i)_{i \in [n]})$ with $v_i = f(\alpha_i)$ for this. Since f is of degree d, the sensitive value v can be reconstructed from $(v_i)_{i \in I}$ with any subset $I \subset [n]$ with $|I| > d$ and $(v_i)_{i \in I}$ is independent of v if $|I| \leq d$.

An important fact that we will make use of throughout this paper is the fact that a sharing $(F_i)_{i \in [n]}$ of a non-zero polynomial with many zero entries corresponds to a polynomial of high degree, as captured by the following well-known fact.

Lemma 2 (Fundamental Lemma). *Let $f \in \mathbb{F}[x]$ be a polynomial of non-zero degree. If f has k distinct roots, $\deg(f) \geq k$.*

Circuit Model. We represent the computation via a circuit on the field $(\mathbb{F}, \oplus, \odot)$, i.e., we consider directed acyclic graphs G where each node is labeled as (i) input gate, (ii) output gate, (iii) random gate, (iv) addition gate, (v) multiplication gate, or (vi) constant (transformation) gate. To compute the circuit on given inputs $x_1, x_2, \ldots$ we first initialize the input gates with the according inputs. Then, at each time step, we evaluate all gates that only have parents that are already evaluated. Random gates are evaluated by sampling an element uniformly at random from $\mathbb{F}$. Constant transformation gates have two constants a and b and evaluate $a \cdot x + b$ on input x. For $a = 0$ it is the usual constant gate initialized with b. We denote the resulting output distribution $y_1, y_2, \ldots$ of circuit C with inputs $x_1, x_2, \ldots$ by $(y_1, y_2, \ldots) \leftarrow \mathsf{C}(x_1, x_2, \ldots)$. In order to simplify notation, we also write $\mathsf{C}^R(x_1, x_2, \ldots)$ for the output of C if the samples from the random gates are taken according to the *random values R*. A *gadget* is simply a subgraph of a circuit. We stress that our definition allows for an arbitrary out-degree of a gate. Hence, there is no need for copy gates or similar. Instead of outputting the result of the computation, a circuit can also *abort* the computation by returning the abort signal $\perp$.

Compiler. A *compiler* $\mathfrak{C}$ is a function transforming a circuit C into another circuit C′. We are interested in compilers that output fault- and leakage-resilient circuits C′. This can be done with polynomial sharing $(\mathsf{Enc}(\cdot), \mathsf{Dec}(\cdot))$ described above such that the circuit C′ only computes on encoded values. Therefore, each gate is transformed into a sub-circuit, a so-called *gadget*, that takes as input the encoded inputs of the gate and outputs encodings such that the decoded output represents the outputs of the gate. For security reasons, additional randomness can be injected by so-called refresh gadgets that take as input an encoding and outputs a randomized encoding in such a way that the decoded value of the input and output is the same. For any circuit $\mathsf{C} : \mathbb{F}^n \to \mathbb{F}^m$ with n inputs and m outputs, the resulting compiler $\mathfrak{C}$ generates $\mathsf{C}' \leftarrow \mathfrak{C}(\mathsf{C})$ such that for any input $x^0, x^1, \ldots x^{n-1}$ and $(y_i^0)_{i \in [n]}, (y_i^1)_{i \in [n]}, \ldots (y_i^{m-1})_{i \in [n]} \leftarrow \mathsf{C}'(\mathsf{Enc}(x^0), \mathsf{Enc}(x^0) \ldots, \mathsf{Enc}(x^{n-1}))$ it holds that $\mathsf{Dec}((y_i^0)_{i \in [n]}), \mathsf{Dec}((y_i^1)_{i \in [n]}), \ldots, \mathsf{Dec}((y_i^{m-1})_{i \in [n]}) = \mathsf{C}(x^0, x^1, \ldots x^{n-1})$. In this case we also write that C and C′ are arithmetic circuits over $\mathbb{F}$ and $\mathbb{F}^n$, respectively to highlight the fact that C′ is working on the shared representation. Further, we say that C′ is a *masked circuit* and has the same functionality as C. Section 4 gives a more detailed construction of the compiler and defines all the required gadgets.

Security Notions. When the adversary has access to a device to perform side-channel and fault attacks, we assume that the adversary can run the device and probe up to d intermediate values. The first and simplest security definition, d-*probing security* requires that the observation of up to d intermediate values in a masked circuit does not reveal anything about the unmasked variables.

Definition 1. *A masked circuit* C *with k inputs* $(x_i^j)_{i \in [n]} \leftarrow \mathsf{Enc}(x^j)$ *and* $j \in [k]$ *is d-probing secure if for any set $\mathcal{L}$ of d probes in*

$$\mathsf{C}((x_i^0)_{i \in [n]}, (x_i^1)_{i \in [n]}, \ldots, (x_i^{k-1})_{i \in [n]}))$$

there is a simulator Sim *only having access to* $\mathsf{C}(\cdot)$ *without the k secrets x^j such that $\mathcal{L} \equiv \mathsf{Sim}(\mathsf{C}(\cdot))$ for any secret $x^0, x^1, \ldots x^{k-1}$.*

Note that Sim has only access to the circuit C but not to the secrets $x^1, x^2, \ldots x^k$. In other words, the probes $\mathcal{L}$ are independent of the unmasked values. A stronger security definition is the d-region-probing model that also takes the circuit size into account. In detail it allows d-probes in each gadget of the masked circuit.

Definition 2. *A masked circuit* C *with k inputs* $(x_i^j)_{i \in [n]} \leftarrow \mathsf{Enc}(x^j)$ *and* $j \in [k]$ *is d-region-probing secure if for any set $\mathcal{L}$ of d probes in each gadget of*

$$\mathsf{C}((x_i^1)_{i \in [n]}, (x_i^2)_{i \in [n]}, \ldots, (x_i^k)_{i \in [n]}))$$

there is a simulator Sim *only having access to* $\mathsf{C}(\cdot)$ *without the k secrets x^j such that $\mathcal{L} \equiv \mathsf{Sim}(\mathsf{C}(\cdot))$ for any secret $x^1, x^2, \ldots x^k$.*

It turned out that probing security of two circuits does not always imply probing security of its composition. Since composition results are very useful and allow the construction of compilers that work on a gate-by-gate basis, stronger definitions were subsequently developed. In the following, we give some stronger security definitions, well suited to masked circuits (or gadgets). To simplify presentation, we consider only gadgets having a single output sharing $(y_i)_{i \in [n]}$. We refer to Cassiers and Standaert for discussion of gadgets with multiple outputs [CS20]. An important notion to achieve composability in the presence of probing attacks is the notion of d-*Non-Interference* (d-NI) and d-*Strong-Non-Interference* (d-SNI) [BBD+16]. Both definitions guarantee that the leakage of up to d probes is independent of the shared secret.

Definition 3 (d-NI [BBD+15, BBD+16]). *A gadget G with one output sharing is d-non-interfering (d-NI) if and only if every set of $d' \leq d$ internal probes can be (perfectly) simulated with at most d' shares of each input sharing.*

The stronger d-SNI notion requires to distinguish between intermediate and output probes and guarantees that only the number of intermediate probes affects the number of inputs required by the simulator, easing the compilation of circuits.

Definition 4 (d-SNI [BBD+16]). *A gadget with one output sharing is d-strong-non-interfering (d-SNI) if and only if for every set I of d_1 internal probes and every set O of d_2 output probes such that $d_1 + d_2 \leq d$, the set of probes $I \cup O$ can be (perfectly) simulated with d_1 shares of each input sharing.*

Note PINI is another useful security notion for compositions in the threshold model. We omit this definition in the main body since it is vulnerable to horizontal attacks, and thus does not provide good properties for proofs in the region probing model. A detailed analysis is given in the full version.

3   Combined Security Model

As mentioned in the introduction, many countermeasures defending against fault attacks *or* probing attacks have been studied in the literature, but the task to protect against both attacks at the same time has only received more attention in the last few years. In this section we analyze the combined security of both fault resilience and probe resilience. To understand the influence of different kind of faults, we will model these faults as set of functions. An adversary with access to the class of faults $\mathcal{F}$ is able to change the value x to $\zeta(x)$ for $\zeta \in \mathcal{F}$ during the computation. For the sake of simplicity, we always assume that the identity function id is part of every class $\mathcal{F}$. A fault attack now applies several of these faults to different wires of $\mathsf{C}^R : \mathbb{F}^k \to \mathbb{F}^l$. More formally, if the wires of the circuit C^R are numbered by $1, \ldots, W$, a *fault attack* T is a tuple of functions $T = (\zeta_1, \ldots, \zeta_W)$ with $\zeta_i \in \mathcal{F}$ for all $i = 1 \ldots W$ that describes how the value of each wire i is faulted. This means that such a wire i gets a value z_i from its output gate, but the following gate gets as input the faulted value $\zeta_i(z_i, \boldsymbol{u}_i)$, where ζ_i is the ith function in $T = (\zeta_1, \ldots, \zeta_W)$ and $\boldsymbol{u}_i$ are the values already revealed by probes. We write $\mathsf{A}(\mathcal{F})$ to refer to the set of all possible fault attacks using the fault-functions $\mathcal{F}$. To simplify notation, we will often only use the ordering of the wires implicitly. If we tamper the circuit C^R with a fault attack $T \in \mathsf{A}(\mathcal{F})$ we write $T[\mathsf{C}^R]$. Due to physical constraints, a typical attacker cannot fault arbitrary many wires and is thus restricted (for example, [SFRES18] considers at most 3 faults and [RDB+18] at most 8 faults). For a fault attack $T \in \mathsf{A}(\mathcal{F})$, we write $|T|$ for the number of non-identity faults used, i.e., $|T| = |\{i \in \{1, \ldots, W\} \mid \zeta_i \neq \mathrm{id}\}|$ with $T = (\zeta_1, \ldots, \zeta_W)$. In the following we often consider different types of fault sets. In the most general case, we use *wire independent faults* $\mathcal{F}^{ind} := \{$all functions $\zeta \colon \mathbb{F} \times \mathbb{F}^* \to \mathbb{F}\}$ to show that the attacker can fault arbitrarily. We stress here that our model implies that the faults performed on different wires are somewhat *independent*, as they each only consider a single wire. An often studied restriction are *additive faults* $\mathcal{F}^+ := \{\zeta : \zeta(x, \boldsymbol{u}) = x + a$ for all $a \in \mathbb{F}\}$ that fault the wires value by adding an arbitrary value. We give a detailed discussion about the fault sets in the full version.

Security Experiment. We are now ready to give a formal description of the underlying security experiment where an attacker is able to perform combined attacks. Therefore, we adjusted the security game of Dhooge and Nikova [DN20b] to allow adaptive faults and region probes. Let $\mathsf{C} \colon \mathbb{F}^k \to \mathbb{F}^l$ be a circuit with wires $W = \{w_i\}_i$ that is split into *regions* $R_1, \ldots, R_r$ with wires $W_1, \ldots, W_r$.

An (d, e)-*attacker* A with respect to a fault class $\mathcal{F}$ takes part in the following experiment:

- The experiment chooses $b \leftarrow_\$ \{0, 1\}$ uniformly at random
- A is given input C and outputs the following:
    - a fault-attack $T \in \mathsf{A}(\mathcal{F})$ with $|T| \leq e$
    - for each region R_j, a subset $W_j' \subseteq W_j$ of wires with $|W_j'| \leq d$
    - two possible circuit inputs $x_0, x_1 \in \mathbb{F}^k$
- The experiment runs $\widetilde{y_b} \leftarrow T[\mathsf{C}](x_b)$ and the wire values corresponding to $W' = \bigcup_{j=1}^r W_j'$ are given to A. The attacker outputs a bit b'.

We say that C is ϵ-secure if $\Pr[b = b'] = 1/2$ and $\Pr[\widetilde{y_b} \in \{\perp, y_b\}] \geq 1 - \epsilon$ for any (d, e)-*attacker* A, where $y_b \leftarrow \mathsf{C}(x_b)$ is the output of a non-faulted run of C on x_b. In other words, the circuit is ϵ-secure if it is information-theoretic secure against leakage and detects erroneous values with probability at least $1 - \epsilon$.

In this work, we assume leakage-free encoding and decoding gadgets as defined in Definition 1. As a consequence, it is sufficient to prove that the probes can be simulated with less than d values of each masked input, if the circuit is masked with a degree d masking. The existence of such gadgets is commonly used and goes back to Ishai, Sahai, and Wagner [ISW03].

3.1   Privacy

First, we give a property that guarantees the (S)NI property of a gadget even in the presence of fault attacks. We emphasize that this property only gives probing security in the presence of faults, but ignores fault security notions such as error preservation and detection. For the general fault resilience we refer to Sect. 3.2. Next, we extend the probing security by requiring that a gadget is d-(S)NI even if the adversary inserts faults into the computation.

Definition 5 (fault resilient SNI). *A gadget* G *is* d fault resilient (strong-) non-interfering (d-fr(S)NI) *with respect to* $\mathcal{F}$ *if* $T[\mathsf{G}]$ *is* d-(S)NI *for any fault attack* $T \in \mathsf{A}(\mathcal{F})$.

Note that an (S)NI gadget is not always (S)NI in the presence of faults. In the full version, we give a detailed discussion and some examples. fr(S)NI is a relative strong property and in some cases it might be sufficient (or needed) to slightly weaken this notion. To do so, we will consider the situation introduced before where (a) the number of faults are bounded and, furthermore, (b) we will treat these faults additionally as probes. This is justified, e.g., in the context of constant fault functions (also called *stuck faults*) that might set a random value to a fixed value known by the adversary, as this can easily be seen to be strictly stronger than a probe on this random value. If a circuit is fault resilient under these restrictions, we say that the circuit is wfr(S)NI.

Definition 6 (weak fault resilient NI). *A gadget* G *is* d weak fault resilient non-interfering (d-wfrNI) *with respect to* $\mathcal{F}$ *if every set of* d' *probes in* $T[\mathsf{G}]$ *can be (perfectly) simulated with* $d' + |T|$ *shares of each input sharing for any fault attack* $T \in \mathsf{A}(\mathcal{F})$ *with* $|T| + d' \leq d$.

Definition 7 (weak fault resilient SNI). *A gadget* G *is d* weak fault resilient strong-non-interfering *(d-wfrSNI) with respect to $\mathcal{F}$ if every set of d_1 internal probes and d_2 output probes in $T[G]$ can be (perfectly) simulated with $d_1 + \epsilon_1$ shares of each input sharing for any fault attack $T \in A(\mathcal{F})$ with ϵ_1 internal faults and ϵ_2 output faults such that $d_1 + d_2 + \epsilon_1 + \epsilon_2 \leq d$.*

Note that this weaker notion does not imply that the faulted gadget $T[G]$ is $(d - \epsilon) - (S)NI$ with $\epsilon = |T|$, as our d-wfr(S)NI definition gives ϵ more input values to the simulator for the simulation. This new security notions allows us to use the same composition results as the standard (S)NI gadgets even in the presence of faults. For example, the composition of two d-frSNI gadgets is easily seen to be d-frSNI again.

Theorem 1. *The composition of two d-frSNI (or d-wfrSNI) gadgets with respect to $\mathcal{F}$ is d-frSNI (or d-wfrSNI) with respect to $\mathcal{F}$ if $\mathcal{F} \subseteq \mathcal{F}^{ind}$.*

We write adaptive if the security still holds under the assumption that the adversary can choose the function with the knowledge of the probes (before). Theorem 1 implies that the composition of an arbitrary number of SNI gadgets is SNI again. This easily follows by the fact that composed SNI gadgets can be seen as SNI gadgets again, and we can compose step-by-step arbitrary many gadgets together. Theorem 1 is only an example composition for SNI. Next, we give a general proof that also implies this theorem[2] and shows that all d-(S)NI composition rules apply as well to the d-frSNI and d-wfrSNI.

Theorem 2. *The composition rules for (S)NI also apply to d-fr(S)NI and d-wfr(S)NI.*

Proof. We start with the proof for the stronger security notion. The faults $\mathcal{F} \subseteq \mathcal{F}^{ind}$ only allow independent faults on each wire, and this allows us to split the adversary in multiple adversaries that tamper each gadget independently. So let C be an arbitrary composed circuit only using d-fr(S)NI gadgets $G_0, G_1, \ldots, G_m$ with respect to $\mathcal{F}$ and let T be any fault attack $T \in A(\mathcal{F})$. Since we keep the proof as general as possible we just assume that C has some security properties (e.g. SNI) that follow from the (S)NI properties of G_0, G_1. Now we show that the property also holds for any T. Since we can split the circuit attack T to gadget-wise attacks $T_0, T_1, \ldots, T_m$ it holds that $T[C]$ can be also described as the composition of the (independently) faulted gadgets $T_0[G_0], T_1[G_1], \ldots, T_m[G_m]$. The fr(S)NI properties still guarantees that each faulted gadget $T_j[G_j]$ has the same (S)NI property as its unfaulted version G_j. Hence, the faulted gadgets $T_0[G_0], T_1[G_1], \ldots, T_m[G_m]$ have the same composition properties as the unfaulted (S)NI gadgets $G_0, G_1, \ldots, G_m$ and the faulted circuit $T[C]$ has the same (S)NI properties as the original one C. Note that this holds for any fault attack $T \in A(\mathcal{F})$, and it follows that the same composition rules apply for fr(S)NI as for (S)NI. The proof for the weaker notion is similar, only the fault attack is limited and the faults are counted as probes. □

---

[2] Alternatively, we give a straight forward proof of Theorem 1 in the full version.

Remember that d-(S)NI gadgets are also d-probing secure as defined in Definition 1. Similarly to Theorem 2 it easily follows that any d-frSNI circuit C with respect to $\mathcal{F}$ is also d-probing secure for any fault attack $T \in A(\mathcal{F})$. More formally, $T[C]$ is d-probing secure for any $T \in A(\mathcal{F})$. The probing security of d-wfrSNI circuits is slightly weaker. Since the number of allowed probes in d-wfrSNI circuits is reduced by the number of faults, a d-wfrSNI circuit C with respect to $\mathcal{F}$ is only $(d - e)$-probing secure for any fault attack $T \in A(\mathcal{F})$ with $|T| = e \leq d$.

Privacy analyzes. Analyzing the (S)NI property in itself is often tedious and to study the (w)f-(S)NI notion means we also need to consider all possible fault attacks. To avoid the combinatorial explosion, we present an additional property such that the classical (S)NI property directly implies the faulty one. This property is called *fault-invariance*, as the amount of information that a probe gives is independent of the faults. As the internal values z_i of a circuit only depend on the internal randomness R and the inputs $x_0, x_i, \ldots, x_{l-1}$ we can also write them as functions $z_i = f_i^R(x_0, x_1, \ldots x_{k-1})$.

Definition 8 (fault-invariance). *A circuit C is fault-invariant with respect to a fault set $\mathcal{F}$ if for any $T \in A(\mathcal{F})$, any intermediate value f in C^R and the according value $\tilde{f}$ in $T[C^R]$ there are $\zeta, \zeta_0, \zeta_1, \ldots \zeta_{k-1} \in \mathcal{F}$ such that it holds*

$$\tilde{f}^R(x_0, x_1, \ldots x_{m-1}) = \zeta(f^R(\zeta_0(x_0), \zeta_1(x_1), \ldots \zeta_{m-1}(x_{m-1})))$$

for any input $(x_0, x_1, \ldots x_{m-1})$ and randomness R.

In other words, Definition 8 says that all faults in $\mathcal{F}$ applied to a gadget can be pushed to the input or the output of the gadget.

Gadgets that are (S)NI and also have this property are directly (S)NI in the presence of faults.

Corollary 1. *If a gadget is d-(S)NI and fault-invariant with respect to $\mathcal{F} \subseteq \mathcal{F}^{ind}$, the gadget is d-fr(S)NI with respect to $\mathcal{F}$.*

Proof. We will prove that we can take the classical leakage simulator of the non-faulted gadget and transform it according to the faults due to the fault invariance. Fix a gadget G and some probed values $(p_0, p_1, \ldots, p_{d-1})^T$. Due to the d-(S)NI property there is a simulator $S(a_0, a_1, \ldots)$ that perfectly simulates the leakage with some input values $(a_0, a_1, \ldots)$. This means it holds that

$$S(a_0, a_1, \ldots) = (S_0(a_0, a_1, \ldots), S_1(a_0, a_1, \ldots), \ldots S_{d-1}(a_0, a_1, \ldots))^T$$

has the same distribution as $(p_0, p_1, \ldots, p_{d-1})^T$, where $S_i(a_0, a_1, \ldots)$ is the projection of the output of S to the wire indexed by probe p_i. Further, let any $T \in A(\mathcal{F})$ be a fault-attack and $(p'_0, p'_1, \ldots, p'_{d-1})^T$ be the according probes on the same wires in $T[G]$. Due to the fault-invariance we know that there exist functions $\zeta_{i,j}, \zeta'_i \in \mathcal{F}$ such that the values

$$S'(a_0, a_1, \ldots) = \begin{pmatrix} \zeta'_0(S_0(\zeta_{0,0}(a_0), \zeta_{0,1}(a_1), \ldots)) \\ \zeta'_1(S_1(\zeta_{1,0}(a_0), \zeta_{1,1}(a_1), \ldots)), \\ \vdots \\ \zeta'_{p-1}(S_{p-1}(\zeta_{p-1,0}(a_0), \zeta_{p-1,1}(a_1), \ldots)) \end{pmatrix}$$

have the same distribution as $(p'_0, p'_1, \ldots, p'_{d-1})^T$. Hence, the simulator S' can simulate the faulted gadget and with the same inputs as the simulator S of the unfaulted (S)NI gadget. This proves that $T[\mathsf{G}]$ is also (S)NI for any $T \in \mathsf{A}(\mathcal{F})$. □

In the following, we show that the stronger definition with regard to the additive faultset $\mathcal{F}^+$ directly implies the weaker definition for the more general independent $\mathcal{F}^{ind}$, if we consider fault-invariant gadgets.

Corollary 2. *If a gadget is d-fr(S)NI and fault-invariant with respect to $\mathcal{F}^+$, it is adaptively d-wfr(S)NI with respect to $\mathcal{F}^{ind}$.*

Proof. Let C be an d-fr(S)NI and fault-invariant circuit with respect to $\mathcal{F}^+$. We give a reduction and prove that any simulator Sim for d-wfr(S)NI with respect to $\mathcal{F}^{ind}$ can be simulated by a simulator $\widetilde{\mathsf{Sim}}$ for d-fr(S)NI with respect to $\mathcal{F}^+$ if the according gadget is fault-invariant with respect to $\mathcal{F}^+$.

So let Sim simulate a fault attack $T \in \mathsf{A}(\mathcal{F}^{ind})$ with $|T| = s$ and $d-s$ probes. Now we show that Sim can be simulated with a Simulator $\widetilde{\mathsf{Sim}}$ with fault attack $\widetilde{T} \in \mathsf{A}(\mathcal{F}^+)$ with $|\widetilde{T}| = s$ and d probes. Here, we use the fact that $\widetilde{\mathsf{Sim}}$ can simulate d values, and we can also simulate the faulted values to transform all faults into additive faults. In detail, let $v_1, v_2, \ldots v_s$ the values faulted by the fault functions $\zeta_1, \zeta_2, \ldots, \zeta_s \in \mathcal{F}^{ind}$ due to T and $v_{s+1}, v_{s+2}, \ldots, v_d$ the $d-s$ values simulated by Sim in $T[\mathsf{C}]$. Now $\widetilde{\mathsf{Sim}}$ can simulate the according values $\tilde{v}_1, \tilde{v}_2, \ldots, \tilde{v}_d$ in the unfaulted C. Next, it computes for all fault functions ζ_j with $a_j = \zeta_j(v_j) - v_j$ and constructs the new additive fault function $\tilde{\zeta}_j(x) = x + a_j$. It follows that for all faults it holds $\zeta_j(v_j) = \tilde{\zeta}_j(v_j)$. Due to the invariance $\widetilde{\mathsf{Sim}}$ can move all additive faults to the inputs and outputs. In other words $\widetilde{\mathsf{Sim}}$ can compute how the additive faults affect the simulated probes $\tilde{v}_1, \tilde{v}_2, \ldots, \tilde{v}_d$, and can compute the according probes $v'_1, v'_2, \ldots, v'_d$ in the circuit faulted with the fault functions $\tilde{\zeta}_j(x)$. Since the faults are the same as $\zeta_j(x)$, the values $v'_{s+1}, v'_{s+2}, \ldots, v'_d$ and $v_{s+1}, v_{s+2}, \ldots, v_d$ have the same distribution. This implies the claim of the corollary because it shows that if we have $\widetilde{\mathsf{Sim}}$, we also have Sim. In other words if the gadget is d-fr(S)NI and fault-invariant with respect to $\mathcal{F}^+$, it is d-wfr(S)NI with respect to $\mathcal{F}^{ind}$.

Note that the simulator can choose the fault function with the knowledge of the probes. This also means that if the adversary chooses the function adaptively, it does not affect the simulator. Hence the adversary can be adaptive.   □

3.2   Error Preservation and Detection

As described before, a general way to understand the countermeasures against passive and active attacks, can be viewed as *encodings*. For a concrete (randomized) encoding scheme $\mathsf{Enc} \colon \mathbb{F} \to \mathbb{F}^n$, a value $y \in \mathbb{F}^n$ is a *valid* encoding if there is an $x \in \mathbb{F}$ and some randomness such that $\mathsf{Enc}(x; r) = y$. Similar to the fr(S)NI property we are interested in a property that guarantees that errors can be detected even when we compose multiple gadgets. In our case, we want to guarantee that errors are detected by the fact that the resulting encodings are invalid. More concretely, if y and y' are valid encodings, we want to increase their Hamming distance, denoted by $d(y, y')$. To argue about the behavior of a gadget in the presence of faults that can introduce computation errors, we need to guarantee that errors already present in the computation (a) stay present in the computation (to detect them) and (b) that these errors cannot accumulate over time to lead to a valid encoding of an *incorrect* value. To model this, we assume that the inputs $(x_i)_{i \in [n]}$ of our gadgets might already be faulted by a *fault vector* $(v_i)_{i \in [n]}$, i.e., the inputs will always be $(x_i)_{i \in [n]} + (v_i)_{i \in [n]}$, where $(x_i)_{i \in [n]}$ is a valid encoding. In a first approach, one might require that the input of an invalid encoding, i.e., one where $(v_i)_{i \in [n]} \neq 0$, always leads to an invalid output encoding. But this is a very strict requirement that is nearly impossible to fulfill if we consider an addition gadget: The attacker might add $(v_i)_{i \in [n]}$ to one of the inputs and then later add $-(v_i)_{i \in [n]}$ to the output. Clearly, this gives a valid encoding although the input was invalid. We thus also allow that our gadget on input $(x_i)_{i \in [n]} + (v_i)_{i \in [n]}$ with $(v_i)_{i \in [n]} \neq 0$ can produce a valid encoding of the *correct value* but this effect has to be independent of input $(x_i)_{i \in [n]}$.

Definition 9 (e-f-robust). *A gadget* G *with one output sharing and two input sharings is* e-*fault-robust with respect to* $\mathcal{F}$, *if for any valid encoding* $(x_i^{(0)})_{i \in [n]}$ *and* $(x_i^{(1)})_{i \in [n]}$, *the output* $(y_i)_{i \in [n]} \leftarrow G((x_i^{(0)})_{i \in [n]}, (x_i^{(1)})_{i \in [n]})$ *is also valid. Further, it holds for any fault vectors* $(v_i^{(0)})_{i \in [n]}$, $(v_i^{(1)})_{i \in [n]}$, *and* $T \in A(\mathcal{F})$ *with*
$$(y_i)_{i \in [n]} + (w_i^{(1)})_{i \in [n]} + (w_i^{(2)})_{i \in [n]} \leftarrow T[G]((x^{(0)} + v_i^{(0)})_{i \in [n]}, (x^{(1)} + v_i^{(1)})_{i \in [n]}),$$
that there are numbers t_1 *and* t_2 *with* $t_1 + t_2 \leq |T|$ *such that*

(i) weight$(w') \leq t_1$ *with* $(w_i')_{i \in [n]} = (v_i^{(0)})_{i \in [n]} + (v_i^{(1)})_{i \in [n]} - (w_i^{(1)})_{i \in [n]}$;
(ii) and $(w_i^{(2)})_{i \in [n]}$ *is the zero vector or produced by the following random experiment: A polynomial* $p_w \in \mathbb{F}[x]$ *is chosen such that the coefficients of* x^{d+1}, $x^{d+2}, \ldots, x^{n-t_2}$ *are drawn uniformly at random from* $\mathbb{F}$. *Then,* $w_i^{(2)} = p_w(\alpha_i)$.

Note that any valid encoding $(y_i)_{i \in [n]}$ and any fault vector $(w_i)_{i \in [n]}$ with weight$(w) \leq e$ cannot result in a valid encoding with $(y_i)_{i \in [n]} + (w_i)_{i \in [n]}$ in our setting, as we use $d + 1 + e$ shares of a polynomial of degree d. Hence, weight$((y_i)_{i \in [n]} - (y'_i)_{i \in [n]}) \geq e + 1$ for all valid sharings y and y'. Next we give a useful composition result for e-f-robustness.

Theorem 3. *The composition of two* e-*fault-robust gadgets with respect to* $\mathcal{F}$ *is* e-*fault-robust with respect to* $\mathcal{F}$ *if* $\mathcal{F} \subseteq \mathcal{F}^{ind}$.

Proof. Let G and G' be two gadgets such that G is given inputs $(x_i^{(0)})_{i \in [n]}$ and $(x_i^{(1)})_{i \in [n]}$ and produces output $(y_i^{(0)})_{i \in [n]}$. Furthermore, let G' have the inputs $(y_i^{(0)})_{i \in [n]}$ (i.e., the output of G) and $(y_i^{(1)})_{i \in [n]}$ and output $(z_i)_{i \in [n]}$. Let $\tilde{G}$ be the complete construction and $v_{x^{(0)}}, v_{x^{(1)}}, v_{y^{(0)}}, v_{y^{(1)}}, v_z$ be the fault vectors.

Fix any $\tilde{T} \in A(\mathcal{F})$. Due to the independence of these faults, we can split them into two parts T and T', where T corresponds to the faults introduced in G and T' corresponds to the faults introduced in G'.

As G is e-fault-robust, its output fault vector $v_{y^{(0)}}$ is of the form $v_{y^{(0)}} = v_{x^{(0)}} + v_{x^{(1)}} + w^{(1)} + w^{(2)}$ where $\text{weight}(w^{(1)}) \leq t_1$ and $w^{(2)}$ is the zero vector or drawn randomly with highest coefficient x^{n-t_2} for some numbers t_1 and t_2 with $t_1 + t_2 \leq |T|$. Furthermore, as G' is e-fault-robust, its output fault vector v_z is of the form $v_z = v_{y^{(0)}} + v_{y^{(1)}} + w'^{(1)} + w'^{(2)}$ where $\text{weight}(w'^{(1)}) \leq t_1'$ and $w'^{(2)}$ is drawn randomly with highest coefficient $x^{n-t_2'}$ for some numbers t_1' and t_2' with $t_1' + t_2' \leq |T'|$. Hence, $v_z = v_{x^{(0)}} + v_{x^{(1)}} + w^{(1)} + w^{(2)} + v_{y^{(1)}} + w'^{(1)} + w'^{(2)}$, where $\text{weight}(w^{(1)} + w'^{(1)}) \leq t_1 + t_1'$ and $w^{(2)} + w'^{(2)}$ corresponds to a random polynomial with highest coefficient $x^{n-\min\{t_2, t_2'\}}$.   □

The definition of e-fault-robustness can be simplified for non-adaptive attackers: We can then guarantee that either $w^{(1)}$ or $w^{(2)}$ are zero. The proof of composability is similar, but uses the fact that the sum of a random polynomial and a deterministic, *independent* polynomial is again a random polynomial.

The notion of e-fault-robustness now directly allows us to give a bound on the probability that a valid encoding of an invalid value is generated by a circuit.

Theorem 4. *If a circuit is e-fault-robust, the probability that $s \leq e$ faults can produce a valid encoding of an invalid value is at most q^{s-e-1} in the case of non-adaptive attackers and $q^{s-e} \cdot (d+e+1)^{t_1}$ for all $t_1 \leq s$ in the case of adaptive attackers.*

Proof. Let $w^{(1)}$ and $w^{(2)}$ be as in the definition of e-fault-robustness and let $p^{(1)}$ and $p^{(2)}$ be the corresponding polynomials. Lemma 2 implies that the fault polynomial $p^{(1)}$ has degree at least $n - t_1$. Hence, if $p^{(2)}$ is identical to zero, the attacker can not produce a valid encoding of an invalid value. Furthermore, if $p^{(1)}$ is identical to zero, the sharing is valid if and only if all coefficients of x^{d+1}, $x^{d+2}, \ldots, x^{n-s}$ of $p^{(1)}$ are zero, which happens with probability q^{s-e-1}.

If $p^{(2)}$ is not identical to zero, the polynomial $p = p^{(1)} + p^{(2)}$ corresponding to $w = w^{(1)} + w^{(2)}$ needs to have degree at most d. As $p^{(2)}$ has degree at most $n - t_2$, this is only possible if $n - t_1 \leq n - t_2$, i.e., if $t_1 \geq t_2$ holds. We will now show that the number of different polynomials $p^{(1)}$ and $p^{(2)}$ such that p has degree at most d is very small. Clearly, the number of different polynomials possible for $p^{(2)}$ is q^{e-t_2} due to the fact that $p^{(2)}$ is randomly generated. Furthermore, the number of different polynomials possible for $p^{(1)}$ is $\binom{n}{t_1} \cdot q^{t_1} \leq n^{t_1} \cdot q^{t_1}$. Hence, the probability that there is a vector $w^{(1)}$ matching to the random vector $w^{(2)}$ is at most

$$\frac{q^{t_1}}{q^{e-t_2}} \cdot n^{t_1} = q^{t_1 + t_2 - e} \cdot n^{t_1}.$$

Hence, the probability that $s \leq e$ faults can produce a valid encoding of an invalid value is at most $q^{s-e} \cdot (d+e+1)^{t_1}$.   □

3.3   Combined Security

Equipped with our new notions of d-fr(S)NI and e-fault-robustness, it is easy to see that the combination of these notions directly implies security against (d, e)-attackers.

Theorem 5. *If the circuit* C *is d-frSNI (or d-wfr(S)NI) and e-fault-robust, it is q^{s-e-1}-secure against any non-adaptive (d,s)-attacker (or $(d-s,s)$-attacker) with $s \le e$. Furthermore, it is $q^{s-e} \cdot (d+e+1)^{t_1}$-secure against any adaptive (d,s)-attacker (or $(d-s,s)$-attacker) with $t_1 \le s \le e$.*

Proof. The perfect security with regard to the leakage (i.e., that the attacker is not able to determine the challenge bit b) directly follows from the fact that the circuit is d-SNI even in the presence of at most e faults. Furthermore, Theorem 4 directly implies that the probability that a valid encoding of an invalid value is ever output is at most q^{s-e-1} in the non-adaptive case and $q^{s-e} \cdot (d+e+1)^{t_1}$ in the adaptive case. □

4   Compiler

This section gives a compiler transforming an unprotected circuit into a fault and probe resilient circuit using a polynomial sharing with an optimal number of shares. As described in the previous section, the sensitive data v is masked with a $d+1$-out-of-n polynomial sharing. Therefore, a polynomial f with degree d such that $f(0) = v$ is generated, and the shares are given by $f(\alpha_i)$ for pairwise different non-zero inputs $\alpha_0, \ldots, \alpha_{n-1}$. The main goal of the compiler is now to take an ordinary circuit and transform it into a circuit operating on shares such that d probes and e faults do not reveal any sensitive data, i.e., into a circuit that is ϵ-secure against (d,e)-attackers. As usual, this is done by replacing gates of the original circuit with gadgets. For security reasons, refresh gadgets are also inserted that guarantee that intermediate sharings become independent. Refresh gadgets take as input an encoded secret and output a re-randomized encoding of the same secret. This procedure reduces the dependencies that might occur when one value is used as input for multiple gadgets.

In the following, let $n = d + e + 1$. Unary gates (such as addition or multiplication with a constant) taking only a single input can be handled easily, as these operations are linear and can thus be computed locally on the shares. We thus only need to focus on binary gates, i.e., addition and multiplication gates that take two inputs. Let us consider two $d+1$-out-of-n sharings $(F_i)_{i\in[n]}$ and $(G_i)_{i\in[n]}$ of secrets f_0, respectively g_0. Similar to the unary gates, Algorithm 1 computes a *share-wise* addition such that its output $(Q_i)_{i\in[n]}$ represents the addition $f_0 + g_0$. This algorithm is a gadget computing an addition since it outputs a $d+1$-out-of-n sharing again, as the addition of two degree d polynomials also has degree d.

Algorithm 1 (n,d)-**SWAdd** for $n = d + \epsilon + 1$

Input: Shares of f_0 as $(F_i)_{i\in[n]}$ and g_0 as $(G_i)_{i\in[n]}$ with degree d
Output: Shares of $f_0 + g_0$ as $(Q_i)_{i\in[n]}$ with degree d.

1: **for** $i = 0$ to $n - 1$ **do**
2:    $Q_i \leftarrow F_i + G_i$

3: **return** $(Q_i)_{i\in[n]}$

Due to our attack model, all faults added to the input of any such share-wise (linear) gadget can also be added to the output without any change in the computation. Furthermore, as $n \geq d$, these gadgets are secure against d probes, as d values of a $d + 1$-out-of-n sharing do not reveal any information. We can thus state the following fact.

Theorem 6. *Share-wise affine gadgets are d-frNI with respect to $\mathcal{F}^+$ (or d-wfrNI with respect to $\mathcal{F}^{ind}$) and e-fault-robust with respect to $\mathcal{F}^{ind}$.*

Proof. The e-fault-robustness immediately follows from Definition 9(i). Next, we prove the frNI property. It is sufficient to show that a share-wise linear gadget is NI and fault invariant with respect to $\mathcal{F}^+$ because Corollary 1 shows that this implies d-frNI with respect to $\mathcal{F}^+$. Further, Corollary 2 shows that this also implies d-wfrNI with respect to $\mathcal{F}^{ind}$. Hence, it remains to prove that a share-wise linear gadget is (i) NI and (ii) fault invariant with respect to $\mathcal{F}^+$.

(i) It is well known that any share-wise gadget is NI, as all output (and intermediate) values only depend on input shares with the same index. For example, the share-wise addition with $c_i \leftarrow a_i + b_i$ only depends on the ith share a_i and b_i for any $i \in [n]$. It follows that any d probes can be simulated by at most d shares of each input sharing because we never need more than one share of each input sharing for each probe. This implies the NI property.

(ii) The invariance w.r.t $\mathcal{F}^+$ follows from the linearity. Since an additive fault ζ only adds a constant value x on a wire, we can move the addition x to the output or input due to the linearity. For example it holds for the share-wise addition $c_i \leftarrow a_i + b_i$ that $(a_i + b_i) + x = a_i + (b_i + x) = (a_i + x) + b_i$. In the first term, the fault is moved to the output $\zeta(c_i) = c_i + x$ and in the second two terms it is moved to the inputs $\zeta(b_i)$, and $\zeta(a_i)$, respectively. This is the property required for fault invariance. We give a more general proof in the full version. With (i) and (ii) we can conclude the proof. □

As usual, the remaining gate, the binary multiplication gate is the most complicated gate, as it does not behave linearly. Nevertheless, Algorithm 2 computes a share-wise multiplication such that its output $(Q_i)_{i \in [n]}$ represents the multiplication $f_0 \cdot g_0$. Unfortunately, the multiplication of two polynomials of degree d results in a polynomial of degree $2d$. Therefore, Algorithm 2 outputs a $2d$ degree polynomial. For $n < 2d$, this means that the shares can not represent this polynomial properly and we thus lose the information about the shared value. Furthermore, even if $n > 2d$, the next multiplication gadget in the circuit could possibly lead to a polynomial of degree $4d$ and so on. Hence, Algorithm 2 can not be used as a multiplication gadget alone and further work is required. The classical approach due to Ben-Or, Goldwasser, and Wigderson [BGW88] performs a *degree reduction* to reduce the polynomial to degree d after the share-wise multiplication to prevent the exponential blowup of the degrees. Nevertheless, the polynomial of degree $2d$ needs to be stored and their approach thus requires at least $2d$ shares.

Algorithm 2 (n, d)-**SWMult** for $n = d + \epsilon + 1$

Input: Shares of f_0 as $(F_i)_{i \in [n]}$ and g_0 as $(G_i)_{i \in [n]}$ with degree d
Output: Shares of $f_0 g_0$ as $(Q'_i)_{i \in [n]}$ with degree $2d$.

1: **for** $i = 0$ to $n - 1$ **do**
2:    $Q'_i \leftarrow F_i \cdot G_i$

3: **return** $(Q'_i)_{i \in [n]}$

To construct a multiplication gadget, the state-of-the-art gadget due to Seker, Fernandez-Rubio, Eisenbarth, and Steinwandt [SFRES18] also follows the general approach of Ben-Or, Goldwasser, and Wigderson: They first apply the share-wise multiplication (Alg. 2) to compute sharing of degree $2d$ and then reduce the degree back to d afterwards such that subsequent operations can be performed. However, the degree reduction is relatively expensive and complex. We will discuss this strategy in more depth in the following section, Sect. 4.1. But due to the need to store a polynomial of degree $2d$, their approach can not need less than $2d$ shares. Furthermore, they also need an additional e shares to handle faults. Our solution circumvents the need for this large number of shares. Section 4.2 presents a new compiler that needs at most $d + e + 1$ shares.

4.1 Fixed State-of-the-Art

Here, we give a more thorough explanation of the binary multiplication gadget construction due to Seker, Fernandez-Rubio, Eisenbarth, and Steinwandt [SFRES18]. We note here that this gadget can only handle *additive* faults.

Figure 1b illustrates the high-level idea of the gadget. It first performs the share-wise multiplication which outputs sharing $(Q'_i)_{i \in [n]}$ of degree $2d$ that encodes the product of the secrets of $(F_i)_{i \in [n]}$ and $(G_i)_{i \in [n]}$ and then reduces the degree of $(Q'_i)_{i \in [n]}$ such that $(Q_i)_{i \in [n]}$ carries the same secret as $(Q'_i)_{i \in [n]}$ but has degree d. This construction was proven to be d-SNI secure. As mentioned above, this multiplication leads to the intermediate $2d$ degree sharing $(Q'_i)_{i \in [n]}$ that requires $n = 2d + e + 1$ shares. To handle faults, the following idea is used: Any attacker that can add e additive faults to the shares adds a polynomial of degree at least $n - e = d + 1$ to the sharing. As a valid sharing has degree at most d, this means that the higher-order monomial $d + 1$ is set to a non-zero value iff a fault was added. These higher-order monomials are kept unchanged by share-wise additions and by careful design, are also kept unchanged with probability at least $1 - (1/q)$ in the multiplication gadget (or, more generally $1 - q^{-e+s-1}$ for $s \leq e$ faults). Unfortunately, their refresh gadget is not (S)NI, as shown in the full version, and an alternative refresh is required. We remark that such a refresh gadget can be seen as multiplication with a fresh sharing of the value 1. It is thus sufficient to focus on addition and multiplication gadgets here. We refer to [BBD+16] for more detailed explanations. The result by Seker, Fernandez-Rubio, Eisenbarth, and Steinwandt [SFRES18] can thus be summed up via the following informal theorem:

Theorem 7 (Fixed SotA). *For any $d, e \in \mathbb{N}$ there is a compiler that is given an arithmetic circuit $\mathcal{C}$ over $\mathbb{F}$ and outputs an arithmetic circuit $\mathcal{C}'$ on $\mathbb{F}^n$ where $n = 2d + e + 1$ with*

- *$\mathcal{C}'$ has the same functionality as $\mathcal{C}$*
- *$\mathcal{C}'$ is d-probing-secure,*
- *$\mathcal{C}'$ is e-fault-robust with respect to $\mathcal{F}^+$.*

The proof follows from [SFRES18] with the multiplication use as SNI refresh, and the compiler presented in [BBD+16]. The idea is that the multiplication and refresh gadgets are error preserving and d-SNI and the addition gadget is error preserving and d-NI. Applying the compiler of [BBD+16] results in a d-probing secure circuit with error preserving gadgets and, consequently, the compiler outputs an error preserving circuit that is information-theoretic secure against d probes.

4.2   LaOla Compiler

We improve our compiler in two steps. We first improve the (fr)SNI refresh, and we give a new multiplication gadget to reduce the number of shares from $2d + e + 1$ to $d + e + 1$.

Refresh. We construct a new SNI refresh gadget only using d^2 random values. Therefore, we transform this problem to a gadget that generates a zero encoding. Assuming a "secure" zero encoding $(e_i)_{i \in [n]} \leftarrow \mathsf{Enc}(0)$ it is easy to see that the refreshed output $(y_i)_{i \in [n]}$ of a sharing $(x_i)_{i \in [n]}$ with $y_i = x_i + e_i$ is SNI. Any probe y_i is uniform random, and only the (additional) internal probe e_i requires the input x_i for a perfect simulation. However, we still ignored the internal probes in $(e_i)_{i \in [n]} \leftarrow \mathsf{Enc}(0)$ to generate the zero encoding. **sZEnc** depicted in Algorithm 4 is such a gadget that is SNI secure even in the presence of internal probes and faults (Theorem 11).

Further, we can show that the resulting refresh gadget even gives region probing security (Theorem 12). Using our new refresh gadget we can improve the compiler of [SFRES18]. The improved compiler (Imp. SotA, listed in Table 3) requires less randomness and guarantees higher security due to region probing security.

Multiplication. In order to avoid the dependency on $2d$, a trivial (insecure) approach is to *switch* the order of operations: I.e., we first reduce the degree of the input shares $(G_i)_{i \in [n]}, (F_i)_{i \in [n]}$ to sharings $(G'_i)_{i \in [n]}, (F'_i)_{i \in [n]}$ of degree $d/2$. The output of the share-wise multiplication **SWMult**$((G'_i)_{i \in [n]}, (F'_i)_{i \in [n]})$ then has the right degree d again. However, it is easy to see that $(G'_i)_{i \in [n]}, (F'_i)_{i \in [n]}$ would reveal their secrets with $d/2 + 1 \leq d$ probes. Hence, this approach does not guarantee privacy against d probes.

While a naive implementation of this idea is insecure, our new construction depicted in Fig. 1a still guarantees security. Instead of performing a simple degree

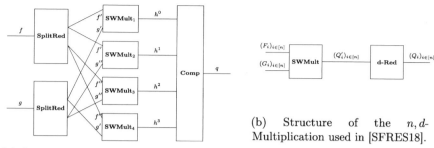

(a) Structure of the n, d-Multiplication defined in Algorithm 6

(b) Structure of the n, d-Multiplication used in [SFRES18].

Fig. 1: Our n, d-Multiplication and the multiplication in [SFRES18]

reduction, our gadget **SplitRed** *simultaneously* constructs an *additive* sharing of the polynomials. Hence, an application of **SplitRed** on an input sharing described by the polynomial f produces *two* polynomials f' and f'' both of degree d such that the polynomial $f' + f''$ has only degree $d/2$. In other words, we produce two polynomials f' and f'' where the coefficients of the monomials $x^0, x^1, \ldots x^{d/2}$ are additive sharings of the corresponding coefficients of f and the coefficients of the monomials $x^{d/2+1}, \ldots, x^d$ are additive sharings of the all-zero vector. We compute g' and g'' similarly such that each polynomial $f', f'',$ $g',$ and g'' considered individually is still a polynomial of degree d. Now we can apply the share-wise multiplication four times to compute $f' \cdot g', f' \cdot g'',$ $f'' \cdot g',$ and $f'' \cdot g''$ and sum all four outputs with our gadget **Comp**. It follows that the output $(H_i)_{i \in [n]}$ describes a polynomial h of degree d again because $f' \cdot g' + f' \cdot g'' + f'' \cdot g' + f'' \cdot g'' = (f' + f'') \cdot (g' + g'')$ is again a polynomial of degree d. The formal description of the algorithm is given in Sect. 6 and the full version provides a detailed security analysis against probes and faults.

Compiler The multiplication, and refresh, together with the share-wise addition, lead to a compiler using only $n = d + e + 1$ shares against additive faults.

Theorem 8 (laOla (additive)). *For any $d, e \in \mathbb{N}$ there is a circuit compiler that is given an arithmetic circuit $\mathcal{C}$ over $\mathbb{F}$ and outputs an arithmetic circuit $\mathcal{C}'$ over $\mathbb{F}^n$ where $n = d + e + 1$ with*

- *$\mathcal{C}'$ has the same functionality as $\mathcal{C}$,*
- *$T[\mathcal{C}']$ is probing secure for any $T \in \mathsf{A}(\mathcal{F}^+)$ and*
  (i) up to d probes in $T[\mathcal{C}']$ (threshold probing security), or
  (ii) up to $d/2$ probes in every gadget of $T[\mathcal{C}']$ (region probing security).
- *$\mathcal{C}'$ is e-fault-robust with respect to $\mathcal{F}^+$.*

Furthermore, we also show that our approach can handle more general faults, although this comes at the cost of needing more shares.

Theorem 9 (laOla-Compiler (general)). *For any $d, e \in \mathbb{N}$ there is a circuit compiler that is given an arithmetic circuit $\mathcal{C}$ over $\mathbb{F}$ and outputs an arithmetic circuit $\mathcal{C}'$ over $\mathbb{F}^n$ where $n = d + e + 1$ with*

- *$\mathcal{C}'$ has the same functionality as $\mathcal{C}$,*
- *$T[\mathcal{C}']$ is probing secure for any $T \in \mathsf{A}(\mathcal{F}^+)$ with $|T| \leq e$ and*
  - *(i) up to $d - e$ probes in $T[\mathcal{C}']$ (threshold probing security), or*
  - *(ii) with up to $d/2$ probes in every gadget of $T[\mathcal{C}']$ when the faults are counted as probes (region probing security).*
- *$T[\mathcal{C}']$ is $d - e$ probing secure for any $T \in \mathsf{A}(\mathcal{F}^{ind})$ with $|T| \leq e$,*
- *$\mathcal{C}'$ is e-fault-robust with respect to $\mathcal{F}^{ind}$.*

In both cases, Theorem 5 implies q^{s-e-1}-security against (d, s)-attackers.

Table 3: A concrete comparison with the compiler [SFRES18] fixed in this work, the constuction in [DN19], and our new compiler.

Compiler	# Shares	Randomness Cost		Comb. Sec. in the Reg	Opt. for affine
		Mult. Gadget	SNI Refresh	Prob. Model	Circuits
[DN19]	$d+e+1$	$\Theta(n^3)$	$\Theta(n^3)$	✘	✔
Fixed SotA [SFRES18]	$2d+e+1$	$2d^2 + d(e+1)$	$2d^2 + d(e+1)$	✘	✘
Imp. SotA[This Work]	$2d+e+1$	$2d^2 + d(e+1)$	d^2	(✔)	✘
laOla [This Work]	$d+e+1$	$3d^2 + 2d(e+1)$	d^2	✔	✔

In the full version, we also prove that our compiler is optimal for affine circuits and it is inherently impossible to use a lower number of shares.

Theorem 10. *The number of shares n of any sharing procedure that protects against d probes and e faults is at least $n \geq d + e + 1$.*

5   Refresh Gadget

To construct a refresh gadget with input sharing $(x_i)_{i \in [n]}$ it is sufficient to generate a zero encoding $(e_i)_{i \in [n]}$ and output its sum $(y_i)_{i \in [n]} = (x_i)_{i \in [n]} + (e_i)_{i \in [n]}$. In this section we give two different gadgets to generate zero encodings. The first one is sufficient to inject randomness in our multiplication gadget. The latter gadget uses the weaker one and results in a d-SNI refresh gadget. Further we show that the gadget is even stronger, and we can use it to transform our d-probing secure circuit into a $d/2$-region-probing secure circuit.

ZEroenc *Gadget.* The gadget **ZEnc** depicted in Algorithm 3 generates a random zero encoding. We use the polynomial representation to describe the high level idea of the gadget. Since g is a random polynomial with $g(0) = 0$, it holds $g(x) = \sum_{i=1}^{d} r_j x^j$ with $r_1, r_2, \ldots r_d \in \mathbb{F}$. Our gadget generates such polynomials by choosing each r_i uniform at random and outputs g. More precisely, we use the polynomial masking where each polynomial is described by n points $g(\alpha_0), g(\alpha_1), \ldots g(\alpha_{n-1})$. Therefore, the algorithm does not compute $g(x)$ but each $g(\alpha_i) = \sum_{i=1}^{d} r_j \alpha_i$, separately. Hence, the final output of Algorithm 3 represent an encoding of zero with $(g_i)_{i \in [n]} := (g(\alpha_i))_{i \in [n]}$.

Algorithm 3 $\mathbf{ZEnc}_n^d$

Output: A randomized (n, d)-Encoding of zero $(g_i)_{i \in [n]}$.

1: **for** $j = 1$ **to** d **do**
2:      $r_j \leftarrow_\$ \mathbb{F}$
3:      **for** $i = 0$ **to** $n - 1$ **do**
4:          $g_{i+1} \leftarrow g_i \oplus r_j \alpha_i^j$
5: **return** $(g_i)_{i \in [n]}$

In the full version, we show that this encoding does not suffice for an SNI refresh. However, next we show how to use **ZEnc** to construct an SNI secure refresh.

sZEroenc *Gadget.* The gadget **sZEnc** depicted in Algorithm 4 generates a zero encoding because the sum of zero encodings is a zero encoding again.

Algorithm 4 $\mathbf{sZEnc}_n^d$

Output: A randomized (n, d)-Encoding of zero $(g_i)_{i \in [n]}$.

1: **for** $j = 0$ **to** d **do**
2:      $(g_i)_{i \in [n]} \leftarrow \mathbf{ZEnc}_n^d$
3:      $(y_i)_{i \in [n]} \leftarrow (y_i)_{i \in [n]} + (g_i)_{i \in [n]}$
4: **return** $(y_i)_{i \in [n]}$

Lemma 3 (Probing security). *For any set P with $d' \leq d$ probes it holds for $(e_i)_{i \in [n]} \leftarrow \mathbf{sZEnc}_n^d$: There is a sub set $A \subset [n]$ with $|A| = n - d'$ such that*

(i) $(e_i)_{i \in A}$ are still $(d - d')$-wise independent, independent from P and $(e_i)_{i \in [n] \setminus A}$,
(ii) P can be perfectly simulated with $(e_i)_{i \in [n] \setminus A}$

The proof is given in the full version. It is easy to see that a gadget with input sharing $(x_i)_{i \in [n]}$ and output sharing $(x_i + e_i)_{i \in [n]}$ with $(e_i)_{i \in [n]} \leftarrow \mathbf{sZEnc}_n^d$ is an SNI refresh:

Theorem 11 (Refresh). *The gadget G'_G (Alg. 5) with identity G is a d-frSNI w.r.t. $\mathcal{F}^+$ (or d-wfrSNI w.r.t. $\mathcal{F}^{ind}$) and e-fault-robust w.r.t. $\mathcal{F}^{ind}$ refresh gadget*

Proof. In the full version we give a detailed proof for fault-robustness, SNI and fault-invariance w.r.t. $\mathcal{F}^+$. With Theorem 1 we get frSNI, and with Theorem 2 follows wfrSNI.   □

Algorithm 5 G'_G with $n \geq d + e + 1$

Input: The same input sharings as G. E.g., $(x_i)_{i \in [n]}$ and $(x'_i)_{i \in [n]}$, or only $(x_i)_{i \in [n]}$.
Output: A randomized output of $\mathsf{G}((x_i)_{i \in [n]}, (x'_i)_{i \in [n]})$ (or $\mathsf{G}((x_i)_{i \in [n]})$).

1: $(e_i)_{i \in [n]} \leftarrow \mathbf{sZEnc}_n^d$
2: $(y'_i)_{i \in [n]} \leftarrow \mathsf{G}((x_i)_{i \in [n]}, (x'_i)_{i \in [n]})$ (or $(y'_i)_{i \in [n]} \leftarrow \mathsf{G}((x_i)_{i \in [n]})$)
3: $(y_i)_{i \in [n]} \leftarrow (y'_i)_{i \in [n]} + (e_i)_{i \in [n]}$
4: **return** $(y_i)_{i \in [n]}$

However, this refresh gadget is even more secure. Next, we show how to construct a region-probing secure compiler with the gadget depicted in Algorithm 5.

Theorem 12. *A d probing secure composition with d-NI and d-SNI secure gadgets G_i is $d/2$ region probing secure if each gadget is transformed into G'_G (Alg. 5), and outputs refreshed sharings.*

It immediately follows from Lemma 3, and the detailed proof is given in the full version. Assuming a (w)frSNI and error preserving multiplication, this theorem directly implies both Theorem 8 and Theorem 9. Using Theorem 5 then implies q^{s-e-1}-security against (d, s)-attackers. Next, we give our frSNI and error preserving multiplication gadget only using $n = d + e + 1$ shares.

6 Multiplication Gadget

In this section we introduce our new improved gadget which securely performs a masked multiplication on a polynomial sharing with just $n = d + e + 1$ shares, whereas the state-of-the-art requires $2d + e + 1$ shares.

6.1 Concept and Overview

In the following we formally introduce the new multiplication gadget depicted in Fig. 1a, its formal description is given in Algorithm 6.

For a better intuition of the gadget **Mult** with inputs $(F_i)_{i \in [n]}$ and $(G_i)_{i \in [n]}$, we use the polynomial representation f and g such that $f(\alpha_i) = F_i$ and $g(\alpha_i) = G_i$. As depicted in Fig. 1a, the gadget **SplitRed** first splits the inputs g and f with secrets $f(0) = f_0$ and $g(0) = g_0$ into polynomials f', f'', g', and g'' such that each polynomial is uniform random with degree d but $f' + f'$ and $g' + g''$ have degree $\frac{d}{2}$ each and, furthermore, $f'(0) + f'(0) = f_0$ and $g'(0) + g'(0) = g_0$. This allows to avoid the intermediate polynomials that require $2d$ shares. Furthermore, we can use $\mathbf{SWMult}_i$ to compute<s the four polynomials $h^0(x) = f'(x)g'(x)$, $h^1(x) = f'(x)g''(x)$, $h^2(x) = f''(x)g'(x)$, and $h^3(x) = f''(x)g''(x)$. The last gadget $\mathbf{Comp}$ refreshes the polynomials and sums them up into $f'(x)g'(x) + f'(x)g''(x) + f''(x)g'(x) + f''(x)g''(x)$. The sum results in a polynomial $q(x)$ with $(Q_i)_{i \in [n]} = q(\alpha_i)$ which encodes the correct value $q(0) = f_0 \cdot g_0$, as

$$q(0) = f'(0) \cdot g'(0) + f'(0) \cdot g''(0) + f''(0) \cdot g'(0) + f''(0) \cdot g''(0)$$
$$= (f'(0) + f''(0)) \cdot (g'(0) + g''(0)) = g(0) \cdot f(0).$$

The next sections introduce the sub-gadgets $\mathbf{SplitRed}$ (Sect. 6.2), $\mathbf{SWMult}$, and $\mathbf{Comp}$ (Sect.6.3) needed for our multiplication gadget.

Algorithm 6 $(n, d) - \mathbf{Mult}$

Input: Shares of f_0 as $(F_i)_{0 \leq i < n}$ and shares of g_0 as $(G_i)_{0 \leq i < n}$.
Output: Shares of $f_0 g_0$ as $(Q_i)_{0 \leq i < n}$.

1: $\left((F_i')_{i \in [n]}, (F_i'')_{i \in [n]}\right) \leftarrow \mathbf{SplitRed}((F_i)_{i \in [n]})$
2: $\left((G_i')_{i \in [n]}, (G_i'')_{i \in [n]}\right) \leftarrow \mathbf{SplitRed}((G_i)_{i \in [n]})$

3: $(H_i^0)_{i \in [n]} \leftarrow \mathbf{SWMult}((F_i')_{i \in [n]}, (G_i')_{i \in [n]})$
4: $(H_i^1)_{i \in [n]} \leftarrow \mathbf{SWMult}((F_i')_{i \in [n]}, (G_i'')_{i \in [n]})$
5: $(H_i^2)_{i \in [n]} \leftarrow \mathbf{SWMult}((F_i'')_{i \in [n]}, (G_i')_{i \in [n]})$
6: $(H_i^3)_{i \in [n]} \leftarrow \mathbf{SWMult}((F_i'')_{i \in [n]}, (G_i'')_{i \in [n]})$

7: $(Q_i)_{i \in [n]} \leftarrow \mathbf{Comp}((H_i^0)_{i \in [n]}, (H_i^1)_{i \in [n]}, (H_i^2)_{i \in [n]}, (H_i^3)_{i \in [n]})$

8: **return** $(Q_i)_{i \in [n]}$

6.2   SplitRedGadget

The general idea of $\mathbf{SplitRed}$-LAOLA is best understood in the polynomial representation, on which we focus here. We are given a sharing $(F_i)_{i \in [n]}$ of a polynomial $f = \sum_i f_i x^i$, where f_0 encodes the sensitive information. We now want to split f into two polynomials f' and f''. To understand the general idea behind the algorithm, we will first focus on the case that no faults are present and later show how to adapt to faults. In this scenario, we aim for the following two properties.

(*) The sum of the sensitive information of f' and f'' is an *additive* sharing of the sensitive information of f, i.e., $(f' + f'')_0 = f_0$ (which is the *split* part of the gadget).
(**) The degrees of both f' and f'' are equal to $d = \deg(f)$, but the degree of the sum $f' + f''$ is only equal to $\frac{d}{2}$ (which is the *reduce* part of the gadget).

To obtain these properties, we proceed roughly as follows:
   (i) We generate a random polynomial $g = \sum_i g_i x^i$ of degree d with $g_0 = 0$, i.e., all coefficients g_i are drawn uniformly at random for $i > 0$.

(ii) We generate another polynomial $g' = \sum_i g'_i x^i$ of degree d with $g'_0 = 0$. For $i \in [1, \frac{d}{2}]$, the coefficients g'_i are drawn uniformly at random. For $i > \frac{d}{2}$, we set $g'_i = -g_i$. This means that $\deg(g) = \deg(g') = d$, but $\deg(g + g') = \frac{d}{2}$.

(iii) Now, the second property (**) is fulfilled, but we still need to share the sensitive information of f into g and g'. Now, remember that share j holds the value $f(\alpha_j)$. We now set $g_0 = \sum_{j<n/2} \lambda_j^{(0)} f(\alpha_j)$ and $g'_0 = \sum_{j \geq n/2} \lambda_j^{(0)} f(\alpha_j)$. The interpolation lemma then implies the correctness, as $g_0 + g'_0 = \sum_j \lambda_j^{(0)} f(\alpha_j) = f(0) = f_0$.

While the correctness of this idea directly follows from the interpolation lemma, we need to be careful to secure the algorithm against both probes and faults. To obtain probing security, we simply need to generate more random polynomials and include the values $\lambda_j^{(0)} f(\alpha_j)$ more carefully over time. More concretely, for $j = 1, \ldots, n/2$, we first generate random polynomials $\hat{g}^{(j)}$ of degree d (with absolute term 0), and for $j = 1, \ldots, n$, we first generate random polynomials $\tilde{g}^{(j)}$ of degree $\frac{d}{2}$ (with absolute term 0). For $j < n/2$, we compute $g^{(j)} = \tilde{g}^{(j)} + \hat{g}^{(j)}$ and for $j \geq n/2$, we compute $g^{(j)} = \tilde{g}^{(j)} - \hat{g}^{(j-n/2)}$. Then, for $j = 1, \ldots, n$, we set $g^{(j)} = g^{(j)} + \lambda_j^{(0)} f(\alpha_j)$ and finally, obtain $f' = \sum_{j<n/2} g^{(j)}$ and $f'' = \sum_{j \geq n/2} g^{(j)}$. A careful inspection of the construction shows that the sensitive information is always sufficiently hidden against up to d probes.

To handle faults, we need to make sure that the error coefficients of f are also preserved. To do so, we do not only incorporate the terms $\lambda_j^{(0)} f(\alpha_j)$, but the term $\left(\lambda_j^{(0)} + \sum_{k>d} \lambda_j^{(k)} \alpha_i^k \right) f(\alpha_j)$, which we will denote by $\hat{\lambda}_j^{(i)} \cdot f(\alpha_j)$ in the following. Note that the interpolation lemma implies that $\sum_j \sum_i \hat{\lambda}_j^{(i)} f(\alpha_j) = f_0 + \sum_{k>d} f_k x^k$.

We show in the full version that **SplitRed** is d-NI and transfers faults from its inputs to the output.

6.3   Share-wise Multiplication and Compression Gadgets

The share-wise multiplication **SWMult** (Algorithm 2) works similar to the addition. Remember that **SplitRed** shares two polynomials $f(x)$ and $g(x)$ into $f'(x)$, $f''(x)$, $g'(x)$, and $g''(x)$ such that for $\tilde{f}(x) = f'(x) + f''(x)$ and $\tilde{g}(x) = g'(x) + g''(x)$ it holds $\tilde{f}(x)$ and $\tilde{g}(x)$ have degree $\frac{d}{2}$ and $f(0) = \tilde{f}(0)$, $g(0) = \tilde{g}(0)$. The share-wise multiplication now might lead to degrees larger than d when they compute $h^0(x) = f'(x) \cdot g'(x)$, $h^1(x) = f'(x) \cdot g''(x)$, $h^2(x) = f''(x) \cdot g'(x)$, $h^3(x) = f''(x) \cdot g''(x)$, but the final gadget **Comp** sums up all h^i and this results into a polynomial $\sum_{i=0}^3 h^i$ with degree d. This follows from the fact that we can alternatively write $\sum_{i=0}^3 h^i(x) = (f'(x) + f''(x)) \cdot (g'(x) + g''(x)) = \tilde{f}(x) \cdot \tilde{g}(x)$. Since $\tilde{f}(x)$ and $\tilde{g}(x)$ have degree $\frac{d}{2}$, the product $\tilde{f}(x) \cdot \tilde{g}(x)$ has degree d. Hence the sum of the h^i results in a degree d polynomial with secret $f_0 \cdot g_0$. Note that we also add an encoding of zero in **Comp** to re-randomize the values, but this does not change the correctness of the gadget. We show in the full version that

Algorithm 7 (n, d)-**SplitRed** for $n = d + \epsilon + 1$.

Input: Shares of f_0 as $(F_i)_{i \in [n]}$.
Output: Shares of f_0' as $(F'_i)_{i \in [n]}$ and shares of f_0'' as $(F''_i)_{i \in [n]}$, such that $f_0 = f_0' + f_0''$.

1: **for** $j \in [\frac{n}{2}]$ **do**
2:     $(\hat{g}_i^j)_{i \in [n]} \leftarrow \mathbf{ZEnc}_n^d$

3: **for** $j \in [\frac{n}{2}]$ **do**
4:     $(\tilde{g}_i^j)_{i \in [n]} \leftarrow \mathbf{ZEnc}_n^{\frac{d}{2}}$
5:     $(g_i^j)_{i \in [n]} \leftarrow (\tilde{g}_i^j)_{i \in [n]} + (\hat{g}_i^j)_{i \in [n]}$

6: **for** $j \in [\frac{n}{2}]$ **do**
7:     **for** $i \in [n]$ **do**
8:         $\mathcal{F}_i'^j \leftarrow \hat{\lambda}_j^i \cdot F_j$

9: **for** $j \in [\frac{n}{2}]$ **do**
10:     $(\mathcal{F}_i^j)_{i \in [n]} \leftarrow (\mathcal{F}_i'^j)_{i \in [n]} + (g_i^j)_{i \in [n]}$

11: **for** $j \in [\frac{n}{2}]$ **do**
12:     $(F'_i)_{i \in [n]} \leftarrow (F'_i)_{i \in [n]} + (\mathcal{F}_i^j)_{i \in [n]}$

13: **for** $j \in [\frac{n}{2}]$ **do**
14:     $(\tilde{g}_i^{j + \frac{n}{2}})_{i \in [n]} \leftarrow \mathbf{ZEnc}_n^{\frac{d}{2}}$
15:     $(g_i^{j + \frac{n}{2}})_{i \in [n]} \leftarrow (\tilde{g}_i^j)_{i \in [n]} - (\hat{g}_i^j)_{i \in [n]}$

16: **for** $j \in [\frac{n}{2}]$ **do**
17:     **for** $i \in [n]$ **do**
18:         $\mathcal{F}_i'^{j + \frac{n}{2}} \leftarrow \hat{\lambda}_{j + \frac{n}{2}}^i \cdot F_{j + \frac{n}{2}}$

19: **for** $j \in [\frac{n}{2}]$ **do**
20:     $(\mathcal{F}_i^{j + \frac{n}{2}})_{i \in [n]} \leftarrow (\mathcal{F}_i'^{j + \frac{n}{2}})_{i \in [n]} + (g_i^{j + \frac{n}{2}})_{i \in [n]}$

21: **for** $j \in [\frac{n}{2}]$ **do**
22:     $(F''_i)_{i \in [n]} \leftarrow (F''_i)_{i \in [n]} + (\mathcal{F}_i^{j + \frac{n}{2}})_{i \in [n]}$

23: **return** $(F'_i)_{i \in [n]}, (F''_i)_{i \in [n]}$

---

all values of **Comp** can be simulated from a few inputs and both **SWMult** and **Comp** transfer faults from their inputs to their outputs.

Algorithm 8 Comp for $n = d + \epsilon + 1$

Input: 4 Sharings $(H_i^j)_{i \in [n]}$ of h^j
Output: Sharing $(Q_i)_{i \in [n]}$ with $h^0 + h^1 + h^2 + h^3$

1: $(Q_i)_{i \in [n]} \leftarrow \mathbf{sZEnc}_n^d$
2: $(Q_i)_{i \in [n]} \leftarrow [[[(Q_i)_{i \in [n]} + (H_i^0)_{i \in [n]}] + (H_i^1)_{i \in [n]}] + (H_i^2)_{i \in [n]}] + (H_i^3)_{i \in [n]}$
3: **return** $(Q_i)_{i \in [n]}$

6.4   Security Analysis of the Multiplication Gadget

In this section we show that the multiplication **Mult** is frSNI and e-fault-robust. Corollary 1 shows that SNI and fault-invariance implies frSNI. Due to space constraints, all security proofs can be found in the full version.

Theorem 13. *The multiplication gadget **Mult** depicted in Algorithm 6 is d-fr(S)NI with respect to $\mathcal{F}^+$ or (d-wfr(S)NI with respect to $\mathcal{F}^{ind}$) and e-fault-robust with respect to $\mathcal{F}^{ind}$.*

Proof (sketch). In the full version we prove e-fault-robustness with respect to $\mathcal{F}^{ind}$. It remains to prove the frSNI property. Due to Corollary 1, it is sufficient to show that the multiplication gadget is SNI and fault invariant with respect to $\mathcal{F}^+$ because this implies d-frSNI with respect to $\mathcal{F}^+$. Further, Corollary 2 shows that this also implies d-wfrSNI with respect to $\mathcal{F}^{ind}$. Hence, it remains to prove that the gadget **Mult** is (i) SNI and (ii) fault invariant with respect to $\mathcal{F}^+$.

(i) In the full version we first analyze the different subroutines of **Mult** separately. Combining these results shows that the complete gadget is t-SNI.
(ii) The proof is similar to the fault-invariance proof of linear gadgets. The only difference is that the gadget has (only) one non-linear layer – the share-wise multiplication. The idea is that all faults before the non-linear layer can be moved to the inputs, and the faults after the non-liner layer can be moved to the outputs.

Acknowledgment. This work was partly supported by the German Research Foundation (DFG) via the DFG CRC 1119 CROSSING (project S7), by the German Federal Ministry of Education and Research (BMBF) and the Hessen State Ministry for Higher Education, Research and the Arts within their joint support of the National Research Center for Applied Cybersecurity ATHENE, and by the European Commission(ERCEA), ERC Grant Agreement 101044770 CRYPTOLAYER. This work has been partially supported by BMBF through the VE-Jupiter project. We thank the anonymous reviewers for the helpful support.

References

[AAB+20] Aly, A., Ashur, T., Ben-Sasson, E., Dhooghe, S., Szepieniec, A.: Design of symmetric-key primitives for advanced cryptographic protocols. IACR Trans. Symm. Cryptol. **2020**(3), 1–45 (2020)

[ADF16] Andrychowicz, M., Dziembowski, S., Faust, S.: Circuit compilers with $O(1/\log(n))$ leakage rate. In: Fischlin, M., Coron, J.-S. (eds.) EUROCRYPT 2016. Part II, volume 9666 of LNCS, pp. 586–615. Springer, Heidelberg (2016). https://doi.org/10.1007/978-3-662-49896-5_21

[AGR+16] Albrecht, M., Grassi, L., Rechberger, C., Roy, A., Tiessen, T.: MiMC: efficient encryption and cryptographic hashing with minimal multiplicative complexity. In: Cheon, J.H., Takagi, T. (eds.) ASIACRYPT 2016. LNCS, vol. 10031, pp. 191–219. Springer, Heidelberg (2016). https://doi.org/10.1007/978-3-662-53887-6_7

[ARS+15] Albrecht, M.R., Rechberger, C., Schneider, T., Tiessen, T., Zohner, M.:
          Ciphers for MPC and FHE. In: Oswald, E., Fischlin, M. (eds.) EURO-
          CRYPT 2015. LNCS, vol. 9056, pp. 430–454. Springer, Heidelberg (2015).
          https://doi.org/10.1007/978-3-662-46800-5_17

[BBD+15] Barthe, G., Belaïd, S., Dupressoir, F., Fouque, P.-A., Grégoire, B., Strub,
          P.-Y.: Verified proofs of higher-order masking. In: Oswald, E., Fischlin,
          M. (eds.) EUROCRYPT 2015. LNCS, vol. 9056, pp. 457–485. Springer,
          Heidelberg (2015). https://doi.org/10.1007/978-3-662-46800-5_18

[BBD+16] Barthe, G.: Strong non-interference and type-directed higher-order mask-
          ing. In: Weippl, E.R., Katzenbeisser, S., Kruegel, C., Myers, A.C., Halevi,
          S., (eds.) ACM CCS 2016, pp. 116–129. ACM Press (October 2016)

[BCPZ16] Battistello, A., Coron, J.-S., Prouff, E., Zeitoun, R.: Horizontal side-
          channel attacks and countermeasures on the ISW masking scheme. In:
          Gierlichs, B., Poschmann, A.Y. (eds.) CHES 2016. LNCS, vol. 9813, pp. 23–
          39. Springer, Heidelberg (2016). https://doi.org/10.1007/978-3-662-53140-
          2_2

[BDPA13] Bertoni, G., Daemen, J., Peeters, M., Van Assche, G.: Keccak. In: Johans-
          son, T., Nguyen, P.Q. (eds.) EUROCRYPT 2013. LNCS, vol. 7881, pp.
          313–314. Springer, Heidelberg (2013). https://doi.org/10.1007/978-3-642-
          38348-9_19

[BGW88]   Ben-Or, M., Goldwasser, S., Wigderson, A.: Completeness theorems
          for non-cryptographic fault-tolerant distributed computation (extended
          abstract). In: 20th ACM STOC, pp. 1–10. ACM Press (May 1988)

[BS97]   Biham, E., Shamir, A.: Differential fault analysis of secret key cryptosys-
          tems. In: Kaliski, B.S. (ed.) CRYPTO 1997. LNCS, vol. 1294, pp. 513–525.
          Springer, Heidelberg (1997). https://doi.org/10.1007/BFb0052259

[BS21]   Bronchain, O., Standaert, F.X.: Breaking masked implementations with
          many shares on 32-bit software platforms. IACR TCHES 2021(3), 202–
          234 (2021). https://tches.iacr.org/index.php/TCHES/article/view/8973

[CFG+10] Clavier, C., Feix, B., Gagnerot, G., Roussellet, M., Verneuil, V.: Horizontal
          correlation analysis on exponentiation. In: Soriano, M., Qing, S., López, J.
          (eds.) ICICS 10. LNCS, vol. 6476, pp. 46–61. Springer, Heidelberg (2010).
          https://doi.org/10.1007/978-3-642-17650-0_5

[Cla07]   Clavier, C.: Secret external encodings do not prevent transient fault anal-
          ysis. In: Paillier, P., Verbauwhede, I. (eds.) CHES 2007. LNCS, vol. 4727,
          pp. 181–194. Springer, Heidelberg (2007). https://doi.org/10.1007/978-3-
          540-74735-2_13

[CN16]   De Cnudde, T., Nikova, S.: More efficient private circuits II through thresh-
          old implementations. In: FDTC 2016, pp. 114–124. IEEE Computer Society
          (2016)

[CPR12]   Coron, J.-S., Prouff, E., Roche, T.: On the use of shamir's secret sharing
          against side-channel analysis. In: Mangard, S. (ed.) CARDIS 2012. LNCS,
          vol. 7771, pp. 77–90. Springer, Heidelberg (2013). https://doi.org/10.1007/
          978-3-642-37288-9_6

[CS20]   Cassiers, G., Standaert, F.-X.: Trivially and efficiently composing masked
          gadgets with probe isolating non-interference. IEEE Trans. Inf. Forensics
          Secur. 15, 2542–2555 (2020)

[DDF14]   Duc, A., Dziembowski, S., Faust, S.: Unifying leakage models: from probing
          attacks to noisy leakage. In: Nguyen, P.Q., Oswald, E. (eds.) EUROCRYPT
          2014. LNCS, vol. 8441, pp. 423–440. Springer, Heidelberg (2014). https://
          doi.org/10.1007/978-3-642-55220-5_24

[DEK+18] Dobraunig, C., Eichlseder, M., Korak, T., Mangard, S., Mendel, F., Primas, R.: SIFA: Exploiting ineffective fault inductions on symmetric cryptography. IACR TCHES **2018**(3), 547–572 (2018). https://tches.iacr.org/index.php/TCHES/article/view/7286

[DN19] Dhooghe, S., Nikova, S.: My gadget just cares for me - how NINA can prove security against combined attacks. Cryptology ePrint Archive, Report 2019/615 (2019). https://eprint.iacr.org/2019/615

[DN20a] Dhooghe, S., Nikova, S.: Let's tessellate: tiling for security against advanced probe and fault adversaries. In: Liardet, P.-Y., Mentens, N. (eds.) CARDIS 2020. LNCS, vol. 12609, pp. 181–195. Springer, Cham (2021). https://doi.org/10.1007/978-3-030-68487-7_12

[DN20b] Dhooghe, S., Nikova, S.: My gadget just cares for me - how NINA can prove security against combined attacks. In: Jarecki, S. (ed.) CT-RSA 2020. LNCS, vol. 12006, pp. 35–55. Springer, Heidelberg (2020). https://doi.org/10.1007/978-3-030-40186-3_3

[FRSG22] Feldtkeller, J., Richter-Brockmann, J., Sasdrich, P., Güneysu, T.: CINI MINIS: domain isolation for fault and combined security. In: CCS, pp. 1023–1036. ACM (2022)

[GKR+21] Grassi, L., Khovratovich, D., Rechberger, C., Roy, A., Schofnegger, M.: Poseidon: A new hash function for zero-knowledge proof systems. In: Bailey, M., Greenstadt, R., (eds.) USENIX Security 2021, pp. 519–535. USENIX Association (August 2021)

[GLR+20] Grassi, L., Lüftenegger, R., Rechberger, C., Rotaru, D., Schofnegger, M.: On a generalization of substitution-permutation networks: The HADES design strategy. In: Canteaut, A., Ishai, Y. (eds.) EUROCRYPT 2020. LNCS, vol. 12106, pp. 674–704. Springer, Cham (2020). https://doi.org/10.1007/978-3-030-45724-2_23

[GM11] Goubin, L., Martinelli, A.: Protecting AES with shamir's secret sharing scheme. In: Preneel, B., Takagi, T. (eds.) CHES 2011. LNCS, vol. 6917, pp. 79–94. Springer, Heidelberg (2011). https://doi.org/10.1007/978-3-642-23951-9_6

[GPRV21] Goudarzi, D., Prest, T., Rivain, M., Vergnaud, D.: Probing security through input-output separation and revisited quasilinear masking. IACR Trans. Cryptogr. Hardw. Embed. Syst. **2021**(3), 599–640 (2021)

[HKL+22] Ha, J., Kim, S., Lee, B., Lee, J., Son, M.: Rubato: Noisy ciphers for approximate homomorphic encryption. In: Dunkelman, O., Dziembowski, S., (eds) EUROCRYPT 2022, Part I. LNCS, vol. 13275, pp. 581–610. Springer, Heidelberg (May/June 2022). https://doi.org/10.1007/978-3-031-06944-4_20

[IPSW06] Ishai, Y., Prabhakaran, M., Sahai, A., Wagner, D.: Private Circuits II: keeping secrets in tamperable circuits. In: Vaudenay, S. (ed.) EUROCRYPT 2006. LNCS, vol. 4004, pp. 308–327. Springer, Heidelberg (2006). https://doi.org/10.1007/11761679_19

[ISW03] Ishai, Y., Sahai, A., Wagner, D.: Private circuits: securing hardware against probing attacks. In: Boneh, D. (ed.) CRYPTO 2003. LNCS, vol. 2729, pp. 463–481. Springer, Heidelberg (2003). https://doi.org/10.1007/978-3-540-45146-4_27

[LFZD14] Luo, P., Fei, Y., Zhang, L., Ding, A.A.: Side-channel power analysis of different protection schemes against fault attacks on AES. In: ReConFig 2014, pp. 1–6. IEEE (2014)

[ORSW12] Oren, Y., Renauld, M., Standaert, F.-X., Wool, A.: Algebraic side-channel attacks beyond the hamming weight leakage model. In: Prouff, E., Schaumont, P. (eds.) CHES 2012. LNCS, vol. 7428, pp. 140–154. Springer, Heidelberg (2012). https://doi.org/10.1007/978-3-642-33027-8_9

[RDB+18] Reparaz, O., De Meyer, L., Bilgin, B., Arribas, V., Nikova, S., Nikov, V., Smart, N.P.: CAPA: The spirit of beaver against physical attacks. In: Shacham, H., Boldyreva, A. (eds.) CRYPTO 2018. Part I, volume 10991 of LNCS, pp. 121–151. Springer, Heidelberg (2018). https://doi.org/10.1007/978-3-319-96884-1_5

[REB+08] Regazzoni, F., Eisenbarth, T., Breveglieri, L., Ienne, P., Koren, I.: Can knowledge regarding the presence of countermeasures against fault attacks simplify power attacks on cryptographic devices? In: Bolchini, C., Kim, Y.-B., Gizopoulos, D., Tehranipoor, M., (eds.) DFT 2008, pp. 202–210. IEEE Computer Society (2008)

[RFSG22] Richter-Brockmann, J., Feldtkeller, J., Sasdrich, P., Güneysu, T.: VERICA - verification of combined attacks automated formal verification of security against simultaneous information leakage and tampering. IACR Trans. Cryptogr. Hardw. Embed. Syst. 2022(4), 255–284 (2022)

[RP12] Roche, T., Prouff, E.: Higher-order glitch free implementation of the AES using secure multi-party computation protocols - extended version. J. Cryptogr. Eng. 2(2), 111–127 (2012)

[SFRES18] Seker, O., Fernandez-Rubio, A., Eisenbarth, T., Steinwandt, R.: Extending glitch-free multiparty protocols to resist fault injection attacks. IACR TCHES 2018(3), 394–430 (2018). https://tches.iacr.org/index.php/TCHES/article/view/7281

[SMG16] Schneider, T., Moradi, A., Güneysu, T.: ParTI – towards combined hardware countermeasures against side-channel and fault-injection attacks. In: Robshaw, M., Katz, J. (eds.) CRYPTO 2016. LNCS, vol. 9815, pp. 302–332. Springer, Heidelberg (2016). https://doi.org/10.1007/978-3-662-53008-5_11

[VGS14] Veyrat-Charvillon, N., Gérard, B., Standaert, F.-X.: Soft analytical side-channel attacks. In: Sarkar, P., Iwata, T. (eds.) ASIACRYPT 2014. LNCS, vol. 8873, pp. 282–296. Springer, Heidelberg (2014). https://doi.org/10.1007/978-3-662-45611-8_15

Learning with Physical Rounding for Linear and Quadratic Leakage Functions

Clément Hoffmann[1], Pierrick Méaux[2(✉)], Charles Momin[1], Yann Rotella[3], François-Xavier Standaert[1], and Balazs Udvarhelyi[1]

[1] Crypto Group, ICTEAM Institute, UCLouvain, Louvain-la-Neuve, Belgium
fstandae@uclouvain.be
[2] Luxembourg University, SnT, Esch-sur-Alzette, Luxembourg
pierrick.meaux@uni.lu
[3] Université Paris-Saclay, UVSQ, CNRS, Laboratoire de mathématiques de Versailles, 78000 Versailles, France

Abstract. Fresh re-keying is a countermeasure against side-channel analysis where an ephemeral key is derived from a long-term key using a public random value. Popular instances of such schemes rely on key-homomorphic primitives, so that the re-keying process is easy to mask and the rest of the (e.g., block cipher) computations can run with cheaper countermeasures. The main requirement for these schemes to be secure is that the leakages of the ephemeral keys do not allow recovering the long-term key. The Learning with Physical Rounding (LWPR) problem formalizes this security in a practically-relevant model where the adversary can observe noise-free leakages. It can be viewed as a physical version of the Learning With Rounding (LWR) problem, where the rounding is performed by a leakage function and therefore does not have to be computed explicitly. In this paper, we first consolidate the intuition that LWPR cannot be secure in a serial implementation context without additional countermeasures (like shuffling), due to attacks exploiting worst-case leakages that can be mounted with practical data complexity. We then extend the understanding of LWPR in a parallel implementation setting. On the one hand, we generalize its robustness against cryptanalysis taking advantage of any (i.e., not only worst-case) leakage. A previous work claimed security in the specific context of a Hamming weight leakage function. We clarify necessary conditions to maintain this guarantee, based on the degree of the leakage function and the accuracy of its coefficients. On the other hand, we show that parallelism inherently provides good security against attacks exploiting worst-case leakages. We finally confirm the practical relevance of these findings by validating our assumptions experimentally for an exemplary implementation.

1 Introduction

Hard learning problems have been shown to be an important source of cryptographic hardness [Reg10, Pie12]. Popular instances of such problems include Learning Parity with Noise (LPN), Learning With Errors (LWE), which is a

© International Association for Cryptologic Research 2023
H. Handschuh and A. Lysyanskaya (Eds.): CRYPTO 2023, LNCS 14083, pp. 410–439, 2023.
https://doi.org/10.1007/978-3-031-38548-3_14

generalization to larger moduli [Reg05], and Learning With Rounding (LWR), which is a deterministic version [BPR12]. They have found many applications for the design of basic cryptographic primitives such as efficient authentication protocols [HB01, HKL+12] or pseudorandom functions [YS16], and advanced cryptographic primitives such as identity-based [GPV08, CHKP10] or fully homomorphic [Gen09, BV11] encryption. They have also gained particular interest in the context of post-quantum cryptography, as witnessed by the signature scheme CRYSTALS-Dilithium [DKL+18] and the encryption scheme CRYSTALS-Kyber [BDK+18], which have been selected by the NIST to become future standards.[1] Furthermore, their algebraic structure makes a (key-homomorphic) part of their implementation quite amenable to masking against side-channel attacks. Yet, protecting the error generation part remains a challenge, whether in the case of probabilistic (e.g., LPN-based) or deterministic (LWR-based) designs. This is because the noise generation itself can become the target of a side-channel attack [GLS14], and the rounding functions needed for the deterministic designs to be secure are non-linear and therefore more difficult to mask [BGL+14].

Hard *physical* learning problems have been introduced as a possible remedy to these implementation issues. Conceptually, their goal is to leverage the physical features of an implementation in order to generate errors or to round, as required to implement primitives based on hard learning problems. A typical application of such physical problems is fresh re-keying against side-channel attacks [MSGR10], of which the goal is to generate an ephemeral (e.g., block cipher) key thanks to an easy-to-protect operation. Various pieces of work studied the cryptanalysis of such schemes instantiated with a binary field multiplication [BFG14, BCF+15, PM16, GJ19]. Dziembowski et al. proved the security of binary re-keying based on a Learning Parity with Leakage (LPL) problem that reduces to the standard LPN problem [DFH+16]. Unfortunately, the concrete level of noise in the leakages needed for their proof that LPL is secure was shown to be quite high. More recently, Duval et al. showed that it is possible to design re-keying schemes based on a Learning With Physical Rounding (LWPR) problem [DMMS21]. Here, the main observation is that many practical leakage functions, such as the Hamming weight one [MOP07], are non-injective. It is therefore tempting to let the leakage function perform the rounding, removing the hassle of computing this rounding explicitly and protecting it against side-channel attacks. Non-injectivity alone (i.e., without noise nor further constraints on the field in which computations take place) is known to be insufficient. For example, in binary fields the Hamming weight of a secret value provides a linear equation of its bits. But combining a non-injective leakage function with computations in a prime field was suggested as a possible source of "crypto-physical" hardness, emulating Boneh et al.'s cryptographic dark matter [BIP+18].

It is easy to see that practically-relevant secure LWPR instances could be a game changer for the secure implementations of cryptographic algorithms. First, masked block ciphers usually incur performance overheads that are quadratic in the number of shares [ISW03, GR17]. By contrast, the cost of masked key-homomorphic primitives scales linearly in this number and can benefit from simple refreshing schemes (with linear randomness requirements) [BDF+17].

---

[1] https://csrc.nist.gov/Projects/post-quantum-cryptography.

Second, the analysis of key-homomorphic primitives in the probing model is trivial and does not raise composability issues since, as for linear functions, their computation can be implemented share by share and is therefore probe-isolating non-interferent [CS20]. Third, they intrinsically mitigate the risks of security flaws caused by physical defaults like glitches [MPG05] or transitions [CGP+12] that can lead to shares re-combinations, thanks to the independent manipulation of the shares they allow [CS21]. Eventually, is was recently hinted that they also have good potential to significantly improve the performance vs. side-channel security tradeoff of CCA-secure public key encryption schemes [HLM+23]. The latter is well-motivated given the acknowledged difficulty to protect schemes like CRYSTALS-Kyber against side-channel attacks [RRCB20, NDGJ21, UXT+22].

All these reasons give a strong incentive for understanding the security of the LWPR assumption under realistic leakage functions. The CHES 2021 work of Duval et al. made a first step in this direction by analyzing LWPR in the meaningful though specific case of Hamming weight leakages, and proposed parallel (FPGA) implementations processing 124 bits per cycle as a first cryptanalysis target. This investigation therefore suggested as fundamental problem the analysis of leakage functions that (even slightly) deviate from the Hamming weight case, while also leaving doubts regarding the possibility to ensure the security of LWPR in a serial (e.g., 32-bit software) implementation context.

In this paper, we contribute to these problems in three main directions.

As an appetizer, we confirm the intuition that securing LWPR in a serial implementation context requires additional side-channel countermeasures. This is because attacks exploiting so-called worst-case leakages can then be mounted with practical data complexity. By worst-case leakages, we mean the most informative values provided by the leakage function (e.g., the extreme ones in the Hamming weight case). This observation suggests the use of shuffling as a natural complement to serial LWPR which, if well implemented, has the effect of emulating a parallel implementation [HOM06, VMKS12, UBS21]. It also allows us to focus the rest of our investigations on parallel LWPR instances.

Next, we generalize the security of the LWPR assumption beyond the Hamming weight function. For this purpose, we first consider attacks taking advantage of any value of the leakage function, which we denote as "any-case leakages" in the paper. We show that security against algebraic cryptanalysis is preserved in the practical context of linear leakage functions (i.e., functions that can be expressed as a weighted sum of the bits manipulated by an implementation) [SLP05], under reasonable conditions on the accuracy of the weights. We also argue that these guarantees can be extended towards higher-order (e.g., quadratic) leakage functions. We then show that attacks exploiting worst-case leakages (used to rule out unprotected serial LWPR instances) can be prevented in the parallel case, with similar assumptions as to resist any-case leakages.

We combine these investigations with experiments confirming the practical relevance of our assumptions for realistic hardware implementations. As a result, we make a crucial step towards making deterministic hard physical learning problems a credible alternative to secure cryptographic implementations. And we conclude the paper by identifying interesting scopes for further research.

We note that the security of LWPR with linear or quadratic leakage functions relies on different arguments than previously used for similar constructions. For example in [DMMS21], the high-level idea behind the hardness of LWPR with Hamming weight leakages is that the composition of linear functions in different structures is sufficient to provide security. This holds since the composition gives functions with good cryptographic parameters in both initial structures. It corresponds to the main conclusion of Boneh et al.'s cryptographic dark matter [BIP+18] which proposes PRF constructions by only combining additions modulus p and modulus q for any pair of different primes p and q. The same general idea has been reused recently in [DGH+21]. In the case of LWPR with linear or quadratic leakage functions, additionally to the composition of functions over two different structures, good cryptographic properties are obtained directly from the non-injectivity of one of the functions. This new insight allows us to generalize the results to more functions and to strengthen their connection to practice, since the non-injectivity of a leakage function is typically something that can be characterized by existing side-channel evaluation setups & tools.

2   Background

2.1   Learning with Physical Rounding

We first define the LWPR assumption introduced in [DMMS21]. For this purpose, let us consider a secret matrix $\boldsymbol{K} \in \mathbb{F}_2^{m \times n}$ and a public vector $\boldsymbol{r} \in \mathbb{F}_2^n$. The work of Boneh et al. on cryptographic dark matter showed that a low-complexity wPRF $\mathsf{F}_K(\boldsymbol{r})$ can be obtained by computing the product $\boldsymbol{K} \cdot \boldsymbol{r}$, interpreting its output as a vector of $0/1$ values over $\mathbb{F}_3$ and rounding it. Precisely:

$$\mathsf{F}_K(\boldsymbol{r}) := \mathsf{map}(\boldsymbol{K} \cdot \boldsymbol{r}),$$

where the proposed mapping was the sum of this vector of $0/1$ values modulo 3 [BIP+18]. The idea of Duval et al. is to replace this mathematical mapping by a physical one (the leakage function) that is formalized as follows.

First, it is assumed that the leaking device computes on binary-represented data: each value in $\mathbb{F}_p$ is therefore represented with (at least) $\lceil \log p \rceil$ bits. We denote as $\mathsf{g} : \mathbb{F}_p \to \{0,1\}^{\lceil \log p \rceil}$ the function associating to each element y of $\mathbb{F}_p$ the binary representation of its representative in $[0, p-1]$. We also define $\mathsf{g}_m : \mathbb{F}_p^m \to \{0,1\}^{m\lceil \log p \rceil}$ as: $\mathsf{g}_m(\boldsymbol{y}) := \mathsf{g}(\boldsymbol{y}_1)\|\mathsf{g}(\boldsymbol{y}_2)\| \ldots \|\mathsf{g}(\boldsymbol{y}_m)$. This assumption is quite generic and captures the reality of most embedded computing devices deployed in current applications. Next, a more specialized assumption is required to define how the physical (noise-free) leakages depend on the $m\lceil \log p \rceil$ bits provided by g_m. This role will be played by the leakage function. We denote the leakage function computed on the binary representation of the manipulated data as $\mathsf{L}_\mathsf{g}(.)$. The generic LWPR problem is then defined as follows:

Definition 1 (Learning with physical rounding). *Let $p, n, m \in \mathbb{N}^*$, p prime, for $\boldsymbol{K} \in \mathbb{F}_p^{m \times (n+1)}$. The $\mathrm{LWPR}_{\mathsf{L}_\mathsf{g}, p}^{n,m}$ sample distribution is given by:*

$\mathcal{D}_{\mathrm{LWPR}_{\mathsf{L_g},p}^{n,m}} := \big(r, \mathsf{L_g}(K \boxdot r)\big)$ *for* $r \in \mathbb{F}_p^n$ *uniformly random, where* $K \boxdot r = K \cdot (r, 1)$ *and* $\mathsf{L_g} : \mathbb{F}_p^m \to \mathbb{R}^{n_d}$ *is the physical rounding function. Given query access to* $\mathcal{D}_{\mathrm{LWPR}_{\mathsf{L_g},p}^{n,m}}$ *for a uniformly random* K, *the* $\mathrm{LWPR}_{\mathsf{L_g},p}^{n,m}$ *problem is* (q, τ, μ, ϵ)-*hard to solve if after the observation of* q *LWPR samples, no adversary can recover the key* K *with time complexity* τ, *memory complexity* μ *and probability higher than* ϵ.

Duval et al. analyzed the case of Hamming weight leakages as a first step. The Hamming weight function is defined on any vector v of length $t \in \mathbb{N}^*$ with coefficients in $\{0,1\}$ as $\mathsf{M_h}(v) = \sum_{i=1}^{t} v_i$, where the sum is performed in $\mathbb{Z}$. They additionally considered two implementation contexts. In the serial case, the adversary is provided with m leakages on $\lceil \log p \rceil$ bits:

$$\mathsf{M_h^s}(y) : y \mapsto \Big(\mathsf{M_h}\big(\mathsf{g}(y_1)\big), \mathsf{M_h}\big(\mathsf{g}(y_2)\big), \ldots, \mathsf{M_h}\big(\mathsf{g}(y_m)\big)\Big).$$

In the parallel case, she receives the sum of these m values, denoted as $\mathsf{M_h^p}(y)$.

The LWPR instance proposed by Duval et al. uses a Mersenne prime $p = 2^{31} - 1$. It aims at the generation of 124-bit fresh keys in the parallel case and therefore considers $m = 4$. As for the main security parameter n, their analysis suggested $(n + 1)\log(p) + 3\log(n) \geq 124$ as a lower bound. This led the authors to select $n = 4$ as a first target for further cryptanalytic investigations.

2.2   Regression-Based Side-Channel Analysis

Linear regression is among the most popular tools for profiling a side-channel leakage model. Originally introduced by Schindler et al. [SLP05], it has been rapidly established as an efficient alternative to template attacks [GLP06]. Its main idea is to approximate the deterministic part of the leakage function as a weighted sum of n_b well-chosen basis function that we denote as β_i:

$$\mathsf{M_r}(v) = \sum_{i=1}^{n_b} a_i \cdot \beta_i(v),$$

with the a_i's $\in \mathbb{R}$. For a t-bit value v, a typical choice is to consider $n_b = t$ and to use the bits of v as basis functions.[2] We will denote the resulting class of leakage functions as linear models $\mathsf{M_{r1}}(v)$, which generalizes Hamming weight leakages where $a_i = 1 \ \forall \ 1 \leq i \leq n_b$. The model can be refined by adding more basis functions. Typically, we can add the $\binom{t}{\delta}$ basis functions of degree δ, which we denote as quadratic leakage models $\mathsf{M_{r2}}(v)$ when $\delta = 2$, cubic leakage models $\mathsf{M_{r3}}(v)$ when $\delta = 3$, $\ldots$, until the bijective model $\mathsf{M_{rt}}$ where $\delta = t$ and $n_b = 2^t$.

Profiling a leakage model then essentially boils down to estimate the vector of coefficients a, by applying the least square method. For this purpose, the evaluator first collects a vector of n_p profiling traces $l = [l^1, l^2, \ldots, l^{n_p}]$, corresponding

---

[2] Or $n_b = t + 1$, with a constant term to capture DC effects in the measurements.

to values $\boldsymbol{v}^1, \boldsymbol{v}^2, \ldots, \boldsymbol{v}^{n_p}$. She then builds a $n_p \times n_b$ matrix:

$$B = \begin{pmatrix} \beta_1(\boldsymbol{v}^1) & \beta_2(\boldsymbol{v}^1) & \cdots & \beta_{n_b}(\boldsymbol{v}^1) \\ \beta_1(\boldsymbol{v}^2) & \beta_2(\boldsymbol{v}^2) & \cdots & \beta_{n_b}(\boldsymbol{v}^2) \\ \vdots & \vdots & \ddots & \vdots \\ \beta_1(\boldsymbol{v}^{n_p}) & \beta_2(\boldsymbol{v}^{n_p}) & \cdots & \beta_{n_b}(\boldsymbol{v}^{n_p}) \end{pmatrix}.$$

Eventually, the vector of coefficients minimizing the means square error is:

$$\hat{\boldsymbol{a}} = [\hat{a_1}, \hat{a_2}, \ldots, \hat{a_{n_b}}] = (B^T \cdot B)^{-1} \cdot B^T \cdot \boldsymbol{l}.$$

We note that the analysis in [SLP05] considers noisy leakages and therefore adds a probabilistic component to the previous deterministic function. We do not detail this part since LWPR (conservatively) assumes noise-free leakages.

2.3   Correlation-Based Security Evaluations

Given a leakage model, the main question of a side-channel security evaluation is to determine the number of attack traces needed to recover a key [SMY09]. In the context of univariate leakage functions that we consider in this paper, Pearson's correlation is among the most popular evaluation tools [BCO04]. We next describe the basic approximations we will use in our empirical analyses.

Let us first denote a vector of n_a attack values $\overline{\boldsymbol{v}} = [\boldsymbol{v}^1, \boldsymbol{v}^2, \ldots, \boldsymbol{v}^{n_a}]$. From those values, an evaluator can compute the modeled leakage vector:

$$\boldsymbol{m} = [\mathsf{M_r}(\boldsymbol{v}^1), \mathsf{M_r}(\boldsymbol{v}^2), \ldots, \mathsf{M_r}(\boldsymbol{v}^{n_a})].$$

Similarly, she can measure a vector of actual leakage traces $\boldsymbol{l} = [l^1, l^2, \ldots, l^{n_a}]$. Viewing these vectors as n_a samples of random variables M and L, the data complexity of a Correlation Power Analysis (CPA) is given by [Man04]:

$$N = \frac{c}{\hat{\rho}(M, L)^2},$$

where c is a small constant and $\hat{\rho}$ denotes Pearson's correlation coefficient.

In our experimental evaluations, we will in particular be interested by the comparison between different leakage models, with the goal to evaluate whether simplifying a model (e.g., by limiting its degree or quantizing it) results in a significant information loss. Pearson's correlation is convenient for this purpose. For example, let us assume a model M_1 that is a simplification of a model M_2, leading to model errors captured by a random variable E so that $M_1 = M_2 + E$. Then, thanks to the correlation chain rule given in [SPRQ06] we have:

$$\hat{\rho}(M_1, L) = \hat{\rho}(M_1, M_2) \cdot \hat{\rho}(M_2, L).$$

As a result, the increase of data complexity that is due to simplifying the model M_2 into M_1 is reflected by the factor $f = \frac{1}{\hat{\rho}(M_1, M_2)^2}$: if $f \approx 1$ the attack using the simplified model is close to the one using the complex model; if $f > 1$ the simpler model misses some leakage features and the attack using this model requires f times more traces than the attack using the more complex model.

2.4   Cryptographic Criteria and p-Ary Functions

Since the re-keying scheme we consider in this paper is linear over $\mathbb{F}_p$, we will study the properties of the leakage function embedded in $\mathbb{F}_p$ that a side-channel adversary can obtain. For this purpose, we adapt tools from the analysis of cryptographic criteria for Boolean functions from $\mathbb{F}_2^n$ to $\mathbb{F}_2$ (e.g., [Car21]) and study the cryptographic properties of functions from $\mathbb{F}_p^n$ to $\mathbb{F}_p$.

Definition 2 (p-ary function). *For p a prime, a p-ary function f in n variables (an n-variable p-ary function) is a function from $\mathbb{F}_p^n$ to $\mathbb{F}_p$. The set of all p-ary functions in n variables is denoted by $\mathcal{F}_{p,n}$, and $|\mathcal{F}_{p,n}| = p^{p^n}$.*

Definition 3 (Algebraic normal form and degree (e.g., [Hou18])). *We call Algebraic Normal Form (ANF) of a p-ary function f its n-variable polynomial representation over $\mathbb{F}_p$ belonging to $\mathbb{F}_p[x_1, \ldots, x_n]/(x_1^p - x_1, \ldots, x_n^p - x_n)$:*

$$f(x) = \sum_{S \subset [0,p-1]^n} a_S \left(\prod_{i \in [1,n]} x_i^{S_i} \right) = \sum_{S \subset [0,p-1]^n} a_S x^S,$$

where $a_S \in \mathbb{F}_p$. The ANF of f is unique, and the algebraic degree of f is defined as $\deg(f) = \max\limits_{\{S \mid a_S \neq 0\}} \sum\limits_{i=1}^{n} S_i$ (with the convention that $\deg(0) = 0$).

Definition 4 (Nonlinearity). *The nonlinearity $\mathsf{nl}(f)$ of a p-ary function $f \in \mathcal{F}_{p,n}$, is the minimum Hamming distance between f and all the affine functions in $\mathcal{F}_{p,n}$:*

$$\mathsf{nl}(f) = \min_{g, \deg(g) \leq 1} \{d_H(f,g)\},$$

where $d_H(f,g)$ is the Hamming distance $|\{x \in \mathbb{F}_p^n \mid f(x) \neq g(x)\}|$ between f and g.

3   Appetizer: Threat Model and Serial LWPR

Before describing our technical contributions, we quickly recall the threat model we consider, which is illustrated in Fig. 1. We also come back on the impact of an attack against serial LWPR instances outlined in the appendix of [DMMS21], by specializing it to the case of a Hamming weight function for simplicity. We use this example for two purposes: first, confirming that securing serial LWPR instances requires additional countermeasures; second: introducing the difference between attacks using worst-case leakages and any-case leakages.

In brief, the idea of fresh re-keying schemes is that it is possible to efficiently mask their key-homomorphic part (i.e., the product between the secret matrix $\boldsymbol{K}$ and the public vector $\boldsymbol{r}$) and to recombine the output of this product for which the adversary can only observe the leakage. In other words, the multiplication we consider in Definition 1 will be performed on the shares $\boldsymbol{K}^1, \boldsymbol{K}^2, \ldots, \boldsymbol{K}^q$ and then recombined such that the fresh key is $\boldsymbol{K} \boxdot \boldsymbol{r} = \sum_{i=1}^{q} (\boldsymbol{K}^i \boxdot \boldsymbol{r})$.

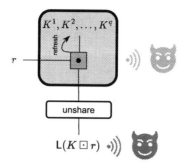

Fig. 1. Fresh re-keying with LWPR: threat model.

This fresh key will then be used without masking for a single (e.g., block cipher) encryption, which is expected to be significantly harder to break than if using the long-term key multiple times with the same cipher. As a result, there are two natural attack paths against such re-keying schemes. The first one (depicted in gray on Fig. 1) is to target the masked product. Evaluating it can be done with standard side-channel analysis techniques, enjoying the advantages listed in introduction (linear overheads, no composability issues, resistance against glitches). The analysis of this attack path given in [DMMS21] remains identical and we therefore do not repeat it. The second option (depicted in red on Fig. 1) is to target the output of the product after its shares have been recombined. Evaluating it requires less standard techniques and can be done in different models. Binary fresh re-keying schemes like [MSGR10] require noisy leakages to be secure. We consider a more conservative model where the adversary obtains noise-free leakages. As a result, the analysis of this attack path becomes conceptually similar to the analysis of a stream cipher, the product playing the role of an LFSR and the leakage function the one of a filter.

Given this threat model, the attack against serial LWPR implementations is pretty simple. Say we have an instance of LWPR with $p = 2^{31} - 1$ where the adversary can observe the Hamming weight of every 31-bit word of $K \boxdot r$. Then, she can filter the leakages and retain the ones with (worst-case) value 0, which has a single preimage. Every such event gives a linear equation in the key elements of the corresponding line of K, and each such line can be recovered with $(n + 1)$ linear equations. Since p is only mid-size, these events happen with a concretely reachable probability $\frac{1}{p}$. As a result, after the generation $p(n + 1)$ LWPR samples, the full key is compromised with good probability.

Since it is hard to rule out that (close to) Hamming weight leakages can be observed in practice (as Sect. 6 will confirm experimentally), this attack suggests that serial instances of LWPR cannot be secure without additional side-channel countermeasures. Various candidates can be considered for this purpose. As it is argued in [DMMS21], exploiting extreme Hamming weights becomes difficult when the level of parallelism increases (since they become exponentially less likely), and shuffling therefore appears as the most natural one. Indeed, if well implemented, shuffling makes the m intermediate computations of a serial implementation hard to distinguish so that the adversary does not gain more information than if she was provided with the sum of these leakages, which emulates a parallel implementation [HOM06, VMKS12, UBS21].[3] We show in Sect. 5 that attacks exploiting worst-case leakages can be generalized, and that a security argument can be given based on the degree of the (linear) leakage function and the accuracy of its coefficients. Beforehand, we consider another important class of (algebraic) attacks where the adversary exploits any-case leakages (i.e., where the leakages are not filtered and all the measurements are used). For this purpose, we generalize the former security analysis of Duval et al. from the specialized Hamming weight leakage function towards any linear leakage function. Interestingly, for those attacks we are even able to give a security argument for serial implementations, which then easily extends to parallel ones.

4   LWPR for Linear Leakage Functions

While reasonable as a first step, considering security against Hamming weight leakages is oversimplifying since the different bits of an implementation can consume more or less power, due to different load capacitances. This is precisely what is modeled by regression-based attacks [SLP05]. In this section, we therefore analyze the security of LWPR in this generalized context.

For this purpose, we first observe that the product $K \boxdot r$ is linear over $\mathbb{F}_p$. As a result, we focus on the (linear invariant) cryptographic criteria of the remaining function $\mathsf{L_g}$ considered as a function over $\mathbb{F}_p$. If the adversary can approximate well the real function $\mathsf{L_g}$ by a p-ary function, she obtains a system of equations over $\mathbb{F}_p$ where the unknowns are (affine combinations of) the key elements.

This gives a modeling of $\mathsf{L_g}(K \boxdot r)$ as equations over $\mathbb{F}_p$ where the only unknowns are the $\mathbb{F}_p$ elements of K. We next carry out such an analysis for a linear leakage model in the serial case, by considering these models as functions over $\mathbb{F}_p$, which we define as s-bounded pseudo-linear functions.

Definition 5 (s-bounded pseudo-linear functions). *We denote as F_a the function characterized by $a \in \mathbb{F}_p^t$, where $t = \lceil \log p \rceil$ and defined as:*

$$\mathsf{F}_a : \ \mathbb{F}_p \to \mathbb{F}_p, \ y \mapsto \sum_{i=0}^{t-1} a_i \cdot \mathsf{g}(y)_i. \tag{1}$$

We call F_a s-bounded pseudo-linear if each a_i belongs to $[0, s]$, with $s \in \mathbb{F}_p$ a security parameter, and we call C_1^s the class of s-bounded pseudo-linear functions.

We recall that the g function associates elements of $\mathbb{F}_p$ to their binary representation. The name pseudo-linear comes from the fact that this function is linear in the bits of the binary representation of a. However, it corresponds to a much higher degree p-ary function. This increase of the degree when projecting

---

[3] Increasing the size of p could provide similar security benefits at higher cost.

a binary representation into a prime field is the root of the LWPR hardness. We next consider that an s-bounded F_a is the p-ary function used to approximate L_g.

We note that this definition implicitly relies on two assumptions: one on the degree of the physical leakage function and another one on the number of values taken by the coefficients a_i. The practical relevance of these two assumptions is discussed in Sect. 6. We also note that the proposed analysis captures an important class of (algebraic) attacks against LWPR. We will show that the non-injectivity of a one-variable p-ary function is sufficient to prove a lower bound on its degree and its nonlinearity. On the one hand, the high algebraic degree of a p-ary function allows thwarting the attacks based on solving a linearized algebraic system. On the other hand, the high nonlinearity prevents the attacks based on solving noisy linear algebraic systems, which use the best approximation of a p-ary function by an affine function. But as usual in cryptanalysis, nothing prevents that other characterizations or attack vectors lead to better results.

Definition 6 (Preimage sets & main preimage). *Let $f \in \mathcal{F}_{p,m}$, we call:*

- $\mathcal{A}_f(y) = \{x \in \mathbb{F}_p^m \mid f(x) = y\}$ *for $y \in \mathbb{F}_p$, the set of preimages of y through f.*
- $u_f \in \mathbb{F}_p$ *a main image of f defined as $\forall y \in \mathbb{F}_p, |\mathcal{A}_f(u_f)| \geq |\mathcal{A}_f(y)|$.*
- $v_f \in [1, p^m]$ *the main preimage size of f, defined as $v_f = |\mathcal{A}_f(u_f)|$.*
- $w_f \in [0, p-1]$ *the no preimage set's size of f, defined as*

$$w_f = |\{y \in \mathbb{F}_p \mid \mathcal{A}_f(y) = \emptyset\}|$$

We first show a bound on the degree of f based on its main preimage size.

Proposition 1 (Main preimage size and algebraic degree). *Let $f \in \mathcal{F}_{p,1}$, if its main preimage $v_f < p$ then its algebraic degree $\deg(f) \geq v_f$.*

Proof. Since $v_f < p$, f is not a constant function and $f - u_f$ is not the null function. Accordingly, the function $f - u_f$ admits v_f different zeros in $\mathbb{F}_p$, and there exists v_f terms $(x - z_i)$ dividing f. Therefore its degree is at least v_f and, since the algebraic degree is affine invariant, $\deg(f) = \deg(f - u_f) \geq v_f$. $\square$

Furthermore, when f is not enough non-injective, composing the function can be used to determine better its degree as shown in the following corollary:

Corollary 1. *Let $f \in \mathcal{F}_{p,1}$ and $r \in \mathbb{N}^*$, we denote $f^{\circ r} = f \circ f \circ \cdots \circ f$ the composition of f r times. If $v_{f^{\circ r}} < p$ then $\deg(f) \geq (v_{f^{\circ r}})^{1/r}$.*

We next show a bound on the nonlinearity of f.

Proposition 2 (Main preimage size, no preimage set's size and non-linearity). *Let $f \in \mathcal{F}_{p,1}$ such that its main preimage size $v_f < p$, then:*

$$nl(f) \geq \min\left(p - v_f, \max\left(v_f - 1, w_f\right)\right).$$

Proof. We derive the bound on the nonlinearity by first considering the distance to constant functions, and then to any affine function. Since $v_f < p$, f is not constant, and it will agree on at most v_f values with a constant function c. Hence $d_H(f,c) \geq p - v_f$. Besides, p-ary affine (not constant) functions in one variable are bijective. Accordingly, each element of $\mathbb{F}_p$ is the image of exactly one element. Therefore, for any affine (not constant) function in $\mathcal{F}_{p,1}$, there exists at least $v_f - 1$ elements of $\mathbb{F}_p$ where the image of f is different from the affine function's one (all except one of the preimages of u_f). Moreover, since w_f elements are not in the image of f, f disagrees at least w_f times with any affine (not constant) function, which give the final bound. $\qquad\square$

Finally, we bound the main preimage size of s-bounded pseudo-linear functions.

Proposition 3 (Properties of s-bounded pseudo-linear functions). *Let $f \in C_1^s$ with $ts < p$, where $t = \lceil \log p \rceil$, then the following holds:*

- $v_f \geq \lceil \frac{p}{ts+1} \rceil$,
- $w_f \geq p - ts - 1$.

And assuming $v_f \neq p$, we further have:

- $\deg(f) \geq \lceil \frac{p}{ts+1} \rceil$,
- $\mathsf{nl}(f) \geq \min \left(p - v_f, \max \left(\lceil \frac{p}{ts+1} \rceil - 1, p - ts - 1 \right) \right)$.

Proof. Since $ts < p$, we obtain that for all $x \in \mathbb{F}_p$, $0 \leq f(x) \leq ts$, hence $w_f \geq p - ts - 1$. Thereafter, $f(x)$ can take at most $ts + 1$ values, hence there exists at least a preimage set with cardinal $\lceil \frac{p}{ts+1} \rceil$ or more. The last two items are obtained using Proposition 1, Proposition 2 and two first items. $\qquad\square$

Note that the condition $ts < p$ guarantees that no reduction takes place independent of the input of the pseudo-linear leakage function in Eq. 1.

For a given $a \in \mathbb{F}_p^t$, the output of F_a gives a system of equations where the key elements are the unknowns. Therefore, solving the algebraic system given by images of F_a allows retrieving the key. We next explore two methods for solving such a system over $\mathbb{F}_p$, and demonstrate that the time and data complexity of these methods are sufficiently high for our instances in Sect. 6.5.

Concretely, an adversary can either solve the system of k variables directly or use the higher-order correlation approach presented in [Cou02]. Higher-order correlation attacks consist in approximating F_a by a degree-d function h, and then solving systems of equations until one is such that F_a and h coincide on all these equations. An adversary can create additional equations if needed, for instance through a linear combination of the existing ones. Hence, the time complexity of solving a noisy degree-d system of equations over $\mathbb{F}_p$ can be written as $C(1-\varepsilon)^{-D}$ with C the time complexity to solve a degree-d system of equations in k' variables over $\mathbb{F}_p$, $(1-\varepsilon)$ the probability of the approximation to be correct for one equation, k' the number of variables (i.e., at least the number of key variables k, but it can be more if techniques introducing new variables are used), and D the quantity of data necessary (at least the number of variables k').

Exact algebraic system attack path. Let us for now fix the security parameter s to 2^{12} (the practical relevance of this value will be discussed in Sect. 6). Trying to solve the system directly given by the output of the function F_a with this value and a modulus $p = 2^{31} - 1$, we find $v_f \geq \lceil \frac{2^{31}-1}{31 \cdot 2^{12}+1} \rceil \geq 2^{14}$ (since $t = \lceil \log(p) \rceil$). Therefore, the adversary would have to solve a system of equations of degree at least 2^{14} in $n + 1$ variables over $\mathbb{F}_{2^{31}-1}$ to recover the first row of K. There are usually two main families of algorithms considered to solve polynomial systems of equations: the XL algorithms and Gröbner bases algorithms such as F4 [Fau99] or F5 [Fau02]. The complexities of these families of algorithms are studied in different works. We refer to [YC04] for the XL family and to [BFS15] for F4/F5. For clarity, we first discuss the results given by the simpler approach of linearization. Let V_d denote the number of monomials over $\mathbb{F}_p$ with degree at most d in the k variables of the system. The linearization attacks consists in considering each of these monomials as a new variable, and then in inverting the linear system using Gaussian elimination. Thereafter, the corresponding time complexity to solve a system with this approach is simply $\mathcal{O}(V_d^3)$. XL algorithms or Gröbner bases algorithms should improve over this complexity. However, Gaussian elimination algorithms give a convenient estimate of the complexity to solve a linear system, that is sufficient for our purposes and which can be combined with mild security margins if needed. For example, XL and F4/F5 can be much faster when more polynomials are available, leading to a time complexity reduced to $\mathcal{O}(V_d^\omega)$, where $2 \leq \omega \leq 3$ is a linear algebra constant that depends on the algorithm used. We make the conservative choice to consider the complexity $\mathcal{O}(V_d^2)$ for our concrete security estimations.

Noisy linear system attack path. We also consider the complexity of linearizing the d-degree system, then solving the resulting linear system. For this purpose, we use a similar argument as the one given in [DMMS21]. Namely, we first observe that the number of variables after linearization is $V_d = |\{v \in [0, p-1]^k, 0 \leq \sum_{i=1}^k v_i \leq d\}| = \sum_{l=0}^d \binom{l+k-1}{l} = \binom{k+d}{k}$ (using the stars and bars theorem) and again assume $C = \mathcal{O}(V_d^\omega)$. The noisy linear system approach then just implies considering a probability of error $\varepsilon = \mathsf{nl}(F_a)/p$ for the equation approximation. In this case, with a degree $d = 1$, we have $V_1 = k + 1$ and the time complexity is at least $\mathcal{O}((k+1)^\omega (p/(p - \mathsf{nl}(F_a)))^k)$. Using the bound of Proposition 3 therefore provides the required security estimation.

These theoretical bounds will be made concrete in Sect. 6.5, where actual instances of F_a are given, with their associated values v_f and w_f.

Adaptation to the parallel case. In the serial case above, we studied the properties of the function an adversary can obtain from the leakage corresponding to one ($\mathbb{F}_p$) element of the ephemeral key, each element of y depending on a different row of the long term key. In the parallel case, the adversary gets less information since she obtains the leakage on the whole y and not independently on each coefficient. In this case, the leakage is the sum of the leakages obtained in the serial case. Therefore, in terms of p-ary functions, calling f_i the functions considered in the serial case, the one in the parallel case is $f' \in \mathcal{F}_{p,m}$:

$$f'(\boldsymbol{y}) = \sum_{i=1}^{m} f_i(y_i).$$

Since f' is a direct sum of functions (sum of functions acting on different variables) its properties can be derived from the ones of the f_i's. Namely, $\deg(f_i)$ and $\mathsf{nl}(f_i)$ can be obtained from Proposition 3, $\deg(f') = \max_i \deg(f_i)$ and the nonlinearity of f' can be derived from the following result:

Property 1 (Adapted from [CHMS22], Proposition 1). Let $\mathbb{G}$ be a group, Let $h = f + g$ be the direct sum of the functions f and g with n and m $\mathbb{G}$-variables respectively. Then, $\mathsf{nl}_{\mathbb{G}}(h) \geq \max(|\mathbb{G}|^n \mathsf{nl}_{\mathbb{G}}(g), |\mathbb{G}|^m \mathsf{nl}_{\mathbb{G}}(f))$.

Accordingly, we also obtain $\mathsf{nl}(f') \geq \max_i p^{m-1} \mathsf{nl}(f_i)$. The complexity of the attacks against parallel LWPRG implementations is therefore increased thanks to this higher nonlinearity and the higher number of variables km.

5   Security Against Worst-Case Leakages

We now extend the approach of [DMMS21] for attacks taking advantage of worst-case leakages (intuitively outlined in Sect. 3). Precisely, we investigate the complexity of attacks that benefit from the existence of leakages with small preimage sets. In the parallel case, the adversary obtains images z such that:

$$z = f'(\boldsymbol{y}) = \sum_{i=1}^{m} f_i(y_i) = \sum_{i=1}^{m} f_i(\boldsymbol{k}_i \boxdot \boldsymbol{r}),$$

where $\boldsymbol{k}_i$ denotes the i-th row of $\boldsymbol{K}$. For $z = f'(\boldsymbol{y})$, the m-variable p-ary function f' has $|\mathcal{A}_{f'}(z)|$ preimages that we denote $(y_1^{(j)}, \ldots, y_m^{(j)})$, for $j \in [1, |\mathcal{A}_{f'}(z)|]$. From an image z, the adversary obtains that a linear system of m equations, namely $\{\boldsymbol{k}_i \boxdot \boldsymbol{r} = y_i^{(j)}, \text{ for } i \in [1, m]\}$, is correct for one j. She can then collect $n + 1$ samples $z_1, \ldots, z_{n+1}$ and solve the $\prod_{i=1}^{n+1} |\mathcal{A}_{f'}(z_i)|$ possible linear systems in $m(n + 1)$ variables (in order to retrieve $\boldsymbol{K}$). Only one of these systems is the correct one, and the correct solution can be verified with more samples. Since by definition $|\mathcal{A}_{f'}(z_i)| \leq v_{f'}$, the time complexity of this attack is upper bounded by $\mathcal{O}(v_{f'}^{n+1} \cdot (m(n+1))^{\omega})$ (following the analysis of Sect. 4).

We extend this attack by considering algebraic systems of higher degree rather than linear systems. When z gives $|\mathcal{A}_{f'}(z)|$ preimages, instead of considering $m \cdot |\mathcal{A}_{f'}(z)|$ linear equations, we can build the m equations:

$$\prod_{j=1}^{|\mathcal{A}_{f'}(z)|} (\boldsymbol{k}_i \boxdot \boldsymbol{r} - y_i^{(j)}) = 0, \text{ for } i \in [1, m],$$

where the m equations have degree $|\mathcal{A}_{f'}(z)|$. We first observe that the cases we previously described, with $m \cdot |\mathcal{A}_{f'}(z)|$ equations of degree 1 and $m \cdot 1$ equations of degree $|\mathcal{A}_{f'}(z)|$, are two extreme cases. We can also create $m \cdot b$ equations of degree c such that $bc = |\mathcal{A}_{f'}(z)|$, where only one of the b system of equations is correct. As a result, the attack becomes a tradeoff between the number of polynomial systems of fixed degree and their algebraic degree, since it corresponds to the resolution of b^{n+1} polynomial systems of degree c, with $bc = |\mathcal{A}_{f'}(z)|$.

The complexity of the attack relies on two main factors: first, the size of the preimage sets considered $|\mathcal{A}_{f'}(z)|$, intervening in the number of systems and the degree of the polynomial systems; second, the probability to get samples z_i with small preimage sets. We argue that this attack is not a threat since either the time complexity is higher than the security level targeted when $\mathcal{A}_{f'}(z)$ is large, or the data complexity is too high when $\mathcal{A}_{f'}(z)$ is small. To do so, we first give the expression of $|\mathcal{A}_{f'}(z)|$ when f' is the direct sum of m p-ary functions. Then, we show how the complexity of the attack can be bounded from the values of $|\mathcal{A}_{f'}(z_i)|$ from the samples z_i an adversary obtains. Finally, we give a proposition to bound the probability of getting z_i such that the preimage set is small, and we conclude by applying these results to a practical example.

Concretely, when f' is the direct sum of m p-ary functions f_i, the expression of $|\mathcal{A}_{f'}(z)|$ is given by:

$$|\mathcal{A}_{f'}(z)| = \sum_{\substack{y_1,\ldots,y_m \in \mathbb{F}_p \\ y_1+\cdots+y_m=z}} \prod_{i=1}^{m} |\mathcal{A}_{f_i}(y_i)|.$$

Then, since the time complexity of the attack comes from the resolution of b^{n+1} polynomial systems of degree c such that $bc = |\mathcal{A}_{f'}(z)|$, using the analysis of Sect. 4 the complexity is $\mathcal{O}(b^{n+1} \cdot (mV_c)^\omega)$. We rewrite $b^{n+1} \cdot (mV_c)^\omega$ to express it relatively to $|\mathcal{A}_{f'}(z)|$ as follows:

$$b^{n+1} \cdot (mV_c)^\omega = \left(\frac{|\mathcal{A}_{f'}(z)|}{c}\right)^{n+1} \left(\frac{n+1+c}{n+1}\right)^\omega m^\omega,$$

$$\geq \left(\frac{|\mathcal{A}_{f'}(z)|}{c}\right)^{n+1} \frac{c^{n+1}}{(n+1)!} \left(\frac{n+1+c}{n+1}\right)^{\omega-1} m^\omega,$$

$$\geq \frac{|\mathcal{A}_{f'}(z)|^{n+1}}{(n+1)!}.$$

Finally, we use the following proposition in order to bound the probability of getting images coming from small preimage sets:

Proposition 4 (Probability of getting images from small preimage sets). *Let $f' \in \mathcal{F}_{p,m}$ and $B \in \mathbb{N}$ such that $B < p^m/|\mathrm{Im}(f')|$ where $\mathrm{Im}(\cdot)$ denotes the image, the probability $p_{f',B}$ of choosing at random $z \in \mathbb{F}_p^m$ such that $|\mathcal{A}_{f'}(z)| \leq B$ follows:*

$$p_{f',B} \leq \frac{(|\mathrm{Im}(f')| - 1)B}{p^m}.$$

In particular, if f' is the direct sum of m p-ary functions with C_1^s and $mts < p$ (where $t = \lceil \log p \rceil$), the probability becomes:

$$p_{f',B} \le \frac{mstB}{p^m}.$$

Proof. First, we show the result in the general case. By definition, the preimage sets $\mathcal{A}_{f'}(z)$ for $z \in \mathbb{F}_p$ are a partition of $\mathbb{F}_p^m$, Therefore:

$$p^m = \sum_{z \in \mathbb{F}_p} |\mathcal{A}_{f'}(z)| = \sum_{z \in \text{Im}(f')} |\mathcal{A}_{f'}(z)|.$$

Since $B < \frac{p^m}{|\text{Im}(f')|}$, at least one of the images is such that $|\mathcal{A}_{f'}(z)| > B$. Hence, at most $|\text{Im}(f')| - 1$ images are such that $|\mathcal{A}_{f'}(z)| \le B$, and the corresponding number of corresponding preimages is therefore at most $(|\text{Im}(f')| - 1)B$, which allows us to conclude on $p_{f',B}$. For the particular case where f' is a direct sum of m p-ary functions from C_1^s, since $mst < p$ we have that $f(y) \in [0, st]$ since $f \in C_1^s$ and $f'(\boldsymbol{y}) \in [0, mst]$, hence $|\text{Im}(f')| \le mst + 1$. $\square$

Using the same parameters as in Sect. 5, namely $p = 2^{31} - 1$, $s = 2^{12}$, $n = 4$ and $m = 4$, we obtain that preimage sizes $|\mathcal{A}_{f'}(z)|$ larger than $\sqrt[5]{5!2^{124}} \approx 2^{26}$ lead to a time complexity larger than 2^{124}. We can then take the value $B = 2^{26}$ and apply Proposition 4, leading to a probability to get a sample z with at most B preimages lower than $\frac{4 \cdot 2^{12} \cdot 31 \cdot 2^{26}}{(2^{31}-1)^4)} \approx 2^{-79}$. Hence, our analysis shows that attacks exploiting worst-case leakages cannot succeed for adversaries with a data complexity bounded by 2^{79}, whereas side-channel security generally requires preventing attacks with data complexity in the 2^{50} range. As a result, we conclude that such attacks are not a concrete threat to the proposed instance.

6   Empirical Validation

The previous sections showed that the LWPR assumption can remain secure in the generalized context of linear leakage functions. Yet, as illustrated in Fig. 2, it is based on an adversarial strategy that interprets the leakages in $\mathbb{F}_p$ and security against adversaries following this strategy relies on two assumptions. Namely, it requires a bound on the degree of the leakage function and another bound on the quantization of the coefficients of this leakage function.

In the following, we therefore evaluate the validity of our assumptions based on a prototype hardware implementation (in Sect. 6.2 and Sect. 6.4) and discuss the applicability and relevance of our attack strategy (in Sect. 6.3). We conclude in Sect. 6.5, by confirming that the concrete leakage models we estimated from real measurements are covered by our security analysis. Beforehand, we describe the prototype implementation we considered in Sect. 6.1

	domain	codomain	degree	model coefficients
physical leakages	$\mathbb{F}_p^m$	$\mathbb{R}$	1 to δ	$\emptyset$
measured leakages	$\mathbb{F}_p^m$	$\{0, 1, \ldots, s'\} \in \mathbb{Z}$	1 to δ	$\emptyset$
s-bounded leakages	$\mathbb{F}_p^m$	at most $\{0, 1, \ldots, st\} \in \mathbb{F}_p$	1 (or more) Sect. 6.2 (& 5)	$\{0, 1, \ldots, s\} \in \mathbb{F}_p$ Sect. 6.4

SCA model
Sect. 6.3

Fig. 2. Adversarial strategy & leakage assumptions.

6.1   Prototype Hardware Implementation

We measured a parallel hardware implementation operating on 31-bit words running on a FPGA. The architecture of the computational core of our masked LWPR-based re-keying scheme is depicted in Fig. 3. Concretely, the complete computation is performed by processing each share sequentially and the matrix multiplication for the share index d is split in $(N + 1) \times M = (4 + 1) \times 4 = 20$ modular multiplications over $\mathbb{F}_p$. More precisely, the core implements 4 modular multiplications in parallel (i.e., the results of the multiplications between the j-th column of a key share denoted $K_{*,0 \leq j < 5}^d$ and the j-th element of the nonce denoted r_j, where $r_4 = 1$). We used the efficient modular multiplication architecture based on DSPs proposed in [KSHS17] for this purpose. The results obtained for the multiplications are then added in 4 accumulators (i.e., one for each row) dedicated to the reconstruction of the resulting fresh key.

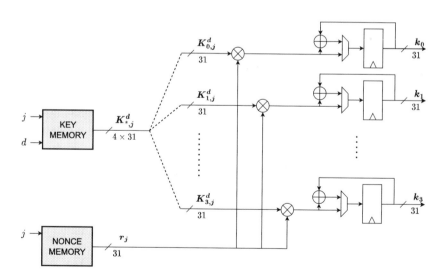

Fig. 3. Masked LWPR-based re-keying: prototype hardware implementation.

As shown in Fig. 4, the architecture of the key memory is designed to limit the impact of physical defaults on the implementation's security. In particular, the key shares are stored in independent physical memory units (i.e., BRAMs in the context of our FPGA implementation) and a register barrier is used before selecting the appropriate memory output. The latter is needed to avoid shares' recombinations that may be caused by glitches. Finally, a dedicated multiplexer at the input of the register barrier is used to drive the shares' values that are not currently processed to zero. Together with the fact that the shares are processed sequentially, this mechanism ensures the independence of the key shares.

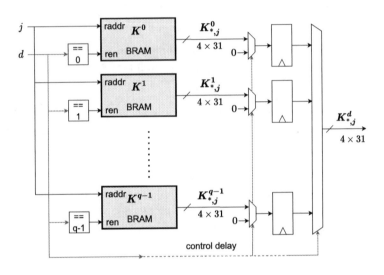

Fig. 4. Key material memory architecture.

Overall, our prototype implementation matches the parallelism requirements of our security analysis since it recombines a full (124-bit) fresh key in a single clock cycle, the leakage of which we analyze in the rest of this section. Besides, we note that when analyzing the second (red) attack path described in the threat model of Fig. 1, we are only interested in the value of the recombined fresh key.[4] Concretely, we therefore choose to measure an implementation with a single share (i.e., $q = 1$). This gives the most favorable leakages to the evaluator and therefore puts us as close as possible to the noise-free setting considered in our analyzes. This is because the implementation with $q = 1$ is the smallest one and a limited use of resources in turn reduces the noise in the leakages.

Our measurements were performed on the Sakura-G evaluation board, which embeds a XC6SLX75-2CSG484C Spartan6 FPGA. The traces were collected using a Picoscope 5244D with a Tektronix CT-1 current probe, following the

---

[4] The first attack path (leveraging the leakages of the shared multiplications) was analyzed in [DMMS21] and the arguments of this previous work apply similarly.

guidelines given in [BUS21]. In order to take into account the effect of conges-
tion that can take place during the place-and-route step of a dense design, we
performed three different syntheses using the ISE14.7 design toolchain. The first
one is unconstrained. The second one is constrained in order to achieve 95%
of resources' utilization density (using a PBLOCK area constraint). The last
one further constraints the design by (artificially) enforcing that higher-capacity
routing elements are included in the path of some bits. We next refer to these
different syntheses as unconstrained, constrained and amplified. The layout of
the unconstrained and constrained syntheses are illustrated in Fig. 5.

6.2   Bounded Degree of the Leakage Function

The first (and main) physical assumption used to rule out algebraic attacks in
our previous analysis is that the leakage function has a bounded degree. More
precisely, we claim security for linear leakage functions in Sects. 4 and 5 and will
generalize to higher-order (e.g., quadratic) functions in Sect. 7.

We next study whether this assumption can be reasonably fulfilled in practice. As detailed in Sect. 2.2, regression-based models are a natural tool for this
purpose, since they can be estimated for different, more or less complex, basis
functions. A simple case, considered in the previous sections, is to take the bits
of the target intermediate value as basis functions. But higher-degree models
can be built, culminating with the exhaustive model which corresponds to a
(worst-case) profiling where all the mean leakage values are exhaustively estimated [CRR02]. Our goal is to therefore show that a simple linear model does
not lead to significant information losses compared to the exhaustive one.

For this purpose, we analyzed the 4 leakage functions f_i of our target implementation. We analyzed them independently to reduce the noise. They all gave
similar results. For the exhaustive model, and since building 2^{31} templates is
computationally intensive, we rather estimated a subset of n_a average leakage traces (with $n_a = 10,000$), and stored them in a vector of average leak-
age traces $\bar{l} = [\bar{l^1}, \bar{l^2}, \ldots, \bar{l^{n_a}}]$. We then computed the vectors corresponding to
our regression-based linear models for the three different syntheses, evaluated
on the same values. In each case, we first estimated the 31-element vector of
coefficients $\hat{a}$ using $n_p = 10,000$ profiling traces (meaning $\approx \frac{10,000}{31}$ traces per
coefficient, which was sufficient for good estimation given the low noise level of
our measurements). As a result, we obtained model predictions:

$$m_{r1}^u = [\mathsf{M}_{r1}^u(v^1), \mathsf{M}_{r1}^u(v^2), \ldots, \mathsf{M}_{r1}^u(v^{n_a})],$$

for the unconstrained synthesis, and similarly m_{r1}^c & m_{r1}^a for the constrained and
amplified syntheses. Viewing these vectors as the samples of random variables
$\bar{L}$, M_{r1}^u, M_{r1}^c and M_{r1}^a, we finally computed the correlation between the true
(averaged) leakages and the models: $\hat{\rho}(M_{r1}^u, \bar{L})$, $\hat{\rho}(M_{r1}^c, \bar{L})$ and $\hat{\rho}(M_{r1}^a, \bar{L})$.

These correlation coefficients are reported in Fig. 6 in function of the number
of traces used to obtain the average traces $\bar{l^i}$. We additionally report the estimates obtained when correlating the real leakage vectors with a Hamming weight

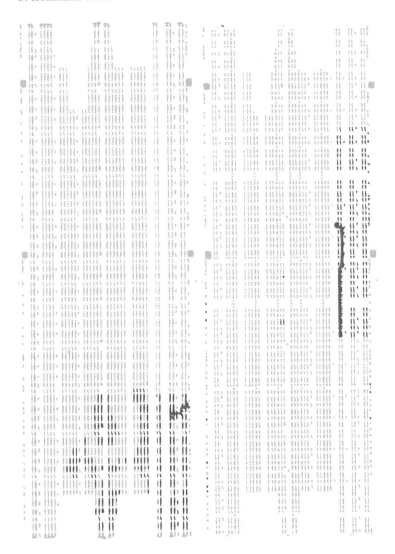

Fig. 5. Layout of unconstrained (left) and constrained (right) syntheses. Unused resources are in white. Used resources are in blue. Routing is in red. (Color figure online)

leakage model, and each curve in the figure is accompanied by a 95% bootstrap confidence interval. These results confirm that unconstrained syntheses (at the top of the figure) lead to high correlations already with the Hamming weight leakage model. By contrast, for constrained and amplified syntheses reflecting congestioned designs (at the middle and bottom of the figure) the correlation with the Hamming weight leakage model decreases while it remains close to one for the linear models. These experiments show that the generalization we propose indeed captures practically-relevant implementations. Admittedly, reaching such high correlation values does not preclude that higher-degree terms can be characterized and exploited. But it shows that most of the information leaked by our target implementation can be extracted with a simple linear model. So combined with (*i*) the generalization of Sect. 7 showing that security does not collapse as long as the leakage function remains sufficiently non-injective, and (*ii*) the fact that our modeling is conservative (since it assumes noise-free leakages), we conjecture that the bounded-degree assumption we require can be matched sufficiently well to provide practically secure LWPR instances.

6.3   Practical Application of the Attack

The attacks we study in this paper work by interpreting physical leakages as functions in $\mathbb{F}_p$. So far, we showed that such attacks are hard if the leakage function has a bounded degree and its coefficients have limited accuracy. We also assessed empirically that the bounded degree assumption can be reasonably matched in practice. We now describe how to mount these attacks thanks to

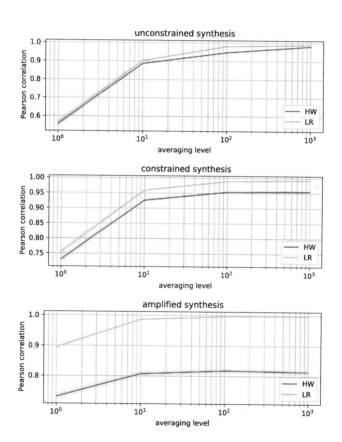

Fig. 6. Correlation between real traces with different levels of averaging (on the X axis) and Hamming weight vs. regression-based linear models.

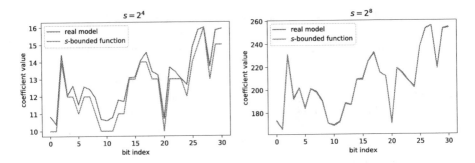

Fig. 7. Discretization of the linear regression models (unconstrained synth.).

standard side-channel analysis tools, which will incidentally lead us to provide good indications that limiting the coefficient's accuracy is also reasonable.

Precisely, and as illustrated in Fig. 2, we show how to move from measured leakages to s-bounded leakages thanks to the linear regression-based model of Sect. 2.2. For this purpose, we re-use the 31-element vectors of coefficients $\hat{a}$ estimated using $n_p = 10,000$ profiling traces, for each of our three syntheses. We next observe that the value of Pearson's correlation is not affected if one of its variables is multiplied by a constant value. As a result, the following simple discretization process for the coefficients $\hat{a}$ can be used:

$$\hat{a}_{\mathsf{d}} = \left\lceil \hat{a} \cdot \frac{s}{\max(\hat{a})} \right\rceil .$$

We finally illustrate the coefficients of the linear models estimated from the unconstrained synthesis measurements together with the coefficients of the corresponding s-bounded functions in Fig. 7. We can observe that already for $s = 2^8$ the matching between both is quite accurate. We further estimated the correlation $\hat{\rho}(M_{\mathsf{r}1}^s, M_{\mathsf{r}1})$ which was worth $1 - \phi$ with $\phi < 10^{-6}$ for $s = 2^8$.[5] We conclude that a quantization corresponding to $s = 2^{12}$ offers a sufficient granularity to discretize our linear leakage models nearly perfectly. In other words, while we cannot rule out that other strategies than interpreting the leakages in $\mathbb{F}_p$ as we consider can lead to better results, this section shows that if this is the best strategy, then the move from measured leakages to s-bounded ones does not imply a significant information loss for the values of s (e.g., 2^{12}) that our theoretical investigations tolerate. The results for the quantization of the models for moderately constrained and amplified syntheses are similar. We illustrate their respective coefficients in Figs. 8 and 9 for completeness.

6.4 Bounded Measurement Accuracy

The previous sections suggested that using linear regression-based models is sufficient to accurately capture concretely-relevant leakage functions and that

---

[5] With a relative error of below 1%, which is easy to reach since the estimation is performed from modeled samples (rather than measured ones in Sect. 6.2).

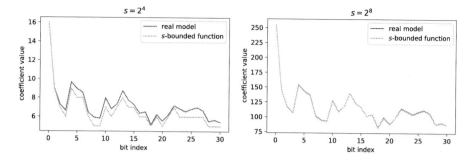

Fig. 8. Discretization of the linear regression models (constrained synthesis).

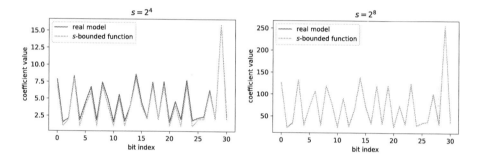

Fig. 9. Discretization of the linear regression models (amplified synthesis).

increasing the coefficient accuracy of the s-bounded pseudo-linear functions beyond 2^{12} does not lead to significant improvements of their informativeness in our case study. Quite naturally, such assessments remain limited by their heuristic nature. For the analysis of the degree, this is unavoidable (since absence of evidence is not evidence of absence) and the only option to make it more robust is to consider higher-degree functions that could theoretically show up, which we will do in Sect. 7. But for the bounded coefficient accuracy, there is a complementary argument that could be given. For this purpose, the starting observation is that physical leakages are measured by converting an analog signal into a digital one. Concretely, the "vertical resolution" s' of modern oscilloscopes typically ranges from 8 to 12 bits, meaning that the measured leakage can take between 2^8 and 2^{12} values (possibly a bit more thanks to oversampling, at the cost of a reduced "horizontal" resolution). So if the increase of the s parameter from Definition 5 leads to a pseudo-linear function having a codomain with more than s' elements, it implies that the s-bounded leakage function is more informative than the measured one, which contradicts the data processing inequality. So for such leakage functions, the bounded coefficient accuracy can be directly connected to an assumption on the adversary's measurement apparatus.

However, increasing the s parameter does not always increase the cardinality of the leakage functions (e.g., think about the case where $t = 1$ for an increasing s). So one cannot directly bound the coefficient accuracy s based on the resolution of the oscilloscope s'. Yet, we note that most of the security claims in Sects. 4 (resp., 5) depend on the product ts (resp., mts) which bounds the cardinality of the functions' co-domain and where t corresponds to the $\binom{t}{1}$ basis functions of a linear leakage model. So if the security analysis could be improved in order to rely only on this cardinality of the leakage functions, independent of the value of s (i.e., getting rid of the $ts < p$ and $mts < p$ conditions), we could replace the assumption on the bounded coefficient accuracy by an assumption on the resolution of the oscilloscope used to mount the attack. We leave the investigation of such an improved analysis as an interesting open problem.

6.5   Concrete Security Level

The three aforementioned implementations gave us three sets of real parameters, namely $\hat{a}^u, \hat{a}^c$ and $\hat{a}^a$. Each of them can be discretized using the method of Sect. 6.3, resulting in three sets of $\mathbb{F}_p$ coefficients a_d^u, a_d^c and a_d^a, themselves associated to an s-bounded pseudo-linear function $\mathsf{F}_{a_d^u}, \mathsf{F}_{a_d^c}$ and $\mathsf{F}_{a_d^a}$.

Table 1. $\deg(\mathsf{F}_{a_d^*})$ and $\mathsf{nl}(\mathsf{F}_{a_d^*})$ bounds of s-bounded pseudo-linear functions for the different implementations (computed using Proposition 3).

	$v_{\mathsf{F}_{a_d^*}}$	$w_{\mathsf{F}_{a_d^*}}$	$\deg(\mathsf{F}_{a_d^*})$	$\mathsf{nl}(\mathsf{F}_{a_d^*})$
Unconstrained	101748	1073657388	≥ 101748	≥ 2147381899
Constrained	213852	1073692455	≥ 213852	≥ 2147269795
Amplified	160593	1073709374	≥ 160593	≥ 2147323054

The results of Table 1 show the very high values of the degree and nonlinearity reached by these s-bounded pseudo-linear functions. As a result, algebraic attacks appear to be impracticable against the corresponding LWPR instances. The time complexities being several order of magnitude larger than the 124 bits of security we target, even more advanced approach (e.g., solving algebraic systems with Gröbner bases, using code-based techniques to approximate by smaller-degree functions) should not lead to successful attacks.

7   Further Generalizations

The previous section confirmed the security that can be offered by concrete LWPR instances. It also showed that linear models are good abstractions to capture the features of actual leakage measurements. In this section, we show that the positive results obtained for s-bounded pseudo-linear functions extend naturally to higher-order leakage models, taking the quadratic case as an example. Despite not directly motivated by practice (as linear leakage models offered high level of correlation with real leakages in the previous section), we deem this result important to confirm that even in the hypothetical presence of such higher-order dependencies, the security of LWPR would not collapse.

Definition 7 (s-bounded pseudo-quadratic functions). *We denote* $Q_{a,b}$ *the function defined by a vector* $a \in \mathbb{F}_p^t$ *and a strictly upper triangular matrix* $b \in \mathbb{F}_p^{t \times t}$, *where* $t = \lceil \log p \rceil$, *as:*

$$Q_{a,b} : \mathbb{F}_p \to \mathbb{F}_p$$

$$y \mapsto \sum_{i=0}^{t-1} a_i \mathbf{g}(y)_i + \sum_{0 \le i < j < t} b_{i(t+1)+j} \mathbf{g}(y)_i \mathbf{g}(y)_j.$$

We call $Q_{a,b}$ *s-bounded pseudo-quadratic when each* $a_i, b_{i,j}$ *belongs to* $[0, s]$, *with security parameter* $s \in \mathbb{F}_p$ C_2^s *the class of s-bounded pseudo-quadratic functions.*

We give the following result for attacks exploiting any-case leakages.

Proposition 5 (Properties of s-bounded pseudo-quadratic functions). *Let* $f \in C_2^s$ *with* $\frac{t(t+1)}{2}s < p$ *and* $t = \lceil \log p \rceil$, *then the following holds:*

- $\mathsf{v}_f \ge \left\lceil \frac{p}{st(t+1)/2+1} \right\rceil$,
- $\mathsf{w}_f \ge p - st(t+1)/2 - 1$.

And assuming $\mathsf{v}_f \ne p$, *we further have:*

- $\deg(f) \ge \left\lceil \frac{p}{st(t+1)/2+1} \right\rceil$,
- $\mathsf{nl}(f) \ge \min \left(p - \mathsf{v}_f, \max \left(\left\lceil \frac{p}{st(t+1)/2+1} \right\rceil - 1, p - st(t+1)/2 - 1 \right) \right)$.

Proof. Since $\frac{t(t+1)}{2}s < p$, we obtain that for all $x \in \mathbb{F}_p$, $0 \le f(x) \le \frac{t(t+1)}{2}s$, hence $\mathsf{w}_f \ge p - \frac{t(t+1)}{2}s - 1$. Thereafter, $f(x)$ can take at most $\frac{t(t+1)}{2}s + 1$ values, hence there exists at least a preimage set with cardinal $\left\lceil \frac{p}{st(t+1)/2+1} \right\rceil$ or more. Finally, the last items are obtained by using Proposition 1 and Proposition 2 respectively, combined with the two first items.   □

Note that the condition $ts < p$ which avoids the reduction when computing the leakage function in the analysis of the linear case is replaced by a condition $\frac{t(t+1)}{2}s < p$, where $\frac{t(t+1)}{2} = \binom{t}{1} + \binom{t}{2}$ is the number of basis functions in the quadratic model. This last result shows that s-bounded pseudo-quadratic functions behave similarly to s-bounded pseudo-linear functions. The only difference is that the security parameter s is a bit more constrained, so that $\frac{t(t+1)}{2}s < p$. Yet, with $p = 2^{31} - 1$ and $t = \lceil \log p \rceil$, security remains guaranteed for $s = 2^{12}$ (with a large security margin). In a similar manner, it could be shown that the estimated cost of algebraic attacks against LWPR is maintained for larger degrees, if the leakage function it relies on remains sufficiently non-injective, with a constraint on s evolving with the number of basis functions in the model.

As for attacks using worst-case leakages as studied in Sect. 5, the condition is slightly more restricted since we need $m\frac{t(t+1)}{2}s < p$ in order to apply Proposition 4. It nevertheless remains sufficient in the quadratic case. Besides, it could again be that an improved analysis leads to relaxed conditions (or tighter bounds), which we leave as an interesting scope for further research.

8   Conclusions and Open Problems

By showing that the LWPR assumption remains secure for a wide class of practically-relevant leakage functions, this work makes an important step in improving its usability. As a result, it strengthens the motivation for using re-keying schemes operating in prime fields, since they provide significant security improvements over their binary counterparts. Concretely, our investigations suggest that parallel instances of LWPR have good potential to be secure. The generalization of Sect. 7 further shows that increasing the degree of the leakage function is not a direct threat, so that the main assumption for LWPR to be hard is the quite natural requirement that the leakages are sufficiently non-injective.

Our results open several interesting avenues for further research. First, Sect. 3 recalled the challenge of securing serial LWPR implementations against leakage and suggested shuffling as a possible option for this purpose. Its concrete investigation is therefore a natural next step. Second, our analyzes could be improved in order to rely only on the degree of the leakage functions and the cardinality of their co-domain. As discussed in Sect. 6.4, this could lead to formally connect the bouned coefficient accuracy hypothesis with the resolution of the adversary's measurement apparatus. Third, we for now consider univariate leakages. They reasonably match the hardware implementation context we evaluated, where it is possible to implement the un-masking of the ephemeral key in a single cycle. But multivariate generalizations are an important scope for further investigations and will be especially relevant in a software implementation context where (for example) the reduction that has to take place after the un-masking may take several cycles. Dealing with more leaky software implementations (even with shuffling) may also motivate stepping back to a less conservative model, where security is argued based on the difficulty for the adversary to infer leakage values without errors, possibly formalized by a Learning With Physical Rounding and Errors problem. LWPR being an aggressive and new physical assumption, improving the understanding of the best cryptanalysis techniques to break it naturally remains needed as well. For example, our current attacks do not exploit key guessing strategies (which should at least imply a slight increase of the security parameters). Eventually, it would be worth studying the conditions upon which hard physical learning problems can be connected and reduced to standard (mathematical) hard learning problems.

Acknowledgments. Pierrick Méaux was supported by the ERC project 787390 (acronym CLOUDMAP). François-Xavier Standaert is a senior research associate of the Belgian Fund for Scientific Research (FNRS-F.R.S.). This work has been funded in parts by the European Union through the ERC project 724725 (acronym SWORD) and by the Walloon Region Win2Wal project PIRATE.

References

BCF+15. Belaïd, S., Coron, J.-S., Fouque, P.-A., Gérard, B., Kammerer, J.-G., Prouff, E.: Improved side-channel analysis of finite-field multiplication. In: Güneysu, T., Handschuh, H. (eds.) CHES 2015. LNCS, vol. 9293, pp. 395–415. Springer, Heidelberg (2015). https://doi.org/10.1007/978-3-662-48324-4_20

BCO04. Brier, E., Clavier, C., Olivier, F.: Correlation power analysis with a leakage model. In: Joye, M., Quisquater, J.-J. (eds.) CHES 2004. LNCS, vol. 3156, pp. 16–29. Springer, Heidelberg (2004). https://doi.org/10.1007/978-3-540-28632-5_2

BDF+17. Barthe, G., Dupressoir, F., Faust, S., Grégoire, B., Standaert, F.-X., Strub, P.-Y.: Parallel implementations of masking schemes and the bounded moment leakage model. In: Coron, J.-S., Nielsen, J.B. (eds.) EUROCRYPT 2017. LNCS, vol. 10210, pp. 535–566. Springer, Cham (2017). https://doi.org/10.1007/978-3-319-56620-7_19

BDK+18. Bos, J.W., et al.: CRYSTALS - Kyber: a CCA-secure module-lattice-based KEM. In: EuroS&P, pp. 353–367. IEEE (2018)

BFG14. Belaïd, S., Fouque, P.-A., Gérard, B.: Side-channel analysis of multiplications in GF(2^{128}). In: Sarkar, P., Iwata, T. (eds.) ASIACRYPT 2014. LNCS, vol. 8874, pp. 306–325. Springer, Heidelberg (2014). https://doi.org/10.1007/978-3-662-45608-8_17

BFS15. Bardet, M., Faugère, J.-C., Salvy, B.: On the complexity of the F5 gröbner basis algorithm. J. Symb. Comput. **70**, 49–70 (2015)

BGL+14. Brenner, H., Gaspar, L., Leurent, G., Rosen, A., Standaert, F.-X.: FPGA implementations of SPRING. In: Batina, L., Robshaw, M. (eds.) CHES 2014. LNCS, vol. 8731, pp. 414–432. Springer, Heidelberg (2014). https://doi.org/10.1007/978-3-662-44709-3_23

BIP+18. Boneh, D., Ishai, Y., Passelègue, A., Sahai, A., Wu, D.J.: Exploring crypto dark matter: new simple PRF candidates and their applications. In: Beimel, A., Dziembowski, S. (eds.) TCC 2018. LNCS, vol. 11240, pp. 699–729. Springer, Cham (2018). https://doi.org/10.1007/978-3-030-03810-6_25

BPR12. Banerjee, A., Peikert, C., Rosen, A.: Pseudorandom functions and lattices. In: Pointcheval, D., Johansson, T. (eds.) EUROCRYPT 2012. LNCS, vol. 7237, pp. 719–737. Springer, Heidelberg (2012). https://doi.org/10.1007/978-3-642-29011-4_42

BUS21. Bellizia, D., Udvarhelyi, B., Standaert, F.-X.: Towards a better understanding of side-channel analysis measurements setups. In: Grosso, V., Pöppelmann, T. (eds.) CARDIS. LNCS, vol. 13173, pp. 64–79. Springer, Cham (2021). https://doi.org/10.1007/978-3-030-97348-3_4

BV11. Brakerski, Z., Vaikuntanathan, V.: Fully homomorphic encryption from ring-LWE and security for key dependent messages. In: Rogaway, P. (ed.) CRYPTO 2011. LNCS, vol. 6841, pp. 505–524. Springer, Heidelberg (2011). https://doi.org/10.1007/978-3-642-22792-9_29

Car21. Carlet, C.: Boolean Functions for Cryptography and Coding Theory. Cambridge University Press (2021)

CGP+12. Coron, J.-S., Giraud, C., Prouff, E., Renner, S., Rivain, M., Vadnala, P.K.: Conversion of security proofs from one leakage model to another: a new issue. In: Schindler, W., Huss, S.A. (eds.) COSADE 2012. LNCS, vol. 7275, pp. 69–81. Springer, Heidelberg (2012). https://doi.org/10.1007/978-3-642-29912-4_6

CHKP10. Cash, D., Hofheinz, D., Kiltz, E., Peikert, C.: Bonsai trees, or how to delegate a lattice basis. In: Gilbert, H. (ed.) EUROCRYPT 2010. LNCS, vol. 6110, pp. 523–552. Springer, Heidelberg (2010). https://doi.org/10.1007/978-3-642-13190-5_27

CHMS22. Cosseron, O., Hoffmann, C., Méaux, P., Standaert, F.-X.: Towards case-optimized hybrid homomorphic encryption - featuring the Elisabeth stream cipher. In: Agrawal, S., Lin, D. (eds.) ASIACRYPT (3). LNCS, vol. 13793, pp. 32–67. Springer, Cham (2022). https://doi.org/10.1007/978-3-031-22969-5_2

Cou02. Courtois, N.T.: Higher order correlation attacks, XL algorithm and cryptanalysis of Toyocrypt. In: Lee, P.J., Lim, C.H. (eds.) Information Security and Cryptology - ICISC 2002, 5th International Conference Seoul, Korea, 28–29 November 2002, Revised Papers. LNCS, vol. 2587, pp. 182–199. Springer, Heidelberg (2002). https://doi.org/10.1007/3-540-36552-4_13

CRR02. Chari, S., Rao, J.R., Rohatgi, P.: Template attacks. In: Kaliski, B.S., Koç, K., Paar, C. (eds.) CHES 2002. LNCS, vol. 2523, pp. 13–28. Springer, Heidelberg (2003). https://doi.org/10.1007/3-540-36400-5_3

CS20. Cassiers, G., Standaert, F.-X.: Trivially and efficiently composing masked gadgets with probe isolating non-interference. IEEE Trans. Inf. Forensics Secur. 15, 2542–2555 (2020)

CS21. Cassiers, G., Standaert, F.-X.: Provably secure hardware masking in the transition- and glitch-robust probing model: better safe than sorry. IACR Trans. Cryptogr. Hardw. Embed. Syst. 2021(2), 136–158 (2021)

DFH+16. Dziembowski, S., Faust, S., Herold, G., Journault, A., Masny, D., Standaert, F.-X.: Towards sound fresh re-keying with hard (physical) learning problems. In: Robshaw, M., Katz, J. (eds.) CRYPTO 2016. LNCS, vol. 9815, pp. 272–301. Springer, Heidelberg (2016). https://doi.org/10.1007/978-3-662-53008-5_10

DGH+21. Dinur, I., et al.: MPC-friendly symmetric cryptography from alternating moduli: candidates, protocols, and applications. In: Malkin, T., Peikert, C. (eds.) CRYPTO 2021. LNCS, vol. 12828, pp. 517–547. Springer, Cham (2021). https://doi.org/10.1007/978-3-030-84259-8_18

DKL+18. Ducas, L., et al.: Crystals-Dilithium: a lattice-based digital signature scheme. IACR Trans. Cryptogr. Hardw. Embed. Syst. 2018(1), 238–268 (2018)

DMMS21. Duval, S., Méaux, P., Momin, C., Standaert, F.-X.: Exploring crypto-physical dark matter and learning with physical rounding towards secure and efficient fresh re-keying. IACR Trans. Cryptogr. Hardw. Embed. Syst. 2021(1), 373–401 (2021)

Fau99. Faugère, J.-C.: A new efficient algorithm for computing Groebner bases. J. Pure Appl. Algebra, 61–88 (1999)

Fau02. Faugère, J.C.: A new efficient algorithm for computing Gröbner bases without reduction to zero (F5). In: Proceedings of the 2002 International Symposium on Symbolic and Algebraic Computation, ISSAC 2002, pp. 75–83 (2002)

Gen09. Gentry, C.: Fully homomorphic encryption using ideal lattices. In: STOC, pp. 169–178. ACM (2009)

GJ19. Guo, Q., Johansson, T.: A new birthday-type algorithm for attacking the fresh re-keying countermeasure. Inf. Process. Lett. 146, 30–34 (2019)

GLP06. Gierlichs, B., Lemke-Rust, K., Paar, C.: Templates vs. stochastic methods. In: Goubin, L., Matsui, M. (eds.) CHES 2006. LNCS, vol. 4249, pp. 15–29. Springer, Heidelberg (2006). https://doi.org/10.1007/11894063_2

GLS14. Gaspar, L., Leurent, G., Standaert, F.-X.: Hardware implementation and side-channel analysis of lapin. In: Benaloh, J. (ed.) CT-RSA 2014. LNCS, vol. 8366, pp. 206–226. Springer, Cham (2014). https://doi.org/10.1007/978-3-319-04852-9_11

GPV08. Gentry, C., Peikert, C., Vaikuntanathan, V.: Trapdoors for hard lattices and new cryptographic constructions. In: STOC, pp. 197–206. ACM (2008)

GR17. Goudarzi, D., Rivain, M.: How fast can higher-order masking be in software? In: Coron, J.-S., Nielsen, J.B. (eds.) EUROCRYPT 2017. LNCS, vol. 10210, pp. 567–597. Springer, Cham (2017). https://doi.org/10.1007/978-3-319-56620-7_20

HB01. Hopper, N.J., Blum, M.: Secure human identification protocols. In: Boyd, C. (ed.) ASIACRYPT 2001. LNCS, vol. 2248, pp. 52–66. Springer, Heidelberg (2001). https://doi.org/10.1007/3-540-45682-1_4

HKL+12. Heyse, S., Kiltz, E., Lyubashevsky, V., Paar, C., Pietrzak, K.: Lapin: an efficient authentication protocol based on ring-LPN. In: Canteaut, A. (ed.) FSE 2012. LNCS, vol. 7549, pp. 346–365. Springer, Heidelberg (2012). https://doi.org/10.1007/978-3-642-34047-5_20

HLM+23. Hoffmann, C., Libert, B., Momin, C., Peters, T., Standaert, F.-X.: POLKA: towards leakage-resistant post-quantum CCA-secure public key encryption. In: Boldyreva, A., Kolesnikov, V. (eds.) Public Key Cryptography (1). LNCS, vol. 13940, pp. 114–144. Springer, Cham (2023). https://doi.org/10.1007/978-3-031-31368-4_5

HOM06. Herbst, C., Oswald, E., Mangard, S.: An AES smart card implementation resistant to power analysis attacks. In: Zhou, J., Yung, M., Bao, F. (eds.) ACNS 2006. LNCS, vol. 3989, pp. 239–252. Springer, Heidelberg (2006). https://doi.org/10.1007/11767480_16

Hou18. Hou, X.-D.: Lectures on Finite Fields, vol. 190. American Mathematical Society (2018)

ISW03. Ishai, Y., Sahai, A., Wagner, D.: Private circuits: securing hardware against probing attacks. In: Boneh, D. (ed.) CRYPTO 2003. LNCS, vol. 2729, pp. 463–481. Springer, Heidelberg (2003). https://doi.org/10.1007/978-3-540-45146-4_27

KSHS17. Koppermann, P., De Santis, F., Heyszl, J., Sigl, G.: Automatic generation of high-performance modular multipliers for arbitrary Mersenne primes on FPGAs. In: HOST, pp. 35–40. IEEE Computer Society (2017)

Man04. Mangard, S.: Hardware countermeasures against DPA – a statistical analysis of their effectiveness. In: Okamoto, T. (ed.) CT-RSA 2004. LNCS, vol. 2964, pp. 222–235. Springer, Heidelberg (2004). https://doi.org/10.1007/978-3-540-24660-2_18

MOP07. Mangard, S., Oswald, E., Popp, T.: Power Analysis Attacks - Revealing the Secrets of Smart Cards. Springer, New York (2007). https://doi.org/10.1007/978-0-387-38162-6

MPG05. Mangard, S., Popp, T., Gammel, B.M.: Side-channel leakage of masked CMOS gates. In: Menezes, A. (ed.) CT-RSA 2005. LNCS, vol. 3376, pp. 351–365. Springer, Heidelberg (2005). https://doi.org/10.1007/978-3-540-30574-3_24

MSGR10. Medwed, M., Standaert, F.-X., Großschädl, J., Regazzoni, F.: Fresh re-keying: security against side-channel and fault attacks for low-cost devices. In: Bernstein, D.J., Lange, T. (eds.) AFRICACRYPT 2010. LNCS, vol. 6055, pp. 279–296. Springer, Heidelberg (2010). https://doi.org/10.1007/978-3-642-12678-9_17

NDGJ21. Ngo, K., Dubrova, E., Guo, Q., Johansson, T.: A side-channel attack on a masked IND-CCA secure saber KEM implementation. IACR Trans. Cryptogr. Hardw. Embed. Syst. **2021**(4), 676–707 (2021)

Pie12. Pietrzak, K.: Cryptography from learning parity with noise. In: Bieliková, M., Friedrich, G., Gottlob, G., Katzenbeisser, S., Turán, G. (eds.) SOFSEM 2012. LNCS, vol. 7147, pp. 99–114. Springer, Heidelberg (2012). https://doi.org/10.1007/978-3-642-27660-6_9

PM16. Pessl, P., Mangard, S.: Enhancing side-channel analysis of binary-field multiplication with bit reliability. In: Sako, K. (ed.) CT-RSA 2016. LNCS, vol. 9610, pp. 255–270. Springer, Cham (2016). https://doi.org/10.1007/978-3-319-29485-8_15

Reg05. Regev, O.: On lattices, learning with errors, random linear codes, and cryptography. In: STOC, pp. 84–93. ACM (2005)

Reg10. Regev, O.: The learning with errors problem (invited survey). In: Computational Complexity Conference, pp. 191–204. IEEE Computer Society (2010)

RRCB20. Ravi, P., Roy, S.S., Chattopadhyay, A., Bhasin, S.: Generic side-channel attacks on CCA-secure lattice-based PKE and KEMs. IACR Trans. Cryptogr. Hardw. Embed. Syst. **2020**(3), 307–335 (2020)

SLP05. Schindler, W., Lemke, K., Paar, C.: A stochastic model for differential side channel cryptanalysis. In: Rao, J.R., Sunar, B. (eds.) CHES 2005. LNCS, vol. 3659, pp. 30–46. Springer, Heidelberg (2005). https://doi.org/10.1007/11545262_3

SMY09. Standaert, F.-X., Malkin, T.G., Yung, M.: A unified framework for the analysis of side-channel key recovery attacks. In: Joux, A. (ed.) EUROCRYPT 2009. LNCS, vol. 5479, pp. 443–461. Springer, Heidelberg (2009). https://doi.org/10.1007/978-3-642-01001-9_26

SPRQ06. Standaert, F.-X., Peeters, E., Rouvroy, G., Quisquater, J.-J.: An overview of power analysis attacks against field programmable gate arrays. Proc. IEEE **94**(2), 383–394 (2006)

UBS21. Udvarhelyi, B., Bronchain, O., Standaert, F.-X.: Security analysis of deterministic re-keying with masking and shuffling: application to ISAP. In: Bhasin, S., De Santis, F. (eds.) COSADE 2021. LNCS, vol. 12910, pp. 168–183. Springer, Cham (2021). https://doi.org/10.1007/978-3-030-89915-8_8

UXT+22. Ueno, R., Xagawa, K., Tanaka, Y., Ito, A., Takahashi, J., Homma, N.: Curse of re-encryption: a generic power/EM analysis on post-quantum KEMs. IACR Trans. Cryptogr. Hardw. Embed. Syst. **2022**(1), 296–322 (2022)

VMKS12. Veyrat-Charvillon, N., Medwed, M., Kerckhof, S., Standaert, F.-X.: Shuffling against side-channel attacks: a comprehensive study with cautionary note. In: Wang, X., Sako, K. (eds.) ASIACRYPT 2012. LNCS, vol. 7658, pp. 740–757. Springer, Heidelberg (2012). https://doi.org/10.1007/978-3-642-34961-4_44

YC04. Yang, B.-Y., Chen, J.-M.: All in the XL family: theory and practice. In: Park, C., Chee, S. (eds.) ICISC 2004. LNCS, vol. 3506, pp. 67–86. Springer, Heidelberg (2005). https://doi.org/10.1007/11496618_7

YS16. Yu, Yu., Steinberger, J.: Pseudorandom functions in almost constant depth from low-noise LPN. In: Fischlin, M., Coron, J.-S. (eds.) EUROCRYPT 2016. LNCS, vol. 9666, pp. 154–183. Springer, Heidelberg (2016). https://doi.org/10.1007/978-3-662-49896-5_6

Unifying Freedom and Separation for Tight Probing-Secure Composition

Sonia Belaïd[1]([✉]), Gaëtan Cassiers[3], Matthieu Rivain[1],
and Abdul Rahman Taleb[1,2]

[1] CryptoExperts, Paris, France
{sonia.belaid,matthieu.rivain,abdul.taleb}@cryptoexperts.com
[2] Sorbonne Université, CNRS, LIP6, 75005 Paris, France
[3] TU Graz, Graz, Austria
gaetan.cassiers@iaik.tugraz.at

Abstract. The masking countermeasure is often analyzed in the probing model. Proving the probing security of large circuits at high masking orders is achieved by composing gadgets that satisfy security definitions such as non-interference (NI), strong non-interference (SNI) or free SNI. The region probing model is a variant of the probing model, where the probing capabilities of the adversary scale with the number of regions in a masked circuit. This model is of interest as it allows better reductions to the more realistic noisy leakage model. The efficiency of composable region probing secure masking has been recently improved with the introduction of the input-output separation (IOS) definition.

In this paper, we first establish equivalences between the non-interference framework and the IOS formalism. We also generalize the security definitions to multiple-input gadgets and systematically show implications and separations between these notions. Then, we study which gadgets from the literature satisfy these. We give new security proofs for some well-known arbitrary-order gadgets, and also some automated proofs for fixed-order, special-case gadgets. To this end, we introduce a new automated formal verification algorithm that solves the open problem of verifying free SNI, which is not a purely simulation-based definition. Using the relationships between the security notions, we adapt this algorithm to further verify IOS. Finally, we look at composition theorems. In the probing model, we use the link between free SNI and the IOS formalism to generalize and improve the efficiency of the tight private circuit (Asiacrypt 2018) construction, also fixing a flaw in the original proof. In the region probing model, we relax the assumptions for IOS composition (TCHES 2021), which allows to save many refresh gadgets, hence improving the efficiency.

Keywords: Masking · Probing model · Region probing model ·
Non-interference · Input output separation · Tight private circuit

1 Introduction

The security of cryptographic algorithms is mainly studied in the *black-box* model, where an adversary is restricted to the knowledge of inputs and outputs

© International Association for Cryptologic Research 2023
H. Handschuh and A. Lysyanskaya (Eds.): CRYPTO 2023, LNCS 14083, pp. 440–472, 2023.
https://doi.org/10.1007/978-3-031-38548-3_15

to recover the secret key. However, the discovery of *side-channel attacks* in the late nineties [29] opened the door for a new field of security study. These attacks can break cryptosystems by exploiting the device's physical leakage (power consumption, electromagnetic emanations, ...) that executes the implementation.

Many countermeasures have since been studied to protect against this class of attacks. The *masking* countermeasure is the most widely deployed one. The concept was introduced in 1999 by Chari et al. [19] and by Goubin and Patarin [23], and suggests splitting a sensitive variable x of the implementation into n shares, such that an adversary must get information on all the shares to recover the secret. This can be easily achieved by generating $n-1$ shares uniformly at random $x_1, \ldots, x_{n-1}$ and computing the last share x_n so that $x = x_1 * \ldots * x_{n-1} * x_n$ according to some group law $*$. An implementation then manipulates the sharing $\vec{x} = (x_1, \ldots, x_n)$ instead of the secret itself. While being easy to manipulate for affine operations, which can be computed on each share separately (sharewise), it is not trivial to securely manipulate sharings for non-linear operations without recombining the secrets.

To theoretically evaluate the security of a circuit against side-channel attacks, Ishai, Sahai, and Wagner (ISW) [27] introduced the *t-probing leakage model*. A circuit is secure in the t-probing model if the exact values of any set of t intermediate variables do not reveal any information on the secrets. This definition is motivated by the increasing difficulty of recovering information on the combination of $t + 1$ variables from the leakage traces that contain noisy functions of the manipulated data, as t grows. Furthermore, this model corresponds to the practically-relevant notion of masking security order [6]. Many works have since built and analyzed masking schemes with respect to their security in the probing model [10,20,34].

Meanwhile, probing security is only partially satisfactory. Indeed, there is a mismatch between the fixed number of probes and the amount of real-world leakage, which grows with the number of performed computations. For instance, the authors of [7] show that the repeated manipulation of identical values can be exploited to retrieve the secrets in the context of *horizontal side-channel attacks*. This led to the formalization of the *noisy leakage model* in [33] as a specialization of the *only computation leaks* model [31]. In this model, the adversary can retrieve a noisy function of each intermediate variable of the computation. Because of the inconvenience of the noisy model for security proofs, Duc, Dziembowski, and Faust [22] proposed a reduction from the noisy model to the t-probing model. Reducing to the t-region probing model, where the whole computation is split into regions and the adversary can chose t probes in each region, improves significantly the security of this bound since this model increases the number of probes with respect to the size of the circuit/region.

Even in the simple probing model, proving the security of large masked circuits is a challenging problem, due to the combinatorial number of possible sets of probes. The most common solution is to build circuits from smaller sub-circuits named gadgets that implement a simple computation on masked data. Then, these gadgets can be composed to implement more complex computations, and the security proof only needs to care about the properties of the gadgets and their composition. In their seminal work [27], ISW introduced such gadgets for a field multiplication and addition. These gadgets can be arbitrarily composed, but this scheme requires masking with $n = 2t + 1$ shares. For performance reasons, the follow-up works mostly focused on using the optimal number of shares $n = t + 1$. The first composition security notion which is known as t-*strong non-interference* (SNI) was introduced by Barthe, Belaïd, Dupressoir, Fouque, Grégoire, Strub and Zucchini in [5]. In a nutshell, t-SNI ensures that probes inside a gadget and on its output shares can be perfectly simulated with knowledge of a limited number of input shares of a gadget. It follows that one can simulate all the probes in a composition of t-SNI gadgets by knowing t shares of each input sharing, which is independent of the secret input values. The SNI gadgets for affine operations are however not very efficient, was solved by the t-PINI definition (at the expense of slightly less efficient multiplication) [17].

Another direction to improve efficiency is to drop the requirement of arbitrary composition: while direct application of the ISW construction with $n = t + 1$ is not secure [34], it can be fixed by adding refresh gadgets (which implement the identity function but re-randomize the sharings). This has instance been proposed in [5] with the `maskComp` tool that can compose weaker non-interferent (NI) gadgets by inserting SNI refresh gadgets (which can be derived from the ISW multiplication) in the circuit. Later, Belaïd, Goudarzi and Rivain [12], introduced tight private circuits (TPC), which is another variant of the ISW scheme with $n = t+1$ and additional refresh gadgets. The set of refresh gadgets inserted by their `tightProve` tool is tight in the sense that removing one of these gadgets is guaranteed to break t-probing security.

A stronger version of the probing model has been considered in the literature which is known as the *region probing model* [1]. In this model, the adversary is not limited to t probes on the circuit but gets t probes per gadget (or *region*) of the circuit. This model is relevant in practice as being closer to actual side-channel leakages (providing information on all the gadgets of an implementation) which is formally captured by a reduction to the noisy leakage model [22,33]. In a recent work [25], Goudarzi, Prest, Rivain and Vergnaud introduce the *input-output separation* (IOS) notion for simple composition in the region probing model. This notion acts as probing-composition scissors: the circuit is divided into regions separated by IOS gadgets whose probes can then be simulated separately.

A complementary line of research has been considering the optimization of the masked gadgets themselves. This culminated in the design of a $(n - 1)$-NI multiplication gadget with randomness usage $n^2/4 + \mathcal{O}(n)$ [9] (while the ISW multiplication is $(n - 1)$-SNI and has $n^2/2 + \mathcal{O}(n)$ randomness usage) and a $(n - 1)$-SNI refresh gadget with complexity $\mathcal{O}(n \log n)$ [8]. Besides these arbitrary-order gadgets, there have been many optimizations for low-order gadgets. Manually verifying the security properties of such small gadgets is tedious and error-prone [20], which naturally led to the development of automatic formal verification tools for these security properties [2,4,5,13,15,28].

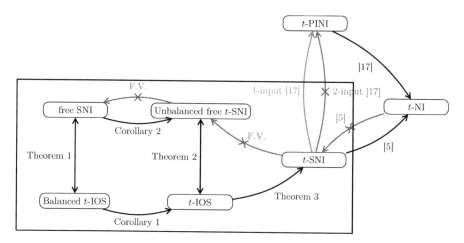

Fig. 1. Relations between security notions. Plain black arrows represent mathematical implications whereas red crossed out arrows mean that a counterexample demonstrates the absence of implication. The orange plain arrow represents an implication from t-SNI to t-PINI only for 1-input gadgets. The black rectangle frames the security notions that are focused on in this paper. F.V. means that a counterexample is given in the full version of the paper. (Color figure online)

Our Contributions. In this paper, we unify and extend existing probing composition notions, we analyze gadget constructions under these unified notions, we provide efficient verification methods for these notions, and we extend existing composition approaches in the probing and region probing model. In more details, our contributions are as follows:

- We show that the composition approach of tight private circuits (TPC) introduced in [12] actually requires a stronger notion than the SNI notion initially considered by the authors. The required notion happens to be the *free SNI* notion introduced by Coron and Spignoli in [21]. In a nutshell, the free SNI notion requires that the non-simulated output shares of a gadget be uniformly distributed and mutually independent of the simulated wires. We generalize the free SNI notion to two input gadgets and patch the composition proof of TPC.[1] Our proof also generalizes the TPC composition approach to any gadget circuit based on $(n-2)$-free SNI multiplication gadgets, $(n-1)$-free SNI refresh gadget and sharewise affine gadgets (which encompasses a wide number of masked circuits used in practice).
- We show strong connections between the free SNI notion and the IOS notion introduced in [25] for easy composition in the region probing model. Specif-

---

[1] We note that, while the composition proof is flawed, the TPC construction considered in [12] which relies on ISW multiplication and refresh gadgets is still secure since these gadgets achieve the necessary free SNI notion as we further show in the present paper.

ically, we show that these notions are essentially equivalent. More precisely, the IOS notion is equivalent to a *unbalanced* version of the free SNI notion which relaxes some constraints on the input and output shares involved in the simulation. On the other hand, the free SNI notion is equivalent to a *balanced* version of the IOS notion which adds the latter constraints to IOS. We further show that free SNI and IOS (for either the balanced or unbalanced version) both imply the SNI notion. This notably answers the questions left open in [26]: (1) IOS (resp. free SNI) is strictly stronger than SNI: IOS implies SNI while the converse is not true, (2) IOS (resp. free SNI) is strictly stronger than PINI for one-input gadget but it is separated from PINI for two-input gadgets. These relations are depicted on Fig. 1 which summarizes the current state of affairs in terms of (most common) probing composition notions.

- We then investigate gadget constructions under the strong unified notions of free SNI and balanced IOS. We propose generic constructions of gadgets achieving these notions from simpler building blocks. We further demonstrate that common gadgets satisfy these properties. Specifically, we prove that the well known ISW multiplication gadget is free-$(n-2)$-SNI (or equivalently balanced $(n-2)$-IOS) and not free-$(n-1)$-SNI. We further show that the ISW refresh gadget as well as the quasilinear refresh gadget from [8] both satisfy the free-$(n-1)$-SNI security notion (or equivalently balanced $(n-1)$-IOS).

- While the verification of probing composition notions such as, *e.g.*, NI, SNI, PINI, is today relatively well understood and engineered [2,4,13], it is not yet clear how to verify notions such as free SNI or IOS which are different in nature. Verifying such notions not only means checking that a given tuple of wires can be perfectly simulated from at most t input shares, it further requires showing that a set of output wires is uniform and mutually independent of this simulation. In this paper, we tackle this issue and provide an efficient verification method for these notions. We present a set of algorithms to efficiently verify common gadgets under these notions which we implemented in the IronMask tool.[2] We further report applications of these algorithms to several gadgets of the literature and hence (in)validate their free SNI / IOS features.

- Finally, we extend the IOS composition framework proposed in [25]. We show a general composition theorem for circuits made of IOS gadgets and share-wise affine gadgets. Compared to the original IOS composition framework, we consider IOS gadgets which are not necessarily refresh gadgets, which allows us to take advantage of the IOS property of *e.g.* the ISW multiplication gadgets. Moreover, our composition result does not require to insert an IOS refresh gadget between any two non-IOS gadgets which allows to save many refresh gadgets, hence improving the global efficiency of the underlying masked circuit.

---

[2] This augmented version of IronMask is available at https://github.com/CryptoExperts/IronMask.

2   Preliminaries

Along the paper, $\mathbb{K}$ shall denote a finite field. For any tuple $\vec{x} = (x_1, \ldots, x_n) \in \mathbb{K}^n$ and any set $I \subseteq [1 : n]$, we shall denote $\vec{x}|_I = (x_i)_{i \in I}$. We use $\stackrel{\text{id}}{=}$ to refer to the equality of the distributions of random variables.

2.1   Additive Sharing, Circuits and Gadgets

In the following, the n-*additive decoding* mapping, denoted AddDec, refers to the function $\bigcup_n \mathbb{K}^n \to \mathbb{K}$ defined as

$$\mathsf{AddDec} : (x_1, \ldots, x_n) \mapsto x_1 + \cdots + x_n \ ,$$

for every $n \in \mathbb{N}$ and $(x_1, \ldots, x_n) \in \mathbb{K}^n$. We shall further consider that, for every $n, \ell \in \mathbb{N}$, on input $(\vec{x}_1, \ldots, \vec{x}_\ell) \in (\mathbb{K}^n)^\ell$ the n-additive decoding mapping acts as

$$\mathsf{AddDec} : (\vec{x}_1, \ldots, \vec{x}_\ell) \mapsto (\mathsf{AddDec}(\vec{x}_1), \ldots, \mathsf{AddDec}(\vec{x}_\ell)) \ .$$

Definition 1 (Additive Sharing). *Let* $n, \ell \in \mathbb{N}$. *For any* $x \in \mathbb{K}$, *an* n-additive *sharing of* x *is a random vector* $\vec{x} \in \mathbb{K}^n$ *such that* $\mathsf{AddDec}(\vec{x}) = x$. *It is said to be* uniform *if for any set* $I \subseteq [1 : n]$ *with* $|I| < n$ *the tuple* $\vec{x}|_I$ *is uniformly distributed over* $\mathbb{K}^{|I|}$. *A* n-additive encoding *is a probabilistic algorithm* AddEnc *which on input a tuple* $(x_1, \ldots, x_\ell) \in \mathbb{K}^\ell$ *outputs a tuple* $(\vec{x}_1, \ldots, \vec{x}_\ell) \in (\mathbb{K}^n)^\ell$ *such that* $\vec{x}_i$ *is a uniform* n-additive sharing of x_i for every $i \in [1 : \ell]$.

An *arithmetic circuit* on a field $\mathbb{K}$ is a labeled directed acyclic graph whose edges are *wires* and vertices are *arithmetic gates* processing operations on $\mathbb{K}$. We consider circuits composed of addition gates, $(x_1, x_2) \mapsto x_1 + x_2$, multiplication gates, $(x_1, x_2) \mapsto x_1 \cdot x_2$, and copy gates, $x \mapsto (x, x)$. A *randomized arithmetic circuit* is equipped with an arithmetic circuit additional random gate which outputs a fresh uniform random value of $\mathbb{K}$.

In the following, we shall call an (n-share, ℓ-to-m) *gadget*, a randomized arithmetic circuit that maps an input $(\vec{x}_1, \ldots, \vec{x}_\ell) \in (\mathbb{K}^n)^\ell$ to an output $(\vec{y}_1, \ldots, \vec{y}_m) \in (\mathbb{K}^n)^m$ such that $(x_1, \ldots, x_\ell) = \mathsf{AddDec}(\vec{x}_1, \ldots, \vec{x}_\ell) \in \mathbb{K}^\ell$ and $(y_1, \ldots, y_m) = \mathsf{AddDec}(\vec{y}_1, \ldots, \vec{y}_m) \in \mathbb{K}^m$ satisfy $(y_1, \ldots, y_m) = g(x_1, \ldots, x_\ell)$ for some function g. A *refresh gadget* is a gadget for which g is the identity function, while a *multiplication gadget* implements the multiplication function. Affine functions g can be implemented with *sharewise affine gadgets*: such gadgets apply the underlying linear function to all the shares, except for the last one where the affine function is applied.

Some gadgets are said *probing complete*: for all the combinations of one share from each of their input sharings they contain a wire which depends on all the shares of the combination. For example, a multiplication gadget that computes $a_i \cdot b_j$ (if $\vec{a}$ and $\vec{b}$ are its input sharings) for all i and j is probing complete. For single-input gadgets, probing completeness is a trivial notion.

2.2   Probing Security

An *assign-wires sampler* takes as input a randomized arithmetic circuit C, a set of wire labels W (subset of the wire labels of C), and an input $(\vec{x_1}, \ldots, \vec{x_\ell})$, and it outputs a $|W|$-tuple $(w_1, \ldots, w_{|W|}) \in (\mathbb{K} \cup \{\bot\})^{|W|}$, denoted as

$$(w_1, \ldots, w_{|W|}) \leftarrow \mathsf{AssignWires}(C, W, (\vec{x_1}, \ldots, \vec{x_\ell})) ,$$

where $(w_1, \ldots, w_{|W|})$ corresponds to the assignments of the wires of C with label in W for an evaluation on input $(\vec{x_1}, \ldots, \vec{x_\ell})$.

Definition 2 (Probing Security). *A randomized arithmetic circuit C equipped with an encoding Enc[3] is t-probing secure if there exists a simulator Sim which, for any input $(x_1, \ldots, x_\ell) \in \mathbb{K}^\ell$, for every set of wires W such that $|W| \leq t$, satisfies*

$$\mathsf{Sim}(C, W) \stackrel{\mathrm{id}}{=} \mathsf{AssignWires}(C, W, \mathsf{Enc}(x_1, \ldots, x_\ell)).$$

Definition 3 (Region Probing Security). *Let r be an integer. A randomized arithmetic circuit C equipped with an encoding Enc is r-region probing secure if there exists a circuit partition $C = (C_1, \ldots, C_m)$ such that for any input $(x_1, \ldots, x_\ell) \in \mathbb{K}^\ell$ and for any sets of wires $W_1 \subseteq W_{C_1}, \ldots, W_m \subseteq W_{C_m}$ such that $|W_1| \leq \lceil r|C_1| \rceil, \ldots, |W_m| \leq \lceil r|C_m| \rceil$, there exists a simulator Sim which satisfies*

$$\mathsf{Sim}(C, W) \stackrel{\mathrm{id}}{=} \mathsf{AssignWires}(C, W, \mathsf{Enc}(x_1, \ldots, x_\ell))$$

where $W = W_1 \cup \cdots \cup W_m$.

3   Advanced Probing Composition Notions

Several security notions have been introduced in the literature to efficiently compose gadgets in the (region) probing model. This section aims to recall them, to specify or relax them for our purposes, and to demonstrate how they are connected to each other.

3.1   Existing Notions

First, most common gadgets that use randomness are expected to be uniform in the sense of Definition 4 (to not be confused with the uniformity definition of Threshold Implementations [32]), which is the most basic requirement for a refresh gadget.

Definition 4 (Uniformity from [25]). *An (n-share, ℓ-to-m) gadget G implementing a function g is uniform if, for every $(\vec{x_1}, \ldots, \vec{x_\ell}) \in (\mathbb{K}^n)^\ell$, the output $G(\vec{x_1}, \ldots, \vec{x_\ell})$ is a uniform additive sharing (see Definition 1) of $g(x_1, \ldots, x_\ell)$.*

---

[3] In this paper, we restrict ourselves to additive encodings as recalled in Definition 1.

Then, we recall the notions of strong non-interference (or SNI), input-output separative (or IOS) and free SNI that were chronologically introduced in various contexts to compose gadgets in the (region) probing model.

SNI was the first security notion introduced to securely compose n-share gadgets into a $(n - 1)$-probing secure circuit. In a nutshell, a gadget is t-SNI if any set of t_i internal probes and t_o output probes can be perfectly simulated from at most t_i shares of each input sharing for any $t_i + t_o \leq t$. Composition of SNI gadgets is then straightforward. Probes of one gadget can be simulated by its input shares which are the output shares of the incoming gadget(s). The latter inherited probes can then be simulated *for free*.

Definition 5 (Strong Non-Interference [5]). *Let G be an (n-share, ℓ-to-1) gadget. G is said t-Strong Non-Interferent (t-SNI), if for every set W of internal wires of G such that $|W| \leq t_i$, and every set $J \subseteq [1:n]$ of output share indices such that $|J| \leq t_o$ and $t_i + t_o \leq t$, there exists a (two-stage) simulator $\mathsf{Sim} = (\mathsf{Sim}_1, \mathsf{Sim}_2)$ such that for every input $(\vec{x_1}, \ldots, \vec{x_\ell}) \in (\mathbb{K}^n)^\ell$,*

1. $\mathsf{Sim}_1(W, J) = (I_1, \ldots, I_\ell)$ where $I_1, \ldots, I_\ell \subseteq [1:n]$, with $|I_1|, \ldots, |I_\ell| \leq |W|$,

2. $\mathsf{Sim}_2(W, J, (\vec{x_1}|_{I_1}, \ldots, \vec{x_\ell}|_{I_\ell})) \stackrel{\text{id}}{=} (\mathsf{AssignWires}(G, W, (\vec{x_1}, \ldots, \vec{x_\ell})), \vec{y}|_J)$

where $\vec{y} = G(\vec{x_1}, \ldots, \vec{x_\ell})$. A gadget is simply said to be SNI if it is $(n - 1)$-SNI.

A few years after SNI, the IOS security notion was introduced for 1-to-1 refresh gadgets. The latter are meant to be inserted between gadgets satisfying the classical probing security notion (which does not yield a secure composition on its own) in order to obtain a region probing secure circuit. In a nutshell, a gadget is t-IOS if it is uniform and if any set of t probes can be perfectly simulated from at most t input shares and t output shares.

In the following, we shall say that a pair of vector $(\vec{x}, \vec{y}) \in (\mathbb{K}^n)^2$ is *admissible* for a gadget G if there exists a random tape $\vec{\rho}$ (*i.e.* an assignment of the random gates' outputs) such that $\vec{y} = G^{\vec{\rho}}(\vec{x})^4$. For an admissible pair $(\vec{x}, \vec{y})$ and a set W of wires of G, the wire assignment distribution of G in W *induced* by $(\vec{x}, \vec{y})$, denoted $\mathsf{AssignWires}(G, W, \vec{x}, \vec{y}) \in \mathbb{K}^{|W|}$, is the random vector $\mathsf{AssignWires}(G, W, \vec{x})$ constrained to $\vec{y} = G^{\vec{\rho}}(\vec{x})$, *i.e.* the wire assignment distribution obtained for a uniform drawing of $\vec{\rho}$ among $\{\vec{\rho}; G^{\vec{\rho}}(\vec{x}) = \vec{y}\}$. We note that for a uniform gadget, an admissible pair is any $(\vec{x}, \vec{y}) \in (\mathbb{K}^n)^2$ such that $\sum_{i=1}^n x_i = \sum_{i=1}^n y_i$. Based on this definition, we recall the IOS security notion for any 1-to-1 gadget.

Definition 6 (IOS [25]). *Let G be an (n-share, 1-to-1) gadget. G is said t-input-output separative (t-IOS), if it is uniform and if there exists a (two-stage) simulator $\mathsf{Sim} = (\mathsf{Sim}_1, \mathsf{Sim}_2)$ such that for every admissible pair $(\vec{x}, \vec{y})$ for G and for every set of wires W of G with $|W| \leq t$, we have*

1. $\mathsf{Sim}_1(W) = (I, J)$ where $I, J \subseteq [1:n]$, with $|I| \leq |W|$ and $|J| \leq |W|$, and

---

[4] This notion of *admissible pair* can be trivially extended to the notion of *admissible tuple* for any number of inputs.

2. $\mathsf{Sim}_2(W, \vec{x}|_I, \vec{y}|_J) \overset{\mathrm{id}}{=} \mathsf{AssignWires}(G, W, \vec{x}, \vec{y})$.

A gadget is simply said to be IOS *if it is* n-IOS.

Finally, the free SNI notion was introduced for 1-to-1 refresh gadgets as well to strengthen the existing SNI property and produce probing secure circuits in the stateful model. In addition to the SNI features, the free SNI security notion ensures that a strict subset of the output shares which are not indexed by the input shares involved in the probes' simulation is uniformly and independently distributed, even conditioned on the probes and the other output shares.

Definition 7 (Free SNI [21]). *Let* G *be an* (n-share, 1-to-1) *gadget.* G *is said free* t-SNI, *if for every set* W *of internal wires of* G *such that* $|W| \leq t$, *there exists a* (two-stage) *simulator* $\mathsf{Sim} = (\mathsf{Sim}_1, \mathsf{Sim}_2)$ *such that for every input* $\vec{x} \in \mathbb{K}^n$,

1. $\mathsf{Sim}_1(W) = I$ *where* $I \subseteq [1 : n]$, *with* $|I| \leq |W|$,
2. $\mathsf{Sim}_2(W, \vec{x}|_I) \overset{\mathrm{id}}{=} (\mathsf{AssignWires}(G, W, \vec{x}), \vec{y}|_I)$,

where $\vec{y} = G(\vec{x})$, *and for every set* $O \subsetneq [1 : n] \setminus I$, $\vec{y}|_O$ *is uniformly and independently distributed, conditioned on* $\mathsf{AssignWires}(G, W, \vec{x})$ *and* $\vec{y}|_I$. *A gadget is simply said to be free* SNI *if it is free* $(n-1)$-SNI.

3.2 Extending and Balancing IOS

We now generalize the IOS property for 2-input gadgets[5]. In a nutshell, any set of at most t probes is now simulated from *two* subsets of input shares and a subset of output shares.

Definition 8 (Two-Input IOS). *Let* G *be an* (n-share, 2-to-1) *gadget.* G *is said* t-input-output separative (t-IOS), *if it is uniform and if there exists a* (two-stage) *simulator* $\mathsf{Sim} = (\mathsf{Sim}_1, \mathsf{Sim}_2)$ *such that for every admissible triple* $(\vec{x_1}, \vec{x_2}, \vec{y})$ *for* G *and for every set of wires* W *of* G *with* $|W| \leq t$, *we have*

1. $\mathsf{Sim}_1(W) = (I_1, I_2, J)$ *where* $I_1, I_2, J \subseteq [1 : n]$, *with* $|I_1| \leq |W|$, $|I_2| \leq |W|$ *and* $|J| \leq |W|$, *and*
2. $\mathsf{Sim}_2(W, \vec{x_1}|_{I_1}, \vec{x_2}|_{I_2}, \vec{y}|_J) \overset{\mathrm{id}}{=} \mathsf{AssignWires}(G, W, (\vec{x_1}, \vec{x_2}), \vec{y})$.

We then define a balanced version of the IOS property in which the output set of shares used for the simulation is entirely defined together with the input sets of shares used for the simulation. This tweaked notion is already satisfied by the refresh gadget introduced in [25] and is advantageously equivalent to the free SNI notion (as proven later in Theorem 1).

Definition 9 (Two-Input Balanced IOS). *Let* G *be an* (n-share, 2-to-1) *gadget.* G *is said balanced* t-input-output separative (balanced t-IOS), *if it is uniform and if there exists a* (two-stage) *simulator* $\mathsf{Sim} = (\mathsf{Sim}_1, \mathsf{Sim}_2)$ *such that for every admissible triple* $(\vec{x_1}, \vec{x_2}, \vec{y})$ *for* G *and for every set of wires* W *of* G *with* $|W| \leq t$, *we have*

---

[5] The definition for ℓ-input gadgets is given in the full version of the paper.

1. $\mathsf{Sim}_1(W) = (I_1, I_2)$ *where* $I_1, I_2 \subseteq [1:n]$, *with* $|I_1| \leq |W|$, $|I_2| \leq |W|$ *and*
2. $\mathsf{Sim}_2(W, \vec{x_1}|_{I_1}, \vec{x_2}|_{I_2}, \vec{y}|_{I_1 \cap I_2}) \overset{\text{id}}{=} \mathsf{AssignWires}(G, W, (\vec{x_1}, \vec{x_2}), \vec{y})$.

A gadget is simply said to be balanced IOS *if it is* balanced $(n-1)$-IOS.

Corollary 1. *An (n-share, 2-to-1) balanced t-IOS gadget is t-IOS.*

For the above corollary, it is indeed enough to use the first simulator of the balanced IOS definition and to fix the J set to the intersection of I_1 and I_2.

The (balanced) IOS notion can also be naturally extended to 1-to-2 gadgets, *e.g.* to cover copy gadgets which are useful in the context of region probing composition (see Sect. 7). We give a formal definition of IOS for 1-to-2 gadgets in the full version of the paper.

3.3   Extending and Unbalancing Free SNI

As for the IOS property, we generalize the free SNI security notion for 2-input gadgets[6]. In a nutshell, *two* subsets of input shares are now involved in the simulation and the output shares to be simulated are defined from the intersection of their indices.

Definition 10 (Two-Input Free SNI). *Let G be an (n-share, 2-to-1) gadget. G is said* free t-SNI, *if for every set W of internal wires of G such that $|W| \leq t$, there exists a (two-stage) simulator $\mathsf{Sim} = (\mathsf{Sim}_1, \mathsf{Sim}_2)$ such that for every input $(\vec{x_1}, \vec{x_2}) \in \mathbb{K}^n \times \mathbb{K}^n$,*

1. $\mathsf{Sim}_1(W) = (I_1, I_2)$ *where* $I_1, I_2 \subseteq [1:n]$, *with* $|I_1| \leq |W|$ *and* $|I_2| \leq |W|$,
2. $\mathsf{Sim}_2(W, \vec{x_1}|_{I_1}, \vec{x_2}|_{I_2}) \overset{\text{id}}{=} (\mathsf{AssignWires}(G, W, (\vec{x_1}, \vec{x_2})), \vec{y}|_{I_1 \cap I_2})$,

where $\vec{y} = G(\vec{x_1}, \vec{x_2})$, and for every set $O \subsetneq [1:n] \setminus (I_1 \cap I_2)$, $\vec{y}|_O$ is uniformly and independently distributed, conditioned on $\mathsf{AssignWires}(G, W, (\vec{x_1}, \vec{x_2}))$ and $\vec{y}|_{I_1 \cap I_2}$. A gadget is simply said to be free SNI *if it is* free $(n-1)$-SNI.

In the reverse direction compared to IOS (see Fig. 1), we define an unbalanced variant of free SNI for which the first simulator outputs different sets of indices. It has the advantage of being equivalent to the IOS security property (as proven later in Theorem 2).

Definition 11 (Two-Input Unbalanced Free SNI). *Let G be an (n-share, 2-to-1) gadget. G is said* unbalanced free t-SNI, *if for every set W of internal wires of G such that $|W| \leq t$, there exists a (two-stage) simulator $\mathsf{Sim} = (\mathsf{Sim}_1, \mathsf{Sim}_2)$ such that for every input $(\vec{x_1}, \vec{x_2}) \in \mathbb{K}^n \times \mathbb{K}^n$,*

1. $\mathsf{Sim}_1(W) = (I_1, I_2, J)$ *where* $I_1, I_2, J \subseteq [1:n]$, *with* $|I_1| \leq |W|$, $|I_2| \leq |W|$ *and* $|J| \leq |W|$, *and*
2. $\mathsf{Sim}_2(W, \vec{x_1}|_{I_1}, \vec{x_2}|_{I_2}) \overset{\text{id}}{=} (\mathsf{AssignWires}(G, W, (\vec{x_1}, \vec{x_2})), \vec{y}|_J)$,

---

[6] The definition for ℓ-input gadgets is given in the full version of the paper.

where $\vec{y} = G(\vec{x_1}, \vec{x_2})$, *and for every set* $O \subsetneq [1:n] \setminus J$, $\vec{y}|_O$ *is uniformly and independently distributed, conditioned on* AssignWires$(G, W, (\vec{x_1}, \vec{x_2}))$ *and* $\vec{y}|_J$. *A gadget is simply said to be* unbalanced free SNI *if it is* unbalanced free $(n-1)$-SNI.

Corollary 2. *An (n-share, 2-to-1) free t-SNI gadget is unbalanced free t-SNI.*

As for IOS (see Corollary 1), the free t-SNI property trivially implies the unbalanced free t-SNI property by fixing the output set of indices J to the intersection of sets I_1 and I_2.

Also, unbalanced free t-SNI implies t-SNI: the unbalanced free-SNI can simulate any strict subset of the output (more formally, this is a consequence of Theorem 3).

Corollary 3. *An (n-share, 2-to-1) unbalanced free t-SNI gadget is t-SNI.*

3.4   Relations Between Security Notions

In this section, we draw and prove the relations between the different security notions recalled or introduced above for (n-share, 2-to-1) gadgets. They are summarized in Fig. 1.

We first demonstrate the equivalence between the free t-SNI and balanced t-IOS notions. This result is somehow surprising given the different natures of the two notions: Free SNI requires the ability to simulate the probed wires from some input shares with the feature that non-simulated output wires are mutually independent of the simulation. On the other hand, IOS requires the ability to simulate the probed wires from some input *and* output shares where the simulation must be consistent with any given (admissible) values of the input and output sharings. The following theorem show that these two requirements are essentially equivalent.

Theorem 1. *Let G be a (n-share, 1-to-1 or 2-to-1) gadget and let t be an integer strictly less than n. G is free t-SNI if and only if G is t-balanced IOS.*

The complete proof is given in the full version of the paper. For both implications, we demonstrate how to build the new simulators from the existing ones. For the right-to-left implication, we additionally show that some part of the output sharing is uniform and independent conditioned on the probes and the remaining outputs using a contradiction. While the first simulators of both properties are always built the same way, the construction of the second simulators is trickier. For the left-to-right implication, we need to run the second free t-SNI simulator until its second output matches the third value of the admissible triple for the balanced IOS property. For the right-to-left implication, any uniformly random chunk of output forms an admissible triple to be used in the second balanced t-IOS simulator to build the free t-SNI one.

Similarly, Theorem 2 gives the equivalence between the unbalanced free SNI and IOS notions. Its proof follows exactly the same steps as the proof of Theorem 1 (see complete proof in the full version of the paper).

Theorem 2. *Let G be a (n-share, 1-to-1 or 2-to-1) gadget and let t be an integer strictly less than n. G is unbalanced free t-SNI if and only if G is t-IOS.*

Finally, the t-IOS security property implies the t-SNI security property, as stated in Theorem 3 and formally proven in the full version of the paper. In a nutshell, the first t-SNI simulator is built from the two first outputs of the first t-IOS simulator. Then, the second t-SNI simulator is built from the second t-IOS simulator using an admissible triple in which the output additionally integrates the output probes authorized by the SNI property.

Theorem 3. *Let G be an (n-share, 1-to-1 or 2-to-1) gadget and let t be an integer strictly less than n. If G is t-IOS then G is t-SNI.*

From Theorem 1 on the equivalence between t-IOS and unbalanced free t-SNI, it follows that unbalanced free t-SNI also directly implies t-SNI.

Meanwhile, unbalanced free t-SNI (or equivalently t-IOS) does not imply free t-SNI (or equivalently balanced t-IOS) and t-SNI does not imply t-unbalanced SNI (or equivalently t-IOS). Counterexamples are given in the full version of the paper.

3.5 Additional Relations for ZE-Refresh Gadgets

In the literature, it can be noticed that most efficient refresh gadgets are built from a refresh on a sharing of zero. We thus properly define such constructions and we show how to use them to build free SNI gadgets.

In the following, we call a *ZE-refresh gadget* (*ZE* for *zero-encoding*) a gadget G which, for any input $\vec{x} \in \mathbb{K}^n$ computes $\vec{y} = G(\vec{x})$ as follows (*i.e.*, respecting the order of operations)

$$\vec{y} \leftarrow \vec{x} + \mathsf{ZeroEnc}() \ ,$$

where $\mathsf{ZeroEnc}$ is a randomized circuit which takes no input and outputs a sharing of 0. We note that G is uniform if and only if $\mathsf{ZeroEnc}$ outputs a uniform sharing of 0, *i.e.* $\vec{z} \leftarrow \mathsf{ZeroEnc}()$ is such that $\vec{z}|_O$ is uniformly distributed over $\mathbb{K}^{|O|}$ for every $O \subsetneq [1:n]$. Definition 12 introduces a security property on $\mathsf{ZeroEnc}$ that, if satisfied, yields free t-SNI ZE-refresh gadgets.

Definition 12 (Free Encoding of Zero). *Let $\mathsf{ZeroEnc}$ be an (n-share, 0-to-1) gadget performing a refresh on a sharing of zero. $\mathsf{ZeroEnc}$ is said to be t-free if for every set W of (internal and output) wires on $\mathsf{ZeroEnc}$ with $|W| \leq t$, there exists a set J of cardinality $|J| \leq |W|$ such that for every set $O \subsetneq [1:n] \setminus J$, $\vec{z}|_O$ is uniformly distributed and mutually independent of $\mathsf{AssignWires}(\mathsf{ZeroEnc}, W, \emptyset, \vec{z})$, and $\vec{z}|_J$, where $\vec{z} = \mathsf{ZeroEnc}()$.*

Then we obtain the following result, whose proof is given in the full version of the paper.

Proposition 1. *Let G be an n-share uniform ZE-refresh gadget. The inner gadget $\mathsf{ZeroEnc}$ is t-free if and only if G is free t-SNI.*

Let us remark that a result similar to Proposition 1 for SNI refresh gadgets has been introduced by Cassiers et al. [16]. Indeed, our ZE-refresh gadgets are the same construction as their "off-path" refresh gadgets. Moreover, they define the notion of Strong Output Independence (t-SOI) for ZeroEnc gadgets, which is a weaker variant of free encoding: ZeroEnc is t-SOI if, for every $t_1 + t_2 \leq t$, every set of wires in ZeroEnc with $|W| \leq t_1$ and every set $O \subset [1:n]$ such that $|O| \leq t_2$, there exists a set $J \subseteq O$ such that $|J| \leq t_1$ and $\vec{z}|_{O \setminus J}$ is uniformly distributed and mutually independent of AssignWires(ZeroEnc, $W, \emptyset, \vec{z}$), and $\vec{z}|_J$, where $\vec{z} = \mathsf{ZeroEnc}()$. A ZE-Refresh gadget is t-SNI if and only if the inner ZeroEnc is t-SOI.

4   Gadgets Under New Notions for Arbitrary Orders

This section is dedicated to the construction of free t-SNI or t-IOS gadgets at arbitrary orders. We first demonstrate useful propositions to build strong generic gadgets from ZE-refresh gadgets, and then we explore the properties satisfied by the most deployed gadgets from the literature.

4.1   Generic Constructions

ZE-refresh gadgets can be used to build free t-SNI and t-IOS gadgets with larger t, like multiplication or copy gadgets for instance, as illustrated on Fig. 2.

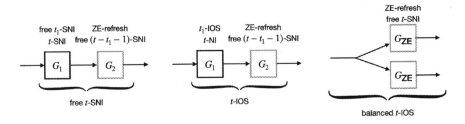

Fig. 2. Illustration of Generic Constructions of Propositions 2, 3 and 4

In particular, Proposition 2 and Proposition 3 demonstrate how to compose free t_1-SNI gadgets which are additionally t-SNI or t-NI (with $t > t_1$) with free $(t - t_1)$-SNI ZE-refresh gadgets to obtain free t-SNI refresh gadgets. Their proofs are given in the full version of the paper.

Proposition 2. *Let G_1 be an (n-share, 2-to-1) gadget and let G_2 be an n-share ZE-refresh gadget. Let $G = G_2 \circ G_1$. For $t > t_1 \geq 1$, if G_1 is t-SNI and free t_1-SNI, and G_2 is free $(t - t_1 - 1)$-SNI, then G is free t-SNI.*

Proposition 3. *Let G_1 be an (n-share, 2-to-1) gadget and let G_2 be an n-share ZE-refresh gadget. Let $G = G_2 \circ G_1$. For $t > t_1 \geq 1$, if G_1 is t-NI and t_1-IOS, and G_2 is free $(t - t_1 - 1)$-SNI, then G is t-IOS.*

In the same vein, Proposition 4 claims that a copy gadget built from the double application of a free t-SNI ZE-refresh gadget is balanced t-IOS. Its proof is given in the full version of the paper.

Proposition 4. *Let G_{ZE} be an n-share ZE-refresh gadget. Let $G_{cp} = (G_{ZE}, G_{ZE})$. If G_{ZE} is free t-SNI, then G_{cp} is balanced t-IOS.*

From Theorem 1, this copy gadget is equivalently free t-SNI (and trivially unbalanced free t-SNI and t-IOS). We state the result for the IOS notion here since such copy gadgets are useful in the context of the IOS composition framework for region probing security (see Sect. 7).

4.2 Known Gadgets

We now demonstrate that common gadgets satisfy the strong unified notions of free SNI and IOS. Specifically, we prove that the well known ISW multiplication gadget (named after its authors Ishai, Sahai, and Wagner, from [27]) is free-$(n-2)$-SNI (or equivalently balanced $(n-2)$-IOS) and not free-$(n-1)$-SNI and that the subsequent ISW refresh gadget is free-$(n-1)$-SNI. Then, we show that the $\mathcal{O}(n \log n)$ refresh gadget from [8,30] and the copy gadget built from it are both free $(n-1)$-SNI.

4.3 ISW Multiplication and Refresh Gadgets

We recall the ISW multiplication gadget in Algorithm 1.

Algorithm 1: ISW Multiplication [27]

> **Input** : $(a_1, \ldots, a_n), (b_1, \ldots, b_n)$ input sharings, $\{r_{i,j}\}_{1 \leq i < j \leq n}$ random values
> **Output:** $(c_1, \ldots, c_n)$ sharing of $a \cdot b$

1 **for** $i \leftarrow 1$ **to** n **do**
2 $\quad$ $c_i \leftarrow a_i \cdot b_i$;
3 **end**
4 **for** $i \leftarrow 1$ **to** n **do**
5 $\quad$ **for** $j \leftarrow i + 1$ **to** n **do**
6 $\quad\quad$ $c_i \leftarrow c_i + r_{i,j}$;
7 $\quad\quad$ $r_{ji} \leftarrow (a_i \cdot b_j - r_{i,j}) + a_j \cdot b_i$;
8 $\quad\quad$ $c_j \leftarrow c_j + r_{j,i}$;
9 $\quad$ **end**
10 **end**
11 **return** $(c_1, \ldots, c_n)$;

Our main result for the n-share ISW multiplication gadget is provided in Proposition 5 whose proof is given in the full version of the paper. The n-share ISW multiplication gadget can thus be used as a building block of a tight composition in the probing model, as proven in Sect. 6.

Proposition 5. *The n-share ISW multiplication gadget is free-$(n-2)$-SNI.*

Note that from Theorem 1, the ISW multiplication is equivalently balanced $(n-2)$-IOS and it is also $(n-2)$-IOS, which is enough to act as a building block of a tight composition in the region probing model described in Sect. 7. However it is not free-$(n-1)$-SNI, as claimed in Proposition 6 whose proof is given in the full version of the paper. In a nutshell, the proof exhibits the following set of $n-1$ probes on the gadget $W = \{a_1 \cdot b_2 - r_{1,2}, \ldots, a_1 \cdot b_n - r_{1,n}\}$ as a counterexample. One can check that a linear combination between all the probes in W and the output share c_1 gives the value $a_1 \cdot (b_1 + \ldots + b_n)$ which involves all of the shares of the second input, leading to a failure.

Proposition 6. *The n-share ISW multiplication gadget is not free $(n-1)$-SNI.*

Remark 1. Note that the ISW multiplication gadget satisfies a security notion slightly weaker than free $(n-1)$-SNI for which the output shares indexed by $I_1 \cap I_2$ do not need to be simulated.

Even though the ISW multiplication gadget is not free $(n-1)$-SNI, we can use the fact that it is free $(n-2)$-SNI and $(n-1)$-SNI to construct a new free $(n-1)$-SNI gadget, by applying the result of Proposition 2. Since the ISW gadget is free $(n-2)$-SNI, then the ZE-refresh gadget must be free 1-SNI. Hence, we can use any refresh gadget which simply outputs a uniform sharing. For this, we can choose a linear refresh gadget, for instance Algorithm 3 from [18] or the circular refresh gadget from [6].

Corollary 4. *The composition of the n-share ISW multiplication gadget with a free 0-SNI ZE-refresh gadget (like Algorithm 3 from [18] or the circular refresh gadget from [6]) is free $(n-1)$-SNI.*

The proof of Corollary 4 follows directly from Proposition 2.

From the ISW multiplication gadget, one can build the ISW refresh gadget by simply fixing the second input to the constant vector $(1, 0, \ldots, 0)$. Following Proposition 5, the gadget is trivially free $(n-2)$-SNI. Interestingly, it is even free $(n-1)$-SNI as stated in Lemma 1. In fact, the failure sets of probes of size $n-1$ in the case of the ISW multiplication gadget essentially failed because of the manipulation of two input sharings. This is no longer the case in the ISW refresh gadget, which is why it becomes free $(n-1)$-SNI. The full proof is given in the full version of the paper.

Lemma 1. *The n-share ISW refresh gadget is free-$(n-1)$-SNI.*

Like the ISW multiplication gadget, the ISW refresh gadget can be used as a building block of a tight composition in the probing or in the region probing model (as shown in Sects. 6 and 7).

4.4 $\mathcal{O}(n \log n)$ Refresh and Copy Gadgets

In the following, we present the optimized version of the $\mathcal{O}(n \log n)$ refresh gadget from [8], as improved in [30], by removing one layer of randomness. This ZE-refresh gadget relies on the ZeroEnc gadget that we recall in Algorithm 2.

Algorithm 2: QuasiLinearZeroEnc

Input   : Number of shares n
Output: $(d_1, \ldots, d_n)$ such that $d_1 + \cdots + d_n = 0$
1 **if** $n = 1$ **then return** 0;
2 **if** $n = 2$ **then**
3 $\quad$ $r \leftarrow \$$;
4 $\quad$ **return** $(r, -r)$;
5 **end**
6 $(c_1, \ldots, c_{\lfloor n/2 \rfloor}) \leftarrow$ QuasiLinearZeroEnc($\lfloor n/2 \rfloor$);
7 $(c_{\lfloor n/2 \rfloor + 1}, \ldots, c_n) \leftarrow$ QuasiLinearZeroEnc($\lceil n/2 \rceil$);
8 **for** $i \leftarrow 1$ **to** $\lfloor n/2 \rfloor$ **do**
9 $\quad$ $r \leftarrow \$$;
10 $\quad$ $d_i \leftarrow c_i + r$;
11 $\quad$ $d_{\lfloor n/2 \rfloor + i} \leftarrow c_{\lfloor n/2 \rfloor + i} - r$;
12 **end**
13 **if** $n \mod 2 = 1$ **then** $d_n \leftarrow c_n$;
14 **return** $(d_1, \ldots, d_n)$;

Our next proposition states that the ZeroEnc gadget recalled in Algorithm 2 is a $(n - 1)$-free encoding of zero. The proof is given in the full version of the paper.

Proposition 7. *Algorithm 2 is an $(n - 1)$-free encoding of zero.*

From Proposition 1 and Proposition 7, we conclude that the corresponding ZE-refresh gadget is free $(n - 1)$-SNI.

Corollary 5. *The $\mathcal{O}(n \log n)$ n-share ZE-refresh gadget instantiated with Algorithm 2 as ZeroEnc is free $(n - 1)$-SNI.*

From Theorem 1, this $\mathcal{O}(n \log n)$ n-share ZE-refresh gadget is equivalently balanced IOS and thus trivially IOS (see Corollary 1). This result confirms (and even generalizes) the proven statement from [26] stating that the gadget is IOS when the number n of shares is a power of two.

Following this result and Proposition 4, the copy gadget built from the double application of the $\mathcal{O}(n \log n)$ ZE-refresh gadget described above is directly balanced t-IOS (or equivalently free t-SNI).

Corollary 6. *Let $G_{ZE, \mathcal{O}(n \log n)}$ be the $\mathcal{O}(n \log n)$ n-share ZE-refresh gadget recalled above. Then the copy gadget defined as $G_{cp} = (G_{ZE, \mathcal{O}(n \log n)}, G_{ZE, \mathcal{O}(n \log n)})$ is balanced t-IOS.*

5   Efficient Verification of Free SNI and IOS

Verification tools for probing security/composition notions such as maskVerif [2, 4] or IronMask [13] usually work by enumerating possible tuples of probed wires (for a given number of probes depending on the security notion) and for each of them analyze the number of input shares which are necessary for a perfect simulation. The latter analysis is done by considering linear combinations of the probed variables to eliminate the randomness (assuming linearly introduced randomness) and by listing the input shares involved in the random-free symbolic expressions (which are hence necessary for a perfect simulation). While this approach is sound to verify usual probing composition notions (*e.g.* NI, SNI, PINI) and the random probing notions (RPC, RPE) recently introduced in [11], it is not clear how to extend it to notions such as free SNI or IOS. Indeed, free SNI requires the ability to simulate the probed wires but also to demonstrate that each subset of non-simulated output wires is mutually independent of the simulation. On the other hand, IOS constrains the simulation to be consistent with any given (admissible) values of the input and output sharings and to simulate the probed wires not only from input shares but also with some output shares.

In this section, we show how to extend the existing probing verification approach to the free SNI and IOS notions recalled and generalized in Sect. 3. We present a set of algorithms to efficiently verify common gadgets under these notions. We then show a few applications of these algorithms as implemented in IronMask.

5.1   Verification Algorithms

Notations. In the following, we consider (n-share, 2-to-1) gadgets, and denote $\overrightarrow{x_1}, \overrightarrow{x_2}$ the input sharings, $\overrightarrow{r}$ the internal randomness, and $\overrightarrow{y}$ the output sharing. Throughout this section, the coordinates of $\overrightarrow{x_1}, \overrightarrow{x_2}$ and $\overrightarrow{r}$ are considered as symbolic variables and we denote W the set of symbolic *arithmetic* expressions in these symbolic variables (by *arithmetic* we mean with operations and/or constants from $\mathbb{K}$). Under this formalism, any wire w_i in the gadget and any output share y_j lies in W. We note that the verification algorithms presented hereafter can easily be adapted to cover gadgets with a single input.

We exclusively focus on LR-gadgets (as defined in [14]), *i.e.* gadgets for which all random values are additively introduced to compute the output shares. For these common gadgets (see *e.g.* [9,10,20,27]), each wire computes a variable of the form:

$$w = f_w(\overrightarrow{x_1}, \overrightarrow{x_2}) + \overrightarrow{r}^T \cdot \overrightarrow{s_w},$$

for some arithmetic function $f_w : (\mathbb{K}^n)^2 \to \mathbb{K}$, the input sharings $\overrightarrow{x_1}, \overrightarrow{x_2} \in \mathbb{K}^n$, the vector $\overrightarrow{r}$ of all random values used by the gadget which is uniformly drawn from $\mathbb{K}^\rho$ (with ρ the number of random gates in the gadget), and some constant vector $\overrightarrow{s_w} \in \mathbb{K}^\rho$.

In the following, we assume that we have access to the following function:

$$\text{Gaussian} : \mathcal{W}^k \to \mathcal{W}^k$$
$$\overrightarrow{W} = (w_1, \dots, w_k)^T \mapsto \overrightarrow{W'} = (w'_1, \dots, w'_k)^T$$

such that $\overrightarrow{W'} = N \cdot \overrightarrow{W}$ where N is an invertible matrix in $\mathbb{K}^{k \times k}$ such that $S' = N \cdot S$ with S' the row reduced form (after Gaussian elimination) of the matrix $S := (\overrightarrow{s_{w_1}} | \overrightarrow{s_{w_2}} | \dots | \overrightarrow{s_{w_k}})^T$ which satisfies $S' = (\overrightarrow{s_{w'_1}} | \overrightarrow{s_{w'_2}} | \dots | \overrightarrow{s_{w'_v}} | \overrightarrow{0} | \dots | \overrightarrow{0})^T$ for some $v \in [1 : k]$.

After Gaussian elimination, the expression of each w'_i can be written as

$$w'_i = c_1 \cdot w_{j_1} + \dots + c_t \cdot w_{j_t} = f_{w'_i}(\overrightarrow{x_1}, \overrightarrow{x_2}) + \overrightarrow{r}^T \cdot \overrightarrow{s_{w'_i}}$$

for $(c_1, \dots, c_t) \in \mathbb{K}^t$, such that $N_{i,j} \neq 0$ for any $j \in \{j_1, \dots, j_t\}$ and $N_{i,j} = 0$ for all other coefficients on the same row i of matrix N.

We denote by I_{1,w'_i} (resp. I_{2,w'_i}) the indices of the first input (resp. second input) shares that are contained in the symbolic expression of w'_i, i.e. in $f_{w'_i}(\overrightarrow{x_1}, \overrightarrow{x_2})$.

We also denote $\overline{I_{1,w'_i}}$ (resp. $\overline{I_{2,w'_i}}$) the indices of the first input (resp. second input) shares that are involved in the symbolic expression of $f_{w'_i}(\overrightarrow{x_1}, \overrightarrow{x_2}) - g(\overrightarrow{x_1}, \overrightarrow{x_2})$, where $g(\overrightarrow{x_1}, \overrightarrow{x_2}) := \sum_{i=1}^{n} y_i$ is the (unshared) output of the considered gadget G. For instance, if G is a single input refresh gadget, then we have, $g(\overrightarrow{x_1}) = \sum_{i=1}^{n} x_{1,i}$, and $\overline{I_{1,w'_i}} = [1 : n] \setminus I_{1,w'_i}$. In the case where G is a multiplication gadget, the products of input shares must be considered in each symbolic expression, i.e. $g(\overrightarrow{x_1}, \overrightarrow{x_2}) = \left(\sum_{i=1}^{n} x_{1,i}\right)\left(\sum_{i=1}^{n} x_{2,i}\right)$.

Finally, given $\overrightarrow{W} = (w_1, \dots, w_k)^T$ and $\overrightarrow{W'} = (w'_1, \dots, w'_k)^T$ such that $\overrightarrow{W} = N \cdot \overrightarrow{W}$ (obtained through a call to Gaussian), we define

$$O_{w'_i} := \{j \in [1 : n] \mid \exists \ell \in [1 : k] \text{ s.t. } N_{i,\ell} \neq 0 \text{ and } w_\ell = y_j\} .$$

Namely, following the Gaussian elimination, the output share $w_\ell = y_j$ appears in the linear combination defining w'_i. We further define $\overline{O_{w'_i}} := [1 : n] \setminus O_{w'_i}$.

Preliminary Results. We present hereafter the sub-algorithms used to verify the main security notions defined or recalled in Sect. 3. These sub-algorithms take as input a given set of probes $\overrightarrow{W}$ and verify the free SNI or IOS notion for this set. These sub-algorithms have been implemented in the IronMask tool (see [13]) and called on all possible sets of probes $\overrightarrow{W}$ of the target gadget to check that it satisfies the free SNI or IOS notion.

First, we present an efficient method to check that an n-share gadget G is uniform. Namely, this method checks that for any $O \subsetneq [1 : n]$, the output shares in $\overrightarrow{y}|_O$ are all independent and uniform (with $\overrightarrow{y}$ denoting the output sharing of the gadget). The method is described in Algorithm 3.

Algorithm 3: Verification of Output independence and Uniformity

---

Input   : Symbolic expressions $\overrightarrow{y} \in W^n$ of the output sharing of an LR-gadget
G.

Output: success if G is uniform, failure otherwise.

1 $(w_1', \ldots, w_n') \leftarrow \mathsf{Gaussian}(y_1, \ldots, y_n)$;

2 $v \leftarrow$ index in $[1:n]$ such that $\forall j > v,\ \overrightarrow{s_{w_j'}} = \overrightarrow{0}$;

3 **if** $v \neq n-1$ **then**

4 $\quad \mid$ **return** failure;

5 **end**

6 **return** success;

Proposition 8. *Algorithm 3 is correct.*

The proof of Proposition 8 is given in the full version of the paper. In a nutshell, it states that if the gadget is indeed uniform and we perform a Gaussian elimination on the vectors of randomness for the output shares $\overrightarrow{y}$, then we get at most one row which is a linear combination of all of the others outputs in the matrix of the Gaussian procedure. This is exactly the check performed by Algorithm 3.

In the rest of this section, we assume a gadget G on which Algorithm 3 does not fail. If Algorithm 3 fails, then we do not need to go further in the verification since both the free SNI and IOS properties require that the gadget G satisfy uniformity.

Before presenting the full verification algorithm, we state the following useful result. Namely, a set $I \subseteq [1:n]$ satisfies the *free property* for some probes $\overrightarrow{W} \in \mathcal{W}^k$ if, for any $O \subsetneq [1:n] \setminus I$, the output shares $\overrightarrow{y}|_O$ are independent and uniform conditioned on the probes in $\overrightarrow{W}$ and output shares $\overrightarrow{y}|_I$. The proof is given in the full version of the paper.

Lemma 2. *Let G be a uniform n-share LR-gadget for the base field $\mathbb{K} = \mathbb{F}_2$. Let $\overrightarrow{W} = (w_1, \ldots, w_k)$ be a tuple of internal probes on G and let*

$$(f_1, \ldots, f_{n+k-1}) \leftarrow \mathsf{Gaussian}(w_1, \ldots, w_k, y_1, \ldots, y_{n-1}) \ .$$

Let $v \in [0:n+k-1]$ such that $\overrightarrow{s_{f_i}} \neq \overrightarrow{0}$ for all $i \leq v$ and $\overrightarrow{s_{f_i}} = \overrightarrow{0}$ for all $i > v$ and denote $P = \{f_{v+1}, \ldots, f_{n+k-1}\}$.

For any partition $P_1 \cup P_2 = P$ (with $P_1 \cap P_2 = \emptyset$), the set

$$I = \left(\bigcup_{f_i \in P_1} O_{f_i} \right) \cup \left(\bigcup_{f_i \in P_2} \overline{O_{f_i}} \right) , \tag{1}$$

with $\overline{O_{f_i}} = [1:n] \setminus O_{f_i}$, satisfies the free property for $\overrightarrow{W}$.

Moreover, any set I' which is not a superset of a set I in the form of (1) does not satisfy the free property for $\overrightarrow{W}$.

Verification Algorithms. We present hereafter the verification algorithms which check whether a given set of probes on a gadget represents a failure for free SNI or IOS property. The complete procedure is described in Algorithms 4, 5, and 6. They are implemented in the IronMask verification tool, which iterates over all possible sets of probes on the gadget and calls the procedure on each of them. The exploration of the different sets of probes uses the optimizations already integrated in the tool and presented in [13]. As in Lemma 2, the description assumes that the base field is $\mathbb{K} = \mathbb{F}_2$. We later discuss the general case of any base field $\mathbb{K}$.

Algorithm 4 performs the preliminary steps common to the verification of free SNI and IOS. Namely, it determines the sets of input shares necessary to simulate the given set of probes $\overrightarrow{W}$. This is done through the Gaussian elimination $(g_1, \ldots, g_t) \leftarrow \mathsf{Gaussian}(w_1, \ldots, w_t)$ performed on line 2 and then constructing the sets of input shares

$$I_1 = \bigcup_{i \in [v+1:t]} I_{1,g_i} \quad \text{and} \quad I_2 = \bigcup_{i \in [v+1:t]} I_{2,g_i}$$

on lines 3 to 6, where, as introduced above, I_{j,g_i} is the set of shares from $\overrightarrow{x_j}$ which are involved in the expression g_i. At this point, we already have a failure if at least one of the sets I_1 or I_2 is of size larger than $|\overrightarrow{W}|$. This indeed consists in an SNI failure, which is automatically a failure for free SNI and IOS. This test is performed on line 7. Next, on lines 8 and 9, the algorithm prepares the inputs to the inner algorithm, which either checks free SNI or IOS by performing the Gaussian elimination described in Lemma 2. Depending on the property, Algorithm 4 then calls one of Algorithms 5 or 6. In both algorithms, we perform a direct application of Lemma 2. In other words, we try to find a set of output shares that satisfies free SNI or IOS requirements using the Lemma result. The correctness of this procedure is proved in Lemmas 3 and 4. The full proof of the lemmas are given in the full version of the paper.

Lemma 3. *Algorithms 4 and 5 are correct when checking free t-SNI property.*

Lemma 4. *Algorithms 4 and 6 are correct when checking t-IOS property.*

Optimization. We can optimize the execution time of Algorithms 5 and 6 by reducing the number of sets to test, *i.e.* the number of subsets to consider in the main loop on line 2 in both algorithms.

Observe that in Algorithm 5, for each $i \in C = \{v + 1, \ldots, n + t - 1\}$, if $|I_{1,f_i} \cup O_{f_i}| > t$ or $|I_{2,f_i} \cup O_{f_i}| > t$, then for any subset C' of C such that $i \in C'$, the constructed sets I_1' and I_2' will be of size bigger than t, which means

---

Algorithm 4: Verification Algorithm for free-t-SNI or t-IOS for a single set of probes

---

Input : $\overrightarrow{W} = (w_1, \ldots, w_t) \in \mathcal{W}^t$ a tuple of t internal probes on an (n-share, 2-to-1) LR-gadget G.

    property $\in$ {freeSNI, IOS} to check.

Output: false if $\overrightarrow{W}$ is a failure for property, true otherwise.

1   $I_1 \leftarrow \{\}, \quad I_2 \leftarrow \{\}$;

2   $(g_1, \ldots, g_t) \leftarrow$ Gaussian$(w_1, \ldots, w_t)$;

3   $v \leftarrow$ index in $[1 : t]$ such that $\forall j > v, \; \overrightarrow{s_{g_j}} = \overrightarrow{0}$;

4   **for** $i \in [v + 1 : t]$ **do**

5 | $I_1 \leftarrow I_1 \cup I_{1,g_i}, \quad I_2 \leftarrow I_2 \cup I_{2,g_i}$;

6   **end**

7   **if** $|I_1| > t$ **or** $|I_2| > t$ **then return** false;

8   $(f_1, \ldots, f_{n+t-1}) \leftarrow$ Gaussian$(w_1, \ldots, w_t, y_1, \ldots, y_{n-1})$;

9   $v \leftarrow$ index in $[1 : n + t - 1]$ such that $\forall j > v, \; \overrightarrow{s_{f_j}} = \overrightarrow{0}$;

10 **return** check$\_$\{property\}$(t, I_1, I_2, (f_{v+1}, \ldots, f_{n+t-1}))$;

Algorithm 5: check$\_$freeSNI	**Algorithm 6:** check$\_$IOS
Input : $t, I_1, I_2, (f_{v+1}, ..., f_{n+t-1})$ from Algorithm 4	**Input** : $t, I_1, I_2, (f_{v+1}, ..., f_{n+t-1})$ from Algorithm 4
Output: false if failure for free-t-SNI, true otherwise.	**Output:** false if failure for t-IOS, true otherwise.

1 $C \leftarrow \{v + 1, \ldots, n + t - 1\}$;	1 $C \leftarrow \{v + 1, \ldots, n + t - 1\}$;
2 **for** each C' such that $C' \subseteq C$ **do**	2 **for** each C' such that $C' \subseteq C$ **do**
3 $I_1' \leftarrow I_1, \quad I_2' \leftarrow I_2$;	3 $I_1' \leftarrow I_1, \quad I_2' \leftarrow I_2, \quad J' \leftarrow \{\}$;
4 **for** $i \in C'$ **do**	4 **for** $i \in C'$ **do**
5 $I_1' \leftarrow I_1' \cup I_{1,f_i} \cup O_{f_i}$;	5 $I_1' \leftarrow I_1' \cup I_{1,f_i}$;
6 $I_2' \leftarrow I_2' \cup I_{2,f_i} \cup O_{f_i}$;	6 $I_2' \leftarrow I_2' \cup I_{2,f_i}$;
	7 $J' \leftarrow J' \cup O_{f_i}$;
7 **end**	8 **end**
8 **for** $i \in C \setminus C'$ **do**	9 **for** $i \in C \setminus C'$ **do**
9 $I_1' \leftarrow I_1' \cup \overline{I_{1,f_i}} \cup \overline{O_{f_i}}$;	10 $I_1' \leftarrow I_1' \cup \overline{I_{1,f_i}}$;
10 $I_2' \leftarrow I_2' \cup \overline{I_{2,f_i}} \cup \overline{O_{f_i}}$;	11 $I_2' \leftarrow I_2' \cup \overline{I_{2,f_i}}$;
	12 $J' \leftarrow J' \cup \overline{O_{f_i}}$;
11 **end**	13 **end**
12 **if** $|I_1'| \leq t$ **and** $|I_2'| \leq t$ **then** **return** true;	14 **if** $|I_1'| \leq t$ **and** $|I_2'| \leq t$ **and** $|J'| \leq t$ **then return** true;
13 **end**	15 **end**
14 **return** false;	16 **return** false;

---

that we cannot use them to satisfy the free SNI property. In this case, we have no choice but to use $\overline{I_{1,f_i}} \cup \overline{O_{f_i}}$ and $\overline{I_{2,f_i}} \cup \overline{O_{f_i}}$ to add to the sets I_1' and I_2' respectively. The observation works analogously in the case where $|\overline{I_{1,f_i}} \cup \overline{O_{f_i}}| > t$ or $|\overline{I_{2,f_i}} \cup \overline{O_{f_i}}| > t$. We hence apply this in a preprocessing phase to the algorithm, where for each such $i \in C = \{v+1, \ldots, n+t-1\}$, we update the sets I_1 and I_2 correspondingly, and remove the index i from C. Then, in the loop afterwards, we only consider a subset of C. In fact, in the case where $t < n/2$, we always have either $|I_{1,f_i} \cup O_{f_i}| \leq t$ or $|\overline{I_{2,f_i}} \cup \overline{O_{f_i}}| \leq t$ for each $i \in C$, hence there is only one possible partition that could work for the property. This means that we do not need to loop on all possible subsets of C anymore but only go through all indices once. In the case where $t \geq n/2$, the experimental results in the next section show that with the optimization, we end up considering, on average, only 1 or 2 subsets of C in the loop before finding the partition that satisfies the property. In other words, Algorithm 5 for checking the free SNI property is in $\mathcal{O}(n+t)$ whenever $t < n/2$ while it might be exponential in $\mathcal{O}(2^{n+t})$ otherwise to explore all the subsets $C' \subseteq C$. But interestingly in practice, this exploration does not explode for tested gadgets for which the overhead is at most a factor 2.

Finally, we can also apply the same optimization for Algorithm 6 where instead of considering the sizes of the sets $I_{1,f_i} \cup O_{f_i}$ and $I_{2,f_i} \cup O_{f_i}$, we have to consider the sets I_{1,f_i}, I_{2,f_i}, and O_{f_i} independently.

Generalization to Any Base Field $\mathbb{K}$. The verification technique presented in this section can be generalized from $\mathbb{F}_2$ to any base field $\mathbb{K}$. First, Algorithm 3 which tests if the output sharing of the gadget is uniform can be applied in the exact same way. Then, to verify free SNI and IOS properties, we can also apply Algorithm 4 without any changes by correctness of the verification procedure of IronMask on any base field as proven in [14]. Next, we need to slightly modify Algorithms 5 and 6. For each $i \in C$, where C is the set defined on the first line of the algorithms, instead of considering the equation f_i (i.e. the sets I_{1,f_i}, I_{2,f_i} and O_{f_i}), and $f_i + \sum_j y_j$ (i.e. the sets $\overline{I_{1,f_i}}$, $\overline{I_{2,f_i}}$ and $\overline{O_{f_i}}$), we need to consider substracting from f_i different multiples of $\sum_j y_j$ by constant factors of $\mathbb{K}$. In general, we need to consider the $|\mathbb{K}|$ different multiples of $\sum_j y_j$ (where $|\mathbb{K}|$ is the size of the field). However, we can observe that each f_i can be written as

$$f_i = c_{1,f_1} \cdot w_1 + \ldots + c_{t,f_1} \cdot w_t + d_{1,f_1} \cdot y_1 + \ldots d_{n-1,f_1} \cdot y_{n-1}$$

for coefficients $(c_{1,f_1}, \ldots, c_{t,f_1}, d_{1,f_1}, \ldots, d_{n-1,f_1}) \in \mathbb{K}^{t+n-1}$ (on $\mathbb{F}_2$, all of these coefficients are either 0 or 1). Hence, for each $i \in C$, we only need to consider the n equations $f_i, f_i - d_{1,f_1} \cdot \sum_j y_j, \ldots, f_i - d_{n-1,f_1} \cdot \sum_j y_j$. The correctness of this procedure can be proven in a similar way to the result of Lemma 2. Indeed, the cost of Algorithms 5 and 6 becomes more exponential: in the case of $\mathbb{F}_2$, the algorithms perform at most $2^{n+t-v-2}$ iterations of the main loop, while on a larger base field $\mathbb{K}$, the algorithms perform at most $n^{n+t-v-2}$ iterations to find the sets satisfying the free SNI or IOS property.

5.2 Application to Concrete Gadgets

We now demonstrate the verification of the recalled or newly defined properties of Sect. 3 for the most common multiplication and refresh gadgets used in the literature for a reasonable number of shares. We execute the IronMask tool extended with Algorithm 4 on a single core of a 2.4 GHz Intel Core i9 8 cores with a 16 GB RAM. Our results are given in Table 1.

The first column displays the number of shares n (or the range when applicable) for which the gadget is tested. The second column gives the complexity of the gadget with its number of random variables and its number of intermediate variables. Then, the three properties SNI, IOS, and free SNI are tested for $t = n - 1$, and the verification result is given in the Res. column. Finally, the last column displays the verification time and the highest t for which the property is verified when it is not for $t = n - 1$.

First, Table 1 confirms for small numbers of shares that refresh gadgets from Sect. 4, *i.e.* the ISW refresh gadget and the optimized $\mathcal{O}(n \log n)$ ZE-refresh gadget, are free $(n-1)$-SNI and $(n-1)$-IOS. The table also shows the verification result for the ISW multiplication gadget, which is $(n-1)$-SNI for up to 7 shares, and confirms that the gadget is only free $(n-2)$-SNI and $(n-2)$-IOS. Conversely, the multiplication gadget from Corollary 4 is free $(n-1)$-SNI for up to 7 shares, as expected.

As an additional multiplication gadget, we test the parallel construction from [6, SNI gadgets from Table 4] for up to 8 shares.[7] The results in the table show that the gadget is always $(n-1)$-SNI, but depending on the number of shares, is free t-SNI and t'-IOS for different values of $t, t' \geq 1$. Interestingly, the values of t and t' change differently depending on the number of shares in the construction. Also, the gadget is only free $(n-1)$-SNI and $(n-1)$-IOS for $n = 4$.

Finally, we test the optimized 8-shares refresh gadget from [16], which is slightly more efficient than the 8-shares $\mathcal{O}(n \log n)$ refresh gadget from Corollary 5, and uses one less random value. The gadget is confirmed to be free 7-SNI and 7-IOS. We also test the circular refresh gadget as constructed in [3] as a ZE-refresh and confirm that it is free $(n-1)$-SNI and $(n-1)$-IOS for n up to 11 shares.

In all of the tests, we evaluate the impact of the optimization on Algorithms 5 and 6. In order to do this, for each checked gadget, we compute the total number of iterations performed in the loops of Algorithm 5 for free SNI, or Algorithm 6 for IOS, for all of the tuples, divided by the total number of tuples which require at least one iteration of the loop. We observe that for any of the tested gadgets, this ratio does not exceed 1.2, which means that for each tuple of probes, we need, on average, one or at most two iterations of the loop of Algorithm 5 or 6 before finding the sets that satisfy the respective property. This shows that with the optimization introduced to the algorithms, the cost is not exponential anymore, meaning that we do not need to test all possible partitions as described in Lemma 2, but only at most one or two before finding the right one.

---

[7] When we implemented the parallel multiplication gadgets from [6, SNI gadgets from Table 4], we detected a correctness flaw for the case $n \mod 4 = 2$. That is why we could not test such a gadget with six shares.

Table 1. IronMask verification results and execution time.

# shares	Complexity # rand. - # var.	Property	Res.	Verification time
Multiplication Gadgets				
ISW multiplication from [27]				
$n \leq 7$	≤ 21, ≤ 161	SNI	✓	≤ 10 s
		IOS	✗	≤ 10 s ($t_{max} = n - 2$)
		Free SNI	✗	≤ 10 s ($t_{max} = n - 2$)
Multiplication from Corollary 4				
$n \leq 7$	≤ 27, ≤ 179	SNI	✓	≤ 1 min30 s
		IOS	✓	≤ 3 min
		Free SNI	✓	≤ 3 min
Parallel multiplication from [6, SNI gadgets from Table 4]				
*3	3, 27	SNI	✓	≤ 1 s
		IOS	✗	≤ 1 s ($t_{max} = 1$)
		Free SNI	✗	≤ 1 s ($t_{max} = 1$)
4	8, 56	SNI	✓	≤ 1 s
		IOS	✓	≤ 1 s
		Free SNI	✓	≤ 1 s
5	10, 80	SNI	✓	≤ 1 s
		IOS	✓	≤ 1 s
		Free SNI	✗	≤ 1 s ($t_{max} = 3$)
7	21, 161	SNI	✓	7 s
		IOS	✗	4 s ($t_{max} = 5$)
		Free SNI	✗	4 s ($t_{max} = 5$)
8	24, 200	SNI	✓	6 min
		IOS	✗	11 s ($t_{max} = 5$)
		Free SNI	✗	≤ 1 s ($t_{max} = 3$)
Refresh Gadgets				
ISW refresh gadget from [27]				
$n \leq 8$	≤ 28, ≤ 84	SNI	✓	≤ 30 s
		IOS	✓	≤ 2 min30 s
		Free SNI	✓	≤ 2 min30 s
$\mathcal{O}(n \log n)$ refresh gadget from Corollary 5				
$n \leq 11$	≤ 17, ≤ 51	SNI	✓	≤ 1 min
		IOS	✓	≤ 3 min
		Free SNI	✓	≤ 3 min
Optimized 8-share refresh gadget from [16]				
8	11, 33	SNI	✓	≤ 1 s
		IOS	✓	≤ 1 s
		Free SNI	✓	≤ 1 s
Circular refresh gadget (RefreshBlock1; RefreshBlock3) from [3]				
$n \leq 11$	≤ 22, ≤ 66	SNI	✓	≤ 6 min
		IOS	✓	≤ 76 min
		Free SNI	✓	≤ 71 min

6 Probing Model Composition

In this section, we revisit the security proof of the tight private circuits (TPC) [12]. We begin with an overview of this proof, and then show that there is a flaw in one of its lemmas. We however remark that the security of the standard circuits verified by tightPROVE still holds, since the ISW multiplication gadgets are free $(n-2)$-SNI. We are actually able to leverage the new security notions to generalize the tight private circuits to circuits using other types of gadgets (*i.e.* not only ISW multiplication/refresh and additions). This generalization allows, for example, to use the $\mathcal{O}(n \log n)$ refresh gadget from Algorithm 2 in TPCs, instead of the less efficient ISW refresh gadget.

6.1 TPC Security Proof

The TPCs [12] are *standard shared circuits*, that is, masked circuits obtained by composing sharewise addition gadgets, ISW multiplication gadgets and ISW refresh gadgets (next collectively denoted as ISW gadgets). The security proof for TPCs is composed of two parts: the equivalence between t-probing security and a simpler leakage model (Game 3), and a technique to verify the security of a circuit in this model (instantiated with the tightPROVE tool).

In this paper, we focus on the first part of the proof, which is carried by showing the successive equivalence of four different security games. In each of these games, an adversary $\mathcal{A}$ selects some probes and secret inputs, and a simulator $\mathcal{S}$ has to perfectly simulate the set of probes in the circuit. A simulator wins the game if the simulation $\mathsf{ExpSim}_i(\mathcal{A}, \mathcal{S}, C)$ has the same distribution as the true set of probes $\mathsf{ExpReal}_i(\mathcal{A}, C)$, and a circuit is secure in a game if for all adversaries, there exists a simulator that wins the game.

The first game of the reduction (Game 0, see Fig. 4) is the t-probing security game. Next, Game 1 is a variant of Game 0 where the adversary cannot put probes inside RNL ("refresh or non-linear") gadgets, and instead of a probe in a ISW gadget, can get a probe on one share of each of its input sharings. The two following games (see Fig. 5) operate on a flattened circuit $C' = \mathsf{Flatten}(C)$, in which the output sharing of each ISW gadget is replaced by a new input sharing of the circuit. In Game 2, the adversary probes C', and the constraints on the probes are the same as in Game 1. Finally, in Game 3, the set of probes follow the same rules, but is additionally limited to probes on the input shares of two-input ISW gadgets (i.e., the multiplication gadgets).

The reduction between the games is illustrated in Fig. 3, and we next present the main ideas of the reductions. First, the equivalence between Game 0 and Game 1 is based, in one direction, on the simulation of the internal probes using knowledge of the input shares, and in the other direction by exploiting the probing completeness of the ISW gadgets. Next, the equivalence between Game 1 and Game 2 is a consequence of [12, Lemma 1], which states that the output sharing of any SNI gadget, hence of ISW gadgets, is uniform. Finally, the equivalence of Game 2 and Game 3 relies on the observation that without probes on the multiplication gadgets, any standard circuit would be secure, and we can actually show that the other probes are redundant with the ones in multiplication gadgets.

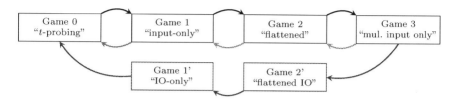

Fig. 3. Representation of the flawed and fixed TPC proofs (an arrow Game $i \to$ Game j means "Security for Game i implies security for Game j."). The flawed implication is in red and the new reductions are in blue. (Color figure online)

$\mathsf{ExpReal}_i(\mathcal{A}, C)$
1. $(\mathcal{P}_i, x_1, \ldots, x_m) \leftarrow \mathcal{A}()$
2. $\overrightarrow{x_1} \leftarrow \mathsf{Enc}(x_1), \ldots, \overrightarrow{x_m} \leftarrow \mathsf{Enc}(x_m)$
3. $(v_1, \ldots, v_q) \leftarrow C(\overrightarrow{x_1}, \ldots, \overrightarrow{x_m})_{\mathcal{P}_i}$
4. Return $(v_1, \ldots, v_q)$

$\mathsf{ExpSim}_i(\mathcal{A}, \mathcal{S}, C)$
1. $(\mathcal{P}_i, x_1, \ldots, x_m) \leftarrow \mathcal{A}()$
2. $(v_1, \ldots, v_q) \leftarrow S(\mathcal{P}_i)$
3. Return $(v_1, \ldots, v_q)$

Fig. 4. Game 0, Game 1 and Game 1' ($i = 0, 1, 1'$ respectively). For Game 0, $\mathcal{P}_0$ can be any set of $q = t$ probes in C. For Game 1, the probes in ISW or RNL gadgets are moved to their input shares while for Game 1', the corresponding output probes (following the balanced IOS definition) are also included.

6.2 Proof Flaw

The reduction of security w.r.t. Game 0 to the security w.r.t. Game 1 (security implication from Game 1 to Game 0 in Fig. 3, [12, Proposition 4]) has a flawed proof. This proof relies on a simulation argument. At a gadget level, a probe in a ISW multiplication gadget can be simulated when one share of each input is known, since the gadget is SNI. However, when handling the composition, the simulation may need the values of output shares of a multiplication gadget. Thanks to [12, Lemma 1]), any set of $n - 1$ output shares of the ISW multiplication is uniform and independent of the input sharings. This observation is used in the proof of the proposition to claim that the output shares can be simulated as fresh randomness. However, this is not correct in presence of probes in the multiplication gadget, whose value may not be independent of the output shares.

Let us now show with a counter-example that the proof cannot be easily fixed, $i.e.$ that it cannot be fixed while relying only on the SNI security of the ISW multiplication. We consider the circuit described in Algorithm 7. In the first multiplication gadget, the adversary can probe the last intermediate sum in

$\mathsf{ExpReal}_i(\mathcal{A}, C)$
 1. $C' \leftarrow \mathsf{Flatten}(C)$
 2. $(\mathcal{P}_i, x_1, \ldots, x_M) \leftarrow \mathcal{A}()$
 3. $\vec{x_1} \leftarrow \mathsf{Enc}(x_1), \ldots, \vec{x_M} \leftarrow \mathsf{Enc}(x_M)$
 4. $(v_1, \ldots, v_q) \leftarrow C(\vec{x_1}, \ldots, \vec{x_M})_{\mathcal{P}_i}$
 5. Return $(v_1, \ldots, v_q)$

$\mathsf{ExpSim}_i(\mathcal{A}, \mathcal{S}, C)$
 1. $C' \leftarrow \mathsf{Flatten}(C)$
 2. $(\mathcal{P}_i, x_1, \ldots, x_M) \leftarrow \mathcal{A}()$
 3. $(v_1, \ldots, v_q) \leftarrow S(\mathcal{P}_i)$
 4. Return $(v_1, \ldots, v_q)$

Fig. 5. Game 2, Game 2' and Game 3 ($i = 2, 2', 3$ respectively). For Game 2, the probes are the same as in Game 1, and for Game 2' we add probes on the new input shares that correspond to probes on output shares of RNL gadgets in $\mathcal{P}_{1'}$. For Game 3, $\mathcal{P}_3$ contains only probes on input shares of the two-input ISW/RNL gadgets.

Algorithm 7: Broken ISW composition

  Input : sharings $(a_1, \ldots, a_4)$ and $(b_1, \ldots, b_4)$
 1 $(c_1, \ldots c_4) \leftarrow \mathsf{ISW\text{-}MUL}((a_1, \ldots, a_4), (b_1, \ldots, b_4))$;   // Uses randomness $r_{i,j}$
 2 $(d_1, d_2, d_3, d_4) \leftarrow (c_2, c_3, c_4, c_1)$
 3 **for** $i \leftarrow 1$ **to** 4 **do**
 4 $\quad\mid\quad e_i \leftarrow a_i \oplus d_i$;
 5 **end**
 6 $(f_1, \ldots f_4) \leftarrow \mathsf{ISW\text{-}MUL}((e_1, \ldots, e_4), (a_1, \ldots, a_4))$

---

the computation of c_2: $p_1 = S$ with $c_2 = S \oplus r_{2,3}$, and $p_2 = (a_2 b_3 \oplus r_{2,3}) \oplus a_3 b_2$. It can also probe $p_3 = e_1 a_4$ in the second multiplication. Since $p_3 = (a_1 \oplus c_2) a_4$, the adversary may compute $p_1 \oplus p_2 \oplus p_3 = (S \oplus r_{2,3})(a_4 \oplus 1) \oplus a_2 b_3 \oplus a_3 b_2 \oplus a_1 a_4$. When S, b_2 and b_3 are uniform randomness, and (a_1, a_2, a_3, a_4) is a uniform sharing of a, the value of previous expression depends on a, therefore the circuit is not 3-probing secure.

Let us remark that the presence of the rotation between the sharing $(c_1, \ldots, c_4)$ and the sharing $(d_1, \ldots, d_4)$ is needed the exhibit the attack. If we consider this rotation as part of the first multiplication gadget, it remains $(n-1)$-SNI (as the size of a set of output shares is not impacted by the rotation), showing that, for the proof to work, we have to rely on a stronger property. However, a rotation break the free SNI property, and indeed, we next show that, since the ISW multiplication is free $(n-2)$-SNI, the TPC proof can be repaired.

6.3 Generalized Proof

We now fix the above flaw and generalize the proof of [12] to cover more types of gadgets. Namely, we allow any probing complete gadget that is free $(n-2)$-SNI and $(n-1)$-NI instead of only ISW multiplication and refresh gadgets. Moreover, instead of only additions, our proof works with arbitrary affine sharewise gadgets.

Definition 13 (GTPC). *An n-generalized tight private circuit (GTPC) is an n-share masked circuit composed of SA gadgets and RNL gadgets (standing for refresh or non-linear). A gadget is SA if it is sharewise affine, and a gadget is*

RNL if it is $(n-1)$-probing complete, $(n-1)$-NI, free $(n-2)$-SNI, and has one or two input shares.

Let us remark that this definition covers the standard shared circuits, since ISW multiplication and refresh gadgets are free $(n-2)$-SNI and $(n-1)$-NI.

Theorem 4 (All games are equivalent). *Let G be any of the games of Fig. 3. A n-GTPC is $(n-1)$-probing secure if and only if for every adversary $\mathcal{A}$ there exists a simulator $\mathcal{S}$ that wins G.*

The proof idea is as follows (the full proof is given in the full version of the paper): we introduce two new intermediate games (Game 1' and Game 2', shown in Fig. 3) for the reduction of Game 0 security to Game 3 security, while for the tightness (reduction of Game 3 security to Game 0) we discuss the minor changes needed to generalize the proofs of [12] to the generalized circuit assumptions.

In a nutshell, with the two new games, we introduce the output probes needed to simulate the probes in the RNL gadgets, using a balanced IOS simulator, as shown in Fig. 4 and Fig. 5. Security in Game 1' therefore implies security in Game 0 thanks to the balanced IOS simulation, while, as previously, the reduction of Game 1' to Game 2' is a consequence of the uniformity of output sharings of RNL gadgets. Finally, the reduction of Game 2' to Game 3 has to deal with the additional probes on the circuit inputs and the more general affine gadgets, but the core proof idea remain the same: any attack in Game 2' has its source in a probe in a 2-input RNL gadget.

Let us remark that we only require free $(n-2)$-SNI and not free $(n-1)$-SNI, which allows us to cover ISW gadgets with our proof. This relaxed requirement is only significant when the adversary puts all its $n-1$ probes in a single gadget. In that case, the part of the circuit that uses the output of this gadget is not probed, hence we do not care about the output shares distribution, which is why $(n-1)$-NI is a sufficient requirement.

7 Region Probing Model Composition

In this section, we revisit the IOS composition framework introduced in [25] to achieve security in the region probing model. As recalled in Sect. 2, the region probing model is a strong version of the probing model in which the adversary gets to place t probes in each gadget (or region) of the circuit. This model is relevant in practice as being closer to actual side-channel leakages (providing information on all the gadgets of an implementation) which is formally captured by a reduction from the *noisy leakage model* [22,33].

We show hereafter that another generalized version of tight private circuits (TPC), which we name *region tight private circuit* (RTPC), enjoys a tight security in the region probing model.

Composing several sharewise affine gadgets yields a larger sharewise affine gadget which we shall call a *sharewise affine region* (or SA region) hereafter when it is delimited by IOS gadgets. Consider such an SA region

$$G : (\overrightarrow{x_1}, \ldots, \overrightarrow{x_\ell}) \mapsto (\overrightarrow{y_1}, \ldots, \overrightarrow{y_m})$$

computing a function $g : (x_1, \ldots, x_\ell) \to (g_1(x_1, \ldots, x_\ell), \ldots, g_m(x_1, \ldots, x_\ell))$. We say that this SA region is *full rank* if the computed coordinate functions g_i's are linearly independent, *i.e.*, there exist no constant $\alpha \in \mathbb{K}^m$ and $\beta \in \mathbb{K}$ such that $\langle \alpha, g(x_1, \ldots, x_\ell) \rangle = \beta$ (for all $x_1, \ldots, x_\ell$).

Definition 14 (RTPC). *An n-region tight private circuit (RTPC) is an n-share masked circuit composed of SA gadgets and RCNL gadgets (standing for refresh, copy or non-linear). A gadget is SA if it is sharewise affine while a gadget is RCNL if it is $\lfloor (n-1)/3 \rfloor$-IOS. Moreover, all the SA regions of an RTPC are full rank.*

We stress that for $n \geq 3$, a generalized tight private circuit (GTPC) under Definition 13 is also an RTPC under the above definition provided that its SA regions are full rank. Moreover, the common example of masked circuits composed of ISW multiplications, $\mathcal{O}(n \log n)$ refresh gadgets and sharewise affine gadgets are both GTPC and RTPC (once again provided that their SA regions are full rank).

Remark 2. We note that an SA region which is not full rank can be split into smaller full rank SA regions by introducing IOS refresh and/or copy gadgets. Consider for example the function:

$$g(x_1, x_2, x_3) \mapsto \begin{pmatrix} y_1 \\ y_2 \\ y_3 \end{pmatrix} = \begin{pmatrix} x_1 + x_2 \\ x_2 + x_3 \\ x_1 + x_3 \end{pmatrix}.$$

An SA region composed of three addition gadgets computing this function is not full rank. By introducing IOS copies of x_1 and x_3 (*e.g.* using the copy gadget of Sect. 4.4), this SA region can be split into two full rank SA regions, the first one computing (y_1, y_2) and the second one computing y_3.

An RTPC tolerates up to $t = \lfloor (n-1)/3 \rfloor$ probes per IOS gadget and per (full rank) SA region, which gives a probing rate r of $\lfloor (n-1)/3 \rfloor$ over the size of the largest region (IOS gadget or SA region). This is formalized in the following theorem (the proof is given in the full version of the paper).

Theorem 5. *An n-region tight private circuit is r-region probing secure with*

$$r = \min \left(\frac{\lfloor (n-1)/3 \rfloor}{|\mathsf{SAR}|}, \frac{\lfloor (n-1)/3 \rfloor}{|\mathsf{RCNL}|} \right)$$

with $|\mathsf{SAR}|$ the size of the largest SA region in the circuit and $|\mathsf{RCNL}|$ the size of the largest RCNL gadget in the circuit.

The above theorem generalizes the composition result from [25] to RTPC. Compared to this previous result, the above theorem is more general in several aspects:

- We consider IOS gadgets which are not necessarily refresh gadgets. We can thus take advantage of the IOS property of multiplication gadgets, such as the ISW multiplication gadget, and use IOS copy gadgets.
- We do not require the underlying circuit to insert an IOS refresh gadget between any two non-IOS gadgets whereas the *standard circuit compilers* defined in [25] impose this requirement (which is needed by the composition theorem). As a result, we can use large sharewise affine regions and save many refresh gadgets.
- The underlying circuit can use IOS copy gadgets where a standard circuit compiler from [25] would use a copy gadget surrounded by three IOS refreshes. Our construction of IOS copy gadget (see Sect. 4.4) is slightly more efficient (*i.e.* equivalent to 2 IOS refreshes).
- We do not consider probing secure gadgets (besides sharewise affine gadgets) which seemingly is a loss of generality but is actually not as we show hereafter.

Probing Secure Gadgets in Our Framework. The power of the IOS framework introduced in [25] resides in the fact that it enables to securely compose gadgets which only satisfy probing security and no further probing composition notions. Sharewise affine gadgets are an example of probing-secure gadgets (which are not *e.g.* SNI or IOS) but other probing secure gadgets exist which are not sharewise affine. An example is the multiplication gadget considered in [25] (previously introduced in [24]) which achieves quasilinear complexity $\mathcal{O}(n \log n)$ (with some constraints on the underlying field $\mathbb{K}$). While such gadgets are seemingly out of the scope of RTPC circuits they can be augmented to fit into it thanks to the following proposition (the proof is given in the full version of the paper).

Proposition 9. Let $G : (x_1, x_2) \mapsto y$ be a t-probing secure gadget and G_{ref} be a t-IOS refresh gadget. The gadget G' defined as

$$G' : (x_1, x_2) \mapsto G_{ref}\big(G\big(G_{ref}(\overrightarrow{x_1}), G_{ref}(\overrightarrow{x_2})\big)\big)$$

is (balanced) t-IOS.

The above proposition shows that any probing secure gadget can be made IOS by surrounding it with IOS refreshes (which is the principle of the composition from [25]). This way, we can include non-sharewise affine probing secure gadgets (such as the quasilinear multiplication gadget) in our extended IOS framework by first composing them with IOS refreshes.

Acknowledgements. This work is partly supported by SGS and the French FUI-AAP25 VeriSiCC project. The authors would also like to thank Benjamin Grégoire for his insightful comments and constructive discussions.

References

1. Andrychowicz, M., Dziembowski, S., Faust, S.: Circuit compilers with $O(1/\log(n))$ leakage rate. In: Fischlin, M., Coron, J.-S. (eds.) EUROCRYPT 2016, Part II. LNCS, vol. 9666, pp. 586–615. Springer, Heidelberg (2016). https://doi.org/10.1007/978-3-662-49896-5_21

2. Barthe, G., Belaïd, S., Cassiers, G., Fouque, P.-A., Grégoire, B., Standaert, F.-X.: maskVerif: automated verification of higher-order masking in presence of physical defaults. In: Sako, K., Schneider, S., Ryan, P.Y.A. (eds.) ESORICS 2019, Part I. LNCS, vol. 11735, pp. 300–318. Springer, Cham (2019). https://doi.org/10.1007/978-3-030-29959-0_15

3. Barthe, G., et al.: Improved parallel mask refreshing algorithms: generic solutions with parametrized non-interference and automated optimizations. J. Cryptogr. Eng. **10**(1), 17–26 (2020)

4. Barthe, G., Belaïd, S., Dupressoir, F., Fouque, P.-A., Grégoire, B., Strub, P.-Y.: Verified proofs of higher-order masking. In: Oswald, E., Fischlin, M. (eds.) EURO-CRYPT 2015, Part I. LNCS, vol. 9056, pp. 457–485. Springer, Heidelberg (2015). https://doi.org/10.1007/978-3-662-46800-5_18

5. Barthe, G., et al.: Strong non-interference and type-directed higher-order masking. In: Weippl, E.R., Katzenbeisser, S., Kruegel, C., Myers, A.C., Halevi, S. (eds.) ACM CCS 2016: 23rd Conference on Computer and Communications Security, Vienna, Austria, October 24–28, 2016, pp. 116–129. ACM Press (2016)

6. Barthe, G., Dupressoir, F., Faust, S., Grégoire, B., Standaert, F.-X., Strub, P.-Y.: Parallel implementations of masking schemes and the bounded moment leakage model. In: Coron, J.-S., Nielsen, J.B. (eds.) EUROCRYPT 2017, Part I. LNCS, vol. 10210, pp. 535–566. Springer, Cham (2017). https://doi.org/10.1007/978-3-319-56620-7_19

7. Battistello, A., Coron, J.-S., Prouff, E., Zeitoun, R.: Horizontal side-channel attacks and countermeasures on the ISW masking scheme. In: Gierlichs, B., Poschmann, A.Y. (eds.) CHES 2016. LNCS, vol. 9813, pp. 23–39. Springer, Heidelberg (2016). https://doi.org/10.1007/978-3-662-53140-2_2

8. Battistello, A., Coron, J.-S., Prouff, E., Zeitoun, R.: Horizontal side-channel attacks and countermeasures on the ISW masking scheme. Cryptology ePrint Archive, Report 2016/540 (2016). https://eprint.iacr.org/2016/540

9. Belaïd, S., Benhamouda, F., Passelègue, A., Prouff, E., Thillard, A., Vergnaud, D.: Randomness complexity of private circuits for multiplication. In: Fischlin, M., Coron, J.-S. (eds.) EUROCRYPT 2016, Part II. LNCS, vol. 9666, pp. 616–648. Springer, Heidelberg (2016). https://doi.org/10.1007/978-3-662-49896-5_22

10. Belaïd, S., Benhamouda, F., Passelègue, A., Prouff, E., Thillard, A., Vergnaud, D.: Private multiplication over finite fields. In: Katz, J., Shacham, H. (eds.) CRYPTO 2017, Part III. LNCS, vol. 10403, pp. 397–426. Springer, Cham (2017). https://doi.org/10.1007/978-3-319-63697-9_14

11. Belaïd, S., Coron, J.-S., Prouff, E., Rivain, M., Taleb, A.R.: Random probing security: verification, composition, expansion and new constructions. In: Micciancio, D., Ristenpart, T. (eds.) CRYPTO 2020, Part I. LNCS, vol. 12170, pp. 339–368. Springer, Cham (2020). https://doi.org/10.1007/978-3-030-56784-2_12

12. Belaïd, S., Goudarzi, D., Rivain, M.: Tight private circuits: achieving probing security with the least refreshing. In: Peyrin, T., Galbraith, S. (eds.) ASIACRYPT 2018, Part II. LNCS, vol. 11273, pp. 343–372. Springer, Cham (2018). https://doi.org/10.1007/978-3-030-03329-3_12

13. Belaïd, S., Mercadier, D., Rivain, M., Taleb, A.R.: IronMask: versatile verification of masking security. In: 43rd IEEE Symposium on Security and Privacy, SP 2022, San Francisco, CA, USA, May 22–26, 2022, pp. 142–160. IEEE (2022)

14. Belaïd, S., Mercadier, D., Rivain, M., Taleb, A.R.: IronMask: versatile verification of masking security. In: 2022 IEEE Symposium on Security and Privacy, San Francisco, CA, USA, 22–26 May 2022. IEEE Computer Society Press, pp. 142–160

15. Bordes, N., Karpman, P.: Fast verification of masking schemes in characteristic two. In: Canteaut, A., Standaert, F.-X. (eds.) EUROCRYPT 2021, Part II. LNCS, vol. 12697, pp. 283–312. Springer, Cham (2021). https://doi.org/10.1007/978-3-030-77886-6_10

16. Cassiers, G., Grégoire, B., Levi, I., Standaert, F.-X.: Hardware private circuits: from trivial composition to full verification. IEEE Trans. Comput. **70**(10), 1677–1690 (2021)

17. Cassiers, G., Standaert, F.-X.: Trivially and efficiently composing masked gadgets with probe isolating non-interference. IEEE Trans. Inf. Forensics Secur. **15**, 2542–2555 (2020)

18. Cassiers, G., Standaert, F.-X.: Provably secure hardware masking in the transition- and glitch-robust probing model: better safe than sorry. IACR Trans. Cryptogr. Hardw. Embed. Syst. **2021**(2), 136–158 (2021). https://tches.iacr.org/index.php/TCHES/article/view/8790

19. Chari, S., Jutla, C.S., Rao, J.R., Rohatgi, P.: Towards sound approaches to counteract power-analysis attacks. In: Wiener, M. (ed.) CRYPTO 1999. LNCS, vol. 1666, pp. 398–412. Springer, Heidelberg (1999). https://doi.org/10.1007/3-540-48405-1_26

20. Coron, J.-S., Prouff, E., Rivain, M., Roche, T.: Higher-order side channel security and mask refreshing. In: Moriai, S. (ed.) FSE 2013. LNCS, vol. 8424, pp. 410–424. Springer, Heidelberg (2014). https://doi.org/10.1007/978-3-662-43933-3_21

21. Coron, J.-S., Spignoli, L.: Secure wire shuffling in the probing model. In: Malkin, T., Peikert, C. (eds.) CRYPTO 2021, Part III. LNCS, vol. 12827, pp. 215–244. Springer, Cham (2021). https://doi.org/10.1007/978-3-030-84252-9_8

22. Duc, A., Dziembowski, S., Faust, S.: Unifying leakage models: from probing attacks to noisy leakage. In: Nguyen, P.Q., Oswald, E. (eds.) EUROCRYPT 2014. LNCS, vol. 8441, pp. 423–440. Springer, Heidelberg (2014). https://doi.org/10.1007/978-3-642-55220-5_24

23. Goubin, L., Patarin, J.: DES and differential power analysis the "Duplication" method. In: Koç, Ç.K., Paar, C. (eds.) CHES 1999. LNCS, vol. 1717, pp. 158–172. Springer, Heidelberg (1999). https://doi.org/10.1007/3-540-48059-5_15

24. Goudarzi, D., Joux, A., Rivain, M.: How to securely compute with noisy leakage in quasilinear complexity. In: Peyrin, T., Galbraith, S. (eds.) ASIACRYPT 2018, Part II. LNCS, vol. 11273, pp. 547–574. Springer, Cham (2018). https://doi.org/10.1007/978-3-030-03329-3_19

25. Goudarzi, D., Prest, T., Rivain, M., Vergnaud, D.: Probing security through input-output separation and revisited quasilinear masking. IACR Trans. Cryptogr. Hardw. Embed. Syst. **2021**(3), 599–640 (2021). https://tches.iacr.org/index.php/TCHES/article/view/8987

26. Goudarzi, D., Prest, T., Rivain, M., Vergnaud, D.: Probing security through input-output separation and revisited quasilinear masking. Cryptology ePrint Archive, Report 2022/045 (2022). https://eprint.iacr.org/2022/045

27. Ishai, Y., Sahai, A., Wagner, D.: Private circuits: securing hardware against probing attacks. In: Boneh, D. (ed.) CRYPTO 2003. LNCS, vol. 2729, pp. 463–481. Springer, Heidelberg (2003). https://doi.org/10.1007/978-3-540-45146-4_27

28. Knichel, D., Sasdrich, P., Moradi, A.: SILVER – statistical independence and leakage verification. In: Moriai, S., Wang, H. (eds.) ASIACRYPT 2020, Part I. LNCS, vol. 12491, pp. 787–816. Springer, Cham (2020). https://doi.org/10.1007/978-3-030-64837-4_26

29. Kocher, P., Jaffe, J., Jun, B.: Differential power analysis. In: Wiener, M. (ed.) CRYPTO 1999. LNCS, vol. 1666, pp. 388–397. Springer, Heidelberg (1999). https://doi.org/10.1007/3-540-48405-1_25

30. Mathieu-Mahias, A.: Securisation of implementations of cryptographic algorithms in the context of embedded systems (2021)

31. Micali, S., Reyzin, L.: Physically observable cryptography. In: Naor, M. (ed.) TCC 2004. LNCS, vol. 2951, pp. 278–296. Springer, Heidelberg (2004). https://doi.org/10.1007/978-3-540-24638-1_16

32. Nikova, S., Rechberger, C., Rijmen, V.: Threshold implementations against side-channel attacks and glitches. In: Ning, P., Qing, S., Li, N. (eds.) ICICS 2006. LNCS, vol. 4307, pp. 529–545. Springer, Heidelberg (2006). https://doi.org/10.1007/11935308_38

33. Prouff, E., Rivain, M.: Masking against side-channel attacks: a formal security proof. In: Johansson, T., Nguyen, P.Q. (eds.) EUROCRYPT 2013. LNCS, vol. 7881, pp. 142–159. Springer, Heidelberg (2013). https://doi.org/10.1007/978-3-642-38348-9_9

34. Rivain, M., Prouff, E.: Provably secure higher-order masking of AES. In: Mangard, S., Standaert, F.-X. (eds.) CHES 2010. LNCS, vol. 6225, pp. 413–427. Springer, Heidelberg (2010). https://doi.org/10.1007/978-3-642-15031-9_28

Symmetric Constructions

Twin Column Parity Mixers and Gaston
A New Mixing Layer and Permutation

Solane El Hirch[1]($\boxtimes$), Joan Daemen[1], Raghvendra Rohit[2],
and Rusydi H. Makarim[3]

[1] Radboud University, Nijmegen, The Netherlands
solane.elhirch@ru.nl, joan@cs.ru.nl
[2] Cryptography Research Centre, Technology Innovation Institute, Abu Dhabi, UAE
raghvendra.rohit@tii.ae
[3] Jakarta, Indonesia
rusydi@makarim.id

Abstract. We introduce a new type of mixing layer for the round function of cryptographic permutations, called circulant twin column parity mixer (CPM), that is a generalization of the mixing layers in Keccak-f and Xoodoo. While these mixing layers have a bitwise differential branch number of 4 and a computational cost of 2 (bitwise) additions per bit, the circulant twin CPMs we build have a bitwise differential branch number of 12 at the expense of an increase in computational cost: depending on the dimension this ranges between 3 and 3.34 XORs per bit. Our circulant twin CPMs operate on a state in the form of a rectangular array and can serve as mixing layer in a round function that has as non-linear step a layer of S-boxes operating in parallel on the columns. When sandwiched between two ShiftRow-like mappings, we can obtain a columnwise branch number of 12 and hence it guarantees 12 active S-boxes per two rounds in differential trails. Remarkably, the linear branch numbers (bitwise and columnwise alike) of these mappings is only 4. However, we define the *transpose* of a circulant twin CPM that has linear branch number of 12 and a differential branch number of 4. We give a concrete instantiation of a permutation using such a mixing layer, named Gaston. It operates on a state of 5×64 bits and uses χ operating on columns for its non-linear layer. Most notably, the Gaston round function is lightweight in that it takes as few bitwise operations as the one of NIST lightweight standard Ascon. We show that the best 3-round differential and linear trails of Gaston have much higher weights than those of Ascon. Permutations like Gaston can be very competitive in applications that rely for their security exclusively on good differential properties, such as keyed hashing as in the compression phase of Farfalle.

Keywords: Mixing layer · Permutations · Branch number · Column parity mixer (CPM) · Ascon

R. H. Makarim—Independent Researcher.

© International Association for Cryptologic Research 2023
H. Handschuh and A. Lysyanskaya (Eds.): CRYPTO 2023, LNCS 14083, pp. 475–506, 2023.
https://doi.org/10.1007/978-3-031-38548-3_16

1   Introduction

Over the last decades there has been extensive research on lightweight crypto-graphic primitives, where lightweight means with the objective of being imple-mented on resource-constrained platforms, e.g., for the Internet of Things (IoT), Radio Frequency ID (RFID) and sensors. Those platforms require a careful trade-off between efficiency and security. A major challenge is to achieve excellent per-formance results on a wide spectrum of target devices while providing a good security margin, and this at reasonable implementation cost. In hardware imple-mentations and in bit-sliced software implementations a good estimate of the cost is the total number of binary Boolean operations (XOR, (N)AND, (N)OR, NOT) required to execute the primitive. We will refer to this as the *gate cost*.

In recent years, iterated cryptographic permutations have become increas-ingly popular, but their design is very similar to that of the data path of block ciphers. In so-called substitution-permutation networks (SPN), the round func-tion has a linear layer and a non-linear S-box layer. In an SPN block cipher the rounds are typically alternated with the addition of a round key, derived from the cipher key by means of a key schedule. The linear layer often consists of the composition of a mixing layer and a bit shuffle moving the bits around.

Many SPNs are designed according to the *wide trail strategy* and the best know example of this is the Advanced Encryption Standard (AES) [12]. With this strategy, one can easily prove strong upper bounds for the expected differential probability of differential trails and for the correlation contribution of linear trails. The simplicity of the strategy and this ability to prove trail bounds have made it one of the most widely used design approaches for block ciphers and permutations.

AES [12] operates on a state that can be represented as a 4×4 byte array. Its mixing layer is called MixColumns and it considers each column of the state as a 4-byte vector and it multiplies them by a 4×4-byte matrix. These matrices are maximum-distance-separable (MDS): they have (differential and linear) branch number 5. The AES linear layer also has a byte shuffle, called ShiftRows. Their combination allows to prove that the number of active S-boxes in any 4-round trail is 25, or in general, the square of the branch number [12]. In the context of lightweight cryptography, there has been ample research about construct-ing MDS matrices with low gate cost, see [2,17,23–25,27,33,35]. While most research is about 4×4 matrices, the first MixColumn-like MDS matrices for use in cryptographic round functions were 8×8, introduced in the block cipher SHARK [32]. Later 8×8 MDS matrices were used in the compression function of hash functions such as Whirlpool [1] and there has also been research on reduc-ing the gate cost of such mappings [23]. Constructions that combine 8×8 MDS matrices with an appropriate ShiftRows mapping have at least $9^2 = 81$ active S-boxes in any 4-round trail. Still, it would be a stretch to call such mappings and ciphers that make use of them lightweight.

A different flavor of the wide trail strategy we find in ASCON-p, the per-mutation underlying ASCON [16], KECCAK-f, the permutation underlying KEC-CAK [5], and the permutation XOODOO [11]. The former two have a mixing layer of the type *column parity mixer* (CPM) that cannot be split into a number of parallel mappings but operates on the state as a whole. The mixing layer of ASCON-p consists of separate mix mappings operating on the 5 rows of the state independently, combined with two mixing steps that act as enforcements of the low-diffusion linear step in the S-box layer. The latter is the χ mapping borrowed from KECCAK-f, but then operating on 5-bit columns rather than rows.

In all three permutations the mixing layer has a branch number of 4 and hence they have relatively low worst-case diffusion. Moreover, they do not lend themselves to easy proofs for strong lower bounds on the number of active S-boxes over 4 or more rounds. Still, with computer-aided techniques, strong bounds have been achieved for KECCAK-f [30], XOODOO [14] and ASCON-p [18,28].

A study in [8] provides evidence that this approach outperforms MDS-based designs in that they achieve lower upper bounds on the probability of differential trails and the correlation contribution of linear trails for the same amount of computation, often due to lighter rounds. Moreover, the paper shows that they suffer less from clustering of trails.

The mixing layers in XOODOO and KECCAK-f both require 2 binary XOR operations per bit of the state. In the permutation underlying ASCON, winner of the NIST lightweight cryptography cipher competition [31], the mixing layer p_L costs similarly 2 binary XOR operations per bit. However, the part of the mixing layer in the S-boxes p_S has an additional cost of 1.2 binary XOR operations per bit, totaling to 3.2 binary XOR operations per bit. In this split-up, the gate cost of the non-linear layer is equal in all three permutations as all use the χ mapping: 1 XOR, 1 AND and 1 NOT gate per state bit.

Our Contribution. In this work, we explore the possibility of using the mixing budget of 3.2 binary XOR operations per bit, allocated for ASCON-p, differently. We define a new type of mixing layer, the *circulant twin CPM*, a generalization of the column parity mixers in KECCAK-f and XOODOO. Whereas the latter have differential branch number 4, our twin CPM achieves differential branch number 12. Remarkably, its linear branch number is equal to that of the mixing layer of KECCAK-f, XOODOO and ASCON-p, namely 4. We show that we can *transpose* a twin CPM resulting in linear branch number of 12 and differential branch number of 4 with no effect on the gate cost. We provide a proof-of-concept permutation that uses the twin CPM as its mixing layer that we name Gaston. This permutation is lightweight in the sense that it takes the same number of bitwise Boolean operations per round as ASCON-p. We show that Gaston achieves very good differential trail behaviour for both differential, and even linear, trails over 2 and 3 rounds.

Related Work. There is a lot of research that focuses on finding MDS matrices that have low implementation cost. The efficiency of MDS matrices can be defined in terms of several criteria such as the overall gate cost, latency or circuit depth [2,21,22,26,27,33]. Implementing an MDS matrix with branch number 9 (dimension 8) requires more than 6 XORs per bit. We know of no work that investigates the gate cost of MDS matrices or other mixing layers with branch number above 9. At least for MDS matrices existing research suggests that the number of XORs per bit increases with the branch number. In Table 1, we compare various types of mixing layers.

Table 1. A comparison of different types of mixing layers. For MDS, the dimensions in the second column represent the dimension of the matrix (defined over the finite field) while for the rest it denotes the state size in bits. The symbols d, m and n denote the degree of the field defining polynomial, the number of rows and number of columns, respectively. For the first row of CPM, w represents the number of 5×5 slices and $w \in \{8, 16, 32, 64\}$ based on the variant of KECCAK-f.

Mixing layer type	Dimensions	XORs per bit	Branch number		Source
			Diff.	Linear	
MDS	3×3, $GF(2^d)$	$\frac{5}{3} + \frac{1}{3d}$	4	4	[17]
	4×4, $GF(2^d)$	$2 + \frac{3}{4d}$ †	5	5	[17]
	8×8, $GF(2^4)$	6.06	9	9	[23]
	8×8, $GF(2^8)$	6.125	9	9	[23]
CPM	$5 \times 5 \times w$, $GF(2)$	2	4	4	[5]
	$3 \times 4 \times 32$, $GF(2)$	2	4	4	[11]
	$m \times n$, $GF(2)$	$2 + \frac{h-2}{m}$ ‡	4	4	[34]
ASCON p_L	5×64, $GF(2)$	2	4	4	[16]
Twin CPM	$m \times n$, $GF(2)$	$3 + \frac{1}{m}$	12	4	This work
Transpose of Twin CPM	$m \times n$, $GF(2)$	$3 + \frac{1}{m}$	4	12	This work

† : For $d = 4, 8$ this bound is tight as shown in [35]. A 4×4 matrix over $GF(2^4)$ with cost 35 XORs is used in Saturnin [9].

‡ : h is the Hamming weight of the parity-folding polynomial as defined in [34].

Outline. In Sect. 2, we recall different diffusion metrics for linear layers. The circulant twin CPM and the bit shuffles which make up the linear layer are defined in Sect. 3. The study of the differential diffusion properties of twin CPMs is given in Sect. 4 while in Sect. 5 we discuss the equivalence relations that partition the sets of the shift offsets that define the linear layer. We investigate the linear mask properties of twin CPMs in Sect. 6. In Sect. 7, we describe the search strategy for the shift offsets in the twin CPM mixing layer and row shifts of lightweight permutation Gaston and further provide upper bounds on the weight of trails over 2 and 3 rounds of Gaston using general-purpose solvers. In Sect. 8 we finalize the specifications of Gaston and discuss how Gaston and variants can be used in the Farfalle construction. In Sect. 9 we provide conclusions and open problems.

2   Diffusion Metrics for Linear Layers

We will study iterated permutations with a round function R consisting of a linear layer that we will denote by λ and a non-linear layer that we will denote by γ. We will assume $R = \gamma \circ \lambda$. The other option would be $R = \lambda \circ \gamma$. When investigating difference (and mask) propagation through the round function the variant can be addressed by a simple re-phasing.

We assume the round function operates on a state A that consists of bits arranged in an array of rows of equal length. We denote the set of all possible states by $\mathcal{A}$. Note that $\mathcal{A}$ forms a vector space with bitwise addition.

Orthogonal to the rows we have *columns*. We assume the non-linear layer operates in parallel on the columns, as in ASCON-p [15] and XOODOO [11].

Iterating such a round function provides resistance against differential (DC) and linear cryptanalysis (LC) by the alternation of λ and γ. In particular, their combination targets the avoidance of differential trails with high probability and/or linear trails with high correlation contribution.

Within the linear layer there typically is a mixlayer that ensures that a bit at its output depends on multiple bits at its input and that a difference in few input bits propagates to multiple bits at its output. The mixlayer mixes bits *close to each other in the state* and the role of the shuffles is to move bits close to each other to positions that are far from each other. We call the mixlayer θ.

In this section we recall the basics of difference and linear propagation and list some metrics for λ and θ such as the branch number and the branch histogram to provide an indicator of their performance in the round function of a cryptographic permutation or block cipher.

2.1   Difference Propagation

Differential cryptanalysis exploits high-probability differentials [7]. Let f be a transformation over $\mathbb{F}_2^n$ and let a be an input difference to f and b its output difference. The combination of input difference and output difference (a, b) is called a differential over f and its differential probability (DP) is defined as the fraction of all possible input pairs with difference a that exhibit the difference b after application of f to its members:

$$\mathrm{DP}(a, b) = \frac{\#\{x \in \mathbb{F}_2^n \mid f(x) \oplus f(x \oplus a) = b\}}{2^n}.$$

The *restriction weight* $\mathrm{w_r}$ of a differential relates to its DP as $\mathrm{DP} = 2^{-\mathrm{w_r}}$.

We call a differential over the round function R a *round differential*. Round differentials can be chained to form a *differential trail*. An r-round differential trail Q is determined by the sequence of difference patterns before and after each round $(q^0, q^1, \ldots, q^r)$. The DP of a trail is the fraction of all possible input pairs with difference q^0 that exhibit difference q^i after i rounds for all $i \leq r$.

The DP of a trail is in general hard to compute and often approximated by its expected DP (EDP). The EDP of a differential trail is the product of the DP values of its round differentials and is what you would get if the round differentials would act independently: $\mathrm{EDP}(Q) = \prod_{0 < i \leq r} \mathrm{DP}(q^{i-1}, q^i)$. The restriction weight of a trail is defined as the sum of the restriction weights of its round differentials and hence $2^{-\mathrm{w_r}(Q)} = \mathrm{EDP}(Q)$.

2.2   Linear Propagation

Linear cryptanalysis exploits linear approximations with high correlation [29]. Let a be a mask that defines the linear Boolean function of input bits $a^\mathrm{T}x$ of a transformation f and b one that defines the linear Boolean function of output bits $b^{\mathrm{T}} f(x)$. The combination of input mask and output mask (a, b) is called a *linear approximation* over f and its correlation is determined as the probability p over all inputs x that the linear function defined by a and the linear function defined by b are equal, namely $2p - 1$:

$$\mathrm{C}(a, b) = \frac{\#\{x \in \mathbb{F}_2^n \mid a^{\mathrm{T}} x + b^{\mathrm{T}} f(x) = 0\}}{2^{n-1}} - 1 .$$

The *correlation weight* $\mathrm{w_c}$ of a linear approximation is defined by $\mathrm{C}^2 = 2^{-\mathrm{w_c}}$.

We call a linear approximation over the round function R a *round linear approximation*. Round linear approximations can be chained to form a *linear trail*. An r-round linear trail Q is determined by the sequence of masks before and after each round $(q^0, q^1, \ldots, q^r)$. The correlation contribution C of a trail is defined as the product of the correlations of its round linear approximations: $\mathrm{C}(Q) = \prod_{0 < i \leq r} \mathrm{C}(q^{i-1}, q^i)$. The correlation weight of a linear trail relates to its correlation C as $\mathrm{C}^2 = 2^{-\mathrm{w_c}}$ and is therefore the sum of the correlation weights of its constituent round linear approximations.

2.3   Diffusion Metrics Related to Differences

In this section we discuss diffusion metrics for the propagation of differences. We will indicate differences of state dimensions by the term *state* and its non-zero bits or columns as *active*. Let $w_b(A)$ be the number of active bits in state A and $w_c(A)$ its number of active columns. We call $w_b(A)$ the *bit weight*, $w_c(A)$ the *column weight* of A and denote by L the linear layer.

The concept of branch number is an important metric for the diffusion power of mixing layers. It was introduced in [13] and popularized through [12]. We will generalize it to individual states. For simplicity, we will implicitly assume we are dealing with differential branch numbers and omit the qualification "differential". We discuss the propagation of linear masks in Sect. 6.

Definition 1 (Bit branch number of a state). *The bit branch number of state A with respect to L is the sum of the bit weight of A and that of $L(A)$:*

$$\mathcal{B}_{b,L}(A) = w_b(A) + w_b(L(A)) .$$

Definition 2 (Column branch number of a state). *The column branch number of state A with respect to L is the sum of the column weight of A and that of $L(A)$:*

$$\mathcal{B}_{c,L}(A) = w_c(A) + w_c(L(A)) .$$

The well-known branch numbers of a linear mapping are the minimum of the corresponding branch number over all non-zero states. The bit and column branch numbers are given by:

$$\mathcal{B}_b(L) = \min_{A \in \mathcal{A} \setminus \{0\}} \mathcal{B}_{b,L}(A) \quad \text{and} \quad \mathcal{B}_c(L) = \min_{A \in \mathcal{A} \setminus \{0\}} \mathcal{B}_{c,L}(A) .$$

The branch numbers of a mapping give only limited information about its diffusion power. We wish to compare several linear mappings according to their diffusion power. High diffusion power means few states with low branch number. In that respect, a more informative quantitative measure of the "immediate" diffusion power is given by the *branch histograms*.

Definition 3 (Bit branch histogram). *The bit branch histogram of L is the histogram indicating the number of states per bit branch number:*

$$H_{b,L}(w) = \#\{A \in \mathcal{A} \text{ with } \mathcal{B}_{b,L}(A) = w\}.$$

The bit branch histogram is the appropriate measure for a mixlayer like θ: a mixlayer strives to minimize the number of states with low bit branch number.

Definition 4 (Column branch histogram). *The column branch histogram of L is the histogram indicating the number of states per column branch number:*

$$H_{c,L}(w) = \#\{A \in \mathcal{A} \text{ with } \mathcal{B}_{c,L}(A) = w\}.$$

The column branch histogram is the appropriate measure for a linear layer λ: it says something about the number of 2-round trails with a given number of active columns and that lower bounds their weight. Good diffusion corresponds to branch histograms with a *low left tail*.

2.4   Diffusion Metrics Related to Masks

As was shown in [13], the linear branch of a linear mapping specified by a matrix M is equal to the differential branch number of M^{T}, the transpose of M. When talking about linear branch numbers of a linear mapping we will speak about the (differential) branch number of its transpose.

Using the bit and column Hamming weight, we define the linear branch number of a state A with respect to a linear layer L as the sum of the weights of A and that of $L^{\mathrm{T}}(A)$. Depending on the type of weight, we have two types of linear branch number:

$$\mathcal{B}_{b,L^{\mathrm{T}}}(A) = w_b(A) + w_b(L^{\mathrm{T}}(A)) \quad \text{and} \quad \mathcal{B}_{c,L^{\mathrm{T}}}(A) = w_c(A) + w_c(L^{\mathrm{T}}(A)).$$

The linear bit and column branch numbers of a mapping L are defined by

$$\mathcal{B}_b(L^{\mathrm{T}}) = \min_{A \in \mathcal{A} \setminus \{0\}} \mathcal{B}_{b,L^{\mathrm{T}}}(A) \quad \text{and} \quad \mathcal{B}_c(L^{\mathrm{T}}) = \min_{A \in \mathcal{A} \setminus \{0\}} \mathcal{B}_{c,L^{\mathrm{T}}}(A).$$

The histograms are defined analogously.

3   Circulant Twin Column Parity Mixers and Row Shifts

The round function operates on a state A with m rows and n columns, that we denote as A_i with $0 \le i < m$. The bit in row i and column j is denoted as $a_{i,j}$.

As we wish our round function to be suited for software implementations, we will assume the row length n is a power of two: $n = 2^\ell$. Still, some of the lemmas we prove are also valid if that is not the case.

We limit our choice of the steps of the round function, except for the round constant addition, to mappings that commute with a cyclic shift of the state in the horizontal direction. Such a property has been called shift-invariant, translation-invariant or rotation-invariant but we will use the term *circulant*. More formally, if τ is a mapping that shifts the state one position to the left, then a mapping α is circulant if $\tau \circ \alpha = \alpha \circ \tau$. Circulance partitions the state space into classes where a class contains all shifted versions of a given state. For the vast majority of states these classes contain n members. In our investigations on propagation, we can restrict ourselves to one representative of each class. We adopt a convention how to choose that representative and call that *canonical*.

For γ, circulance simply means that it applies the same S-box to all columns. For λ we assume it is a mixlayer sandwiched between two cyclic row shift steps as in XOODOO [11] and all three are circulant.

3.1   Cyclic Row Shifts

Similar to ShiftRows in Rijndael [12], the round function of Gaston has two bit shuffles that cyclically shift the bits within the rows. We call them ρ_{west} and ρ_{east} and we specify them as follow:

$$\rho_{\text{west}} : A_i \leftarrow (A_i \lll w_i), \text{ for } 0 \leq i < m$$
$$\rho_{\text{east}} : A_i \leftarrow (A_i \lll e_i), \text{ for } 0 \leq i < m .$$

Here $(C \lll r)$ denotes row C shifted over offset r, i.e., moving the bit in position j to position $j + r \bmod n$. Sometimes we write $\tau^r(C)$ for $(C \lll r)$.

Each row shift step is parameterized by m offsets, hence there are $2m$ shift offset parameters: w_0 to w_{m-1} and e_0 to e_{m-1}. In the diffusion properties only the differences between the offsets of ρ_{west} (or ρ_{east}) matter and therefore we can fix one offset for each of them to 0. We set $w_0 = 0$ and $e_0 = 0$, and hence to fully specify the row shift steps we must specify $2(m-1)$ offsets. We will denote the array of shift offsets for ρ_{west} by $\mathbf{R}_w$, the array of shift offsets for ρ_{east} by $\mathbf{R}_e$ and their combination by $\mathbf{R}_\rho$.

3.2   Circulant Twin Column Parity Mixers

The mixlayer θ is what we call a *circulant twin column parity mixer* or twin CPM for short. This is a variant of the column parity mixers as in XOODOO and KECCAK-f. A circulant column parity mixer applied to our two-dimensional state would look like this:

$$A_i \leftarrow A_i + (E \lll u) \text{ for } 0 \leq i < m, \text{ with } E \leftarrow (P + (P \lll r)) \text{ and } P \leftarrow \sum_{i=0}^{m-1} A_i . \quad (1)$$

This mapping computes the bitwise sum of all rows, called the *column parity* P, *folds* it to the θ-effect E and adds that to each row after shifting over some offset u. Here folding consists of adding P and a shifted copy of P. The two shift offsets r and u would be parameters. The CPM of (1) has a computational cost of two XORs per bit. CPMs and their properties were studied in [34].

A circulant twin column parity mixer looks like this:

$$A_i \leftarrow A_i + (E \lll u) \text{ for } 0 \leq i < m$$
$$\text{with } E \leftarrow (P + (P \lll r)) + (Q + (Q \lll s)),$$
$$\text{and } P \leftarrow \sum_{i=0}^{m-1} A_i \text{ and } Q \leftarrow \sum_{i=0}^{m-1} (A_i \lll t_i). \tag{2}$$

In (2), next to the column parity P, there is an additional column parity Q, obtained by adding the rows where each one is first shifted over a row-specific offset t_i. Both parities P and Q are folded and the θ-effect E consists of the sum of the two folded parities. The twin CPM of (2) has a computational cost of $3+1/m$ XORs per bit, hence 3.2 for 5 rows and 3.333 for 3 rows. Like the row shift steps, the twin CPM (2) is also a parameterized mapping. Its parameters are: the two folding offsets r and s, the θ-effect addition offset u, and the m offsets t_i for computing parity Q. This totals to $m + 3$ shift offset parameters. We denote the array of shift offsets for θ by $\mathbf{R}_\theta$ and the combination of $\mathbf{R}_\theta$ with those of the row shift steps $\mathbf{R}_\rho$ by $\mathbf{R}_\lambda$. We divide $\mathbf{R}_\theta$ into two parts: the ones that determine the distribution of the bit weight of the θ-effect that we group in $\mathbf{R}_E = (s, t_0, t_1, t_2, t_3, t_4)$ and u.

3.3   Polynomial Representation

The mixlayer θ and the row shifts ρ_{west} and ρ_{east} are specified in terms of two operations: bitwise addition of rows and cyclic shifts. These operations lend themselves to a representation of the rows of the state as polynomials with coefficients in $\mathbb{F}_2$. We denote row i of a state by

$$A_i(X) = \sum_j a_{i,j} X^j \text{ for } 0 \leq i < m.$$

These are elements of $\mathbb{F}_2[X]$, the ring of binary polynomials. Bitwise addition of rows is just the addition of polynomials in $\mathbb{F}_2[X]$. A cyclic shift of a row A_i over an offset r corresponds with the multiplication of A_i by the polynomial X^r modulo $1 + X^n$. It follows that we are working in the ring of binary polynomials modulo $1 + X^n$: $\mathbb{F}_2[X]/(1 + X^n)$ and a state is a vector of m polynomials, hence the state space $\mathcal{A}$ is $(\mathbb{F}_2[X]/(1 + X^n))^m$.

In polynomial representation, the column parity mixer of (1) becomes:

$$A_i \leftarrow A_i + \sum_{j=0}^{m-1} (X^u + X^{u+r}) A_j \text{ for } 0 \leq i < m.$$

Here $(X^u + X^{u+r}) A_j$ denotes the multiplication of the constant polynomial $(X^u + X^{u+r})$ by a variable polynomial A_j modulo $1 + X^n$.

The circulant twin CPM of (2) becomes:

$$A_i \leftarrow A_i + X^u \sum_{j=0}^{m-1} \left(1 + X^r + X^{t_j} + X^{s+t_j}\right) A_j \text{ for } 0 \le i < m.$$

We will denote the constant polynomials in this expression as ρ_j, hence

$$A_i \leftarrow A_i + X^u E \text{ with } E = \sum_{j=0}^{m-1} \rho_j A_j \text{ and } \rho_j = 1 + X^r + X^{t_j} + X^{s+t_j}. \quad (3)$$

The polynomial representation of state and linear mappings can be quite convenient in demonstrating properties. For example, $A_i(x)$ is divisible by $1+X$ iff $A_i(1) = 0$, that is, it has an even number of active bits.

3.4   The Inverse of a Circulant Twin CPM

Equation (3) represents m equations, one for each row A_i of the state. We can rewrite it as a matrix equation where we represent the state A as an m-dimensional vector with coordinates the rows polynomials. We denote the vector containing the polynomials $R_i = X^u \rho_i$ by R and write $\mathbf{1}$ for an m-dimensional vector with all coordinates equal to 1. Denoting the image by B, this gives:

$$B = A + \mathbf{1}R^{\mathrm{T}} A = (\mathbf{I} + \mathbf{1}R^{\mathrm{T}})A,$$

with $\mathbf{I}$ an $m \times m$ unit matrix. For symmetry reasons, the inverse has a similar shape: $A = (\mathbf{I} + \mathbf{1}R'^{\mathrm{T}})B$, where R' is the vector of polynomials for the inverse. Substitution results in: $B = (\mathbf{I}+\mathbf{1}R^{\mathrm{T}})(\mathbf{I}+\mathbf{1}R'^{\mathrm{T}})B$ or simplified $\mathbf{I} = (\mathbf{I}+\mathbf{1}R^{\mathrm{T}})(\mathbf{I}+\mathbf{1}R'^{\mathrm{T}})$. Working this out yields:

$$0 = \mathbf{1}R^{\mathrm{T}} + \mathbf{1}R'^{\mathrm{T}} + \mathbf{1}R^{\mathrm{T}}\mathbf{1}R'^{\mathrm{T}} = \mathbf{1}R^{\mathrm{T}} + \mathbf{1}R'^{\mathrm{T}} + \mathbf{1}\left(\sum_j R_j\right) R'^{\mathrm{T}}$$

$$= \mathbf{1}R^{\mathrm{T}} + \mathbf{1}\left(1 + \sum_j R_j\right) R'^{\mathrm{T}}.$$

Taking the i-th component yields $R_i = \left(1 + \sum_j R_j\right) R'_i$, hence R'_i is given by

$$R'_i = \left(1 + X^u \sum_j \rho_j\right)^{-1} X^u \rho_i .$$

As the polynomials ρ_j are divisible by $1+X$, the expression between the brackets is coprime to $1 + X$ and hence to $1 + X^n$, hence its inverse exists for any choice of the shift offsets if $n = 2^\ell$. Moreover, this inverse is in general dense, similar to the inverse of θ in KECCAK-p.

4 Differential Diffusion Properties of Twin CPMs

In this section we study structural properties of twin CPMs that are a function of their shift offsets. This leads to necessary conditions for achieving branch number of 12 and suggests choices leading to a low left tail in the branch histogram. We will group these conditions in a number of condition sets governing the shift offsets. They have the form of inequalities and are always modulo n.

For a state A that has $E = 0$ in (2), a twin CPM acts like the identity. Its bit branch number is simply its number of active bits times two. The set of states with $E = 0$ forms a subspace of $\mathcal{A}$ and plays an important role in this section.

Definition 5 (θ-effect kernel). *The subspace of $\mathcal{A}$ of states that have $E = 0$ in (2) for a twin CPM is its θ-effect kernel.*

We will refer to the θ-effect kernel simply as the kernel. States in the kernel with few active bits have a low branch number and are therefore undesirable.

In this section we start by characterizing the kernel, then we discuss unavoidable states in the kernel, followed by states that are avoidable by a good choice of shift offsets and finally states with low branch number outside the kernel.

4.1 The Kernel and Its Dimension

We define the P-kernel as the subspace of $\mathcal{A}$ for which $P = 0$ in (2) and the Q-kernel analogously. The dimension of the P-kernel is $(m - 1)n$. It is namely the subspace of $\mathcal{A}$ that satisfies n independent linear equations: the parity of each column shall be 0. The dimension of the Q-kernel is likewise $(m - 1)n$ as it is also a subspace of $\mathcal{A}$ that satisfies n independent linear equations.

We call the intersection of the P-kernel and the Q-kernel the PQ-kernel. Clearly the PQ-kernel is a subspace of the θ-kernel. Its dimension depends on the offsets t_i but is at least $(m-2)n+1$. This is because the sum of all conditions of the P-kernel is the sum of all conditions of the Q-kernel.

We call states in P-kernel with the lowest number of active bits, namely 2, P-orbitals and similar states in the Q-kernel we call Q-orbitals.

Definition 6 (P-orbital). *A P-orbital is a state with 2 active bits that are in the same column: it has $A_i = X^q$ and $A_j = X^q$ for some q.*

Definition 7 (Q-orbital). *A Q-orbital is a state with 2 active bits contributing to the same bit in Q: it has $A_i = X^{q+t_j}$ and $A_j = X^{q+t_i}$ for some q.*

If for two rows i and j, we have $t_i = t_j$, then the state with two active rows $A_i = 1$ and $A_j = 1$ is at the same time a P-orbital and a Q-orbital, and therefore in the kernel. A 2-bit state in the kernel implies a branch number of at most 4 and clearly we want to avoid it. Therefore, we will take all offsets t_i different.

Condition set 1. *Conditions to avoid single-orbital states in the kernel:*

$$t_i \neq t_j, \forall\{i, j\} \subset \{0, 1, \ldots, m - 1\} .$$

The following lemma says something about the dimension of the kernel if the number of columns is a power of two: $n = 2^\ell$.

Lemma 1. *Let* $(1 + X)^d = \gcd(\rho_0, \rho_1, \ldots, \rho_{m-1}, 1 + X^n)$ *with* $n = 2^\ell$, *then the dimension of the kernel is* $(m - 1)n + d$.

Proof. As $n = 2^\ell$ we have $1 + X^n = 1 + X^{2^\ell} = (1 + X)^{2^\ell} = (1 + X)^n$. Then there exists a j such that $(1 + X)^d = \gcd(\rho_j, 1 + X^n)$. We can do a renumbering such that $\gcd(\rho_0, 1 + X^n) = (1 + X)^d$, therefore this is without loss of generality. We now rewrite

$$\sum_{j>0} \rho_j A_j = \rho_0 A_0. \tag{4}$$

The number of different solutions of (4) determines the dimension of the kernel. We can choose A_j in the lefthand side freely, resulting in some value B and try to solve $B = \rho_0 A_0$ for A_0. As all ρ_j are divisible by $1 + X^d$, so is B. Hence, we can divide both sides by $1 + X^d$ resulting in an equation $B' = \pi A_0$ with $B' = B/(1 + X)^d$ and $\pi = \rho_0/(1 + X)^d$. As π is coprime to $1 + X^n$ it has an inverse and the solution is given by $A_0 = \pi^{-1} B'$. Moreover, if C is a solution for A_0 in (4), then $C + \beta(X)(1 + X)^{n-d}$ is also a solution as $\rho_0(1 + X)^{n-d} = 0$. The term $\beta(X)(1 + X)^{n-d}$ can take on 2^d possible values, namely those obtained by taking for β the polynomials of degree less than d. Hence, the choice of the A_j in the lefthand side accounts for dimension $(m - 1)n$ and the 2^d values of A_0 per element of that vector space adds d to the dimension. $\square$

4.2   Minimizing the Kernel

By choosing our offsets well, we can ensure that all states in the kernel have an even number of active bits. First in Lemma 2, we link the shape of the polynomials ρ_j with the number of factors $1 + X$ they contain. Then in Lemma 3 we prove that the kernel contains only states with an even number of bits if the polynomials ρ_i satisfy a certain condition.

Lemma 2. *Let* $n = 2^\ell$ *and* $0 \le a < b < c < d < n$. *Then*

$$\gcd(X^a + X^b + X^c + X^d, 1 + X^n) = 1 + X \iff a + b + c + d \bmod 2 = 1,$$

i.e., if $\{a, b, c, d\}$ *has an odd number of odd integers.*

Proof. Dividing $X^a + X^b + X^c + X^d$ by $1 + X$ gives $\sum_{a \le i < b} X^i + \sum_{c \le i < d} X^i$. This polynomial is only divisible by $1 + X$ if it has an even number of terms. This expression has an even number of terms iff $b - a$ and $d - c$ are both odd or both even, or equivalently iff $a + b + c + d$ is even. $\square$

Lemma 3. *If* $n = 2^\ell$ *and for all polynomials* ρ_j *the GCD with* $1 + X^n$ *is the same:* $\gcd(\rho_j, 1 + X^n) = 1 + X^d$ *with* $d < n$, *all states in the kernel have an even number of active bits.*

Proof. If $\gcd(\rho_j, 1 + X^n) = (1 + X)^d$ then $\rho_j \bmod (1 + X)^{d+1} = (1 + X)^d$. We now have

$$E \bmod (1 + X)^{d+1} = \left(\sum_i \rho_i A_i \right) \bmod (1 + X)^{d+1}$$

$$= \left(\sum_i (1 + X)^d A_i \right) \bmod (1 + X)^{d+1}$$

$$= \left((1 + X)^d \sum_i A_i \right) \bmod (1 + X)^{d+1}$$

$$= (1 + X)^d \left(\left(\sum_i A_i \right) \bmod (1 + X) \right).$$

If A has odd bit weight, $(\sum_j A_j) \bmod (1 + X) = 1$ and therefore $E \neq 0$. □

We now give a corollary with a sufficient condition for minimizing the kernel.

Corollary 1. *For $n = 2^\ell$, if in θ we have $r + s \bmod 2 = 1$, then the dimension of kernel is $(m - 1)n + 1$ and only contains states with an even number of active bits.*

Proof. If $r + s \bmod 2 = 1$, then for all polynomials ρ_j we have $(0 + r + t_j + (s + t_j)) \bmod 2 = 1$. Due to Lemma 2 this implies that for all ρ_j we have $\gcd(\rho_j, 1 + X^n) = 1 + X$. It follows from Lemma 3 that the kernel only contains states with an even number of active bits and from Lemma 1 that the dimension of the kernel is $(m - 1)n + 1$. □

4.3 Row Twins

Irrespective of the choice of shift offsets, the kernel contains states with 8 active bits. These states have a specific structure and we call them *row twins*.

Definition 8. *A state A is a row twin if it only has two active rows with indices in $\{i, j\} \subset \{0, 1, \ldots, m - 1\}$ and*

$$A_i = \rho_j = 1 + X^r + X^{t_i} + X^{s+t_i}, \ A_j = \rho_i = 1 + X^r + X^{t_j} + X^{s+t_j},$$

or if it is a shifted version of such a state.

Lemma 4. *Row twins are in the kernel.*

Proof. From (3) we have $E = \rho_i A_i + \rho_j A_j = \rho_i \rho_j + \rho_j \rho_i = 0$. □

There are $\binom{m}{2} = m(m - 1)/2$ canonical row twins. To avoid row twins with less than 8 active bits, each row in a row twins shall have 4 active bits implying that the 4 powers in ρ_j shall be different. This results in a number of conditions for the shift offsets of θ.

Condition set 2. *Conditions to avoid row twins with less than 8 active bits:*

$$r \neq 0, \ s \neq 0$$

$$t_i \neq 0, \ t_i \neq r, \ t_i \neq -s, \ t_i \neq r - s \qquad \forall i \in \{0, 1, \ldots, m - 1\}$$

4.4   Vortices

Irrespective of the choice of shift offsets, the kernel contains states with 6 active bits. We call these *vortices*, after states with similar structure in KECCAK-f.

Definition 9. *A state A is a vortex if it only has three active rows with indices in $\{i, j, k\} \subset \{0, 1, \ldots, m - 1\}$ and*

$$A_i = X^{t_j} + X^{t_k}, \ A_j = X^{t_k} + X^{t_i}, \ A_k = X^{t_i} + X^{t_j},$$

or if it is a shifted version of such a state.

Lemma 5. *Vortices are in the kernel.*

Proof. As $P = A_i + A_j + A_k = 0$, the vortex is in the P-kernel, and as $Q = X^{t_i} A_i + X^{t_j} A_j + X^{t_k} A_k = 0$, it is in the Q-kernel. Hence it is in the θ- kernel. $\square$

As the indices of the active rows completely determine the shape of a vortex, there are $\binom{5}{3} = 10$ canonical vortices. Due to the existence of vortices, the binary branch number of any circulant twin CPM is at most 12.

4.5   Avoiding States in the Kernel with Less Than 6 Active Bits

The Condition sets 1 are covered by a more general set of conditions to avoid states in the kernel with 4 active bits. There are three types of such states and we will cover them in the following three lemmas.

Lemma 6. *For even n, let $\{i, j\} \subset \{0, 1, \ldots, m - 1\}$ and $t_I = t_j + n/2$, then the state A with two active rows $A_i = A_j = 1 + X^{n/2}$ is in the kernel.*

Proof. The state is in the P kernel as $P = (1 + X^{n/2}) + (1 + X^{n/2}) = 0$. It is also in the Q-kernel as $Q = X^{t_j}(1 + X^{n/2}) + (X^{t_j+n/2})(1 + X^{n/2}) = 0$. $\square$

Lemma 7. *Let $\{i, j, k\} \subset \{0, 1, \ldots, m - 1\}$ and $t_I + t_j = 2t_k$, then the state A with three active rows $A_i = X^{t_k}, \ A_j = X^{t_i}$ and $A_k = X^{t_k} + X^{t_i}$ is in the kernel.*

Proof. The state is in the P-kernel as $P = X^{t_k} + X^{t_i} + X^{t_k} + X^{t_i} = 0$. It is also in the Q-kernel as $Q = X^{t_i+t_k} + X^{t_j+t_i} + X^{t_k+t_k} + X^{t_k+t_i} = 0$. $\square$

Lemma 8. *Let $\{i, j, k, l\} \subset \{0, 1, \ldots, m - 1\}$ and $t_I + t_j = t_k + t_l$, then the state with 4 active rows $A_i = 1, \ A_j = X^{t_k - t_j}, \ A_k = 1$ and $A_l = X^{t_i - t_l}$ is in the kernel.*

Proof. The state is in the P-kernel as $1 + X^{t_k - t_j} + 1 + X^{t_i - t_l} = 0$. It is also in the q-kernel as $A_i = X^{t_i} + X^{t_k} + X^{t_k} + X^{t_i} = 0$. $\square$

These three lemmas combined with Condition sets 1 result in three types of conditions that we group in the following set.

Condition set 3. *To avoid in-kernel states with 4 active bits (or 2 active bits). For any set $\{i,j\} \subset \{0,1,\ldots,m-1\}$ (for even n):*

$$2t_i \neq 2t_j \,.$$

For any sets $\{i,j\} \subset \{0,1,\ldots,m-1\}$ and $k \in \{0,1,\ldots,m-1\}$ with $k \notin \{I,j\}$:

$$t_i + t_j \neq 2t_k \,.$$

For any two sets $\{i,j\} \subset \{0,1,\ldots,m-1\}$ and $\{K,l\} \subset \{0,1,\ldots,m-1\}$ and $\{I,j\} \cap \{k,l\} = \varnothing$:

$$t_i + t_j \neq t_k + t_l \,.$$

4.6   States with Low Branch Number Outside the Kernel

We now discuss structures that result in states outside the kernel with low branch number. If the θ-effect E of a state has d active bits, the state has (bit) branch number of at least md.

This is because each active bit in E is added to m rows and if in a row it is added to a passive bit, that bit is active after θ and vice versa, hence it will always contribute 1 to the bit branch number. As the polynomials ρ_j all have even parity, so does E and therefore the smallest non-zero value of d is 2. In that case the branch number is at least $2m$. If E has more than 2 active bits, it has at least 4 and the branch number is at least $4m$. In the following, we discuss states with a low number of active bits before θ with 2 active bits in E.

Each of the polynomials ρ_j has 4 active bits and therefore for any single-bit state A, E has 4 active bits. A state A outside the kernel with two active bits may have $2, 4, 6$ or 8 active bits in E. P- and Q-orbitals lead to at most 4 active bits in E.

A P-orbital with active bits in $(0,i)$ and $(0,j)$ has $A_i = 1$ and $A_j = 1$ and 0 in other rows, and yields:

$$E = \rho_i + \rho_j = X^{t_i} + X^{s+t_i} + X^{t_j} + X^{s+t_j} \,. \tag{5}$$

A Q-orbital with active bits in (t_i, j) and (t_j, i) has $A_i = X^{t_j}$ and $A_j = X^{t_i}$ and 0 in the other rows and yields:

$$E = X^{t_j}\rho_i + X^{t_i}\rho_j = X^{t_j} + X^{r+t_i} + X^{t_i} + X^{r+t_j} \,. \tag{6}$$

If two exponents in (5) collide, we obtain an E with two active bits. The same holds for (6) and this leads to $2\binom{n}{2}$ more conditions.

Condition set 4. *Conditions for P-orbitals or Q-orbitals having E with two active bits. For all $\{i,j\} \in \{0,1,\ldots,m-1\}$:*

$$t_i \neq t_j + r$$
$$t_i \neq t_j + s \,.$$

Notice that we can build a state with 3 active bits that has at most 4 active bits in E by taking for the first two bits a Q-orbital and the last two bits a P-orbital, or vice versa. For example, let the 3 active bits be at (t_j, i), (t_i, j) and (t_i, k), then we have:

$$E = X^{t_j}\rho_i + X^{t_i}\rho_j + X^{t_i}\rho_k = X^{t_j} + X^{r+t_j} + X^{t_k+t_i} + X^{s+t_k+t_i}. \tag{7}$$

This can be seen as a chain: a Q-orbital followed by a P-orbital. Note that k can be equal to i.

A P-orbital followed by a Q-orbital: (t_k, i), (t_k, j) and (t_j, k), gives:

$$E = X^{t_k}\rho_i + X^{t_k}\rho_j + X^{t_j}\rho_k = X^{t_j} + X^{r+t_j} + X^{t_i+t_k} + X^{s+t_i+t_k}. \tag{8}$$

These chains can be generalized by building longer sequences of alternating P-orbitals and Q-orbitals. The number of active bits grows with the chain length and hence the longer the chains are, the less threatening.

5   Equivalence Classes of Shift Offset Vectors

In this section we discuss two equivalence relations that partition the sets of shift offset vectors $\mathbf{R}_\lambda$. The equivalence stems from alternative representations of the state that lead to linear mappings λ with the same bit branch and column branch histograms. These representations change the indexes of the bits, but preserve grouping of bits in columns.

If we denote the alternative representation of a state A by A', then we have $A' = \sigma(A)$ with σ a bit shuffle. Clearly, $B = \lambda(A)$ implies $B' = \sigma(B) = \sigma(\lambda(A)) = \sigma(\lambda(\sigma^{-1}(A')))$. In other words, $B' = \lambda'(A')$ with $\lambda' = \sigma \circ \lambda \circ \sigma^{-1}$. As σ is a bit shuffle, the bit branch number of A with respect to λ is equal to that of A' with respect to λ'. Moreover, if σ preserves the grouping of bits in columns, this is also true for the column branch number.

We will now describe two groups of bit shuffles whose elements convert a mapping $\lambda = \rho_{\text{west}} \circ \theta \circ \rho_{\text{east}}$ characterized by some offset vector $\mathbf{R}_\lambda$ to a linear mapping of the same shape but with a different offset vector.

5.1   Multiplicative Factor Equivalence

The first group of bit shuffles rearranges the bits within the rows of a state by multiplying their horizontal indexes with a fixed constant q modulo n. Expressions in the horizontal index shall be taken modulo n.

Definition 10 (Multiplicative shuffle). *Let* $q \in (\mathbb{Z}/n\mathbb{Z})^*$, *then* π_q *is the permutation over domain* $\mathbb{F}_2^n$ *defined by:*

$$A' = \pi_q(A) \Leftrightarrow \forall j \in \mathbb{Z}/n\mathbb{Z} : a'_{qj} = a_j,$$

with A *a row and* a_j *its component at index* j. *We call* π_q *the multiplicative shuffle with shuffling factor* q *(operating on* n-*bit vectors).*

Clearly, as q is coprime to n, π_q has an inverse. It is $\pi_{q^{-1}}$ with q^{-1} the multiplicative inverse of q in $(\mathbb{Z}/n\mathbb{Z})^*$.

Lemma 9. *Let $A' = \pi_q(A)$ and $B' = \pi_q(B)$. Then, if $B = (A \lll t)$ we have $B' = (A' \lll qt)$, or equivalently, $\pi_q \circ \tau^t \circ \pi_{q^{-1}} = \tau^{qt}$.*

Proof. Using $A' = \pi_q(A)$, $B' = \pi_q(B)$ and $B = (A \lll t)$ yields:

$$\forall i \in \mathbb{Z}/n\mathbb{Z} : b'_{qi} = b_i = a_{i+t} = a'_{q(i+t)} = a'_{qi+qt}.$$

A change of variable $j \leftarrow qi$ results in $\forall j \in \mathbb{Z}/n\mathbb{Z} : b'_j = a'_{j+qr}$, in other words $B' = (A' \lll qt)$. $\qquad\square$

We can define a multiplicative shuffle on a rectangular state with m rows by applying it to all its rows. Clearly, it preserves the grouping of bits in columns.

A linear layer λ with some offset vector $\mathbf{R}_\lambda$ only makes use of cyclic shifts and row additions and therefore $\pi_q \circ \lambda \circ \pi_{q^{-1}}$ is of the same type but has an offset vector that is given by $q\mathbf{R}_\lambda$, i.e., $\mathbf{R}_\lambda$ with all entries multiplied by q modulo n.

As offset vectors $\mathbf{R}_\lambda$ and $q\mathbf{R}_\lambda$ with q coprime to n are equivalent, we can limit investigating variants with a given entry fixed to some constant value. In this respect the following lemma is useful.

Lemma 10. *Assume $n = 2^\ell$ and q is coprime to n. Then if r is of the form $u2^d$ with u odd, $qr \bmod n$ is of the form $v2^d$ with v odd.*

Proof. We have:

$$qu2^d \bmod 2^\ell = (qu \bmod 2^\ell)(2^d \bmod 2^\ell) \bmod 2^\ell = (qu \bmod 2^\ell)2^d \bmod 2^\ell$$

The group $(\mathbb{Z}/2^\ell\mathbb{Z})^*$ consists of the odd integers $< 2^\ell$. As the product of two group elements is a group element, $qu \bmod 2^\ell \in (\mathbb{Z}/2^\ell\mathbb{Z})^*$ and hence odd. $\qquad\square$

Corollary 2. *Multiplication of shift offset by an invertible factor q modulo $n = 2^\ell$ preserves its parity: it maps odd to odd and even to even.*

5.2   Implications for $\mathbf{R}_\theta$

Let us now focus on θ, in particular $\mathbf{R}_E$. According to Corollary 1, the kernel is minimized by taking r odd and s even or vice versa. Let us assume r is odd. Then we can fix its value to 1 in the offset vector $\mathbf{R}_E$ without loss of generality: we can obtain an offset vector with any possible odd value q for r by just multiplying by q. We can limit s to even values in the interval $[2, n/2]$. It starts at 2 as according to Condition sets 2 we wish $s \neq 0$. The end of the interval is $n/2$ due to the following reason. The two terms in ρ_i that depend on s are X^{t_i} and X^{s+t_i}. Assuming the offsets t_i range over all possible values, X^a and X^b can be obtained in two different ways: $t_i = a$ and $s = b - a \bmod n$ or $t_i = b$ and $s = a - b \bmod n$. The values of $b - a$ and $a - b$ cannot both be above n and hence without loss of generality we can set the limit $s \leq n/2$.

These restrictions on r and s reduce the number of options for $\mathbf{R}_E$ from n^7 to less than $n^6/2$. When we add u to $\mathbf{R}_E$, we obtain $\mathbf{R}_\theta$ and it turns out that there are pairs of offset vectors $\mathbf{R}_\theta$ that result in equivalent mappings θ.

Lemma 11. *The following offset vectors yield θ mappings that are equivalent*

$$\mathbf{R}_\theta = [1, a, b_0, \ldots, b_{m-1}, c]$$
$$\mathbf{R}'_\theta = [1, a, 1 - b_0 - a, \ldots, 1 - b_{m-1} - a, -c - 1].$$

Proof. Consider $R_j = X^u \rho_j = X^u + X^{u+r} + X^{u+t_j} + X^{u+s+t_j}$. Filling in $\mathbf{R}_\theta$:

$$R_j = X^c + X^{c+1} + X^{c+b_j} + X^{c+a+b_j},$$

and filling in $\mathbf{R}'_\theta$:

$$R'_j = X^{-c-1} + X^{-c} + X^{-c-1+1-b_j-a} + X^{-c-1+1-b_j}$$
$$= X^{-c} + X^{-c-1} + X^{-c-b_j} + X^{-c-b_j-a}.$$

Composition with π_{-1} yields $R''_j = X^c + X^{c+1} + X^{c+b_j} + X^{c+b_j+a} = R_j.$ □

Note that the offset t_i in $\mathbf{R}'_\theta$ is even if t_i in $\mathbf{R}_\theta$ is odd and vice versa. For the case of odd m, we can avoid investigating equivalent offset vectors by requiring the number of odd t_i values in a canonical offset vector to be odd.

5.3   Row Order Equivalence

A row shuffle is a bit shuffle that keeps the order of the bits in the rows intact but changes the order of the rows. Naturally it preserves both bit and column branch numbers. As there are $m!$ ways to shuffle m rows, this creates classes of shift offsets of size up to $m!$ that are equivalent.

As a canonical representation we can adopt the one where the offsets t_i are ordered by increasing value. Moreover, according to Condition sets 1 we should take all t_i different, thus we can adopt $\forall 0 < i < m : t_i > t_{i-1}$. This reduces the number of offset vectors $\mathbf{R}_E$ to investigate to less than $n/4\binom{n}{m}$.

Corollary 3. *All interesting classes of offset vectors $\mathbf{R}_E$ are represented by the lists with the following features*

- $r = 1$ *and* $s \in [2, n]$ *and even,*
- *For all* $i > 0$, $t_i > t_{i-1}$,
- $t_{n-1} \bmod 2 = \sum_{i<n-1} t_i \bmod 2.$

6   Linear Mask Propagation Properties

The propagation of linear masks through a linear mapping, important in the context of linear cryptanalysis, can be easily described with the matrix representation of the linear map. If we denote the matrix of L by M, we have $U = \mathsf{M}^\mathsf{T} V$ with V the mask at the output and U the mask at its input.

For a twin CPM we wish to express its transpose in terms of row additions and cyclic shifts. This allows expressing masks at the input as a function of masks at the output. This is more convenient with the polynomial representation.

6.1   Representing Masks as Polynomials

In linear cryptanalysis, a mask defines a linear function of state bits, i.e., a sum of the state bits in positions where the mask is 1. If a state A has the shape of a binary vector, the shape of the mask u is a binary vector of the same dimension A and the linear function corresponding to mask u is given by $u^{\mathrm{T}}A$. In our case the state is an array of m rows A_i and we can represent masks similarly, where the linear function corresponding to a mask U is $\sum_i U_i^{\mathrm{T}}A_i$.

We will express the m rows of a mask by polynomials $(U_0, U_1, \ldots, U_{m-1})$ and its propagation through θ in polynomial form.

Definition 11 (transpose of a polynomial). *The transpose of a polynomial* $P(X) \in \mathbb{F}_2[X]/(1 + X^n)$ *is given by the polynomial* $P(X^{-1})$. *Therefore, if* $P = \sum_j p_j X^j$ *then* $P^{\mathrm{T}}(X) = \sum_i p_j X^{n-j \bmod n}$.

With this we can express linear functions of a state using polynomials.

Lemma 12 (Expression for a linear function). *The linear function of a state* $A \in (\mathbb{F}_2[X]/(1+X^n))^m$ *defined by a mask* $U \in (\mathbb{F}_2[X]/(1+X^n))^m$ *is given by* $U^{\mathrm{T}}A \bmod X$. *In other words, it is the coefficient of* X^0 *in* $U^{\mathrm{T}}A$.

Proof. The coefficient of X^0 in $U_i^{\mathrm{T}}(X)A_i(X) \bmod 1 + X^n = U_i(-X)A_i(X) \bmod 1 + X^n$ is $\sum_j u_{i,j}a_{i,j}$. Taking the sum over all rows gives $\sum_{i,j} u_{i,j}a_{i,j}$.   □

6.2   Mask Propagation Through a Twin CPM

We will now show how input and output masks are related over a generalization of a circulant twin CPM in polynomial representation.

Lemma 13 (Mask propagation throught a circulant mapping). *Let* L *be determined by a square matrix of polynomials* $\rho_{i,j}$ *with* $B_j \leftarrow A_j + \sum_i \rho_{i,j}A_i$. *An input mask* $V \in (\mathbb{F}_2[X]/(1+X^n))^m$ *depends on an output mask* $U \in (\mathbb{F}_2[X]/(1+X^n))^m$ *as:*

$$V_i = U_i + \sum_j \rho_{j,i}^{\mathrm{T}}U_j .$$

Proof. We can compute an input mask V from the output mask U as follows:

$$\sum_i U_i^{\mathrm{T}}B_i = \sum_i U_i^{\mathrm{T}}\left(A_i + \sum_j \rho_{i,j}A_j\right) = \sum_i U_i^{\mathrm{T}}A_i + \sum_j \sum_i U_i^{\mathrm{T}}\rho_{i,j}A_j$$

$$= \sum_i U_i^{\mathrm{T}}A_i + \sum_i \sum_j U_j^{\mathrm{T}}\rho_{j,i}A_i = \sum_i \left(U_i^{\mathrm{T}} + \sum_j U_j^{\mathrm{T}}\rho_{j,i}\right)A_i$$

$$= \sum_i \left(U_i + \sum_j \rho_{j,i}^{\mathrm{T}}U_j\right)^{\mathrm{T}}A_i .$$

hence, we have $\sum_i U_i^{\mathrm{T}}B_i = \sum_i V_i^{\mathrm{T}}A_i$ with $V_i = U_i + \sum_j \rho_{j,i}^{\mathrm{T}}U_j$.   □

Therefore, the polynomial representation of the transpose of θ is given by:

$$A_i \leftarrow A_i + \sum_{j=0}^{4} X^{-u} \left(1 + X^{-r} + X^{-t_i} + X^{-s-t_i}\right) A_j .$$

This translates readily to:

$$A_i \leftarrow A_i + ((E + (F \ggg t_i)) \ggg u) \text{ for } 0 \leq i < m \text{ with}$$

$$E \leftarrow P + (P \ggg r) , \quad F \leftarrow P + (P \ggg s) \text{ and } P \leftarrow \sum_{i=0}^{4} A_i . \tag{9}$$

We see two θ-effects, E and F with different folding offsets: r and s. They are both added to the rows, where the second one is shifted over different offsets t_i.

6.3   Low-Weight 3-Round Linear Trails

The P-kernel of θ^{T} consists of all states with an even number of active bits in each column. It has elements with only two active bits, namely P-orbitals, in total $n\binom{m}{2}$ of them. It follows that the bit branch number of θ^{T} is at most 4. It is also at least 4 because for any state A with a single active bit $\theta^{\mathrm{T}}(A)$ and $\left(\theta^{\mathrm{T}}\right)^{-1}(A)$ have more than 3 bits.

If all shift offsets in $\mathbf{R}_w$ are different and similarly all shift offsets in $\mathbf{R}_e$, the bit branch number of θ^{T} translates to a column branch number of 4 for λ^{T}. As an active column has at least weight (and minimum reverse weight) 2, it follows that there are 2-round trails with weight 8.

For three rounds we consider a particular type of linear trails. We know a single-bit mask at the output of χ, restricted to a single column, is correlated to the same single-bit mask at its input with correlation 1/2. Therefore, with respect to masks with at most a single active bit per column, χ can act as the identity. The type of 3-round linear trails we consider are those where this is the case for the middle χ.

An orbital at θ of the second round is transformed by $\rho_{\mathrm{west}}^{-1}$, goes through χ unchanged and is then transformed by $\rho_{\mathrm{east}}^{-1}$ to end up at the output of θ of the first round. If these bits are in the same column, they form again an orbital and are in the kernel, implying that we see it unchanged at the input of θ. This would mean a 3-round trail that has in each χ-step only two active bits, thus with weight only 12.

We can avoid these by having conditions on the shift offsets formed by the combination of ρ_{west} and ρ_{east}. We will denote them by $c_i = e_i + w_i$.

From the example above, we should ensure $\forall i, j : c_i \neq c_j$. These are the rules of Condition sets 1, applied to c_i. Similarly, violation of the rules in Condition sets 3 applied to c_i would lead to trails with 4-bit states in the kernel of θ^{T} in two consecutive rounds, and thus to 3-round linear trails with weight only 24.

We cannot avoid the existence of linear trails with 6-bit states in the kernel of θ^{T} in two consecutive rounds, and these result in 3-round linear trails with weight at most 36. In particular, they are like the vortices of Definition 9, but with c_i taking the place of t_i. In total there are $\binom{m}{3}$ canonical vortices and there may be additional trails with 6-bit states in the kernel of θ^T in two consecutive rounds. If the 6 active bits of the masks at input/output of the χ steps in these trails are not in 6 different columns, the weight goes under 36.

6.4   Transpose of Twin CPMs

Twin CPMs have stronger diffusion for the propagation of differences than for the propagation of masks. In some use cases we may wish to have the inverse. For those cases we can use the transpose of a twin CPM as specified in (9).

7   Application: The Design of **Gaston**

In this section we will illustrate the power of circulant twin CPMs by building a concrete iterated permutation using it as the mixing layer in its round function. Our permutation operates on a two-dimensional state with the same dimensions as ASCON-p and we decided to call it Gaston.

7.1   The Structure of the Round Function and Shape of the State

Gaston operates on 320-bit states with $m = 5$ rows and $n = 64$ columns. Its round function consists of a linear layer followed by a non-linear layer. As in the iterated permutation XOODOO [11], the linear layer consists of the mixlayer θ, preceded and followed by row shift steps ρ_{west} and ρ_{east} respectively and a round constant addition ι. The non-linear layer consists of the application of the χ-mapping that operates in parallel on the 5-bit columns. The main differences with the XOODOO round function are that θ is a circulant twin CPM rather than a circulant CPM and that the state has 5-bit columns rather than 3-bit columns.

After fixing the round function structure, the design effort mainly consists of determining the shift offsets of the mixlayer and the row shift steps. We discuss our search strategy to find shift offsets for the mixlayer as well as for the two row shuffles in Sect. 7.2, the procedure we followed for $\mathbf{R}_\theta$ in Sect. 7.3 and for $\mathbf{R}_\rho$ in Sects. 7.4 and 7.5.

7.2   General Search Strategy

As discussed in Sect. 3, the shift offsets of the linear layer λ are gathered in a shift offset vector $\mathbf{R}_\lambda = (\mathbf{R}_\theta, \mathbf{R}_\rho)$. We aim to find a shift offset vector $\mathbf{R}_\lambda$ that minimizes the maximum DP value of differentials over a fixed round version of Gaston, say with 4 rounds. Determining the maximum DP value of 4-round differentials is actually a huge task, even for a single value of $\mathbf{R}_\lambda$. Moreover, the number of $\mathbf{R}_\lambda$ values is astronomical: It has $3m + 1$ entries each in the range $[0, 63]$, thus for Gaston there are $64^{16} = 2^{96}$ possible values. Taking into account the equivalence classes discussed in Sect. 5 this reduces to $16\binom{64}{5}64^9 \approx 2^{81}$, but it remains astronomical.

With minimization of the maximum DP of differentials over 4-round Gaston being infeasible, we turn to local optimization. In particular, we will choose a value for $\mathbf{R}_\lambda$ that gives rise to a linear layer λ with a column branch number of 12. There are many such values of $\mathbf{R}_\lambda$ and as secondary criterion we look at the left tail in the column branch histogram of the corresponding mappings λ.

For λ to have a column branch number of 12, θ must have a bit branch number of 12. Moreover, the height of the tail of the column branch histogram of λ depends strongly on that of the bit branch histogram of θ. Both the bit branch number and the height of the tail of the bit branch histogram of θ are fully determined by $\mathbf{R}_\theta$. Therefore, we opt for a two-phase approach: we first determine $\mathbf{R}_\theta$ and then only $\mathbf{R}_\rho$, where we choose $\mathbf{R}_\theta$ based on quantitative bit-level diffusion properties of θ and $\mathbf{R}_\rho$ is chosen to translate this bit-level diffusion to the column level for λ.

Our two phases are each divided into a number of steps. In particular, for $\mathbf{R}_\rho$ we first find a suitable candidate for $\mathbf{R}_w$ before making a choice on $\mathbf{R}_e$.

7.3   Selecting the Offsets of $\mathbf{R}_\theta$

To find the offsets for $\mathbf{R}_\theta$, the steps are the following:

1. $\mathbf{R}_E$-condition-filtering: we eliminate all $\mathbf{R}_E$ candidates leading to avoidable in-kernel states with less than 6 active bits. This phase reduces the $16\binom{64}{5} \approx 2^{27}$ $\mathbf{R}_E$ candidates that move on to the next phase to $14\,282\,988 \approx 2^{23}$ candidates.
2. $\mathbf{R}_E$-kernel-filtering: we keep the $\mathbf{R}_E$ candidates that have no in-kernel states with less than 6 active bits and count the number of in-kernel states with 6 active bits. There are 828 candidates for $\mathbf{R}_E$ with 11 6-bit states.
3. $\mathbf{R}_E$-candidate-pool: for each $\mathbf{R}_E$ candidate we compute the θ-effect E of all states with 3 active bits and keep those that minimize the number of 3-bit states that result in E having 2 active bits. This minimum turns out to be 1 and there are 3 such candidates for $\mathbf{R}_E$.
4. u-selection: we exhaustively test all u candidates and select the value that moves all active bits to different columns for states outside the kernel with 5 active bits or less. After this phase $\mathbf{R}_\theta$ is fully determined.

$\mathbf{R}_E$-*Condition-Filtering.* Several cases of in-kernel and out-of-kernel states with bit branch number less than 12 are avoidable by discarding shift offsets defined in Sect. 4. More specifically, we discard candidates leading to single-orbital states (Condition sets 1) as well as 2-bit and 4-bit states in the kernel (Condition sets 3). Offsets that result in in-kernel states with an odd number of active bits, in-kernel row twins states with less that 8 active bits (Condition sets 2) and 2-bit states that have a θ-effect E with 2 active bits (Condition sets 4) are also eliminated.

$\mathbf{R}_E$-*Kernel-Filtering.* For each $\mathbf{R}_E$ candidate we generate all states up to 6 active bits and discard any candidate that leads to in-kernel states with 4 active bits as well as 2-bit states with 2 bits in E that were not caught during the $\mathbf{R}_E$-condition-filtering phase. We keep those that result in the minimum number of in-kernel states with bit branch number of 12.

$\mathbf{R}_E$-*Candidate-Pool.* For each $\mathbf{R}_E$ candidate we look at the θ-effect E of all out-of-kernel states with less than 6 active input bits. For a θ-effect E with 2 active bits the bitwise branch number is at least 10. If E has 4 active bits then states have a bitwise branch number of at least 20. During this phase we discard $\mathbf{R}_E$ candidates that do not minimize the number of 3-bit states with 2 bits in E. We report in Table 2 the histograms for the chosen candidate (right table) and we also give an example of a discarded $\mathbf{R}_E$ candidate (left table).

Table 2. 2-dimensional histograms giving the number of states according to the number of active bits in the θ-effect (vertical axis) and the number of active bits at the input (horizontal axis). We have $\mathbf{R}_E = (1, 20, 4, 6, 21, 33, 61)$ at the left and $\mathbf{R}_E = (1, 18, 25, 32, 52, 60, 63)$ at the right.

	3	4	5	6		3	4	5	6
0				11	0				11
2	6	28	168	868	2	1	24	158	686

u-Selection. For the 3 $\mathbf{R}_E$ candidates, we generate the histogram listing the number of states according to the bit weight at input and output for all u values. We generate all states with at most 6 active input bits and at most 2 active bits in the θ-effect E. In the generated histograms, we see that u impacts an effect that we call *affected-loss* that we now explain. An active bit in an unaffected column contributes 2 to the branch number and an active bit in an affected column does not contribute to it. We choose the u candidate that minimizes that affected-loss. As the offset u shifts the θ-effect E before it is added to the rows, we only need to look at out-of-kernel states. We chose to look only at those with few active bits that have two active bits in E as that is where the risk of getting a branch number below 12 is. We select the u value where active bits do not overlap with affected columns for all states up to 5 active bits. We report in Table 4 the histogram associated to the chosen candidate and we also give an example of a u candidate that can be discarded in Table 3. In particular, there are 24 4-bit states with 2 bits in E and a bit overlapping with a affected column costs 2 bits. If u is fixed to 29 then out of these 24 states there are 3 states that have an image with 10 active bits. It means that there are 2 bits at the input that are overlapping with an affected column. Moreover, 2 states have an image with 12 active bits which means that 1 bit is overlapping with an affected column. For $u = 23$ all 24 4-bit states will have an image with 14 active bits. We report in Table 4 the bit branch histogram associated to the chosen candidate.

Table 3. 2-dimensional bit weight histograms for $\mathbf{R}_E = (1, 18, 25, 32, 52, 60, 63)$ with offset $u = 29$.

	6	7	8	9	10	11	12	13	14	15
3							1			
4					3		2		19	
5						6		2		150
6	11		2	3			40		73	

Table 4. 2-dimensional bit weight histogram for $\mathbf{R}_E = (1, 18, 25, 32, 52, 60, 63)$ with offset $u = 23$.

	6	7	8	9	10	11	12	13	14	15	16	17	18	19	20	21	22	23
1																5		
2																	29	
3								1								5		149
4									24				1		14		67	
5										158		3		17		289		506
6	11							18		15	653		42		132		3012	
7		1							200		143	4447		578		1930		29567
8			346		18		25		1421		1432		25849		7119		24174	
9						94		303		12900		16428		207062		81499		284023
10					10952		1247		3139		94506		141168		1313837		894509	
11			17		58			10545		39889		842033		1492497		10832247		9631128

7.4 Selecting the Offsets of $\mathbf{R}_w$

The mixlayer θ being set, we can generate low-branch number in-kernel and out-of-kernel states. The role of the row shuffle $\mathbf{R}_w$ is to move bits that are in the same column in a state at the output of θ to different columns at the output of λ. To determine $\mathbf{R}_w$ we proceed with the following steps:

1. $\mathbf{R}_w$-kernel-filtering: for each $\mathbf{R}_w$ candidate we apply ρ_{west} to the 11 in-kernel states with 6 active bits, see Table 4. We keep those that shift all 6 bits to different columns at the output of λ. This phase reduces the $63 * 62 * 61 * 60 \approx 2^{24}$ candidates for $\mathbf{R}_w$ to $3\,943\,564 \approx 2^{22}$.
2. $\mathbf{R}_w$-condition-filtering: we reduce the set of $\mathbf{R}_w$ candidates by keeping those that for the 10 bits in any 2 affected columns are moved to at least 9 different columns. This reduces the set of 2^{22} candidates for $\mathbf{R}_w$ candidates to $1\,362\,650 \approx 2^{20}$ candidates.
3. $\mathbf{R}_w$-kernel-filtering: we apply each $\mathbf{R}_w$ candidate to all in-kernel states with 8 active bits, see Table 4. We keep those that shift at most 2 active bits to the same column. We are left with 9212 candidates.
4. $\mathbf{R}_w$-candidate-pool: we apply each $\mathbf{R}_w$ candidate to out-of-kernel states with at most bit branch number 18. We keep those where at most one column will have two active bits at the output of λ. There are 24 candidates.

$\mathbf{R}_w$-*Kernel-Filtering.* The desired effect of ρ_{west} is the following. For low-branch-number states, the row shuffle ρ_{west} should move active bits in the state after θ

to different columns at the output of λ. When bits cluster in columns it results in a state having a column branch number under λ smaller than the bit branch number under θ. The effect of active bits at the output of θ ending up in the same column after λ is called *bit huddling* [8]. In this phase, for all $\mathbf{R}_w$ values we check whether for the 11 states with bit branch number 12 there is bit huddling at the output of λ and keep only those where there is none.

$\mathbf{R}_w$-*Condition-Filtering.* For states outside the kernel, the state at the output of θ will have a number of affected columns. For low-branch-number states, typically an affected column will have most of its bits active, most often all of them. Now, if we have a state consisting of two affected columns at the output of θ, the positions of these affected columns can be chosen such that there are at least 2 bits in the same column after ρ_{west}: the 10 bits huddle to 9 columns. By a judicious choice of the shift offsets in $\mathbf{R}_w$ this number can be limited to not be lower than 9 for any two affected column position. The conditions on the shift offsets to limit this bit huddling coincide with Condition sets 3.

$\mathbf{R}_w$-*Kernel-Filtering.* We keep any $\mathbf{R}_w$ that moves the 8 active bits before ρ_{west} to at least 7 different columns after ρ_{west}.

$\mathbf{R}_w$-*Candidate-Pool.* We require that a $\mathbf{R}_w$ candidate moves active bits in the state before ρ_{west} to different columns after ρ_{west}. We minimize the bit huddling effect to one column having at most 2 active bits.

7.5   Selecting the Offsets of $\mathbf{R}_e$

Following the procedure to determine a suitable $\mathbf{R}_w$, for each of the 24 $\mathbf{R}_w$ candidates we go through the following steps to make a choice on $\mathbf{R}_e$:

1. $\mathbf{R}_e$-kernel-filtering: the $\mathbf{R}_e$ candidates are selected from the set of $\mathbf{R}_w$ candidates passing the $\mathbf{R}_w$-kernel-filtering phase.
2. $\mathbf{R}_e$-condition-filtering: for each $\mathbf{R}_e$ candidate we take into account $\mathbf{R}_w$. We eliminate any $\mathbf{R}_e$ that results in vortices with less than 4 bits remaining in the kernel of θ^{T} for two successive rounds.
3. $\mathbf{R}_e$-vortices-filtering: we apply each $(\mathbf{R}_w, \mathbf{R}_e)$ candidate to the 10 canonical vortices obtained by the combination of ρ_{west} and ρ_{east}. Candidates that result in vortices with less than 6 bits in the kernel of θ^{T} for two successive rounds when χ acts as the identity are discarded.
4. $\mathbf{R}_\rho$-tie-break: we check the minimum squared correlation C^2 of 3-round linear trails in the kernel of θ^{T} for the $(\mathbf{R}_w, \mathbf{R}_e)$ candidates.

$\mathbf{R}_e$-*Kernel-Filtering.* The conditions for a $\mathbf{R}_e$ candidate in this step are the same as the conditions for a $\mathbf{R}_w$ candidate in the $\mathbf{R}_w$-kernel-filtering step, but applied to the additive inverses of the ρ_{east} shift offsets that we denote as $-\mathbf{R}_e$. A $\mathbf{R}_e$ candidate passes the step if it moves all bits of the 11 6-bit states at the input of θ to different columns after $\rho_{\text{east}}{}^{-1}$. As all these 6-bit states are in-kernel, the bits before and after θ are the same. Thus, the list of candidates for $-\mathbf{R}_e$ is the same as the list of candidates generated during the $\mathbf{R}_w$-kernel-filtering step.

$\mathbf{R}_e$-*Condition-Filtering.* As described in Sect. 6.3, we eliminate all candidates leading up to low-weight 3-round linear trails with 4-bit states in the kernel of θ^T in two consecutive rounds when χ acts as the identity. The conditions to discard those offsets coincide with Condition sets 3 applied to $\rho_{west} + \rho_{east}$ and ensure that we don't obtain a 3-round in-kernel linear trail with weight 24 when χ acts as the identity.

$\mathbf{R}_e$-*Vortices-Filtering.* As stated in Sect. 6.3, we can generate all 10 canonical vortices obtained from the combination of $\mathbf{R}_w$ and $\mathbf{R}_e$. For each candidate, we apply ρ_{east}^{-1}, ρ_{west} as well as $\rho_{west} \circ \rho_{east} \circ \rho_{west}$ and require that all 6 bits in the 10 vortices are moved to different columns after each operation. Doing so ensures that we avoid vortices with 6 active bits in the kernel of θ^T in two consecutive rounds which lead to 3-round linear trails with weight less than 36.

$\mathbf{R}_\rho$-*Tie-Break.* For a $(\mathbf{R}_w, \mathbf{R}_e)$ candidate, we model the linear propagation behavior of the permutation with SMT and we check the minimum weight of 3-round linear trails in the kernel of θ^T. We select a candidate that maximizes the minimum squared correlation C^2 of trails over 3 rounds in the kernel of θ^T. The parameters for the linear layer are given in Table 6 in Sect. 8.

7.6   Trail Search and Bounds

Several of the steps in the selection process for the linear layer require the generation of states up to some branch number. To generate these states, we use the tree traversal technique and we make use of the two-level tree search as well as canonicity and a *score* function, both defined in [18]. We further use Satisfiability Modulo Theories (SMT) and Mixed-Integer Linear Programming (MILP) in a hybrid manner [28] to obtain bounds on the differential and linear trails. We then discuss our results in Table 5.

Two-Level Tree Search. The two-level tree traversal strategy introduced in [18] allows efficiently generating all states with branch number below a given target. The strategy arranges the states in a tree with nodes identified by a row list, that specifies the active rows of the state. The parent of a state is the row list with the last row removed and the root of the tree is the empty list. The active rows are lists of active bits, indicated by their x-coordinates. When traversing the tree, going to the first child of a node corresponds to adding the smallest possible active row after its last active row in the list. Going to the sibling of a node corresponds to iterating the last active row to the next value. Lastly, going to the parent of a node is done by removing the last active row from the row list.

Canonicity. The linear layer λ and the non-linear layer χ are both shift invariant with respect to translation along the horizontal axis. This symmetry property partitions the state space into equivalence classes and we only need to visit one node per class. The representative of such a class is called a *canonical* state and corresponds to the *smallest* state of its class, for some order relation. We adopt an order relation where a non-canonical state has no canonical descendants. Hence, we can safely prune complete subtrees of non-canonical state in the tree.

Score. We denote by *score* the function that gives a lower bound on the branch number of a node and all its descendants. It allows us to safely prune complete subtrees from nodes with score higher than the target branch number. Moreover, we are only interested in low-branch number states and thus the states generation can be limited by the number of active bits in the θ-effect E. Since the addition of a bit in a state at the input of θ always adds 4 active bits at the output of θ with the number of affected columns, it is enough to generate all states with a score below 4 times the limit weight at the input.

SMT and MILP Models for Analysis of Trails in Gaston. Since the automated methods for searching differential and linear trails are well known, we omit their description due to space limitation.

Results. We use the parameters from Table 6 to compute the differential and linear properties of Gaston and compare them with ASCON in Table 5.

Table 5. Differential and linear bounds of Gaston where kernel of E and P are taken at the first round. The exact numbers in the table represents the minimum values.

Differential			
	Gaston		ASCON
	$\mathrm{Ker}(E) = 0$	$\mathrm{Ker}(E) \neq 0$	
Column-wise branch number	12	$13 - 16$	4
Weight of 2-round trail	24	$26 - 34$	8
Weight of 3-round trail	≤ 106	-	40
Linear			
	$\mathrm{Ker}(P) = 0$	$\mathrm{Ker}(P) \neq 0$	
Column-wise branch number	4	21	4
Weight of 2-round trail	8	42	8
Weight of 3-round trail	34	≥ 44	28

From Table 5, we observe that the column-wise branch number (differential) of Gaston's mixing layer is three times larger than that of ASCON, while the linear column-wise branch number of both mixing layers are the same. The best 3-round differential trail we find for Gaston has weight 106, much higher than ASCON's 3-round differential trail with weight 40. Moreover, the optimal weight of Gaston's 3-round linear trail is 34 while it is 28 for ASCON.

Algorithm 1. Definition of Gaston

Parameters: Number q of rounds
for Round index i from $1 - q$ up to 0 **do** $A = \mathrm{R}_i(A)$

The round function R:
for index j from 0 to 4 **do** $A_j \leftarrow (A_j \lll e_j)$ $\qquad\qquad\qquad\qquad\quad \triangleright \rho_{\text{east}}$
$E \leftarrow (\sum A_j + (\sum A_j \lll r)) + (\sum (A_j \lll t_j) + (\sum (A_j \lll t_j) \lll s))$
for index j from 0 to 4 **do** $A_j \leftarrow A_j + (E \lll u)$ $\qquad\qquad\qquad\qquad\qquad\; \triangleright \theta$
for index j from 0 to 4 **do** $A_j \leftarrow (A_j \lll w_j)$ $\qquad\qquad\qquad\qquad\quad\; \triangleright \rho_{\text{west}}$
$A_0 \leftarrow A_0 + \mathrm{C}_i$ $\qquad\qquad\qquad\qquad\qquad\qquad\qquad\qquad\qquad\qquad\quad \triangleright \iota$
for index j from 0 to 4 **do** $A_j \leftarrow A_j + \overline{A_{j+1}} \cdot A_{j+2}$ $\qquad\qquad\qquad\quad \triangleright \chi$

---

8 Specifications of Gaston and Use Case

In this section we provide a non-ambiguous specification of the Gaston family of permutations and present a concrete use case.

As in ASCON-p and XOODOO, the number of rounds in Gaston is not fixed but depends on the use case. The round function is the same for all rounds, except for the round constants. As in XOODOO and ASCON-p, the round constants are numbered from the last round backwards, therefore, the last round always has the same round constant, irrespective of the number of rounds and likewise the penultimate round, etc. The round constants used in Gaston correspond to those used in ASCON-p . Algorithm 1 describes Gaston and uses the shift offset parameters alongside the round constants that are specified in Table 6. We denote by $A_j \cdot A_{j'}$ the bitwise product (AND) of rows A_j and $A_{j'}$ while $\overline{A_j}$ denotes the bitwise complement of row A_j. A reference implementation of Gaston is available at https://gitlab.science.ru.nl/selhirch/circulanttwincpm.

Table 6. List of parameters for the linear diffusion layer of Gaston at the left and the round constants C_i with $-11 \leq i \leq 0$, in hexadecimal notation at the right.

Index	$\mathbf{R}_\theta = $	(r	s	t_j	u)	$\mathbf{R}_w$	$\mathbf{R}_e$
0		1	18	25	23	0	0
1				32		56	60
2				52		31	22
3				60		46	27
4				63		43	4

i	C_i	i	C_i	i	C_i	i	C_i
-11	0xf0	-8	0xc3	-5	0x96	-2	0x69
-10	0xe1	-7	0xb4	-4	0x87	-1	0x5a
-9	0xd2	-6	0xa5	-3	0x78	0	0x4b

A permutation by itself does not constitute as a cryptographic primitive, it must be used in a construction to be cryptographically useful. Constructions include Even-Mansour [19] to build a block cipher, Farfalle [3] to build a deck function (a variable-input-length variable-output-length pseudorandom function), sponge to build a hash function or an extendable output function (XOF) [4] and (monkey)duplex [6] as a basis for authenticated encryption schemes like ASCON. There is a actually quite a list of permutation-based constructions and modes and this list is still growing.

We believe Gaston, and in some cases a similar permutation using a transpose twin CPM, are competitive in most of these constructions but choosing the required number of rounds would require some more comprehensive cryptanalysis. In Farfalle however the security depends mostly on differential and correlation properties and the number of rounds is easier to choose based on existing analysis. Therefore we will concentrate on that use case in this subsection.

Farfalle makes use of 4 permutations that in the case of XOOFFF all are 6-round XOODOO. When instantiated with Gaston, we propose the following:

p_c in the compression layer. In [20] it has been shown that the strength against inner collisions in Farfalle is given by $\max_a \sum_b \mathrm{DP}^2(a, b) \leq \max_{a,b} \mathrm{DP}(a, b)$ under reasonable assumptions. To achieve 128 bits of security with respect to this, it is sufficient that $\max_{a,b} \mathrm{DP}(a, b) \leq 2^{-128}$. With the current bounds we are confident that 4 rounds are sufficient.

p_e in the expansion layer. This permutation needs to protect against state/key-recovery attacks using output only and to avoid biases in the output. For the latter the input-output correlations are important and therefore a Gaston variant with a transpose twin CPM would be the logical choice. Assuming the squared correlation of the best linear trails for this variant would be similar to the DP of differential trails for Gaston, 4 rounds would be sufficient to avoid detectable biases in the output. Moreover, based on the cryptanalysis of [10], the high diffusion of the twin CPM in Gaston in comparison to that of the CPM of XOODOO would make 4 rounds sufficient to offer a comfortable security margin with respect to state/key-recovery attacks.

p_d between the compression and expansion layer. Its role is to protect against input/output attacks. Here the algebraic degree of the concatenation of p_d and p_e is relevant rather than difference propagation and correlation. Here a Gaston variant with a classical CPM would be the logical choice, thanks to its low gate cost of 2 XORs per state bit. We believe again 4 rounds would be sufficient, resulting in an algebraic degree close to 256.

p_b for deriving the initial mask from the key K. The purpose of this permutation is to diffuse the key bits to the mask in case of a biased key. Here we propose to take Gaston with 4 rounds where the reduction in rounds with respect to XOODOO is motivated by the higher diffusion of the twin CPM as compared to the CPM.

Thus, all 4 permutations have 4 rounds instead of 6 rounds. The rounds of Gaston are slightly more expensive per bit than those of XOODOO but this is still compensated by the decrease in number of rounds. Additionally, the Gaston-based Farfalle instance operates on smaller blocks than XOOFFF, 320 bits instead of 384. This is an advantage on constrained platforms. We believe this provides a promising perspective for the future adoption of Gaston and its variants.

9   Conclusions

Circulant twin CPMs are a generalization of CPMs used as mixing layer in KEC-CAK-f and XOODOO. Together with their transpose, they form a new category of mixing layer that has very high local diffusion in the form of a differential branch number (linear branch number for the transpose) not seen before for such a low cost. The optimization for differential or linear branch number is a new feature that allows to get a much higher specific branch number for the same amount of computation than MDS matrices.

We use a twin CPM in a proof-of-concept lightweight permutation Gaston that has a round function that has the same width, shape and gate cost as that of ASCON-p. Due to its high branch number, the best 2-round differential trails in Gaston have weight 24 vs. 8 in ASCON-p. Even though the linear branch number of our mixing layer in Gaston is only 4, the best 3-round linear trails of Gaston have weight 34 vs. 28 in ASCON-p. No 3-round differential trails were found with weight less than 106 while in ASCON-p there are 3-round differential trails with weight 40.

Open Problems. For Gaston it would be interesting to have tighter bounds for the weight of differential trails over more than 2 rounds and linear trails over more than 3 rounds. This will require the introduction of new techniques. Moreover, interesting aspects to investigate are clustering of differential trails in differentials, clustering of linear trails in linear approximations and the validation of the approximation of the DP of differential trails by $\mathrm{DP}(Q) \approx 2^{-\mathrm{w_r}(Q)}$. Another direction for future research is to explore permutations operating on states with other dimensions such as those of XOODOO.

Finally, it would be interesting to more closely investigate the use of Gaston-like permutations within constructions like Farfalle, (monkey)-duplex such as ASCON or XOODYAK and others and do a comprehensive analysis of the permutation in that context.

Acknowledgements. Solane El Hirch is supported by the Cryptography Research Center of the Technology Innovation Institute (TII), Abu Dhabi (UAE), under the TII-Radboud project with title *Evaluation and Implementation of Lightweight Cryptographic Primitives and Protocols.* Joan Daemen is supported by the European Research Council under the ERC advanced grant agreement under grant ERC-2017-ADG Nr. 788980 ESCADA. Rusydi H. Makarim did this work while he was at the Cryptography Research Center of the Technology Innovation Institute (TII), Abu Dhabi (UAE). We would also like to thank the reviewers of CRYPTO 2023 and our shepherd Bart Preneel for their insightful suggestions which helped us in significantly improving the quality of paper.

References

1. Barreto, P., Rijmen, V.: The WHIRLPOOL hashing function. Submitted to NESSIE, Sept 2000, revised May 2003. https://citeseerx.ist.psu.edu/document?repid=rep1&type=pdf&doi=664b5286124b28abf2d30a07ba6f9e020f4138fe

2. Beierle, C., Kranz, T., Leander, G.: Lightweight multiplication in $GF(2^n)$ with applications to MDS matrices. In: Robshaw, M., Katz, J. (eds.) CRYPTO 2016. LNCS, vol. 9814, pp. 625–653. Springer, Heidelberg (2016). https://doi.org/10.1007/978-3-662-53018-4_23

3. Bertoni, G., Daemen, J., Hoffert, S., Peeters, M., Van Assche, G., Van Keer, R.: Farfalle: parallel permutation-based cryptography. IACR Trans. Symmetric Cryptol. **2017**(4), 1–38 (2017). https://tosc.iacr.org/index.php/ToSC/article/view/801

4. Bertoni, G., Daemen, J., Peeters, M., Van Assche, G.: Sponge functions. Ecrypt Hash Workshop 2007 (2007)

5. Bertoni, G., Daemen, J., Peeters, M., Van Assche, G.: The Keccak reference (2011). https://keccak.team/papers.html

6. Bertoni, G., Daemen, J., Peeters, M., Van Assche, G.: Permutation-based encryption, authentication and authenticated encryption. In: Directions in Authenticated Ciphers (2012)

7. Biham, E., Shamir, A.: Differential cryptanalysis of DES-like cryptosystems. In: Menezes, A.J., Vanstone, S.A. (eds.) CRYPTO 1990. LNCS, vol. 537, pp. 2–21. Springer, Heidelberg (1991). https://doi.org/10.1007/3-540-38424-3_1

8. Bordes, N., Daemen, J., Kuijsters, D., Van Assche, G.: Thinking outside the Superbox. In: Malkin, T., Peikert, C. (eds.) CRYPTO 2021. LNCS, vol. 12827, pp. 337–367. Springer, Cham (2021). https://doi.org/10.1007/978-3-030-84252-9_12

9. Canteaut, A., et al.: Saturnin: a suite of lightweight symmetric algorithms for post-quantum security. IACR Trans. Symmetric Cryptol. **2020**(S1), 160–207 (2020). https://doi.org/10.13154/tosc.v2020.iS1.160-207

10. Cui, T., Grassi, L.: Algebraic key-recovery attacks on reduced-round Xoofff. In: Dunkelman, O., Jacobson, Jr., M.J., O'Flynn, C. (eds.) SAC 2020. LNCS, vol. 12804, pp. 171–197. Springer, Cham (2021). https://doi.org/10.1007/978-3-030-81652-0_7

11. Daemen, J., Hoffert, S., Van Assche, G., Van Keer, R.: The design of Xoodoo and Xoofff. IACR Trans. Symmetric Cryptol. **2018**(4), 1–38 (2018). https://tosc.iacr.org/index.php/ToSC/article/view/7359

12. Daemen, J., Rijmen, V.: The Design of Rijndael: AES - The Advanced Encryption Standard. Information Security and Cryptography, Springer, Heidelberg (2002). https://doi.org/10.1007/978-3-662-04722-4

13. Daemen, J.: Cipher and hash function design, strategies based on linear and differential cryptanalysis, Ph D. Thesis, K.U.Leuven (1995). http://jda.noekeon.org/

14. Daemen, J., Mella, S., Van Assche, G.: Tighter trail bounds for Xoodoo. IACR Cryptol. ePrint Arch., p. 1088 (2022). https://eprint.iacr.org/2022/1088

15. Dobraunig, C., Eichlseder, M., Mendel, F., Schläffer, M.: Ascon v1.2. submission to NIST Lightweight Cryptography Standardization Process (round 2) (2019). https://ascon.iaik.tugraz.at/

16. Dobraunig, C., Eichlseder, M., Mendel, F., Schläffer, M.: Ascon v1.2: lightweight authenticated encryption and hashing. J. Cryptol. **34**(3), 1–42 (2021). https://doi.org/10.1007/s00145-021-09398-9

17. Duval, S., Leurent, G.: MDS matrices with lightweight circuits. IACR Trans. Symmetric Cryptol. **2018**(2), 48–78 (2018). https://doi.org/10.13154/tosc.v2018.i2.48-78

18. El Hirch, S., Mella, S., Mehrdad, A., Daemen, J.: Improved differential and linear trail bounds for ASCON. IACR Trans. Symmetric Cryptol. **2022**(4), 145–178 (2022). https://doi.org/10.46586/tosc.v2022.i4.145-178

19. Even, S., Mansour, Y.: A construction of a cipher from a single pseudorandom permutation. In: Imai, H., Rivest, R.L., Matsumoto, T. (eds.) ASIACRYPT 1991. LNCS, vol. 739, pp. 210–224. Springer, Heidelberg (1993). https://doi.org/10.1007/3-540-57332-1_17

20. Fuchs, J., Rotella, Y., Daemen, J.: On the security of keyed hashing based on an unkeyed block function. IACR Cryptol. ePrint Arch, p. 1172 (2022). https://eprint.iacr.org/2022/1172

21. Guo, J., Peyrin, T., Poschmann, A.: The PHOTON family of lightweight hash functions. In: Rogaway, P. (ed.) CRYPTO 2011. LNCS, vol. 6841, pp. 222–239. Springer, Heidelberg (2011). https://doi.org/10.1007/978-3-642-22792-9_13

22. Guo, J., Peyrin, T., Poschmann, A., Robshaw, M.: The LED block cipher. In: Preneel, B., Takagi, T. (eds.) CHES 2011. LNCS, vol. 6917, pp. 326–341. Springer, Heidelberg (2011). https://doi.org/10.1007/978-3-642-23951-9_22

23. Kranz, T., Leander, G., Stoffelen, K., Wiemer, F.: Shorter linear straight-line programs for MDS matrices. IACR Trans. Symmetric Cryptol. 2017(4), 188–211 (2017). https://doi.org/10.13154/tosc.v2017.i4.188-211

24. Li, C., Wang, Q.: Design of lightweight linear diffusion layers from near-MDS matrices. IACR Trans. Symmetric Cryptol. 2017(1), 129–155 (2017). https://doi.org/10.13154/tosc.v2017.i1.129-155

25. Li, S., Sun, S., Shi, D., Li, C., Hu, L.: Lightweight iterative MDS matrices: How small can we go? IACR Trans. Symmetric Cryptol. 2019(4), 147–170 (2019). https://doi.org/10.13154/tosc.v2019.i4.147-170

26. Li, Y., Wang, M.: On the construction of lightweight circulant involutory MDS matrices. In: Peyrin, T. (ed.) FSE 2016. LNCS, vol. 9783, pp. 121–139. Springer, Heidelberg (2016). https://doi.org/10.1007/978-3-662-52993-5_7

27. Liu, M., Sim, S.M.: Lightweight MDS generalized circulant matrices. In: Peyrin, T. (ed.) FSE 2016. LNCS, vol. 9783, pp. 101–120. Springer, Heidelberg (2016). https://doi.org/10.1007/978-3-662-52993-5_6

28. Makarim, R.H., Rohit, R.: Towards tight differential bounds of Ascon: a hybrid usage of SMT and MILP. IACR Trans. Symmetric Cryptol. 2022(3), 303–340 (2022). https://doi.org/10.46586/tosc.v2022.i3.303-340

29. Matsui, M., Yamagishi, A.: A new method for known plaintext attack of FEAL cipher. In: Rueppel, R.A. (ed.) EUROCRYPT 1992. LNCS, vol. 658, pp. 81–91. Springer, Heidelberg (1993). https://doi.org/10.1007/3-540-47555-9_7

30. Mella, S., Daemen, J., Van Assche, G.: New techniques for trail bounds and application to differential trails in Keccak. IACR Trans. Symmetric Cryptol. 2017(1), 329–357 (2017)

31. National Institute of Standards and Technology: Lightweight Cryptography (LWC) Standardization project (2019). https://csrc.nist.gov/projects/lightweight-cryptography

32. Rijmen, V., Daemen, J., Preneel, B., Bosselaers, A., De Win, E.: The cipher SHARK. In: Gollmann, D. (ed.) FSE 1996. LNCS, vol. 1039, pp. 99–111. Springer, Heidelberg (1996). https://doi.org/10.1007/3-540-60865-6_47

33. Sim, S.M., Khoo, K., Oggier, F., Peyrin, T.: Lightweight MDS involution matrices. In: Leander, G. (ed.) FSE 2015. LNCS, vol. 9054, pp. 471–493. Springer, Heidelberg (2015). https://doi.org/10.1007/978-3-662-48116-5_23

34. Stoffelen, K., Daemen, J.: Column parity mixers. IACR Trans. Symmetric Cryptol. 2018(1), 126–159 (2018). https://doi.org/10.13154/tosc.v2018.i1.126-159

35. Venkateswarlu, A., Kesarwani, A., Sarkar, S.: On the lower bound of cost of MDS matrices. IACR Trans. Symmetric Cryptol. 2022(4), 266–290 (2022). https://doi.org/10.46586/tosc.v2022.i4.266-290

New Design Techniques for Efficient Arithmetization-Oriented Hash Functions: Anemoi Permutations and Jive Compression Mode

Clémence Bouvier[1,2]([✉]), Pierre Briaud[1,2], Pyrros Chaidos[3], Léo Perrin[2], Robin Salen[4], Vesselin Velichkov[5,6], and Danny Willems[7,8]

[1] Sorbonne University, Paris, France
[2] Inria, Paris, France
[3] National & Kapodistrian University of Athens, Athens, Greece
[4] Toposware, Inc., Boston, USA
[5] University of Edinburgh, Edinburgh, Scotland
[6] Clearmatics, London, England
[7] Nomadic Labs, Paris, France
[8] LIX, Paris, France
anemoi@inria.fr

Abstract. Advanced cryptographic protocols such as Zero-knowledge (ZK) proofs of knowledge, widely used in cryptocurrency applications such as Zcash, Monero, Filecoin, Tezos, Topos, demand new cryptographic hash functions that are efficient not only over the binary field $\mathbb{F}_2$, but also over large fields of prime characteristic $\mathbb{F}_p$. This need has been acknowledged by the wider community and new so-called *Arithmetization-Oriented* (AO) hash functions have been proposed, e.g. MiMC-Hash, Rescue–Prime, POSEIDON, Reinforced Concrete and GRIFFIN to name a few.

In this paper we propose Anemoi: a new family of ZK-friendly permutations, that can be used to construct efficient hash functions and compression functions. The main features of these algorithms are that 1) they are designed to be efficient within multiple proof systems (e.g. Groth16, Plonk, etc.), 2) they contain dedicated functions optimised for specific applications (namely Merkle tree hashing and general purpose hashing), 3) they have highly competitive performance e.g. about a factor of 2 improvement over POSEIDON and Rescue–Prime in terms of R1CS constraints, a 21%–35% Plonk constraint reduction over a highly optimized POSEIDON implementation, as well as competitive native performance, running between two and three times faster than Rescue–Prime, depending on the field size.

On the theoretical side, Anemoi pushes further the frontier in understanding the design principles that are truly entailed by arithmetization-orientation. In particular, we identify and exploit a previously unknown relationship between CCZ-equivalence and arithmetization-orientation. In addition, we propose two new standalone components that can be easily reused in new designs. One is a new S-box called Flystel, based

© International Association for Cryptologic Research 2023
H. Handschuh and A. Lysyanskaya (Eds.): CRYPTO 2023, LNCS 14083, pp. 507–539, 2023.
https://doi.org/10.1007/978-3-031-38548-3_17

on the well-studied butterfly structure, and the second is Jive – a new mode of operation, inspired by the "Latin dance" symmetric algorithms (Salsa, ChaCha and derivatives). Our design is a conservative one: it uses a very classical Substitution-Permutation Network structure, and our detailed analysis of algebraic attacks highlights can be of independent interest.

Keywords: Anemoi · Flystel · Jive · Arithmetization-oriented · Hash functions · CCZ-equivalence · Plonk · R1CS · AIR · Merkle tree · Zero-knowledge · Arithmetic circuits · Algebraic attacks

1   Introduction

In recent years we have seen a rapid surge of interest in the practical application of an old cryptographic construction known as zero-knowledge (ZK) proofs of knowledge. Such protocols allow a prover P to convince a verifier V that a certain statement x is true without revealing any additional information beyond the fact that it is verifiably correct. Such a piece of information may, for example, be that the result of a specified complex computation is 1. ZK proofs of knowledge, and more generally computational integrity proofs, allow V to verify that the result of the proven computation is correct without having to perform the computation herself. In fact, to verify correctness, V does not even need to know some of the details of the computation e.g., its intermediate values or any potentially secret inputs.

ZK proof systems have been introduced with the seminal work of Micali, Goldwasser and Rackoff back in 1989 [27]. Traditionally, ZK protocols were deployed to allow a prover to keep some elements of a computation secret (e.g. a private key). More recently, the blockchain ecosystem has witnessed a rise of a category of ZK protocols, namely Succinct Non-Interactive Arguments of Knowledge (ZK-SNARKs), that leverages their succinctness property to relieve the verifier from the necessity to perform an expensive computation for which it may not have sufficient resources (in terms of space as well as computational power). The increased interest in such protocols today is largely driven by the latest advancements in digital currencies such as Bitcoin, Ethereum, Tezos, Topos, etc. In particular, ZK proofs make it possible to add privacy on a public blockchain (e.g. Zcash [7]) and to perform off-chain computation verifiable by network nodes with significantly limited resources, improving scalability.

The computation performed by P and verified by V in a ZK proof is often expressed as an arithmetic circuit composed of *gates* (algebraic operations e.g. multiplication or addition) connected by *wires*. The quantities that pass over the wires and are operated on by the gates are elements of a field $\mathbb{F}_q$, where $q \geq 2$.

Cryptographic hash functions are fundamental to practical ZK applications. They are often used for testing membership of some element(s) by means of Merkle trees. They can also be used as part of the ZK protocol itself e.g. by compressing multiple public inputs to a single hash. The modified protocol has a reduced input footprint, and the collision resistance of the hash function implies that security is not impacted. This is relevant in proof systems where the verifier's costs are proportional to the number of public inputs such as Groth16 [32].

Modern cryptographic hash functions such as SHA2, SHA3 and BLAKE are designed over vector spaces of the binary field $\mathbb{F}_2$ (i.e. they work over bits), while ZK protocols often operate over $\mathbb{F}_q$ for a large q – usually a prime number. Therefore the efficient execution of ZK protocols in applications such as Zcash or Filecoin, that aim to process millions of transactions per day, imposes the need for new hash functions designed to be natively efficient in $\mathbb{F}_q$ – the so-called *Arithmetization-Oriented* (AO) designs. The need for new arithmetization-oriented hash functions has been acknowledged by both researchers and engineers. As a result, the past couple of years have seen a surge of new proposals of hash functions that operate natively in $\mathbb{F}_q$ for q prime, enabling efficient verification: MiMC-Hash [2], POSEIDON [30], Rescue–Prime [3,41] and GRIFFIN [28] to name a few. Another line of work, including Reinforced Concrete [29] and Tip5 [42], aims at exploiting lookup tables for more efficient native computations, while remaining practical inside proving systems. This additional requirement for lookup tables however reduces the compatibility of these hash functions within the space of proving systems, and hence limiting the chances of global adoption.

The Design Requirements of Arithmetization-Orientation. Building upon the works mentioned above as well as on the study of practical use cases, we have identified several properties and design requirements that are expected from arithmetization-oriented hash functions.

Evaluation vs. Verification. The operation for which the efficiency of an AO primitive is the most crucial is not its *evaluation*, but rather its *verification*. Concretely, while the cost of evaluating $y = F(x)$ given x remains important, the step with the harshest constraints is a verification: given both x and y, checking if y is indeed equal to $F(x)$ should be "efficient", where the exact meaning of "efficient" depends on the proof system considered.

b-**to-1 compression.** One of the main use cases for AO hash functions is in Merkle trees. In this context, rather than a hash function taking arbitrarily long inputs, protocol designers need a compression function mapping bm to m finite field elements, meaning a compression factor of b (often, $b = 2$).

Primitive Factories. Rather than a single primitive or a small family of primitives (such as for instance AES-128/192/256), AO hash functions are defined for a vast number of field sizes and security levels. In fact, we would argue that algorithms like POSEIDON are *primitive factories*[1], and that the task of the cryptanalysts is not only to assess whether specific instances are secure. Rather, it is to verify if such factories can return weak algorithms. Furthermore, since the protocols and arithmetization techniques vary, a factory should be able to output primitives optimized for each use case.

---

[1] "Factory" is here used in the sense of the programming design pattern, i.e. it is an object returning functions.

Performance constraints. The space and time complexities of proving systems depend on the size (i.e. the number of gates) of the arithmetized program that is being verified. Therefore, it is crucial for practical applications to minimize the number of gates. Otherwise, the cost of a proof may be so high as to make it unusable, as the computational cost of the prover is often the bottleneck of an entire system. AIR-based systems additionally require keeping constraint degrees low for practical applications. Furthermore, good conventional CPU architecture performance is still required as real world applications tend to use the primitives both outside and inside the circuit.

Outline of Our Contributions. In this paper, we study each of the specific design requirements of AO, and provide new tools to satisfy them. First, we present the necessary theoretical background in Sect. 2.

We then present two building blocks. First, in Sect. 3 we introduce a new mode of operation, Jive, which turns a public permutation into a t-to-1 compression function. Its main advantage is that it compresses an input consisting of tu words using a permutation operating on a state consisting of tu words, unlike the sponge structure which needs a bigger state in order to accomodate a capacity. Then, in Sect. 4, we argue that the asymmetry between the evaluation and the verification of a function is best framed in terms of *CCZ-equivalence*. Using this insight, we propose a new family of non-linear components (S-boxes) operating on $\mathbb{F}_q^2$ which we call Flystel: they allow both a high degree evaluation, and a low degree verification.

In a natural progression, we use the Flystel structure to construct a new permutation factory: Anemoi. It uses the familiar Substitution-Permutation Network (SPN) structure, which simplifies our security analysis. Its specification is given in Sect. 5, and our initial cryptanalysis is presented in Sect. 6. We combine all these results together in Sect. 7, where we show via detailed benchmarks that combining the Anemoi permutations with the Jive mode of operation allows us to compete with the best AO hash functions in the literature in terms of performance, and to substantially outclass them in some contexts. In particular, in the case of Plonk, we can compute more than twice as many hashes for a fixed number of constraints as is possible with POSEIDON, which to the best of our knowledge was the best until now. We conclude the paper in Sect. 8.

2   Theoretical Background

In what follows, q is an integer corresponding to the size of the field $\mathbb{F}_q$, so that $q = p$ for some prime number p or $q = 2^n$. In particular, for binary fields $\mathbb{F}_{2^n}$, we focus on the case where n is odd as it is harder to build low degree permutations otherwise. As usual, the symbols "+" and "×" denote respectively the addition and multiplication operations over $\mathbb{F}_q$. We also let $m \geq 1$ be an integer corresponding to the number of field elements we are operating on. We denote by $\langle a, b \rangle$ the usual scalar product of $a \in \mathbb{F}_q^m$ and $b \in \mathbb{F}_q^m$ which is such that $\langle a, b \rangle = \sum_{i=0}^{m-1} a_i b_i$.

Below, we consider a function $F : \mathbb{F}_q^m \to \mathbb{F}_q^m$, and recall some of the concepts behind the use and analysis of functions to design symmetric cryptographic primitives. We first recall the definitions of their differential and linear properties, and then that of *CCZ-equivalence*. While the latter has seldom been used in practice so far, it plays a crucial role in our work.

Differential Properties. The *Difference Distribution Table (DDT)* of function F is the two dimensional array δ_F, where $\delta_F[a, b] = \#\{x \in \mathbb{F}_q^m \,|\, F(x+a) - F(x) = b\}$. The maximum value of $\delta_F[a, b]$ for $a \neq 0$ is the *differential uniformity* [39] of F.

Linear Properties. While a general formula that works both when q is a power of two and a prime can be given, it is simpler to treat the two cases separately, especially given that the reader is probably familiar with the case of characteristic 2. If $q = 2^n$, then the Walsh transform of the component $\langle b, F \rangle : \mathbb{F}_q \to \mathbb{F}_2$ for any $b \in \mathbb{F}_q \setminus \{0\}$ is $\mathcal{W}_{\langle b, F \rangle}(a) = \sum_{x \in \mathbb{F}_{2^n}^m} (-1)^{\langle a, x \rangle + \langle b, F(x) \rangle}$.

Otherwise, when $q = p$ the Fourier transform of a function $f : \mathbb{F}_p^m \to \mathbb{F}_p$ is the function $\mathcal{W}_f : \mathbb{F}_p^m \to \mathbb{C}$ such that

$$\mathcal{W}_f(a) = \sum_{x \in \mathbb{F}_p^m} \exp\left(\frac{2\pi i \left(\langle a, x \rangle - f(x) \right)}{p} \right) .$$

For a vectorial function $F : \mathbb{F}_q^m \to \mathbb{F}_q^m$, we consider the Fourier transform of each of its components, i.e. of all the linear combinations $\langle b, F \rangle$.

CCZ-Equivalence [19]. Let $F : \mathbb{F}_q^m \to \mathbb{F}_q^m$ and $G : \mathbb{F}_q^m \to \mathbb{F}_q^m$ be two functions. They are *affine-equivalent* if there exist two affine permutations $\mu : \mathbb{F}_q^m \to \mathbb{F}_q^m$ and $\eta : \mathbb{F}_q^m \to \mathbb{F}_q^m$ such that $F = \eta \circ G \circ \mu$. This can alternatively be written using the *graphs* of these functions:

$$\underbrace{\Gamma_F = \left\{ (x, F(x)) \mid x \in \mathbb{F}_q^m \right\}}_{\text{graph of } F} = \mathcal{L}(\Gamma_G) = \left\{ \mathcal{L}(x, G(x)) \mid x \in \mathbb{F}_q^m \right\},$$

where $\mathcal{L}$ is the affine permutation defined by $\mathcal{L}(x, y) = (\eta(x), \mu^{-1}(y))$. If we allow $\mathcal{L}$ to be any affine permutation,[2] we obtain *CCZ-equivalence*.

Definition 1 (CCZ-Equivalence). *Let F and G be functions of $\mathbb{F}_q^m$. We say that they are* CCZ-equivalent *if there exists an affine permutation $\mathcal{L} : (\mathbb{F}_q^m)^2 \to (\mathbb{F}_q^m)^2$ such that $\Gamma_F = \mathcal{L}(\Gamma_G)$.*

An important property of CCZ-equivalence that is instrumental in our work is that it preserves the differential spectrum and the squared Walsh coefficients.

---

[2] Starting from a given function F, applying any affine permutation of $\mathbb{F}_q^2$ to its graph is unlikely to yield the graph of another function G. Indeed, this would require that the left hand side of $\mathcal{L}(x, F(x))$ takes all the values in $\mathbb{F}_q$ as x goes through $\mathbb{F}_q$, which is a priori not the case. A mapping $\mathcal{L}$ that does yield the graph of another function is called "admissible", a concept that was extensively studied in [18].

In other words, all functions within the same CCZ-equivalence class share the same differential and linear properties and hence offer the same resilience against differential and linear attacks. It also means that it is sufficient to investigate these properties for a single member of a CCZ-equivalence class.

Another relevant property of CCZ-equivalence is that it does *not* preserve the degree of the function. In fact, there are known cases where a low-degree function is CCZ-equivalent to a higher-degree one. It is most notably the case of the so-called *butterfly structure*, originally introduced in [40], and then further generalized in two different ways in [16] and [34].

3   Modes of Operation

In advanced protocols, hash functions are used for two purposes. The first is to emulate a random oracle, in particular to return the "fingerprint" or digest of a message of arbitrary length. The idea is that this fixed length digest is simpler to sign than the full message. The second use is as a compression function within a Merkle-tree: in this case, the hash function H is used to map two inputs of size n to an output of size n, and the security of the higher level scheme relies on its collision resistance. While a general purpose hash function like SHA-3 [10, 22] or an arithmetization-friendly one can safely be used for both cases, for improved efficiency we chose a full hash function only for the random oracle case (Sect. 3.1). Indeed, the specific constraints of the Merkle-tree case can be satisfied more efficiently using a dedicated structure that remains permutation-based, and which we introduce in Sect. 3.2. SAGE implementations of both modes are provided in [14, App. C].

3.1   Random Oracle: The Sponge Structure

A random oracle is essentially a theoretical function that picks each output uniformly at random while keeping track of its previous outputs in order to remain a deterministic function. The sponge construction is a convenient approach to try to emulate this behaviour. First introduced by Bertoni et al. in [11], this method was most notably used to design SHA-3. It is also how most arithmetization-oriented hash functions have been designed, e.g. Rescue–Prime, gMiMC-Hash, POSEIDON [30], and Reinforced Concrete. Such hash functions can easily be tweaked into eXtendable Output Functions (XOF) [22] should the need arise.

The overall principle of the sponge construction is best explained by the diagram in Fig. 1. In this paper, we slightly modify the original approach to operate on elements of $\mathbb{F}_q$ instead of $\mathbb{F}_2$. The main component of the structure is a permutation P operating on $\mathbb{F}_q^{r+c}$, where both r and c are non-zero integers. The *rate* r is the size of the *outer part* of the state, while c is the *capacity* and corresponds to the size of the *inner part* of the state. The digest consists of h elements of $\mathbb{F}_q$. Then, to process a message m consisting of elements of $\mathbb{F}_q$, we apply the following operations.

Padding. A basic padding works as follows: append $1 \in \mathbb{F}_q$ to the message followed by enough zeroes so that the total length is a multiple of r, and then divide the result into blocks $m_0,...,m_{\ell-1}$ of r elements.

However, with this approach, we may end up using one more call to P in the case where the length of the message was already a multiple of r. A more efficient approach is presented in [33]: if the length of the message is already a multiple of r, then we do not append further blocks to it. Instead, we add a constant to the capacity before squeezing. This is summarized as the addition of σ which is equal to 0 if the message length is not a multiple of r, and to 1 otherwise (see Fig. 1). This variant also has the advantage of gracefully handling the case where $r = 1$.

Absorption. For each message block m_i, we add it into the outer part of the state, and then apply P on the full state.

Squeezing. We extract $\min(h, r)$ elements from the outer part of the state to generate the first elements of the digest. If $h > r$, we apply P and then extract additional elements again from the rate registers, repeating this process until the desired digest length is reached.

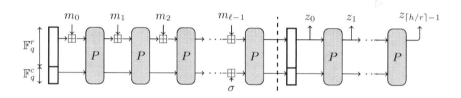

Fig. 1. Sponge construction with the modification of [33].

The security of a sponge rests on the properties of its permutation. Informally, the only special property of the permutation should be the existence of an efficient implementation. Its differential, linear, algebraic, etc. properties should be similar to those expected from a permutation picked uniformly at random from the set of all permutations.

Following a *flat sponge claim* [11], the designers of such an algorithm can essentially claim that any attack against it will have a complexity equivalent to at least $q^{c/2}$ calls to the permutation (provided $h \geq c$, $h \log_2 q \geq 2s$ and $c \log_2 q \geq 2s$). Thus, a flat sponge claim states that a sponge-based hash function provides $c \lfloor \log_2 q \rfloor / 2$ bits of security.

3.2   Merkle Compression Function: The Jive Mode

One of the main use cases for an arithmetization-oriented hash function is as a compression function in a Merkle tree. This case could be easily handled using a regular hashing mode, such as the sponge structure discussed above. However, due to the specifics of this use case, it is possible to use a more efficient mode.

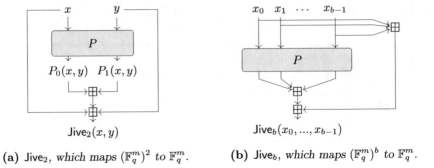

(a) Jive$_2$, which maps $(\mathbb{F}_q^m)^2$ to $\mathbb{F}_q^m$. **(b)** Jive$_b$, which maps $(\mathbb{F}_q^m)^b$ to $\mathbb{F}_q^m$.

Fig. 2. The Jive mode turning a permutation into a compression function.

In a Merkle tree, the elements considered are in $\mathbb{F}_q^m$, where m is chosen so that $m\lfloor \log_2 q \rfloor \geq n$, where n is the intended security level. We then need to hash two such elements to obtain a new one. As a consequence, unlike in the usual case, the input size is fixed, and is equal to exactly twice the digest size. Given a permutation of $(\mathbb{F}_q^m)^2$, we can thus construct a suitable hash function by plugging it into the following mode.

Definition 2 (Jive). *Consider a permutation P defined as follows:*

$$P : \begin{cases} (\mathbb{F}_q^m)^b & \rightarrow (\mathbb{F}_q^m)^b \\ (x_0, ..., x_{b-1}) & \mapsto (P_0(x_0, ..., x_{b-1}), ..., P_{b-1}(x_0, ..., x_{b-1})) \end{cases},$$

so that it operates on bm elements of $\mathbb{F}_q$, where $P_i(x_0, \ldots, x_{b-1}) : 0 \leq i < b$ refers to the i-th element in $\mathbb{F}_q^m$ of the output $P(x_0, \ldots, x_{b-1})$ from P. The Jive mode is built from P by defining the following one way function $\text{Jive}_b(P)$:

$$\text{Jive}_b(P) : \begin{cases} (\mathbb{F}_q^m)^b & \rightarrow \mathbb{F}_q^m \\ (x_0, ..., x_{b-1}) & \mapsto \sum_{i=0}^{b-1} (x_i + P_i(x_0, ..., x_{b-1})) \end{cases}.$$

This approach, also described in Fig. 2 can be seen as a permutation-based variant of the Davies-Meyer mode which, like the latter, crucially relies on a feedforward to ensure one-wayness. Alternatively, it can be interpreted as a truncated instance of the mode used in the "Latin dance" ciphers ChaCha and Salsa [9], which is also based on a public permutation combined with a feedforward. Incidentally, we called it Jive after another Latin dance.

If used inside a Merkle tree, this mode can save some computations. For example, in the case where the fan-in b is equal to 2, a sponge would use a permutation operating on $(\mathbb{F}_q^m)^3$ in order to leave one vector of $\mathbb{F}_q^m$ free for the capacity. Using Jive$_2$ instead, we only need a permutation of $(\mathbb{F}_q^m)^2$. The trade-off of course is that, unlike a sponge-based approach, the relevance of Jive is restricted to some specific cases.

4   The Flystel Structure

The performance metrics for AO algorithms differ substantially from the usual ones in symmetric cryptography. Neither the number of CPU cycles, nor the RAM consumption or the code size are the dominant factors. Pin-pointing exactly what is needed for the various protocols relying on arithmetization is a difficult task as each protocol has its own subtleties. For example, Plonk offers custom gates, which add complexity and a small overall overhead but can drastically decrease the cost of a particular operation, while other proof systems might not. On the other hand, additions are essentially free for R1CS or AIR, but not for Plonk. In addition, permutations of a sequence of elements are likely to incur cost in Plonk or AIR (via copy-constraints), but are free in R1CS.

In this section, we present a family of non-linear components that provide both the cryptographic properties that we need to ensure the security of our primitives, and efficient implementations across proof systems, which we call *open Flystel*. It uses—and highlights—the connection between arithmetization-orientation and CCZ-equivalence.

4.1   On CCZ-Equivalence and Arithmetization-Orientation

In order for a function F to be arithmetization-oriented, it is necessary that verifying whether $y = F(x)$ can be done using few multiplications in a specific field (whose size is dictated by other parts of the protocol). A very straightforward initial approach is to use a function F which, itself, can be evaluated using a small number of multiplications: both MiMC-Hash [2] and POSEIDON [30] work in this way. The downside is that using a low degree round function may imply vulnerability to attacks based on polynomial solving, known as *algebraic attacks*. As a consequence, these algorithms have to use a high number of rounds.

A first breakthrough on this topic was made by the designers of Rescue–Prime [3]. They noticed that for a permutation F, checking if $y = F(x)$ is equivalent to checking if $x = F^{-1}(y)$. It allows them to use both x^α and $x^{1/\alpha}$ (where $x \mapsto x^\alpha$ is a permutation of the field used) in their round function, with α chosen so as to minimize the number of multiplications. It means that both can be verified using a (cheap) evaluation of x^α, and at the same time that the degree of the round function is very high as $1/\alpha$ is a dense integer of $\mathbb{Z}/(q-1)\mathbb{Z}$. As a consequence, much fewer rounds are needed to prevent algebraic attacks.

We go further and propose a generalization of this insight. So far, we have seen that AO implies that a function or its inverse must have a particular implementation property (low number of multiplications). In fact, we claim the following:

A subfunction is arithmetization-oriented if it is **CCZ-equivalent** to a function that can be verified efficiently.

The above should come as no surprise since a permutation and its inverse are known to be CCZ-equivalent [15]. In that sense, this insight is a natural generalization of the one of the Rescue–Prime designers.

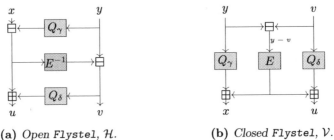

(a) *Open* Flystel, $\mathcal{H}$.   (b) *Closed* Flystel, $\mathcal{V}$.

Fig. 3. The Flystel structure (both variants are CCZ-equivalent).

Exploiting this idea is simple: suppose that F and G are such that $\Gamma_F = \mathcal{L}(\Gamma_G)$, where $\mathcal{L} : (x, y) \mapsto (\mathcal{L}_L(x, y), \mathcal{L}_R(x, y))$ is an affine permutation, and where G can be efficiently verified. Then we can use F to construct an AO algorithm: checking if $y = F(x)$ is equivalent to checking if $\mathcal{L}_R(x, y) = G(\mathcal{L}_L(x, y))$, which only involves G and linear functions: it is efficient.

Below, we present a first component based on this idea: the Flystel. Nevertheless, we hope that further research in discrete mathematics will lead to new non-linear components that are even better suited to this use case: we need more permutations with good cryptographic properties (including a high degree) that are CCZ-equivalent to functions with a low number of multiplications.

4.2   High Level View of the Flystel Structure

Let $Q_\gamma : \mathbb{F}_q \to \mathbb{F}_q$ and $Q_\delta : \mathbb{F}_q \to \mathbb{F}_q$ be two quadratic functions, and let $E : \mathbb{F}_q \to \mathbb{F}_q$ be a permutation. Then, the Flystel is a pair of functions relying on Q_γ, Q_δ and E. The *open* Flystel is the permutation of $(\mathbb{F}_q)^2$ obtained using a 3-round Feistel network with Q_γ, E^{-1}, and Q_δ as round functions, as depicted in Fig. 3a. It is denoted $\mathcal{H}$, so that $\mathcal{H}(x, y) = (u, v)$ is evaluated as follows:

1. $x \leftarrow x - Q_\gamma(y)$,   3. $x \leftarrow x + Q_\delta(y)$,
2. $y \leftarrow y - E^{-1}(x)$,   4. $u \leftarrow x, \ v \leftarrow y$.

We define by $\mathcal{V} : (y, v) \mapsto (R_\gamma(y, v), R_\delta(y, v))$ the *closed* Flystel function over $\mathbb{F}_q^2$, where $R_\gamma : (y, v) \mapsto E(y-v)+Q_\gamma(y)$ and $R_\delta : (y, v) \mapsto E(y-v)+Q_\delta(v)$.

Our terminology of "open" for the permutation and "closed" for the function is based on the relation between the Flystel and the butterfly structure, as detailed later. In particular, the two Flystels are linked in the following way.

Proposition 1. *For a given tuple (Q_γ, E, Q_δ), the corresponding closed and open Flystel are CCZ-equivalent.*

Proof. Let $(u, v) = \mathcal{H}(x, y)$. Then it holds that $v = y - E^{-1}(x - Q_\gamma(y))$, so that we can write $x = E(y-v)+Q_\gamma(y)$. Similarly, we have that $u = Q_\delta(v)+E(y-v)$.

Consider now the set $\Gamma_{\mathcal{H}} = \{((x,y), \mathcal{H}(x,y)), (x,y) \in \mathbb{F}_q^2\}$. By definition, we have

$$\Gamma_{\mathcal{H}} = \{((x,y),(u,v)), (x,y) \in \mathbb{F}_q^2\} = \mathcal{L}\big(\{((y,v),(x,u)), (x,y) \in \mathbb{F}_q^2\}\big)$$

where $\mathcal{L}$ is the permutation of $(\mathbb{F}_q^2)^2$ such that $\mathcal{L}^{-1}((x,y),(u,v)) = ((y,v),(x,u))$, which is linear. Using the equalities we established at the beginning of this proof, we can write:

$$\mathcal{L}^{-1}(\Gamma_{\mathcal{H}}) = \{((y,v),(x,u)), (x,y) \in \mathbb{F}_q^2\}$$
$$= \{((y,v),(Q_\gamma(y) + E(y-v), Q_\delta(v) + E(y-v))), (y,v) \in \mathbb{F}_q^2\} = \Gamma_{\mathcal{V}}.$$

We deduce that $\Gamma_{\mathcal{H}} = \mathcal{L}(\Gamma_{\mathcal{V}})$, so the two functions are CCZ-equivalent. □

This simple proposition has two crucial corollaries on which we will rely in the remainder of the paper. The first is that it suffices to investigate the differential and linear properties of the closed butterfly to obtain results on the open one.

Corollary 1. *The open and closed* Flystel *structures have identical differential and linear properties. More precisely, the set of the values in the DDT of both functions is the same, and the set of the square of the Fourier coefficients of the components is also the same.*

The second corollary is the key reason behind the relevance of the Flystel structure in the arithmetization-oriented setting and is stated below.

Corollary 2. *Verifying that* $(u,v) = \mathcal{H}(x,y)$ *is equivalent to verifying that* $(x,u) = \mathcal{V}(y,v)$.

Indeed, Corollary 2 means that it is possible to encode the verification of the evaluation of the high degree open Flystel using the polynomial representation of the low degree closed Flystel.

In characteristic 2, quadratic mappings correspond to different exponents than in the general case. As a consequence, when giving concrete instantiations of the Flystel structure, we need to treat this case separately. To highlight the difference, we call Flystel$_2$ the instances used in characteristic 2, and Flystel$_p$ the instances used in odd prime characteristic.

4.3   Characteristic 2

Let $q = 2^n$, with n odd. Furthermore, let $\alpha = 2^i + 1$ be such that $\gcd(i,n) = 1$, so that $x \mapsto x^\alpha$ is a permutation of $\mathbb{F}_q$. In this case, the Flystel$_2$ structure with $Q_\gamma(x) = Q_\delta(x) = \beta x^\alpha$, with $\beta \neq 0$, and with $E(x) = x^\alpha$ is a degenerate generalized butterfly structure. It was studied in [34] as a generalization of the structure introduced in [40], which was also refined in [16]. We recall the following particular case[3] in Theorems 3, 4 and 5 of [34].

---

[3] The result of Li et al. covers all generalized butterflies, not just those corresponding to Flystel structures. In a Flystel, the first parameter (which we will denote a)

Proposition 2 ([34]). *Let $q = 2^n$ with n odd, $E = x \mapsto x^\alpha$, where $\alpha = 2^i + 1$ is such that $\gcd(i, n) = 1$, and $Q_\gamma = Q_\delta = x \mapsto \beta x^\alpha$, where $\beta \neq 0$ Then the* Flystel$_2$ *structures defined by the functions $Q_\gamma, E,$ and Q_δ have differential uniformity equal to 4, linearity equal to 2^{n+1}, and algebraic degree of n.*

In practice, to prevent some attacks (see [13, App. A.3]), we instead use $Q_\gamma(x) = \beta x^3 + \gamma$ and $Q_\delta(x) = \beta x^3 + \delta$, where β, γ, δ are constants in $\mathbb{F}_q$ such that $\gamma \neq \delta$ and $\beta \neq 0$. The particular values of those constants are not essential to the properties of the construction as long as the noted requirements are satisfied. For simplicity we set $\beta = g, \gamma = g^{-1}$ and $\delta = 0$ with g being a generator of the multiplicative subgroup of the field $\mathbb{F}_q$. This results in $Q_\gamma : x \mapsto gx^3 + g^{-1}$ and $Q_\delta : x \mapsto gx^3$ as depicted in Fig. 4a.

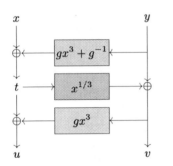
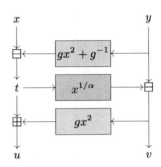

(a) Flystel$_2$ *in characteristic 2.*   **(b)** Flystel$_p$ *in odd prime characteristic.*

Fig. 4. The two variants of the open Flystel, mapping (x, y) to (u, v).

4.4 Odd Characteristic

When $q = p$, the three functions of the Flystel$_p$ structure are resp.: $Q_\gamma : x \mapsto gx^2 + g^{-1}$, $E : x \mapsto x^\alpha$, and $Q_\delta : x \mapsto gx^2$, where $\alpha, g \in \mathbb{F}_q$ and g again is a generator of the multiplicative subgroup of the field $\mathbb{F}_q$.

Differential Properties. Such structures have a low differential uniformity.

Proposition 3. *Let $q = p$ be a prime number, $E = x \mapsto x^\alpha$, where α is such that $\gcd(\alpha, p - 1) = 1$, and $Q_\gamma = x \mapsto gx^2 + g^{-1}$, $Q_\delta = x \mapsto gx^2$. Then the* Flystel$_p$ *structures defined by the functions $Q_\gamma, E,$ and Q_δ has a differential uniformity equal to $\alpha - 1$.*

---

is set to 1. Their results for the differential uniformity and the linearity hold only when $\beta \neq (1 + a)^\alpha$, meaning that we simply need to make sure that $\beta \neq 0$. For the algebraic degree, the condition they give in their Theorem 5 to have a degree equal to $n + 1$ degenerates into $\beta^{2^{i+1}} = \beta^{2^i+1}$, which is never the case as $i > 0$.

Proof. Let a, b, c, d be elements of $\mathbb{F}_p$ such that $(a, b) \neq (0, 0)$. To investigate the differential uniformity of $\mathcal{V} : (y, v) \mapsto (R_\gamma(y, v), R_\delta(y, v))$, we look at the number of solutions (y, v) of (1).

$$\begin{cases} R_\gamma(y + a, v + b) - R_\gamma(y, v) = c \\ R_\delta(y + a, v + b) - R_\delta(y, v) = d \ . \end{cases} \tag{1}$$

We have:

$$\begin{cases} (y + a - (v + b))^\alpha + g^{-1} + g(y + a)^2 - (y - v)^\alpha - g^{-1} - gy^2 &= c \\ (y + a - (v + b))^\alpha + g(v + b)^2 - (y - v)^\alpha - gv^2 &= d \ . \end{cases}$$

We get:

$$c - d = g(y + a)^2 - gy^2 + gv^2 - g(v + b)^2 \ ,$$

which is equivalent to:

$$v = (2b)^{-1} \left(2ay + a^2 - b^2 - g^{-1}(c - d)\right) \ .$$

As a consequence, we know that v can be expressed as an affine polynomial in y. We then have that the first equation is an equation in y of degree $\alpha - 1$ (since the terms y^α cancel out), and thus has at most $\alpha - 1$ solutions for y. In the end, we have at most $\alpha - 1$ solutions (y, v) for the system (since for each value of y, there is one v). $\qquad \square$

Linear Properties. We do not have a theoretical bound on the correlation for the `Flystel`$_p$ structure, but we provide informal arguments supporting its security against linear cryptanalysis attacks. Notice first that `Flystel`$_p$ is defined by the functions Q_γ, E^{-1} and Q_δ, where Q_γ and Q_δ are quadratic. Given that the function x^2 is bent (i.e. its correlations are the lowest possible), we argue that a linear trail which would activate just one of these functions should be expected to have a very low correlation. In [13, App. A], we give a conjecture supported by experimental results, stating that the linearity of `Flystel`$_p$ is lower than $p \log p$.

Invariant Subset. Regardless of the characteristic, it holds that $\mathcal{H}(Q_\gamma(x), x) = (Q_\delta(x), x)$. Thus, setting $Q_\gamma = Q_\delta$ would mean that `Flystel` is the identity over a subset of size q, which is why we use constant additions to ensure $Q_\gamma \neq Q_\delta$. Nevertheless, this only ensures that the open `Flystel` is a translation over the set $\{(Q_\gamma(x), x), x \in \mathbb{F}_q\}$, which remains cryptographically weak. While a priori undesirable, the impact of this property can be mitigated. First, the subset over which it has a simple expression is not an affine space. Second, as we show in [13, App. A.3], the propagation of such patterns can be broken via the linear layer.

Degree. Given the structure of the open `Flystel`$_p$, its degree is lower bounded by the inverse of α modulo $p - 1$, a quantity which in practice corresponds to a dense integer of $\mathbb{Z}/(p - 1)\mathbb{Z}$. We deduce that one call to the open `Flystel`$_p$ is likely to be of maximum degree and is therefore sufficient to thwart attacks that exploit the low degree of a component, such as higher order differentials.

4.5   Implementation Aspects

For direct computation, or witness calculation, one can simply implement the open Flystel. For the verification however, we also have the option to use the closed Flystel structure, since there is no requirement for the various verification steps to be performed in a particular order as long as consistency is enforced. In this case, the cost is one multiplication for Q_γ and Q_δ, and as many as are needed to compute $x \mapsto x^\alpha$. This can be implemented using a technique slightly more subtle than basic fast exponentiation, instead relying on addition chains as discussed for example in [12]. Good addition chains can be found using the addChain tool [37]. They are also particularly useful for implementing $x \mapsto x^{1/\alpha}$.

5   Description of Anemoi

In this section, we present new primitives, and the way to deterministically construct all of their variants. At their core are the Anemoi permutations, that operate on $\mathbb{F}_q^{2\ell}$ for any field size q that is either a prime number or a power of two, and for positive integer ℓ. The round function of these permutations is presented in Sect. 5.1: for each value of ℓ, and for each value of q, there is a unique round function.

In order to build the primitives themselves, we need also to consider the security level required as it will influence the number of rounds of the permutation (note that the security level will also influence the size of the internal state). The procedures to follow to define higher level algorithms are described in Sect. 5.2. We then provide some specific instances in Sect. 5.3.

5.1   Round Function

A round function is a permutation of $\mathbb{F}_q^{2\ell}$, where $\ell > 0$ is an integer, and where q is either a prime number or a power of 2 with a bitlength of at least 10.[4]

In order to define it, we organize its state into a rectangle of elements of $\mathbb{F}_q$ of dimension $2 \times \ell$. The elements in the first row are denoted $(x_0, ..., x_{\ell-1})$, and those in the second row are $(y_0, ..., y_{\ell-1})$ (see Fig. 5a). We refer to vectors of $\mathbb{F}_q^\ell$ using the same upper-case letters, e.g. $(x_0, ..., x_{\ell-1})$ is denoted X. Subscripts correspond to indices within a vector of $\mathbb{F}_q^\ell$, and superscripts to round indices, so X^i is the top part of the state at the start of round i. We let g be a specific generator of the multiplicative subgroup of the field $\mathbb{F}_q$. If q is prime, then g is the smallest such generator using the usual integer ordering. Otherwise, we have that $\mathbb{F}_q = \mathbb{F}_{2^n} = \mathbb{F}_2[x]/p(x)$, where p is an irreducible polynomial of degree n, in which case we let g be one of its roots.

The function applied during round r is denoted R_r. It has the structure of a classical Substitution-Permutation Network, whose components are described

---

[4] The field order must have a bitlength of at least 10 bits. The aim of this restriction is to ensure that e.g. MDS matrices can be found as those might not be defined for small field sizes.

below: first the linear layer, then the S-box layer, and finally the constant addition. The overall action of each of these operations on the state is summarized in Fig. 5, and a complete round is represented in Fig. 6.

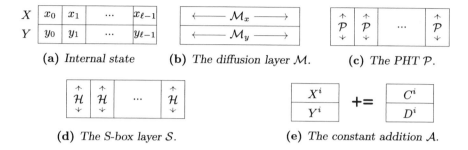

(a) *Internal state*   **(b)** *The diffusion layer* $\mathcal{M}$.   **(c)** *The PHT* $\mathcal{P}$.

(d) *The S-box layer* $\mathcal{S}$.   **(e)** *The constant addition* $\mathcal{A}$.

Fig. 5. The internal state of `Anemoi` and its basic operations.

Constant Additions $\mathcal{A}$. We let $x_j \leftarrow x_j + c_j^i$ and $y_j \leftarrow y_j + d_j^i$, where $c_j^i \in \mathbb{F}_q$ and $d_j^i \in \mathbb{F}_q$ are round constants that depend on both the position (index j) and the round (index i). The aim is to increase the complexity of the algebraic expression of multiple rounds of the primitive and to prevent the appearance of patterns that an attacker could leverage in their attack.

They are derived using the digits of π using the following procedure. We let

$(\pi_0, \pi_1) =$

(1415926535897932384626433832795028841971693993751058209749445923078164062862089986280348253421170679,

8214808651328230664709384460955058223172535940812848111745028410270193852110555964462294895493038196)

be the first and second blocks of 100 digits of π. We derive the round constants c_j^i and d_j^i by applying an open `Flystel` with the same parameters as in the round function on the pair (π_0^i, π_1^j), where superscripts are exponents, so that

$$\begin{cases} c_j^i = g(\pi_0^i)^2 + \left(\pi_0^i + \pi_1^j\right)^\alpha \\ d_j^i = g(\pi_1^j)^2 + \left(\pi_0^i + \pi_1^j\right)^\alpha + g^{-1} \,, \end{cases}$$

where the computations are done in $\mathbb{F}_q$. When $q = 2^n$, π_0 and π_1 are cast to field elements using the usual mapping sending $\sum_{k=0}^{n-1} x_i 2^i$ to $\sum_{k=0}^{n-1} x_i g^i$, where $(x_0, ..., x_{n-1})$ is the binary representation of x modulo 2^n.

Diffusion Layer $\mathcal{M}$. If $\ell > 1$, then the diffusion layer $\mathcal{M}$ operates on X and Y separately, so that

$$\mathcal{M}(X, Y) = \left(\mathcal{M}_x(X), \mathcal{M}_y(Y)\right) \,,$$

as summarized in Fig. 5b. The linear permutations $\mathcal{M}_x$ and $\mathcal{M}_y$ are closely related, but differ in order to break the column structure imposed by the non-linear layer (see below). More precisely, we impose that $\mathcal{M}_x$ is a matrix of size

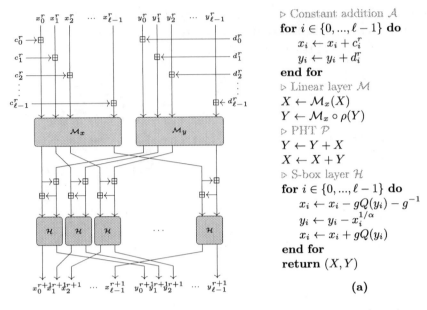

$$\rhd \text{ Constant addition } \mathcal{A}$$
$$\textbf{for } i \in \{0, ..., \ell - 1\} \textbf{ do}$$
$$\quad x_i \leftarrow x_i + c_i^r$$
$$\quad y_i \leftarrow y_i + d_i^r$$
$$\textbf{end for}$$
$$\rhd \text{ Linear layer } \mathcal{M}$$
$$X \leftarrow \mathcal{M}_x(X)$$
$$Y \leftarrow \mathcal{M}_x \circ \rho(Y)$$
$$\rhd \text{ PHT } \mathcal{P}$$
$$Y \leftarrow Y + X$$
$$X \leftarrow X + Y$$
$$\rhd \text{ S-box layer } \mathcal{H}$$
$$\textbf{for } i \in \{0, ..., \ell - 1\} \textbf{ do}$$
$$\quad x_i \leftarrow x_i - gQ(y_i) - g^{-1}$$
$$\quad y_i \leftarrow y_i - x_i^{1/\alpha}$$
$$\quad x_i \leftarrow x_i + gQ(y_i)$$
$$\textbf{end for}$$
$$\textbf{return } (X, Y)$$

(a)

Fig. 6. R_r, the r-th round of Anemoi, applied on the state $(X, Y) \in \mathbb{F}_q^\ell \times \mathbb{F}_q^\ell$, where $X = (x_0, ..., x_{\ell-1})$ and $Y = (y_0, ..., y_{\ell-1})$.

$\ell \times \ell$ of $\mathbb{F}_q$ with maximum diffusion, i.e. such that its branching number is equal to $\ell + 1$.[5] We then construct $\mathcal{M}_y$ as $\mathcal{M}_y = \mathcal{M}_x \circ \rho$, where ρ is a simple word permutation: $\rho(x_0, ..., x_{\ell-1}) = (x_1, ..., x_{\ell-1}, x_0)$.

The specifics of the linear permutation $\mathcal{M}_x$ then depend on the value of ℓ. Furthermore, in order for our permutation to best satisfy different proof systems, we use different techniques to construct them. At a high level, there are two different situations:

- if ℓ is small, then the field size is expected to be large in order for the permutation to operate on a state large enough to offer security against generic attacks, meaning that this case is expected to happen when using pairing-based proof systems like Groth16 or standard Plonk which require large scalar fields for security.
- if ℓ is large, then the situation is the opposite, meaning that we would expect the field size to be smaller and thus to correspond to e.g. fields used in FRI-based proving systems.

In the Plonk case, additions have a non-negligible cost during verification. As a consequence, when ℓ is at most equal to 4, we use linear layers requiring a number of additions as small as possible. To this end, we adapt results from [21] where Duval and Leurent present generic matrix constructions with a minimal number

---

[5] Recall that the branching number of a linear permutation L is the minimum over $x \neq 0$ of $\text{hw}(x) + \text{hw}(L(x))$, where $\text{hw}(x)$ denotes the Hamming weight of x.

of additions. Their goal was to limit the number of XORs needed to implement a linear layer, which was especially welcome in the context of lightweight cryptography. In fact, one of their matrices has been used by the designers of Saturnin [17] precisely for this reason. More generally, we think this surprising connection between lightweight and arithmetization-oriented symmetric cryptography is interesting in itself: limiting the total number of additions can be important in both cases. As the approach of [21] is general enough that their matrices can work in most fields, we thus opt to use their matrices. In practice, when $\ell \in \{2, 3, 4\}$, we use the matrix $\mathcal{M}_x^\ell$ where

$$\mathcal{M}_x^2 = \begin{bmatrix} 1 & g \\ g & g^2+1 \end{bmatrix}, \ \mathcal{M}_x^3 = \begin{bmatrix} g+1 & 1 & g+1 \\ 1 & 1 & g \\ g & 1 & 1 \end{bmatrix}, \ \mathcal{M}_x^4 = \begin{bmatrix} 1 & g^2 & g^2 & 1+g \\ 1+g & g+g^2 & g^2 & 1+2g \\ g & 1+g & 1 & g \\ g & 1+2g & 1+g & 1+g \end{bmatrix}.$$

If $\ell = 1$, then there is a unique column in the internal state, so $\mathcal{M}_x^1$ is the identity.

Low-addition implementations are shown in [13, App. C], and the corresponding diagrams are given in Fig. 7. As [21] contains several different matrices for each number of inputs, we based our matrices on their candidates that have the lowest number of additions, and the least symmetries.

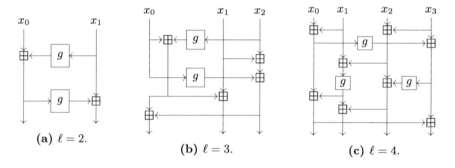

(a) $\ell = 2$.

(b) $\ell = 3$.

(c) $\ell = 4$.

Fig. 7. Diagram representations of $\mathcal{M}_x$.

In the AIR (STARK) case, linear operations are essentially free. Thus, the dominating constraint on a linear layer is its native implementation cost, i.e. the time it takes for a C or Rust program to evaluate $\mathcal{M}_x(x)$. To minimize this cost, we need to minimize the value of the coefficients appearing in the matrix. To this end, we use the circulant matrix where the first row is the smallest in the lexicographic order, and such that the overall matrix is MDS. A script implementing this generation method is provided in [13, App. C].

Pseudo-Hadamard Transform $\mathcal{P}$. To destroy some undesirable involutive patterns at the S-box level, we use a linear layer, namely the Pseudo-Hadamard transform (PHT), to have diffusion on the rows. In particular, this means that we still have a linear layer when $\ell = 1$. The PHT has good properties since it can be easily implemented with: $Y \leftarrow Y + X$ and $X \leftarrow X + Y$ and is also relevant against algebraic attacks (see Sect. 6.2).

S-box Layer $\mathcal{S}$. Let $\mathcal{H}$ be an open `Flystel` operating over $\mathbb{F}_q^2$. Then we let

$$\mathcal{S}(X,Y) = \big(\mathcal{H}(x_0, y_0), ..., \mathcal{H}(x_{\ell-1}, y_{\ell-1})\big) ,$$

as summarized in Fig. 5d. A `Flystel` instance is defined by 4 parameters, regardless of whether it is a `Flystel`$_p$ or `Flystel`$_2$: the exponent α, the multiplier β, and the two added constants γ and δ. First, as mentioned in Sect. 4.3, we let $\beta = g$: setting $\beta = 1$ would lead to the invariant space (see [13, App. A.3]) having equation (x^2, x), which we deem too simple; g is then the most natural non-trivial constant. Furthermore, in order to break the symmetry of the `Flystel`, we impose that $\gamma \neq \delta$. We thus let $\gamma = 0$ and $\delta = g^{-1}$ as this value is both different from 1 and g while retaining a simple definition.

All that remains is to choose the exponent α. If $q = 2^n$, then we let $\alpha = 3$: we have to use a Gold exponent (i.e. of the shape $2^k + 1$), and 3 always works since n is odd. Otherwise, when q is prime, the process is a bit more involved as a higher value allows using fewer rounds to thwart Gröbner-basis-based attacks, but is also more expensive. Users should use the value of α that yields the most efficient algorithm according to their metrics.

5.2   Higher Level Algorithms

Anemoi. The `Anemoi` permutation iterates n_r rounds of the round function described in Fig. 6, followed by a call to the linear layer $\mathcal{M}$:

$$\texttt{Anemoi}_{q,\alpha,\ell} = \mathcal{M} \circ \mathsf{R}_{n_r-1} \circ ... \circ \mathsf{R}_0 .$$

In symmetric cryptography, we usually *remove* outer linear layers, e.g. in the AES. That is because they don't contribute to the cryptographic strength of a block cipher (e.g. can be removed "for free" by an adversary). In the case of a sponge construction however, the adversary only controls a part of the state, namely the outer part (the rate). Thus, starting/finishing with a diffusion layer ensures that this control is spread across the full state in a way which is not aligned with the non-linear layer. A similar goal could be achieved using *indirect injection*, as is done in `Esch` [5].

The number of rounds n_r is computed using the following rule that is derived from our security analysis in Sect. 6.

More precisely, we focus on algebraic attacks since it appears to be the bottleneck. Indeed, we only need to activate few S-boxes to prevent statistical attacks. In prime characteristic we have an upper bound that is $(\alpha - 1)/p^2$ for the probability of a differential transition for one S-box, and that is conjectured to be $\log p/p$ for a linear transition. In the case where $q = 2^n$, similar arguments hold: the best differential probability is $4/2^{2n}$, and the best linear probability is around

2^{-n} (see [13, App. A] for more details). Let s be the required security level, and (q, ℓ, α) be the parameters imposed by the use case. As we believe that a construction with more branches gives more freedom to the attacker, we choose a security margin that increases with the size of the internal state, but setting a maximum of 5 additional rounds. In Sect. 6.2, we study two models for algebraic attacks. We fix the number of rounds by considering the first model, which is easier to study, and add a security margin of 2 rounds to take into account the second model. Whilst it is not clear whether the second model actually outperforms the first, its complexity is more difficult to estimate and we opt to increase the safety margin as a conservative measure. Then the number of rounds n_r is the smallest value satisfying both of the following conditions:

$$n_r \;\geq\; \max\left\{ 8 \;,\; \underbrace{\min(5, 1 + \ell)}_{\text{security margin}} \;+\; \underbrace{2 + \min\left\{ r \in \mathbb{N} \;\middle|\; \mathcal{C}_{alg(r)} \geq 2^s \right\}}_{\text{to prevent algebraic attacks, see Sect. 6.2}} \right\} \;,\;\; (2)$$

where $\mathcal{C}_{alg(r)} = \binom{4\ell r + \kappa_\alpha}{2\ell r}^2$ when $q = p$ and $\mathcal{C}_{alg(r)} = \ell r \cdot 9^{2\ell r}$ when $q = 2^n$.

We compute the number of rounds needed both for a security level of 128 bits (Table 1a), and of 256 bits (Table 1b). Note that the values of the digest size h and of the state size $2\ell n = 2\ell \log_2(q)$ must be coherent with the desired security level.

Table 1. Number of Rounds of Anemoi.

α	3	5	7	11
$\ell = 1$	21	21	20	19
$\ell = 2$	14	14	13	13
$\ell = 3$	12	12	12	11
$\ell = 4$	12	12	11	11
$\ell = 6$	10	10	10	10
$\ell = 8$	10	10	9	9

(a) When $s = 128$.

α	3	5	7	11
$\ell = 1$	37	37	36	35
$\ell = 2$	22	22	21	21
$\ell = 3$	17	17	17	17
$\ell = 4$	16	16	15	15
$\ell = 6$	13	13	13	13
$\ell = 8$	12	12	11	11

(b) When $s = 256$.

AnemoiSponge. This function is a "regular" hash function, in the sense that it should be able to process messages of arbitrary length. We therefore rely on the sponge construction detailed in Sect. 3, where r words are used as the rate, c are used as the capacity, and where the permutation is the Anemoi instance operating on $\mathbb{F}_q^{r+c}$. Note that the inner workings of Anemoi imply that $r+c$ must be even.

AnemoiJive. We can construct a compression function mapping b-to-1 vectors of $\mathbb{F}_q^m$ elements, using Jive_b and an Anemoi instance operating on bm elements of $\mathbb{F}_q$. The only constraint is, again, that bm must be even.

Security Claims. All the Anemoi permutations generated as defined above can be used safely to construct cryptographic primitives with the given security level. In particular, we make a "hermetic sponge" claim about all the hash functions AnemoiSponge generated as above, and we claim that all the AnemoiJive functions are secure b-to-1 compression functions (provided of course that the state size is chosen correctly).

5.3   Specific Instances

In this section, we present some examples of functions in the Anemoi family that are defined over different fields, aim for different APIs (both AnemoiSponge and AnemoiJive), and for a security level of 127 bits.

We consider the case of the BLS12-381 curve, in which case $(\lceil \log_2(q) \rceil, \alpha, g) = (255, 5, 7)$, and the case of the BN-254 curve, in which case $(\lceil \log_2(q) \rceil, \alpha, g) = (254, 5, 2)$. In both cases, we aim for 127 bits of security. We decided to consider these two curves because they have been historically used in SNARKs and have been deployed in production in projects that use Arithmetization-Oriented hash functions like ZCash or Ethereum.

AnemoiJive.   AnemoiJive-BLS12-381 and AnemoiJive-BN-254 are Merkle Compression functions mapping two elements of $\mathbb{F}_q$ to a unique one. In order to reach a security level of 127 bits, $\ell = 1$ is sufficient in both cases. The underlying permutations of the compression functions then use the following components.

S-box. $\mathcal{H}$ uses the parameters g and α corresponding to the elliptic curve.
Linear layer. As $\ell = 1$, we use the Pseudo-Hadamard transform:

$$\begin{bmatrix} 2 & 1 \\ 1 & 1 \end{bmatrix} \tag{3}$$

Round Constants. These are generated as described in Section 5.1.
Number of Rounds. Using Eq. (2), we obtain that 19 rounds are needed for a security level of 127 bits.

Round r is then defined as $\mathsf{R}_r : (x, y) \mapsto \mathcal{H} \circ \mathcal{M}(x + c_r, y + d_r)$, and we define the compression functions as follows. Let (x, y) be the input, and P be the Anemoi instance defined by $P := \mathcal{M} \circ \mathsf{R}_{18} \circ \ldots \circ \mathsf{R}_0$. Then $\mathsf{AnemoiJive}(x, y)$ is evaluated as follows: first, let $(u, v) \leftarrow P(x, y)$, then, return $x + y + u + v$.

Security Claims. The best way to find collisions in AnemoiJive-BLS12-381 (respectively AnemoiJive-BN-254) is to rely on a generic collision search. Since the output is an element of $\mathbb{F}_q$ with $\log_2(q) \geq 254$, this is expected to require about 2^{127} function calls on average.

AnemoiSponge. AnemoiSponge-BLS12-381 and AnemoiSponge-BN-254 are hash functions mapping a sequence $\{x_i\}_{0 \le i < m}$ of elements of $\mathbb{F}_q$ to an element of $\mathbb{F}_q$, where m is a positive integer. It is constructed using a sponge which relies on Anemoi as the permutation. We aim to provide about 127 bits of security, meaning that a capacity of 1 word of $\mathbb{F}_q$ is enough in both cases. We then pick an identical rate, so that $r = c = 1$, and thus $\ell = 1$. The permutations used are then the same as for AnemoiJive-BLS12-381 and AnemoiJive-BN-254.

Security Claims. We claim that AnemoiSponge-BLS12-381 and AnemoiSponge-BN-254 provide 127 bits of security against all known attacks.

6 Security Analysis

The security of AnemoiSponge and AnemoiJive is reduced to the security of their inner permutation, namely the Anemoi family. In this section, we argue that the latter has sufficient security level.

6.1 "Classical" Attacks

We call "classical" attacks those that have been used to target algorithms designed over $(\mathbb{F}_2)^n$. As we argue below, we do not expect those to be a significant problem. More detailed arguments are provided in [13, App. A].

Statistical attacks like differential and linear cryptanalysis exploit patterns that exist at the S-box level, and which are then propagated through the linear layers to form so-called "trails". As the Flystel has excellent differential and linear properties, we do not expect those to pose a threat (especially given that our linear layers are MDS).

For integral attacks and invariant subspaces, we rely on the fact that our round structure is not "aligned", meaning that the non-linear and linear layers operate over different alphabets (the columns and the rows). As a consequence, the propagation of the patterns exploited by these attacks is hindered. Similarly, thanks to the MDS matrix, truncated differentials, boomerang attacks and MitM attacks also do not pose a threat.

We refer the reader to [13, App. A] for a more detailed security analysis of the proposed constructions with respect to classical attacks.

6.2 Algebraic Attacks

Gröbner basis attacks may constitute the main threat as is usually the case for this type of primitives. Since we are mainly interested in a minimal condition on the number of rounds to reach a security of 2^s bits, we allow ourselves to *underestimate* complexity in several places, out of caution. We focus on the following version of the CICO (Constrained Input Constrained Output) problem, stated for $\ell = 1$:

Definition 3. *Let* $P : \mathbb{F}_q^2 \to \mathbb{F}_q^2$ *be a permutation. The* CICO *problem consists in finding* $(y_{in}, y_{out}) \in \mathbb{F}_q^2$ *such that* $P(0, y_{in}) = (0, y_{out})$.

Intermediate Variables. There are plenty of ways to model CICO as an algebraic system. We start from the one which consists in introducing equations and variables at each round. Such an approach was already proposed to study similar arithmetization-oriented primitives [8,20,31]. It applies to `Anemoi` for any $\ell \geq 1$ but for practical reasons a large part of our experiments has been restricted to $\ell = 1$. We now present our analysis of this particular case but we will also indicate how to deal with several columns. For $0 \leq j \leq n_r - 1$, let us define f_j and g_j by

$$(x_{j+1}, y_{j+1}) = \mathsf{R}_j(x_j, y_j) \Leftrightarrow \begin{cases} f_j := f(x_j, y_j, x_{j+1}, y_{j+1}) = 0 \\ g_j := g(x_j, y_j, x_{j+1}, y_{j+1}) = 0, \end{cases}$$

where R_j is the round function and where f and g are closely related to the verification equations.

Modeling 1. *We consider the system* $\mathcal{F} \subset \mathbb{F}_q[x_0, \ldots, x_{n_r}, y_0, \ldots, y_{n_r}]$ *containing the round equations* f_j *and* g_j *for* $0 \leq j \leq n_r - 1$.

The CICO system $\mathcal{F}_{\mathsf{CICO}}$ is simply Modeling 1 in which we fix $x_0 = 0$ and $x_{n_r} = 0$. This system can be seen as containing $2n_r$ equations and variables when $\ell = 1$ and $2\ell n_r$ in the general case. To solve it, we apply the standard *zero-dimensional* strategy:

1. Compute a Gröbner basis $\mathcal{G}_{\mathrm{drl}}$ for a DRL ordering [36, Definition 1.4.3],
2. Compute a new Gröbner basis $\mathcal{G}_{\mathrm{lex}}$ for the LEX ordering by using the FGLM algorithm [23] on $\mathcal{G}_{\mathrm{drl}}$.

For Step 1, the running time of Gröbner basis algorithms such as F4 [24] or F5 [25] is usually estimated by evaluating the *solving degree* of the system denoted by d_{solv}. This degree can be informally defined as the maximal degree of a polynomial which occurs during the Gröbner basis computation. Once d_{solv} is known, a generic estimate for the cost of F4/F5 is

$$\mathcal{O}\left(\binom{d_{\mathrm{solv}} + n_v}{n_v}^{\omega}\right) \tag{4}$$

field operations, where n_v is our number of variables and where $2 \leq \omega \leq 3$ is a linear algebra constant. We stress that this estimation is heuristic and it is an upper bound that does not take into account the structure or the sparsity of the given Macaulay matrices. In particular, to use it as a guidance, we will adopt the conservative $\omega = 2$ for the linear algebra constant. Regarding Step 2, the complexity of FGLM is in $\mathcal{O}(n_v \cdot \deg(I_{\mathsf{CICO}})^{\omega})$, where $I_{\mathsf{CICO}} := \langle \mathcal{F}_{\mathsf{CICO}} \rangle$ is the ideal generated by the system and where $\deg(I_{\mathsf{CICO}})$ is the *degree* of this ideal.

Characteristic 2. In even characteristic, we derive the number of rounds from the following Estimate 1.

Estimate 1. *We estimate the cost of solving* $\mathcal{F}_{\mathsf{CICO}}$ *in even characteristic by one of the FGLM steps. This step has complexity*

$$\mathcal{O}(\ell n_r \cdot 9^{\omega \ell n_r}),$$

where ℓ *is the number of columns and* ω *is the linear algebra exponent from the FGLM algorithm.*

More details are provided in [13, App. B.1] the full version of this work, where we focus on the case $\ell = 1$. In short, Estimate 1 comes from the fact that the cost of the Gröbner basis computation on $\mathcal{F}_{\mathsf{CICO}}$ is mostly independent from the number of rounds and that the cost of FGLM can be approximated by the one on a generic system containing $2\ell n_r$ cubic equations.

Odd Characteristic. The $\mathcal{F}_{\mathsf{CICO}}$ system behaves differently in odd characteristic since the dominant cost corresponds to the Gröbner basis computation. We derive the number of rounds from the following Estimate 2, where $d_{\exp}$ is the experimental solving degree of $\mathcal{F}_{\mathsf{CICO}}$ given in Conjecture 1.

Conjecture 1 (From experiments for $\ell = 1$**).** *We have*

$$d_{exp} \geq 2n_r + \kappa_\alpha,$$

where κ_α *is a constant depending only on* α*. We found* $\kappa_3 = 1$*,* $\kappa_5 = 2$*,* $\kappa_7 = 4$*,* $\kappa_9 = 7$ *and* $\kappa_\alpha = 9$ *for*[6] $\alpha \geq 11$*.*

Estimate 2. *In odd characteristic, we estimate the cost of solving* $\mathcal{F}_{\mathsf{CICO}}$ *for* $\ell = 1$ *by one of the Gröbner basis steps. By using Equation* (4)*, it has complexity*

$$\mathcal{O}\left(\left(\binom{d_{exp} + 2n_r}{2n_r}\right)^\omega\right),$$

where d_{exp} *is given in Conjecture 1 and where* ω *is a linear algebra constant.*

[13, App. B.2] contains more details on Conjecture 1 and Estimate 2. There, we also compare $\mathcal{F}_{\mathsf{CICO}}$ to another system denoted by $\mathcal{P}_{\mathsf{CICO}}$ which seems to take advantage of the particularities of our design but which does not seem to bring an improvement, at least asymptotically. Still, we add 2 extra rounds on top of Estimate 2 to ensure that these equations will not jeopardize security if exploited in a more ingenious way. We find it interesting that the complexities corresponding to the resolution of each system are extremely similar, despite their a priori significantly different structures.

When $\ell > 1$, the number of equations and variables in $\mathcal{F}_{\mathsf{CICO}}$ is naturally multiplied by ℓ and thus experiments were extremely difficult to conduct. We generalize Conjecture 1 to $\ell > 1$ by replacing $2n_r$ by $2\ell n_r$ everywhere, which is natural when looking at the expressions of the Macaulay bound. Similarly, we note that the bounds given for Rescue in [8] exhibit this extra ℓ factor. We adjust the number of variables $n_v := 2\ell n_r$ accordingly to obtain the final estimate.

---

[6] We would expect the value of κ_α to keep increasing with α but the computations needed to estimate it become too costly as α increases.

7 Benchmarks

In this section, we compare various instances of Rescue–Prime, POSEIDON, GRIFFIN and Anemoi with respect to SNARK metrics: R1CS (Sect. 7.1) and Plonk (Sect. 7.2), and STARK: AIR (Sect. 7.3). For Plonk performance, we will also conduct a comparison with Reinforced Concrete.

Due to the increasing number of projects revolving around zk-STARKs, which do not require an algebraic group with large underlying fields, we also illustrate native performance comparison of 2-to-1 compression functions based on Rescue–Prime, POSEIDON and Anemoi on a 64-bit field used in various projects [1,43].

To do so, we need to set the parameters. Then, let $\mathbb{F}_q$, where $q = p$, be a prime field, and let t be the number of field elements we operate on ($t = 2\ell$ for Anemoi). Besides, let s denote the security level in bits, n_r the number of rounds, and $\mathcal{C}_\alpha$ the cost of an exponentiation $x \mapsto x^\alpha$.

Rescue–Prime requires $1.5 \cdot \max\{5, \lceil (s + 2)/4t \rceil\}$ rounds when $\alpha = 3$ and $1.5 \cdot \max\{5, \lceil (s + 3)/5.5t \rceil\}$ rounds when $\alpha = 5$ (see [3,41]). POSEIDON has $n_r = \mathsf{RF} + \mathsf{RP}$ rounds. While the bound is a complex expression, in our setting and for the safety margin recommended by the authors, it holds that $\mathsf{RF} = 8$, and that RP must be higher than (or equal to) $1.075 \cdot (\lceil \log_\alpha(2) \cdot \min\{s, \log_2(p)\} \rceil + \lceil \log_\alpha t \rceil - \mathsf{RF})$. GRIFFIN requires at least $\lceil 1.2 \max\{6, 1 + R_{\mathsf{GB}}\} \rceil$ rounds where R_{GB} is the smallest integer such that $\min\left\{ \binom{R_{\mathsf{GB}} \cdot (\alpha+t)+1}{1+t \cdot R_{\mathsf{GB}}}, \binom{\alpha^{R_{\mathsf{GB}}}+1+R_{\mathsf{GB}}}{1+R_{\mathsf{GB}}} \right\} \geq 2^{s/2}$.

In the following, we use the n_r values from Sect. 5.2.

7.1 R1CS Systems

We first estimate the number of constraints for R1CS. Using the *closed Flystel* of Fig. 3b, we obtain the following verification equations for the S-Box:

$$\begin{cases} (y - v)^\alpha + \beta y^2 + \gamma - x = 0 \\ (y - v)^\alpha + \beta v^2 + \delta - u = 0 \ . \end{cases} \tag{5}$$

Then, evaluating one S-Box costs $\mathcal{C}_\alpha$ constraints to obtain $(y - v)^\alpha$, and 1 constraint for each of the two quadratics. For Rescue–Prime and POSEIDON, each S-Box costs $\mathcal{C}_\alpha$ constraints. For GRIFFIN, each S-Box costs $2 \cdot \mathcal{C}_\alpha$ constraints for the first two words, and 1 constraint for each squaring of L and each word of the remaining state. As a consequence, when using Rescue–Prime, POSEIDON, GRIFFIN and Anemoi as hash functions in sponge mode, the number of constraints is respectively $\mathcal{C}_\alpha \cdot 2t \cdot n_r$, $\mathcal{C}_\alpha \cdot (t\mathsf{RF} + \mathsf{RP})$, $(\mathcal{C}_\alpha + t - 2) \cdot 2n_r$ and $(\mathcal{C}_\alpha + 2) \cdot (\frac{t}{2} \cdot n_r)$.

We compare the number of constraints for those four schemes in Table 2. As we can see, the Anemoi permutations are consistently much more efficient than both POSEIDON and Rescue–Prime by about a factor 2. Anemoi and GRIFFIN are on par, and Anemoi takes the advantage for $\alpha = 3$.

Table 2. Total R1CS, Plonk and AIR cost for several hash functions ($s = 128$).

	t	$Rescue'$	POSEIDON	GRIFFIN	Anemoi
	2	208	198	-	76
	3	216	214	96	-
R1CS	4	224	232	112	96
	6	216	264	-	120
	8	256	296	176	160
	2	312	380	-	189
	3	432	594	197	-
Plonk	4	560	824	260	308
	6	756	1344	-	444
	8	1152	1920	574	624
	2	156	300	-	126
	3	162	324	144	-
AIR	4	168	348	168	168
	6	162	396	-	216
	8	192	480	264	288

(a) when $\alpha = 3$.

	t	$Rescue'$	POSEIDON	GRIFFIN	Anemoi
	2	240	216	-	95
	3	252	240	96	-
R1CS	4	264	264	110	120
	6	288	315	-	150
	8	384	363	162	200
	2	320	344	-	210
	3	420	512	173	-
Plonk	4	528	696	222	336
	6	768	1125	-	480
	8	1280	1609	492	672
	2	200	360	-	210
	3	210	405	180	-
AIR	4	220	440	220	280
	6	240	540	-	360
	8	320	640	360	480

(b) when $\alpha = 5$.

7.2 Plonk

For ease of exposition, we will consider rounds to be shifted so that constant additions and linear operations come after the S-box. As for R1CS, we again investigate Eq. (5). In standard Plonk (i.e. 3 wires and no custom gates), evaluating an S-Box costs 1 constraint to derive $w = y - v$ and $\mathcal{C}_\alpha$ constraints to obtain w^α, 1 constraint for each of the two quadratics, and 1 each for the sums on x, u. The total cost for the S-box layer with 3 wires is $(\mathcal{C}_\alpha + 5)\frac{t}{2}$.

The constant additions can be folded into the $n_r + 1$ linear layers and can thus be disregarded. For $t = 2$, the linear layer consists of the PHT, which requires 2 constraints. For $t > 2$, the linear layer itself consists of 2 separate matrix-vector multiplications, each producing $\frac{t}{2}$ sums of $\frac{t}{2}$ terms, requiring $t \cdot (\frac{t}{2} - 1)$ constraints, in addition to a cost of t constraints for the PHT. However, the number of constraints per matrix multiplication can be reduced by choosing MDS matrices lowering the number of additions. For the matrices given for $t = 6$ and $t = 8$ in Sect. 5.1, we have respectively a cost of 10 and 16 per linear layer.

POSEIDON uses simpler S-Boxes, each costing $\mathcal{C}_\alpha$ constraints. Full rounds use t S-boxes whereas partial ones use only one. Using the optimisation described in the Supplementary Material of [30], the linear layer costs $t \cdot (t - 1)$ constraints for the full rounds and $2t - 2$ constraints for the partial rounds. Rescue–Prime uses t standard and t inverted S-Boxes, each costing $\mathcal{C}_\alpha$. Each round also utilizes 2 independent linear layers each costing $t \cdot (t - 1)$ constraints for all rounds.

For GRIFFIN, the cost of the S-BOX is $2 \cdot \mathcal{C}_\alpha + 3 + 4 \cdot (t - 3)$. Regarding the linear layer, the matrix used for $t = 3$ can be computed in 5 constraints. For $t = 4$, the cost of one multiplication by the matrix they chose is 8. By observing intermediate variables from the S-BOX computation which can be reused in the linear layer computation, GRIFFIN gives 222 constraints for $t = 4$ (resp. 492 for $t = 8$).

We then compare the number of constraints for these four schemes in Table 2. Anemoi is consistently ahead of Rescue–Prime and POSEIDON with a significant margin, but for larger t, our performances are slightly worse than GRIFFIN, since our strategy to compute the security margin is different: we try to take into account the greater freedom given by the larger number of branches, which impacts our number of rounds.

Plonk Optimizations. One of the more fruitful, but also challenging aspects of Plonk is its ability to extend the expressive power of the constraints at a reasonable cost. In the analysis, the linear layer cost dominates that of the S-Boxes. This is particularly impactful for POSEIDON, as the efficiency benefit of its partial rounds is negated. The recent work of Ambrona et al. [4] presents a set of generic and tailored optimizations for Plonk applicable to POSEIDON.

While an exhaustive comparison of optimization options is beyond the scope of this work, real-world usage implies that a reasonable set of optimizations have been applied before deployment. For this reason, we perform a minimal comparison between: POSEIDON as optimized by Ambrona et al., and Reinforced Concrete [29] which was built with Plonk optimizations in mind, and Anemoi. As POSEIDON and Reinforced Concrete are sponge based we use $s = 128, \alpha = 5$ and $t = 3$ to represent popular deployment choices, while we set $t = 2$ for Anemoi, using the Jive$_2$ mode For comparison we also extrapolate a Jive$_2$ version of POSEIDON with the optimizations of [4], and Reinforced Concrete.

We use one of the constraint systems used by Ambrona et al. [4]: a 3-wire constraint system with a x^5, as well as selectors for the next constraint wires:

$$q_L.a + q_R.b + q_O.c + q_M.a.b + q_5.c^5 + q_{L'}.a' + q_{R'}.b' + q_{O'}.c' .$$

At a base level, the relations we need to express for one AnemoiJive$_2$ round are

1. $y - v - w = 0$
2. $w^5 + \beta yy + \gamma - x = 0$
3. $w^5 + \beta vv + \delta - u = 0$

4. $\tilde{u} - 2u - v - \rho = 0$

5. $\tilde{v} - u - v - \kappa = 0$

where $\tilde{u}, \tilde{v}$ are the values of u, v after the linear layer and ρ, κ are derived from round constants. We can save one constraint by calculating $\tilde{u}$ directly and eliminating u. We also need to make sure that the relations fit into the available wires, and make sure that the last constraint leaves the "next constraint" wires free, so that each set of round constraints can be followed by any constraint without restriction. To accomplish this, we also need to perform some reordering. Setting $\rho' = \rho + 2\delta$ and $\kappa' = \kappa - \rho$, the end result is:

1. $w^5 + \beta yy + \gamma - x = 0$,   for: $(a, b, c) = (y, y, w)$, $(a', b,' c') = (x, \_, \_)$,
2. $y - v - w = 0$,   for: $(a, b, c) = (x, y, w)$, $(a', b,' c') = (v, \_, \_)$,
3. $2w^5 + 2\beta vv + \rho' + v - \tilde{u} = 0$, for: $(a, b, c) = (v, v, w)$, $(a', b,' c') = (\tilde{u}, \_, \_)$,
4. $\tilde{v} - \tilde{u} + u - \kappa' = 0$,   for: $(a, b, c) = (\tilde{u}, \tilde{v}, u)$, $(a', b,' c') = (\_, \_, \_)$.

Thus, we are able to perform one AnemoiJive round in 4 constraints, and 2 additional constraints to account for the initial linear layer. We can fold the final

Jive$_2$ addition into the final constraint (using the "next" wires), and ensuring the initial layer constraints are directly below it. With four wires, we can eliminate w, by having the 5th power gate operate on $y - v$. Rounds are reduced to 3 constraints, and we need only 1 extra constraint for the first linear layer as we handle x_0 inline.

Table 3. Constraints comparison of several hash functions for Plonk with an additional custom gate to compute x^5. We fix $s = 128$, and prime field sizes of 256.

	t	Constraints
POSEIDON	3	110
	2	88
Reinforced Concrete	3	378
	2	236
GRIFFIN	3	125
AnemoiJive	2	86

(a) With 3 wires.

	t	Constraints
POSEIDON	3	98
	2	82
Reinforced Concrete	3	267
	2	174
GRIFFIN	3	111
AnemoiJive	2	64

(b) With 4 wires.

We summarize our findings in Table 3. We extrapolate the $t = 2$ costs for POSEIDON and Reinforced Concrete by assuming a Jive$_2$ mode of operation is feasible at no additional overhead or increase in rounds. Against the next-best proposed system, POSEIDON for $t = 3$ as optimized by [4] we achieve a 21% reduction when using 3 wires and 35% when using 4. We note that while the costs between POSEIDON, Anemoi and GRIFFIN are directly comparable as they use the same features (namely x^5 and "next constraint" selectors), Reinforced Concrete leverages lookup tables [26, 29] instead. We do note that by [4, Table 2], the additional overhead (compared to standard Plonk) for the custom gates we describe is between 10% and 40%.

Plonk Optimisations with an Additional Quadratic Custom Gate. We can go further in the optimisation given above by extending Plonk with a custom gate to compute the square of a wire, which adds a negligible overhead to the prover and the verifier time. In the 3-wires setting, having the quadratic custom gate on the wire b frees a wire in the constraints given above and allow us to compute two rounds in 5 constraints as described below[7], giving a total number of constraints of 56.

1. $w_0^2 + w_0 y_0 + w_0 - x_0 - y_0 + y_1 + q_c,$ where: $(a, b, c) = (y_0, w_0, x_0)$
   and $(a', b,' c') = (y_1, \_, \_)$,

2. $w_1^2 + w_1 y_1 - w_0 + w_1 + x_2 + y_0 - y_1 + q_c,$ where: $(a, b, c) = (y_1, w_1, w_0)$
   and $(a', b,' c') = (y_0, x_2, \_)$,

---

[7] For readability, the selectors values have been omitted.

3. $w_1 - x_2 - y_1 + y_2 - q_c,$ where: $(a, b, c) = (y_0, x_2, y_2)$
     and $(a', b,' c') = (w_1, y_1, \_)$,

4. $w_1^5 + y_1^2 - w_0 + y_0 - y_1 + q_c,$ where: $(a, b, c) = (w_1, y_1, \_)$
     and $(a', b,' c') = (w_0, y_0, \_)$.

5. $w_0^5 + y_0^2 - x_0 + q_c,$ where: $(a, b, c) = (w_0, y_0, x_0)$
     and $(a', b,' c') = (\_, \_, \_)$.

7.3   AIR

Finally, we also study the performance of `Anemoi` in the Algebraic Intermediate Representation (AIR) arithmetization used in STARKs [6]. Here, the relevant quantities are: the width of the computation state w, the number of computation steps T, and the maximum degree of the constraints $d_{\max}$. While there are several ways to estimate the cost of a given AIR program given the above quantities, we will consider the total cost to be expressed as $w \cdot T \cdot d_{\max}$, following [3].

For Rescue–Prime, GRIFFIN and `Anemoi`, we have $w = t$, $T = n_r$ and $d_{\max} = \alpha$. For POSEIDON, we have $w = t$, $T = \mathsf{RF} + \lceil \mathsf{RP}/t \rceil$ and $d_{\max} = \alpha$.

We then compare the total cost for these four schemes in Table 2. `Anemoi` and GRIFFIN are quite similar, and close to Rescue–Prime.

7.4   Native Performance

Outside of proving systems, `Anemoi` performance can challenge other algebraic hash functions, especially in Merkle trees thanks to its Jive mode. In particular in STARKs settings where one can use small cryptographic fields, `Anemoi` offers the best balance in terms of native evaluation and number of constraints. In Table 4, we illustrate the running time of a 2-to-1 compression method with `Anemoi` Jive, Rescue–Prime, POSEIDON and GRIFFIN over the 64 bits prime field $\mathbb{F}_p$ with $p = 2^{64} - 2^{32} + 1$. Each instantiation has a 4 field elements (32 bytes) digest size to ensure 128 bits security[8]. Rescue–Prime, POSEIDON and GRIFFIN have been evaluated with two instantiations: a regular of width 12 with rate 8, capable of compressing two digests with one permutation using the sponge construction, and an instantiation of width 8 with rate 4 using Jive as compression mode. All experiments were performed on an *Intel(R) Core(TM) i7-9750H CPU @ 2.60 GHz*. We present average times in microseconds of each experiment running for 5 s. Standard deviations are negligible. All instantiations have been implemented in Rust.

In Table 5, we compare the native performance with Rescue–Prime, POSEIDON and GRIFFIN with a state size useful for applications like Merkle tree over the scalar field of BLS12-381. For small state size, the dominant computation for `Anemoi` (like Rescue–Prime and GRIFFIN) is $x^{1/d}$ and can be implemented using an appropriate addition chain. All experiments were performed on an *Intel(R)*

---

[8] We refer here to original instantiations, in opposition to a common practice in the industry to tweak parameters (typically the MDS matrix layer). All instantiations here are original, paper versions for fair comparison.

Table 4. Native performance comparison of 2-to-1 compression functions for $\mathbb{F}_p$ with $p = 2^{64} - 2^{32} + 1$. We fix $s = 128$. Times are given in μs. Rescue–Prime is denoted by RP.

RP-12	RP-8	POSEIDON-12	POSEIDON-8	GRIFFIN-12	GRIFFIN-8	Anemoi-8
15.67	9.13	5.87	2.69	2.87	2.59	4.21

Core(TM) i7-8565U CPU @ 1.80 GHz. We present average times in microseconds of each experiment running for 2 s. Standard deviations are in the order of tens of nanoseconds. Our implementation uses C via FFI through an OCaml binding, but this introduces a negligible overhead.

Table 5. Native performance comparison of a permutation for the scalar field of $BLS12 - 381$. We fix $s = 128$. GRIFFIN is instantiated with a state size of 3 and Anemoi, Rescue–Prime and POSEIDON with a state size of 2. Times are in μs.

Rescue–Prime	POSEIDON	GRIFFIN	Anemoi
206	9.2	74.18	128.29

8   Conclusion

We have made several contributions towards both the theoretical understanding and the practical use of arithmetization-oriented hash functions. Our main contribution is of course Anemoi, a family of permutations that are efficient across various arithmetization methods, yielding gains from 10% up to more than 50% depending on the context, over existing designs. Furthermore, in order to be able to design its main component, the Flystel structure, we had to first identify the link between arithmetization-orientation and CCZ-equivalence. We hope that functions such as the Flystel construction as well as similar ones will be studied by mathematicians as we believe those to be of independent interest.

Finally, we provided a new simple mode, Jive$_b$, which adds to the growing list of permutation-based modes of operation providing a b-to-1 compression function, of particular relevance in Merkle trees. It allows us to further improve upon the state-of-the-art, so that AnemoiJive requires only 56 Plonk constraints in total (when 3 wires and 2 custom gates are used), compared to the best sponge-based instance of POSEIDON which requires 98 constraints with 4 wires (or 110 with 3) and 1 custom gate. With only one custom gate, AnemoiJive requires 64 constraints for 4 wires (or 86 with 3).

Recent work by Liu et al. [35] has demonstrated the potential for further optimizations leveraging our design: by using 4 custom gates they are able to reduce the cost of a 4-to-1 Jive instance to just over 1 constraint per round (16 constraints for 14 rounds)[9]. This compares favorably to the highly optimized and customized version of POSEIDON specified in Mina [38] which performs 2:1 compression using 15 wires and 11 constraints (at 55 rounds, 5 rounds per constraint).

Acknowledgements. We thank the reviewers of CRYPTO 2023 for providing insightful comments which helped improve the clarity of this paper. In particular, we would like to thank the shepherd for their assistance in finalizing the paper. We are also grateful to Markulf Kohlweiss, Antoine Rondelet and Duncan Tebbs for proofreading an earlier draft of this paper, and for providing insightful comments and suggestions. Additionally, we extend our thanks to Duncan Tebbs for providing an independent estimation of the Flystel circuit cost in terms of R1CS constraints. The work of Léo Perrin is supported by the European Research Council (ERC, grant agreement no. 101041545 "ReSCALE"). We thank Tomer Ashur for pointing out a mistake in Fig. 1 in a previous version of the paper. We also thank Miguel Ambrona and Raphaël Toledo for the idea of the quadratic custom gate and their contribution to the Plonk implementation.

References

1. Polygon Miden. Repository, September 2022. https://github.com/maticnetwork/miden

2. Albrecht, M., Grassi, L., Rechberger, C., Roy, A., Tiessen, T.: MiMC: efficient encryption and cryptographic hashing with minimal multiplicative complexity. In: Cheon, J.H., Takagi, T. (eds.) ASIACRYPT 2016, Part I. LNCS, vol. 10031, pp. 191–219. Springer, Heidelberg (2016). https://doi.org/10.1007/978-3-662-53887-6_7

3. Aly, A., Ashur, T., Ben-Sasson, E., Dhooghe, S., Szepieniec, A.: Design of symmetric-key primitives for advanced cryptographic protocols. IACR Trans. Symm. Cryptol. **2020**(3), 1–45 (2020). https://doi.org/10.13154/tosc.v2020.i3.1-45

4. Ambrona, M., Schmitt, A.L., Toledo, R.R., Willems, D.: New optimization techniques for PlonK's arithmetization. Cryptology ePrint Archive, Paper 2022/462 (2022). https://eprint.iacr.org/2022/462

5. Beierle, C., et al.: Lightweight AEAD and hashing using the Sparkle permutation family. IACR Trans. Symm. Cryptol. **2020**(S1), 208–261 (2020). https://doi.org/10.13154/tosc.v2020.iS1.208-261

6. Ben-Sasson, E., Bentov, I., Horesh, Y., Riabzev, M.: Scalable, transparent, and post-quantum secure computational integrity. Cryptology ePrint Archive, Report 2018/046 (2018). https://eprint.iacr.org/2018/046

7. Ben-Sasson, E., et al.: Zerocash: decentralized anonymous payments from bitcoin. In: 2014 IEEE Symposium on Security and Privacy, pp. 459–474. IEEE Computer Society Press, May 2014. https://doi.org/10.1109/SP.2014.36

---

[9] Liu et al. originally utilized an earlier version of this work specifying 12 rounds in this setting.

8. Ben-Sasson, E., Goldberg, L., Levit, D.: Stark friendly hash - survey and recommendation. Cryptology ePrint Archive, Report 2020/948 (2020). https://ia.cr/2020/948

9. Bernstein, D.J.: The Salsa20 family of stream ciphers. In: Robshaw, M., Billet, O. (eds.) New Stream Cipher Designs. LNCS, vol. 4986, pp. 84–97. Springer, Heidelberg (2008). https://doi.org/10.1007/978-3-540-68351-3_8

10. Bertoni, G., Daemen, J., Peeters, M., Van Assche, G.: Keccak. In: Johansson, T., Nguyen, P.Q. (eds.) EUROCRYPT 2013. LNCS, vol. 7881, pp. 313–314. Springer, Heidelberg (2013). https://doi.org/10.1007/978-3-642-38348-9_19

11. Bertoni, G., Daemen, J., Peeters, M., Van Assche, G.: Sponge functions. In: ECRYPT Hash Workshop, vol. 9. Citeseer (2007)

12. Bos, J., Coster, M.: Addition chain heuristics. In: Brassard, G. (ed.) CRYPTO 1989. LNCS, vol. 435, pp. 400–407. Springer, New York (1990). https://doi.org/10.1007/0-387-34805-0_37

13. Bouvier, C., Briaud, P., Chaidos, P., Perrin, L., Salen, R., Velichkov, V., Willems, D.: New design techniques for efficient arithmetization-oriented hash functions: Anemoi permutations and Jive compression mode. Cryptology ePrint Archive, Paper 2022/840 (2022). https://eprint.iacr.org/2022/840

14. Bouvier, C., Briaud, P., Chaidos, P., Perrin, L., Velichkov, V.: Anemoi: exploiting the link between arithmetization-orientation and CCZ-equivalence. Cryptology ePrint Archive, Report 2022/840 (2022). https://eprint.iacr.org/2022/840

15. Budaghyan, L., Carlet, C., Pott, A.: New classes of almost bent and almost perfect nonlinear polynomials. IEEE Trans. Inf. Theor. $52(3)$, 1141–1152 (2006)

16. Canteaut, A., Duval, S., Perrin, L.: A generalisation of Dillon's APN permutation with the best known differential and nonlinear properties for all fields of size 2^{4k+2}. IEEE Trans. Inf. Theor. $63(11)$, 7575–7591 (2017). https://doi.org/10.1109/TIT.2017.2676807

17. Canteaut, A., et al.: Saturnin: a suite of lightweight symmetric algorithms for post-quantum security. IACR Trans. Symm. Cryptol. 2020(S1), 160–207 (2020). 10.13154/tosc.v2020.iS1.160-207

18. Canteaut, A., Perrin, L.: On CCZ-equivalence, extended-affine equivalence, and function twisting. Finite Fields Appl. 56, 209–246 (2019). https://doi.org/10.1016/j.ffa.2018.11.008

19. Carlet, C., Charpin, P., Zinoviev, V.: Codes, bent functions and permutations suitable for DES-like cryptosystems. Des. Codes Crypt. $15(2)$, 125–156 (1998)

20. Dobraunig, C., Grassi, L., Guinet, A., Kuijsters, D.: CIMINION: symmetric encryption based on Toffoli-gates over large finite fields. In: Canteaut, A., Standaert, F.-X. (eds.) EUROCRYPT 2021. LNCS, vol. 12697, pp. 3–34. Springer, Cham (2021). https://doi.org/10.1007/978-3-030-77886-6_1

21. Duval, S., Leurent, G.: MDS matrices with lightweight circuits. IACR Trans. Symm. Cryptol. $2018(2)$, 48–78 (2018). https://doi.org/10.13154/tosc.v2018.i2.48-78

22. Dworkin, M.: SHA-3 standard: permutation-based hash and extendable-output functions (2015-08-04 2015). https://doi.org/10.6028/NIST.FIPS.202

23. Faugère, J., Gianni, P., Lazard, D., Mora, T.: Efficient computation of zero-dimensional gröbner bases by change of ordering. J. Symbolic Comput. $16(4)$, 329–344 (1993). https://doi.org/10.1006/jsco.1993.1051. https://www.sciencedirect.com/science/article/pii/S0747717183710515

24. Faugère, J.C.: A new efficient algorithm for computing gröbner bases (f4). J. Pure Appl. Algebra $139(1)$, 61–88 (1999). https://doi.org/10.

1016/S0022-4049(99)00005-5. https://www.sciencedirect.com/science/article/pii/S0022404999000055

25. Faugère, J.C.: A new efficient algorithm for computing gröbner bases without reduction to zero (f5). In: Proceedings of the 2002 International Symposium on Symbolic and Algebraic Computation, ISSAC 2002, pp. 75–83. Association for Computing Machinery, New York (2002). https://doi.org/10.1145/780506.780516. https://doi.org/10.1145/780506.780516

26. Gabizon, A., Williamson, Z.J.: plookup: a simplified polynomial protocol for lookup tables. Cryptology ePrint Archive, Report 2020/315 (2020). https://eprint.iacr.org/2020/315

27. Goldwasser, S., Micali, S., Rackoff, C.: The knowledge complexity of interactive proof systems. SIAM J. Comput. **18**(1), 186–208 (1989). https://doi.org/10.1137/0218012

28. Grassi, L., Hao, Y., Rechberger, C., Schofnegger, M., Walch, R., Wang, Q.: A new Feistel approach meets fluid-SPN: Griffin for zero-knowledge applications. Cryptology ePrint Archive, Report 2022/403 (2022). https://eprint.iacr.org/2022/403

29. Grassi, L., Khovratovich, D., Lüftenegger, R., Rechberger, C., Schofnegger, M., Walch, R.: Reinforced concrete: a fast hash function for verifiable computation. In: Proceedings of the 2022 ACM SIGSAC Conference on Computer and Communications Security, CCS 2022, pp. 1323–1335. Association for Computing Machinery (2022). https://doi.org/10.1145/3548606.3560686

30. Grassi, L., Khovratovich, D., Rechberger, C., Roy, A., Schofnegger, M.: Poseidon: a new hash function for zero-knowledge proof systems. In: Bailey, M., Greenstadt, R. (eds.) USENIX Security 2021, pp. 519–535. USENIX Association, August 2021

31. Grassi, L., Øygarden, M., Schofnegger, M., Walch, R.: From farfalle to MEGAFONO via Ciminion: the PRF HYDRA for MPC applications. In: Hazay, C., Stam, M. (eds.) EUROCRYPT 2023, Part IV. LNCS, vol. 14007, pp. 255–286. Springer, Heidelberg, April 2023. https://doi.org/10.1007/978-3-031-30634-1_9

32. Groth, J.: On the size of pairing-based non-interactive arguments. In: Fischlin, M., Coron, J.S. (eds.) EUROCRYPT 2016, Part II. LNCS, May 2016, vol. 9666, pp. 305–326. Springer, Heidelberg (2016). https://doi.org/10.1007/978-3-662-49896-5_11

33. Hirose, S.: Sequential hashing with minimum padding. In: NIST Workshop on Lightweight Cryptography 2016. National Institute of Standards and Technology (NIST) (2016)

34. Li, Y., Tian, S., Yu, Y., Wang, M.: On the generalization of butterfly structure. IACR Trans. Symm. Cryptol. **2018**(1), 160–179 (2018). https://doi.org/10.13154/tosc.v2018.i1.160-179

35. Liu, J., et al.: An efficient verifiable state for zk-EVM and beyond from the Anemoi hash function. Cryptology ePrint Archive, Paper 2022/1487 (2022). https://eprint.iacr.org/2022/1487

36. Loustaunau, W.: An Introduction to Grobner Bases. American Mathematical Society (1994). https://books.google.is/books?id=Caoxi78WaIAC

37. McLoughlin, M.B.: addchain: cryptographic addition chain generation in go. Repository, October 2021. https://github.com/mmcloughlin/addchain. https://doi.org/10.5281/zenodo.5622943

38. Meckler, I., Rao, V., Ryan, M., Querol, A., Spadavecchia, J., Wong, D.: Mina book, kimchi specification. https://o1-labs.github.io/proof-systems/specs/kimchi.html#poseidon

39. Nyberg, K.: Differentially uniform mappings for cryptography. In: Helleseth, T. (ed.) EUROCRYPT 1993. LNCS, vol. 765, pp. 55–64. Springer, Heidelberg (1994). https://doi.org/10.1007/3-540-48285-7_6

40. Perrin, L., Udovenko, A., Biryukov, A.: Cryptanalysis of a theorem: decomposing the only known solution to the big APN problem. In: Robshaw, M., Katz, J. (eds.) CRYPTO 2016, Part II. LNCS, vol. 9815, pp. 93–122. Springer, Heidelberg (2016). https://doi.org/10.1007/978-3-662-53008-5_4

41. Szepieniec, A., Ashur, T., Dhooghe, S.: Rescue-prime: a standard specification (SoK). Cryptology ePrint Archive, Report 2020/1143 (2020). https://eprint.iacr.org/2020/1143

42. Szepieniec, A., Lemmens, A., Sauer, J.F., Threadbare, B.: The tip5 hash function for recursive starks. Cryptology ePrint Archive, Paper 2023/107 (2023). https://eprint.iacr.org/2023/107

43. Zero, P.: Plonky2. Repository, September 2022. https://github.com/mir-protocol/plonky2

Coefficient Grouping for Complex Affine Layers

Fukang Liu[1(✉)], Lorenzo Grassi[2], Clémence Bouvier[3,4], Willi Meier[5], and Takanori Isobe[6,7]

[1] Tokyo Institute of Technology, Tokyo, Japan
liu.f.ad@m.titech.ac.jp
[2] Ruhr University Bochum, Bochum, Germany
Lorenzo.Grassi@ruhr-uni-bochum.de
[3] Sorbonne University, Paris, France
clemence.bouvier@inria.fr
[4] Inria, Paris, France
[5] FHNW, Windisch, Switzerland
willi.meier@fhnw.ch
[6] University of Hyogo, Hyogo, Japan
takanori.isobe@ai.u-hyogo.ac.jp
[7] NICT, Tokyo, Japan

Abstract. Designing symmetric-key primitives for applications in Fully Homomorphic Encryption (FHE) has become important to address the issue of the ciphertext expansion. In such a context, cryptographic primitives with a low-AND-depth decryption circuit are desired. Consequently, quadratic nonlinear functions are commonly used in these primitives, including the well-known χ function over $\mathbb{F}_2^n$ and the power map over a large finite field $\mathbb{F}_{p^n}$. In this work, we study the growth of the algebraic degree for an SPN cipher over $\mathbb{F}_{2^n}^m$, whose S-box is defined as the combination of a power map $x \mapsto x^{2^d+1}$ and an $\mathbb{F}_2$-linearized affine polynomial $x \mapsto c_0 + \sum_{i=1}^{w} c_i x^{2^{h_i}}$ where $c_1, \ldots, c_w \neq 0$. Specifically, motivated by the fact that the original coefficient grouping technique published at EUROCRYPT 2023 becomes less efficient for $w > 1$, we develop a variant technique that can efficiently work for arbitrary w. With this new technique to study the upper bound of the algebraic degree, we answer the following questions from a theoretic perspective:

1. can the algebraic degree increase exponentially when $w = 1$?
2. what is the influence of w, d and $(h_1, \ldots, h_w)$ on the growth of the algebraic degree?

Based on this, we show (i) how to efficiently find $(h_1, \ldots, h_w)$ to achieve the exponential growth of the algebraic degree and (ii) how to efficiently compute the upper bound of the algebraic degree for arbitrary $(h_1, \ldots, h_w)$. Therefore, we expect that these results can further advance the understanding of the design and analysis of such primitives.

Keywords: Degree evaluation · Coefficient grouping technique · Finite fields

© International Association for Cryptologic Research 2023
H. Handschuh and A. Lysyanskaya (Eds.): CRYPTO 2023, LNCS 14083, pp. 540–572, 2023.
https://doi.org/10.1007/978-3-031-38548-3_18

1 Introduction

Since the birth of the first Fully Homomorphic Encryption (FHE) scheme by Gentry [24], various improved schemes [8,10–13,26,39] have been proposed to push the FHE technique closer to practice. Especially, the transciphering framework [39] is an important technique to address the issue of computational overload and the ciphertext expansion, which suggests to use a symmetric-key primitive to encrypt the data on the client side and then to perform the homomorphic decryption and additional homomorphic operations on the server side. It is soon observed that standard symmetric-key primitives may be not the best in such a framework due to the high AND-depth, e.g., the widely-deployed and well-studied encryption algorithm AES is inefficient [25]. Hence, this opens a new direction to design FHE-friendly symmetric-key primitives and many proposals have emerged, currently including Kreyvium [9], LowMC [3], FiLIP [38], RASTA [19], DASTA [28], MASTA [27], PASTA [20], HERA [13] Chaghri [4], and Elisabeth [15].

As one may expect, these new designs differ from the traditional ones in several aspects. As a result, new dedicated attacks (especially based on algebraic techniques) have been recently developed for breaking these primitives. Especially, it is found that for some proposals, there are undesirable or fatal weaknesses in the used components, which can even allow a complete break of the cipher [1,5,17,18,22,23,30,32–36]. Despite these successful attacks, it is still challenging to further understand their security after they are patched to resist against the corresponding attacks.

1.1 Our Target: The Studied Constructions

In this work, we consider SPN ciphers over $\mathbb{F}_{2^n}^m$ for $n \geq 3$ and $m \geq 1$ as illustrated in Fig. 1, where

- the invertible S-box is defined as the composition of a power map $S(x) = x^{2^d+1}$ for $d \geq 1$ and of an $\mathbb{F}_2$-linearized affine polynomial $B(x) = c_0 + \sum_{i=1}^{w} c_i x^{2^{h_i}}$ where $c_1, \ldots, c_w \neq 0$. In the following, we call $B(x)$ the affine layer and w **the density of** $B(x)$;
- the linear transformation is defined via the multiplication with an arbitrary invertible matrix $M \in \mathbb{F}_{2^n}^{m \times m}$.

Examples include MiMC [2] and Chaghri. MiMC is a special case of this construction for which $m = 1, B(x) = x$ and M is the identity matrix of size 1×1, i.e. $M = (1)$. For the original parameter of Chaghri, we have $m = 3, B(x) = c_0 + c_1 x^{2^{h_1}}$. Just to clarify that the designers of Chaghri have revised their design by choosing $w = 3$. For convenience, in the following, Chaghri refers to the original design Chaghri where $w = 1$. If we instead consider $S(x) = x^{2^n-2}$, then the MPC-friendly cipher Rain [21] and the well-known block cipher AES also follow this SPN structure.

Although M can be any invertible matrix, to keep the number of secure rounds as small as possible, it is better to choose an MDS matrix. The reason

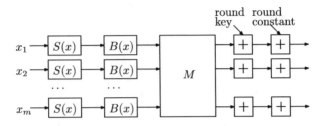

Fig. 1. The round function of SPN ciphers over $\mathbb{F}_{2^n}^m$

to only consider this nonlinear power map $S(x) = x^{2^d+1}$ is that its algebraic degree is the lowest, i.e. 2, and that it has good cryptographic properties [40], i.e. resistance against differential and linear attacks.

1.2 Related Works

Higher-order differential (HD) attacks [29] form a prominent class of attacks exploiting the low algebraic degree of a nonlinear transformation. Given a function F of degree $\deg(F)$ over $\mathbb{F}_2^n$, the attack exploits the fact that $\bigoplus_{x \in \mathcal{V}} F(x) = 0$ for each affine subspace $\mathcal{V} \subseteq \mathbb{F}_2^n$ whose dimension $\dim(\mathcal{V})$ satisfies $\dim(V) \geq \deg(F) + 1$. This version of the attack has been extended to a large finite field of any characteristics at CRYPTO 2020 [5], and it was refined for the extension field $\mathbb{F}_{2^n}$ at ASIACRYPT 2020 [23] via the link between $\mathbb{F}_{2^n}$ and $\mathbb{F}_2^n$. The two techniques are successfully applied to MiMC-based constructions. E.g., for MiMC over $\mathbb{F}_{2^n}$ (an iterated Even-Mansour cipher instantiated via $x \mapsto x^3$), it is found that the algebraic degree increases linearly rather than exponentially.

Since evaluating the degree is essential to mount the HD attack, several follow-up works have appeared. In [14], the authors also studied the algebraic degree for SPN ciphers over $\mathbb{F}_{2^n}^m$ where a general nonlinear map $x \mapsto \sum_{i=0}^{j} c_i' x^i$ over $\mathbb{F}_{2^n}$ and a binary matrix over $\mathbb{F}_2^{nm \times nm}$ are used as the nonlinear and linear components, respectively. (This binary matrix can be decomposed as the combination of m $\mathbb{F}_2$-linearized polynomials $(B_1, \ldots, B_m)$ over $\mathbb{F}_{2^n}$ and a matrix over $\mathbb{F}_{2^n}^{m \times m}$.) In [7], MiMC over $\mathbb{F}_{2^n}$ with $S(x) = x^j$ was studied. In both works, the underlying idea to bound the algebraic degree is similar to [23] where the upper bound of the algebraic degree is computed as $\lfloor \log_2(j^r + 1) \rfloor$.

However, the techniques in [7,14,23] are basically inefficient when targeting the construction proposed in Fig. 1 if $(2^d + 1) \cdot 2^{\max\{h_1, \ldots, h_w\}}$ (equivalently, $\max\{d, d \cdot \max\{h_1, \ldots, h_w\}\}$) is large and n is small. As a concrete example, the bounds obtained with these techniques do *not* violate the designers' claim for Chaghri that the algebraic degree increases exponentially. This fact has been recently disproved via the new "coefficient grouping technique" [30]. Compared with the techniques proposed in [7,14,23], the coefficient grouping technique allows to efficiently handle the case when $((2^d + 1) \cdot 2^{\max\{h_1, \ldots, h_w\}})^r > 2^n$ for the case $w = 1$. With this new technique, it is shown that the algebraic degree of Chaghri indeed increases linearly [30].

As a parallel work to the coefficient grouping technique, the division property [42] has been also extended to $\mathbb{F}_{2^n}$ and successfully applied to MiMC-based constructions [16]. However, this method completely relies on a blackbox solver and it has the feature to model the heavy monomial transitions round by round as in the division property [42]. Hence, its performance for complex affine layers is questionable. More importantly, with this technique, we seem to have little insight into the main factors to influence the growth of the algebraic degree.

1.3   Our Contributions

Problems to Be Addressed. One notable feature of the coefficient grouping technique for the case $w = 1$ is that the problem to upper bound the algebraic degree can be reduced to a well-structured optimization problem. However, while it works quite efficiently [37] and accurately for the case $w = 1$, its performance and accuracy become low for $w > 1$, though it has been used to patch Chaghri for $w > 1$. For these reasons, we are interested to answer the following problems:

Problem 1: For $w = 1$, can we prove that the algebraic degree will *never* increase exponentially for any d, even for the first few rounds? Note that with the techniques in [7,14,23], we cannot conclude whether the algebraic degree will increase exponentially at the first few rounds if d is large.

Problem 2: Chaghri has been revised by replacing $w = 1$ with $w = 3$. However, we are still lacking theories regarding the influence of w on the growth of the algebraic degree. Can we build such a theory?

Problem 3: Are there equivalent $(h_1, \ldots, h_w)$ from the point of view of the growth of the algebraic degree?

Problem 4: It has been demonstrated in [30] that using $B(x)$ with $w > 1$ allows to achieve the exponential growth of the algebraic degree. However, it is an open problem to efficiently find concrete parameter sets of $(h_1, \ldots, h_w)$ for reaching this goal. We emphasize that the method in [30] is inefficient and the accuracy is sacrificed for the efficiency.

Problem 5: Can we efficiently provide meaningful upper bounds of the growth of the degree for a cipher that uses arbitrary $B(x)$? Note that no result about upper bounds when $w > 1$ has been proposed in [30].

Our Results. To address the above problems, we first deeply analyse the set of all monomials that will possibly appear in the polynomial representation of the internal state after any rounds. Our analysis shows that such a set is well-structured, which directly allows us to systematically study the above problems. Based on our theoretical analysis, we obtain the following results:

Answer 1: When $w = 1$, for any (n, d), the algebraic degree will *never* increase exponentially after the 1st round and it is always below the quadratic growth.

Answer 2: Necessary conditions on w and the concrete parameter $(h_1, \ldots, h_w)$ are derived to ensure the exponential growth of the algebraic degree. Especially, we found that for $w = 2, 3, 4$, the algebraic degree can *never* increase exponentially at the 4th, 7th and 10th round for any $(h_1, \ldots, h_w)$, respectively.

Answer 3: With our new technique, some equivalent $(h_1, \ldots, h_w)$ are derived. With the equivalent relations, we only need to consider about $\frac{1}{w} \cdot \binom{n}{w-1}$ possible candidates of $(h_1, \ldots, h_w)$ when aiming to find one that can achieve the exponential growth of the algebraic degree.

Answer 4: We build a very light model to check whether the exponential growth can be achieved for a concrete $(h_1, \ldots, h_w)$. It is found that this problem can be reduced to the problem whether it is possible to select 2^r different numbers from $r + 1$ sets under some special conditions.

Answer 5: For arbitrary $B(x)$, we show how to reduce the problem to upper bound the algebraic degree to a well-structured optimization problem. However, the well-structured problem is constructed at the sacrifice of using relaxed constraints. Hence, the upper bound may be not tight, but it is still useful for many cases as shown in our practical tests.

Comparison with Previous Works. Similar to the analysis proposed in [7,14,23,30], our work exploits the link between the degree of the functions over $\mathbb{F}_{2^n}$ and over $\mathbb{F}_2^n$, making it different from e.g. the well-known technique proposed in [6]. Still, our analysis differs from [7,14,23], since such methods become completely inefficient when $\max\{d, d \cdot \max\{h_1, \ldots, h_w\}\}$ is large.

Compared with the division property [16,42], our technique does not require to model the heavy propagation of monomials round by round, i.e. we can directly identify the relations between the polynomial representation of the input and polynomial representation of the output after any rounds, where the propagation of monomials in the middle rounds are simply captured by some conditions.

Similar to [30], our strategy aims to capture the properties of the polynomial representation for determining the growth of the algebraic degree. However, while the original coefficient grouping technique and the technique proposed in this paper almost overlap for the case $w = 1$, the former one becomes completely inefficient for $w > 1$, as we are going to discuss in details in the following. As a concrete example, in [30], authors discuss a possible way to choose the affine layer in Chaghri for guaranteeing the exponential growth of the degree. In this paper, we show that the suggested choice is *not* optimal, in the sense that the fastest growth of the algebraic degree may *not* be achieved. This is related to the fact that the technique proposed in [30] requires several approximation for being efficient in practice, with a consequent lost in precision. By exploiting our new technique proposed in this paper, we show how to choose the affine layer for ensuring the fastest growth of the algebraic degree.

Outline of This Paper. In Sect. 2, we briefly recall the higher-order differential attacks over $\mathbb{F}_{2^n}$ and the original coefficient grouping technique [30]. In Sect. 3, we build the most important theory for complex affine layers, which is the basis of all the results in this paper. In Sect. 4, we aim to answer Problem 1, 2 and 3. In Sect. 5 and 6, we try to solve Problem 4 and 5 in the univariate setting respectively, and will report some practical applications and experiments[1]. Finally, we mention some problems worth further study in Sect. 7.

2 Preliminaries

2.1 Notation

In this paper, variables and/or parameters are denoted via lower letters and/or Greek letters, while functions and/or arrays are denoted via capital letters. We use the calligraphic notation for denoting sets. Given two integers a and b, we use the notation $a|b$ to denote the fact that a divides b, while we denote the rest of the division as $a\%b := a \bmod b$. $[a, b]$ is a set of integers i satisfying $a \le i \le b$. $|\mathcal{S}|$ denotes the size of the set $\mathcal{S}$. $\mathrm{Hw}(a)$ is the hamming weight of $a \in \mathbb{N}$, i.e. the number of 1 in its binary representation.

Furthermore, similar to [30], we introduce the function $M_n : \mathbb{N} \to \mathbb{N}$ defined as follows:

$$M_n(x) := \begin{cases} 2^n - 1 & \text{if } 2^n - 1 | x \text{ and } x \ge 2^n - 1, \\ x\%(2^n - 1) & \text{otherwise.} \end{cases}$$

The symbol $\binom{a}{\le b}$ where $a \ge b$ is defined as:

$$\binom{a}{\le b} := \begin{cases} \binom{a}{0} + \cdots + \binom{a}{b} & \text{if } b \ge 0, \\ 0 & \text{otherwise.} \end{cases}$$

By definition of $M_n(x)$, we get the following lemma:

Lemma 1. *For each $x_1, x_2, i, x \in \mathbb{N}$, we have:*

1. $M_n(x_1 + x_2) = M_n(M_n(x_1) + M_n(x_2))$;
2. $M_n(2^i) = 2^{i\%n}$;
3. $M_n(2^i \cdot x) = M_n(2^{i\%n} \cdot M_n(x))$.

The definition of $M_n(x)$ is mainly to capture the following facts:

$$\begin{cases} x^{p^n} = x \ \forall x \in \mathbb{F}_{p^n}, \\ x^{p^n - 1} = 1 \ \forall x \in \mathbb{F}_{p^n} \text{ and } x \ne 0, \\ (x + y)^{p^i} = x^{p^i} + y^{p^i} \ \forall x, y \in \mathbb{F}_{p^n}, i \in \mathbb{N}. \end{cases}$$

---

[1] The code is available at https://github.com/LFKOKAMI/degreeEva.

2.2   Algebraic Degree for Polynomials over $\mathbb{F}_{2^n}^m$

To mount the HD attack, the first step is to find the upper bound of the algebraic degree of the polynomial representation of the output in terms of the input. In order to do this, in the following we heavily exploit the link between the algebraic degree of the functions over $\mathbb{F}_{2^n}$ and over $\mathbb{F}_2^n$. We recall that even if such a link is well established, it has not been widely used for attacking ciphers until recently [7,14,23,30].

Given a polynomial $F \in \mathbb{F}_{2^n}[x_1,\ldots,x_t]$, in this paper we call it (i) a *univariate polynomial* if $t = 1$, and (ii) *multivariate polynomial* if $t \geq 2$. As is well-known, e.g. [7,14,23,30], the algebraic degree of polynomials over $\mathbb{F}_{2^n}$ is defined as follows:

– for a *univariate* polynomial $F = \sum_{i=0}^{2^n-1} \mu_i x^i \in \mathbb{F}_{2^n}[x]$, its algebraic degree δ_F is defined as

$$\delta_F = \max\{\mathrm{Hw}(i) \mid i \in [0, 2^n - 1] \text{ and } \mu_i \neq 0\}.$$

This definition is mainly based on how to convert a function over $\mathbb{F}_{2^n}$ into a vectorial function over $\mathbb{F}_2^n$, e.g., as shown in Chap. 6 in [41].

– for a *multivariate* polynomial

$$F = \sum_{i_1=0}^{2^n-1} \sum_{i_2=0}^{2^n-1} \cdots \sum_{i_t=0}^{2^n-1} \mu_{i_1,i_2,\ldots,i_t} x_1^{i_1} \cdots x_t^{i_t} \in \mathbb{F}_{2^n}[x_1,\ldots,x_t],$$

its algebraic degree δ_F is defined as

$$\delta_F = \max\left\{\sum_{j=1}^{t} \mathrm{Hw}(i_j) \mid i_j \in [0, 2^n - 1] \text{ and } \mu_{i_1,i_2,\ldots,i_t} \neq 0\right\}.$$

To mount the HD attack on ciphers over $\mathbb{F}_{2^n}$, it is paramount to know the growth of δ_F. E.g., if δ_F is smaller than $t \cdot n$ when considering polynomials in t variables, it is possible to mount a HD attack with time and data complexity 2^{δ_F+1}.

2.3   The Coefficient Grouping Technique

For our studied SPN ciphers, the coefficient grouping technique can be classified into two settings: the univariate setting and the multivariate setting. This technique is very efficient for $w = 1$, i.e., $B(x) = c_0 + c_1 x^{2^{h_1}}$, as stated below.

The Univariate Setting. In this case, the attacker considers $(x_1, x_2, \ldots, x_m)$ of the form $x_i = \lambda_{1,i} \cdot z + \lambda_{2,i}$ for each $i \in \{1, 2, \ldots, m\}$, where $\lambda_{1,i}, \lambda_{2,i} \in \mathbb{F}_{2^n}$ are randomly chosen constants and $z \in \mathbb{F}_{2^n}$ is the variable. Computing the upper bound for the algebraic degree after r rounds reduces to solving the following optimization problem, which we denote by **OP-1**:

$$\text{maximize } \mathrm{Hw}\left(M_n\left(\sum_{i=0}^{n-1} 2^i a_i\right)\right),$$

$$\text{subject to } 0 \leq a_i \leq \nu_{r,i} \text{ for } i \in [0, n-1],$$

where the parameter $\nu_r = (\nu_{r,n-1}, \ldots, \nu_{r,0}) \in \mathbb{N}^n$ is computed with the following recursive relation:

$$\begin{cases} \nu_{0,0} = 1, \nu_{0,i} = 0 & \text{for } i \in [1, n-1], \\ \nu_{j,i} = \nu_{j-1,(i-d-h_1)\%n} + \nu_{j-1,(i-h_1)\%n} & \text{for } j \in [1, r], i \in [0, n-1]. \end{cases} \quad (1)$$

The Multivariate Setting. In this case, the attacker considers such $(x_1, x_2, \ldots, x_m)$ that $x_i = \sum_{j=1}^t \lambda_{j,i} z_j$ for each $i \in \{1, 2, \ldots, m\}$, where $\lambda_{j,i} \in \mathbb{F}_{2^n}$ are randomly chosen constants and $(z_1, \ldots, z_t) \in \mathbb{F}_{2^n}^t$ are t variables. Computing the upper bound after r rounds reduces to solving the following problem denoted by **OP-t**:

$$\text{maximize} \sum_{j=1}^t \text{Hw}\left(M_n\left(\sum_{i=0}^{n-1} 2^i a_{j,i}\right)\right),$$

$$\text{subject to } 0 \leq \sum_{j=1}^t a_{j,i} \leq \nu_{r,i} \text{ for } i \in [0, n-1],$$

where the parameter $\nu_r = (\nu_{r,n-1}, \ldots, \nu_{r,0})$ is still computed with the recursive relation specified in Eq. 1. Note that **OP-t** $(t \geq 1)$ can always be solved in time $\mathcal{O}(n)$ via the reduction algorithm in [37].

Weaknesses and Open Problems. When $w = 1$, there is always only one parameter vector ν_r and it can be computed in time $\mathcal{O}(n)$ with Eq. 1. This implies that we only need to solve the optimization problem once. However, for $w > 1$, after r rounds, there will be a set of parameter vectors denoted by $\mathcal{P}_r$, i.e. $\nu_r \in \mathcal{P}_r$ where $\mathcal{P}_0 = \{(0, \ldots, 0, 1)\}$. Moreover, $\mathcal{P}_r$ $(r \geq 1)$ is updated as follows:

$$\mathcal{P}_r = \{(e_{n-1}, \ldots, e_0) \in \mathbb{N}^n \mid \forall \nu_{r-1}, \nu'_{r-1} \in \mathcal{P}_{r-1}, \forall j \in [1, w], \forall i \in [0, n-1],$$

$$e_i = \nu_{r-1,(i-d-h_j)\%n} + \nu'_{r-1,(i-h_j)\%n}\}. \quad (2)$$

We point out that some redundant elements can be removed when constructing $\mathcal{P}_r$ via Eq. 2 (note that $\nu''_r = (\nu''_{r,n-1}, \ldots, \nu''_{r,0})$ is *redundant* if $\exists \nu_r \in \mathcal{P}_r$ such that $\nu_{r,i} \geq \nu''_{r,i}$ holds for $\forall i \in [0, n-1]$). Still, this does not have an impact on the size of $\mathcal{P}_r$, since the number of redundant elements is – in general – relatively small compared to its size.

In order to get an accurate upper bound for the case $w > 1$:

- in the worst case, one has to solve all the corresponding optimization problems by enumerating all $\nu_r \in \mathcal{P}_r$;
- in the best case, when one vector for which the solution of the corresponding optimization problem is $\min\{2^r, t \cdot n\}$ is found, one can stop enumerating the remaining vectors, since the highest upper bound $\min\{2^r, t \cdot n\}$ has been already reached.

The best case has been used to find proper $B(x)$ that can realize the (almost) exponential growth of the algebraic degree, as shown in [30].

Limitations When $w > 1$ and Our Solutions. Roughly speaking, the time and memory complexity to construct $\mathcal{P}_r$ can be estimated as $\mathcal{O}(w^{2^{r-1}})$. It is easy to observe that the inefficiency comes from that $\mathcal{P}_r$ has to be computed round by round, which is crucial for determining the upper bound after r rounds. E.g., in [30], to find proper $B(x)$ achieving the (almost) exponential growth of the algebraic degree, it is suggested to store at most 2^{13} desired elements for each $\mathcal{P}_r$ and hence the time complexity becomes $2^{26} \times r$. However, too much accuracy is sacrificed because many possible ν_r are ignored.

In the following, we present an analogous approach exploited by the coefficient grouping technique for the case $w = 1$, which will allow to avoid the problem to construct $\mathcal{P}_r$ round by round because we can directly identify many crucial properties of $\mathcal{P}_r$ without explicitly computing it. This will significantly improve the efficiency and accuracy for $w > 1$.

3   On the Polynomial Representation for Complex $B(x)$

In this section, we aim to build a theory to capture the features of the polynomial representation of the analyzed cipher. We start by working in the univariate setting defined as before.

This will give us a necessary condition for the growth of the degree. Indeed, we recall that, if the degree does not increase exponentially in such setting in which the inputs $(x_1, \ldots, x_m)$ depend on a single variable, then it cannot increase exponentially in general.

Initial Remarks. We start by pointing out some preliminary observations.

Remark 1. We recall that our theory covers also the case where $S(x) = x^{2^{d_1}+2^{d_2}}$ for $(d_2 > d_1)$. Indeed, it is sufficient to notice that

$$S(x) = x^{2^{d_1}+2^{d_2}} = (x^{2^{d_2-d_1}+1})^{2^{d_1}} = B' \circ S'(x)$$

where $B'(x) = x^{2^{d_1}}$ and $S'(x) = x^{2^{d_2-d_1}+1}$.

Remark 2. Since we are only interested in an upper bound of the growth of the degree, our goal is to predict which monomials do *not* appear in the polynomial representation of the analyzed cipher. Equivalently, we are not interested in the details of the coefficients of the monomials that appear. For this reason, from now on, we set them to 1. We emphasize that the same approach has been used in almost all the previous papers that cover the same topic, including [6,7,14, 16,23,30,42].

Based on this, since the invertible matrix M only changes the coefficients of the monomials in the polynomial representation, we can omit its influence on the value of the coefficients of the monomial, exactly as in [30]. Note that a bad choice of M may affect the tightness of our upper bound and tracing its influence requires non-trivial work, i.e. how to detect the cancellations in the monomials for our technique is quite challenging. This is an interesting open problem and we emphasize that the cipher is defined over $\mathbb{F}_{2^n}$, which makes detecting cancellations much more difficult, i.e. the coefficient of a monomial can take 2^n different possible values.

Tracing the Evolution of Polynomials. In the univariate setting, each input state word x_i ($i = 1, \ldots, m$) can be written as a certain polynomial $x_i = P_0(x) = u_1 \cdot x + u_0$, where we fix $u_0 = u_1 = 1$ due to the argument just given. (Note that each internal state word will have the same polynomial representation if we treat the coefficients of all possible monomials as 1, as already shown in the coefficient grouping technique [30].) In the following, we denote the polynomial representation of each state word after r rounds by $P_r(x)$ and the polynomial representation after $S(x)$ in the r-th round by $P_r^S(x)$.

Based on these considerations, we simply have that

$$P_r(x) = (B \circ S)^r (P_0(x)), \qquad \text{and} \qquad P_r^S(x) = S(P_{r-1}(x)).$$

For the particular case $r = 1$:

$$P_1^S(x) = (x + 1)^{2^d} (x + 1) = x^{2^d} + x^{2^d + 1} + x + 1,$$

$$P_1(x) = 1 + \sum_{i=1}^{w} \left(P_1^S(x) \right)^{2^{h_i}} = 1 + \sum_{i=1}^{w} x^{2^{d+h_i}} + x^{2^{d+h_i}+2^{h_i}} + x^{2^{h_i}}.$$

It follows that only the monomials

$$\left\{ x^{2^d}, x^{2^d + 1}, x, x^0 \right\}$$

can possibly appear in $P_1^S(x)$, and that only the monomials

$$\left\{ x^{2^{d+h_i}}, x^{2^{d+h_i}+2^{h_i}}, x^{2^{h_i}}, x^0 \mid 1 \le i \le w \right\}$$

can possibly appear in $P_1(x)$.

Working iteratively, our goal is to find similar sets of possible monomials that can appear in $P_r^S(x)$. Denote such a set by $\mathcal{M}_r^S$. Given this set, the upper bound – denoted by δ_r – on the algebraic degree in the univariate setting after r rounds can be simply obtained as follows:

$$\delta_r = \max \left\{ \mathrm{Hw}(M_n(e)) \mid x^e \in \mathcal{M}_r^S \right\}.$$

Since each monomial is uniquely identified by its degree, we can simply introduce the set $\mathcal{W}_r^S$ for the exponents, that is,

$$\mathcal{W}_r^S = \left\{ e \in \mathbb{N} \mid x^e \in \mathcal{M}_r^S \right\}, \quad \delta_r = \max \left\{ \mathrm{Hw}(M_n(e)) \mid e \in \mathcal{W}_r^S \right\}.$$

One more time, we recall that some of the monomials present in the previous set $\mathcal{M}_r^S$ do not necessarily appear for some particular values of the key and/or of the linear layer M. At the same time, if a monomial that does *not* appear in such set, then it does *not* appear independently of the values of the key and/or of the linear layer M. This is sufficient for setting up an upper bound. Obviously, such bound is tight if the cancellation due to the key and/or of the linear layer M is almost null.

Given such definitions, we have the following results:

– case $r = 0$:
$$\mathcal{W}_0 = \{0, 1\};$$

– case $r = 1$:
$$\mathcal{W}_1^S = \left\{2^d, 2^d + 1, 1, 0\right\} = \left\{a_{1,1}2^d + a_{1,2} \mid 0 \le a_{1,1}, a_{1,2} \le 1\right\}$$
$$\mathcal{W}_1 = \left\{2^{d+h_i}, 2^{h_i} + 2^{d+h_i}, 2^{h_i}, 0 \mid 1 \le i \le w\right\}$$
$$= \left\{a_{1,1}2^{d+h_i} + a_{1,2}2^{h_i} \mid 0 \le a_{1,1}, a_{1,2} \le 1, 1 \le i \le w\right\},$$

– case $r = 2$:
$$\mathcal{W}_2^S = \left\{a_{2,1}2^{2d+h_{i_0}} + a_{2,2}2^{d+h_{i_0}} + a_{2,3}2^{d+h_{i_1}} + a_{2,4}2^{h_{i_1}}\right.$$
$$\left. \mid 0 \le a_{2,j} \le 1, 1 \le i_0, i_1 \le w, 1 \le j \le 4\right\},$$
$$\mathcal{W}_2 = \left\{a_{2,1}2^{2d+h_{i_0}+h_{i_2}} + a_{2,2}2^{d+h_{i_0}+h_{i_2}} + a_{2,3}2^{d+h_{i_1}+h_{i_2}} + a_{2,4}2^{h_{i_1}+h_{i_2}}\right.$$
$$\left. \mid 0 \le a_{1,j} \le 1, 1 \le i_0, i_1, i_2 \le w, 1 \le j \le 4\right\},$$

and so on. The case $r = 2$ may be not obvious, especially for $\mathcal{W}_2^S$. This can be explained using the following remark:

Remark 3. We have $y^{2^d+1} = y^{2^d} \cdot y$ where y is a polynomial whose monomials can always be represented as $x^{a_{1,1}2^{d+h_i}+a_{1,2}2^{h_i}}$. Hence, for the left part in $y^{2^d} \cdot y$, i.e. y^{2^d}, we can choose any possible monomial $x^{a_{1,1}2^{d+h_{i_0}}+a_{1,2}2^{h_{i_0}}}$ for y, while for the right part in $y^{2^d} \cdot y$, we can also independently choose any possible monomial $x^{a'_{1,1}2^{d+h_{i_1}}+a'_{1,2}2^{h_{i_1}}}$ for y. Hence, we have $x^{a_{1,1}2^{2d+h_{i_0}}+a_{1,2}2^{d+h_{i_0}}+a'_{1,1}2^{d+h_{i_1}}+a'_{1,2}2^{h_{i_1}}}$ is a possible monomial in $y^{2^d+1} = y^{2^d} \cdot y$.

Hence, we can deduce the following theorem.

Theorem 1. *For each $r \ge 1$, let $\mathcal{V}_{r,w}$ be the set defined as*

$$\mathcal{V}_{r,w} = \left\{e \in \mathbb{N} \mid e = \sum_{i=1}^{w} b_i h_i, \sum_{i=1}^{w} b_i = r - 1, b_i \ge 0\right\}, \tag{3}$$

which represents all possible values by summing up $r - 1$ elements from the set $\{h_1, \ldots, h_w\}$. The set $\mathcal{W}_r^S$ can then be described as follows:

$$\mathcal{W}_r^S = \left\{\sum_{i=0}^{r} \sum_{j=1}^{\binom{r}{i}} a_{r,v}2^{(r-i)d+f_v}, v = j + \binom{r}{\le i - 1}, 0 \le a_{r,v} \le 1, f_v \in \mathcal{V}_{r,w}\right\},$$

where

$$f_{\binom{r}{\le i}+\ell} = f_{\binom{r}{\le i}-\binom{r-1}{i}+\ell} \text{ for } 0 \le i \le r - 1, 1 \le \ell \le \binom{r-1}{i}. \tag{4}$$

Proof. We prove it by induction. Based on the above deduction, this has been proved for $r \in \{1, 2\}$. For example, $\mathcal{W}_2^S$ can be rewritten as the form in this theorem:

$$\mathcal{W}_2^S = \{a_{2,1}2^{2d+f_1} + a_{2,2}2^{d+f_2} + a_{2,3}2^{d+f_3} + a_{2,4}2^{f_4}, 0 \le a_{2,1}, a_{2,2}, a_{2,3}, a_{2,4} \le 1\},$$

$$f_2 = f_1, \quad f_4 = f_3,$$

$$f_1, f_2, f_3, f_4 \in \mathcal{V}_{2,w} = \left\{ e \in \mathbb{N} \mid e = \sum_{i=1}^{w} b_i h_i, \sum_{i=1}^{w} b_i = 1, b_i \ge 0 \right\} = \{h_i \mid 1 \le i \le w\}.$$

Assuming the theorem holds for $r = q$, we now prove that it also holds for $r = q + 1$. According to the assumption, we have

$$\mathcal{W}_q^S = \left\{ \sum_{i=0}^{q} \sum_{j=1}^{\binom{q}{i}} a_{q,v} 2^{(q-i)d+f_v}, v = j + \binom{q}{\le i-1}, 0 \le a_{q,v} \le 1, f_v \in \mathcal{V}_{q,w} \right\},$$

where

$$f_{\binom{q}{\le i}+\ell} = f_{\binom{q}{\le i}-\binom{q-1}{i}+\ell} \text{ for } 0 \le i \le q-1, 1 \le \ell \le \binom{q-1}{i}.$$

Then, after applying the affine transformation $B(x)$, the $\{h_u\}_{1 \le u \le w}$ appear in the power of 2, as described below:

$$\mathcal{W}_q = \left\{ \sum_{i=0}^{q} \sum_{j=1}^{\binom{q}{i}} a_{q,v} 2^{(q-i)d+f_v+h_u}, v = j + \binom{q}{\le i-1}, 0 \le a_{q,v} \le 1, f_v \in \mathcal{V}_{q,w}, 1 \le u \le w \right\},$$

Consider the set $\{f_v + h_u \mid f_v \in \mathcal{V}_{q,w}, 1 \le u \le w\}$. Then we have

$$\{f_v + h_u \mid f_v \in \mathcal{V}_{q,w}, 1 \le u \le w\} = \mathcal{V}_{q+1,w} = \left\{ e \mid e = \sum_{i=1}^{w} b_i h_i, \sum_{i=1}^{w} b_i = q, b_i \ge 0 \right\},$$

by definition of $\mathcal{V}_{q,w}$. Hence, $\mathcal{W}_q$ can be rewritten as

$$\mathcal{W}_q = \left\{ \sum_{i=0}^{q} \sum_{j=1}^{\binom{q}{i}} a_{q,v} 2^{(q-i)d+f_v}, v = j + \binom{q}{\le i-1}, 0 \le a_{q,v} \le 1, f_v \in \mathcal{V}_{q+1,w} \right\}$$

and there is still $f_{\binom{q}{\le i}+\ell} = f_{\binom{q}{\le i}-\binom{q-1}{i}+\ell}$ for $0 \le i \le q-1, 1 \le \ell \le \binom{q-1}{i}$.

Based on this new representation of $\mathcal{W}_q$, and using the idea of Remark 3, by introducing another 2^q variables $(f_1', \ldots, f_{2^q}')$ satisfying:

$$f'_{\binom{q}{\le i}+\ell} = f'_{\binom{q}{\le i}-\binom{q-1}{i}+\ell} \text{ for } 0 \le i \le q-1, 1 \le \ell \le \binom{q-1}{i},$$

we can write $\mathcal{W}_{q+1}^S$ as follows:

$$\mathcal{W}_{q+1}^S = \left\{ \sum_{i=0}^{q} \sum_{j=1}^{\binom{q}{i}} a_{q,v} 2^{(q-i+1)d+f_v} + \sum_{i=0}^{q} \sum_{j=1}^{\binom{q}{i}} a'_{q,v} 2^{(q-i)d+f'_v}, \right.$$

$$\left. 0 \le a_{q,v}, a'_{q,v} \le 1, v = j + \binom{q}{\le i-1}, f_v, f'_v \in \mathcal{V}_{q+1,w} \right\}$$

$$= \left\{ a_{q+1,1} 2^{q+1d+g_1} + \sum_{i=1}^{q} \sum_{j=1}^{\binom{q}{i-1}+\binom{q}{i}=\binom{q+1}{i}} a_{q+1,v} 2^{(q+1-i)d+g_v} + a_{q+1,2^{q+1}} 2^{g_2 q+1}, \right.$$

$$\left. 0 \le a_{q+1,v} \le 1, v = j + \binom{q+1}{\le i-1}, g_v \in \mathcal{V}_{q+1,w} \right\}$$

$$= \left\{ \sum_{i=0}^{q+1} \sum_{j=1}^{\binom{q+1}{i}} a_{q+1,v} 2^{(q+1-i)d+g_v}, 0 \le a_{q+1,v} \le 1, v = j + \binom{q+1}{\le i-1}, g_v \in \mathcal{V}_{q+1,w} \right\}$$

In the deduction, we replace $a_{q,1}$ and $a'_{q,2^r}$ with $a_{q+1,1}$ and $a_{q+1,2^{q+1}}$, respectively, i.e. $g_1 = f_1$ and $g_{2^{q+1}} = f'_{2^q}$.

Moreover, for $i \in [0, q-1]$, we make such changes:

$$\left(a_{q,\binom{q}{\le i}+1}, \ldots, a_{q,\binom{q}{\le i}+\binom{q-1}{i}}, a_{q,\binom{q}{\le i}+\binom{q-1}{i}+1}, \ldots, a_{q,\binom{q}{\le i}+\binom{q-1}{i}+\binom{q-1}{i+1}} \right)$$

$$= \left(a_{q+1,\binom{q+1}{\le i}+1}, \ldots, a_{q+1,\binom{q+1}{\le i}+\binom{q-1}{i}}, a_{q+1,\binom{q+1}{\le i}+\binom{q}{i}+1}, \ldots, a_{q+1,\binom{q+1}{\le i}+\binom{q}{i}+\binom{q-1}{i+1}} \right),$$

In addition, we make $a_{q+1,\binom{q+1}{\le 1}} = a'_1$. For $i \in [1, q-1]$, we make such changes:

$$\left(a'_{q,\binom{q}{\le i-1}+1}, \ldots, a'_{q,\binom{q}{\le i-1}+\binom{q-1}{i-1}}, a'_{q,\binom{q}{\le i-1}+\binom{q-1}{i-1}+1}, \ldots, a'_{q,\binom{q}{\le i-1}+\binom{q-1}{i-1}+\binom{q-1}{i}} \right)$$

$$= \left(a_{q+1,\binom{q+1}{\le i}+\binom{q-1}{i}+1}, \ldots, a_{q+1,\binom{q+1}{\le i}+\binom{q}{i}}, a_{q+1,\binom{q+1}{\le i}+\binom{q}{i}+\binom{q-1}{i+1}+1}, \ldots, a_{q+1,\binom{q+1}{\le i+1}} \right).$$

By this construction, we have

$$g_{\binom{q+1}{\le i}+j} = f_{\binom{q}{\le i}+j} \text{ for } 0 \le i \le q-1, \ 1 \le j \le \binom{q-1}{i},$$

$$g_{q+2} = f'_1, g_{\binom{q+1}{\le i}+\binom{q-1}{i}+j} = f'_{\binom{q}{\le i-1}+j} \text{ for } 1 \le i \le q-1, \ 1 \le j \le \binom{q-1}{i-1},$$

$$g_{\binom{q+1}{\le i}+\binom{q}{i}+j} = f_{\binom{q}{\le i}+\binom{q-1}{i}+j} \text{ for } 0 \le i \le q-2, \ 1 \le j \le \binom{q-1}{i+1},$$

$$g_{\binom{q+1}{\le i}+\binom{q}{i}+\binom{q-1}{i+1}+j} = f'_{\binom{q}{\le i-1}+\binom{q-1}{i-1}+j} \text{ for } 0 \le i \le q-1, \ 1 \le j \le \binom{q-1}{i},$$

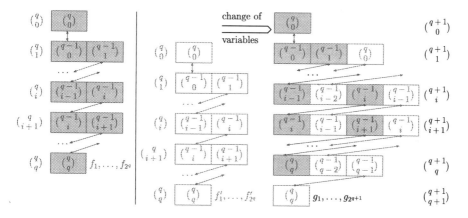

Fig. 2. The change of variables, where arrows represent the identical relation

For better understanding, Fig. 2 illustrates these changes of variables. Therefore, for $1 \le i \le q-1$ and $1 \le \ell \le \binom{q-1}{i}$, we have

$$g_{\binom{q+1}{\le i}+\ell} = f_{\binom{q}{\le i}+\ell} = f_{\binom{q}{\le i}-\binom{q-1}{i}+\ell} = f_{\binom{q}{\le i-1}+\binom{q-1}{i-1}+\ell} = g_{\binom{q+1}{\le i}-\binom{q}{i}+\ell}.$$

For $2 \le i \le q-1$ and $\binom{q-1}{i}+1 \le \ell \le \binom{q-1}{i}+\binom{q-1}{i-1} = \binom{q}{i}$, we have

$$g_{\binom{q+1}{\le i}+\ell} = f'_{\binom{q}{\le i-1}-\binom{q-1}{i}+\ell} = f'_{\binom{q}{\le i-2}+\binom{q-1}{i-2}-\binom{q-1}{i}+\ell} = g_{\binom{q+1}{\le i}-\binom{q}{i}+\ell}.$$

Moreover, we have $g_2 = f_2 = f_1 = g_1$, $g_{2q+2} = f'_2 = f'_1 = g_{q+2}$ and $g_{2q+1} = f_{2q} = f_{2q-1} = g_{2q+1-1}$. Therefore, for $0 \le i \le q$ and $1 \le \ell \le \binom{q}{i}$, we have

$$g_{\binom{q+1}{\le i}+\ell} = g_{\binom{q+1}{\le i}-\binom{q}{i}+\ell}. \qquad \square$$

Based on Theorem 1, we can give a well-structured description of the monomials that will possibly appear after r rounds. Especially, from its current form, we immediately observe that the exponent of each possible monomial is a linear combination of $\sum_{i=0}^{r}\binom{r}{i} = 2^r$ numbers $(2^{j_1},\dots,2^{j_{2^r}})$ satisfying certain properties. In the following, we show how to use this well-structured description to study several problems relevant to the growth of the algebraic degree.

4   Implications on the Growth of the Algebraic Degree

As next step, we exploit the result proposed in Theorem 1 to study the growth of the algebraic degree for complex affine layers in a systematic way. In the following, we will separately study (i) the growth of the algebraic degree for the special case $w = 1$, (ii) necessary conditions to achieve the exponential growth and (iii) equivalent affine layers.

4.1 Special Case: $w = 1$

Let us start by pointing out the connection between Theorem 1 and the results proposed via the coefficient grouping technique developed for the case $w = 1$. In this case,

$$\mathcal{W}_r^S = \left\{ \sum_{i=0}^{r} \sum_{j=1}^{\binom{r}{i}} a_{r,v} 2^{(r-i)d+f_v}, v = j + \binom{r}{\leq i-1}, 0 \leq a_{r,v} \leq 1, f_v \in \mathcal{V}_{r,1} \right\},$$

where $\mathcal{V}_{r,1} = \{(r-1)h_1\}$. By definition, this means that $f_v = (r-1)h_1$ for each $v \in [1, 2^r]$. Hence, we have $\mathcal{W}_r^S = \{\sum_{i=0}^{r} a_i 2^{(r-i)d+(r-1)h_1}, 0 \leq a_i \leq \binom{r}{i}\}$, which implies $\mathcal{W}_r = \{\sum_{i=0}^{r} a_i 2^{(r-i)d+rh_1}, 0 \leq a_i \leq \binom{r}{i}\}$ when $w = 1$.

According to the definition of δ_r, it follows that

$$\delta_r = \max \left\{ \mathrm{Hw}(M_n(e)) \mid e \in \mathcal{W}_r^S \right\} = \max\{\mathrm{Hw}(M_n(e)) \mid e \in \mathcal{W}_r\}.$$

In order to efficiently compute δ_r, we suggest to iteratively construct a vector $\nu_r = (\nu_{r,n-1}, \dots, \nu_{r,0}) \in \mathbb{N}^n$ via Algorithm 1. By the construction of this vector ν_r, we can equivalently describe $\{M_n(e) \mid e \in \mathcal{W}_r\}$ as follows:

$$\{M_n(e) \mid e \in \mathcal{W}_r\} = \left\{ M_n(e) \mid e = \sum_{i=0}^{n-1} 2^i a_i, a_i \in [0, \nu_{r,i}] \right\}$$

In this way, computing δ_r for the case $w = 1$ is converted into solving **OP-1** parameterized by the constructed vector $(\nu_{r,n-1}, \dots, \nu_{r,0})$.

Algorithm 1. Constructing $(\nu_{r,n-1}, \dots, \nu_{r,0}) \in \mathbb{N}^n$ when $w = 1$

1: **procedure** CONVERSION(ν_r, r, n)
2:     initialize $(\nu_{r,n-1}, \dots, \nu_{r,0})$ as all 0
3:     **for all** $i \in [0, r]$ **do**
4:         $j = ((r - i) \times d + r \times h_1)\%n$
5:         $\nu_{r,j} = \nu_{r,j} + \binom{r}{i}$

By induction, it is possible to prove that the vector ν_r constructed via Algorithm 1 is indeed the same as that computed with the recursive relation specified in Eq. 1. The main difference is that the recursive relation in Eq. 1 computes the vector ν_r round by round, while we no more compute it in such a round-by-round way. If interpreting this from a mathematic perspective, we now deal with the modular addition in the exponent at the last round, while it is handled round by round in the recursive relation when tracing the polynomial representation. This reveals that the original coefficient grouping technique [30] developed for the case $w = 1$ can be fully interpreted via this new representation of $\mathcal{W}_r$.

4.2 (At Most) Quadratic Growth for $w = 1$

Meanwhile, our new representation allows us to show that *the algebraic degree in the univariate setting will never increase exponentially after the 1st round if $w = 1$.* In particular, we can prove that it can increase at most quadratically.

Specifically, for $0 \leq a_i \leq \nu_{r,i}$, based on the inequality $\mathrm{Hw}(M_n(a + b)) \leq \mathrm{Hw}(M_n(a)) + \mathrm{Hw}(M_n(b))$ [37], the following inequality always holds:

$$\mathrm{Hw}\left(M_n\left(\sum_{i=0}^{n-1} 2^i a_i\right)\right) \leq \sum_{i=0}^{n-1} \mathrm{Hw}\left(M_n(2^i a_i)\right) \leq \sum_{i=0}^{n-1} \mathrm{Hw}(a_i) \leq \sum_{i=0}^{n-1} \lfloor \log_2(\nu_{r,i} + 1)\rfloor.$$

Denote the nonzero elements in ν_r by $(\nu_{r,i_1}, \ldots, \nu_{r,i_\tau})$. With Algorithm 1 to construct such ν_r, for each $1 \leq j \leq \tau$, we have

$$\nu_{r,i_j} = \binom{r}{\ell_{i_j,1}} + \ldots + \binom{r}{\ell_{i_j,k_j}} \quad \text{where } k_j \geq 1. \tag{5}$$

In this way, we have $k_1 + \ldots + k_\tau = r + 1$ and

$$\{\ell_{i_1,1}, \ldots, \ell_{i_1,k_1}, \ldots, \ell_{i_\tau,1}, \ldots, \ell_{i_\tau,k_\tau}\} = \{0, \ldots, r\}. \tag{6}$$

Since $k_j \geq 1$ for $j \in [1, \tau]$, we have

$$\delta_r \leq \sum_{i=0}^{n-1} \lfloor \log_2(\nu_{r,i}+1)\rfloor = \sum_{j=1}^{\tau} \lfloor \log_2(\nu_{r,i_j}+1)\rfloor \leq \sum_{j=1}^{\tau} \log_2(\nu_{r,i_j}+1) \leq \sum_{j=1}^{\tau} \log_2(\nu_{r,i_j}+k_j).$$

Since $\log_2(a + b) \leq \log_2 a + \log_2 b$ for each $a, b \geq 2$, due to Eq. 5 and Eq. 6, we further have

$$\delta_r \leq \sum_{j=1}^{\tau} \log_2\left(\nu_{r,i_j} + k_j\right) = \sum_{j=1}^{\tau} \log_2\left(\sum_{u=1}^{k_j}\left(\binom{r}{\ell_{i_j,u}} + 1\right)\right) \leq \sum_{j=0}^{r} \log_2\left(\binom{r}{j} + 1\right),$$

which implies $\delta_1 \leq 2$ and $\delta_2 \leq 3$. Since $\binom{r}{i} + 1 \leq 2^{r-1}$ if $r \geq 3$, for $r \geq 3$, we have

$$\delta_r \leq 2 + \sum_{j=1}^{r-1} \log_2\left(\binom{r}{j} + 1\right) \leq 2 + (r - 1) \cdot \log_2 2^{r-1} = r^2 - 2r + 3.$$

As can be noted, these bounds are not tight. Still, *since $r^2 - 2r + 3 < 2^r$ for each $r \geq 2$*, it follows that the algebraic degree will never increase exponentially after the 1st round, and that it is always below the quadratic growth $r^2 - 2r + 3$ for any d when $w = 1$. Only for completeness, we emphasize that the accurate bound for the case $w = 1$ can be computed via the $\mathcal{O}(n)$ reduction algorithm in [37]. Compared with the results in [7,14,23], we point out that:

- the upper bounds proposed in such papers is exponential for the first r_0 rounds where $\lfloor \log_2(2^d + 1)^{r_0} + 1\rfloor > 2^{r_0}$ (roughly speaking, $d \cdot r_0 > 2^{r_0}$), while here we proved that it is always at most quadratic for any rounds and any d.
- although the upper bounds $\approx d \cdot r$ proposed in such papers become linear in the remaining rounds, it is still possible that our quadratic bound is better for some d in some of these rounds, e.g. this is obvious for large d.

4.3   Necessary Conditions for the Exponential Growth for $w > 1$

In the above, we have proved that the algebraic degree will never increase exponentially when $w = 1$. It is then natural to ask whether similar conclusions can be derived for complex affine layers, i.e., the case $w > 1$. Here, we answer this question.

Observations on $\mathcal{W}_r^S$. First, focus on the new representation of $\mathcal{W}_r^S$, as shown below:

$$\mathcal{W}_r^S = \left\{ \sum_{i=0}^{r} \sum_{j=1}^{\binom{r}{i}} a_{r,v} 2^{(r-i)d+f_v}, v = j + \binom{r}{\leq i-1}, 0 \leq a_{r,v} \leq 1, f_v \in V_{r,w} \right\},$$

Observe that each element in $e \in \mathcal{W}_r^S$ is a linear combination of 2^r numbers specified as:

$$\underbrace{2^{rd+f_1}}_{i=0}, \underbrace{2^{(r-1)d+f_{1+1}}, \ldots, 2^{(r-1)d+f_{1+\binom{r}{1}}}}_{i=1}, \ldots,$$

$$\underbrace{2^{(r-i)d+f_{\binom{r}{\leq i-1}+1}}, \ldots, 2^{(r-i)d+f_{\binom{r}{\leq i-1}+\binom{r}{i}}}}_{i}, \ldots, \underbrace{2^{f_{2^r}}}_{i=r}.$$

For each valid assignment to $(f_1, \ldots, f_{2^r})$, we can obtain a subset $\mathcal{W}_r^{S,f} \subseteq \mathcal{W}_r^S$ defined as:

$$\mathcal{W}_r^{S,f} = \left\{ \sum_{i=0}^{r} \sum_{j=1}^{\binom{r}{i}} a_{r,v} 2^{(r-i)d+f_v}, v = j + \binom{r}{\leq i-1}, 0 \leq a_{r,v} \leq 1 \right\}.$$

For this subset $\mathcal{W}_r^{S,f}$, computing $\max\{\mathrm{Hw}(M_n(e)) \mid e \in \mathcal{W}_r^{S,f}\}$ is equivalent to solving **OP-1** parameterized by the vector $\nu_r = (\nu_{r,n-1}, \ldots, \nu_{r,0})$, which is computed according to Algorithm 2. The underlying reason is that with the vector ν_r constructed with Algorithm 2, we have $\{M_n(e) \mid e \in \mathcal{W}_r^{S,f}\} = \{M_n(e) \mid e = \sum_{i=0}^{n-1} 2^i a_i, 0 \leq a_i \leq \nu_{r,i} \text{ for } 0 \leq i \leq n-1\}$.

Based on this, we can derive the following theorem.

Theorem 2. *For each valid assignment to $(f_1, \ldots, f_{2^r})$, the corresponding vector $\nu_r = (\nu_{r,n-1}, \ldots, \nu_{r,0})$ computed with Algorithm 2 satisfies the following property:*

$$\sum_{i=0}^{n-1} \nu_{r,i} = 2^r.$$

Especially, if there exists (i_1, v_1) and (i_2, v_2) where $i_1, i_2 \in [0, r]$ and $v_1, v_2 \in [1, 2^r]$ such that $(r - i_1) \times d + f_{v_1} = (r - i_2) \times d + f_{v_2}$, there are at most $2^r - 1$ nonzero elements in the vector ν_r.

Algorithm 2. Constructing $(\nu_{r,n-1}, \ldots, \nu_{r,0}) \in \mathbb{N}^n$ for the subset $\mathcal{W}_r^{S,f}$

```
1: procedure CONVERSION_SUBSET(νr, r, n)
2:     initialize (νr,n−1, . . . , νr,0) as all 0
3:     v = 1
4:     for all i ∈ [0, r] do
5:         for all j ∈ [1, (ri)] do
6:             u = ((r − i) × d + fv)%n
7:             νr,u = νr,u + 1
8:             v = v + 1
```

Proof. The first sum property directly follows from Algorithm 2 because there are 2^r iterations and in each iteration, one $\nu_{r,u}$ will be increased by 1. The second part can be observed from the formula to compute the index u, i.e. $u = ((r - i) \times d + f_v)\%n$. Specifically, if there exists such a pair (i_1, v_1) and (i_2, v_2), the same index u will appear at least twice and hence there are at most $2^r - 1$ different elements in ν_r that will be updated. $\qquad\square$

Necessary Condition for Exponential Growth. Based on this, we can deduce a necessary condition for ensuring the exponential growth.

Theorem 3. *To ensure that the sharp exponential growth can occur for the first r rounds, i.e. the algebraic degree 2^r can be reached after r rounds, one necessary condition is that there exists a valid assignment to $(f_1, \ldots, f_{2^r})$ such that the following 2^r elements are all different:*

$$
\underbrace{(rd + f_1)\%n,}_{i=0} \underbrace{((r-1)d + f_{1+1})\%n, \ldots, ((r-1)d + f_{1+\binom{r}{1}})\%n,}_{i=1} \ldots,
$$

$$
\underbrace{((r-i)d + f_{\binom{r}{\leq i-1}+1})\%n, \ldots, ((r-i)d + f_{\binom{r}{\leq i-1}+\binom{r}{i}})\%n,}_{i} \ldots, \underbrace{f_{2^r}\%n}_{i=r}.
$$

Proof. For each valid assignment to $(f_1, \ldots, f_{2^r})$ and the corresponding subset $\mathcal{W}_r^{S,f}$, we always have

$$
\max\left\{\mathrm{Hw}(M_n(e)) \mid e \in \mathcal{W}_r^{S,f}\right\} \leq \sum_{i=0}^{n-1} \lfloor \log_2(\nu_{r,i} + 1) \rfloor.
$$

If there does not exist an assignment to make the above 2^r numbers different, according to Theorem 2, there will be at most $2^r - 1$ nonzero elements in ν_r and we denote them by $(\nu_{r,j_1}, \ldots, \nu_{r,j_\tau})$ where $\tau \leq 2^r - 1$ and $\sum_{i=1}^{\tau} \nu_{r,j_i} = 2^r$. Due to $\lfloor \log_2(a + 1) \rfloor \leq a$ for $a \geq 1$ and $\lfloor \log_2(a + 1) \rfloor \leq a - 1$ for $a \geq 2$, we have $\sum_{i=0}^{n-1} \lfloor \log_2(\nu_{r,i} + 1) \rfloor = \sum_{i=1}^{\tau} \lfloor \log_2(\nu_{r,j_i} + 1) \rfloor \leq \sum_{i=1}^{\tau} \nu_{r,j_i} - 1 = 2^r - 1$, which implies $\delta_r \leq 2^r - 1$. If there exists such an assignment, we trivially have $\delta_r = 2^r$. $\qquad\square$

Corollary 1. *For a given* $(h_1, \ldots, h_w)$, *a necessary condition to ensure that the exponential growth can occur is*

$$|\mathcal{V}_{r,w}^R| \geq \binom{r}{\lceil \frac{r}{2} \rceil}$$

where

$$\mathcal{V}_{r,w}^R = \{e \% n \mid e \in \mathcal{V}_{r,w}\} = \left\{ e \% n \mid e = \sum_{i=1}^{w} b_i h_i, \sum_{i=1}^{w} b_i = r - 1, b_i \geq 0 \right\}.$$

Proof. To ensure the necessary condition in Theorem 3, then at least the following $\binom{r}{i}$ numbers must be different from each other for $i = \lceil \frac{r}{2} \rceil$:

$$\left((r-i)d + f_{\binom{r}{\leq i-1}+1} \right) \% n, \quad \ldots, \quad \left((r-i)d + f_{\binom{r}{\leq i-1}+\binom{r}{i}} \right) \% n,$$

which implies

$$\left(f_{\binom{r}{\leq i-1}+1} \right) \% n, \quad \ldots, \quad \left(f_{\binom{r}{\leq i-1}+\binom{r}{i}} \right) \% n$$

must be different. □

4.4   Choosing the Affine Layer $B(x)$ for the Exponential Growth

Impact of Theorem 3 on the Choice of $B(x)$. Let $\mathcal{B}_{r,w}$ be the set of tuples $(b_1, \ldots, b_w)$ defined as:

$$\mathcal{B}_{r,w} = \left\{ (b_1, \ldots, b_w) \mid \sum_{i=1}^{w} b_i = r, b_i \geq 0 \right\}.$$

Note that by definition, we have

$$|\mathcal{B}_{r,w}| = |\mathcal{B}_{r,w-1}| + |\mathcal{B}_{r-1,w-1}| + |\mathcal{B}_{r-2,w-1}| + \ldots + |\mathcal{B}_{0,w-1}|$$
$$= |\mathcal{B}_{r,w-1}| + |\mathcal{B}_{r-1,w}|.$$

Given such a set, we can deduce the following result.

Corollary 2. *A necessary condition for the exponential growth in the first r rounds is that*

$$|\mathcal{B}_{r-1,w}| \geq \binom{r}{\lceil \frac{r}{2} \rceil}.$$

Proof. For any given $(h_1, h_2, \ldots, h_w) \in \mathbb{N}^w$, by definition, we have

$$|\mathcal{V}_{r,w}^R| \leq |\mathcal{V}_{r,w}| \leq |\mathcal{B}_{r-1,w}|. \tag{7}$$

The necessary condition $|\mathcal{B}_{r-1,w}| \geq \binom{r}{\lceil \frac{r}{2} \rceil}$ directly follows Corollary 1 by involving the condition on $|\mathcal{B}_{r-1,w}| \geq |\mathcal{V}_{r,w}| \geq |\mathcal{V}_{r,w}^R|$ specified in Eq. 7. □

By simple computation:

$$|\mathcal{B}_{2,2}| = 3 \ge \binom{3}{2} = 3, \qquad |\mathcal{B}_{3,2}| = 4 < \binom{4}{2} = 6.$$

According to Corollary 2, the above inequality implies that it is impossible to achieve the sharp exponential growth of the algebraic degree at the 4th round when $w = 2$. In a similar way,

$$|\mathcal{B}_{5,3}| = 21 \ge \binom{6}{3} = 20, \qquad\qquad |\mathcal{B}_{6,3}| = 28 < \binom{7}{4} = 35,$$

$$|\mathcal{B}_{8,4}| = 165 \ge \binom{9}{5} = 126, \qquad\qquad |\mathcal{B}_{9,4}| = 220 < \binom{10}{5} = 252,$$

(and so on). As before, these imply that it is impossible to achieve the sharp exponential growth of the algebraic degree at the 7th and 10th round when $w = 3$ and $w = 4$, respectively (and so on). In other words, the sharp exponential growth can be achieved for at most the first 3, 6 and 9 rounds when $w = 2, 3, 4$, respectively.

In summary, even without considering the concrete affine layers, i.e., the concrete values of $(h_1, \ldots, h_w)$, the above results have revealed the influence of the density (w) of the affine layers on the growth of the algebraic degree from a pure theoretical perspective.

Equivalent Affine Layers. Corollary 1 and Corollary 2 can work as efficient filters to decide whether a specific $B(x)$ can achieve the exponential growth of the algebraic degree. To further reduce the number of candidates, it will be helpful if we can identify equivalent affine layers with the same influence on the growth of the algebraic degree with our techniques.

The following results hold:

Corollary 3. *Given an integer* $\varepsilon \ge 0$, *the following two affine layers have the same effect on the growth of the algebraic degree:*

$$B(x) = c_0 + \sum_{i=1}^{w} c_i x^{2^{h_i}}, \quad B'(x) = c_0' + \sum_{i=1}^{w} c_i' x^{2^{(h_i + \varepsilon) \% n}}.$$

Proof. First, let us introduce the set $\mathcal{V}'_{r,w}$ for a given integer $\varepsilon \ge 0$. Given $\mathcal{V}_{r,w}$ defined as in Eq. 3, let $\mathcal{V}'_{r,w}$ and $\mathcal{W}'^{S}_{r}$ be defined as:

$$\mathcal{V}'_{r,w} = \left\{ e \mid e = \sum_{i=1}^{w} b_i(h_i + \varepsilon), \sum_{i=1}^{w} b_i = r - 1, b_i \ge 0 \right\} = \{(r-1)\varepsilon + e \mid e \in \mathcal{V}_{r,w}\},$$

$$\mathcal{W}'^{S}_{r} = \left\{ \sum_{i=0}^{r} \sum_{j=1}^{\binom{r}{i}} a_{r,v} 2^{(r-i)d + f_v}, v = j + \binom{r}{\le i - 1}, 0 \le a_{r,v} \le 1, f_v \in \mathcal{V}'_{r,w} \right\},$$

where $(f_1, \ldots, f_{2^r})$ also satisfy Eq. 4. Then, we have $\{e \mid e \in \mathcal{W}'^S_r\} = \{2^{(r-1)\varepsilon} \cdot e \mid e \in \mathcal{W}^S_r\}$. Since $\mathrm{Hw}(M_n(e)) = \mathrm{Hw}(M_n(2^j \cdot e))$ for $j \in \mathbb{N}$, we have

$$\max\left\{\mathrm{Hw}(M_n(e)) \mid e \in \mathcal{W}^S_r\right\} = \max\left\{\mathrm{Hw}(M_n(e)) \mid e \in \mathcal{W}'^S_r\right\}.$$

$\square$

Corollary 4. *The following two affine layers have the same effect on the growth of the algebraic degree:*

$$B(x) = c_0 + \sum_{i=1}^{w} c_i x^{2^{h_i}}, \quad B'(x) = c'_0 + \sum_{i=1}^{w} c'_i x^{2^{h'_i}}$$

where $(h_{i+1} - h_i)\%n = (h'_{i+1} - h'_i)\%n$ for $i \in [1, w-1]$

Proof. First, according to Corollary 3, $B(x)$ is equivalent to $B_1(x) = c_{0,1} + \sum_{i=1}^{w} c_{i,1} x^{2^{(h_i - h_1)\%n}}$. Similarly, $B'(x)$ is equivalent to $B_2(x) = c_{0,2} + \sum_{i=1}^{w} c_{i,2} x^{2^{(h'_i - h'_1)\%n}}$. Moreover, we also have

$$(h'_i - h'_1)\%n = ((h'_i - h'_{i-1}) + (h'_{i-1} - h'_{i-2}) + \ldots + (h'_2 - h'_1))\%n$$
$$= ((h_i - h_{i-1}) + (h_{i-1} - h_{i-2}) + \ldots + (h_2 - h_1))\%n = (h_i - h_1)\%n.$$

This implies that $B_1(x)$ and $B_2(x)$ are equivalent and hence $B(x)$ and $B'(x)$ are equivalent. $\square$

As a concrete consequence, the two previous Corollaries imply that about $\frac{1}{w} \cdot \binom{n}{w-1}$ candidates out of $\binom{n}{w}$ have a different impact on the growth of the algebraic degree. Indeed, Corollary 3 indicates that we only need to consider such $(h_1, \ldots, h_w)$ that $0 \in \{h_1, \ldots, h_w\}$. For simplicity, let $0 = h_1 < \ldots < h_w$. Corollary 4 further suggests that even if we only need to consider such $(h_1, \ldots, h_w)$, there are still w equivalent cases, i.e. $(0, h_2, \ldots, h_w)$ is equivalent to $((0 - h_i)\%n, (h_2 - h_i)\%n, \ldots, (h_w - h_i)\%n)$ for $\forall i \in [1, w]$.

Consistency with Previous Works [7,14,23]. Let $h' = \max\{h_1, \ldots, h_w\}$. With the techniques proposed in these papers, an upper bound of δ_r is given by

$$\delta_r \leq \lfloor \log_2((2^d + 1)^r \cdot (2^{h'})^{r-1} + 1) \rfloor.$$

Here, we point out that this result can also be derived via the set $\mathcal{W}^S_r$. Specifically, since we always have $2^{(r-i)d+f_v} \leq 2^{(r-i)d} \cdot 2^{(r-1)h'}$, it follows that

$$\max\{e \mid e \in \mathcal{W}^S_r\} = 2^{(r-1)h'} \cdot \left(\sum_{i=0}^{r} \binom{r}{i} \cdot (2^d)^{r-i}\right) = 2^{(r-1)h'} \cdot (1 + 2^d)^r.$$

Hence, we have $\delta_r = \max\{\mathrm{Hw}(M_n(e)) \mid e \in \mathcal{W}^S_r\} \leq \lfloor \log_2((2^d+1)^r \cdot (2^{h'})^{r-1}+1) \rfloor$, which is exactly the same bound given before. While $\lfloor \log_2((2^d + 1)^r \cdot (2^{h'})^{r-1} + 1) \rfloor$ is an absolute upper bound, it may be loose because it corresponds to $\max\{\mathrm{Hw}(e) \mid e \in \mathcal{W}^S_r\}$ rather than $\max\{\mathrm{Hw}(M_n(e)) \mid e \in \mathcal{W}^S_r\}$, i.e. the modular addition cannot be handled. In our technique, we will deal with the modular operation.

5   Finding Affine Layers for the Exponential Increase

In the previous sections, we presented necessary conditions for the exponential growth of the algebraic degree. As next step, we analyze how to efficiently find $(h_1, \ldots, h_w)$ that satisfies such a requirement. We point out that this problem is nontrivial, since – as stated in Theorem 3 – we have to guarantee that there exists a valid assignment to $(f_1, \ldots, f_{2^r})$ for a given $(h_1, \ldots, h_w)$ such that the following 2^r numbers are all different, where we define $r + 1$ classes for these 2^r numbers and there are $\binom{r}{i-1}$ numbers in Class i:

Class 1 : $(rd + f_1)\%n$,

Class 2 : $((r - 1)d + f_{1+1})\%n, \ldots, \left((r - 1)d + f_{1+\binom{r}{1}}\right)\%n$,

$\ldots$,

Class $i + 1$: $\left((r - i)d + f_{\binom{r}{\leq i-1}+1}\right)\%n, \ldots, \left((r - i)d + f_{\binom{r}{\leq i-1}+\binom{r}{i}}\right)\%n$,

$\ldots$,

Class $r + 1$: $f_{2^r}\%n$.

Remark 4. We point out that giving a sufficient condition is a much more difficult task. Indeed, even giving the capability to write down the accurate polynomial representation after r rounds, many more factors play a role. E.g., the coefficients in the polynomial representation depend on the concrete value of the secret key, hence, the maximum algebraic degree could be different for different keys (remember that it is defined by the monomials with nonzero coefficients).

Let us recall that there are some special inner conditions on $(f_1, \ldots, f_{2^r})$:

$$f_{\binom{r}{\leq i}+\ell} = f_{\binom{r}{\leq i}-\binom{r-1}{i}+\ell} \quad \text{for } 0 \leq i \leq r - 1, 1 \leq \ell \leq \binom{r-1}{i}. \tag{8}$$

Specifically, the inner conditions on $(f_1, \ldots, f_{2^r})$ state that for two consecutive classes, the last $\binom{r-1}{i} = \binom{r}{i} - \binom{r-1}{i-1}$ different f_v in Class $i+1$ have to be identical to the first $\binom{r-1}{i}$ different f_v in Class $i + 2$, respectively. This can be observed from Fig. 2 by replacing q with r.

5.1   The Pre-processing Phase

To efficiently check the conditions in Theorem 3, we first precompute $r + 1$ arrays of size n, which are denoted by $A_1, \ldots, A_{r+1}$ where $A_i = (A_i[n-1], \ldots, A_i[0]) \in \mathbb{F}_2^n$. Specifically, A_{i+1} corresponds to the Class $i + 1$, and it is computed via the following rule:

$$\text{Set } A_{i+1} \text{ as all zero}$$
$$\text{for all } u \in \mathcal{V}_{r,w}^R :$$
$$j = ((r - i) \times d + u)\%n$$
$$A_{i+1}[j] = 1$$

In other words, $A_{i+1}[j] = 1$ means that the value j can appear in the Class $i+1$, while $A_{i+1}[j] = 0$ means that the value j does not appear in the Class $i+1$. By simple computation, we also have that

$$A_{i+1}[j] = A_i[(j+d)\%n], \ \forall j \in [0, n-1].$$

Given these $r+1$ precomputed arrays, we can build a model to decide whether there exists an assignment to $(f_1, \ldots, f_{2^r})$ such that all the 2^r elements in the $r+1$ classes are different. This corresponds to finding $\binom{r}{i}$ nonzero positions from A_{i+1} for each $i \in [0, r]$ – by taking the inner conditions in Eq. 8 into account – such that all these 2^r positions are different.

Before going on, we introduce an important set $\mathcal{Z}$. With these $r+1$ arrays $(A_1, \ldots, A_{r+1})$, we can construct a set $\mathcal{Z}$ defined as:

$$\mathcal{Z} := \{j \mid \exists i \in [1, r+1], \ A_i[j] \neq 0\}. \tag{9}$$

This set $\mathcal{Z}$ stores all possible numbers that can be chosen for the 2^r numbers in the $r+1$ classes. The following necessary condition trivially follows:

Corollary 5. *A necessary condition for the exponential growth in the first r rounds is $|\mathcal{Z}| \geq 2^r$.*

Different from Corollary 1 and Corollary 2, the influence of d on the growth of the algebraic degree can be reflected by Corollary 5.

5.2   Building the Model

Given the arrays A_i defined as before, we can now construct our model. First, we introduce two binary arrays for each A_i denoted by A_i^{up} and A_i^{dw}, respectively. A_i^{up} records the choices for the first $\binom{r-1}{i-2}$ elements in the Class i, while A_i^{dw} records the choices for the last $\binom{r-1}{i-1} = \binom{r}{i-1} - \binom{r-1}{i-2}$ elements in the Class i. Note that:

- if $A_i^{up}[j] = 1$ or $A_i^{dw}[j] = 1$, then the position j will be chosen from A_i as a number in the first $\binom{r-1}{i-2}$ (or the last $\binom{r-1}{i-1}$) elements in Class i;
- the inner conditions in Eq. 8 imply that

$$A_{i+1}^{up}[j] = A_i^{dw}[(j+d)\%n], \ \forall i \in [1, r], \forall j \in [0, n-1]; \tag{10}$$

- the arrays A_1^{up} and A_{r+1}^{dw} should always be set to 0 because A_1 and A_{r+1} represent the first and last class, respectively. This implies that the following conditions are necessary:

$$A_1^{up}[j] = 0, \quad A_{r+1}^{dw}[j] = 0, \forall j \in [0, n-1]; \tag{11}$$

- the arrays A_i^{up} and A_i^{dw} have to satisfy

$$A_i^{up}[j] = A_i^{dw}[j] = 0 \ \text{if} \ A_i[j] = 0, \ \forall i \in [1, r+1], \forall j \in [0, n-1], \tag{12}$$

because we can only choose positions from nonzero positions in A_i.

– the arrays A_i^{dw} have to satisfy

$$\sum_{j=0}^{n-1} A_i^{dw}[j] \leq \binom{r-1}{i-1}, \ \forall i \in [1, r], \tag{13}$$

because we can choose at most $\binom{r-1}{i-1}$ positions from A_i for the last $\binom{r-1}{i-1}$ elements in Class i, i.e. it is possible that some elements in Class i will be the same. Note that combined with Eq. 10, there is always:

$$\sum_{j=0}^{n-1} A_i^{up}[j] = \sum_{j=0}^{n-1} A_{i-1}^{dw}[j] \leq \binom{r-1}{i-2}, \ \forall i \in [2, r+1], \tag{14}$$

i.e. we can choose at most $\binom{r-1}{i-2}$ positions from A_i for the first $\binom{r-1}{i-2}$ elements in Class i. In other words, the constraint in Eq. 14 can be omitted.

Finally, we introduce another binary array $X = (X[n-1], \ldots, X[0]) \in \mathbb{F}_2^n$, where $X[j] = 1$ (resp., $X[j] = 0$) means j has (resp., not) been chosen for the 2^r numbers. Hence, $X[j] = 1$ holds if and only if there exists (i, j) such that $A_i^{up}[j] + A_i^{dw}[j] \geq 1$. As a result, the following constraints can be derived:

$$X[j] \geq A_i^{up}[j], \ \forall i \in [1, r+1], \forall j \in [0, n-1],$$
$$X[j] \geq A_i^{dw}[j], \ \forall i \in [1, r+1], \forall j \in [0, n-1],$$
$$X[j] \leq \sum_{i=1}^{r+1} (A_i^{up}[j] + A_i^{dw}[j]), \ \forall j \in [0, n-1].$$

The objective function can be set to

$$\text{maximize} \sum_{i=0}^{n-1} X[i].$$

Interpretation of the Objective Function. The objective function indeed corresponds to the maximal number of different elements in the $r+1$ classes under all possible valid assignments to $(f_1, \ldots, f_{2^r})$. Let us denote the solution of the objective function by π. Taking Algorithm 2 into account, π indeed means that under all possible assignments to $(f_1, \ldots, f_{2^r})$, the corresponding vectors $(\nu_{r,n-1}, \ldots, \nu_{r,0})$ must satisfy

$$|\{i \mid \nu_{r,i} \neq 0, 0 \leq i \leq n-1\}| \leq \pi. \tag{15}$$

According to Theorem 3, $\pi = 2^r$ has to hold to ensure the sharp exponential growth of the algebraic degree, in which case we can find a valid assignment to $(f_1, \ldots, f_{2^r})$ such that all the 2^r elements in the $r+1$ classes are different.

Remark 5. To ensure the maximal degree n can be reached at round r, we can turn to testing whether $\pi = n$ holds. Of course, this is not a necessary condition but it greatly simplifies the problem and helps designers efficiently pick proper $(h_1, \ldots, h_w)$ for the fastest growth of the algebraic degree.

5.3   Practical Tests

For the efficiency of ciphers, w should be kept as small as possible while it can still ensure the exponential/fastest growth of the algebraic degree. In our following experiments, we find that the model is very light and can be efficiently solved. Our aim is to find proper $(h_1, \ldots, h_w)$ for any specified (n, d) with small w. All the experiments in this paper are performed on a PC by using 4 threads. The processor is 11th Gen Intel(R) Core(TM) i7-1195G7 and the RAM is 32 GB.

The Case $(n, d) = (63, 32)$. For example, for $(n, d) = (63, 32)$ which is the parameter used in Chaghri, according to Corollary 2, $w \geq 3$ has to hold to ensure the sharp exponential growth. With our new technique, we found in total 80 desired solutions of (h_1, h_2, h_3) without equivalent relations that can make $\delta_5 = 32$ and $\delta_6 = 63$. The details can be referred to the full version [31]. For the running time, we observed that for each possible candidate of (h_1, h_2, h_3), it takes about 0.01–0.07 s to output the solution π. This is definitely much better than the previous coefficient grouping technique by the plain enumeration [30].

It is found that the recommended parameter $(h_1, h_2, h_3) = (0, 2, 8)$ to patch Chaghri in [30] is not included, which implies that $(h_1, h_2, h_3) = (0, 2, 8)$ is probably not a good choice.

The Case $(n, d) = (129, 1)$. According to Corollary 2, for $(n, d) = (129, 1)$ which is the parameter used in MiMC, to ensure the sharp exponential growth, $w \geq 4$ has to hold. There are so many possible such (h_1, h_2, h_3, h_4) that can reach this goal, i.e. $\delta_7 = 128$ and $\delta_8 = 129$ can be achieved with these $(h_1, \ldots, h_4)$. For the running time, we observed that for each possible candidate of (h_1, h_2, h_3, h_4), it takes about 0.02–0.15 s to output the solution π.

To summarize, we presented a light strategy for efficiently determining whether a complex affine layer can be used to achieve the goal of the exponential/fastest growth of the algebraic degree. It is found that this problem can be converted into checking whether it is possible to select $\min\{2^r, n\}$ numbers from $r + 1$ sets under several constraints. As a result, we no more need to enumerate the set $\mathcal{P}_r$ as in [30], and test whether the best case occurs.

6   Degree Evaluation for Arbitrary Affine Layers

Until now, we mainly consider the problem from the designers' perspective, i.e. how to efficiently find proper $B(x)$ to achieve the fastest growth of the algebraic degree. If we consider the attackers' perspective, we then need to give an upper bound for δ_r for any $B(x)$.

The main obstacle here is how to avoid the enumeration of all possible $(f_1, \ldots, f_{2^r})$ and the corresponding vectors ν_r constructed with Algorithm 2. Once we can overcome it, we will be closer to efficiently finding a meaningful upper bound for δ_r for any $B(x)$.

6.1   Three Common Features

We avoid the enumeration of all possible $(\nu_{r,n-1}, \ldots, \nu_{r,0})$ by capturing the common features in them.

Feature 1. The first feature has been given by Theorem 2, i.e., each vector $\nu_r = (\nu_{r,n-1}, \ldots, \nu_{r,0})$ satisfies $\sum_{i=0}^{n-1} \nu_{r,i} = 2^r$.

Feature 2. The second feature is given by Eq. 15, i.e. each such vector $\nu_r = (\nu_{r,n-1}, \ldots, \nu_{r,0})$ satisfies $|\{i \mid \nu_{r,i} \neq 0, \ 0 \leq i \leq n-1\}| \leq \pi$.

Feature 3. By the definition of $\mathcal{Z}$ as in Eq. 9, we also know that the positions i for which $\nu_{r,i}$ can be different from zero must belong to $\mathcal{Z}$, that is, $\{i \mid \nu_{r,i} \neq 0, \ 0 \leq i \leq n-1\} \subseteq \mathcal{Z}$.

6.2   The Problem Reduction

To give an upper bound for δ_r for any $B(x)$, we use the problem reduction, i.e. finding an equivalent problem to upper bound δ_r. With the above common features in all possible $(\nu_{r,n-1}, \ldots, \nu_{r,0})$, the problem reduces to

$$\text{maximize Hw}\left(M_n\left(\sum_{i=0}^{n-1} 2^i a_i\right)\right)$$

subjectto :

$$\forall i \in [0, n-1] : a_i \leq \nu_{r,i}; \ \sum_{i=0}^{n-1} \nu_{r,i} = 2^r; \ |\{i \mid \nu_{r,i} \neq 0\}| \leq \pi; \ \{i \mid \nu_{r,i} \neq 0\} \subseteq \mathcal{Z}.$$

For convenience, let $\mathcal{Z} = \{p_1, \ldots, p_{|\mathcal{Z}|}\}$. Then, we can obtain an equivalent description of the above optimization problem by omitting the variables $(\nu_{r,n-1}, \ldots, \nu_{r,0})$, as shown below:

$$\text{maximize Hw}\left(M_n\left(\sum_{i=1}^{|\mathcal{Z}|} 2^{p_i} a_{p_i}\right)\right),$$

$$\text{subjectto } \forall i \in [1, |\mathcal{Z}|] : a_{p_i} \geq 0; \ \sum_{i=1}^{|\mathcal{Z}|} a_{p_i} \leq 2^r; \ |\{p_i \mid a_{p_i} \neq 0\}| \leq \pi.$$

Hence, to upper bound δ_r for any given $B(x)$, the first step is to compute the set $\mathcal{Z}$ and the solution of the objective function π as shown in the above section. The next step is to solve the above optimization problem. It can be observed that this optimization problem is very similar to **OP-1**. The differences are (i) there is only a trivial upper bound for each a_{p_i}, i.e. $a_{p_i} \leq 2^r$; (ii) there is a concrete upper bound for the sum $\sum_{i=1}^{|\mathcal{Z}|} a_{p_i}$; and (iii) there is an upper bound for the number of nonzero a_{p_i}. In this sense, this optimization problem is more general and should be more difficult to solve. However, by using off-the-shelf solvers like Gurobi[2], we can still efficiently solve it. Modelling this optimization problem is almost the same as modelling **OP-1**, which has been fully described in [30]. The pseudo-code for this general optimization problem can be referred to the full version [31].

Remark 6. It can be observed that we consider all possible vectors ν_r satisfying the 3 common features. It is possible that some of them will not appear in the actual set of all possible ν_r obtained by the naive enumeration. Hence, the solution of the optimization problem is a possibly loose upper bound of δ_r.

6.3   Practical Tests

One interesting experiment is to see how the upper bound of the algebraic degree increases in the univariate setting when $w = 2$. We tried some (n, d, h_1, h_2) and the results are shown in Table 1. A graphic illustration is given in Fig. 3. Note that with the method [30] to enumerate $\mathcal{P}_r$ to find the upper bound, it can work for at most the first 6 rounds since the time complexity is $w^{2^{r-1}} = 2^{2^{r-1}}$ when $w = 2$. However, in the experiments with our technique, testing this even for 20 rounds takes less than 1 min.

In particular, it is found that upper bound of the algebraic degree increases linearly for $(n, d, h_1, h_2) = (129, 1, 0, 63)$ and it increases by 7 each round after the 7th round. This is difficult to explain since $\log_2((2^1 + 1) \cdot 2^{63}) \approx 64.6$ is much larger than 7. We thus believe that more theoretic interpretations should be developed to understand this, which is left as an interesting problem.

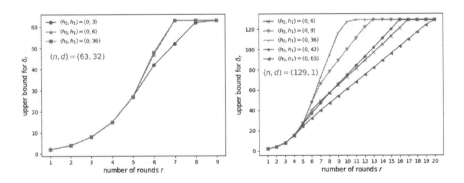

Fig. 3. Graphic illustration of the growth of the algebraic degree

As for the multivariate case, we should emphasize that once the maximal degree is reached for the univariate case, we will reach the maximal degree for the

---

[2] www.gurobi.com.

Table 1. Some experimental results for upper bounding the algebraic degree

(n,d,h_1,h_2)	r	≤ 3	4	5	6	7	8	9	10	11	12	13	14	15	16	17	18	19	20
(63,32,0,3)	δ_r	2^r	15	27	42	52	62	63	–	–	–	–	–	–	–	–	–	–	–
time (seconds)		≤ 0.1	0.1	0.1	0.4	0.2	0.3	5.2	–	–	–	–	–	–	–	–	–	–	–
(63,32,0,6)	δ_r	2^r	15	27	47	63	–	–	–	–	–	–	–	–	–	–	–	–	–
time (seconds)		≤ 0.1	0.11	0.1	0.5	1.6	–	–	–	–	–	–	–	–	–	–	–	–	–
(63,32,0,36)	δ_r	2^r	15	27	48	63	–	–	–	–	–	–	–	–	–	–	–	–	–
time (seconds)		≤ 0.1	0.1	0.1	1.0	4.3	–	–	–	–	–	–	–	–	–	–	–	–	–
(129,1,0,6)	δ_r	2^r	15	27	40	49	$49 + 8 \times (r-7)$									129	–	–	–
time (seconds)		< 0.1	0.1	0.1	0.3	0.1	0.5	0.7	0.3	0.3	1.7	1.9	1.5	1.9	2.3	5.8	–	–	–
(129,1,0,9)	δ_r	2^r	15	27	48	66	78	89	100	111	122	129	–	–	–	–	–	–	–
time (seconds)		< 0.1	0.1	0.1	0.2	1.5	1.4	2.4	1.3	1.7	1.9	5	–	–	–	–	–	–	–
(129,1,0,36)	δ_r	2^r	15	27	48	72	94	116	127	129	–	–	–	–	–	–	–	–	–
time (seconds)		< 0.1	0.1	0.1	0.3	0.6	5.1	18.3	23.3	13.9	–	–	–	–	–	–	–	–	–
(129,1,0,42)	δ_r	2^r	15	26	37	47	57	66	75	84	93	102	111	120	129	–	–	–	–
time (seconds)		< 0.1	0.1	0.1	0.2	0.3	0.4	0.7	0.5	8.9	1.5	4.2	8.3	23.6	11.1	–	–	–	–
(129,1,0,63)	δ_r	2^r	15	24	32	40	$40 + 7 \times (r-7)$												129
time (seconds)		< 0.1	0.1	0.1	0.1	0.3	0.2	0.5	0.9	0.9	1.0	1.1	29.2	4.8	8.6	32.9	70.7	23.2	48.9

multivariate degree very fast, which can be seen from the attacks on Chaghri [30] and can also be seen from the relations between **OP-1** and **OP-t** which share the same vector ν_r. Details can be referred to the full version [31].

7 Future Works

In this paper, we have developed a new technique to evaluate the growth of the algebraic degree for a special SPN cipher over $\mathbb{F}_{2^n}$. With this technique, we are able to answer some important related questions. Still, there are still some problems worth further investigating.

First of all, as mentioned several times, the reduced well-structured optimization problems are solved via blackbox solvers. It is meaningful to develop efficient algorithms for them to further understand the efficiency of the new technique.

Secondly, we have mainly discussed how to efficiently find $B(x)$ such that the fastest growth of the algebraic degree can be reached and how to upper bound the algebraic degree for arbitrary $B(x)$. It is natural to ask how tight the upper bounds are.

In order to answer this question, we performed some practical experiments[3] on the studied SPN cipher parameterized with $m = 3$, where the coefficients $(c_1, \ldots, c_w)$ in $B(x)$ and the round constants/keys will vary in each experiment. For the matrix M, we considered three cases:

case1: *M* is a simple non-MDS matrix fixed as $[[0, 1, \beta], [\beta, 0, 1], [1, \beta, 0]]$ for the efficiency of the experiments, where β here denotes the root of the irreducible polynomial over $\mathbb{F}_{2^n}$.

---

[3] The source code is available at https://github.com/LFKOKAMI/CG_test.

Table 2. Comparison between the algebraic degree (obtained experimentally via "AZP" or "OZP") with the upper bound obtained with the strategy proposed in this paper ("our bound") for case1/case2/case3.

(n,d,h_1,h_2)	methods	case	# rounds				
			1	2	3	4	5
(129,1,0,6)	our bound		2	4	8	15	27
	AZP/OZP	case1	2	4	8	14	23
		case2	2	4	8	13	23
		case3	2	4	8	14	23
(129,1,0,9)	our bound		2	4	8	15	27
	AZP/OZP	case1	2	4	8	14	23
		case2	2	4	8	13	23
		case3	2	4	8	14	23
(129,1,0,36)	our bound		2	4	8	15	27
	AZP/OZP	case1	2	4	8	14	23
		case2	2	4	8	13	23
		case3	2	4	8	14	23
(129,1,0,42)	our bound		2	4	8	15	26
	AZP/OZP	case1	2	4	8	14	22
		case2	2	4	8	13	21
		case3	2	4	8	14	22
(129,1,0,63)	our bound		2	4	8	15	24
	AZP/OZP	case1	2	4	8	14	20
		case2	2	4	8	13	20
		case3	2	4	8	14	20
(63,32,0,3)	our bound		2	4	8	15	27
	AZP/OZP	case1	2	4	8	14	25
		case2	2	4	8	14	24
		case3	2	4	8	14	25
(63,32,0,6)	our bound		2	4	8	15	27
	AZP/OZP	case1	2	4	8	14	25
		case2	2	4	8	14	24
		case3	2	4	8	14	25
(63,32,0,36)	our bound		2	4	8	15	27
	AZP/OZP	case1	2	4	8	14	25
		case2	2	4	8	14	24
		case3	2	4	8	14	25

case2: M is a simple MDS matrix fixed as $[[\beta, 1, 1 + \beta], [1, 1, 1], [1 + \beta, \beta, 1]]$ for the efficiency of the experiments.

case3: M is a randomly generated invertible matrix.

For finding the actual growth of the algebraic degree, we simply choose subspaces of dimension dim, and test whether the corresponding sums of the outputs are zero. In this way, we can deduce that the algebraic degree is dim -1 for the smallest dim that can make the sums of the outputs zero. For completeness, we test two different zero-sum properties:

- all-zero property (AZP): all the sums of the output words are zero;
- one-zero property (OZP): one of the sums of the output words is zero.

First, we test the parameters to achieve the exponential growth of the algebraic degree as discussed in Sect. 5. In case1/case2/case3, we obtain that the algebraic degree at round i is exactly 2^i for $1 \leq i \leq 4$, no matter if it is detected by AZP or OZP. Due to the limitation of our computing resources[4], we could only verify this for the first 4 rounds.

Second, to bound the algebraic degree for arbitrary $B(x)$, we test the parameters considered in Sect. 6 for up to 5 rounds. It is found that the upper bounds are tight for the first 3 rounds and become loose in the 4th and 5th rounds, though the gap is not so large, as shown in Table 2. This result is expected, since the model used to evaluate the upper bound of the algebraic degree for arbitrary $B(x)$ is not perfect due to the usage of relaxed constraints. We leave the problem to improve it without affecting its efficiency too much open for future work.

Moreover, it can also be observed from Table 2 that the same algebraic degree is obtained by detecting AZP or OZP. We also observe that the algebraic degree obtained in the 3 cases is only slightly different, which somehow demonstrates the influence of M on the growth of the algebraic degree, though we could not capture it with our technique. This is also an interesting problem for further study.

Acknowledgments. We thank the reviewers of CRYPTO 2023 for providing many insightful comments. Fukang Liu is supported by Grant-in-Aid for Research Activity Start-up (Grant No. 22K21282). Lorenzo Grassi is supported by the German Research Foundation (DFG) within the framework of the Excellence Strategy of the Federal Government and the States - EXC 2092 CaSa - 39078197. Takanori Isobe is supported by JST, PRESTO Grant Number JPMJPR2031. These research results were also obtained from the commissioned research (No.05801) by National Institute of Information and Communications Technology (NICT), Japan.

---

[4] It turns out that case3 consumes much more time than case1/case2. Encrypting 2^{23} inputs takes about 1 h in case1/case2, while encrypting 2^{21} inputs takes about 1 h in case3.

References

1. Albrecht, M.R., et al.: Algebraic cryptanalysis of STARK-friendly designs: application to MARVELLOUS and MiMC. In: Galbraith, S.D., Moriai, S. (eds.) ASIACRYPT 2019. LNCS, vol. 11923, pp. 371–397. Springer, Cham (2019). https://doi.org/10.1007/978-3-030-34618-8_13

2. Albrecht, M., Grassi, L., Rechberger, C., Roy, A., Tiessen, T.: MiMC: efficient encryption and cryptographic hashing with minimal multiplicative complexity. In: Cheon, J.H., Takagi, T. (eds.) ASIACRYPT 2016. LNCS, vol. 10031, pp. 191–219. Springer, Heidelberg (2016). https://doi.org/10.1007/978-3-662-53887-6_7

3. Albrecht, M.R., Rechberger, C., Schneider, T., Tiessen, T., Zohner, M.: Ciphers for MPC and FHE. IACR Cryptol. ePrint Arch., Paper 2016/687 (2016)

4. Ashur, T., Mahzoun, M., Toprakhisar, D.: Chaghri - a FHE-friendly Block Cipher. In: CCS, pp. 139–150. ACM (2022)

5. Beyne, T., et al.: Out of oddity – new cryptanalytic techniques against symmetric primitives optimized for integrity proof systems. In: Micciancio, D., Ristenpart, T. (eds.) CRYPTO 2020. LNCS, vol. 12172, pp. 299–328. Springer, Cham (2020). https://doi.org/10.1007/978-3-030-56877-1_11

6. Boura, C., Canteaut, A., De Cannière, C.: Higher-order differential properties of KECCAK and *Luffa*. In: Joux, A. (ed.) FSE 2011. LNCS, vol. 6733, pp. 252–269. Springer, Heidelberg (2011). https://doi.org/10.1007/978-3-642-21702-9_15

7. Bouvier, C., Canteaut, A., Perrin, L.: On the algebraic degree of iterated power functions. Des. Codes Cryptogr. **91**(3), 997–1033 (2023)

8. Brakerski, Z., Gentry, C., Vaikuntanathan, V.: (Leveled) fully homomorphic encryption without bootstrapping. ACM Trans. Comput. Theor. **6**(3), 13:1-13:36 (2014)

9. Canteaut, A., et al.: Stream ciphers: a practical solution for efficient homomorphic-ciphertext compression. J. Cryptol. **31**(3), 885–916 (2018). https://doi.org/10.1007/s00145-017-9273-9

10. Cheon, J.H., Kim, A., Kim, M., Song, Y.: Homomorphic encryption for arithmetic of approximate numbers. In: Takagi, T., Peyrin, T. (eds.) ASIACRYPT 2017. LNCS, vol. 10624, pp. 409–437. Springer, Cham (2017). https://doi.org/10.1007/978-3-319-70694-8_15

11. Chillotti, I., Gama, N., Georgieva, M., Izabachène, M.: Faster fully homomorphic encryption: bootstrapping in less than 0.1 seconds. In: Cheon, J.H., Takagi, T. (eds.) ASIACRYPT 2016. LNCS, vol. 10031, pp. 3–33. Springer, Heidelberg (2016). https://doi.org/10.1007/978-3-662-53887-6_1

12. Chillotti, I., Gama, N., Georgieva, M., Izabachène, M.: TFHE: fast fully homomorphic encryption over the torus. J. Cryptol. **33**(1), 34–91 (2020)

13. Cho, J., et al.: Transciphering framework for approximate homomorphic encryption. In: Tibouchi, M., Wang, H. (eds.) ASIACRYPT 2021. LNCS, vol. 13092, pp. 640–669. Springer, Cham (2021). https://doi.org/10.1007/978-3-030-92078-4_22

14. Cid, C., Grassi, L., Gunsing, A., Lüftenegger, R., Rechberger, C., Schofnegger, M.: Influence of the linear layer on the algebraic degree in SP-networks. IACR Trans. Symmetric Cryptol. **2022**(1), 110–137 (2022)

15. Cosseron, O., Hoffmann, C., Méaux, P., Standaert, F.-X.: Towards globally optimized hybrid homomorphic encryption - featuring the Elisabeth stream cipher. Cryptology ePrint Archive, Paper 2022/180 (2022). https://eprint.iacr.org/2022/180

16. Cui, J., Hu, K., Wang, M., Wei, P.: On the field-based division property: applications to MiMC, Feistel MiMC and GMiMC. In: Agrawal, S., Lin, D. (eds.) Advances in Cryptology, ASIACRYPT 2022. LNCS, vol. 13793, pp. 241–270. Springer, Cham (2022). https://doi.org/10.1007/978-3-031-22969-5_9

17. Dinur, I.: Cryptanalytic applications of the polynomial method for solving multivariate equation systems over GF(2). In: Canteaut, A., Standaert, F.-X. (eds.) EUROCRYPT 2021. LNCS, vol. 12696, pp. 374–403. Springer, Cham (2021). https://doi.org/10.1007/978-3-030-77870-5_14

18. Dinur, I., Liu, Y., Meier, W., Wang, Q.: Optimized interpolation attacks on LowMC. In: Iwata, T., Cheon, J.H. (eds.) ASIACRYPT 2015. LNCS, vol. 9453, pp. 535–560. Springer, Heidelberg (2015). https://doi.org/10.1007/978-3-662-48800-3_22

19. Dobraunig, C., et al.: Rasta: a cipher with low ANDdepth and few ANDs per bit. In: Shacham, H., Boldyreva, A. (eds.) CRYPTO 2018. LNCS, vol. 10991, pp. 662–692. Springer, Cham (2018). https://doi.org/10.1007/978-3-319-96884-1_22

20. Dobraunig, C., Grassi, L., Helminger, L., Rechberger, C., Schofnegger, M., Walch, R.: Pasta: a case for hybrid homomorphic encryption. Cryptology ePrint Archive, Paper 2021/731 (2021). https://eprint.iacr.org/2021/731

21. Dobraunig, C., Kales, D., Rechberger, C., Schofnegger, M., Zaverucha, G.: Shorter signatures based on Tailor-made minimalist symmetric-key crypto. In: CCS, pp. 843–857. ACM (2022)

22. Duval, S., Lallemand, V., Rotella, Y.: Cryptanalysis of the FLIP family of stream ciphers. In: Robshaw, M., Katz, J. (eds.) CRYPTO 2016. LNCS, vol. 9814, pp. 457–475. Springer, Heidelberg (2016). https://doi.org/10.1007/978-3-662-53018-4_17

23. Eichlseder, M., et al.: An algebraic attack on ciphers with low-degree round functions: application to full MiMC. In: Moriai, S., Wang, H. (eds.) ASIACRYPT 2020. LNCS, vol. 12491, pp. 477–506. Springer, Cham (2020). https://doi.org/10.1007/978-3-030-64837-4_16

24. Gentry, C.: Fully homomorphic encryption using ideal lattices. In: STOC, pp. 169–178. ACM (2009)

25. Gentry, C., Halevi, S., Smart, N.P.: Homomorphic evaluation of the AES circuit. In: Safavi-Naini, R., Canetti, R. (eds.) CRYPTO 2012. LNCS, vol. 7417, pp. 850–867. Springer, Heidelberg (2012). https://doi.org/10.1007/978-3-642-32009-5_49

26. Gentry, C., Sahai, A., Waters, B.: Homomorphic encryption from learning with errors: conceptually-simpler, asymptotically-faster, attribute-based. In: Canetti, R., Garay, J.A. (eds.) CRYPTO 2013. LNCS, vol. 8042, pp. 75–92. Springer, Heidelberg (2013). https://doi.org/10.1007/978-3-642-40041-4_5

27. Ha, J., et al.: Masta: an HE-friendly cipher using modular arithmetic. IEEE Access 8, 194741–194751 (2020)

28. Hebborn, P., Leander, G.: Dasta - alternative linear layer for Rasta. IACR Trans. Symmetric Cryptol. 2020(3), 46–86 (2020)

29. Lai, X.: Higher order derivatives and differential cryptanalysis. In: Blahut, R.E., Costello, D.J., Maurer, U., Mittelholzer, T. (eds.) Communications and Cryptography. The Springer International Series in Engineering and Computer Science, vol. 276, pp. 227–233. Springer, Boston (1994). https://doi.org/10.1007/978-1-4615-2694-0_23

30. Liu, F., Anand, R., Wang, L., Meier, W., Isobe, T.: Coefficient grouping: breaking Chaghri and more. In: Hazay, C., Stam, M. (eds.) Advances in Cryptology, EUROCRYPT 2023. LNCS, vol. 14007. Springer, Cham (2023). https://doi.org/10.1007/978-3-031-30634-1_10

31. Liu, F., Grassi, L., Bouvier, C., Meier, W., Isobe, T.: Coefficient grouping for complex affine layers. Cryptology ePrint Archive, Paper 2023/782 (2023). https://eprint.iacr.org/2023/782

32. Liu, F., Isobe, T., Meier, W.: Cryptanalysis of full LowMC and LowMC-M with algebraic techniques. In: Malkin, T., Peikert, C. (eds.) CRYPTO 2021. LNCS, vol. 12827, pp. 368–401. Springer, Cham (2021). https://doi.org/10.1007/978-3-030-84252-9_13

33. Liu, F., Meier, W., Sarkar, S., Isobe, T.: New low-memory algebraic attacks on LowMC in the picnic setting. IACR Trans. Symmetric Cryptol. **2022**(3), 102–122 (2022)

34. Liu, F., Sarkar, S., Meier, W., Isobe, T.: Algebraic attacks on Rasta and Dasta using low-degree equations. In: Tibouchi, M., Wang, H. (eds.) ASIACRYPT 2021. LNCS, vol. 13090, pp. 214–240. Springer, Cham (2021). https://doi.org/10.1007/978-3-030-92062-3_8

35. Liu, F., Sarkar, S., Meier, W., Isobe, T.: The inverse of χ and its applications to Rasta-like ciphers. J. Cryptol. **35**(4), 28 (2022)

36. Liu, F., Sarkar, S., Wang, G., Meier, W., Isobe, T.: Algebraic meet-in-the-middle attack on LowMC. In: Agrawal, S., Lin, D. (eds.) Advances in Cryptology, ASIACRYPT 2022. LNCS, vol. 13791, pp. 225–255. Springer, Cham (2022). https://doi.org/10.1007/978-3-031-22963-3_8

37. Liu, F., Wang, L.: An $\mathcal{O}(n)$ algorithm for coefficient grouping. Cryptology ePrint Archive, Paper 2022/992 (2022). https://eprint.iacr.org/2022/992

38. Méaux, P., Journault, A., Standaert, F.-X., Carlet, C.: Towards stream ciphers for efficient FHE with low-noise ciphertexts. In: Fischlin, M., Coron, J.-S. (eds.) EUROCRYPT 2016. LNCS, vol. 9665, pp. 311–343. Springer, Heidelberg (2016). https://doi.org/10.1007/978-3-662-49890-3_13

39. Naehrig, M., Lauter, K.E., Vaikuntanathan, V.: Can homomorphic encryption be practical? In: CCSW, pp. 113–124. ACM (2011)

40. Nyberg, K.: Differentially uniform mappings for cryptography. In: Helleseth, T. (ed.) EUROCRYPT 1993. LNCS, vol. 765, pp. 55–64. Springer, Heidelberg (1994). https://doi.org/10.1007/3-540-48285-7_6

41. Rodríguez-Henríquez, F., Pérez, A.D., Saqib, N.A., Koç, Ç.K.: Cryptographic Algorithms on Reconfigurable Hardware. Springer, New York (2007). https://doi.org/10.1007/978-0-387-36682-1

42. Todo, Y.: Structural evaluation by generalized integral property. In: Oswald, E., Fischlin, M. (eds.) EUROCRYPT 2015. LNCS, vol. 9056, pp. 287–314. Springer, Heidelberg (2015). https://doi.org/10.1007/978-3-662-46800-5_12

Horst Meets *Fluid*-SPN: Griffin for Zero-Knowledge Applications

Lorenzo Grassi[1], Yonglin Hao[2], Christian Rechberger[3],
Markus Schofnegger[4(⊠)], Roman Walch[3,5,6], and Qingju Wang[7]

[1] Ruhr University Bochum, Bochum, Germany
`lorenzo.grassi@ruhr-uni-bochum.de`
[2] State Key Laboratory of Cryptology, P.O. Box 5159, Beijing 100878, China
`haoyonglin@yeah.net`
[3] Graz University of Technology, Graz, Austria
`christian.rechberger@iaik.tugraz.at`
[4] Horizen Labs, Austin, USA
`mschofnegger@horizenlabs.io`
[5] Know-Center GmbH, Graz, Austria
[6] TACEO GmbH, Graz, Austria
[7] Telecom Paris, Institut Polytechnique de Paris, Paris, France
`qingju.wang@telecom-paris.fr`

Abstract. Zero-knowledge (ZK) applications form a large group of use cases in modern cryptography, and recently gained in popularity due to novel proof systems. For many of these applications, cryptographic hash functions are used as the main building blocks, and they often dominate the overall performance and cost of these approaches.

Therefore, in the last years several new hash functions were built in order to reduce the cost in these scenarios, including POSEIDON and *Rescue* among others. These hash functions often look very different from more classical designs such as AES or SHA-2. For example, they work natively over prime fields rather than binary ones. At the same time, for example POSEIDON and *Rescue* share some common features, such as being SPN schemes and instantiating the nonlinear layer with invertible power maps. While this allows the designers to provide simple and strong arguments for establishing their security, it also introduces crucial limitations in the design, which may affect the performance in the target applications.

In this paper, we propose the `Horst` construction, in which the addition in a Feistel scheme $(x, y) \mapsto (y + F(x), x)$ is extended via a multiplication, i.e., $(x, y) \mapsto (y \times G(x) + F(x), x)$.

By carefully analyzing the performance metrics in SNARK and STARK protocols, we show how to combine an expanding `Horst` scheme with a *Rescue*-like SPN scheme in order to provide security and better efficiency in the target applications. We provide an extensive security analysis for our new design GRIFFIN and a comparison with all current competitors.

Keywords: Hash Functions · GRIFFIN · Zero-Knowledge · `Horst` · *Fluid*-SPN

Author list in alphabetical order.

© International Association for Cryptologic Research 2023
H. Handschuh and A. Lysyanskaya (Eds.): CRYPTO 2023, LNCS 14083, pp. 573–606, 2023.
https://doi.org/10.1007/978-3-031-38548-3_19

1   Introduction

Concepts like multi-party computation (MPC), homomorphic encryption (HE), post-quantum signature schemes, and zero-knowledge (ZK) proof systems have recently grown in popularity. Some of these applications favor cryptographic schemes with specific properties, such as a small number of multiplications. Considering $\mathbb{F}_p^t$ for a prime $p \geq 3$ and $t \geq 1$, examples include Feistel-MiMC [3], GMiMC [2], POSEIDON[32], *Rescue* [4,59], *Grendel* [58], Reinforced Concrete [31], NEPTUNE [35], and Anemoi [15], among others.

The performance metrics vary between the different use cases. While the cost in e.g. MPC is well-studied [3,34,36], ZK protocols often have more sophisticated optimization targets. The two major classes of ZK proof systems are *zero-knowledge succinct non-interactive arguments of knowledge* (zk-SNARKs) and *zero-knowledge scalable transparent arguments of knowledge* (zk-STARKs), which are also the ones we focus on in this paper.

Recent hash functions proposed for these protocols differ substantially from each other, however their internal permutations are usually SPN constructions. While this approach may have advantages for arguing security, it can also have various limitations affecting the performance in ZK protocols.

1.1   Hash and Compression Functions in ZK Settings

Cost Metrics in ZK Protocols. In many ZK applications, the prover uses ZK proofs to convince a verifier that they know a preimage x of a given hash or compression output $y = \mathcal{H}(x)$ without revealing anything about x. The efficiency of these protocols depends on the details of $\mathcal{H}$. In zk-SNARKs, the cost of the proof is proportional to the number of nonlinear operations one has to perform, and in some cases (e.g., Plonk [28]) the number of linear operations must also be considered. In zk-STARKs, the cost is related to the degree and the depth of the circuit that must be verified. In both cases, it is not required to recompute $\mathcal{H}$ in order to determine if $y = \mathcal{H}(x)$. Indeed, one can verify any equivalent cheaper representation $\mathcal{F}(x,y) = 0$ which is satisfied if and only if $y = \mathcal{H}(x)$.

Most previous designs focused only on a subset of cost metrics. For example, the idea of MiMC, HADESMiMC, and POSEIDON was to minimize the number of multiplications. As a result, they can be efficient in SNARKs, but their comparatively large round numbers lead to disadvantages in other proof systems. In contrast, *Rescue* has an inner structure tailored for STARKs, which results in comparatively low round numbers and decent Plonk performance. However, the efficiency in other SNARKs and the plain performance suffer from this structure.

SPN Schemes and Power Maps. Competitive hash functions for ZK protocols include *Rescue* and POSEIDON. Both schemes are instantiated via an SPN permutation, whose round function $\mathcal{R} : \mathbb{F}_p^t \to \mathbb{F}_p^t$ is defined as

$$\mathcal{R}(\cdot) = c + M \times S(\cdot), \tag{1}$$

where c is a round constant, $M \in \mathbb{F}_p^{t \times t}$ is an MDS matrix, and $S : \mathbb{F}_p^t \to \mathbb{F}_p^t$ is an S-box layer defined as

$$S(x_0, x_1, \ldots, x_{t-1}) = S_0(x_0) \parallel S_1(x_1) \parallel \cdots \parallel S_{t-1}(x_{t-1}) \qquad (2)$$

for invertible maps $S_i : \mathbb{F}_p \to \mathbb{F}_p$ ($\cdot \parallel \cdot$ denotes concatenation). Every round of *Rescue* consists of two steps, one in which all S_i correspond to $x \mapsto x^{1/d}$ and one in which all S_i correspond to $x \mapsto x^d$. POSEIDON uses two different rounds, one in which $S_i(x) = x^d$ and one in which $S_0(x) = x^d$ and $S_{i \neq 0}(x) = x$ (identity).

1.2   Our Contribution

SPN Schemes in ZK. An SPN scheme usually allows for simple and strong security arguments regarding statistical attacks, including the (classical) differential [11] and linear [46] attacks. For example, the combination of a linear layer with a high branch number and an S-box layer with a good maximum differential probability allows to efficiently use the wide trail design strategy [21].

However, SPN schemes over $\mathbb{F}_p^t$ have a crucial limitation in our setting. Indeed, a common way to instantiate the nonlinear layer for ZK use cases is to use invertible power maps $x \mapsto x^d$ (hence, $\gcd(d, p-1) = 1$). Since the square function is not a permutation over $\mathbb{F}_p$, one has to use a function of degree $d \geq 3$, which affects the performance. This is true for every state element, and hence the number of multiplications is at least $2t$ for a t-element state, and $3t$ for the particular ZK settings we are interested in (due to the specification of p).

Horst Schemes. Together with an SPN, another popular cryptographic construction is the Feistel one, represented e.g. by GMiMC in the case of ZK-friendly schemes. Given a function F over a generic field $\mathbb{F}$, a Feistel scheme is defined as the map $(x, y) \mapsto (y + F(x), x)$ over $\mathbb{F}_p^2$. Several generalizations over $\mathbb{F}_p^t$ are proposed in the literature [38,52,61].

Inspired by the results presented in [12] and in [20], in Sect. 3.2 we propose a modified Feistel scheme, called Horst, in which the linear relation between y and $F(x)$ is combined with a nonlinear one, i.e., $(y, x) \mapsto (x, y \times G(x) + F(x))$.[1] To guarantee invertibility, we require that $G(x) \neq 0$ for each input x.

In Sect. 3.2, we show how to construct such a low-degree (non-trivial) function over any prime field $\mathbb{F}_p$ independently of the size of p, and we propose an initial security analysis regarding the indifferentiability/indistinguishability of a generic iterated Horst construction.

Besides that, our experiments suggest that the strength against algebraic attacks such as Gröbner basis [16,19] attacks is easier to argue by using Horst instead of the classical Feistel, resulting in another advantage of the new structure. We explore this direction in Sect. 6.3.

---

[1] The name Horst (due to the cryptographer Horst Feistel) has been chosen in order to emphasize the link between $(x, y) \mapsto (y + F(x), x)$ and $(y, x) \mapsto (x, y \times G(x) + F(x))$.

Griffin. In Sect. 5 we specify a new family of sponge hash and compression functions called GRIFFIN, using the internal permutation GRIFFIN-π.[2] GRIFFIN-π cannot be rewritten as in Eqs. (1) and (2) since its nonlinear layer is not divided into independent nonlinear S-boxes. Instead, it is composed of two nonlinear sublayers defined via three different nonlinear functions. Two of them are defined via the invertible power maps $x \mapsto x^d$ and $x \mapsto x^{1/d}$, which is inspired by *Rescue*. The final one is defined by our proposed Horst strategy, using the map $(x, y) \mapsto (x, y \cdot G(x))$ for a quadratic function G s.t. $G(z) \neq 0$ for each z.

Since the cost metrics in our target use cases are mainly related to the number of nonlinear operations, a linear layer with an MDS matrix may be the simplest choice. However, for a $t \times t$ matrix this usually requires $\mathcal{O}(t^2)$ multiplications. Hence, we propose a matrix which can be implemented with a small number of operations, but still offers a decent branch number for better diffusion.

As a result, similarly to the SPN wide trail design strategy and thanks to the details of the linear layer, we have simple arguments against statistical attacks. Moreover, due to the *Rescue*-like construction, we gain efficient verifiability and a high degree both in the forward and the backward direction. Finally, with our Horst construction, we have minimal multiplicative complexity and good security against algebraic attacks.

Modes of Operation. Our proposed permutation GRIFFIN-π can be used both in a sponge mode and in a compression mode. The former is more versatile while the latter can be more efficient in specific settings (for example, when only compression for small fixed-sized inputs is needed). We also compare our construction with other compression modes used in the literature, in particular those in Haraka [42] and Jive [15].

Security Analysis. A security analysis of the proposed design is given in Sect. 6. From the algebraic perspective, Gröbner basis attacks at the round level are the most efficient ones. We present several strategies considering the details of the function. Further, we compare GRIFFIN-π instantiated with Feistel and with Horst in Sect. 6.3, observing that security is easier to argue with Horst.

From the statistical perspective, well-known techniques like the wide trail design strategy do not apply since our design does not have an SPN structure. For this reason, we apply a simple bound against classical differential and linear attacks, which is sufficient for our purposes. For rebound attacks, an advanced form of a (truncated) differential attack, we propose an analysis using dedicated tools that help us to provide the bound on the minimal number of rounds needed.

Efficiency in Plain and ZK Settings. Following the cost metrics from Sect. 1.1, with GRIFFIN we aim to find a beneficial tradeoff between all of them.

---

[2] The griffin is a legendary creature with the body, tail, and back legs of a lion, and the head and wings of an eagle. The name GRIFFIN has been chosen since our design merges ideas of a *Fluid*-SPN and a construction as the Horst one.

We evaluate the performance of GRIFFIN in SNARKs using R1CS and compare it to various other constructions in Sect. 7.2. Our evaluation shows that GRIFFIN is better suited for these zk-SNARKs than any previously proposed design. In the case of zk-STARKs and Plonk (a SNARK with different arithmetization), GRIFFIN provides similar performance as the currently best hash functions for STARKs, the best performance for many configurations in Plonk (especially larger state sizes) and is only slightly less efficient for smaller state sizes in some Plonk configurations compared to the recent design Anemoi proposed in [15]. We show a comparison of GRIFFIN and similar constructions in Plonk in Sect. 7.3. We show the comparison between GRIFFIN and its competitors in zk-STARKs in [30, App. A]. As was our goal, GRIFFIN provides an efficient tradeoff between the plain performance and the performance across different ZK proof systems.

2   Cost Metrics for Zero-Knowledge Proof Systems

In this section, we analyze the cost metrics for R1CS-based SNARKs and Plonk [28]. For a similar analysis for AIR-based STARKs we refer to the full version [30, App. A.1], where we also discuss the relations between these three cost metrics in [30, App. A.2]. We start by providing a brief introduction to arithmetization techniques used in various ZK proof systems. We directly focus on iterative functions to give an intuition on how to describe a hash function in this context.

2.1   Zero-Knowledge Proofs

A ZK proof system is a two-player protocol between a prover and a verifier, allowing the prover to convince the verifier that they know a witness w to a statement x without revealing anything about the witness beyond what can be implied by x. For example, the prover can use ZK proofs to convince a verifier that they know a preimage w of a given hash $y = \mathcal{H}(w)$ without revealing anything about w. The proof system needs to be complete and sound with a negligible soundness error ϵ, and it must fulfill the zero-knowledge property, which informally states that the proof is independent of the witness w.

The two major classes of ZK proof systems are zk-SNARKs and zk-STARKs, where zk-SNARKs require a trusted setup and are not post-quantum secure. Recently, many use cases involving ZK proofs have emerged, two of them mainly relying on hash functions: *set membership proofs* based on Merkle tree accumulators and *verifiable computation* based on recursive proofs. In both cases one has to prove the knowledge of preimages of hashes, and thus the overall performance mainly depends on the efficiency of the hash function used in the protocol.

2.2   Arithmetization

To prove a solution of a computational problem, one has to translate the problem into an algebraic representation. This step is known as arithmetization and it differs between the various proof systems. Many algebraic representations have been proposed in the literature, with rank-1 constraint satisfaction systems (R1CS) and Plonk gates being the most widely used representations in zk-SNARKs, and the algebraic intermediate representation (AIR) being used in zk-STARKs [7].

Concretely, in applications involving preimage proofs, the algebraic representation describes the relation between the preimage and the final hash. The witness of the ZK proof captures all intermediate values (including the preimage) required to satisfy this representation for a given instance of the problem (i.e., a specific hash). For this purpose, let $q = p^n$ for a prime $p \geq 2$ and $n \geq 1$, and let $\mathcal{H} : \mathbb{F}_q^t \to \mathbb{F}_q^t$, where $\mathbb{F}_q$ is a field and $t \geq 1$. We focus on an iterative function $\mathcal{H}(a) = \mathcal{F}_{r-1} \circ \cdots \circ \mathcal{F}_1 \circ \mathcal{F}_0(a)$, where $\mathcal{F}_0, \mathcal{F}_1, \ldots, \mathcal{F}_{r-1} : \mathbb{F}_q^t \to \mathbb{F}_q^t$. Given $a, b \in \mathbb{F}_q^t$, the goal is to prove $\mathcal{H}(a) = b$ without revealing a. To efficiently determine whether $\mathcal{H}(a) = b$, the prover can use the intermediate values $x_0 \equiv a, x_1, x_2, \ldots, x_{r-1} \equiv b$ such that $\mathcal{F}_i(x_i) - x_{i+1} = 0$ for $i \in \{0, 1, \ldots, r-1\}$. In particular, they can prove any *equivalent system of equations*, i.e., they can introduce functions $\mathcal{G}_0, \mathcal{G}_1, \ldots, \mathcal{G}_{s-1} : (\mathbb{F}_q^t)^r \to \mathbb{F}_q^t$ such that the previous system of equations is satisfied if and only if $\mathcal{G}_j(x_0, x_1, \ldots, x_{r-1}) = 0$ for $j \in \{0, 1, \ldots, s-1\}$.

Definition 1 (Zero-Equivalence). *Let $q = p^n$ for a prime $p \geq 2$ and $n \geq 1$. Let $\mathcal{F}_0, \ldots, \mathcal{F}_{r-1} : \mathbb{F}_q^t \to \mathbb{F}_q^t$ be $r \geq 1$ functions. Let $\mathcal{G}_0, \ldots, \mathcal{G}_{s-1} : (\mathbb{F}_q^t)^r \to \mathbb{F}_q^t$ be $s \geq 1$ functions. We say that $\mathcal{G}_0, \ldots, \mathcal{G}_{s-1}$ are **zero-equivalent** to $\mathcal{F}_0, \ldots, \mathcal{F}_{r-1}$ if for each $x_0, x_1, x_2, \ldots, x_{r-1} \in \mathbb{F}_q^t$ the following holds:*

$$\forall i \in \{0, \ldots, r-1\} : x_{i+1} = \mathcal{F}_i(x_i) \iff \forall j \in \{0, \ldots, s-1\} : \mathcal{G}_j(x_0, \ldots, x_{r-1}) = 0.$$

This strategy is based on the notion of *non-procedural computation* introduced in [4], which describes the idea of not only evaluating schemes in the plain direction, but using intermediate relations instead.

The choice of the equivalent functions $\mathcal{G}_0, \ldots, \mathcal{G}_{s-1}$ depends on the cost metric of the given proof system. For the following, we say that a scheme is *fluid* if it admits an equivalent representation which can be proven and/or verified more efficiently.[3] As an example for $r = s$, we report the ones given in [4].

Example 1. *An invertible function $\mathcal{F}(x) = x^{1/d}$ over $\mathbb{F}_q$ can be proven via $\mathcal{G} : \mathbb{F}_q^2 \to \mathbb{F}_q$ defined as $\mathcal{G}(x, y) = x - y^d$ by imposing $\mathcal{G}(x, y) = 0$. Similarly, given $\mathcal{F}(x) = 1/x$ over $\mathbb{F}_q \setminus \{0\}$, one can choose $\mathcal{G} : (\mathbb{F}_q \setminus \{0\})^2 \to \mathbb{F}_q$ as $\mathcal{G}(x, y) = xy - 1$.*

A scheme that satisfies the condition just given is a fluid scheme. In [15], the authors noticed that $y = x^{1/d}$ and $y^d = x$ are CCZ-equivalent. For this reason, in [15, Sect. 4.1] they deduce that a function is arithmetization-oriented if it is CCZ-equivalent to a function that can be verified efficiently.

Definition 2 (CCZ Equivalence). *Two functions $\mathcal{F}, \mathcal{G} : \mathbb{F}_q^t \to \mathbb{F}_q^t$ are CCZ-equivalent if there exists an affine permutation $\mathcal{A}$ over $(\mathbb{F}_q^t)^2$ such that $\{(x, \mathcal{F}(x)) \mid \forall x \in \mathbb{F}_q^t\} = \{\mathcal{A} \circ (x, \mathcal{G}(x)) \mid \forall x \in \mathbb{F}_q^t\}$.*

Restricting to CCZ equivalence is not necessary, and there exist fluid schemes that do not satisfy any CCZ equivalence condition, as shown in the following.

---

[3] A fluid material continuously deforms (flows) under an applied external force. In our case, the scheme adapts its algebraic representation to the target protocol.

Example 2. Consider $y = \mathcal{F}(x) = x^{e/d}$ over $\mathbb{F}_q$ such that $d, e \geq 3$ and $\gcd(q - 1, e) = \gcd(q - 1, d) = \gcd(e, d) = 1$. This permutation can be easily verified via $\mathcal{G}(x, y) = y^d - x^e = 0$, but we are not aware of any CCZ equivalence between $y = x^{e/d}$ and $y^d = x^e$.

Example 3. Let $\mathcal{F}_0, \mathcal{F}_1 : \mathbb{F}_q \to \mathbb{F}_q$ be defined as $y = \mathcal{F}_0(x) = \gamma + x^d$ and $z = \mathcal{F}_1(y) = y^{1/d}$, where $\gamma \neq 0$ and where $x \mapsto x^d$ is assumed to be invertible. Then $\mathcal{H} = \mathcal{F}_1 \circ \mathcal{F}_0$ can be efficiently proven via a single function $\mathcal{G} : \mathbb{F}_q^3 \to \mathbb{F}_q$ defined as $\mathcal{G}(x, y, z) = z^d - (\gamma + x^d)$, which is independent of y.

This resembles the arithmetization of *Rescue* in zk-STARKs. Both representations are valid and require the same number of multiplications, but they have different degrees when chained together. In this sense, *Rescue* is a *Fluid*-SPN.

2.3   Rank-1 Constraint Satisfaction Systems (R1CS)

Many proof systems (e.g., Groth16 [37], Ligero [5], Aurora [8], Bulletproofs [17]) require to translate the circuit into an R1CS, with Groth16 being the fastest proof system with the smallest proofs to date. An R1CS is a set of η equations (i.e., η constraints) on the variables $a_0, \ldots, a_m \in \mathbb{F}_q$ (with $a_0 = 1$) such that

$$\forall j \in \{0, 1, \ldots, \eta - 1\} : \quad \left(\sum_i u_{i,j} \cdot a_i \right) \cdot \left(\sum_i v_{i,j} \cdot a_i \right) = \left(\sum_i w_{i,j} \cdot a_i \right),$$

where $u_{i,j}, v_{i,j}, w_{i,j} \in \mathbb{F}_q$ are constants describing the j-th constraint. These are derived from the hash or compression function when proving the knowledge of an input and are independent of the given output value. An assignment to the variables $a_0, \ldots, a_m$ is the witness of the ZK proof and captures all intermediate values (including the preimage) when computing a given output value. The role of the zk-SNARK is to prove that the witness satisfies the R1CS system without revealing the witness itself. The efficiency then depends on the number of constraints η in the constraint system, i.e., the prover complexity is in $\mathcal{O}(\eta)$.

In R1CS constraints, every statement needs to be translated into multiplications of linear combinations of the witness variables. Consequently, linear operations can be embedded into subsequent constraints and do not require additional constraints. For nonlinear operations, the designer has to find a representation which fully captures the relation between the input and the output of the operation, while minimizing the number of degree-2 equations.

Cost Metric. We measure the number of R1CS constraints, i.e., the minimum number of nonlinear operations of linear combinations of witness variables required to fully represent any (equivalent) relation between the input and its output (e.g., a preimage and the corresponding hash). In order to perform an efficient verification, we therefore suggest to work with the *zero-equivalent functions* that can be computed with the minimum number of nonlinear operations.

2.4 Plonk Arithmetization

Plonk [28] is a zk-SNARK which does not use R1CS constraints. Its arithmetization is based on Plonk gates with constraints of the form

$$q_{L_i} \cdot a_{L_i} + q_{R_i} \cdot a_{R_i} + q_{O_i} \cdot a_{O_i} + q_{M_i} \cdot (a_{L_i} \cdot a_{R_i}) + q_{C_i} = 0, \qquad (3)$$

where the a values are again the witness variables and the q values describe a given constraint. Using this equation, one can either describe a 2-fan-in addition (setting $q_{M,i} = 0$) or a 2-fan-in multiplication (setting $q_{L,i} = q_{R,i} = 0$). Thus, to use the Plonk proof system one needs to describe the given circuit using 2-fan-in addition and multiplication gates. As a result, contrary to R1CS constraints, additions cannot be embedded into subsequent multiplication constraints anymore and require separate Plonk gates.

Cost Metric. We measure the number of Plonk gates, i.e., the minimum number of 2-fan-in additions and multiplications of witness variables required to fully represent any (equivalent) relation between the input and its output.

Remark 1. The Plonk proof system can be modified to use constraints different from Eq. (3). Some implementations of the Plonk system extend Eq. (3) to allow 3-fan-in addition gates which are beneficial in various use cases. In this case the cost metric changes accordingly, i.e., the cost is then the minimum number of 2-fan-in multiplications and 3-fan-in additions of witness variables required to fully represent any (equivalent) relation between the input and the output.

3 The Road to Griffin

3.1 Related Work: SPN Schemes for ZK Applications

We first recall some of the SPN schemes proposed in the literature for zero-knowledge applications, focusing on the evolution of their designs from POSEIDON and *Rescue* to NEPTUNE and Anemoi.

Poseidon and *Rescue*. Two well-known examples of SPN schemes for ZK settings are POSEIDON and *Rescue*. Their round function is defined as in Eq. (1), where all S-boxes $S_0, \ldots, S_{t-1}$ operate over $\mathbb{F}_p$ independently of the others, i.e.,

$$S(x_0, x_1, \ldots, x_{t-1}) = S_0(x_0) \ || \ S_1(x_1) \ || \cdots || \ S_{t-1}(x_{t-1}).$$

An important advantage of these SPN schemes is that several techniques such as the wide trail design strategy [21] have been developed in order to study their security. For example, using the branch number of the linear layer and the maximum differential probability of the S-boxes, it is possible to provide a simple and strong security argument against classical differential (and linear) attacks.

At the same time, a strong limitation on the choice of the S-box arises for these schemes. Indeed, as already recalled in the introduction, when working over a prime field the designer is restricted to S-box functions of degree $d \geq 3$ in order to build permutations. At the current state of the art, invertible nonlinear maps over $\mathbb{F}_p$ include only power maps $x \mapsto x^d$ for $\gcd(d, p-1) = 1$ and the Dickson polynomials $D_\alpha(x) = \sum_{i=0}^{\lfloor \frac{d}{2} \rfloor} \frac{d}{d-i} \binom{d-i}{i} (-\alpha)^i x^{d-2i}$ for $\gcd(d, p^2-1) = 1$, besides other invertible functions constructed via the Legendre function and the $x \mapsto (-1)^x$ operator proposed in [33]. In particular, quadratic nonlinear components cannot be used. This may not be an issue in more classical use cases, but it leads to performance limitations in the settings we consider.

Neptune and Anemoi. One way to gain more flexibility regarding the degree is by considering S-boxes over $\mathbb{F}_p^n$ for $n \geq 2$, that is, SPN schemes in which the nonlinear layer is defined as

$$S(x_0, \ldots, x_{t-1}) = S_0(x_0, \ldots, x_{n-1}) \,\|\, S_1(x_n, \ldots, x_{2n-1}) \,\|\, \cdots \,\|\, S_{t'-1}(x_{t-n}, \ldots, x_{t-1})$$

for a certain $n \geq 2$ such that $t = nt'$, where $S_0, \ldots, S_{t'-1}$ over $\mathbb{F}_{p^n} \equiv \mathbb{F}_p^n$ are invertible functions. Naturally, it is still possible to instantiate such S-boxes over $\mathbb{F}_{p^n}$ via the power maps or the other invertible maps previously recalled. However, the algebraic representation over $\mathbb{F}_p^n$ becomes more complicated, and the number of multiplications in $\mathbb{F}_p$ increases exponentially. Other invertible degree-2 functions over $\mathbb{F}_p^n$ constructed via a local map have recently been presented in [35], and they include e.g. the Lai–Massey one [43] as a special case.

Examples of such SPN schemes are NEPTUNE and Anemoi. The hash function NEPTUNE is inspired by POSEIDON, but the power maps in the external rounds are replaced by the concatenation of independent S-boxes over $\mathbb{F}_{p^2} \equiv \mathbb{F}_p^2$ based on quadratic Lai–Massey functions. In the Anemoi scheme, the S-boxes over $\mathbb{F}_{p^2} \equiv \mathbb{F}_p^2$ are based on a particular instantiation of the Feistel scheme called Flystel and defined as $(x, y) \mapsto (u, v) := \left(x - 2yz^{1/d} + z^{2/d}, y - z^{1/d}\right)$ for $z := x - y^2$, where $d \geq 3$ satisfies $\gcd(d, p-1) = 1$.[4] Exploiting its CCZ-equivalent function, this can be efficiently verified via $(y^2 + (y-v)^d - x, v^2 + (y-v)^d - u) = (0, 0)$.

3.2 Non-SPN Schemes: From Feistel to Horst

While the strategy exploited by the previous SPN schemes is indeed appealing for designing ZK-friendly schemes, here we explore a different approach. In order to be invertible, the low-degree (quadratic) S-boxes of both NEPTUNE and Anemoi are constructed via a function that is affine equivalent to a Feistel scheme (we recall that [29] recently proved the affine equivalent relation existing between Feistel and Lai–Massey schemes). Hence, given the functions $\tilde{F}_0, \tilde{F}_1, \ldots, \tilde{F}_{t-2}$ over $\mathbb{F}_p$, we may also directly consider a Feistel scheme, such as Type-I/-II/-III Feistel schemes [38,52,61] defined respectively as

$$(x_0, x_1, \ldots, x_{t-1}) \mapsto (x_1 + \tilde{F}(x_0), x_2, x_3, \ldots, x_{t-1}, x_0),$$
$$(x_0, x_1, \ldots, x_{t-1}) \mapsto (x_1 + \tilde{F}_0(x_0), x_2, x_3 + \tilde{F}_2(x_2) \ldots, x_{t-1} + \tilde{F}_{t-2}(x_{t-2}), x_0),$$
$$(x_0, x_1, \ldots, x_{t-1}) \mapsto (x_1 + \tilde{F}_0(x_0), x_2 + \tilde{F}_1(x_1), \ldots, x_{t-1} + \tilde{F}_{t-2}(x_{t-2}), x_0),$$

---

[4] The constants β, γ, and δ are omitted in this description.

in which the circular shift is replaced by a multiplication with an invertible linear layer that accelerates the full diffusion.

An example of a ZK-friendly generalized Feistel scheme is GMiMC (broken in [10]). In order to prevent internal collisions, the round functions of GMiMC are instantiated via invertible power maps. We considered variants of it instantiated via quadratic maps $\tilde{F}_i(x) = x^2$ and with the circular shifts being replaced by multiplications with invertible matrices. As we are going to explain in more detail in the following, practical tests suggest that these schemes may not provide the expected security level against some algebraic attacks like the Gröbner basis one. A possible reason for that could be the strong arrangement/alignment/structure existing in the Feistel network. To solve this issue, we propose the following.

Let $q = p^n$ for a prime $p \geq 2$ and $n \geq 1$ as before. Given a function $F : \mathbb{F}_q \to \mathbb{F}_q$, the nonlinear layer of a Feistel scheme over $\mathbb{F}_q^2$ is defined as $(x, y) \mapsto (x, y + F(x))$, which is invertible independently of F. Instead of considering a linear relation between y and $F(x)$, here we combine y and $F(x)$ in a nonlinear way without losing the advantageous properties of Feistel schemes. The simplest way is to replace the sum with a multiplication, but then the invertibility cannot be guaranteed anymore. We solve this with a stronger assumption on the function.

Definition 3 (Horst Scheme). *Let $G : \mathbb{F}_q \to \mathbb{F}_q \setminus \{0\}$ and $F : \mathbb{F}_q \to \mathbb{F}_q$. We define the* **Horst** *scheme over $\mathbb{F}_q^2$ as in Fig. 1a, i.e.,*

$$(y, x) \mapsto (x, y \cdot G(x) + F(x)).$$

In particular, we call this scheme

(1) Feistel or **Horst$^+$** *if G is identically equal to 1, i.e., $G(x) \equiv 1$,*
(2) **Horst$^\times$** *if $F(x) = \alpha \cdot G(x) + \beta$ for certain $\alpha, \beta \in \mathbb{F}_q$ (hence, $y \cdot G(x) + F(x) \equiv (\alpha + y) \cdot G(x) + \beta$).*

Since $\mathbb{F}_q$ is a field and $G(x) \neq 0$ for each $x \in \mathbb{F}_q$, Horst is invertible.

Feistel Schemes with Nonlinear Diffusion for Constructing S-Boxes. The idea behind Horst is not entirely new in the literature. In the case $F(x) = 0$ for each $x \in \mathbb{F}_q$, we note that a Feistel scheme based on a nonlinear relation between the branches was allegedly also used in order to set up the 8-bit S-boxes of Streebog [24] and Kuznyechik [26], two Russian standards of a hash function and a block cipher, respectively. This was discovered in [12], where the authors reconstructed the design of the S-box from its lookup table definition. The nonlinear diffusion in this case consists of multiplications in $\mathbb{F}_{2^4}$ between the two branches.

Similarly, in [20] the authors construct S-boxes over small fields by a modified version of a Feistel network instantiated with a nonlinear operation between the branches. Also in this case, the components of the round are chosen randomly and tested against various criteria, in order to ensure that the resulting construction is invertible. This approach is feasible when working over small finite fields.

However, to the best of our knowledge, no generalization from e.g. $\mathbb{F}_{2^4}$ to larger binary extension fields or larger prime fields is publicly available. Indeed,

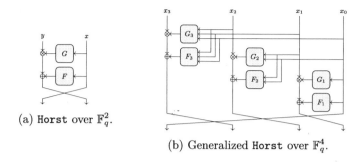

(a) Horst over $\mathbb{F}_q^2$.

(b) Generalized Horst over $\mathbb{F}_q^4$.

Fig. 1. The generalized Horst scheme over $\mathbb{F}_q^t$.

given $(x, y) \mapsto x \cdot G(y)$, while a brute-force approach may be sufficient to achieve invertibility (i.e., $G(y) \neq 0$ for each y) and efficiency in terms of linear or non-linear operations for small fields, this does not seem feasible when considering larger fields. We solve this problem in the following, by showing how to construct G in an efficient way for the Horst approach given above.

Generalized Feistel Constructions over Groups. Various independent works [39, 55] discuss generalized Feistel constructions over generic groups $(\mathfrak{G}, \#)$. We emphasize that those are not compatible with our result presented here, due to the simple reason that $(\mathbb{F}_q, \times)$, where $q = p^n$ and $\times$ is the multiplication, is not a group (e.g., 0 does not admit any inverse with respect to the multiplication).

Initial Security Considerations. The security of Feistel schemes [45] has been heavily analyzed both from the indistinguishability point of view [48,53,54] and from the indifferentiability one [18,22]. Here we make an initial analogous security analysis for the Horst scheme. In the following, $F^{(i)} : \mathbb{F}_q \to \mathbb{F}_q$ and $G^{(i)} : \mathbb{F}_q \to \mathbb{F}_q$ denote the functions in the i-th round for $i \in \{0, \dots, r - 1\}$.

It is always possible to set up a distinguisher for one (trivial) and two rounds of the Horst scheme. Consider three inputs of the form $(y_i, x) \in \mathbb{F}_q^2$ and the corresponding outputs $(z_i, w_i) \in \mathbb{F}_q^2$ for $i \in \{0, 1, 2\}$, where $z_i := y_i \cdot G^{(0)}(x) + F^{(0)}(x)$ and for unknown $w_0, w_1, w_2 \in \mathbb{F}_q$. In the case of 2-round Horst, we have $(y_2 - y_0) \cdot (z_1 - z_0) = (z_2 - z_0) \cdot (y_1 - y_0)$ with probability 1, while this occurs with probability $1/q$ in the case of a pseudo-random permutation (PRP).

In the full version [30, App. B], we present distinguishers for 3 and 4 rounds of Horst$^\times$, by adapting the analogous attacks on Feistel schemes proposed by Patarin in e.g. [54]. For the particular Horst$^\times$ defined as $(y, x) \mapsto (x, y \cdot G(x))$ (i.e., F is identically equal to zero), we point out that it is possible to set up a distinguisher on an arbitrary number of rounds, by noting that $(0, x) \in \mathbb{F}_q^2$ is always mapped in $(x, 0) \in \mathbb{F}_q^2$ after one round and in $(0, x) \in \mathbb{F}_q^2$ after two rounds, for each $x \in \mathbb{F}_q$ and for each $G : \mathbb{F}_q \to \mathbb{F}_q \setminus \{0\}$.

The problems of setting up distinguishers for more than 2 rounds of Horst and for more than 6 rounds of Feistel or Horst$^{\times}$ are open for future research.

Generalized Horst. Next, we generalize the Horst scheme over $\mathbb{F}_q^t$ for $t \geq 2$.

Definition 4 (Generalized Horst). *Let $t \geq 2$. For each $i \in \{1, 2, \ldots, t-1\}$, let $G_i : \mathbb{F}_q^i \to \mathbb{F}_q \setminus \{0\}$ and $F_i : \mathbb{F}_q^i \to \mathbb{F}_q$. We define the Generalized Horst scheme over $\mathbb{F}_q^t$ as $x = (x_0, \ldots, x_{t-1}) \mapsto y = (y_0, \ldots, y_{t-1})$, where*

$$y_i := \begin{cases} x_{i+1} \cdot G_{i+1}(x_0, x_1, \ldots, x_i) + F_{i+1}(x_0, x_1, \ldots, x_i) & \text{if } i \in \{0, 1, \ldots, t-2\}, \\ x_0 & \text{otherwise } (i = t-1). \end{cases} \quad (4)$$

We refer to Fig. 1b for $t = 4$. The final circular shift is crucial for achieving full diffusion (as in the case of any Feistel scheme), but it can be replaced with a different linear diffusion. The invertibility follows from the fact that

$$x_i := \begin{cases} y_{t-1} & \text{if } i = 0, \\ \frac{y_{i-1} - F_i(x_0, x_1, \ldots, x_{i-1})}{G_i(x_0, x_1, \ldots, x_{i-1})} & \text{otherwise } (i \in \{1, 2, \ldots, t-1\}). \end{cases}$$

We point out that the case $G_1 = G_2 = \cdots = G_{t-1} = 1$ corresponds to the T-function proposed and analyzed in [41]. Moreover, based on [38,52,61], we highlight the possibility to set up Type-I/-II/-III, expanding, contracting Horst schemes analogous to Type-I/-II/-III, expanding, contracting Feistel schemes. We give the following concrete examples.

- A Type-I Feistel scheme is characterized by $G_i = 1$ for $i \in \{1, \ldots, t-1\}$, $F_j = 0$ for $j \in \{2, \ldots, t-1\}$, and without a condition on F_1. Hence, if $G_i = 1, F_i = 0$ for $i \in \{2, \ldots, t-1\}$, and without a condition on G_1 and F_1, the scheme resembles a Type-I Horst.
- A Type-III Feistel scheme is characterized by $G_i = 1$ for $i \in \{1, \ldots, t-1\}$ and $F_j(x_0, \ldots, x_{j-1}) = \tilde{F}_j(x_{j-1})$ for $j \in \{1, \ldots, t-1\}$. Hence, if $G_j(x_0, \ldots, x_{j-1}) = \tilde{G}_j(x_j)$ and $F_j(x_0, \ldots, x_{j-1}) = \tilde{F}_j(x_{j-1})$ for $j \in \{1, \ldots, t-1\}$, the scheme resembles a Type-III Horst.

3.3   Constructing Nonzero Functions G

One way of instantiating G is to exploit the following result.

Lemma 1. *Let $G : \mathbb{F}_q \to \mathbb{F}_q$ such that $G'(x) := G(x) \cdot x$ is a permutation over $\mathbb{F}_q$ and $G(0) \neq 0$. Then, $G(x) \neq 0$ for each $x \in \mathbb{F}_q$.*

Proof. By definition, $G'(0) = 0 \cdot G(0) = 0$. Since G' is a permutation by assumption, it follows that $G'(x) \neq 0$ for each $x \neq 0$. Hence, $G(x) = G'(x)/x \neq 0$ for each $x \in \mathbb{F}_q \setminus \{0\}$. Since $G(0) \neq 0$, it follows that $G(x) \neq 0$ for each $x \in \mathbb{F}_q$. $\square$

Let $d \geq 3$ be the smallest integer such that $x \mapsto x^d$ is invertible over $\mathbb{F}_q$, hence $\gcd(d, q - 1) = 1$. Let $\alpha \in \mathbb{F}_q \setminus \{0\}$. A concrete example of G over $\mathbb{F}_q$ is

$$G(z) = \frac{(z \pm \alpha)^d \mp \alpha^d}{z} = \sum_{i=1}^{d} \binom{d}{i} z^{i-1} \cdot (\pm \alpha)^{d-i},$$

which satisfies Lemma 1. Indeed, $G(0) = d \cdot (\pm \alpha)^{d-1} \neq 0$ by assumption on α and $z \mapsto G(z) \cdot z = (z \pm \alpha)^d \mp \alpha^d$ is invertible by assumption on d.

Result for Binary Fields. In the case of binary fields $\mathbb{F}_{2^n}$, Lemma 1 can be exploited by noting that $x \mapsto x^{2^i}$ are linear operations over $\mathbb{F}_2^n$. Indeed, by defining $G(x) = \sum_{i=0}^{d} \alpha_i \cdot x^{2^i - 1}$ for $\alpha_0 \in \mathbb{F}_{2^n} \setminus \{0\}$ and $\alpha_1, \alpha_2, \ldots, \alpha_d \in \mathbb{F}_{2^n}$, due to Lemma 1, G satisfies the required property if and only if the matrix corresponding to $G'(x) = x \cdot G(x) = \sum_{i=0}^{d} \alpha_i \cdot x^{2^i}$ rewritten over $\mathbb{F}_2^n$ is invertible.

Result for Prime Fields. In the case of a prime field $\mathbb{F}_p$ for $p \geq 3$, we can also exploit the fact that the quadratic map $x \mapsto x^2$ is not invertible over $\mathbb{F}_p$ in order to construct G. Let $\alpha, \beta \in \mathbb{F}_p$ such that $\alpha^2 - 4\beta$ is a quadratic nonresidue modulo p, that is, $\alpha^2 - 4\beta \neq w^2$ for each $w \in \mathbb{F}_p$. In this case, $G(x) = x^2 + \alpha x + \beta$ satisfies the required property. Indeed, the solutions of $x^2 + \alpha x + \beta = 0$ are given by $x_\pm = -(\alpha \pm \sqrt{\alpha^2 - 4\beta})/2$. Since $\alpha^2 - 4\beta$ is a quadratic nonresidue, no solution $x_\pm$ exists. Note that the function G just given does in general not satisfy the requirement of Lemma 1. Indeed, a function $H(x) = \eta x^3 + \psi x^2 + \varphi x$ over $\mathbb{F}_p$ is invertible if and only if $p = 2 \mod 3$ and $\psi^2 = 3\eta\varphi \mod p$ (we refer to [50, Corollary 2.9] for the proof). As a result, $G'(x) = G(x) \cdot x = x^3 + \alpha x^2 + \beta x$ is not a permutation either if (i) $p = 1 \mod 3$ or if (ii) $p = 2 \mod 3$ and $\alpha^2 = 3\beta$ does not satisfy the condition that $\alpha^2 - 4\beta$ is a quadratic nonresidue modulo p.

3.4   Combining Horst with a *Rescue*-like SPN: The Birth of GRIFFIN

A *Fluid*-SPN scheme whose nonlinear layer uses both $x \mapsto x^d$ and $x \mapsto x^{1/d}$ (where $d \geq 3$ is the smallest integer ensuring invertibility) can be efficiently proven/verified in ZK protocols. Further, the overall degree of the function increases quickly due to the degree-$(1/d)$ S-boxes, while the round-level constraints remain of degree d. This prevents attacks exploiting the degree of the entire function. However, while this representation is efficient in STARKs, such a nonlinear layer may be too expensive for SNARKs and for the plain performance.

An unarranged scheme based on generalized Horst seems beneficial since it provides diffusion in the nonlinear layer. To minimize the multiplicative complexity, we work with quadratic functions G_j in Definition 4, while we fix all F_i functions to zero for efficiency reasons. Further, we work with $G_j(x_0, x_1, \ldots, x_{j-1}) = G'_j(\sum_{l=0}^{j-1} \lambda_l \cdot x_l)$, where $G'_j : \mathbb{F}_p \to \mathbb{F}_p$ for each $j \in \{2, \ldots, t-1\}$.

Nonlinear Layer. By combining a *Fluid*-SPN scheme and `Horst` in a single nonlinear layer, we get $S : \mathbb{F}_p^t \to \mathbb{F}_p^t$ defined as $S(\cdot) = S'' \circ S'(\cdot)$, where

$$(S'(x_0, \dots, x_{t-1}))_i = \begin{cases} x_0^{1/d} & \text{if } i = 0, \\ x_1^{d} & \text{if } i = 1, \\ x_i & \text{otherwise,} \end{cases}$$

$$(S''(x_0, \dots, x_{t-1}))_i = \begin{cases} x_i & \text{if } i \in \{0, 1\}, \\ x_i \cdot (z_{i-1}^2 + \alpha_i z_{i-1} + \beta_i) & \text{otherwise,} \end{cases}$$

such that $\alpha_i^2 - 4\beta_i$ is a quadratic nonresidue and z_i is a linear combination of the inputs and outputs $\{x_0, \dots, x_{t-1}\} \cup \{x_0^{1/d}, x_1^{d}\}$. Clearly, S' is inspired by the nonlinear layer of *Rescue*, while S'' is based on the `Horst` function. Further, note that both S' and S'' are invertible if $\gcd(d, p-1) = 1$ and by choosing (α_i, β_i) such that $\alpha_i^2 - 4\beta_i$ is a quadratic nonresidue.

Number of Multiplications. The number of multiplications per round for the verification process is $2(\text{hw}(d) + \lfloor \log_2(d) \rfloor - 1)$ for S' and $2(t-2)$ for S'', i.e.,

$$2t + 2(\text{hw}(d) + \lfloor \log_2(d) \rfloor - 3) \in \mathcal{O}(t)$$

multiplications are needed per round.[5] Hence, for large t, the cost of our design is almost independent of the value of d.

Table 1. Number of multiplication per round for the verification process of several ZK-friendly hash functions (instantiated with $d = 5$) proposed in the literature over $\mathbb{F}_p^t$. (*The number given for POSEIDON refers to the external full rounds.)

GRIFFIN	Anemoi	POSEIDON*	*Rescue*
$2t + 2$	$2.5t$	$3t$	$6t$

For comparison, each external round of POSEIDON and each step of *Rescue* costs $t(\text{hw}(d) + \lfloor \log_2(d) \rfloor - 1)$ multiplications, while each round of Anemoi costs $\frac{t}{2}(\text{hw}(d) + \lfloor \log_2(d) \rfloor - 1 + 2)$ multiplications, where t is even. A comparison of the number of multiplication for the most-used case $d = 5$ is given in Table 1.

Griffin with Feistel. To highlight the advantages of `Horst`, we consider a variant of GRIFFIN instantiated with a classical Feistel, where S'' is replaced by

$$(\widehat{S''}(x_0, \dots, x_{t-1}))_i = \begin{cases} x_i & \text{if } i \in \{0, 1\}, \\ x_i + (z_{i-1}^2 + \alpha_i \cdot z_{i-1} + \beta_i) & \text{otherwise,} \end{cases} \tag{5}$$

---

[5] Note that $x \mapsto x^d$ costs $\text{hw}(d) + \lfloor \log_2(d) \rfloor - 1$ multiplications (see [35] for details).

where as before $\alpha_i^2 - 4\beta_i$ is a quadratic nonresidue for each i, while z_i is a linear combination of the inputs and outputs $\{x_0, \ldots, x_{i-1}\} \cup \{y_0, y_1\}$. As we discuss in Sect. 6.3, the security of this variant against algebraic attacks is smaller and more difficult to argue than in GRIFFIN. Moreover, the diffusion is slower, which leads to a crucial impact on the performance in the target ZK applications. This highlights the importance of the nonlinear combination in the Horst scheme.

Linear Layer. In many recent SNARK/STARK-friendly designs, an MDS matrix is used for every state size t, and hence the number of linear operations is an element in $\mathcal{O}(t^2)$ in general. Since our target applications mostly use large primes for a security level of 128 or 256 bits, an MDS matrix for large t is not required from a statistical point of view. For example, security against (classical) differential and linear attacks can also be provided with smaller branch numbers.

In GRIFFIN we only use an MDS matrix for $t \in \{3, 4\}$, and we use a more efficient linear layer for $t > 4$. Still, we want to achieve full diffusion over a single round to obtain stronger security against statistical attacks. For this goal and for the case $t = 4 \cdot t' \geq 8$, we reconsider the linear layer of AES written over $\mathbb{F}_{2^8}^{16}$ as the multiplication of two matrices, namely $M = M_{\mathrm{MC}} \times M_{\mathrm{SR}}$ where

$$M_{\mathrm{SR}} = \mathrm{diag}(I, I_2, I_3, I_4), \qquad M_{\mathrm{MC}} = \mathrm{circ}(2 \cdot I, 3 \cdot I, I, I),$$

where I is the 4×4 identity matrix, $I_2 = \mathrm{circ}(0, 1, 0, 0)$, $I_3 = \mathrm{circ}(0, 0, 1, 0)$, and $I_4 = \mathrm{circ}(0, 0, 0, 1)$. As is well-known, $M = M_{\mathrm{MC}} \times M_{\mathrm{SR}}$ does not provide full diffusion over a single round, due to the fact that each I_i is sparse.

As we will show in detail in Sect. 5.1, we replaced every I_i with an MDS matrix M_4 and we generalize the matrix M_{MC} via the circulant matrix $\mathrm{circ}(2 \cdot I, I, \ldots, I)$. This achieves full diffusion over a single round and efficiency. Indeed, for $t \geq 8$ (and similarly for $t \in \{3, 4\}$), the multiplication with M_4 only needs 12 arithmetic operations, resulting in $12t' = 12(t/4) \approx 3t$ operations for all M_4 matrices. Further, $\mathrm{circ}(2 \cdot I, I, \ldots, I) \cdot x$ can be computed with $4(t/4) + t = 2t$ additions. Hence, our linear layer M only requires around $5t \in \mathcal{O}(t)$ operations.

4   Modes of Operation

For our setting, we build a hash function with the sponge construction and a compression function with the feed-forward operation and the truncation. Both use the GRIFFIN-π permutation proposed in the following section.

The generic hash function using a sponge construction can be used in all parts of modern protocols where hash functions are needed, for example to compute a digest of a message or as a pseudo-random oracle. At the same time, these protocols are instantiated with Merkle trees, where t input elements are mapped into $n < t$ output elements. When building a Merkle tree via a single-call sponge hash function for this purpose, the state needs to be increased in order to include the capacity part, which negatively affects the performance. Hence, we also propose a compression function to be used in Merkle tree constructions.

4.1 Sponge Hash Functions

The sponge construction (Fig. 2) introduced in [9] builds upon an internal permutation and can be used to achieve various goals such as encryption, authentication, and hashing. Both the input and the output may be of arbitrary size. The state size is split into $t = r + c$, where r and c denote the number of elements in the rate (outer) and capacity (inner) part, respectively. Given an input message m, we assume the padding rule proposed for POSEIDON in [32, Section 4.2], consisting of adding the smallest number $< r$ of zeros such that the size of $m \mid\mid 0^*$ is a multiple of r and of replacing the initial value $IV \in \mathbb{F}_p^c$ instantiating the inner part with $|m| \mid\mid IV' \in \mathbb{F}_p^c$, where $|m| \in \mathbb{F}_p$ is the size of the input message m and $IV' \in \mathbb{F}_p^{c-1}$ is an initial value.

Security. As proven in [9], if the inner permutation resembles a random one, the sponge construction is indifferentiable from a random oracle up to around $p^{c/2}$ queries. Equivalently, to provide κ bits of security, $p^{c/2} \geq 2^\kappa$, i.e., $c \geq \lceil 2\kappa \cdot \log_p(2) \rceil$. For such a hash function $\mathcal{H} : \mathbb{F}_p^\star \to \mathbb{F}_p^\infty$, it is hard to find

(collision resistance) $x, x' \neq x$ such that $\mathcal{H}(x) = H(x')$,
(preimage resistance) x given y such that $\mathcal{H}(x) = y$, or
(second-preimage resistance) x' given $x \neq x'$ such that $\mathcal{H}(x') = \mathcal{H}(x)$.

We assume an output of at least $\lceil 2\kappa/\log_2(p) \rceil$ elements to prevent birthday bound attacks. Further, we require $c \geq \lceil 2\kappa/\log_2(p) \rceil$ for a κ-bit security level.

4.2 Compression Functions

Let $p \geq 2$ be a prime and let $1 \leq n < t$. A cryptographic compression function $\mathcal{C} : \mathbb{F}_p^t \to \mathbb{F}_p^n$ takes t-element inputs and compresses them to n-element outputs such that collision resistance and (second-)preimage resistance defined as before are guaranteed. One possible way to set up a compression function via a permutation is to combine the truncation function with the feed-forward operation, i.e.,

$$x \in \mathbb{F}_p^t \mapsto \mathcal{C}(x) := \mathrm{Tr}_n(\mathcal{P}(x) + x) \in \mathbb{F}_p^n,$$

where $\mathcal{P}$ is a permutation over $\mathbb{F}_p^t$ and Tr_n yields the first n elements, i.e., $\mathrm{Tr}_n(x_0, x_1, \ldots, x_{t-1}) := x_0 \mid\mid x_1 \mid\mid \cdots \mid\mid x_{n-1}$.

Security. Let $\mathcal{E}_k : \mathbb{F}_p^t \to \mathbb{F}_p^t$ be a cipher for a key $k \in \mathbb{F}_p^t$. Assume that for a particular $IV \in \mathbb{F}_p^t$, $\mathcal{E}_{IV}(x) = \mathcal{P}(x)$ for each $x \in \mathbb{F}_p^t$. Then $x \mapsto \mathcal{P}(x) + x$ over $\mathbb{F}_p^t$ corresponds to the first round of the Davies–Meyer construction $(x, IV) \mapsto \mathcal{E}_{IV}(x) + x$. As shown in [13,57], this compression function provides κ-bit security against collision and (second-)preimage attacks if $p^t \geq 2^{2\kappa}$. The final truncation does not decrease the security if $p^n \geq 2^{2\kappa}$ (due to the birthday bound).

In the following, we consider $t = 2n$ for the case we have in mind. From now on, we impose $n = t/2 \geq \lceil 2\kappa/\log_2(p) \rceil$. Note that $p^{t-n} \geq 2^\kappa$ guarantees that it is infeasible to find the truncated part by exhaustive search.

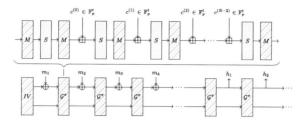

Fig. 2. GRIFFIN-π (top) and the GRIFFIN sponge (bottom), where $\boxplus$ and $\oplus$ denote the element-wise addition of two vectors in $\mathbb{F}_p^t$ and $\mathbb{F}_p^r$, respectively.

Related Work. A similar compression function has been used in several schemes in the literature, including Haraka [42] and Jive [15]. With respect to the one just defined, the compression function used in there is defined as

$$x \in \mathbb{F}_q^t \mapsto \mathrm{Tr}_n(M_{\mathcal{C}}' \times \mathcal{P}(x) + M_{\mathcal{C}} \times x) \in \mathbb{F}_p^n,$$

where $M_{\mathcal{C}}, M_{\mathcal{C}}' \in \mathbb{F}_p^{t \times t}$ are two invertible functions. For example, in the case of Jive instantiated via $t = 4$ and $n = 2$,

$$M_{\mathcal{C}} = M_{\mathcal{C}}' = \begin{pmatrix} 1 & 0 & 1 & 0 \\ 0 & 1 & 0 & 1 \\ 0 & 0 & 1 & 0 \\ 0 & 0 & 0 & 1 \end{pmatrix}.$$

If no condition is imposed on the inputs of the compression function, the matrix multiplications via $M_{\mathcal{C}}, M_{\mathcal{C}}'$ do not affect the security. Indeed, assume the permutation $\mathcal{P}'$ over $\mathbb{F}_p^t$ defined as $\mathcal{P}'(x) := M_{\mathcal{C}}' \times \mathcal{P}(M_{\mathcal{C}}^{-1} \times x)$. Since

$$\mathrm{Tr}_n(M_{\mathcal{C}}' \times \mathcal{P}(x) + M_{\mathcal{C}} \times x) = \mathrm{Tr}_n(\mathcal{P}'(x') + x')$$

for $x' = M_{\mathcal{C}} \times x$, the security of these constructions is identical.

5   Griffin and Griffin-π

GRIFFIN-Sponge and GRIFFIN-Compression are respectively a sponge hash function and a compression function over $\mathbb{F}_p^t$ instantiated with the permutation GRIFFIN-π, where $p > 2^{63}$ (i.e., $\lceil \log_2(p) \rceil > 63$) for a prime p and $t \in \{3, 4t'\}$ for a positive integer $t' \in \{1, 2, \ldots, 6\}$, i.e., t is either 3 or a multiple of 4. We limit ourselves to $t \leq 24$, since this is sufficient for the applications we have in mind. For the sponge case we assume that the rate r satisfies $r \geq t/3$.

The security level is κ bits, where $80 \leq \kappa \leq \min\{256, \lfloor \log_2(p) \cdot t/3 \rfloor\}$. The condition $2^\kappa \leq p^{t/3}$ follows from (i) the analysis just given regarding the security of the sponge hash function and of the compression one, and (ii) the condition on the rate for the sponge case.[6] We assume there exists $d \in \{3, 5, 7, 11\}$ such

---

[6] The condition $2^{3\kappa} \leq p^t$ implies the condition $2^{2\kappa} \leq p^t$ for the compression case, since $2^{2\kappa} \leq 2^{3\kappa} \leq p^t$. For the sponge case, the combination of $c \geq \lceil 2\kappa/\log_2(p) \rceil$ and $c \leq 2t/3$ implies $2t/3 \geq \lceil 2\kappa/\log_2(p) \rceil$, that is, $2^\kappa \leq p^{t/3}$.

that $\gcd(d, p-1) = 1$.[7] In the following, we refer to GRIFFIN when we do not distinguish between the modes of operation.

5.1   Specification of Griffin-π

The GRIFFIN-π permutation $\mathcal{G}^\pi : \mathbb{F}_p^t \to \mathbb{F}_p^t$ is defined by

$$\mathcal{G}^\pi(\cdot) := \mathcal{F}_{R-1} \circ \cdots \circ \mathcal{F}_1 \circ \mathcal{F}_0(M \times \cdot),$$

where $M \in \mathbb{F}_p^{t\times t}$ is an invertible matrix and $\mathcal{F}_i : \mathbb{F}_p^t \to \mathbb{F}_p^t$ is a round function of the form $\mathcal{F}_i(\cdot) = c^{(i)} + M \times S(\cdot)$ for a round constant $c^{(i)} \in \mathbb{F}_p^t$, a nonlinear layer $S : \mathbb{F}_p^t \to \mathbb{F}_p^t$, and $i \in \{0, 1, \ldots, R-1\}$. The same matrix M is applied to the input and in every round. We assume $c^{(R-1)} = 0$.

The Nonlinear Layer S. Let $d \in \{3, 5, 7, 11\}$ be the smallest integer such that $\gcd(d, p-1) = 1$. Let $(\alpha_i, \beta_i) \in \mathbb{F}_p^2 \setminus \{(0,0)\}$ be pairwise distinct such that $\alpha_i^2 - 4\beta_i$ is a quadratic nonresidue modulo p for $2 \le i \le t-1$. The nonlinear layer $S(x_0, \ldots, x_{t-1}) = y_0 \,||\, \cdots \,||\, y_{t-1}$ is then defined by

$$y_i = \begin{cases} x_0^{1/d} & \text{if } i = 0, \\ x_1^d & \text{if } i = 1, \\ x_2 \cdot \big((L_i(y_0, y_1, 0))^2 + \alpha_2 \cdot L_i(y_0, y_1, 0) + \beta_2\big) & \text{if } i = 2, \\ x_i \cdot \big((L_i(y_0, y_1, x_{i-1}))^2 + \alpha_i \cdot L_i(y_0, y_1, x_{i-1}) + \beta_i\big) & \text{otherwise,} \end{cases} \tag{6}$$

where $y_0 = x_0^d$, $y_1 = x_1^{1/d}$, and $L_i : \mathbb{F}_p^3 \to \mathbb{F}_p$ are of the form $L_i(z_0, z_1, z_2) = \gamma_i \cdot z_0 + z_1 + z_2$ for arbitrary pairwise distinct $\gamma_i \in \mathbb{F}_p \setminus \{0\}$ (e.g., $\gamma_i = i - 1$).

The Linear Layer M. For $t \in \{3, 4\}$, the matrices must be MDS. We suggest

$$M_3 = \begin{pmatrix} 2 & 1 & 1 \\ 1 & 2 & 1 \\ 1 & 1 & 2 \end{pmatrix}, \quad M_4 = \begin{pmatrix} 5 & 7 & 1 & 3 \\ 4 & 6 & 1 & 1 \\ 1 & 3 & 5 & 7 \\ 1 & 1 & 4 & 6 \end{pmatrix},$$

where M_4 corresponds to $M_{4,4}^{8,4}$ from [25], setting $\alpha = 2$.[8] This allows for an efficient implementation, as further shown in [25, Figure 13]. Indeed, the multiplication by M_4 can be computed with only 8 additions and 4 multiplications.

For $t = 4t' \ge 8$, M is defined as

$$M = M'' \times M' \equiv M' \times M'' = \begin{pmatrix} 2 \cdot M_4 & M_4 & \cdots & M_4 \\ M_4 & 2 \cdot M_4 & \cdots & M_4 \\ \vdots & \vdots & \ddots & \vdots \\ M_4 & M_4 & \cdots & 2 \cdot M_4 \end{pmatrix}, \tag{7}$$

where $M' = \mathrm{diag}(M_4, M_4, \ldots, M_4) \in \mathbb{F}_p^{t\times t}$ and $M'' = \mathrm{circ}(2 \cdot I, I, \ldots, I) \in \mathbb{F}_p^{t\times t}$ for a 4×4 MDS matrix M_4 and the 4×4 identity matrix I.

---

[7] GRIFFIN-π may be used also with $d \notin \{3, 5, 7, 11\}$. However, the security analysis and the number of rounds must be adapted for this case.

[8] We use the smallest $\alpha \ge 2$ such that the resulting matrix is MDS.

Table 2. Instances of GRIFFIN-π with security margin. We focus on the most common cases, namely $d \in \{3, 5\}$, $\kappa = 128$, $p \approx 2^{256}$, and $c = \lceil 2\kappa / \log_2(p) \rceil$.

	$t = 3$	$t = 4$	$t = 8$	$t \in \{12, 16, 20, 24\}$
R ($d = 3$)	16	14	11	10
R ($d = 5$)	12	11	9	9

Choosing the Constants. We use a pseudo-random number generator based on SHAKE [51] in order to choose our round constants $\{c^{(i)}\}_{i=0}^{R-2}$ and the constants $\{(\alpha_2, \beta_2)\}$ that define the nonlinear layer. The other constants $\{(\alpha_i, \beta_i)\}_{i=3}^{t-1}$ are defined as $\alpha_i = (i-1) \cdot \alpha_2$ and $\beta_i = (i-1)^2 \cdot \beta_2$. Note that $L_p(\alpha_i^2 - 4 \cdot \beta_i) = L_p((i-1)^2 \cdot (\alpha_2^2 - 4 \cdot \beta_2)) = L_p(\alpha_2^2 - 4 \cdot \beta_2) = -1$.

5.2 Number of Rounds of Griffin-π

For κ-bit security, the round number R including a margin of 20% must satisfy

$$R \geq \left\lceil 1.2 \cdot \max \left\{ 6, \left\lceil \frac{2.5 \cdot \kappa}{\log_2(p) - \log_2(d-1)} \right\rceil, 1 + R_{\mathrm{GB}} \right\} \right\rceil,$$

where $R_{\mathrm{GB}} \geq 1$ is the smallest integer such that

$$\min \left\{ \binom{R_{\mathrm{GB}} \cdot (d+t) + 1}{1 + t \cdot R_{\mathrm{GB}}}, \binom{d^{R_{\mathrm{GB}}} + 1 + R_{\mathrm{GB}}}{1 + R_{\mathrm{GB}}} \right\} \geq 2^{\kappa/2}.$$

These numbers are supported by our security analysis given in Sect. 6. Some instances for GRIFFIN-π are given in Table 2.

6 Security of Griffin and Griffin-π

We aim for GRIFFIN-π instances that prevent attacks on the hash and compression function. Distinguishers on GRIFFIN-π that cannot be exploited for an attack on the entire construction (e.g., zero sum partitions) are not taken into account. This approach is largely applied in the literature and similar designs.

6.1 Statistical Attacks on Griffin-π

The best statistical attacks against GRIFFIN-π include the differential [11] and the rebound attack [47,49]. Our security analysis is supported by dedicated automatic MILP tools which we designed in order to search for bounds on the minimal number of rounds against rebound attacks. Other attacks such as linear cryptanalysis, impossible differential, zero-correlation, integral/square, multiple-of-n, and mixture differential attacks are analyzed in the full version [30, App. F.1].

Differential Cryptanalysis. Differential cryptanalysis [11] and its variations are the most widely used techniques to analyze symmetric-key primitives. Given pairs of inputs with fixed input differences, differential cryptanalysis considers the probability distribution of the corresponding output differences. Let $\Delta_I, \Delta_O \in \mathbb{F}_p^t$ be respectively the input and the output differences through a permutation $\mathcal{P}$ over $\mathbb{F}_p^t$. The differential probability (DP) for Δ_O given Δ_I is

$$\text{Prob}(\Delta_I \to \Delta_O) = (|\{x \in \mathbb{F}_p^t \mid \mathcal{P}(x + \Delta_I) - \mathcal{P}(x) = \Delta_O\}|)/p^t.$$

Its maximum DP is $\text{DP}_{\max} = \max_{\Delta_I, \Delta_O \in \mathbb{F}_p^t \setminus \{0\}} \text{Prob}(\Delta_I \to \Delta_O)$. As GRIFFIN-$\pi$ is an iterated scheme, we search for ordered sequences of differences over any number of rounds, i.e., differential characteristics/trails. Assuming independent rounds, the DP of a differential trail is the product of the DPs of its one-round differences. Our goal is to find the minimum number of rounds such that each characteristic's probability is smaller than $2^{-2.5\kappa}$ in order to also prevent clustering effects. Based on other works published in the literature, we chose this arbitrary value since more characteristics can be used simultaneously to set up a differential attack, and hence each probability must be significantly smaller than $2^{-\kappa}$ for security. For this purpose, we first compute $\text{DP}_{\max}$ of the components of the nonlinear layer S, and the branch number of the matrix M.

Lemma 2. *Let $d \geq 3$ be an integer such that $\gcd(d, p - 1) = 1$. Then,*
$\text{DP}_{\max}(x \mapsto x^d) = \text{DP}_{\max}(x \mapsto x^{1/d}) = (\min\{d, 1/d\} - 1)/p.$[9]

Lemma 3. *Let $\alpha, \beta \in \mathbb{F}_p \setminus \{0\}$ such that $\alpha^2 - 4\beta$ is a quadratic nonresidue modulo p. Let $F : \mathbb{F}_p^2 \to \mathbb{F}_p$ be defined as $F(x, \ell) = x \cdot (\ell^2 + \alpha \cdot \ell + \beta)$. Given an input difference $\Delta_I = (\delta_x, \delta_\ell) \neq (0, 0)$ and an output difference Δ_O, the maximum differential probability of F is given by*

$$Prob(\Delta_I \to \Delta_O) \leq \begin{cases} 0 & \text{if } \delta_\ell = 0 \text{ and } \Delta_O \neq 0, \\ \frac{2}{p} & \text{if } \delta_\ell = 0 \text{ or } \delta_x = \Delta_O = 0, \\ \frac{p-1}{p^2} \leq \frac{1}{p} & \text{otherwise.} \end{cases}$$

We emphasize that the probability is zero if $\delta_\ell = 0$ and $\Delta_O \neq 0$ simultaneously.

The previous probabilities are always smaller than d/p for each $d \geq 3$. The proofs for Lemmas 2 and 3 are given in [30, App. C.1].

   Since a nonlinear mixing takes place between the $\mathbb{F}_p$ elements, it is not possible to apply the previous two lemmas directly in order to provide an estimation of the differential probability over a single round. For example, in the case of $(x_i, \ell_i) \mapsto x_i \cdot (\ell_i^2 + \alpha_i \cdot \ell_i + \beta_i)$, where $\ell_i := L_i(y_0, y_1, x_{i-1})$, the values of ℓ_i and of the corresponding difference δ_{ℓ_i} cannot be considered as variables, since they depend on the values of $x_0, x_1, x_{i-1} \in \mathbb{F}_p$ and on the corresponding differences.[10] Still, the previous results imply that the differential probability over a

---

[9] Note that $\min\{d, 1/d\} = d$ in our case.
[10] An analysis for this case is given in [30, Lemma 4].

single round cannot be bigger than $(d-1)/p$. Hence,

$$\left(\frac{d-1}{p}\right)^R \leq 2^{-2.5\kappa} \implies R \geq \frac{2.5\kappa}{\log_2(p) - \log_2(d-1)}$$

rounds are sufficient to achieve a probability smaller than $2^{-2.5\kappa}$ over the entire permutation, where the value 2.5 has been chosen to prevent clustering effect.

We emphasize that we expect that every differential probability has *much smaller probability*, since the activation of many S-boxes is helped by our diffusion matrix (besides the diffusion in the nonlinear layer). For this purpose, we prove the following result regarding the branch number of M in [30, App. C.2].

Proposition 1. *Let $t = 4t' \in \{8, 12, \ldots, 24\}$. The branch number of the matrix $M \in \mathbb{F}_p^{t \times t}$ defined as in Eq. (7) is $t' + 4$.*

We recall that $M \in \mathbb{F}_p^{t \times t}$ is an MDS matrix for $t \in \{3, 4\}$ and its branch number is equal to $t + 1$ in these cases.

Rebound Attacks. In a rebound attack [44,49], the goal of the attacker is to find two (input, output) pairs such that the two inputs and the corresponding outputs satisfy certain (truncated) differences. The approach consists of the *inbound* and the *outbound* phase. According to these phases, the internal permutation $\mathcal{P}$ of the hash function is split into three subparts, that is, $\mathcal{P} = \mathcal{P}_{\text{fw}} \circ \mathcal{P}_{\text{in}} \circ \mathcal{P}_{\text{bw}}$. The inbound phase is placed in the middle of the permutation and the two outbound phases are placed next to the inbound part. In the outbound phase, two high-probability (truncated) differential trails are constructed, which are then connected in the inbound phase. We claim that 6 rounds are sufficient against this attack. From our analysis, we know that there exist truncated differentials with probability 1 over a single round, but they cannot be extended over more rounds, and any classical differential characteristic over 2 rounds has a probability smaller than $2^{-\kappa}$ (for common d). Hence, by using an inside-out approach, the attacker can cover less than 4 rounds in the inbound phase. Since one round can be covered with a truncated differential characteristic of probability 1, the attacker can cover two rounds (one in each direction) in the outbound phase. Thus, no rebound attack on 6 rounds of GRIFFIN-π can be set up.

Verification with a Dedicated Tool. Our results have been verified via a dedicated mixed integer linear programming (MILP) tool. The results obtained with the tool for rebound attacks are presented in the full version [30, App. D]. The tool deduces all necessary word conditions of differential characteristics for making a successful rebound attack and traversing all possible settings of the inbound phase, assuming that the single inbound phase state can be used to modify word conditions of two S layers for free (without costing any degree of freedom). Even under such an impractical assumption, the tool cannot find a feasible rebound attack for 3 or more GRIFFIN-π rounds, which supports the conclusion that 6 rounds are sufficient against rebound attacks.

6.2   Algebraic Attacks

Algebraic attacks exploit weak algebraic properties of the design (e.g., low degrees or low density). Our analysis suggests that interpolation attacks and Gröbner basis attacks are the most efficient ones against GRIFFIN. For this purpose, we analyze the algebraic properties of the obtained equation systems and also practically implement GRIFFIN-π to obtain better estimates.

We also claim security against higher-order differentials, which is implied by the security against interpolation attacks. We do not claim security against zero-sum partitions [14]. We refer to [30, App. F.2] for more details.

Interpolation Attacks. The goal of an interpolation attack [40] is to construct an interpolation polynomial describing the function. In the case of a hash function, an interpolation polynomial can potentially be exploited to set up collisions or forgery attacks. The cost of the attack grows with the number of different monomials in the interpolation polynomial, where (an upper/lower bound of) the number of different monomials can be estimated given the degree of the function. If the number of unknown monomials is sufficiently large, this cannot be done faster than by exhaustive search. Roughly speaking, if the interpolation polynomial is dense and if its degree is maximum, this attack does not work.

In our case, 3 rounds are sufficient to reach the maximum degree. Indeed, due to Fermat's little theorem, $1/d \equiv d'$ where $(d \cdot d' - 1) \mod (p-1) = 0$. Since $d \geq 3$ is the smallest integer s.t. $\gcd(d, p-1) = 1$, d' is of the same order as p. In order to frustrate variants of the interpolation attack like MitM approaches or inside-out approaches starting from the middle of the construction, we double the number of rounds, conjecturing that $2 \cdot 3 = 6$ rounds are sufficient to prevent interpolation attacks and their variants. We further refer to the full version [30, App. E.1] for a more detailed analysis about the density of GRIFFIN-π.

Gröbner Basis Attacks. A Gröbner basis [16,19] allows to solve the system of equations that represent the cryptographic construction in a set of variables depending on the attack goals. In general, a Gröbner basis attack consists of three steps. First, the attacker needs to set up the equation system and compute a Gröbner basis for it. Secondly, they perform a change of term ordering for the basis, usually going to a term order which makes it easier to eliminate variables and find the solutions. Finally, the attacker uses the system obtained in the second step in order to start solving for the variables. As is usually done in the literature, here we focus on the complexity of the first step (i.e., computing a Gröbner basis), which can be estimated by

$$\mathcal{O}\left(\binom{D_{\text{reg}} + n_v}{n_v}^{\omega}\right),$$

where D_{reg} is the degree of regularity, n_v is the number of variables, and $2 \leq \omega < 3$ is a constant representing the complexity of a matrix multiplication. Theoretical estimations of the degree of regularity are known only for regular and semi-regular equation systems [6]. For example, in the case of a regular system of equations with $n_e = n_v$, where n_e denotes the number of polynomials in the system, the degree of regularity is estimated by $D_{reg} = 1 + \sum_{i=1}^{n_e}(d_i - 1)$, where d_i is the degree of the i-th equation. Since most of our equation systems do not exhibit the properties of regular sequences, we compute the actual degrees reached during the computations (the "practical" degree of regularity) for reduced versions of GRIFFIN-π, and use these estimates for the final round numbers.

As largely done in the literature (e.g., [4,15,32]), here we claim that the security of GRIFFIN with respect to the Gröbner basis attack follows from the infeasibility of solving the CICO problem instantiated by GRIFFIN-π.

Definition 5. *The invertible function* $\mathcal{P} : \mathbb{F}_p^t \to \mathbb{F}_p^t$ *is* κ-*secure against the CICO* (t_1, t_2)-*problem (where* $0 < t_1, t_2 < t$ *and* $t_1 + t_2 = t$*) if no algorithm with expected complexity smaller than* 2^κ *finds* $I_2 \in \mathbb{F}_p^{t_2}$ *and* $O_2 \in \mathbb{F}_p^{t_1}$ *for given* $I_1 \in \mathbb{F}_p^{t_1}$ *and* $O_1 \in \mathbb{F}_p^{t_2}$ *such that* $\mathcal{P}(I_1 \| I_2) = O_1 \| O_2$.

To support this claim, note that e.g. a preimage attack on the sponge hash function corresponds to solving the CICO problem (by simply reordering the elements). Indeed, the attacker cannot control (i) the inner part of a sponge hash function corresponding to I_1 in CICO and (ii) its output O_1, which depends on the element for which we are searching for a preimage, while no condition is imposed on the message (corresponding to I_2) and the truncated part (corresponding to O_2). Analogously, an attack on the CICO problem just given corresponds to a preimage attack on the compression function $\mathcal{P}(I_1 \| I_2) = O_1 + I_1 \| O_2 \equiv O_1' \| O_2$ (where I_1, O_1 are fixed).

Intermediate Variables. Using the inputs and outputs of GRIFFIN-π directly is infeasible since the degree is maximum and the polynomials are dense. A possible strategy to overcome this problem consists of introducing intermediate variables. This is a method to decrease the degrees in the equation system (and thus in general also the number of appearing monomials) at the cost of more variables. For GRIFFIN-π, we can introduce new variables in each round in order to avoid reaching a degree of $1/d$. Let $x = x_0 \| \cdots \| x_{t-1}$ and $y = y_0 \| \cdots \| y_{t-1}$ be respectively the state before and after a nonlinear layer. Then, the relation between x and y can be described by 2 equations of degree d and $t - 2$ equations of degree 3, using the fact that $y_1 = x_1^{1/d}$ can be rewritten as $y_1^d = x_1$ and the definition of our nonlinear layer given in Eq. (6). In order to connect two rounds with this approach, we denote the input of the next nonlinear layer by affine functions in $y_0, \ldots, y_{t-1}$, depending on the linear layer matrix M and the round constants. Hence, we add t variables in each round, except for the last one, where we simply use the desired output values. We then have $n_v = r + Rt$ variables (where r is the rate) and the same number of equations $n_e = n_v$. Of these equations, $2R$ equations are of degree d and $(t-2)R$ equations are of degree 3. The degree of the remaining equations depends on r. We focus on $r = 1$, since by experiments this is the easiest case from the attacker's point of view.

When implementing this system in Sage and Magma, the observed degrees of regularity are $\geq D_{\text{est}}^{(1)} = dR$ for a degree-d nonlinear layer after R rounds (see [30, App. E.2] for details). Using $D_{\text{est}}^{(1)}$, we obtain an estimated complexity of $\left(\frac{D_{\text{est}}^{(1)} + n_v}{n_v}\right)^{\omega} = \left(\frac{dR + n_v}{n_v}\right)^{\omega}$ operations. By setting $\omega = 2$ (optimistic from the attacker's point of view) and for a security level of κ bits, R must satisfy

$$\log_2\left(\binom{D_{\text{est}}^{(1)} + n_v}{n_v}\right) = \log_2\left(\binom{dR + 1 + tR}{1 + tR}\right) \geq \frac{\kappa}{2}. \tag{8}$$

Partial Intermediate Variables. Another strategy consists in introducing only a single intermediate variable for each round in order to avoid the high degree growth in the second word. The other state words go through the nonlinear layer without adding any more variables. In particular, we introduce a single new equation $y_1{}^d - x_1 = 0$ in each round, where y_1 is the new variable. Hence, we have $r + R$ variables in total, and we again focus on $r = 1$. The degree of the equations increases in each round, however not as fast as it would without adding a variable for the second word. By practical experiments, we found that the degree of regularity can be estimated conservatively by $D_{\text{est}}^{(2)} = d^R$ for this strategy (see [30, App. E.2] for details). Even if the equations here have a higher degree than in the first strategy, the number of variables and equations is smaller, since only one relation is added in each round (instead of t). Still, there is one crucial difference. Adding intermediate variables for all state words leads to a complexity which scales significantly with t. In this case, we add only one variable in each round, regardless of t. This means that we require

$$\log_2\left(\binom{D_{\text{est}}^{(2)} + n_v}{n_v}\right) = \log_2\left(\binom{d^R + 1 + R}{1 + R}\right) \geq \frac{\kappa}{2}. \tag{9}$$

Gröbner Basis Summary. Given the results just presented, we require that Eq. (8) and Eq. (9) are fulfilled for a κ-bit security level. However, due to the particular structure of our nonlinear layer, it is possible to choose the input such that the degrees in the first round are lower than expected. In particular, an attacker may choose the input such that $y_0 = x_0^{1/d} = u_1$ and $y_1 = x_1^d = u_2$, where u_1, u_2 are two fixed constants chosen by the attacker. This can be done by simply solving a linear equation system with these constraints. Consequently, the first two words are constant, the third word is linear, and only then the degree starts to grow. In order to protect from this attack, we add 1 round to the final round number needed for preventing Gröbner basis attacks.

For completeness, we also describe two additional attack strategies in [30, App. E.3]. They are both less efficient than the ones just presented.

6.3   Feistel Versus Horst: Security of GRIFFIN Instantiated with Feistel

We consider the security of GRIFFIN instantiated with a Feistel scheme as in Eq. (5) with respect to the two Gröbner basis approaches discussed in Sect. 6.2.

In the first Gröbner basis strategy we introduce intermediate variables for the whole state, i.e., we add t new variables and equations per round. In our experiments with Sage and Magma we could observe that the practical degree of regularity was constant regardless of the number of rounds in our tests for $R \geq 2$. Indeed, we were able to compute Gröbner bases in practice for the round numbers proposed for GRIFFIN (with Horst). We emphasize that this does not necessarily mean that the complexity of an attack changes only slightly with increased round numbers, but rather that it is harder for the designer to argue security. A similar behaviour was reported in [1, Section 6.1] for MiMC, where computing the Gröbner basis is efficient with intermediate variables, but the other steps in the full attack (monomial reordering, factorization) are not.

For the second strategy, where we only introduce intermediate variables to avoid the degree-$(1/d)$ growth in each round, it is easier to argue security. Still, the maximum degree in each round is reduced due to the missing multiplication. In particular, the difference is $\deg(R_{i-1})$ in each round, where $\deg(R_i)$ is the degree in the i-th round. Additionally, we could observe faster Gröbner basis computations for the Feistel version compared to the Horst version. Concretely, the difference is about a factor of 8 between the two versions.

Hence, even with a detailed analysis of the first strategy, the number of rounds would have to be increased due to the second strategy. This suggests that using the multiplication instead of the addition is better when aiming for security and efficiency in the applications discussed in this paper.

7   Performance Evaluation

In this section, we evaluate the performance of GRIFFIN and compare it to POSEIDON, *Rescue*-Prime [59] (a newer variant of *Rescue* with less security margin), GMiMC$_{\mathrm{erf}}$, *Grendel*, and NEPTUNE. Since GMiMC$_{\mathrm{erf}}$ was broken in [10], we use the updated round numbers proposed in [23, App. G]. *Grendel* has been broken too [33], leading to an adaptation of the round numbers by the designers. Our evaluation includes the updated numbers. Further, we compare GRIFFIN to the follow-up design Anemoi [15].

First we evaluate the plain performance, then we compare the efficiency when used in R1CS-based SNARKs and Plonk. For an evaluation in STARKs we refer to [30, App. A.3]. We instantiate all hash functions to provide 128 bits of security. All benchmarks were obtained on Linux using an Intel Xeon E5-2699 v4 CPU (2.2 GHz, turboboost up to 3.6 GHz) using stable Rust version 1.59 and the target-cpu=native flag. Each of the individual benchmarks has only access to one thread. We refer to our repository for the source code.[11]

Remark 2. The target use case plays a crucial role for the state size t. Indeed, while large primes are used in SNARK-based proof systems (and hence t can be small for a certain desired level of security), smaller primes are often preferred in STARK-based proof systems due to efficiency. For example, in Plonky2 [56]

---

[11] https://extgit.iaik.tugraz.at/krypto/zkfriendlyhashzoo/-/tree/master/bellman.

Table 3. Plain performance of different permutations in Rust (measured in μs).

Permutation	State size t								
	3	4	5	8	9	12	16	20	24
BLS12 ($d = 5$)									
GRIFFIN	113.97	105.45	–	89.32	–	93.76	98.19	**103.78**	**107.96**
GMiMC$_{\mathrm{erf}}$	20.14	20.70	**21.65**	**26.07**	26.44	**37.72**	**65.94**	107.45	167.75
NEPTUNE	–	19.54	–	30.87	–	60.20	93.14	128.95	171.97
POSEIDON	**18.61**	24.36	30.60	55.52	63.10	95.84	149.61	212.85	286.75
Rescue-Prime	412.91	434.13	451.49	645.79	739.24	1005.20	1363.40	1759.10	2147.80
Grendel	822.54	959.92	1001.30	1154.60	1215.60	1283.30	1425.30	1411.90	1459.20
BN254 ($d = 5$)									
GRIFFIN	106.90	99.33	–	84.97	–	88.21	92.08	**96.85**	**100.10**
GMiMC$_{\mathrm{erf}}$	18.67	19.34	**20.08**	**23.44**	24.63	**34.05**	**69.49**	107.82	156.35
NEPTUNE	–	17.38	–	29.83	–	58.41	89.89	125.87	166.11
POSEIDON	**17.56**	23.23	29.37	51.06	58.96	89.20	139.68	196.64	267.80
Rescue-Prime	379.78	400.87	411.16	598.86	683.81	929.89	1275.50	1639.30	2006.10
Grendel	703.36	808.78	849.89	994.20	1034.30	1094.20	1213.30	1196.00	1253.50

a 64-bit prime is used. Therefore, we emphasize that the efficiency with larger state sizes (e.g., $t \geq 12$) is as important as the efficiency with smaller ones.

Remark 3. The Pedersen hash function [60, Sec. 5.4.1.7] is also relevant for ZK proof systems. However, since it is not preimage-resistant, uses hardness assumptions vulnerable to quantum computers, and requires more R1CS constraints than POSEIDON and *Rescue* (see [31]), we do not consider it in our benchmarks.

7.1   Plain Performance

In Table 3, we compare the plain performance of the permutations when instantiated with the scalar fields of the commonly used BLS12 and BN254 elliptic curves.[12] In both of these fields $d = 5$ is the smallest value for which x^d is a permutation.

As the table shows, the fastest permutation for $t \leq 16$ is GMiMC$_{\mathrm{erf}}$. However, as we show later, it has the worst performance when used with SNARKs and STARKs. *Rescue*-Prime and *Grendel* have the worst plain performance due to having t high-degree $x^{1/d}$ or Legendre symbol evaluations per round. GRIFFIN also uses $x^{1/d}$, but only once per round. Thus, GRIFFIN scales significantly better with larger t than the other designs. Indeed, for small t GRIFFIN is slower than POSEIDON and NEPTUNE, but the differences get smaller for larger t, until GRIFFIN is faster than POSEIDON and NEPTUNE if $t \geq 16$.

Regarding the recent follow-up work Anemoi, we expect that it has a slower plain performance compared to GRIFFIN due to having more of the expensive $x^{1/d}$ evaluations per round (which dominate plain performance) while having a similar number of rounds. Furthermore, since in GRIFFIN the number of $x^{1/d}$

---

[12] $p_{\mathrm{BLS381}} = $ 0x73eda753299d7d483339d80809a1d80553bda402fffe5bfefffffff00000001,
$p_{\mathrm{BN254}} = $ 0x30644e72e131a029b85045b68181585d2833e84879b9709143e1f593f0000001.

Table 4. Bellman_ce performance of various hash functions in the sponge mode of operation (one permutation per call) for different state sizes t. Performance numbers are for proving the knowledge of preimages of hashes (`Perm`) and for proving the membership of a Merkle tree accumulator with 2^{24} elements (`MT`). Proving times are given in ms.

Hash		State size t (MT arity)										
		3 (2 : 1)		4 (2 : 1)		5 (4 : 1)		8 (4 : 1)		9 (8 : 1)		12 (8 : 1)	
		Prove	R1CS	Prove	R1CS	Prove	R1CS	Prove	R1CS	Prove	R1CS	Prove	R1CS
BLS12 ($d = 5$)													
GRIFFIN	Perm	**39.08**	**96**	**42.46**	**110**	–	–	**60.54**	**162**	–	–	**82.29**	**234**
	MT	**451.88**	**2637**	**495.74**	**2712**	–	–	**422.50**	**2136**	–	–	**424.07**	**2192**
NEPTUNE	Perm	–	–	71.53	228	–	–	95.54	264	–	–	120.55	306
	MT	–	–	969.71	5544	–	–	728.11	3360	–	–	747.22	2768
POSEIDON	Perm	75.31	240	88.29	264	93.43	288	108.40	363	114.35	387	132.54	459
	MT	1013.70	5832	1093.00	6408	654.85	3648	877.17	4548	630.17	3416	719.52	3992
Rescue-Prime	Perm	75.12	252	77.55	264	78.01	270	96.71	384	106.61	432	138.93	576
	MT	851.56	6120	872.26	6408	512.97	3432	726.84	4800	541.93	3776	737.59	4928
GMiMC$_{erf}$	Perm	173.71	678	176.91	684	180.20	690	190.01	708	193.76	714	253.53	942
	MT	3060.80	16344	2842.40	16488	1537.40	8472	1640.80	8688	1118.20	6032	1535.60	7856
Grendel	Perm	148.76	870	160.50	1000	191.33	1050	216.12	1200	223.85	1260	231.53	1320
	MT	2297.70	20952	2535.40	24072	1403.20	12792	1505.40	14592	1249.70	10400	1268.00	10880
Anemoi	Perm	–	–	n/a	140	–	–	n/a	240	–	–	n/a	300
	MT	–	–	n/a	3432	–	–	n/a	3072	–	–	n/a	2720
BN254 ($d = 5$)													
GRIFFIN	Perm	**22.48**	**96**	**24.24**	**110**	–	–	**35.08**	**162**	–	–	**48.05**	**234**
	MT	**266.77**	**2637**	**294.07**	**2712**	–	–	**251.90**	**2136**	–	–	**257.31**	**2192**
NEPTUNE	Perm	–	–	42.75	228	–	–	61.30	264	–	–	86.31	306
	MT	–	–	621.76	5544	–	–	512.69	3360	–	–	569.48	2768
POSEIDON	Perm	43.47	240	51.58	264	54.35	288	64.46	363	70.82	387	79.86	459
	MT	604.91	5832	656.77	6408	391.55	3648	542.02	4548	385.03	3416	446.87	3992
Rescue-Prime	Perm	43.54	252	44.36	264	44.87	270	54.52	384	61.51	432	80.97	576
	MT	510.03	6120	520.01	6408	306.12	3432	436.83	4800	323.67	3776	445.66	4928
GMiMC$_{erf}$	Perm	101.81	678	104.95	684	107.36	690	115.99	708	119.02	714	164.38	942
	MT	2148.60	16344	1791.20	16488	952.34	8472	1049.80	8688	717.61	6032	1046.70	7856
Grendel	Perm	86.85	870	94.12	1000	113.33	1050	127.31	1200	131.54	1260	135.80	1320
	MT	1401.20	20952	1523.60	24072	854.51	12792	920.43	14592	759.53	10400	776.86	10880
Anemoi	Perm	–	–	n/a	140	–	–	n/a	240	–	–	n/a	300
	MT	–	–	n/a	3432	–	–	n/a	3072	–	–	n/a	2720

evaluations is fixed to only one per round while it depends on the statesize t in Anemoi, we expect the performance difference to grow even further in favour of GRIFFIN. These expectations are confirmed by the benchmarks given in [15].

7.2 R1CS-Based SNARKs with GRIFFIN

Here we evaluate the efficiency of GRIFFIN when used in R1CS-based zk-SNARKs and compare it to its competitors by giving the number of R1CS constraints, as well as concrete runtimes for proving the knowledge of preimages and membership witnesses for Merkle tree accumulators. Our implementation is written in Rust using the bellman_ce library for creating Groth16 [37] proofs.[13]

---

[13] https://docs.rs/bellman_ce/0.3.5/bellman_ce/.

Describing GRIFFIN as a R1CS system is straightforward. The first two words of the nonlinear layer (i.e., y_0, y_1 in Eq. (6)) each require $\lfloor \log_2(d) \rfloor + \text{hw}(d) - 1$ constraints (2 constraints if $d = 3$, 3 constraints if $d = 5$). The squaring of each $L(\cdot)$ and each word of the remaining state require an additional constraint each. Since the linear layers can be incorporated into the constraints of the subsequent nonlinear layers (see Sect. 2.3), the total number of R1CS constraints for describing the whole GRIFFIN-π permutation is

$$(2 \cdot \lfloor \log_2(d) \rfloor + 2 \cdot \text{hw}(d) + 2 \cdot t - 6) \cdot R,$$

i.e., $2 \cdot R \cdot t$ R1CS constraints if $d = 3$ and $R \cdot (2 \cdot t + 2)$ ones if $d = 5$. In Table 4 we compare the number of R1CS constraints and the concrete runtime to create a ZK proof using the bellman_ce library when instantiated with two different elliptic curves (BLS12-381, BN254) which require d to be $d \geq 5$. We compare the performance of the hash functions when proving the knowledge of a preimage of a specific hash and when proving membership of a Merkle tree accumulator with 2^{24} elements. For these benchmarks we instantiate all permutations in a sponge mode of operations. Consequently, when constructing Merkle trees with arity $(x : 1)$ we require a state size t which is at least one word larger than x. In all cases, verifying the created ZK proof took < 4 ms which is why we do not explicitly list this runtime in Table 4.

Remark 4. As mentioned above, the hash functions in Table 4 are instantiated using the sponge mode of operation. One can, however, also read the benchmarks from Table 4 when using the compression function from Sect. 4.2. For a $(x : 1)$ compression we require a state size of $t = x$. As an example, the GRIFFIN benchmark with $t = 8$ is a valid benchmark for a $(4 : 1)$ compression using the sponge mode of operation and a $(8 : 1)$ compression using the compression function from Sect. 4.2. Or, when considering 64-bit field elements and a 128-bit security, a $(2 : 1)$ compression with GRIFFIN can be achieved either with a sponge and $t = 12$ or with a compression function and $t = 8$.

Table 4 shows that GRIFFIN requires the smallest number of R1CS constraints to prove the knowledge of a preimage of a hash for several state sizes t. However, since GRIFFIN is defined for $t \in \{3, 4t'\}$, it cannot be instantiated with $t = 5$ or $t = 9$ (the smallest state sizes for Merkle trees with arities 4 and 8, respectively). Thus, to create trees of this arity, GRIFFIN either requires a larger state size with a sponge compared to its competitors (e.g., more words in the inner part of the sponge), or it has to be used together with the compression function from Sect. 4.2. As shown in Table 4, even the first approach results in significantly fewer R1CS constraints and smaller proving times compared to the other hash functions. Concretely, using GRIFFIN results in nearly half of the required constraints compared to POSEIDON and *Rescue* and two third of the constraints compared to the recently proposed NEPTUNE. Only Anemoi comes close, however, it scales worse than GRIFFIN for larger t. Consequently, GRIFFIN has the fastest proving times which also lead to the fastest membership proving times when used as a hash function in Merkle tree accumulators.

7.3 Plonk Performance of GRIFFIN

Describing GRIFFIN with Plonk gates can be done as follows. Each affine layer usually requires $t \cdot (t - 1)$ addition gates. However, due to the specific structure of our linear layers which are optimized for a low number of additions, the number gets reduced significantly (similar to POSEIDON and NEPTUNE where the affine layers can be represented with fewer addition gates as well). Regarding the nonlinear layer, the first two words require $\lfloor \log_2(d) \rfloor + \mathrm{hw}(d) - 1$ multiplication gates. Computing $L(\cdot)$ requires one addition gate for $i = 2$ and two gates for $i > 2$. Computing $z_i = L_i(\cdot)^2 + \alpha_i L_i(\cdot) + \beta_i$ requires one gate plus an additional multiplication gate for $y_i = x_i \cdot z_i$. Summing up, GRIFFIN requires

$$(R + 1) \cdot \#\mathrm{mat} + R \cdot (2 \cdot \lfloor \log_2(d) \rfloor + 2 \cdot \mathrm{hw}(d) + 4t - 11)$$

Plonk gates, i.e., $(R + 1) \cdot \#\mathrm{mat} + R \cdot (4t - 5)$ gates if $d = 3$ and $(R + 1) \cdot \#\mathrm{mat} + R \cdot (4t - 3)$ gates if $d = 5$. Depending on t, the gates per linear layer $\#\mathrm{mat}$ varies: $\#\mathrm{mat} = 5$ for $t = 3$, $\#\mathrm{mat} = 8$ for $t = 4$, $\#\mathrm{mat} = 24$ for $t = 8$, and $\#\mathrm{mat} = \frac{8t}{4} + 2t - 4$ otherwise. Further, an intermediate constraint from the nonlinear layer can be reused in the subsequent linear layer calculations, and hence the total number of constraints gets reduced by R for $t \geq 4$.

Remark 5. Considering 3-fan-in addition gates (see Remark 1), GRIFFIN requires $(R+1) \cdot \#\mathrm{mat} + R \cdot (2 \cdot \lfloor \log_2(d) \rfloor + 2 \cdot \mathrm{hw}(d) + 3t - 8)$ Plonk gates, with $\#\mathrm{mat} = 3$ for $t = 3$, $\#\mathrm{mat} = 6$ for $t = 4$, $\#\mathrm{mat} = 20$ for $t = 8$, and $\#\mathrm{mat} = \frac{6t}{4} + 4 \cdot \left\lfloor \frac{t/4 - 1}{2} \right\rfloor + t$ otherwise. As above, one intermediate constraint from the nonlinear layer can be reused in the subsequent linear layer calculations, and hence the total number of constraints gets reduced by R for $t \geq 4$.

In Table 5, we compare the efficiency of different hash functions in Plonk by counting the number of gates required for one permutation. Compared to POSEIDON and *Rescue*, GRIFFIN always requires the smallest number of Plonk gates due to having a small number of multiplications (Sect. 7.2) and a small number of rounds implying a small number of linear layers. Only Anemoi requires a smaller number of gates for $d = 3$ and small state sizes, due to having more efficient linear layers requiring fewer addition gates. However, GRIFFIN's linear layer becomes more efficient with larger state sizes until GRIFFIN is more efficient than Anemoi in these configurations as well at around $t \geq 12$. We also compare GRIFFIN to Reinforced Concrete [31], a hash function with a fixed state size $t = 3$ introducing novel techniques to use lookup tables in $\mathbb{F}_p$ designs. This leads to fast plain performances, but potentially also introduces the risk of side-channel attacks. Further, this prevents Reinforced Concrete from (efficiently) being used in R1CS-based SNARKs or AIR-based STARKs. However, it is usable and specifically designed for Plookup [27], an extension to Plonk allowing lookup tables. Interestingly though, GRIFFIN requires fewer Plonk gates than Reinforced Concrete when using Plonk with the Plookup extension.

Table 5. Number of Plonk gates to describe various hash functions when instantiated with a 256-bit prime field. Numbers are given for Plonk implementations using either 2-fan-in addition gates or 3-fan-in addition gates.

| Hash | State size t | | | | | | | | | | | |
| | 2-fan-in addition gates | | | | | | 3-fan-in addition gates | | | | | |
	3	4	5	8	9	12	3	4	5	8	9	12
$d = 3$												
GRIFFIN	**197**	260	–	574	–	**904**	**163**	216	–	471	–	704
Reinforced Concrete	372	–	–	–	–	–	270	–	–	–	–	–
Rescue-Prime	432	560	**720**	1152	**1440**	2496	324	448	**480**	768	**864**	1536
POSEIDON	600	844	1100	1976	2304	3420	407	640	674	1256	1308	2030
NEPTUNE	–	687	–	1435	–	2451	–	534	–	1074	–	1812
Grendel	1485	1792	2040	2560	2835	3456	1386	1680	1800	2176	2295	2736
GMiMC$_{erf}$	1312	1650	1992	3042	3400	4498	984	1320	1328	2028	2040	2768
Anemoi	–	**256**	–	**544**	–	1080	–	**200**	–	**396**	–	**696**
$d = 5$												
GRIFFIN	**173**	**222**	–	**492**	–	**836**	**147**	**193**	–	**407**	–	**655**
Reinforced Concrete	378	–	–	–	–	–	276	–	–	–	–	–
Rescue-Prime	420	528	**630**	1280	**1584**	2688	336	440	**450**	896	**1008**	1728
POSEIDON	518	708	916	1665	1947	2901	379	560	602	1107	1167	1791
NEPTUNE	–	755	–	1507	–	2529	–	602	–	1146	–	1890
Grendel	1392	1700	1890	2520	2772	3300	1305	1600	1680	2160	2268	2640
GMiMC$_{erf}$	1130	1368	1610	2360	2618	4396	904	1140	1150	1652	1666	2826
Anemoi	–	284	–	592	–	1140	–	228	–	444	–	756

Acknowledgments. The authors thank all reviewers for their suggestions on how to improve the quality of the paper. We also thank them for the suggestion of the name Horst, for pointing out the similarity between Horst and the S-box used in Streebog, and for pointing out a mistake in the differential security analysis of GRIFFIN. We thank Danny Willems for pointing out an optimization in the Plonk arithmetization for GRIFFIN. Lorenzo Grassi is supported by the German Research Foundation (DFG) within the framework of the Excellence Strategy of the Federal Government and the States - EXC 2092 CaSa - 39078197. Roman Walch is supported by the "DDAI" COMET Module within the COMET – Competence Centers for Excellent Technologies Programme, funded by the Austrian Federal Ministry for Transport, Innovation and Technology (bmvit), the Austrian Federal Ministry for Digital and Economic Affairs (bmdw), the Austrian Research Promotion Agency (FFG), the province of Styria (SFG) and partners from industry and academia. The COMET Programme is managed by FFG. Yonglin Hao is supported by National Natural Science Foundation of China (Grant No. 62002024), National Key Research and Development Program of China (No. 2018YFA0306404). Qingju Wang was funded, in part, by Huawei Technologies Co., Ltd (Agreement No.: YBN2020035184) when she was working at the University of Luxembourg.

References

1. Albrecht, M.R., et al.: Algebraic cryptanalysis of STARK-friendly designs: application to MARVELLOUS and MiMC. In: Galbraith, S.D., Moriai, S. (eds.) ASIACRYPT 2019. LNCS, vol. 11923, pp. 371–397. Springer, Cham (2019). https://doi.org/10.1007/978-3-030-34618-8_13

2. Albrecht, M.R., et al.: Feistel structures for MPC, and more. In: Sako, K., Schneider, S., Ryan, P.Y.A. (eds.) ESORICS 2019. LNCS, vol. 11736, pp. 151–171. Springer, Cham (2019). https://doi.org/10.1007/978-3-030-29962-0_8

3. Albrecht, M., Grassi, L., Rechberger, C., Roy, A., Tiessen, T.: MiMC: efficient encryption and cryptographic hashing with minimal multiplicative complexity. In: Cheon, J.H., Takagi, T. (eds.) ASIACRYPT 2016. LNCS, vol. 10031, pp. 191–219. Springer, Heidelberg (2016). https://doi.org/10.1007/978-3-662-53887-6_7

4. Aly, A., Ashur, T., Ben-Sasson, E., Dhooghe, S., Szepieniec, A.: Design of symmetric-key primitives for advanced cryptographic protocols. IACR Trans. Symmetric Cryptol. **2020**(3), 1–45 (2020)

5. Ames, S., Hazay, C., Ishai, Y., Venkitasubramaniam, M.: Ligero: lightweight sublinear arguments without a trusted setup. In: CCS, pp. 2087–2104. ACM (2017)

6. Bardet, M., Faugére, J.C., Salvy, B., Yang, B.Y.: Asymptotic behaviour of the degree of regularity of semi-regular polynomial systems. In: Proceedings of MEGA, vol. 5 (2005)

7. Ben-Sasson, E., Bentov, I., Horesh, Y., Riabzev, M.: Scalable, transparent, and post-quantum secure computational integrity. Cryptology ePrint Archive, Report 2018/46 (2018)

8. Ben-Sasson, E., Chiesa, A., Riabzev, M., Spooner, N., Virza, M., Ward, N.P.: Aurora: transparent succinct arguments for R1CS. In: Ishai, Y., Rijmen, V. (eds.) EUROCRYPT 2019. LNCS, vol. 11476, pp. 103–128. Springer, Cham (2019). https://doi.org/10.1007/978-3-030-17653-2_4

9. Bertoni, G., Daemen, J., Peeters, M., Van Assche, G.: On the indifferentiability of the sponge construction. In: Smart, N. (ed.) EUROCRYPT 2008. LNCS, vol. 4965, pp. 181–197. Springer, Heidelberg (2008). https://doi.org/10.1007/978-3-540-78967-3_11

10. Beyne, T., et al.: Out of oddity – new cryptanalytic techniques against symmetric primitives optimized for integrity proof systems. In: Micciancio, D., Ristenpart, T. (eds.) CRYPTO 2020. LNCS, vol. 12172, pp. 299–328. Springer, Cham (2020). https://doi.org/10.1007/978-3-030-56877-1_11

11. Biham, E., Shamir, A.: Differential cryptanalysis of DES-like cryptosystems. In: Menezes, A.J., Vanstone, S.A. (eds.) CRYPTO 1990. LNCS, vol. 537, pp. 2–21. Springer, Heidelberg (1991). https://doi.org/10.1007/3-540-38424-3_1

12. Biryukov, A., Perrin, L., Udovenko, A.: Reverse-engineering the S-Box of Streebog, Kuznyechik and STRIBOBr1. In: Fischlin, M., Coron, J.-S. (eds.) EUROCRYPT 2016. LNCS, vol. 9665, pp. 372–402. Springer, Heidelberg (2016). https://doi.org/10.1007/978-3-662-49890-3_15

13. Black, J., Rogaway, P., Shrimpton, T.: Black-box analysis of the block-cipher-based hash-function constructions from PGV. In: Yung, M. (ed.) CRYPTO 2002. LNCS, vol. 2442, pp. 320–335. Springer, Heidelberg (2002). https://doi.org/10.1007/3-540-45708-9_21

14. Boura, C., Canteaut, A., De Cannière, C.: Higher-order differential properties of KECCAK and *Luffa*. In: Joux, A. (ed.) FSE 2011. LNCS, vol. 6733, pp. 252–269. Springer, Heidelberg (2011). https://doi.org/10.1007/978-3-642-21702-9_15

15. Bouvier, C., et al.: New design techniques for efficient arithmetization-oriented hash functions: Anemoi Permutations and Jive Compression Mode. IACR Cryptology ePrint Archive, p. 840 (2022)
16. Buchberger, B.: Ein Algorithmus zum Auffinden der Basiselemente des Restklassenringes nach einem nulldimensionalen Polynomideal. Ph.D. thesis, University of Innsbruck (1965)
17. Bünz, B., Bootle, J., Boneh, D., Poelstra, A., Wuille, P., Maxwell, G.: Bulletproofs: short proofs for confidential transactions and more. In: IEEE Symposium on Security and Privacy, pp. 315–334. IEEE Computer Society (2018)
18. Coron, J.-S., Patarin, J., Seurin, Y.: The random oracle model and the ideal cipher model are equivalent. In: Wagner, D. (ed.) CRYPTO 2008. LNCS, vol. 5157, pp. 1–20. Springer, Heidelberg (2008). https://doi.org/10.1007/978-3-540-85174-5_1
19. Cox, D.A., Little, J., O'Shea, D.: Ideals, Varieties, and Algorithms - An Introduction to Computational Algebraic Geometry and Commutative Algebra, 2nd edn. Undergraduate Texts in Mathematics. Springer, Cham (1997). https://doi.org/10.1007/978-3-319-16721-3
20. de la Cruz Jiménez, R.A.: On some methods for constructing almost optimal s-boxes and their resilience against side-channel attacks. IACR Cryptology ePrint Archive, p. 618 (2018)
21. Daemen, J., Rijmen, V.: The wide trail design strategy. In: Honary, B. (ed.) Cryptography and Coding 2001. LNCS, vol. 2260, pp. 222–238. Springer, Heidelberg (2001). https://doi.org/10.1007/3-540-45325-3_20
22. Dai, Y., Steinberger, J.: Indifferentiability of 8-round Feistel networks. In: Robshaw, M., Katz, J. (eds.) CRYPTO 2016. LNCS, vol. 9814, pp. 95–120. Springer, Heidelberg (2016). https://doi.org/10.1007/978-3-662-53018-4_4
23. Dobraunig, C., Grassi, L., Guinet, A., Kuijsters, D.: CIMINION: symmetric encryption based on Toffoli-Gates over large finite fields. In: Canteaut, A., Standaert, F.-X. (eds.) EUROCRYPT 2021. LNCS, vol. 12697, pp. 3–34. Springer, Cham (2021). https://doi.org/10.1007/978-3-030-77886-6_1
24. Dolmatov, V., Degtyarev, A.: GOST R 34.11-2012: Hash function. RFC 6986, pp. 1–40 (2013)
25. Duval, S., Leurent, G.: MDS matrices with lightweight circuits. IACR Trans. Symmetric Cryptol. 2018(2), 48–78 (2018)
26. Federal Agency on Technical Regulation and Metrology: GOST R 34.12-2015: Block cipher (2015)
27. Gabizon, A., Williamson, Z.J.: plookup: a simplified polynomial protocol for lookup tables. IACR Cryptology ePrint Archive, p. 315 (2020)
28. Gabizon, A., Williamson, Z.J., Ciobotaru, O.: PLONK: permutations over Lagrange-bases for Oecumenical noninteractive arguments of knowledge. Cryptology ePrint Archive, Report 2019/953 (2019)
29. Grassi, L.: On Generalizations of the Lai-Massey scheme: the blooming of amaryllises. IACR Cryptology ePrint Archive, p. 1245 (2022)
30. Grassi, L., Hao, Y., Rechberger, C., Schofnegger, M., Walch, R., Wang, Q.: Horst meets Fluid-SPN: Griffin for zero-knowledge applications. IACR Cryptology ePrint Archive, p. 403 (2022)
31. Grassi, L., Khovratovich, D., Lüftenegger, R., Rechberger, C., Schofnegger, M., Walch, R.: Reinforced concrete: fast hash function for zero knowledge proofs and verifiable computation. Cryptology ePrint Archive, Report 2021/1038 (2021). Accepted at ACM CCS 2022

32. Grassi, L., Khovratovich, D., Rechberger, C., Roy, A., Schofnegger, M.: Poseidon: a new hash function for zero-knowledge proof systems. In: USENIX Security Symposium, pp. 519–535. USENIX Association (2021)

33. Grassi, L., Khovratovich, D., Rønjom, S., Schofnegger, M.: The Legendre symbol and the Modulo-2 operator in symmetric schemes over Fnp preimage attack on full Grendel. IACR Trans. Symmetric Cryptol. **2022**(1), 5–37 (2022)

34. Grassi, L., Lüftenegger, R., Rechberger, C., Rotaru, D., Schofnegger, M.: On a generalization of substitution-permutation networks: the HADES design strategy. In: Canteaut, A., Ishai, Y. (eds.) EUROCRYPT 2020. LNCS, vol. 12106, pp. 674–704. Springer, Cham (2020). https://doi.org/10.1007/978-3-030-45724-2_23

35. Grassi, L., Onofri, S., Pedicini, M., Sozzi, L.: Invertible quadratic non-linear layers for MPC-/FHE-/ZK-friendly schemes over Fnp: application to Poseidon. IACR Trans. Symmetric Cryptol. **2022**(3), 20–72 (2022)

36. Grassi, L., Rechberger, C., Rotaru, D., Scholl, P., Smart, N.P.: MPC-friendly symmetric key primitives. In: CCS, pp. 430–443. ACM (2016)

37. Groth, J.: On the size of pairing-based non-interactive arguments. In: Fischlin, M., Coron, J.-S. (eds.) EUROCRYPT 2016. LNCS, vol. 9666, pp. 305–326. Springer, Heidelberg (2016). https://doi.org/10.1007/978-3-662-49896-5_11

38. Hoang, V.T., Rogaway, P.: On generalized Feistel networks. In: Rabin, T. (ed.) CRYPTO 2010. LNCS, vol. 6223, pp. 613–630. Springer, Heidelberg (2010). https://doi.org/10.1007/978-3-642-14623-7_33

39. Hougaard, H.B.: 3-round Feistel is not superpseudorandom over any group. IACR Cryptology ePrint Archive, p. 675 (2021)

40. Jakobsen, T., Knudsen, L.R.: The interpolation attack on block ciphers. In: Biham, E. (ed.) FSE 1997. LNCS, vol. 1267, pp. 28–40. Springer, Heidelberg (1997). https://doi.org/10.1007/BFb0052332

41. Klimov, A., Shamir, A.: Cryptographic applications of T-functions. In: Matsui, M., Zuccherato, R.J. (eds.) SAC 2003. LNCS, vol. 3006, pp. 248–261. Springer, Heidelberg (2004). https://doi.org/10.1007/978-3-540-24654-1_18

42. Kölbl, S., Lauridsen, M.M., Mendel, F., Rechberger, C.: Haraka V2 - efficient short-input hashing for post-quantum applications. IACR Trans. Symmetric Cryptol. **2016**(2), 1–29 (2016)

43. Lai, X., Massey, J.L.: A proposal for a new block encryption standard. In: Damgård, I.B. (ed.) EUROCRYPT 1990. LNCS, vol. 473, pp. 389–404. Springer, Heidelberg (1991). https://doi.org/10.1007/3-540-46877-3_35

44. Lamberger, M., Mendel, F., Rechberger, C., Rijmen, V., Schläffer, M.: Rebound distinguishers: results on the full whirlpool compression function. In: Matsui, M. (ed.) ASIACRYPT 2009. LNCS, vol. 5912, pp. 126–143. Springer, Heidelberg (2009). https://doi.org/10.1007/978-3-642-10366-7_8

45. Luby, M., Rackoff, C.: How to construct pseudorandom permutations from pseudorandom functions. SIAM J. Comput. **17**(2), 373–386 (1988)

46. Matsui, M.: Linear cryptanalysis method for DES cipher. In: Helleseth, T. (ed.) EUROCRYPT 1993. LNCS, vol. 765, pp. 386–397. Springer, Heidelberg (1994). https://doi.org/10.1007/3-540-48285-7_33

47. Matusiewicz, K., Naya-Plasencia, M., Nikolić, I., Sasaki, Yu., Schläffer, M.: Rebound attack on the full LANE compression function. In: Matsui, M. (ed.) ASIACRYPT 2009. LNCS, vol. 5912, pp. 106–125. Springer, Heidelberg (2009). https://doi.org/10.1007/978-3-642-10366-7_7

48. Maurer, U., Pietrzak, K.: The security of many-round Luby-Rackoff pseudorandom permutations. In: Biham, E. (ed.) EUROCRYPT 2003. LNCS, vol. 2656, pp. 544–561. Springer, Heidelberg (2003). https://doi.org/10.1007/3-540-39200-9_34

49. Mendel, F., Rechberger, C., Schläffer, M., Thomsen, S.S.: The Rebound attack: cryptanalysis of reduced whirlpool and Grostl. In: Dunkelman, O. (ed.) FSE 2009. LNCS, vol. 5665, pp. 260–276. Springer, Heidelberg (2009). https://doi.org/10.1007/978-3-642-03317-9_16

50. Mollin, R.A., Small, C.: On permutation polynomials over finite fields. Int. J. Math. Math. Sci. **10**, 535–543 (1987)

51. National Institute of Standards and Technology: SHA-3 Standard: Permutation-based hash and extendable-output functions. Federal Information Processing Standards Publication (FIPS) (2015)

52. Nyberg, K.: Generalized Feistel networks. In: Kim, K., Matsumoto, T. (eds.) ASIACRYPT 1996. LNCS, vol. 1163, pp. 91–104. Springer, Heidelberg (1996). https://doi.org/10.1007/BFb0034838

53. Patarin, J.: About Feistel schemes with six (or more) rounds. In: Vaudenay, S. (ed.) FSE 1998. LNCS, vol. 1372, pp. 103–121. Springer, Heidelberg (1998). https://doi.org/10.1007/3-540-69710-1_8

54. Patarin, J.: Generic attacks on Feistel schemes. In: Boyd, C. (ed.) ASIACRYPT 2001. LNCS, vol. 2248, pp. 222–238. Springer, Heidelberg (2001). https://doi.org/10.1007/3-540-45682-1_14

55. Patel, S., Ramzan, Z., Sundaram, G.S.: Luby-Racko. ciphers: why XOR is not so exclusive. In: Nyberg, K., Heys, H. (eds.) SAC 2002. LNCS, vol. 2595, pp. 271–290. Springer, Heidelberg (2003). https://doi.org/10.1007/3-540-36492-7_18

56. Polygon: Introducing Plonky2 (2022). https://blog.polygon.technology/introducing-plonky2/

57. Preneel, B., Govaerts, R., Vandewalle, J.: Hash functions based on block ciphers: a synthetic approach. In: Stinson, D.R. (ed.) CRYPTO 1993. LNCS, vol. 773, pp. 368–378. Springer, Heidelberg (1994). https://doi.org/10.1007/3-540-48329-2_31

58. Szepieniec, A.: On the use of the Legendre symbol in symmetric cipher design. IACR Cryptology ePrint Archive, p. 984 (2021)

59. Szepieniec, A., Ashur, T., Dhooghe, S.: Rescue-prime: a standard specification (SoK). Cryptology ePrint Archive, Report 2020/1143 (2020)

60. Zcash: ZCash protocol specification (2021). https://github.com/zcash/zips/blob/master/protocol/protocol.pdf

61. Zheng, Y., Matsumoto, T., Imai, H.: On the construction of block ciphers provably secure and not relying on any unproved hypotheses. In: Brassard, G. (ed.) CRYPTO 1989. LNCS, vol. 435, pp. 461–480. Springer, New York (1990). https://doi.org/10.1007/0-387-34805-0_42

On the Security of Keyed Hashing Based on Public Permutations

Jonathan Fuchs[1]([✉]) [iD], Yann Rotella[2], and Joan Daemen[1] [iD]

[1] Radboud University, Nijmegen, The Netherlands
{jonathan.fuchs,joan.daemen}@ru.nl
[2] Université Paris-Saclay, UVSQ, CNRS, Versailles, France
yann.rotella@uvsq.fr

Abstract. Doubly-extendable cryptographic keyed functions (deck) generalize the concept of message authentication codes (MAC) and stream ciphers in that they support variable-length strings as input and return variable-length strings as output. A prominent example of building deck functions is Farfalle, which consists of a set of public permutations and rolling functions that are used in its compression and expansion layers. By generalizing the compression layer of Farfalle, we prove its universality in terms of the probability of differentials over the public permutation used in it. As the compression layer of Farfalle is inherently parallel, we compare it to a generalization of a serial compression function inspired by Pelican-MAC. The same public permutation may result in different universalities depending on whether the compression is done in parallel or serial. The parallel construction consistently performs better than the serial one, sometimes by a big factor. We demonstrate this effect using XOODOO[3], which is a round-reduced variant of the public permutation used in the deck function Xoofff.

Keywords: keyed hashing · public permutations · universal hashing · parallel · serial · differential probability

1 Introduction

The doubly-extendable cryptographic keyed (deck) function is a relatively recent cryptographic primitive introduced by Daemen et al. [12]. A deck function generalizes a MAC function and a stream cipher in that it supports variable-length strings as input and returns variable-length strings as output.

Farfalle is a construction for building deck functions from a set of b-bit public permutations and rolling functions and was introduced in 2017 by Bertoni et al. [5]. It consists of a compression phase followed by an expansion phase. The compression phase has two steps, namely, the generation of a variable-length sequence of b-bits secret masks followed by the parallel compression of strings. Each b-bit secret mask is added to a b-bit input string block using a group addition. A public permutation is then applied to each block of the resulting string. The output of all the permutation calls are added together, resulting in a variable called the *accumulator*.

© International Association for Cryptologic Research 2023
H. Handschuh and A. Lysyanskaya (Eds.): CRYPTO 2023, LNCS 14083, pp. 607–627, 2023.
https://doi.org/10.1007/978-3-031-38548-3_20

Farfalle is a type of function called *protected hash* (also called hash-then-encrypt). The goal of such a function is to achieve pseudorandom function (PRF) security. This is defined in terms of the advantage of an optimal attacker of distinguishing it from a random oracle, when keyed with a uniformly random key unknown to the attacker. Protected hash functions can be described as follows. For a keyed compression function F_k and a fixed-input length cryptographic function $P_{k'}$, the output Z for a given input m is defined as $Z = P_{k'}(F_k(m))$. We can now isolate the contribution of the compression function F_k to the PRF security of the protected hash function by assuming that $P_{k'}$ is PRP secure. Then the PRF advantage of the protected hash function is upper bound by the sum of the PRF advantage and the success probability, taken over the key space of k of an optimal attacker to generate collisions in the output of F_k: distinct m, m' such that $F_k(m) = F_k(m')$.

This probability is in turn upper bound by the so called ε-universality [25] of F. This is the maximum taken over all distinct message pairs of the probability taken over all keys k, that two distinct messages result in the same output. A typical application of protected hash functions is message authentication code (MAC) computation. Another mainstream approach of building a MAC is the so called Wegman-Carter(-Shoup) (WC(S)) [24,26], that requires a nonce in the input. Given a fixed-input-length cryptographic function $P_{k'}$, a nonce n, a keyed compression function F_k and an input string m, the output is a tag T that corresponds to the input m and is given by $T = P_{k'}(n) + F(m)$. In the case of Wegman-Carter, the function $P_{k'}$ is assumed to satisfy some level of PRF security. In the case of Wegman-Carter-Shoup, $P_{k'}$ should be hard to distinguish from a random permutation, i.e., it is a pseudo-random permutation (PRP). The security of WC(S) depends on the ability of an attacker to generate forgeries, i.e., creating a valid (m', n, T') tuple whereby the attacker may have obtained one or more valid (m, n, T) tuple from a tag generation oracle. The probability of generating a successful forgery is upper bound by the so called ε-Δuniversality [25] of F. This is an upper bound on the probability taken over all keys k of two distinct input strings having a specific output difference.

Both approaches make use of a keyed compression function which we refer to as *keyed hash functions*. When looking at the proposed keyed hash functions in cryptographic literature, we can divide them into three categories. The first category makes use of strong cryptographic primitives. Notable examples are block-cipher-based modes such as CBC-MAC [2], CMAC [21], PMAC [7], Protected Counter Sums [3] and LightMAC [22]. For these modes PRF advantages can be expressed in terms of the PRP advantage of the underlying block cipher. Other examples are hash-function-based constructions such as NMAC [1] and HMAC [1] that also follow a reductionist security approach. In most of these constructions there is actually no clear separation between the keyed hashing component and PRF/PRP component and both are built using the same primitive and use the same key.

The second category are simple functions built from multiplication and addition, often in a large finite field. The best known examples are GMAC, used in the authentication encryption mode GCM [23], and poly1305 [4]. The universality of these functions can be derived using simple mathematical arguments. This approach gives functions that are more efficient than those in the first category in many modern CPUs thanks to the presence of dedicated instructions for efficient big integer multiplication of even multiplication in binary fields, e.g., the CLMUL instruction set.

The third category uses fixed-length public permutations. Examples include Farfalle, and the compression phase of Pelican MAC [16], which compresses a variable length input in a serial way using a CBC-MAC like construction, but with a public permutation taking the place of the block cipher. This approach leads also to improved performance. For example per 16-byte input block compression in Pelican MAC requires 4 unkeyed AES rounds while CBC-MAC and PMAC require a full 10-round keyed AES. On platforms where there is no dedicated hardware support for efficient multiplication, like the ARM cortex M3/M4, it is even competitive with functions in the second category. In dedicated hardware this approach is likely to lead to more efficient compression for the same security level as functions making use of multiplication as despite its mathematical simplicity, fast multiplication has a large footprint in hardware.

The problem with this third category is that their security cannot be reduced to the PRP or PRF security of some underlying primitive as in the first category and also the simple mathematical arguments of the second category do not apply. For the serial case there is some analysis by Daemen et al. in [15] and [17] and by Dobraunig et al. in [19] but they assume a random permutation. For the parallel case there is some analysis in [5] and [12] but these are not rigorous and seem to be meant more as design rationale.

1.1 Our Contributions

In this paper we provide a rigorous security analysis of permutation-based keyed hashing without relying on a random permutation. We propose a framework that idealizes the compression phases of Farfalle and Pelican MAC in order to derive upper bounds on their universalities, under the assumption of long independent keys. This framework is meaningful in the same way that cryptanalysis of block ciphers under the assumption of independent round keys is meaningful, or in the same way that proofs on bounds for the distinguishing/differentiating advantage in the random permutation model, like for sponge [6], duplex [14] or Even-Mansour [20] are meaningful.

We express the ε-universality and ε-Δuniversality of the constructions we present as a function of the probability of differentials of the underlying permutations.

Our main contributions are:

- In Sect. 2 we introduce the notion of *key-then-hash* functions and we generalize the concept of differentials over them. By using this generalization, we are able to define the differential probability of a differential over such keyed hash functions.

- In Sects. 3 and 4 we prove that the universality of serial and parallel key-then-hash functions using a public permutation can be expressed in terms of the probability of differentials over the underlying permutation using the new notion of differential probability over keyed hash functions.
  - We show that serial universal hashing using a public permutation f is both $\max_{a,\Delta} \mathsf{DP}_f(a, \Delta)$-universal and $\max_{a,\Delta} \mathsf{DP}_f(a, \Delta)$-$\Delta$universal. This result is given in Theorem 1.
  - We show that the ε-universality of parallel hashing using a public permutation f is $\max_a \sum_\Delta \mathsf{DP}_f^2(a, \Delta)$-universal and as such has the potential to result in better bounds than the ε-universality of serial hashing using the same f. This result is given in Theorem 2 and Theorem 3.
- In Sect. 5 we apply these results on XOODOO[3], a round-reduced version of the public permutation used in Xoofff [12], i.e., XOODOO[6].

2   Preliminaries

In this section we define the basic notation and definitions required to follow the analysis presented in this paper.

2.1   Notation

Our hash functions operate on strings of elements of an abelian group $\langle G, + \rangle$ with the neutral element written as 0. We call the elements of G *blocks*, denote the set of ℓ-block strings as G^ℓ and the set of strings of length 1 up to κ as $\mathsf{BS}(G, \kappa) = \cup_{\ell=1}^\kappa G^\ell$. We denote strings in bold, like $\mathbf{m}$, their blocks by m_i, with indexing starting from 1 and the length of a string $\mathbf{m}$ as $|\mathbf{m}|$. For a string of ℓ zeroes we write 0^ℓ.

In this paper we work with variables $x \in G$ that have a value that depends on the key $\mathbf{k}$. We denote the probability that a variable x has value X by $\Pr(x = X)$. In words, $\Pr(x = X)$ is the fraction of the keyspace for which variable x has value X. We call two variables independent if $\Pr(x = X, x' = X') = \Pr(x = X) \Pr(x' = X')$ for all $X, X' \in G$.

The probability mass function (PMF) of a variable x, denoted as g_x, is the array of values $\Pr(x = X)$ over all values X. We have $g_x(X) = \Pr(x = X)$, with the probability taken over the key space. Clearly, $\forall X : 0 \le g_x(X) \le 1$ and $\sum_X g_x(X) = 1$. As such, a PMF can be seen as a mapping $g : G \to [0, 1]$.

The convolution of two PMFs g_x, g_y, denoted as $g_x * g_y$, is given by:

$$g_z = g_x * g_y \iff \forall Z : g_z(Z) = \sum_X g_x(X) g_y(Z - X),$$

with $-$ determined by the group operation of G and the summation done over $\mathbb{R}$.

We denote the uniform PMF over G by U: so $\forall X \in G \; U(X) = \frac{1}{\#G}$. When we have two independent variables $x, y \in G$ then the PMF of their sum (in G) is the convolution of their PMFs. Moreover, if $z = x + y$ with x and y independent, then $\max_Z g_z(Z) \leq \min\left(\max_X g_x(X), \max_Y g_y(Y)\right)$. It immediately follows that convolution with an independent uniform variable results in a uniform variable.

2.2 ε-Universality and ε-ΔUniversality

As discussed in Sect. 1, the security of our keyed hash functions in their relevant use cases is determined by their ε-universality and ε-Δuniversality [25]. We adapt these definitions to our notation in this section.

Definition 1 (ε-universality[25]). *A keyed hash function F is said to be ε-universal if for any distinct strings $\mathbf{m}, \mathbf{m}^*$*

$$\Pr[F_{\mathbf{k}}(\mathbf{m}) = F_{\mathbf{k}}(\mathbf{m}^*)] \leq \varepsilon \,.$$

Definition 2 (ε-Δuniversality[25]). *A keyed hash function F is said to be ε-Δ universal if for any distinct strings $\mathbf{m}, \mathbf{m}^*$ and for all $\Delta \in G$*

$$\Pr[F_{\mathbf{k}}(\mathbf{m}) - F_{\mathbf{k}}(\mathbf{m}^*) = \Delta] \leq \varepsilon \,.$$

We will prove upper bounds on the universalities of our constructions in Sects. 3.2 and 4.2.

2.3 Key-Then-Hash Functions

We study keyed hash functions that take as input elements of $\mathrm{BS}(G, \kappa)$ and return an element of G. The keys are elements of G^κ. When processing an input, the key is first added to the input and then an unkeyed function is applied to the result. We refer to this special case of keyed hash functions as *key-then-hash* functions. A key-then-hash function is denoted as F and is defined as $F\colon G^\kappa \times \mathrm{BS}(G, \kappa) \to G$ with $F_{\mathbf{k}}(\mathbf{m}) = F(\mathbf{k} + \mathbf{m})$. The addition of two strings $\mathbf{m}, \mathbf{m}^*$ with $|\mathbf{m}| \leq |\mathbf{m}^*|$ is defined as $\mathbf{m}' = \mathbf{m} + \mathbf{m}^* = m_1 + m_1^*, m_2 + m_2^*, \ldots, m_{|\mathbf{m}|} + m_{|\mathbf{m}|}^*$, so the sum of two strings is as long as the shortest of the two.

In Sects. 3 we show a construction for serial key-then-hash functions whose primitive is a public permutation and in Sect. 4 we show a parallel construction for key-then-hash functions which also makes use of a public permutation as its underlying primitive.

2.4 Differential Probability over Fixed-length Functions

Definition 3 (Differential probability). *The differential probability of a differential (a, b) over a permutation $f\colon G \to G$, denoted as $\mathsf{DP}_f(a, b)$, is:*

$$\mathsf{DP}_f(a, b) = \frac{\#\{x \in G \mid f(x + a) - f(x) = b\}}{\#G} \,.$$

We say that input difference a propagates to output difference b with probability $\mathsf{DP}_f(a, b)$.

If $\mathsf{DP}_f(a, b) > 0$, we call input difference a and output difference b *compatible* through f. In our bounds $\max_{a \neq 0, b} \mathsf{DP}_f(a, b)$ plays an important role and we denote it by MDP_f. The differential probabilities of all differentials with a common input difference a form a PMF that we denote as DP_a, so we have $\mathsf{DP}_a(b) = \mathsf{DP}_f(a, b)$.

A useful quantity is the square of the Euclidean norm of DP_a given by $\sum_b \mathsf{DP}_a^2(b)$. We denote it by $\mathsf{NDP}_f(a)$ and denote the maximum of this quantity over all input differences by MNDP_f, hence $\mathsf{MNDP}_f = \max_{a \neq 0} \sum_b \mathsf{DP}_f^2(a, b)$.

2.5   Differentials over Key-Then-Hash Functions and Their Differential Probability

Classically, the definition of a differential is defined over fixed-length functions. The introduction of variable-length input makes the definition of a differential non-trivial due to the fact that two strings may differ in value but also in length. In this section, we generalize the concept of differentials to variable-length functions and define the differential probably of such differentials over key-then-hash functions. The core of our proofs in Sects. 3.3, 4.3 and 4.4 relies on understanding the relationship between the probability of differentials of the keyed hash function and those of its underlying permutation.

Proposition 1. *For a key-then-hash function, the probability that two messages* $\mathbf{m}, \mathbf{m}^*$ *with* $|\mathbf{m}| \leq |\mathbf{m}^*|$ *result in an output difference* Δ *through* $F_{\mathbf{k}}$ *is given by the following ratio:*

$$\Pr\left[F_{\mathbf{k}}(\mathbf{m}) - F_{\mathbf{k}}(\mathbf{m}^*) = \Delta\right] = \frac{\#\{\mathbf{k} \in \mathrm{G}^\kappa \mid F(\mathbf{a} + \mathbf{k}) - F(0^{|\mathbf{a}| + \lambda} + \mathbf{k}) = \Delta\}}{\#\mathrm{G}^\kappa},$$

where $\lambda = |\mathbf{m}'| - |\mathbf{m}|$ *and* $\mathbf{a}$ *is taken as* $\mathbf{a} \in \mathrm{G}^{|\mathbf{m}|}$ *such that* $\mathbf{m} = \mathbf{a} + \mathbf{m}^*$.

Proof. We start by looking at the probability of any pair of strings $\mathbf{m}, \mathbf{m}^*$ leading to an output difference Δ:

$$\Pr\left[F_{\mathbf{k}}(\mathbf{m}) - F_{\mathbf{k}}(\mathbf{m}^*) = \Delta\right] = \frac{\#\{\mathbf{k} \in \mathrm{G}^\kappa \mid F(\mathbf{m} + \mathbf{k}) - F(\mathbf{m}^* + \mathbf{k})\}}{\#\mathrm{G}^\kappa}.$$

Now we prove that given an offset $\mathbf{o} \in \mathrm{G}^\kappa$ the following holds:

$$\Pr\left[F(\mathbf{m} + \mathbf{k}) - F(\mathbf{m}^* + \mathbf{k}) = \Delta\right] = \Pr\left[F(\mathbf{m} + \mathbf{o} + \mathbf{k}) - F(\mathbf{m}^* + \mathbf{o} + \mathbf{k}) = \Delta\right].$$

We denote $\mathcal{S} = \{\mathbf{k} \in \mathrm{G}^\kappa \mid F(\mathbf{m} + \mathbf{k}) - F(\mathbf{m}^* + \mathbf{k}) = \Delta\} \subseteq \mathrm{G}^\kappa$ and we note the following property. Since G^κ is an abelian group, adding an offset $\mathbf{o}$ to every element of $\mathcal{S}$ does not change its size. Furthermore, since string addition is associative, offsetting $\mathbf{m}, \mathbf{m}^*$ by $\mathbf{o}$ is equivalent to adding $\mathbf{o}$ to every element of $\mathcal{S}$. Therefore, by choosing $\mathbf{o}$ such that $\mathbf{m}^* + \mathbf{o} = 0^{|\mathbf{m}^*|}$, we get the expression in Proposition 1.

The tuple $(\mathbf{a}, \lambda)$ can be seen as the string equivalent of an input difference. This leads us to the following definition of a difference.

Definition 4 (Difference between two strings). *We define the difference between two strings* $\mathbf{m}, \mathbf{m}^*$ *with* $|\mathbf{m}| \leq |\mathbf{m}^*|$ *as the pair* $(\mathbf{a}, \lambda) \in G^{|\mathbf{m}|} \times \mathbb{Z}_{\geq 0}$ *where* $\mathbf{a} = m_1 - m_1^*, m_2 - m_2^*, \ldots, m_{|\mathbf{m}|} - m_{|\mathbf{m}|}^*$ *and* $\lambda = |\mathbf{m}^*| - |\mathbf{m}|$.

When $\lambda = 0$ we say a difference is *equal-length* and otherwise we say it is *unequal-length*. Now, we define the probability of differentials over F.

Definition 5 (Generalized differentials and their DP). *Given an input difference* $(\mathbf{a}, \lambda)$ *and an output difference* Δ, *the differential probability of the differential* $(\mathbf{a}, \lambda, \Delta)$ *over* F, *denoted as* $\mathsf{DP}_F(\mathbf{a}, \lambda, \Delta)$ *is given by:*

$$\mathsf{DP}_F(\mathbf{a}, \lambda, \Delta) = \frac{\#\{\mathbf{k} \in G^\kappa \mid F(\mathbf{a} + \mathbf{k}) - F(0^{|\mathbf{a}|+\lambda} + \mathbf{k}) = \Delta\}}{\#G^\kappa}.$$

In order to simplify notation, when $\lambda = 0$ we omit it from the differential. Note that if we take $\lambda = 0$ and $\mathbf{a} = a \in G$ we get the classical definition of differential probability.

As for fixed-length functions, the differential probabilities of all differentials with a common input difference $(\mathbf{a}, \lambda)$ form a PMF that we denote as $\mathsf{DP}_{F(\mathbf{a},\lambda)}$, so we have $\mathsf{DP}_{F(\mathbf{a},\lambda)}(\Delta) = \mathsf{DP}_F(\mathbf{a}, \lambda, \Delta)$. From Definitions 1 and 2, we can say that a keyed hash function F is $\max_{\mathbf{a},\lambda} \mathsf{DP}_F(a, \lambda, 0)$-universal and $\max_{\mathbf{a},\lambda,\Delta} \mathsf{DP}_F(a, \lambda, \Delta)$-$\Delta$universal. We focus for the rest of the paper on proving upper bounds on the differential probability of our constructions.

3 Serial Key-Then-Hash Construction

We will consider the universality of serial key-then-hash functions based on an unkeyed permutation f. The construction is described in Sect. 3.1. The main theorem is provided in Sect. 3.2. We show that the universality of such construction is equal to the maximum differential probability over all non-trivial differentials of the underlying permutation. We prove Theorem 1 in Sect. 3.3.

3.1 Construction

We define the serialization of a public permutation in Algorithm 1 and depict it in Fig. 1. The construction takes as parameters a public permutation $f : G \to G$ and a maximum string length κ. Its inputs are a key $\mathbf{k} \in G^\kappa$ and a message $\mathbf{m} \in \mathrm{BS}(G, \kappa)$ and it returns a digest $h \in G$.

3.2 Security of the Serial Construction

In this section we express the universality of the serialization of a public permutation f in terms of the probability of differentials over f. Furthermore, we prove that $\mathrm{Serial}[f]$ is ε-universal and ε-Δuniversal for the same value of ε.

Theorem 1 (Universality of $\mathrm{Serial}[f]$**).** *The serialization of a public permutation* f, $\mathrm{Serial}[f]$, *is* MDP_f-*universal and* MDP_f-Δuniversal.

Algorithm 1: The serialization Serial[f]

Parameters: A public permutation $f\colon \mathrm{G} \to \mathrm{G}$ and a maximum length κ
Inputs   : A key $\mathbf{k} \in \mathrm{G}^{\kappa}$ and a message $\mathbf{m} \in \mathrm{BS}(\mathcal{A}, \kappa)$
Output   : A digest $h \in \mathrm{G}$

Processing :
$\mathbf{x} \leftarrow \mathbf{m} + \mathbf{k}$
$h \leftarrow 0$
for $i \leftarrow 1$ **to** $|\mathbf{m}|$ **do**
 | $h \leftarrow f(x_i + h)$
end
return h

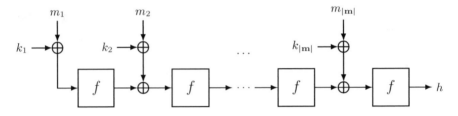

Fig. 1. The serialization Serial[f]

3.3   Proof of Theorem 1

In order to determine the probability of differentials over Serial[f], denoted as $\mathrm{DP_S}$, we have to consider both equal-length and unequal-length differences. We show in Lemma 1 that differentials with unequal-length input differences all have $\mathrm{DP_S} = \frac{1}{\#\mathrm{G}}$ regardless of $\mathbf{a}$ and Δ. In Lemma 2 we prove a recursive expression for $\mathrm{DP_S}$ for equal-length differences with $|\mathbf{a}| > 1$. By combining these two lemmas we are able to construct a proof for Theorem 1.

Lemma 1 (DP$_\mathrm{S}$ of unequal-length differences). *For any differential* $(\mathbf{a}, \lambda, \Delta)$ *with* $\lambda > 0$, $\mathrm{DP_S} = \frac{1}{\#\mathrm{G}}$.

Proof. Let $\mathbf{m}, \mathbf{m}^*$ be two strings with length $|\mathbf{m}| < |\mathbf{m}^*|$ and difference $(\mathbf{a}, \lambda, b)$. The probability that Serial[f]$(\mathbf{m} + \mathbf{k}) = x$ is $\frac{1}{\#\mathrm{G}}$ since it is the result of $f(\mathrm{cv} + k_{|\mathbf{m}|} + m_{|\mathbf{m}|})$, where cv is the intermediate value accumulating the first $|\mathbf{m}| - 1$ blocks. Since we take the probability over all keys, and therefore over all values of $k_{|\mathbf{m}|}$, the probability distribution of the permutation input is uniform and hence also its output. Similarly, the probability that Serial[f]$(\mathbf{m}^* + \mathbf{k}) = y$ is $\frac{1}{\#\mathrm{G}}$ since it is the result of $f(\mathrm{cv}^* + k_{|\mathbf{m}^*|} + m_{|\mathbf{m}^*|})$, where cv^* is the intermediate value accumulating the first $|\mathbf{m}^*| - 1$ blocks. The value of y is independent of the value of x since they result from f being computed under the addition of $k_{|\mathbf{m}|}$ and $k_{|\mathbf{m}^*|}$ respectively and they are two secret key blocks chosen independently of each other from a uniform distribution. We get that the output difference is Δ if $x = \Delta + y$. Hence, we can partition the sample space. We use the following condition. $\mathrm{Serial}[f](\mathbf{m}+\mathbf{k}) = \Delta + y$ given the event $\mathrm{Serial}[f](\mathbf{m}^* + \mathbf{k}) = y$. Each partition has probability $\frac{1}{\#\mathrm{G}^2}$. By applying the law of total probability we obtain the expression in Lemma 1.

Lemma 2 (DP$_\mathrm{S}$ of an extra message block with $\lambda = 0$). *Let $(\mathbf{a}, a)$ be the concatenation of $\mathbf{a} \in \mathrm{BS}(\mathrm{G}, \kappa)$ and $a \in \mathrm{G}$. The differential probability of the differential $((\mathbf{a}, a), \Delta)$ over $\mathrm{Serial}[f]$ is given by:*

$$\mathrm{DP}_\mathrm{S}((\mathbf{a}, a), \Delta) = \sum_{t \in \mathrm{G}} \mathrm{DP}_\mathrm{S}(\mathbf{a}, t)\mathrm{DP}_f(a + t, \Delta).$$

Proof. We prove this using the law of total probability. We start by looking at the conditional probability that $a + t$ propagates to Δ through f given that $\mathbf{a}$ propagates to t through $\mathrm{Serial}[f]$ for any value $t \in \mathrm{G}$. Since the key blocks are chosen independently and at random from a uniform distribution these two events are independent from each other. Therefore, it happens with probability $\mathrm{DP}_\mathrm{S}(\mathbf{a}, t)\mathrm{DP}_f(a + t, \Delta)$. By applying the law of total probability we get the expression in Lemma 2.

Proof (Theorem 1). Using Lemma 2, we first show that the DP of an equal-length differential $((\mathbf{a}, a), \Delta)$ is upper bounded by $\max_{\Delta'} \mathrm{DP}_\mathrm{S}(\mathbf{a}, \Delta')$:

$$\mathrm{DP}_\mathrm{S}((\mathbf{a}, a), \Delta) = \sum_{t \in \mathrm{G}} \mathrm{DP}_\mathrm{S}(\mathbf{a}, t)\mathrm{DP}_f(a + t, \Delta)$$

$$\leq \sum_{t \in \mathrm{G}} (\max_t \mathrm{DP}_\mathrm{S}(\mathbf{a}, t))\mathrm{DP}_f(a + t, \Delta)$$

$$= \max_{\Delta'} \mathrm{DP}_\mathrm{S}(\mathbf{a}, \Delta') \sum_t \mathrm{DP}_f(t, \Delta).$$

Since f is a permutation, we have $\sum_t \mathrm{DP}_f(t, \Delta) = \sum_t \mathrm{DP}_{f^{-1}}(\Delta, t) = 1$ and we obtain:

$$\mathrm{DP}_\mathrm{S}((\mathbf{a}, a), \Delta) = \max_\Delta \mathrm{DP}_\mathrm{S}(\mathbf{a}, \Delta). \tag{1}$$

As (1) holds for any input difference $(\mathbf{a}, a)$ and output difference Δ we have:

$$\max_{(\mathbf{a}, a), \Delta} \mathrm{DP}_\mathrm{S}((\mathbf{a}, a), \Delta) \leq \max_{\mathbf{a}, \Delta} \mathrm{DP}_\mathrm{S}(\mathbf{a}, \Delta).$$

It follows that the maximum DP over all equal-length differentials with an input difference of length ℓ is upper bounded by the maximum DP over all equal-length differentials with an input difference of length $\ell - 1$. This can be applied recursively until we reach $\ell = 1$, yielding $\max_{a_1, \Delta} \mathrm{DP}_\mathrm{S}(a_1, \Delta) = \max_{a_1, \Delta} \mathrm{DP}_f(a_1, \Delta) = \mathrm{MDP}_f$. So the maximum DP over all equal-length differentials is MDP_f.

For unequal-length differentials Lemma 1 states that the DP equals $\frac{1}{\#\mathrm{G}}$. As $\mathrm{MDP}_f > \frac{1}{\#\mathrm{G}}$, this finishes the proof.

4   Parallel Key-Then-Hash Construction

Similarly to Sect. 3, we consider the universality of a construction based on an unkeyed permutation f. However, in this construction, strings are compressed in a parallel way. In Sect. 4.1 we define the construction. The main theorems of this section are provided in Sect. 4.2. In Sects. 4.3 and 4.4 we prove Theorems 2 and 3 respectively.

4.1   Construction

We describe the parallelization of a public permutation in Algorithm 2 and depict it in Fig. 2. The construction takes as parameters a public permutation $f \colon \mathrm{G} \to \mathrm{G}$ and a maximum string length κ. The inputs are a key $\mathbf{k} \in \mathrm{G}^\kappa$ and a string $\mathbf{m} \in \mathrm{BS}(\mathrm{G}, \kappa)$ and it returns a digest $h \in \mathrm{G}$.

Algorithm 2: The parallelization Parallel[f]

Parameters: A public permutation $f \colon \mathrm{G} \to \mathrm{G}$ and a maximum length κ
Inputs   : A key $\mathbf{k} \in \mathrm{G}^\kappa$ and a message $\mathbf{m} \in \mathrm{BS}(\mathrm{G}, \kappa)$
Output   : A digest $h \in \mathrm{G}$

$\mathbf{x} \leftarrow \mathbf{m} + \mathbf{k}$
$h \leftarrow 0$
for $i \leftarrow 1$ **to** $|\mathbf{m}|$ **do**
$\quad |\quad h \leftarrow h + f(x_i)$
end
return h

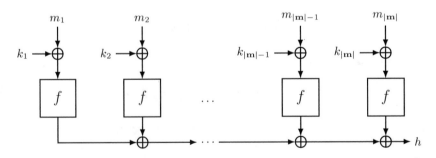

Fig. 2. The parallelization Parallel[f]

4.2   Security of Parallel Construction

In this section we describe the universality of the parallelization of a public permutation f in terms of the differential probability of f. Unlike the serialization of a public function, the ε-universality and ε-Δ universality of Parallel[f] are in general different.

Theorem 2 (Δ-Universality of Parallel[f]**).** *The parallelization of a public permutation f, Parallel[f], is* MDP_f-$\Delta universal$.

Theorem 3 Universality of Parallel[f]**).** *The parallelization of a public permutation f, Parallel[f], is* MNDP_f-$universal$.

4.3   Proof of Theorem 2

In Lemma 3 we show that the PMF of an input difference to Parallel[f], denoted as $\mathsf{DP}_{\mathrm{P}(\mathbf{a},\lambda)}$, can be obtained by convolution of the PMFs DP_{a_i} and the uniform distribution U.

Lemma 3 (DP of differentials over Parallel[f]**).** *The PMF of an input difference $(\mathbf{a}, \lambda)$ to Parallel[f] is given by:*

$$\mathsf{DP}_{\mathrm{P}}(\mathbf{a}, \lambda) = \mathsf{DP}_{a_1} * \mathsf{DP}_{a_2} * \ldots * \mathsf{DP}_{a_\ell} * \mathrm{U}.$$

Proof. Assume we process from left to right. We will express the PMF of the chaining value after processing a new block with difference a as a function of the PMF of the chaining value before processing that new block. We denote the difference in the partial message by $\mathbf{a}$. Per definition we have for the PMF of that chaining value $\mathsf{DP}_{\mathrm{P}(\mathbf{a})}$. The PMF of the difference in the new block is DP_a. The new value of the chaining value is the sum of these two variables. If the PMFs are independent, then the resulting PMF is given by the convolution of the two. These PMFs are indeed independent, as the two PMFs are governed by non-overlapping key blocks and their distribution is over all possible keys. This can be applied recursively and we obtain for any two partial messages of equal length that $\mathsf{DP}_{\mathrm{P}(\mathbf{a})} = \mathsf{DP}_{a_1} \mathsf{DP}_{a_2} \ldots \mathsf{DP}_{a_{|\mathbf{a}|}}$.

Now we will absorb a new block that is only present in one of the two messages. The difference between the two messages is now simply the value of the output of the permutation for the input block in the longest message. The PMF of this value is the U distribution as its input due to the presence of a key block. The new value of the chaining value is the sum of these two variables. These PMFs are independent, as the two PMFs are here also governed by non-overlapping key blocks. Therefore the PMF of the sum is the convolution of the PMFs. Convolution with the uniform distribution gives again the uniform distribution.

Combining the two results proves the lemma.

Proof (Theorem 2). Similarly to the proof of Theorem 1, we will prove an upper bound on $\max_{\mathbf{a},\lambda,\Delta} \mathsf{DP}_{\mathrm{P}}(\mathbf{a}, \lambda, \Delta)$.

By applying Lemma 3, we get the following upper bounds:

$$\max_{\mathbf{a},\lambda,\varDelta} \mathsf{DP}_\mathsf{P}(\mathbf{a},\lambda,\varDelta) \leq \max\left\{ \max_{\mathbf{a},\varDelta\in G} \mathsf{DP}_\mathsf{P}(\mathbf{a},\varDelta), \max_{\mathbf{a},\lambda,\varDelta} \mathsf{DP}_\mathsf{P}(\mathbf{a},\lambda,\varDelta) \right\}$$

$$= \max\left\{ \max_{a,\varDelta\in G} \mathsf{DP}_f(a,\varDelta), \max_{x\in G} \mathrm{U}(x) \right\}$$

$$= \max_{a,\varDelta\in G} \mathsf{DP}_f(a,\varDelta).$$

4.4 Proof of Theorem 3

In this section we will prove Theorem 3 by using the same technique used in the proof of Theorem 2 but on two-block equal-length differentials.

Proof Theorem 3). Since f is a permutation, it is impossible to achieve a 0 output difference with single block equal-length differences. From the proof of Theorem 2, we know that the following holds:

$$\max_{\mathbf{a},\lambda} \mathsf{DP}_\mathsf{P}(\mathbf{a},\lambda,0) \leq \max_{a_1,a_2,\varDelta\in G} \mathsf{DP}_\mathsf{P}((a_1,a_2),\varDelta) \tag{2}$$

$$= \max_{a_1,a_2,\varDelta\in G} \sum_{t\in G} \mathsf{DP}_f(a_1,t)\mathsf{DP}_f(a_2,\varDelta - t). \tag{3}$$

The right-hand part of (3) can be seen as a scalar product of vectors with components indexed by t. The scalar product of two vectors is upper bound by the square of the maximum of the norm of the two vectors where the norm of a vector is square root of the sum of squares of its coordinates, i.e., the Euclidian norm. Hence, we have the following upper-bound.

$$\max_{\mathbf{a},\lambda} \mathsf{DP}_\mathsf{P}(\mathbf{a},\lambda,0) \leq \max\left\{ \sum_{t\in G} \mathsf{DP}_f^2(a_1,t), \sum_{t\in G} \mathsf{DP}_f^2(a_2,\varDelta-t) \right\}$$

$$= \max\left\{ \sum_{t\in G} \mathsf{DP}_f^2(a_1,t), \sum_{t\in G} \mathsf{DP}_f^2(a_2,t) \right\}.$$

This is true for any a_1 or a_2, hence we have:

$$\max_{\mathbf{a},\lambda} \mathsf{DP}_\mathsf{P}(\mathbf{a},\lambda,0) \leq \max_{a\in G} \sum_{t\in G} \mathsf{DP}_f^2(a,t).$$

Equality is achieved by taking $a_2 = -a_1$.

We summarize the results of the Theorems 1, 2 and 3 in Table 1.

5 Application to Xoodoo

In this section we determine, bound and estimate the quantities of Xoodoo that determine the universalities in our keyed hash constructions: MDP_f and MNDP_f.

Table 1. ϵ-Δuniversality and ϵ-universality of Serial[f] and Parallel[f] based on Theorems 1, 2 and 3.

	Serial[f]	Parallel[f]
Δuniversality	MDP$_f$	MDP$_f$
universality	MDP$_f$	MNDP$_f$

The specification for the round function of XOODOO can be found in the Appendix Sect. A.

In Sects. 5.1 and 5.2 we provide some the background knowledge required to understand this section. In Sects. 5.3 and 5.4 we discuss MDP$_f$ and MNDP$_f$ of XOODOO[3] and XOODOO[4] respectively.

By Theorem 1 it immediately implies the MDP$_f$-universality and MDP$_f$-Δuniversality of Serial[XOODOO[3]] and Serial[XOODOO[4]], and by Theorems 2 and 3 the MDP$_f$-Δuniversality and MNDP$_f$-universality of Parallel[XOODOO[3]] and Parallel[XOODOO[4]].

5.1 Differential Propagation Basics

As we will only discuss differential probabilities over f, we will just write DP for DP$_f$. Determining the DP of differentials over an iterated permutation passes via *differential trails*: a chaining of differentials over a sequence of successive rounds.

Definition 6 (Differential trail). *An r-round differential trail, denoted as Q, is a sequence of $r + 1$ differences: an input difference, $r - 1$ intermediate differences and an output difference, where the round differentials (q_{i-1}, q_i) have non-zero DP, namely,*

$$Q = (q_0, q_1, q_2, \ldots, q_{r-1}, q_r) \text{ with } \mathsf{DP}(q_{i-1}, q_i) > 0 \text{ for all } i.$$

The differential probability of a trail, denoted DP(Q), is the probability that a random pair with input difference q_0 propagates via intermediate differences $q_1, q_2, \ldots$ to output difference q_r.

A useful concept when studying differential propagation is the *restriction weight*.

Definition 7 (Restriction weight of a differential [9]). *The restriction weight of a differential* $\mathsf{DP}(a, b) > 0$ *is defined as* $w(a, b) = -\log_2 \mathsf{DP}(a, b)$.

Definition 8 (Restriction weight of a differential trail [9]). *The restriction weight of a differential trail* $Q = (q_0, q_1, \ldots, q_{r-1})$ *is defined as* $w(Q) = \sum_i w(q_{i-1}, q_i)$, *hence the sum of the restriction weights if its round differentials.*

In the following we will omit the qualification "restriction" and simply speak of weight. We use the term *weight profile* of a trail for the sequence of weights of its round differentials. The weight of any given round differential is in general easy to compute and hence so is the weight of any given trail. Often $2^{-w(Q)}$ is a good approximation for $DP(Q)$. If the propagation through the round differentials of a trail are independent, we call it a *Markov trail* and it satisfies $DP(Q) = 2^{-w(Q)}$. This is not the case in general and an attention point that must be verified. Trails are linked to differentials: the DP of an r-round differential is the sum of the DPs of all trails connecting input difference and output difference:

$$DP(a, b) = \sum_{Q \text{ with } q_0 = a, q_r = b} DP(Q).$$

Trails with common input and output difference contribute to the same differential and are said to *cluster*. We call a trail that is the only one in its differential a *lone trail*.

Papers on trail search often report on large sets of trails with common features rather than individual trails. These sets are called *trail cores*.

Definition 9 (Differential trail core [18]**).** *An r-round differential trail core, denoted as $\widetilde{Q}$, is a set of differential trails over r rounds with a shared core of intermediate differences $(q_1, q_2, \ldots, q_{r-1})$ with $DP(q_i, q_{i+1}) > 0$ for all $1 \leq i < r - 1$.*

Given an r-round trail core $\widetilde{Q}$ and an r-round differential (a, b), the trail core will contribute to $DP(a, b)$ if a is compatible with q_1 and q_{r-1} with b.

Determining $NDP_f(a)$ requires computing of $DP(a, b)$ for all output differences b and in typical iterated permutations this is infeasible. However, it is reasonable to assume that for a given input difference a all output differences b with $DP(a, b) > T$ are known. Then we can use the following lemma to upper bound $NDP_f(a)$.

Lemma 4. *For any limit T, we have:*

$$NDP_f(a) \leq \sum_{b \text{ with } DP(a,b)>T} DP^2(a, b) + T.$$

Proof. Partitioning the differentials gives:

$$\sum_b DP^2(a, b) = \sum_{\substack{b \text{ with} \\ DP(a,b)>T}} DP^2(a, b) + \sum_{\substack{b \text{ with} \\ DP(a,b)\leq T}} DP^2(a, b).$$

The second sum in the right-hand side is at most T, namely, using

$$\sum_b DP(a, b) = 1$$

gives

$$\sum_{\substack{b \text{ with} \\ DP(a,b)\leq T}} DP^2(a, b) = \sum_{\substack{b \text{ with} \\ DP(a,b)\leq T}} DP(a, b)DP(a, b) \leq T \sum_{\substack{b \text{ with} \\ DP(a,b)\leq T}} DP(a, b) \leq T.$$

This proves the lemma.

5.2   Differential Propagation in XOODOO

XOODOO is a family of 384-bit permutations with a classical iterated structure: it iteratively applies a round function to a state. It is parameterized by its number of rounds: XOODOO with r rounds is denoted XOODOO$[r]$. The round function consist of a linear layer that we will call λ followed by a non-linear layer called χ. The non-linear layer has algebraic degree two. A consequence of this is that in round differentials the value of $\mathsf{DP}(a, b)$ is fully determined by the input difference a and hence the same for all compatible output differences b [12]. Moreover, the inverse of χ also has algebraic degree 2 and therefore in round differentials the value of $\mathsf{DP}(a, b)$ is also fully determined by the output difference b and hence the same for all compatible input differences a. The consequence of these two properties is that all trails in a trail core have the same weight and we can speak about $w(\widetilde{Q})$ without ambiguity, with $w(\widetilde{Q})$ the weight of any trail in the core.

Thanks to the shift-invariance of the XOODOO round function, trails (and trail cores) occur in classes with members that are equivalent under horizontal shifts. These classes have size 2^d with d ranging from 0 to 7. The vast majority of trail cores are in classes of size $2^7 = 128$.

The non-linear layer χ operates in parallel and independently on 3-bit parts of the state, the so-called *columns*: it is a layer of invertible non-linear S-boxes. This has its implications for clustering. A trail core $\widetilde{Q}$ contributes to a differential (a, b) if a and q_1 are compatible. The input difference a fully determines the difference at the input of χ of the first round: it is $\lambda(a)$. So $\lambda(a)$ and q_1 must be compatible over χ.

A non-zero difference in a column at the input of χ can only propagate to a non-zero difference at its output and a zero difference in a column at its input can only propagate to a zero difference at its output. So $\lambda(a)$ must be active in exactly the same columns as q_1. We say that $\lambda(a)$ and q_1 must have the same *column activity pattern*. Similarly, $\lambda(q_{r-1})$ and b must have the same column activity pattern.

From this follows that a trail in trail cores $\widetilde{Q}$ can only cluster with a trail in trail core $\widetilde{Q}'$ if q_1 and q'_1 have the same column activity pattern and if q_{r-1} and q'_{r-1} have the same column activity pattern.

5.3   MDP$_f$ and MNDP$_f$ of XOODOO$[3]$

In the Xoodoo GitHub repository [11] there is a list available of all 3-round trail core classes of XOODOO$[3]$ with weight up to 52. The list has 201 entries. In [8] it is reported that all 3-round trails with weight up to 50 are lone Markov trails. The lowest weight, 36, is attained by 4 trail core classes, hence under reasonable assumptions, we have $\mathsf{MDP}_f = 2^{-36}$. The assumptions are that there are no trail cores with weight above 50 clustering to form a differential with $\mathsf{DP} > 2^{-36}$. This would require the clustering of at least $2^{54-36} = 2^{18}$ Markov trails. The fact that there are only 201 trail core classes with weight below 52 that contain only lone Markov trails makes this extremely unlikely.

For estimating MNDP_f it is interesting to make use of Lemma 4. For its application, we need to make a reasonable assumption on the limit T. If trails remain to be lone Markov trails up to some weight, e.g., 70, the DP of differentials coincides with the values predicted by the weights of trails and we can take $T = 2^{-54}$. Clearly, as the weight of trails increases, the likelihood of clustering and dependence of round differentials does increase. Still, as discussed in [8], it is unlikely these effects are noticeable for trails with relatively low weight in permutations with round functions in which no superboxes can be identified. XOODOO is such a permutation and any trails leading to the best collision attacks would have weight well below the permutation width that is 384.

Lemma 5. *Assuming that all differentials with $\mathsf{DP}(a, b) > T$ for $T > 2^{-54}$ correspond to lone Markov trails, we can upper bound MNDP_f as*

$$\mathsf{MNDP}_f \leq T + \max_a \sum_{\substack{\widetilde{Q} \text{ with } w(\widetilde{Q}) < 54 \\ \text{and } \mathsf{DP}(a, q_1) > 0}} 2^{w(q_{r-1}) - 2w(\widetilde{Q})}.$$

Proof. The contribution of a trail core $\widetilde{Q}$ to $\mathsf{NDP}_f(a)$ is only non-zero if q_1 is compatible with a, and in that case it is $2^{w(q_{r-1}) - 2w(\widetilde{Q})}$. Namely, in a trail core with q_1 compatible with a given input difference a there are $2^{w(q_{r-1})}$ trails, that each have DP equal to $2^{-w(\widetilde{Q})}$.

For two trail cores to contribute to $\mathsf{NDP}_f(a)$ for some value of a, they must have equal column activity patterns in q_1. Or in other words, two trail cores that have different column activity patterns in q_1 cannot both contribute to $\mathsf{NDP}_f(a)$ for some a. We can partition the trail cores in the 201 trail core classes per their activity pattern in q_1: we call these *activity classes*. Then for each partition we just add the contributions of the trail cores as in Lemma 5.

Over all 3-round trail cores in [11] the ones that have highest contribution to $\mathsf{MNDP}_f(a)$ for some input difference a have weight profile $(4, 4, 28)$ and they contribute $2^{28 - 2 \times 36} = 2^{-44}$. There are three of them and they are described in [12] and called *single-orbital fans*. For each single-orbital fan, there are 4 other trail cores with the same column activity pattern in q_1, that contribute to $\mathsf{MNDP}_f(a)$ respectively $2^{-54}, 2^{-54}, 2^{-56}$ and 2^{-58}, resulting in $2^{-44} + 2^{-53} + 2^{-56} + 2^{-58} + T = (1.00226) \times 2^{-44} + T$. All other classes of trail core classes result in lower values for $\mathsf{NDP}_f(a)$. We see that the value of $\mathsf{NDP}_f(a)$ is dominated by its "lightest" trail core and that additional trail cores make it go up only slightly. We think it is reasonable to expect that this is also the case for the (unknown) trail cores with weight above 52. Still, for MNDP_f to deviate significantly from 2^{-44}, T would have to go up to 2^{-45} or so, which would imply considerable clustering and/or non-Markov trails.

So we conclude that $\mathsf{MNDP}_f \approx 2^{-44}$ and this value reflects the contribution of the single-orbital fan as dominant trail core. We see that for XOODOO[3], MDP_f is a factor 2^8 larger than MNDP_f.

5.4   MDP$_f$ and MNDP$_f$ of Xoodoo[4]

The trail cores of Xoodoo[4] are far less documented than those of Xoodoo[3]. Still, [13] reports that the 4-round trails with lowest weight have weight 80 and documents these trail core classes, only 2 of them.

It is not known whether the trails in these trail cores classes are Markov trails. Moreover, they have a high degree of symmetry and the trail cores in the classes cluster two-by-two. Assuming Markov trails and no more clustering occurs this would yield MDP$_f = 2^{-79}$. Based on arguments in [8] we do not expect non-Markov behaviour and/or additional clustering trails to affect this value significantly.

For MNDP$_f$ we need again to look at the weight profiles of the trail cores. Those of two trail core classes are respectively $(32, 24, 16, 8)$ and $(8, 16, 24, 32)$.

If we approximate MNDP$_f$ by the contribution of single trail cores, the former would give NDP$_f(a) \approx 2^{-160+32} = 2^{-128}$ and the latter NDP$_f(a) \approx 2^{-160+8} = 2^{-152}$. However, as said, the trail cores cluster two-by-two: the clustering trail cores have equal differences q_1 and different differences q_3, but with equal activity patterns. When fixing an input difference a, in each trail core there are 2^{32} trails to different output differences b, all with weight 80. Among those 2^{33} output differences, there are exactly 2^{16} where two trails arrive and therefore they have DP$(a, b) = 2^{-79}$. So assuming all these trails are Markov trails, their contribution to NDP$_f(a)$ is $(2^{33} - 2^{16})2^{-160} + 2^{16}2^{-158} = (2^{33} + 2^{16}3)2^{-160} = 1.00005 \times 2^{-127}$.

Due to the limited knowledge about 4-round trails we cannot tell whether there are no trail cores that lead to a lower value of MNDP$_f$. Still, an interesting observation is that the preliminary value of MDP$_f$ is a factor 2^{48} higher than that of MNDP$_f$.

We summerize the results on Sect. 5 in Table 2.

Table 2. Initial results on MDP$_f$ and MNDP$_f$ of Xoodoo[3] and Xoodoo[4].

	MDP$_f$	MNDP$_f$
Xoodoo[3]	2^{-36}	2^{-44}
Xoodoo[4]	2^{-79}	1.00005×2^{-127}

6   Conclusion

By assuming long independent keys, we are able to idealize the compression phase of Farfalle. The assumption allowed us to study a class of keyed hash functions that first add a key to the input string and then do unkeyed processing. We study it by first generalizing the notion of differentials over said class of keyed hash functions by also taking into account the difference in length between two input strings. We then show that it is possible to express the universality of our constructions in terms of the probability of differentials over the underlying public permutation. In the case of serial key-then-hash functions, we show that the universality and Δuniversality is given by MDP_f of the public permutation. These upper bounds are tight and are achieved by equal-length message pairs with a message difference of length 1. For parallel key-then-hash functions, we show that the universality is given by MNDP_f and the Δuniversality is given by MDP_f. These upper bounds are once again tight and are achieved by equal-length message pairs with a message difference of length 2 and 1 respectively. While MDP_f is a very well known property of public permutations, MNDP_f is still not well studied. For many public permutations, MNDP_f is significantly smaller than MDP_f thus making it a very compelling case to use them in parallel key-then-hash instead of serial in the proteced hash setting.

Acknowledgments. The authors would like to thank Bart Mennink for his valuable inputs during the finalization of this paper. Joan Daemen and Jonathan Fuchs are supported by the European Research Council under the ERC advanced grant agreement under grant ERC-2017-ADG Nr. 788980 ESCADA.

A   Xoodoo Specification

We quote the specification of the Xoodoo round function, taken verbatim from the Xoodoo Cookbook [10].

Xoodoo is a family of permutations parameterized by its number of rounds r and denoted Xoodoo[r].

Xoodoo has a classical iterated structure: It iteratively applies a round function to a state. The state consists of 3 equally sized horizontal *planes*, each one consisting of 4 parallel 32-bit *lanes*. Similarly, the state can be seen as a set of 128 *columns* of 3 bits, arranged in a 4×32 array. The planes are indexed by y, with plane $y = 0$ at the bottom and plane $y = 2$ at the top. Within a lane, we index bits with z. The lanes within a plane are indexed by x, so the position of a lane in the state is determined by the two coordinates (x, y). The bits of the state are indexed by (x, y, z) and the columns by (x, z). *Sheets* are the arrays of three lanes on top of each other and they are indexed by x. The Xoodoo state is illustrated in Fig. 3.

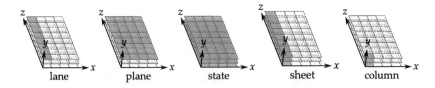

Fig. 3. Toy version of the Xoodoo state, with lanes reduced to 8 bits, and different parts of the state highlighted. [10]

The permutation consists of the iteration of a round function R_i that has 5 steps: a mixing layer θ, a plane shifting ρ_{west}, the addition of round constants ι, a non-linear layer χ and another plane shifting ρ_{east}.

Table 3. Notational conventions [10]

A_y	Plane y of state A
$A_y \lll (t, v)$	Cyclic shift of A_y moving bit in (x, z) to position $(x + t, z + v)$
$\overline{A_y}$	Bitwise complement of plane A_y
$A_y + A_{y'}$	Bitwise sum (XOR) of planes A_y and $A_{y'}$
$A_y \cdot A_{y'}$	Bitwise product (AND) of planes A_y and $A_{y'}$

Algorithm 3: Definition of XOODOO$[r]$ with r the number of rounds [10]

Parameters: Number of rounds r
for Round index i from $1 - r$ to 0 **do**
$\quad A = R_i(A)$
end for

Here R_i is specified by the following sequence of steps:

θ :
$$P \leftarrow A_0 + A_1 + A_2$$
$$E \leftarrow P \lll (1, 5) + P \lll (1, 14)$$
$$A_y \leftarrow A_y + E \text{ for } y \in \{0, 1, 2\}$$

ρ_{west} :
$$A_1 \leftarrow A_1 \lll (1, 0)$$
$$A_2 \leftarrow A_2 \lll (0, 11)$$

ι :
$$A_0 \leftarrow A_0 + C_i$$

χ :
$$B_0 \leftarrow \overline{A_1} \cdot A_2$$
$$B_1 \leftarrow \overline{A_2} \cdot A_0$$
$$B_2 \leftarrow \overline{A_0} \cdot A_1$$
$$A_y \leftarrow A_y + B_y \text{ for } y \in \{0, 1, 2\}$$

ρ_{east} :
$$A_1 \leftarrow A_1 \lll (0, 1)$$
$$A_2 \leftarrow A_2 \lll (2, 8)$$

Table 4. The round constants c_i with $-11 \le i \le 0$, in hexadecimal notation (the least significant bit is at $z = 0$) [10].

i	c_i	i	c_i	i	c_i	i	c_i
-11	0x00000058	-8	0x000000D0	-5	0x00000060	-2	0x000000F0
-10	0x00000038	-7	0x00000120	-4	0x0000002C	-1	0x000001A0
-9	0x000003C0	-6	0x00000014	-3	0x00000380	0	0x00000012

We specify XOODOO in Algorithm 3, completely in terms of operations on planes and use thereby the notational conventions we specify in Table 3 and 4.

References

1. Bellare, M., Canetti, R., Krawczyk, H.: Keying hash functions for message authentication. In: Koblitz, N. (ed.) CRYPTO 1996. LNCS, vol. 1109, pp. 1–15. Springer, Heidelberg (1996). https://doi.org/10.1007/3-540-68697-5_1
2. Bellare, M., Kilian, J., Rogaway, P.: The security of cipher block chaining. In: Desmedt, Y.G. (ed.) CRYPTO 1994. LNCS, vol. 839, pp. 341–358. Springer, Heidelberg (1994). https://doi.org/10.1007/3-540-48658-5_32
3. Bernstein, D.J.: How to stretch random functions: The security of protected counter sums. J. Cryptol. **12**(3), 185–192 (1999). https://doi.org/10.1007/s001459900051
4. Bernstein, D.J.: The Poly1305-AES message-authentication code. In: Gilbert, H., Handschuh, H. (eds.) FSE 2005. LNCS, vol. 3557, pp. 32–49. Springer, Heidelberg (2005). https://doi.org/10.1007/11502760_3
5. Bertoni, G., Daemen, J., Hoffert, S., Peeters, M., Van Assche, G., Van Keer, R.: Farfalle: parallel permutation-based cryptography. IACR Trans. Symmetric Cryptol. **2017**(4), 1–38 (2017). https://tosc.iacr.org/index.php/ToSC/article/view/801
6. Bertoni, G., Daemen, J., Peeters, M., Van Assche, G.: On the indifferentiability of the sponge construction. In: Smart, N. (ed.) EUROCRYPT 2008. LNCS, vol. 4965, pp. 181–197. Springer, Heidelberg (2008). https://doi.org/10.1007/978-3-540-78967-3_11
7. Black, J., Rogaway, P.: A block-cipher mode of operation for parallelizable message authentication. In: Knudsen, L.R. (ed.) EUROCRYPT 2002. LNCS, vol. 2332, pp. 384–397. Springer, Heidelberg (2002). https://doi.org/10.1007/3-540-46035-7_25
8. Bordes, N., Daemen, J., Kuijsters, D., Van Assche, G.: Thinking outside the superbox. In: Malkin, T., Peikert, C. (eds.) CRYPTO 2021. LNCS, vol. 12827, pp. 337–367. Springer, Cham (2021). https://doi.org/10.1007/978-3-030-84252-9_12
9. Daemen, J.: Cipher and hash function design, strategies based on linear and differential cryptanalysis, PhD Thesis. K.U.Leuven (1995). http://jda.noekeon.org/
10. Daemen, J., Hoffert, S., Peeters, M., Assche, G.V., Keer, R.V.: Xoodoo cookbook. Cryptology ePrint Archive, Paper 2018/767 (2018). https://eprint.iacr.org/2018/767
11. Daemen, J., Hoffert, S., Van Assche, G., Van Keer, R.: DC-Xoodoo-3r.txt (2018). https://github.com/KeccakTeam/Xoodoo/blob/master/XooTools/Trails/DC-Xoodoo-3r.txt/
12. Daemen, J., Hoffert, S., Van Assche, G., Van Keer, R.: The design of Xoodoo and Xoofff. IACR Trans. Symmetric Cryptol. 2018(4), 1–38 (2018), https://doi.org/10.13154/tosc.v2018.i4.1-38
13. Daemen, J., Mella, S., Van Assche, G.: Tighter trail bounds for Xoodoo. Cryptology ePrint Archive, Paper 2022/1088 (2022). https://eprint.iacr.org/2022/1088
14. Daemen, J., Mennink, B., Van Assche, G.: Full-State Keyed Duplex with Built-In Multi-user Support. In: Takagi, T., Peyrin, T. (eds.) ASIACRYPT 2017. LNCS, vol. 10625, pp. 606–637. Springer, Cham (2017). https://doi.org/10.1007/978-3-319-70697-9_21
15. Daemen, J., Rijmen, V.: A new MAC construction ALRED and a specific instance ALPHA-MAC. In: Gilbert, H., Handschuh, H. (eds.) FSE 2005. LNCS, vol. 3557, pp. 1–17. Springer, Heidelberg (2005). https://doi.org/10.1007/11502760_1
16. Daemen, J., Rijmen, V.: The Pelican MAC Function. IACR Cryptol. ePrint Arch. **2005**, 88 (2005). http://eprint.iacr.org/2005/088
17. Daemen, J., Rijmen, V.: Refinements of the ALRED construction and MAC security claims. IET Inf. Secur. 4(3), 149–157 (2010). https://doi.org/10.1049/iet-ifs.2010.0015

18. Daemen, J., Van Assche, G.: Differential propagation analysis of keccak. In: Canteaut, A. (ed.) FSE 2012. LNCS, vol. 7549, pp. 422–441. Springer, Heidelberg (2012). https://doi.org/10.1007/978-3-642-34047-5_24

19. Dobraunig, C., Mennink, B.: Security of the Suffix Keyed Sponge. IACR Trans. Symmetric Cryptol. **2019**(4), 223–248 (2019). https://doi.org/10.13154/tosc.v2019.i4.223-248

20. Even, S., Mansour, Y.: A construction of a cipher from a single pseudorandom permutation. J. Cryptol. **10**(3), 151–162 (1997). https://doi.org/10.1007/s001459900025

21. Iwata, T., Kurosawa, K.: OMAC: one-key CBC MAC. In: Johansson, T. (ed.) FSE 2003. LNCS, vol. 2887, pp. 129–153. Springer, Heidelberg (2003). https://doi.org/10.1007/978-3-540-39887-5_11

22. Luykx, A., Preneel, B., Tischhauser, E., Yasuda, K.: A MAC mode for lightweight block ciphers. In: Peyrin, T. (ed.) FSE 2016. LNCS, vol. 9783, pp. 43–59. Springer, Heidelberg (2016). https://doi.org/10.1007/978-3-662-52993-5_3

23. McGrew, D.A., Viega, J.: The use of galois message authentication code (GMAC) in IPsec ESP and AH. RFC **4543**, 1–14 (2006). https://doi.org/10.17487/RFC4543

24. Shoup, V.: On fast and provably secure message authentication based on universal hashing. In: Koblitz, N. (ed.) CRYPTO 1996. LNCS, vol. 1109, pp. 313–328. Springer, Heidelberg (1996). https://doi.org/10.1007/3-540-68697-5_24

25. Stinson, D.R.: On the connections between universal hashing, combinatorial designs and error-correcting codes. Electron. Colloquium Comput. Complex. **2**(52) (1995). http://eccc.hpi-web.de/eccc-reports/1995/TR95-052/index.html

26. Wegman, M.N., Carter, L.: New hash functions and their use in authentication and set equality. J. Comput. Syst. Sci. **22**(3), 265–279 (1981). https://doi.org/10.1016/0022-0000(81)90033-7

Revisiting the Indifferentiability
of the Sum of Permutations

Aldo Gunsing[1](✉), Ritam Bhaumik[2](✉), Ashwin Jha[3](✉), Bart Mennink[1](✉),
and Yaobin Shen[4](✉)

[1] Digital Security Group, Radboud University, Nijmegen, The Netherlands
aldo.gunsing@ru.nl, b.mennink@cs.ru.nl
[2] EPFL, Lausanne, Switzerland
ritam.bhaumik@epfl.ch
[3] CISPA Helmholtz Center for Information Security, Saarbrücken, Germany
ashwin.jha@cispa.de
[4] UCLouvain, ICTEAM/ELEN/Crypto Group, Louvain-la-Neuve, Belgium
yaobin.shen@uclouvain.be

Abstract. The sum of two n-bit pseudorandom permutations is known to
behave like a pseudorandom function with n bits of security. A recent line
of research has investigated the security of two public n-bit permutations
and its degree of indifferentiability. Mandal et al. (INDOCRYPT 2010)
proved $2n/3$-bit security, Mennink and Preneel (ACNS 2015) pointed out
a non-trivial flaw in their analysis and re-proved $(2n/3 - \log_2(n))$-bit security. Bhattacharya and Nandi (EUROCRYPT 2018) eventually improved
the result to n-bit security. Recently, Gunsing at CRYPTO 2022 already
observed that a proof technique used in this line of research only holds for
sequential indifferentiability. We revisit the line of research in detail, and
observe that the strongest bound of n-bit security has two other serious
issues in the reasoning, the first one is actually the same non-trivial flaw
that was present in the work of Mandal et al., while the second one discards biases in the randomness influenced by the distinguisher. More concretely, we introduce two attacks that show limited potential of different
approaches. We (i) show that the latter issue that discards biases only holds
up to $2^{3n/4}$ queries, and (ii) perform a differentiability attack against their
simulator in $2^{5n/6}$ queries. On the upside, we revive the result of Mennink
and Preneel and show $(2n/3 - \log_2(n))$-bit regular indifferentiability security of the sum of public permutations.

Keywords: indifferentiability · sum of permutations · attacks ·
resolutions

1 Introduction

The question of how to achieve a secure pseudorandom function (PRF) from
a pseudorandom permutation (PRP) has played a central role in symmetric
cryptography. After all, we have the availability of many cryptographic primitives such as AES [10] that behave – or are at least claimed to behave – like

© International Association for Cryptologic Research 2023
H. Handschuh and A. Lysyanskaya (Eds.): CRYPTO 2023, LNCS 14083, pp. 628–660, 2023.
https://doi.org/10.1007/978-3-031-38548-3_21

a pseudorandom permutation, whereas for, e.g., stream encryption or message authentication, we would like to have a primitive that behaves like a pseudorandom function. Dedicated pseudorandom functions, in turn, are scarce [1,6,25]. Instead, over the last decades, the question of PRF design has mostly been dominated by approaches of building them generically from PRPs.

An n-bit PRP behaves like an n-bit PRF, but only as long as the number of evaluations is below $2^{n/2}$, a result known as the PRP-PRF switch [3,5,8, 14,17,18]. As this birthday bound could be restrictive in case of small block ciphers, various beyond birthday bound constructions have been analyzed. One such construction is the sum of PRPs:

$$F_{K_0, K_1}(x) = \mathcal{E}(K_0, x) \oplus \mathcal{E}(K_1, x),$$

where $\mathcal{E}$ is a PRP with a block size of n bits. The construction was first introduced by Bellare et al. [4]. Lucks [20] proved around $2^{2n/3}$ security, Bellare and Impagliazzo [2] around $2^n/n$ security, and Patarin [27–29] proved optimal 2^n security, up to constant, albeit using the mirror theory. Dai et al. [11] proved around 2^n security using the chi-squared method.

These results were all in the case where the underlying primitive was a PRP, i.e., a building block $\mathcal{E}$ that, when instantiated with a secret key, behaves like a secret random permutation. A natural related question is to what degree the sum of two *public* permutations behaves like a *public* random function. In other words, suppose we are given two n-bit permutations Π_0, Π_1, to what degree

$$F^{\Pi_0, \Pi_1}(x) = \Pi_0(x) \oplus \Pi_1(x)$$

behaves like a random function. As this function is keyless, we cannot rely on conventional indistinguishability (as we considered the sum of PRPs in), but instead, we should consider this function in the indifferentiability framework of Maurer et al. [23], or more specifically the version of Coron et al. [9] tailored towards symmetric cryptographic primitives. In this framework, one compares the function F in conjunction with the primitives Π_0, Π_1 with a random function $\mathcal{R}$ in conjunction with a simulator ensemble $\mathcal{S}_0, \mathcal{S}_1$, and one says that F *behaves like* $\mathcal{R}$ if there exists a simulator ensemble such that these two worlds are hard to distinguish.

In the indifferentiability framework, Mandal et al. [21] proved that the sum of permutations behaves like a random function up to $2^{n/2}$ queries, and even up to $2^{2n/3}$ queries with a slightly more involved simulator. Mennink and Preneel identified a flaw in the reasoning of Mandal et al. [21] and re-proved $(2n/3 - \log_2(n))$ security. Bhattacharya and Nandi [7] proved optimal 2^n indifferentiability of F, using a simulator that is slightly more involved than that of Mandal et al. and Mennink and Preneel. Lee [19] proved $2^{(r-1)n/r}$ security for the sum of r permutations, but only for even integers $r \geqslant 4$. Our focus is on the sum of two permutations. A more detailed description of the earlier security analyses is given in Sect. 3.

1.1   Issues with Existing Security Analyses

This state of the art suggests that the case of the sum of permutations is closed: there is a proof of optimal 2^n security both in the case of secret permutations as in the case of public permutations. However, nothing is further from the truth.

First of all, Gunsing [15] recently discussed a faulty reasoning in a proof technique used in the indifferentiability of tree hashing. In a nutshell, this proof technique consists of replacing the distinguisher by a slightly stronger distinguisher for which the security analysis was easier. The author also observed that the same technique was used for the indifferentiability of the sum of permutations. As a matter of fact, all four indifferentiability results on the sum of permutations [7,19,21,26] use this proof technique. Concretely, it turns out that this proof technique *only* works in the case of sequential indifferentiability (i.e., where the distinguisher should first make its primitive queries before making construction queries, cf., Sect. 2.3). Concluding, all indifferentiability results on the sum of permutations known to date *only hold for sequential indifferentiability*. This issue of 'sequentiality' is discussed in detail in Sect. 3.1.

Inspired by this, we aimed to fix the proof of Bhattacharya and Nandi [7] to reattain 2^n (regular) indifferentiability, but while doing so, we observed that this was not easily done. To the contrary, we observed two additional issues in the security proof of Bhattacharya and Nandi that made it impossible for us to reattain optimal 2^n security.

The first issue, dubbed 'fresh oracle', is about the fact that the proof assumes that any query to the random oracle returns a uniform random value. This is not the case when the inverse simulator tries a value and rejects it when it is not a suitable value, as this rejection leads to a bias in future values. The ideal world could be modified to have the more uniform behavior, but this comes at the cost of $3n/4$-bit security, diminishing the optimal n-bit security bound. We show this as an attack described in Sect. 5. Interestingly, this difference does not lead to an attack on the real construction, as the real world behaves more like the regular ideal world and not the modified one. So this bias is a feature, not a bug, and it is necessary to prove more than $3n/4$-bit security, even in the sequential setting.

The second issue, dubbed 'random range', centers around the problem that the proof assumes that the ranges of the primitives are randomly sampled. This is not the case as the adversary can freely choose this by making inverse queries with a desired range. This is a fundamental error that basically ignores the inverse queries. (The problem is of the same vein as what Mennink and Preneel identified for the proof of Mandal et al., though more ingenious.) The issue is not solvable, except by removing the inverse query direction. The issue is discussed in detail in Sect. 3.3.

To conclude, whereas Gunsing [15] already suggested that the entire line of research on the indifferentiability of the sum of permutations only holds in the case of sequential indifferentiability, we go even further to state that the proof of 2^n indifferentiability contains two fundamental and seemingly unsolvable gaps. A summary of these issues is given in Table 1. In short, the only result remaining that is not fundamentally problematic is that of Mennink and Preneel [26], which proves $(2n/3 - \log_2(n))$ bits of security, but its result has to be reduced to the weaker sequential indifferentiability setting. There is no known result for the normal indifferentiability setting.

Table 1. Overview of the previous results with the claimed security level and the different errors they contain.

paper	security level	sequentiality (Sect. 3.1)	fresh oracle (Sect. 3.2)	random range (Section 3.3)
[21]	$2n/3$	[15]	—	[26]
[26]	$2n/3 - \log_2(n)$	[15]	—	—
[7]	n	[15]	now	now
Sect. 4	$2n/3 - \log_2(n)$	—	—	—

1.2 New Indifferentiability Proof

Taking all issues in earlier analyses into account, the best result to date is $2^{2n/3}/n$ sequential indifferentiability, i.e., the result of Mennink and Preneel [26] but only for the case of sequential indifferentiability. As this state of affairs is rather unsatisfactory, we reconsider the (regular) indifferentiability of the sum of permutations in Sect. 4, and manage to prove $2^{2n/3}/n$ (regular) indifferentiability. The idea of the proof is to extend the analysis of Mennink and Preneel. We make use of its result in the sequential setting as a black box and extend it to the (regular) indifferentiability setting by proving that queries of the simulator can be swapped at a cost of $2^{2n/3}$, maintaining the same bound. The new security result is also included in Table 1.

1.3 Generic Attack

Inspired by the fact that we managed to restore the proof of Mennink and Preneel [26] in the (regular) indifferentiability setting, one might be tempted to investigate the possibility to restore the proof of Bhattacharya and Nandi [7] in the (regular) indifferentiability setting. However, it turns out that this is not possible: in Sect. 5 we describe an attack in $2^{3n/4}$ queries that show that the 'fresh oracle' simplification cannot be made and in Sect. 6 we describe a generic differentiability attack in $2^{5n/6}$ queries, that succeeds against the simulator of Bhattacharya and Nandi, which is in fact the most logical choice of simulator and all previous works use a variant of it.

   Our generic attack implies that the best 'one can hope for' is $2^{5n/6}$ indifferentiability, except for possibly expanding the simulator to a much more advanced one. Admittedly, this still exposes a gap between the $2^{2n/3}/n$ indifferentiability bound of Sect. 4, but it turns out (as also testified by the multiple issues found in earlier analyses) that proving tightness for the indifferentiability of the sum of permutations is very hard, and we leave tightness of the indifferentiability of the sum of permutations as an open problem.

1.4   Applications

Besides being of general theoretical interest, the sum of two public random permutations has important implications for the design of cryptographic schemes. Examples include as a building block to construct beyond-birthday-bound domain extender [24], as a building block to construct collision-resistant compression function [30,31], and as a building block to construct variable input length random oracle [12].

2   Preliminaries

2.1   Notation

Let $n \geqslant 1$ be an integer. Let $\{0,1\}^n$ be the set of all n-bit strings. Let $\mathrm{func}(n)$ be the set of all functions from $\{0,1\}^n \to \{0,1\}^n$ and $\mathrm{perm}(n)$ the set of permutations on $\{0,1\}^n$. For a set $\mathcal{X}$, we denote by $x \xleftarrow{\$} \mathcal{X}$ the uniformly random sampling of an element from $\mathcal{X}$. If x and y are two bit-strings of the same length, we denote by $x \oplus y$ their bit-wise XOR.

2.2   Sum of Permutations

We will restrict our focus to the sum of two independent public permutations.[1] Let $\Pi_0, \Pi_1 \in \mathrm{perm}(n)$ be two n-bit permutations. The sum of permutations is the construction $F : \{0,1\}^n \to \{0,1\}^n$ defined as

$$F^{\Pi_0, \Pi_1}(x) = \Pi_0(x) \oplus \Pi_1(x). \tag{1}$$

The output of Π_0 will typically be denoted y_0, the output of Π_1 will typically be denoted y_1, and the output of F will be denoted $z = y_0 \oplus y_1$. See also Fig. 1. In the remainder, we will drop the superscript access of F for brevity.

2.3   Indifferentiability

Maurer et al. [23] introduced indifferentiability as an extension of indistinguishability, in order to measure the degree in which a keyless function behaves like its random counterpart. Coron et al. [9] applied the model to cryptographic hash functions, and we will adopt their model. In fact, in our work, we will restrict our focus to the construction $F : \{0,1\}^n \to \{0,1\}^n$ built on top of two permutations $\Pi_0, \Pi_1 : \{0,1\}^n \to \{0,1\}^n$.

Before stating what we mean when a construction is indifferentiable, we first pose the differentiability setup.

---

[1] It is possible to describe a variant based on one permutation $\Pi \in \mathrm{perm}(n)$ using domain separation, as in $\Pi(x\|0) \oplus \Pi(x\|1)$.

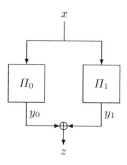

Fig. 1. The sum of permutations.

Definition 1 (Differentiability Setup). *Let $F : \{0,1\}^n \rightarrow \{0,1\}^n$ be the construction of (1) based on ideal permutations $\Pi_0, \Pi_1 \xleftarrow{\$} \mathrm{perm}(n)$. Denote $\Pi = (\Pi_0, \Pi_1)$ for brevity. Let $\mathcal{R} \xleftarrow{\$} \mathrm{func}(n)$ be a random function with the same domain and range as F. Let $\mathcal{S} = (\mathcal{S}_0, \mathcal{S}_1)$ be a simulator with the same domain and range as $\Pi = (\Pi_0, \Pi_1)$ that has access to $\mathcal{R}$. The advantage of an indifferentiability distinguisher $\mathcal{D}$ against F with respect to simulator $\mathcal{S}$ is defined as*

$$\mathbf{Adv}_{F,\mathcal{S}}(\mathcal{D}) = \left| \mathbb{P}\left[\mathcal{D}^{F,\Pi,\Pi^{-1}} = 1\right] - \mathbb{P}\left[\mathcal{D}^{\mathcal{R},\mathcal{S},\mathcal{S}^{-1}} = 1\right] \right|. \tag{2}$$

The differentiability setup is depicted in Fig. 2. We will refer to (F, Π, Π^{-1}) as the *real world* and to $(\mathcal{R}, \mathcal{S}, \mathcal{S}^{-1})$ as the *ideal world*. The attacker can make a *construction* query to $\mathcal{C}$ (F in the real world and $\mathcal{R}$ in the ideal world) and it can make a *primitive* query to $\mathcal{P}$ ($\Pi^{\pm}$ in the real world and $\mathcal{S}^{\pm}$ in the ideal world).

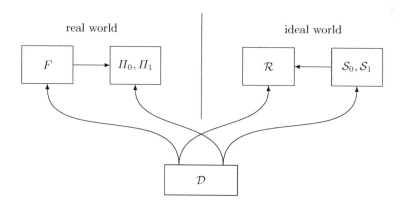

Fig. 2. The indifferentiability setup.

In (regular) indifferentiability as formalized by Coron et al. [9], the distinguisher has full freedom in the order in which it makes the queries.

Definition 2 ((Regular) Indifferentiability). *The construction* F : $\{0,1\}^n \to \{0,1\}^n$ *of* (1) *built on ideal permutations* $\Pi_0, \Pi_1 \xleftarrow{\$} \text{perm}(n)$ *is regularly* ε-*indifferentiable from a random oracle* $\mathcal{R} \xleftarrow{\$} \text{func}(n)$ *if there exists a simulator* $\mathcal{S} = (\mathcal{S}_0, \mathcal{S}_1)$ *such that*

$$\mathbf{Adv}_{F,\mathcal{S}}^{\text{indif}}(\mathcal{D}) < \varepsilon$$

for any distinguisher $\mathcal{D}$ *that can make its construction and primitive queries in a fully adaptive manner.*

We will also discuss a weaker variant of indifferentiability, called public indifferentiability as introduced by Yoneyama et al. [32] and Dodis et al. [13]. Here, the queries made by the distinguisher to the construction oracle are *public* and known to the simulator. Canonically, the simulator will internally execute its own queries corresponding to the given input to deduce the result given by the construction oracle.

Definition 3 (Public Indifferentiability). *A construction* F : $\{0,1\}^n \to \{0,1\}^n$ *of* (1) *built on ideal permutations* $\Pi_0, \Pi_1 \xleftarrow{\$} \text{perm}(n)$ *is publicly* ε-*indifferentiable from a random oracle* $\mathcal{R} \xleftarrow{\$} \text{func}(n)$ *if there exists a simulator* $\mathcal{S} = (\mathcal{S}_0, \mathcal{S}_1, \mathcal{S}_{\text{con}})$ *such that*

$$\mathbf{Adv}_{F,\mathcal{S}}^{\text{seq-indif}}(\mathcal{D}) < \varepsilon$$

for any distinguisher $\mathcal{D}$ *that can make its construction and primitive queries in a fully adaptive manner. The procedure* $\mathcal{S}_{\text{con}}(x)$ *is executed whenever* $\mathcal{D}$ *makes the query* $\mathcal{R}(x)$.

We also look at another variant, sequential indifferentiability as introduced by Mandal et al. [22]. Sequential indifferentiability differs from (regular) indifferentiability only in the sense that the distinguisher *cannot make its queries in a fully adaptive manner*. Instead, it is restricted to *first* making its primitive queries and *then* its construction queries. It turns out that sequential indifferentiability is equivalent to public indifferentiability for stateless ideal primitives [22], which includes the sum of permutations.

Definition 4 (Sequential Indifferentiability). *A construction* F : $\{0,1\}^n \to \{0,1\}^n$ *of* (1) *built on ideal permutations* $\Pi_0, \Pi_1 \xleftarrow{\$} \text{perm}(n)$ *is sequentially* ε-*indifferentiable from a random oracle* $\mathcal{R} \xleftarrow{\$} \text{func}(n)$ *if there exists a simulator* $\mathcal{S} = (\mathcal{S}_0, \mathcal{S}_1)$ *such that*

$$\mathbf{Adv}_{F,\mathcal{S}}^{\text{seq-indif}}(\mathcal{D}) < \varepsilon$$

for any distinguisher $\mathcal{D}$ *that is restricted to first making its primitive queries and then making its construction queries.*

Algorithm 1. Definition of the uniform simulator with parameter ℓ

1: **function** $\mathcal{S}_b(x)$
2:     **if** $x \in \text{domain}(\mathsf{P}_b)$ **then**
3:         **return** $\mathsf{P}_b(x)$
4:     $z \leftarrow \mathcal{R}(x)$
5:     $y_b \xleftarrow{\$} \{0,1\}^n \setminus (\text{range}(\mathsf{P}_b) \cup (\text{range}(\mathsf{P}_{1-b}) \oplus z))$
6:     $\mathsf{P}_b(x) \leftarrow y_b$
7:     $\mathsf{P}_{1-b}(x) \leftarrow y_b \oplus z$
8:     **return** y_b

1: **function** $\mathcal{S}_b^{-1}(y_b)$
2:     **if** $y_b \in \text{range}(\mathsf{P}_b)$ **then**
3:         **return** $\mathsf{P}_b^{-1}(y_b)$
4:     **for** ℓ times **do**
5:         $x \xleftarrow{\$} \{0,1\}^n \setminus \text{domain}(\mathsf{P}_0)$
6:         $z \leftarrow \mathcal{R}(x)$
7:         **if** $y_b \oplus z \notin \text{range}(\mathsf{P}_{1-b})$ **then**
8:             $\mathsf{P}_b(x) \leftarrow y_b$
9:             $\mathsf{P}_{1-b}(x) \leftarrow y_b \oplus z$
10:            **return** x
11:    **return** $\perp$

Clearly, sequential indifferentiability is a weaker variant than (regular) indifferentiability in the sense that it significantly restricts the power of the distinguisher. Intuitively, in sequential indifferentiability, the queries that matter most are the primitive queries, and the construction queries made afterwards are only made to verify consistency in the primitive queries. The distinguisher has no possibility to use these construction queries to smartly select upcoming primitive queries.

The definition of indifferentiability requires the existence of a simulator $\mathcal{S}$. For a lower bound this means that providing an explicit one is sufficient. However, for an upper bound one would have to show attacks for *any* simulator, which is very difficult to do. Instead, for our attacks we focus on the most logical definition of the simulator, which we call the uniform simulator as it selects its values uniformly at random. It has a parameter ℓ determining how many times a loop should be executed. All previous works [7,21,26] use essentially this simulator with varying ℓ.

Definition 5 (Uniform Simulator). *The* uniform simulator *with parameter ℓ is defined in Algorithm 1.*

The uniform simulator internally keeps two partial permutations P_0 and P_1 consisting of the previously made queries. Additionally, on input $\mathcal{S}_b(x)$ (with $b \in \{0,1\}$) it not only sets $\mathsf{P}_b(x)$, but also $\mathsf{P}_{1-b}(x)$ and similarly for $\mathcal{S}_b^{-1}(y_b)$ it sets both $\mathsf{P}_b(x) = y_b$ and $\mathsf{P}_{1-b}(x)$ for some x.

The forward simulator simply samples uniformly from all possible outputs $\{0,1\}^n \setminus (\text{range}(\mathsf{P}_b) \cup (\text{range}(\mathsf{P}_{1-b}) \oplus z))$, where b denotes the selected permutation and $z = \mathcal{R}(x)$ is the output of random oracle for the input x.

The backward simulator is slightly more involved. It chooses a new input x uniformly at random (note that $\mathsf{domain}(\mathsf{P}_0) = \mathsf{domain}(\mathsf{P}_1)$), consults the random oracle to get $z = \mathcal{R}(x)$ and checks whether this x is possible as the condition $y_b \oplus z \notin \mathsf{range}(\mathsf{P}_{1-b})$ is required. It repeats this process up to ℓ times. If there is still no suitable x found, the simulator fails by returning $\perp$.

The parameter ℓ determines how many times the simulator tries an x. If $\ell = 1$ the simulator never retries, leading to a failure probability equal to the birthday bound. For larger ℓ the simulator can try multiple times, making the failure probability smaller and smaller. On the other hand, ℓ should not be too large as the simulator makes at most ℓq queries to the random oracle for q primitive queries. The first two works [21, 26] set $\ell = 2$ and [7] sets $\ell = n$.

Remark 1. The simulator given in [7] is slightly different, as they do not resample previously selected guesses: let x_i be chosen at iteration i of the loop ($1 \leqslant i \leqslant \ell$), then $x_i \xleftarrow{\$} \{0,1\}^n \backslash (\mathsf{domain}(\mathsf{P}_0) \cup \{x_1, \ldots, x_{i-1}\})$. This difference is negligible and only influences the failure probability. In fact, the selection of the parameter ℓ does not influence the outputs of the simulator at all, conditioned on the fact that it did not fail. Only the failure probability is impacted, which has a probability of $\mathcal{O}\left(q^{\ell+1}/2^{\ell n}\right)$.

3   Earlier Security Analysis

The sum of *secret* permutations has a long history, dating back to Impagliazzo and Rudich in 1988 [18]. A long sequence of research [2, 4, 11, 20, 27–29] has lead to a final conclusion that the sum of two *secret* permutations is hard to distinguish from a random function up to 2^n queries.

In this work, we are however concerned with the sum of *public* permutations, a problem that is more recent. In 2010, Mandal et al. [21] gave two indifferentiability results, one proving $2^{n/2}$ with a naive simulator (the simulator of Definition 5 with $\ell = 1$), and one result with a more involved simulator (the simulator of Definition 5 with $\ell = 2$) achieving $2^{2n/3}$ security. However, later, Mennink and Preneel observed that the latter result was flawed. In detail, the analysis of Mandal et al. relied on the premise that if the distinguisher makes q primitive queries, for any value $z \in \{0,1\}^n$ there are not more than $O(q^2/2^n)$ tuples $\{(x_0, y_0), (x_1, y_1)\}$ satisfying $y_0 \oplus y_1 = z$, a premise that was obviously false as the distinguisher can make inverse queries to the primitive. (Refer to [26, Sect. 4.3] for a more detailed discussion of the issue.) A noteworthy proof technique used by Mandal et al. was that the proof started with a transition of the distinguisher $\mathcal{D}$ to a more powerful distinguisher $\mathcal{D}'$ to make the security analysis easier (this transition is explained in more detail in Sect. 3.1).

In 2015, Mennink and Preneel re-proved $2^{2n/3}/n$ security [26], with the same simulator (the simulator of Definition 5 with $\ell = 2$) and a comparable proof technique as Mandal et al., but with a different bad event in the security analysis. In 2018, Bhattacharya and Nandi [7] proved optimal 2^n indifferentiability of F. The simulator of Bhattacharya and Nandi only marginally changed from the simulator of Mandal et al., the only difference being that the simulator would potentially redraw up to $\ell = n$. In 2017, Lee [19] proved $2^{(r-1)n/r}$ security for the sum of r permutations for even integers $r \geqslant 4$.

It is important to mention that all these results adopted the proof technique used by Mandal et al. to start the proof by replacing the distinguisher $\mathcal{D}$ by a more powerful distinguisher $\mathcal{D}'$, or a similar technique, to make the security analysis easier. In the context of tree hashing, Gunsing [15] pointed out that this reasoning is faulty, and only holds in the case of sequential indifferentiability. We elaborate on this 'sequentiality' in detail in Sect. 3.1. In addition, we observe two additional issues in the proof of Bhattacharya and Nandi, namely the 'fresh oracle' problem (in Sect. 3.2) and the 'random range' problem (in Sect. 3.3).

3.1   Sequentiality

As shown in [15] all known results only hold for sequential indifferentiability. We explain the problem specifically for the case of the sum of permutations. In all previous works [7,19,21,26] the error appears in a similar form.

Moving from $\mathcal{D}$ to $\mathcal{D}'$. The works [21,26] make an explicit modification to the distinguisher. For any distinguisher $\mathcal{D}$ another distinguisher $\mathcal{D}'$ is constructed that behaves as follows:

1. Interact like $\mathcal{D}$;
2. At the end of the interaction, query $\mathcal{P}_0(x)$ and $\mathcal{P}_1(x)$ for any construction query $\mathcal{C}(x)$ made in the previous step (if not already done);
3. Output the same decision as $\mathcal{D}$.

As $\mathcal{D}'$ outputs the same decision as $\mathcal{D}$ and its extra queries happen at the end of the interaction, its advantage is the same as that of $\mathcal{D}$. Furthermore, as $\mathcal{C}(x)$ can be derived from $\mathcal{P}_0(x)$ and $\mathcal{P}_1(x)$, we can ignore the construction queries from the transcript and focus just on the primitive queries of the form $\mathcal{P}_0(x)$ and $\mathcal{P}_1(x)$. However, this last reasoning where the construction queries are ignored is incorrect and cannot be done. It ignores the fact that future queries can *depend* on the output of these construction queries. For example, let $\mathcal{D}$ be the distinguisher that generates two arbitrary inputs x_1 and x_2 and interacts as follows:

1. Make the construction query $z_1 = \mathcal{C}(x_1)$;
2. Make the construction query $z_2 = \mathcal{C}(x_2)$;
3. Compare z_1 and z_2 lexicographically and define $x^{\min}$ and $x^{\max}$ as:
    - If $z_1 \leqslant z_2$, then $x^{\min} = x_1$ and $x^{\max} = x_2$;
    - Otherwise, $x^{\min} = x_2$ and $x^{\max} = x_1$;
4. Make the primitive queries $y_0^{\min} = \mathcal{P}_0(x^{\min})$ and $y_1^{\min} = \mathcal{P}_1(x^{\min})$;
5. Make the primitive queries $y_0^{\max} = \mathcal{P}_0(x^{\max})$ and $y_1^{\max} = \mathcal{P}_1(x^{\max})$.

Here, the final transcript looks like

$$\Big((x_1, \mathcal{C}(x_1)), (x_2, \mathcal{C}(x_2)), (x^{\min}, \mathcal{P}_0(x^{\min}), \mathcal{P}_1(x^{\min})), (x^{\max}, \mathcal{P}_0(x^{\max}), \mathcal{P}_1(x^{\max}))\Big).$$

While it is the case that $\mathcal{C}(x_1) = \mathcal{P}_0(x_1) \oplus \mathcal{P}_1(x_1)$ and $\mathcal{C}(x_2) = \mathcal{P}_0(x_2) \oplus \mathcal{P}_1(x_2)$ can be derived from the full transcript (as x_1 and x_2 are either $x^{\min}$ or $x^{\max}$), they cannot simply be dropped, simplifying the transcript to

$$\Big((x^{\min}, \mathcal{P}_0(x^{\min}), \mathcal{P}_1(x^{\min})), (x^{\max}, \mathcal{P}_0(x^{\max}), \mathcal{P}_1(x^{\max}))\Big),$$

as this transcript is not well-defined. The input to the first query is $x^{\min}$, but this definition only makes sense given $\mathcal{C}(x_1)$ and $\mathcal{C}(x_2)$, whose values are still unknown.

One way to salvage the results is to consider the weaker notion of sequential indifferentiability, where all primitive queries have to be made before the construction queries. In this setting this dependence is not present as the construction queries happen last. Hence, we can downgrade a proof containing this flaw to the sequential indifferentiability setting.

Public Construction Queries. The works [7,19] do not make an explicit modification to $\mathcal{D}$ but they make a similar mistake. Again, at the end of the interaction we give the outputs $\mathcal{P}_0(x)$ and $\mathcal{P}_1(x)$ for every made construction query $\mathcal{C}(x)$. Furthermore, if $\mathcal{P}_0(x)$ is made, then $\mathcal{P}_1(x)$ is given and vice versa. This means that for query i, the tuple

$$(x_i, \mathcal{P}_0(x_i), \mathcal{P}_1(x_i))$$

is known, from which the construction output $\mathcal{C}(x_i) = \mathcal{P}_0(x_i) \oplus \mathcal{P}_1(x_i)$ can be derived immediately. However, this step implicitly reorders some primitive queries. Consider the same interaction as before, where the final transcript looks like

$$\Big((x_1, \mathcal{C}(x_1)), (x_2, \mathcal{C}(x_2)), (x^{\min}, \mathcal{P}_0(x^{\min}), \mathcal{P}_1(x^{\min})), (x^{\max}, \mathcal{P}_0(x^{\max}), \mathcal{P}_1(x^{\max}))\Big).$$

Now, with the 'additional' information added this becomes

$$\Big((x_1, \mathcal{P}_0(x_1), \mathcal{P}_1(x_1)), (x_2, \mathcal{P}_0(x_2), \mathcal{P}_1(x_2))\Big).$$

Whenever $x^{\min} = x_2$, this reorders the primitive queries made. In the real world this does not matter, but in the ideal world the primitive is a simulator for which the order can be important. In general, for stateless primitives, like random functions and permutations, the order of the queries does not matter as there is no state to be influenced. However, most simulators are stateful, in which case the queries influence the state and with that the distribution of future queries as well. Ideally, the simulator should behave like a stateless primitive as much as possible. We quantify this notion by looking at what influence swapping two queries has on the distribution of the outputs. The core of our new indifferentiability proof in Sect. 4 is to show that we can reorder the simulator queries up to $\mathcal{O}\left(2^{2n/3}\right)$ queries. Additionally, we also show an impossibility result in Sect. 6 where we make use of the fact that for the uniform simulator the order does matter, leading to an attack on it using $\mathcal{O}\left(2^{5n/6}\right)$ queries.

This reordering of the simulator queries has more in common with the notion of public indifferentiability. In this setting, which is equivalent to the previously mentioned sequential indifferentiability, the queries made by the distinguisher to the construction are publicly available to the simulator. The simplest way the simulator can make use of this is by making the queries $\mathcal{S}_0(x)$ and $\mathcal{S}_1(x)$ internally whenever the distinguisher queries $\mathcal{R}(x)$. This does correspond to the transformation made in [7], but it only holds for public indifferentiability. Note that it is true that the simulator can internally execute $\mathcal{S}_1(x)$ whenever $\mathcal{S}_0(x)$ is made as this is a query to the simulator. However, it can only execute these when $\mathcal{R}(x)$ happens if the construction queries are public. This is the case for public indifferentiability, but in (regular) indifferentiability they are not.

Reording Simulator Queries. We use this reordering idea in our new indifferentiability proof. In essence, we use many intermediate worlds in which the verification are step-wise moved to the end to convert the transcript corresponding to the public indifferentiability setting to the regular one. Instead of directly verifying the construction queries, we delay by a predetermined number of queries. We illustrate this using the example above. We start with the world corresponding to the case of public indifferentiability, where the verification queries of construction queries happen immediately. We denote them just before the construction queries, but this does not matter and is an arbitrary choice.

$$\Big((x_1, \mathcal{P}_0(x_1), \mathcal{P}_1(x_1)), (x_1, \mathcal{C}(x_1)), (x_2, \mathcal{P}_0(x_2), \mathcal{P}_1(x_2)), (x_2, \mathcal{C}(x_2)),$$
$$(x^{\min}, \mathcal{P}_0(x^{\min}), \mathcal{P}_1(x^{\min})), (x^{\max}, \mathcal{P}_0(x^{\max}), \mathcal{P}_1(x^{\max}))\Big),$$

where we do denote duplicate queries. We start with delaying the second verification query. We do this one step at a time. After three steps (one swap with the construction query, two with primitive queries) it will be verified at the end:

$$\Big((x_1, \mathcal{P}_0(x_1), \mathcal{P}_1(x_1)), (x_1, \mathcal{C}(x_1)), (x_2, \mathcal{C}(x_2)), (x^{\min}, \mathcal{P}_0(x^{\min}), \mathcal{P}_1(x^{\min})),$$
$$(x^{\max}, \mathcal{P}_0(x^{\max}), \mathcal{P}_1(x^{\max})), (x_2, \mathcal{P}_0(x_2), \mathcal{P}_1(x_2))\Big).$$

Now that the second query is completed, we move to the first query. After four delaying steps (two over a construction queries two over primitive queries), we get the following:

$$\Big((x_1, \mathcal{C}(x_1)), (x_2, \mathcal{C}(x_2)), (x^{\min}, \mathcal{P}_0(x^{\min}), \mathcal{P}_1(x^{\min})),$$
$$(x^{\max}, \mathcal{P}_0(x^{\max}), \mathcal{P}_1(x^{\max})), (x_1, \mathcal{P}_0(x_1), \mathcal{P}_1(x_1)), (x_2, \mathcal{P}_0(x_2), \mathcal{P}_1(x_2))\Big).$$

This corresponds to the normal transcript resulting from the indifferentiability setting, completing the process. We use the same idea in our proof, in reverse, to convert a normal transcript to one used in public indifferentiability. Furthermore, as there the construction queries can be derived from the primitive queries, they can essentially be ignored. In general they still have to be executed at the end to verify consistency, resulting in a sequential transcript. What is left to show is that this swapping of simulator queries has limited influence on its output distribution, which is a major part of the proof requiring a lot of computation.

3.2   Fresh Oracle

Even if we still consider [7] and restrict our focus to sequential indifferentiability, there is another problem, giving at most $3n/4$ bits of security. The problem is that for every query in the ideal world, the output of the construction oracle $\mathcal{R}$ is considered to be uniformly random. However, the inverse simulator can have a candidate output x, query the random oracle $z = \mathcal{R}(x)$, reject x as an output based on z and continue with a new candidate x'. This means that when $\mathcal{R}(x)$ for the same candidate x is queried later, its output will not be uniformly random, as it was rejected earlier and it is known what values are rejected. While it is not known what the candidate outputs were, it will still give a bias. Consider the following example:

1. Suppose there is some earlier interaction, giving non-empty domain D and ranges R_0 and R_1, all of size q. There is no bias in $\mathcal{R}$ yet;
2. Make the inverse query $x_1 = \mathcal{S}_0^{-1}(y_1)$ for an arbitrary $y_1 \notin R_0$;
3. Make the construction query $z_2 = \mathcal{R}(x_2)$ for an arbitrary $x_2 \notin D \cup \{x_1\}$.

In [7] the distribution of z_2 is considered to be uniformly random over $\{0, 1\}^n$. However, there is the possibility that x_2 was a rejected candidate in step (2), making the probability that $z_2 \in R_1 \oplus y_1$ slightly more likely. More precisely, we can consider the outputs of $\mathcal{R}(x)$ to be determined just before step (2). As all values are independently and uniformly chosen, the probability that $\mathcal{R}(x) \in R_1 \oplus y_1$ is $q/2^n$. For $X = \{x \in \{0, 1\}^n \setminus D | \mathcal{R}(x) \in R_1 \oplus y_1\}$ we have $\mathbb{E}\left[\|X\|\right] = (2^n - |D|)q/2^n$. Before step (2) there are trivially $|X|$ values $x \in \{0, 1\}^n \setminus D$ such that $\mathcal{R}(x) \in R_1 \oplus y_1$. After step (2) this value stays the same, because $x_1 \notin X$ as the simulator would reject x_1 otherwise and redraw. Therefore there are still $|X|$ values in $\{0, 1\}^n \setminus D \cup \{x_1\}$ such that $\mathcal{R}(x) \in R_1 \oplus y_1$ while the size of possible values for x decreased by one. This means that at step (3), conditioned on that the simulator did not fail, we have that

$$\mathbb{P}\left[z_2 \in R_1 \oplus y_1\right] = \mathbb{E}\left[\frac{|X|}{2^n - |D| - 1}\right] = \frac{(2^n - |D|)q}{2^n(2^n - |D| - 1)}$$

$$= \frac{q}{2^n}\frac{2^n - q}{2^n - q - 1} = \frac{q}{2^n}\left(1 + \frac{1}{2^n - q - 1}\right),$$

which is slightly higher than the uniform probability of $q/2^n$. Note that it actually does not matter for the distribution how many times the simulator retries.

Given the fact that it did not fail, the probabilities will always be the same. The only influence that the number of retries gives is the probability for failure, which is roughly $q^{\ell+1}/2^{\ell n}$ for ℓ attempts.

As a consequence, z_2 is not uniformly distributed but has a slight positive bias towards the set $R_1 \oplus y$ and a slight negative bias towards the other values. The earlier works [21,26] circumvent this problem by adding a bad event for repeated evaluations of $\mathcal{R}(x)$, contributing to limiting the proven security level to $(2n/3 - \log_2(n))$ bits. A way to view the flaw is that the proof in [7] does not consider the regular ideal world, but that it implicitly considers a modified ideal world. This modified world, which we will call 'fresh ideal world', is similar to the regular ideal world, but when the random function $\mathcal{R}(x)$ is asked for an output on input x, it will always output a uniformly random value from $\{0,1\}^n$, even when it was queried x before. The only exception is when it was queried by the distinguisher or when it can be derived from the primitive queries, then it will be consistent with the previous values. We formalize this in Algorithm 2, where the modified random function is denoted by $\mathcal{R}'$ and the modified simulator by $\mathcal{S}'$. The latter is based on the existing simulator $\mathcal{S}[\mathcal{R}']$, with its oracle access to $\mathcal{R}'$ made explicit. Although the change is small, this 'fresh ideal world' is significantly different from the regular ideal world. We formally show this as an attack between these two worlds in Sect. 5 using $\mathcal{O}\left(2^{3n/4}\right)$ queries. This attack works in the sequential indifferentiability setting, so even there the simplification of (implicitly) replacing the regular ideal world with the fresh ideal world is not possible when a security level of more than $3n/4$ bits is desired.

Algorithm 2. The 'fresh ideal world'

1: **function** $\mathcal{R}'(x)$
2:      **if** $x \in \mathsf{domain}(\mathsf{F})$ **then**
3:          **return** $\mathsf{F}(x)$
4:      $z \xleftarrow{\$} \{0,1\}^n$
5:      **if** query from distinguisher **then**
6:          $\mathsf{F}(x) \leftarrow z$
7:      **return** z

1: **function** $\mathcal{S}'_b[\mathcal{R}'](x)$
2:      $y_b \leftarrow \mathcal{S}_b[\mathcal{R}'](x)$
3:      $y_{1-b} \leftarrow \mathcal{S}_{1-b}[\mathcal{R}'](x)$
4:      $\mathsf{F}(x) \leftarrow y_b \oplus y_{1-b}$
5:      **return** y_b

1: **function** $\mathcal{S}'^{-1}_b[\mathcal{R}'](y_b)$
2:      $x \leftarrow \mathcal{S}^{-1}_b[\mathcal{R}'](y_b)$
3:      $y_{1-b} \leftarrow \mathcal{S}_b[\mathcal{R}'](x)$
4:      $\mathsf{F}(x) \leftarrow y_b \oplus y_{1-b}$
5:      **return** x

3.3 Random Range

The final problem we describe is that the ranges R_0 and R_1 cannot be considered to be random subsets of $\{0,1\}^n$ as by using inverse queries (halve of) these sets can basically be constructed as desired. These sets were actually considered to be random in [21] as highlighted and fixed in [26]. We note that this same problem is actually again present in [7] as their Lemma 1 considers these sets to be random and independent subsets of $\{0,1\}^n$. This is a fundamental problem in the proof and cannot be salvaged, bare the disallowance of any inverse queries.

4 New (Regular) Indifferentiability Proof

In this section we show that the F construction is regularly indifferentiable from a random oracle $\mathcal{R}$. Surprisingly, we show that the Mennink-Preneel's simulator [26], identical to the uniform simulator from Definition 5 with $\ell = 2$, suffices to provide security up to $2^{2n/3}/n$ queries.

In what follows, we first give a general security lifting lemma in the context of F. Specifically, we characterize the indifferentiability advantage into three terms: (1) the sequential indifferentiability advantage, (2) the failure probability and (3) the sequential difference. As the proof in [26] does hold in the sequential indifferentiability setting, we can directly use this result for term (1). This work also implicitly bounds the failure probability, but, again, only in the sequential setting. We show an upper bound for (2) that also holds in the regular indifferentiability setting by using straightforward computations. The sequential difference is more involved and highly non-trivial. It is the part that is ignored in previous papers. Our approach is generic with the potential of allowing similar resolutions for other works with the same issue. We argue that we can swap two consecutive primitive queries with only receiving a loss of $\mathcal{O}\left(q/2^{2n}\right)$. We use this fact to move the primitive queries corresponding to construction queries around. Instead of having them at the end of the interaction, we move them to just before their construction companions. By doing this, we are able to put the construction queries at the end, as we already know their output, making the transcript suitable for the sequential setting. As there are most q such queries that we have to swap at most q times, this results in an extra $\mathcal{O}\left(q^3/2^{2n}\right)$ term for (3), maintaining the proven security level.

4.1 Assumptions

In order to simplify our analysis, we make the following assumptions on the indifferentiability game, none of which result in a loss of generality for our subsequent derivation of an upper bound for the indifferentiability advantage (b will always denote an unspecified bit):

- The simulator never aborts on a forward primitive query.

- Every forward primitive query x is broadcast to both primitives immediately, and the adversary receives both $y_0 = \mathcal{P}_0(x)$ and $y_1 = \mathcal{P}_1(x)$ as response; as such we think of a forward query as just an input x without specifying one of the two primitives.
- After every inverse primitive query y_b to $\mathcal{P}_b^{-1}$, the response x is immediately fed to the other primitive, and the adversary receives both x and $y_{1-b} = \mathcal{P}_{1-b}(x)$ (the only exception being when $x = \bot$); this along with the first assumption means that every primitive query can be represented in the transcript as a triple (x, y_0, y_1).
- For every construction query x made by the adversary, the transcript contains a corresponding primitive query-response triple (x, y_0, y_1) for some y_0, y_1; this can be enforced by processing all the missing x's as forward primitive queries at the end of the game and appending the generated triples at the end of the transcript.
- Every primitive query-response triple (x, y_0, y_1) in the transcript corresponds to some construction query x; this can similarly be enforced by querying all the missing x's to the construction (or random oracle) at the end of the game.
- The adversary never makes a repeated construction query or a *pointless* primitive query (i.e., a primitive query which has already been settled while processing a previous primitive query).

A construction query-response pair (x, z) and a primitive query-response triple (x, y_0, y_1) which share the same x will be called *companion queries*; the above assumptions then imply that the queries in the transcript always occur in such companion pairs. When needed, we will write a primitive query-response triple as $(x, y_0, y_1)^+$ and $(x, y_0, y_1)_b^-$ to denote a query to $\mathcal{S}^+$ and $\mathcal{S}_b^-$ respectively. Aborted queries to $\mathcal{S}_b^-$ will be denoted as $(y_b, \bot)_b^-$ or simply as $(y_b, \bot)$ when b is either irrelevant or clear from the context.

4.2   Transcript

A transcript τ of length σ is a sequence $(\tau_1, \ldots, \tau_\sigma)$, where for all $j \in [\sigma]$, τ_j is one of the following:

- a construction query-response pair (x, z);
- a completed primitive query-response triple (x, y_0, y_1);
- an aborted primitive query $(y_b, \bot)$.

Accordingly, we partition $[\sigma]$ into three sets $c(\tau)$, $p(\tau)$, and $a(\tau)$, which correspond respectively to the three cases for τ_j above.

Definition 6 (Sequential Transcript). *A transcript τ is said to be sequential when all the construction queries are at the end, i.e., when $c(\tau)$ exactly coincides with $[i..\sigma]$ for some i.*

We can transform each transcript $\tau = (\tau_1, \ldots, \tau_\sigma)$ to a sequential transcript through the following steps:

1. for each $i \in c(\tau)$, look at the companion $i' \in p(\tau)$ (i.e., the i' such that τ_i and $\tau_{i'}$ share the same x), and if $i < i'$, put $\tau_{i'}$ at position i while pushing each of $\tau_i, \ldots, \tau_{i'-1}$ one place to the right;
2. once all construction queries are to the right of their companion primitive queries, push all the construction queries to the end of the transcript without changing their order.

We denote by $\widehat{\tau}$ the output of the above transformation on τ, and treat $\tau \mapsto \widehat{\tau}$ as a mapping from transcripts to sequential transcripts. Algorithm 3 gives an algorithmic description of this transformation. We use the array-indexing notation $\widehat{\tau}[i]$ to indicate the current i-th element of the array $\widehat{\tau}$, to emphasise the dynamic nature of $\widehat{\tau}$ while the algorithm is running.

Algorithm 3. Sequentialising a transcript

1: **function** $\mathrm{SEQ}(\tau)$
2:     $q \leftarrow |\tau|$
3:     $\widehat{\tau} \leftarrow \tau$
4:     **for** $i \leftarrow 1$ to $q - 1$ **do**   ▷ Step 1
5:         **if** $\widehat{\tau}[i]$ is a construction query **then**
6:             $(x, \_) \leftarrow \widehat{\tau}[i]$
7:             **for** $i' \leftarrow i + 1$ to q **do**   ▷ Companion search
8:                 **if** $\widehat{\tau}[i']$ is a primitive query **then**
9:                     $(x', \_, \_) \leftarrow \widehat{\tau}[i']$
10:                     **if** $x = x'$ **then**   ▷ Companion detection
11:                         temp $\leftarrow \widehat{\tau}[i']$
12:                         **for** $j \leftarrow 1$ to $i' - i$ **do**
13:                             $\widehat{\tau}[i' - j + 1] \leftarrow \widehat{\tau}[i' - j]$
                              $\widehat{\tau}[i] \leftarrow$ temp
14:     **for** $i \leftarrow 1$ to $q - 1$ **do**   ▷ Step 2
15:         **if** $\widehat{\tau}[i]$ is a construction query **then**
16:             **for** $i' \leftarrow i + 1$ to q **do**
17:                 **if** $\widehat{\tau}[i']$ is a primitive query **then**
18:                     temp $\leftarrow \widehat{\tau}[i']$
19:                     **for** $j \leftarrow 1$ to $i' - i$ **do**
20:                         $\widehat{\tau}[i' - j + 1] \leftarrow \widehat{\tau}[i' - j]$
                          $\widehat{\tau}[i] \leftarrow$ temp
21:     **return** $\widehat{\tau}$

4.3   Additional Notation

Any adversary $\mathcal{D}$ can be viewed as a two-stage algorithm $(\mathcal{D}_{\mathrm{int}}, \mathcal{D}_{\mathrm{dist}})$, where $\mathcal{D}_{\mathrm{int}}$ and $\mathcal{D}_{\mathrm{dist}}$ represent $\mathcal{D}$'s interactive and distinguishing phases, respectively. Formally, $\mathcal{D}_{\mathrm{int}}$ is an interactive oracle algorithm that outputs a transcript of its interaction with its oracle, and $\mathcal{D}_{\mathrm{dist}}$ is an algorithm that takes as input the transcript generated by $\mathcal{D}_{\text{int}}$'s interaction with its oracle and outputs a guess bit.

Fix q and a simulator $\mathcal{S}$. Let $\mathcal{T}^{\mathcal{D}}$ denote the set of all possible transcripts consisting of exactly q construction queries and q primitive queries (in companion pairs) that can be realized by $\mathcal{D}$ in an interaction with $(\mathcal{R}, \mathcal{S})$ (we call such a game a (q, q)-query game). For all $\tau \in \mathcal{T}$, we write $\mathbb{P}_{\text{re}}[\tau]$ and $\mathbb{P}_{\text{id}}[\tau]$ to denote the probability of realizing τ by an interaction with (F, Π) (the real world) and $(\mathcal{R}, \mathcal{S})$ (the ideal world) respectively; since we are considering only deterministic adversaries, this probability only depends on the random coins of the oracles and not on $\mathcal{D}$. By extending this notation, we write $\mathbb{P}_{\text{re}}[\mathcal{T}']$ to denote $\sum_{\tau \in \mathcal{T}'} \mathbb{P}_{\text{re}}[\tau]$ for any $\mathcal{T}' \subseteq \mathcal{T}^{\mathcal{D}}$. More generally, for an event E, we also use $\mathbb{P}_{\text{re}}[\mathsf{E}]$ and $\mathbb{P}_{\text{id}}[\mathsf{E}]$ to denote the probability of E in the real world and the ideal world respectively. Let

- $\mathcal{T}^{\mathcal{D} \hookrightarrow 1} := \left\{ \tau \in \mathcal{T}^{\mathcal{D}} \mid \mathcal{D}_{\text{dist}}(\tau) = 1 \right\}$;
- $\mathcal{T}^{\mathcal{D} \hookrightarrow 0} := \left\{ \tau \in \mathcal{T}^{\mathcal{D}} \mid \mathcal{D}_{\text{dist}}(\tau) = 0 \right\} = \mathcal{T}^{\mathcal{D}} \setminus \mathcal{T}^{\mathcal{D} \hookrightarrow 1}$;
- $\mathcal{T}^{\mathcal{D} \geqslant} := \left\{ \tau \in \mathcal{T}^{\mathcal{D}} \mid \mathbb{P}_{\text{id}}[\tau] \geqslant \mathbb{P}_{\text{re}}[\tau] \right\}$;
- $\mathcal{T}^{\mathcal{D}}_{\text{bad}} := \left\{ \tau \in \mathcal{T}^{\mathcal{D}} \mid \alpha(\tau) \neq \varnothing \right\}$;
- $\mathcal{T}^{\mathcal{D}}_{\text{good}} := \left\{ \tau \in \mathcal{T}^{\mathcal{D}} \mid \alpha(\tau) = \varnothing \right\} = \mathcal{T}^{\mathcal{D}} \setminus \mathcal{T}^{\mathcal{D}}_{\text{bad}}$.

For brevity, we also let $\mathcal{T}^{\mathcal{D} \geqslant}_{\text{good}} = \mathcal{T}^{\mathcal{D} \geqslant} \cap \mathcal{T}^{\mathcal{D}}_{\text{good}}$ and $\mathcal{T}^{\mathcal{D} \geqslant}_{\text{bad}} = \mathcal{T}^{\mathcal{D} \geqslant} \cap \mathcal{T}^{\mathcal{D}}_{\text{bad}}$.

Remark 2. We note that $\mathcal{T}^{\mathcal{D}}$ and its various subsets defined above depend on q and $\mathcal{S}$, and $\mathbb{P}_{\text{id}}[\tau]$ also depends on $\mathcal{S}$; when we need to make this dependence explicit, we will add the relevant symbols to the notation—for instance, $\mathcal{T}^{\mathcal{D}}$ becomes $\mathcal{T}^{\mathcal{D}}(q, \mathcal{S})$, and $\mathbb{P}_{\text{id}}[\tau]$ becomes $\mathbb{P}^{\mathcal{S}}_{\text{id}}[\tau]$. Fortunately, most often q and $\mathcal{S}$ will be clear from context, allowing us to drop these explicit references and keep the notation cleaner. We always assume that the adversary $\mathcal{D}$ adapts to q; this could for instance be realised by letting $\mathcal{D}$ be a collection of several instances $\mathcal{D}^q$ for different choices of q, such that $\mathcal{D}^q$ is specifically tailored for playing a (q, q)-query game.

Definition 7 (Failure Probability). *We define the failure probability of $\mathcal{S}$ in a (q, q)-query game as*

$$\mathsf{FP}(q, \mathcal{S}) := \max_{\mathcal{D}} \mathbb{P}^{\mathcal{S}}_{\text{id}} \left[\mathcal{T}^{\mathcal{D}}_{\text{bad}}(q, \mathcal{S}) \right].$$

Definition 8 (Sequential Difference). *We define the sequential difference of $\mathcal{S}$ in a (q, q)-query game as*

$$\mathsf{SD}(q, \mathcal{S}) := \max_{\mathcal{D}} \sum_{\tau \in \mathcal{T}^{\mathcal{D} \geqslant}_{\text{good}}(q, \mathcal{S})} \left(\mathbb{P}^{\mathcal{S}}_{\text{id}}[\tau] - \mathbb{P}^{\mathcal{S}}_{\text{id}}[\widehat{\tau}] \right).$$

In the full version [16] we show that for any q and any simulator $\mathcal{S}$ we have

$$\mathbf{Adv}^{\text{indif}}_{F, \mathcal{S}}(q, q) \leqslant \mathbf{Adv}^{\text{seq-indif}}_{F, \mathcal{S}}(q, q) + \mathsf{SD}(q, \mathcal{S}) + \mathsf{FP}(q, \mathcal{S}). \tag{3}$$

4.4   Mennink-Preneel Simulator

We aim to employ (3) with the same simulator used in [26] to achieve security up to $2^{2n/3}/n$ queries. This simulator is identical to the uniform simulator from Definition 5 with $\ell = 2$. From now on, we denote this simulator by $\mathcal{S}$.

First we show in the full version [16] that the simulator has a limited probability to fail. That is, for the simulator $\mathcal{S}$ we have

$$\mathsf{FP}\,(q,\mathcal{S}) \leqslant \frac{2q}{2^n} + \frac{13q^3}{2^{2n}}. \tag{4}$$

We continue with the main part of the proof, showing that the sequential difference of $\mathcal{S}$ is bounded by $\mathcal{O}\left(q^3/2^{2n}\right)$.

Lemma 1. *For Mennink-Preneel's simulator $\mathcal{S}$, we have*

$$\mathsf{SD}\,(q,\mathcal{S}) \leqslant \frac{46q^3}{2^{2n}}.$$

Proof. Fix an adversary $\mathcal{D}$. For any $\tau = (\tau_1, \ldots, \tau_{2q}) \in \mathcal{T}_{\mathrm{good}}^{\mathcal{D}\geqslant}$, let C^τ denote the partially sampled $\mathcal{R}$ as revealed to the adversary through all the construction queries in the game, and let $\mathsf{D}_{\mathsf{C}^\tau}$ and $\mathsf{R}_{\mathsf{C}^\tau}$ be respectively the domain and range of C^τ.

For some $\tau = (\tau_1, \ldots, \tau_{2q}) \in \mathcal{T}_{\mathrm{good}}^{\mathcal{D}\geqslant}$, consider primitive queries $\tau_i = (x, y_0, y_1), \tau_j = (x', y_0', y_1')$ with $i < j$, and let R_0 and R_1 respectively denote the range of P_0 and the range of P_1 right before the i-th query. We call the pair (τ_i, τ_j) *erratic* when it satisfies one of the following:

- τ_j is queried to $\mathcal{S}^+$, and $\{\mathsf{C}^\tau(x) \oplus y_1', y_1 \oplus \mathsf{C}^\tau(x')\} \cap \mathsf{R}_0 \neq \varnothing$;
- τ_j is queried to $\mathcal{S}^+$, and $\{\mathsf{C}^\tau(x) \oplus y_0', y_0 \oplus \mathsf{C}^\tau(x')\} \cap \mathsf{R}_1 \neq \varnothing$;
- τ_j is queried to $\mathcal{S}_b^-$, and $y_b \oplus y_{1-b}' \in \mathsf{R}_{\mathsf{C}^\tau}$.

As y_0, y_1, y_0' and y_1' are all sampled uniformly from at most $2^n - 2q$ values and y_{1-b}' is sampled from $2^n - q$ values when $x' \notin \mathsf{D}_{\mathsf{C}^\tau}$, and the event $x' \in \mathsf{D}_{\mathsf{C}^\tau}$ happens with probability at most $q/(2^n - q)$, we can bound the probability by

$$\mathbb{P}_{\mathrm{id}}\left[(\tau_i, \tau_j)\ \mathrm{erratic}\right] \leqslant \max\left(\frac{2q}{2^n - 2q} + \frac{2q}{2^n - 2q}, \frac{q}{2^n - q} + \frac{q}{2^n - q}\right)$$

$$\leqslant \max\left(\frac{4q}{2^n} + \frac{4q}{2^n}, \frac{2q}{2^n} + \frac{2q}{2^n}\right) = \frac{8q}{2^n}, \tag{5}$$

using that $q \leqslant 2^{n-2}$. We partition $\mathcal{T}_{\mathrm{good}}^{\mathcal{D}\geqslant}$ into the set $\mathcal{T}_{\mathrm{ill}}^{\mathcal{D}\geqslant}$ of *ill-behaved* transcripts, and the set $\mathcal{T}_{\mathrm{well}}^{\mathcal{D}\geqslant}$ of *well-behaved* transcripts, based on the following criterion: $\tau \in \mathcal{T}_{\mathrm{ill}}^{\mathcal{D}\geqslant}$ if for some $x, x', x'' \in \mathsf{D}_{\mathsf{C}^\tau}$, $\mathsf{C}^\tau(x) = \mathsf{C}^\tau(x') = \mathsf{C}^\tau(x'')$. We have that

$$\sum_{\tau \in \mathcal{T}_{\mathrm{ill}}^{\mathcal{D}\geqslant}} \mathbb{P}_{\mathrm{id}}\,[\tau] \leqslant \frac{q^3}{2^{2n}}. \tag{6}$$

Fix a transcript $\tau \in \mathcal{T}^{\mathcal{D}\geqslant}_{\text{well}}$, and let $\mathsf{C} := \mathsf{C}^\tau$. We first observe that responses obtained from the random oracles are sampled independent of the rest of the game, and $\mathcal{D}$ (eventually) sees the random oracle outputs of all x that occur in primitive query-response triples, so we can always condition on the outputs of all the construction queries when computing the probabilities of simulator responses. In the analysis that follows we assume that all the probabilities are implicitly conditioned on the random oracle outputs (which is the same as assuming that the random oracle output $\mathsf{C}(x)$ is known for each triple (x, y_0, y_1)).

We will find it useful to derive expressions for $\mathbb{P}_{\text{id}}[\tau_i \mid \tau_1, \ldots, \tau_{i-1}]$ for any $i \in \mathit{p}(\tau)$. Fix i, and define $\tau_{\text{head}} := (\tau_1, \ldots, \tau_{i-1})$. First let $\tau_i = (x, y_0, y_1)^+$. Let R_0 and R_1 be the ranges of the partial permutations P_0 and P_1 respectively just before the i-th query. Writing $z := \mathsf{C}(x)$, we have

$$\mathbb{P}_{\text{id}}[\tau_i \mid \tau_{\text{head}}] = \frac{1}{2^n - |\mathsf{R}_0 \cup (\mathsf{R}_1 \oplus z)|}. \tag{7}$$

Next let $\tau_i = (x, y_0, y_1)^-_0$. For arbitrary $\mathsf{G} \subseteq \mathsf{D}_\mathsf{C}$ and $\mathsf{H} \subseteq \{0,1\}^n$ define

$$\mathsf{S}_{\mathsf{G} \to \mathsf{H}} := \{x \in \mathsf{G} \mid \mathsf{C}(x) \in \mathsf{H} \cap \mathsf{R}_\mathsf{C}\},$$

the set of elements in G which have an image under C in H. Finally, let $\mathsf{D} \subseteq \mathsf{D}_\mathsf{C}$ be the shared domain of P_0 and P_1 just before the i-th query. (Note that all these sets are functions of τ_{head}.) In the full version [16] we show that

$$\mathbb{P}_{\text{id}}[\tau_i \mid \tau_{\text{head}}] = \frac{\left|\mathsf{S}_{\mathsf{D}_\mathsf{C} \setminus \mathsf{D} \to \mathsf{R}_1 \oplus y_0}\right| + 2^n - q|\mathsf{D}|/2^n}{(2^n - |\mathsf{D}|)^2}. \tag{8}$$

We are now ready to derive the bound claimed in the lemma statement. Define

$$\Delta_\tau := \mathbb{P}_{\text{id}}[\tau] - \mathbb{P}_{\text{id}}[\widehat{\tau}].$$

For each construction-query index $i \in \mathit{c}(\tau)$, let i^* denote the companion primitive-query index in $\mathit{p}(\tau)$ (i.e., $\tau_i = (x, z)$ and $\tau_{i^*} = (x, y_0, y_1)$ for some x, y_0, y_1, z). We recall that we construct $\widehat{\tau}$ from τ as follows:

- for each $i \in \mathit{c}(\tau)$, if $i < i^*$ then put τ_{i^*} at position i while pushing each of $\tau_i, \ldots, \tau_{i^*-1}$ one place to the right.
- once all construction queries are to the right of their companion primitive queries, push all the construction queries to the end.

We first observe that the second step above does not affect the probability of the transcript, because the output of the construction queries is already fixed from the companion primitive queries. (Note that this may not hold for certain simulators which try to cheat by returning a query-response triple (x, y_0, y_1) without ensuring that $y_0 \oplus y_1 = \mathcal{R}(x)$, but it holds for our simulator.) Thus, when computing $\mathbb{P}_{\text{id}}[\widehat{\tau}]$ we can pretend that the second step did not happen.

In the first step, we can assume that we check each $i \in \mathit{c}(\tau)$ in order. Consider the smallest $i \in \mathit{c}(\tau)$ satisfying $i < i^*$. Then, τ_{i^*} moves $i^* - i$ places to the left.

This can be seen as a sequence of $i^* - i$ adjacent transpositions, where the j-th transposition consists of swapping τ_{i^*} with τ_{i^*-j}. Let $\tau^{(i,j)}$ denote the transcript obtained after j transpositions, with the convention that $\tau^{(i,0)} = \tau$; also let $\tau^{[i]} := \tau^{(i,i^*-i)}$ denote the transcript at the moment when τ_{i^*} has reached the target position. We also add i to a (mutable) set $\mathcal{I}$, initialised as empty, which will eventually hold all the indices which need to be *processed* as above through a sequence of adjacent transpositions.

We can inductively extend this notation for the rest of the transpositions as follows: having obtained $\tau^{[i']}$ for the latest (and largest) $i' \in \mathcal{I}$, we look for the smallest $i \in c(\tau^{[i']})$ satisfying $i < i^*$; we then move $\tau^{[i']}_{i^*}$ $i^* - i$ places to the left through $i^* - i$ adjacent transpositions, the j-th of which swaps $\tau^{[i']}_{i^*}$ with $\tau^{[i']}_{i^*-j}$; and finally, i is added to $\mathcal{I}$. $\tau^{(i,j)}$ continues to denote the transcript obtained after j transpositions, with the convention that $\tau^{(i,0)} = \tau^{[i']}$, and $\tau^{[i]} := \tau^{(i,i^*-i)}$ now denotes the transcript at the moment when $\tau^{[i']}_{i^*}$ has reached the target position. For the last i to be added to $\mathcal{I}$, $\tau^{[i]} = \widehat{\tau}$.

Remark 3. We point out that it would be difficult to define the notation by listing out at the outset all the $i \in c(\tau)$ satisfying $i < i^*$ and going through them one by one; this is because processing the i-th entry changes the positions of the next $i^* - i$ entries, which could contain the next candidate to be processed. We further point out that the above notation is nevertheless well-defined, because the positions of the candidate entries can only increase during the handling of previous candidates, and we process them in increasing order, thus ensuring the same i is never repeated.

Remark 4. One part of the notation we abuse is i^*, which we assume is defined at every stage in accordance with the transcript $\tau^{(i,0)} = \tau^{[i']}$ for the immediate predecessor i' of i in $\mathcal{I}$, i.e., it shows the position of a query in $p(\tau^{[i']})$. Making its dependence on τ explicit would make the notation more cumbersome, so we deem it best for the sake of clarity to leave this dependence implicit and add this clarifying remark. It may be worth noting that the condition $i < i^*$ is invariant under the processing of previous entries, even with the lazy definition of i^*.

For an $i \in \mathcal{I}$ and a $j \in [i^* - i]$, we observe that the first $i^* - j - 1$ entries are identical in $\tau^{(i,j-1)}$ and $\tau^{(i,j)}$; we call this common prefix $\tau^{(i,j)}_{\text{head}}$. Similarly, the last $\sigma - i^* + j - 1$ entries of the transcripts are also identical, forming a common suffix we call $\tau^{(i,j)}_{\text{tail}}$. Then we see that

$$
\mathbb{P}_{\text{id}}\left[\tau^{(i,j-1)}\right] = \mathbb{P}_{\text{id}}\left[\tau^{(i,j)}_{\text{head}}\right] \cdot \mathbb{P}_{\text{id}}\left[\tau_{i^*-j} \mid \tau^{(i,j)}_{\text{head}}\right]
$$
$$
\cdot \mathbb{P}_{\text{id}}\left[\tau_{i^*} \mid \tau_{i^*-j}, \tau^{(i,j)}_{\text{head}}\right] \cdot \mathbb{P}_{\text{id}}\left[\tau^{(i,j)}_{\text{tail}} \mid \tau_{i^*}, \tau_{i^*-j}, \tau^{(i,j)}_{\text{head}}\right],
$$
$$
\mathbb{P}_{\text{id}}\left[\tau^{(i,j)}\right] = \mathbb{P}_{\text{id}}\left[\tau^{(i,j)}_{\text{head}}\right] \cdot \mathbb{P}_{\text{id}}\left[\tau_{i^*} \mid \tau^{(i,j)}_{\text{head}}\right]
$$
$$
\cdot \mathbb{P}_{\text{id}}\left[\tau_{i^*-j} \mid \tau_{i^*}, \tau^{(i,j)}_{\text{head}}\right] \cdot \mathbb{P}_{\text{id}}\left[\tau^{(i,j)}_{\text{tail}} \mid \tau_{i^*-j}, \tau_{i^*}, \tau^{(i,j)}_{\text{head}}\right].
$$

We define

$$\rho_\tau^{(i,j)} := \frac{\mathbb{P}_{\mathrm{id}}\left[\tau^{(i,j-1)}\right]}{\mathbb{P}_{\mathrm{id}}\left[\tau^{(i,j)}\right]} = \frac{\mathbb{P}_{\mathrm{id}}\left[\tau_{i^*-j} \mid \tau_{\mathrm{head}}^{(i,j)}\right] \cdot \mathbb{P}_{\mathrm{id}}\left[\tau_{i^*} \mid \tau_{i^*-j}, \tau_{\mathrm{head}}^{(i,j)}\right]}{\mathbb{P}_{\mathrm{id}}\left[\tau_{i^*} \mid \tau_{\mathrm{head}}^{(i,j)}\right] \cdot \mathbb{P}_{\mathrm{id}}\left[\tau_{i^*-j} \mid \tau_{i^*}, \tau_{\mathrm{head}}^{(i,j)}\right]}. \quad (9)$$

For each $i \in \mathcal{I}$, we further define

$$\rho_\tau^{[i]} := \prod_{j \in [i^*-i]} \rho_\tau^{(i,j)} = \frac{\mathbb{P}_{\mathrm{id}}\left[\tau^{(i,0)}\right]}{\mathbb{P}_{\mathrm{id}}\left[\tau^{[i]}\right]},$$

and finally, we define

$$\rho_\tau := \prod_{i \in \mathcal{I}} \rho_\tau^{[i]} = \frac{\mathbb{P}_{\mathrm{id}}\left[\tau\right]}{\mathbb{P}_{\mathrm{id}}\left[\widehat{\tau}\right]}.$$

Using this, and the fact that $1/(1+x) \geqslant 1 - x$ for all x, we can write

$$\Delta_\tau = \left(1 - \frac{1}{\rho_\tau}\right) \cdot \mathbb{P}_{\mathrm{id}}\left[\tau\right] = \left(1 - \prod_{i \in \mathcal{I}} \prod_{j \in [i^*-i]} \frac{1}{\rho_\tau^{(i,j)}}\right) \cdot \mathbb{P}_{\mathrm{id}}\left[\tau\right]$$

$$\leqslant \left(1 - \prod_{i \in \mathcal{I}} \prod_{j \in [i^*-i]} \left(1 - (\rho_\tau^{(i,j)} - 1)\right)\right) \cdot \mathbb{P}_{\mathrm{id}}\left[\tau\right]$$

$$\leqslant \sum_{i \in \mathcal{I}} \sum_{j \in [i^*-i]} (\rho_\tau^{(i,j)} - 1) \cdot \mathbb{P}_{\mathrm{id}}\left[\tau\right].$$

We next try to to find a suitable upper bound for ρ_τ. Fix an $i \in \mathcal{I}$ and a $j \in [i^* - i]$. Our first task will be to find an upper bound for $\rho_\tau^{(i,j)}$. In the full version [16] we find one depending on whether $(\tau_{i^*-j}, \tau_{i^*})$ is an erratic pair or not. We get

$$\rho_\tau^{(i,j)} \leqslant \Phi^{(i,j)}(\tau) := \begin{cases} 1 + \frac{5}{2^{2n}} & \text{if } (\tau_{i^*-j}, \tau_{i^*}) \text{ is erratic,} \\ 1 + \frac{5q}{2^{2n}} & \text{otherwise,} \end{cases}$$

for all $\tau \in \mathcal{T}_{\mathrm{well}}^{\mathcal{D}\geqslant}$. Furthermore, as the probability that $(\tau_{i^*-j}, \tau_{i^*})$ is an erratic pair is at most $8q/2^n$ by (5) we derive for $\Phi^{(i,j)}$ that

$$\mathbb{E}_{\mathrm{id}}\left[\Phi^{(i,j)}(\tau)\right] \leqslant \left(1 + \frac{5}{2^n}\right) \mathbb{P}_{\mathrm{id}}\left[(\tau_i, \tau_j) \text{ erratic}\right]$$

$$+ \left(1 + \frac{5q}{2^{2n}}\right) \mathbb{P}_{\mathrm{id}}\left[(\tau_i, \tau_j) \text{ not erratic}\right]$$

$$\leqslant 1 + \frac{40q}{2^{2n}} + \frac{5q}{2^{2n}} = 1 + \frac{45q}{2^{2n}},$$

Using this bound and the one in (6), and extending the definition of Δ_τ to all of $\mathcal{T}_{\text{good}}^{\mathcal{D}\geqslant}$, we have

$$
\begin{aligned}
\mathrm{SD}\,(q, \mathcal{S}) = \max_{\mathcal{D}} \sum_{\tau \in \mathcal{T}_{\text{good}}^{\mathcal{D}\geqslant}} \Delta_\tau &= \max_{\mathcal{D}} \left(\sum_{\tau \in \mathcal{T}_{\text{well}}^{\mathcal{D}\geqslant}} \Delta_\tau + \sum_{\tau \in \mathcal{T}_{\text{ill}}^{\mathcal{D}\geqslant}} \Delta_\tau \right) \\
&\leqslant \max_{\mathcal{D}} \left(\sum_{\tau \in \mathcal{T}_{\text{well}}^{\mathcal{D}\geqslant}} \sum_{i \in \mathcal{I}} \sum_{j \in [i^* - i]} (\rho_\tau^{(i,j)} - 1) \cdot \mathbb{P}_{\text{id}}\left[\tau\right] + \sum_{\tau \in \mathcal{T}_{\text{ill}}^{\mathcal{D}\geqslant}} \mathbb{P}_{\text{id}}\left[\tau\right] \right) \\
&\leqslant \max_{\mathcal{D}} \left(\sum_{i \in \mathcal{I}} \sum_{j \in [i^* - i]} \mathbb{E}_{\text{id}}\left[\varPhi^{(i,j)}(\tau) - 1\right] + \sum_{\tau \in \mathcal{T}_{\text{ill}}^{\mathcal{D}\geqslant}} \mathbb{P}_{\text{id}}\left[\tau\right] \right) \\
&\leqslant \max_{\mathcal{D}} \left(\frac{45 q^3}{2^{2n}} + \frac{q^3}{2^{2n}} \right) = \frac{46 q^3}{2^{2n}},
\end{aligned}
$$

thus establishing Lemma 1.   □

Using Eqs. (3), (4) and Lemma 1, and the observation from [15] that [26, Theorem 2] implies sequential indifferentiability with the same advantage, we get the following full indifferentiability bound.

Corollary 1. *For $9n \leqslant q \leqslant 2^{n-2}$, there exists a simulator $\mathcal{S}$ making at most $2q$ queries to $\mathcal{R}$ such that*

$$
\mathbf{Adv}_{F,\mathcal{S}}^{\text{indif}}(q, q) \leqslant \sqrt{\frac{9nq^3}{2^{2n}}} + \frac{2q}{2^n} + \frac{59 q^3}{2^{2n}}.
$$

5   Sequential Difference 'Fresh Ideal World'

In this section, we show an attack with complexity $\mathcal{O}\left(2^{3n/4}\right)$ that can distinguish the ideal world from the 'fresh ideal world' as described in Sect. 3.2. It works for any uniform simulator as described in Definition 5. Moreover, the attack makes primitive queries before making construction queries, meaning that the simplification of considering random oracle outputs fresh is even problematic when considering the weaker sequential indifferentiability setting.

The intuition behind this attack is that in the regular ideal world the construction oracle output $\mathcal{C}(x)$ is uniformly at random and independently selected from $\{0, 1\}^n$ at start and does not change during the interaction. However, in the fresh ideal world the output $\mathcal{C}(x)$ is not fixed at the start but is redrawn every time. Consequently, some biases introduced when making well-tailored backward queries, where the simulator does not select values with specific construction oracle outputs, are not present. We can exploit this flaw to differentiate between these worlds using $\mathcal{O}\left(2^{3n/4}\right)$ queries as shown below.

5.1   Attack Setup

Let $q = 2^k$ for some k with $q \leqslant 2^{n-1}$. We make at most $2q$ queries to the primitive oracle and at most q queries to the construction oracle. We define the distinguisher $\mathcal{D}$ as follows:

1. Let $X \subseteq \{0,1\}^n$ be an arbitrary set of size q;
2. Call $\mathcal{P}_0^{-1}(0^{n-k} \parallel y)$ for all $y \in \{0,1\}^k$;
3. Call $\mathcal{P}_1^{-1}(0^{n-k} \parallel y)$ for all $y \in \{0,1\}^k$;
4. Call $\mathcal{C}(x)$ for all $x \in X$;
5. Count the number of $x \in X$ such that $\lfloor \mathcal{C}(x) \rfloor_{n-k} = 0^{n-k}$ and call it c;
6. Return 1 when c is lower than some cutoff d and 0 otherwise.

Note that as pointless queries are not made, the value of $\mathcal{C}(x)$ can be determined in either step (2), (3) or (4). The cutoff d is the midpoint between the expected values in the two different worlds. The distinguisher $\mathcal{D}$ is formally given in Algorithm 4, with implicit calls by the simulator made explicit.

   We will compute the expectation and variance of c in both the regular ideal world (μ_1 and σ_1^2) and the fresh ideal world (μ_2 and σ_2^2). These values will be used to determine the advantage.

5.2   Ideal World

In the regular ideal world, we can view $\mathcal{C}(x)$ to be fixed at the start for all x. It does not matter whether the attacker retrieves it in step (2), (3) or (4), the probability that $\lfloor \mathcal{C}(x) \rfloor_{n-k} = 0^{n-k}$ for a fixed $x \in X$ is always $1/2^{n-k} = q/2^n$. As every x is also independent from the other values, the total count is distributed as the binomial distribution $B(q, q/2^n)$, leading to

$$\mu_1 = \frac{q^2}{2^n},$$

$$\sigma_1^2 = \frac{q^2}{2^n}\left(1 - \frac{q}{2^n}\right) \leqslant \frac{q^2}{2^n}.$$

5.3   Fresh Ideal World

In the fresh ideal world, however, $\mathcal{C}(x)$ is not fixed at the start but is sampled fresh at every invocation. This means that we have to separate the different steps. Let $c_2^{(2)}$, $c_2^{(3)}$ and $c_2^{(4)}$ denote the subcounts in step (2), (3) and (4), respectively, so that $c_2 = c_2^{(2)} + c_2^{(3)} + c_2^{(4)}$. We compute them separately.

   For $c_2^{(2)}$ we consider the output of an arbitrary query made in step (2). As the simulator samples x uniformly from all possibilities, the probability that $x \in X$ is $q/2^n$. Furthermore, the simulator samples $\mathcal{C}(x)$ uniformly over all possibilities such that $\mathcal{C}(x) \notin R_1 \oplus (0^{n-k} \parallel y)$. As the previous queries are also sampled fresh, R_1 is uniformly distributed over all possible subsets, hence there is no bias

Algorithm 4. Distinguisher between the normal and 'fresh ideal world'

1: **function** $\mathcal{D}^{\mathcal{P},\mathcal{C}}$
2:     $X \leftarrow \{0^{n-k} \parallel x : x \in \{0,1\}^k\}$
3:     $c^{(2)} \leftarrow$ COUNTINVERSE(0)
4:     $c^{(3)} \leftarrow$ COUNTINVERSE(1)
5:     $c^{(4)} \leftarrow$ COUNTCONSTRUCTION$()$
6:     $c \leftarrow c^{(2)} + c^{(3)} + c^{(4)}$
7:     **if** $c \leqslant d$ **then**
8:         **return** 1
9:     **else**
10:        **return** 0

1: **function** COUNTINVERSE(b)
2:     $c \leftarrow 0$
3:     **for** $y \in \{0,1\}^k$ **do**
4:         $y_b \leftarrow 0^{n-k} \parallel y$
5:         **if** $y_b \notin$ range$(\mathcal{P}_b)$ **then**
6:             $x \leftarrow \mathcal{P}_b^{-1}(y_b)$
7:             $y_{1-b} \leftarrow \mathcal{P}_{1-b}(x)$
8:             $z \leftarrow y_b \oplus y_{1-b}$
9:             **if** $x \in X$ and $\lfloor z \rfloor_{n-k} = 0^{n-k}$ **then**
10:                $c \leftarrow c + 1$
11:    **return** c

1: **function** COUNTCONSTRUCTION
2:     $c \leftarrow 0$
3:     **for** $x \in X$ **do**
4:         **if** $x \notin$ domain$(\mathcal{P}_0)$ **then**
5:             $z \leftarrow \mathcal{C}(x)$
6:             **if** $\lfloor z \rfloor_{n-k} = 0^{n-k}$ **then**
7:                 $c \leftarrow c + 1$
8:     **return** c

---

leading to $q/2^n$ for the probability that $\lfloor \mathcal{C}(x) \rfloor_{n-k} = 0^{n-k}$ happens. Finally, as there are always q queries made in step (2), we get

$$\mathbb{E}\left[c_2^{(2)}\right] = q \cdot \frac{q}{2^n} \cdot \frac{q}{2^n} = \frac{q^3}{2^{2n}}.$$

For $c_2^{(3)}$ we simply have that $\lfloor \mathcal{C}(x) \rfloor_{n-k} = 0^{n-k}$ is not possible, as the simulator rejects any x with $\mathcal{C}(x) \in R_0 \oplus (0^{n-k} \parallel y')$ and $\{0^{n-k} \parallel y : y \in \{0,1\}^k\} \subseteq R_0$. As a consequence,

$$c_2^{(3)} = 0.$$

Note that the number of queries made in step (3) is not always q as there can pointless queries that are already made in step (2). This happens whenever the simulator sets $\mathcal{P}_1(x)$ as $0^{n-k} \parallel y'$ for a $y' \in \{0,1\}^k$, which happens exactly when $\lfloor \mathcal{C}(x) \rfloor_{n-k} = 0^{n-k}$ which has a probability of $q/2^n$. Therefore, the number of queries made in step (3) has an expected value of $q - q^2/2^n$.

For $c_2^{(4)}$ we have that $\mathcal{C}(x)$ is freshly sampled, hence the probability that $\lfloor \mathcal{C}(x) \rfloor_{n-k} = 0^{n-k}$ happens is $q/2^n$. We still have no bias in the chosen x, so the probability that $x \in X$ for a specific x is also still $q/2^n$. However, we do not necessarily make the maximum possible number of q queries as we ignore pointless queries. Let $q^{(2)}$ and $q^{(3)}$ denote the number of queries made in step (2) and (3), respectively, of which the output lies within X. Then, we have that

$$\mathbb{E}\left[c_2^{(4)} \;\middle|\; q^{(2)}, q^{(3)} \right] = (q - q^{(2)} - q^{(3)}) \frac{q}{2^n}.$$

As $\mathbb{E}\left[q^{(2)} \right] = q^2/2^n$ and $\mathbb{E}\left[q^{(3)} \right] = (q - q^2/2^n)q/2^n = q^2/2^n - q^3/2^{2n}$, we get by the law of total expectation that

$$\mathbb{E}\left[c_2^{(4)} \right] = \left(q - \mathbb{E}\left[q^{(2)} \right] - \mathbb{E}\left[q^{(3)} \right] \right) \frac{q}{2^n} = \left(q - \frac{2q^2}{2^n} + \frac{q^3}{2^{2n}} \right) \frac{q}{2^n}$$

$$= \frac{q^2}{2^n} - \frac{2q^3}{2^{2n}} + \frac{q^4}{2^{3n}}.$$

Combining all this gives

$$\mu_2 = \mathbb{E}\left[c_2^{(2)} + c_2^{(3)} + c_2^{(4)} \right] = \frac{q^3}{2^{2n}} + 0 + \frac{q^2}{2^n} - \frac{2q^3}{2^{2n}} + \frac{q^4}{2^{3n}}$$

$$= \frac{q^2}{2^n} - \frac{q^3}{2^{2n}} + \frac{q^4}{2^{3n}} \leqslant \frac{q^2}{2^n} - \frac{q^3}{2^{2n+1}},$$

using that $q \leqslant 2^{n-1}$. For the variance we have that every single query is a Bernoulli variable. In step (2) the probability is $q^2/2^{2n}$ and in step (3) the probability is $q/2^n$, giving variances of $q^2/2^{2n}(1 - q^2/2^{2n}) \leqslant q^2/2^{2n}$ and $q/2^n(1 - q/2^n) \leqslant q/2^n$, respectively. The variance of a sum of variables is the sum of the variances of the individual variables with the covariances between the variables added. But in our case the variables in step (2) negatively influence future queries and variables in step (3) have no influence, leading to a negative correlation, hence

$$\sigma_2^2 \leqslant \frac{q^3}{2^{2n}} + \frac{q^2}{2^n} \leqslant \frac{2q^2}{2^n},$$

where we additionally use the fact that at most q queries are made in both step (2) and (4).

5.4   Advantage

In the full version [16] we show, directly from the means and variances, that the advantage is at least

$$\mathbf{Adv}_{(\mathcal{R},\mathcal{S}),(\mathcal{R}',\mathcal{S})}^{\text{seq-indif}}(\mathcal{D}) \geqslant 1 - \frac{4(\sigma_1^2 + \sigma_2^2)}{(\mu_1 - \mu_2)^2} \geqslant 1 - \frac{12q^2}{2^n} \frac{2^{4n+2}}{q^6} \geqslant 1 - \frac{2^{3n+6}}{q^4},$$

where $\mathbf{Adv}_{(\mathcal{R},\mathcal{S}),(\mathcal{R}',\mathcal{S})}^{\text{seq-indif}}(\cdot)$ denotes the sequential indifferentiability advantage between the ideal world $(\mathcal{R},\mathcal{S})$ and the fresh ideal world $(\mathcal{R}',\mathcal{S})$ with $\mathcal{R}'$ the modified random oracle that always gives fresh results.

6   Generic Differentiability Attack

In this section, we show an attack with complexity $\mathcal{O}\left(2^{5n/6}\right)$ that can distinguish the ideal world with the uniform simulator from the real world. The intuition behind this attack is that the uniform forward simulator returns a value uniformly sampled from all possibilities. While this sounds reasonable it turns out that this actually does not exactly match the real world for all interactions. This uniformity changes the distribution of outputs when the order of the queries is changed in the ideal world, while the order does not matter in the real world. We can exploit this flaw to attack the uniform simulator using $\mathcal{O}\left(2^{5n/6}\right)$ queries as shown below.

6.1   Attack Setup

Let $q = 2^k$ for some k with $q \leqslant 2^{n-3}$. We make at most $3q$ queries to the primitive oracle and at most q queries to the construction oracle.

1. Call $\mathcal{P}_1^{-1}(0^{n-k} \parallel y)$ for all $y \in \{0,1\}^k$;
2. Call $\mathcal{C}(x_i) = z_i$ for q fresh x_i;
3. Let I be the index set consisting of all i such that $\lfloor z_i \rfloor_{n-k} = 0^{n-k}$ in the previous step;
4. Call $\mathcal{P}_0(x_i)$ for all $i \in I$ (optional);
5. Call $\mathcal{P}_0(x_j) = y_j$ for q fresh x_j;
6. Count the number of j such that $\lfloor y_j \rfloor_{n-k} = 0^{n-k}$ and call it c;
7. Return 1 when c is lower than some cutoff d and 0 otherwise.

Step (4) is denoted as optional. We define two related distinguishers depending on whether step (4) is executed or not. We denote $\mathcal{D}_\varnothing$ for the distinguisher that skips (4) and $\mathcal{D}_I$ for the distinguisher that executes (4). Again, the cutoff d is the midpoint between the expected values in the two different worlds. The distinguishers $\mathcal{D}_\varnothing$ and $\mathcal{D}_I$ are formally given in Algorithm 5, with again implicit calls by the simulator made explicit.

By the triangle inequality we get that

$$\left| \mathbb{P}\left[\mathcal{D}_\varnothing^{R,S,S^{-1}} = 1 \right] - \mathbb{P}\left[\mathcal{D}_I^{R,S,S^{-1}} = 1 \right] \right| \tag{10}$$

$$\leqslant \left| \mathbb{P}\left[\mathcal{D}_\varnothing^{R,S,S^{-1}} = 1 \right] - \mathbb{P}\left[\mathcal{D}_\varnothing^{F,\Pi,\Pi^{-1}} = 1 \right] \right|$$

$$+ \left| \mathbb{P}\left[\mathcal{D}_\varnothing^{F,\Pi,\Pi^{-1}} = 1 \right] - \mathbb{P}\left[\mathcal{D}_I^{F,\Pi,\Pi^{-1}} = 1 \right] \right|$$

$$+ \left| \mathbb{P}\left[\mathcal{D}_I^{F,\Pi,\Pi^{-1}} = 1 \right] - \mathbb{P}\left[\mathcal{D}_I^{R,S,S^{-1}} = 1 \right] \right|$$

$$= \mathbf{Adv}_{F,S}^{\mathrm{indif}}(\mathcal{D}_\varnothing) + 0 + \mathbf{Adv}_{F,S}^{\mathrm{indif}}(\mathcal{D}_I)$$

$$\leqslant 2 \max\left(\mathbf{Adv}_{F,S}^{\mathrm{indif}}(\mathcal{D}_\varnothing), \mathbf{Adv}_{F,S}^{\mathrm{indif}}(\mathcal{D}_I) \right),$$

where the reasoning for the 0 is given in Sect. 6.2. This means that if we show that there is a non-negligible difference between adding the queries I or not in

Algorithm 5. Distinguisher on the uniform simulator, with the highlighted lines 9–11 included in $\mathcal{D}_I$ but not in $\mathcal{D}_\varnothing$

```
1: function 𝒟^{P,𝒞}
2:     for y ∈ {0,1}^k do
3:         y₁ ← 0^{n-k} ‖ y
4:         x ← 𝒫₁^{-1}(y₁)
5:         y₀ ← 𝒫₀(x)
6:     for 1 ⩽ i ⩽ q do
7:         x ←$ {0,1}^n \ (domain(𝒫₀) ∪ domain(𝒞))
8:         z ← 𝒞(x)
9:         if ⌊z⌋_{n-k} = 0^{n-k} then
10:            y₀ ← 𝒫₀(x)
11:            y₁ ← 𝒫₁(x)
12:    c ← 0
13:    for 1 ⩽ j ⩽ q do
14:        x ←$ {0,1}^n \ (domain(𝒫₀) ∪ domain(𝒞))
15:        y₀ ← 𝒫₀(x)
16:        y₁ ← 𝒫₁(x)
17:        if ⌊y₀⌋_{n-k} = 0^{n-k} then
18:            c ← c + 1
19:    if c ⩽ d then
20:        return 1
21:    else
22:        return 0
```

the ideal world, i.e., there is a non-trivial lower bound for (10), there is a distinguisher (either $\mathcal{D}_\varnothing$ or $\mathcal{D}_I$) that has a non-negligible advantage on the original construction. In Sect. 6.3 we will derive such a lower bound on (10), leading to

$$2 \max \left(\mathbf{Adv}_{F,\mathcal{S}}^{\mathrm{indif}}(\mathcal{D}_\varnothing), \mathbf{Adv}_{F,\mathcal{S}}^{\mathrm{indif}}(\mathcal{D}_I) \right) \geqslant 1 - \mathcal{O}\left(\frac{2^{5n}}{q^6} \right).$$

6.2 Real World

In the real world, the construction oracle is defined as $F(x) = \Pi_0(x) \oplus \Pi_1(x)$. This means that a construction query $F(x)$ will behave the same as the two primitive queries $\Pi_0(x)$ and $\Pi_1(x)$. Therefore, the primitive queries $\Pi_0(x_i)$ optionally made in step (4) have no influence as they are already implicitly executed in the construction query $F(x_i)$ in step (3). As the only difference between $\mathcal{D}_\varnothing$ and $\mathcal{D}_I$ are these 'extra' primitive queries, their output probabilities do not differ, and hence

$$\mathbb{P}\left[\mathcal{D}_\varnothing^{F,\Pi,\Pi^{-1}} = 1 \right] - \mathbb{P}\left[\mathcal{D}_I^{F,\Pi,\Pi^{-1}} = 1 \right] = 0.$$

6.3   Ideal World

In this section we focus on finding a lower bound for

$$\left| \mathbb{P}\left[\mathcal{D}_{\varnothing}^{\mathcal{R},\mathcal{S},\mathcal{S}^{-1}} = 1 \right] - \mathbb{P}\left[\mathcal{D}_{I}^{\mathcal{R},\mathcal{S},\mathcal{S}^{-1}} = 1 \right] \right|.$$

In order to do this, we will compute the expectation and variance of c for both $\mathcal{D}_{\varnothing}$ ($\mu_{\varnothing}$ and $\sigma_{\varnothing}^2$) and $\mathcal{D}_I$ (μ_I and σ_I^2). These values will be used to determine the advantage. We are mostly interested in the difference between the expectations which we can denote as

$$\mu_I - \mu_{\varnothing} = \sum_j \delta_j,$$

$$\delta_j = p_{I,j} - p_{\varnothing,j},$$

where $p_{\varnothing,j} = \mathbb{P}_{\varnothing}\left[\lfloor y_j \rfloor_{n-k} = 0^{n-k} \right]$ and $p_{I,j} = \mathbb{P}_I\left[\lfloor y_j \rfloor_{n-k} = 0^{n-k} \right]$, where $\mathbb{P}_{\varnothing}[\cdot]$ (resp., $\mathbb{P}_I[\cdot]$) denotes the probability is taken when interacting with distinguisher $\mathcal{D}_{\varnothing}$ (resp., $\mathcal{D}_I$).

Now we will look at the probability that $\lfloor y_j \rfloor_{n-k} = \lfloor \mathcal{S}_0(x_j) \rfloor_{n-k} = 0^{n-k}$ for a fixed j when I is excluded or included. By the behavior of the simulator, the probability is of the form

$$p_j = \mathbb{P}\left[\lfloor y_j \rfloor_{n-k} = 0^{n-k} \right] = \mathbb{E}\left[\frac{q - W_j}{2^n - V_j} \right],$$

where W_j denotes the number of elements that exclude $\lfloor y_j \rfloor_{n-k} = 0^{n-k}$ from occurring and V_j denotes the number of excluded values to draw. This notation is more generic and we denote $W_{\varnothing,j}$ and $V_{\varnothing,j}$ when interacting with $\mathcal{D}_{\varnothing}$ and similar for $\mathcal{D}_I$.

In the full version [16] we show that

$$\delta_j \geqslant \frac{q^3}{2^{3n+2}} + \mathcal{O}\left(\frac{q^4}{2^{4n}} \right).$$

The intuition behind this difference is that the queries $i \in I$ satisfy $\lfloor z_i \rfloor_{n-k} = 0^{n-k}$, which means that $\lfloor \mathcal{S}_0(x_i) \rfloor_{n-k} \neq 0^{n-k}$. Therefore, these queries do not directly exclude possibilities for $\lfloor y_j \rfloor_{n-k}$ to hit 0^{n-k}, while excluding other options. This slightly increases the probability of $\lfloor y_j \rfloor_{n-k} = 0^{n-k}$, leading to the difference. As $\mu_I - \mu_{\varnothing} = \sum_j \delta_j$, this implies that

$$\mu_I - \mu_{\varnothing} \geqslant \frac{q^4}{2^{3n+2}} + \mathcal{O}\left(\frac{q^5}{2^{4n}} \right) = \Omega\left(\frac{q^4}{2^{3n}} \right),$$

$$\frac{1}{(\mu_I - \mu_{\varnothing})^2} = \mathcal{O}\left(\frac{2^{6n}}{q^8} \right).$$

Furthermore, in the full version [16] we show that the expectation for a single event in both cases is

$$p_{\varnothing,j}, p_{I,j} = \frac{q}{2^n} + \mathcal{O}\left(\frac{q^3}{2^{3n}} \right),$$

immediately giving its variance of at most the same value. Furthermore, the variance of a sum of variables is the sum of the variables, with the pairwise correlations added. In our case the variables are negatively correlated as when $\lfloor y_j \rfloor_{n-k} = 0^{n-k}$ happens one more possibility to hit is discarded for future queries, reducing its probability. This means that we can upper bound the variances as

$$\sigma_I^2, \sigma_\varnothing^2 \leqslant \frac{q^2}{2^n} + \mathcal{O}\left(\frac{q^4}{2^{3n}}\right) = \mathcal{O}\left(\frac{q^2}{2^n}\right).$$

Finally, in the full version [16] we show, directly from the means and variances, that the advantage is at least

$$(10) \geqslant 1 - \frac{4(\sigma_I^2 + \sigma_\varnothing^2)}{(\mu_I - \mu_\varnothing)^2} = 1 - \mathcal{O}\left(\frac{q^2}{2^n}\right) \mathcal{O}\left(\frac{2^{6n}}{q^8}\right) = 1 - \mathcal{O}\left(\frac{2^{5n}}{q^6}\right),$$

as desired.

7   Conclusion

The contributions of this work are both negative and positive. On the negative side, we demonstrated that previous best security result on the sum of permutations is flawed and not easily fixed as there is an attack in $2^{5n/6}$ queries. On the positive side, the security claim of the second-best result, guaranteeing $2^{2n/3}/n$ security, can be reattained. The two results, albeit highly technical and non-trivial, admit a gap. We expect that security beyond $2^{2n/3}/n$ may still be possible but that such result will require resorting to a more sophisticated simulator and/or following an entirely different proof approach. Indeed, to be precise, our $2^{2n/3}/n$ security result for the simulator of Definition 5 with $\ell = 2$ took the result of Mennink and Preneel, with $2^{2n/3}/n$ sequential indifferentiability, as a black box and performed a query shuffling approach that was valid as long as the number of queries is at most $2^{2n/3}/n$. Going beyond this security bound thus requires resolving *both* bottlenecks.

Acknowledgements. This work was partly performed while the authors were visiting Dagstuhl Seminar 22141 "Symmetric Cryptography". Aldo Gunsing is supported by the Netherlands Organisation for Scientific Research (NWO) under TOP grant TOP1.18.002 SCALAR. Ritam Bhaumik carried out part of this research while affiliated to Inria Paris, funded by the European Research Council (ERC) under the European Union's Horizon 2020 research and innovation programme (grant agreement no. 714294 - acronym QUASYModo). Ashwin Jha carried out this work in the framework of the French-German-Center for Cybersecurity, a collaboration of CISPA and LORIA. Bart Mennink is supported by the Netherlands Organisation for Scientific Research (NWO) under grant VI.Vidi.203.099. Yaobin Shen is supported by the European Union through the ERC consolidator grant SWORD (num. 724725).

References

1. Banik, S., Isobe, T., Liu, F., Minematsu, K., Sakamoto, K.: Orthros: a low-latency PRF. IACR Trans. Symmetric Cryptol. **2021**(1), 37–77 (2021). https://doi.org/10.46586/tosc.v2021.i1.37-77
2. Bellare, M., Impagliazzo, R.: A tool for obtaining tighter security analyses of pseudorandom function based constructions, with applications to PRP to PRF conversion. Cryptology ePrint Archive, Report 1999/024 (1999). http://eprint.iacr.org/1999/024
3. Bellare, M., Kilian, J., Rogaway, P.: The security of cipher block chaining. In: Desmedt, Y.G. (ed.) CRYPTO 1994. LNCS, vol. 839, pp. 341–358. Springer, Heidelberg (1994). https://doi.org/10.1007/3-540-48658-5_32
4. Bellare, M., Krovetz, T., Rogaway, P.: Luby-Rackoff backwards: increasing security by making block ciphers non-invertible. In: Nyberg, K. (ed.) EUROCRYPT 1998. LNCS, vol. 1403, pp. 266–280. Springer, Heidelberg (1998). https://doi.org/10.1007/BFb0054132
5. Bellare, M., Rogaway, P.: The security of triple encryption and a framework for code-based game-playing proofs. In: Vaudenay, S. (ed.) EUROCRYPT 2006. LNCS, vol. 4004, pp. 409–426. Springer, Heidelberg (2006). https://doi.org/10.1007/11761679_25
6. Bernstein, D.J.: SURF: simple unpredictable random function. https://cr.yp.to/papers.html#surf (1997)
7. Bhattacharya, S., Nandi, M.: Full indifferentiable security of the xor of two or more random permutations using the χ^2 method. In: Nielsen, J.B., Rijmen, V. (eds.) EUROCRYPT 2018. LNCS, vol. 10820, pp. 387–412. Springer, Cham (2018). https://doi.org/10.1007/978-3-319-78381-9_15
8. Chang, D., Nandi, M.: A Short Proof of the PRP/PRF Switching Lemma. Cryptology ePrint Archive, Report 2008/078 (2008). http://eprint.iacr.org/2008/078
9. Coron, J.-S., Dodis, Y., Malinaud, C., Puniya, P.: Merkle-Damgård revisited: how to construct a hash function. In: Shoup, V. (ed.) CRYPTO 2005. LNCS, vol. 3621, pp. 430–448. Springer, Heidelberg (2005). https://doi.org/10.1007/11535218_26
10. Daemen, J., Rijmen, V.: The Design of Rijndael: AES - The Advanced Encryption Standard. Information Security and Cryptography. Springer, Heidelberg (2002). https://doi.org/10.1007/978-3-662-04722-4
11. Dai, W., Hoang, V.T., Tessaro, S.: Information-theoretic indistinguishability via the chi-squared method. In: Katz, J., Shacham, H. (eds.) CRYPTO 2017. LNCS, vol. 10403, pp. 497–523. Springer, Cham (2017). https://doi.org/10.1007/978-3-319-63697-9_17
12. Dodis, Y., Puniya, P.: Getting the best out of existing hash functions; or what if we are stuck with SHA? In: Bellovin, S.M., Gennaro, R., Keromytis, A., Yung, M. (eds.) ACNS 2008. LNCS, vol. 5037, pp. 156–173. Springer, Heidelberg (2008). https://doi.org/10.1007/978-3-540-68914-0_10
13. Dodis, Y., Ristenpart, T., Shrimpton, T.: Salvaging Merkle-Damgård for practical applications. In: Joux, A. (ed.) EUROCRYPT 2009. LNCS, vol. 5479, pp. 371–388. Springer, Heidelberg (2009). https://doi.org/10.1007/978-3-642-01001-9_22
14. Freedman, D.: A remark on the difference between sampling with and without replacement. J. Am. Stat. Assoc. **72**(359), 681–681 (1977). https://doi.org/10.1080/01621459.1977.10480637

15. Gunsing, A.: Block-cipher-based tree hashing. In: Dodis, Y., Shrimpton, T. (eds.) Advances in Cryptology - CRYPTO 2022–42nd Annual International Cryptology Conference, CRYPTO 2022, Santa Barbara, CA, USA, 15–18 August 2022, Proceedings, Part IV. Lecture Notes in Computer Science, vol. 13510, pp. 205–233. Springer, Heidelberg (2022). https://doi.org/10.1007/978-3-031-15985-5_8

16. Gunsing, A., Bhaumik, R., Jha, A., Mennink, B., Shen, Y.: Revisiting the indifferentiability of the sum of permutations. Cryptology ePrint Archive, Paper 2023/840 (2023). https://eprint.iacr.org/2023/840

17. Hall, C., Wagner, D., Kelsey, J., Schneier, B.: Building PRFs from PRPs. In: Krawczyk, H. (ed.) CRYPTO 1998. LNCS, vol. 1462, pp. 370–389. Springer, Heidelberg (1998). https://doi.org/10.1007/BFb0055742

18. Impagliazzo, R., Rudich, S.: Limits on the provable consequences of one-way permutations. In: Goldwasser, S. (ed.) CRYPTO 1988. LNCS, vol. 403, pp. 8–26. Springer, New York (1990). https://doi.org/10.1007/0-387-34799-2_2

19. Lee, J.: Indifferentiability of the sum of random permutations toward optimal security. IEEE Trans. Inf. Theory **63**(6), 4050–4054 (2017). https://doi.org/10.1109/TIT.2017.2679757

20. Lucks, S.: The sum of PRPs is a secure PRF. In: Preneel, B. (ed.) EUROCRYPT 2000. LNCS, vol. 1807, pp. 470–484. Springer, Heidelberg (2000). https://doi.org/10.1007/3-540-45539-6_34

21. Mandal, A., Patarin, J., Nachef, V.: Indifferentiability beyond the birthday bound for the Xor of two public random permutations. In: Gong, G., Gupta, K.C. (eds.) INDOCRYPT 2010. LNCS, vol. 6498, pp. 69–81. Springer, Heidelberg (2010). https://doi.org/10.1007/978-3-642-17401-8_6

22. Mandal, A., Patarin, J., Seurin, Y.: On the public indifferentiability and correlation intractability of the 6-round feistel construction. In: Cramer, R. (ed.) TCC 2012. LNCS, vol. 7194, pp. 285–302. Springer, Heidelberg (2012). https://doi.org/10.1007/978-3-642-28914-9_16

23. Maurer, U., Renner, R., Holenstein, C.: Indifferentiability, impossibility results on reductions, and applications to the random oracle methodology. In: Naor, M. (ed.) TCC 2004. LNCS, vol. 2951, pp. 21–39. Springer, Heidelberg (2004). https://doi.org/10.1007/978-3-540-24638-1_2

24. Maurer, U., Tessaro, S.: Domain extension of public random functions: beyond the birthday barrier. In: Menezes, A. (ed.) CRYPTO 2007. LNCS, vol. 4622, pp. 187–204. Springer, Heidelberg (2007). https://doi.org/10.1007/978-3-540-74143-5_11

25. Mennink, B., Neves, S.: Optimal PRFs from blockcipher designs. IACR Trans. Symmetric Cryptol. **2017**(3), 228–252 (2017). https://doi.org/10.13154/tosc.v2017.i3.228-252

26. Mennink, B., Preneel, B.: On the XOR of multiple random permutations. In: Malkin, T., Kolesnikov, V., Lewko, A.B., Polychronakis, M. (eds.) ACNS 2015. LNCS, vol. 9092, pp. 619–634. Springer, Cham (2015). https://doi.org/10.1007/978-3-319-28166-7_30

27. Patarin, J.: A proof of security in $O(2^n)$ for the Xor of Two Random Permutations. In: Safavi-Naini, R. (ed.) ICITS 2008. LNCS, vol. 5155, pp. 232–248. Springer, Heidelberg (2008). https://doi.org/10.1007/978-3-540-85093-9_22

28. Patarin, J.: Introduction to Mirror Theory: Analysis of Systems of Linear Equalities and Linear Non Equalities for Cryptography. Cryptology ePrint Archive, Report 2010/287 (2010). http://eprint.iacr.org/2010/287

29. Patarin, J.: Security in $O(2^n)$ for the Xor of Two Random Permutations - Proof with the standard H technique-. Cryptology ePrint Archive, Report 2013/368 (2013). http://eprint.iacr.org/2013/368
30. Shrimpton, T., Stam, M.: Building a collision-resistant compression function from non-compressing primitives. In: Aceto, L., Damgård, I., Goldberg, L.A., Halldórsson, M.M., Ingólfsdóttir, A., Walukiewicz, I. (eds.) ICALP 2008. LNCS, vol. 5126, pp. 643–654. Springer, Heidelberg (2008). https://doi.org/10.1007/978-3-540-70583-3_52
31. Stam, M.: Beyond uniformity: better security/efficiency tradeoffs for compression functions. In: Wagner, D. (ed.) CRYPTO 2008. LNCS, vol. 5157, pp. 397–412. Springer, Heidelberg (2008). https://doi.org/10.1007/978-3-540-85174-5_22
32. Yoneyama, K., Miyagawa, S., Ohta, K.: Leaky random oracle. IEICE Trans. Fundam. Electron. Commun. Comput. Sci. **92-A**(8), 1795–1807 (2009). https://doi.org/10.1587/transfun.E92.A.1795

When Messages Are Keys: Is HMAC a Dual-PRF?

Matilda Backendal[1]($\boxtimes$) (iD), Mihir Bellare[2] (iD), Felix Günther[1] (iD), and Matteo Scarlata[1] (iD)

[1] Department of Computer Science, ETH Zurich, Zurich, Switzerland
{mbackendal,scmatteo}@inf.ethz.ch, mail@felixguenther.info
[2] Department of Computer Science and Engineering, University of California, San Diego, USA
mbellare@ucsd.edu

Abstract. In Internet security protocols including TLS 1.3, MLS and Noise, HMAC is being assumed to be a dual-PRF, meaning a PRF not only when keyed conventionally (through its first input), but also when "swapped" and keyed (unconventionally) through its second (message) input. We give the first in-depth analysis of the dual-PRF assumption on HMAC. For the swap case, we note that security does not hold in general, but completely characterize when it does; we show that HMAC is swap-PRF secure if and only if keys are restricted to sets satisfying a condition called feasibility, that we give, and that holds in applications. The sufficiency is shown by proof and the necessity by attacks. For the conventional PRF case, we fill a gap in the literature by proving PRF security of HMAC for keys of arbitrary length. Our proofs are in the standard model, make assumptions only on the compression function underlying the hash function, and give good bounds in the multi-user setting. The positive results are strengthened through achieving a new notion of variable key-length PRF security that guarantees security even if different users use keys of different lengths, as happens in practice.

1 Introduction

HMAC [8] is a hash-function-based construct taking two inputs to return a fixed-length output. It was designed to be PRF-secure, a usage in which the first input is the key and the second is the message. It is standardized by the IETF [37] and NIST [47] and widely used, including in IPsec, SSH, and TLS. However, its conventional use as a PRF is now being supplemented with another type of use, as a key combiner, which (additionally) assumes that it is a swap-PRF, meaning a PRF when keyed by the second input, with the first input regarded as the message. This is happening in various Internet security protocols including TLS 1.3 [22,25], KEMTLS [46], hybrid key-exchange designs [16,49], post-quantum versions of WireGuard [33] and Noise [1], and Message Layer Security (MLS) [21]. Overall, then, HMAC is being assumed to be a dual-PRF; as defined in [5,6] this means being both a PRF and a swap-PRF.

But is this assumption well-founded? The extensive real-world usage represented by the above protocols makes this question crucial. Yet, it has not been

© International Association for Cryptologic Research 2023
H. Handschuh and A. Lysyanskaya (Eds.): CRYPTO 2023, LNCS 14083, pp. 661–693, 2023.
https://doi.org/10.1007/978-3-031-38548-3_22

seriously investigated. And as an indication that the gap is more than academic, we note that there are concerns on *both* sides of the dual-PRF coin, meaning for both swap-PRF and conventional PRF security, as follows.

▷ HMAC is not swap-PRF secure, but may be for restricted inputs. Simple attacks (described below) show that HMAC is actually *not* swap-PRF secure. Luckily, due to the specific inputs used, these attacks do not endanger the protocols listed above. But that doesn't mean these usages are secure. We want to know for what inputs one can prove security and under what assumptions, and whether current usage assuming swap-PRF security can be validated with proofs.

▷ PRF security of HMAC has only been proved for one key length. Meanwhile, our work lead us to realize that there is a gap in the literature even with regard to the conventional PRF security of HMAC, namely that it has only been proven for keys of length equal to the block length [5,6]. Yet, in practice, and in the above applications, HMAC is often used with keys shorter than the block length, and the standards allow keys of any length. We want to know whether proofs of PRF security are possible for all allowed key lengths, and under what assumptions.

CONTRIBUTIONS IN BRIEF. Our contribution is to identify and fill the above gaps. To capture restrictions on inputs, we let HMAC[$\mathcal{S}$] denote HMAC restricted to keys being drawn from a subset $\mathcal{S}$ of its keyspace. As the more novel and interesting case, we first consider swap-PRF security, in which case $\mathcal{S}$ is a subset of the message space. We give necessary and sufficient conditions on $\mathcal{S}$ for HMAC[$\mathcal{S}$] to be swap-PRF secure, justifying the sufficiency by proof and the necessity by attack. Sets used in current applications meet our sufficient conditions, hence our proofs provide guarantees for these usages. Turning to the conventional PRF security of HMAC, we prove it for keys of *any* (sufficiently large) length. Our results hold even when different users use keys of different and adaptively-chosen lengths, as captured formally by a new definition, of a variable key-length PRF (vkl-PRF), that we give as an auxiliary contribution. In summary, we emerge with a full picture of the security of HMAC as a dual-PRF.

We stress that all our proofs for HMAC are in the standard model (no idealized assumptions) and make assumptions only on the compression function underlying the hash function. Also, for the first time for HMAC, we prove multi-user security with good bounds, for all of our results. We now look at all this in more detail. A summary of our and prior results is in Table 1; notation used there is explained below.

1.1   Background

THE FUNCTIONS. The starting point is a compression function $h\colon \{0,1\}^c \times \{0,1\}^b \to \{0,1\}^c$, taking a c-bit chaining variable and b-bit block to return a c-bit result, where $c < b$. Briefly, one starts with the cascade h^* [9], which takes a c-bit key, and message whose length is a multiple of b, and iterates h to return a c-bit result. (See Fig. 3 later in Sect. 4 for full details.) The hash function $H\colon \{0,1\}^* \to \{0,1\}^c$ associated to h by the **MD** transform [23,42] is $H(M) = h^*(\text{IV}, \overline{M})$ where $\text{IV} \in \{0,1\}^c$ is a fixed initial vector and $\overline{M}$ pads M out to a length that is a multiple of b bits. (The details of the padding, which do matter, are in Sect. 4.) This is the design underlying the SHA-2 function family [48], including SHA-256 ($c = 256$, $b = 512$), SHA-384 ($c = 384$, $b = 1024$), and SHA-512 ($c = 512$, $b = 1024$). The simplest version of HMAC is $\mathsf{HMAC}_b \colon \{0,1\}^b \times \{0,1\}^* \to \{0,1\}^c$, taking a b-bit key and defined by $\mathsf{HMAC}_b(K_b, M) = \mathsf{H}((K_b \oplus \mathsf{opad}) \| \mathsf{H}((K_b \oplus \mathsf{ipad}) \| M))$, where $\mathsf{ipad}, \mathsf{opad} \in \{0,1\}^b$ are distinct constants specified in the standards. The "full" HMAC: $\{0,1\}^* \times \{0,1\}^* \to \{0,1\}^c$ as standardized [8,37,47] takes a key of arbitrary length and is defined by $\mathsf{HMAC}(K, M) = \mathsf{HMAC}_b(\mathsf{PoH}_b(K), M)$, where the "Pad or Hash" function $\mathsf{PoH}_b \colon \{0,1\}^* \to \{0,1\}^b$ returns $K \| 0^{b-|K|}$ if $|K| \le b$ and $\mathsf{H}(K) \| 0^{b-c}$ otherwise.

To facilitate analysis, Sect. 4 unravels the above definitions of HMAC_b and HMAC to view the functions in a more modular way. The core is NMAC [8], which is applied to the message with keys derived from the given key via a subkey derivation function HSKD.

PRFs, SWAP-PRFs AND DUAL-PRFs. Recall that the definition of a function family $\mathsf{F} \colon \mathcal{X} \times \mathcal{Y} \to \mathcal{Z}$ being a PRF views the first input as a key and the second input as a message: we ask that oracles for $\mathsf{F}(X, \cdot)$ and a random function $g \colon \mathcal{Y} \to \mathcal{Z}$ be indistinguishable when $X \leftarrow_\$ \mathcal{X}$ is not known to the attacker [29]. The *swap* of F is the function family $\mathsf{F}^{\leftrightharpoons} \colon \mathcal{Y} \times \mathcal{X} \to \mathcal{Z}$ defined by $\mathsf{F}^{\leftrightharpoons}(Y, X) = \mathsf{F}(X, Y)$. We say that F is a swap-PRF if $\mathsf{F}^{\leftrightharpoons}$ is a PRF. (That is, F is a PRF when keyed by the second, or message, input.) The concept of a dual PRF was introduced in [5,6]. F is a dual-PRF if F is both a PRF *and* a swap-PRF. That is, it is a PRF when keyed as usual by the first input, but also if keyed by the second input.

PRIOR WORK. A primary line of work has focused on proving PRF security of HMAC-related functions in the standard model and making assumptions only on the compression function. First, BCK [8] showed that NMAC is PRF-secure if the compression function h is PRF-secure and collision resistant. Bellare [5,6] showed that PRF security of h alone suffices for the conclusion, and better bounds were given by GPR [28]. Further [5,6] showed that HMAC_b is PRF-secure assuming NMAC is PRF-secure and h is swap-PRF secure under a simple form of related-key attack. (This prior work is summarized in Table 1.) We briefly note some gaps that will be addressed below. Namely, there are no proofs (1) of swap-PRF security for any of NMAC, HMAC_b, HMAC, (2) of PRF security of HMAC itself (only of HMAC_b), (3) with good bounds in the multi-user setting.

USAGE. Key derivation in some prominent Internet security protocols involves combining a pair of keys K_1, K_2 into a single key via $K \leftarrow \mathsf{HMAC}(K_1, K_2)$. The intent is that (1) if K_1 is good (uniformly random and unknown to the attacker) then so is K regardless of K_2 and (2) vice versa. Requirement (1) is satisfied if HMAC is a PRF, and requirement (2) if HMAC is a swap-PRF. That is, jointly, the assumption is that HMAC is a dual-PRF. Specifically, this is happening in TLS 1.3 [22,25], KEMTLS [46], hybrid key-exchange designs [16,49], post-quantum versions of WireGuard [33] and Noise [1], and Message Layer Security (MLS) [21], representing a large number of real-world use cases. In light of this, it is crucial to evaluate the dual-PRF security of HMAC.

1.2   Swap-PRF Security of HMAC

ATTACKS. We first note that there are simple attacks showing HMAC is in fact *not* swap-PRF secure. The issue is the well-known fact that the "Pad or Hash" function PoH_b is not collision resistant. (This is also the source of attacks on the indifferentiability of HMAC for arbitrary keys [24], and the reason for an erratum filed for the HMAC RFC [27,41].) For example if K_1, K_1' are keys of length strictly less than b bits such that $K_1' = K_1 \| 0^\ell$ for some $\ell \geq 1$, then $PoH_b(K_1) = K_1 \| 0^{b-|K_1|} = K_1' \| 0^{b-|K_1'|} = PoH_b(K_1')$, so $HMAC(K_1, K_2) = HMAC(K_1', K_2)$ for any K_2. An adversary can now violate PRF security of $HMAC^{\leftrightarrows}$ by using K_1, K_1' as messages: it calls its oracle on K_1 and K_1' and declares "real" if the outputs are the same and "random" otherwise.

While this disallows an unqualified assumption of swap-PRF security on HMAC, it does not negatively impact the security of any of the aforementioned usages of HMAC as a swap-PRF. This is because, in those uses, the HMAC keys (messages for $HMAC^{\leftrightarrows}$) are limited in some way, for example prescribed to be of a fixed length, and this precludes the trivial weak-key pairs exploited above. So the question of practical significance that emerges is whether we can prove security in these cases.

SWAP-PRF SECURITY OF HMAC[$\mathcal{S}$]. To formalize the question, let HMAC[$\mathcal{S}$]: $\mathcal{S} \times \{0,1\}^* \rightarrow \{0,1\}^c$ denote the restriction of HMAC to keys from a set $\mathcal{S} \subseteq \{0,1\}^*$. Then the question is, for what choices of $\mathcal{S}$ can we prove swap-PRF security of HMAC[$\mathcal{S}$]? We answer this question by giving a complete characterization of the class of sets $\mathcal{S}$ for which swap-PRF security of HMAC[$\mathcal{S}$] holds. We restrict the attention to sets that are length closed, meaning if $L \in \mathcal{S}$ then $\{0,1\}^{|L|} \subseteq \mathcal{S}$, a natural condition desirable for applications. Now define $\mathcal{S}$ to be *feasible* if either (1) $\mathcal{S} = \{0,1\}^\ell$ for some $\ell \leq b$ or (2) $\mathcal{S}$ contains no strings of length $\leq b$. Then, in Sect. 6, we show:

> HMAC[$\mathcal{S}$] is swap-PRF secure **if and only if** $\mathcal{S}$ is feasible.

The "if" is proven (Theorem 9), under assumptions on h discussed below, and the "only if" is shown by attacks (in the full version [3]).

ASSUMPTIONS. Indifferentiability results on HMAC [24] will imply swap-PRF security of HMAC[$\mathcal{S}$] for $\mathcal{S}$ the set of all keys of a fixed length $\ell < b$, but these results are in the random-oracle model, meaning they assume a truly random compression function. However, as noted above, prior proofs [5,6,8,28] have shown (conventional) PRF security of NMAC and $HMAC_b$ in the *standard model* while making assumptions *only on the compression function* h. Ideally, one would do the same in proofs of swap-PRF security. Our proofs for the "if" above meet this bar. For any feasible $\mathcal{S}$, Theorem 9 establishes swap-PRF security of HMAC[$\mathcal{S}$] under three assumptions on h. The first two are from the prior works [5,6,8,28] and can be considered standard, namely that h is PRF secure and collision resistant (CR). Now recall that the proof of PRF security of $HMAC_b$ from [5,6] assumes $h^{\leftrightarrows}$ is a PRF under related-key attack (rka) as defined in [10], for a related-key-deriving (RKD) function we denote Φ_{io}. Our third assumption,

Table 1. Summary of prior results (in the single-user setting) and our (multi-user) results proving security for HMAC_b, HMAC, $\mathsf{HMAC}[\mathcal{S}]$, and NMAC, as well as results supporting assumptions made for these.

Function	Goal	Assumptions	Comments
HMAC_b	PRF	h is PRF, $\mathsf{h}^{\leftrightarrows}$ is $\varPhi_{\mathsf{io}}$-rka-PRF	[5,6]
HMAC	vkl-PRF	h is PRF, $\mathsf{h}^{\leftrightarrows}$ is PRF, $\mathsf{h}^{\leftrightarrows}$ is $\varPhi_{\mathsf{zio},a}$-rka-PRF	Theorem 8
$\mathsf{HMAC}[\mathcal{S}]^{\leftrightarrows}$ (for $\mathcal{S}$ feasible)	vkl-PRF	h is PRF, $\mathsf{h}^{\leftrightarrows}$ is $\varPhi_{\mathsf{pad},a}$-rka-PRF, h is CR	Theorem 9
NMAC	PRF	h is PRF	[5,6,28], Theorem 4
$\mathsf{NMAC}^{\leftrightarrows}$	vkl-PRF	h is PRF, $\mathsf{h}^{\leftrightarrows}$ is $\varPhi_{\mathsf{pad},a}$-rka-PRF	Theorem 3
$\mathsf{h}^{\leftrightarrows}$	$\varPhi$-rka-PRF	E is $\varPhi$-rka-PRP	[3]

in the same vein, also assumes rka-PRF security of $\mathsf{h}^{\leftrightarrows}$, but for a different RKD function $\varPhi_{\mathsf{pad},a}$. Roughly, the function $\varPhi_{\mathsf{pad},a}$ allows the adversary to overwrite a suffix of length at most $b - a$ bits of the b-bit key with padding. The assumption is new but we will validate it through auxiliary proofs. Intuitively it arises because key material of length $\ell < b$ can now be part of the message, which is padded to block length. We summarize the assumptions in Table 1.

1.3   PRF Security of HMAC

We turn next to the other side of dual-PRF security, asking about the (conventional) PRF security of HMAC.

THE GAP. There appears at first to be no question here; PRF security of HMAC is broadly assumed and seen as established in prior work [5,6,8,28]. There is, however, a noteworthy gap in prior results, namely that they only prove security with keys of full block length. More precisely, in the notation introduced above, what is proved in [5,6] is PRF security of HMAC_b, not HMAC itself. Yet, in practice, HMAC is almost never used with b bit keys. Take for example HMAC-256, i.e., HMAC instantiated with SHA-256: Its output is $c = 256$ bits long. When using it in a protocol for key derivation, it is hence natural to use 256-bit keys throughout. However, the block length of SHA-256 is $b = 512$, meaning that 256-bit keys lead to HMAC being keyed with keys of length *less* than the block length. This is precisely what is done in protocols like TLS [44], meaning that even their usage of HMAC as a regular PRF falls outside of the security guarantees provided in the literature.

FILLING THE GAP. Theorem 8 proves PRF security of HMAC with keys of *any* (sufficiently large, of course) length. With regard to assumptions, recall that those made for PRF security of HMAC_b were that h is PRF secure and $\mathsf{h}^{\leftrightarrows}$ is $\varPhi_{\mathsf{io}}$-rka-PRF secure. We likewise assume that h is PRF secure and $\mathsf{h}^{\leftrightarrows}$ is $\varPhi_{\mathsf{zio},a}$-rka-PRF secure, for a function $\varPhi_{\mathsf{zio},a}$ that allows the adversary to overwrite an at most $b - a$ bits long suffix of the b-bit key with zeroes (cf. $\varPhi_{\mathsf{pad},a}$ for our $\mathsf{HMAC}^{\leftrightarrows}$ result) and then to XOR with ipad or opad. This again arises because of key material of length $\ell < b$ bits, to which (in contrast to $\mathsf{HMAC}^{\leftrightarrows}$) the XOR is applied in HMAC. As before we will validate the new assumption through auxiliary proofs. We clarify that unlike in the swap-PRF case, here there is no restriction of the keys or messages to some subset $\mathcal{S}$; for both keys and messages, any length is allowed, as per the definition of the full HMAC.

1.4   Auxiliary Contributions and Technical Overview

We obtain the above results via a modular approach that treats swap and conventional PRF security in a unified way. Along the way we give some definitions and auxiliary results of independent interest.

VKL-PRFS, A NEW DEFINITION. Recall that the definition of $\mathsf{F}\colon \mathcal{X} \times \mathcal{Y} \to \mathcal{Z}$ being PRF secure picks a key $X \leftarrow_\$ \mathcal{X}$ at random. But for $\mathsf{HMAC}\colon \{0,1\}^* \times \{0,1\}^* \to \{0,1\}^c$, the keyspace, $\{0,1\}^*$, contains keys of many different lengths and it is not clear under what distribution a random one would be chosen. The first and natural answer, and the one assumed above, is that one has fixed a key length ℓ and is drawing a key from $\{0,1\}^\ell$ at random. But this fails to capture different users using HMAC with keys of different lengths, which occurs in practice. These considerations lead us to introduce (in Sect. 3) a new definition, of a *variable key-length* PRF (vkl-PRF). The definition is inherently in the multi-user setting. The adversary can, for each user, adaptively pick a key length, and the game initializes the key for that user to a uniformly random string of the chosen length. The rest is as one would expect from the usual multi-user PRF setting [9]. (A subtle point is that we cannot expect security for too-short keys. This is handled by having theorems assume a minimum key length.)

Our proof of PRF security for HMAC (Theorem 8) actually proves vkl-PRF security. For swap-PRF security for $\mathsf{HMAC}[\mathcal{S}]$, Theorem 9 likewise proves vkl-PRF security of $\mathsf{HMAC}[\mathcal{S}]^{\leftrightarrows}\colon \{0,1\}^* \times \mathcal{S} \to \{0,1\}^c$. This means that in both cases we give a guarantee that is strong and better models real-world usage, namely that security holds even when different users use keys of different and adaptively-chosen lengths.

RESULTS FOR NMAC. As in prior works, we start with NMAC (Sect. 5). Beginning with the swap case, we prove in Theorem 3 that $\mathsf{NMAC}^{\leftrightarrows}\colon \{0,1\}^* \times \{0,1\}^{2c} \to \{0,1\}^c$ is vkl-PRF secure. Unlike for $\mathsf{HMAC}[\mathcal{S}]^{\leftrightarrows}$, this NMAC result involves no restrictions of inputs to any set $\mathcal{S}$, but rather holds for all inputs for which the function is defined. The assumptions made are PRF security of h and $\varPhi_{\mathsf{pad},a}$-rka-PRF security of $\mathsf{h}^{\leftrightarrows}$, with the proof leveraging a lemma (Lemma 1) that we give on the strong multi-user PRF security of the 2-tier cascade defined in [7]. Due to targeting vkl-PRF security, the result is directly in the multi-user setting, and the bound in Theorem 3 is good. That is, it does not degrade with the number of users.

Turning now to the conventional PRF security of NMAC, the proofs in prior works [5,6,8,28] are for the single-user setting, and it has remained open if one can show security in the multi-user setting with a bound that does not degrade with the number of users. We resolve this and give such a proof (Theorem 4). We follow the approach used in GPR [28] to prove single-user security, but while the latter relied on a lemma on random systems from [40], we give a quite simple, self-contained game-playing proof, establishing multi-user security.

A DUAL COMPOSITION THEOREM. To lift the above results to HMAC, we give a dual composition theorem (Theorem 5, in Sect. 6). $\mathsf{HMAC}(X, Y)$ can be seen as deriving keys $X_i \| X_o \leftarrow \mathsf{HSKD}(X)$ for NMAC via a key-derivation function HSKD (shown in Fig. 3) and then returning $\mathsf{NMAC}(X_i \| X_o, Y)$. We write this as HMAC $= \mathbf{Comp}[\mathsf{NMAC}, \mathsf{HSKD}]$. Theorem 5 implies that (1) if NMAC is PRF secure and HSKD is a variable seed-length (vsl) PRG, then $\mathsf{HMAC} = \mathbf{Comp}[\mathsf{NMAC}, \mathsf{HSKD}]$ is vkl-PRF secure, and (2) if $\mathsf{NMAC}^{\leftrightarrows}$ is vkl-PRF secure, and the restriction $\mathsf{HSKD}[\mathcal{S}]$ of HSKD to inputs in set $\mathcal{S}$ is collision resistant, then $\mathsf{HMAC}[\mathcal{S}]^{\leftrightarrows} = \mathbf{Comp}[\mathsf{NMAC}, \mathsf{HSKD}[\mathcal{S}]]^{\leftrightarrows}$ is vkl-PRF secure.

Let us explain. It is folklore understanding that the composition preserves PRF security assuming PRG security of the key-derivation. Result (1) casts this in our variable key-length setting, which involves introducing the definition of a vsl-PRG, but we see the result as expected. Result (2) is more interesting, saying that the composition equally well preserves swap-PRF security if we switch the assumption on key-derivation to collision resistance Put together, we get a simply-stated, unified result, saying that the composition preserves dual-PRF security assuming key-derivation is a collision-resistant PRG.

SECURITY OF THE HSKD KEY-DERIVATION FUNCTION. To complete the circle we need to establish the security assumed of HSKD in the composition theorems, which we also do in Sect. 6. Proposition 6 shows vsl-PRG security of HSKD assuming PRF security of h and $\mathsf{h}^{\leftrightarrows}$, and $\Phi_{\mathsf{zio},a}$-rka-PRF security of $\mathsf{h}^{\leftrightarrows}$. The function is *not* collision resistant on its full domain (leading to the above-discussed attacks on the swap-PRF security of HMAC), but Proposition 7 shows collision resistance of $\mathsf{HSKD}[\mathcal{S}]$ for all feasible $\mathcal{S}$, assuming collision resistance of h. Putting all the above together gives our results on the PRF and swap-PRF security of HMAC.

VALIDATION OF RKA-PRF ASSUMPTIONS ON $\mathsf{h}^{\leftrightarrows}$. HMAC is mainly used with the SHA-256, SHA-384, and SHA-512 hash functions. Here the compression function is a Davies–Meyer one, $\mathsf{h}(X, L) = \mathsf{E}(L, X) \oplus X$ for a block cipher $\mathsf{E}: \{0,1\}^b \times \{0,1\}^c \to \{0,1\}^c$. Resistance to related-key attacks is a commonly studied goal for block ciphers, see e.g. [4,10,13–15,17,18,26,32,34–36,43,51], so we ask if this assumption implies ours. Curiously, being in the swap setting helps us here and enables such a reduction, because the key when considering rka-PRF security of $\mathsf{h}^{\leftrightarrows}$ is L, which is the message for h, which then becomes the key for E. Exploiting this, we show in the full version [3] that if E is Φ-rka-PRP secure, then $\mathsf{h}^{\leftrightarrows}$ is also Φ-rka-PRF secure.

These results are strengthened by introducing (in Sect. 3) an extension of the single-user rka-PRF/PRP definitions of [10] to a multi-user setting; the novel element is that the RKD functions have a user-dependent input. Finally, one must be careful that, due to attacks from [10], Φ-rka-PRP security of the block cipher E does not hold for all Φ, so we need to verify it for the functions we introduce and use. This final step is done through an analysis that models E as an ideal cipher. We stress that idealized assumptions are made only on E and limited to this one step; all other security proofs are in the standard model.

Organization. Sect. 2 provides a more extensive discussion of related work. Section 3 introduces notation and definitions (including our new vkl-PRF notion). Section 4 introduces the modularization of HMAC functions we use in our analysis, as well as some basic results on cascades of h. We then turn to our main results. Section 5 studies the dual-PRF security of NMAC. Based on this, Sect. 6 takes on the dual-PRF security of HMAC, along the way establishing the necessary properties of the subkey derivation function HSKD, including the characterization of the feasible key sets for which HMAC is swap-PRF secure.

2   Related Work

DUAL-PRF ASSUMPTIONS ON HMAC. Several works [16,21,22,25,33,46,49] (as indicated above) have explicitly or implicitly assumed dual-PRF security of HMAC. For example, for TLS 1.3, [25, Section 2.4] says "we however need to deploy stronger assumptions which we recap here. The first assumption is concerned with the use of HMAC as a dual PRF (cf. [5,6])." While the cited paper [5,6] introduces dual-PRF security, it does not establish swap-PRF security for HMAC, and as we noted, not even conventional PRF security for all key sizes. For KEMTLS, SSW [46], in the context of their proof of Theorem 4.1, perform game hops "under the PRF-security or dual-PRF-security [5,6] of HKDF", the latter in this mode is HMAC. In the full version [3], we give an account of where dual-PRF assumptions on HMAC show up in prior work and when they are supported by our results.

HKDF. The extraction mode of Krawczyk's HKDF [38] uses HMAC with a salt as first input and key material as second input. This has computational extraction properties under certain assumptions, including that the first input (the salt) is random [38]. However, it does not justify key-combiner usage of HMAC in protocols, because here the first input to HMAC may be adversarially influenced. Swap-PRF security of HMAC, in contrast, allows the first input to be adversarially chosen. This is where swap and dual-PRF security shows up in protocols built on HKDF, motivating our study.

We note that in HKDF's extraction mode, the key-material in the second input may be a non-uniformly-distributed source of entropy such as a Diffie–Hellman shared secret in a key exchange protocol, and HMAC is supposed to return a computationally uniform key. Our results do not cover such usage; in dual-PRF security, keys are assumed to be uniformly distributed.

MULTI-USER SECURITY. The setting of protocols like TLS involves many users and it is well understood that this is better modeled by multi-user (mu) security than by single-user security (su). For most primitives, su implies mu via a hybrid argument, but the adversary advantage grows by a factor of the number u of users [39]. This has led to dedicated analyses and schemes for many primitives, aiming to show mu security with good bounds, meaning degradation of the advantage with u is avoided [7,20,31]. Our work follows this, aiming for, and obtaining, good bounds in the mu setting. In particular we fill a gap in the literature by showing PRF security of NMAC with good mu bounds in Theorem 4. We also show vkl-prf of HMAC with good mu bounds in Theorem 8.

UNIFORM AND NON-UNIFORM ASSUMPTIONS. The conference version of Bellare's work [5] showed (su) PRF security of NMAC and HMAC (with good bounds) assuming PRF security of the compression function against non-uniform adversaries. The journal version [6] added proofs under uniform assumptions but with a degraded bound. The gap was filled by Gaži, Pietrzak and Rybár [28], who showed (su) PRF security with bounds as good as in [5] but under uniform assumptions. All our results use uniform assumptions and are shown with black-box reductions. The proofs explicitly build adversaries against the assumptions from the given adversary against the target.

BUILDING NEW DUAL-PRFS. A new template for building dual-PRFs was given in BL [11]. It combines a computational extractor with a collision-resistant function and can be instantiated to obtain dual-PRFs assuming collision-resistant functions or One-Way Permutations (OWP)s. The BL template was extended in ADKPRY [2] to add an output transformation, leading to further instantiations. However, what is in use in the real world as a dual-PRF is HMAC and thus we focus on it rather than on new constructions. We note that determining the dual-PRF security of HMAC is stated as an open question in ADKPRY [2] and resolved in our work.

On the theoretical side, while the existence of One-Way Functions (OWF)s is known to imply the existence of PRFs [30], it is not known whether OWFs imply dual-PRFs. This is an intriguing open question.

3   Notation and Definitions

We recall some notation, including for game-playing, recap some standard definitions, and then give our new ones, namely variable key-length PRFs (vkl-PRFs), variable seed-length PRGs (vsl-PRGs) and multi-user rka-PRF security.

3.1   Notation and Conventions

Let $\mathbb{N} = \{0, 1, 2, \ldots\}$ be the set of non-negative integers. Let ε be the empty string. For $n \in \mathbb{N}$ let $\{0,1\}^n$ be the set of all strings of length n, $\{0,1\}^{>n}$ the set of all strings of length greater than n, and let $\{0,1\}^*$ be the set of all strings of any length $n \geq 0$. For $b \in \mathbb{N}$ let $\{0,1\}^{b*} = \{X \in \{0,1\}^* : |X| \bmod b = 0\}$ be the set of all strings whose length is a multiple of b. If a is a string, then $|a|$ denotes its length, $a[i]$ denotes its i-th bit and $a[i..j] = a[i]\ldots a[j]$. (The last is the empty string ε when $j < i$.) Similarly, if $\mathbf{X}$ is a vector then $|\mathbf{X}|$ denotes its length (the number of its coordinates) and $\mathbf{X}[i]$ its i-th element. The empty vector has length 0 and is also written ε. We let $\mathbf{X}[1..i]$ denote $(\mathbf{X}[1], \ldots, \mathbf{X}[i])$ for $1 \leq i \leq |\mathbf{X}|$. If $i = 0$ then $\mathbf{X}[1..i] = \varepsilon$. For a string $A \in \{0,1\}^{b*}$ the operator $\xleftarrow{b}$ splits it into b-bit blocks and places them in a vector. For example, if $|A| \geq 2b$, then $\mathbf{X} \xleftarrow{b} A$ results in $\mathbf{X}[1] = A[1..b]$ and $\mathbf{X}[2] = A[b+1..2b]$, etc.

We say that a set $\mathcal{S} \subseteq \{0,1\}^*$ is *length closed* if for every $n \in \mathbb{N}$ it is the case that $\mathcal{S} \cap \{0,1\}^n$ is either $\{0,1\}^n$ or $\emptyset$. This condition is made on key and message spaces. For sets $\mathcal{S}_1$ and $\mathcal{S}_2$, let $\mathsf{FUNC}[\mathcal{S}_1, \mathcal{S}_2]$ denote the set of all functions $f \colon \mathcal{S}_1 \to \mathcal{S}_2$ and $\mathsf{PERM}[\mathcal{S}_1]$ the set of all permutations on $\mathcal{S}_1$. The shorthand $\mathcal{S}_1 \xleftarrow{\cup} \mathcal{S}_2$ denotes $\mathcal{S}_1 \leftarrow \mathcal{S}_1 \cup \mathcal{S}_2$.

For a finite set S, we let $x \leftarrow_\$ S$ denote sampling x uniformly at random from S. We let $y \leftarrow A(x_1, \ldots; r)$ denote executing algorithm A on inputs $x_1, \ldots$ and coins r and letting y be the result. We let $y \leftarrow_\$ A(x_1, \ldots)$ be the result of picking r at random and letting $y \leftarrow A(x_1, \ldots; r)$. Algorithms are randomized unless otherwise indicated. Running time is worst case.

We use the code-based game playing framework of [12]. (See Fig. 1 for an example.) Games have procedures, also called oracles, with INIT and FINALIZE being optional. In executing an adversary $\mathcal{A}$ with a game G, oracle INIT, if present, executes first. Then the adversary, given the outputs of INIT, can query other oracles at will. If FINALIZE is present, only one query to it is allowed, and this must be the last query the adversary makes. The output of the execution is defined as the output of FINALIZE if the latter is present and the output of the adversary otherwise. By $\mathrm{G}(\mathcal{A}) \Rightarrow y$ we denote the event that the execution of game G with adversary $\mathcal{A}$ results in output y. We write $\Pr[\mathrm{G}(\mathcal{A})]$ as shorthand for $\Pr[\mathrm{G}(\mathcal{A}) \Rightarrow 1]$, the probability that the execution returns 1. We write $\mathbf{Q}^{\mathrm{OR}}(\mathcal{A})$ for the number of queries made by adversary $\mathcal{A}$ to an oracle OR in the game with which $\mathcal{A}$ is executed. Our convention is that running time of an adversary executed with some game includes the time for the game procedures to respond to oracle queries.

In writing game or adversary pseudocode, it is assumed that Boolean variables are initialized to 0, integer variables are initialized to 0, and set-valued variables are initialized to the empty set $\emptyset$. The distinguished symbol $\perp$ stands for "undefined" and is used as a placeholder value for uninitialized variables and to signal errors. Table entries are assumed initialized to $\perp$. Let $[[\mathrm{cond}]]$ denote the boolean (1 or 0) result of evaluating condition cond. For example, $[[d^* = 1]]$ returns 1 if variable d^* equals 1, and 0 otherwise.

3.2   Standard Definitions

COLLISION RESISTANCE. A collision for a function $\mathsf{F} \colon \mathcal{X} \to \mathcal{Y}$ is a pair of distinct points $X, X' \in \mathcal{X}$ such that $\mathsf{F}(X) = \mathsf{F}(X')$. Let game $\mathbf{G}_\mathsf{F}^{\mathrm{CR}}$ consist only of procedure FINALIZE that given $X, X' \in \mathcal{X}$, returns 1 if X, X' are a collision for F, and 0 otherwise. We define the advantage of an adversary $\mathcal{A}$ against the CR security of F as $\mathbf{Adv}_\mathsf{F}^{\mathrm{CR}}(\mathcal{A}) = \Pr[\mathbf{G}_\mathsf{F}^{\mathrm{CR}}(\mathcal{A})]$. The probability is over the coins of the adversary.

To accurately model cryptographic hash functions like SHA-256, SHA-384, SHA-512, which are keyless, our syntax is also keyless. The theoretical issue of

Game $\mathbf{G}_F^{\text{PRF-}d}$:	Game $\mathbf{G}_F^{\text{vkl-PRF-}d}$:	Game $\mathbf{G}_G^{\text{vsl-PRG-}d}$:
NEW	NEW(ℓ)	FN(ℓ)
1 $n \leftarrow n + 1$	1 Assert: $\ell \in \text{F.KL}$	1 Assert $\ell \in \text{G.KL}$
2 $X_n \leftarrow\!\!\$\; \mathcal{X}$	2 $n \leftarrow n + 1$	2 $s \leftarrow\!\!\$\; \{0,1\}^\ell$;
	3 $\ell_n \leftarrow \ell$; $X_n \leftarrow\!\!\$\; \{0,1\}^\ell$	$r_1 \leftarrow G(s)$
		3 $r_0 \leftarrow\!\!\$\; \mathcal{R}$
FN(i, Y)	FN(i, Y)	4 Return r_d
3 If $T[i, Y] = \bot$ then:	4 If $T[i, Y] = \bot$ then:	
4 If $d = 1$ then:	5 If $d = 1$ then:	
5 $T[i, Y] \leftarrow F(X_i, Y)$	6 $T[i, Y] \leftarrow F(X_i, Y)$	
6 Else $T[i, Y] \leftarrow\!\!\$\; \mathcal{Z}$	7 Else $T[i, Y] \leftarrow\!\!\$\; \mathcal{Z}$	
7 Return $T[i, Y]$	8 Return $T[i, Y]$	

Fig. 1. Left and middle: PRF and variable key-length PRF security games ($d \in \{0,1\}$) for function family $F: \mathcal{X} \times \mathcal{Y} \to \mathcal{Z}$. **Right:** Variable seed-length PRG games ($d \in \{0,1\}$) for PRG $G: \mathcal{S} \to \mathcal{R}$.

existence of an adversary that violates CR security by hard-wiring a collision into its code is circumvented in the usual way. Namely, those of our results which assume CR of some F give explicit constructions of CR adversaries based on the given adversary, so a practical attack against the scheme leads to a practical attack against F. This was popularized as the "human ignorance" approach in [45].

PRFs. Let $F: \mathcal{X} \times \mathcal{Y} \to \mathcal{Z}$ be a function: family, where $\mathcal{X}$ and $\mathcal{Y}$ are length closed sets. We recall the definition of it being a PRF via the games on the left of Fig. 1. They are parameterized by a bit $d \in \{0,1\}$, with $d = 1$ indicating the "real" game and $d = 0$ the "random" game. We let $\mathbf{Adv}_F^{\text{PRF}}(\mathcal{A}) = \Pr[\mathbf{G}_F^{\text{PRF-1}}(\mathcal{A})] - \Pr[\mathbf{G}_F^{\text{PRF-0}}(\mathcal{A})]$ be its advantage. This definition is in the multi-user setting [9], with the original single-user setting [29] recovered by considering adversaries making only one NEW query.

3.3 New Definitions

VKL-PRFs. We extend the usual definition of PRF security to allow keys of variable, adversary-determined length, in the multi-user setting. Let $F: \mathcal{X} \times \mathcal{Y} \to \mathcal{Z}$ be a function family as above, where $\mathcal{X}$ and $\mathcal{Y}$ are length closed sets. Consider games $\mathbf{G}_F^{\text{vkl-PRF}}$ in the middle of Fig. 1, parameterized by $d \in \{0,1\}$ as above. The advantage of an adversary $\mathcal{A}$ is defined as $\mathbf{Adv}_F^{\text{vkl-PRF}}(\mathcal{A}) = \Pr[\mathbf{G}_F^{\text{vkl-PRF-1}}(\mathcal{A})] - \Pr[\mathbf{G}_F^{\text{vkl-PRF-0}}(\mathcal{A})]$. Let us now explain. The game is in the multi-user setting. By calling NEW with a length ℓ, the adversary initializes a new user with a key whose length ℓ is determined by the adversary. The game checks that ℓ is in the set of *allowed key lengths* F.KL, which we define to be $\text{F.KL} = \{\ell : \{0,1\}^\ell \cap \mathcal{X} \neq \emptyset\}$. That is, F.KL is the set of integers which appears as lengths of keys in the key space of F. The FN oracle as usual allows the adversary to obtain either results of F on a chosen message under a previously initialized key, or random strings. Note that the lengths of keys can be determined by the adversary adaptively.

MINIMAL AND MAXIMAL KEY LENGTH. The vkl-PRF game allows keys of any length. In particular, it does not preclude even a one-bit key, as long as such keys are in the keyspace of F. But clearly, if very short keys are allowed, no practically useful security is achieved. This is not a problem with the definition or to be dealt with here; it is handled, rather, in theorems. There, we will as usual consider various resource parameters for an adversary $\mathcal{A}$, such as the number of queries to the oracles. Now, additionally, there will be a *minimal key length* $\ell_{min}(\mathcal{A})$, defined as the shortest ℓ for which it makes a NEW(ℓ) query. Bounds in the theorem statement will be a function of $\ell_{min}(\mathcal{A})$. In practice, we would then ask that applications use key lengths for which the bounds are good, which in particular will dictate large-enough choices of minimal key length. We may also speak of a *maximal key length*, denoted $\ell_{max}(\mathcal{A})$, of a given adversary, which affects the resources of adversaries constructed from it.

VSL-PRGS. A variable seed-length pseudorandom generator (PRG) is a function $G : \mathcal{S} \to \mathcal{R}$. We assume that the seed space $\mathcal{S}$ is length closed and let the set of allowed seed lengths of G be $G.KL = \{\ell : \{0,1\}^\ell \cap \mathcal{S} \neq \emptyset\}$.

Analogously to vkl-PRF security, we extend the usual definition of PRG security [19,50] to allow seeds of variable, adversary-determined length. The games defining this new notion are on the right of Fig. 1, again for $d \in \{0,1\}$. We let the advantage of an adversary $\mathcal{A}$ against the vsl-PRG security of G be defined as $\mathbf{Adv}_G^{vsl\text{-}PRG}(\mathcal{A}) = \Pr[\mathbf{G}_G^{vsl\text{-}PRG\text{-}1}(\mathcal{A})] - \Pr[\mathbf{G}_G^{vsl\text{-}PRG\text{-}0}(\mathcal{A})]$.

As for vkl-PRFs, the vsl-PRG security provided by G in some usage will depend crucially on the length of the shortest allowed seed. To quantify, we define the *minimal seed length* $\ell_{min}(\mathcal{A})$ of an adversary $\mathcal{A}$ to be the shortest ℓ for which the adversary makes a FN(ℓ) query. Also the *maximal seed length* $\ell_{max}(\mathcal{A})$, defined as the longest ℓ for which the adversary makes a FN(ℓ) query, will arise in resource considerations.

RKA DEFINITIONS. We extend the definitions of PRF and PRP security under related-key attacks [10] (rka-PRF resp. rka-PRP) to the multi-user setting, beginning with rka-PRF.

Let $F: \mathcal{X} \times \mathcal{Y} \to \mathcal{Z}$ be a function family, and $\Phi : \Lambda_1 \times \Lambda_2 \times \mathcal{X} \to \mathcal{X} \cup \{\bot\}$ a function. We call Φ the *related-key-deriving* function. It takes as input two parameters, which specify the transformation that will be applied to the key $X \in \mathcal{X}$. The multi-user aspect is captured by the first parameter, $\alpha \in \Lambda_1$, which will depend on the user. The second parameter $\beta \in \Lambda_2$ in turn specifies the function within the function family belonging to each user. Mapping back to [10], for each $\alpha \in \Lambda_1$ and $\beta \in \Lambda_2$, we let $\Phi_{\alpha,\beta} : \mathcal{X} \to \mathcal{X}$ be the related-key deriving function $\Phi(\alpha, \beta, \cdot)$.

The rka-PRF security game $\mathbf{G}_{\Phi,F}^{rka\text{-}PRF\text{-}d}$ ($d \in \{0,1\}$) shown in Fig. 2, provides the adversary with two oracles: NEW and FN. Oracle NEW takes as input $\alpha \in \Lambda_1$, setting the RKD parameter α_i associated to the new user instance i. Oracle FN

Game $\mathbf{G}_{\Phi,\mathsf{F}}^{\text{rka-PRF-}d}$:	Game $\mathbf{G}_{\Phi,\mathsf{E}}^{\text{rka-PRP-}d}$:
NEW(α)	NEW(α)
1 $n \leftarrow n+1$; $X_n \leftarrow\!\!\$\ \mathcal{X}$; $\alpha_n \leftarrow \alpha$	1 $n \leftarrow n+1$; $L_n \leftarrow\!\!\$\ \mathcal{K}$; $\alpha_n \leftarrow \alpha$
	2 For all $L \in \mathcal{K}$ do:
FN(i, β, Y)	3 $\quad \Pi_{n,L} \leftarrow\!\!\$\ \mathsf{PERM}[\mathcal{X}]$
2 Assert: $\Phi_{\alpha_i,\beta}(X_i) \neq \bot$	
3 $X' \leftarrow \Phi_{\alpha_i,\beta}(X_i)$ // Derived key	FN(i, β, X)
4 If $\mathrm{T}[i, X', Y] \neq \bot$ then:	4 Assert: $\Phi_{\alpha_i,\beta}(L_i) \neq \bot$
5 $\quad$ Return $\mathrm{T}[i, X', Y]$	5 $L' \leftarrow \Phi_{\alpha_i,\beta}(L_i)$ // Derived key
6 If $d = 1$ then: $\mathrm{T}[i, X', Y] \leftarrow \mathsf{F}(X', Y)$	6 If $d = 1$ then:
7 Else $\mathrm{T}[i, X', Y] \leftarrow\!\!\$\ \mathcal{Z}$	7 $\quad$ Return $\mathsf{E}(L', X)$
8 Return $\mathrm{T}[i, X', Y]$	8 Else return $\Pi_{i,L'}(X)$

Fig. 2. Left: Related-key attack PRF security game ($d \in \{0,1\}$) for function family $\mathsf{F}: \mathcal{X} \times \mathcal{Y} \to \mathcal{Z}$ and RKD function Φ. **Right:** Related-key attack PRP security game ($d \in \{0,1\}$) for a block cipher $\mathsf{E}: \mathcal{K} \times \mathcal{X} \to \mathcal{X}$ and RKD function Φ.

takes as input a user index i, a $\beta \in \Lambda_2$, and a function input $Y \in \mathcal{Y}$. It returns $\mathsf{F}(\Phi_{\alpha_i,\beta}(X_i), Y)$, if $d = 1$ or a consistently sampled random string from $\mathcal{Z}$ if $d = 0$. We define the advantage of an adversary $\mathcal{A}$ against the PRF security under Φ-restricted related-key attacks as $\mathbf{Adv}_{\Phi,\mathsf{F}}^{\text{rka-PRF}}(\mathcal{A}) = \Pr[\mathbf{G}_{\Phi,\mathsf{F}}^{\text{rka-PRF-1}}(\mathcal{A})] - \Pr[\mathbf{G}_{\Phi,\mathsf{F}}^{\text{rka-PRF-0}}(\mathcal{A})]$.

Analogously, we extend the single-user rka-PRP definition from [10] to the multi-user/key setting. For a block cipher $\mathsf{E}: \mathcal{K} \times \mathcal{X} \to \mathcal{X}$, the resulting game $\mathbf{G}_{\Phi,\mathsf{E}}^{\text{rka-PRP-}d}$ ($d \in \{0,1\}$) is shown on the right in Fig. 2, and the corresponding advantage of an adversary $\mathcal{A}$ defined as $\mathbf{Adv}_{\Phi,\mathsf{E}}^{\text{rka-PRP}}(\mathcal{A}) = \Pr[\mathbf{G}_{\Phi,\mathsf{E}}^{\text{rka-PRP-1}}(\mathcal{A})] - \Pr[\mathbf{G}_{\Phi,\mathsf{E}}^{\text{rka-PRP-0}}(\mathcal{A})]$.

4 Background and Modularization of HMAC

Our analyses rely on seeing HMAC as built from lower-level functions in a particular modular way. Here we present this view of HMAC. Then we state results on some tools that we will use in our proofs.

PADDING. We fix integers c, b representing the chaining-variable length and block length, respectively, and assume $b > c$. HMAC-related functions may pad inputs to lengths a multiple of b. We discuss the padding in some detail because it matters to ensure that the modular and standard definitions of HMAC are indeed the same. Also it needs to be handled explicitly in analyses of swap-PRF security. (This was not the case for prior analyses of PRF security [5,6,8,28].)

We fix a padding function pad, parameterized by a maximum encoding length $le \in \mathbb{N}$. Function pad takes as input a length $\ell < 2^{le}$ and returns a string $\mathsf{pad}(\ell)$ such that $\ell + |\mathsf{pad}(\ell)|$ is a positive multiple of b. The canonical method is $\mathsf{pad}(\ell) = 10^*\langle\ell\rangle$ where $\langle\ell\rangle$ is the encoding of integer ℓ in le bits and 0^* denotes the minimum number i of zeros to ensure that $\ell + 1 + i + le$ is a multiple of b, where the length encoding le is another parameter. Thus $|\mathsf{pad}(\ell)|$ is always in the range $\{1 + le, \ldots, b + le\}$. For $X \in \{0,1\}^*$ we denote by $\overline{X} = X \| \mathsf{pad}(|X|) \in \{0,1\}^{b*}$.

Concretely, for SHA-256, the parameters are $(c, b, le) = (256, 512, 64)$ and for SHA-384 and SHA-512 they are $(c, b, le) = (512, 1024, 128)$. We assume $b - c > le$, as is true for SHA-256, SHA-384, and SHA-512, so that if $|M| \bmod b \leq c$ then for any ℓ its padded version $M \| \mathsf{pad}(\ell)$ is $\lceil |M|/b \rceil$ blocks long, meaning no extra block of padding is created. In particular, if $|M| \leq c$ then $M \| \mathsf{pad}(\ell)$ is just one block, which is relevant in ensuring that the modular form of HMAC written below matches with the original.

MESSAGE AND KEY LENGTHS. The upper limit of le on the binary length of an input ℓ to pad means that the maximum length of an input to the hash function H is $Le = 2^{le}$. This translates into restrictions on the maximum length of both keys and messages for HMAC. However in practice Le is very large (at least 2^{64} in the above examples), making this a theoretical limitation. Thus, in the remainder of this paper we write $\{0,1\}^*$ for domains of functions that are actually limited to inputs of lengths Le. It is understood that in any theorems about these functions, there is an implicit assumption that adversary queries do not exceed the maximum allowed lengths.

MODULARIZATION OF HMAC FUNCTIONS. The starting point is a compression function $\mathsf{h} \colon \{0,1\}^c \times \{0,1\}^b \to \{0,1\}^c$ taking a c-bit chaining variable and b-bit block to return a c-bit result. Figure 3 now specifies various functions that we will consider; for an illustration of how we modularize HMAC, see also Fig. 4.

The cascade $\mathsf{h}^* \colon \{0,1\}^c \times \{0,1\}^{b*} \to \{0,1\}^c$ [9] takes a c-bit key L and an input S whose length is assumed a multiple of b, and returns a c-bit output as shown. Note that $S = \varepsilon$ could be the empty string, in which case $n = 0$ in the code and thus what is returned is C_0, meaning $\mathsf{h}^*(L, \varepsilon) = L$.

Fixing an initial vector $\mathtt{IV} \in \{0,1\}^c$, one can then define the hash function $\mathsf{H} \colon \{0,1\}^* \to \{0,1\}^c$ as per the Merkle–Damgård transform [23,42].

Next is NMAC: $\{0,1\}^{2c} \times \{0,1\}^{b*} \to \{0,1\}^c$ [8], an abstraction useful in the study of HMAC. Its $2c$-bit key is viewed as split into an "inner" key K_i and "outer" key K_o. Here $M \in \{0,1\}^*$ needs to be padded to length a multiple of b to run h^*. The obvious padding $\overline{M}$ would append $\mathsf{pad}(|M|)$. Instead, we define NMAC to pad M with $\mathsf{pad}(b + |M|)$ and similarly pad X with $\mathsf{pad}(b + c)$ rather than $\mathsf{pad}(c)$. As explained below, this is to accurately capture HMAC_b and HMAC, where the b-bit keys are prepended to the message resp. X, adding to the overall hash function input length. We note that traditionally NMAC has been defined and analyzed as taking unpadded messages in $\{0,1\}^{b*}$ [5,6,8,28], which is sufficient when considering PRF security, but for swap-PRF security the padding will matter.

The first, basic version of HMAC is $\mathsf{HMAC}_b \colon \{0,1\}^b \times \{0,1\}^* \to \{0,1\}^c$ which takes a b-bit key K_b. It is defined as $\mathsf{HMAC}_b(K_b, M) = \mathsf{H}((K_b \oplus \mathsf{opad}) \| \mathsf{H}((K_b \oplus \mathsf{ipad}) \| M))$, where $\mathsf{ipad}, \mathsf{opad} \in \{0,1\}^b$ are distinct constants defined in [8,37, 47]. The modular rendition first applies the shown subkey derivation function $\mathsf{HSKD}_b \colon \{0,1\}^b \to \{0,1\}^{2c}$ to the key and then calls NMAC on the derived keys

---

$\underline{h^*(L, S)}$ // **Cascade of compression function h**

▷ $h^* : \{0,1\}^c \times \{0,1\}^{b*} \to \{0,1\}^c$

$S \xleftarrow{b} S$; $n \leftarrow |S|$
$C_0 \leftarrow L$; For $i = 1$ to n do: $C_i \leftarrow h(C_{i-1}, S[i])$
Return C_n

$\underline{H(M)}$ // **Hash function H = MD[h]** [23,42]

▷ $H : \{0,1\}^* \to \{0,1\}^c$

Return $h^*(\text{IV}, M \| \text{pad}(|M|))$

$\underline{\text{NMAC}(K_i \| K_o, M)}$ // **NMAC** [8]

▷ $\text{NMAC} : \{0,1\}^{2c} \times \{0,1\}^* \to \{0,1\}^c$

$X \leftarrow h^*(K_i, M \| \text{pad}(b + |M|))$; Return $h(K_o, X \| \text{pad}(b + c))$

$\underline{\text{HSKD}_b(K_b)}$ // **Subkey derivation function of HMAC$_b$**

▷ $\text{HSKD}_b : \{0,1\}^b \to \{0,1\}^{2c}$

$K_i \leftarrow h(\text{IV}, K_b \oplus \text{ipad})$; $K_o \leftarrow h(\text{IV}, K_b \oplus \text{opad})$; Return $K_i \| K_o$

$\underline{\text{HMAC}_b(K_b, M)}$ // **HMAC with b-bit keys** [8]

▷ $\text{HMAC}_b : \{0,1\}^b \times \{0,1\}^* \to \{0,1\}^c$

$K_i \| K_o \leftarrow \text{HSKD}_b(K_b)$; Return $\text{NMAC}(K_i \| K_o, M)$

$\underline{\text{PoH}_b(K)}$ // **Derive a b-bit key for HSKD$_b$ from an HMAC key $K \in \{0,1\}^*$**

▷ $\text{PoH}_b : \{0,1\}^* \to \{0,1\}^b$

If $|K| \le b$ then $K_b \leftarrow K \| 0^{b-|K|}$ else $K_b \leftarrow H(K) \| 0^{b-c}$
Return K_b

$\underline{\text{HSKD}(K)}$ // **Subkey derivation function of HMAC**

▷ $\text{HSKD} : \{0,1\}^* \to \{0,1\}^{2c}$

$K_b \leftarrow \text{PoH}_b(K)$; $K_i \| K_o \leftarrow \text{HSKD}_b(K_b)$; Return $K_i \| K_o$

$\underline{\text{HMAC}(K, M)}$ // **"Full" HMAC** [37,47]

▷ $\text{HMAC} : \{0,1\}^* \times \{0,1\}^* \to \{0,1\}^c$

$K_i \| K_o \leftarrow \text{HSKD}(K)$; Return $\text{NMAC}(K_i \| K_o, M)$

Fig. 3. HMAC and friends built from compression function $h : \{0,1\}^c \times \{0,1\}^b \to \{0,1\}^c$.

---

and the message, again as shown. It is in order for the main and modular forms here to indeed be the same function that NMAC is carefully defined to pad in a way that accommodates an extra first block.

Finally, to obtain "full" HMAC, consider the subkey derivation function $\text{HSKD} : \{0,1\}^* \to \{0,1\}^{2c}$. It first maps an arbitrary-length key K down to a b-bit key K_b via PoH_b and then maps K_b to an NMAC key $K_i \| K_o$ via HSKD_b. The definition of $\text{HMAC} : \{0,1\}^* \times \{0,1\}^* \to \{0,1\}^c$ from [8,37,47] is

676   M. Backendal et al.

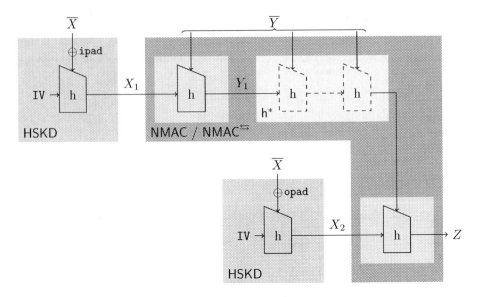

Fig. 4. Illustration of how we modularize $\mathsf{HMAC}(X,Y)$ and its swap $\mathsf{HMAC}^{\leftrightarrows}(Y,X)$ as the composition of subkey derivation function HSKD (highlighted in orange) and $\mathsf{NMAC}(X_1 \| X_2, Y)$ resp. $\mathsf{NMAC}^{\leftrightarrows}(Y, X_1 \| X_2)$ (in blue). In turn, NMAC and $\mathsf{NMAC}^{\leftrightarrows}$ are modularized as the composition of h (in green) and h^* (in yellow). The dashed h invocations may be omitted depending on the length of $\overline{Y}$. (Color figure online)

$\mathsf{HMAC}(K,M) = \mathsf{HMAC}_b(\mathsf{PoH}_b(K), M) = \mathsf{H}((\mathsf{PoH}_b(K) \oplus \mathsf{opad})\|\mathsf{H}((\mathsf{PoH}_b(K) \oplus \mathsf{ipad})\|M))$. Figure 3 shows the modular form. Again, the choice of padding in the definition of NMAC is important to ensure that the modular and standard forms of HMAC are indeed the same function.

LEMMAS ON CASCADE AND 2-TIER CASCADE. Our proofs will use the 2-tier cascade, a generalization of the cascade from [7]. In addition to the function family $\mathsf{h} \colon \{0,1\}^c \times \{0,1\}^b \to \{0,1\}^c$ underlying h^*, we have another function family $\mathsf{f} \colon \mathcal{K} \times \mathcal{X} \to \{0,1\}^c$. The 2-tier cascade associated to f, h is the function family $\mathsf{2CSC}[\mathsf{f}, \mathsf{h}] \colon \mathcal{K} \times (\mathcal{X} \times \{0,1\}^{b*}) \to \{0,1\}^c$ defined as follows:

$\underline{\mathsf{2CSC}[\mathsf{f},\mathsf{h}](J,(A,S))} \ /\!/ \ J \in \mathcal{K}$ and $(A,S) \in \mathcal{X} \times \{0,1\}^{b*}$
$L \leftarrow \mathsf{f}(J,A) \ ; \ X \leftarrow \mathsf{h}^*(L,S) \ ; \ \text{Return } X$

Let $\mathcal{A}$ be a PRF adversary attacking $\mathsf{2CSC}[\mathsf{f},\mathsf{h}]$. We say that it is prefix-free if for all i there do not exist distinct (A,S) and (A',S') among the $\mathrm{FN}(i, \cdot)$ queries such that $A = A'$ and S is a prefix of S'. (Note that there are no restrictions on queries across different users i.) This is a necessary condition for PRF security. The following says that it is also sufficient, and furthermore the result is in the multi-user setting with good bounds, meaning security does not degrade linearly with the number of users. The proof is a simple extension of a proof in [7] and is given in the full version [3].

Lemma 1 (PRF security of 2CSC). *Let* $f\colon \mathcal{K} \times \mathcal{X} \to \{0,1\}^c$ *and* $h\colon \{0,1\}^c \times \{0,1\}^b \to \{0,1\}^c$ *be function families. Let* 2CSC$\colon \mathcal{K} \times (\mathcal{X} \times \{0,1\}^{b*}) \to \{0,1\}^c$ *be the 2-tier cascade function family associated to* f, h *as above. Let* $\mathcal{A}_{2CSC}$ *be a prefix-free adversary against the PRF security of* 2CSC. *Assume the second components of each pair in the second argument of its queries to* FN *have at most* n *blocks. Then we can construct adversaries* $\mathcal{A}_f, \mathcal{A}_h$ *such that*

$$\mathbf{Adv}_{2CSC}^{PRF}(\mathcal{A}_{2CSC}) \leq \mathbf{Adv}_{f}^{PRF}(\mathcal{A}_f) + n \cdot \mathbf{Adv}_{h}^{PRF}(\mathcal{A}_h). \tag{1}$$

Adversary $\mathcal{A}_f$ *makes* $\mathbf{Q}^{NEW}(\mathcal{A}_{2CSC})$ *queries to* NEW *and* $\mathbf{Q}^{FN}(\mathcal{A}_{2CSC})$ *to* FN. *Adversary* $\mathcal{A}_h$ *makes at most* $\mathbf{Q}^{FN}(\mathcal{A}_{2CSC})$ *queries to* NEW *and* $\mathbf{Q}^{FN}(\mathcal{A}_{2CSC})$ *to* FN. *The running times of the constructed adversaries are about the same as that of* $\mathcal{A}_{2CSC}$.

The cascade h* itself is known to be a PRF under prefix-free queries assuming h is a PRF [9]. (And attacks show prefix-freeness is necessary.) This is in the single-user setting, which implies multi-user security with a loss in advantage that is a factor of the number of users. The following lemma gives instead a good bound, not degrading with the number of users. Here a PRF adversary $\mathcal{A}$ against h* is said to be prefix-free if for all i there do not exist distinct X and X' among the FN$(i, \cdot)$ queries such that X is a prefix of X'. This is obtained as a simply corollary of Lemma 1 using the technique of [7] of setting the first tier of the 2-tier cascade to a random function. For completeness details are in the full version [3], where we also discuss related work and techniques.

Lemma 2 (Multi-user PRF security of h*). *Let* h$\colon \{0,1\}^c \times \{0,1\}^b \to \{0,1\}^b$ *be a function family. Let* h*$\colon \{0,1\}^c \times \{0,1\}^{b*} \to \{0,1\}^c$ *be the cascade function family associated to* h *as per Fig. 3. Let* $\mathcal{A}_{h*}$ *be a prefix-free adversary against the PRF security of* h*. *Assume that the second arguments of its queries to* FN *have at most* n *blocks. Then we can construct an adversary* $\mathcal{A}_h$ *such that*

$$\mathbf{Adv}_{h*}^{PRF}(\mathcal{A}_{h*}) \leq n \cdot \mathbf{Adv}_{h}^{PRF}(\mathcal{A}_h). \tag{2}$$

Adversary $\mathcal{A}_h$ *makes* $\mathbf{Q}^{FN}(\mathcal{A}_{h*})$ *queries to* NEW *and* $\mathbf{Q}^{FN}(\mathcal{A}_{h*})$ *to* FN. *The running time of* $\mathcal{A}_h$ *is about the same as that of* $\mathcal{A}_{h*}$.

5 Dual-PRF Security of NMAC

We now have all the definitions and modularizations in place to turn to our main results, on NMAC (in this section) and, based on these, HMAC (in the next). To understand the PRF security of HMAC$^{\leftrightarrows}$ and HMAC, it is instructive to start with their (swapped) core, i.e., NMAC$^{\leftrightarrows}$ and NMAC. Recall from Fig. 3 that NMAC takes two keys $K_i \parallel K_o$ of length c bits each and a message $M \in \{0,1\}^*$ as input. It first processes the padded message using the cascade h* keyed with K_i, then applies h keyed with K_o to the cascade's padded output.

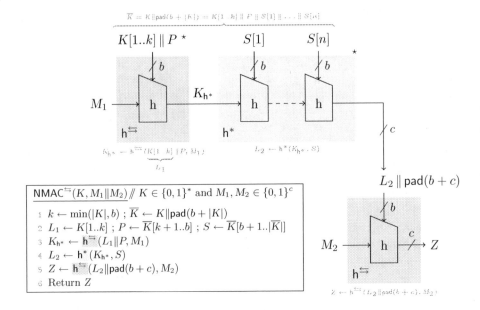

Fig. 5. Illustration of and code for $\mathsf{NMAC}^{\leftrightarrows}$, viewed as the composition of $\mathsf{h}^{\leftrightarrows}$ (highlighted in green) and h^* (in yellow). The purple asterisks ⋆ indicate that the P part of the key padding may be empty (namely, if $k = b$) or that the cascade G may be omitted (if $|\overline{K}| = b$). (Color figure online)

5.1   vkl-PRF Security of $\mathsf{NMAC}^{\leftrightarrows}$

Swapping key and message input means that $\mathsf{NMAC}^{\leftrightarrows}$ takes as input a single arbitrary-length key K and two (concatenated) messages $M_1 \parallel M_2$ of length c bits each. The latter "key" the upper and the lower cascade, the former is padded to $K \parallel \mathsf{pad}(b + |K|)$ and enters the upper cascade through the block inputs.

It is conducive to single out the first and last invocation of h: the first takes the leading (up to b) bits of the key K (possibly padded), the last the (padded) output of the cascade, through the block input. In our security analysis, we will treat both as invocations of $\mathsf{h}^{\leftrightarrows}$ and rely on rka-PRF security to capture the padding. Figure 5 shows $\mathsf{NMAC}^{\leftrightarrows}$ modularized in this way.

SECURITY OF $\mathsf{NMAC}^{\leftrightarrows}$. We show that $\mathsf{NMAC}^{\leftrightarrows}$ is a vkl-PRF if $\mathsf{h}^{\leftrightarrows}$ is rka-PRF secure and h is a PRF. The RKD functions of interest for $\mathsf{h}^{\leftrightarrows}$ are those which allow the adversary to overwrite a suffix of the full, block-length key with padding. In the reduction, we will use this to simulate the padding in lines 3 and 5 of Fig. 5.

We define $\Phi_{\mathsf{pad},a} : \{0,\dots,b\} \times \{\varepsilon\} \times \{0,1\}^b \to \{0,1\}^b \cup \{\bot\}$, on input ℓ, ε, K, to return $\bot$ if $\ell < a$ and $K[1..\ell] \parallel \mathsf{pad}(b+\ell)[1..b-\ell]$ otherwise. In more detail:

$\underline{\Phi_{\mathsf{pad},a}(\ell, \varepsilon, K)}$

If $\ell < a$ then return $\bot$

Games G_0–G_5:

$\text{New}(\ell)$ // Game G_0

1 $n \leftarrow n + 1$
  // Pre-computation of $\text{NMAC}^{\leftrightarrows}$ key values; cf. Figure 5, lines 1–2
2 $K_n \leftarrow_\$ \{0,1\}^\ell$; $k \leftarrow \min(\ell, b)$; $\overline{K}_n \leftarrow K_n \parallel \text{pad}(b + \ell)$
3 $L_{n,1} \leftarrow K_n[1..k]$; $P_n \leftarrow \overline{K}_n[k + 1..b]$; $S_n \leftarrow \overline{K}_n[b + 1..|\overline{K}_n|]$

$\text{New}(\ell)$ // Games G_1, G_2, G_3

4 $n \leftarrow n + 1$; $k \leftarrow \min(\ell, b)$
5 $K_n \leftarrow_\$ \{0,1\}^\ell$; $\overline{K}_n \leftarrow K_n \parallel \text{pad}(b + \ell)$; $S_n \leftarrow \overline{K}_n[b + 1..|\overline{K}_n|]$

$\text{New}(\ell)$ // Games G_4, G_5

6 $n \leftarrow n + 1$

Fig. 6. The New oracles for games in the proof of Theorem 3.

$P \leftarrow \text{pad}(b + \ell)[1..b - \ell]$; $L \leftarrow K[1..\ell] \parallel P$
Return L

That is, $\Phi_{\text{pad},a}(\ell, \varepsilon, K)$ overwrites the suffix of K with the first $b - \ell$ bits of padding specified by $\text{pad}(b + \ell)$, where pad is defined as per Sect. 4. The function requires that $\ell \geq a$, otherwise the output is $\bot$. That is, at least a bits of key prefix are left intact in the transformation. Note that the second input to $\Phi_{\text{pad},a}$ is empty, meaning that for each user, there is only a single RKD function; namely, the one applying the appropriate-length padding.

We justify the assumption that $h^{\leftrightarrows}$ is a PRF under related-key attacks when restricted to $\Phi_{\text{pad},a}$ in the full version [3].

Theorem 3 (vkl-PRF security of $\text{NMAC}^{\leftrightarrows}$). *Let c, b, and pad be as in Sect. 4, let h, h^* be defined as in Fig. 3. Let $\mathcal{A}$ be an adversary against the vkl-PRF security of $\text{NMAC}^{\leftrightarrows}$ whose New queries have minimal and maximal key length $\ell_{\min}(\mathcal{A})$ resp. $\ell_{\max}(\mathcal{A})$. Let $n = \lceil \ell_{\max}(\mathcal{A})/b \rceil$ be the block length of the maximum-length key used by $\mathcal{A}$ and let $a = \min(c, \ell_{\min}(\mathcal{A}))$. Then we can construct adversaries $\mathcal{A}_{h^{\leftrightarrows}}, \mathcal{A}_h$ such that*

$$\mathbf{Adv}_{\text{NMAC}^{\leftrightarrows}}^{\text{vkl-PRF}}(\mathcal{A}) \leq 2 \cdot \mathbf{Adv}_{\Phi_{\text{pad},a},h^{\leftrightarrows}}^{\text{rka-PRF}}(\mathcal{A}_{h^{\leftrightarrows}}) + n \cdot \mathbf{Adv}_h^{\text{PRF}}(\mathcal{A}_h) . \qquad (3)$$

Adversary $\mathcal{A}_{h^{\leftrightarrows}}$ makes at most $\max(\mathbf{Q}^{\text{New}}(\mathcal{A}), \mathbf{Q}^{\text{Fn}}(\mathcal{A}))$ to oracle New and at most $\mathbf{Q}^{\text{Fn}}(\mathcal{A})$ to oracle Fn. $\mathcal{A}_h$ makes $\mathbf{Q}^{\text{Fn}}(\mathcal{A})$ queries to each of oracle New and Fn. The running times of both adversaries are approximately that of $\mathcal{A}$.

Proof of Theorem 3. We use a sequence of games G_0–G_5. All are executed with $\mathcal{A}$, and hence provide the oracles named in game $\mathbf{G}_{\text{NMAC}^{\leftrightarrows}}^{\text{vkl-PRF-}d}$. The New oracles of the games are shown in Fig. 6. This allows further descriptions to focus on the Fn oracle.

▷ *Replacing the first invocation of* $\mathsf{h}^{\leftrightarrows}$ *with a random function.* We begin with game G_0 being $\mathbf{G}_{\mathrm{NMAC}^{\leftrightarrows}}^{\mathrm{vkl\text{-}PRF\text{-}1}}(\mathcal{A})$. That is, G_0 is the "real" vkl-PRF game.

The first game hop, to game G_1, replaces the first evaluation of $\mathsf{h}^{\leftrightarrows}$ in $\mathrm{NMAC}^{\leftrightarrows}$ (on line 3 of Fig. 5) by consistent random sampling. Consequently, $L_{n,1}$ is not used anymore and the corresponding first k bits of K_n become superfluous in the NEW oracle (Fig. 6). The FN oracles of games G_0, G_1 reflecting this change are in Fig. 7. They differ only in that line 4 is only in G_0 and line 5 is only in G_1. By standard equation rewriting

$$\Pr[\mathbf{G}_{\mathrm{NMAC}^{\leftrightarrows}}^{\mathrm{vkl\text{-}PRF\text{-}1}}(\mathcal{A})] = \Pr[G_0(\mathcal{A})] = \Pr[G_1(\mathcal{A})] + (\Pr[G_0(\mathcal{A})] - \Pr[G_1(\mathcal{A})]). \quad (4)$$

We build an adversary $\mathcal{A}_{\mathsf{h}^{\leftrightarrows},1}$ such that

$$\Pr[G_0(\mathcal{A})] - \Pr[G_1(\mathcal{A})] \le \mathbf{Adv}_{\varPhi_{\mathrm{pad},a},\mathsf{h}^{\leftrightarrows}}^{\mathrm{rka\text{-}PRF}}(\mathcal{A}_{\mathsf{h}^{\leftrightarrows},1}). \quad (5)$$

Adversary $\mathcal{A}_{\mathsf{h}^{\leftrightarrows},1}$ simulates G_0 for $\mathcal{A}$, with two changes: First, it does not sample K_n itself in the NEW oracle of G_0, but instead issues a NEW(k) query to its $\mathbf{G}_{\varPhi_{\mathrm{pad},a},\mathsf{h}^{\leftrightarrows}}^{\mathrm{rka\text{-}PRF}}$ game, where $k = \min(\ell, b)$. This initializes a b-bit key for $\mathsf{h}^{\leftrightarrows}$ and fixes the RKD parameter for user n to $\alpha_n = k$. If $\ell > b$, adversary $\mathcal{A}_{\mathsf{h}^{\leftrightarrows},1}$ then samples the remaining $\ell - b$ bits of K_n uniformly at random. It then applies the (remaining) padding to compute S_n. Second, instead of computing $\mathsf{h}^{\leftrightarrows}$ in line 4 of G_0 (Fig. 7) in response to a query FN$(i, M_1 \| M_2)$ from $\mathcal{A}$, adversary $\mathcal{A}_{\mathsf{h}^{\leftrightarrows},1}$ queries its FN oracle on (i, ε, M_1) and uses the result for $T_{\mathsf{h}^{\leftrightarrows},1}[i, M_1]$. Note that for each user index i, the same RKD function $\varPhi_{\mathrm{pad},a}(\alpha_i, \varepsilon, \cdot)$ is always applied. Hence it is sufficient to index the table by (i, M_i), as these uniquely determine the output from oracle FN in the rka-PRF game. Furthermore, since $\mathsf{h}^{\leftrightarrows}(L_{i,1} \| P_i, M_1)$ on line 4 of Fig. 7 is computed only once per pair (i, M_1), $\mathcal{A}_{\mathsf{h}^{\leftrightarrows},1}$ makes at most one FN query for each of the $\mathbf{Q}^{\mathrm{FN}}(\mathcal{A})$ FN queries made by $\mathcal{A}$. Its NEW queries are all with an input $k \ge a$, since the minimal k on which NEW is called is $k = \min(\ell_{\min}(\mathcal{A}), b) \ge \min(\ell_{\min}(\mathcal{A}), c) = a$. This is by virtue of $\ell_{\min}(\mathcal{A})$ being the smallest key length ℓ queried by $\mathcal{A}$, and the assumption that $b > c$ (see Sect. 4). Adversary $\mathcal{A}_{\mathsf{h}^{\leftrightarrows},1}$ soundly simulates $G_{(1-d)}$ when playing game $\mathbf{G}_{\varPhi_{\mathrm{pad},a},\mathsf{h}^{\leftrightarrows}}^{\mathrm{rka\text{-}PRF\text{-}}d}$, for $d \in \{0,1\}$, which yields the bound in Equation (5).

▷ *Replacing* h^* *with a random function.* We simplify the FN oracle from G_1 to G_2. Note that storing the values $L_{i,2}$ in $T_{\mathsf{h}^*}[i, M_1]$ and computing them only once (lines 4 and 5 of G_2) is sound since S_i is fixed per key i, so for each $T_{\mathsf{h}^{\leftrightarrows},1}[i, M_1]$, the inputs to h^* are fixed.

In G_3 (Fig. 7), we replace the computation of $\mathsf{h}^*(T_{\mathsf{h}^{\leftrightarrows},1}[i, M_1], S_i)$, originally in line 4 of Fig. 5, by (consistent) random sampling. We construct an adversary $\mathcal{A}_{\mathsf{h}^*}$ such that

$$\Pr[G_2(\mathcal{A})] - \Pr[G_3(\mathcal{A})] \le \mathbf{Adv}_{\mathsf{h}^*}^{\mathrm{PRF}}(\mathcal{A}_{\mathsf{h}^*}). \quad (6)$$

Observe that in game G_2, values $T_{\mathsf{h}^{\leftrightarrows},1}[i, M_1]$ in the FN oracle are random c-bit strings. Adversary $\mathcal{A}_{\mathsf{h}^*}$ simulates G_2, except for two differences: Instead of sampling $T_{\mathsf{h}^{\leftrightarrows},1}[i, M_1] \leftarrow_{\$} \{0,1\}^c$ in line 3 of G_2 (Fig. 7), $\mathcal{A}_{\mathsf{h}^*}$ issues a NEW query

---

$\text{FN}(i, M)$ // Games G_0, G_1

1 If $T[i, M] \neq \perp$ then return $T[i, M]$
2 $M_1 \| M_2 \leftarrow M$ // $|M_1| = |M_2| = c$
3 If $T_{h^{\leftrightarrows},1}[i, M_1] = \perp$ then
4      $T_{h^{\leftrightarrows},1}[i, M_1] \leftarrow h^{\leftrightarrows}(L_{i,1} \| P_i, M_1)$ // G_0
5      $T_{h^{\leftrightarrows},1}[i, M_1] \leftarrow\!\!\$ \{0, 1\}^c$ // G_1
6 $L_{i,2} \leftarrow h^*(T_{h^{\leftrightarrows},1}[i, M_1], S_i)$
7 $T[i, M] \leftarrow h^{\leftrightarrows}(L_{i,2} \| \mathsf{pad}(b + c), M_2)$; Return $T[i, M]$

$\text{FN}(i, M)$ // Games G_2, G_3

1 If $T[i, M] \neq \perp$ then return $T[i, M]$
2 $M_1 \| M_2 \leftarrow M$ // $|M_1| = |M_2| = c$
3 If $T_{h^{\leftrightarrows},1}[i, M_1] = \perp$ then $T_{h^{\leftrightarrows},1}[i, M_1] \leftarrow\!\!\$ \{0, 1\}^c$
4 If $T_{h^*}[i, M_1] = \perp$ then
5      $T_{h^*}[i, M_1] \leftarrow h^*(T_{h^{\leftrightarrows},1}[i, M_1], S_i)$ // G_2
6      $T_{h^*}[i, M_1] \leftarrow\!\!\$ \{0, 1\}^c$ // G_3
7 $T[i, M] \leftarrow h^{\leftrightarrows}(T_{h^*}[i, M_1] \| \mathsf{pad}(b + c), M_2)$; Return $T[i, M]$

$\text{FN}(i, M)$ // Games G_4, G_5

1 If $T[i, M] \neq \perp$ then return $T[i, M]$
2 $M_1 \| M_2 \leftarrow M$ // $|M_1| = |M_2| = c$
3 If $T_{h^*}[i, M_1] = \perp$ then $T_{h^*}[i, M_1] \leftarrow\!\!\$ \{0, 1\}^c$
4 If $T_{h^{\leftrightarrows},2}[i, M_1, M_2] = \perp$ then
5      $T_{h^{\leftrightarrows},2}[i, M_1, M_2] \leftarrow h^{\leftrightarrows}(T_{h^*}[i, M_1] \| \mathsf{pad}(b + c), M_2)$ // G_4
6      $T_{h^{\leftrightarrows},2}[i, M_1, M_2] \leftarrow\!\!\$ \{0, 1\}^c$ // G_5
7 $T[i, M] \leftarrow T_{h^{\leftrightarrows},2}[i, M_1, M_2]$; Return $T[i, M]$

Fig. 7. The FN oracles for games G_0–G_5 in the proof of Theorem 3.

---

to set up a new key with index j in its $\mathbf{G}_{h^*}^{\text{PRF-}d}$ game and stores $T_{h^{\leftrightarrows},1}[i, M_1] \leftarrow j$. Further, instead of computing $h^*(T_{h^{\leftrightarrows},1}[i, M_1], S_i)$ itself in line 5 of G_2, it queries $(T_{h^{\leftrightarrows},1}[i, M_1], S_i)$ to its FN oracle, using the result as $T_{h^*}[i, M_1]$. It thus makes at most $\mathbf{Q}^{\text{FN}}(\mathcal{A})$ queries to its NEW oracle, and one FN query under each key (since each $T_{h^*}[i, M_1]$ is only computed once), each of whose second component is at most $n = \lceil \ell_{\max}(\mathcal{A})/b \rceil$ blocks long. (Note that $n + 1$ is an upper bound on the number of blocks of the *padded* key $\overline{K}$ of $\mathsf{NMAC}^{\leftrightarrows}$. The input S to the cascade in any FN query is hence at most n blocks.) Depending on the challenge bit d in $\mathbf{G}_{h^*}^{\text{PRF-}d}$, $\mathcal{A}_{h^*}$ soundly simulates either G_2 or G_3, yielding Equation (6).

▷ *Replacing the second $h^{\leftrightarrows}$ with a random function.* We again first simplify the FN oracle from G_3 to G_4 (cf. Fig. 7), sampling $T_{h^*}[i, M_1]$ directly and omitting the no longer needed table $T_{h^{\leftrightarrows},1}$. Next, in G_5 (also Fig. 7), we sample the output of the second call to $h^{\leftrightarrows}$ (Fig. 5, line 5), stored in $T_{h^{\leftrightarrows},2}[i, M_1, M_2]$, (consistently) at random instead of computing it as $h^{\leftrightarrows}(T_{h^*}[i, M_1] \| \mathsf{pad}(b + c), M_2)$.

We bound the introduced probability difference via an adversary $\mathcal{A}_{\mathsf{h}^{\leftrightarrows},2}$ as

$$\Pr[G_4(\mathcal{A})] - \Pr[G_5(\mathcal{A})] \leq \mathbf{Adv}_{\Phi_{\mathsf{pad},a},\mathsf{h}^{\leftrightarrows}}^{\mathrm{rka\text{-}PRF}}(\mathcal{A}_{\mathsf{h}^{\leftrightarrows},2}). \tag{7}$$

Adversary $\mathcal{A}_{\mathsf{h}^{\leftrightarrows},2}$ acts as the challenger in G_4 with the following two modifications: First, for any $T_{\mathsf{h}^*}[i, M_1]$ value sampled in line 3 of Fig. 7, $\mathcal{A}_{\mathsf{h}^{\leftrightarrows},2}$ queries NEW(c) and stores the key index in a table $T_{\mathsf{h}^*}[i, M_1]$. Second, instead of computing $\mathsf{h}^{\leftrightarrows}(T_{\mathsf{h}^*}[i, M_1] \| \mathsf{pad}(b + c), M_2)$ in line 5, $\mathcal{A}_{\mathsf{h}^{\leftrightarrows},2}$ queries its FN oracle on $(T_{\mathsf{h}^*}[i, M_1], \varepsilon, M_2)$. Note that $\Phi_{\mathsf{pad},a}$ will never return $\perp$ here since by definition $a = \min(\ell_{\min}(\mathcal{A}), c)$, so $c \geq a$. This results in at most $\mathbf{Q}^{\mathrm{FN}}(\mathcal{A})$ queries to each of $\mathcal{A}_{\mathsf{h}^{\leftrightarrows},2}$'s oracles NEW and FN. Depending on bit d in $\mathbf{G}_{\Phi_{\mathsf{pad},a},\mathsf{h}^{\leftrightarrows}}^{\mathrm{rka\text{-}PRF\text{-}}d}$, $\mathcal{A}_{\mathsf{h}^{\leftrightarrows},2}$ soundly simulates either G_4 ($d = 1$) or G_5 ($d = 0$), yielding Eq. 7.

Finally we claim that

$$\Pr[G_5(\mathcal{A})] = \Pr[\mathbf{G}_{\mathsf{NMAC}^{\leftrightarrows}}^{\mathrm{vkl\text{-}PRF\text{-}0}}(\mathcal{A})], \tag{8}$$

which results from observing that $T_{\mathsf{h}^*}[i, M_1]$ is not used anymore in G_5, and the FN oracle in G_5 responds with (consistently-sampled) random strings. Hence G_5 equals $\mathbf{G}_{\mathsf{NMAC}^{\leftrightarrows}}^{\mathrm{vkl\text{-}PRF\text{-}0}}$.

Combining Eqs. (4)–(8) gives

$$\mathbf{Adv}_{\mathsf{NMAC}^{\leftrightarrows}}^{\mathrm{vkl\text{-}PRF}}(\mathcal{A}) \leq 2 \cdot \mathbf{Adv}_{\Phi_{\mathsf{pad},a},\mathsf{h}^{\leftrightarrows}}^{\mathrm{rka\text{-}PRF}}(\mathcal{A}_{\mathsf{h}^{\leftrightarrows}}) + \mathbf{Adv}_{\mathsf{h}^*}^{\mathrm{PRF}}(\mathcal{A}_{\mathsf{h}^*}), \tag{9}$$

where $\mathcal{A}_{\mathsf{h}^{\leftrightarrows}}$ is formed by picking $\gamma \leftarrow_\$ \{1, 2\}$ and running $\mathcal{A}_{\mathsf{h}^{\leftrightarrows},\gamma}$. Adversary $\mathcal{A}_{\mathsf{h}^{\leftrightarrows}}$ makes at most $\max(\mathbf{Q}^{\mathrm{NEW}}(\mathcal{A}), \mathbf{Q}^{\mathrm{FN}}(\mathcal{A}))$ to oracle NEW and at most $\mathbf{Q}^{\mathrm{FN}}(\mathcal{A})$ to oracle FN.

▷ *Applying Lemma 2.* Lastly, we invoke Lemma 2 on the multi-user PRF security of the cascade. This gives us an adversary $\mathcal{A}_{\mathsf{h}}$ such that

$$\mathbf{Adv}_{\mathsf{h}^*}^{\mathrm{PRF}}(\mathcal{A}_{\mathsf{h}^*}) \leq n \cdot \mathbf{Adv}_{\mathsf{h}}^{\mathrm{PRF}}(\mathcal{A}_{\mathsf{h}}), \tag{10}$$

where $\mathcal{A}_{\mathsf{h}}$ makes $\mathbf{Q}^{\mathrm{FN}}(\mathcal{A}_{\mathsf{h}^*}) = \mathbf{Q}^{\mathrm{FN}}(\mathcal{A})$ queries to each of oracle NEW and FN. □

5.2   Strong Multi-user PRF Security of NMAC

PRF security for NMAC was already established in [5,6,8,28] for the single user setting. By the usual hybrid argument [9] one can conclude multi-user PRF security with advantage degraded by the number of NEW queries. We are interested in strong multi-user PRF security, meaning bounds that do not suffer such degradation and instead are as good as in the single-user setting.

Let us first review the proof of single-user PRF security of GPR [28]. Here the starting point is the proof of BCK [8] which first exploits PRF security of the outer application of h to reduce to the hidden-key collision-resistance of h^*. Now, if h^* was a general PRF, it would imply it is also hidden-key collision resistant. But it is only a prefix-free PRF. The technique of GPR [28] is to exploit a random systems lemma by Maurer [40] that allows us to first reduce to a non-adaptive setting. Then, one can use a trick of appending a new block to colliding messages. This preserves collisions but breaks prefix-ness.

We give a simple, direct proof that establishes strong multi-user security with good bounds: The bound in Equation (11) below shows no degradation with the number of NEW queries. We do not use the random systems lemma. Instead we directly use game playing to move to a non-adaptive game. Finally we exploit our Lemma 2 showing strong multi-user PRF security of the cascade. The proof , given in the full version [3], is quite simple and it is surprising this was not noted before.

Theorem 4. *Let* $h: \{0,1\}^c \times \{0,1\}^b \to \{0,1\}^c$ *and let* NMAC *be as defined in Fig. 3. Let* $\mathcal{A}$ *be an adversary against the PRF security of* NMAC. *Assume each of its* FN *queries has length at most* L, *and let* $m = 1 + \lceil L/b \rceil$. *Let* $q_f = \mathbf{Q}^{\mathrm{FN}}(\mathcal{A})$ *and assume* $m \cdot q_f < 2^b$. *Then we can construct an adversary* $\mathcal{A}_h$ *such that*

$$\mathbf{Adv}^{\mathrm{PRF}}_{\mathsf{NMAC}}(\mathcal{A}) \le (m+2) \cdot \mathbf{Adv}^{\mathrm{PRF}}_{\mathsf{h}}(\mathcal{A}_h) + \frac{q_f(q_f - 1)}{2^{c+1}} . \tag{11}$$

Adversary $\mathcal{A}_h$ *makes* $\mathbf{Q}^{\mathrm{FN}}(\mathcal{A})$ *queries to* FN *and* $\max(\mathbf{Q}^{\mathrm{NEW}}(\mathcal{A}), \mathbf{Q}^{\mathrm{FN}}(\mathcal{A}))$ *to* NEW, *and its running time is about the same as that of* $\mathcal{A}$.

6 Dual-PRF Security of HMAC

Here we obtain what we consider our main result, namely to settle the dual-PRF security of the full HMAC via two, complementary results. (1) In the swap-PRF case, we give necessary and sufficient conditions on the set $\mathcal{S}$ of keys (messages for HMAC$^{\leftrightarrows}$) for which HMAC$^{\leftrightarrows}$ is vkl-PRF secure. (2) For the PRF case, we prove vkl-PRF security of HMAC for all (long enough) key lengths.

As illustrated in Fig. 4, we can see HMAC (resp. HMAC$^{\leftrightarrows}$) as the composition of a subkey derivation function HSKD deriving the keys for NMAC (resp. NMAC$^{\leftrightarrows}$). We leverage this to reduce the security of HMAC to that of NMAC and HSKD. The first step below is a general composition theorem. The second step below is to analyze HSKD to show the attributes asked for by the composition theorem. Then we can conclude by applying our results for NMAC from Sect. 5.

For the PRF security of HMAC, this approach is not new; it is the same taken in [5,6,8]. But we will see that it is also handy for analyzing HMAC$^{\leftrightarrows}$. See Table 2 for an overview and Fig. 8 for an illustration of the details for HMAC$^{\leftrightarrows}$.

6.1 Composition Theorem

Let MAC: $\{0,1\}^{2c} \times \{0,1\}^* \to \{0,1\}^c$ be a given function family. (In our application it will be NMAC.) Let $\mathcal{F}$ be a length closed-set and let SKD: $\mathcal{F} \to \{0,1\}^{2c}$ be a function that we call the subkey derivation function. We define their composition $\mathsf{F} = \mathbf{Comp}[\mathsf{MAC}, \mathsf{SKD}]: \mathcal{F} \times \{0,1\}^* \to \{0,1\}^c$ by

Table 2. Overview of the composition results for HMAC_b, HMAC, and $\mathsf{HMAC}^{\leftrightarrows}$, modularly obtained by viewing them as composition of a function family MAC and a subkey derivation function SKD.

Function	Goal	Assumption	Comments
Comp[MAC, SKD] ($\mathsf{HMAC}_b = \mathbf{Comp}[\mathsf{NMAC}, \mathsf{HSKD}_b]$)	PRF	MAC is PRF, SKD is PRG	[6]
Comp[MAC, SKD] ($\mathsf{HMAC} = \mathbf{Comp}[\mathsf{NMAC}, \mathsf{HSKD}]$)	vkl-PRF	MAC is vkl-PRF, SKD is vsl-PRG	Theorem 5.1
Comp[MAC, SKD] ($\mathsf{HMAC}^{\leftrightarrows} = \mathbf{Comp}[\mathsf{NMAC}^{\leftrightarrows}, \mathsf{HSKD}]$)	vkl-PRF	$\mathsf{MAC}^{\leftrightarrows}$ is vkl-PRF, SKD is CR	Theorem 5.2
HSKD	vsl-PRG	h is PRF, $\mathsf{h}^{\leftrightarrows}$ is PRF, $\mathsf{h}^{\leftrightarrows}$ is $\Phi_{\mathsf{zio},a}$-rka-PRF	Proposition 6
HSKD	CR	h is CR	Proposition 7

$$\underline{\mathsf{F}(K,M)} \; /\!/ \; K \in \mathcal{F} \text{ and } M \in \{0,1\}^*$$
$$K_i \| K_o \leftarrow \mathsf{SKD}(K) \; /\!/ \text{ Derive a } 2c\text{-bit subkey}$$
$$\text{Return } \mathsf{MAC}(K_i\|K_o, M)$$

The following allows us to deduce both normal and swap-PRF security of F from the corresponding security of MAC. What differs is the assumption on the subkey derivation function SKD: (1) If SKD is a vsl-PRG then the transform preserves PRF security and (2) if SKD is CR then the transform preserves swap-PRF security. Notably, we can show both results for *variable-key length* (swap-)PRF security. This is made precise in Theorem 5. Through (1), our result fills a gap left in prior work, namely HMAC's security for keys of non–full block length.

We first state the composition result and then study the assumptions on SKD in Sect. 6.2.

Theorem 5 (Composition theorem). *Let* $\mathsf{MAC}\colon \{0,1\}^{2c} \times \{0,1\}^* \to \{0,1\}^c$ *be a function family and* $\mathsf{SKD}\colon \mathcal{F} \to \{0,1\}^{2c}$ *a function. Let* $\mathsf{F} = \mathbf{Comp}[\mathsf{MAC}, \mathsf{SKD}]\colon \mathcal{F} \times \{0,1\}^* \to \{0,1\}^c$ *be their composition as above.*

1. **[Composition transfers vkl-PRF security if** SKD **is a vsl-PRG]** *Let* $\mathcal{A}_\mathsf{F}$ *be an adversary against the vkl-PRF security of* F. *Then we can construct adversaries* $\mathcal{A}_\mathsf{MAC}, \mathcal{A}_\mathsf{SKD}$ *such that*

$$\mathbf{Adv}^{\text{vkl-PRF}}_{\mathsf{F}}(\mathcal{A}_\mathsf{F}) \leq \mathbf{Adv}^{\text{PRF}}_{\mathsf{MAC}}(\mathcal{A}_\mathsf{MAC}) + \mathbf{Adv}^{\text{vsl-PRG}}_{\mathsf{SKD}}(\mathcal{A}_\mathsf{SKD}). \tag{12}$$

Also $\mathbf{Q}^{\text{FN}}(\mathcal{A}_\mathsf{SKD}) = \mathbf{Q}^{\text{NEW}}(\mathcal{A}_\mathsf{F})$ *and* $\mathcal{A}_\mathsf{SKD}$ *has minimal (resp. maximal) seed length* $\ell_{\min}(\mathcal{A}_\mathsf{F})$ *(resp.* $\ell_{\max}(\mathcal{A}_\mathsf{F})$*).*

2. **[Composition transfers swap-vkl-PRF security if** SKD **is CR]** *Let* $\mathcal{A}_\mathsf{F}$ *be an adversary against the vkl-PRF security of* $\mathsf{F}^{\leftrightarrows}$. *Then we can construct adversaries* $\mathcal{A}_\mathsf{MAC}, \mathcal{A}_\mathsf{SKD}$ *such that*

$$\mathbf{Adv}^{\text{vkl-PRF}}_{\mathsf{F}^{\leftrightarrows}}(\mathcal{A}_\mathsf{F}) \leq \mathbf{Adv}^{\text{vkl-PRF}}_{\mathsf{MAC}^{\leftrightarrows}}(\mathcal{A}_\mathsf{MAC}) + \mathbf{Adv}^{\text{CR}}_{\mathsf{SKD}}(\mathcal{A}_\mathsf{SKD}). \tag{13}$$

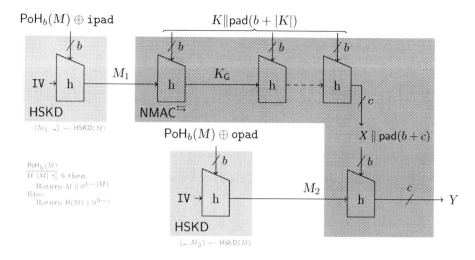

Fig. 8. Illustration of how $\mathsf{HMAC}^{\leftrightarrows}(K,M)$ can be seen as the composition of HSKD (highlighted in orange) and $\mathsf{NMAC}^{\leftrightarrows}$ (in blue). (Color figure online)

In both cases, adversary $\mathcal{A}_{\mathsf{MAC}}$ has the same query counts and in 2. the same minimal/maximal key lengths as $\mathcal{A}_{\mathsf{F}}$. The constructed adversaries have about the same running time as $\mathcal{A}_{\mathsf{F}}$.

We give proof sketches for each sub-theorem. See the full version [3] for the detailed proofs.

Proof sketch of Theorem 5.1. The proof proceeds via two game hops, starting with the "real-world" vkl-PRF game $\mathbf{G}_{\mathsf{F}}^{\text{vkl-PRF-1}}(\mathcal{A}_{\mathsf{F}})$, in which the adversary sees real evaluations of F using uniformly random keys (as input to SKD).

In the first game hop, we replace the outputs $K_i \| K_o$ of SKD in the NEW oracle by randomly sampled $2c$-bit keys. We bound the advantage difference introduced by this step by the vsl-PRG security of SKD, via a reduction $\mathcal{A}_{\mathsf{SKD}}$ obtaining these keys through its vsl-PRG FN oracle.

In the second game hop, in oracle FN, we replace the output of MAC in the response to each query by a consistent, randomly sampled string in $\{0,1\}^c$. This change we bound by the PRF security of MAC, with the reduction $\mathcal{A}_{\mathsf{MAC}}$ simulating the FN via its own FN.

The final game is then equivalent to $\mathbf{G}_{\mathsf{F}}^{\text{vkl-PRF-0}}(\mathcal{A}_{\mathsf{F}})$, yielding the claim. $\square$

Proof sketch of Theorem 5.2. The proof again proceeds via two game hops, starting with the "real-world" vkl-PRF game $\mathbf{G}_{\mathsf{F}^{\leftrightarrows}}^{\text{vkl-PRF-1}}(\mathcal{A}_{\mathsf{F}})$, with the functionality of $\mathsf{F}^{\leftrightarrows} = \mathbf{Comp}[\mathsf{MAC}^{\leftrightarrows}, \mathsf{SKD}]$ made explicit.

The first game hop replaces the evaluation of $\mathsf{MAC}^{\leftrightarrows}$ on input $M_1 \| M_2 = \mathsf{SKD}(M)$ within oracle FN by consistent random sampling. We bound this step by the vkl-PRF security of $\mathsf{MAC}^{\leftrightarrows}$, via a reduction $\mathcal{A}_{\mathsf{MAC}}$ that forwards queries to the corresponding oracles, evaluating the $\mathsf{SKD}(M)$ part of $\mathsf{F}^{\leftrightarrows}$ itself.

In the second hop, the new game samples a fresh random output for oracle FN for every new input $M \in \mathcal{F}$ to SKD. It additionally introduces a bad event, which is triggered when two distinct inputs $M \neq M'$ to SKD yield the same output $M_1 \| M_2$. This game is equivalent to the previous unless the bad event occurs, so we bound the probability difference by the probability of bad being triggered, which in turn is bounded by the collision resistance of SKD.

The final game is then equivalent to $\mathbf{G}_{\mathsf{F}^{\leftrightarrows}}^{\mathrm{vkl\text{-}PRF\text{-}0}}(\mathcal{A}_\mathsf{F})$, yielding the claim. □

6.2 Analysis of HSKD

In order to deduce security for HMAC and HMAC$^{\leftrightarrows}$ via the composition result from Theorem 5, we need to analyze the properties of HMAC's subkey derivation function HSKD shown in Fig. 3. We rewrite it, unfolding PoH$_b$ and HSKD$_b$:

$\underline{\mathsf{HSKD}(K)}$ ▷ HSKD: $\{0,1\}^* \to \{0,1\}^{2c}$

If $|K| \leq b$ then $K_b \leftarrow K \| 0^{b-|K|}$ else $K_b \leftarrow \mathsf{H}(K) \| 0^{b-c}$ // PoH$_b$
$K_i \leftarrow \mathsf{h}(\mathtt{IV}, K_b \oplus \mathtt{ipad})$; $K_o \leftarrow \mathsf{h}(\mathtt{IV}, K_b \oplus \mathtt{opad})$ // HSKD$_b$
Return $K_i \| K_o$

We will next justify HSKD both as a variable seed-length PRG (for HMAC) and as a collision-resistant function under restricted inputs (for HMAC$^{\leftrightarrows}$).

HSKD IS A VSL-PRG. To prove that HSKD is a variable-seed-length PRG, we rely on properties of its two building blocks, H and h. First, H is the MD hash function defined as $\mathsf{H}(K) = \mathsf{h}^*(\mathtt{IV}, K \| \mathsf{pad}(|K|))$, which, given that it is only applied in the case that $|K| > b$, can be viewed as an instantiation of the 2-tier cascade 2CSC, where the first tier is $\mathsf{h}^{\leftrightarrows}$. Viewed this way, we have

---

$\underline{\mathsf{H}(K)}$ ▷ H: $\{0,1\}^* \to \{0,1\}^c$
$\overline{K} \leftarrow K \| \mathsf{pad}(|K|); S \leftarrow \overline{K}[b+1..|\overline{K}|]$
Return $\mathsf{2CSC}[\mathsf{h}^{\leftrightarrows}, \mathsf{h}](K[1..b], (\mathtt{IV}, S))$

We will use the result from Lemma 1 to bound the probability of distinguishing the replacement of the output of $\mathsf{H}(K)$ by a random c-bit string by the advantage of an adversary against the PRF security of $\mathsf{h}^{\leftrightarrows}$ and h, respectively.

Next, we study the remaining invocations of h in $K_i \leftarrow \mathsf{h}(\mathtt{IV}, K_b \oplus \mathtt{ipad}) = \mathsf{h}^{\leftrightarrows}(K_b \oplus \mathtt{ipad}, \mathtt{IV})$ and $K_o \leftarrow \mathsf{h}(\mathtt{IV}, K_b \oplus \mathtt{opad}) = \mathsf{h}^{\leftrightarrows}(K_b \oplus \mathtt{opad}, \mathtt{IV})$. Here, we reduce the distinguishing probability of replacing K_i and K_o by uniformly sampled random strings in $\{0,1\}^c$ to the advantage of an adversary against the PRF security of $\mathsf{h}^{\leftrightarrows}$ under related-key attacks.

The RKD function of interest is $\Phi_{\mathsf{zio},a} : \{0, \ldots, b\} \times \{\mathtt{ipad}, \mathtt{opad}\} \times \{0,1\}^b \to \{0,1\}^b \cup \{\bot\}$ defined as follows: on inputs ℓ, io, K, it returns $\bot$ if $\ell < a$ and $(K[1..\ell] \| 0^{b-\ell}) \oplus \mathsf{io}$ otherwise. In more detail:

$\underline{\Phi_{\mathsf{zio},a}(\ell, \mathsf{io}, K)}$

If $\ell < a$ then return $\bot$
$K' \leftarrow K[1..\ell] \| 0^{b-\ell}$
$L \leftarrow K' \oplus \mathsf{io}$; Return L

That is, $\Phi_{\mathsf{zio},a}$ is the related-key-deriving function that overwrites a $b - \ell$-bit long suffix of the key with zeros, and then XORs the result with ipad or opad. The parameter a specifies the length of the shortest prefix of the key which must be left unchanged before the XOR, otherwise the function returns $\bot$. We obtain the result below, the proof of which is in the full version [3].

Proposition 6 (vsl-PRG security of HSKD). *Let* $\mathsf{HSKD} \colon \{0,1\}^* \to \{0,1\}^{2c}$ *be as defined in Fig. 3. Let* $\mathcal{A}$ *be an adversary against the* vsl-PRG *security of* HSKD. *Let* $n = \lceil \ell_{\max}(\mathcal{A})/b \rceil$ *be the block length of the maximal-length seed queried by* $\mathcal{A}$ *and let* $a = \min(c, \ell_{\min}(\mathcal{A}))$. *Then we can construct adversaries* $\mathcal{A}_{\mathsf{f}}$, $\mathcal{A}_{\mathsf{h}}$ *and* $\mathcal{A}_{\mathsf{h}^{\leftrightarrows}}$ *such that*

$$
\begin{aligned}
\mathbf{Adv}^{\text{vsl-PRG}}_{\mathsf{HSKD}}(\mathcal{A}) \leq & \mathbf{Adv}^{\text{PRF}}_{\mathsf{h}^{\leftrightarrows}}(\mathcal{A}_{\mathsf{f}}) \\
& + n \cdot \mathbf{Adv}^{\text{PRF}}_{\mathsf{h}}(\mathcal{A}_{\mathsf{h}}) + \mathbf{Adv}^{\text{rka-PRF}}_{\Phi_{\mathsf{zio},a},\mathsf{h}^{\leftrightarrows}}(\mathcal{A}_{\mathsf{h}^{\leftrightarrows}}) \,.
\end{aligned}
\tag{14}
$$

Adversaries $\mathcal{A}_{\mathsf{f}}$ *and* $\mathcal{A}_{\mathsf{h}}$ *each make at most* $\mathbf{Q}^{\text{FN}}(\mathcal{A})$ *queries to* NEW *and at most* $\mathbf{Q}^{\text{FN}}(\mathcal{A})$ *queries to* FN. *Adversary* $\mathcal{A}_{\mathsf{h}^{\leftrightarrows}}$ *makes* $\mathbf{Q}^{\text{FN}}(\mathcal{A})$ *queries to oracle* NEW *and* $2 \cdot \mathbf{Q}^{\text{FN}}(\mathcal{A})$ *queries to oracle* FN.

HSKD IS COLLISION RESISTANT FOR FEASIBLE INPUT SPACES.   As already pointed out in the introduction, it is easy to find colliding messages for $\mathsf{HMAC}^{\leftrightarrows}$, due to how short key inputs (now messages, under adversarial control) are padded with zeros and long key inputs are hashed down (then padded). Indeed, these trivial collisions are instances of bigger classes of collisions that exist for HSKD, which for $\mathsf{HMAC}^{\leftrightarrows}$ is applied to the message input. Since such collisions in HSKD immediately yield PRF attacks on $\mathsf{HMAC}^{\leftrightarrows}$, the natural question thus is: for which input spaces is HSKD collision resistant?

Let $\mathsf{HSKD}[\mathcal{S}] \colon \mathcal{S} \to \{0,1\}^{2c}$ be the restriction of HSKD to the input space $\mathcal{S}$, corresponding to $\mathsf{HMAC}[\mathcal{S}]$, i.e., restricting the key space of HMAC to $\mathcal{S}$. Focusing on length-closed sets, we now give a complete characterization of the class of *feasible* sets for which we will show $\mathsf{HSKD}[\mathcal{S}]$ to be collision resistant (enabling swap-PRF security of $\mathsf{HMAC}[\mathcal{S}]$). For all other sets, we will give attacks against swap-PRF security of $\mathsf{HMAC}[\mathcal{S}]$. Together with our attack results on $\mathsf{HMAC}^{\leftrightarrows}$ below, this will establish that $\mathsf{HMAC}[\mathcal{S}]^{\leftrightarrows}$ is vkl-PRF secure *if and only if* $\mathcal{S}$ is feasible.

We can write any finite length-closed set as $\mathcal{S} = \{0,1\}^{\ell_1} \cup \cdots \cup \{0,1\}^{\ell_n}$, $\ell_1 < \cdots < \ell_n$, for $n, \ell_1, \ldots, \ell_n \in \mathbb{N}$. Then $\mathcal{S}$ belongs to (exactly) one of the following classes:

1. $\mathcal{S} \subseteq \{0,1\}^{>b}$: The class of *feasible* sets of only "long" keys (of lengths $> b$), denoted $\mathcal{S}_L$.

2. $\mathcal{S} \subseteq \{0,1\}^{\leq b}$: We distinguish between
   (2a) $n = 1$: The class of *feasible* sets of the form $\{0,1\}^{\ell}$ (for some $\ell \leq b$) of "short", fixed-length keys, denoted $\mathcal{S}_S$.
   (2b) $n > 1$: We give *0-padding* attacks for these sets.

3. $\exists i, j \in [1, n] : \ell_i \leq b \wedge \ell_j > b$: We distinguish between
   (3a) $c \leq \ell_i \leq b$: We give *hash-confusion* attacks for these sets.
   (3b) $\ell_i < c$: We give *hash-suffix* attacks for these sets. (Note that a key length smaller than the c-bit output length of the compression function is an unnatural choice of keys. We nevertheless discuss attacks.)

We now first establish that HSKD[$\mathcal{S}$] is collision resistant for the classes of *feasible* sets of "short", fixed-length keys $\mathcal{S}_S = \{0,1\}^\ell$ (for some $\ell \leq b$) and only "long" keys $\mathcal{S}_L \subseteq \{0,1\}^{>b}$, assuming collision resistance of the compression function h. Essentially, keys from feasible sets colliding under HSKD requires a collision under one of the internal h calls; see the proof in the full version [3]. Notably, our results for feasible sets mean that HSKD is collision-resistant whenever *fixed-length* keys are used (no matter the length). This in particular covers the dual-PRF usage of HMAC in practice, since protocols like TLS 1.3 [44], KEMTLS [46] and MLS [21] use fixed-length key inputs.

In the full version, we complete this characterization by giving attacks on the PRF security of HMAC$^\leftrightarrows$ for all other (*infeasible*) input sets, which generically emerge through finding collisions in HSKD.

Proposition 7 (CR security of HSKD[$\mathcal{S}$]). *Let* h *and* HSKD *be defined as in Fig. 3. Let* HSKD[$\mathcal{S}$]$: \mathcal{S} \to \{0,1\}^{2c}$ *be the restriction of* HSKD *to a feasible set* $\mathcal{S}$ *of type* $\mathcal{S}_S$ *or* $\mathcal{S}_L$ *defined above. Let* $\mathcal{A}$ *be a CR adversary for* HSKD[$\mathcal{S}$]. *Then we can construct an adversary* $\mathcal{A}_h$ *such that*

$$\mathbf{Adv}^{\mathrm{CR}}_{\mathsf{HSKD}[\mathcal{S}]}(\mathcal{A}) = \mathbf{Adv}^{\mathrm{CR}}_{\mathsf{h}}(\mathcal{A}_h) . \tag{15}$$

The running time of the constructed adversary is about the same as that of $\mathcal{A}$.

6.3   vkl-PRF Security of HMAC

Existing proofs of PRF security of HMAC assume a b-bit key [5,6,8], i.e., they actually only hold for HMAC$_b$. As standardized [37,47], HMAC however allows keys of varying length. Combining Theorem 5.1 with our results on multi-user PRF security of NMAC (Theorem 4) and vsl-PRG security of HSKD (Proposition 6), we establish vkl-PRF security for HMAC through the composition HMAC = **Comp**[NMAC, HSKD], assuming dual-PRF security of h and rka-PRF security of h$^\leftrightarrows$. The proof mechanically leverages these results, we give it in the full version [3].

Theorem 8 (vkl-PRF security of HMAC). *Let* c, b, *and* pad *be as in Sect. 4, and functions* h, HMAC *be as defined in Fig. 3. Let* $\mathcal{A}$ *be an adversary against the vkl-PRF security of* HMAC. *Assume each of its* FN *queries has length at most* L, *and let* $m = 1 + \lceil L/b \rceil$. *Let* $q_f = \mathbf{Q}^{\mathrm{FN}}(\mathcal{A})$ *and assume* $m \cdot q_f < 2^b$. *Assume* $\mathcal{A}$'s *queries to* NEW *have minimal and maximal key length* $\ell_{\mathsf{min}}(\mathcal{A})$ *resp.* $\ell_{\mathsf{max}}(\mathcal{A})$. *Let* $n = \lceil \ell_{\mathsf{max}}(\mathcal{A})/b \rceil$, $a = \min(c, \ell_{\mathsf{min}}(\mathcal{A}))$, *and* $\Phi_{\mathsf{zio},a}$ *be the "zero-pad-then-xor"*

RKD function defined in Sect. 6.2. Then we can construct adversaries $\mathcal{A}_h$, $\mathcal{A}_f$ and $\mathcal{A}_{h\leftrightarrows}$ such that

$$\mathbf{Adv}_{\mathsf{HMAC}}^{\mathsf{vkl\text{-}PRF}}(\mathcal{A}) \leq (m+2+n)\cdot\mathbf{Adv}_{\mathsf{h}}^{\mathsf{PRF}}(\mathcal{A}_h) + \frac{q_f(q_f-1)}{2^{c+1}}$$
$$+ \mathbf{Adv}_{\mathsf{h}\leftrightarrows}^{\mathsf{PRF}}(\mathcal{A}_f) + \mathbf{Adv}_{\Phi_{\mathsf{zio},a},\mathsf{h}\leftrightarrows}^{\mathsf{rka\text{-}PRF}}(\mathcal{A}_{h\leftrightarrows}). \tag{16}$$

Adversary $\mathcal{A}_h$ makes $\max(\mathbf{Q}^{\mathrm{NEW}}(\mathcal{A}), \mathbf{Q}^{\mathrm{FN}}(\mathcal{A}))$ queries to each of NEW and FN. Adversaries $\mathcal{A}_f$, $\mathcal{A}_{h\leftrightarrows}$ make $\mathbf{Q}^{\mathrm{NEW}}(\mathcal{A})$ queries to NEW, $\mathcal{A}_f$ makes at most $\mathbf{Q}^{\mathrm{NEW}}(\mathcal{A})$ queries to FN, and $\mathcal{A}_{h\leftrightarrows}$ makes $2\cdot\mathbf{Q}^{\mathrm{NEW}}(\mathcal{A})$ to FN. The running times of adversaries $\mathcal{A}_h, \mathcal{A}_f$ and $\mathcal{A}_{h\leftrightarrows}$ are about the same as that of $\mathcal{A}$.

6.4 vkl-PRF Security of HMAC$^\leftrightarrows$

We finally turn to the swap-PRF security of HMAC. Letting $\mathsf{HMAC}[\mathcal{S}]^\leftrightarrows : \{0,1\}^* \times \mathcal{S} \to \{0,1\}^c$ denote the restriction of $\mathsf{HMAC}^\leftrightarrows$ to keys from a set $\mathcal{S}$, we establish vkl-PRF security of $\mathsf{HMAC}[\mathcal{S}]^\leftrightarrows$ for the *feasible* key input spaces of the forms $\mathcal{S}_S = \{0,1\}^\ell$ (for some $\ell \leq b$) and $\mathcal{S}_L \subseteq \{0,1\}^{>b}$.

Again, we obtain this result via Theorem 5.2 for the composition $\mathsf{HMAC}[\mathcal{S}]^\leftrightarrows = \mathbf{Comp}[\mathsf{NMAC}^\leftrightarrows, \mathsf{HSKD}[\mathcal{S}]]$. Leveraging our vkl-PRF security result of $\mathsf{NMAC}^\leftrightarrows$ (Theorem 3) and collision resistance of HSKD for feasible $\mathcal{S}$ (Proposition 7), we establish vkl-PRF security for $\mathsf{HMAC}[\mathcal{S}]^\leftrightarrows$ assuming PRF security of h, rka-PRF security of $\mathsf{h}^\leftrightarrows$, and collision resistance of h. We give a proof in the full version [3].

One might note that CR of h is *not* assumed in the proofs of PRF security for HMAC_b [5,28]. So why extra assumptions for $\mathsf{HMAC}^\leftrightarrows$? The answer is that collisions in the hash function H lead to attacks violating PRF security of $\mathsf{HMAC}^\leftrightarrows$, as mentioned before and detailed in Sect. 6.2. Collision resistance of h rules this out.

Theorem 9 (vkl-PRF security of HMAC$[\mathcal{S}]^\leftrightarrows$). Let c, b, and pad be as in Sect. 4, and functions h, $\mathsf{HMAC}^\leftrightarrows$ be as defined in Fig. 3. Let $\mathcal{S}$ be a feasible key input space as defined in Sect. 6.2 and $\mathsf{HMAC}[\mathcal{S}]^\leftrightarrows : \{0,1\}^* \times \mathcal{S} \to \{0,1\}^c$ be the swap of HMAC restricted to keys from $\mathcal{S}$. Let $\mathcal{A}$ be an adversary against the vkl-PRF security of $\mathsf{HMAC}[\mathcal{S}]^\leftrightarrows$ whose NEW queries have minimal and maximal key length $\ell_{\min}(\mathcal{A})$ resp. $\ell_{\max}(\mathcal{A})$. Let $n = \lceil \ell_{\max}(\mathcal{A})/b \rceil$, $a = \min(c, \ell_{\min}(\mathcal{A}))$, and $\Phi_{\mathsf{pad},a}$ be the "padding" RKD function defined in Sect. 5.1. Then we can construct adversaries $\mathcal{A}_{h\leftrightarrows}$, $\mathcal{A}_{h,1}$, $\mathcal{A}_{h,2}$ such that

$$\mathbf{Adv}_{\mathsf{HMAC}[\mathcal{S}]^\leftrightarrows}^{\mathsf{vkl\text{-}PRF}}(\mathcal{A}) \leq 2\cdot\mathbf{Adv}_{\Phi_{\mathsf{pad},a},\mathsf{h}\leftrightarrows}^{\mathsf{rka\text{-}PRF}}(\mathcal{A}_{h\leftrightarrows})$$
$$+ n\cdot\mathbf{Adv}_{\mathsf{h}}^{\mathsf{PRF}}(\mathcal{A}_{h,1}) + \mathbf{Adv}_{\mathsf{h}}^{\mathsf{CR}}(\mathcal{A}_{h,2}). \tag{17}$$

Adversary $\mathcal{A}_{h\leftrightarrows}$ makes at most $\max(\mathbf{Q}^{\mathrm{NEW}}(\mathcal{A}), \mathbf{Q}^{\mathrm{FN}}(\mathcal{A}))$ queries to NEW and at most $\mathbf{Q}^{\mathrm{FN}}(\mathcal{A})$ to FN. $\mathcal{A}_{h,1}$ makes $\mathbf{Q}^{\mathrm{FN}}(\mathcal{A})$ queries to each of NEW and FN. The running times of the constructed adversaries are about the same as that of $\mathcal{A}$.

Acknowledgments. Bellare was supported in part by NSF grant CNS-2154272 and KACST.

References

1. Angel, Y., Dowling, B., Hülsing, A., Schwabe, P., Weber, F.: Post quantum noise. In: Yin, H., Stavrou, A., Cremers, C., Shi, E. (eds.) ACM CCS 2022, pp. 97–109. ACM Press (2022). https://doi.org/10.1145/3548606.3560577
2. Aviram, N., Dowling, B., Komargodski, I., Paterson, K.G., Ronen, E., Yogev, E.: Practical (post-quantum) key combiners from one-wayness and applications to TLS. Cryptology ePrint Archive, Report 2022/065 (2022). https://eprint.iacr.org/2022/065
3. Backendal, M., Bellare, M., Günther, F., Scarlata, M.: When messages are keys: Is HMAC a dual-PRF? (full version). Cryptology ePrint Archive, Paper 2023/861 (2023). https://eprint.iacr.org/2023/861
4. Barbosa, M., Farshim, P.: The related-key analysis of Feistel constructions. In: Cid, C., Rechberger, C. (eds.) FSE 2014. LNCS, vol. 8540, pp. 265–284. Springer, Heidelberg (2015). https://doi.org/10.1007/978-3-662-46706-0_14
5. Bellare, M.: New proofs for NMAC and HMAC: security without collision-resistance. In: Dwork, C. (ed.) CRYPTO 2006. LNCS, vol. 4117, pp. 602–619. Springer, Heidelberg (2006). https://doi.org/10.1007/11818175_36
6. Bellare, M.: New proofs for NMAC and HMAC: security without collision resistance. J. Cryptol. **28**(4), 844–878 (2014). https://doi.org/10.1007/s00145-014-9185-x
7. Bellare, M., Bernstein, D.J., Tessaro, S.: Hash-function based PRFs: AMAC and its multi-user security. In: Fischlin, M., Coron, J.-S. (eds.) EUROCRYPT 2016. LNCS, vol. 9665, pp. 566–595. Springer, Heidelberg (2016). https://doi.org/10.1007/978-3-662-49890-3_22
8. Bellare, M., Canetti, R., Krawczyk, H.: Keying hash functions for message authentication. In: Koblitz, N. (ed.) CRYPTO 1996. LNCS, vol. 1109, pp. 1–15. Springer, Heidelberg (1996). https://doi.org/10.1007/3-540-68697-5_1
9. Bellare, M., Canetti, R., Krawczyk, H.: Pseudorandom functions revisited: the cascade construction and its concrete security. In: 37th FOCS, pp. 514–523. IEEE Computer Society Press (1996). https://doi.org/10.1109/SFCS.1996.548510
10. Bellare, M., Kohno, T.: A theoretical treatment of related-key attacks: RKA-PRPs, RKA-PRFs, and applications. In: Biham, E. (ed.) EUROCRYPT 2003. LNCS, vol. 2656, pp. 491–506. Springer, Heidelberg (2003). https://doi.org/10.1007/3-540-39200-9_31
11. Bellare, M., Lysyanskaya, A.: Symmetric and dual PRFs from standard assumptions: A generic validation of an HMAC assumption. Cryptology ePrint Archive, Report 2015/1198 (2015). https://eprint.iacr.org/2015/1198
12. Bellare, M., Rogaway, P.: The security of triple encryption and a framework for code-based game-playing proofs. In: Vaudenay, S. (ed.) EUROCRYPT 2006. LNCS, vol. 4004, pp. 409–426. Springer, Heidelberg (2006). https://doi.org/10.1007/11761679_25
13. Biham, E.: New types of cryptanalytic attacks using related keys. In: Helleseth, T. (ed.) EUROCRYPT 1993. LNCS, vol. 765, pp. 398–409. Springer, Heidelberg (1994). https://doi.org/10.1007/3-540-48285-7_34
14. Biham, E., Dunkelman, O., Keller, N.: Related-key impossible differential attacks on 8-round AES-192. In: Pointcheval, D. (ed.) CT-RSA 2006. LNCS, vol. 3860, pp. 21–33. Springer, Heidelberg (2006). https://doi.org/10.1007/11605805_2
15. Biham, E., Dunkelman, O., Keller, N.: A simple related-key attack on the full SHACAL-1. In: Abe, M. (ed.) CT-RSA 2007. LNCS, vol. 4377, pp. 20–30. Springer, Heidelberg (2006). https://doi.org/10.1007/11967668_2

16. Bindel, N., Brendel, J., Fischlin, M., Goncalves, B., Stebila, D.: Hybrid key encapsulation mechanisms and authenticated key exchange. In: Ding, J., Steinwandt, R. (eds.) PQCrypto 2019. LNCS, vol. 11505, pp. 206–226. Springer, Cham (2019). https://doi.org/10.1007/978-3-030-25510-7_12

17. Biryukov, A., Khovratovich, D.: Related-key cryptanalysis of the full AES-192 and AES-256. In: Matsui, M. (ed.) ASIACRYPT 2009. LNCS, vol. 5912, pp. 1–18. Springer, Heidelberg (2009). https://doi.org/10.1007/978-3-642-10366-7_1

18. Biryukov, A., Khovratovich, D., Nikolić, I.: Distinguisher and related-key attack on the full AES-256. In: Halevi, S. (ed.) CRYPTO 2009. LNCS, vol. 5677, pp. 231–249. Springer, Heidelberg (2009). https://doi.org/10.1007/978-3-642-03356-8_14

19. Blum, M., Micali, S.: How to generate cryptographically strong sequences of pseudorandom bits. SIAM J. Comput. **13**(4), 850–864 (1984)

20. Bose, P., Hoang, V.T., Tessaro, S.: Revisiting AES-GCM-SIV: multi-user security, faster key derivation, and better bounds. In: Nielsen, J.B., Rijmen, V. (eds.) EUROCRYPT 2018. LNCS, vol. 10820, pp. 468–499. Springer, Cham (2018). https://doi.org/10.1007/978-3-319-78381-9_18

21. Brzuska, C., Cornelissen, E., Kohbrok, K.: Security analysis of the MLS key derivation. In: 2022 IEEE Symposium on Security and Privacy, pp. 2535–2553. IEEE Computer Society Press (2022). https://doi.org/10.1109/SP46214.2022.9833678

22. Brzuska, C., Delignat-Lavaud, A., Egger, C., Fournet, C., Kohbrok, K., Kohlweiss, M.: Key-schedule security for the TLS 1.3 standard. In: Agrawal, S., Lin, D. (eds.) ASIACRYPT 2022, Part I. LNCS, vol. 13791, pp. 621–650. Springer, Heidelberg (2022). https://doi.org/10.1007/978-3-031-22963-3_21

23. Damgård, I.B.: A design principle for hash functions. In: Brassard, G. (ed.) CRYPTO 1989. LNCS, vol. 435, pp. 416–427. Springer, New York (1990). https://doi.org/10.1007/0-387-34805-0_39

24. Dodis, Y., Ristenpart, T., Steinberger, J., Tessaro, S.: To hash or not to hash again? (in)differentiability results for H^2 and HMAC. In: Safavi-Naini, R., Canetti, R. (eds.) CRYPTO 2012. LNCS, vol. 7417, pp. 348–366. Springer, Heidelberg (2012). https://doi.org/10.1007/978-3-642-32009-5_21

25. Dowling, B., Fischlin, M., Günther, F., Stebila, D.: A cryptographic analysis of the TLS 1.3 handshake protocol. J. Cryptol. **34**(4), 1–69 (2021). https://doi.org/10.1007/s00145-021-09384-1

26. Dunkelman, O., Keller, N., Kim, J.: Related-key rectangle attack on the full SHACAL-1. In: Biham, E., Youssef, A.M. (eds.) SAC 2006. LNCS, vol. 4356, pp. 28–44. Springer, Heidelberg (2007). https://doi.org/10.1007/978-3-540-74462-7_3

27. Farrell, S.: [Cfrg] erratum for hmac what do we think... IRTF Crypto Forum Research Group mailing list. https://mailarchive.ietf.org/arch/msg/cfrg/hxj9UM2LdBy2eipAJX2idjQuxhk/ (2017)

28. Gaži, P., Pietrzak, K., Rybár, M.: The exact PRF-security of NMAC and HMAC. In: Garay, J.A., Gennaro, R. (eds.) CRYPTO 2014. LNCS, vol. 8616, pp. 113–130. Springer, Heidelberg (2014). https://doi.org/10.1007/978-3-662-44371-2_7

29. Goldreich, O., Goldwasser, S., Micali, S.: How to construct random functions. J. ACM **33**(4), 792–807 (1986)

30. Håstad, J., Impagliazzo, R., Levin, L.A., Luby, M.: A pseudorandom generator from any one-way function. SIAM J. Comput. **28**(4), 1364–1396 (1999)

31. Hoang, V.T., Tessaro, S., Thiruvengadam, A.: The multi-user security of GCM, revisited: tight bounds for nonce randomization. In: Lie, D., Mannan, M., Backes, M., Wang, X. (eds.) ACM CCS 2018, pp. 1429–1440. ACM Press (2018). https://doi.org/10.1145/3243734.3243816

32. Hong, S., Kim, J., Lee, S., Preneel, B.: Related-key rectangle attacks on reduced versions of SHACAL-1 and AES-192. In: Gilbert, H., Handschuh, H. (eds.) FSE 2005. LNCS, vol. 3557, pp. 368–383. Springer, Heidelberg (2005). https://doi.org/10.1007/11502760_25

33. Hülsing, A., Ning, K.C., Schwabe, P., Weber, F., Zimmermann, P.R.: Post-quantum WireGuard. In: 2021 IEEE Symposium on Security and Privacy, pp. 304–321. IEEE Computer Society Press (2021). https://doi.org/10.1109/SP40001.2021.00030

34. Kelsey, J., Schneier, B., Wagner, D.: Related-key cryptanalysis of 3-WAY, Biham-DES, CAST, DES-X, NewDES, RC2, and TEA. In: Han, Y., Okamoto, T., Qing, S. (eds.) ICICS 97. LNCS, vol. 1334, pp. 233–246. Springer, Heidelberg (Nov 1997)

35. Kim, J., Hong, S., Preneel, B.: Related-key rectangle attacks on reduced AES-192 and AES-256. In: Biryukov, A. (ed.) FSE 2007. LNCS, vol. 4593, pp. 225–241. Springer, Heidelberg (2007). https://doi.org/10.1007/978-3-540-74619-5_15

36. Knudsen, L.R.: Cryptanalysis of LOKI 91. In: Seberry, J., Zheng, Y. (eds.) AUSCRYPT 1992. LNCS, vol. 718, pp. 196–208. Springer, Heidelberg (1993). https://doi.org/10.1007/3-540-57220-1_62

37. Krawczyk, H., Bellare, M., Canetti, R.: HMAC: Keyed-Hashing for Message Authentication. RFC 2104 (Informational) (1997). https://doi.org/10.17487/RFC2104. https://www.rfc-editor.org/rfc/rfc2104.txt, updated by RFC 6151

38. Krawczyk, H.: Cryptographic extraction and key derivation: the HKDF scheme. In: Rabin, T. (ed.) CRYPTO 2010. LNCS, vol. 6223, pp. 631–648. Springer, Heidelberg (2010). https://doi.org/10.1007/978-3-642-14623-7_34

39. Luykx, A., Mennink, B., Paterson, K.G.: Analyzing multi-key security degradation. In: Takagi, T., Peyrin, T. (eds.) ASIACRYPT 2017. LNCS, vol. 10625, pp. 575–605. Springer, Cham (2017). https://doi.org/10.1007/978-3-319-70697-9_20

40. Maurer, U.: Indistinguishability of random systems. In: Knudsen, L.R. (ed.) EUROCRYPT 2002. LNCS, vol. 2332, pp. 110–132. Springer, Heidelberg (2002). https://doi.org/10.1007/3-540-46035-7_8

41. Memisyazici, E.: RFC Erratum on RFC 2104, "HMAC: Keyed-Hashing for Message Authentication". RFC Errata, Errata ID: 4809. https://www.rfc-editor.org/errata_search.php?rfc=2104&eid=4809 (2016)

42. Merkle, R.C.: A certified digital signature. In: Brassard, G. (ed.) CRYPTO 1989. LNCS, vol. 435, pp. 218–238. Springer, New York (1990). https://doi.org/10.1007/0-387-34805-0_21

43. Phan, R.C.-W.: Related-key attacks on triple-DES and DESX variants. In: Okamoto, T. (ed.) CT-RSA 2004. LNCS, vol. 2964, pp. 15–24. Springer, Heidelberg (2004). https://doi.org/10.1007/978-3-540-24660-2_2

44. Rescorla, E.: The Transport Layer Security (TLS) Protocol Version 1.3. RFC 8446 (Proposed Standard) (2018). https://doi.org/10.17487/RFC8446. https://www.rfc-editor.org/rfc/rfc8446.txt

45. Rogaway, P.: Formalizing human ignorance. In: Nguyen, P.Q. (ed.) VIETCRYPT 2006. LNCS, vol. 4341, pp. 211–228. Springer, Heidelberg (2006). https://doi.org/10.1007/11958239_14

46. Schwabe, P., Stebila, D., Wiggers, T.: Post-quantum TLS without handshake signatures. In: Ligatti, J., Ou, X., Katz, J., Vigna, G. (eds.) ACM CCS 2020, pp. 1461–1480. ACM Press (2020). https://doi.org/10.1145/3372297.3423350

47. of Standards, N.I., Technology: The keyed-hash message authentication code (HMAC). Tech. Rep. Federal Information Processing Standards Publications (FIPS PUBS) 198–1, U.S. Department of Commerce, Washington, D.C. (2008). https://doi.org/10.6028/NIST.FIPS.198-1

48. of Standards, N.I., Technology: Secure hash standard (SHS). Tech. Rep. Federal Information Processing Standards Publications (FIPS PUBS) 180–4, U.S. Department of Commerce, Washington, D.C. (2015). https://doi.org/10.6028/NIST.FIPS.180-4
49. Stebila, D., Fluhrer, S., Gueron, S.: Hybrid key exchange in TLS 1.3 - draft-ietf-tls-hybrid-design-05. https://datatracker.ietf.org/doc/html/draft-ietf-tls-hybrid-design-05 (2022)
50. Yao, A.C.C.: Theory and applications of trapdoor functions (extended abstract). In: 23rd FOCS, pp. 80–91. IEEE Computer Society Press (1982). https://doi.org/10.1109/SFCS.1982.45
51. Zhang, W., Wu, W., Zhang, L., Feng, D.: Improved related-key impossible differential attacks on reduced-round AES-192. In: Biham, E., Youssef, A.M. (eds.) SAC 2006. LNCS, vol. 4356, pp. 15–27. Springer, Heidelberg (2007). https://doi.org/10.1007/978-3-540-74462-7_2

Layout Graphs, Random Walks and the t-Wise Independence of SPN Block Ciphers

Tianren Liu[1]([✉])(ⅅ), Angelos Pelecanos[2](ⅅ), Stefano Tessaro[3](ⅅ),
and Vinod Vaikuntanathan[4](ⅅ)

[1] Peking University, Beijing, China
liutianren@gmail.com
[2] UC Berkeley, Berkeley, USA
[3] University of Washington, Seattle, USA
[4] MIT CSAIL, Cambridge, USA

Abstract. We continue the study of t-wise independence of substitution-permutation networks (SPNs) initiated by the recent work of Liu, Tessaro, and Vaikuntanathan (CRYPTO 2021).

Our key technical result shows that when the S-boxes are *randomly and independently chosen* and kept secret, an r-round SPN with input length $n = b \cdot k$ is $2^{-\Theta(n)}$-close to t-wise independent within $r = O(\min\{k, \log t\})$ rounds for any t almost as large as $2^{b/2}$. Here, b is the input length of the S-box and we assume that the underlying mixing achieves maximum branch number. We also analyze the special case of AES parameters (with random S-boxes), and show it is 2^{-128}-close to pairwise independent in 7 rounds. Central to our result is the analysis of a random walk on what we call the *layout graph*, a combinatorial abstraction that captures equality and inequality constraints among multiple SPN evaluations.

We use our technical result to show concrete security bounds for SPNs with actual block cipher parameters and *small-input S-boxes*. (This is in contrast to the large body of results on ideal-model analyses of SPNs.) For example, for the censored-AES block cipher, namely AES with most of the mixing layers removed, we show that 192 rounds suffice to attain 2^{-128}-closeness to pairwise independence. The prior such result for AES (Liu, Tessaro and Vaikuntanathan, CRYPTO 2021) required more than 9000 rounds.

1 Introduction

The design of block ciphers like the Advanced Encryption Standard (AES) is one of the most central topics in practical cryptography. Our confidence in their security stems from decades of cryptanalysis, spanning a wide range of attacks including linear [38] and differential [4] cryptanalysis, higher-order [33], truncated [31] and impossible [30] differential attacks, interpolation [25] and algebraic attacks [13], integral cryptanalysis [32], biclique attacks [5], and so on. These attacks have so far failed to make a dent in the conjectured security of AES as a (fixed-parameter) pseudorandom permutation. Nonetheless, we remain very

ⓒ International Association for Cryptologic Research 2023
H. Handschuh and A. Lysyanskaya (Eds.): CRYPTO 2023, LNCS 14083, pp. 694–726, 2023.
https://doi.org/10.1007/978-3-031-38548-3_23

far from rigorously justifying that security actually holds. Crucially, the design methodology behind most block ciphers iterates a very weak round function (too weak to achieve any meaningful security notion). It is not clear whether it is even possible to formulate a meaningful non-tautological assumption that implies the security of a block cipher within the classical framework of provable security.

t-wise independent ciphers. Facing the above limitations, this paper continues a line of work justifying the security of block ciphers against *restricted* classes of attacks, with a focus on *substitution permutation networks* (SPNs), an important class of block ciphers that includes AES. In particular, we build on top of recent work by Liu, Tessaro, and Vaikuntanathan (LTV) [37] that studies the t-wise independence of SPNs as a "catch-all" security property that prevents all t-input statistical attacks. (The notion was already studied earlier [7,24] for less standard block cipher constructions.)

We take a *quantitative* angle where, for a given t, we aim to know the smallest $\epsilon = \epsilon(r)$ for which an r-round SPN is $\epsilon(r)$-close to a t-wise independent permutation. The case $t = 2$ already implies, for a small enough ϵ, security against *linear* [38] and *differential* [4] attacks, which have (on their own) been the subject of hundreds of works. Similarly, security against degree-d higher-order differential attacks [33] follows when $t = 2^d$.

The results from [37] suffer however from two major limitations, which we aim to address here: First, they only prove *pairwise* independence of SPNs. Second, for AES-like parameters, their pairwise-independence bound effectively requires *thousands of rounds* to achieve meaningful security matching practical expectations. (Concretely, more than 9000.[1])

Our Contributions, in a Nutshell. In this work, we study the t-wise independence of SPNs when the S-boxes are *randomly chosen, independent,* and *secret,* and thus act as the actual secret keys. Unlike a number of recent works in the random S-box model (e.g., [10,18,40]), which assume the S-box inputs to be as large as the security parameter, here we target a scenario with *small-input* S-boxes (e.g., 8 bits, as in AES), which presents a unique challenge. Random S-box SPNs were for instance also studied by Baignères and Vaudenay [3], who quantified the linear and differential probabilities in the limit as the number of rounds goes to infinity. Here, instead, we prove *concrete* bounds for the *stronger* property of t-wise independence. A summary of our results is given in Table 1.

While it is interesting to study random S-boxes in their own right, as they have been used in actual ciphers (e.g., GOST [41] and AES variants [45]), we really want to derive conclusions for block ciphers with fixed S-boxes (as [37] did) from our results. An *optimistic* interpretation of our results is that random, secret, S-boxes yield a good heuristic approximation of the behavior of SPNs with a concrete S-box (e.g., the inversion map $x \mapsto x^{2^b-1}$ as in AES). But we also offer a more *pragmatic* interpretation, based on the fact that a random S-box can be approximated by the sequential composition of an actual S-box (where a key is XORed prior to each call). Our analyses in the random S-box model

---

[1] LTV prove that $6r$-round AES is $2^{r-1}(0.472)^r$-close to pairwise independent, which becomes smaller than 2^{-128} for $r \geq 1528$.

Table 1. Results for the t-wise independence of SPN* and AES*. Here, b is the length of the input to the S-box (the word length or block size), and k is the width for SPN* (equivalently, the number of parallel S-box invocations). All of the SPN* results assume a linear mixing layer with maximum branch number. The AES* result uses the AES mixing layer, $k = 16$, $b = 8$.

	Rounds	t		Closeness	Theorem
SPN*	2	$O(1)$		$2^{-\Omega(kb)}$	Theorem 2
	2	$2^{(0.499-1/(4k))b}$	2^{-b}	Theorem 3
	$O(k)$	$2^{(0.499-1/(4k))b}$	$2^{-\Omega(kb)}$	Theorem 3 + [28,39]
	$O(\log t)$	$2^{0.499b}$	$2^{-\Omega(kb)}$	Theorem 4
AES*	7	2		2^{-128}	Theorem 6
censored AES	192	2		2^{-128}	Theorem 7

therefore carry over to a *concrete* block cipher which can be thought of as an SPN with a number of mixing layers removed (what we refer to as a "censored" SPN or SPN*).

We now go back to our contributions in a bit more in detail.

Substitution-permutation Networks. To state our results more concretely, recall that a substitution permutation network (SPN) with *word length* b, *width* k, and r *rounds*, is defined by an invertible *substitution box* (or S-box) $S : \mathbb{F} \to \mathbb{F}$, where $\mathbb{F} = \mathbb{F}_{2^b}$, and an invertible *mixing layer* $M : \mathbb{F}^k \to \mathbb{F}^k$. (One usually focuses on *linear* mixing functions as we do in this paper.) Computation proceeds in r rounds, given input vector $\mathbf{x}^{(\mathrm{in})} = \mathbf{y}^{(0)} \in \mathbb{F}^k$ and round keys $\mathbf{k}^{(0)}, \ldots, \mathbf{k}^{(r)} \in \mathbb{F}^k$. For $i = 1, \ldots, r+1$ we compute

$$\mathbf{x}^{(i)} = \left[S\left(\mathbf{y}^{(i-1)}[1] + \mathbf{k}^{(i-1)}[1]\right), \ldots, S\left(\mathbf{y}^{(i-1)}[k] + \mathbf{k}^{(i-1)}[k]\right) \right] .$$

$$\mathbf{y}^{(i)} = M\mathbf{x}^{(i)}$$

The final output is $\mathbf{y}^{(\mathrm{out})} = \mathbf{x}^{(r+1)}$. See Fig. 1 for an illustration. (Note that in this representation, the final operation is the application of S-boxes, with no further mixing. This differs from some of the literature; however, the difference is inconsequential to our results.) In an actual block cipher, one would compute the round keys from a short key via a suitable key-scheduling algorithm, but here we follow the convention from prior works of using independent keys for the analysis.

Typical choices for the above parameters are those from AES, where $k = 16$ and $b = 8$, and one should think of these when assessing whether a result is meaningful.

t-wise Independence for Random S-Boxes. The bulk of our results will be concerned with the analysis of SPNs in a model where the S-boxes are ideal, i.e.,

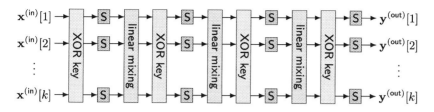

Fig. 1. Illustration of a 3-round SPN.

randomly chosen and secret. In other words, we replace the step

$$\mathbf{x}^{(i)}[j] \leftarrow S(\mathbf{y}^{(i-1)}[j] \oplus \mathbf{k}^{(i-1)}[j])$$

for $i = 1, \ldots, r+1$ and $j = 1, \ldots, k$ with

$$\mathbf{x}^{(i)}[j] \leftarrow S_j^{(i-1)}(\mathbf{y}^{(i-1)}[j])$$

where $S_j^{(i-1)}$ is a uniformly chosen random permutation on $\mathbb{F}$. Here, we can think of the S-box descriptions as part of a longer key, and following the notation from [3], we refer to this variant as SPN*.

Formally, we measure the proximity to t-wise independence by picking t arbitrary distinct input vectors and obtain the t output vectors processed by the r-round SPN* construction. We then give an upper bound on the statistical distance of these output vectors from t uniformly sampled, but distinct, vectors. As observed in [37], such a distance bound also gives explicit concrete bounds for the linear and differential probabilities. (In particular, our result gives concrete bounds for such quantities, as opposed to [3] which only shows eventual convergence to a particular probability as the number of rounds goes to infinity.)

Layouts and Random Walks. At the core of our results is the formalization of the concept of a *layout*, which allows us to reduce the question of t-wise independence to the analysis of a random walk which is entirely defined by the mixing layer M. Concretely, if we are given a t-tuple of vectors $(\mathbf{y}_1, \ldots, \mathbf{y}_t)$, and map them to $(\mathbf{x}_1, \ldots, \mathbf{x}_t)$ by applying the same k random S-boxes to each of the vectors, we observe that the mapping respects equality and inequality constraints. For example, if $\mathbf{y}_i[j] = \mathbf{y}_{i'}[j]$ for $i \neq i'$, then $\mathbf{x}_i[j] = \mathbf{x}_{i'}[j]$. Inequalities are also similarly preserved. A t-wise *layout* I is, formally, a description of equality/inequality constraints among t k-dimensional vectors over $\mathbb{F}$. Crucially, applying random S-boxes to *any* t-tuple $(\mathbf{y}_1, \ldots, \mathbf{y}_t)$ satisfying the layout I results in a t-tuple picked *uniformly at random* from the set of *all* t-tuples that satisfy the same layout I. For the special case of $t = 2$, a layout is equivalent to an *activity pattern* formulated and studied in the AES literature [1].

This means in particular that the evaluation of an r-round SPN* on t inputs corresponds to taking r random steps on the *layout* graph. We start with an arbitrary layout I_0, and step $i = 1, \ldots, r$ consists of:

- Picking a random t-tuple $(\mathbf{x}_1^{(i)}, \ldots, \mathbf{x}_t^{(i)})$ that lies in layout I_{i-1};
- Compute $\mathbf{y}_j^{(i)} = M\mathbf{x}_j^{(i)}$ for all $j = 1, \ldots, t$; and
- Set I_i to be the (unique) layout satisfied by $(\mathbf{y}_1^{(i)}, \ldots, \mathbf{y}_t^{(i)})$.

The convergence of this walk to the distribution over layouts induced by a uniformly sampled t-tuple of distinct vectors directly yields t-wise independence of the r-round SPN*. For the case $t = 2$, this random walk was also described in [3] without any explicit convergence guarantees, which we provide here.

We provide a careful analysis of this random walk by first characterizing the transition probability of going from a layout I to a layout J and then derive an upper bound on the distance from the stationary distribution after one single step, provided we start from a nice enough layout, i.e., one that does not induce too many collisions. Then, very roughly, one shows that a nice layout is reached in one round with very high probability. We use this analysis to derive a number of theorems, which all assume that the mixing layer achieves maximum branch number, i.e., for all $\mathbf{x} \in \mathbb{F}^k \setminus \{0\}$, we have $\mathsf{wt}(\mathbf{x}) + \mathsf{wt}(M\mathbf{x}) \geq k + 1$, where $\mathsf{wt}(\cdot)$ denotes Hamming weight, i.e., the number of non-zero components.

Our first two theorems give the smallest ϵ depending on whether t is small or large.

Theorem 2. 2-round SPN* is ε-close to t-wise independent, for $\varepsilon = \frac{t^2 \cdot 2^{k+1}}{(2^b)^{k/(2t)}} + t \cdot \left(\frac{8 \cdot t^3}{2^b}\right)^{k/2}$.

Theorem 3. For any $\alpha \in (0, 1]$, 2-round SPN* is ε-close to t-wise independent, where $\varepsilon = \frac{t^2}{\alpha \cdot 2^b} + t \cdot \left(\frac{(2t)^{2-\alpha}}{(2^b)^{1-\alpha}}\right)^k$.

A standard goal is to make ϵ equal $2^{-\Omega(k \cdot b)}$, as $n = k \cdot b$ is the input length of the SPN, and the first theorem implies that for small constant $t = O(1)$, we achieve distance $2^{-\Omega(n)}$ already after two rounds. In contrast, by picking the suitable α, the second theorem allows t to become almost as large as $2^{b/2}$ (concretely, we require $t < 2^{(0.499-1/(4k))b}$, which is as large as 14 for AES-like parameters), but only gives $\epsilon = 2^{-\Omega(b)}$. However, one can then amplify this using existing amplification results [28,39] to achieve $\epsilon = 2^{-\Omega(bk)}$ after $2k$ rounds.

We also show an alternative theorem that also yields $\epsilon = 2^{-\Omega(bk)}$, but this time using $O(\log t)$ rounds, instead of $O(k)$. This follows from the following.

Theorem 4. Let $t = 2^r$. Then, r-round SPN* is ε-close to 2^r-wise independent for $\varepsilon = \frac{t \cdot 2^{\frac{11}{4}}}{1 - 2^{-\frac{k}{4}}} \cdot \left(\frac{8 \cdot t^2}{2^b}\right)^{k/4}$ if $k > 4$.

The Case of AES. The specific case of AES is interesting because its mixing layer does not achieve the maximal branch number. One could in fact extend some of our techniques above to a more relaxed branch number. However, we give a more precise analysis of a variant of AES with random S-boxes which, unlike the above SPN*, uses the *actual* AES mixing layer (alternating the ShiftRows and MixColumn operations). It also sets $k = 16$ and $b = 8$. We refer to this variant as AES*. We show that AES* is 2^{-128}-close to pairwise independent already for *seven* rounds. To achieve these results, we combine experimental computations with our random walk framework. We note that this result could have been obtained computationally also using results from [3], in particular their description of the random walk on layouts for the special case of AES* and $t = 2$. (Their description is however not sufficient to yield the results in the other sections of this paper, nor do they actually carry out the computation, or target a security property as strong as pairwise-independence.)

Concrete S-Boxes and Censored SPNs. For the special case of pairwise independence, one can easily transform our results for random S-boxes into results for concrete S-boxes if we are willing to replace the application of a *single* random S-box $S_j^{(i)}$ with the repeated application of the AES S-box (namely, the patched inversion function over $\mathbb{F}$) alternated with the addition of a key value prior to each S-box call. We refer to the resulting cipher as *censored SPN* (or *censored* AES), because it is equivalent to an SPN where a fraction of mixing layers have been removed (i.e., "censored"). We give a censored variant of AES which is 2^{-128}-close to pairwise independent after 192 rounds. We conjecture that 192-round of AES itself is also 2^{-128}-close to pairwise independent, i.e., the censoring mixing layers never increases security.

This should be contrasted with [37], which shows that AES is 2^{-128}-close to pairwise independent after (more than) 9000 rounds.

1.1   Related Work: The "Large" S-Box Model

A number of works [10, 18, 40] have considered SPNs with random S-boxes when the input length b is large (i.e., it can be thought of as the security parameter), and aims to prove an r-round SPN to be a (strong) pseudorandom permutation. Miles and Viola [40] deal with *secret* S-boxes (as we do here), whereas [10, 18] consider a single public S-box (accessible as a random oracle) which is then keyed within the construction. (But clearly, this implies an analysis in a model where the S-box is secret.) These works fit within the bigger scope of a long line of works [2, 6, 8, 9, 11, 12, 15, 16, 19–23, 35, 36, 44]) analyzing block cipher constructions in ideal models. A recent paper by Dodis, Karthikeyan, and Wichs [17] then suggests conjectures under which these large S-box analyses could imply security in the small S-box regime (for full pseudorandomness).

While the result is not explicitly stated, one can, in fact, apply the toolkit from [10], which in turn relies on the H-coefficient method [43], to show that a 1-round SPN is ϵ-close to t-wise independent for $\epsilon = O(kt^2/2^b)$. For $b = 8$ and $k = 16$, one might hope to achieve $\epsilon = 1/2$ for $t = 2$ (and in turn, this can be boosted using [39]), but the involved constants prevent that. In addition, we observe that this bound has the unnatural feature that it *degrades* as a function of the width parameter k, which is exactly what we show *not to be the case*. Our results adopt completely different techniques, that rely on the analysis of random walks on the layout graph, and indeed also indicate an improvement of the achievable ϵ as k grows, as intuition would suggest.

While (almost) t-wise independent permutations can be constructed in many other ways (see, e.g. [29]), that is not the point of this paper. Our goal is to analyze natural constructions, in this case following the substitution-permutation paradigm, which are *provably* almost t-wise independent and *plausibly* pseudorandom.

1.2   Technical Overview

In this overview, we briefly explain how our technique works in the special case of 2-wise (or pairwise) independence of SPN* (i.e., SPN with random S-boxes). A more detailed analysis of the pairwise setting can be found in Sect. 4. The more involved analysis of the general t-wise setting follows the same framework, and is presented in Sect. 5. Concrete bounds for censored AES are given in Sect. 6.

Differences and Layouts. As we only consider two inputs, we can follow the standard differential cryptanalysis approach of working with *differences*. For any input difference $\mathbf{x}_{\Delta}^{(\mathrm{in})} = \mathbf{x}_1^{(\mathrm{in})} - \mathbf{x}_2^{(\mathrm{in})}$, we need to show that the corresponding distribution of the output difference $\mathbf{y}_{\Delta}^{(\mathrm{out})} = \mathbf{y}_1^{(\mathrm{out})} - \mathbf{y}_2^{(\mathrm{out})}$ is close to uniform. We consider a two-round SPN*, so we can define analogously differences $\mathbf{x}_{\Delta}^{(1)}$, $\mathbf{y}_{\Delta}^{(1)}$, $\mathbf{x}_{\Delta}^{(2)}$, $\mathbf{y}_{\Delta}^{(2)}$, and $\mathbf{y}_{\Delta}^{(\mathrm{out})}$. See Fig. 2 for an illustration.

Let $I^{(0)}$ denote the layout of $(\mathbf{x}_1^{(\mathrm{in})}, \mathbf{x}_2^{(\mathrm{in})})$. In the pairwise setting, the layout can be defined as a subset $I^{(0)} \subseteq [k]$ including the coordinates where $\mathbf{x}_1^{(\mathrm{in})}, \mathbf{x}_2^{(\mathrm{in})}$ collide, or, equivalently, $I^{(0)}$ consists of all the coordinates where $\mathbf{x}_{\Delta}^{(\mathrm{in})}$ is zero. In general, we say $I \subseteq [k]$ is the layout of $\mathbf{x} \in \mathbb{F}^k$, or $\mathbf{x}$ is in layout I, if I consists precisely of the zero coordinates of $\mathbf{x}$. That is,

$$\mathbf{x} \text{ in } I \quad \text{means} \quad \forall i \in [k],\ i \in I \iff \mathbf{x}[i] = 0.$$

Due to the randomness of the S-boxes, $\mathbf{x}_{\Delta}^{(1)}$ is distributed uniformly among all vectors in layout $I^{(0)}$. Similarly, if we let $I^{(1)}$ (resp. $I^{(2)}$) denote the layout of $\mathbf{y}_{\Delta}^{(1)}$ (resp. $\mathbf{y}_{\Delta}^{(2)}$), then $\mathbf{x}_{\Delta}^{(2)}$ (resp. $\mathbf{y}_{\Delta}^{(\mathrm{out})}$) is distributed uniformly among all vectors in layout $I^{(1)}$ (resp. $I^{(2)}$).

It is easy to show that if $I^{(2)}$ is close to the distribution on layouts induced by a random (non-zero) vector, then the distribution of $\mathbf{y}_{\Delta}^{(\mathrm{out})}$ is close to uniform. Thus the heart of the analysis is to understand how the distribution of $I^{(r)}$ depends on that of $I^{(r-1)}$. Evidently, this depends on the characteristics of the linear mixing layer. In particular, we show the following lemma.

Lemma 3 (informal). If $I^{(r-1)}$ is *nice* in the sense that $|I^{(r-1)}| \leq k/2$, then $I^{(r)}$ is $2^{-\Omega(kb)}$-close in variation distance to the layout of a random vector.

The Blueprint. We now use the above lemma to prove that 2-round SPN* is close to 2-wise independent using the following blueprint. All the error terms in the analysis have magnitude $2^{-\Omega(kb)}$.

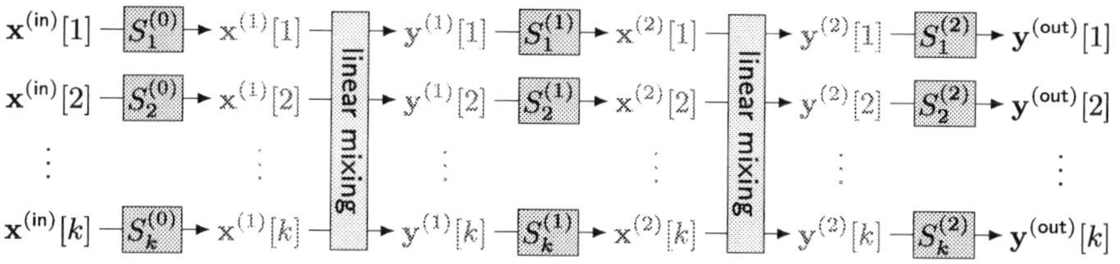

Fig. 2. Illustration of a 2-round SPN* Network. Each S-box is a uniformly random permutation from $\mathbb{F}$ to $\mathbb{F}$. These S-boxes form the key of the SPN* network.

In the first round: If $I^{(0)}$ is nice, then $I^{(1)}$ is statistically close to the layout of a random vector by Lemma 3 above, so $I^{(1)}$ is nice with high probability. If $I^{(0)}$ is not nice, then we claim that $I^{(1)}$ must be nice due to the fact that the linear mixing matrix M has maximal branch number. Recall that this guarantees $\mathsf{wt}(\mathbf{x}) + \mathsf{wt}(M\mathbf{x}) \geq k + 1$ for all $\mathbf{0} \neq \mathbf{x} \in \mathbb{F}^k$. Thus, if $I^{(0)}$ is not nice, $I^{(1)}$ must be nice. In either case, $I^{(1)}$ is very likely to be nice.

In the second round: Since $I^{(1)}$ is very likely to be nice, $I^{(2)}$ is close to the layout of a random vector again by Lemma 3, which implies that $\mathbf{y}^{(\mathsf{out})}_\Delta$ is close to uniform.

Our analysis of the t-wise setting in Sect. 5 follows the same high-level framework, which requires in particular generalizing the notion of a layout and its niceness.

Proof Sketch of Lemma 3. The rest of this overview provides a proof sketch of the lemma. The transition probability from $I^{(r-1)}$ to $I^{(r)}$ can be written as

$$\Pr\left[I^{(r)} = J \mid I^{(r-1)} = I\right] = \Pr_{\mathbf{x} \in I}\left[M\mathbf{x} \text{ in } J\right] = \frac{\#\{\mathbf{x} \text{ s.t. } \mathbf{x} \text{ in } I \wedge M\mathbf{x} \text{ in } J\}}{\#\{\mathbf{x} \text{ s.t. } \mathbf{x} \text{ in } I\}} .$$

Define an indicator function $\mathbb{1}_M$ where $\mathbb{1}_M(\mathbf{x}, \mathbf{y}) = 1$ if and only if $M\mathbf{x} = \mathbf{y}$. Then

$$\Pr\left[I^{(r)} = J \mid I^{(r-1)} = I\right] = \frac{\sum_{\mathbf{x} \text{ in } I} \sum_{\mathbf{y} \text{ in } J} \mathbb{1}_M(\mathbf{x}, \mathbf{y})}{\sum_{\mathbf{x} \text{ in } I} 1} . \tag{1}$$

To compute the numerator, it turns out that it is convenient to relax the notion of being in a layout. In particular, we say that $\mathbf{x}$ *satisfies* layout I as follows:

$$\mathbf{x} \text{ SAT } I \quad \text{means} \quad \forall i \in [k], \ i \in I \implies \mathbf{x}[i] = 0.$$

In particular, if $\mathbf{x}$ is in layout I, it satisfies layout I, but not vice versa.

Note that if M has the maximal branch number, then one can show that

$$\sum_{\mathbf{x} \text{ SAT } I} \sum_{\mathbf{y} \text{ SAT } J} \mathbb{1}_M(\mathbf{x}, \mathbf{y}) = \begin{cases} (2^b)^{k-|I|-|J|} & \text{if } |I| + |J| \leq k , \\ 1 & \text{if } |I| + |J| > k . \end{cases} \tag{2}$$

Also, note that

$$\sum_{\mathbf{x}\, \text{SAT}\, I} \sum_{\mathbf{y}\, \text{SAT}\, J} \frac{1}{(2^b)^k} = (2^b)^{k-|I|-|J|} \tag{3}$$

is very close to (2), off by at most 1 for any I and J. In order to express the numerator of (1) in closed form, we first note that (2) and (3) should remain close if the sum operator is replaced by $\sum_{\mathbf{x}\, \text{in}\, I} \sum_{\mathbf{y}\, \text{in}\, J}$. That is

$$\sum_{\mathbf{x}\, \text{in}\, I} \sum_{\mathbf{y}\, \text{in}\, J} \left(\mathbb{1}_M(\mathbf{x},\mathbf{y}) - \frac{1}{(2^b)^k} \right) = O(2^{2k}).$$

This can be verified by the inclusion-exclusion principle (details in Sect. 4.1).

Plugging it in (1) gives a good bound on the transition probability

$$\Pr\left[I^{(r)} = J \mid I^{(r-1)} = I \right] = \frac{\displaystyle\sum_{\mathbf{x}\, \text{in}\, I} \sum_{\mathbf{y}\, \text{in}\, J} \frac{1}{(2^b)^k} + O(2^k)}{\displaystyle\sum_{\mathbf{x}\, \text{in}\, I} 1} = \overbrace{\sum_{\mathbf{y}\, \text{in}\, J} \frac{1}{(2^b)^k}}^{=\Pr_{\mathbf{y}}[\mathbf{y}\, \text{in}\, J]} + \overbrace{\frac{O(2^{2k})}{(2^b-1)^{k-|I|}}}^{\text{err}}.$$

The error term is of the order of $2^{-\Omega(kb)}$ if I is nice (i.e., $|I| \le k/2$). The transition probability is close to $\sum_{\mathbf{y}\, \text{in}\, J} \frac{1}{(2^b)^k}$, which is the probability that a random vector lies in J. This can then be turned into a bound on the statistical distance to conclude the proof of the lemma.

2   Preliminaries

For any positive integer n, let $[n]$ denote the set $\{1, 2, \ldots, n\}$. We will use bold-face letters such as $\mathbf{x}$ to denote vectors and will denote the ith coordinate of such a vector by $\mathbf{x}[i]$. For an integer $b \ge 1$, we let $\mathbb{F}_{2^b}$ denote the finite field of size 2^b. We also denote a finite field by $\mathbb{F}$ when the field size is clear from the context.

2.1   Substitution-Permutation Networks (SPN)

A *Substitution-Permutation Network* (SPN) is parameterized by the number of rounds, denoted by r; the word length, denoted by b; the width parameter, denoted by k; the linear mixing permutation, a full rank matrix $M : (\mathbb{F}_{2^b})^k \to (\mathbb{F}_{2^b})^k$; and an S-box permutation $S : \mathbb{F}_{2^b} \to \mathbb{F}_{2^b}$. All these parameters are public. The network is a keyed permutation over $\mathbb{F}_{2^b}^k$, so every input (output) vector is bk-bit long. The key is a tuple of $r+1$ (meant to be uniformly random) vectors $\mathbf{k}_0, \mathbf{k}_1, \ldots, \mathbf{k}_r \in (\mathbb{F}_{2^b})^k$. The "independent round keys" assumption here is very common and rooted in the model of Markov Ciphers from the seminal works of Lai, Massey, and Murphy [34], Nyberg [42] and follow-ups. We follow the convention that the number of rounds is the same as the number of mixing layers. In Fig. 1, we give an illustration of a 3-round SPN.

SPN with Random Secret S-boxes (SPN*). Much of this work will deal with SPN networks where each S-box is chosen independently at random from the set of all permutations on $\mathbb{F} := \mathbb{F}_{2^b}$, and kept secret. In this case, the set of S-boxes acts as the key, and there is no reason to have a separate addition of round keys. Thus, the key of the network consists of $k(r+1)$ permutations $S_j^{(i)} : \mathbb{F} \to \mathbb{F}$ (for $0 \leq i \leq r, 1 \leq j \leq k$).

Given input $\mathbf{x}^{(\mathsf{in})} = \mathbf{y}^{(0)} \in \mathbb{F}^k$ and the key, the output $\mathbf{y}^{(\mathsf{out})} = \mathbf{x}^{(r+1)} \in \mathbb{F}^k$ is determined by alternating the following two steps, as illustrated in Fig. 2. For consistency, we let $\mathbf{y}^{(0)}$ be another name for $\mathbf{x}^{(\mathsf{in})}$ and let $\mathbf{x}^{(r+1)}$ be another name for $\mathbf{y}^{(\mathsf{out})}$.

Substitution Step-i $(0 \leq i \leq r)$ For $1 \leq j \leq k$, let $\mathbf{x}^{(i+1)}[j] = S_{i,j}(\mathbf{y}^{(i)}[j])$,
Permutation Step-i $(1 \leq i \leq r)$ Let $\mathbf{y}^{(i)} = M\mathbf{x}^{(i)}$.

We call $\mathbf{x}^{(i)}$ and $\mathbf{y}^{(i)}$ the intermediate values of the i-th round. Then the input $\mathbf{x}^{(\mathsf{in})}$, also called $\mathbf{y}^{(0)}$, is in "the 0-th round". This gets fed into the substitution step-0 which produces $\mathbf{x}^{(1)}$. Permutation step-i is inside the i-th round. Substitution step-i is the boundary between the i-th round and the $(i+1)$-th round. The output $\mathbf{y}^{(\mathsf{out})}$, also called $\mathbf{x}^{(r+1)}$, is in "the $(r+1)$-th round".

Branch number. We use the definition of the branch number of a matrix that quantifies how well the linear layer "mixes" its input.

Definition 1. *The branch number of a matrix* $M \in (\mathbb{F}_{2^b})^{k \times k}$ *is defined to be*

$$\mathsf{br}(M) = \min_{0 \neq \alpha \in (\mathbb{F}_{2^b})^k} (\mathsf{wt}(\alpha) + \mathsf{wt}(M\alpha))$$

where wt *denotes the Hamming weight.*

Having the maximal branch number (namely, $k+1$) is considered a desirable feature for mixing functions [14, 27].

Summary of notations. The intermediate states in an SPN (or SPN*) network are denoted by boldface letters $\mathbf{x}$ or $\mathbf{y}$. The notation $\mathbf{x}^{(r)}$ (resp. $\mathbf{y}^{(r)}$) is used to denote the state at round r; and $\mathbf{x}^{(r)}[s]$ denotes the sth coordinate of $\mathbf{x}^{(r)}$. When dealing with multiple inputs, we let the subscript denote which input we are referring to: i.e., $\mathbf{x}_i^{(r)}$ denotes round-r state of the ith input. We let $\mathbf{x}_{1:t}^{(r)} = (\mathbf{x}_i^{(r)})_{i \in [t]} = (\mathbf{x}_1^{(r)}, \dots, \mathbf{x}_t^{(r)})$ be a shorthand for a tuple of vectors.

3   Layouts

This section introduces *layout*, a key notion of this paper. In the pairwise setting, layout is similar to the notions of an activity pattern [26] or support [3] of an input that have been formulated in the literature in the context of differential and linear cryptanalysis. Our notion considers the generalized setting and deals with t-tuples of inputs for an arbitrary t.

Motivation. Given t inputs $\mathbf{x}_1^{(\text{in})}, \ldots, \mathbf{x}_t^{(\text{in})}$ to an SPN* network, we want to characterize the joint distribution of the outputs $\mathbf{y}_1^{(\text{out})}, \ldots, \mathbf{y}_t^{(\text{out})}$ when all the S-boxes are i.i.d. uniform. The evaluation of the SPN* on these t inputs is essentially a Markov chain. The dependency between the intermediate values can be illustrated by the following Bayesian network.

$$\mathbf{x}_{1:t}^{(\text{in})} \longrightarrow \mathbf{x}_{1:t}^{(1)} \longrightarrow \mathbf{y}_{1:t}^{(1)} \longrightarrow \mathbf{x}_{1:t}^{(2)} \longrightarrow \mathbf{y}_{1:t}^{(2)} \longrightarrow \cdots$$

Here $\mathbf{x}_{1:t}^{(r)}$ denotes the tuple of t vectors $(\mathbf{x}_1^{(r)}, \ldots, \mathbf{x}_t^{(r)})$, and so does $\mathbf{y}_{1:t}^{(r)}$.

The tuple $\mathbf{y}_{1:t}^{(r)}$ depends deterministically on $\mathbf{x}_{1:t}^{(r)}$ via the permutation step. The substitution step is more interesting. The randomness of the substitution step-r consists of k S-boxes $S_1^{(r)}, \ldots, S_k^{(r)}$. Each S-box $S_s^{(r)}$ is applied to the corresponding coordinate for all inputs, namely, $\mathbf{y}_i^{(r)}[s]$ for all $i \in [t]$. The substitution step erases most information, but some are preserved. In particular,

– $\mathbf{y}_i^{(r)}[s] = \mathbf{y}_j^{(r)}[s]$ if and only if $\mathbf{x}_i^{(r+1)}[s] = \mathbf{x}_j^{(r+1)}[s]$.

And it is not hard to verify that this is the only information preserved. In particular, the distribution of $\mathbf{x}_{1:t}^{(r+1)}$ is uniform among all tuples that satisfy

$$\forall i, j \in [t], \ \forall s \in [k], \ \mathbf{x}_i^{(r+1)}[s] = \mathbf{x}_j^{(r+1)}[s] \iff \mathbf{y}_i^{(r)}[s] = \mathbf{y}_j^{(r)}[s].$$

To capture and formalize these constraints, we introduce the notion of a *layout* below. The layout of t vectors $\mathbf{x}_{1:t}$ should specify whether $\mathbf{x}_i[s] = \mathbf{x}_j[s]$, for any $i, j \in [t], s \in [k]$.

Definition 2 (layouts). *A t-wise layout I is defined as $I = (I_{i,j})_{1 \le i < j \le t}$. Each $I_{i,j}$ is a subset of $[k]$. For a tuple of t vectors $\mathbf{x}_{1:t} = (\mathbf{x}_1, \ldots, \mathbf{x}_t) \in (\mathbb{F}^k)^t$, we say that the tuple is in a layout I, denoted by $\mathbf{x}_{1:t}$ in I, if*

$$\forall 1 \le i < j \le t, \ \forall s \in [k], \ s \in I_{i,j} \iff \mathbf{x}_i[s] = \mathbf{x}_j[s].$$

We say I is the layout of $\mathbf{x}_{1:t}$, denoted by $\text{layout}(\mathbf{x}_{1:t}) = I$, if $\mathbf{x}_{1:t}$ is in layout I.

We also define a weaker notion: say $\mathbf{x}_{1:t}$ satisfies a layout I, denoted by $\mathbf{x}_{1:t}$ SAT I, if and only if

$$\forall 1 \le i < j \le t, \ \forall s \in [k], \ s \in I_{i,j} \implies \mathbf{x}_i[s] = \mathbf{x}_j[s].$$

Given another layout $J = (J_{i,j})_{1 \le i < j \le t}$, we say J is stricter or equal to I, denoted by $J \supseteq I$ or $I \subseteq J$, if

$$\forall 1 \le i < j \le t, \ J_{i,j} \supseteq I_{i,j}.$$

Example 1. Consider the 3-wise layout $I = (I_{1,2}, I_{1,3}, I_{2,3}) = (\{1\}, \{2\}, \{3\})$. Then, the tuple of vectors $\mathbf{x}_1 = [a, b, c']$, $\mathbf{x}_2 = [a, b', c]$, and $\mathbf{x}_3 = [a', b, c]$ lay in the layout I a long as $a \ne a'$, $b \ne b'$, $c \ne c'$.

Note that not all layouts are "valid". For example,

$$I = (I_{1,2}, I_{1,3}, I_{2,3}) = (\{1\}, \varnothing, \{1\}).$$

is not the layout of any 3-tuple. Because $1 \in I_{1,2}$ means the first two vectors agree on coordinate 1, and $1 \in I_{2,3}$ means the last two vectors agree on coordinate 1, by transitivity, these imply $1 \in I_{1,3}$. We say a layout I is *valid* if for all $s \in [k]$ and for all $i < i' < i''$, if any two of $I_{i,i'}, I_{i,i''}, I_{i',i''}$ contain s, so does the third one.

Random Walks on Layouts. Using the notion of layouts, the distribution of $\mathbf{x}_{1:t}^{(r+1)}$ conditioned on $\mathbf{y}_{1:t}^{(r)}$ can be described more concisely: the substitution step simply samples a random $\mathbf{x}_{1:t}^{(r+1)}$ who is in the same layout as $\mathbf{y}_{1:t}^{(r)}$. In other words, the substitution step is equivalent to a two-step process: first extract the layout of $\mathbf{y}_{1:t}^{(r)}$, then sample a random tuple from the layout. If letting $I^{(r)}$ denote the layout of $\mathbf{y}_{1:t}^{(r)}$ (and also $\mathbf{x}_{1:t}^{(r+1)}$, since they are in the same layout), the Bayesian network of the SPN* evaluation can also be written in the following way:

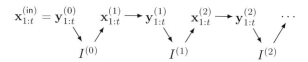

This Bayesian network view through the lens of layouts suggests that the right problem to study is the transition probability from $I^{(r)}$ to $I^{(r+1)}$ (induced by the linear mixing layer). This transition probability could be easier to characterize since the space of all layouts is much smaller than the space of all t-tuples.

All theorems in this paper follow this framework. They essentially prove the following statement: Starting from any layout $I^{(0)}$, after some r rounds, the distribution of $I^{(r)}$ is close to t-wise independent. To complete the framework, we need to answer two questions: 1) What is the definition of a layout being close to t-wise independent; and 2) How does a layout being close to t-wise independent imply that a random tuple in the layout is close to t-wise independent?

Definition 3 (closeness to t-wise independence). *Let $\mathbf{z}_1, \dots, \mathbf{z}_t$ be sampled uniformly at random from $\mathbb{F}^k$ with (resp. without) replacement. Then we say the tuple $(\mathbf{z}_1, \dots, \mathbf{z}_t)$ is t-wise independent with (resp. without) replacement.*

Let $(\mathbf{x}_1, \dots, \mathbf{x}_t)$ be sampled from a distribution. We say $(\mathbf{x}_1, \dots, \mathbf{x}_t)$ is ε-close to t-wise independent with (resp. without) replacement if

$$\Delta_{TV}\Big((\mathbf{x}_1, \dots, \mathbf{x}_t)(\mathbf{z}_1, \dots, \mathbf{z}_t)\Big) \le \varepsilon.$$

Let layout I be sampled from a distribution. We say I is ε-close to t-wise independent with (resp. without) replacement if

$$\Delta_{TV}\Big(I, \text{layout}(\mathbf{z}_1, \dots, \mathbf{z}_t)\Big) \le \varepsilon.$$

We say a keyed permutation (e.g., a SPN*) is ε-close to t-wise independent with (resp. without) replacement if for any t distinct input $\mathbf{x}_{1:t}^{(in)}$, the joint distribution of the t corresponding output $\mathbf{y}_{1:t}^{(out)}$ is ε-close to t-wise independent with (resp. without) replacement, assuming the key is sampled properly.

The following lemma and its corollary show how the distribution of t-tuples is related to the distribution of their layouts, and justify why this 'layout' analysis suffices for our purposes of proving t-wise independence. Their proofs are deferred to the full version of the paper.

Lemma 1. *Assume I and $\mathbf{x}_{1:t} = (\mathbf{x}_1, \ldots, \mathbf{x}_t)$ jointly come from a distribution where $\mathbf{x}_{1:t}$ is a random tuple in I when conditioning on I, and similarly for J and $\mathbf{z}_{1:t}$. Then*

$$\Delta_{TV}(I, J) = \Delta_{TV}(\mathbf{x}_{1:t}, \mathbf{z}_{1:t}).$$

Corollary 1. *Suppose I is sampled from a distribution and $\mathbf{x}_{1:t} = (\mathbf{x}_1, \ldots, \mathbf{x}_t)$ is sampled uniformly within layout I. Then $\mathbf{x}_{1:t}$ is ε-close to t-wise independent if and only if I is ε-close to t-wise independent.*

4 Warm-Up: 2-Wise Independence of 2-Round SPN*

In this section, we present the core idea of our new technique and demonstrate its power by showing that a 2-round SPN* is $2^{-\Theta(kb)}$-close to 2-wise independent. That is, we show that for any two distinct inputs $(\mathbf{x}_1^{(in)}, \mathbf{x}_2^{(in)})$ (which is the same as $(\mathbf{y}_1^{(0)}, \mathbf{y}_2^{(0)})$) the joint distribution of their corresponding outputs $(\mathbf{y}_1^{(out)}, \mathbf{y}_2^{(out)})$ (which is the same as $(\mathbf{x}_1^{(3)}, \mathbf{x}_2^{(3)})$) is close to 2-wise independent.

Theorem 1. *2-round SPN* is ε-close to 2-wise independent, where*

$$\varepsilon \leq \frac{3^k}{(2^{b-1})^{k/2}},$$

if its linear mixing function has maximal branch number (see Definition 1).

The theorem will be proved in Sect. 4.2. At a high level, the proof is the combination of the following two statements.

- **After the first round, the layout is nice w.h.p.** That is, starting from any pair of inputs, the intermediate layout is "nice" with overwhelmingly high probability. A layout is nice if the number of collisions (i.e., coordinates where the two vectors agree) is relatively small.
- **If the layout is nice before the second round, the output is close to 2-wise independent.** That is, conditioning on the intermediate layout being any nice layout, the pair of outputs will be close to 2-wise independent

Let $I^{(r)}$ denote the layout of $(\mathbf{y}_1^{(r)}, \mathbf{y}_2^{(r)})$ and $(\mathbf{x}_1^{(r+1)}, \mathbf{x}_2^{(r+1)})$. Since the section only discusses the 2-wise setting, the representation of a layout can be simplified. A layout is represented by a subset $I \subseteq [k]$, such that $i \in I$ means the two vectors agree on the i-th position.

As pointed out by the standard differential cryptanalysis, it would be helpful to consider the difference between each pair of vectors

$$\mathbf{x}_\Delta^{(r)} := \mathbf{x}_1^{(r)} - \mathbf{x}_2^{(r)}, \qquad \mathbf{y}_\Delta^{(r)} := \mathbf{y}_1^{(r)} - \mathbf{y}_2^{(r)}.$$

Note that for each $s \in [k]$

$$\mathbf{y}_\Delta^{(r)}[s] = 0 \iff (\mathbf{y}_1^{(r)}[s] = \mathbf{y}_2^{(r)}[s]) \iff s \in I^{(r)}.$$

This suggests that $\mathbf{y}_\Delta^{(r)}[s]$ is also "in" $I^{(r)}$. This can be formalized by introducing the following simplified definition for the pairwise setting.

Definition 4. *A (pairwise) layout I is a subset of $[k]$. For any vector $\mathbf{x}_\Delta$ and layout I, define*

$$\mathbf{x}_\Delta \ \mathsf{SAT} \ I \iff (\forall s \in [k], \ s \in I \implies \mathbf{x}[s] = 0),$$
$$\mathbf{x}_\Delta \ \mathsf{in} \ I \iff (\forall s \in [k], \ s \in I \iff \mathbf{x}[s] = 0).$$

And we say I is the layout of $\mathbf{x}_\Delta$, denoted by $\mathrm{layout}(\mathbf{x}_\Delta) = I$, if $\mathbf{x}_\Delta$ in I.

Then for any vector difference $\mathbf{x}_\Delta = \mathbf{x}_1 - \mathbf{x}_2$, we have

$$\mathbf{x}_\Delta \ \mathsf{SAT} \ I \iff (\mathbf{x}_1, \mathbf{x}_2) \ \mathsf{SAT} \ I, \qquad \mathbf{x}_\Delta \ \mathsf{in} \ I \iff (\mathbf{x}_1, \mathbf{x}_2) \ \mathsf{in} \ I,$$

and $\mathrm{layout}(\mathbf{x}_\Delta) = \mathrm{layout}(\mathbf{x}_1, \mathbf{x}_2)$.

Therefore it suffices to *only* consider the difference vectors, since the whole analysis can ignore the original pair of vectors.

- Permutation step: $\mathbf{y}_\Delta^{(r)} = M\mathbf{x}_\Delta^{(r)}$.
- Substitution step: $\mathbf{x}_\Delta^{(r+1)}$ is a random tuple whose layout is the same as $\mathbf{y}_\Delta^{(r)}$.
- Output: The pair of output vectors is ε-close to 2-wise independent if and only if $I^{(2)} = \mathrm{layout}(\mathbf{y}_\Delta^{(2)})$ is ε-close to 2-wise independent (Corollary 1).

4.1   The Layout Transition Probability

This section computes the transition probability from layout $I^{(r)}$ to $I^{(r+1)}$. Their dependency can be captured by the following Bayesian network.

$$I^{(r-1)} \longrightarrow \mathbf{x}_\Delta^{(r)} \xrightarrow{\ \mathsf{M}\ } \mathbf{y}_\Delta^{(r)} \longrightarrow I^{(r)}$$

Let trans-prob(I, J) denote the probability $I^{(r)} = J$ conditioning on $I^{(r-1)} = I$. Formally, trans-prob(I, J) is the probability layout$(M\mathbf{x}) = J$ when the (difference) vector $\mathbf{x}$ is sampled uniformly from layout I. By definition

$$\text{trans-prob}(I, J) = \Pr_{\mathbf{x} \text{ in } I}\left[M\mathbf{x} \text{ in } J\right] = \frac{\#\{\mathbf{x} : \mathbf{x} \text{ in } I \text{ and } M\mathbf{x} \text{ in } J\}}{\#\{\mathbf{x} : \mathbf{x} \text{ in } I\}}.$$

To simplify this expression, we introduce some new notations.

For the denominator, we define free$(I) = k - |I|$, which stands for the number of "free" coordinates. Then $\#\{\mathbf{x} : \mathbf{x} \text{ in } I\} = (2^b - 1)^{\text{free}(I)}$.

Denote the numerator by trans-count(I, J). Define indicator function $\mathbb{1}_M$ as

$$\mathbb{1}_M(\mathbf{x}, \mathbf{y}) := \begin{cases} 1 & \text{if } M\mathbf{x} = \mathbf{y}, \\ 0 & \text{otherwise.} \end{cases}$$

Then the numerator can be written as

$$\text{trans-count}(I, J) = \#\{\mathbf{x} : \mathbf{x} \text{ in } I \text{ and } M\mathbf{x} \text{ in } J\} = \sum_{\mathbf{x} \text{ in } I} \sum_{\mathbf{y} \text{ in } J} \mathbb{1}_M(\mathbf{x}, \mathbf{y}).$$

The core idea is to also consider another sum operator $\sum_{\mathbf{x} \text{ SAT} I}$. For any function f, we have

$$\sum_{\mathbf{x} \text{ SAT} I} f(\mathbf{x}) = \sum_{I' \supseteq I} \sum_{\mathbf{x} \text{ in } I'} f(\mathbf{x}).$$

Then by the inclusion-exclusion principle,

$$\sum_{\mathbf{x} \text{ in } I} f(\mathbf{x}) = \sum_{I' \supseteq I} (-1)^{|I' \setminus I|} \sum_{\mathbf{x} \text{ SAT} I'} f(\mathbf{x}).$$

Consider the following sum

$$\sum_{\mathbf{x} \text{ SAT} I} \sum_{\mathbf{y} \text{ SAT} J} \mathbb{1}_M(\mathbf{x}, \mathbf{y}) = \#\{\mathbf{x} : \mathbf{x} \text{ SAT } I \text{ and } M\mathbf{x} \text{ SAT } J\} \tag{4}$$

that looks similar to trans-count(I, J). The only difference is whether to enumerate vectors *in* I, J or *satisfying* I, J. The value of (4) is easier to compute. It is the number of solutions of a linear system, which must be a power of $|\mathbb{F}| = 2^b$. In particular, if the matrix M has the maximal branch number, we have

$$\sum_{\mathbf{x} \text{ SAT} I} \sum_{\mathbf{y} \text{ SAT} J} \mathbb{1}_M(\mathbf{x}, \mathbf{y}) = \begin{cases} (2^b)^{\text{free}(I)+\text{free}(J)-k} & \text{if } \text{free}(I) + \text{free}(J) \geq k, \\ 1 & \text{if } \text{free}(I) + \text{free}(J) < k. \end{cases} \tag{5}$$

Then by the inclusion-exclusion principle,

$$\begin{aligned}
\text{trans-count}(I, J) &= \sum_{\mathbf{x} \text{ in } I} \sum_{\mathbf{y} \text{ in } J} \mathbb{1}_M(\mathbf{x}, \mathbf{y}) \\
&= \sum_{I' \supseteq I} \sum_{J' \supseteq J} (-1)^{|I' \setminus I|+|J' \setminus J|} \sum_{\mathbf{x} \text{ SAT} I'} \sum_{\mathbf{y} \text{ SAT} J'} \mathbb{1}_M(\mathbf{x}, \mathbf{y}) \tag{6} \\
&= \sum_{I' \supseteq I} \sum_{J' \supseteq J} (-1)^{|I' \setminus I|+|J' \setminus J|} (2^b)^{\max(\text{free}(I')+\text{free}(J')-k,0)}.
\end{aligned}$$

Now we are ready to present our results about the layout transition probability. They are essentially polishing (6).

Lemma 2. *If M has the maximal branch number, the layout transition probability* trans-prob$(I, J) := \Pr_{\mathbf{x} \text{ in } I}[M\mathbf{x} \text{ in } J]$ *is bounded by*

$$\left| \text{trans-prob}(I, J) - \frac{(2^b - 1)^{\text{free}(J)}}{(2^b)^k} \right| \leq \frac{2^{\text{free}(I)+\text{free}(J)}}{(2^b - 1)^{\text{free}(I)}}.$$

Proof. Consider function $u(\mathbf{x}, \mathbf{y}) = \frac{1}{(2^b)^k}$. If we view $u(\mathbf{x}, \mathbf{y})$ as the conditional probability of $\mathbf{y}$ given $\mathbf{x}$, then it captures the process that $\mathbf{y}$ is sampled uniformly at random and is independent of $\mathbf{x}$. Notice that

$$\sum_{\mathbf{x} \text{ SAT } I} \sum_{\mathbf{y} \text{ SAT } J} u(\mathbf{x}, \mathbf{y}) = \sum_{\mathbf{x} \text{ SAT } I} \sum_{\mathbf{y} \text{ SAT } J} \frac{1}{(2^b)^k} = (2^b)^{\text{free}(I)+\text{free}(J)-k}$$

is very similar to (5). The difference is no more than 1 for any I, J. Therefore, in some sense, u is a very good approximation of $\mathbb{1}_M$. With this intuition in mind, we expect

$$\sum_{\mathbf{x} \text{ in } I} \sum_{\mathbf{y} \text{ in } J} \mathbb{1}_M(\mathbf{x}, \mathbf{y}) \quad - \quad \sum_{\mathbf{x} \text{ in } I} \sum_{\mathbf{y} \text{ in } J} u(\mathbf{x}, \mathbf{y}) \tag{7}$$

to be very small. The difference between them is bounded by

$$\left| \text{trans-count}(I, J) - \sum_{\mathbf{x} \text{ in } I} \sum_{\mathbf{y} \text{ in } J} \frac{1}{(2^b)^k} \right| = \left| \sum_{\mathbf{x} \text{ in } I} \sum_{\mathbf{y} \text{ in } J} \left(\mathbb{1}_M(\mathbf{x}, \mathbf{y}) - \frac{1}{(2^b)^k} \right) \right|$$

$$= \left| \sum_{I' \supseteq I} \sum_{J' \supseteq J} (-1)^{|I' \setminus I| + |J' \setminus J|} \sum_{\mathbf{x} \text{ SAT } I'} \sum_{\mathbf{y} \text{ SAT } J'} \left(\mathbb{1}_M(\mathbf{x}, \mathbf{y}) - \frac{1}{(2^b)^k} \right) \right|$$

$$\leq \sum_{I' \supseteq I} \sum_{J' \supseteq J} 1 = 2^{\text{free}(I)+\text{free}(J)}.$$

So we can approximate the transition probability by

$$\text{trans-prob}(I, J) = \frac{\sum_{\mathbf{x} \text{ in } I} \sum_{\mathbf{y} \text{ in } J} \frac{1}{(2^b)^k} + \text{term (7)}}{\sum_{\mathbf{x} \text{ in } I} 1} = \underbrace{\sum_{\mathbf{y} \text{ in } J} \frac{1}{(2^b)^k}}_{\text{approximation}} + \underbrace{\frac{\text{term (7)}}{\sum_{\mathbf{x} \text{ in } I} 1}}_{\text{error}}.$$

The approximation term is particularly nice, as it can be interpreted as the probability that a random vector lies in layout J. It equals to

$$\sum_{\mathbf{y} \text{ in } J} \frac{1}{(2^b)^k} = \Pr_{\mathbf{y} \in \mathbb{F}^k}[\mathbf{y} \text{ in } J] = \frac{(2^b - 1)^{\text{free}(J)}}{(2^b)^k}.$$

The absolute value of the error term is at most $2^{\text{free}(I)+\text{free}(J)}/(2^b - 1)^{\text{free}(I)}$. □

Lemma 3. *Let $M : \mathbb{F}^k \to \mathbb{F}^k$ be a matrix with maximal branch number. For any layout I. Let J denote the layout of I after one round of SPN. That is,* trans-prob(I, J) *is the probability mass function of J. Then J is ε-close to 2-wise independent, where $\varepsilon \leq 3^k/2(2^{b-1})^{\text{free}(I)}$.*

4.2   The Niceness of a Layout

Implied by Lemma 3, if the starting input difference is in a layout I with large free(I), then after one round it will be very close to 2-wise independent. However, consider the extreme case when free(I) = 1, that is, the input difference $\mathbf{x}_\Delta$ is zero on all but one coordinate. Then after one round of SPN with maximal branch number mixing, the difference must be non-zero on every coordinate, which is about $(k/2^b)$ away from 2-wise independence.

So for proving 2-wise independent, a layout I with larger free(I) is "easier" to analyze. We formalize this by defining the *niceness* of a layout. We say a layout I is α-nice if $|I| = k - \text{free}(I) \le \alpha k$.

To prove Theorem 1, we show that after one round, the layout is likely to be nice, then after one more round, it will be close to 2-wise independent.

Lemma 4. *Assume the mixing function has maximal branch number. For any 2-wise layout I, let J be sampled according to* trans-prob(I, J). *Then for any $\alpha \in [0, 1]$,*

$$\Pr[J \text{ is } \alpha\text{-nice}] \ge 1 - \frac{e \cdot 2^k}{(2^b - 1)^{\alpha k}}.$$

Proof. The proof starts with an upper bound on the transition probability trans-prob(I, J) that does not depend on I.

$$\text{trans-prob}(I, J) = \frac{\sum_{\mathbf{x} \text{ in } I} \sum_{\mathbf{y} \text{ in } J} \mathbb{1}_M(\mathbf{x}, \mathbf{y})}{(2^b - 1)^{\text{free}(I)}}$$

$$\le \frac{\sum_{\mathbf{x} \text{ SAT} I} \sum_{\mathbf{y} \text{ SAT} J} \mathbb{1}_M(\mathbf{x}, \mathbf{y})}{(2^b - 1)^{\text{free}(I)}} = \frac{(2^b)^{\max(\text{free}(I)+\text{free}(J)-k, 0)}}{(2^b - 1)^{\text{free}(I)}}.$$

Focus on the case that free(I)+free(J) > k, since otherwise trans-prob(I, J) = 0.

$$\text{trans-prob}(I, J) \le \frac{(2^b)^{\text{free}(I)+\text{free}(J)-k}}{(2^b - 1)^{\text{free}(I)}}$$

$$\le \left(\frac{2^b}{2^b - 1}\right)^k \cdot \frac{1}{(2^b - 1)^{k-\text{free}(J)}} \le \frac{e}{(2^b - 1)^{k-\text{free}(J)}}.$$

The last inequality holds because the mixing function has maximal branch number inherently implies $k \le 2^b$.

We finish the proof by applying the union bound over all layouts J that are not α-nice. The number of not-α-nice layouts is no more than 2^k. □

Proof (Theorem 1). Let $I^{(0)}, I^{(1)}, I^{(2)}$ denote the layout of the inputs, the layout of the middle vectors, the layout of the outputs respectively.

By Lemma 4,

$$\Pr[I^{(1)} \text{ is } \alpha\text{-nice}] \ge 1 - \frac{e \cdot 2^k}{(2^b - 1)^{\alpha k}}.$$

Conditioning on $I^{(1)}$ being an α-nice layout, $I^{(2)}$ is $(3^k/2(2^{b-1})^{(1-\alpha)k})$-close to 2-wise independent, as shown by Lemma 3. Adding up all the errors, $I^{(2)}$ is ε-close to 2-wise independent, where

$$\varepsilon \leq \frac{3^k}{2 \cdot (2^{b-1})^{(1-\alpha)k}} + \frac{e \cdot 2^k}{(2^b - 1)^{\alpha k}}.$$

Set $\alpha = 1/2$ to minimize the statistical distance bound.

$\square$

5 The General Case of t-Wise Independence

In this section, we generalize our analysis of 2-wise independence in Sect. 4 to the t-wise setting. The high-level framework is mostly the same:

- Introducing the proper notion of *nice* layouts.
- Starting from any t distinct inputs $(\mathbf{x}_1^{(in)}, \ldots, \mathbf{x}_t^{(in)})$, after one round (or a few rounds), the tuple will fall into some nice layout with high probability.
- Core lemma: For any nice layout I, if t inputs $(\mathbf{x}_1, \ldots, \mathbf{x}_t)$ are uniformly sampled from layout I, then after the linear mixing, the layout of $(\mathbf{y}_1, \ldots, \mathbf{y}_1) :=$ $(M\mathbf{x}_1, \ldots, M\mathbf{x}_t)$ is close to t-wise independent.

We define *nice* layouts as follows: For any t-wise layout $I = \{I_{i,j}\}_{1 \leq i < j \leq t}$, we say I is α-*nice* if and only if for all $1 < j \leq t$,

$$\left| \bigcup_{i<j} I_{i,j} \right| < \alpha k.$$

Here $\alpha \in [0, 1]$ is a parameter quantifying the niceness of the layout. An equivalent definition is as follows: For any t-tuple $\mathbf{x}_{1:t} = (\mathbf{x}_1, \ldots, \mathbf{x}_t)$, say $\mathbf{x}_j$ collides with $\mathbf{x}_{1:j-1} = (\mathbf{x}_1, \ldots, \mathbf{x}_{j-1})$ on coordinate s if and only if there exists $i < j$ such that $\mathbf{x}_i[s] = \mathbf{x}_j[s]$. Then $\mathbf{x}_{1:t}$ is in an α-nice layout if and only if for every $1 < j \leq t$, $\mathbf{x}_j$ collides with $\mathbf{x}_{1:j-1}$ on at most αk coordinates.

If a t-tuple is sampled from a nice layout, it will be close to t-wise independent after one more round, as shown by our core lemma (Lemma 5). At a high level, the proof inductively uses the technique of its pairwise analog in Sect. 4.

Thanks to this core lemma, in order to show a r-round SPN* is close to t-wise independent, it suffices to show that after the first $r - 1$ rounds, the tuple falls into some nice layout with high probability. We present three different results of this flavor. They differ in the following three criteria

- How large t can be (the core lemma supports t up to $2^{0.499b}$);
- How small the statistical error is (we are aiming for $2^{-\Theta(bk)}$ error); and
- How many rounds are required (ideally 2 rounds).

Each of our results optimizes two of the criteria, and compromises on the third criterion. Section 5.2 can only handle small t. Section 5.3 supports t up to $2^{0.499b}$ but the statistical error is slightly larger. Section 5.4 supports large t and keeps the statistical error $2^{-\Theta(bk)}$, but it requires $O(\log t)$ rounds.

5.1   Core Lemma and Conditional Transition Probability

Lemma 5. *For $\alpha \in [0,1]$ and any α-nice t-wise layout I, if tuple $(\mathbf{x}_1, \ldots, \mathbf{x}_t)$ is sampled uniformly from layout I and let $(\mathbf{y}_1, \ldots, \mathbf{y}_t) = (M\mathbf{x}_1, \ldots, M\mathbf{x}_t)$, then the layout of $(\mathbf{y}_1, \ldots, \mathbf{y}_t)$ is ε-close to t-wise independence with replacement, where*

$$\varepsilon \le t \cdot \left(\frac{2t}{2^b}\right)^{(1-\alpha)k} (2t)^k = t \cdot \left(\frac{(2t)^{2-\alpha}}{(2^b)^{1-\alpha}}\right)^k$$

and we assume the mixing function M has maximal branch number.

This section proves Lemma 5, which is the core of our analysis. The lemma says, if the tuple is in a nice layout at the beginning of a round (must be uniform within this layout due to the S-boxes), then the tuple will become very close to t-wise independent after this round.

The lemma is proved by induction. Assume the lemma holds for smaller t. Say $I = \{I_{a,b}\}_{1 \le a < b \le t}$ is a nice layout, $\mathbf{x}_{1:t}$ is sampled uniformly from layout I and $\mathbf{y}_{1:t} = M\mathbf{x}_{1:t}$, as in the lemma statement. By the definition of niceness, $\mathbf{x}_{1:t-1}$ is sampled uniformly from a nice $(t-1)$-wise layout $I' = \{I_{a,b}\}_{1 \le a < b \le t-1}$. By the induction hypothesis, layout$(\mathbf{y}_{1:t-1})$ is close to $(t-1)$-wise independent. To complete the induction, we need to show that the "conditional layout" of $\mathbf{y}_t$ is close to uniform. First, we need to formalize "conditional layout".

We want to analyze the distribution of $(\mathbf{x}_t, \mathbf{y}_t)$ conditioning on the value of $\mathbf{x}_{1:t-1}, \mathbf{y}_{1:t-1}$. Let's start with a simpler question: What is the conditional distribution of $\mathbf{x}_t$? Since the tuple is sampled from layout I, any constraint in I saying $\mathbf{x}_a[i] = \mathbf{x}_t[i]$ (i.e., if $i \in I_{a,t}$) affects the conditional distribution of $\mathbf{x}_t$. In more detail, the constraints on $\mathbf{x}_t$ can be formalized as[2]

$$I_c(i) = \begin{cases} \mathbf{x}_a[i] & \text{if } i \in I_{a,t} \text{ for some } a < t, \\ \bot & \text{otherwise.} \end{cases} \tag{8}$$

For each $i \in [k]$, if $I_c(i) \ne \bot$ then $\mathbf{x}_t[i]$ must equal to $I_c(i)$, otherwise $\mathbf{x}_t[i]$ is uniform in $\mathbb{F} \setminus \{\mathbf{x}_1[i], \ldots, \mathbf{x}_{t-1}[i]\}$.

Inspired by the above discussion, we formally define *conditional layouts*. When conditioning on $\mathbf{x}_{1:t-1}$ and $\mathbf{y}_{1:t-1} = M\mathbf{x}_{1:t-1}$. For any $i, j \in [k]$, define

$$S_i = \{\mathbf{x}_a[i] \mid a < t\}, \qquad T_j = \{\mathbf{y}_a[j] \mid a < t\}.$$

A *conditional layout* for $\mathbf{x}_t$ is specified by a function $I_c : [k] \to \mathbb{F} \cup \{\bot\}$ such that $I_c(i) \in S_i \cup \{\bot\}$ for every $i \in [k]$. Define $\mathbf{x}_t$ is in I_c (denoted by $\mathbf{x}_t$ in I_c) and $\mathbf{x}_t$ satisfies I_c (denoted by $\mathbf{x}_t$ SAT I_c) as

$$\mathbf{x}_t \text{ in } I_c \iff \forall i \in [k], \left(\begin{matrix} I_c(i) \ne \bot \implies \mathbf{x}_t[i] = I_c(i), \\ I_c(i) = \bot \implies \mathbf{x}_t[i] \notin S_i \end{matrix}\right),$$

$$\mathbf{x}_t \text{ SAT } I_c \iff \forall i \in [k], \left(I_c(i) \ne \bot \implies \mathbf{x}_t[i] = I_c(i)\right).$$

---

[2] Even if there exists distinct a, a' such that $i \in I_{a,t} \cap I_{a',t}$, I_c is still well-defined. Because in such case, we must have $i \in I_{a,a'}$ (otherwise I is not a valid layout), then $\mathbf{x}_a[i] = \mathbf{x}_{a'}[i]$.

We say I_c is the layout of $\mathbf{x}_t$, denoted by $\mathrm{layout}_c(\mathbf{x}^{(t)}) = I_c$, if $\mathbf{x}_t \in I_c$. Define

$$\mathrm{free}(I_c) := |I_c^{-1}(\bot)| = \#\{i \in [k] \text{ s.t. } I_c(i) = \bot\}$$

as the number of coordinates that I_c outputs $\bot$. Note that, if I_c is derived from an α-nice layout I as in (8), then

$$\mathrm{free}(I_c) = k - \left| \bigcup_{a<t} I_{a,t} \right| \geq (1-\alpha)k.$$

Define I_c' is stricter or equal to I_c, denoted by $I_c' \supseteq I_c$, as

$$I_c' \supseteq I_c \iff \forall i \in [k], \left(I_c(i) \neq \bot \implies I_c'(i) = I_c(i) \right).$$

Symmetrically, a conditional layout for $\mathbf{y}_t$ is specified by a function $J_c : [k] \to \mathbb{F} \cup \{\bot\}$ such that $J_c(j) \in T_j \cup \{\bot\}$ for every $j \in [k]$. We adopt the same notations and terminology from the conditional layout of $\mathbf{x}_t$.

Let $\mathbf{y}^*$ be sampled uniformly at random from $\mathbb{F}^k$. Then

$$\Pr\left[\mathrm{layout}_c(\mathbf{y}^*) = J_c\right] = \sum_{\mathbf{y} \text{ in } J_c} \frac{1}{2^{bk}} = \frac{\prod_{j \in [k] \text{ s.t. } J_c(j)=\bot}(2^b - |T_j|)}{2^{bk}}. \tag{9}$$

We hope $\mathrm{layout}_c(\mathbf{y}_t)$ is close to $\mathrm{layout}_c(\mathbf{y}^*)$ by distribution. So we analyze the transition probability from I_c to J_c. That is, if $\mathbf{x}$ is sampled from layout I_c, what is the distribution of the layout of $\mathbf{y} = M\mathbf{x}$. We found that, if $\mathrm{free}(I_c)$ is large enough, the layout of $\mathbf{y}$ is close to the layout of random $\mathbf{y}^*$ by distribution.

Lemma 6. *Assume the linear mixing M has maximal branch number. Conditioning on any sets $S_1, \ldots, S_k, T_1, \ldots, T_k$, each of size at most $t-1$. For any conditional layout I_c, if $\mathbf{x}$ is sampled uniformly at random from layout I_c and let $\mathbf{y} := M\mathbf{x}$, then the statistical distance between $\mathrm{layout}_c(\mathbf{y})$ and the conditional layout of a random vector is no greater than*

$$\left(\frac{2t-1}{2^b}\right)^{\mathrm{free}(I_c)} (2t-1)^k.$$

We start by bounding the transition probability. For any conditional layouts I_c, J_c, the transition probability from I_c to J_c, denoted by $\mathrm{trans\text{-}prob}(I_c, J_c)$, is the probability $M\mathbf{x}$ in J_c when $\mathbf{x}$ is sampled from layout I_c. By definition,

$$\mathrm{trans\text{-}prob}(I_c, J_c) = \frac{\mathrm{trans\text{-}count}(I_c, J_c)}{\text{size of layout } I_c} = \frac{\displaystyle\sum_{\mathbf{x} \text{ in } I_c} \sum_{\mathbf{y} \text{ in } J_c} \mathbb{1}_M(\mathbf{x}, \mathbf{y})}{\displaystyle\sum_{\mathbf{x} \text{ in } I_c} 1} \tag{10}$$

where $\mathbb{1}_M$ is defined as

$$\mathbb{1}_M(\mathbf{x}, \mathbf{y}) = \begin{cases} 1 & \text{if } M\mathbf{x} = \mathbf{y}, \\ 0 & \text{otherwise.} \end{cases}$$

We show that if $\mathrm{free}(I_c)$ is sufficiently large, then the transition probability $\mathrm{trans\text{-}prob}(I_c, J_c)$ is close to the probability that random $\mathbf{y}^*$ lies in layout J_c.

Lemma 7. *Assume the linear mixing has maximal branch number. Condition-ing on any sets $S_1, \ldots, S_k, T_1, \ldots, T_k$, each of size at most $t - 1$. For any (con-ditional) layouts I_c, J_c, the transition probability from I_c to J_c is bounded by*

$$\left| \text{trans-prob}(I_c, J_c) - \sum_{\mathbf{y} \text{ in } J_c} \frac{1}{2^{bk}} \right| \leq \left(\frac{2t - 1}{2^b} \right)^{\text{free}(I_c)} t^{\text{free}(J_c)}.$$

Proof. In the definition of transition probability (Eq. (10)), the sum is over $\mathbf{x}$ in I_c, which is hard to analyze. But we know how $\sum_{\mathbf{x} \text{ SAT } I_c}$ and $\sum_{\mathbf{x} \text{ in } I_c}$ are closely connected. On the easy direction, we have

$$\sum_{\mathbf{x} \text{ SAT } I_c} \equiv \sum_{I_c' \supseteq I_c} \sum_{\mathbf{x} \text{ in } I_c'}, \qquad \sum_{\mathbf{y} \text{ SAT } J_c} \equiv \sum_{J_c' \supseteq J_c} \sum_{\mathbf{y} \text{ in } J_c'}.$$

Then by the inclusion-exclusion principle

$$\sum_{\mathbf{x} \text{ in } I_c} \equiv \sum_{I_c' \supseteq I_c} (-1)^{\Delta(I_c', I_c)} \sum_{\mathbf{x} \text{ SAT } I_c'}, \qquad \sum_{\mathbf{y} \text{ in } J_c} \equiv \sum_{J_c' \supseteq J_c} (-1)^{\Delta(J_c', J_c)} \sum_{\mathbf{y} \text{ SAT } J_c'},$$

where Δ denotes the Hamming distance. Since $I_c' \supseteq I_c$, the Hamming distance can also be written as $\Delta(I_c', I_c) = \text{free}(I_c) - \text{free}(I_c')$.

We can apply the inclusion-exclusion principle to the numerator of (10),

$$\text{trans-count}(I_c, J_c) = \sum_{\mathbf{x} \text{ in } I_c} \sum_{\mathbf{y} \text{ in } J_c} \mathbb{1}_M(\mathbf{x}, \mathbf{y})$$

$$= \sum_{I_c' \supseteq I_c} \sum_{J_c' \supseteq J_c} (-1)^{\Delta(I_c', I_c) + \Delta(J_c', J_c)} \sum_{\mathbf{x} \text{ SAT } I_c'} \sum_{\mathbf{y} \text{ SAT } J_c'} \mathbb{1}_M(\mathbf{x}, \mathbf{y}).$$

As we have observed in previous sections, $\sum_{\mathbf{x} \text{ SAT } I_c'} \sum_{\mathbf{y} \text{ SAT } J_c'} \mathbb{1}_M(\mathbf{x}, \mathbf{y})$ is easy to bound. Since the linear mixing has maximal branch number,

$$\sum_{\mathbf{x} \text{ SAT } I_c'} \sum_{\mathbf{y} \text{ SAT } J_c'} \mathbb{1}_M(\mathbf{x}, \mathbf{y}) = \begin{cases} (2^b)^{\text{free}(I_c') + \text{free}(J_c') - k} & \text{if } \text{free}(I_c') + \text{free}(J_c') \geq k \\ 0 \text{ or } 1 & \text{otherwise.} \end{cases}$$

It can be approximated by

$$\sum_{\mathbf{x} \text{ SAT } I_c'} \sum_{\mathbf{y} \text{ SAT } J_c'} \frac{1}{2^{bk}} = (2^b)^{\text{free}(I_c') + \text{free}(J_c') - k},$$

such that the absolute value of the error is no more than 1 for any I_c', J_c'.

As $\sum_{\mathbf{x} \text{ SAT } I_c'} \sum_{\mathbf{y} \text{ SAT } J_c'} \frac{1}{2^{bk}}$ is a good approximation of $\sum_{\mathbf{x} \text{ SAT } I_c'} \sum_{\mathbf{y} \text{ SAT } J_c'} \mathbb{1}_M(\mathbf{x}, \mathbf{y})$ and the inclusion-exclusion principle has small coefficients, $\sum_{\mathbf{x} \text{ in } I_c'} \sum_{\mathbf{y} \text{ in } J_c'}$

$\frac{1}{2^{bk}}$ should also be a fairly good approximation of trans-count(I_c, J_c).

$$\left| \text{trans-count}(I_c, J_c) - \sum_{\mathbf{x} \, \text{in} \, I_c} \sum_{\mathbf{y} \, \text{in} \, J_c} \frac{1}{2^{bk}} \right| = \left| \sum_{\mathbf{x} \, \text{in} \, I_c} \sum_{\mathbf{y} \, \text{in} \, J_c} \left(\mathbb{1}_M(\mathbf{x}, \mathbf{y}) - \frac{1}{2^{bk}} \right) \right|$$

$$= \left| \sum_{I_c' \supseteq I_c} \sum_{J_c' \supseteq J_c} (-1)^{\Delta(I_c', I_c) + \Delta(J_c', J_c)} \sum_{\mathbf{x} \, \text{SAT} \, I_c'} \sum_{\mathbf{y} \, \text{SAT} \, J_c'} \left(\mathbb{1}_M(\mathbf{x}, \mathbf{y}) - \frac{1}{2^{bk}} \right) \right| \quad (11)$$

$$\leq \sum_{I_c' \supseteq I_c} \sum_{J_c' \supseteq J_c} 1 \leq t^{\text{free}(I_c) + \text{free}(J_c)}.$$

This can be translated into a bound on the transition probability,

$$\left| \text{trans-prob}(I_c, J_c) - \frac{\displaystyle\sum_{\mathbf{x} \, \text{in} \, I_c} \sum_{\mathbf{y} \, \text{in} \, J_c} \frac{1}{2^{bk}}}{\displaystyle\sum_{\mathbf{x} \, \text{in} \, I_c} 1} \right| \leq \frac{t^{\text{free}(I_c) + \text{free}(J_c)}}{\displaystyle\sum_{\mathbf{x} \, \text{in} \, I_c} 1}.$$

In the fraction on the left-hand side, the $\sum_{\mathbf{x} \, \text{in} \, I_c} 1$ in the numerator and in the denominator can cancel out. So

$$\left| \text{trans-prob}(I_c, J_c) - \sum_{\mathbf{y} \, \text{in} \, J_c} \frac{1}{2^{bk}} \right| \leq \frac{t^{\text{free}(I_c) + \text{free}(J_c)}}{\displaystyle\sum_{\mathbf{x} \, \text{in} \, I_c} 1}$$

$$\leq \frac{t^{\text{free}(I_c) + \text{free}(J_c)}}{(2^b - (t-1))^{\text{free}(I_c)}} \leq \left(\frac{2t - 1}{2^b} \right)^{\text{free}(I_c)} t^{\text{free}(J_c)}.$$

The last inequality assumes $t \leq 2^{b-1}$, we can assume this without loss of generality, because the lemma is trivialized otherwise. $\qquad\square$

Now we can prove Lemma 6, by adding up the error term over all layouts J_c.

Proof (Lemma 6). The statistical distance between the conditional layout of $\mathbf{y}$ and the conditional layout of a random $\mathbf{y}^* \in \mathbb{F}^k$ is bounded by

$$\sum_{J_c} \left(\frac{2t - 1}{2^b} \right)^{\text{free}(I_c)} t^{\text{free}(J_c)} \leq \left(\frac{2t - 1}{2^b} \right)^{\text{free}(I_c)} (2t - 1)^k.$$

The inequality holds because

$$\sum_{J_c} t^{\text{free}(J_c)} = \sum_i \sum_{\substack{J_c \, \text{s.t.} \\ \text{free}(J_c) = i}} t^i \leq \sum_i \binom{k}{i} (t - 1)^{k-i} t^i = (2t - 1)^k.$$

$\qquad\square$

We are now ready to complete our inductive proof of the core lemma (Lemma 5).

Proof (Lemma 5). Let $\mathbf{x}_{1:t} = (\mathbf{x}_1, \ldots, \mathbf{x}_t)$ be sampled uniformly from an α-nice layout I. We need to show that the layout of $\mathbf{y}_{1:t} := (M\mathbf{x}_1, \ldots, M\mathbf{x}_t)$ is statistically close to the layout of t random vectors.

Consider $\mathbf{x}_{1:t}^{(\text{next})} = (\mathbf{x}_1^{(\text{next})}, \ldots, \mathbf{x}_t^{(\text{next})})$, which is obtained by applying k independent random S-boxes on $\mathbf{y}_{1:t}$. By Corollary 1, it is equivalent to study the statistical distance between $\mathbf{x}_{1:t}^{(\text{next})}$ and t random vectors. Denote this statistical distance by $\varepsilon(t)$. Clearly $\varepsilon(1) = 0$.

For $t > 1$, assume the lemma holds for smaller t. By our definition of niceness, $\mathbf{x}_{1:t-1}$ is sampled from an α-nice layout I'. By the induction hypothesis, $\mathbf{x}_{1:t-1}^{(\text{next})}$ is $\varepsilon(t-1)$-close to uniform by distribution. Implied by Lemma 6, the distribution of $\mathbf{x}_t^{(\text{next})}$ conditioning on the values of $\mathbf{x}_{1:t-1}, \mathbf{y}_{1:t-1}, \mathbf{x}_{1:t-1}^{(\text{next})}$ is very close to uniform. The (conditional) statistical distance is at most $(\frac{2t-1}{2^b})^{\text{free}(I_c)}(2t-1)^k$ where I_c is determined by (8). Since I is α-nice, free$(I_c) \geq (1-\alpha)k$. Therefore, the statistical distance between $\mathbf{x}_{1:t}^{(\text{next})}$ and t random vectors is bounded by

$$\varepsilon(t) \leq \varepsilon(t-1) + \left(\frac{2t-1}{2^b}\right)^{(1-\alpha)k}(2t-1)^k.$$

By induction on t,

$$\varepsilon(t) \leq \sum_{t'=2}^{t} \left(\frac{2t'-1}{2^b}\right)^{(1-\alpha)k}(2t'-1)^k \leq t \cdot \left(\frac{2t}{2^b}\right)^{(1-\alpha)k}(2t)^k.$$

$\square$

5.2   2-Round SPN* is $2^{-\Theta(bk)}$-Close to $O(1)$-Wise Independence

In this section, we use the core lemma (Lemma 5) to prove that a 2-round SPN* is $2^{-\Theta(bk)}$-close to t-wise independent, for constant t.

Theorem 2. *The 2-round SPN* is ε-close to t-wise independent, where*

$$\varepsilon = \frac{t^2 \cdot 2^{k+1}}{(2^b)^{k/(2t)}} + t \cdot \left(\frac{8 \cdot t^3}{2^b}\right)^{k/2},$$

if the linear mixing has maximal branch number.

When t is a constant, the distance satisfies $\varepsilon = 2^{-\Theta(bk)}$.

The proof follows the high-level framework introduced at the beginning of Sect. 5. Lemma 8 shows that for constant t, the first-round tuple $\mathbf{y}_{1:t}^{(1)}$ will be in an α-nice layout with high probability. Thus, the core lemma (Lemma 5) implies that the layout of the second-round tuple $\mathbf{y}_{1:t}^{(2)}$ is exponentially close to t-wise independent.

Lemma 8. *For any $\alpha \in [0,1]$ and any t-wise layout I, if tuple $\mathbf{x}_{1:t}$ is sampled uniformly from layout I, and let $\mathbf{y}_{1:t} = M\mathbf{x}_{1:t}$, then $J = \text{layout}(\mathbf{y}_{1:t})$ is α-nice with probability*

$$\Pr[J \text{ is } \alpha\text{-nice}] \geq 1 - \frac{2^{k+1} \cdot t^2}{(2^b)^{\alpha k/t}}.$$

Proof. We will upper bound the probability that J is α-nice by requiring that each pair of vectors collide in at most $\alpha k/(t-1)$ coordinates. Then every vector collides with other vectors on at most αk coordinates, which implies that the layout of the tuple is α-nice.

The number of collisions between each pair of vectors can be bounded by Lemma 4, which does not depend on the starting layout. The probability $|J_{i,j}| > \alpha k/t$ is no more than $e \cdot 2^k/(2^b - 1)^{\alpha k/t}$.

$$\Pr\left[J \text{ is not } \alpha\text{-nice} \right] \leq \Pr\left[\bigwedge_{1 \leq i < j \leq t} |J_{i,j}| > \frac{\alpha k}{t} \right] \leq \frac{t^2 \cdot 2^{k+1}}{(2^b - 1)^{\alpha k/t}}$$

The last inequality is obtained by applying the union bound inequality over all $\binom{t}{2} \leq \frac{t^2}{2}$ pairs of vectors. $\qquad\square$

We are now ready to present the proof of the main theorem of this section.

Proof (Theorem 2). Lemma 8 shows that

$$\varepsilon_1 := \Pr[J \text{ is not } \alpha\text{-nice}] \leq \frac{t^2 \cdot 2^{k+1}}{(2^b - 1)^{\alpha k/t}}.$$

Conditioning on J being α-nice, consider the (conditional) distribution of $\mathbf{y}_{1:t}^{(2)}$. The core lemma (Lemma 5) shows that the conditional distribution is ε_2-close to t-wise independent, for

$$\varepsilon_2 \leq t \cdot \left(\frac{(2t)^{2-\alpha}}{(2^b)^{1-\alpha}} \right)^k.$$

In conclusion, the output tuple $\mathbf{x}_{1:t}^{(3)}$, alias $\mathbf{y}_{1:t}^{(\text{out})}$, is $(\varepsilon_1 + \varepsilon_2)$-close to t-wise independent. If we set $\alpha = \frac{1}{2}$, the statistical distance is bounded by

$$\varepsilon_1 + \varepsilon_2 \leq \frac{t^2 \cdot 2^{k+1}}{(2^b)^{k/(2t)}} + t \cdot \left(\frac{8 \cdot t^3}{2^b} \right)^{k/2}.$$

$\qquad\square$

5.3 2-Round SPN* is $2^{-\Theta(b)}$-Close to t-Wise independent

This section shows a similar result for larger t. In particular, we prove that 2-round SPN* with a maximal-branch-number mixing is $2^{-\Theta(b)}$-close to t-wise independent, for t almost up to $2^{0.499b}$.

By applying the amplification result of Maurer, Pietrzak, and Renner [39], we can reduce the error to $2^{-\Theta(bk)}$ by having $O(k)$ rounds.

Theorem 3. *For any $\alpha \in (0, 1]$, the 2-round SPN* is ε-close to t-wise independent, where*

$$\varepsilon = \frac{t^2}{\alpha \cdot 2^b} + t \cdot \left(\frac{(2t)^{2-\alpha}}{(2^b)^{1-\alpha}} \right)^k,$$

if the mixing function has the maximal branch number.
If $t < 2^{(0.499 - 1/(4k))b}$, the distance is $\varepsilon = 2^{-\Theta(b)}$ by choosing the optimal α.

Corollary 2. *Assuming $t < 2^{(0.499-1/(4k))b}$, $\Theta(k)$-round SPN* with maximal-branch-number linear mixing is $2^{-\Theta(bk)}$-close to t-wise independent.*

The proof of this theorem is in the full version of the paper.

5.4 $(\log t)$-Rounds SPN* is $2^{-\Theta(bk)}$-Close to t-Wise Independent

In this section, we discuss how to achieve $2^{-\Theta(bk)}$-closeness to t-wise independent, for t up to $2^{0.499b}$, at the cost of a slightly larger number of rounds.

This result is proved by induction. The base case is closeness to 2-wise independent in 2 rounds. Assume that we have already shown ε-closeness to t-wise independent in r rounds. As the inductive step, we will prove the closeness to $(2t-1)$-wise independent in $r+1$ rounds.

As for notations, let $\mathbf{x}_{1:2t-1}^{(in)}$ denote $2t-1$ distinct inputs, let $\mathbf{y}_{1:2t-1}^{(out)}$ denote their corresponding outputs, and let $\mathbf{x}_{1:2t-1}^{(last)}, \mathbf{y}_{1:2t-1}^{(last)}$ denote the intermediate values in the last round (as illustrated in Fig. 3).

$$\mathbf{x}^{(in)} \xrightarrow{\quad} \boxed{S} \rightarrow \mathbf{x}^{(1)} \dashrightarrow \mathbf{y}^{(r)} \xrightarrow{\quad} \boxed{S} \rightarrow \mathbf{x}^{(last)} \xrightarrow{\mathbf{M}} \mathbf{y}^{(last)} \xrightarrow{\quad} \boxed{S} \rightarrow \mathbf{y}^{(out)}$$

$$\underbrace{\qquad\qquad\qquad}_{\text{the first } r \text{ rounds}} \qquad \underbrace{\qquad\qquad\qquad}_{\text{the last round}}$$

Fig. 3. Illustration of a $(r+1)$-round SPN

Due to the core lemma (Lemma 5), it suffices to show that: With overwhelming probability, $(\mathbf{x}_{1:2t-1}^{(last)})$ lies in a α-nice layout for some $\alpha \in (0,1)$ of our choice.

By the induction hypothesis, we know that the distribution of $\mathbf{x}_{1:t}^{(last)}$ is $\varepsilon(t)$-close to t-wise independent. If they are actually t-wise independent, then the probability $\mathbf{x}_t^{(last)}$ collides with $\mathbf{x}_{1:t-1}^{(last)}$ in more than $\alpha k/2$ coordinates is exponentially small due to Chernoff bound. The same argument also bounds the probability that $\mathbf{x}_t^{(last)}$ collides with $\mathbf{x}_{t+1:2t-1}^{(last)}$ in more than $\alpha k/2$ coordinates. Then the probability $\mathbf{x}_t^{(last)}$ collides with the other $2t-2$ vectors in at most αk coordinates is bounded by the union bound. Due to the symmetry and the union bound, $\mathbf{x}_{1:2t-1}^{(last)}$ is α-nice with good probability. Then we can finish the induction step by Lemma 5.

Such analysis can show $\varepsilon(t)$-closeness to t-wise independent in $O(\log t)$ rounds, where $\varepsilon(t)$ is inductively bounded by

$$\varepsilon(2t-1) \leq O(t) \cdot \left(\varepsilon(t) + \underbrace{\text{a small term}}_{\text{from Chernoff bound}}\right) + \underbrace{\text{another small term.}}_{\text{from Lemma 5}}$$

The $O(t)$ multiplicative factor before $\varepsilon(t)$ turns out to be problematic. It results in a multiplicative blow-up of order $t^{O(\log t)}$. When $t = 2^{\Theta(b)}$, this blow-up is about $2^{O(b^2)}$, which is unacceptable especially if $b = \Omega(k)$. In the actual proof of our result (Theorem 4), we conduct a more sophisticated analysis, though the high-level inductive idea is the same.

Theorem 4. *If $k > 4$, r-round SPN* is ε-close to 2^r-wise independent for*

$$\varepsilon = \frac{2^{r+\frac{3}{4}}}{1 - 2^{-\frac{k}{4}}} \cdot \left(\frac{2^{2r+3}}{2^b}\right)^{k/4} = \frac{t \cdot 2^{\frac{11}{4}}}{1 - 2^{-\frac{k}{4}}} \cdot \left(\frac{8 \cdot t^2}{2^b}\right)^{k/4}.$$

As usual, let $\mathbf{x}_{1:t}^{(r)}, \mathbf{y}_{1:t}^{(r)}$ denote the intermediate values in the r-th round. We also introduce a new notation $\mathbf{x}_{i,\times 2^\rho}^{(r)}$

$$\mathbf{x}_{i,\times 2^\rho}^{(r)} := \mathbf{x}_{i2^\rho+1:i2^\rho+2^\rho}^{(r)} = (\mathbf{x}_{i2^\rho+1}^{(r)}, \ldots, \mathbf{x}_{i2^\rho+2^\rho}^{(r)})$$

to denote 2^ρ consecutive vectors. Similarly we define $\mathbf{y}_{i,\times 2^\rho}^{(r)}$.

In the ρ-th round, for $0 \leq i < j < 2^{r-\rho}$, define $A_{i,j}^{(\rho)}$ as the event that

$$\Big(\underbrace{\mathbf{x}_{i2^{\rho-1}+1}^{(\rho)}, \ldots, \mathbf{x}_{i2^{\rho-1}+2^{\rho-1}}^{(\rho)}}_{\mathbf{x}_{i,\times 2^{\rho-1}}^{(\rho)}}, \underbrace{\mathbf{x}_{j2^{\rho-1}+1}^{(\rho)}, \ldots, \mathbf{x}_{j2^{\rho-1}+2^{\rho-1}}^{(\rho)}}_{\mathbf{x}_{j,\times 2^{\rho-1}}^{(\rho)}}\Big) \tag{12}$$

is in an α_ρ-nice layout. For $0 \leq i < j < 2^{r-\rho+1}$, define $B_{i,j}^{(\rho)}$ as the event that

$$\Big(\underbrace{\mathbf{x}_{i2^{\rho-2}+1}^{(\rho)}, \ldots, \mathbf{x}_{i2^{\rho-2}+2^{\rho-2}}^{(\rho)}}_{\mathbf{x}_{i,\times 2^{\rho-2}}^{(\rho)}}, \underbrace{\mathbf{x}_{j2^{\rho-2}+1}^{(\rho)}, \ldots, \mathbf{x}_{j2^{\rho-2}+2^{\rho-2}}^{(\rho)}}_{\mathbf{x}_{j,\times 2^{\rho-2}}^{(\rho)}}\Big) \tag{13}$$

is in a $\frac{1}{3}\alpha_\rho$-nice layout. The value of α_ρ will be fixed later.

The proof of Theorem 4 is inductive. The induction hypothesis is that with overwhelming probability $\bigwedge_{0 \leq i < j < 2^{r-\rho}} A_{i,j}^{(\rho)}$ holds. Then by Lemma 5, the joint distribution of $\mathbf{x}_{i,\times 2^{\rho-1}}^{(\rho)}, \mathbf{x}_{j,\times 2^{\rho-1}}^{(\rho)}$ is close to 2^ρ-wise uniform, for each $0 \leq i < j < 2^{r-\rho}$. Then by the following Lemma 9, they are very likely to be $\frac{1}{3}\alpha_{\rho+1}$-nice, that is, $B_{i,j}^{(\rho+1)}$ is likely to hold. To complete the induction step, we bridge the remaining gap by proving the following statement for $\rho > 2$,

$$\bigwedge_{0 \leq i < j < 2^{r-\rho+1}} B_{i,j}^{(\rho)} \implies \bigwedge_{0 \leq i < j < 2^{r-\rho}} A_{i,j}^{(\rho)}. \tag{14}$$

Lemma 9. *Assume $\mathbf{x}_{1:t}$ are uniformly sampled from $(\mathbb{F}^k)^t$, for any $\alpha > \frac{t-1}{2^b}$,*

$$\Pr\big[\text{layout}(\mathbf{x}_1, \ldots, \mathbf{x}_t) \text{ is } \alpha\text{-nice}\big] \geq 1 - \frac{t \cdot 2^k}{1 + \alpha k} \cdot \left(\frac{t}{2^b}\right)^{\alpha k}.$$

The proofs of statement (14) and of Lemma 9 are deferred to the full version of the paper.

Now we are nearly ready to prove Theorem 4. We introduce a few additional notations. For $\rho \geq 1$, define

$$A_\rho := \bigwedge_{0 \leq i < j < 2^{r-\rho}} A_{i,j}^{(\rho)}, \qquad \qquad \delta_\rho := 1 - \Pr[A_\rho].$$

Define $\varepsilon_{\rho,i,j}$ as the statistical distance between the uniform distribution and the distribution of $\mathbf{x}_{i,\times 2^\rho - 1}^{(\rho+1)}, \mathbf{x}_{j,\times 2^\rho - 1}^{(\rho+1)}$ (the vectors in the definition of $B_{i,j}^{(\rho+1)}$) *conditioning on event* A_ρ. Lemma 5 shows that

$$\varepsilon_{\rho,i,j} \leq 2^\rho \cdot \left(\frac{2^{\rho+1}}{2^b}\right)^{(1-\alpha_\rho)k} (2^{\rho+1})^k.$$

for all $\rho \geq 2$. Define $\varepsilon_\rho = \sum_{0 \leq i < j < 2^{r-\rho}} \varepsilon_{\rho,i,j}$.

Note that $\varepsilon_r = \varepsilon_{r,1,2}$ is the statistical distance between the 2^r output vectors and uniform, conditioning on A_r. So r-round SPN* is $(\delta_r + \varepsilon_r)$-close to 2^r-wise independent.

Proof (Theorem 4). For each $2 < \rho \leq r$, conditional on $A_{\rho-1}$, the (conditional) distribution of $\mathbf{x}_{i,\times 2^{\rho-2}}^{(\rho)}, \mathbf{x}_{j,\times 2^{\rho-2}}^{(\rho)}$ is $\varepsilon_{\rho-1,i,j}$-close to uniform. Then by Lemma 9

$$\Pr\left[\neg B_{i,j}^{(\rho)} \,\Big|\, A_{\rho-1}\right] \leq \varepsilon_{\rho-1,i,j} + 2^{\rho-1} \cdot 2^k \cdot \left(\frac{2^{\rho-1}}{2^b}\right)^{\frac{1}{3}\alpha_\rho k}.$$

By the union bound,

$$\Pr\left[\neg \bigwedge_{0 \leq i < j < 2^{r-\rho+1}} B_{i,j}^{(\rho)} \,\Big|\, A_{\rho-1}\right] \leq \varepsilon_{\rho-1} + \frac{(2^{r-\rho+1})^2}{2} \cdot 2^{\rho-1} \cdot 2^k \cdot \left(\frac{2^{\rho-1}}{2^b}\right)^{\frac{1}{3}\alpha_\rho k}.$$

By (14), the left-hand side is lower bounded by $\Pr\left[\neg A_\rho \mid A_{\rho-1}\right]$. And we know

$$\Pr\left[\neg A_\rho \mid A_{\rho-1}\right] \geq \Pr\left[\neg A_\rho \wedge A_{\rho-1}\right] \geq \delta_\rho - \delta_{\rho-1}.$$

So

$$\delta_\rho \leq \delta_{\rho-1} + \varepsilon_{\rho-1} + \frac{(2^{r-\rho+1})^2}{2} 2^{\rho-1} \cdot 2^k \cdot \left(\frac{2^{\rho-1}}{2^b}\right)^{\frac{1}{3}\alpha_\rho k}.$$

For the base case $\rho = 2$, Lemma 4 directly bounds the probability of $B_{i,j}^{(2)}$ by $\frac{e \cdot 2^k}{(2^b-1)^{\frac{1}{3}\alpha_2 k}}$. Then by the union bound

$$\delta_2 \leq \Pr\left[\neg \bigwedge_{i,j} B_{i,j}^{(2)}\right] \leq \frac{(2^r)^2}{2} \frac{e \cdot 2^k}{(2^b - 1)^{\frac{1}{3}\alpha_2 k}}.$$

As the final goal is to bound $\delta_r + \varepsilon_r$, we are interested in how $\delta_\rho + \varepsilon_\rho$ depends on $\delta_{\rho-1} + \varepsilon_{\rho-1}$,

$$(\delta_\rho + \varepsilon_\rho) - (\delta_{\rho-1} + \varepsilon_{\rho-1})$$

$$\leq \frac{(2^{r-\rho})^2}{2} 2^\rho \cdot \left(\frac{2^{\rho+1}}{2^b}\right)^{(1-\alpha_\rho)k} (2^{\rho+1})^k + \frac{(2^{r-\rho+1})^2}{2} 2^{\rho-1} \cdot 2^k \cdot \left(\frac{2^{\rho-1}}{2^b}\right)^{\frac{1}{3}\alpha_\rho k}$$

$$= 2^{2r-\rho-1}\left(\left(\frac{2^{\rho+1}}{2^b}\right)^{(1-\alpha_\rho)k} (2^{\rho+1})^k + 2^{k+1} \cdot \left(\frac{2^{\rho-1}}{2^b}\right)^{\frac{1}{3}\alpha_\rho k}\right). \tag{15}$$

Table 2. Statistical (TV) distance from pairwise independence of the r-round AES* given two inputs that differ in exactly one coordinate. This corresponds to starting from a layout I with Hamming weight 1, e.g. $I = \{1, \ldots, k-1\}$.

Number of rounds r	$\log_2$(TV distance from 2-wise ind.)
3	-23.4275
4	-48.9916
5	-117.1745
6	-126.3073
7	-141.2575

The value of α_ρ should be chosen so that (15) is minimized. Note that

$$\text{Right-hand side of (15)} \approx \left(\frac{2^\rho}{2^b}\right)^{-\alpha_\rho k} \left(\frac{2^{2\rho}}{2^b}\right)^k + \left(\frac{2^\rho}{2^b}\right)^{\frac{1}{3}\alpha_\rho k}$$

so (15) is minimized when $\alpha \approx \frac{3}{4}\frac{b-2\rho}{b-\rho}$, and the minimum value is about $\left(\frac{2^{2\rho}}{2^b}\right)^{k/4}$. If we tune the value of α_ρ, we get

$$(\delta_\rho + \varepsilon_\rho) - (\delta_{\rho-1} + \varepsilon_{\rho-1}) \leq 2^{2r-\rho} \cdot 2^{\frac{1}{2}k\rho - \frac{1}{4}kb + \frac{3}{4}k + \frac{3}{4}} = 2^{2r-\rho+\frac{3}{4}} \cdot \left(\frac{2^{2\rho+3}}{2^b}\right)^{k/4}.$$

We defer the analysis of the base case to the full version.

$$\delta_r + \varepsilon_r \leq \delta_2 + \varepsilon_2 + \sum_{\rho=3}^{r} 2^{2r-\rho+\frac{3}{4}} \cdot \left(\frac{2^{2\rho+3}}{2^b}\right)^{k/4} \leq \frac{2^{r+\frac{3}{4}}}{1 - 2^{-\frac{k}{4}}} \cdot \left(\frac{2^{2r+3}}{2^b}\right)^{k/4}.$$

$\square$

6 Pairwise Independence of AES* and Censored AES

In this section, we obtain concrete bounds on the pairwise independence of (1) an SPN cipher with random, independent S-boxes and the *actual* AES mixing (we refer to this as AES*) as well as (2) a "censored" version of the actual AES block cipher (with the *actual* AES S-box, but some mixing layers removed). We will use partially computational methods for our theorems. The source code for our computations is available at https://github.com/AnPelec/t-wise-ind-SPN.

6.1 Pairwise Independence of AES*

We can represent the evaluation of AES* as a Markov chain over $2^{16} - 1$ layouts. Our goal is to describe this random walk exactly, and then use numerical calculations to infer an upper bound on the statistical distance of an output pair after a certain number of rounds. To compute the transition probabilities, we start with an exact version of Lemma 2. A similar lemma was already proved in [3], by relating the number of transitions to the number of codewords of specific weight in an MDS code.

Lemma 10. *If M has the maximal branch number, the layout transition probability* $\text{trans-prob}(I, J) := \Pr_{\mathbf{x} \text{ in } I}\left[M\mathbf{x} \text{ in } J\right]$ *equals*

$$\text{trans-prob}(I, J) = \sum_{i=0}^{\text{free}(I)+\text{free}(J)-k-1} (-1)^i \, \frac{\binom{k-1+i}{k-1}}{(2^b - 1)^{k-\text{free}(J)+i}}. \qquad (16)$$

Lemma 10 assumes however a full-branch mixing layer, which is not the case for AES mixing. Another issue is that the number of layouts is still quite high and poses a non-trivial computational challenge. Thankfully, we can overcome this obstacle by representing the AES mixing layer in terms of permutations and full-branch mixings, an observation first made by [3]. More details can be found in the full version of this paper.

As our starting point, we numerically compute the total variation distance from uniform after r rounds starting with a pair of inputs that differ in exactly one 8-bit word. The results are summarized in Table 2, and are obtained by computing the corresponding r-th power of the transition matrix of the random walk. (This requires leveraging a number of symmetries to be computationally feasible.)

We then derive conjectures on the maximum distance over all possible input layouts and verify that our conjectures hold by computing the statistical distance for all input layouts. As a result of this, we obtain the following theorems.

Theorem 5. *The 3-round AES* is $2^{-23.42}$-close to pairwise independent.*

Theorem 6. *The 7-round AES* is 2^{-128}-close to pairwise independent.*

6.2 Censored AES

To translate our results from the random S-box setting to the AES S-box, we replace a random S-box by consecutive applications of the AES one, namely the patched inverse function over $\mathbb{F}_{2^8}$ where the input is XOR with a fresh key byte. Note that the resulting SPN which we refer to as "censored" AES is simply AES with several mixing layers removed.

We numerically compute the closeness to pairwise independence of the sequential composition of AES S-boxes over $\mathbb{F}_{2^8}$, where a fresh key byte is XORed into the input prior to each call. These distances can be found in the full version of this paper. Note that analytical bounds were obtained in [37], however here we obtain tighter numerical bounds for our parameter settings. We defer the implementation details to the full version of this paper.

Overall, we prove the following theorem. It considers what we (informally) refer to as "192-round censored AES." One should think of this as a 191-round SPN (thus with 192 layers of S-boxes), with independent keys, using the true AES S-box (patched inverse) and the AES mixing layer, but with a subset of mixing layers removed. Which mixing layers remain can be inferred from the proof below.

Theorem 7. *192-round censored AES is 2^{-128}-close to pairwise independent.*

Proof. First off, Theorem 5 implies that 3-round AES* (that is, 4 layers of random S-boxes) is $\varepsilon_{ideal} = 2^{-23.42}$-close to pairwise independent. We then replace each random S-box with the sequential composition of c consecutive AES S-boxes (and xoring an independent uniform key byte to each call) and show that the resulting construction (which consists of $4c$ layers of S-boxes) is ϵ-close to pairwise independent, for some suitable ϵ. This value of ϵ will be then amplified, via further sequential composition. By the amplification theorem of [28,39], the resulting $4cr$-round censored AES is in particular $(2^{r-1}\epsilon^r)$-close to pairwise independent. The exact constants c and r are chosen to optimize the final number of rounds required to reach 2^{-128}-closeness.

First of all, we pick $c = 8$. Indeed, according to our findings in the full version, the 8-fold sequential composition of the S-box (with independent key bytes XORed to each S-box input) is $\varepsilon_{sim} \leq 2^{-29.39}$-close to pairwise independent, and hence to the behavior of a random S-box. Recall that the random S-box in AES* is applied to $k = 16$ blocks in parallel, hence by the triangle inequality we deduce that we can simulate 4 random S-box layers with an error of at most $16 \cdot 4 \cdot \varepsilon_{sim} \leq 2^{-23.39}$.

Therefore, we conclude that this partial 32-round censored AES is ϵ-close to pairwise independent for

$$\epsilon \leq \varepsilon_{ideal} + 16 \cdot 4 \cdot \varepsilon_{sim} \leq 2^{-23.42} + 2^{-23.39} < 2^{-22.39} .$$

Then, amplification for $r = 6$ repetitions gives that the 192-round censored AES is

$$2^5 \cdot (2^{-22.39})^6 = 2^{5-22.39 \cdot 6} < 2^{-128}$$

close to pairwise independent. □

If one believes that the mixing layers are useful for AES to achieve pseudorandomness, then it is natural to expect that removing a large fraction of them should only hurt the convergence to pairwise independence. This leads us to conjecture that 192-round AES is 2^{-128}-close to pairwise independent. We view proving this conjecture formally to be an outstanding open problem.

Acknowledgements. Pelecanos was supported by DARPA under Agreement No. HR00112020023. Tessaro was supported in part by NSF grants CNS-2026774, CNS-2154174, a JP Morgan Faculty Award, a CISCO Faculty Award, and a gift from Microsoft. Vaikuntanathan was supported by DARPA under Agreement No. HR00112020023, NSF CNS-2154149, and a Thornton Family Faculty Research Innovation Fellowship.

References

1. Advanced Encryption Standard (AES). National Institute of Standards and Technology, NIST FIPS PUB 197, U.S. Department of Commerce (Nov 2001)
2. Andreeva, E., Bogdanov, A., Dodis, Y., Mennink, B., Steinberger, J.P.: On the indifferentiability of key-alternating ciphers. In: Canetti, R., Garay, J.A. (eds.) CRYPTO 2013. LNCS, vol. 8042, pp. 531–550. Springer, Heidelberg (2013). https://doi.org/10.1007/978-3-642-40041-4_29

3. Baignères, T., Vaudenay, S.: Proving the security of AES substitution-permutation network. In: Preneel, B., Tavares, S. (eds.) SAC 2005. LNCS, vol. 3897, pp. 65–81. Springer, Heidelberg (2006). https://doi.org/10.1007/11693383_5

4. Biham, E., Shamir, A.: Differential cryptanalysis of des-like cryptosystems. J. Cryptol. 4(1), 3–72 (1991)

5. Bogdanov, A., Khovratovich, D., Rechberger, C.: Biclique cryptanalysis of the full AES. In: Lee, D.H., Wang, X. (eds.) ASIACRYPT 2011. LNCS, vol. 7073, pp. 344–371. Springer, Heidelberg (2011). https://doi.org/10.1007/978-3-642-25385-0_19

6. Bogdanov, A., Knudsen, L.R., Leander, G., Standaert, F.-X., Steinberger, J., Tischhauser, E.: Key-alternating ciphers in a provable setting: encryption using a small number of public permutations. In: Pointcheval, D., Johansson, T. (eds.) EUROCRYPT 2012. LNCS, vol. 7237, pp. 45–62. Springer, Heidelberg (2012). https://doi.org/10.1007/978-3-642-29011-4_5

7. Brodsky, A., Hoory, S.: Simple permutations mix even better. Random Struct. Algorithms 32(3), 274–289 (2008). https://doi.org/10.1002/rsa.20194

8. Chen, S., Lampe, R., Lee, J., Seurin, Y., Steinberger, J.: Minimizing the two-round even-mansour cipher. In: Garay, J.A., Gennaro, R. (eds.) CRYPTO 2014. LNCS, vol. 8616, pp. 39–56. Springer, Heidelberg (2014). https://doi.org/10.1007/978-3-662-44371-2_3

9. Chen, S., Steinberger, J.: Tight security bounds for key-alternating ciphers. In: Nguyen, P.Q., Oswald, E. (eds.) EUROCRYPT 2014. LNCS, vol. 8441, pp. 327–350. Springer, Heidelberg (2014). https://doi.org/10.1007/978-3-642-55220-5_19

10. Cogliati, B., et al.: Provable security of (tweakable) block ciphers based on substitution-permutation networks. In: Shacham, H., Boldyreva, A. (eds.) CRYPTO 2018. LNCS, vol. 10991, pp. 722–753. Springer, Cham (2018). https://doi.org/10.1007/978-3-319-96884-1_24

11. Cogliati, B., Seurin, Y.: On the Provable Security of the Iterated Even-Mansour Cipher Against Related-Key and Chosen-Key Attacks. In: Oswald, E., Fischlin, M. (eds.) EUROCRYPT 2015. LNCS, vol. 9056, pp. 584–613. Springer, Heidelberg (2015). https://doi.org/10.1007/978-3-662-46800-5_23

12. Coron, J.S., Holenstein, T., Künzler, R., Patarin, J., Seurin, Y., Tessaro, S.: How to build an ideal cipher: The indifferentiability of the Feistel construction. J. Cryptol. 29(1), 61–114 (2016). https://doi.org/10.1007/s00145-014-9189-6

13. Courtois, N.T., Pieprzyk, J.: Cryptanalysis of block ciphers with overdefined systems of equations. In: Zheng, Y. (ed.) ASIACRYPT 2002. LNCS, vol. 2501, pp. 267–287. Springer, Heidelberg (2002). https://doi.org/10.1007/3-540-36178-2_17

14. Daemen, J.: Cipher and hash function design strategies based on linear and differential cryptanalysis. Ph.D. Thesis, KU Leuven (1995)

15. Dai, Y., Seurin, Y., Steinberger, J., Thiruvengadam, A.: Indifferentiability of iterated even-mansour ciphers with non-idealized key-schedules: five rounds are necessary and sufficient. In: Katz, J., Shacham, H. (eds.) CRYPTO 2017. LNCS, vol. 10403, pp. 524–555. Springer, Cham (2017). https://doi.org/10.1007/978-3-319-63697-9_18

16. Dai, Y., Steinberger, J.: Indifferentiability of 8-round feistel networks. In: Robshaw, M., Katz, J. (eds.) CRYPTO 2016. LNCS, vol. 9814, pp. 95–120. Springer, Heidelberg (2016). https://doi.org/10.1007/978-3-662-53018-4_4

17. Dodis, Y., Karthikeyan, H., Wichs, D.: Small-box cryptography. In: Braverman, M. (ed.) 13th Innovations in Theoretical Computer Science Conference, ITCS 2022, January 31 - February 3, 2022, Berkeley, CA, USA. LIPIcs, vol. 215, pp. 56:1–56:25. Schloss Dagstuhl - Leibniz-Zentrum für Informatik (2022)

18. Dodis, Y., Katz, J., Steinberger, J., Thiruvengadam, A., Zhang, Z.: Provable security of substitution-permutation networks. Cryptology ePrint Archive, Report 2017/016 (2017). https://eprint.iacr.org/2017/016

19. Dodis, Y., Stam, M., Steinberger, J., Liu, T.: Indifferentiability of confusion-diffusion networks. In: Fischlin, M., Coron, J.-S. (eds.) EUROCRYPT 2016. LNCS, vol. 9666, pp. 679–704. Springer, Heidelberg (2016). https://doi.org/10.1007/978-3-662-49896-5_24

20. Even, S., Mansour, Y.: A construction of a cipher from a single pseudorandom permutation. J. Cryptol. **10**(3), 151–162 (1997). https://doi.org/10.1007/s001459900025

21. Farshim, P., Procter, G.: The related-key security of iterated even–mansour ciphers. In: Leander, G. (ed.) FSE 2015. LNCS, vol. 9054, pp. 342–363. Springer, Heidelberg (2015). https://doi.org/10.1007/978-3-662-48116-5_17

22. Guo, C., Lin, D.: On the indifferentiability of key-alternating feistel ciphers with no key derivation. In: Dodis, Y., Nielsen, J.B. (eds.) TCC 2015. LNCS, vol. 9014, pp. 110–133. Springer, Heidelberg (2015). https://doi.org/10.1007/978-3-662-46494-6_6

23. Hoang, V.T., Tessaro, S.: Key-alternating ciphers and key-length extension: exact bounds and multi-user security. In: Robshaw, M., Katz, J. (eds.) CRYPTO 2016. LNCS, vol. 9814, pp. 3–32. Springer, Heidelberg (2016). https://doi.org/10.1007/978-3-662-53018-4_1

24. Hoory, S., Magen, A., Myers, S.A., Rackoff, C.: Simple permutations mix well. Theor. Comput. Sci. **348**(2–3), 251–261 (2005)

25. Jakobsen, T., Knudsen, L.R.: The interpolation attack on block ciphers. In: FSE. Lecture Notes in Computer Science, vol. 1267, pp. 28–40. Springer (1997). https://doi.org/10.1007/bfb0052332

26. Joan, D., Vincent, R.: The design of rijndael: Aes-the advanced encryption standard. Information Security and Cryptography (2002)

27. Kang, J.S., Hong, S., Lee, S., Yi, O., Park, C., Lim, J.: Practical and provable security against differential and linear cryptanalysis for substitution-permutation networks. Etri J. **23** (02 2002). https://doi.org/10.4218/etrij.01.0101.0402

28. Kaplan, E., Naor, M., Reingold, O.: Derandomized constructions of k-wise (almost) independent permutations. In: APPROX-RANDOM. Lecture Notes in Computer Science, vol. 3624, pp. 354–365. Springer (2005). https://doi.org/10.1007/s00453-008-9267-y

29. Kaplan, E., Naor, M., Reingold, O.: Derandomized constructions of k-wise (almost) independent permutations. Algorithmica **55**(1), 113–133 (2009). https://doi.org/10.1007/s00453-008-9267-y

30. Knudsen, L.: Deal - a 128-bit block cipher. In: NIST AES Proposal (1998)

31. Knudsen, L.R.: Truncated and higher order differentials. In: Preneel, B. (ed.) FSE 1994. LNCS, vol. 1008, pp. 196–211. Springer, Heidelberg (1995). https://doi.org/10.1007/3-540-60590-8_16

32. Knudsen, L., Wagner, D.: Integral cryptanalysis. In: Daemen, J., Rijmen, V. (eds.) FSE 2002. LNCS, vol. 2365, pp. 112–127. Springer, Heidelberg (2002). https://doi.org/10.1007/3-540-45661-9_9

33. Lai, X.: Higher Order Derivatives and Differential Cryptanalysis, pp. 227–233. Springer, US, Boston, MA (1994). https://doi.org/10.1007/978-1-4615-2694-0_23

34. Lai, X., Massey, J.L., Murphy, S.: Markov ciphers and differential cryptanalysis. In: Davies, D.W. (ed.) EUROCRYPT 1991. LNCS, vol. 547, pp. 17–38. Springer, Heidelberg (1991). https://doi.org/10.1007/3-540-46416-6_2

35. Lampe, R., Patarin, J., Seurin, Y.: An asymptotically tight security analysis of the iterated even-mansour cipher. In: Wang, X., Sako, K. (eds.) ASIACRYPT 2012. LNCS, vol. 7658, pp. 278–295. Springer, Heidelberg (2012). https://doi.org/10.1007/978-3-642-34961-4_18

36. Lampe, R., Seurin, Y.: Security Analysis of Key-Alternating Feistel Ciphers. In: Cid, C., Rechberger, C. (eds.) FSE 2014. LNCS, vol. 8540, pp. 243–264. Springer, Heidelberg (2015). https://doi.org/10.1007/978-3-662-46706-0_13

37. Liu, T., Tessaro, S., Vaikuntanathan, V.: The t-wise independence of substitution-permutation networks. In: Malkin, T., Peikert, C. (eds.) CRYPTO 2021. LNCS, vol. 12828, pp. 454–483. Springer, Cham (2021). https://doi.org/10.1007/978-3-030-84259-8_16

38. Matsui, M., Yamagishi, A.: A new method for known plaintext attack of FEAL cipher. In: Rueppel, R.A. (ed.) EUROCRYPT 1992. LNCS, vol. 658, pp. 81–91. Springer, Heidelberg (1993). https://doi.org/10.1007/3-540-47555-9_7

39. Maurer, U., Pietrzak, K., Renner, R.: Indistinguishability Amplification. In: Menezes, A. (ed.) CRYPTO 2007. LNCS, vol. 4622, pp. 130–149. Springer, Heidelberg (2007). https://doi.org/10.1007/978-3-540-74143-5_8

40. Miles, E., Viola, E.: Substitution-permutation networks, pseudorandom functions, and natural proofs. In: Safavi-Naini, R., Canetti, R. (eds.) CRYPTO 2012. LNCS, vol. 7417, pp. 68–85. Springer, Heidelberg (2012). https://doi.org/10.1007/978-3-642-32009-5_5

41. National Soviet Bureau of Standards: Information processing system - cryptographic protection - cryptographic algorithm gost 28147–89 (1989)

42. Nyberg, K.: Differentially uniform mappings for cryptography. In: Helleseth, T. (ed.) EUROCRYPT 1993. LNCS, vol. 765, pp. 55–64. Springer, Heidelberg (1994). https://doi.org/10.1007/3-540-48285-7_6

43. Patarin, J.: A proof of security in $O(2^n)$ for the Benes scheme. In: Vaudenay, S. (ed.) AFRICACRYPT 08. LNCS, vol. 5023, pp. 209–220. Springer, Heidelberg (Jun (2008)

44. Tessaro, S.: Optimally secure block ciphers from ideal primitives. In: Iwata, T., Cheon, J.H. (eds.) ASIACRYPT 2015. LNCS, vol. 9453, pp. 437–462. Springer, Heidelberg (2015). https://doi.org/10.1007/978-3-662-48800-3_18

45. Tiessen, T., Knudsen, L.R., Kölbl, S., Lauridsen, M.M.: Security of the AES with a secret S-box. In: Leander, G. (ed.) FSE 2015. LNCS, vol. 9054, pp. 175–189. Springer, Heidelberg (Mar 2015). https://doi.org/10.1007/978-3-662-48116-5_9

Isogenies

CSI-Otter: Isogeny-Based (Partially) Blind Signatures from the Class Group Action with a Twist

Shuichi Katsumata[1,2]($\boxtimes$), Yi-Fu Lai[3], Jason T. LeGrow[4], and Ling Qin[3]

[1] PQShield, Ltd., Oxford, UK
shuichi.katsumata@pqshield.com
[2] AIST, Tokyo, Japan
[3] Department of Mathematics, University of Auckland, Auckland, New Zealand
{ylai276,lqin276}@aucklanduni.ac.nz
[4] Department of Mathematics, Virginia Polytechnic Institute and State University,
Blacksburg, USA
jlegrow@vt.edu

Abstract. In this paper, we construct the first provably-secure isogeny-based (partially) blind signature scheme. While at a high level the scheme resembles the Schnorr blind signature, our work does not directly follow from that construction, since isogenies do not offer as rich an algebraic structure. Specifically, our protocol does not fit into the *linear identification protocol* abstraction introduced by Hauck, Kiltz, and Loss (EURO-CYRPT'19), which was used to generically construct Schnorr-like blind signatures based on modules such as classical groups and lattices. Consequently, our scheme does not seem susceptible to the recent efficient ROS attack exploiting the linear nature of the underlying mathematical tool.

In more detail, our blind signature exploits the *quadratic twist* of an elliptic curve in an essential way to endow isogenies with a strictly richer structure than abstract group actions (but still more restrictive than modules). The basic scheme has public key size 128 B and signature size 8 KB under the CSIDH-512 parameter sets—these are the smallest among all provably secure post-quantum secure blind signatures. Relying on a new *ring* variant of the group action inverse problem (rGAIP), we can halve the signature size to 4 KB while increasing the public key size to 512 B. We provide preliminary cryptanalysis of rGAIP and show that for certain parameter settings, it is essentially as secure as the standard GAIP. Finally, we show a novel way to turn our blind signature into a partially blind signature, where we deviate from prior methods since they require hashing into the set of public keys while hiding the corresponding secret key—constructing such a hash function in the isogeny setting remains an open problem.

1 Introduction

Blind signatures, introduced by Chaum [14], allow a user to obtain a signature on a message from a signer, while the signer is *blind* to the message it signed.

Author list in alphabetical order; see https://ams.org/profession/leaders/Culture Statement04.pdf.

© International Association for Cryptologic Research 2023
H. Handschuh and A. Lysyanskaya (Eds.): CRYPTO 2023, LNCS 14083, pp. 729–761, 2023.
https://doi.org/10.1007/978-3-031-38548-3_24

One can think of the physical analogy where a user puts a letter—acting as the message—to be signed into a special carbon paper envelope. The signer can sign the envelope without opening it; his signature is transferred to the letter by the carbon paper, and the letter is never visible to the signer. In practice, it is sometimes necessary to consider the extension of *partially* blind signatures, introduced by Abe and Fujisaki [1], that further allow embedding a message agreed by both the signer and the user into the signature. The messages can now be divided into public and private parts, where the public part can include, for instance, the expiration date of the signature. While (partially) blind signatures[1] were originally used to construct e-cash [14,16,35], anonymous credentials [10,12], and e-voting [15,24], the notion has recently seen renewed interest due to applications in blockchains [11,44] and privacy-preserving authentication tokens [29,42].

Currently, the most promising class of efficient blind signatures known to withstand quantum attacks is those based on lattices. We have recently encountered significant progress in lattice-based blind signatures, such as [3,21,28,34], where the signature size currently sits around 50 KB to 10 MB. However, this is still an order of magnitude larger than their classical counterparts, with a signature size ranging from a few hundred bytes to 1 KB. As we see a continuous surge of interest in post-quantum security and better user privacy, we aim to investigate a post-quantum blind signature with a smaller signature size.

One potentially promising path to a post-quantum blind signature with a short signature is to rely on *isogeny*-based constructions. This is because while their signing and verification times are less efficient, standard isogeny-based signature schemes [8,19,20] are known to produce comparable or even smaller signatures compared to lattices. In fact, for a more advanced form of signature schemes such as ring signatures and group signatures, isogenies can produce much shorter signatures compared to their lattice counterparts [6,7].

Unfortunately, at first glance this path seems difficult to follow. Very roughly, there are two approaches to constructing a blind signature. The first approach is based on the Schnorr blind signature [17]. This approach builds on a sigma (or an identification) protocol with a "nice" algebraic property and boosts it into a blind signature by appropriately randomizing the interaction. This nice algebraic property has recently been stated informally to be *modules* [27,28], where isogenies are not known to be endowed with: isogenies are only *group actions* that are strictly less structured than modules (see Sect. 1.2 for more details). The second approach is based on the generic construction proposed by Fischlin [23] that requires proving, at the minimum, possession of a valid signature of a standard signature scheme using a non-interactive zero-knowledge proof (NIZK). While del Pino and Katsumata [21] and Agrawal, Kirshanova, Stehlé and Yadav [3] recently used this approach to construct more efficient lattice-based blind signatures than were previously known, this seems impractical

---

[1] For readability, we focus on blind signatures below when the distinction between the partial and non-partial difference is insignificant.

to translate to the isogeny setting due to the lack of efficient NIZKs for such complex languages.

In summary, while isogenies have the potential to produce the shortest post-quantum blind signatures, it is unclear how we can leverage known approaches to build them. This brings us to the main question of this work:

> *Can we construct an efficient post-quantum (partially) blind signature scheme from isogenies?*

1.1   Our Contribution

In this work, we answer the above question in the affirmative through four contributions. Our first contribution is to construct the first post-quantum blind signature based on isogenies (or CSIDH group actions to be more specific) called CSI-Otter, short for <u>CSI</u>-fish with <u>O</u>r-proof <u>T</u>wisted <u>ThreE</u>-<u>R</u>ound protocol. The construction is akin to the Schnorr blind signature [17] but follows a slightly different approach. Unlike previous constructions that required the underlying mathematical tool to be a module [27, 28], we bypass this requirement. The crux of our construction is to effectively use the *quadratic twist* of an elliptic curve, or in layman's terms, we use the fact that isogenies are *slightly* more expressive than a group action. We build a basic blind signature with public key size 128 B and signature size 8 KB based on the standard group action inverse problem (GAIP) over the CSIDH-512 parameter sets. We formally prove that our basic blind signature is secure in the (classical) random oracle model with poly-logarithmically many concurrent signing sessions following the recent work by Kastner, Loss, and Xu [30]. That is, the security proof permits a poly-logarithmic number of signatures to be issued per public key in a concurrent manner. However, we note that due to the lack of algebraic structures in isogenies, there seems to be no ROS[2] problem underlying the security of our blind signature [40, 43], and hence, it may be secure even for polynomially many concurrent signing sessions. This is in contrast to the Schnorr blind signature that admits a concrete attack in such a regime [5]. A formal analysis of our blind signature in the more desirable polynomial regime is left for future work.

Our second contribution is to provide an optimization of our basic blind signature using a new hardness assumption called the ζ_d-*ring* group action inverse problem (ζ_d-rGAIP), where ζ_d denotes a *d-th primitive root of unity* over $\mathbb{Z}_N$. Informally, ζ_d-rGAIP asserts that given $([\mathfrak{g}^{s \cdot \zeta_d^j}] * E_0)_{j \in [d]}$ for a random exponent $s \xleftarrow{\$} \mathbb{Z}_N$ and base elliptic curve $E_0 : y^2 = x^3 + x$, it is difficult to solve for s. Note that when $d = 2$, we have $\zeta_2 = -1$ and we recover the standard GAIP, where $[\mathfrak{g}^{-s}] * E_0$ is the (efficiently computable) quadratic twist of $[\mathfrak{g}^s] * E_0$. At a high level, ζ_d-rGAIP allows us to use a larger challenge space for the underlying sigma protocol by increasing the public key. This in turn implies that the number of parallel repetitions can be lowered compared to our basic blind signature, and

---

[2] ROS stands for for Random inhomogenities in an Overdetermined, Solvable system of linear equations.

effectively, we obtain a public key size of $(128 \cdot d)$ B and signature size of roughly $(8/\log_2 d)$ KB based on ζ_d-rGAIP. Our construction is generic and works for any group actions for which the ζ_d-rGAIP is hard, however, we must show that such group actions exist for it to be useful.

Our third contribution complements our second contribution: we provide a preliminary cryptanalysis on the hardness of ζ_d-rGAIP for the CSIDH-512 parameter sets. We first show that the set of values $\left\{ \gcd(\zeta_d^i - 1, N) \right\}_{i \in [d]}$ relates to the hardness of ζ_d-rGAIP. Informally, we create new GAIP instances over a series of subgroups of the class group, where the size of these subgroups relate to each $\gcd(\zeta_d^i - 1, N)$. Using known attacks against GAIP in a Pohlig-Hellman manner, we can break this newly generated GAIP instances that has a smaller order compared to the GAIP with CSIDH-512. For instance with CSIDH-512, when $d = 7$ or 8, this attack shows that ζ_d-rGAIP only has half the security of GAIP over CSIDH-512. On the other hand, for other values of d such as $d = 2, 3, 4, 5, 9, \ldots$, this attack is no more effective than trying to break GAIP over CSIDH-512. In fact, when $\gcd(\zeta_d^i - 1, N) = N/\mathsf{poly}(n)$ for n the security parameter, we show a reduction from the ζ_d-rGAIP to GAIP, thus establishing the optimality of our attack for certain parameters such as $d = 3, 5, 9, \ldots$. In the end, due to other correctness constraints, we are only able to instantiate the above optimized blind signature with $d = 4$, which leads to a public key of size 512 B and signature size of 4 KB. While our preliminary cryptanalysis shows that ζ_4-rGAIP is presumably as hard as GAIP over CSIDH-512, we leave further cryptanalysis for future work as it is not covered by our reduction to GAIP.

Our final contribution is extending our basic blind signature into a *partially* blind signature. While it is straightforward to construct a partially bind signature from a Schnorr-style blind signature in the classical group or the lattice settings, this approach fails in the isogeny setting.[3] For example, Abe and Okamoto [2] constructed the first partially blind signature, where the main idea was to hash the public message (also known as a *tag*) info to a group element $h_{\mathsf{info}} \in \mathbb{G}$ and let the signer prove that it knows either the exponent of its public key $h = g^a$ or the hashed tag h_{info}. In particular, the underlying sigma protocol proves a 1-out-of-2 (or an OR) relation. In the security proof, the reduction samples $a_{\mathsf{info}} \xleftarrow{\$} \mathbb{Z}_p$, programs the random oracle so that $h_{\mathsf{info}} = g^{a_{\mathsf{info}}}$, and uses a_{info} to simulate the signing algorithm. Unfortunately, this approach is inapplicable in the isogeny setting since we do not know how to map into the set of elliptic curves while simultaneously hiding the exponent. Note that if the exponent is known, any real-world adversary can use the reduction algorithm to forge a signature, thus rendering the scheme insecure.

To this end, we provide a new general approach to constructing partially blind signatures that may be of an independent interest. At the core of our approach is devising a sigma protocol for a *2-out-of-3* relation and embedding the tag info into the signature differently. Since the sigma protocol must also be

---

[3] We note that *proving* the security of a partially blind signature is more subtle and difficult. Indeed, it was only recently that Kastner, Loss, and Xu [30] provided a corrected proof of the Abe-Okamoto (partially) blind signature [2].

compatible with the blind signature, we are not able to rely on any 2-out-of-3 sigma protocols for threshold relations such as Cramer-Damgård-Schnoemakers' sigma protocol [18] using Shamir's secret-sharing scheme [41]. One downside of our partially blind signature is that compared to our blind signature, it requires a signature size roughly three times as large. However, we note that even then, we still achieve a smaller signature size than the lattice-based counterparts.

1.2   Technical Overview

We now explain our contributions in detail. We first review the Schnorr blind signature and see where it fails when translating the construction to the isogeny setting. We then explain our basic blind signature CSI-Otter that uses the quadratic twist and further show how to extend it to the partially blind setting. Finally, we explain the optimization using the newly introduced rGAIP assumption.

Reviewing the Schnorr Blind Signature. We first recall the Schnorr sigma/identification protocol between a prover with $(\mathsf{pk}, \mathsf{sk}) = (h = g^a, a) \in \mathbb{G} \times \mathbb{Z}_p$ and a verifier with pk. The prover samples $y \xleftarrow{\$} \mathbb{Z}_p$ and sends $Y = g^y$ to the verifier. The verifier sends a random challenge $c \xleftarrow{\$} \mathbb{Z}_p$ to the prover, where the prover replies with $r = y - a \cdot c$. The verifier is convinced that it was communicating with a prover in possession of $\mathsf{sk} = a$ if $g^r \cdot h^c = Y$. Here, if the verifier sets the challenge as $c = \mathsf{H}(Y \| \mathsf{M})$ for a message M and a hash function H modeled as a random oracle, then $\sigma = (c, r)$ serves as a signature based on the Fiat-Shamir transform [22], where the prover is the *signer* and the verifier is the *user with* M.

Clearly, this interactive signing protocol does not satisfy *blindness*, which roughly stipulates that a signature cannot be traced back to a specific signing session. In particular, when the user outputs the pair (M, σ), the signer will know in which session it signed σ—or equivalently, the signature σ can be traced back to the user—by simply checking when the hash value c included in σ was used.

The main idea of the Schnorr blind signature [17] is to let the user randomize the interaction so the session transcript becomes independent of the final signature. More explicitly, the user randomizes the interaction so that the final signature becomes $\sigma' = (c+d, r+z)$, where (d, z) is uniform over $\mathbb{Z}_p^2$ from the view of the signer. The Schnorr blind signature accomplishes this as follows: When the user receives Y as the first-sender message, it samples $(d, z) \xleftarrow{\$} \mathbb{Z}_p^2$ and sets $Y' := g^z \cdot Y \cdot h^d$. It then computes $c' = \mathsf{H}(Y' \| \mathsf{M})$ and sends $c := c' - d$ to the signer, where the signer replies with $r = y - a \cdot c$ as before. Since we have $g^r \cdot h^c = Y$, the user can multiply g^z and h^d on each side to obtain $g^{r+z} \cdot h^{c+d} = Y'$. Thus, $\sigma' = (c', r') := (c + d, r + z)$ is a valid signature for the message M. Moreover, it can be checked that this satisfies (perfect) blindness since any signature $\sigma' = (c', r')$ has an equal chance of being generated from a transcript (Y, c, r), where the probability is taken over the randomness sampled by the user.

Difficulty with Group Actions. In the above, the user is implicitly using a specific structure of the underlying Schnorr sigma protocol to randomize the interaction. Specifically, it is using the fact that $\mathbb{G}$ is a $\mathbb{Z}_p$-*module*. This allows the user to randomize the first-signer message $Y \in \mathbb{G}$ by multiplying it with the generator $g \in \mathbb{G}$ raised to the power of $z \in \mathbb{Z}_p$ and the public key $h = g^a \in \mathbb{G}$ lifted to the power of $d \in \mathbb{Z}_p$. This property has been more formally abstracted as a *linear identification protocol* [27,28], which covers schemes based on classical groups and lattices.

Unfortunately, this does not extend to the isogeny setting since isogenies are only a *group action*. Concretely, the CSIDH group action is defined as $* : G \times \mathcal{E} \to \mathcal{E}$, where G is an ideal class group and $\mathcal{E}$ is a set of elliptic curves, and we further assume the structure of G is known and can be expressed as $G = \langle [\mathfrak{g}] \rangle \cong \mathbb{Z}_N$ for some $N \in \mathbb{N}$, where $\mathfrak{g}$ is the generator [8]. Let us make an attempt to construct an isogeny-based Schnorr-style blind signature where the public key is $\mathsf{pk} = A = [\mathfrak{g}^a] * E_0 \in \mathcal{E}$ for a random $a \xleftarrow{\$} \mathbb{Z}_N$ and a fixed curve E_0. While the analogy of setting the first-signer message as $Y = [\mathfrak{g}^y] * E_0$ for $y \xleftarrow{\$} \mathbb{Z}_N$ works, it seems this is as far as we can get. Unlike the Schnorr blind signature, the user can only randomize Y *once from the left side*. That is, while computing $[\mathfrak{g}^z] * Y$ for a random $z \in G$ is possible, combining Y with $[\mathfrak{g}^d] * A$ is not possible since they are both set elements. We note that in the Schnorr blind signature setting, the former and latter correspond to $g^z \cdot Y$ and $Y \cdot h^d$, respectively. Since the blindness of the Schnorr blind signature hinged on the fact that the first-sender message Y can be randomized *twice*; one randomness d to hide the challenge c and another randomness z to hide the second-signer message r, it is unclear how to use isogenies to construct a blind signature while having only one way to randomize Y.

Using the Quadratic Twist. Our main observation to overcome this problem is to rely on the property that isogenies are slightly more expressive than a group action due to the *quadratic twist*. Given any $A = [\mathfrak{g}^a] * E_0$ for an unknown $a \in \mathbb{Z}_N$, we can efficiently compute its quadratic twist $[\mathfrak{g}^{-a}] * E_0$, which we denote[4] by A^{-1}.

We first explain the underlying isogeny-based sigma protocol, where we assume for now that the challenge space is $\mathcal{C} = \{-1, 1\}$. As above, the prover sends $Y = [\mathfrak{g}^y] * E_0$ for $y \xleftarrow{\$} \mathbb{Z}_N$. The verifier then sends a random challenge $c \xleftarrow{\$} \{-1, 1\}$, and the prover replies with $r = y - a \cdot c$. The verifier then verifies the "signature" $\sigma = (c, r)$ by checking whether $[\mathfrak{g}^r] * A^c = Y$, where note that A^c is well-defined for $c \in \{-1, 1\}$ even though A comes from

---

[4] The notation for the quadratic twist is not totally uniform in the literature. When $E/k : y^2 = x^3 + Ax^2 + x$ and $c \in k^\times \setminus k^{\times 2}$ one sometimes denotes $E^c/k : cy^2 = x^3 + Ax^2 + x$. In this work we will always have $-1 \in k^\times \setminus k^{\times 2}$ (since $k = \mathbb{F}_p$ and $p \equiv 3 \pmod 4$), and we will have $E^{-1} \cong E' : y^2 = x^3 - Ax^2 + x$ by the change of variables $(x, y) \mapsto (-x, y)$. So this notation—while not usually used in the CSIDH literature—is reasonable, and will be convenient for our protocol description.

the set of elliptic curves. For an honest execution of the protocol, we have $[\mathfrak{g}^r] * A^c = [\mathfrak{g}^r] * ([\mathfrak{g}^{a \cdot c}] * E_0) = [\mathfrak{g}^{r+a \cdot c}] * E_0 = Y$ as desired.[5]

Our idea is to randomize this sigma protocol so that the signature $\sigma = (c, r)$ becomes $\sigma' = (c \cdot d, r \cdot d + z)$, where (d, z) is uniform over $\{-1, 1\} \times \mathbb{Z}_N$ from the view of the signer. Concretely, given the first-sender message Y, the user randomizes Y by sampling random $(d, z) \xleftarrow{\$} \{-1, 1\} \times \mathbb{Z}_N$ and sets $Y' := [\mathfrak{g}^z] * Y^d$. It then computes $c' = \mathsf{H}(Y' \| \mathsf{M})$ and sends $c := c' \cdot d$. The signer replies with $r = y - a \cdot c$ as before. Since we have $[\mathfrak{g}^r] * A^c = Y$, the user can first compute $[\mathfrak{g}^{r \cdot d}] * A^{c \cdot d} = Y^d$. Namely, it performs nothing if $d = 1$, and computes the quadratic twist of both sides if $d = -1$. It then acts by $[\mathfrak{g}^z]$ to obtain $[\mathfrak{g}^{r \cdot d + z}] * A^{c \cdot d} = [\mathfrak{g}^z] * Y^d$. Since the right-hand side is Y', $\sigma' = (c', r') := (c \cdot d, r \cdot d + z)$ is a valid signature for the message M as desired. Moreover, it can be checked that we have perfect blindness since c and r are both randomized; the (multiplicative) randomness $d \in \{-1, 1\}$ hides the challenge c and the (additive) randomness $z \in \mathbb{Z}_N$ hides the response r. Put differently, any signature $\sigma' = (c', r')$ has an equal chance of being generated from a transcript (Y, c, r), where the probability is taken over the randomness sampled by the user.

Finally, to turn this basic idea into a secure blind signature, we enlarge the challenge space to be exponentially large, i.e., $\mathcal{C} = \{-1, 1\}^n$ where n is the security parameter. All the above arguments naturally extend to this enlarged challenge space by running the protocol n times in parallel.

Formal Security Proof. A knowledgeable reader may recall that the Schnorr blind signature is not known to be secure in the random oracle model [4]. This is also the case for our described isogeny-based blind signature. The Schnorr blind signature has been generalized by Pointcheval and Stern [37, 38] and Abe and Okamoto [2] in similar but different ways to have a security proof in the random oracle model. The latter Abe-Okamoto blind signature is compatible with our isogeny-based construction, where the public key is modified to a tuple $\mathsf{pk} = (A_0, A_1) = ([\mathfrak{g}_0^a] * E_0, [\mathfrak{g}_1^a] * E_0) \in \mathcal{E}^2$ for a random $(a_0, a_1) \xleftarrow{\$} \mathbb{Z}_N^2$, and the secret key to $\mathsf{sk} = (\delta, a_\delta)$ for a random $\delta \xleftarrow{\$} \{0, 1\}$. The construction uses the OR composition of the underlying sigma protocol and works well with our idea using the quadratic twist. While the original proof of Abe and Okamoto [2] contained a subtle but non-trivially fixable bug, Kastner, Loss, and Xu [30] recently provided a somewhat generic proof for Abe-Okamoto style blind signatures. The security proof of our blind signature is established by adapting their result to our setting.

Turning It Partially Blind. As explained in Sect. 1.1, there is no analog of the Abe-Okamoto *partially* blind signature in the isogeny setting. The only reason why we could replicate the Abe-Okamoto (non-partial) blind signature in the isogeny setting was that both (A_0, A_1) in pk were set up in a way that the user did not know the secret exponents. Generating $A_1 \in \mathcal{E}$ as a hash of the tag

---

[5] Note that this is a standard (optimized variant of an) isogeny-based sigma protocol where 0 is removed from the challenge space (see for instance [8]).

info, i.e., $A_1 = H(\text{info})$, would have failed in the isogeny setting since we cannot do so without letting the computation of $H(\cdot)$ reveal the secret exponent a_1. If a_1 is public, then the scheme becomes trivially forgeable.

Our main approach in constructing a partially blind signature is to keep the same public key $\text{pk} = (A_0, A_1)$ as before but to generate another curve $A_2 = H(\text{info})$ *with the secret exponent* a_2. We then modify the signer to prove that it knows at least *two of the three* exponents of (A_0, A_1, A_2). The reduction will be able to extract either a secret key pair (a_0, a_2), (a_1, a_2), or (a_0, a_1) from the forgery: we can rely on the proof for the standard blind signature that the first two pairs occur with an almost equal probability independent of the secret key used by the reduction, and the third case always allows the reduction to win.

The question is then how to construct a base sigma protocol for this 2-out-of-3 relation that is compatible with the above randomization technique using the quadratic twist. For instance, we cannot use the well-known Cramer-Damgård-Schnoemakers' sigma protocol [18] using Shamir's secret-sharing scheme [41] since the challenge space $\mathcal{C} = \{-1, 1\}$ is used as a multiplicative group in our construction, rather than a field as required by Shamir's secret-sharing scheme.[6] To this end, we use a 2-out-of-3 *multiplicative* secret-sharing scheme as follows: Given a secret $c \in \{-1, 1\}$, sample $(c_0, c_1, c_2) \in \{-1, 1\}^3$ uniformly random conditioned on $c_0 \cdot c_1 \cdot c_2 = c$. We then view (c_0, c_1), (c_1, c_2), and (c_2, c_0) as the three shares. One can check that any two of the three shares allow reconstructing c, while c is information-theoretically hidden when only one share is known.

We now construct a sigma protocol for a 2-out-of-3 relation using this secret-sharing scheme as follows: the high-level idea is to assign the secret shares (c_0, c_1), (c_1, c_2), and (c_2, c_0) to the exponents a_0, a_1, and a_2, respectively. In more detail, assume the prover knows the exponents a_0 and a_2. It first samples two shares $(c_1, c_2) \xleftarrow{\$} \{-1, 1\}^2$ and runs the honest-verifier zero-knowledge simulator to simulate the knowledge of the unknown exponent a_1. Specifically, it samples $(r_{1,0}, r_{1,1}) \xleftarrow{\$} \mathbb{Z}_N^2$ and sets $(Y_{1,0}, Y_{1,1}) = ([\mathfrak{g}^{r_{1,0}}] * A_1^{c_1}, [\mathfrak{g}^{r_{1,1}}] * A_1^{c_2})$. It then sets $(Y_{b,0}, Y_{b,1}) = ([\mathfrak{g}^{y_{b,0}}] * A_b, [\mathfrak{g}^{y_{b,1}}] * A_b)$ for $b \in \{0, 2\}$ by sampling the y's as before. Upon receiving $(Y_{b,0}, Y_{b,1})_{b \in \{0,1,2\}}$, the verifier returns a random $c \in \{-1, 1\}$. The prover sets the final share $c_0 = c \cdot c_1 \cdot c_2$ and computes $(r_{0,0}, r_{0,1}) = (y_{0,0} - a_0 \cdot c_0, y_{0,1} - a_0 \cdot c_1)$ and $(r_{2,0}, r_{2,1}) = (y_{2,0} - a_2 \cdot c_2, y_{2,1} - a_2 \cdot c_0)$, where recall a_2 is the publicly known exponent associated with the tag info. Finally, the prover replies with $(r_{b,0}, r_{b,1})_{b \in \{0,1,2\}}$. The verifier can check the validity of the proof by a similar check as before and will be convinced that the prover knows at least two secret exponents of $\text{pk} = (A_0, A_1, A_2)$.

Building on a similar argument using the quadratic twist, we turn this 2-out-of-3 sigma protocol into a partially blind signature by allowing the user to appropriately randomize the first-signer message Y's. The user samples three randomness from $\{-1, 1\}$ to randomize the challenge (c_0, c_1, c_2) and six randomness from $\mathbb{Z}_N$ to randomize the second-signer message $(r_{b,0}, r_{b,1})_{b \in \{0,1,2\}}$. We

---

[6] Since parallel repetition is not required to show blindness, we only focus on the small challenge space for simplicity.

show that the proof of Kastner, Loss, and Xu [30] can be slightly modified to work for this partially blind signature.

Optimization Using Higher Degree Roots of Unity. Finally, we show how to optimize our blind signature. One of the implicit reasons why the randomization of the sigma protocol worked was because the challenge space $\mathcal{C} = \{-1, 1\}$ was a multiplicative subgroup of the ring $\mathbb{Z}_N$. We generalize this observation and consider a larger challenge space $\mathcal{C}_d = \left\{ \zeta_d^j \right\}_{j \in [d]}$, where ζ_d is the d-th primitive root of unity over $\mathbb{Z}_N$,[7] i.e., $\zeta_d^d = 1$ and $\zeta_d^j \neq 1$ for any $j \in [d-1]$. $\mathcal{C}_d$ is indeed a larger multiplicative subgroup of the ring $\mathbb{Z}_N$, where setting $d = 2$ recovers the challenge space $\mathcal{C}_2 = \mathcal{C}$. The goal of the optimized scheme remains the same: we want to randomize the signature $\sigma = (c, r) \in \mathcal{C}_d \times \mathbb{Z}_N$ by $\sigma' = (c \cdot d, r \cdot d + z)$ for a random $(d, z) \xleftarrow{\$} \mathcal{C}_d \times \mathbb{Z}_N$. However, unfortunately, when we use a larger challenge space $\mathcal{C}_d$ for $d > 2$, the underlying sigma protocol no longer satisfies correctness. Recall in the most simple sigma protocol, the verifier receives $Y = [\mathfrak{g}^y] * E_0$, outputs a challenge $c \in \{-1, 1\}$, receives $r = y - a \cdot c$ and checks if $[\mathfrak{g}^r] * A^c = Y$. The final check by the verifier was computable since computing the quadratic twist (i.e., A^{-1}) was efficient. This is no longer the case for a more general $c \in \mathcal{C}_d$ since we do not know how to compute $A^j := [\mathfrak{g}^{a \cdot \zeta_d^j}] * E_0$ given only the curve $A = [\mathfrak{g}^a] * E_0 \in \mathcal{E}$, $j \in [d-1]$, and ζ_d with $d \geq 3$. To this end, we extend the public key to $\mathsf{pk} = (A^j)_{j \in [d]}$ to aid the verifier's computation and modify the sigma protocol to address this extension. This is where we rely on the new ζ_d-*ring* group action inverse problem (ζ_d-rGAIP) which states that given pk, it is difficult to recover the exponent $a \in \mathbb{Z}_N$. Before getting into the hardness of ζ_d-rGAIP, we finish the overview of our optimized blind signature below.

Although we are now able to construct a sigma protocol with a larger challenge space, it does not yet naturally extend to blind signatures due to the extra structure. In particular, the main issue is that when the signer sends $Y = [\mathfrak{g}^y] * E_0$ as the first message, our idea was to let the user randomize this by $[\mathfrak{g}^z] * Y^w$, where $Y^w := [\mathfrak{g}^{y \cdot \zeta_d^w}] * E_0$ for $(z, w) \xleftarrow{\$} \mathbb{Z}_N \times \mathcal{C}_d$. However, due to the same reason as above, this cannot be efficiently computed from only Y. To this end, we further extend the sigma protocol so that the prover includes all $(Y^j)_{j \in [d]}$ in the first message. While this structure cannot be efficiently checked by the verifier/user, we modify the sigma protocol so that it performs some consistency checks on these Y^j's. We show that this check is sufficient to argue blindness of the resulting blind signature even when the malicious signer is using a malformed public key, i.e., $(A^j)_{j \in [d]}$ does not have the correct ring structure.

Cryptanalysis of ζ_d-rGAIP. We have explained how to construct an optimized blind signature assuming the hardness of ζ_d-rGAIP. We complement our result by providing a preliminary cryptanalysis of ζ_d-rGAIP for the CSIDH-512 parameter. We provide an attack that exploits the additional structure of ζ_d-rGAIP

---

[7] For the overview, we will ignore when such ζ_d exists and how to find them (see Sect. 7.1 for more details).

for specific choices of d. The insight is the difference of each curves in the public key always has a factor of $(\zeta_d^i - \zeta_d^j)$ for distinct $i, j \in [d]$ which constitutes a non-injective endomorphism over the secret key space $\mathbb{Z}_N$. By investigating these differences, we can reduce an ζ_d-rGAIP instance to a GAIP instance with a possibly smaller group than $\mathbb{Z}_N$ and recover partial information. Then, we can integrate these partial information in a Pohlig-Hellman sense. As a consequence, we can evaluate the upper bound security strength of ζ_d-rGAIP using known attacks against GAIP. For some choices of ζ_d, ζ_d-rGAIP only has half the security compared with GAIP for the CSIDH-512 parameters. On the other hand, for some instances of ζ_d, we show that ζ_d-rGAIP is as hard as GAIP, which demonstrates that the upper bounds obtained via our cryptanalysis are also the lower bounds. There are some instances of ζ_d-rGAIP for which our attack does not apply while also having no reduction to GAIP. We leave analysis of such instances of ζ_d-rGAIP for the CSIDH-512 parameter set as an interesting future work.

2 Background

2.1 (Partially) Blind Signature

We define partially blind signatures consisting of three moves, which is sufficient to capture many known protocols, e.g., [2,30,31]. Below, we retrieve the standard definition of (three-move) blind signatures by ignoring the tag info or alternatively setting info to a predefined value.

Definition 2.1 (Partially Blind Signature Scheme). *A three-move partially blind signature* PBS = (PBS.KGen, PBS.S, PBS.U, PBS.Verify) *with an efficiently decidable public key space* $\mathcal{PK}$ *consists of the following PPT algorithms:*

PBS.KGen(1^n) $\rightarrow$ (pk, sk): *On input the security parameter* 1^n, *the key generation algorithm outputs a pair of public and secret keys* (pk, sk).

PBS.S = (PBS.S$_1$, PBS.S$_2$): *The interactive signer algorithm consists of two phases:*

> PBS.S$_1$(sk, info) $\rightarrow$ (state$_S$, $\rho_{S,1}$): *On input a secret key* sk *and a tag* info, *it outputs an internal signer state* state$_S$ *and a first-sender message* $\rho_{S,1}$.[8]
>
> PBS.S$_2$(state$_S$, ρ_U)) $\rightarrow \rho_{S,2}$: *On input a signer state* state$_S$ *and a user message* ρ_U, *it outputs a second-sender message* $\rho_{S,2}$.

PBS.U = (PBS.U$_1$, PBS.U$_2$): *The interactive user algorithm consists of two phases:*

> PBS.U$_1$(pk, info, M, $\rho_{S,1}$) $\rightarrow$ (state$_U$, ρ_U): *On input a public key* pk $\in \mathcal{PK}$, *a tag* info, *a message* M, *and a first-sender message* $\rho_{S,1}$, *it outputs an internal user state* state$_U$ *and a user message* ρ_U.

---

[8] We assume without loss of generality that sk includes pk and state$_S$ includes (pk, sk) and omit it when the context is clear. Below, we also assume that state$_U$ includes M.

PBS.U_2($\text{state}_U, \rho_{S,2}$)) → σ: *On input a user state* state_U *and a second-signer message* $\rho_{S,2}$, *it outputs a signature* σ.

PBS.Verify(pk, info, M, σ) → 1 *or* 0: *In input a public key* pk, *a tag* info, *a message* M, *and a signature* σ, *the verification algorithm outputs* 1 *to indicate the signature is valid, and* 0 *otherwise.*

If the partially blind signature only accepts a unique tag info, we drop the "partially" and simply call it a *blind signature* (BS) and omit info from the syntax.

We require a partially blind signature to be complete, blind against malicious signer, and one-more unforgeable. We first define correctness.

Definition 2.2 (Perfect Correctness). *A three-move partially blind signature scheme* PBS *is perfectly correct if for all public and secret key pairs* (pk, sk) ∈ PBS.KGen(1^n) *and every tag and message pair* (info, M), *we have*

$$\Pr\left[\text{PBS.Verify(pk, info, M, }\sigma) = 1 \left| \begin{array}{l} (\text{state}_S, \rho_{S,1}) \xleftarrow{\$} \text{PBS.S}_1(\text{sk, info}) \\ (\text{state}_U, \rho_U) \xleftarrow{\$} \text{PBS.U}_1(\text{pk, info, M}, \rho_{S,1}) \\ \rho_{S,2} \xleftarrow{\$} \text{PBS.S}_2(\text{state}_S, \rho_U) \\ \sigma \xleftarrow{\$} \text{PBS.U}_2(\text{state}_U, \rho_{S,2}) \end{array} \right. \right] = 1$$

The following definitions are taken from [30,31]. Partial blindness roughly requires the transcript to be independent of the signature even if the signer choses the keys maliciously.

Definition 2.3 (Partial Blindness Under Chosen Keys). *We define partial blindness of a three-move partially blind signature scheme* PBS *via the following game between a challenger and an adversary* $\mathcal{A}$:

Setup. *The challenger samples* coin ∈ {0, 1} *and runs* $\mathcal{A}$ *on input* 1^n.

Online Phase. *When* $\mathcal{A}$ *outputs a tag* info, *messages* $\widetilde{M}_0$ *and* $\widetilde{M}_1$, *and a public key* pk ∈ $\mathcal{PK}$, *it assigns* $(M_0, M_1) := (\widetilde{M}_{\text{coin}}, \widetilde{M}_{1-\text{coin}})$. $\mathcal{A}$ *is then given access to oracles* U_1, U_2, *which behave as follows:*

> **Oracle** U_1. *On input* b ∈ {0, 1}, *and a first-signer message* $\rho_{S,1,b}$, *if the session* b *is not yet open, the oracle marks session* b *as* **opened** *and runs* ($\text{state}_{U,b}, \rho_{U,b}$) $\xleftarrow{\$}$ PBS.U_1 (pk, info, M_b, $\rho_{S,1,b}$). *It returns* $\rho_{U,b}$ *to* $\mathcal{A}$.
>
> **Oracle** U_2. *On input* b ∈ {0, 1} *and a second-signer message* $\rho_{S,2,b}$, *if the session* b *is* **opened**, *the oracle creates a signature* σ_b $\xleftarrow{\$}$ PBS.U_2 ($\text{state}_{U,b}, \rho_{S,2,b}$). *It marks session* b *as* **closed**. *Oracle* U_2 *does not output anything.*

Output Determination. *When both sessions are closed and* PBS.Verify (pk, info, M_b, σ_b) = 1 *for* b ∈ {0, 1}, *the oracle returns the two signatures* ($\sigma_{\text{coin}}, \sigma_{1-\text{coin}}$) *to* $\mathcal{A}$, *where note that* σ_{coin} *(resp.* $\sigma_{1-\text{coin}}$*) is a valid signature for* $\widetilde{M}_0$ *(resp.* $\widetilde{M}_1$*) regardless of the choice of* coin. $\mathcal{A}$ *outputs a guess* coin* *for* coin. *We say* $\mathcal{A}$ *wins if* coin* = coin.

We say PBS *is partially blind under chosen keys if the advantage of* $\mathcal{A}$ *defined as* Pr[$\mathcal{A}$ *wins*] *is negligible.*

One-more unforgeability roughly ensures that at most one valid signature is generated after each execution of PBS.Sign. Formally, we have the following.

Definition 2.4 (One-More-Unforgeability). *We define ℓ-one-more unforgeability (ℓ-OMUF) for any $\ell \in \mathbb{N}$ of a three-move partially blind signature scheme PBS via the following game between a challenger and an adversary $\mathcal{A}$:*

Setup. *The challenger samples* $(\mathsf{pk}, \mathsf{sk}) \xleftarrow{\$} \mathsf{PBS.KGen}(1^n)$ *and runs $\mathcal{A}$ on input* pk. *It further initializes* $\ell_{\mathsf{closed}} = 0$ *and* $\mathsf{opened}_{\mathsf{sid}} = \mathtt{false}$ *for all* $\mathsf{sid} \in \mathbb{N}$.

Online Phase. *$\mathcal{A}$ is given access to oracles S_1 and S_2, which behave as follows.*

> **Oracle S_1:** *On input a tag* info, *the oracle samples a fresh session identifier* sid. *It sets* $\mathsf{opened}_{\mathsf{sid}} \leftarrow \mathtt{true}$ *and generates* $(\mathsf{state}_{\mathsf{S},\mathsf{sid}}, \rho_{\mathsf{S},1}) \xleftarrow{\$} \mathsf{PBS.S}_1(\mathsf{sk}, \mathsf{info})$. *Then it returns* sid *and the first-sender message* $\rho_{\mathsf{S},1}$ *to $\mathcal{A}$.*

> **Oracle S_2:** *On input a user message* ρ_{U} *and a session identifier* sid, *if* $\ell_{\mathsf{closed}} \geq \ell$ *or* $\mathsf{opened}_{\mathsf{sid}} = \mathtt{false}$, *then it returns* $\bot$. *Otherwise, it sets* $\ell_{\mathsf{closed}} + +$ *and* $\mathsf{opened}_{\mathsf{sid}} = \mathtt{false}$. *It then computes the second-signer message* $\rho_{\mathsf{S},2} \xleftarrow{\$} \mathsf{PBS.S}_2(\mathsf{state}_{\mathsf{S},\mathsf{sid}}, \rho_{\mathsf{U}})$ *and returns* $\rho_{\mathsf{S},2}$ *to $\mathcal{A}$.*

Output Determination. *When $\mathcal{A}$ outputs distinct tuples* $(\mathsf{M}_1, \sigma_1, \mathsf{info}_1), \ldots, (\mathsf{M}_k, \sigma_k, \mathsf{info}_k)$, *we say $\mathcal{A}$ wins if* $k \geq \ell_{\mathsf{closed}} + 1$ *and for all* $i \in [k]$, $\mathsf{PBS.Verify}(\mathsf{pk}, \mathsf{info}_i, \mathsf{M}_i, \sigma_i) = 1$.

We say PBS *is ℓ-one-more unforgeable if the advantage of $\mathcal{A}$ defined as* $\Pr[\mathcal{A} \ wins]$ *is negligible.*

3   Generic Proofs for Blind Schnorr-Type Signatures

In this section, we review the recent work of Kastner, Loss, and Xu [30] that provided a proof of the Abe-Okamoto (partially) blind signature [2]. The original security proof of the one-more unforgeability in [2] contained a leap of logic in the security proof (i.e., the scheme was correct but the security proof was not), and Kastner, Loss, and Xu provided a somewhat generic proof that works for many of the blind Schnorr-type signatures [17].[9] For reference, we provide an overview of the proof by Kastner, Loss, and Xu in the full version of this paper.

3.1   Key Definitions, Lemmas, and Theorems

We extract the minimal definitions and lemmas from [30] in a self-contained manner so that the security of our (partially) blind signatures is established through several easy-to-state lemmas. For a more full exposition, we refer the readers to [30].

---

[9] Note that the proof in [30] relies on the fact that there are two possible signing keys per public key. Therefore, their proof does not work for the original Schnorr blind signature [17], which is known to be secure if we further rely on the algebraic group model [31].

Preparation. We first assume the adversary against the one-more unforgeability game is restricted to make only $\ell + 1$ distinct hash queries to the random oracle, where $\ell + 1$ is the number of forgeries the adversary outputs. Moreover, as with any blind Schnorr-type signature, we assume each signature in the forgery is associated with a distinct hash query.[10] We also assume the public key of the (partially) blind signature has exactly two corresponding secret keys. More specifically, we assume the underlying sigma protocol is for the **NP** OR-relation R defined with respect to another **NP** relation R'. That is, $(X := (X'_0, X'_1), W := (\delta, W'_\delta)) \in R$, where $(X'_0, W'_0), (X'_1, W'_1) \in R'$, X is the public key and W is the secret key. Finally, we assume the adversary's user-message ρ_U queried to the signing algorithm $\mathsf{PBS.S_2}$ satisfies $\rho_U \in \mathcal{C}$, where $\mathcal{C}$ is the challenge space of the underlying sigma protocol for relation R (and R').

We first define the notion of *instances*. Roughly, an instance defines the signer's key and randomness. We present a variant of the definition of instances in [30, Definition 4] that is agnostic to the underlying sigma protocol. We provide an explicit description of instances, analogous to [30, Definition 4], when we detail our construction of (partial) blind signatures.

Definition 3.1 (Instances). *Assume the public key of a blind Schnorr-type signature has exactly two corresponding secret keys* $\mathsf{sk_0} = (0, W'_0)$ *and* $\mathsf{sk_1} = (1, W'_1)$. *We define two types of* instances **I**: *A 0-side (resp. 1-side) instance consists of* $\mathsf{sk_0}$ *(resp.* $\mathsf{sk_1}$*) and the randomness used by the honest signer algorithm when the secret key is fixed to* $\mathsf{sk_0}$ *(resp.* $\mathsf{sk_1}$*), i.e., randomness excluding those used by the key generation algorithm.*

The main argument of Kastner, Loss, and Xu boils down to arguing that the output of the extraction algorithm (i.e., forking algorithm) explained above is independent of the instances.

Let $\overrightarrow{h}$ be the vector of responses returned by the random oracle, where $|\overrightarrow{h}| = \ell + 1$, and let rand be the randomness used by the one-more unforgeability adversary. We define a deterministic wrapper algorithm $\mathcal{W}$ that simulates the interaction between the signer and the adversary given input $(\mathbf{I}, \mathsf{rand}, \overrightarrow{h})$. $\mathcal{W}$ invokes the signer and the adversary on inputs $\mathbf{I}$ and rand, respectively, and uses $\overrightarrow{h}$ to answer the random oracle queries made by the adversary. We define $\mathcal{W}(\mathbf{I}, \mathsf{rand}, \overrightarrow{h})$ to output $\perp$ if the adversary aborts prematurely or fails to win the one-more unforgeability game, and otherwise, output what the adversary outputs. We then define the notion of *successful tuples* as follows.

Definition 3.2 (Successful Tuples). *We define the set of* successful tuples *as follows:*

$$\mathsf{Succ} := \{(\mathbf{I}, \mathsf{rand}, \overrightarrow{h}) \mid \mathcal{W}(\mathbf{I}, \mathsf{rand}, \overrightarrow{h}) \neq \perp\}.$$

We next define a sufficient condition to invoke the extraction algorithm of the underlying sigma protocol. This is a standard definition (often implicitly) used even for Fiat-Shamir based signatures.

---

[10] For those unfamiliar with Schnorr-type signatures, we encourage to look at our concrete construction, where the meaning would be clear from context.

Definition 3.3 (Successful Forking [30, Definition 7]). *We say two success-ful input tuples* $(\mathbf{I}, \mathsf{rand}, \overrightarrow{h}), (\mathbf{I}, \mathsf{rand}, \overrightarrow{h}') \in \mathsf{Succ}$ *fork from each other at index* $i \in [\ell+1]$ *if* $\overrightarrow{h}_{[i-1]} = \overrightarrow{h}'_{[i-1]}$ *but* $h_i \neq h_i'$. *We denote the set of hash vector pairs* (h_i, h_i') *such that* $(\mathbf{I}, \mathsf{rand}, \overrightarrow{h}), (\mathbf{I}, \mathsf{rand}, \overrightarrow{h}') \in \mathsf{Succ}$ *fork at index* i *as* $\mathrm{F}_i(\mathbf{I}, \mathsf{rand})$.

We next define the notion of transcripts. A *query transcript* denotes the user messages queried to the signer. A *full transcript* denotes the entire transcript produced by the signer and the adversary, including the final forgery.

Definition 3.4 (Query Transcript [30, Definition 5]). *Consider the wrapper* $\mathcal{W}$ *running on input* $(\mathbf{I}, \mathsf{rand}, \overrightarrow{h})$. *The* query transcript, *denoted* $\overrightarrow{e}(\mathbf{I}, \mathsf{rand}, \overrightarrow{h})$, *is the vector of user message* (ρ_U) *queries made to the signing algorithm* $\mathsf{PBS.S_2}$ *(simulated by* $\mathcal{W}$*) by the adversary, ordered by* sid.

Definition 3.5 (Full Transcript [30, Definition 6]). *Consider the wrapper* $\mathcal{W}$ *running on input* $(\mathbf{I}, \mathsf{rand}, \overrightarrow{h})$. *The* full transcript, *denoted* $\mathsf{trans}(\mathbf{I}, \mathsf{rand}, \overrightarrow{h})$, *is the transcript produced between the signer and the adversary, i.e., all messages sent between the signer and user played by the adversary, including the forgeries.*

We now define *partners*, which plays a key role in the analysis of [2,30]. Informally, two tuples $(\mathbf{I}, \mathsf{rand}, \overrightarrow{h}), (\mathbf{I}, \mathsf{rand}, \overrightarrow{h}') \in \mathsf{Succ}$ are partners at i if they fork at this index i and produce the same query transcript. Note that this does not necessarily imply that each tuple results in the same full transcript.

Definition 3.6 (Partners [30, Definition 8]). *We say two successful tuples* $(\mathbf{I}, rand, \overrightarrow{h}), (\mathbf{I}, rand, \overrightarrow{h}')$ *are partners at index* $i \in [\ell+1]$ *if the followings hold:*

- $(\mathbf{I}, \mathsf{rand}, \overrightarrow{h})$ *and* $(\mathbf{I}, \mathsf{rand}, \overrightarrow{h}')$ *fork at index* i.
- $\overrightarrow{e}(\mathbf{I}, \mathsf{rand}, \overrightarrow{h}) = \overrightarrow{e}(\mathbf{I}, \mathsf{rand}, \overrightarrow{h}')$

We denote the set of $(\overrightarrow{h}, \overrightarrow{h}')$ *such that* $(\mathbf{I}, \mathsf{rand}, \overrightarrow{h})$ *and* $(\mathbf{I}, \mathsf{rand}, \overrightarrow{h}')$ *are partners at index* i *by* $\mathsf{prt}_i(\mathbf{I}, \mathsf{rand})$.

A *triangle* is another key tool introduced in [2,30] in order to enhance the standard forking tuples with the nice properties of partners. A triangle consists of three vectors $\overrightarrow{h}, \overrightarrow{h}', \overrightarrow{h}''$ such that each two vectors fork at the same index, and additionally, $(\overrightarrow{h}, \overrightarrow{h}')$ are partners.

Definition 3.7 (Triangles [30, Definition 9]). *A triangle at index* $i \in [\ell+1]$ *with respect to* $\mathbf{I}$, rand *is a tuple of three successful tuples in the following set:*

$$\triangle_i(\mathbf{I}, \mathsf{rand}) = \left\{ \begin{array}{l} ((\mathbf{I}, \mathsf{rand}, \overrightarrow{h}), \\ (\mathbf{I}, \mathsf{rand}\,\overrightarrow{h}'), \\ (\mathbf{I}, \mathsf{rand}\,\overrightarrow{h}'')) \end{array} \middle| \begin{array}{l} (\overrightarrow{h}, \overrightarrow{h}') \in \mathsf{prt}_i(\mathbf{I}, \mathsf{rand}) \\ (\overrightarrow{h}, \overrightarrow{h}'') \in \mathrm{F}_i(\mathbf{I}, \mathsf{rand})) \\ (\overrightarrow{h}', \overrightarrow{h}'') \in \mathrm{F}_i(\mathbf{I}, \mathsf{rand}) \end{array} \right\}$$

For a triangle $((\mathbf{I}, \mathsf{rand}, \overrightarrow{h}), (\mathbf{I}, \mathsf{rand}, \overrightarrow{h}'), (\mathbf{I}, \mathsf{rand}, \overrightarrow{h}'')) \in \triangle_i(\mathbf{I}, \mathsf{rand})$, *we call the pair of tuples* $((\mathbf{I}, \mathsf{rand}, \overrightarrow{h}), (\mathbf{I}, \mathsf{rand}, \overrightarrow{h}'))$ *the* base, *and* $((\mathbf{I}, \mathsf{rand}, \overrightarrow{h}), (\mathbf{I}, \mathsf{rand}, \overrightarrow{h}''))$ *and* $((\mathbf{I}, \mathsf{rand}, \overrightarrow{h}'), (\mathbf{I}, \mathsf{rand}, \overrightarrow{h}''))$ *the* sides.

We next define a map that transforms a b-side instance into a $(1 - b)$-side instance for $b \in \{0, 1\}$. Roughly, the map allows us to relate the number of triangles with a 0-side instance to those with a 1-side instance. We present a variant of the definition of instances in [30, Definition 12] that is agnostic to the underlying sigma protocol. We provide an explicit description of the map, analogous to [30, Definition 12], when we detail our construction of (partial) blind signatures.

Definition 3.8 (Mapping Instances via Transcript). *For* $(\mathbf{I}, \mathsf{rand}, \overrightarrow{h}) \in$ Succ, *we define* $\Phi_{\mathsf{rand}, \overrightarrow{h}}(\mathbf{I})$ *as a function that maps a 0-side instance* $\mathbf{I}$ *(resp. 1-side instance* $\mathbf{I}$) *to a 1-side instance* $\mathbf{I}'$ *(resp. 0-side instance* $\mathbf{I}'$).

Finally, we formally define the witness extractor used by the reduction. We present a variant of the definition of witness extractor in [30, Definition 13] that is agnostic to the underlying sigma protocol. This is because the witness extractor's concrete description is defined using the special soundness extractor of the underlying sigma protocol, which we will do when we detail our construction of (partial) blind signatures.

Definition 3.9 (Witness Extraction). *Fix* $\mathbf{I}, \mathsf{rand}$ *and let* $\overrightarrow{h}, \overrightarrow{h}' \in$ $\mathsf{F}_i(\mathbf{I}, \mathsf{rand})$ *for some* $i \in [\ell + 1]$. *Moreover, denote* σ_i, σ_i' *the signatures that correspond to* h_i, h_i', *respectively. We say deterministic algorithms* $(\mathsf{Ext}_0, \mathsf{Ext}_1)$ *are witness extractors if* $(\mathsf{Ext}_0(\sigma_i, \sigma_i'), \mathsf{Ext}_1(\sigma_i, \sigma_i')) \in \{(\mathsf{sk}_0, \bot), (\bot, \mathsf{sk}_1), (\mathsf{sk}_0, \mathsf{sk}_1)\}$.[11] *For* $b \in \{0, 1\}$, *we say that the b-side witness can be extracted from* $(\mathbf{I}, \mathsf{rand}, \overrightarrow{h})$ *and* $(\mathbf{I}, \mathsf{rand}, \overrightarrow{h}')$ *at index* i *if* $\mathsf{Ext}_b(\sigma_i, \sigma_i')$ *outputs* sk_b.

Sufficient Condition for One-More Unforgeability. We are now prepared to formally present the main result of Kastner, Loss, and Xu [30]. Let us prepare the following two lemmas.

Lemma 3.1 ([30, Lemma 2]). *Fix* $\mathsf{rand}, \overrightarrow{h}$. *For all tuples* $(\mathbf{I}, \mathsf{rand}, \overrightarrow{h}) \in$ Succ, $\Phi_{\mathsf{rand}, \overrightarrow{h}}$ *is a self-inverse bijection and* $\mathsf{trans}(\mathbf{I}, \mathsf{rand}, \overrightarrow{h}) = \mathsf{trans}(\Phi_{\mathsf{rand}, \overrightarrow{h}}(\mathbf{I}), \mathsf{rand}, \overrightarrow{h})$.

Lemma 3.2 ([30, Corollary 3]). *Fix* $\mathbf{I}, \mathsf{rand}$ *and let* $(\overrightarrow{h}, \overrightarrow{h}', \overrightarrow{h}'') \in \triangle_i(\mathbf{I},$ $\mathsf{rand})$, *for some* $i \in [\ell + 1]$. *If the 0-side (1-side) witness can be extracted from the base* $(\mathbf{I}, \mathsf{rand}, \overrightarrow{h}), (\mathbf{I}, \mathsf{rand}, \overrightarrow{h}')$ *of the triangle at index* i, *then one can also extract the 0-side (1-side) witness from at least one of the sides* $(\mathbf{I}, \mathsf{rand}, \overrightarrow{h}), (\mathbf{I}, \mathsf{rand}, \overrightarrow{h}'')$ *or* $(\mathbf{I}, \mathsf{rand}, \overrightarrow{h}), (\mathbf{I}, \mathsf{rand}, \overrightarrow{h}'')$ *at index* i.

---

[11] [30] defined the witness extractors in such a way that it outputs only $(\mathsf{sk}_0, \bot)$ or $(\bot, \mathsf{sk}_1)$. However, this restriction is not required as long as Lemma 3.1 (i.e., [30, Corollary 3]) holds. We note that we need this extra relaxation for it to be useful in our *partially* blind signature. Moreover, note that the extractors are only required to output W_b' included in $\mathsf{sk}_b = (b, \mathsf{W}_b')$. We use W_b' and sk_b interchangeably for readability.

Kastner, Loss, and Xu showed that if the above two lemmas hold, then we can perform a fine-grained analysis of the reduction's success probability. For completeness, we provide some intuition on the above lemmas in the full version of this paper. The following is the main theorem of Kastner, Loss, and Xu [30, Theorem 1] casted slightly generally to be agnostic to the underlying hardness assumption.

Theorem 3.1. *Let the (partially) blind Schnorr-type signature* (P)BS *be as defined in the preparation of Sect. 3.1. In particular, assume the public key consists of two instances of the **NP** relation R' generated by a corresponding hard instance generator* IG *and the underlying sigma protocol has challenge space* $\mathcal{C}$.

If Lemmas 3.1 and 3.2 hold, then for all $\ell \in \mathbb{N}$, if there exists an adversary $\mathcal{A}$ that makes Q hash queries to the random oracle and breaks the ℓ-one more unforgeability of (P)BS *with advantage $\epsilon_{\mathcal{A}} \geq \frac{C_1}{|\mathcal{C}|} \cdot \binom{Q}{\ell+1}$, then there exists an algorithm $\mathcal{B}$ that breaks the hard instance generator with advantage $\epsilon_{\mathcal{B}} \geq C_2 \cdot \frac{\epsilon_{\mathcal{A}}^2}{\binom{Q}{\ell+1}^2 \cdot (\ell+1)^3}$ for some universal positive constants C_1 and C_2.*

We note that Kastner, Loss, and Xu only show the above theorem for blind signatures. They then show that it can be extended to a proof for their particular partially blind signature with a loss of $1/T$, where T is the number of the distinct tag info queries by the adversary (see [30, Theorem 2]). However, as explained in the introduction, we cannot follow their approach since our partially blind signature must deviate from prior constructions. To this end, we notice that the same proofs and theorem above can be applied to the partially blind setting if the instances in Definition 3.1 can be defined independently from the tags info used by the adversary. See Sect. 5 for more details.

4   Constructing Isogeny-Based Blind Signatures

In this section, we provide our isogeny-based blind signature. We first explain the sigma protocol that underlies our isogeny-based blind signature and then show how to compile it into a blind signature.

4.1   Base Sigma Protocol for an OR Relation

To begin, we consider a sigma protocol to prove that the prover knows at least *one of the two secrets* corresponding to the public statement $\mathsf{X} = (A_0, A_1) = ([\mathfrak{g}^{a_0}] * E_0, [\mathfrak{g}^{a_1}] * E_0)$. The sigma protocol is depicted in Fig. 1. Note that this is a standard isogeny-based sigma protocol where 0 is removed from the challenge space (see for instance [8]). As explained in Sect. 1.2, the main reason for this slight modification is to make the (non-soundness amplified) challenge space $\{-1, 1\}$ to be a (multiplicative) subgroup of $\mathbb{Z}_N^\times$.

$$P: \begin{array}{l} \mathsf{X} = (A_0, A_1) = ([\mathfrak{g}^{a_0}] * E_0, [\mathfrak{g}^{a_1}] * E_0) \\ \mathsf{W} = (\delta, a_\delta) \in \{0,1\} \times \mathbb{Z}_N \end{array} \qquad\qquad V: \mathsf{X} = (A_0, A_1)$$

$$\mathbf{y}_\delta \xleftarrow{\$} \mathbb{Z}_N^n$$
$$\mathbf{Y}_\delta = [\mathfrak{g}^{\mathbf{y}_\delta}] * E_0$$
$$(\mathbf{c}_{1-\delta}, \mathbf{r}_{1-\delta}) \xleftarrow{\$} \{-1,1\}^n \times \mathbb{Z}_N^\delta \qquad \xrightarrow{\quad (\mathbf{Y}_0, \mathbf{Y}_1) \quad}$$
$$\mathbf{Y}_{1-\delta} = [\mathfrak{g}^{\mathbf{r}_{1-\delta}}] * A_{1-\delta}^{\mathbf{c}_{1-\delta}}$$

$$\xleftarrow{\qquad \mathbf{c} \qquad} \qquad \mathbf{c} \xleftarrow{\$} \{-1,1\}^n$$

$$\mathbf{c}_\delta = \mathbf{c} \odot \mathbf{c}_{1-\delta}$$
$$\mathbf{r}_\delta = \mathbf{y}_\delta - a_\delta \cdot \mathbf{c}_\delta \qquad \xrightarrow{\quad (\mathbf{r}_0, \mathbf{r}_1, \mathbf{c}_0, \mathbf{c}_1) \quad} \qquad \begin{array}{l} \text{Accept if } \mathbf{c} = \mathbf{c}_0 \odot \mathbf{c}_1 \text{ and} \\ \forall b \in \{0,1\}, [\mathfrak{g}^{\mathbf{r}_b}] * A_b^{\mathbf{c}_b} = \mathbf{Y}_b \end{array}$$

Fig. 1. The base OR sigma protocol underlying our blind signature scheme.

4.2   Description of Our Blind Signature

We present our isogeny-based blind signature building on top of the base sigma protocol in Sect. 4.1. Let (p, N, E_0) be the public parameter specified as the underlying prime, the order of the group and the distinguished element, resp. Let $\mathfrak{g}$ be a generator of the ideal class group $\mathcal{C}\ell(\mathcal{O})$. We assume these parameters are provided to all algorithms. Let $\mathsf{H} : \{0,1\}^* \to \{-1,1\}^n$ be a hash function modeled as a random oracle in the security proof.

BS.KGen (1^n): On input the security parameter 1^n, it samples a bit $\delta \xleftarrow{\$} \{0,1\}$, $(a_0, a_1) \xleftarrow{\$} \mathbb{Z}_N^2$ and outputs a public key $\mathsf{pk} = (A_0, A_1) = ([\mathfrak{g}^{a_0}] * E_0, [\mathfrak{g}^{a_1}] * E_0)$ and secret key $\mathsf{sk} = (\delta, a_\delta)$.

BS.$S_1(\mathsf{sk})$: The signer first samples $\mathbf{y}_\delta^* \xleftarrow{\$} \mathbb{Z}_N^n$ and sets $\mathbf{Y}_\delta^* = [\mathfrak{g}^{\mathbf{y}_\delta^*}] * E_0$. It then samples $(\mathbf{c}_{1-\delta}^*, \mathbf{r}_{1-\delta}^*) \xleftarrow{\$} \{-1,1\}^n \times \mathbb{Z}_N^n$ and sets $\mathbf{Y}_{1-\delta}^* = [\mathfrak{g}^{\mathbf{r}_{1-\delta}^*}] * A_{1-\delta}^{\mathbf{c}_{1-\delta}^*}$. It then outputs the signer state $\mathsf{state}_S = (\mathbf{y}_\delta^*, \mathbf{c}_{1-\delta}^*, \mathbf{r}_{1-\delta}^*)$ and the first-sender message $\rho_{S,1} = (\mathbf{Y}_0^*, \mathbf{Y}_1^*)$.

BS.$U_1(\mathsf{pk}, \mathsf{M}, \rho_{S,1})$: The user parses $(\mathbf{Y}_0^*, \mathbf{Y}_1^*) \leftarrow \rho_{S,1}$, samples $(\mathbf{d}_b, \mathbf{z}_b) \xleftarrow{\$} \{-1,1\}^n \times \mathbb{Z}_N^n$, and computes $\mathbf{Z}_b = [\mathfrak{g}^{\mathbf{z}_b}] * (\mathbf{Y}_b^*)^{\mathbf{d}_b}$ for $b \in \{0,1\}$. It then computes $\mathbf{c} = \mathsf{H}(\mathbf{Z}_0 \| \mathbf{Z}_1 \| \mathsf{M}) \in \{-1,1\}^n$ and outputs the user state $\mathsf{state}_U = (\mathbf{d}_b, \mathbf{z}_b)_{b \in \{0,1\}}$ and user message $\rho_U = \mathbf{c}^* = \mathbf{c} \odot \mathbf{d}_0 \odot \mathbf{d}_1$.

BS.$S_2(\mathsf{state}_S, \rho_U)$: The signer parses $(\mathbf{y}_\delta^*, \mathbf{c}_{1-\delta}^*, \mathbf{r}_{1-\delta}^*) \leftarrow \mathsf{state}_S$, $\mathbf{c}^* \leftarrow \rho_U$, sets $\mathbf{c}_\delta^* = \mathbf{c}^* \odot \mathbf{c}_{1-\delta}^* \in \{-1,1\}^n$, and computes $\mathbf{r}_\delta^* = \mathbf{y}_\delta^* - a_\delta \cdot \mathbf{c}_\delta^* \in \mathbb{Z}_N^n$.[12] It then outputs the second-signer message $\rho_{S,2} = (\mathbf{c}_b^*, \mathbf{r}_b^*)_{b \in \{0,1\}}$.

BS.$U_2(\mathsf{state}_U, \rho_{S,2})$: The user parses $(\mathbf{d}_b, \mathbf{z}_b)_{b \in \{0,1\}} \leftarrow \mathsf{state}_U$, $(\mathbf{c}_b^*, \mathbf{r}_b^*)_{b \in \{0,1\}} \leftarrow \rho_{S,2}$ and sets $(\mathbf{c}_b, \mathbf{r}_b) = (\mathbf{c}_b^* \odot \mathbf{d}_b, \mathbf{z}_b + \mathbf{r}_b^* \odot \mathbf{d}_b)$ for $b \in \{0,1\}$. It then checks if

$$\mathbf{c}_0 \odot \mathbf{c}_1 = \mathsf{H}\Big([\mathfrak{g}^{\mathbf{r}_0}] * A_0^{\mathbf{c}_0} \big\| [\mathfrak{g}^{\mathbf{r}_1}] * A_1^{\mathbf{c}_1} \big\| \mathsf{M}\Big). \qquad (1)$$

If it holds, it outputs a signature $\sigma = (\mathbf{c}_b, \mathbf{r}_b)_{b \in \{0,1\}} \in \big(\{-1,1\}^n \times \mathbb{Z}_N^n\big)^2$, and otherwise a $\perp$.

---

[12] Recall that we assume state_S includes sk (cf. Footnote 8).

BS.Verify($\mathsf{pk}, \mathsf{M}, \sigma$): The verifier outputs 1 if Eq. (1) holds, and otherwise 0.

Correctness, blindness, and one-more unforgeability of our blind signature are subsumed by those in Sect. 5. We give the details in the full version of this paper.

5   Extension to Partially Blind Signatures

In this section, we provide our isogeny-based partially blind signature. We first explain the sigma protocol that underlies our isogeny-based partially blind signature and then show how to compile it into a partially blind signature.

5.1   Base Sigma Protocol for a 2-Out-of-3 Relation

We consider a sigma protocol to prove that the prover knows at least *two out of the three* secrets corresponding to the public statement $\mathsf{X} = (A_0, A_1, A_2) = ([\mathfrak{g}^{a_0}] * E_0, [\mathfrak{g}^{a_1}] * E_0, [\mathfrak{g}^{a_2}] * E_0)$. The sigma protocol is depicted in Fig. 2. Since the secret a_2 for A_2 will be known by the signer *and* user in our partially blind signature, we assume the prover always knows the secret a_2 and proves knowledge of one other secret a_0 or a_1 in our sigma protocol.

P: $\quad \mathsf{X} = (A_0, A_1, A_2) = ([\mathfrak{g}^{a_0}] * E_0, [\mathfrak{g}^{a_1}] * E_0, [\mathfrak{g}^{a_2}] * E_0)$ $\quad$ V: $\mathsf{X} = (A_0, A_1, A_2)$
$\quad \mathsf{W} = (\delta, a_\delta, a_2) \in \{0, 1\} \times \mathbb{Z}_N^2$

For $j \in \{0, 1\}$
$\quad (\mathbf{y}_{\delta,j}, \mathbf{y}_{2,j}) \xleftarrow{\$} (\mathbb{Z}_N^n)^2$
$\quad \mathbf{Y}_{\delta,j} = [\mathfrak{g}^{\mathbf{y}_{\delta,j}}] * E_0$
$\quad \mathbf{Y}_{2,j} = [\mathfrak{g}^{\mathbf{y}_{2,j}}] * E_0 \qquad\qquad (\mathbf{Y}_{k,j})_{k \in [0:2]}$
$\quad (\mathbf{c}_{[1-\delta+j]_3}, \mathbf{r}_{1-\delta,j}) \xleftarrow{\$} \{-1, 1\}^n \times \mathbb{Z}_N^n \xrightarrow{\qquad\qquad j \in \{0,1\}\qquad}$
$\quad \mathbf{Y}_{1-\delta,j} = [\mathfrak{g}^{\mathbf{r}_{1-\delta,j}}] * A_{1-\delta}^{\mathbf{c}_{[1-\delta+j]_3}}$

$\qquad\qquad\qquad\qquad\qquad\qquad\qquad \mathbf{c} \qquad\qquad \mathbf{c} \xleftarrow{\$} \{-1, 1\}^n$
$\qquad\qquad\qquad\qquad\qquad\qquad \xleftarrow{\qquad\qquad}$

$\mathbf{c}_{[3-\delta]_3} = \mathbf{c} \odot \mathbf{c}_{[1-\delta]_3} \odot \mathbf{c}_{[2-\delta]_3}$
For $j \in \{0, 1\}$ $\qquad\qquad\qquad\qquad (\mathbf{r}_{k,j})_{k \in [0:2]}$, $\quad$ Accept if $\mathbf{c} = \mathbf{c}_0 \odot \mathbf{c}_1 \odot \mathbf{c}_2$
$\quad \mathbf{r}_{\delta,j} = \mathbf{y}_{\delta,j} - a_\delta \cdot \mathbf{c}_{[\delta+j]_3} \qquad\qquad j \in \{0,1\} \qquad \wedge \forall (k, j) \in [0:2] \times \{0, 1\}$,
$\quad \mathbf{r}_{2,j} = \mathbf{y}_{2,j} - a_2 \cdot \mathbf{c}_{[2+j]_3} \qquad (\mathbf{c}_k)_{k \in [0:2]} \qquad\quad [\mathfrak{g}^{\mathbf{r}_{k,j}}] * A_k^{\mathbf{c}_{[k+j]_3}} = \mathbf{Y}_{k,j}$
$\qquad\qquad\qquad\qquad\qquad\qquad \xrightarrow{\qquad\qquad}$

Fig. 2. The base 2-out-of-3 sigma protocol underlying our partially blind signature scheme. Recall $[0:2]$ denotes the set $\{0, 1, 2\}$ and $[x]_3$ is a shorthand for $x \bmod 3$.

5.2   Description of Our Partially Blind Signature

We are now able to present our isogeny-based partially blind signature. Let (p, N, E_0) be the public parameters, $\mathfrak{g}$ be a generator in $\mathcal{C}\ell(\mathcal{O})$, and H :

$\{0,1\}^* \to \{-1,1\}^n$ as defined in Sect. 4. We also require another hash function $\mathsf{G} : \{0,1\}^* \to \mathbb{Z}_N$ that is modeled as a random oracle. Note that H and G can be implemented by a single random oracle by using domain separation.

$\mathsf{PBS.KGen}\,(1^n)$: On input the security parameter 1^n, it samples a bit $\delta \xleftarrow{\$} \{0,1\}$, $(a_0, a_1) \xleftarrow{\$} \mathbb{Z}_N^2$ and outputs a public key $\mathsf{pk} = (A_0, A_1) = ([\mathfrak{g}^{a_0}] * E_0, [\mathfrak{g}^{a_1}] * E_0)$ and secret key $\mathsf{sk} = (\delta, a_\delta)$.

$\mathsf{PBS.S}_1(\mathsf{sk}, \mathsf{info})$: The signer performs the following for $j \in \{0,1\}$: It samples $(\mathbf{y}_{\delta,j}^*, \mathbf{y}_{2,j}^*) \xleftarrow{\$} (\mathbb{Z}_N^n)^2$ and sets $(\mathbf{Y}_{\delta,j}^*, \mathbf{Y}_{2,j}^*) = ([\mathfrak{g}^{\mathbf{y}_{\delta,j}^*}] * E_0, [\mathfrak{g}^{\mathbf{y}_{2,j}^*}] * E_0)$. It then samples $(\mathbf{c}_{[1-\delta+j]_3}^*, \mathbf{r}_{1-\delta,j}^*) \xleftarrow{\$} \{-1,1\}^n \times \mathbb{Z}_N^n$ and sets $\mathbf{Y}_{1-\delta,j}^* = [\mathfrak{g}^{\mathbf{r}_{1-\delta,j}^*}] * A_{1-\delta}^{\mathbf{c}_{[1-\delta+j]_3}^*}$. Finally, it outputs the signer state $\mathsf{state}_\mathsf{S} = (\mathbf{y}_{\delta,j}^*, \mathbf{y}_{2,j}^*, \mathbf{c}_{1-\delta,j}^*, \mathbf{r}_{1-\delta,j}^*)_{j \in \{0,1\}}$ and the first-sender message $\rho_{\mathsf{S},1} = (\mathbf{Y}_{k,j}^*)_{(k,j) \in [0:2] \times \{0,1\}}$.

$\mathsf{PBS.U}_1(\mathsf{pk}, \mathsf{info}, \mathsf{M}, \rho_{\mathsf{S},1})$: The user parses $(\mathbf{Y}_{k,j}^*)_{(k,j) \in [0:2] \times \{0,1\}} \leftarrow \rho_{\mathsf{S},1}$. It then samples $\mathbf{d}_k \xleftarrow{\$} \{-1,1\}^n$, $\mathbf{z}_{k,j} \xleftarrow{\$} \mathbb{Z}_N^n$, and computes $\mathbf{Z}_{k,j} = [\mathfrak{g}^{\mathbf{z}_{k,j}}] * (\mathbf{Y}_{k,j}^*)^{\mathbf{d}_{[k+j]_3}}$ for $(k,j) \in [0:2] \times \{0,1\}$. It then computes $\mathbf{c} = \mathsf{H}\Big((\mathbf{Z}_{k,j})_{(k,j) \in [0:2] \times \{0,1\}} \|\mathsf{info}\|\mathsf{M}\Big) \in \{-1,1\}^n$ and outputs the user state $\mathsf{state}_\mathsf{U} = (\mathbf{d}_k, (\mathbf{z}_{k,j})_{j \in \{0,1\}})_{k \in [0:2]}$ and user message $\rho_\mathsf{U} = \mathbf{c}^* = \mathbf{c} \odot \mathbf{d}_0 \odot \mathbf{d}_1 \odot \mathbf{d}_2$.

$\mathsf{PBS.S}_2(\mathsf{state}_\mathsf{S}, \rho_\mathsf{U})$: The signer computes $a_2 = \mathsf{G}(\mathsf{info}) \in \mathbb{Z}_N$, parses $(\mathbf{y}_{\delta,j}^*, \mathbf{y}_{2,j}^*, \mathbf{c}_{1-\delta,j}^*, \mathbf{r}_{1-\delta,j}^*)_{j \in \{0,1\}} \leftarrow \mathsf{state}_\mathsf{S}$, $\mathbf{c}^* \leftarrow \rho_\mathsf{U}$ and sets $\mathbf{c}_{[3-\delta]_3}^* = \mathbf{c}^* \odot \mathbf{c}_{[1-\delta]_3}^* \odot \mathbf{c}_{[2-\delta]_3}^* \in \{-1,1\}^n$. It then computes $\mathbf{r}_{\delta,j}^* = \mathbf{y}_{\delta,j}^* - a_\delta \cdot \mathbf{c}_{[\delta+j]_3}^* \in \mathbb{Z}_N^n$ and $\mathbf{r}_{2,j}^* = \mathbf{y}_{2,j}^* - a_2 \cdot \mathbf{c}_{[2+j]_3}^* \in \mathbb{Z}_N^n$ for $j \in \{0,1\}$. Finally, it outputs the second-signer message $\rho_{\mathsf{S},2} = (\mathbf{c}_k^*, (\mathbf{r}_{k,j}^*)_{j \in \{0,1\}})_{k \in [0:2]}$.

$\mathsf{PBS.U}_2(\mathsf{state}_\mathsf{U}, \rho_{\mathsf{S},2})$: The user first computes $a_2 = \mathsf{G}(\mathsf{info}) \in \mathbb{Z}_N$ and sets $A_3 = [\mathfrak{g}^{a_2}] * E_0$. It then parses $(\mathbf{d}_k, (\mathbf{z}_{k,j})_{j \in \{0,1\}})_{k \in [0:2]} \leftarrow \mathsf{state}_\mathsf{U}$, $(\mathbf{c}_k^*, (\mathbf{r}_{k,j}^*)_{j \in \{0,1\}})_{k \in [0:2]} \leftarrow \rho_{\mathsf{S},2}$ and sets $\mathbf{c}_k = \mathbf{c}_k^* \odot \mathbf{d}_k$ and $\mathbf{r}_{k,j} = \mathbf{z}_{k,j} + \mathbf{r}_{k,j}^* \odot \mathbf{d}_{[k+j]_3}$ for $(k,j) \in [0:2] \times \{0,1\}$. It then checks if

$$\mathbf{c}_0 \odot \mathbf{c}_1 \odot \mathbf{c}_2 = \mathsf{H}\Big(([\mathfrak{g}^{\mathbf{r}_{k,j}}] * A_k^{\mathbf{c}_{[k+j]_3}})_{(k,j) \in [0:2] \times \{0,1\}} \|\mathsf{info}\|\mathsf{M}\Big). \tag{2}$$

If it holds, it outputs a signature $\sigma = (\mathbf{c}_k, (\mathbf{r}_{k,j})_{j \in \{0,1\}})_{k \in [0:2]} \in (\{-1,1\}^n \times (\mathbb{Z}_N^n)^2)^3$, and otherwise a $\bot$.

$\mathsf{PBS.Verify}(\mathsf{pk}, \mathsf{M}, \sigma)$: The verifier outputs 1 if Eq. (2) holds, and otherwise 0.

The proof of correctness and blindness are straightforward and included in the full version of this paper due to page limitations.

5.3 Proof of One-More Unforgeability

Our proof of OMUF consists of preparing the necessary tools to invoke Theorem 3.1. Specifically, we define instances (see Definition 3.1), the map $\Phi_{\mathsf{rand}, \vec{h}}$ (see Definition 3.8), the witness extractors $(\mathsf{Ext}_0, \mathsf{Ext}_1)$ (see Definition 3.9) and prove that Lemmas 3.1 and 3.2 hold. Below, we denote by $\vec{X}$ a vector $(X^{(1)}, \ldots, X^{(\ell)})$

and endow $\overrightarrow{X}$ with the same operations defined for each $X^{(k)}$ by operating componentwise. Recall that rand denotes the adversary's randomness, and $\overrightarrow{h} = (\mathbf{c}^{(1)}, \ldots, \mathbf{c}^{(\ell)})$ is the random oracle's response vector conditioned on the adversary making only ℓ random oracle queries. Finally, once the instance, adversary's randomness and hash output tuple $(\mathbf{I}, \mathsf{rand}, \overrightarrow{h})$ are fixed, the query transcript $\overrightarrow{e}(\mathbf{I}, \mathsf{rand}, \overrightarrow{h})$—the vector of user message ρ_U queries made to the signing algorithm $\mathsf{BS.S_2}$—is defined. We denote this as $\overrightarrow{\mathbf{c}^*}$ below to be consistent with the notation used in our construction.

Preparation: Instances. Let us first define the **0**-side instance $\mathbf{I}_0$ and the **1**-side instance $\mathbf{I}_1$. Below, we assume the adversary against the one-more unforgeability game makes ℓ signing queries in total.

A **0**-side instance $\mathbf{I}_0 = (0, a_0, A_1, \overrightarrow{\mathbf{y}^*_{0,0}}, \overrightarrow{\mathbf{y}^*_{0,1}}, \overrightarrow{\mathbf{c}^*_1}, \overrightarrow{\mathbf{c}^*_2}, \overrightarrow{\mathbf{r}^*_{1,0}}, \overrightarrow{\mathbf{r}^*_{1,1}}, \overrightarrow{\mathbf{y}^*_{2,0}}, \overrightarrow{\mathbf{y}^*_{2,1}})$ is defined as follows:

- $(0, a_0)$: The secret key sk when $\delta = 0$.
- A_1: The part of the public key $\mathsf{pk} = (A_0, A_1)$ whose secret key is unknown.
- $(\mathbf{y}^{*(k)}_{0,0}, \mathbf{y}^{*(k)}_{0,1})$: The exponent of the commitment $(\mathbf{Y}^{*(k)}_{0,0}, \mathbf{Y}^{*(k)}_{0,1})$ in the k-th $(k \in [\ell])$ first-sender message when $\delta = 0$ such that $(\mathbf{Y}^{*(k)}_{0,0}, \mathbf{Y}^{*(k)}_{0,1}) = ([\mathfrak{g}^{\mathbf{y}^{*(k)}_{0,0}}] * E_0, [\mathfrak{g}^{\mathbf{y}^{*(k)}_{0,1}}] * E_0)$.
- $(\mathbf{c}^{*(k)}_1, \mathbf{c}^{*(k)}_2)$: The simulated challenge in the k-th $(k \in [\ell])$ first-sender message when $\delta = 0$.
- $(\mathbf{r}^{*(k)}_{1,0}, \mathbf{r}^{*(k)}_{1,1})$: The exponent of the commitment $(\mathbf{Y}^{*(k)}_{1,0}, \mathbf{Y}^{*(k)}_{1,1})$ in the k-th $(k \in [\ell])$ first-sender message when $\delta = 0$ such that $(\mathbf{Y}^{*(k)}_{1,0}, \mathbf{Y}^{*(k)}_{1,1}) = ([\mathfrak{g}^{\mathbf{r}^{*(k)}_{1,0}}] * A_1^{\mathbf{c}^{*(k)}_1}, [\mathfrak{g}^{\mathbf{r}^{*(k)}_{1,1}}] * A_1^{\mathbf{c}^{*(k)}_2})$.
- $(\mathbf{y}^{*(k)}_{2,0}, \mathbf{y}^{*(k)}_{2,1})$: The exponent of the commitment $(\mathbf{Y}^{*(k)}_{2,0}, \mathbf{Y}^{*(k)}_{2,1})$ in the k-th $(k \in [\ell])$ first-sender message when $\delta = 0$ such that $(\mathbf{Y}^{*(k)}_{2,0}, \mathbf{Y}^{*(k)}_{2,1}) = ([\mathfrak{g}^{\mathbf{y}^{*(k)}_{2,0}}] * E_0, [\mathfrak{g}^{\mathbf{y}^{*(k)}_{2,1}}] * E_0)$.

A **1**-side instance $\mathbf{I}_1 = (1, a_1, A_0, \overrightarrow{\mathbf{y}^*_{1,0}}, \overrightarrow{\mathbf{y}^*_{1,1}}, \overrightarrow{\mathbf{c}^*_0}, \overrightarrow{\mathbf{c}^*_1}, \overrightarrow{\mathbf{r}^*_{0,0}}, \overrightarrow{\mathbf{r}^*_{0,1}}, \overrightarrow{\mathbf{y}^*_{2,0}}, \overrightarrow{\mathbf{y}^*_{2,1}})$ is defined analogously. In the above, note that the randomness $(\overrightarrow{\mathbf{y}_{2,0}}, \overrightarrow{\mathbf{y}_{2,1}})$ associated with the tags $\overrightarrow{\mathsf{info}}$ are identical for both instances, and moreover, chosen independently of the tags queried by the adversary. This will be a crucial observation when applying Theorem 3.1, which focuses on the one-more unforgeability of blind signatures, to the partially blind signature setting.

Preparation: Map $\Phi_{\mathsf{rand}, \overrightarrow{h}}$. We next define the map $\Phi_{\mathsf{rand}, \overrightarrow{h}}$ that maps a **0**-side instance $\mathbf{I}_0$ into a **1**-side instance $\mathbf{I}_1$ and vice versa. Concretely, a **0**-side instance $\mathbf{I}_0 = (0, a_0, A_1, \overrightarrow{\mathbf{y}^*_{0,0}}, \overrightarrow{\mathbf{y}^*_{0,1}}, \overrightarrow{\mathbf{c}^*_1}, \overrightarrow{\mathbf{c}^*_2}, \overrightarrow{\mathbf{r}^*_{1,0}}, \overrightarrow{\mathbf{r}^*_{1,1}}, \overrightarrow{\mathbf{y}^*_{2,0}}, \overrightarrow{\mathbf{y}^*_{2,1}})$, $\Phi_{\mathsf{rand}, \overrightarrow{h}}(\mathbf{I}_0)$ maps to a **1**-side instance $\mathbf{I}_1$ given by

$$
\mathbf{I}_1 = \left(\begin{array}{c}
1, \\
\begin{array}{ccc}
a_1 \text{ such that } [\mathfrak{g}^{a_1}] * E_0 = A_1, & A_0 = [\mathfrak{g}^{a_0}] * E_0, \\
\overrightarrow{\mathbf{y}^*_{1,0}} = \overrightarrow{\mathbf{r}^*_{1,0}} + a_1 \cdot \overrightarrow{\mathbf{c}^*_1}, & \overrightarrow{\mathbf{y}^*_{1,1}} = \overrightarrow{\mathbf{r}^*_{1,1}} + a_1 \cdot \overrightarrow{\mathbf{c}^*_2}, & \overrightarrow{\mathbf{y}^*_{2,0}}, \overrightarrow{\mathbf{y}^*_{2,1}} \\
\overrightarrow{\mathbf{c}^*_0} = \overrightarrow{\mathbf{c}^*} \odot \overrightarrow{\mathbf{c}^*_1} \odot \overrightarrow{\mathbf{c}^*_2}, & \overrightarrow{\mathbf{c}^*_1}, \\
\overrightarrow{\mathbf{r}^*_{0,0}} = \overrightarrow{\mathbf{y}^*_{0,0}} - a_0 \cdot \overrightarrow{\mathbf{c}^*_0}, & \overrightarrow{\mathbf{r}^*_{0,1}} = \overrightarrow{\mathbf{y}^*_{0,1}} - a_0 \cdot \overrightarrow{\mathbf{c}^*_1},
\end{array}
\end{array}\right),
$$

where recall that $\overrightarrow{\mathbf{c}^*} = \overrightarrow{e}(\mathbf{I}_0, \mathsf{rand}, \overrightarrow{h})$. $\Phi_{\mathsf{rand}, \overrightarrow{h}}(\mathbf{I}_1)$ is defined analogously.

Preparation: Witness Extractors ($\mathsf{Ext}_0, \mathsf{Ext}_1$). Fix $\mathbf{I}$, rand and let $(\overrightarrow{h}, \overrightarrow{h}') \in \overline{F_i(\mathbf{I}, \mathsf{rand})}$ for some $i \in [\ell + 1]$. Let $\sigma = (\mathbf{c}_k, (\mathbf{r}_{k,j})_{j \in \{0,1\}})_{k \in [0:2]}$ and $\sigma' = (\mathbf{c}'_k, (\mathbf{r}'_{k,j})_{j \in \{0,1\}})_{k \in [0:2]}$ be the signatures that correspond to $\mathbf{c}^{(i)}$ and $\mathbf{c}'^{(i)}$, respectively, where $\mathbf{c}^{(i)}$ (resp. $\mathbf{c}'^{(i)}$) is the i-th entry of $\overrightarrow{h}$ (resp. $\overrightarrow{h}'$). In particular, we have $\mathbf{c}_0 \odot \mathbf{c}_1 \odot \mathbf{c}_2 = \mathbf{c}^{(i)}$ and $\mathbf{c}'_0 \odot \mathbf{c}'_1 \odot \mathbf{c}'_2 = \mathbf{c}'^{(i)}$. We define the witness extractors $(\mathsf{Ext}_0, \mathsf{Ext}_1)$ as in Fig. 3.

$\mathsf{Ext}_0(\sigma, \sigma')$	$\mathsf{Ext}_1(\sigma, \sigma')$
$101:$ **if** $\exists t \in [n]$ s.t. $c_{0,t} \neq c'_{0,t}$	$101:$ **if** $\exists t \in [n]$ s.t. $c_{1,t} \neq c'_{1,t}$
$102:$ **return** $a_0 = \dfrac{r_{0,0,t} - r'_{0,0,t}}{c_{0,t} - c'_{0,t}}$	$102:$ **return** $a_1 = \dfrac{r_{1,0,t} - r'_{1,0,t}}{c_{1,t} - c'_{1,t}}$
$103:$ **elseif** $\exists t \in [n]$ s.t. $c_{1,t} \neq c'_{1,t}$	$103:$ **elseif** $\exists t \in [n]$ s.t. $c_{2,t} \neq c'_{2,t}$
$104:$ **return** $a_0 = \dfrac{r_{0,1,t} - r'_{0,1,t}}{c_{1,t} - c'_{1,t}}$	$104:$ **return** $a_1 = \dfrac{r_{1,1,t} - r'_{1,1,t}}{c_{2,t} - c'_{2,t}}$
$105:$ **return** $\perp$	$105:$ **return** $\perp$

Fig. 3. Witness extractors for our partially blind signature. In the above, $\sigma = (\mathbf{c}_k, (\mathbf{r}_{k,j})_{j \in \{0,1\}})_{k \in [0:2]}$ and $\sigma' = (\mathbf{c}'_k, (\mathbf{r}'_{k,j})_{j \in \{0,1\}})_{k \in [0:2]}$, where $\mathbf{c}_k, \mathbf{c}'_k$ live in $\{-1, 1\}^n$ and $\mathbf{r}_{k,j}, \mathbf{r}'_{k,j}$ live in $\mathbb{Z}_N^n$. Non-bold font indicates the entries of a vector.

The following lemma establishes the correctness of the witness extractors.

Lemma 5.1. $(\mathsf{Ext}_0, \mathsf{Ext}_1)$ *in Fig. 3 satisfy Definition 3.9.*

Proof of One-More Unforgeability. We prove the following two lemmas required to invoke the main theorem Theorem 3.1.

Lemma 5.2. *Lemma 3.1 holds for the map $\Phi_{\mathsf{rand}, \overrightarrow{h}}$.*

Lemma 5.3. *Lemma 3.2 holds for the witness extractors $(\mathsf{Ext}_0, \mathsf{Ext}_1)$.*

Combining everything together, we obtain the following.

Theorem 5.1 (One-more Unforgeability). *The partially blind signature scheme is one-more unforgeable. More precisely, for all $\ell \in \mathbb{N}$, if there exists an adversary $\mathcal{A}$ that makes Q hash queries to the random oracle and breaks the ℓ-one more unforgeability of our* PBS *with advantage $\epsilon_{\mathcal{A}} \geq \frac{C_1}{2^n} \cdot \binom{Q}{\ell+1}$, then there exists an algorithm $\mathcal{B}$ that breaks the* GAIP *problem with advantage $\epsilon_{\mathcal{B}} \geq C_2 \cdot \frac{\epsilon_{\mathcal{A}}^2}{\binom{Q}{\ell+1}^2 \cdot (\ell+1)^3}$ for some universal positive constants C_1 and C_2.*

Proof. We define the hard instance generator IG to output a GAIP instance. Then, the proof follows from the above Lemmas 3.1 and 3.2 and by invoking Theorem 3.1, i.e., the main theorem of Kastner, Loss, and Xu [30]. To be precise, [30, Theorem 1] is for blind signatures and not the partially blind variant—however, it can be checked that the same proof applies to our partially blind signature by observing that our definition of **0**-side and **1**-side instances are defined *independently* of the tags $\overrightarrow{\mathsf{info}}$ used by the adversary, where note that $\overrightarrow{\mathsf{info}}$ is implicitly defined by $(\mathbf{I}, \mathsf{rand}, \overrightarrow{h})$. In particular, the probability that the reduction extracts the correct witness (i.e., the witness not used by the reduction), can be bounded following the same argument as [30, Theorem 1].   □

Remark 5.1. (Comparing to the Abe-Okamoto Partially Blind Signature). We note that the reason why the same argument does not hold for the Abe-Okamoto partially blind signature [2] is that the tag info is explicitly required to define the instances. In more detail, the Abe-Okamoto partially blind signature only has one secret key $a_0 \in \mathbb{Z}_p$ attached to the verification key $h_0 = g^{a_0} \in \mathbb{G}$. To sign with respect to a tag info, the signer hashes info to a group element h_{info} and then performs an OR proof that it knows a secret key to either h_0 or h_{info}. In the security proof, the reduction hashes info to a group element $h_{\mathsf{info}} = g^{a_{\mathsf{info}}}$ while knowing the exponent a_{info}. In case the adversary is restricted to use only one tag info, the proof can define the **0**-side and **1**-side instances by using a_0 and a_{info}, respectively, and in particular independently of the adversary's randomness. However, when there is more than one tag, we can no longer define a well-defined **1**-side instance. This is why Kastner, Loss and Xu and Abe and Okamoto first prove the single-tag setting and then prove the multi-tag setting by guessing which tag info the adversary forges on.

6   Optimization Using Higher Degree Roots of Unity

We investigate the possibility of reducing the signature size by exploiting the $\mathbb{Z}$-module structure of the ideal class group. In this section, we present a generalized construction of the blind signature presented in Sect. 4 based on a new assumption, the *ring group action inverse problem* (rGAIP), which is a generalized version of the group action inverse problem (GAIP).

Notations. We summarize some notations unique to this section. We use $\mathbb{Z}_d$ to denote the set $\{0, \ldots, d-1\}$. Moreover, any vector is indexed from 0, e.g., $\mathbf{a} \in \mathbb{Z}_d^{\kappa}$ is expressed as $(a_0, \ldots, a_{\kappa-1})$. With an overload of notations, for any integer j, we define the bold font $\mathbf{j}$ as the length-κ vector $(j, \ldots, j)$. For any positive integer d and $a \in \mathbb{Z}$ or $\mathbb{Z}_d$, we use $[a]_d$ to denote $(a \mod d) \in \mathbb{Z}_d$. For the simplicity of the notations, we use the exponent of $\langle \zeta \rangle$ to represent the challenge space of a sigma protocol with an understanding that $\langle \zeta \rangle$ is the d-th primitive root of unity. That is, we will draw a challenge c from $\mathbb{Z}_d$. The operation between the challenges is thereby the addition $c_0 + c_1$, corresponding to the multiplication of $\zeta^{c_0 + c_1} = \zeta^{c_0} \zeta^{c_1}$.

Preparation. Looking ahead, when we construct a sigma protocol for the rGAIP relation, the special soundness extractor must solve for the secret exponent $a \in \mathbb{Z}_N$, given $c_1, c_2 \in \mathbb{Z}_N^2$ and $r_1 = y + a\zeta^{c_1}$, $r_2 = y + a\zeta^{c_2} \pmod{N}$ for an unknown a and y. If $\mathbb{Z}_N$ is a finite field, then this is trivial. However, in general when $\mathbb{Z}_N$ is a ring, such a may not be efficiently computable. One sufficient condition would be to only use a $d \in \mathbb{Z}_N$ such that $(\zeta^{c_1} - \zeta^{c_2})$ is invertible over $\mathbb{Z}_N$ for all distinct $(c_1, c_2) \in \mathbb{Z}_N^2$. However, this is an overly restrictive requirement and we thus make the following relaxed requirement.

Requirement 1. *We require $\eta_d = \mathsf{lcm}_{i \in [d-1]}(\gcd(\zeta^i - 1, N)) = \mathsf{poly}(n)$.*

The requirement is equivalent to finding a d such that d divides many Euler-values of maximal prime power divisors of the class number (see Sect. 7.1 about the existence and finding a root). Informally, when η_d is polynomial in the security parameter n, then we can brute force all $a \in \mathbb{Z}_N$ such that $a \cdot (\zeta^{c_1} - \zeta^{c_2}) = z$ for a given $(c_1, c_2, z) \in \mathbb{Z}_N^3$. Formally, we have the following.

Lemma 6.1. *Let (N, d, ζ) be a public parameter where the factorization of N is known and let $\eta_d = \mathsf{lcm}_{i \in [d-1]}(\gcd(\zeta^i - 1, N))$. Then, there exists an extractor Ext' that takes as input the public parameter and $(r_1, r_2, c_1, c_2) \in \mathbb{Z}_N^2 \times \mathbb{Z}_d^2$ where c_1, c_2 are distinct with relations $r_1 = y + a\zeta_d^{c_1}$, $r_2 = y + a\zeta_d^{c_2} \pmod{N}$, and outputs a list containing $a \in \mathbb{Z}_N$ of size not greater than η_d in time $\mathsf{poly}(\eta_d)$.*

Proof. By calculating $(r_1 - r_2)\zeta_d^{-c_2} = a(\zeta_d^{c_1 - c_2} - 1)$, the extractor solves a by solving the linear equation lifted to the prime power factor of N, then using the Chinese remainder theorem to obtain a list of candidates of a. The size of the list is the number of solutions for the linear equation, which is at most η_d. $\square$

6.1   Base Sigma Protocol with a Large Challenge Space

We first introduce the base sigma protocol with a larger challenge space assuming Requirement 1. This is depicted in Fig. 4 with the boxed components omitted. We show the special soundness of the protocol assuming that Requirement 1 is satisfied. Correctness and HVZK are shown in the full version of this paper.

$$\begin{aligned}
&\mathsf{X} = ((A_0^j)_{j\in\mathbb{Z}_d}, (A_1^j)_{j\in\mathbb{Z}_d}) \\
\mathsf{P}:\quad &= (([\mathfrak{g}^{a_0\zeta^j}]*E_0)_{j\in\mathbb{Z}_d}, ([\mathfrak{g}^{a_1\zeta^j}]*E_0)_{j\in\mathbb{Z}_d}) \\
&\mathsf{W} = (\delta, a_\delta) \in \{0,1\}\times\mathbb{Z}_N
\end{aligned}$$

$$\mathsf{V}:\ \mathsf{X} = ((A_0^j)_{j\in\mathbb{Z}_d}, (A_1^j)_{j\in\mathbb{Z}_d})$$

$$\mathbf{y}_\delta \xleftarrow{\$} \mathbb{Z}_N^\kappa$$
$$\mathbf{Y}_\delta = [\mathfrak{g}^{\mathbf{y}_\delta}]*E_0$$

$$\boxed{(\mathbf{Y}_\delta^j = [\mathfrak{g}^{\mathbf{y}_\delta\zeta^j}]*E_0)_{j\in\mathbb{Z}_d}}$$

$$(\mathbf{c}_{1-\delta}, \mathbf{r}_{1-\delta}) \xleftarrow{\$} \mathbb{Z}_d^\kappa \times \mathbb{Z}_N^\kappa$$
$$\mathbf{Y}_{1-\delta} = [\mathfrak{g}^{\mathbf{r}_{1-\delta}}]*A_{1-\delta}^{\mathbf{c}_{1-\delta}}$$

$$\boxed{(\mathbf{Y}_{1-\delta}^j = [\mathfrak{g}^{\mathbf{r}_{1-\delta}\zeta^j}]*A_{1-\delta}^{[\mathbf{c}_{1-\delta}+j]_d})_{j\in\mathbb{Z}_d}}$$

$$\xrightarrow{\quad (\mathbf{Y}_0, \mathbf{Y}_1)\quad\boxed{(\mathbf{Y}_0^j, \mathbf{Y}_1^j)_{j\in\mathbb{Z}_d}}\quad}$$

$$\xleftarrow{\qquad\mathbf{c}\qquad}\qquad \mathbf{c}\xleftarrow{\$}\mathbb{Z}_d^\kappa$$

$$\begin{aligned}
\mathbf{c}_\delta &= \mathbf{c}-\mathbf{c}_{1-\delta} \\
\mathbf{r}_\delta &= \mathbf{y}_\delta - a_\delta\zeta^{\mathbf{c}_\delta}
\end{aligned}$$

$$\xrightarrow{\quad (\mathbf{r}_0, \mathbf{r}_1, \mathbf{c}_0, \mathbf{c}_1)\quad}$$

Accept if $\mathbf{c} = \mathbf{c}_0 + \mathbf{c}_1$ and
$$\forall b \in \{0,1\},\ \boxed{\forall j \in \mathbb{Z}_d},$$
$$[\mathfrak{g}^{\mathbf{r}_b}]*A_b^{\mathbf{c}_b} = \mathbf{Y}_b$$
$$\boxed{[\mathfrak{g}^{\mathbf{r}_b\zeta^j}]*A_b^{[\mathbf{c}_b+j]_d} = \mathbf{Y}_b^j}$$

Fig. 4. The base sigma protocol with a large challenge space, where the box is to be ignored. Recall $\mathbb{Z}_d = \{0,1,\ldots,d-1\}$. A_b^j denotes $[\mathfrak{g}^{a_b\zeta^j}]*E_0$ for $j \in \mathbb{Z}_d$ and the vector $A_b^{[\mathbf{c}]_d}$ denotes $(A_b^{[c_0]_d}, \ldots, A_b^{[c_{\kappa-1}]_d})$ where $\mathbf{c} = (c_0,\ldots,c_{\kappa-1}) \in \mathbb{Z}^\kappa$. If $\mathbf{c} \in \mathbb{Z}_d^\kappa$, then $A_b^{[\mathbf{c}]_d}$ is simply $A_b^{\mathbf{c}}$. Other notations are explained in the paragraph above Sect. 6.1. The base sigma protocol can be made compatible with blind signatures by running the boxed lines instead of the preceding non-boxed lines.

Special Soundness. It suffices to show that special soundness holds for $\kappa = 1$. Let $((Y_0,Y_1), c, (r_0,r_1,c_0,c_1))$, and $((Y_0,Y_1), c', (r_0',r_1',c_0',c_1'))$ be two valid transcripts. Since $c = c_0 + c_1$, $c = c_0' + c_1'$ and $c \neq c'$, we assume $c_0 \neq c_0'$ without loss of generality. We have $r_0, r_0' \in \mathbb{Z}_N$, and distinct $c_0, c_0' \in \mathbb{Z}_d$ which satisfy $r_0 = y + a_0\zeta_d^{c_0}$, $r_0' = y + a_0\zeta_d^{c_0'}$ (mod N) where y, a_0 are unknown. Since we assume Requirement 1 holds, we can use the extractor $\mathsf{Ext}'(r_0, r_0', c_0, c_0')$ in Lemma 6.1 to obtain a list of size $\eta = \mathsf{lcm}_{i\in[d-1]}(\gcd(\zeta^i - 1, N)) = \mathsf{poly}(n)$ containing $a_0 \in \mathbb{Z}_N$ in polynomial time. We can find a_0 from the list by running through each element in the list and checking if it maps to the statement $(A_0^j)_{j\in\mathbb{Z}_d}$ or $(A_1^j)_{j\in\mathbb{Z}_d}$.

Before explaining our blind signature, we make a subtle but important modification to our base sigma protocol depicted in Fig. 4 with the boxes. As explained in the introduction, this modification is required since the user of the blind signature is required to randomize $\mathbf{Y}_b = [\mathfrak{g}^{\mathbf{y}_b}]*E_0$ for $b \in \{0,1\}$ to $[\mathfrak{g}^{\mathbf{z}_b}]*([\mathfrak{g}^{\mathbf{y}_b\zeta^{\mathbf{d}_b}}]*E_0)$, where $(\mathbf{z}_b, \mathbf{d}_b) \xleftarrow{\$} \mathbb{Z}_N^\kappa \times \mathbb{Z}_d^\kappa$, which is no longer possible when $d \geq 3$. We will give the details of this construction in the following subsection. This extra components also play a key role when proving blindness with malicious keys.

6.2 Description of Our Optimized Blind Signature

We present our optimized isogeny-based blind signature building upon of the enhanced base sigma protocol in Sect. 6.1. Let (p, N, E_0) be the public parameter and $\mathfrak{g}$ be a generator of the ideal class group $\mathcal{C\ell}(\mathcal{O})$ as in Sect. 4. Let ζ to be a d-th root of unity. We assume these parameters are provided to all algorithms. The parameter $\kappa \in \mathbb{N}$ indicates the number of repetitions of the underlying sigma protocol, chosen so that $d^\kappa \geq 2^n$. Let $\mathsf{H} : \{0,1\}^* \to \mathbb{Z}_d^\kappa$ be a hash function modeled as a random oracle.

BS.KGen (1^n): On input the security parameter 1^n, it samples a bit $\delta \xleftarrow{\$} \{0,1\}$, $(a_0, a_1) \xleftarrow{\$} \mathbb{Z}_N^2$, and outputs a public key pk $= ((A_0^j)_{j \in \mathbb{Z}_d}, (A_1^j)_{j \in \mathbb{Z}_d})$ where $A_b^j = [\mathfrak{g}^{a_b \zeta^j}] * E_0$ for $(b, j) \in \{0,1\} \times \mathbb{Z}_d$, and secret key sk $= (\delta, a_\delta)$.

BS.S$_1$(sk): The signer first samples $\mathbf{y}_\delta^* \xleftarrow{\$} \mathbb{Z}_N^\kappa$ and sets $\mathbf{Y}_\delta^{j*} = [\mathfrak{g}^{\mathbf{y}_\delta^* \zeta^j}] * E_0$ for $j \in \mathbb{Z}_d$. It then samples $(\mathbf{c}_{1-\delta}^*, \mathbf{r}_{1-\delta}^*) \xleftarrow{\$} \mathbb{Z}_d^\kappa \times \mathbb{Z}_N^\kappa$ and sets $\mathbf{Y}_{1-\delta}^{j*} = [\mathfrak{g}^{\mathbf{r}_{1-\delta}^* \zeta^j}] * A_{1-\delta}^{\mathbf{c}_{1-\delta}^*+j}$ for $j \in \mathbb{Z}_d$. It then outputs the signer state state$_{\mathsf{S}} = (\mathbf{y}_\delta^*, \mathbf{c}_{1-\delta}^*, \mathbf{r}_{1-\delta}^*)$ and the first-sender message $\rho_{\mathsf{S},1} = (\mathbf{Y}_0^{j*}, \mathbf{Y}_1^{j*})_{j \in \mathbb{Z}_d}$.

BS.U$_1$(pk, M, $\rho_{\mathsf{S},1}$): The user parses $(\mathbf{Y}_0^{j*}, \mathbf{Y}_1^{j*})_{j \in \mathbb{Z}_d} \leftarrow \rho_{\mathsf{S},1}$, samples $(\mathbf{d}_b, \mathbf{z}_b) \xleftarrow{\$} \mathbb{Z}_d^\kappa \times \mathbb{Z}_N^\kappa$, and computes $\mathbf{Z}_b = [\mathfrak{g}^{\mathbf{z}_b}] * (Y_{b,0}^{d_{b,0}*}, \ldots, Y_{b,\kappa-1}^{d_{b,\kappa-1}*})$ for $b \in \{0,1\}$. Here, note that $Y_{b,j}^{d_{b,j}*}$ denotes the j-th $(j \in \mathbb{Z}_d)$ element of $\mathbf{Y}_b^{d_{b,j}*} \in \mathcal{E}^\kappa$ and $d_{b,j}$ is the j-th element of $\mathbf{d}_b \in \mathbb{Z}_d^\kappa$. It then computes $\mathbf{c} = \mathsf{H}(\mathbf{Z}_0 \| \mathbf{Z}_1 \| \mathsf{M}) \in \mathbb{Z}_d^\kappa$ and outputs the user state state$_{\mathsf{U}} = (\mathbf{d}_0, \mathbf{d}_1, \mathbf{z}_0, \mathbf{z}_1)$ and user message $\rho_{\mathsf{U}} = \mathbf{c}^* = \mathbf{c} - \mathbf{d}_0 - \mathbf{d}_1$.

BS.S$_2$(state$_{\mathsf{S}}$, ρ_{U}): The signer parses $(\mathbf{y}_\delta^*, \mathbf{c}_{1-\delta}^*, \mathbf{r}_{1-\delta}^*) \leftarrow$ state$_{\mathsf{S}}$, $\mathbf{c}^* \leftarrow \rho_{\mathsf{U}}$, sets $\mathbf{c}_\delta^* = \mathbf{c}^* + \mathbf{c}_{1-\delta}^* \in \mathbb{Z}_d^\kappa$, and computes $\mathbf{r}_\delta^* = \mathbf{y}_\delta^* - a_\delta \zeta^{\mathbf{c}_\delta^*} \in \mathbb{Z}_N^\kappa$. It then outputs the second-signer message $\rho_{\mathsf{S},2} = (\mathbf{c}_0^*, \mathbf{c}_1^*, \mathbf{r}_0^*, \mathbf{r}_1^*)$.

BS.U$_2$(state$_{\mathsf{U}}$, $\rho_{\mathsf{S},2}$): The user parses $(\mathbf{d}_0, \mathbf{d}_1, \mathbf{z}_0, \mathbf{z}_1) \leftarrow$ state$_{\mathsf{U}}$, $(\mathbf{c}_0^*, \mathbf{c}_1^*, \mathbf{r}_0^*, \mathbf{r}_1^*) \leftarrow \rho_{\mathsf{S},2}$ and checks if $[\mathfrak{g}^{\mathbf{r}_b^* \zeta^j}] * A_b^{[\mathbf{c}_b^*+j]_d} = \mathbf{Y}_b^{j*}$ holds for all $(b, j) \in \{0,1\} \times \mathbb{Z}_d$. If not, it outputs $\perp$. Otherwise, it sets $(\mathbf{c}_b, \mathbf{r}_b) = (\mathbf{c}_b^* + \mathbf{d}_b, \mathbf{z}_b + \mathbf{r}_b^* \zeta^{\mathbf{d}_b}) \in \mathbb{Z}_d^\kappa \times \mathbb{Z}_N^\kappa$ for $b \in \{0,1\}$. It then checks if

$$\mathbf{c}_0 + \mathbf{c}_1 = \mathsf{H}\left([\mathfrak{g}^{\mathbf{r}_0}] * A_0^{\mathbf{c}_0} \| [\mathfrak{g}^{\mathbf{r}_1}] * A_1^{\mathbf{c}_1} \| \mathsf{M}\right). \tag{3}$$

If it holds, it outputs a signature $\sigma = (\mathbf{c}_0, \mathbf{c}_1, \mathbf{r}_0, \mathbf{r}_1) \in (\mathbb{Z}_d^\kappa)^2 \times (\mathbb{Z}_N^\kappa)^2$, and otherwise $\perp$.

BS.Verify(pk, M, σ): The verifier outputs 1 if Eq. (3) holds, and otherwise 0.

Remark 6.1. One can observe that the only source of overhead in the communication bandwidth compared to the blind signature in Sect. 4 is in BS.S$_1$. The bandwidth is increased by a factor of $\frac{d\kappa}{2n}$.

Remark 6.2. We remark that it is possible to fuse our partial blindness technique and the generalized construction in this section and obtain an optimized PBS variant. By doing so, we can obtain a PBS with a smaller signature size based on the rGAIP. Roughly, there are three sequences of the curves in the public statement $(A_0, A_1, A_2) = (([\mathfrak{g}^{a_0 \zeta_j}] * E_0)_{j \in \mathbb{Z}_d}, ([\mathfrak{g}^{a_1 \zeta_j}] * E_1)_{j \in \mathbb{Z}_d}, ([\mathfrak{g}^{a_2 \zeta_j}] * E_2)_{j \in \mathbb{Z}_d}$ where the secret key of the third public key is derived from the public information. The underlying sigma protocol is to prove for a two-out-of-three secret corresponding to this statement. However, given the proofs in Sect. 5 and in this section, we expect the proof to be highly involved. We leave this as a future work.

The correctness and one-more unforgeability of our optimized blind signature follow identically to those in the previous sections. Proving blindness under chosen keys is slightly more subtle since if a malicious signer uses malformed supersingular curves in $\mathcal{E}$ without the ring structure as the public key, the user cannot detect this. The main reason why we can argue perfect blindness is that if the public key is malformed, then the pair of curves in the first message $(\mathbf{Y}_0^{j*}, \mathbf{Y}_1^{j*})_{j \in \mathbb{Z}_d}$ is also malformed in a controlled manner. If there exists one user state that leads to a valid signature, then we can argue that the first message must be in a specific (but possibly incorrect) form regardless of the user state. Using this, we are able to establish a bijection between an arbitrary user state and a valid signature conditioning on a fixed first and second signature messages and a user message. Namely, any valid signature could have been produced with an equal probability. We give the details in the full version of this paper.

7   Analysis of Ring GAIP

This section analyzes the ζ_d-ring group action inverse problem (ζ_d-rGAIP) over CSIDH-512. Section 7.1 discusses the existence of the root parameter for the assumption and the finding method. Section 7.2 recalls the most efficient classical and quantum algorithms against GAIP and presents a structural attack on ζ_d-rGAIP which effectively reduces ζ_d-rGAIP for a few choices of d to a GAIP instance with a smaller group size compared to the original group considered by ζ_d-rGAIP. In Sect. 7.3, we complement our cryptanalysis by proving that ζ_d-rGAIP for a few choices of d is as hard as GAIP defined over the same group. This shows optimality of our structural attack for ζ_d-rGAIP for some choices of d. We note that the concrete value of d's that admit an attack or a reduction depends on the concrete CSIDH-512 parameter set.

7.1   Finding a Root of Unity and Satisfying Requirement 1

We briefly discuss the existence of and a process for finding a primitive d-th root of unity $\zeta_d \in \mathbb{Z}_N^\times$ which satisfies Requirement 1. Firstly, it is a straightforward consequence of the fundamental theorem of finitely-generated abelian groups and the definition of $\lambda(N)$ that $\mathbb{Z}_N^\times \cong \mathbb{Z}_{n_1} \times \mathbb{Z}_{n_2} \times \cdots \times \mathbb{Z}_{n_r}$ where $n_1 \mid n_2 \mid \cdots \mid n_r$ and $n_r = \lambda(N)$, so that a d-th root of unity exists if and only if d is a divisor of $\lambda(N)$—here, $\lambda(\cdot)$ is the Carmichael function.

To find such a root for a given valid d, the most intuitive method, perhaps, is to start with a primitive $\lambda(N)$-th root of unity $\zeta_{\lambda(N)}$, and compute $\zeta_{\lambda(N)}^{\frac{\lambda(N)}{d}}$, which will have order exactly d. Unfortunately, this may result in a d-th root of unity that does not meet Requirement 1 (even when one exists which satisfies Requirement 1). In particular, we have to ensure that ζ is a generator modulo all but small prime power divisors of N to conclude $\eta_d = \mathsf{lcm}_{i\in[d-1]}(\gcd(\zeta^i-1,N)) = \mathsf{poly}(n)$. To this end, in every Sylow subgroup of $\mathbb{Z}_N^\times$, we find a generator of a cyclic subgroup of order d (if one exists) and use the Chinese remainder theorem to obtain a d-th root of unity. If a root meeting Requirement 1 exists, this method ensures finding such a root.

In the next subsection, we show that the hardness of ζ_d-rGAIP varies with the choice of ζ_d. Since we believe ζ_d-rGAIP may be of independent interest, we waive Requirement 1 when considering the cryptanalysis.

7.2   Cryptanalysis and Structural Attack on rGAIP

In the previous section, we showed how to choose a root ζ_d according to the decomposition of the multiplication group of $\mathbb{Z}_N^\times$. In this section, we show that the underlying structure of ζ_d in each component is related to the security of ζ_d-rGAIP by presenting a concrete cryptanalysis on the overstretched ζ_d-rGAIP with respect to the CSIDH-512 parameters.

Generic Attacks on GAIP. The best known classical algorithm against GAIP is the meet-in-the-middle attack [25, 26] with time complexity $O(\sqrt{|\mathcal{C\ell}(\mathcal{O})|}) = O(\sqrt[4]{p})$ against GAIP.

The best-known quantum algorithm against GAIP is Kuperburg's algorithm [9,32,33,36,39]. Typically, given a challenge E to find $a \in \mathbb{Z}_N$ such that $E_0 = [\mathfrak{g}^a] * E$, we have a hidden shift problem by defining $f(x) = [\mathfrak{g}^x] * E_0$ and $g(x) = [\mathfrak{g}^x] * E$, the permutations f, g over $\mathcal{E}$ are hidden shifted by a. By applying the Kuperburg's algorithm, one can solve GAIP in time complexity $2^{O(\sqrt{\log(|\mathcal{C\ell}(\mathcal{O})|)})}$. It is not clear whether the additional structure can give an advantage to the adversary by reducing the group size *in general*. The subset $\{1, \zeta_d, \ldots, \zeta_d^{d-1}\}$ forms a group with multiplication instead of addition. Modifying the group action by restricting to the multiplication subgroup of $\mathbb{Z}_N^\times$ does not give a feasible g with a hidden shift a. Also, ζ generates the additive group $\mathbb{Z}_N$, so that the quotient group does not help in this case.

Structural Attack on rGAIP. Let ζ_d be a d-th primitive root of unity and N be the class number. We show that the underlying structure of the root in each component of $\mathbb{Z}_N^\times$ is related to security by displaying a structural attack against ζ_d-rGAIP and the efficacy of the attack is related to each $\gcd(\zeta_d^i - 1, N)$.

The high-level strategy of our structural attack is to break down a ζ_d-rGAIP instance into several GAIP instances over smaller subgroups or quotient groups. The idea is to exploit the differential information of any two curves in the instance and launch a Pohlig-Hellman-type attack. Recall that the instance is of the form $(X_0 = [\mathfrak{g}^a] * E_0, X_1 = [\mathfrak{g}^{a\zeta_d}] * E_0, \ldots, X_{d-1} = [\mathfrak{g}^{a\zeta_d^{d-1}}] * E_0)$. For any two curves X_i, X_j in the instance, there exists a unique group element

$[\mathfrak{g}_{ij}] = [\mathfrak{g}^{a\zeta_d^j - a\zeta_d^i}] \in \mathcal{C}\ell(\mathcal{O})$ such that $[\mathfrak{g}_{ij}] * X_i = X_j$. Therefore, recovering differential action $[\mathfrak{g}_{ij}]$ gives the information of a. Typically, it is difficult to recover such $[\mathfrak{g}_{ij}]$ due to the size of the group and considering the GAIP of (X_i, X_j). However, depending on the knowledge of η_d derived from the public ζ_d, the hardness of the GAIP of the structural (X_i, X_j) can be reduced. This is because $G_{ij} := \left\{ [\mathfrak{g}^{n(\zeta_d^j - \zeta_d^i)}] \,|\, , n \in \mathbb{Z}_N \right\}$ possibly constitutes a proper subgroup of $\mathcal{C}\ell(\mathcal{O})$ up to i and j. For any $[\mathfrak{g}'] \in \mathcal{C}\ell(\mathcal{O})$, we have $[\mathfrak{g}'] * X_i = [\mathfrak{g}_{ij}] * X_i = X_j$ if and only if $[\mathfrak{g}']G_{ij} = [\mathfrak{g}_{ij}]G_{ij}$. As a result, recovering $[\mathfrak{g}']G_{ij}$ is exactly a GAIP problem of (X_i, X_j) over the quotient group G/G_{ij}. Then, after obtaining such $[\mathfrak{g}'] \in \mathcal{C}\ell(\mathcal{O})$ such that $[\mathfrak{g}']G_{ij} = [\mathfrak{g}^{a\zeta_d^j - a\zeta_d^i}]G_{ij} = [\mathfrak{g}^a]G_{ij}$, we can recover $[\mathfrak{g}^a]$ by solving $(E_0, (\mathfrak{g}')^{-1} * X_0)$ over G_{ij} for $\mathfrak{g}'^{-1}[\mathfrak{g}^a]$. Therefore, the main strength against our structural attack depends on the GAIP hardness with the group size of $\max(|G_{ij}|, |G/G_{ij}|)$. Choosing a proper subsequence of (i, j), the root ζ_d gives the following ascending chain: $\{1\} = G_1 < G_2 < \ldots < G_k = \mathcal{C}\ell(\mathcal{O})$, where for each $\ell \in [k]$, $G_\ell = G_{ij}$ for some distinct $i, j \in [d]$. Using the aforementioned structural attack, the hardness of ζ_d-rGAIP is determined by the size of the largest quotient group $G_{\ell+1}/G_\ell$ for some $\ell \in [k-1]$.

Remark 7.1. We note that $\gcd(\zeta_d^i - 1, N)$ is divisible by a prime divisor p of N if and only if $\zeta_d^{\frac{d}{\gcd(i,d)}} \equiv 1 \pmod{p}$. Thus we only need to calculate $\gcd(\zeta_d^{d'} - 1, N)$ for every divisor d' of d to find η_d. In particular, when d is prime, we need only compute $\gcd(\zeta_d - 1, N)$ to find η_d. Therefore, we only need to consider $\gcd(\zeta_d - 1, N)$ for $d = 3, 5, 7, 11, 47, 499$ for the CSIDH-512 parameter set.

As a consequence, we reduce each ζ_d-rGAIP instance to a GAIP instance with a group size determined by ζ_d. This is summarized in Table 1. For ζ_8, we have a chain $\{1\} = G_1 < G_2 < G_3 < G_4 < G_5 = \mathcal{C}\ell(\mathcal{O})$ where G_2, G_3, G_4 is of size $\gcd(\zeta_8 - 1, N), \gcd(\zeta_8^2 - 1, N), \gcd(\zeta_8^4 - 1, N)$, respectively, and the largest quotient group is $|G_2/G_1| \approx 2^{134}$, which demonstrates the invulnerability of ζ_8-rGAIP. For instance, for ζ_3 we have a chain $\{1\} = G_1 < G_2 < G_3 = \mathcal{C}\ell(\mathcal{O})$ where G_2 is of size 37 and the largest quotient group is $|G_3/G_2| \approx 2^{251}$. For ζ_4, ζ_{47} and ζ_{499} we have a chain $\{1\} = G_1 < G_2 < G_3 = \mathcal{C}\ell(\mathcal{O})$ where G_2 is of size 1407181 with the largest quotient group $|G_3/G_2| \approx 2^{236}$. Our cryptanalysis gives an upper bound of ζ_d-rGAIP from the perspective of GAIP. Importantly, ζ_4-rGAIP which we use for our optimized blind signature only seems to lose 2 bits of security compared with ζ_2-rGAIP, or equivalently, GAIP over CSIDH-512.

Table 1. The upper row denotes ζ_d-rGAIP over CSIDH-512. Using our cryptanalysis in Sect. 7.2, we reduce each ζ_d-rGAIP instance into a GAIP instance with a group size summarized in the lower row. Note that GAIP over CSIDH-512 is equivalent to ζ_2-rGAIP over CSIDH-512.

ζ_d-rGAIP	ζ_2	ζ_3	ζ_4	ζ_5	ζ_7	ζ_8	ζ_9	ζ_{47}	ζ_{499}
GAIP with Group Size in $\log_2$	257	251	255	236	161	134	251	236	236

7.3   Equivalence Between **GAIP** and **rGAIP**

We complement our cryptanalysis by showing that our attack is optimal for some parameters. Although a few instances of ζ_d-rGAIP were shown to be significantly weaker than the original GAIP over CSIDH-512, we present a surprising condition that allows to reduce ζ_d-rGAIP to the original GAIP. This shows that the attack in Table 1 is optimal for those specific choices of ζ_d. We note that though the condition does not cover all cases (including ζ_4 which meets Requirement 1), the result gives us some guidance of the hardness of ζ_d-rGAIP.

Large gcd$(\zeta_d - 1, N) \approx N$. Note first that in this case we do not know how to have an efficient extractor in our optimized sigma protocol due to the large value of η_d (see Lemma 6.1). Requirement 1 is not satisfied.

It is clear that GAIP is never easier than ζ_d-rGAIP. The key insight of the reverse reduction is that when $\gcd(\zeta_d-1, N) \approx N$ (or $\gcd(\zeta_d-1, N) = N/\mathsf{poly}(n)$ to be precise), given a GAIP instance we can generate a ζ_d-rGAIP instance by trial and error. Additionally, the success rate can also be amplified by repetitively invoking the GAIP oracle and testing the correctness.

Concretely, given $X_0 = [\mathfrak{g}^a] * E_0$ and access to an ζ_d-rGAIP adversary $\mathcal{A}$ for a d-th root of unity ζ_d, we can construct a GAIP adversary $\mathcal{B}$ which invokes $\mathcal{A}$ on input $(X_0, [a'] * X_0, [a'^{\zeta_d}] * X_0, \ldots, [a'^{\zeta_d^{d-1}}] * X_0)$ where a' is sampled uniformly at random from the subgroup $\{r^{\zeta_d-1} | r \in \mathcal{C}\ell(\mathcal{O})\}$. Then, $\mathcal{B}$ outputs whatever $\mathcal{A}$ outputs. Since the subgroup is of size $N/\gcd(\zeta_d - 1, N) = \mathsf{poly}(n)$, the adversary $\mathcal{B}$ invokes $\mathcal{A}$ on a well-formed instance with probability $\gcd(\zeta_d - 1, N)/N$, which is non-negligible. We thus obtain the following theorem.

Theorem 7.1. *Given any ζ_d-rGAIP adversary $\mathcal{A}$ for a known-order effective group action of the group size N, there exists a GAIP adversary $\mathcal{B}$ in time d over the same action such that* $\mathsf{Adv}^{\zeta_d\text{-rGAIP}}(\mathcal{A}) \leq \frac{N}{\gcd(\zeta_d-1,N)} \cdot \mathsf{Adv}^{\mathsf{GAIP}}(\mathcal{B})$.

As a consequence, we know that for CSIDH-512 we have ζ_3, ζ_9, ζ_5, ζ_{47}, ζ_{499}-rGAIPs are as hard as the original GAIP with a reduction loss of factors $37, 37, 1407181, 1407181, 1407181$ respectively. Similarly, $\zeta_{117265} = \zeta_5\zeta_{47}\zeta_{499}$ also has a reduction loss of a factor 1407181.

8   Performance

We present an overall performance in Table 2 for our protocols instantiated using CSIDH-512. As explained in Sect. 7, we instantiate the ζ_d-rGAIP assumption with the 4-th root of unity ζ_4 as it is the only parameter that satisfies Requirement 1 while being presumably as hard as GAIP over CSIDH-512. We also analyze the trade-off between our basic blind signature in Sect. 4 and the optimized blind signature using a d-th primitive root of unity in Sect. 6. This helps us illustrate the effect of the value d on our optimized scheme and may be useful in the future when new group actions where ζ_d-rGAIP is hard are discovered.

The public key is d times larger compared to the basic scheme in general, which can be halved when d is even and $\zeta^{\frac{d}{2}} = -1$. Let $w = \log_2(N)/8$ denote the byte size of a class group element in $\mathbb{Z}_N$ and approximately $2w$ for one elliptic curve in $\mathcal{E}$; for example $w \approx 32$ for a CSIDH-512 group. In Sect. 4, the sender and user bandwidths and the signature size of the basic blind signature are $4wn$ B, $n/8$ B (i.e., one hash), and $2n(w + n/8)$ B, respectively. On the other hand, in Sect. 6 the sender and user bandwidths and the signature size of the optimized blind signature are $2\kappa(wd + w + \log_2 d)$ B, $(\kappa \log_2 d)/8$ B, and $2\kappa(w + \log_2 d)$ B, respectively. Now, given the security parameter n, the number of repetitions κ with a d-th primitive root of unity is required to satisfy $d^\kappa = 2^n$, i.e., $n = \kappa \log_2 d$. Therefore, the communication cost of the signer is increased by roughly $\frac{d\kappa}{2n}$, while the signature is decreased by roughly $\frac{n}{\kappa}$. The computation cost is increased by a factor of $\frac{d\kappa}{2n}$ in group action evaluations for both the signer and the user. Concretely, when $d = 4$, we have $n = 2\kappa$ and thus the signature size is reduced by approximately 50%.

Table 2. The overall performance of our blind signature family regarding the bandwidth, the secret key size, the public size, and the signature size using CSIDH-512. We take $n = 128$ and sk is generated by a seed of n bits. The first two rows are our blind signatures and the final row is our (unoptimized) partially blind signature.

	Bandwidth.S	Bandwidth.U	$|\mathsf{sk}|$	$|\mathsf{pk}|$	$|\sigma|$	Assumption
Basic. (Sect. 4)	16 KB	16 B	16 B	128 B	8 KB	GAIP
Section 6 with ζ_4	64 KB	16 B	16 B	512 B	4 KB	ζ_4-rGAIP
PBS. (Sect. 5)	48 KB	16 B	16 B	128 B	24 KB	GAIP

It takes roughly 40 ms to perform an action on a 2.70 GHz processor [8,13], and we can estimate the running time in terms of the number of the isogeny action. Since the signing (respectively, verifying) process requires 6×128 (respectively, 2×128) actions in Sect. 4, it takes 30 s (respectively, 10 s) for the procedure.

Acknowledgements. Shuichi Katsumata was partially supported by JST, CREST Grant Number JPMJCR22M1 and by JST, AIP Acceleration Research JPMJCR22U5. Yi-Fu Lai, Jason T. LeGrow, and Ling Qin were supported in part by the Ministry for Business, Innovation and Employment of New Zealand. Jason T. LeGrow was supported in part by the Commonwealth of Virginia's Commonwealth Cyber Initiative (CCI), an investment in the advancement of cyber R&D, innovation, and workforce development. For more information about CCI, visit http://www.cyberinitiative.org.

References

1. Abe, M., Fujisaki, E.: How to date blind signatures. In: Kim, K., Matsumoto, T. (eds.) ASIACRYPT 1996. LNCS, vol. 1163, pp. 244–251. Springer, Heidelberg (1996). https://doi.org/10.1007/BFb0034851

2. Abe, M., Okamoto, T.: Provably secure partially blind signatures. In: Bellare, M. (ed.) CRYPTO 2000. LNCS, vol. 1880, pp. 271–286. Springer, Heidelberg (2000). https://doi.org/10.1007/3-540-44598-6_17

3. Agrawal, S., Kirshanova, E., Stehlé, D., Yadav, A.: Practical, round-optimal lattice-based blind signatures. In: ACM CCS 2022, pp. 39–53 (2022)

4. Baldimtsi, F., Lysyanskaya, A.: On the security of one-witness blind signature schemes. In: Sako, K., Sarkar, P. (eds.) ASIACRYPT 2013, Part II. LNCS, vol. 8270, pp. 82–99. Springer, Heidelberg (2013). https://doi.org/10.1007/978-3-642-42045-0_5

5. Benhamouda, F., Lepoint, T., Loss, J., Orrù, M., Raykova, M.: On the (in)security of ROS. In: Canteaut, A., Standaert, F.-X. (eds.) EUROCRYPT 2021, Part I. LNCS, vol. 12696, pp. 33–53. Springer, Cham (2021). https://doi.org/10.1007/978-3-030-77870-5_2

6. Beullens, W., Dobson, S., Katsumata, S., Lai, Y.-F., Pintore, F.: Group signatures and more from isogenies and lattices: generic, simple, and efficient. In: Dunkelman, O., Dziembowski, S. (eds.) EUROCRYPT 2022, Part II. LNCS, vol. 13276, pp. 95–126. Springer, Cham (2022). https://doi.org/10.1007/978-3-031-07085-3_4

7. Beullens, W., Katsumata, S., Pintore, F.: Calamari and Falafl: logarithmic (linkable) ring signatures from isogenies and lattices. In: Moriai, S., Wang, H. (eds.) ASIACRYPT 2020, Part II. LNCS, vol. 12492, pp. 464–492. Springer, Cham (2020). https://doi.org/10.1007/978-3-030-64834-3_16

8. Beullens, W., Kleinjung, T., Vercauteren, F.: CSI-FiSh: efficient isogeny based signatures through class group computations. In: Galbraith, S.D., Moriai, S. (eds.) ASIACRYPT 2019, Part I. LNCS, vol. 11921, pp. 227–247. Springer, Cham (2019). https://doi.org/10.1007/978-3-030-34578-5_9

9. Bonnetain, X., Schrottenloher, A.: Quantum security analysis of CSIDH. In: Canteaut, A., Ishai, Y. (eds.) EUROCRYPT 2020, Part II. LNCS, vol. 12106, pp. 493–522. Springer, Cham (2020). https://doi.org/10.1007/978-3-030-45724-2_17

10. Brands, S.: Untraceable off-line cash in wallet with observers (extended abstract). In: Stinson, D.R. (ed.) CRYPTO 1993. LNCS, vol. 773, pp. 302–318. Springer, Heidelberg (1994). https://doi.org/10.1007/3-540-48329-2_26

11. Buser, M., et al.: A survey on exotic signatures for post-quantum blockchain: challenges and research directions. ACM Comput. Surv. **55**(12), 1–32 (2023)

12. Camenisch, J., Lysyanskaya, A.: An efficient system for non-transferable anonymous credentials with optional anonymity revocation. In: Pfitzmann, B. (ed.) EUROCRYPT 2001. LNCS, vol. 2045, pp. 93–118. Springer, Heidelberg (2001). https://doi.org/10.1007/3-540-44987-6_7

13. Castryck, W., Lange, T., Martindale, C., Panny, L., Renes, J.: CSIDH: an efficient post-quantum commutative group action. In: Peyrin, T., Galbraith, S. (eds.) ASIACRYPT 2018, Part III. LNCS, vol. 11274, pp. 395–427. Springer, Cham (2018). https://doi.org/10.1007/978-3-030-03332-3_15

14. Chaum, D.: Blind signatures for untraceable payments. In: Chaum, D., Rivest, R.L., Sherman, A.T. (eds.) Advances in Cryptology. LNCS, pp. 199–203. Springer, Boston (1983). https://doi.org/10.1007/978-1-4757-0602-4_18

15. Chaum, D.: Elections with unconditionally-secret ballots and disruption equivalent to breaking RSA. In: Barstow, D., et al. (eds.) EUROCRYPT 1988. LNCS, vol. 330, pp. 177–182. Springer, Heidelberg (1988). https://doi.org/10.1007/3-540-45961-8_15

16. Chaum, D., Fiat, A., Naor, M.: Untraceable electronic cash. In: Goldwasser, S. (ed.) CRYPTO 1988. LNCS, vol. 403, pp. 319–327. Springer, New York (1990). https://doi.org/10.1007/0-387-34799-2_25

17. Chaum, D., Pedersen, T.P.: Wallet databases with observers. In: Brickell, E.F. (ed.) CRYPTO 1992. LNCS, vol. 740, pp. 89–105. Springer, Heidelberg (1993). https://doi.org/10.1007/3-540-48071-4_7

18. Cramer, R., Damgård, I., Schoenmakers, B.: Proofs of partial knowledge and simplified design of witness hiding protocols. In: Desmedt, Y.G. (ed.) CRYPTO 1994. LNCS, vol. 839, pp. 174–187. Springer, Heidelberg (1994). https://doi.org/10.1007/3-540-48658-5_19

19. De Feo, L., Galbraith, S.D.: SeaSign: compact isogeny signatures from class group actions. In: Ishai, Y., Rijmen, V. (eds.) EUROCRYPT 2019, Part III. LNCS, vol. 11478, pp. 759–789. Springer, Cham (2019). https://doi.org/10.1007/978-3-030-17659-4_26

20. De Feo, L., Kohel, D., Leroux, A., Petit, C., Wesolowski, B.: SQISign: compact post-quantum signatures from quaternions and isogenies. In: Moriai, S., Wang, H. (eds.) ASIACRYPT 2020, Part I. LNCS, vol. 12491, pp. 64–93. Springer, Cham (2020). https://doi.org/10.1007/978-3-030-64837-4_3

21. del Pino, R., Katsumata, S.: A new framework for more efficient round-optimal lattice-based (partially) blind signature via trapdoor sampling. In: Dodis, Y., Shrimpton, T. (eds.) CRYPTO 2022, Part II. LNCS, vol. 13508, pp. 306–336. Springer, Cham (2022). https://doi.org/10.1007/978-3-031-15979-4_11

22. Fiat, A., Shamir, A.: How to prove yourself: practical solutions to identification and signature problems. In: Odlyzko, A.M. (ed.) CRYPTO 1986. LNCS, vol. 263, pp. 186–194. Springer, Heidelberg (1987). https://doi.org/10.1007/3-540-47721-7_12

23. Fischlin, M.: Round-optimal composable blind signatures in the common reference string model. In: Dwork, C. (ed.) CRYPTO 2006. LNCS, vol. 4117, pp. 60–77. Springer, Heidelberg (2006). https://doi.org/10.1007/11818175_4

24. Fujioka, A., Okamoto, T., Ohta, K.: A practical secret voting scheme for large scale elections. In: Seberry, J., Zheng, Y. (eds.) AUSCRYPT. LNCS, vol. 718, pp. 244–251. Springer, Heidelberg (1993). https://doi.org/10.1007/3-540-57220-1_66

25. Galbraith, S., Stolbunov, A.: Improved algorithm for the isogeny problem for ordinary elliptic curves. Appl. Algebra Eng. Commun. Comput. **24**(2), 107–131 (2013)

26. Galbraith, S.D., Hess, F., Smart, N.P.: Extending the GHS Weil descent attack. In: Knudsen, L.R. (ed.) EUROCRYPT 2002. LNCS, vol. 2332, pp. 29–44. Springer, Heidelberg (2002). https://doi.org/10.1007/3-540-46035-7_3

27. Hauck, E., Kiltz, E., Loss, J.: A modular treatment of blind signatures from identification schemes. In: Ishai, Y., Rijmen, V. (eds.) EUROCRYPT 2019, Part III. LNCS, vol. 11478, pp. 345–375. Springer, Cham (2019). https://doi.org/10.1007/978-3-030-17659-4_12

28. Hauck, E., Kiltz, E., Loss, J., Nguyen, N.K.: Lattice-based blind signatures, revisited. In: Micciancio, D., Ristenpart, T. (eds.) CRYPTO 2020, Part II. LNCS, vol. 12171, pp. 500–529. Springer, Cham (2020). https://doi.org/10.1007/978-3-030-56880-1_18

29. Hendrickson, S., Iyengar, J., Pauly, T., Valdez, S., Wood, C.A.: Private access tokens. internet-draft draft-private-access-tokens-01

30. Kastner, J., Loss, J., Xu, J.: The abe-okamoto partially blind signature scheme revisited. In: Agrawal, S., Lin, D. (eds.) ASIACRYPT 2022, Part IV. LNCS, vol. 13794, pp. 279–309. Springer, Cham (2022). https://doi.org/10.1007/978-3-031-22972-5_10

31. Kastner, J., Loss, J., Xu, J.: On pairing-free blind signature schemes in the algebraic group model. In: Hanaoka, G., Shikata, J., Watanabe, Y. (eds.) PKC. LNCS, vol. 13178, pp. 468–497. Springer, Cham (2022). https://doi.org/10.1007/978-3-030-97131-1_16

32. Kuperberg, G.: A subexponential-time quantum algorithm for the dihedral hidden subgroup problem. SIAM J. Comput. **35**(1), 170–188 (2005)

33. Kuperberg, G.: Another subexponential-time quantum algorithm for the dihedral hidden subgroup problem. arXiv preprint arXiv:1112.3333

34. Lyubashevsky, V., Nguyen, N.K., Plançon, M.: Efficient lattice-based blind signatures via gaussian one-time signatures. In: Hanaoka, G., Shikata, J., Watanabe, Y. (eds.) PKC 2022, Part II. LNCS, vol. 13178, pp. 498–527. Springer, Cham (2022). https://doi.org/10.1007/978-3-030-97131-1_17

35. Okamoto, T., Ohta, K.: Universal electronic cash. In: Feigenbaum, J. (ed.) CRYPTO 1991. LNCS, vol. 576, pp. 324–337. Springer, Heidelberg (1992). https://doi.org/10.1007/3-540-46766-1_27

36. Peikert, C.: He gives C-Sieves on the CSIDH. In: Canteaut, A., Ishai, Y. (eds.) EUROCRYPT 2020, Part II. LNCS, vol. 12106, pp. 463–492. Springer, Cham (2020). https://doi.org/10.1007/978-3-030-45724-2_16

37. Pointcheval, D., Stern, J.: Security proofs for signature schemes. In: Maurer, U. (ed.) EUROCRYPT 1996. LNCS, vol. 1070, pp. 387–398. Springer, Heidelberg (1996). https://doi.org/10.1007/3-540-68339-9_33

38. Pointcheval, D., Stern, J.: Security arguments for digital signatures and blind signatures. J. Cryptol. **13**(3), 361–396 (2000)

39. Regev, O.: A subexponential time algorithm for the dihedral hidden subgroup problem with polynomial space. arXiv preprint quant-ph/0406151

40. Schnorr, C.-P.: Security of blind discrete log signatures against interactive attacks. In: Qing, S., Okamoto, T., Zhou, J. (eds.) ICICS 2001. LNCS, vol. 2229, pp. 1–12. Springer, Heidelberg (2001). https://doi.org/10.1007/3-540-45600-7_1

41. Shamir, A.: How to share a secret. Commun. ACM **22**(11), 612–613 (1979)

42. Vpn by Google one, explained. https://one.google.com/about/vpn/howitworks

43. Wagner, D.: A generalized birthday problem. In: Yung, M. (ed.) CRYPTO 2002. LNCS, vol. 2442, pp. 288–304. Springer, Heidelberg (2002). https://doi.org/10.1007/3-540-45708-9_19

44. Yi, X., Lam, K.-Y.: A new blind ECDSA scheme for bitcoin transaction anonymity. In: ASIACCS 2019, pp. 613–620 (2019)

Weak Instances of Class Group Action Based Cryptography via Self-pairings

Wouter Castryck[1,4](✉)[iD], Marc Houben[1,2,3][iD], Simon-Philipp Merz[5][iD], Marzio Mula[6][iD], Sam van Buuren[1][iD], and Frederik Vercauteren[1][iD]

[1] imec-COSIC, KU Leuven, Leuven, Belgium
{wouter.castryck,marc.houben,sam.vanbuuren,
frederik.vercauteren}@kuleuven.be
[2] Departement Wiskunde, KU Leuven, Leuven, Belgium
[3] Mathematisch Instituut, Universiteit Leiden, Leiden, The Netherlands
[4] Vakgroep Wiskunde: Algebra en Meetkunde, Universiteit Gent, Ghent, Belgium
[5] Information Security Group, Royal Holloway, University of London, Egham, UK
research@simon-philipp.com
[6] Dipartimento di Matematica, Università degli Studi di Trento, Trento, Italy
marzio.mula@unitn.it

Abstract. In this paper we study non-trivial self-pairings with cyclic domains that are compatible with isogenies between elliptic curves oriented by an imaginary quadratic order $\mathcal{O}$. We prove that the order m of such a self-pairing necessarily satisfies $m \mid \Delta_{\mathcal{O}}$ (and even $2m \mid \Delta_{\mathcal{O}}$ if $4 \mid \Delta_{\mathcal{O}}$ and $4m \mid \Delta_{\mathcal{O}}$ if $8 \mid \Delta_{\mathcal{O}}$) and is not a multiple of the field characteristic. Conversely, for each m satisfying these necessary conditions, we construct a family of non-trivial cyclic self-pairings of order m that are compatible with oriented isogenies, based on generalized Weil and Tate pairings.

As an application, we identify weak instances of class group actions on elliptic curves assuming the degree of the secret isogeny is known. More in detail, we show that if $m^2 \mid \Delta_{\mathcal{O}}$ for some prime power m then given two primitively $\mathcal{O}$-oriented elliptic curves (E, ι) and $(E', \iota') = [\mathfrak{a}](E, \iota)$ connected by an unknown invertible ideal $\mathfrak{a} \subseteq \mathcal{O}$, we can recover $\mathfrak{a}$ essentially at the cost of a discrete logarithm computation in a group of order m^2, assuming the norm of $\mathfrak{a}$ is given and is smaller than m^2. We give concrete instances, involving ordinary elliptic curves over finite fields, where this turns into a polynomial time attack.

Finally, we show that these self-pairings simplify known results on the decisional Diffie–Hellman problem for class group actions on oriented elliptic curves.

Keywords: Isogeny based cryptography · class group action · self-pairing

This work was supported in part by the European Research Council (ERC) under the European Union's Horizon 2020 research and innovation programme (grant agreement ISOCRYPT - No. 101020788) and by CyberSecurity Research Flanders with reference number VR20192203.

© International Association for Cryptologic Research 2023
H. Handschuh and A. Lysyanskaya (Eds.): CRYPTO 2023, LNCS 14083, pp. 762–792, 2023.
https://doi.org/10.1007/978-3-031-38548-3_25

1   Introduction

Isogeny based cryptography using class group actions was originally proposed in the works of Couveignes [13] and Rostovtsev–Stolbunov [32] (CRS), and both use ordinary elliptic curves. In particular, let $\mathcal{O}$ be an order in an imaginary quadratic number field K, then there is a natural action of the ideal-class group $\mathrm{Cl}(\mathcal{O})$ on the set of ordinary elliptic curves (up to isomorphism) over a finite field $\mathbb{F}_q$ whose endomorphism ring is isomorphic to $\mathcal{O}$. Since it is difficult to construct ordinary elliptic curves with many small rational subgroups and large enough $\mathrm{Cl}(\mathcal{O})$, computing the class group action in CRS is rather slow. CSIDH [3,5] significantly improved the efficiency of the CRS approach by considering the set of supersingular elliptic curves over a large prime field $\mathbb{F}_p$ and restricting to the $\mathbb{F}_p$-rational endomorphisms. These form a subring of the full endomorphism ring which again is isomorphic to an order $\mathcal{O}$ in an imaginary quadratic number field. Since $\#E(\mathbb{F}_p) = p+1$ for such supersingular elliptic curves, it now becomes trivial to force the existence of small rational subgroups by choosing p such that $p + 1$ has small prime factors. The OSIDH protocol by Colò and Kohel [12] (and more rigorously by Onuki [27]) extended this even further by using oriented elliptic curves: here one considers elliptic curves together with an $\mathcal{O}$-orientation, which is simply an injective ring homomorphism $\iota : \mathcal{O} \hookrightarrow \mathrm{End}(E)$. OSIDH provides a convenient unifying framework for CRS and CSIDH, but also contains many new families of potential cryptographic interest. While the original Colò–Kohel proposal does not seem viable [15], a more recent proposal [16] looks promising.

A different approach to isogeny based cryptography is taken by SIDH [21], which relies on random walks in the isogeny graph of supersingular elliptic curves over $\mathbb{F}_{p^2}$. To make the protocol work however, it needs to reveal the action of the secret isogeny $\phi : E \to E'$ on a basis of $E[m]$, where m typically is a power of 2 or 3. This extra information was recently exploited in a series of papers [4,23,31] resulting in a polynomial time attack on SIDH. This attack not only showed that SIDH is totally insecure, but also added a very powerful technique to the isogeny toolbox: it is possible to recover a secret isogeny $\phi : E \to E'$ between two elliptic curves E and E', all defined over a finite field $\mathbb{F}_q$, in polynomial time if the following information is available:

– the action of ϕ on a basis of $E[m]$ is given where m is sufficiently smooth,
– the degree $d = \deg(\phi)$ is known and coprime with m,
– $m^2 > d$.

The origins of this paper trace back to the simple question: to what extent can the above technique be applied to the class group action setting and are there weak instances where this results in a polynomial time attack? To illustrate which problems need to be solved, we will focus on the CSIDH setting (the more general oriented case is deferred to later sections). In particular, assume E and E' are two supersingular elliptic curves over $\mathbb{F}_p$ connected by a secret isogeny $\phi : E \to E' := [\mathfrak{a}]E$ with $\ker(\phi) = E[\mathfrak{a}]$ and $\mathfrak{a} \subseteq \mathcal{O}$ an invertible ideal. To be able to apply the above technique to recover ϕ, we need to know the degree of ϕ and its action on a basis of $E[m]$ for some smooth m.

Whether the degree of ϕ is known depends on how the class group action is implemented, e.g. in side-channel protected implementations, the degree is sometimes fixed and thus known. For example, this may be the case for the "dummy-free" constant-time variant of CSIDH that was proposed in [9]. In CSIDH variants that employ dummy computations to achieve constant-time, fault attacks that skip isogeny computations could allow an attacker to determine whether an isogeny was a dummy computation or not, and thus deduce information about the private key. In the dummy-free approach the parity of each secret exponent e_i in CSIDH is fixed and sampled from an interval $[-e, e]$. For $e = 1$, which was suggested both in [9] and in [10], the degree of any secret isogeny is thus fixed to a publicly known value, i.e. the product of all the split primes used in the CSIDH group action. In the remainder of the paper, we will assume the degree of ϕ is known. Note that by construction, the degree is automatically smooth, so this does not impose a further restriction.

Determining the action of the secret isogeny ϕ on a basis of $E[m]$ for a chosen m is a somewhat more challenging task, since we only have E, E' and the degree of ϕ at our disposal. To make partial progress, note that we can choose $m = \ell^r$ for some small odd prime ℓ not dividing $d = \deg(\phi)$ that splits in $\mathbb{Q}(\sqrt{-p})$. Then $E[m]$ is spanned by two eigenspaces $\langle P \rangle, \langle Q \rangle$ of the Frobenius endomorphism π_p corresponding to two different eigenvalues. Since ϕ commutes with π_p, $E'[m]$ will also be spanned by two eigenspaces $\langle P' \rangle, \langle Q' \rangle$ of π_p on E' corresponding to these same eigenvalues, so we already have that $\langle P' \rangle = \langle \phi(P) \rangle$ and $\langle Q' \rangle = \langle \phi(Q) \rangle$. In particular, there exist units $\lambda, \mu \in \mathbb{Z}/m\mathbb{Z}$ such that $P' = \lambda\phi(P)$ and $Q' = \mu\phi(Q)$. Using the independence of the points P and Q (resp. P' and Q') and compatibility of the classical Weil pairing e_m with isogenies, we obtain

$$e_m(P', Q') = e_m(\lambda\phi(P), \mu\phi(Q)) = e_m(P, Q)^{\lambda\mu d}.$$

By computing a discrete logarithm (note that ℓ is assumed small, so computing the discrete logarithm is easy), we can therefore eliminate one variable, say μ, since d is assumed known, so we are left with determining λ. It is tempting to use the same trick again by pairing P' with itself, which would lead to

$$e_m(P', P') = e_m(\lambda\phi(P), \lambda\phi(P)) = e_m(P, P)^{\lambda^2 d}.$$

Unfortunately, the classical Weil pairing e_m results in a trivial self-pairing, i.e. we always have $e_m(P, P) = 1$. What we thus require is a non-trivial self-pairing f_m compatible with isogenies, which implies $f_m(\phi(P)) = f_m(P)^d$, and thus $f_m(P') = f_m(P)^{\lambda^2 d}$, with both sides of order m say. We thus recover λ up to sign and as such we can recover $\pm\phi$. The existence of non-trivial self-pairings therefore is crucial to the success of the attack.

Contributions

- We give a self-contained overview of generalized Weil [20] and Tate [2] pairings, filling some gaps in the existing literature and relating both pairings by extending a result in [20]. Although these generalized pairings are more powerful than the classical Weil and Tate pairings, they do not seem to be well known in the cryptographic community.

- We formally define a cyclic self-pairing of order m on an elliptic curve E to be a homogeneous degree-2 function $f_m : C \to \mu_m$ with cyclic domain $C \subseteq E$ such that $\mathrm{im}(f_m)$ spans μ_m. We derive necessary conditions for the existence of non-trivial cyclic self-pairings of order m on $\mathcal{O}$-oriented elliptic curves that are compatible with oriented isogenies. In particular, we show that m cannot be a multiple of the field characteristic and that $m \mid \Delta_{\mathcal{O}}$, with $\Delta_{\mathcal{O}}$ the discriminant of $\mathcal{O}$ (and even $2m \mid \Delta_{\mathcal{O}}$ if $4 \mid \Delta_{\mathcal{O}}$ and $4m \mid \Delta_{\mathcal{O}}$ if $8 \mid \Delta_{\mathcal{O}}$). Note that our results only apply to self-pairings compatible with isogenies, which is required to make the above attack work. This is in stark contrast to considering an individual elliptic curve, where non-trivial cyclic self-pairings of order m always exist (as soon as m is not a multiple of the field characteristic), e.g. by choosing any cyclic order-m subgroup $C = \langle P \rangle$ and simply defining $f_m(\lambda P) = \zeta_m^{\lambda^2}$ with ζ_m some fixed primitive m-th root of unity.
- For m satisfying these necessary conditions we construct cyclic self-pairings of order m compatible with oriented isogenies, based on generalized Weil and Tate pairings.
- Using these non-trivial cyclic self-pairings, we are the first to identify weak instances of class group action based cryptography. In the best case, we obtain a polynomial time attack on the vectorization problem when $\deg(\phi)$ is known and powersmooth, $\ell^{2r} \mid q - 1$, $E(\mathbb{F}_q)[\ell^{\infty}]$ is cyclic of order at least ℓ^{2r}, and $\ell^{2r} > \deg(\phi)$. This for instance would be the case if one would use a setup like SiGamal [26], but using the group action underlying CRS instead of CSIDH. Note however that our attack does not apply to SiGamal itself for two major reasons: here $\Delta_{\mathcal{O}} = -4p$ and the degree of the secret isogeny is not known.
- We present a more elegant version of existing results [6,7] on the decisional Diffie–Hellman problem for class group actions. In particular, in Remark 5.3 we give a conceptual explanation for a phenomenon observed in [6, Appendix A]. This also illustrates why the general framework of oriented elliptic curves can be useful even if one is only interested in elliptic curves over $\mathbb{F}_q$ equipped with the natural Frobenius orientation.

2 Background

Throughout this paper, k denotes a perfect field (e.g., a finite field $\mathbb{F}_q$) with algebraic closure $\overline{k}$, and K is an imaginary quadratic number field with maximal order $\mathcal{O}_K$.

2.1 Oriented Elliptic Curves

Our main references are Colò–Kohel [12] and Onuki [27], although we present matters in somewhat greater generality (in the sense that we also cover non-supersingular elliptic curves). A *K-orientation* on an elliptic curve E/k is an injective ring homomorphism

$$\iota : K \hookrightarrow \text{End}^0(E) := \text{End}(E) \otimes_{\mathbb{Z}} \mathbb{Q},$$

where $\text{End}(E)$ denotes the full ring of endomorphisms of E (i.e., defined over $\overline{k}$). The couple (E, ι) is called a K-*oriented elliptic curve*.

Example 2.1. The standard example to keep in mind is that of an elliptic curve E over a finite field $\mathbb{F}_q$ for which the q-th power Frobenius endomorphism π_q is not a scalar multiplication (that is, we exclude supersingular elliptic curves $E/\mathbb{F}_{p^{2r}}$ on which Frobenius acts as $[\pm p^r]$). In that case we have an orientation

$$\iota : \mathbb{Q}(\sigma) \hookrightarrow \text{End}^0(E) : \sigma \mapsto \pi_q, \qquad \sigma = \frac{t_E + \sqrt{t_E^2 - 4q}}{2} \qquad (1)$$

with t_E the trace of Frobenius of E over $\mathbb{F}_q$. We call this the *Frobenius orientation*. If (and only if) E is ordinary then ι is an isomorphism. If E is supersingular then the image of ι is the subalgebra $\text{End}_q^0(E) = \text{End}_q(E) \otimes_{\mathbb{Z}} \mathbb{Q}$, with $\text{End}_q(E)$ the ring of $\mathbb{F}_q$-rational endomorphisms of E. By abuse of notation, we will occasionally just identify σ with π_q and refer to ι as a $\mathbb{Q}(\pi_q)$-orientation.

Example 2.2. More generally, every endomorphism $\alpha \in \text{End}(E) \setminus \mathbb{Z}$ naturally gives rise to an orientation. Indeed, such an endomorphism necessarily satisfies $\alpha^2 - t\alpha + n = 0$ where the trace $t = \text{Tr}(\alpha)$ and the norm $n = N(\alpha)$ (which we recall is equal to the degree of α) satisfy $t^2 - 4n < 0$. Fixing

$$\sigma = \frac{t + \sqrt{t^2 - 4n}}{2} \in \mathbb{C}$$

we obtain an orientation $\iota : \mathbb{Q}(\sigma) \hookrightarrow \text{End}^0(E)$, which is unique if we impose that $\iota(\sigma) = \alpha$. Every orientation arises in this way.

For an order $\mathcal{O} \subseteq K$, we say that a K-orientation $\iota : K \hookrightarrow \text{End}^0(E)$ is an $\mathcal{O}$-*orientation* if $\iota(\mathcal{O}) \subseteq \text{End}(E)$. If moreover $\iota(\mathcal{O}') \not\subseteq \text{End}(E)$ for every strict superorder $\mathcal{O}' \supsetneq \mathcal{O}$ in K, then we say that it concerns a *primitive* $\mathcal{O}$-orientation. Note that any K-orientation ι is a primitive $\mathcal{O}$-orientation for a unique order $\mathcal{O} \subseteq K$, namely for the order $\iota^{-1}(\text{End}(E))$. We call this order the *primitive order* for the K-orientation. Let us also introduce the following weaker notion:

Definition 2.3. *An $\mathcal{O}$-orientation on an elliptic curve E/k is said to be* locally primitive *at a positive integer m if the index of $\mathcal{O}$ inside the primitive order is coprime to m.*

The following is a convenient sufficient condition for local primitivity:

Lemma 2.4. *Let E/k be an elliptic curve, let $\sigma \in \text{End}(E)$ and let m be a positive integer such that*

(i) $\text{char}(k) \nmid m$,

(ii) $E[\ell, \sigma] \cong \mathbb{Z}/\ell\mathbb{Z}$ *for every prime divisor* $\ell \mid m$.

Then the natural $\mathbb{Z}[\sigma]$-*orientation on* E *is locally primitive at* m. *As a partial converse, we have that this orientation is not locally primitive at* m *as soon as* $E[\ell, \sigma] \cong \mathbb{Z}/\ell\mathbb{Z} \times \mathbb{Z}/\ell\mathbb{Z}$ *for some prime divisor* $\ell \mid m$.

Proof. If the orientation is not locally primitive at m, then we must have $(\sigma - a)/\ell \in \operatorname{End}(E)$ for a prime divisor $\ell \mid m$ and some $a \in \mathbb{Z}$. Thus σ would act as multiplication-by-a on $E[\ell]$. By assumption (ii) we necessarily have $a = 0$, but then $E[\ell, \sigma] = E[\ell] \cong \mathbb{Z}/\ell\mathbb{Z} \times \mathbb{Z}/\ell\mathbb{Z}$ in view of assumption (i): a contradiction. Conversely, if $E[\ell, \sigma] \cong \mathbb{Z}/\ell\mathbb{Z} \times \mathbb{Z}/\ell\mathbb{Z}$ then by [36, Corollary III.4.11] we know that there exists an $\alpha \in \operatorname{End}(E)$ such that $\alpha \circ [\ell] = \sigma$, so the primitive order must contain σ/ℓ, hence the $\mathbb{Z}[\sigma]$-orientation is not locally primitive at m. $\square$

Example 2.5. The Frobenius orientation on an elliptic curve E over a finite field $\mathbb{F}_q$ is also a $\mathbb{Z}[\pi_q]$-orientation. If $E(\mathbb{F}_q)[\ell] \cong \mathbb{Z}/\ell\mathbb{Z}$ for some prime number $\ell \nmid q$, then by Lemma 2.4 applied to $\sigma = \pi_q - 1$ this orientation is locally primitive at ℓ. If $E[\ell] \subseteq E(\mathbb{F}_q)$ then it is not.

If $\phi : E \to E'$ is an isogeny and if ι is a K-orientation on E, then we can define an induced K-orientation $\phi_*(\iota)$ on E' by letting

$$\phi_*(\iota)(\alpha) = \frac{1}{\deg(\phi)} \phi \circ \iota(\alpha) \circ \hat{\phi}, \quad \forall \alpha \in K,$$

where $\hat{\phi}$ denotes the dual isogeny of ϕ. Given two K-oriented elliptic curves (E, ι) and (E', ι'), we say that an isogeny $\phi : E \to E'$ is K-*oriented* if $\iota' = \phi_*(\iota)$; in this case, we write $\phi : (E, \iota) \to (E', \iota')$. The dual of a K-oriented isogeny is automatically K-oriented as well. Two K-oriented elliptic curves (E, ι) and (E', ι') are called *isomorphic* if there exists an isomorphism $\phi : E \to E'$ such that $\phi_*(\iota) = \iota'$.

Example 2.6. Let E, E' be elliptic curves over $\mathbb{F}_q$ with the same trace of Frobenius, so that they can both be viewed as K-oriented elliptic curves with $K = \mathbb{Q}(\sigma)$ as in (1). Then an isogeny $\phi : E \to E'$ is K-oriented if and only if it is $\mathbb{F}_q$-rational.

2.2   Class Group Actions

The set

$$\mathcal{E}\ell\ell_{\overline{k}}^{\mathrm{all}}(\mathcal{O}) = \{ (E, \iota) \mid E \text{ ell. curve over } \overline{k}, \iota \text{ primitive } \mathcal{O}\text{-orientation on } E \}/ \cong$$

of primitively $\mathcal{O}$-oriented elliptic curves over $\overline{k}$ up to isomorphism comes equipped with an action by the ideal class group of $\mathcal{O}$, which we denote by $\mathrm{Cl}(\mathcal{O})$. For elliptic curves over $\mathbb{C}$ with complex multiplication, this is a classical result. The case where k is a finite field and the orientation is by Frobenius is treated in [35, 38]. This group action, which we describe below in more detail, is free, but in general not transitive, see e.g. [35, Theorem 4.5] and [27, Proposition 3.3] for some subtleties. To avoid issues arising from the non-transitivity, we define

$$\mathcal{E}\ell\ell_{\overline{k}}(\mathcal{O}) \subseteq \mathcal{E}\ell\ell_{\overline{k}}^{\mathrm{all}}(\mathcal{O})$$

to be an arbitrary but fixed orbit (in practice, where we want to study a secret relation between two primitively $\mathcal{O}$-oriented elliptic curves, it will concern the orbit containing these two curves.)

The action is defined as follows. Let (E, ι) be a primitively $\mathcal{O}$-oriented elliptic curve and let $[\mathfrak{a}] \in \mathrm{Cl}(\mathcal{O})$ be an ideal class, represented by an invertible ideal $\mathfrak{a} \subseteq \mathcal{O}$ of norm coprime to $\max\{1, \mathrm{char}(k)\}$; every ideal class admits such a representative by [14, Corollary 7.17]. One defines the $\mathfrak{a}$-torsion subgroup as

$$E[\mathfrak{a}] = \bigcap_{\alpha \in \mathfrak{a}} \ker(\iota(\alpha)),$$

which turns out to be finite (of order $N(\mathfrak{a}) = \#(\mathcal{O}/\mathfrak{a})$, to be more precise). Thus there exists an elliptic curve E' and a separable isogeny $\phi_{\mathfrak{a}} : E \to E'$ with $\ker(\phi_{\mathfrak{a}}) = E[\mathfrak{a}]$, which is unique up to post-composition with an isomorphism. The isomorphism class of $(E', \phi_{\mathfrak{a}*}(\iota))$ is independent of the choice of the representing ideal $\mathfrak{a}$. One then lets $[\mathfrak{a}](E, \iota)$ be this isomorphism class, and this turns out to define a free group action.

2.3 Horizontal, Ascending and Descending Isogenies

Let $\ell \neq \mathrm{char}(k)$ be a prime number and consider an ℓ-isogeny $\phi : (E_1, \iota_1) \to (E_2, \iota_2)$ of K-oriented elliptic curves. Let $\mathcal{O}_1 \subseteq K$ be the primitive order of ι_1 and let $\mathcal{O}_2 \subseteq K$ be the primitive order of ι_2. Then one of the following is true:

– $\mathcal{O}_1 \subseteq \mathcal{O}_2$ and $[\mathcal{O}_2 : \mathcal{O}_1] = \ell$, in which case ϕ is called *ascending*,
– $\mathcal{O}_1 = \mathcal{O}_2$, in which case ϕ is called *horizontal*,
– $\mathcal{O}_2 \subseteq \mathcal{O}_1$ and $[\mathcal{O}_1 : \mathcal{O}_2] = \ell$, in which case ϕ is called *descending*.

It is clear that the dual of an ascending isogeny is descending and vice versa. All horizontal isogenies are of the form $\phi_{\mathfrak{a}}$ for some invertible ideal $\mathfrak{a} \subseteq \mathcal{O}_1 = \mathcal{O}_2$ of norm ℓ, with dual $\phi_{\overline{\mathfrak{a}}}$. Ascending isogenies are of the form $\phi_{\mathfrak{a}}$ for some *non-invertible* ideal $\mathfrak{a} \subseteq \mathcal{O}_1$ of norm ℓ, while descending isogenies are not of the form $\phi_{\mathfrak{a}}$ at all.

3   Generalized Weil and Tate Pairings

We review some properties of the generalized Weil and Tate pairings on elliptic curves, with a focus on how the latter can be defined in terms of the former. The main sources of inspiration for this section were papers by Bruin [2] and Garefalakis [20], although now we should highlight the work by Robert [30, Sect. 4], which appeared near the submission time of the current article and takes this discussion to a deeper level. Nevertheless, while the following statements may be well-known to some experts, we did not succeed in pinpointing exact references for all of them, so we take the opportunity to fill some apparent gaps in the existing literature.

3.1 Weil Pairing

Following [20] and [36, Example III.3.15], to any elliptic curve isogeny $\psi : E \to E'$ over a perfect field k such that $\mathrm{char}(k) \nmid \deg(\psi)$ one can associate the ψ-*Weil pairing*

$$e_\psi : \ker(\psi) \times \ker(\hat{\psi}) \to \overline{k}^* : (P, Q) \mapsto \frac{g \circ \tau_P}{g},$$

where $\hat{\psi} : E' \to E$ denotes the dual of ψ. Here, $g \in k(E)$ is any function with divisor $\psi^*(Q) - \psi^*(0_{E'})$ and τ_P denotes the translation-by-P map. It can be argued that $(g \circ \tau_P)/g$ is indeed constant. The ψ-Weil pairing takes values in μ_m, with m any positive integer such that $\ker(\psi) \subseteq E[m]$. When applied to the multiplication-by-m map on an elliptic curve E one recovers the classical m-Weil pairing, as it is defined in [36, Sect. III.8].

Lemma 3.1. *The ψ-Weil pairing is bilinear, non-degenerate, $\mathrm{Gal}(\overline{k}, k)$-invariant and further satisfies:*

1. Skew-symmetry: for any isogeny $\psi : E \to E'$ we have

$$e_\psi(P, Q) = e_{\hat{\psi}}(Q, P)^{-1} \qquad \text{for all } P \in \ker(\psi), Q \in \ker(\hat{\psi}),$$

2. Compatibility Weil-I: for any chain of isogenies $E \xrightarrow{\phi} E' \xrightarrow{\psi} E''$ we have

(a) $\quad e_{\psi \circ \phi}(P, Q) = e_\psi(\phi(P), Q) \qquad \text{for all } P \in \ker(\psi \circ \phi), Q \in \ker(\hat{\psi}),$

(b) $\quad e_{\psi \circ \phi}(P, Q) = e_\phi(P, \hat{\psi}(Q)) \qquad \text{for all } P \in \ker(\phi), Q \in \ker(\hat{\phi} \circ \hat{\psi}),$

3. Compatibility Weil-II: for any positive integer m and any isogeny $\phi : E \to E'$ we have

$$e_m(\phi(P), Q) = e_m(P, \hat{\phi}(Q)) \qquad \text{for all } P \in E[m], Q \in E'[m].$$

Proof. We refer to [20, Sect. 2] and [36, Example III.3.15(c)] for bilinearity, non-degeneracy, Galois invariance and Compatibility Weil-I(a). Compatibility Weil-II is just a restatement of [36, III.Proposition 8.2]. Skew-symmetry is well-known in case $\psi = m$. The general case can be found in [30, Sect. 4.1], although this can also been seen as a consequence of the case $\psi = m$. Indeed, write $m = \deg(\psi)$ and pick any point $R \in E'$ such that $\hat{\psi}(R) = P$ and likewise pick any point $S \in E$ such that $\psi(S) = Q$. Observe that R, S are m-torsion points. Then one checks that

$$e_\psi(P, Q) = e_\psi(\hat{\psi}(R), \psi(S)) = e_m(R, \psi(S)) = e_m(\psi(S), R)^{-1} =$$
$$e_m(S, \hat{\psi}(R))^{-1} = e_{\hat{\psi}}(\psi(S), \hat{\psi}(R))^{-1} = e_{\hat{\psi}}(Q, P)^{-1}$$

as wanted. Here the first and last equality use Compatibility Weil-I(a), the third equality uses skew-symmetry for the classical m-Weil pairing, and the fourth equality uses Compatibility Weil-II. Compatibility Weil-I(b) is an immediate consequence of Compatibility Weil-I(a) and skew-symmetry.   □

For $\psi = m$ there is an equivalent definition of the Weil pairing which is more amenable to computation via Miller's algorithm [24].

Lemma 3.2. *Let $P, Q \in E[m]$. Choose divisors*

$$D_P \sim (P) - (0_E) \qquad and \qquad D_Q \sim (Q) - (0_E)$$

whose supports are disjoint from $\{(Q), (0_E)\}$ and $\{(P), (0_E)\}$, respectively. Let $f_{m,P}, f_{m,Q} \in k(E)$ be such that

$$\mathrm{div}(f_{m,P}) = m(P) - m(0_E), \qquad \mathrm{div}(f_{m,Q}) = m(Q) - m(0_E).$$

Then $e_m(P, Q) = (-1)^m f_{m,P}(D_Q)/f_{m,Q}(D_P)$.

Proof. See e.g. [25].   □

There is no known analogue of this result for the more general ψ-Weil pairing; see [28, Sect. 3.6] for a discussion. Note that it is possible to relax the assumption on the supports of D_P, D_Q by working with normalized functions, along the lines of [25, Definition 4].

3.2   Tate Pairing

The literature describes a number of related pairings on elliptic curves that are all being referred to as the Tate pairing. We focus on the case $k = \mathbb{F}_q$. Following Bruin [2], to any $\mathbb{F}_q$-rational isogeny $\psi : E \to E'$ such that $\ker(\psi) \subseteq E[m] \subseteq E[q-1]$ we associate the ψ-Tate pairing

$$T_\psi : (\ker(\hat{\psi}))(\mathbb{F}_q) \times \frac{E'(\mathbb{F}_q)}{\psi(E(\mathbb{F}_q))} \to \mu_m \subseteq \mathbb{F}_q^*$$

defined by $T_\psi(P, Q) = e_{\hat{\psi}}(P, \pi_q(R) - R)$, where R is arbitrary such that $\psi(R) = Q$. This is sometimes called the *reduced* Tate pairing in order to distinguish it from the Frey–Rück Tate pairing (see below); this terminology is particularly common in case $\psi = m$.

Remark 3.3. Bruin instead writes $e_\psi(\pi_q(R) - R, P)$, so in view of the skew-symmetry we appear to have inverted the pairing value; however, this inversion compensates for the fact that Bruin follows a different convention for the Weil pairing [2, Sect. 4]. In particular, our two definitions of the ψ-Tate pairing match.

Lemma 3.4. *The ψ-Tate pairing is bilinear, non-degenerate, $\mathrm{Gal}(\overline{\mathbb{F}}_q, \mathbb{F}_q)$-invariant and moreover satisfies:*

1. Compatibility Tate-I: *for any chain of $\mathbb{F}_q$-rational isogenies $E \xrightarrow{\phi} E' \xrightarrow{\psi} E''$ we have*

$$T_{\psi \circ \phi}(P, Q) = T_\psi(P, Q) \qquad \text{for all } P \in (\ker(\hat{\psi}))(\mathbb{F}_q), Q \in E''(\mathbb{F}_q),$$

2. Compatibility Tate-II: *for any positive integer m and any $\mathbb{F}_q$-rational isogeny $\phi : E \to E'$ we have*

$$T_m(\phi(P), Q) = T_m(P, \hat{\phi}(Q)) \qquad \text{for all } P \in E[m](\mathbb{F}_q), Q \in E'(\mathbb{F}_q).$$

Proof. For compatibility Tate-I we note that

$$T_{\psi \circ \phi}(P, Q) = e_{\hat{\phi} \circ \hat{\psi}}(P, \pi_q(R) - R) = e_{\hat{\psi}}(P, \pi_q(\phi(R)) - \phi(R))$$

for any R such that $\psi(\phi(R)) = Q$; here we used Compatibility Weil-I(b) and the fact that ϕ is defined over $\mathbb{F}_q$. But this is indeed equal to $T_\psi(P, Q)$, because $\psi(\phi(R)) = Q$. Compatibility Tate-II is an immediate consequence of Compatibility Weil-II. □

Notice that applying Compatibility Tate-I to $E' \xrightarrow{\phi} E \xrightarrow{\psi} E'$, where ϕ is such that $[m] = \psi \circ \phi$ (e.g., $\phi = \hat{\psi}$ in case ψ is cyclic of degree m), shows that

$$T_\psi(P, Q) = T_m(P, Q) \qquad \text{for all } P \in (\ker(\hat{\psi}))(\mathbb{F}_q), Q \in E'(\mathbb{F}_q)$$

from which one sees that the ψ-Tate pairing is just a restriction of the m-Tate pairing. This is in stark contrast with the ψ-Weil pairing, whose relation to the m-Weil pairing is much more convoluted.

The following is an alternative interpretation of the ψ-Tate pairing in terms of the Weil pairing. This generalizes Garefalakis' main observation [20, Sect. 5].

Proposition 3.5. *Consider an $\mathbb{F}_q$-rational isogeny $\psi : E \to E'$ between elliptic curves over $\mathbb{F}_q$ and assume that*

$$\ker(\psi) \subseteq E[q - 1].$$

Then we obtain a well-defined pairing

$$\frac{E'(\mathbb{F}_q)}{\psi(E(\mathbb{F}_q))} \times (\ker(\hat{\psi}))(\mathbb{F}_q) \to \mathbb{F}_q^*$$

from the $(\pi_q - 1)$-Weil pairing

$$e_{\pi_q - 1} : E'(\mathbb{F}_q) \times \ker(\hat{\pi}_q - 1) \to \mathbb{F}_q^*$$

on E', by restricting the domain of the second argument to $\ker(\hat{\pi}_q - 1) \cap \ker(\hat{\psi})$. Moreover,

$$T_\psi(P, Q) = e_{\pi_q - 1}(Q, P)^{-1}$$

for all $P \in (\ker(\hat{\psi}))(\mathbb{F}_q)$ and $Q \in E'(\mathbb{F}_q)$.

Proof. We first show that

$$\ker(\hat{\pi}_q - 1) \cap \ker(\hat{\psi}) = \ker(\pi_q - 1) \cap \ker(\hat{\psi}) = (\ker(\hat{\psi}))(\mathbb{F}_q).$$

Indeed, we have $\ker(\hat{\psi}) \subseteq E'[q-1]$ and $\#\ker(\pi_q - 1) = \#\ker(\hat{\pi}_q - 1) = q - t + 1$, with t the trace of Frobenius. From this it follows that

$$\ker(\pi_q - 1) \cap \ker(\hat{\psi}), \ \ker(\hat{\pi}_q - 1) \cap \ker(\hat{\psi}) \subseteq E'[t-2].$$

Using that $(\hat{\pi}_q - 1) + (\pi_q - 1) = t - 2$, the desired equality follows.

Next, we observe that any point $Q \in (\ker(\hat{\psi}))(\mathbb{F}_q)$ pairs trivially with $\psi(P)$ for any $P \in E(\mathbb{F}_q)$:

$$e_{\pi_q-1}(\psi(P), Q) = e_{(\pi_q-1)\circ\psi}(P, Q) = e_{\psi\circ(\pi_q-1)}(P, Q) = e_{\pi_q-1}(P, \hat{\psi}(Q)) = 1,$$

where the first three equalities use Compatibility Weil-I(a), the rationality of ψ, and Compatibility Weil-I(b), respectively. So we indeed end up with a pairing whose domain coincides with that of T_ψ, up to reordering the factors.

Finally, to see that both pairings are each other's inverses, take $P \in (\ker(\hat{\psi}))(\mathbb{F}_q)$ and $Q \in E'(\mathbb{F}_q)$. From Compatibility Tate-I we know that

$$T_\psi(P, Q) = T_{\psi\circ(\pi_q-1)}(P, Q) = e_{(\hat{\pi}_q-1)\circ\psi}(P, (\pi_q - 1)(R)) = e_{\hat{\psi}\circ(\hat{\pi}_q-1)}(P, (\pi_q - 1)(R))$$

with R such that $\psi \circ (\pi_q - 1)(R) = Q$. Compatibility Weil-I(b) allows us to rewrite this as

$$e_{\hat{\pi}_q-1}(P, \psi((\pi_q - 1)(R))) = e_{\hat{\pi}_q-1}(P, Q)$$

which indeed equals $e_{\pi_q-1}(Q, P)^{-1}$ by skew-symmetry.   □

We will extend this observation to a wider class of pairings in Sect. 5.

Following [18] and [30, Sects. 4.4–4.5] one can also consider the *Frey–Rück* ψ-Tate pairing

$$t_\psi : (\ker(\hat{\psi}))(\mathbb{F}_q) \times \frac{E'(\mathbb{F}_q)}{\psi(E(\mathbb{F}_q))} \to \frac{\mathbb{F}_q^*}{(\mathbb{F}_q^*)^m} : (P, Q) \mapsto f_{m,P}(D_Q)$$

with $f_{m,P}$ and D_Q as in Lemma 3.2.[1] It allows for an efficient evaluation through Miller's algorithm. The Frey-Rück ψ-Tate pairing relates to the reduced ψ-Tate pairing T_m via the rule

$$T_\psi(P, Q) = t_\psi(P, Q)^{(q-1)/m}, \tag{2}$$

see [2, Sect. 4] and [30, Remark 4.14], which is the reason for calling the former reduced. In particular, also T_ψ can be evaluated efficiently.

Remark 3.6. It may be tempting to rephrase Lemma 3.2 as

$$e_m(P, Q) = t_m(P, Q)/t_m(Q, P),$$

however one should be careful with this: other representatives of $t_m(P, Q)$ and $t_m(Q, P)$ may fail to quotient to $e_m(P, Q)$. See [19, Sect. IX.6] for a discussion.

---

[1] It may seem suspicious, at first sight, that $f_{m,P}(D_Q)$ does not depend on ψ. However, here too, the Frey–Rück ψ-Tate pairing is just a restriction of the Frey–Rück m-Tate pairing.

4   Self-pairings

In this section we analyze self-pairings, which we formally define as follows:

Definition 4.1. *A* self-pairing *on a finite subgroup G of an elliptic curve E/k is a homogeneous function*

$$f : G \to \overline{k}^*$$

of degree 2. In other words, for all $P \in G$ and $\lambda \in \mathbb{Z}$ it holds that $f(\lambda P) = f(P)^{\lambda^2}$.

As the terminology suggests, our primary examples come from the application of a bilinear pairing to a point and itself. More generally, it is natural to consider

$$f : G \to \overline{k}^* : P \mapsto e(\tau_1(P), \tau_2(P)) \tag{3}$$

for endomorphisms $\tau_1, \tau_2 \in \mathrm{End}(E)$ (possibly scalar multiplications), with e a bilinear pairing on a group that contains $\tau_1(G) \times \tau_2(G)$.

Example 4.2. Let $m \geq 2$ be an integer. The skew-symmetry of the classical Weil pairing implies that $e_m(P, P) = 1$ for any $P \in E[m]$. More generally, the m-Weil pairing becomes trivial whenever it is evaluated at two points belonging to the same cyclic subgroup $\langle P \rangle \subseteq E[m]$:

$$e_m(\tau_1 P, \tau_2 P) = e_m(P, P)^{\tau_1 \tau_2} = 1 \qquad \text{for any } \tau_1, \tau_2 \in \mathbb{Z}.$$

In particular, if one wants to build non-trivial self-pairings from the classical Weil pairing, then this requires the use of at least one non-scalar τ_i.

Example 4.3. The following example is inspired by [19, p. 193]. Consider the elliptic curve $E : y^2 = x^3 + 1$ over a finite field $\mathbb{F}_q$ with $q \equiv 1 \bmod 3$. It comes equipped with the $\mathbb{F}_q$-rational automorphism $\tau : (x, y) \mapsto (\omega x, y)$, with ω a primitive 3rd root of unity. Let $\ell \mid \#E(\mathbb{F}_q)$ be a prime satisfying $\ell \equiv 2 \bmod 3$. Then the self-pairing

$$E[\ell] \to \mathbb{F}_q^* : P \mapsto e_\ell(P, \tau(P))$$

takes non-trivial values for any $P \neq 0_E$. Indeed, every non-zero $P \in E[\ell]$ is mapped to an independent point because there are no non-trivial eigenvectors for the action of τ on $E[\ell]$: its characteristic polynomial $x^2 + x + 1$ is irreducible mod ℓ. Since τ is defined over $\mathbb{F}_q$, this reasoning also proves that $E[\ell] \subseteq E(\mathbb{F}_q)$.

Example 4.4. As a more interesting example, consider an ordinary elliptic curve $E/\mathbb{F}_q$ with endomorphism ring $\mathbb{Z}[\pi_q]$, and assume $m \mid q-1$. The natural reduction map $E(\mathbb{F}_q) \to E(\mathbb{F}_q)/m(E(\mathbb{F}_q))$ allows us to view the reduced m-Tate pairing as a bilinear map

$$T_m : E(\mathbb{F}_q)[m] \times E(\mathbb{F}_q) \to \mu_m. \tag{4}$$

By doing so, we may give up on the right non-degeneracy, but the pairing is still left non-degenerate, that is, for any non-trivial point $P \in E(\mathbb{F}_q)[m]$ there exists a point $Q \in E(\mathbb{F}_q)$ such that $T_m(P, Q) \neq 1$. Since $\mathrm{End}(E) = \mathbb{Z}[\pi_q]$, the group

$E(\mathbb{F}_q)$ is cyclic (see [22, Theorem 1] or apply Lemma 2.4 to $\sigma = \pi_q - 1$). Thus, in this case, we have an induced self-pairing

$$E(\mathbb{F}_q) \to \mu_m : P \mapsto T_m(\tau P, P), \tag{5}$$

where τ denotes scalar multiplication by the index $[E(\mathbb{F}_q) : E(\mathbb{F}_q)[m]]$. This self-pairing is non-trivial as soon as $E(\mathbb{F}_q)[m]$ is non-trivial. Note that we can restrict the domain $E(\mathbb{F}_q)$ to its m-primary part $E(\mathbb{F}_q)[m^\infty]$ without affecting this property.

Remark 4.5. By the definition of T_m, the image of (5) can be rewritten as

$$e_m\left(\tau P, \frac{\pi_q - 1}{m}(P)\right)$$

which seems to be an instance of (3) with e the m-Weil pairing. However, note that $(\pi_q - 1)/m$ is *not* an endomorphism of E. On the other hand, it *does* descend (or rather ascend) to an endomorphism when considered on $E/\langle P \rangle$ and this is enough for the pairing to be defined unambiguously. Recall from Proposition 3.5 that (5) can also be rewritten as $e_{\pi_q-1}(P, \tau P)^{-1}$.

Our definition of a self-pairing a priori allows for maps that do *not* come from a bilinear pairing. This is indeed possible and, interestingly, a small example has appeared in the literature. Let E be an elliptic curve over a finite field $\mathbb{F}_q$ with $q \equiv 1 \bmod 4$ and $\#E(\mathbb{F}_q) \equiv 2 \bmod 4$. Then the "semi-reduced Tate pairing"

$$E(\mathbb{F}_q)[2] \to \mu_4 : P \mapsto f_{2,P}(D_R)^{\frac{q^2-1}{4}}, \qquad 2R = P \tag{6}$$

from [6, Remark 11] maps 0_E to 1 and it sends the point of order 2 to a primitive 4-th root of unity. Such an increase of order is impossible for self-pairings coming from a bilinear pairing along the recipe (3). Yet it is easy to check that this does concern a self-pairing.

This is essentially the oddest thing that can happen:

Lemma 4.6. *Self-pairings map points of order n to $\gcd(n, 2)n$-th roots of unity.*

Proof. Let $f : G \to \overline{k}^*$ be a self-pairing on an elliptic curve E. Let $P \in G$ have order n. Then from

$$f(P)^{n^2} = f(nP) = f(0_E) = f(0 \cdot 0_E) = f(0_E)^{0^2} = 1$$

and

$$f(P)^{n^2+2n} = \frac{f(P)^{(n+1)^2}}{f(P)} = \frac{f((n+1)P)}{f(P)} = 1$$

it follows that the order of $f(P)$ divides $\gcd(n^2, n^2 + 2n) = \gcd(n, 2)n$. $\square$

Let us now bring isogenies into the picture. Indeed, as discussed in the introduction, self-pairings are only interesting if they are non-trivial and enjoy compatibility with a natural class of isogenies, in the following sense:

Definition 4.7. *Consider two elliptic curves E, E' over k equipped with respective self-pairings $f : G \to \overline{k}^*$, $f' : G' \to \overline{k}^*$ for finite subgroups $G \subseteq E$, $G' \subseteq E'$. Let $\phi : E \to E'$ be an isogeny. We say that f and f' are compatible with ϕ if*

$$\phi(G) \subseteq G', \qquad f'(\phi(P)) = f(P)^{\deg(\phi)}$$

for all $P \in G$.

The most powerful case is where the domains $G = \langle P \rangle$, $G' = \langle P' \rangle$ are cyclic: then we know that $\phi(P) = \lambda P'$ for some $\lambda \in \mathbb{Z}$ and we can conclude

$$f'(P) = f(P)^{\lambda^2 \deg(\phi)},$$

leaking information about λ if $\deg(\phi)$ is known and vice versa. We will sometimes refer to self-pairings with cyclic domains as *cyclic self-pairings*. In the non-cyclic case, extracting such information becomes more intricate, although in certain cases it may still be possible; see Remark 6.8. We note that the self-pairing from Example 4.4 is cyclic, and it follows from Compatibility Tate-II that it is compatible with horizontal $\mathbb{F}_q$-rational isogenies; more specifically (and more generally), if $m \mid q - 1$ and E, E' are elliptic curves over $\mathbb{F}_q$ such that the m-primary parts of $E(\mathbb{F}_q)$, $E'(\mathbb{F}_q)$ are cyclic, then the self-pairings

$$E(\mathbb{F}_q)[m^\infty] \to \mu_m : P \mapsto T_m(\tau P, P), \qquad E'(\mathbb{F}_q)[m^\infty] \to \mu_m : P \mapsto T_m(\tau P, P),$$

with $\tau = [E(\mathbb{F}_q) : E(\mathbb{F}_q)[m]] = [E'(\mathbb{F}_q) : E'(\mathbb{F}_q)[m]]$, are compatible with any $\mathbb{F}_q$-rational isogeny $\phi : E \to E'$.

The focus of the current paper lies, more generally, on non-trivial cyclic self-pairings on $\mathcal{O}$-oriented elliptic curves, for some arbitrary (but fixed) imaginary quadratic order $\mathcal{O}$. If we merely impose compatibility with endomorphisms coming from $\mathcal{O}$, then this already imposes severe restrictions:

Proposition 4.8. *Let $\mathcal{O}$ be an imaginary quadratic order with discriminant $\Delta_\mathcal{O}$ and let (E, ι) be an $\mathcal{O}$-oriented elliptic curve over k. Assume that there exists a self-pairing*

$$f : C \to \overline{k}^*$$

on some finite cyclic subgroup $C \subseteq E$ which is compatible with endomorphisms in $\iota(\mathcal{O})$. In other words, for every $\sigma \in \mathcal{O}$ and every $P \in C$ we have

$$\iota(\sigma)(P) \in C, \qquad f(\iota(\sigma)(P)) = f(P)^{N(\sigma)}.$$

Write $m = \#\langle f(C) \rangle$. Then

(i) $\mathrm{char}(k) \nmid m$,
(ii) $m \mid \Delta_\mathcal{O}$,
(iii) with r the 2-valuation of $\Delta_\mathcal{O}$, we have:
   - *if $r = 2$ then $m \mid \Delta_\mathcal{O}/2$,*
   - *if $r \geq 3$ then $m \mid \Delta_\mathcal{O}/4$.*

Remark 4.9. Note that the image of a self-pairing is not necessarily a group, which is why we write $\langle f(C) \rangle$ rather than $f(C)$.

Proof. Statement *(i)* follows immediately from the fact that $\overline{k}^*$ contains no elements of order $\mathrm{char}(k)$.

As for *(ii)* and *(iii)*, let P be a generator of C. Then $f(P)$ has order m. For any $\sigma \in \mathcal{O}$ we have that $\iota(\sigma)(P) = \lambda_\sigma P$ for some $\lambda_\sigma \in \mathbb{Z}$, and via

$$f(P)^{N(\sigma)} = f(\iota(\sigma)(P)) = f(\lambda_\sigma P) = f(P)^{\lambda_\sigma^2}$$

we see that $N(\sigma) \equiv \lambda_\sigma^2 \bmod m$. Writing s for the 2-valuation of m, we make a case distinction:

- If $s \leq 1$ then from Lemma 4.6 we see that some multiple R of P must have order m. Let σ be such that $\mathcal{O} = \mathbb{Z}[\sigma]$. From

$$(\sigma - \hat{\sigma})^2 R = (\sigma^2 + \hat{\sigma}^2 - 2N(\sigma))R = (\lambda_\sigma^2 + \lambda_{\hat{\sigma}}^2 - 2N(\sigma))R = (2N(\sigma) - 2N(\sigma))R = 0$$

  it follows that $m \mid \Delta_\mathcal{O}$ as wanted.
- If $s \geq 2$ then Lemma 4.6 only shows the existence of a point $R \in C$ of order $m/2$ and we obtain the weaker conclusion $m \mid 2\Delta_\mathcal{O}$. But at least this implies that $\Delta_\mathcal{O}$ is even, so we must have $r \geq 2$. Write $\Delta_\mathcal{O} = -2^r n$ and consider elements in $\mathcal{O}$ of the form

$$\sigma = \frac{\sqrt{\Delta_\mathcal{O}}}{2} + 2^t a \qquad a, t \in \mathbb{Z}_{\geq 0},$$

so that $N(\sigma) = 2^{r-2}n + 2^{2t}a^2$ has to be a square modulo 2^s for every choice of a, t. We distinguish further:
  - If r is odd, then also $r - 2$ is odd and taking $a = 0$ immediately shows that $s \leq r - 2$, as wanted.
  - If r is even, then taking $t = (r-2)/2$ yields that $n + a^2$ must be a square modulo 2^{s-r+2} for all a. If $s \geq r$ then this gives a contradiction both in case $n \equiv 1 \bmod 4$ (take $a = 1$) and in case $n \equiv 3 \bmod 4$ (take $a = 0$). So $s \leq r - 1$.
  It remains to show that if $r \geq 4$ is even then in fact $s \leq r - 2$. But if $s = r - 1$ then taking $t = (r-4)/2$ yields that $4n + a^2$ must be a square modulo 8 for all a, which gives a contradiction (take $a = 0$). $\qquad\square$

We will refer to the quantity $m = \#\langle f(C) \rangle$ as the *order* of the self-pairing f. In the next section, we will show, by explicit construction, that the necessary conditions from Proposition 4.8 are in fact *sufficient* for the existence of a family of cyclic self-pairings

$$f_{(E,\iota)} : C_{(E,\iota)} \to \overline{k}^*, \qquad (E, \iota) \in \mathcal{E}\ell\ell_{\overline{k}}(\mathcal{O}),$$

all satisfying $\#\langle \mathrm{im}(f_{(E,\iota)}) \rangle = m$ and compatible with horizontal isogenies (the family will also cover many non-primitively $\mathcal{O}$-oriented elliptic curves and non-horizontal isogenies; more on that in Sect. 5).

Remark 4.10. One may want to relax the assumptions from Proposition 4.8 and impose compatibility with endomorphisms whose norm is coprime to m only. This is good enough for the applications we have in mind, and the semi-reduced Tate pairing from (6) shows that this is a strict relaxation. Indeed, we know from [6, Theorem 10] that it is compatible with $\mathbb{F}_q$-rational isogenies of odd degree, but there exist $\mathbb{F}_q$-rational endomorphisms of even degree for which compatibility fails: denoting the pairing by f, we see from

$$f(P) = \zeta_4 \quad \text{and} \quad f((\pi_q - 1)P) = f(0_E) = 1$$

that it cannot be compatible with the endomorphism $\pi_q - 1$, since $N(\pi_q - 1) = \#E(\mathbb{F}_q) \equiv 2 \bmod 4$. This concerns a self-pairing of order 4 on a $\mathbb{Z}[\pi_q]$-oriented elliptic curve, so it would not be allowed for by Proposition 4.8 because $\Delta_{\mathbb{Z}[\pi_q]} \equiv 4 \bmod 8$. In the appendix of the full version of this paper we prove a relaxed version of Proposition 4.8 [8, Proposition A.1], and we show (in a non-effective fashion) that the above example is part of a larger class of self-pairings of 2-power order that are compatible with K-oriented isogenies of odd degree only.

5   Constructing Non-trivial Self-pairings

Let $\mathcal{O}$ be an order in an imaginary quadratic number field K and let $m \mid \Delta_{\mathcal{O}}$ be a divisor satisfying the necessary conditions from Proposition 4.8:

- $\mathrm{char}(k) \nmid m$,
- if $4 \mid \Delta_{\mathcal{O}}$ then $m \mid \Delta_{\mathcal{O}}/2$,
- if $8 \mid \Delta_{\mathcal{O}}$ then $m \mid \Delta_{\mathcal{O}}/4$.

We will construct a family of cyclic self-pairings of order m, one for each $(E, \iota) \in \mathcal{Ell}_{\overline{k}}(\mathcal{O})$, which is compatible with all horizontal isogenies. More generally, the construction will apply to all $\mathcal{O}$-oriented elliptic curves (E, ι) for which the orientation is locally primitive at m, in the sense of Definition 2.3. Compatibility will hold for any K-oriented isogeny between two such curves. Our construction is based on a natural generalization of the ψ-Tate pairing to $\mathcal{O}$-oriented elliptic curves, which we discuss first. We will actually only rely on the cases where ψ is a scalar multiplication, but the discussion is fully general for the sake of analogy with the ψ-Tate pairing.

5.1   A Generalization of the ψ-Tate Pairing

Let $m \geq 2$ be any integer that is invertible in k. Consider two $\mathcal{O}$-oriented elliptic curves (E, ι), (E', ι') and let $\psi : E \to E'$ be a K-oriented isogeny between them. Assume that $\ker(\psi) \subseteq E[m]$ and let $\sigma \in \mathcal{O}$ be such that

$$\mathrm{Tr}(\sigma) \equiv 0 \bmod \gcd(m, N(\sigma)). \tag{7}$$

We define

$$T_\psi^\sigma : (\ker(\hat{\psi}))[\sigma] \times \frac{E'[\sigma]}{\psi(E[\sigma])} \to \mu_m \subseteq \overline{k}^* : (P, Q) \mapsto e_{\hat{\psi}}(P, \sigma(R))$$

where $R \in E$ is such that $\psi(R) = Q$ and we abusingly write σ instead of $\iota(\sigma), \iota'(\sigma)$. This is well-defined: indeed,

- we have $(\psi \circ \sigma)(R) = (\sigma \circ \psi)(R) = \sigma(Q) = 0_{E'}$, so $\sigma(R) \in \ker(\psi)$,
- making another choice for R amounts to replacing $R \leftarrow R + T$ for some $T \in \ker(\psi)$, and

$$e_{\hat{\psi}}(P, \sigma T) = e_{\hat{\sigma} \circ \hat{\psi}}(P, T) = e_{\hat{\psi} \circ \hat{\sigma}}(P, T) = e_{\hat{\psi}}(\hat{\sigma}(P), T) = e_{\hat{\psi}}((\mathrm{Tr}(\sigma) - \sigma)(P), T) = 1$$

where the first and third equalities use Compatibility Weil-I and the last equality follows from

$$P \in \ker(\hat{\psi}) \cap \ker(\sigma) \subseteq E'[m] \cap E'[N(\sigma)] = E'[\gcd(m, N(\sigma))].$$

The reader should notice the analogy with the definition of the ψ-Tate pairing from Sect. 3. Indeed, applying the above to elliptic curves over $\mathbb{F}_q$ equipped with the natural Frobenius orientation and to $\sigma = \pi_q - 1$, we exactly recover the ψ-Tate pairing; the assumption $m \mid q - 1$ that was made there indeed implies (7), i.e. $\mathrm{Tr}(\pi_q - 1) \equiv 0 \bmod \gcd(m, N(\pi_q - 1))$.

The pairing T_ψ^σ is bilinear and non-degenerate. Possibly the easiest way to verify this is by noting that the statement and proof of Proposition 3.5 carry over: we have

$$T_\psi^\sigma(P, Q) = e_\sigma(Q, P)^{-1}$$

for all $P \in (\ker(\hat{\psi}))[\sigma]$ and $Q \in E'[\sigma]$, so these properties follow from those of the generalized Weil pairing. Our pairing also satisfies the direct analogues of Compatibilities Tate-I and Tate-II:

1. for any chain of K-oriented isogenies $E \xrightarrow{\phi} E' \xrightarrow{\psi} E''$ between $\mathcal{O}$-oriented elliptic curves we have

$$T_{\psi \circ \phi}^\sigma(P, Q) = T_\psi^\sigma(P, Q) \qquad \text{for all } P \in (\ker(\hat{\psi}))[\sigma], Q \in E''[\sigma],$$

2. for any positive integer m and any K-oriented isogeny $\phi : E \to E'$ between $\mathcal{O}$-oriented elliptic curves we have

$$T_m^\sigma(\phi(P), Q) = T_m^\sigma(P, \hat{\phi}(Q)) \qquad \text{for all } P \in E[m, \sigma], Q \in E'[\sigma].$$

Again the proofs are copies of the corresponding properties of the ψ-Tate pairing.

5.2 Self-pairings from Divisors of the Discriminant

Now consider $m \in \mathbb{Z}_{\geq 2}$ such that $m \mid \Delta_\mathcal{O}$, unless m is even in which case we make the stronger assumptions that $2m \mid \Delta_\mathcal{O}$ in case $4 \mid \Delta_\mathcal{O}$, and $4m \mid \Delta_\mathcal{O}$ in case $8 \mid \Delta_\mathcal{O}$. Furthermore assume that $\mathrm{char}(k) \nmid m$. Pick any generator $\sigma \in \mathcal{O}$ such that

$$m \mid \mathrm{Tr}(\sigma), \tag{8}$$

except in the special case where $v_2(m) = 1$, in which case we want

$$2m \mid \text{Tr}(\sigma) \text{ if } 8 \mid \Delta_{\mathcal{O}}, \qquad m \mid \text{Tr}(\sigma) \text{ but } 2m \nmid \text{Tr}(\sigma) \text{ if } 8 \nmid \Delta_{\mathcal{O}}. \qquad (9)$$

Such a generator always exists. Indeed, if m is odd then we can choose whatever generator $\sigma \in \mathcal{O}$ and replace it by $\sigma - (\text{Tr}(\sigma))/2 \bmod m$ if needed. If m is even and $8 \mid \Delta_{\mathcal{O}}$ then we can just take $\sigma = \sqrt{\Delta_{\mathcal{O}}}/2$, whose trace is exactly zero. If m is even and $8 \nmid \Delta_{\mathcal{O}}$ then we can take $\sigma = \sqrt{\Delta_{\mathcal{O}}}/2 + m/2$, with trace m.

Conditions (8)–(9) trivially imply (7), so from the foregoing it follows that to any elliptic curve E equipped with an $\mathcal{O}$-orientation we can associate the non-degenerate bilinear pairing

$$T_m^\sigma : E[m, \sigma] \times \frac{E[\sigma]}{m(E[\sigma])} \to \mu_m \subseteq \overline{k}^*,$$

and we know that this family of pairings is compatible with K-oriented isogenies. As with the standard reduced Tate pairing in Example 4.4, we can also view T_m^σ as a left non-degenerate bilinear pairing $E[m, \sigma] \times E[m^\infty, \sigma] \to \mu_m$.

Now assume that the orientation is locally primitive at m. Then the group $E[m^\infty, \sigma]$ is cyclic: if it were not cyclic, we would have $E[m'] \subseteq E[m^\infty, \sigma]$ for some positive divisor $m' \mid m$, but this would mean that $\sigma/m' \in \text{End}(E)$, contradicting that σ is a generator of $\mathcal{O}$ and the orientation is locally primitive. Next, note that our assumptions (8)–(9) together with

$$\Delta_{\mathcal{O}} = (\text{Tr}(\sigma))^2 - 4N(\sigma)$$

imply that $m \mid N(\sigma)$. Along with the fact that $E[m^\infty, \sigma]$ is cyclic, this in turn yields that $E[m, \sigma]$ is cyclic of order m. By the left non-degeneracy, we see that T_m^σ is surjective onto μ_m and that, again as in Example 4.4, it can be converted into a self-pairing

$$f_{(E,\iota)} : E[m^\infty, \sigma] \to \mu_m : P \mapsto T_m^\sigma(\tau P, P)$$

still satisfying $\#\langle \text{im}(f_{(E,\iota)}) \rangle = m$; here τ is the index of $E[m, \sigma]$ in $E[m^\infty, \sigma]$. This proves the claims made at the beginning of this section.

5.3   Computing the Self-pairings

For the practical applications we have in mind, our base field k will be a finite field $\mathbb{F}_q$, and then a compelling question is: what is the complexity of evaluating the self-pairings constructed above? Concretely, for an $\mathcal{O}$-oriented elliptic curve (E, ι) such that both E and $\iota(\mathcal{O})$ are defined over $\mathbb{F}_q$, and a divisor $m \mid \Delta_{\mathcal{O}}$ at which the orientation is locally primitive, how efficiently can we find an appropriate $\sigma \in \mathcal{O}$ and compute

$$T_m^\sigma(\tau P, P) = e_\sigma(P, \tau P)^{-1}$$

with P a generator of $E[m^\infty, \sigma]$ and τ the index of $E[m, \sigma]$ inside $E[m^\infty, \sigma]$? Here, by "appropriate" we mean that σ should satisfy conditions (8)–(9), but it is not necessary that σ is a generator of $\mathcal{O}$, as long as the orientation by $\mathbb{Z}[\sigma]$ remains locally primitive at m.

Example 5.1. The situation is particularly nice for the Frobenius orientation in case $m \mid q-1$ and $m \mid \#E(\mathbb{F}_q)$. From the identities $\mathrm{Tr}(\pi_q - 1) = (q-1) - \#E(\mathbb{F}_q)$, $N(\pi_q - 1) = \#E(\mathbb{F}_q)$ and $\Delta_{\mathcal{O}} = \mathrm{Tr}(\pi_q - 1)^2 - 4N(\pi_q - 1)$ it is easy to check that m satisfies our necessary conditions for the existence of an order-m self-pairing. Moreover, they show that $\sigma = \pi_q - 1$ meets conditions (8)–(9). If the orientation by $\mathbb{Z}[\pi_q]$ is locally primitive at m then the resulting order-m self-pairing

$$E(\mathbb{F}_q)[m^\infty] \to \mathbb{F}_q^* : P \mapsto T_m^{\pi_q - 1}(\tau P, P) = T_m(\tau P, P), \qquad \tau = \frac{\#E(\mathbb{F}_q)[m^\infty]}{m}$$

becomes an instance of the reduced m-Tate pairing, so it can be computed via the Frey–Rück Tate pairing t_m as in (2). The latter can be evaluated efficiently using Miller's algorithm, in time $O(\log^2 m \log^{1+\varepsilon} q)$ using fast multiplication.

Example 5.2. An interesting case is where $\sigma = \varsigma/b$ for some integer $b \geq 2$, where ς is some easier endomorphism. Then it suffices to compute $T_m^\varsigma(\tau P, Q)$ for any $Q \in E$ such that $bQ = P$. Indeed:

$$T_m^\varsigma(\tau P, Q) = e_m(\tau P, \varsigma(R)) = e_m(\tau P, \frac{\varsigma}{b}(bR)) = T_m^\sigma(\tau P, P),$$

with R such that $mR = Q$, so that $m(bR) = P$. E.g., if $\varsigma = \pi_q - 1$, then this again allows us to resort to the Frey–Rück Tate pairing.

Remark 5.3. In the previous example the group $E[m^\infty, \varsigma]$, unlike $E[m^\infty, \sigma]$, may not be cyclic. This sheds a new and more conceptual light on the "not walking to the floor" appendix to [6]. There m was taken to be a prime divisor of $q-1$; for the sake of exposition, let us ignore the technical (and less interesting) case $m = 2$ in what follows. It was assumed that E is an ordinary elliptic curve over $\mathbb{F}_q$ not located on the crater of its m-isogeny volcano, and that

$$E[m^\infty, \pi_q - 1] = E(\mathbb{F}_q)[m^\infty] \cong \frac{\mathbb{Z}}{m^r\mathbb{Z}} \times \frac{\mathbb{Z}}{m^s\mathbb{Z}}$$

for some $r > s+1$. For us, the weaker assumptions $r > s$ and $m \mid \Delta_{\mathrm{End}(E)}$ will do. One then simply notes that $\sigma := (\pi_q - 1)/m^s \in \mathrm{End}(E)$ and that, when viewing E as a $\mathbb{Z}[\sigma]$-oriented elliptic curve, the orientation becomes locally primitive at m. By the assumption on $\Delta_{\mathrm{End}(E)}$ we still have

$$m \mid \Delta_{\mathbb{Z}[\sigma]} \qquad \text{and consequently} \qquad \mathrm{Tr}(\sigma) \equiv 0 \bmod m,$$

where the last congruence uses $\Delta_{\mathbb{Z}[\sigma]} = \mathrm{Tr}(\sigma)^2 - 4N(\sigma) = \mathrm{Tr}(\sigma)^2 - 4 \cdot \#E(\mathbb{F}_q)/m^{2s}$. Thus we have a self-pairing

$$E[m^\infty, (\pi_q - 1)/m^s] \to \mu_m : P \mapsto T_m^{(\pi_q - 1)/m^s}(m^{r-s-1}P, P)$$

of order m, with cyclic domain $E[m^\infty, (\pi_q - 1)/m^s] \cong \mathbb{Z}/m^{r-s}\mathbb{Z}$. When computing this self-pairing via the standard m-Tate pairing as in Example 5.2, using $\varsigma = \pi_q - 1$ and $b = m^s$, we recover the pairing discussed in [6, Appendix A].

Unfortunately, for general σ we do not know of an analogue of the Frey–Rück Tate pairing, nor of an analogue of Lemma 3.2 for the generalized Weil pairing. The best methods we can currently think of work by embedding the pairing into a standard Weil pairing, that is, with respect to scalar multiplication. In this way Miller's algorithm becomes available. The embedding is natural via the definition:

$$T_m^\sigma(\tau P, P) = e_m(\tau P, \sigma(R))$$

with $R \in E$ such that $mR = P$. Alternatively, using compatibility Weil-I one can rewrite

$$e_\sigma(P, \tau P)^{-1} = e_{N(\sigma)}(P, \tau R)^{-1}$$

with $R \in E$ a preimage of P under σ. Since m is typically a lot smaller than $N(\sigma)$, and since evaluating σ seems easier than computing a preimage, the first method appears to be preferable in practice.

The complexity then depends heavily on the field of definition of the points in $E[m^\infty, \sigma]$. In the worst case, one may need to unveil the full $N(\sigma)$-torsion to see these points, requiring to switch to $\mathbb{F}_{q^a}$ with a the order of π_q acting on $E[N(\sigma)]$, which is $O(N(\sigma)^2)$. We must also divide P by m to get R, for which we may need to extend further to

$$\mathbb{F}_{q^{aa'}} \quad \text{with } a' = O(m^2).$$

Running Miller's algorithm for the m-Weil pairing over $\mathbb{F}_{q^{aa'}}$ could then cost an atrocious

$$O(\Delta_{\mathcal{O}}^{2+\varepsilon} m^{2+\varepsilon} \log^{1+\varepsilon} q),$$

where we have approximated $N(\sigma) \approx \Delta_{\mathcal{O}}$.

However, this is the absolute worst case: one typically expects $E[m^\infty, \sigma] \subseteq E[m^t]$ for some very small constant t, most likely $t = 1$, and then the estimate becomes

$$O(m^{2t+2+\varepsilon} \log^{1+\varepsilon} q).$$

E.g., in Proposition 6.5 this will be applied to moduli m of sub-exponential size, leading to a sub-exponential workload. We note that the above estimates ignore the cost of determining $\iota(\sigma)$ and evaluating it on R. This heavily depends on how the orientation is given in practice, which is a separate discussion for which we refer to [39].

6   Applications

In this section, we present two applications of the non-trivial self-pairings from Sect. 5. In Sect. 6.1, we show how knowledge of the degree of a secret isogeny together with a non-trivial self-pairing on a large enough subgroup allows us to efficiently attack certain instances of class group action based cryptography. In Sect. 6.2, we use the generalized view of self-pairings to conceptualize previous results on the decisional Diffie–Hellman problem for class group actions [6,7].

6.1   Easy Instances of Class Group Action Inversion

Using the tools developed in the previous sections, we describe a special family of class group actions on oriented elliptic curves for which the vectorization problem is easy, i.e., the class group action can be efficiently inverted. More precisely, we give a high-level recipe for recovering a secret horizontal isogeny ϕ between two primitively $\mathcal{O}$-oriented elliptic curves (E, ι), (E', ι') whenever $d = \deg(\phi)$ is known and smaller than m^2, where m is a prime power satisfying

$$m^2 \mid \Delta_{\mathcal{O}} \text{ if } m \text{ is odd}, \qquad 4m^2 \mid \Delta_{\mathcal{O}} \text{ if } m \text{ is even}.$$

It is also assumed that $\gcd(m, \operatorname{char}(k), d) = 1$. While it has been previously pointed out that factors dividing the discriminant can cause a decrease of security, see e.g. [3, Remark 2] or [6, Sect. 5.1], it was unknown that in special cases they allow for a full break of the vectorization problem.

Attack Strategy. Let $\sigma \in \mathcal{O}$ be such that $\operatorname{Tr}(\sigma) \equiv 0 \bmod m^2$ and the orientation by $\mathbb{Z}[\sigma]$ is locally primitive at m. As discussed in Sect. 5.2 such a σ exists and is easy to find; we can even choose σ to be a generator of $\mathcal{O}$, but in certain cases one may want to take a non-generator for reasons of efficiency.[2]

Recall, again from Sect. 5.2, that the groups $E[m^\infty, \sigma]$ and $E'[m^\infty, \sigma]$ are cyclic and we obtain self-pairings

$$f : E[m^\infty, \sigma] \to \mu_{m^2} \qquad \text{and} \qquad f' : E'[m^\infty, \sigma] \to \mu_{m^2}$$

of order m^2 by mapping $P \mapsto T_{m^2}^\sigma(\tau P, P)$, where

$$\tau = [E[m^\infty, \sigma] : E[m^2, \sigma]] = [E'[m^\infty, \sigma] : E'[m^2, \sigma]].$$

Now, pick respective generators P, P' of $E[m^\infty, \sigma]$, $E'[m^\infty, \sigma]$. Because ϕ is K-oriented and its degree is coprime to m, we know that $P' = \mu\phi(P)$ for some unit $\mu \in \mathbb{Z}/m^2\mathbb{Z}$. The compatibility of f and f' with K-oriented isogenies then implies

$$f'(P') = f(P)^{d\mu^2}.$$

Knowing d, we can determine $\mu^2 \bmod m^2$ using a discrete logarithm computation in μ_{m^2}, which leaves at most four options for $\mu \bmod m^2$: two options if m is odd and four options if m is a power of 2. Given a correct guess for $\mu \bmod m^2$, we obtain knowledge of pair of points

$$Q = \mu\tau P \qquad \text{and} \qquad Q' = \tau P'$$

of order m^2 that are connected via ϕ.

Remark 6.1. Guessing $-\mu$ is in fact equally fine, because it is of course good enough to recover $-\phi = [-1] \circ \phi$. Therefore, only in the case where m is a power of 2 there is an actual need for guessing between $\pm\mu$ and $\pm(1 + m^2/2)\mu$, where we have to repeat the procedure below in case of a wrong guess.

---

[2] For instance, to allow for σ of the form $(\pi_q - 1)/b$ as in Example 5.2.

Using a reduction by De Feo et al.,[3] the problem of recovering ϕ given its images on the cyclic subgroup $\langle Q \rangle$ of order m^2 can be reduced to the problem of recovering a related degree-d isogeny $\phi_0 : E_0 \to E_0'$ given its images on $E_0[m]$. The idea is to compute the isogenies $\psi : E \to E_0$, $\psi' : E' \to E_0'$ with kernels generated by mQ and $m\phi(Q)$, respectively, and complete the diagram:

$$
\begin{array}{ccc}
E_0 & \xrightarrow{\ \phi_0\ } & E_0' \\
\psi \uparrow & & \uparrow \psi' \\
E & \xrightarrow{\ \phi\ } & E'
\end{array}
$$

The points $Q_0 := \psi(Q)$ and $Q_0' := \psi'(Q') = \psi'(\phi(Q))$ are of order m and we have $\phi_0(Q_0) = Q_0'$. Further, by picking any generator R_0 of $\ker(\hat{\psi})$ we obtain a basis $\{Q_0, R_0\}$ of $E_0[m]$. If we choose a generator R_0' of $\ker(\hat{\psi}')$ then it is easy to argue that $R_0' = \lambda\phi_0(R_0)$ for some $\lambda \in \mathbb{Z}$ that is coprime to m. The exact value of $\lambda \bmod m$ can be recovered via a discrete logarithm computation by comparing

$$
e_m(Q_0', R_0') = e_m(\phi_0(Q_0), \lambda\phi_0(R_0)) = e_m(Q_0, R_0)^{\lambda d} \quad \text{with} \quad e_m(Q_0, R_0),
$$

hence we can assume that $\lambda = 1$. Thus, we are given the images of ϕ_0 on a basis of $E_0[m]$. Since $m^2 > d$, we can use Robert's method from [31, Sect. 2], together with the refinement discussed in [31, Sect. 6.4], to evaluate ϕ_0 on arbitrary inputs. In particular, we can evaluate ϕ_0 on a basis of $E_0[d]$ in order to determine the kernel of ϕ_0 explicitly; this kernel can then be pushed through $\hat{\psi}$ to obtain the kernel of ϕ.

Remark 6.2. In our main use cases, namely attacking special instances of CRS, rather than evaluating ϕ_0 on a basis of $E_0[d]$ (which may be defined over a huge field extension only) we want to proceed as follows. For simplicity, let us focus on the dummy-free set-up with $e = 1$ (see Sect. 1). Then we have $d = \ell_1\ell_2\cdots\ell_r$ for distinct small primes ℓ_i that split in $\mathcal{O}$. In this context, recovering ϕ amounts to finding for each $i = 1, 2, \ldots, r$ the prime ideal $\mathfrak{l}_i$ above ℓ_i (one out of two options) for which $E[\mathfrak{l}_i]$ is annihilated by ϕ. Then ϕ is the isogeny corresponding to the invertible ideal $\mathfrak{l}_1\mathfrak{l}_2\cdots\mathfrak{l}_r \subseteq \mathcal{O}$. Since $\gcd(m, d) = 1$ this can be tested directly on E_0 by evaluating ϕ_0 in a generator of $\psi(E[\mathfrak{l}_i])$.

Weak Instances over $\mathbb{F}_q$. Whether or not the above strategy turns into an efficient algorithm depends amongst others on the field arithmetic involved, the cost of evaluating $\iota(\sigma)$, $\iota'(\sigma)$, and the cost of computing discrete logarithms in μ_{m^2}. The following proposition gives instances where it indeed leads to a polynomial-time attack:

Proposition 6.3. *Let E, E' be elliptic curves defined over a finite field $\mathbb{F}_q$, equipped with their Frobenius orientations and connected by an unknown horizontal isogeny ϕ of known degree d, assumed B-powersmooth and coprime to q.*

---

[3] The reduction was presented at the KU Leuven isogeny days in 2022 and an article about this is in preparation [17].

Let $\mathcal{O} \subseteq \mathbb{Q}(\pi_q)$ be their joint primitive order. Assume that there exists a prime power $m = \ell^r$ satisfying $\ell \leq B$, $\ell \nmid qd$, $\ell^{2r} > d$, and

$$\ell^{2r} \mid \Delta_{\mathcal{O}} \text{ if } \ell \text{ is odd}, \qquad \ell^{2r+2} \mid \Delta_{\mathcal{O}} \text{ if } \ell = 2.$$

Further, assume that there exists a positive integer b coprime to q such that $\sigma = (\pi_q - 1)/b \in \mathcal{O}$, $\text{Tr}(\sigma) \equiv 0 \bmod \ell^{2r}$ and $\ell \nmid [\mathcal{O} : \mathbb{Z}[\sigma]]$. Then the invertible ideal $\mathfrak{a} \subseteq \mathcal{O}$ for which $\phi = \phi_{\mathfrak{a}}$ can be computed in time $\text{poly}(\log q, B)$.

Proof. First note that

$$d = O(m^2) = O(|\Delta_{\mathcal{O}}|) \quad \text{and} \quad |\Delta_{\mathcal{O}}| = (4q - \text{Tr}(\pi_q)^2)/[\mathcal{O} : \mathbb{Z}[\pi_q]]^2 = O(q)$$

so any subroutine which runs in time $\text{poly}(d, m)$ also runs in time $\text{poly}(q)$. The orientation by $\mathbb{Z}[\sigma]$ being locally primitive at ℓ, we know that

$$E(\mathbb{F}_q) \cong E'(\mathbb{F}_q) \cong \frac{\mathbb{Z}}{bb'\mathbb{Z}} \times \frac{\mathbb{Z}}{bb'c\mathbb{Z}}$$

for positive integers b', c, where $\ell \nmid b'$, that can be determined in time $\text{poly}(\log q)$ using a point-counting algorithm [34]. Define $\kappa = \gcd(\ell^\infty, c)$, where we note that our assumptions imply that $\ell^{2r} \mid \kappa$: indeed recall from Sect. 5.2 that $E[\ell^{2r}, \sigma] \subseteq E[\sigma] \cong \mathbb{Z}/b'\mathbb{Z} \times \mathbb{Z}/b'c\mathbb{Z}$ has order ℓ^{2r}. A generator $P \in E[\ell^\infty, \sigma]$ is found by repeatedly sampling $X \leftarrow E(\mathbb{F}_q)$ until $P = \frac{bb'c}{\kappa}X$ has order κ. Following Example 5.2, the self-pairing

$$f(P) = T_{\ell^{2r}}^\sigma(\tau P, P) = T_{\ell^{2r}}^{\frac{\pi_q - 1}{b}}(\tau P, P) = T_{\ell^{2r}}\left(\tau P, \frac{b'c}{\kappa}X\right), \qquad \tau = \frac{\kappa}{\ell^{2r}}$$

can then be computed in time $\text{poly}(\log q)$ via the Frey–Rück Tate pairing. Likewise, we can efficiently evaluate f' at a generator $P' \in E'[\ell^\infty, \sigma]$, necessarily satisfying $P' = \mu\phi(P)$ for some μ. As outlined above, via a discrete logarithm computation in $\mu_{\ell^{2r}}$, which can be done in time $\text{poly}(\log q, B)$, we obtain $\mu^2 \bmod \ell^{2r}$. Assuming a correct guess for μ, from this we obtain our order-ℓ^{2r} points $Q, Q' = \phi(Q)$ and we are all set for the torsion-point attack. Note that the points Q, Q' are defined over $\mathbb{F}_q$, hence so are the curves E_0, E_0' and evaluating ϕ_0 at a point in $E_0(\mathbb{F}_{q^a})$ only involves arithmetic over $\mathbb{F}_{q^a}$. We then proceed as outlined in Remark 6.2, with the difference that d need not be square-free: we only require it to be powersmooth. This means that for each prime power $\ell_i^{e_i}$ dividing d, we have to test up to $2^{e_i} - 1 = O(B)$ ideals of norm $\ell_i^{e_i}$ for annihilation by ϕ_0. All arithmetic can be done in an extension of degree $a = \text{poly}(B)$, from which the proposition follows. □

Example 6.4. An example application of Proposition 6.3 is where $\ell^{2r} \mid q - 1$ for a small prime ℓ and $r \geq 1$ and $E(\mathbb{F}_q)[\ell^\infty]$ is cyclic of order at least ℓ^{2r}. Then $m := \ell^r$ and $\sigma := \pi_q - 1$ meet the above requirements. Indeed:

- the orientation by $\mathbb{Z}[\pi_q - 1]$ is locally primitive at ℓ by Lemma 2.4,
- $\text{Tr}(\pi_q - 1) = q - 1 - \#E(\mathbb{F}_q) \equiv 0 \bmod \ell^{2r}$,

– $\Delta_{\mathbb{Z}[\pi_q-1]} = \mathrm{Tr}(\pi_q - 1)^2 - 4\#E(\mathbb{F}_q)$ is divisible by ℓ^{2r}, and by ℓ^{2r+2} if $\ell = 2$.

Here is a baby example with $\ell = 2$. Let E be the ordinary elliptic curve defined by

$$y^2 = x^3 + 106960359001385152381x + 100704579394236675333$$

over $\mathbb{F}_p$ with $p := 2^{30} \cdot 167133741769 + 1$. So here we take $\sigma := \pi_p - 1$ and $m := 2^{15}$. One checks that $E[\sigma] = E(\mathbb{F}_p)$ is a cyclic group of order

$$2^{30} \cdot 5^2 \cdot 7 \cdot 11 \cdot 13 \cdot 17 \cdot 19 \cdot 23 \cdot 29 \cdot 31,$$

in particular its subgroup $E(\mathbb{F}_p)[2^\infty]$ is cyclic of order 2^{30} as wanted. In this case it is easy to check that the $\mathbb{Z}[\sigma]$-orientation is primitive overall, i.e., not just locally at 2. This is a minimal example for a curve one would construct for a SiGamal-type encryption scheme [26] using the group action underlying CRS instead of the CSIDH group action; see below. By Proposition 6.3, one can recover horizontal isogenies of known powersmooth degree $d < 2^{30}$. We implemented the attack in the Magma computer algebra system [1],[4] only skipping the final step, i.e. computing the actual evaluation algorithm as described in [31].

A Generalization. The above recipe can be generalized to the case where multiple squared prime powers $m_1^2, \ldots, m_r^2$ divide $\Delta_\mathcal{O}$ and the degree d of our secret isogeny ϕ is known and smaller than $m_1^2 \cdots m_r^2$. This time we use a cyclic self-pairing of order $m_1^2 \cdots m_r^2$ to recover $\mu^2 \bmod m_1^2 \cdots m_r^2$, with μ as before. Thus, we have 2^r or 2^{r+1} options for μ depending on whether one of the m_i is even (or in fact 2^{r-1} or 2^r options in case we do not care about a global sign). The rest of the recipe follows mutatis mutandis.

Proposition 6.5 (informal). *Let E, E' be elliptic curves defined over a finite field $\mathbb{F}_q$, equipped with their Frobenius orientations and connected by an unknown horizontal isogeny ϕ of known degree d, assumed B-powersmooth and coprime to q. Let $\mathcal{O} \subseteq \mathbb{Q}(\pi_q)$ be their joint primitive order. Assume that there exist $r \approx \sqrt{\log q}$ prime powers $m_1, \ldots, m_r \in L_q(1/2)$ coprime to qd such that $m_1^2 \cdots m_r^2 > d$ and*

$$m_1^2 \cdots m_r^2 \mid \Delta_\mathcal{O} \qquad and \qquad 4m_1^2 \cdots m_r^2 \mid \Delta_\mathcal{O} \text{ if some } m_i \text{ is even.}$$

Then it is expected that the invertible ideal $\mathfrak{a} \subseteq \mathcal{O}$ for which $\phi = \phi_\mathfrak{a}$ can be computed in time $\mathrm{poly}(B) \cdot L_q(1/2)$.

Proof (sketch). Let $\sigma \in \mathcal{O}$ be such that $\mathrm{Tr}(\sigma) \equiv 0 \bmod m_1^2 \cdots m_r^2$ and the orientation by $\mathbb{Z}[\sigma]$ is locally primitive at $m_1 \cdots m_r$. If it so happens that $\sigma = (\pi_q-1)/b$ for some b coprime to q then we can just mimic the previous proof: the main difference is that, this time, there are about $2^r \approx 2^{\sqrt{\log q}} = L_q(1/2)$ possible guesses for the secret scalar μ, from which the stated runtime follows.

---

[4] See https://github.com/KULeuven-COSIC/Weak-Class-Group-Actions for the code.

In general however, it may not be possible to pick σ of the said form, and then the domains $E[(m_1 \cdots m_r)^\infty, \sigma]$ and $E'[(m_1 \cdots m_r)^\infty, \sigma]$ of our self-pairings may be defined over a field extension of degree $L_q(1)$ only, in which case there is no hope for a sub-exponential runtime. For this reason, the attack should be broken up in pieces. Writing $m_1^{t_1} \cdots m_r^{t_r}$ for the order of $E[(m_1 \cdots m_r)^\infty, \sigma] \cong E'[(m_1 \cdots m_r)^\infty, \sigma]$, as discussed in Sect. 5.3 we heuristically expect that $t_i = O(1)$ for all $i = 1, \ldots, r$. If this is indeed the case, then for each i we can find generators $P_i \in E[m_i^\infty, \sigma]$, $P_i' \in E'[m_i^\infty, \sigma]$ over an extension of degree $L_q(1/2)$. The cyclic self-pairings

$$T_{m_i^2}^\sigma(\tau P, P) \quad \text{and} \quad T_{m_i^2}^\sigma(\tau P', P'), \qquad \tau = m_i^{t_i - 2}$$

can thus be computed in time $L_q(1/2)$ and this also accounts for the subsequent discrete logarithm computation. Assuming a correct guess for the scalar μ_i such that $P_i' = \mu_i \phi(P_i)$, we obtain a pair of order-m_i^2 points Q_i, $Q_i' = \phi(Q_i)$. Note that, while these points are defined over an extension of degree $L_q(1/2)$, the groups they generate are $\mathbb{F}_q$-rational because our orientation is by Frobenius. In particular, the isogenies ψ_1, ψ_1' and codomains $E_{0,1}$, $E_{0,1}'$ corresponding to Q_1, Q_1' are defined over $\mathbb{F}_q$. The idea is now to push the points Q_2, Q_2' through ψ_1, ψ_1' and repeat the argument, leading to a diagram

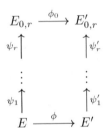

The map ϕ_0 on top comes equipped with its images on a basis of $E_{0,r}[m_i]$ for each $i = 1, \ldots, r$. For the evaluation of ϕ_0 on arbitrary inputs, we can then proceed as in [29, Proposition 2.9] and conclude as before. □

Unaffected Schemes. From the above propositions it follows that a CRS-instantiation using curves whose discriminants are divisible by (large) powers of smallish primes may be vulnerable to a sub-exponential attack. In particular, from a security point of view, walking down the volcano to instantiate CRS is worse than CRS close to the crater. Each descending step on the ℓ-volcano adds a factor ℓ^2 to our discriminant and thus we can recover isogenies of degree ℓ^2 times larger than a level above, using the attack outlined in this section. We examine how some proposed constructions avoid this problem already.

Schemes that use the maximal order as their orientation are not vulnerable to our attack. We need that a prime power, not a prime, divides the discriminant, because the De Feo et al. reduction works only for points of square order. The maximal order has a discriminant that is square-free, at worst after dividing by 4, so the above does not apply. The CSIDH variant CSURF is an example of a scheme that uses the maximal order [3], where the discriminant is not merely square-free but even prime. Similarly, in the original CSIDH proposal the discriminant is four times a large prime and thus there is no factor of the discriminant large enough to enable our attack.

Schemes that are close to the crater are also secure. For instance, the SCAL-LOP scheme [16] uses curves one level underneath the crater in the f-volcano, where f is a large prime. Thus the discriminant is of the form $f^2 \cdot d$, where d is square-free away from 4. Theoretically, we can still use a point of order f^2 to recover an isogeny of degree at most f^2. However, to actually see the f-torsion we would need to pass to an extension of degree $O(f)$, which is infeasible for large enough f.

Another scheme worth mentioning is the higher-degree supersingular group actions [11]. Here the order used is $\mathbb{Z}[\sqrt{-dp}]$ for some square-free d, which has discriminant $-dp$ or $-4dp$. Even if d was a square, d is chosen small relative to p, and as such applying the attack above to these orientations, we could recover an isogeny of degree $2d$ at best.

Pairing-Based Attack Strategy on SiGamal. We end by commenting on a strategy, proposed to us by Luca De Feo and involving self-pairings, to break the IND-CPA security of the SiGamal public-key encryption scheme [26]. In SiGamal, the hardness of the IND-CPA game – i.e., given the encryption of one out of two known plaintexts, guessing which one has been encrypted – relies [26, Theorem 8] on an *ad hoc* assumption called the *P-CSSDDH assumption*.

More precisely, let p be a prime of the form $2^r \ell_1 \cdots \ell_n - 1$, where $r \geq 2$ and $\ell_1, \ldots, \ell_n$ are distinct odd primes. Moreover, let E_0 be the supersingular elliptic curve over $\mathbb{F}_p$ of equation $y^2 = x^3 + x$, P_0 a random generator of $E_0(\mathbb{F}_p)[2^r]$ and $\mathfrak{a}, \mathfrak{b}$ random elements of odd norm in $\mathrm{Cl}(\mathbb{Z}[\pi_p])$. Then the P-CSSDDH assumption is as follows: given the curves $E_0, [\mathfrak{a}]E_0, [\mathfrak{b}]E_0, [\mathfrak{ab}]E_0$ and the points $P_0, P_1 = \phi_{\mathfrak{a}}(P_0)$ and $P_2 = \phi_{\mathfrak{b}}(P_0)$, no efficient algorithm can distinguish $P_3 = \phi_{\mathfrak{ab}}(P_0)$ from a uniformly random 2^r-torsion point $P_3' \in [\mathfrak{a}][\mathfrak{b}]E_0(\mathbb{F}_p)$. Schematically:

$$
\begin{array}{ccc}
(E_0, P_0) & \xrightarrow{\quad\mathfrak{a}\quad} & ([\mathfrak{a}]E_0, P_1 = \phi_{\mathfrak{a}}(P_0)) \\
{\scriptstyle\mathfrak{b}}\big\downarrow & & \big\downarrow{\scriptstyle\mathfrak{b}} \\
([\mathfrak{b}]E_0, P_2 = \phi_{\mathfrak{b}}(P_0)) & \xrightarrow{\quad\mathfrak{a}\quad} & ([\mathfrak{ab}]E_0, P_3 = \phi_{\mathfrak{ab}}(P_0), P_3')
\end{array}
$$

If there existed non-trivial self-pairings f_i on the subgroups $\langle P_i \rangle$, say of order 2^s, compatible with $\mathbb{F}_p$-rational isogenies of odd degree, then one could compute

$$
f_1(P_1) = f_1(\phi_{\mathfrak{a}}(P_0)) = f_0(P_0)^{N(\mathfrak{a})}
$$
$$
f_2(P_2) = f_2(\phi_{\mathfrak{b}}(P_0)) = f_0(P_0)^{N(\mathfrak{b})}
$$
$$
f_3(P_3) = f_3(\phi_{\mathfrak{ab}}(P_0)) = f_0(P_0)^{N(\mathfrak{a})N(\mathfrak{b})}.
$$

Thus, the P-CSSDDH challenge could then be reduced to a decisional Diffie–Hellman problem on μ_{2^s}. However, the existence of such self-pairings f_i is ruled out by Proposition 4.8 and Proposition A.1 in the full version of this paper [8]. Since $\Delta_{\mathcal{O}} = -4p$ and $p \equiv 3 \bmod 4$ by construction, we are condemned to $s = 2$. This is of no use since $\mathfrak{a}$ and $\mathfrak{b}$ are assumed to have odd norm.

6.2   Decisional Diffie–Hellman Revisited

Genus theory [14, Chapter I Sect. 3B] attaches to every imaginary quadratic order $\mathcal{O}$ a list of *assigned characters*, which form a set of generators for the group of quadratic characters $\chi : \mathrm{Cl}(\mathcal{O}) \to \{\pm 1\}$. In detail: if

$$\Delta_{\mathcal{O}} = -2^r m_1^{r_1} m_2^{r_2} \cdots m_n^{r_n}$$

denotes the factorization of $\Delta_{\mathcal{O}}$ into prime powers, then the assigned characters include

$$\chi_{m_i} : [\mathfrak{a}] \mapsto \left(\frac{N(\mathfrak{a})}{m_i} \right), \qquad i = 1, \dots, n, \tag{10}$$

and this list is extended with a subset of

$$\delta : [\mathfrak{a}] \mapsto \left(\frac{-1}{N(\mathfrak{a})} \right), \qquad \epsilon : [\mathfrak{a}] \mapsto \left(\frac{2}{N(\mathfrak{a})} \right), \qquad \delta\epsilon : [\mathfrak{a}] \mapsto \left(\frac{-2}{N(\mathfrak{a})} \right).$$

Concretely, the character δ is included if $r = 2$ and $-\Delta_{\mathcal{O}}/4 \equiv 1 \bmod 4$, or if $r \geq 4$. The character ϵ is included if $r = 3$ and $-\Delta_{\mathcal{O}}/8 \equiv 3 \bmod 4$, or if $r \geq 5$. The character $\delta\epsilon$ is included if $r = 3$ and $-\Delta_{\mathcal{O}}/8 \equiv 1 \bmod 4$, or if $r \geq 5$. In all this, $\left(\frac{\cdot}{\cdot} \right)$ denotes the Legendre/Jacobi symbol and it is assumed that $[\mathfrak{a}]$ is represented by an invertible ideal $\mathfrak{a} \subseteq \mathcal{O}$ of norm coprime with $\Delta_{\mathcal{O}}$.

In the context of breaking the decisional Diffie–Hellman problem for ideal class group actions, it was observed in [6,7] that, given two primitively $\mathcal{O}$-oriented elliptic curves

$$(E, \iota), \ (E', \iota') = [\mathfrak{a}](E, \iota) \ \in \mathscr{Ell}_{\overline{k}}(\mathcal{O})$$

that are connected by an unknown ideal class $[\mathfrak{a}]$, it is possible to compute $\chi([\mathfrak{a}])$ for any assigned character χ, purely from the knowledge of (E, ι), (E', ι'), and at the cost of essentially one discrete logarithm computation (e.g., in the group μ_m in case $\chi = \chi_m$ for an odd prime divisor $m \mid \Delta_{\mathcal{O}}$).

Even though we have not much to add over [6,7] in terms of efficiency or generality, in this section we want to make the nearly obvious remark that cyclic self-pairings are excellently suited for accomplishing this task. Indeed, if m is an odd prime divisor of $\Delta_{\mathcal{O}}$, then we can consider the cyclic self-pairings

$$f : C \to \mu_m \subseteq \overline{k}^*, \qquad f' : C' \to \mu_m \subseteq \overline{k}^*$$

of order m from Sect. 5. Taking any generators $P \in C$, $P' \in C'$, we know that $P' = \lambda\phi_{\mathfrak{a}}(P)$ for some $\lambda \in \mathbb{Z}$ that is invertible mod m and then

$$f'(P') = f(P)^{\lambda^2 N(\mathfrak{a})} \qquad \text{so that} \qquad \chi_m([\mathfrak{a}]) = \left(\frac{\log_{f(P)} f'(P')}{m} \right).$$

None of the methods from [6,7] are literal applications of this simple strategy. Indeed, in the case of [6], which focuses on ordinary elliptic curves over finite fields, the self-pairing step is preceded by a walk to the floor of the m-isogeny volcano truncated at $\mathbb{Z}[\pi_q]$, in order to ensure cyclic rational m^∞-torsion, at which point the usual reduced m-Tate pairing can be used. The method from [7] applies to arbitrary orientations and avoids such walks, but it does not use cyclic self-pairings; rather, it uses self-pairings with non-cyclic domains and, as a result, the argumentation becomes more intricate; see Remark 6.8 for a discussion. So we hope to have convinced the reader that, at least conceptually, this new method is simpler. It is also helpful in understanding and generalizing the "not walking to the floor" phenomenon from [6, Appendix A], as was already discussed in Remark 5.3.

Remark 6.6. If $r \geq 4$ then we can use the cyclic self-pairings of order 2^{r-2} from Sect. 5 for determining $N(\mathfrak{a}) \bmod 2^{r-2}$, and this is enough for evaluating $\delta, \epsilon, \delta\epsilon$ in case they exist. The situation is more subtle if

- $r = 2$ and $-\Delta_{\mathcal{O}}/4 \equiv 1 \bmod 4$ (to evaluate δ),
- $r = 3$ (to evaluate one of $\epsilon, \delta\epsilon$).

Both cases can be handled by descending to elliptic curves that are primitively $(\mathbb{Z} + 2\mathcal{O})$-oriented, similar to the approach from [6, Sect. 3.1]. In the former case this may not be needed: according to [8, Proposition A.1] in the full version of this paper, there may exist cyclic self-pairings that allow us to compute $N(\mathfrak{a}) \bmod 4$ directly. Indeed, for $k = \mathbb{F}_p$ and $\mathcal{O} = \mathbb{Z}[\sqrt{-p}]$ this is handled by the semi-reduced Tate pairing from [6, Remark 11], which was studied precisely for this purpose. But for arbitrary orientations we are currently missing such a pairing.

Remark 6.7. If $m = \mathrm{char}(k)$ then our order-m cyclic self-pairing is not available. However, in view of the character relation [6, Eq. (1)] it is always possible to discard one assigned character, so this concern is usually void.[5] This is in complete analogy with [6,7].

Remark 6.8. In [7] an alternative attack to the DDH problem for oriented curves, that applies to arbitrary orientations, is described, using the Weil pairing rather than the Tate pairing. Here, the situation is slightly more intricate, in the sense that the domain of the self-pairing is no longer cyclic. More specifically, the self-pairing associated to [7, Theorem 1] may be constructed as follows. Let $\mathcal{O}$ be an imaginary quadratic order, let E be an $\mathcal{O}$-oriented elliptic curve, and suppose that $m \mid \Delta_{\mathcal{O}}$ for some odd prime number m. Then we can write $\mathcal{O} = \mathbb{Z}[\sigma]$, for some σ of norm coprime to m [7, Lemma 1]. We define $f : E[m] \rightarrow \mu_m$, $f(P) := e_m(P, \sigma(P))$. One easily checks that this is indeed a non-trivial self-pairing compatible with horizontal isogenies. Interestingly, the proof of [7, Theorem 1] shows that f can still be employed to recover the norm of

---

[5] If $\mathrm{char}(k) = 2$ then it seems like we may be missing more than one assigned character, but see [7, Footnote 1] for why this is not the case.

a connecting ideal up to squares modulo m. A similar phenomenon occurs in [7, Propositions 1 and 2], where the associated self-pairings are maps $E[2] \to \mu_4$ and $E[4] \to \mu_8$ respectively.

7   Conclusions and Open Problems

In this paper we have derived necessary and sufficient conditions for non-trivial cyclic self-pairings that are compatible with oriented isogenies, to exist. We have given examples of such pairings based on the generalized Weil and Tate pairings.

As an application, we have identified weak instances of class group actions assuming the degree of the secret isogeny is known and sufficiently small; some of these instances succumb to a polynomial time attack. We note that these cases are rare, but exist nonetheless; this situation is somewhat reminiscent of anomalous curves for which the ECDLP can be solved in polynomial time [33,37]. These instances can be easily identified in that they require (large) square factors of $\Delta_{\mathcal{O}}$. This also shows that protocols that operate on or close to the crater are immune to this attack. To err on the side of caution it is probably best to limit oneself to (nearly) prime $\Delta_{\mathcal{O}}$.

The following problems remain open:

- In our attack we require square factors m^2 of $\Delta_{\mathcal{O}}$ to be able to derive the action of the secret isogeny on the full $E[m]$, which is required as input to the algorithm from [31]. However, it is well known that a degree d isogeny is uniquely determined if it is specified on more than $4d$ points, so knowing the image of a single point of order $m > 4d$ should suffice. The problem remains to find a method akin to [31] that can handle such one-dimensional input.
- Is it possible to exploit partial information, e.g. how valuable is it to know the action of a secret isogeny on a single point of order $m < 4d$?
- At the moment we have only used the generalized Weil and Tate pairings for endomorphisms, whereas the definition also allows for more general isogenies ψ. Can this somehow be exploited in a more powerful attack?
- Our definition of a self-pairing on cyclic groups of even order allows for instances not derived from a bilinear pairing, e.g. the semi-reduced Tate pairing given in [6, Remark 11]. Proposition A.1 in the full version of this paper [8] shows that such self-pairings indeed exist more generally, but unfortunately the proof is not effective. It would be interesting to find a more direct construction of these self-pairings and thereby genuinely complete the classification from Sects. 4 and 5.
- Are there efficient Miller-type algorithms for computing the generalized Weil and Tate pairings? If not, do they exist for a larger class of endomorphisms than just $\sigma = \pi_q - 1$? At least, can these pairings be computed without needlessly extending the base field?

Acknowledgements. We owe thanks to Luca De Feo, Damien Robert, Katherine Stange and the anonymous reviewers for various helpful comments, discussions and suggestions.

References

1. Bosma, W., Cannon, J., Playoust, C.: The Magma algebra system I: the user language. J. Symb. Comput. **24**(3–4), 235–265 (1997)
2. Bruin, P.: The Tate pairing for Abelian varieties over finite fields. Journal de Théorie des Nombres de Bordeaux **23**(2), 323–328 (2011)
3. Castryck, W., Decru, T.: CSIDH on the surface. In: Ding, J., Tillich, J.-P. (eds.) PQCrypto 2020. LNCS, vol. 12100, pp. 111–129. Springer, Cham (2020). https://doi.org/10.1007/978-3-030-44223-1_7
4. Castryck, W., Decru, T.: An efficient key recovery attack on SIDH. In: Hazay, C., Stam, M. (eds.) Eurocrypt 2023 Part 5. LNCS, vol. 14008, pp. 423–447. Springer, Cham (2023). https://doi.org/10.1007/978-3-031-30589-4_15
5. Castryck, W., Lange, T., Martindale, C., Panny, L., Renes, J.: CSIDH: an efficient post-quantum commutative group action. In: Peyrin, T., Galbraith, S. (eds.) ASIACRYPT 2018 Part 3. LNCS, vol. 11274, pp. 395–427. Springer, Cham (2018). https://doi.org/10.1007/978-3-030-03332-3_15
6. Castryck, W., Sotáková, J., Vercauteren, F.: Breaking the decisional Diffie-Hellman problem for class group actions using Genus theory. In: Micciancio, D., Ristenpart, T. (eds.) CRYPTO 2020 Part 2. LNCS, vol. 12171, pp. 92–120. Springer, Cham (2020). https://doi.org/10.1007/978-3-030-56880-1_4
7. Castryck, W., Houben, M., Vercauteren, F., Wesolowski, B.: On the decisional Diffie-Hellman problem for class group actions on oriented elliptic curves. Res. Number Theory **8**(4), 99 (2022)
8. Castryck, W., Houben, M., Merz, S.-P., Mula, M., van Buuren, S., Vercauteren, F.: Weak instances of class group action based cryptography via self-pairings (2023). Full version on ePrint Archive available at https://eprint.iacr.org/2023/549
9. Cervantes-Vázquez, D., Chenu, M., Chi-Domínguez, J.-J., De Feo, L., Rodríguez-Henríquez, F., Smith, B.: Stronger and faster side-channel protections for CSIDH. In: Schwabe, P., Thériault, N. (eds.) LATINCRYPT 2019. LNCS, vol. 11774, pp. 173–193. Springer, Cham (2019). https://doi.org/10.1007/978-3-030-30530-7_9
10. Chávez-Saab, J., Chi-Domínguez, J.-J., Jaques, S., Rodríguez-Henríquez, F.: The SQALE of CSIDH: sublinear Vélu quantum-resistant isogeny action with low exponents. J. Cryptogr. Eng. **12**(3), 349–368 (2022)
11. Chenu, M., Smith, B.: Higher-degree supersingular group actions. Math. Cryptol. **1**(2), 85–101 (2021)
12. Colò, L., Kohel, D.: Orienting supersingular isogeny graphs. J. Math. Cryptol. **14**(1), 414–437 (2020)
13. Couveignes, J.-M.: Hard homogeneous spaces (2006). Unpublished article. https://eprint.iacr.org/2006/291
14. Cox, D.A.: Primes of the Form $x^2 + ny^2$: Fermat, Class Field Theory, and Complex Multiplication, vol. 116. Pure and Applied Mathematics, 2nd edn. Wiley (2013)
15. Dartois, P., De Feo, L.: On the security of OSIDH. In: Hanaoka, G., Shikata, J., Watanabe, Y. (eds.) PKC 2022 Part 1. LNCS, vol. 13177, pp. 52–81. Springer, Cham (2022). https://doi.org/10.1007/978-3-030-97121-2_3
16. De Feo, L., et al.: SCALLOP: scaling the CSI-FiSh. In: Boldyreva, A., Kolesnikov, V. (eds.) PKC 2023 Part 1. LNCS, vol. 13940, pp. 345–375. Springer, Cham (2023). https://doi.org/10.1007/978-3-031-31368-4_13
17. De Feo, L., et al.: Modular isogeny problems. Private communication
18. Frey, G., Rück, H.-G.: A remark concerning m-divisibility and the discrete logarithm in class groups of curves. Math. Comput. **62**, 865–874 (1994)

19. Galbraith, S.: Pairings. In: Blake, I.F., Seroussi, G., Smart, N.P. (eds.) Advances in Elliptic Curve Cryptography. LMS Lecture Note Series, Chapter 9, vol. 317, pp. 183–213. Cambridge University Press (2005)

20. Garefalakis, T.: The generalized Weil pairing and the discrete logarithm problem on elliptic curves. In: Rajsbaum, S. (ed.) LATIN 2002. LNCS, vol. 2286, pp. 118–130. Springer, Heidelberg (2002). https://doi.org/10.1007/3-540-45995-2_15

21. Jao, D., De Feo, L.: Towards quantum-resistant cryptosystems from supersingular elliptic curve isogenies. In: Yang, B.-Y. (ed.) PQCrypto 2011. LNCS, vol. 7071, pp. 19–34. Springer, Heidelberg (2011). https://doi.org/10.1007/978-3-642-25405-5_2

22. Lenstra, H.W.: Complex multiplication structure of elliptic curves. J. Number Theory 56, 227–241 (1996)

23. Maino, L., Martindale, C., Panny, L., Pope, G., Wesolowski, B.: A direct key recovery attack on SIDH. In: Eurocrypt 2023 Part 5. LNCS, vol. 14008, pp. 448–471. Springer, Cham (2023). https://doi.org/10.1007/978-3-031-30589-4_16

24. Miller, V.S.: Short programs for functions on curves (1986). Unpublished note https://crypto.stanford.edu/miller/miller.pdf

25. Miller, V.S.: The Weil pairing, and its efficient calculation. J. Cryptol. 17(4), 235–261 (2004)

26. Moriya, Tomoki, Onuki, Hiroshi, Takagi, Tsuyoshi: SiGamal: a supersingular isogeny-based PKE and its application to a PRF. In: Moriai, Shiho, Wang, Huaxiong (eds.) ASIACRYPT 2020 Part 2. LNCS, vol. 12492, pp. 551–580. Springer, Cham (2020). https://doi.org/10.1007/978-3-030-64834-3_19

27. Onuki, H.: On oriented supersingular elliptic curves. Finite Fields Appl. 69, Article id 101777 (2021)

28. Robert, D.: Efficient algorithms for Abelian varieties and their moduli spaces. Habilitation à Diriger des Recherches (2021)

29. Robert, D.: Some applications of higher dimensional isogenies to elliptic curves (overview of results) (2022). Preprint https://eprint.iacr.org/2022/1704

30. Robert, D.: The geometric interpretation of the Tate pairing and its applications (2023). Preprint https://eprint.iacr.org/2023/177

31. Robert, D.: Breaking SIDH in polynomial time. In: Hazay, C., Stam, M. (eds.) Eurocrypt 2023 Part 5. LNCS, vol. 14008, pp. 472–503. Springer, Cham (2023). https://doi.org/10.1007/978-3-031-30589-4_17

32. Rostovtsev, A., Stolbunov, A.: Public-key cryptosystem based on isogenies (2006). Unpublished article https://eprint.iacr.org/2006/145

33. Satoh, T., Araki, K.: Fermat quotients and the polynomial time discrete log algorithm for anomalous elliptic curves. Commentarii Mathematici Universitatis Sancti Pauli 47, 81–92 (1998)

34. Schoof, R.: Elliptic curves over finite fields and the computation of square roots mod p. Math. Comput. 44(170), 483–494 (1985)

35. Schoof, R.: Nonsingular plane cubic curves over finite fields. J. Comb. Theory Ser. A 36(2), 183–211 (1987)

36. Silverman, J.H.: The Arithmetic of Elliptic Curves, Graduate Texts in Mathematics, vol. 106, 2nd edn. Springer, Cham (2009). https://doi.org/10.1007/978-0-387-09494-6

37. Smart, N.P.: The discrete logarithm problem on elliptic curves of trace one. J. Cryptol. 12, 193–196 (1999)

38. Waterhouse, W.C.: Abelian varieties over finite fields. Annales scientifiques de l'École Normale Supérieure 2, 521–560 (1969)

39. Wesolowski, B.: The supersingular isogeny path and endomorphism ring problems are equivalent. In: FOCS 2021, pp. 1100–1111. IEEE (2022)

Author Index

A

Aragon, Nicolas 127

B

Backendal, Matilda 661
Beierle, Christof 209
Belaïd, Sonia 440
Bellare, Mihir 661
Berndt, Sebastian 377
Beullens, Ward 101
Bhaumik, Ritam 628
Boura, Christina 240
Bouvier, Clémence 507, 540
Briaud, Pierre 507
Buuren, Sam van 762

C

Cassiers, Gaëtan 440
Castryck, Wouter 762
Chaidos, Pyrros 507

D

Daemen, Joan 475, 607
David, Nicolas 240
Derbez, Patrick 240
Ducas, Léo 37, 150
Dunkelman, Orr 177
Dyseryn, Victor 127

E

Eisenbarth, Thomas 377
El Hirch, Solane 475
Espitau, Thomas 150

F

Faust, Sebastian 377
Felke, Patrick 209
Fuchs, Jonathan 607

G

Gaborit, Philippe 127
Gourjon, Marc 377

**Grassi, Lorenzo 305, 540, 573
Gunsing, Aldo 628
Günther, Felix 661

H

Hao, Yonglin 573
Heninger, Nadia 3
Hoffmann, Clément 410
Hou, Shiqi 273
Houben, Marc 762
Hovd, Martha Norberg 305

I

Isobe, Takanori 540

J

Jha, Ashwin 628

K

Katsumata, Shuichi 729
Keller, Nathan 177

L

Lai, Yi-Fu 729
Leander, Gregor 209, 240
LeGrow, Jason T. 729
Lin, Dongdai 273
Liu, Fukang 540
Liu, Meicheng 273
Liu, Tianren 694

M

Makarim, Rusydi H. 475
Manterola Ayala, Irati 305
Masure, Loïc 343
Méaux, Pierrick 410
Meier, Willi 540
Mennink, Bart 628
Merz, Simon-Philipp 762
Momin, Charles 410
Mula, Marzio 762

© International Association for Cryptologic Research 2023
H. Handschuh and A. Lysyanskaya (Eds.): CRYPTO 2023, LNCS 14083, pp. 793–794, 2023.
https://doi.org/10.1007/978-3-031-38548-3

N
Naya-Plasencia, María 240
Neumann, Patrick 209

O
Orlt, Maximilian 377
Øygarden, Morten 305

P
Pelecanos, Angelos 694
Perrin, Léo 507
Postlethwaite, Eamonn W. 150
Pulles, Ludo N. 37

Q
Qin, Ling 729

R
Raddum, Håvard 305
Rechberger, Christian 573
Rivain, Matthieu 440
Rohit, Raghvendra 475
Rotella, Yann 410, 607
Ryan, Keegan 3

S
Salen, Robin 507
Scarlata, Matteo 661

Schofnegger, Markus 573
Seker, Okan 377
Shen, Yaobin 628
Standaert, François-Xavier 343, 410
Stennes, Lukas 209

T
Taleb, Abdul Rahman 440
Tessaro, Stefano 694

U
Udvarhelyi, Balazs 410

V
Vaikuntanathan, Vinod 694
Velichkov, Vesselin 507
Vercauteren, Frederik 762

W
Walch, Roman 573
Wang, Anyu 70
Wang, Qingju 305, 573
Wang, Shichang 273
Wang, Tianrui 70
Wang, Xiaoyun 70
Weizmann, Ariel 177
Willems, Danny 507

Printed in the United States
by Baker & Taylor Publisher Services